Baking Science & Technology

Fourth Edition

By E.J. Pyler and L.A. Gorton

Volume II

Published by
Sosland Publishing Co.
4800 Main St., Suite 100
Kansas City, MO 64112
United States of America

Library of Congress Control Number: 2008934285
ISBN 978-0-9820239-1-4 Baking Science and Technology, Volume II
ISBN 978-0-9820239-2-1 Baking Science and Technology, 2 Volume Set

Printed in the United States of America

Sosland Publishing Co.
4800 Main St., Suite 100
Kansas City, MO 64112
Telephone: (+1) 816 756 1000
Fax: (+1) 816 756 0494
Web: www.bakingbusiness.com

Permissions
Every effort has been made to ascertain the owners of copyrights for the selections used in this volume and to credit and/or obtain permission to reprint copyrighted information and graphics. Sosland Publishing Co. expresses its gratitude for permissions it has received. Sosland Publishing Co. will be pleased, in subsequent editions to correct any inadvertent errors or omissions that may be pointed out.

Foreword

Preparing Volume II in this 2-volume set of "Baking Science & Technology, 4th edition" was equally as challenging as the extraordinary effort put into Volume I. Completeness, timeliness and accuracy were paramount.

Volume I focused on basic food science, crops and raw materials relating to baking. Although these topics remain somewhat timeless, they still required moderate refreshing and updating for the times. On the other hand, ingredients, testing and applications changed or evolved considerably in the past 20 years. All these were reflected with great detail in Volume I.

Time and technology also have redefined the understanding, design and fundamentals of ingredient interaction, equipment and processing and control systems — the heart of Volume II.

As with Volume I, this work updates the 3rd edition, written by E.J. Pyler. As such, the task was to identify the significant changes and advancements in formulating baked foods as well as changes to the equipment and technology related to processing, handling and packaging of standard, artisan and specialty baked items.

This edition also has been reorganized to better reflect the logical progression of the baking process and the understanding and required knowledge of the various technologies having to do with processing ingredients into finished baked foods. We are honored that "Baking Science & Technology" continues to be used as a textbook by the industry's leading baking schools and as a daily reference for thousands of bakers worldwide. This volume continues and completes the scope for which it is intended.

In addition to updating and reorganizing the content of the previous edition, new sections have been added to reflect significant evolutions of the industry. A whole chapter is dedicated to Artisan baking equipment — once limited to small, manual operations, equipment systems are now capable of producing Old World products at industrial speeds with no loss in quality.

Other specialty equipment such as griddle systems, enrobing and robotics feature new or elaborated sections for this edition. In addition, three appendices have been added covering formulation percentages, automation terminology and industry and governmental resources.

As in Volume I, we relied heavily on Laurie Gorton's experience and expertise to tackle a sizable chunk of the assignment, generating the overall outline and progression of the book as well as tackling the first three chapters, dealing with dough processing and product formulation, as well as the final chapter on artisan processing. She also contributed her knowledge and critical editorial eye to the rest of the book as a primary reviewer.

Because of the breadth and depth of the topics included in this volume, we relied on other experts in the industry to take segmented sections of specific chapters, update them based on their own knowledge as well as pertinent industry materials and organize them in a fashion that reflected the new outline.

Each of the contributing writers and reviewers went above and beyond the call of duty. Each spent many more hours than originally anticipated. But the passion they have for this industry helped them press on to uncompromised excellence. Several commented that they learned valuable knowledge from the research conducted to complete and update the content.

To ensure accuracy, comprehensiveness, quality and an independent critique, each section and chapter was reviewed by Sosland Publishing staff as well as other knowledgeable people in the industry.

Volume II starts with the fundamentals of dough and batter processes from mixing to baking. It proceeds into formulation techniques for 20+ subcategories of baked foods and addresses contemporary formulating issues including staling, allergens, etc.

It then delves deep into each process, starting with mixing and forming equipment, heating and cooling systems, auxiliary and specialty equipment, and finishes up with processing aspects of industrial artisan baking technology.

As noted, this book exists because of help from many individuals. For their work appearing in Volume II, thanks goes to authors Laurie Gorton, Mihaelos N. Mihalos, Sigismondo De Tora, Stephen St. Clair Thompson, Rick Stier, Peter Clark, Jim Kline, Hans van der Maarl, Michael Bakhoum, and Charles Rastle and Nigel Hitchings.

For quality assurance provided by reading and critiquing the work in progress, we relied on Bernie Bruinsma, Bruce Campbell, Theresa Cogswell, Michael Eggebrecht, Larry Evans, Roger Faw, Karen B. Foehse, Mike Hall, Bill Hodgson, Bob Horth, Jian Li, Jason Stricker, Jason Tingley, Tim Trausch, Chuck Walker, Joe Zaleski and Bill Zimmerman.

This entire 4th edition project has taken more than two and a half years from concept to completion. While the planning process and Volume I took nearly 18 months, we pushed hard to get Volume II printed less than one year later. The support of Sosland Publishing Co., including Mark Sabo, president; Paul Lattan, publisher; editorial colleagues Holly Bradley, Kimberlie Clyma, Jennifer Barnett Fox and Shane Whitaker; as well as our design manager, Doni Conarroe and design team assistant Steve Piatt was unfathomable. A huge thank you goes to all involved.

Now that "Baking Science & Technology 4th edition" is complete in print, we foresee the next endeavor — digital formats, updates, online searchability and other advances yet to emerge.

We encourage readers to comment on this edition and its contents as well as to recommend topics and changes for future inclusion.

Steve Berne
Editor, *Baking & Snack*, *Baking & Snack International*, *Snack World*
Project manager, "Baking Science & Technology, 4th ed."
Sosland Publishing Co.
December 2009

Preface

On preparing Volume II
of the 4th edition
of "Baking Science & Technology"

The experts who updated these chapters, the reviewers who critiqued their work and the editors who polished this text did their best to represent baking technology in its state-of-the-art condition at the start of the 21st century. Just as R&D departments constantly push the envelope with their new product development projects, it is also the nature of bakery engineers and their counterparts at bakery equipment manufacturing companies to constantly seek improvement in their machines. Thus, a piece of equipment as familiar as the piston divider or the intermediate proofer can suddenly morph into something altogether new or disappear entirely.

As a reporter who has observed and written about the commercial wholesale baking industry for more than 30 years, I would not have it any other way. I experience constant fascination with where the ingenuity of the equipment designer and the creativity of the formulator are taking the industry. Every bakery I visit, every trade show I attend, every phone conversation brings something new to light.

It was the same with Ernie Pyler, who wrote the earlier editions of this book, published in 1952, 1972 and 1988. Although a chemist and teacher by education and training, he eagerly explored "what's new" in equipment, as well. Often he published the very first look at new bakery machines and technology, and he convinced many of the inventors to write in their own words about the developments they were making. As editor, publisher and owner of *Bakers Digest* for all those years, he wore many hats. His son, Dick Pyler, once told me that his father was as happy to get an article about new technology out of a supplier as sell an advertisement for the magazine, probably happier.

Many of the seminal reports that *Bakers Digest* offered its readers remain informative and figure in the chapter references here. But time marches on, and changes continue to be made in bakery processes and technology. For this reason, the authors referred to current articles in *Baking & Snack, Baking & Snack International*, the *AIB Technical Bulletin*, the *Proceedings of the American Society of Baking, Cereal Chemistry* and *Cereal Foods World*, among other sources, to update this book.

It has been a great honor for me to work on this fourth edition of "Baking Science & Technology." The opportunity was worth all the hard effort it required. I hope you agree that the results live up to their promise.

Laurie Gorton
Executive Editor, *Baking & Snack*
December 2009

E.J. Pyler
(1913-2003)

Table of Contents

CHAPTER 6

Fundamental Bakery Dough Processes

INTRODUCTION

"The baker's perception of breadmaking … is different from a researcher's view," observed Sluimer (2005). Yet the researcher's view helps illuminate the actions and results the baker gets during preparation of doughs and baking of finished products. For this reason, the scientific examination of the processes of doughmaking and bread-making warrant attention from bakery students and bakers. What happens chemically and physically when flour, water, yeast and baking's myriad other ingredients are combined? How do chemical reactions change the characteristics of ingredients during the process of doughmaking? What contributions do the physical actions of mixing, kneading, shaping and baking make to the quality of finished products?

The field of experimental baking deals largely with these concerns. At the commercial level, experimental baking comprises a vital part of the company's research

Complex and varied methods characterize the science and technology of processing yeasted doughs, and each step plays a critical role in overall success.

Perfect loaf after perfect loaf — that happens when dough processes come together correctly at bakeries such as Turano Georgia Bread, Villa Rica, GA, shown here.
(*Baking & Snack*)

and development activities. R&D, as pursued in the baking industry, is an applied science. It encompasses product and process development and also gets involved with specifying and testing ingredients, food safety and regulatory and package labeling matters. Experimental baking supports new product development and ingredient testing, as well as optimizing formulation changes and baking technologies (Doerry 1995b).

Experimental bakers set the standards for how proteins, starch and lipids work in baking. This generally unrecognized and vitally important group of people answers basic questions about chemistry, ingredients and baking. In conjunction with wheat breeders, they set the quality of the wheat crops into the next decade by the varieties that are released to be grown.

Experimental baking is also essential to the work done at academic and research laboratory levels. In these settings, it supplies data to the scientists, chemists and engineers exploring the use of cereals for food and feed. For example, it tests the baking potential of new wheat varieties. To evaluate a theory, a series of doughs or batters can be set to test single or multiple variables. The results help the researcher refine the theory and move to the next stage of the experiment.

The breadmaking process is, as Gould (1998) observed, the interaction of raw materials, equipment and people in a particular environment, and he contrasted the breadmaking practices around the world. The baguette of France, the vollkornbrot of Germany, the pita of Lebanon, the steamed buns of China, the chapattis of India — all qualify as bread, yet they differ markedly. While some pastries are leavened by air, most sweet goods are yeast-raised and follow processes common to the manufacture bread products. The factors of ingredients and equipment determine the end products, but consumer requirements and expectations frame the style and character of finished baked foods.

The breadmaking process has several functions, accomplished at different stages in the preparation and baking of dough. Cauvain (1998a) described these as (a) mixing of flour and water, together with yeast, salt and other ingredients in specified ratios to form the dough; (b) developing the gluten structure of hydrated proteins through application of energy during mixing (a stage often termed "kneading"); (c) incorporating air bubbles within the dough during mixing; (d) continuing the development of the gluten structure after kneading to improve its ability to expand when gas pressures increase (a stage termed "ripening" or "maturing"); (e) creating or modifying flavor compounds in the dough; (f) subdividing the dough mass into unit pieces; (g) modifying the shape of the divided dough pieces; (h) resting to allow further modification of the dough pieces' physical and rheological properties; (i) shaping to achieve required configuration; (j) proofing (fermenting and expanding) the dough; and (k) expanding and fixing the dough into its final shape by baking. As with any process or product using naturally variable ingredients, problems will occur. Cauvain and Young (2001) addressed more than 200 such matters in a question-and-answer format.

Dough chemistry involves a series of interactions between carbohydrates, lipids and proteins. Hamer and Hoseney (1998) assembled a comprehensive examination of these connections as described by current scientific research being done worldwide. The principle physical science involved with doughmaking is rheology. Good baking quality depends on several rheological properties such as extensibility exceeding a minimum level, viscosity, strain hardening and optimal resistance to deformation. Several texts that provide insight into the rheology of dough are available such as Faridi (1985), Bloksma and Bushuk (1988), Hamer and Hoseney (1998) and Faridi and Faubion (1990) and papers written by Bloksma (1990a, 1990b), Weipert (1990), Autio et al. (2001) and Weegels et al. (2003), among others.

Dough is viscoelastic, combining properties of a Hookean solid with those of a non-Newtonian viscous fluid. Physically speaking, doughs are essentially foams, which become sponges after baking. The transformation from the closed cell structure of a foam to the open cells of a sponge is but one of the many changes that occur during dough processing.

Dough formation has been described by many authors, of which Stauffer (1998) provided a succinct description of the chemical, biochemical and physical principals involved. Hamer and Hoseney (1998) dug deep into the ways that proteins, carbohydrates, pentosans, lipids and water interact chemically and physically during preparation and processing of doughs and baked foods. Eliasson and Larson (1993) looked into the colloidal and surface chemistry aspects of dough and doughmaking, using rheological measurements to characterize wheat flour doughs.

The discussions of dough processes in this chapter and batter processes in Chapter 7 are offered to describe the fundamental chemical and physical changes that take place at each stage of the production process. Bread and bun doughs are sufficiently different from cake and chemically-leavened batters that they merit separate coverage. Because some products such as bagels, English muffins and pretzels, among others, employ unique processes, these procedures will be examined in Chapter 8 along with their specific formulating parameters.

The reader will notice that nearly all the discussion here and in most scientific literature concerns white pan bread. The reason is simple: White pan bread is highly standardized, has well-recognized quality characteristics and represents the main product style in North America and many other parts of the world. Some locales, notably France, take the baguette as the standard product.

6.A. Mixing and Doughmaking

Mixing is the act of combining or blending into a homogeneous mass the diverse ingredients that are destined to become part of the processed end product. In the production of bread and other yeast-raised bakery products, mixing initiates the long series of complex changes and interactions of water, starch, protein, lipids, enzymes, salt, sweeteners, yeast, oxidizing and reducing agents and other diverse components by bringing them into intimate contact with each other through the agency of physical work to ultimately result in a dough or batter. Two preconditions must be met for the production of dough with the right properties: (a) appropriate proportioning of the individual ingredients as established in a well-balanced dough formulation and (b) homogenous distribution of these ingredients throughout the dough mass.

In its essentials, dough mixing involves the combining and blending of the formula ingredients and then applying sufficient physical work to the mixture to transform it into a cohesive mass with the requisite viscoelastic properties. In large-scale commercial bakery production, the major ingredients (flour and dry sweeteners) are normally weighed by automatic scales that feed directly into the mixers, while water, liquid shortening and liquid sweeteners are piped into the mixer through meters that can be preset to deliver specified volumes. The small-volume ingredients are usually weighed out individually on small scales or, in the case of yeast foods, enrichment ingredients, dough conditioners, enzymes and other highly reactive materials, they may be added in the form of tablets, wafers or premeasured small packets made of soluble edible films. Increasingly, automated batching systems are being used to deliver such micro ingredients, too. Yeast, depending on the form in which it is used (compressed, active dry or instant active dry) may be added either crumbled, rehydrated as a slurry or in its dry state. Large bread bakeries have almost all converted to cream yeast systems that handle this ingredient as a pumpable liquid.

In addition to achieving a thorough dispersion of the ingredients into a homogeneous mixture, the dough mixing process in breadmaking has the further important objective of physically developing the gluten proteins into a coherent 3-dimensional structure that will impart to the dough the desired degree of plasticity, elasticity and viscosity. The initial mixing phase must physically hydrate the flour particles and incorporate air to nucleate gas cells responsible for leavening. As the dough develops, many complex physical, colloidal and biochemical changes occur that transform the dough into a complex viscoelastic polymer system (Bushuk et al. 1968).

In other words, mixing has three functions: (a) creating a homogenous mass from ingredients of differing characteristics, (b) developing (kneading) the dough sufficiently to ready if for subsequent processing and (c) occluding air into the mass to form the cell structure necessary for finished crumb quality. Also, mixing is the last processing step in which the rheological properties of a dough can be significantly altered by the baker (Spies 1990). Stauffer (1997) summarized the effects of mixing, calling attention to the role that the process plays in hydrating starch and protein, conditioning pentosans, developing gluten and incorporating air.

Batch vs. continuous. No single standard method for mixing ingredients to create doughs is followed by all bakers; instead, more than a half-dozen different procedures can be used (**Table 6.01**). Baker preference, product type and plant practice determine the choice of method (**Table 6.02**). Preparation of the dough can be done in batches or continuously, and fermentation times vary from none to several hours.

Reviewing the history of various doughmaking methods, Sluimer (2005) stated that mixing to full development was so difficult when only manual methods were available that the sponge-and-dough technique was invented to allow resting before adding the rest of the ingredients. "With better mixing equipment presently used in the bakery, straight-dough methods have become more convenient," he observed. Similar bakery needs prompted invention of other methods.

Today, most commercial bakers prepare doughs as separate batches, sized sufficiently to permit an uninterrupted production schedule but not too large to risk over-aging the dough as it waits in the divider hopper. The continuous mix method was developed during the 1950s to automate dough preparation. At one time, it was used by the majority of bakeries producing white pan bread, but this method fell out of favor when consumer demand for variety bread increased starting in the late 1970s. Technologies that grew up around continuous mix such as water brews and liquid sponge, however, remain in wide use for lines dedicated to baking long runs of fast food buns and similar products.

Among mixing methods being practiced commercially, the most prevalent is the sponge-and-dough process that involves two mixing stages, namely one of the sponge and the other of the dough. The sponge mixing stage aims at homogeneous ingredient dispersion and flour hydration and is normally of relatively brief duration,

Table 6.01. Advantages and Disadvantages of Dough Systems

Dough system	Advantages	Disadvantages
Straight dough	Good flavor	Difficult dough handling
	Medium process time	Long mixing times
	Good mixing tolerance	Poor fermentation tolerance
Sponge and dough	Good fermentation tolerance	Poor mixing tolerance
	Superior product score	Long process time
	Good dough handling	High cost of equipment
	Longer product shelf life	Larger space requirement
Liquid sponge	Uniformity of product	High cost of equipment
	Medium process time	Limited to 50 to 60% of flour in sponge
	Good flavor with high amount of flour in the sponge	Lack of flavor and shelf life with low flour in sponge
Continuous mix	Same advantages as liquid sponge if fermented	Limited to 50 to 60% of flour in sponge
	Less equipment, labor and space used	Lack of crumb strength
		Lack of flavor and shelf life with less fermentation
No-time dough	Short production time	Lack of flavor
	Greater flexibility	Lack of shelf life
	Less equipment and space	Higher ingredient costs
	Superior yeast survival in freezing	Problem with floor time
Chorleywood process	Tolerant to low-protein flours	High equipment costs
	Short production time	High energy cost
	Greater flexibility	Lack of flavor
	No floor time problems	Lack of product shelf life
Authentic sourdough process	Sourdough flavor	Very long process times
	Increased shelf life	Nurturing of sponge
	"Blistered" appearance	Less consistency
	Chewy, resilient texture	Increased space requirement

(O'Donnell 1996)

whereas the more critical phase of dough development is reserved for the more extensive mixing of the final dough. In the straight-dough method, as well as in those systems that employ various forms of liquid preferments, there is but one mixing stage in which complete dough development must be achieved.

Chapter 9 of this volume discusses commercial mixing equipment and the mechanical functions that carry out the various methods used to prepare yeast-raised doughs.

6.A.1. Dough preparation

Dough development establishes the major basis for a quality loaf. As Fay (2008) observed, there are many methods for making doughs, and efficiency and preference tend to show the way, but not always.

Bread, in its simplest form, requires but four ingredients: flour, water, yeast and salt. For the most part, however, conventional white pan bread and most specialty

Table 6.02. Products Made with Different Systems

Dough system	Bread and related products produced
Straight dough	Lean formula hearth bread, pita bread, 100% whole-wheat
Sponge and dough	White pan bread, variety pan bread, hamburger/hot dog buns, dinner rolls
Liquid sponge	White pan bread, variety pan bread, hamburger/hot dog buns, dinner rolls, English muffins
Continuous mix	White pan bread, hamburger/hot dog buns
No-time dough	Frozen dough, bagels, hard rolls, pizza crusts, dinner rolls, lean formula hearth bread, variety pan bread, English muffins
Chorleywood process	Hamburger/hot dog buns, variety pan bread
Authentic sourdough process	Lean formula hearth bread, rye bread

(O'Donnell 1996)

Table 6.03. US Standards of Identity for Bread Products

Code of Federal Regulations	
Title 21, Food and Drugs	
Part 136, Bakery Products	
136.6	Definitions
136.110	Bread, rolls and buns
136.115	Enriched bread, rolls and buns
136.130	Milk bread, rolls and buns
136.160	Raisin bread, rolls and buns
136.180	Whole-wheat bread, rolls and buns

breads include additional optional ingredients for the purpose of enhancing the product's overall quality. Thus, attributes such as loaf volume, crumb softness, grain uniformity, silkiness of texture, crust color, flavor and aroma, softness retention, shelf life and, perhaps most important of all, nutritive value can all be improved to varying degrees by the addition of appropriate optional ingredients. The materials that are either required or may be optionally included in the production of various standardized bread products are legally defined in the United States by the Food and Drug Administration (**Table 6.03**) and by the corresponding state agencies. The ingredients for nonstandardized breads are a matter of the baker's choice provided they comply with regulations covering food ingredient use and are handled in a way that promotes food safety.

A representative formula for white pan bread, based on results of a survey of major American bakeries, is shown in **Table 6.04**. About 50% of white pan bread produced in the US is made by the sponge-and-dough process, so the formula is shown in its adaptation to that procedure. In the straight-dough method, a somewhat higher yeast level (about 3.0% or more) is generally used, and all of the listed ingredients are processed as a single batch. It should further be kept in mind that individual bakers introduce minor quantitative variations in their formulations and that the values shown represent weighted averages. Also, most bakers make use of several reactive ingredients as production aids such as oxidizing and reducing agents and enzymes.

The functions of the various optional ingredients have been discussed at some length in Volume I and will, therefore, not be reviewed here. One point that needs stressing, however, is that although water (also referred to as absorption) is shown as a fixed quantity in the formula (a total of 64% based on flour weight in the example here), it is usually the most variable ingredient because its level is determined primarily by the flour's protein content and starch damage, two factors that cannot always be accurately controlled. Too much water, and a slurry results. Too little, and the powder mass is only slightly cohesive. With intermediate amounts, the result is a paste that behaves much like glue. Dough formation is not spontaneous; it requires the mass to be mixed to form a cohesive, viscoelastic material.

Mixing is essentially a hydration process. As the process begins, water wets the outer surfaces of the starch granule (**Figure 6.01**), and fibrils of gluten protein form spontaneously. Contact with the mixer's blades, bowl sides and other flour particles wipes these fibrils off, opening up more surface for water-protein interaction. The process continues, rapidly wearing down the flour particles and creating a continuous system of hydrated protein fibrils with starch granules dispersed throughout. Water, which exists in a free state at the beginning of mixing, decreases steadily and resistance to extension increases. Faubion and Hoseney (1990) related the action of water to the increase in resistance early in mixing and its subsequent decrease past the peak.

Mixing time varies widely for flours from different wheat cultivars, even for the same cultivar from different harvests. Questions about why this happens have occupied the life's work of many cereal scientists over the years. Some speculate that this phenomenon is a matter of the rate of hydration. Millers typically blend flours to achieve given performance specifications to minimize lot-to-lot variation, but the baker must take care to measure mixing time variations during crop year changes and readjust mixing procedures as required.

Mixing also incorporates air into the dough, thus providing nuclei for the cells forming the crumb grain in the final product. Occlusion of air has a significant effect on the mechanical properties of both the dough and the finished product.

At present, new science is illuminating the mixing process, including work being done at the American Institute of Baking using near infrared technology to identify peak dough development in yeast-raised doughs (Dempster et al. 2004).

6.A.1.a. Straight-dough method

The straight-dough method is a single-step process in which all the dough ingredients are mixed into a single batch. At first, the combined ingredients form a mass of wet clumps that exhibit little cohesion. As mixing continues, the dough acquires elastic properties and starts to pull away from the mixer walls. Mixing is carried to the point where the dough becomes smooth in appearance, with a dry surface, and assumes an optimum elastic character. When mixing is continued beyond this stage, the dough undergoes a rather rapid change in its physical character. Its surface takes on a characteristic sheen, and the dough becomes sticky and difficult to handle — the manifestations of an over-mixed dough (Bushuk et al. 1968).

The temperature of correctly mixed dough should fall within the range of 26 to 28°C (78 to 82°F). Higher temperatures will accelerate the rate of yeast fermentation, but they will also make the control of fermentation more difficult and may result in final fermented dough that lacks adequate stability for the subsequent makeup operations. A better way to reduce the fermentation time is to increase the yeast level by an appropriate amount.

The advantages of the straight-dough method are (a) lower requirements in processing time, labor, power and equipment and (b) reduced fermentation losses because of its generally shorter fermentation time compared with the sponge-and-dough process. Some bakers also hold that the straight-dough method enhances bread flavor by subjecting all dough ingredients to the same fermentation treatment;

Table 6.04. Representative White Pan Bread Formula

Ingredients	Sponge %	Dough (remix) %
Essential		
Flour	65.00	35.00
Water	37.00	27.00
Yeast	2.75	
Salt		2.10
Optional		
Yeast food	0.50	
Sweeteners (solids)		7.25
Shortening		2.30
Dairy blend		2.00
Protease enzyme	0.25	
Emulsifier		0.50
Dough strengthener		0.50
Preservative		0.20

(Dubois 1981)

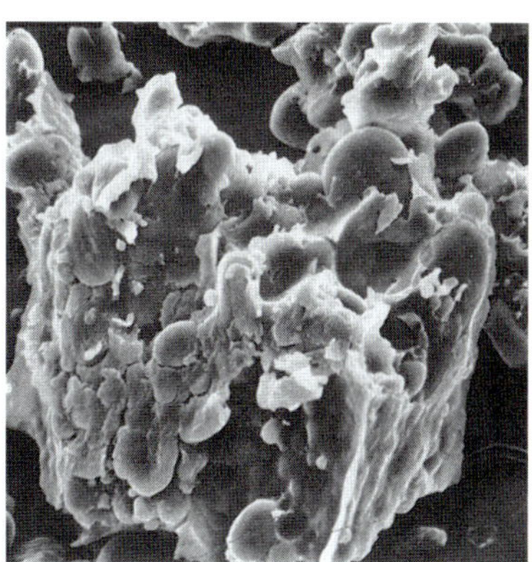

Figure 6.01. The scanning electron microscope reveals the structure of a particle of hard wheat flour and shows the relative size of starch granules to the particle itself.
(Hoseney and Seib 1973)

this view, however, is not universally accepted (Ponte 1971). The major limitation of the straight-dough method is its relative inflexibility with respect to fermentation time and schedule adherence: The dough must be made up when ready, with little leeway in either direction. Even minor schedule disruptions can result in marked differences in product, and little can be done to correct an over-fermented straight dough except to salvage it by incorporating small portions of it into newly mixed doughs.

The sequence of ingredient blending in the straight-dough method makes little difference to final product quality. One recommended procedure with vertical mixers is as follows: Part of the measured dough water, tempered to the correct temperature, is used to prepare a suspension of the yeast. The balance of the water is placed in the mixing bowl, and the small ingredients (sweetener, yeast food, malt, etc.) are stirred in to form a uniform suspension.

The mixer is then set in motion at low speed and about one-half of the flour charge added and mixed for about one-half minute to form a batter. The yeast suspension is then added, together with the remaining flour. Following mixer action for 2 to 3 minutes, the shortening is added, with the mixing continued until the dough begins to clear the sides of the bowl. At this point, salt is added as the final ingredient and mixing is continued for 2 to 3 minutes until smooth, elastic dough is produced. Depending on factors such as mixer speeds and flour strength, this stage is generally reached in 8 to 12 minutes.

With high-speed horizontal mixers, the dry ingredients are generally placed in the bowl first, blended into a uniform mixture by a few turns of the mixer bars, and then the yeast, suspended in a small volume of water at 17 to 21°C (60 to 70°F), and the balance of the dough water are added. Hydration of the flour proceeds rather rapidly under the influence of the mixing action, which serves to uniformly distribute the water throughout the dough mass. After mixing reaches about the halfway point, the shortening is added. Salt addition is normally delayed until the dough begins to clear the back of the mixer bowl. This procedure prevents excessive splashing that may occur when the liquid ingredients are charged into the bowl first.

In most operations, the yeast, yeast food, dough conditioners and other "small" ingredients, plus some water, are blended into a slurry in an "ingrediator," or some other appropriate tank, for pumping into the mixer, to be followed by the flour, other dry ingredients and the remaining dough water. Former concerns that dissolving the yeast with high concentrations of sugar, yeast food, mold inhibitors, etc., would cause extensive plasmolysis of the yeast and reduce its fermentative power have been shown to be groundless. A common practice is to place vital wheat gluten and other highly absorbent ingredients on top of the flour, or to sift them into the flour, to avoid forming lumps if these are first brought into direct contact with the dough water.

Delaying the salt addition during dough mixing until the dough begins to clear the back of the mixer bowl will reduce the mixing time appreciably. Wolfe and Dalby (Wolfe and Dalby 1961) demonstrated that salt in a flour-water dough will increase the mixing time required to reach peak development from 8.5 minutes for the salt-free control dough to 15.5 minutes. Delayed salt addition will not only permit a greater number of doughs to be scheduled within a given time period but will also result in energy savings because salt-free doughs, aside from being more rapidly developed, offer less resistance to mixer action.

6.A.1.b. No-time dough method

Although no-time dough mixing follows the all-in-the-same-bowl approach as straight doughs, this method is specifically aimed at cutting fermentation time to a minimum. Continuous mixing methods, as originally practiced, eliminated fermentation time and deposited doughs directly into pans, ready for final proofing, but the concept of no-time doughmaking is normally associated with batch methods. Although no-time doughs were originally promoted for use with high-speed systems such as the Chorleywood Bread Process, they can be prepared in any bread mixer.

The name "no time" refers to the elimination of bulk fermentation time, and the process must follow formulations and methods assuring that all development and fermentation take place during the mixing and proofing stages. Another term occasionally applied to this process is "flying sponge method."

The no-time dough method, according to Doerry (1995a), developed during the late 1960s as a consequence of changing times, with the advent of high-speed mechanical mixing, cheaper yeast, oxidizing agents and chemical dough development, thus raising the potential to reduce costs through time and labor savings. Prepared concentrates and bases, specifically formulated for no-time methods, also helped spread the use of this process. No-time doughs enabled bakers to produce breads when baked products were in short supply and the time required by the sponge-and-dough and straight-dough methods could not meet market demands (Geigenberger 1985, Reedich 1989). Short- and no-time systems save anywhere from 1 to 3 hours of processing time.

No-time dough systems conserve space in the bakery because a large fermentation room is not required, neither is the employee assigned as a sponge attendant. Breakdowns and line stoppages do not result in the substantial losses as when using processes involving a large number of sponges. Also, no detectable fermentation loss occurs, so dough yield is greater. Mixing time, however, may lengthen in order to get the dough to full development (Shirley 1977).

No-time doughs are mixed to slightly warmer temperatures of 28 to 29°C (82 to 84°F) than straight doughs. They get no bulk fermentation and are delivered to the dough divider within 10 to 20 minutes after mixing. The method employs maturing agents: oxidants (azodicarbonamide and, in open-bowl systems, ascorbic acid), mix-time reducers (L-cysteine and, in closed-bowl systems, ascorbic acid), dough conditioners (monocalcium phosphate and/or calcium sulfate) and enzymes. These functional additive ingredients help develop the gluten to mix the dough in less time and eliminate the need for lengthy fermentation. **Table 6.05** contrasts the formulation needs of a no-time straight dough with a 70% sponge dough.

In the 1950s, a blend of whey and L-cysteine was first offered to bakers as a dough conditioner that could control rapid dough development uniformly. L-cysteine breaks the disulfide bonds that cross-link gluten strands, thus making the gluten more extensible. It works during the mixing stage and continues its activity until subjected to the high heat of baking. It helps the baker achieve fully mechanically developed dough with less mechanical input. Reedich (1989) noted a usage rate of 25 to 50 ppm. Care must be taken in dosing with L-cysteine. Too much will weaken gluten and lead to low loaf volume, dense grain and poor eating quality.

Glover (1975) reported that L-cysteine cut optimum mixing time for dough made from patent flour from its usual 8.75 minutes to 3.5 minutes. Because of the speed with which L-cysteine reacts, the baker's choice of oxidant should be a slow-acting one such as potassium bromate. Should oxidation proceed too quickly or begin during the mixing stage, the oxidant will react directly with the L-cysteine and negate the desired reducing action.

Table 6.05. Formulation Differences Between No-Time Straight Doughs and 70% Sponge Doughs

Ingredient	No-time straight dough (bakers %)	70% Sponge dough (bakers %)
Flour	100	70
Water	60	45
Yeast	4	2
Yeast food	–	0.5
Shortening	3	3
Enzyme fungal protease	–	1 tablet
Enzyme fungal amylase	–	1 tablet
Dough remix		
Flour	–	30
Water	–	15
Sugar	6	8
Milk	3	3
Salt	2	2
Oxidation (potassium bromate and calcium iodate)	–	1 tablet
"No-time dough combination"*	0.25	–

No-time straight doughs are mixed "all in" as a single stage, while sponge doughs go through two mixing stages, separated by a period of bulk fermentation.
** A combination of reducing agents, oxidizers, enzymes, generally in a pre-mix.*

(Glover 1975)

Ascorbic acid acts as a reducing agent in closed systems such as continuous mixers or high-speed sealed-bowl mixers, but it takes on oxidizing properties in batch-type mixers through exposure to air. As explained in Volume I, Chapter 2, Part C.1, ascorbic acid exhibits an intermediate reaction rate as an oxidant, sustaining its action through most of the dough phase. Also, flour is virtually immune to over-treatment with ascorbic acid: Whether dosed at 30 ppm or 120 ppm, its effects are nearly constant.

Yeast seems to act synergistically with oxidation, particularly in no-time doughs, and a minimum fermentation of 15 minutes can improve finished loaf qualities and reduce oxidation needs (Reedich 1989).

Proteolytic enzymes may be used as a "natural" reducing agent. Although they work slower than chemical agents, proteolytic enzymes can cut mixing time by 10 to 20%. These enzymes do not actually "reduce" in the same way a chemical reducing agent would; instead, they catalyze changes in the bonds of gluten protein chains and, thus, cut dough development time. They work on an entirely different type of bond than those ruptured during mixing and those broken by L-cysteine. Without the protease, dough does not develop properly, and crumb structure becomes mealy.

Dough conditioners such as monocalcium phosphate control the dough's pH to maintain the ideal range of 5.1 to 5.2. Yeast nutrients and sources for calcium ions are needed to keep yeast active. Because floor time is so much shorter than conventional bulk fermentation, sugar should be reduced by 1 or 2 percentage points below that required by sponge-and-dough processes, and no more than 6% sugar (flour weight basis) should be used. The amount of yeast in a no-time system must be increased by 1 or 2 percentage points because the limited time allows no significant yeast growth.

Vital wheat gluten is sometimes used in the amounts of 1 to 2%, depending on the variety of bread being made, to give doughs more strength and the finished loaf more volume, better symmetry of form and better slicing (Shirley 1977). Salt may also need to be cut to avoid retarding the dough in the final proofer, but this delay is not a common problem.

Basic rules to follow when converting from the sponge-and-dough method to a no-time straight dough, according to Doerry (1995a), are (a) increase dough water absorption by 2 to 4 percentage points (flour weight basis), (b) increase compressed yeast by 1 percentage point (flour weight basis), (c) increase mixing time and (d) increase dough temperature to 82 to 84°F (28 to 29°C).

This method works well for bread that is sold fresh and consumed shortly after purchase. It is particularly well-suited to frozen dough production. The method works for preparation of white bread, specialty breads, variety breads, hearth breads, sweet doughs, doughnuts, English muffins and many other yeast-raised products.

Compared with bread made using bulk fermentation, no-time bread tends to lose flavor the longer it remains on the shelf. Experimentation with nonfat dry milk at levels of 4 to 8% in short-time systems scored well at the end of 7-day shelf life studies (Reedich 1989).

The crumb of no-time products firms more quickly unless crumb softeners (emulsifiers and stearoyl lactylates) and/or carbohydrase enzymes with extended-shelf-life functionality are included in the formulation.

Deterioration by mold growth can be a problem because, without bulk fermentation, no-time doughs do not contain sufficient acidity to inhibit spoilage microorganisms. Propionate mold inhibitors and/or vinegar (at a dosing level to give pH of 4.9 to 5.1) can solve such problems.

Use of preferments and water brews are a form of no-time dough production and will be discussed later in this chapter.

6.A.1.c. Sponge-and-dough method

In the sponge-and-dough method, the major fermentative action takes place in a preferment, called the sponge, in which normally from 50 to 70% of the total dough flour is subjected to the physical, chemical and biological actions of fermenting yeast. The sponge is subsequently combined with the rest of the dough ingredients, and the entire dough mass receives its final physical development during the dough mixing or remix stage.

The principal objectives of sponge mixing are to (a) bring about the uniform blending of ingredients into a smooth, homogeneous mass, (b) ensure the complete hydration of the flour particles and (c) form enough gluten to retain a sufficient amount of the evolving carbon dioxide gas to produce the characteristic increase in sponge volume as fermentation progresses. Extensive gluten development is undesirable because it leads to excessive sponge volume increases without producing any measurable beneficial effects in the finished bread (Baker 1964). In general, sponge mixing time should not exceed 4 minutes with modern types of high-speed horizontal sponge mixers (**Figure 6.02**). Normal practice calls for mixing at low speed for the first minute and at high speed for an additional 3 minutes. The mixing procedure is the same in all essentials as that of the straight dough, with the exception of its much shorter duration. The aim is to attain a temperature within the range of 25 to 28°C (72 to 78°F) for the sponge out of the mixer. This temperature will rise by about 1.1 C° (2 F°) per hour of fermentation.

Figure 6.02 Spacious mixing areas allow efficient equipment set up, product movement and access for sanitation. (Tom Judd and *Baking & Snack*)

The sponge, as is apparent from the formula in **Table 6.04** (section 6.A.1.) normally contains a major portion of the total flour and most of the yeast, yeast food and enzyme supplements. Modifications in its composition are frequently made in reaction to special problems. Thus, when the flour is deficient in amylolytic activity, the addition of some sweetener will accelerate fermentation. Preston and

Kilborn (1982) showed that the inclusion of 0.5 to 1.0% salt (flour weight basis) will also accelerate the fermentation rate and markedly reduce fermentation time. Dairy products, on the other hand, although rarely used in today's bakeries, inhibit yeast activity because of their buffer action. The same effect is also produced by salt when its level exceeds 1.0%, and because of this activity, salt has a necessary place in controlling the rate of fermentation.

Sponge consistency may vary from stiff to soft or slack. Stiff sponges, obtained by withholding part of the flour's normal absorption water, are known to expand more in volume during fermentation and bring about greater gluten mellowing than do normal sponges. On the other hand, slack or soft sponges, resulting from increased absorption or slight over-mixing, will yield good quality products if properly processed during the later production stages.

The mixed sponge is discharged into a greased trough and set to ferment in a special fermentation room maintained at a temperature of about 27°C (80°F) and a relative humidity of 75 to 80%. The sponge or fermentation time normally lasts 4.5 hours but may vary from 3.5 hours for sponges incorporating 75% of the total flour to 5 hours for sponges with only 50% of the total flour. Increasing the yeast levels will noticeably reduce fermentation time. In the course of fermentation, the volume of the sponge will increase 4- to 5-fold and will ultimately collapse or "break." This "drop" is often taken as a signal that sponge fermentation has achieved two-thirds or more of its full course.

A detailed discussion of the physical, chemical and biochemical reactions and transformations that occur during active fermentation is presented later in this chapter at Part 6.B.

For the second stage of the sponge-and-dough method, the fermented sponge is transferred from the trough to the dough mixer, which normally is larger in capacity than the sponge mixer. Next follows addition of the balance of the flour and water, plus the remaining dough ingredients. The usual procedure is to introduce the dry ingredients first, excepting salt, and start up the mixer at low speed for the mixing bars to break up the sponge. With the mixer at high speed, the liquid ingredients are then added, followed by the shortening in 5 to 6 minutes or about the halfway point of the high-speed mixing cycle. Finally, during the last 2 to 3 minutes of mixing, the salt is added. Some bakers prefer to break up the sponge first with the liquid portion of the dough ingredients to be followed by the addition of the dry ingredients.

In the past, when flour was delivered to bakeries in bags, it was common practice to specify two types of bread flour, namely, strong flour for the sponge and weaker flour for the dough stage. This practice was based on the consideration that the flour in the sponge is subjected to more extensive mixing and fermentative action than is the flour added at the remix stage and, hence, required greater strength for satisfactory performance. With the introduction of bulk flour deliveries to bakeries, most bakers no longer find it practical to carry inventories of two different bread flours. The greater strength requirements of the sponge flour are generally satisfied with supplementary ingredients such as vital wheat gluten and dough strengtheners.

The advantages of the sponge-and-dough method compared with the straight-dough process are, in brief: (a) slightly lower yeast levels may be used (an average of 2.75% vs. 3.0% in straight dough); (b) the method yields bread with good flavor, optimum loaf volume and superior grain and texture and softness retention; and (c) process flexibility is greater in terms of adaptability to minor schedule delays. Its disadvantages include greater equipment demands (for example, the requirement of two mixers instead of one), long processing time (about 7 hours from sponge mixing to oven baking), greater fermentation losses and higher labor costs.

6.A.1.c.i. 100% Sponge method.

In the so-called "100% sponge method," all the flour, about 80% of the dough water, the shortening and malt are combined into a homogeneous dough mass and fermented for about 3.5 hours. During the remix stage, the remaining water, salt and sugar are added, and the dough mixed for 2 minutes at low speed and about 12 minutes at high speed. This procedure yields slightly young doughs, which is claimed to improve the flavor and tenderness in the finished bread. Total fermentation time is less than 4 hours, and the dough pieces exhibit a rather rapid proofing rate, so the final proof is achieved some 10 minutes sooner than in conventional sponge-and-dough processing. A fairly moist oven atmosphere is required to ensure good ovenspring with this system (Silva 1941).

Clark (1985) reviewed contemporary sponge-and-dough practices as used at large-volume bakeries. He reported that finished breads made by this method showed exceptional eating and keeping qualities.

6.A.1.d. High-speed mixing method

Developed in 1961 by the Flour Milling and Baking Research Association at Chorleywood, England, (now part of Campden BRI, located at Chipping-Campden, England), the high-energy, high-speed method for mixing bread dough now known as the Chorleywood Bread Process (CBP) is responsible for preparation of roughly 80% of the UK's bread supply. Bakers in Australia, New Zealand and India and a number of other countries have also adopted this method. Its high-speed, high-intensity approach to mixing suits low-protein wheat flours (10.5 to 11% protein) better than higher-protein flours.

This variation of the straight-dough and no-time dough methods combines low-protein wheat flour with chemical improvers, solid vegetable shortening, water, yeast and salt, under intense mechanical working of the dough by a high-speed mixer operating at 600 rpm or higher, some as much 1,750 rpm. The short mixing time, usually 2 to 5 minutes in all, and intense action raise the dough temperature and shorten fermentation time, thus cutting the start-to-finish time for bread preparation to 3.5 hours or less, saving 1.5 to 2 hours compared with conventional methods. Energy input of about 5 to 7.5 Watt-hours per lb of dough is required, although this will vary with flour strength (Andrews et al. 1989).

The designation of "mechanical dough development" may not be totally appropriate for intensive dough mixing processes because it ignores the essential role played by oxidation. Bushuk et al. (1965) showed, for example, that high-speed mixing will not produce good bread without adequate oxidation. On the other hand, it is possible to produce satisfactory bread with high levels of oxidation and relatively slow mixing speeds. This combination of slow mixing speeds and high levels of oxidants, generally in blends of 30 ppm potassium bromate and 100 ppm ascorbic acid, forms the basis of a "no time" baking process used widely in Australia (Marston 1966). The bread produced by this method is judged to be comparable in quality to bread produced by the conventional bulk fermentation method.

The role of energy during mixing can be seen by its results using UK flour supplies (**Figure 6.03**), but what these high inputs actually do is still widely debated (Cauvain 1998a). High energy input through the action of the high-speed mixer

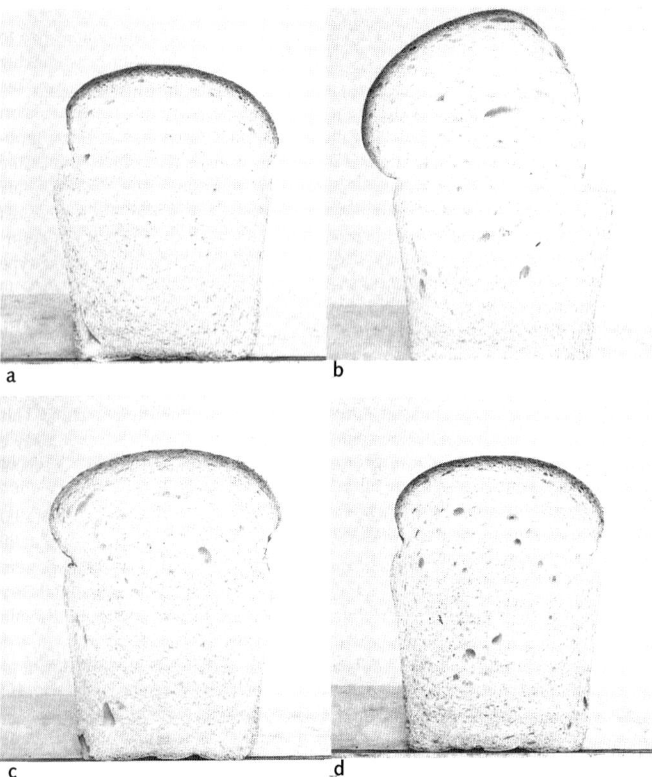

Figure 6.03. Different energy inputs and mixing speeds affect bread quality, with examples (a) at 600 rpm and 5 Watt-hours per kg, (b) 600 rpm and 17 Watt-hours per kg, (c) 250 rpm and 5 Watt-hours per kg and (d) 250 rpm and 17 Watt-hours per kg. (Cauvain 1998a)

is thought to mechanically break the disulfide bonds holding together proteins in their original configurations. If so, then the mechanical action takes the place of natural or chemical reduction to increase the sites available for oxidation.

Chin and Campbell (2004, 2005a, 2005b) investigated the combined effect of the amount and rate of energy input on dough aeration and rheology. Increasing the mixing speed had little effect on the gas-free dough density, they learned, but raising the work input did increase the gas occluded in doughs made with either strong or weak flours (**Figure 6.04**). As mixing proceeded, the air content tended to increase. Rheological values such as the strain hardening index, failure strain and failure stress all initially increased with work input, followed by a decrease.

Functional additives play a big role in this method. Chief among the improvers is ascorbic acid, which oxidizes flour proteins to improve gluten strength. Other such ingredients (and their functions) include azodicarbonamide (oxidizing agent), cysteine (reducing agent), mono- and diglycerides (emulsifiers and anti-staling agents), calcium propionate (mold inhibitor), stearoyl lactylate (dough strengthener), soy flour (crumb whitener), dextrose (fermentable sugar source for the yeast), ammonium chloride (nitrogen source for yeast), enzymes (starch and protein adjustment) and, occasionally, gluten (strengthener).

High-speed dough mixing requires some minor adjustments in other formula components compared with conventional mixing, according to Andrews et al. (1989). An additional 2 to 5% water and 0.5 to 1% yeast (both on a flour weight basis) would be required.

The solid vegetable shortening is also required to bolster structure during baking. Additionally, yeast and water proportions tend to be higher when using this doughmaking method than for conventional mixers. With the bowl sealed during mixing, headspace air becomes the source for gas cells in the dough, and the system is maintained under partial vacuum to prevent the dough from getting "too large."

Doughs are discharged directly to dividers, but because so much energy is imparted to the dough by this method, dough pieces should be rested for at least 8 minutes before further processing.

Cauvain and Young (2006) recently described the development and fundamental characteristics of CBP and how it is applied to making bread. CBP is one of several doughmaking processes identified by Cauvain (1998a) as "activated dough development" methods, all of which use improvers to assist in dough development and reduce fermentation time to less than 1 hour. No-time doughs made in low-speed mixers and continuous mixing are other examples.

High-energy mixers tend to be of smaller capacity than conventional horizontal-bowl mixers, but Fish (1982) argued that the rapidity of mixing (under 5 minutes per batch) yielded smaller, more easily controlled doughs.

By drawing a partial vacuum or adding pressure to the mixer's headspace, the baker can closely control the grain structure of the dough, although there will be a need for extra water (Cauvain 1998a). Similarly, doughs mixed under high pressure will be softer for a given water level. Cell structure as affected by mixing method will be discussed in the Part 6.A.2 of this chapter. The partial vacuum also helps the cooling process during dough mixing.

6.A.1.e. Continuous mixing method

Developed in the 1950s, the continuous mixing method promised — and delivered — the benefits of fast rates, uniform output and good manufacturing economies. Bread formulations changed, however, to answer machining concerns, and some key characteristics of finished baked products differed in subtle ways from conventionally mixed bread. Ultimately, continuous mixing technology for pan-baked bread fell out of common practice by the early 1980s, although some bakers continue to use it to their advantage today, particularly those serving the Southeastern US market.

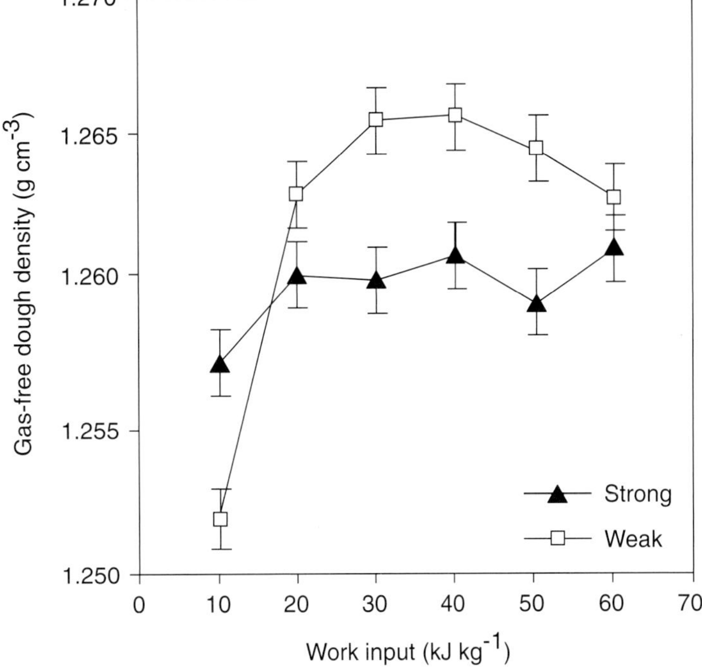

Figure 6.04. Work input changes the density of doughs made from strong and weak flours.
(Chin and Campbell 2004)

Watkins (1985) summarized use of this method for white pan bread as follows. Ingredients are introduced into the first-stage continuous mixer, also termed a pre-mixer, then advanced to and through the second- and final-stage continuous mixer, or developer, and almost immediately extruded and deposited into the pan. At high production rates, the dough is processed in 1 to 2 minutes.

The method requires careful metering of ingredients to assure the correct proportion of each. The ingredients are combined, blended and degassed to form a uniform dough in the pre-mixer. The system advances the raw dough at a controlled rate through the developer where the gluten is conditioned by high-speed mixing to cross-link its proteins. The dough is extruded and shaped with minimal damage to cell structure, cut to suitably sized pieces and dropped directly into the pan.

Application of intensive, high-speed mixing, or energy input, to the dough as it forms in the mixing chamber alters the structure of the flour proteins physically by rupturing their cross-link bonds and simply tearing them apart by force (Glover 1975). The formula, therefore, requires high levels of oxidation to rebuild the protein network. Friction within the mixer causes dough temperatures to rise, thus stimulating yeast activity.

Fermentation is a prerequisite for this method and takes place before the final dough is formed. Liquid preferments evolved as part of the continuous mix process. The fermentation process will be discussed later in this chapter at Part 6.B.

Continuous mixing is well suited for long production runs of similar products, especially white pan bread in open-top and Pullman styles, but it is not useful for open-grain products or short-run items.

As noted above, use of this method of dough mixing is no longer common among most US bread producers. Readers interested in the continuous mixing method and its history of use can consult Authier (1961), Ferrell (1963), Fuhrmann (1955, 1964), Jones (1960), Kamman (1967), Lind (1965), Meyer (1962), Schiller (1968), Trum (1971), Underhill (1966) and Watkins (1985). The rheology of continuously mixed bread doughs was reviewed in detail by Frazier et al. (1975).

Although continuous mixing generally refers to preparation of bread doughs using high-speed, high-energy, small-chamber mixers, the term can also be applied to continuous kneading of cracker, pretzel, pastry and cookie doughs that takes place in screw-style systems. Here, double or single auger screws driven by variable-speed motors carry ingredients through a variety of mixing and kneading conditions, described by Madsen (1994) and Warren (1999).

6.A.1.f. Blended methods

The original continuous-mix process discharged the dough immediately into a pan, with no additional makeup taking place. Bakery engineers refined the process to allow conventional makeup methods (rounding, sheeting and moulding) to be used after the continuous mixer (Beaverson 1968, Cottle 1972, Loudenslager 1974, Watkins 1985).

Because firm dough yielded better results, Carpenter (1977) reported reducing absorption of the continuously mixed dough by cutting water by 2 percentage points at the preferment stage and 3 percentage points on the dough side. When all 5 percentage points were taken out the preferment, it became too stiff for the machinery to handle. The dough-out temperature of 41°C (105°F) was dropped to 27°C (80°F). This reduction was accomplished by running the preferment through a heat exchanger to chill it to 16°C (60°F).

Although bakers prefer that buns be made from stiff cold doughs, these doughs can be produced by continuous mixers. As described by bakers using such methods (Dibble 1977, Watkins 1985), the dough is extruded from the mixer, but not divided, and the developed dough is pumped or conveyed to conventional bun dividing equipment and so processed. A heat exchanger solved the temperature problem and allowed the preferment to be fed into the dough mixer at 10°C (50°F).

Also worth noting is that later bakery engineers took their experience with the continuous mixer's developer section and used its principles to design dough texturizing systems for bun dough handling operations.

Recently, European researchers developed a continuous vacuum dough (COVAD) process that combined a continuous mixing/kneading operation with pressure and vacuum apparatus for modifying the atmospheric conditions during mixing (Alava et al. 2004). This technique allowed modification of dough properties and provided a variety of different final bread structures.

The researchers worked with a standard continuous dough mixer/kneader, adapting its screw auger for production of dough and adding holes along the barrel to allow for addition and subtraction of pressure at various points along the screw.

The improver used was ascorbic acid. Dry ingredients were introduced as the inlet end, along with a solution of salt and yeast. Fat was melted to 57°C (135°F) and pumped separately to the inlet end. A water jacket around the continuous mixer maintained the dough at 24 to 30°C (75 to 86°F). Different dough characteristics were produced by modifying the oxygen availability using pressure during initial stages of processing and by the use of controlled pressure at the end mixing stages.

Additional discussion and detail on continuous mixing can be found at Chapter 9, Part B.

6.A.1.g. Rework

A number of dough processing operations generate considerable amounts of scrap, for example, the die-cutting of laminated or sheeted doughs. Rather than discard this material, many bakers choose to work it back into subsequent batches. In fact, some formulations actually require a certain percentage of "old" dough, deeming it necessary for optimum development of the finished product's flavor. Yeast, which remains active in the dough, continues to generate carbon dioxide, ethanol and flavor compounds that contribute to finished product's taste and texture.

According to processing preference, conveyors or containers catch the scrap dough and then transport it either to the mixing station or to the divider hopper.

When using scrap, the baker must be aware of several factors. First, every pass through the process changes it irreversibly. As Levine (2007) explained, sheeting always results in some breakdown of the dough's viscoelastic structure, while extrusion produces some dextrinization of starch or cross-linking and reduction of proteins in the dough. To gauge the impact of such "aging," he conducted an analysis of dough with a recycle rate of 50%. He rated fresh dough as age 0 and scrap from the first pass as age 1, so a 50:50 blend of fresh and scrap would be age 1.5 at the point it reaches makeup after sheeting. With each pass, the age of the blended dough increases and approaches 2, which means that under steady-state conditions, every piece of dough goes through the sheeting process twice. The expected steady-state age for various levels of recycled dough (with f the fraction recycled) will be:

$$age = 1 \div (1 - f)$$

The matter of dough age has implications for product development, according to Levine (2007). When taking a product out of the lab and running it on the actual production line, company policy usually sets limits to the number of test runs allowed to control costs and minimize interruption to scheduled products. The researcher must optimize doughs to best represent actual production runs. So, instead of testing a product using a 50:50 blend of fresh and old doughs, which only characterizes the second dough in the series, the developer is urged to use as the "old" dough addition one that has passed through the system twice (not just once) or to simply sheet the fresh dough twice.

Absolutely critical when using rework is the practice that "like goes into like" for all products, or else labeling and allergens can become a real issue. Traceability can also be compromised. In addition, consistency and quality can be maintained only if the same amount or percentage of rework is used in each dough.

Not all scrap will be appropriate for rework. The more processed the dough, the less it suits such use. Maintaining scrap as "edible" requires that it be separated from "non-edible" waste. Good sanitation and good housekeeping practices are essential. Misshapen loaves may find use as bread crumbs but not as ingredients for the next batch. Products damaged during packaging are best disposed of through sale to a scrap hauler to be made into animal feed.

6.A.2. Mixing stages

The mixer operator's aim is "getting the dough out in its driest condition, with as high an absorption as possible and, at the same time, of proper consistency so it will machine well" (Daley 1955). The goal is thus to bring about an optimum balance of the rheological properties of the dough. These include, in general terms: (a) plasticity, which enables dough to retain the shape imparted to it by rounding and moulding; (b) viscous flow, or the property of the dough to assume the shape of the pan or other container in which it is placed; (c) elasticity, or the ability of the dough to recover partially from the deformations it undergoes during moulding; and (d) viscoelasticity, which combines viscous and elastic properties and influences dough behavior from makeup to baking.

Mixing blends ingredients into a uniform mixture, dispersing them thoroughly throughout the dough mass. The mixing process also enables development of the dough's proteins by stretching them and orients them in the direction of shear. The physical changes relate to chemical interactions during mixing. In other words, dough mixing has three functions: (a) uniform blending of dough ingredients, (b) hydration of the flour and other dry ingredients and (3) development of the gluten structure.

Hydration overlaps the first stage of mixing (Tipples and Kilborn 1975). After the first half-minute or so, dough consistency levels off before picking up again after about 3 minutes of mixing and increasing to a peak level. This "lag phase" is longer for higher protein flours and at slower mixing speeds, and its existence suggests that hydration must proceed to a sufficient extent before the dough becomes cohesive enough to handle the stretching and kneading action of development.

During the development stage, dough responds to the input of additional work by the mixer. (European researchers and bakers tend to describe this stage as kneading rather than development, but the essential activity is the same: to bring gluten to the optimum condition.) This mixing must take place above a critical speed for gluten to form in an oriented structure consisting of entangled protein fibrils capable of forming the thin, flexible sheets necessary to retain the leavening gases (**Figure 6.05**). If mixer speed is too slow, the dough can relax and will not respond regardless of how long it is mixed.

Bakers often speak of various mixing stages using subjective terms: pickup, cleanup, peak development, letdown and breakdown. Open-bowl systems such as vertical, spiral and wendel mixers and in the McDuffy bowl mixers of the laboratory allow ready observation of these physical stages.

These stages are fairly distinct (Kamman 1970). The objective of the initial stage is merely to ensure the uniform blending of the dough ingredients. The dough at this point is quite slack and rather wet and sticky to the touch. As mixing continues, the dough enters the second, or "pickup" stage, shown in **Figure 6.06**, when the gluten structure begins to form. The "cleanup" stage provides the most definite reference point in the mixing process. As shown in **Figure 6.07**, the developing dough becomes drier and more elastic and forms into a cohesive mass that slaps the back wall of the mixer bowl with each revolution of the mixer arms. This stage is completed when the dough clears or pulls away from the mixer bowl's walls.

The fourth and most critical stage, also referred to as the "development" stage, is

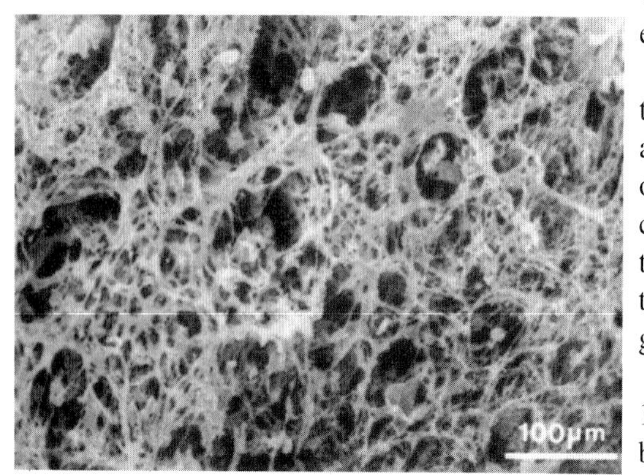
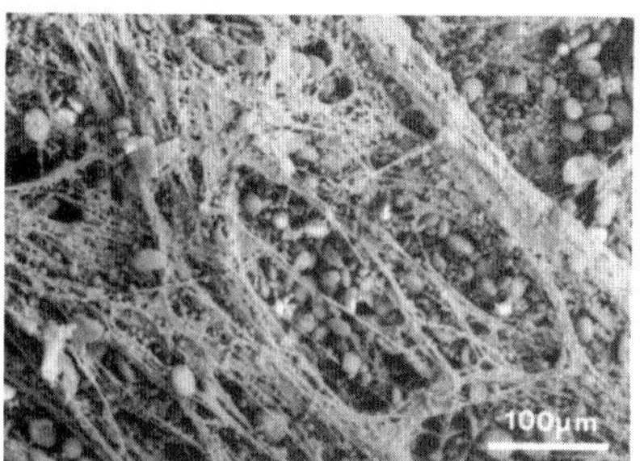
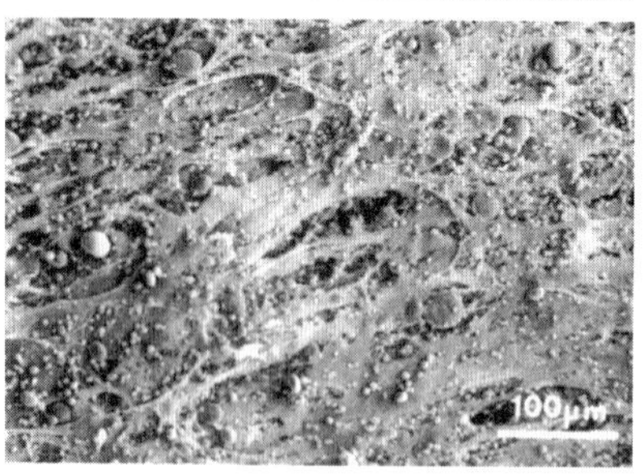

Figure 6.05. Gluten proteins develop into flexible sheets, capable of retaining leavening gases and embedding starch granules. Scanning electron micrographs show (top) a hydrated but minimally mixed dough, (center) a partially developed dough and (bottom) a fully developed dough.
(Stauffer 1997)

shown in **Figure 6.08**. The dough's somewhat dull surface appearance transforms into a smooth, satiny sheen. A dough is said to have "cleared" when a small piece can be stretched into a semitranslucent sheet of uniform thickness, as shown in **Figure 6.09**. Doughs prior to this stage, when subjected to stretching, show strands and lumps and break rather easily (Marston 1971). Fully developed dough exhibits a silky, dry appearance and stretches into smooth, long sheets, as seen in **Figure 6.10**. At this point, it is ready for discharge from the mixer to enter a brief period of recovery, or "floor time," prior to makeup.

Doughs can be mixed too much. After a certain time, additional input of mixing energy harms rather than benefits the dough. The dough will break down, or lose viscosity, with continued mixing. Mixed beyond the development stage, it begins to lose its elastic character and becomea progressively soft, smooth and extensible. The dough now starts to be pulled into long, cohesive strands by the mixer bars. This is the so-called "letdown" stage at which doughs begin to exhibit signs of over-mixing, as illustrated in **Figure 6.11**. Only very strong flours can be safely mixed to this stage without a real risk of subsequent dough failure during the makeup operations.

Carrying the mixing operation beyond this point results in complete disintegration of the dough. It becomes wet, excessively slack and stringy, without any elastic properties, and can no longer be salvaged for breadmaking under practical production conditions. The appearance of such over-mixed dough is shown in **Figure 6.12**.

Also, doughs can become "unmixed," a condition better described as disoriented because it exhibits only random cross-linking, not the highly oriented structure of properly developed gluten. Tipples and Kilborn (1975) found that mixing a dough to peak consistency and beyond at speeds well below the minimum speed required for optimum development changed the character and appearance of the dough, making it appear under-mixed. Bread baked from such doughs resembled that of under-mixed doughs. By speeding up the mixer, they found that "unmixed" doughs redeveloped to peak consistency and made bread of the same quality as that of the initial dough before it was unmixed.

Although bakery scientists have learned much about the rheological aspects of dough, the related science of turbulent flow is also involved, according to Fay (2008), and suggests new areas of study, particularly for examining how mixers form doughs. For example, stratified laminar flow impedes full dispersion and can be a problem in the mechanical design of mixers, leading to poor uniformity of dough temperature or cell structure in large batches. Amplified turbulence at the start of the mixing sequence could lead to better aeration in the early stages of dough formation even before the folding action of pickup and cleanup stages kicks in.

6.A.2.a. Flour hydration

The mixing process promotes hydration by exposing new surfaces of the flour particle to water. Coarse meals and some fiber ingredients need more time for hydration than fine flours, and cold doughs need more time to absorb the dough water than warmer doughs (Doerry

Figure 6.06. Dough during the initial or pickup stage is slack, wet and sticky. (Swortfiguer 1950)

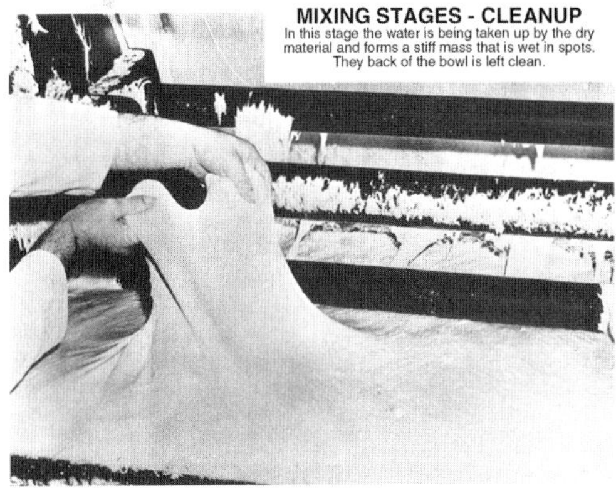

Figure 6.07. At cleanup, hydration of ingredients is completed. (Swortfiguer 1950)

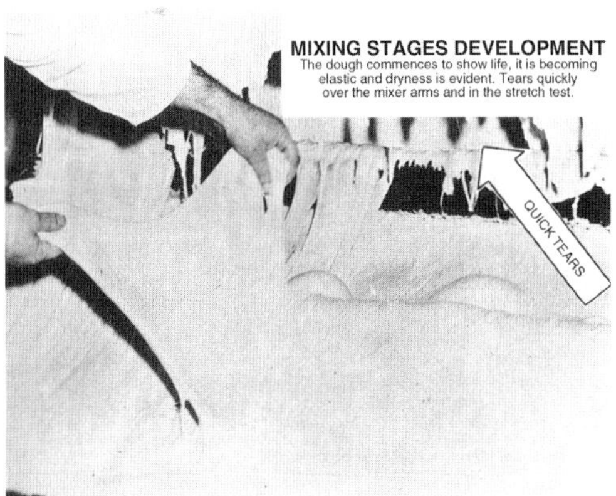

Figure 6.08. During the development stage, dough becomes elastic, with signs of dryness. (Swortfiguer 1950)

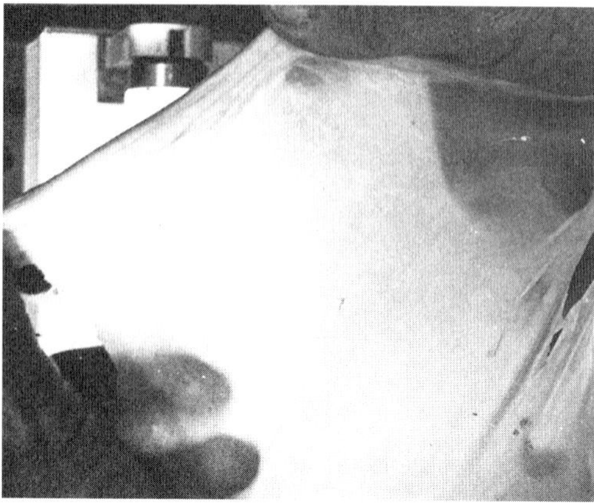

Figure 6.09. A "cleared" dough at full development can be stretched into a thin membrane without breaking. (Marston 1971)

Figure 6.10. At the final stage of mixing, the dough reaches optimum development. (Swortfiguer 1950)

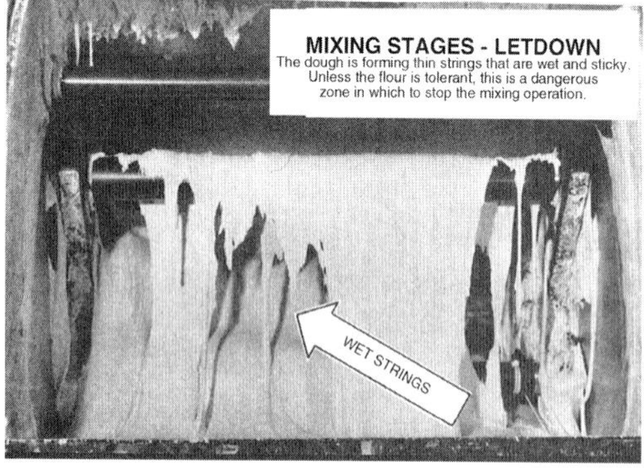

Figure 6.11. Doughs mixed beyond their final stage begin to show signs of letdown. (Swortfiguer 1950)

1995a). It is not possible to make dough without water, and the water content of standard bread dough is about 40%.

Hydration of the flour particles by the dough water weakens the starch-protein bonds and, with the addition of mechanical energy in the form of mixing, gradually transforms the flour-water mass from a wet, sticky mixture into a coherent, smooth and seemingly homogeneous dough.

During mixing, water molecules come into contact with reactive chemical groups in the starch, dextrins, proteins and pentosans with which they interact by means of hydrogen bonds. The actual time required to achieve uniform flour particle hydration depends on factors such as the size and vitreosity of the flour particles, intensity of mixing action and the presence of added ingredients such as salt, dairy products, enzyme supplements, protein additives and so forth. In conventional mixing, the estimated time required to produce a uniform dough is about 10 minutes, while at the ultra-high speeds that prevail in continuous and other mixing systems, complete hydration appears to be achieved within 1 minute. The rate of hydration is closely related to the rapidity with which water can be brought into intimate contact with each flour particle. The tremendous surface area of flour, estimated by Bushuk and Winkler (1957) to be about 235 sq m per g (2,538 sq ft), ensures ready availability of reactive groupings.

Flour particles usually have a diameter of less than 100 μm and immediately start to absorb water as soon as they are wetted. This action takes place very fast, within a few seconds. The amount of water absorbed by a flour particle depends on the availability of the water. At the start of mixing, much water is available to the outer surfaces of the flour particles, and they absorb it easily; however, the first particles to be moistened absorb more than their share of water, leaving a suboptimal amount of water for the other particles. Thus, early in mixing, the moisture is unevenly distributed among the flour particles. One of the functions of the rest of the mixing time is to redistribute the moisture more evenly throughout the dough (Sluimer 2005).

Bushuk (1966) estimated that 45.5% of the total water in dough is held by starch, 31.2% by flour proteins and 23.4% by pentosans. The relative hygroscopicity these flour constituents is evident from their respective proportions of 68%, 14% and 1.5%, respectively, in which they occur in flour. Intact starch granules will absorb about one-half their weight of water, but damaged starch can take up about twice its weight. Flour proteins will similarly absorb about twice their weight of water, while pentosans have a hydration capacity about 15 times their weight. Some changes in water distribution occur during dough fermentation and proofing, mainly as a result of the enzymatic hydrolysis of starch into dextrins of lower hygroscopicity (Bushuk 1966). This reaction may result in the release of 2 to 4% of water that must be absorbed by the flour proteins or else dough slackness and stickiness will occur.

Peak flour absorption precedes the achievement of peak protein development. To determine this, Dempster et al. (2004) used a near infrared spectrometer to monitor lab-scale doughs during mixing through full development. The relationship between absorption and protein development makes sense because gluten cannot form until gliadin and glutenen get wet. Relatively new knowledge indicates that free water exists in the dough longer than previously though, remaining unabsorbed into the flour even 3 to 6 minutes into the mixing cycle.

For a dough to attain optimum consistency, the input of a certain amount of work is required, which can be expressed by the simple equation:

$$W = T \times N \times R$$

where W = the work input, T = mixing time, N = an efficiency factor for the mixer and R = mixer speed (Hoseney and Finney 1974). If the factor N were constant at all mixer speeds, then the work input would be directly proportional to mixing time and mixer speed. Kilborn and Tipples (1972) showed, however, that mixer efficiency increases with mixer speed. Moreover, mixing is accompanied by the phenomenon of dough relaxation that must be taken into account. The original formula thus becomes:

$$W = T \times N \times R - (T \times K)$$

Figure 6.12. Excessively over-mixed dough breaks down and shows signs of liquefaction.
(Swortfiguer 1950)

where K = a relaxation factor.

At high N × R values, the relaxation factor is insignificant, and given a constant efficiency, mixing time varies linearly with mixer speed. With low N × R values, however, the relaxation factor becomes significant and increases the mixing time.

Once the dough mass begins to cohere at the start of mixing, its resistance to extension increases to a peak that characterizes the "mixing time" of the flour and is variously designated as the "point of minimum mobility" or "optimum mixing time" (Hoseney and Finney 1974). Mixing beyond this point greatly alters the dough's structure and eventually leads to its breakdown. Hlynka (1970) theorized that the slackness of over-mixed doughs results from a directional orientation of the long-chain wheat protein molecules that, in turn, promotes laminar flow in the dough.

The resulting increase in protein-to-protein interaction by means of hydrogen bonds causes a release of water, and this imparts a wet, sticky character to the over-mixed dough. More important, the protein network of the dough has been altered to reduce its gas retention capacity and, hence, its loaf volume potential.

Mixing time is further influenced by various dough additives. Salt, for example, increases dough mixing time, as does shortening. On the other hand, cysteine decreases the mixing time. Excessive absorption, by reducing the dough's resistance to extension, increases its mixing time, whereas insufficient absorption decreases it.

Hydration tends to proceed slowly in spiral mixers, and this led Noll (2002) to develop a system to hydrate flour by shooting a high-pressure stream of water at a cascade of falling flour. The rapid jet hydration yields a pre-dough with a random gluten matrix.

6.A.2.b. Gluten development

The rheological and chemical changes that take place when dough is mixed have been extensively investigated in recent years. A comprehensive review of this work has been provided by Bloksma (1971, 1990a, 1990b), Faridi et al. (1985) Faridi and Faubion (1986, 1990), among others, as well as in Volume I, Chapter 1, Parts D and G.

The marked changes in dough appearance and behavior during the development stage of mixing have been attributed by Hlynka (1962) to a basic alteration in the gluten's flow characteristics. During its initial stage of mixing, dough behaves as if it consisted of minute protein units that flow as discrete units. With continued stretching and folding action, these units are transformed into elongated strands and fibrils that exhibit laminar flow and a tendency to form thin, highly extensible films (Bernardin and Kasarda 1973). In fact, proper dough development requires additional mixing after the peak of maximum resistance.

Tsen (1970) proposed the concept of "disaggregation" to explain this change to laminar flow during mixing. Flour has been shown to contain distinct protein aggregates or bodies. In doughmaking, these protein bodies first undergo hydration and disaggregation into smaller protein units that are more susceptible to the molecular orientation required for continuous protein film formation. Disaggregation may result from physical action such as the shearing effect produced by the mixing element or from the chemical scission of disulfide bonds by reducing agents such as cysteine, glutathione and ascorbic acid.

Dough is a complex viscoelastic system that, at the molecular level, may be visualized as a 3-dimensional network made up of long protein chains linked together by various types of chemical bonds or linkages. The most significant of these is the covalent disulfide bond ($-SS-$), which, through sulfhydryl-disulfide interchange reactions, readily adapts to the dynamic requirements imposed by the mixing action. The interchange of disulfide bonds is thought to be initiated by their reduction by thiol, or sulfhydryl (SH), groups. While there is about a 10-fold predominance of $-SS-$ groups over SH groups in wheat protein, a limited number of thiol groups is capable of catalyzing the interchange of a large number of $-SS-$ bonds. The reduction of only 7% of the disulfide bonds in a dough has been shown to produce a profound change in the latter's physical properties (Hlynka 1964). Other major bonds include the hydrogen bonds, hydrophobic bonds, salt linkages and van der Waals forces. Hydrogen bonds are formed primarily by the numerous amide groups of glutamine residues of wheat protein, while such nonpolar amino acid residues as leucine and valine form hydrophobic bonds in the presence of water. Both types of bonds are labile and interchange readily during mixing and thereby facilitate the development of the optimum dough structure (Bushuk 1984).

Farrand (1972) viewed dough formation primarily as an action involving the disaggregation of the protein particles of flour, their hydration to form gluten and the spreading of the gluten over the surface of the free starch granules to form a continuous matrix. In this concept, a principal requirement is that sufficient gluten be formed to adequately cover the surface of the starch, otherwise a claylike dough will result that will lack gas retention. Such a deficient dough is likely to result with flours whose protein content is less than about 7%. Moreover, if excessive amounts of the starch granules are damaged in milling, both their water absorption and particle size will increase. The gluten will not only have to cover a correspondingly enlarged starch surface area but will also have to compete for water of hydration with the highly hygroscopic damaged starch. Hence, there exists a basic relationship between the protein content of flour and the permissible level of starch damage, which has been expressed by Farrand as:

$$(\% \text{ Protein})^2 \div 6$$

or the square of the percent protein content divided by the factor 6. Accordingly, flour with a 12% protein content can tolerate a 24% level of starch damage.

The quality of the flour has a pronounced effect on the mixing behavior of the dough. Using light and transmission electron microscopy to observe the effects of various factors in doughmaking, Bechtel et al. (1978) and Pomeranz (1980a, 1980b) found that an optimally mixed dough made from a good-quality composite flour exhibited an even and continuous gluten matrix. Over-mixing caused the protein matrix to lose its continuity, with the appearance of many large vacuoles and broken protein strands; however, such an over-mixed dough could be restored to its former optimally mixed state by being allowed to relax and then gently remixed. In contrast, doughs from poor-quality flour formed weak protein strands that failed to form a continuous gluten matrix. Thus, the relative tensile strength of hydrated proteins appears to govern the structure of the dough.

Mattern and Sandstedt (1957) attributed the variable mixing requirements of different flours to the water-soluble protein gliadin. When gliadin extracted from flour was added to a dough, it effectively shortened the dough's mixing requirements. On the other hand, replacing part of the normal flour with water-extracted flour extended the dough's mixing requirements. This finding received additional support from the observation that greater quantities of water-soluble protein can be extracted from flour milled from short-mixing wheat varieties than from long-mixing wheat varieties.

Khoo et al. (1975) explored the structural relationships of protein and starch in a good-quality bread flour at various dough stages by scanning electron microscopy. Prior to hydration, flour protein, as shown in **Figure 6.13**, appears in jagged pieces, with some being wedged between the starch granules. When fully hydrated in a mixed dough, the protein forms a veil-like film over the external surface of the starch granules, as seen in **Figure 6.14**. Observed through a fracture in the dough surface (FS), many cleaved starch granules (CSG) are embedded in a protein matrix with numerous microscopic holes. The innate fibrillar form of the protein strands in the matrix is quite apparent.

6.A.2.c. Time aspects

Blending and hydration usually occurs within a few minutes of mixing's starts, but development of the gluten will require significantly more mixing time and the additional energy that is put into the dough by that additional processing time. Bakers must be certain to mix their doughs to optimum gluten development to produce the best finished results.

Gluten protein bonding and alignment advance at a rapid rate for 30 to 60 seconds after the mechanical mixing action has stopped and continue more slowly for several additional minutes (Fay 2008). From this, he suggested that optimal mixing time for yeast-raised doughs is somewhere between 6 and 8 minutes. "Mixing longer only costs money," he observed.

The time required by dough to reach the cleanup stage varies with different flours.

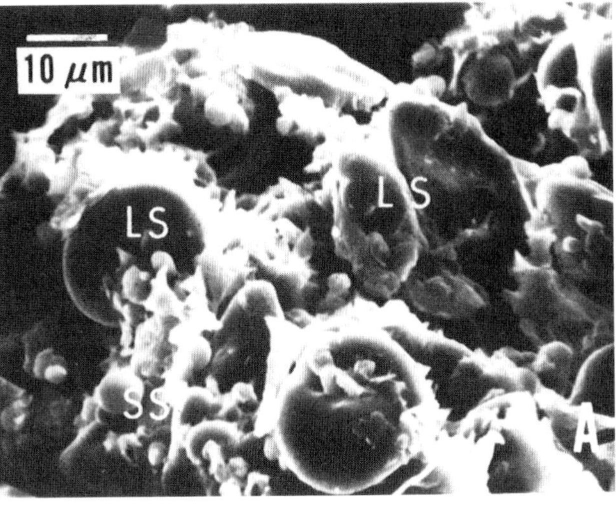

Figure 6.13. At 1,000 × magnification, a scanning electron micrograph of endosperm flour particles reveals lenticular starch (LS) and spherical starch (SS). (Khoo et al. 1975)

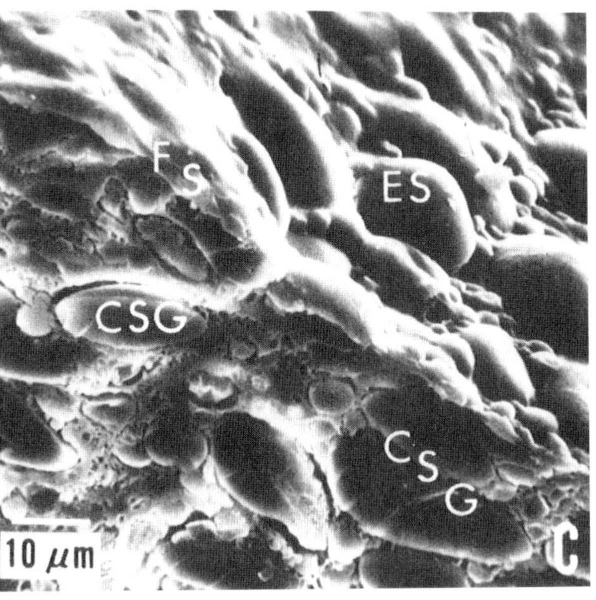

Figure 6.14. At 1,000 × magnification, a scanning electron micrograph of newly mixed dough shows the veil-like coating of protein on starch granules (ES). Through a fracture in the surface (FS), one can see the many cleaved starch granules (CSG) in a protein matrix with microscopic gas cells. (Khoo et al. 1975).

Cleanup in a dough mixer is 2 to 7 minutes under almost any condition. If cleanup takes longer, the baker will generally decrease water, and if shorter, water should be added. According to Clark (1947), the critical point in the mixing cycle that should govern the total mixing operation is the cleanup stage because it denotes "an equilibrium between all the forces of absorption, ingredients, mixing speed, temperature and flour quality. All such forces contending for supremacy up to this point are balanced." Dough appearance at this stage is illustrated in **Figure 6.07** (Section 6.A.2.).

Factors that exert a measurable effect on optimum mixing time include, among others, temperature, absorption level, flour strength, point of salt addition, use of oxidizing and reducing agents, enzyme supplementation and mixer design and speed (Dalby 1960). Baker (1964) reported that an increase of as little as 1.1 C° (2 F°) in the normal temperature of the sponge being returned to the dough mixer may extend the time required for the dough to reach cleanup enough to result in under-mixed doughs if mixing is held to a fixed schedule. Stiff doughs require less time than do slack doughs to reach cleanup. If doughs arrive at cleanup earlier than normal, then a slight increase in the absorption of the dough may be in order.

Fungal enzymes can reduce mixing requirements by as much as 20%, depending on the level used. Delay of the salt addition has a similar effect and may further improve absorption by 1.0%. Low protein or weak flours will often reach their optimum development at the cleanup stage at which point mixing should be ended. Strong flours, on the other hand, may require mixing considerably beyond the clean-up stage.

Sternberg (1968) stated that increasing the surface area of the mixing bars by fluting them not only increased their traction and transferred more mechanical work to the dough to improve mixing efficiency but also promoted more uniform gluten development. Under practical bakery plant conditions, mixers modified in this manner reduced mixing time by as much as 25% at normal water absorption, and by 10% when absorption was increased by 1 to 2%.

An experienced baker will be able to determine how much additional mixing should be imparted to a dough after it has reached the cleanup stage on the basis of "dough feel." As indicated earlier, the transition from clean-up to development, when the dough assumes a smooth and dry appearance and becomes elastic and extensible, takes only a few minutes. For most normal bread flours, this state constitutes the optimum mixing development. The precise time at which to stop mixing is best determined experimentally by running a limited series of trial doughs in which the mixing time following cleanup is extended by 1-minute increments. By comparing the performance of the doughs during subsequent makeup and by scoring the finished bread, the optimum mixing time for a given flour can readily be established. Normally, bread flours have sufficient mixing tolerance to withstand changes of such small magnitude without detracting from final bread quality to an extent that would make the product unsalable.

Serious errors committed in mixing are difficult, and often impossible, to fix during subsequent stages of processing. Under-mixed doughs, with inadequate gluten development, lack smoothness and exhibit stickiness during makeup operations. They produce loaves with caved-in sides, reduced volume, streaky crumb and coarse grain. Over-mixed doughs also are sticky and excessively slack and are difficult to process properly during makeup. The bread made from them exhibits many of the faults that characterize bread from under-mixed doughs.

Daley (1955) reviewed the practical aspects of dough mixing and concluded: (a) the cleanup time is a good reference point for establishing optimum mixing time; (b) sponge temperature, while without effect on cleanup time, influences optimum mixing time; (c) reducing the dough's absorption shortens the mixing time; (d) rich formula doughs require longer mixing than do lean doughs; (e) there is an inverse relation between mixer speed and mixing time; (f) delayed salt addition reduces mixing time, increases water absorption and slightly depresses dough temperatures; (g) the mixing time is positively correlated with the subsequent floor time (longer mixing times call for extended floor times); and (h) the method of dough ejection from the mixer should be standardized to ensure uniform dough treatment at this stage.

Concern over sticky doughs during makeup often causes bakers to use less than optimal absorption, a situation that may not only result in reduced bread yields but also in unsatisfactory product quality. The aim should always be the optimum absorption of which a flour is capable, and that level will yield quality bread. In the US, federal Standards of Identity establish the legal limit for residual moisture in white bread at 38%; however, variety bread, light bread or other types not regulated by such standards will oftentimes exceed 38% residual moisture.

The flour components that govern the amount of water that a flour can absorb and efficiently carry through to the loaf of bread have been discussed by Meredith (1969) and Swortfiguer (1968). The progressive changes in the physical and rheological properties of dough that take place at the various stages of the mixing process were detailed by Swortfiguer (1950).

6.A.2.d. Cell creation

More than 70% of the final volume of bread consists of gas contained in a network of cells, so the incorporation of air into the dough is another important aspect of mixing. Flour itself contains air, representing about 20% of its mass, but additional air must be occluded during mixing. Dough density measurements show that the rate of this incorporation increases as the dough becomes more cohesive. By the time the dough has reached the optimum mixing point, it will have incorporated about one-half the total amount of air it can absorb (Hoseney 1984).

In finished baked foods, gas cells form the small voids in the crumb responsible for the product's grain. The grain, or crumb structure, contributes to texture, eating quality, mechanical strength and perceived product freshness, as well as visual appeal. In general, small voids are preferable to large ones, except in products such as focaccia and rustic breads where large cells are desirable.

When considering dough as a colloidal system, its continuous phase consists essentially of the gluten gel, which acts like a liquid (Eliasson and Larsson 1993). The starch also forms a continuous starch-water phase. Air and leavening gases form the discontinuous phase.

Gas cells resist failure, and thus contribute to the expansion of dough during proofing and baking, by virtue of dual film protection in the form of a primary gluten-starch matrix with a secondary liquid lamella on its inner side, enveloping the gas cells (Gan et al. 1995, Sroan et al. 2009, Sroan and MacRitchie 2009). Gas cell failure, however, results in coalescence of cells and an open crumb grain. Hayman et al. (1998) suggested that such failure was an effect of starch granule size, particularly the large granules in wheat flour. When gas cells coalesce, they do so very quickly taking less than 0.04 (or $^{1}/_{25}$) second (Weegels et al. 2003).

Mixing is solely responsible for formation of the gas cells in dough that create the inviting crumb texture of the finished product (Baker and Mize 1941). The mixer's tumbling and folding actions entrain air from its headspace into the dough and sub-divide it. Carbon dioxide and gaseous ethanol generated by yeast during fermentation do not form new cells; instead, these gases migrate to existing cells, which act as nucleation sites. Air accompanying wheat flour particles also supplies a small portion of cell nuclei (Shimiya and Yano 1987).

Gases produced by the yeast, studied by Hibbert and Parker (1976) as primarily carbon dioxide (CO_2), dissolve in the liquid dough phase. As the concentration of CO_2 reaches 4.3×10^{-2} kmoles per cu m at 27°C (80°F), its rate of evaporation increases and the rate of gas cell growth also rises. When CO_2 reaches equilibrium with gaseous CO_2 in the atmosphere, the liquid dough phase cannot absorb more of this gas. From then on, the evaporation of CO_2 and the expansion of gas cells keep pace with the production of CO_2 (Bloksma 1990a).

Addition of surface-active agents (sodium stearoyl lactylate, ethoxylated mono-glycerides, DATEM, among others) with the dough ingredients was shown by Junge et al. (1981) to impart a fine grain to bread. The surfactants did not so much change the amount of air occluded, but they did help form and stabilize smaller cells during mixing, followed by more subdivision of cells during punching, thus resulting in the fine grain of the finished product.

The growth and function of air cells in doughs involves four key aspects: (a) disappearance of oxygen in the dough as soon as mixing stops, making the dough anaerobic; (b) diffusion of CO_2 from yeast cells to gas nuclei; (c) change by CO_2 from a dissolved to a gaseous state; and (d) generation of excess pressure in gas cells that produces dough expansion (Sluimer 2005).

Through its oxidative action, the oxygen of air causes the accelerated disappearance of the flour's thiol groups and thereby increases the dough's resistance to extension, decreases its mobility and mixing time, and increases its rate of breakdown on continued mixing beyond the optimum point (Tsen and Bushuk 1963). Smith and Andrews (1957) showed a direct relationship between flour grade and rate of oxygen uptake. Thus, doughs made from patent flour were found to absorb 200 parts per million (ppm) of oxygen, compared to 880 ppm absorbed by doughs from second-clear flour. They also found that the oxygen uptake during mixing varied directly with the free fatty acid content of the flour, which suggests a peroxidation of the lipids. The resultant lipid peroxides are then capable of oxidizing the thiol groups and producing an improving effect (Tsen and Hlynka 1963).

Oxidation is essential for optimum dough characteristics. As Baker and Mize (1941) observed, an unoxidized, or "green," dough does not have the capacity to prevent its air cells from coalescing during proofing and baking, yet an over-oxidized dough cannot withstand the action of punching and moulding without breaking existing cells.

The quantity of air incorporated during mixing varies with the type of mixer used (Cauvain et al. 1999), as shown in **Figure 6.15**. These results compare high-speed mixers typical of UK commercial wholesale bakeries and the spiral mixers more commonly found among craft bakers and are in line with the differences seen in loaves made by the two mixer types.

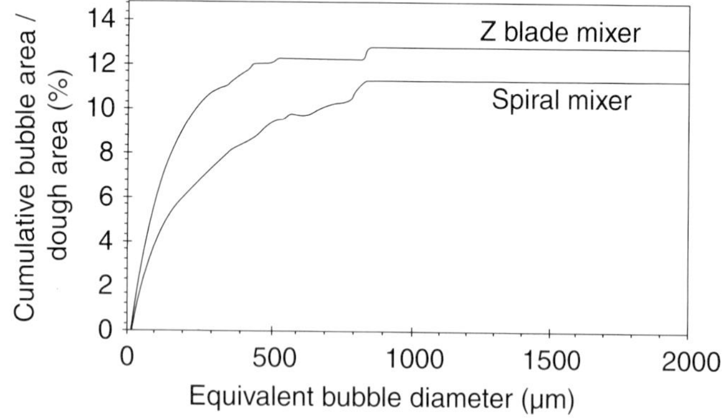

Figure 6.15. A Z-blade mixer (upper curve) produces a different distribution of bubble sizes than does a spiral mixer. (Cauvain et al. 1999)

Under vacuum and/or pressure. Given that the air present in the mixer headspace is the source for the gas cells created in doughs during mixing, how would different proportions of gases change the texture of finished products? Cereal scientists have researched this topic and also examined the effects of mixing under vacuum conditions. Because the Chorleywood Bread Process (CBP) uses a sealed-bowl mixer, its air-tight conditions provide a good way to test such environments.

Bakery researchers have examined the effect of vacuum on doughmaking for many years. Baker and Mize (1937) started their experiment by assuming that a dough mixed under vacuum would have no air occlusions, so all the cells would originate independently by forming around each individual yeast cell or group of cells as the yeast gave off carbon dioxide and ethanol. They expected such doughs to bake out with a very fine cell structure. This theory turned out not to be true. What they got was dough that gassed freely and seemed unable to retain gas. After the first punch, however, the doughs and their baked results became normal in character. They experimented with various mixtures of gases, including nitrogen, oxygen and hydrogen. Dough mixed in hydrogen or nitrogen did absorb the gases, but mixing took more time, and the doughs became soft and sticky but not short. When mixed in pure oxygen, less gas was taken up than when mixed in air, and doughs quickly became soft and short. As they continued to explore cell formation, they discovered that it depended solely on air occluded during mixing (Baker and Mize 1941).

Described by Chamberlain and Collins (1979), a high vacuum intended to remove most of the air bubbles resulted in a few large cells surrounded by waxy cell walls and crumb devoid of the fine bubbles found in normal bread (**Figure 6.16**). When pure oxygen replaced air in the mixer's headspace, results were similar (**Figure 6.17**). Researchers speculated that the yeast removes considerable quantities of oxygen from CBP doughs. Others have since reported the same depletion from gas cells of oxygen taken up by yeast respiration in doughs made by other methods. Nitrogen, present as 78% of air, was theorized as necessary to ensure adequate bubble formation.

A review of the textural effects of mixing bread doughs using the Chorleywood Bread Process under modified atmospheres (air and carbon dioxide) and diverse pressure conditions was provided by Martin et al. (2008). Dough mixed under pure CO_2 resulted in coarse crumb structure, especially at lower pressures. Mixing under air yielded crumb structure that also coarsened as the pressure increased. Sluimer (2005) summarized the effects of mixing doughs under various blends of atmospheric gases.

Cauvain and Young (2001) reported that a partial vacuum produced optimum results in CBP doughs for fine-grained products, while pressures above atmospheric yielded open-grain finished goods. An earlier work (Cauvain 1998a) noted that mixers capable of working sequentially at pressures above and below atmospheric normal gave greater control over dough bubble populations to create a wide range of cell structures, ranging from fine and uniform at partial vacuum to wide open at high pressures. Doughs produced this way retain their larger gas bubbles in the dough without significant damage during processing.

Even though such bubbles are less dense than the dough, they tend not to rise within the dough's interior because of the viscoelastic nature of the gluten structure. Films composed of starch and gluten form the lining of these cells and help the bubbles resist coalescence that would coarsen the texture of the final product.

Although mixing comprises the only processing stage that creates new air cells in the dough, subsequent doughmaking stages enlarge individual cells or subdivide larger ones. **Figure 6.18** shows the cumulative bubble size distribution for doughs mixed in a high-speed CBP-type mixer.

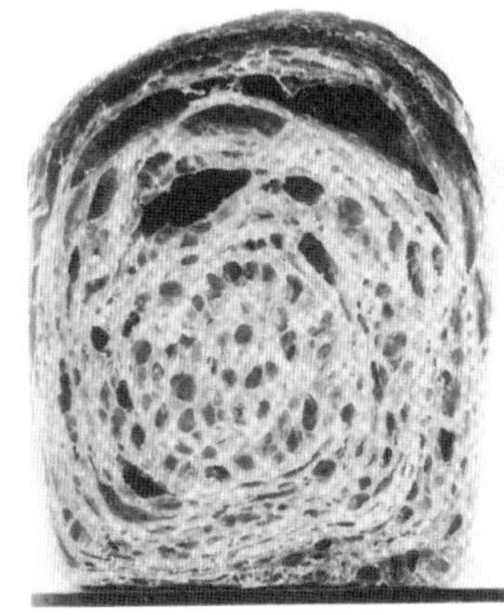

Figure 6.16. Vacuum conditions (28 in. Hg, or 711 mm Hg) in a CBP mixer yields bread with large cells and no fine bubbles in its crumb. (Chamberlain and Collins 1979)

Figure 6.17. Pure oxygen resulted in finished bread lacking fine bubbles. (Chamberlain and Collins 1979)

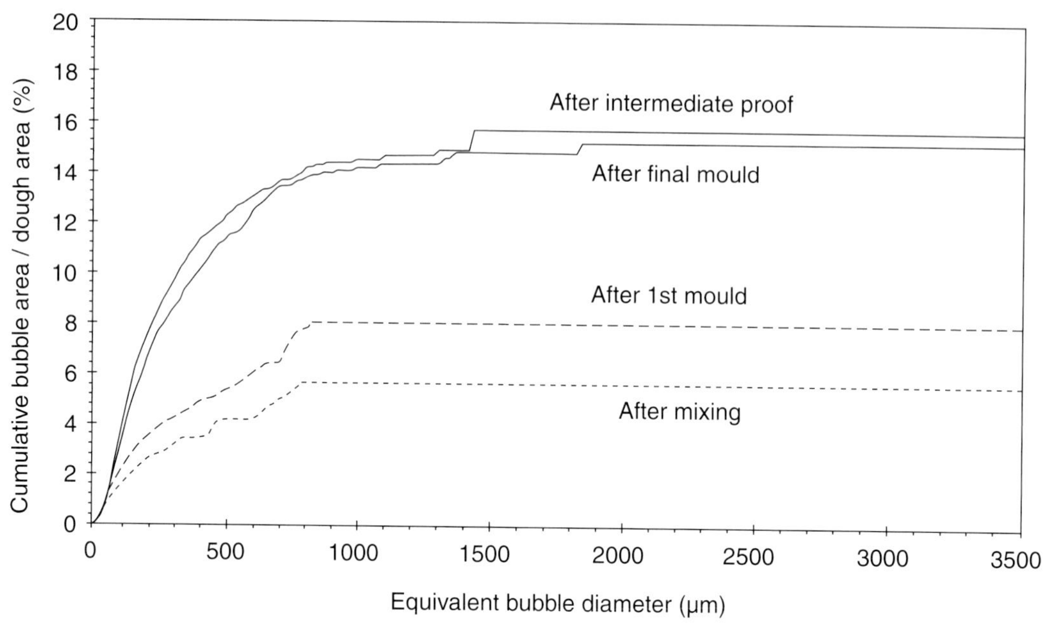

Figure 6.18. Measured at stages from mixing to final makeup ("1st mould" indicates rounding), bubble size distribution changes the most during intermediate proofing. (Whitworth and Alava 1999)

Some baked foods — for example, English muffins, crumpets and pancakes — exhibit an unusual columnar cell structure. The vertical bubbles often penetrate to and through the top surface. As observed by Sadd (2008), this structure is due partly to the manufacturing process (dropping the batter on a heavy hotplate or griddle with a high thermal capacity, which provides high sustained heat flux in the early stages of cooking) and partly to gas phase physics (heat being transferred inside the growing bubbles by the evaporation and condensation of water). The drying base crust releases steam, which collects in the gas cells, and the batter, thus warmed by heat from the condensing steam, releases carbon dioxide into the bubbles. The bubbles expand vertically into the cold batter. To achieve this columnar cell structure, the tops of the bubbles must rise faster than the batter's starch is set by heat from the griddle.

Measuring cell structure and quantifying this essential characteristic of finished product quality has been made easier by modern data analysis methods. Development and use of image analysis systems were detailed in Volume I, Chapter 4, Part H.

6.A.2.e. Heat balance
Dough mixing causes a perceptible rise in the temperature of the dough mass. The two major sources for this increase in temperature are the heat of hydration of flour and the heat generated by the frictional forces of mixing, which is by far the more important factor.

6.A.2.e.i. Heat of hydration
When a substance takes up water, its energy level changes due to the heat of hydration. Quite frequently, hydration involves a release of energy and results in a rise in temperature, as in the case of flour. The heat of hydration produced by flour is influenced by its original moisture content and will average 6.15 Btu (British thermal units) per lb of flour with a normal moisture level of 11 to 12%. One Btu is the quantity of heat required to raise, or to lower, the temperature of 1 lb of water by 0.56 C° (1 F°).

In the case of soluble crystalline substances such as salt and sugar, this change in energy level is termed latent heat of solution. It is often a negative value because energy is absorbed by the dissolving action, and the overall system is thereby cooled. For example, the relative heat-absorbing capacity of sucrose is 10 Btu per lb, and that of glucose, 45.8 Btu, so when these two substances are dissolved, they withdraw corresponding amounts of heat from the system and counteract to some degree the heat generating effects of hydration and frictional forces (Newton 1961).

The specific heat of individual ingredients also exerts an influence on the temperature rise of a dough. It represents the amount of heat, measured in Btus, these substances absorb before their temperatures rise. For example, wetting 1 lb of flour generates 6.5 Btu of heat. Thus, the latent heat of hydrating the flour is often the biggest heat factor in mixing of doughs. This raises issues not only when taking formulations from the lab bench to the plant floor but also when designing the mixer itself.

6.A.2.e.ii. Frictional heat

Dough temperature will rise with the input of work, or energy, by the action of the mixer arms and the rubbing of the dough against bowl surfaces. Frictional heat is produced by the mechanical energy supplied by the mixer motor that is needed to overcome the internal and external frictional forces created whenever dough is worked or kneaded.

The amount of friction so created is related to dough absorption and to the state of gluten development, with the power requirements rising as dough consistency increases. Gluten development requires a relatively high amount of energy, much of which is absorbed by the dough as heat. Most of this heat is surplus and must be dissipated or absorbed by other ingredients such as water.

The amount of heat generated in a dough is also directly proportional to the duration of mixing. Sponges, with their short mixing times, normally accumulate less heat than do doughs. Thus, frictional heat is a product principally of the horsepower rating of the mixer's motor, the degree of water absorption and the duration of the mixing process. In general, the heat produced by the mixer motor is of the order of 42.5 Btu per motor horsepower per minute of mixing time.

6.A.2.e.iii. Heat removal

The heat generated during mixing must be removed by one means or another so that the dough comes out of the mixer at a temperature of 26 to 27°C (78 to 80°F). The reduction in temperature is generally achieved by one or more of three methods: (a) use of ice; (b) use of chilled ingredient water; and (c) application of mechanical refrigeration to the mixer bowl.

When added as ice, water can draw off an enormous amount of this excess heat. Ice at 0°C (32°F) absorbs 144 Btus of latent heat energy before it converts to water. When calculating cooling efficiency, 1 ton of refrigeration provides the cooling effect of melting 2,000 lb of ice at 0°C (32°F) in 24 hours, equaling 288,000 Btu per day or 200 Btu per minute. Ice has a specific heat of 0.5 Btu per lb and at -18°C (0°F) will absorb 16 Btu per lb to reach its melting point, and an additional 8 Btu is absorbed in raising the temperature of the melted ice from 0°C (32°F) to 4.4° (40°F), which is the temperature of the chilled dough water typically added to dough.

When using ice in doughmaking, its weight must be tallied as part of the formula water. Too much ice can inhibit yeast action, unless the yeast is added at the end of the mixing cycle when all ice has melted into water. The use of ice in baking is described in Volume I, Chapter 2, Part A.

To better control dough temperatures, horizontal bread mixers are often equipped with cooling jackets through which glycol or Freon circulates. Bowl sides and beater bars may also have such cooling features. These refrigerated surfaces then absorb some of the excess heat as the dough contacts them. Discussion of these equipment technologies is offered in Chapter 9, Part B, and Chapter 10, Part F.

6.A.2.e.iv. Calculating heat balance

Properly estimating the cooling requirements that will ensure dough of the desired temperature is an important control measure in dough mixing. The procedure for determining the refrigeration requirements under various temperature and mixing conditions have been described by several authors, including Eckstedt (1949), Stribling (1947), and Harrel and Thelen (1959). The following summary is based primarily on the discussion by Valentyne (1959). These principals apply to all doughs, including cake batters and cookie doughs.

Factors include variables such as the sensible heats of flour, dough water and sponge, and of such small ingredients as sugar, salt, yeast, etc. These must be known because the ambient temperatures of these dough components very rarely approach the final dough temperature.

In addition, the amount of heat contributed by more or less constant factors such as heat of hydration and frictional heat, and the specific heats of major ingredients (flour, dough and water) must also be known. These constant factors have all been estimated and the following generally accepted values assigned to them, as noted in **Table 6.06**.

Because the cooling capacity must be adequate for the maximum loads encountered, which occur during the dough-mixing stage of the sponge-and-dough process — the following example of calculating the heat balance is based on a 1,600-lb dough made from the following materials:

Sponge (with 70% of formula flour)	800 lb
Flour	245 lb
Water	355 lb
Small ingredients	200 lb
Total dough weight	1,600 lb

Further assumptions include:

Mixing schedule	4 doughs per hour
Average mixing time	10 minutes each
Final dough temperature	27°C (80°F)
Flour sensible heat	38°C (100°F)
Flour moisture	Heat of hydration of 6.5 Btu per lb per F°
Specific heat of flour, sponge, small ingredients (Btu per lb per F°)	0.42 (flour), 0.60 (sponge), 0.40 (small ingredients)
Sponge temperature	32°C (90°F)

Table 6.06. Heat Factors

Ingredients	Btu per lb per F°
Heat of hydration of flour	6.50
Specific heat of flour	0.42
Specific heat of sponge	0.60
Specific heat of water	1.00
Specific heat of small ingredients	0.40

Mechanical	Btu per minute per hp
Heat generated by motor	42.50
Motor efficiency	90%

Ingredient water temperature   4.4°C (40°F)
Mixer motor rating   60 hp at 90% efficiency
Heat generated by motor   42.5 Btu per minute per hp

Given these assumptions, the heat balance is calculated as follows:

(a) To cool the sponge from 90°F to 80°F — a difference of 10 F° — the heat withdrawn must be equal to the result of the sponge weight (800 lb) multiplied by the specific heat of the sponge (0.6 Btu per lb per F°) and by the 10 F° temperature difference between 90 and 80°F, or $800 \times 0.56 \times 10 = 4{,}800$ Btu.

(b) To remove the heat of hydration of the flour requires subtraction of 1,592 Btu, the result obtained by multiplying the weight of the added flour (245 lb) by its hydration factor (6.5 Btu per lb).

(c) To reduce the sensible heat of the flour from 100°F to 80°F, one must apply cooling equivalent to the result obtained by multiplying the weight of the flour (245 lb) by its specific heat (0.42 Btu per lb per F°) and the temperature difference (20 F°). The result is $245 \times 0.42 \times 20 = 2{,}058$ Btu.

(d) The cooling of the 200 lb of small ingredients, assuming an average temperature reduction of 20 F° and an over-all specific heat of 0.4 Btu per lb per F°, will require heat removal equivalent to $200 \times 0.4 \times 20$, or 1,600 Btu.

(e) The heat load generated by the 60-hp mixer motor running 10 minutes during each mixing cycle is equal to the heat produced per hp per minute multiplied by 10 (for the 10-minute mixing period), by 60 (60-hp motor) and by 0.90 (motor efficiency) or $60 \times 42.5 \times 10 \times 90\%$ (motor efficiency). The result is 22,950 Btu.

The total heat load that needs to be removed from a 1,600-1b dough is thus $4{,}800 + 1{,}592 + 2{,}058 + 1{,}600 + 22{,}950 = 33{,}000$ Btu, which represents the sum total of the individual heat factors.

Some reduction of this load is obtained, however, by using chilled dough water or chilled flour. As the water warms from 4.4°C (40°F) to 27°C (80°F), it removes heat from the dough mass. The extent of this cooling equals the weight of the water, multiplied by its specific heat (1 Btu per lb per F°) and by the temperature differential of 40°F, or $355 \times 1 \times 40$, or 14,200 Btu. Some slight cooling is also obtained when the sugar enters into solution, but this is a negligible factor. Summarizing the heat load of a 1,600-1b dough under the assumed conditions, we obtain the following tabulation shown in **Table 6.07**.

Table 6.07. Heat Calculation

	Btu
Sponge	
800 lb x (90° - 80°) x 0.6	4,800
Flour (heat of hydration)	
245 lb x 6.5	1,592
Flour (sensible heat)	
245 lb x (100° - 80°) x 0.42	2,058
Small ingredients	
200 lb x (100° - 80°) x 0.4	1,600
Motor	
60 hp x 42.5 Btu x 10 minutes x 90% efficiency	22,950
Total heat added to dough	33,000
Heat removed by ingredient water	
355 lb x (80° - 40°)	14,200
Actual cooling load	18,800
Required cooling per minute	
18,800 ÷ 10	1,880
Required cooling per hour	
1,880 x 60	112,800

6.B. Fermentation

Despite all the air bubbles occluded in the dough by mixing, the achievement of desirable light, airy texture for bread, rolls and most pastries would not be possible without the leavening gases produced by yeast and bacteria. Nor would the flavor of such baked foods be acceptable without the fermentation of these micro-organisms that yields flavor precursors, acids and other compounds that mark the many differences between leavened and unleavened breads.

Enough time must be allowed for the yeast and bacteria to consume available carbohydrates and convert them into ethyl alcohol (ethanol, C_2H_5OH) and carbon dioxide (CO_2). In conventional practice, the sponge or dough is discharged from the mixer into a greased dough trough in which it undergoes fermentation in bulk, usually in a temperature-and-humidity-controlled room, as shown in **Figure 6.19**. In liquid ferment systems, yeast fermentation is initiated in preferments, brews or broths, which generally, but not always, contain some of the total formula flour.

The aim of fermentation is to continue the process of dough development that was started during mixing. "The leavening of dough during fermentation, followed by a mechanical treatment, results in better texture (in fact, better eating characteristics) and better flavor development compared with those of a product made without fermentation or with a short fermentation process," stated Sluimer (2005). A comprehensive review of the various factors that influence the functions of yeast in doughs and preferments and of their effects on final product properties was provided by Reed and Nagodawithana (1991).

Figure 6.19. The fermentation room holds sponge doughs at various stages of the process. (Shick USA)

The most apparent physical change marking the course of fermentation in dough is the steady increase in the volume of its mass. The sponge in the dough trough expands to 4 to 5 times its original size before it recedes, assuming at the same time a light, spongy character. According to Jackel (1969a), the fermentation by yeast of 100 lb of carbohydrates such as glucose and fructose will yield 48.6 lb of alcohol, 46.4 lb of carbon dioxide and 15 lb of other organic substances. Assuming an average density of carbon dioxide gas of 8.5 cu ft per lb, the 46.5 lb of carbon dioxide represent about 400 cu ft of gas. This quantity of CO_2 is sufficient to leaven about

Table 6.08. Fermentation Lexicon

Absorption	Expressed on a flour weight basis, absorption is the amount of water added to a preferment or dough to reach the desired dough consistency.
Autolyse	This process, used by some French bakers, combines all or some of the ingredients in a batch of dough, mixing them to incorporation and then letting the dough rest in the mixing bowl for 5 to 10 minutes. The rest period, or autolyse, allows full hydration of the flour and relaxes the gluten. The dough is then mixed fo full development.
Barm	This completely fermented fluid mixture consists of flour, water, yeast and, occasionally, other ingredients such as potato. It is used as a leavener in certain types of bread. In medieval times, bakers concocted barm from a mixture of malt, hops, water and coarse meal, which fermented naturally when colonized by air-borne wild yeast.
Batter sponge	A very soft, pumpable dough or ferment, a batter sponge has a flour-to-water ratio of 1:1.1 or greater and is used in some systems of bread production. Other names include liquid sponge and brew.
Biga	The biga is a sponge starter made from flour, water and a small amount of yeast. It is used to give breads a light, chewy crumb.
Brew (brew dough, broth, concentrated brew, water brew)	A doughmaking process, a brew system carries out its bulk fermentation in a liquid medium or preferment consisting of water, yeast, sugar and a buffer salt. Addition of flour in variable amounts is optional, and the brew remains fluid so it can be pumped or poured into the mixer for final dough mixing.
Bulk fermentation	This term designates fermentation conducted in large doughs, sponges or liquid ferments, in contrast to scaled and moulded dough pieces that are subjected to fermentative action during the final proof stage.
Chef (chef levain, masa madre, Reinzuchtsauer)	This name is given to the original or chief leavening agent. It is usually a natural starter that is given the first of many refreshments and, thereafter, is known as the levain.
Ferment (liquid ferment, liquid preferment, liquid sponge)	The term refers to any of several types of liquid or semi-liquid brews used to initiate yeast fermentation in a medium that contains carbohydrates in the form of flour or sugar, yeast food, salt and, usually, a buffer agent to control the pH. Flour is optional but, when added, may reach a level as high as 70%, based on the liquid in the batch, while still maintaining the ferment's fluid character.
Levain (Anstellgut, mature sour, mother sponge)	The term refers to a natural starter, sourdough or mother dough. The latter is the name given by American bakers to the dough from which all new life is taken. It is usually a stiff, firm material. In France, a levain contains microorganisms that produce both lactic nd acetic acids. A true levain contains no bakers yeast.
Panary fermentation	Literally, "bread" fermentation, a panary fermentation produces alcohol and carbon dioxide through the action of yeast on sugar. This term is commonly found in older texts and covers both bulk fermentation and proofing steps.
Pate fermentee	The French term means "old dough." This starter is similar to a biga except that salt is present.
Poolish	A style of liquid sponge, a poolish is made with commercial yeast and some of the flour and water of a bread formula.
Preferment	A preferment, also referred to as a broth, brew or liquid ferment or liquid sponge, has a liquid or semi-liquid pumpable consistency and forms the preliminary dough stage. It is combined with other ingredients during the final dough mixing stage. It may be either totally flour-free or may contain varying amounts of flour up to about 60%, based on the water portion.
Sponge (plastic sponge)	The preliminary fermentation stage in the sponge-and-dough process of breadmaking contains a major portion of the flour and is subjected to the chemical and biological actions of fermenting yeast. The sponge characteristically contains 50 to 70% of the total dough flour, part of the water and all of the yeast and yeast food. It is generally fermented 3.5 hours to 4.5 hours and combined with the remainder of ingredients to yield the finished dough.

5,000 lb of dough and to increase 5-fold the latter's original volume of about 100 cu ft to a fermented and proofed volume of about 500 cu ft. If it is assumed that 100 lb of flour will yield 180 lb of dough, equal to 3.6 cu ft, then this dough volume should have increased to about 18 cu ft through the proofing stage. On the basis of these values, Jackel (1969a) calculated that this degree of expansion during fermentation and proofing can be sustained by about 3.5% fermentable carbohydrates (flour weight basis). Part of these carbohydrates come from the native sugars of flour, part may result from β-amylase action on damaged starch in the flour, and part may comprise added formula sugar. Any sugar over and beyond the 3.5% level will show up as residual sugar in the finished bread.

Fermentation uses up the available oxygen quickly, and the process turns anaerobic. As the carbon dioxide produced by yeast during fermentation dissolves in the liquid dough phase, it causes a rapid drop in pH. When CO_2 saturates the aqueous phase, any additional gas generated then finds its way into pre-existing air cells, thus leavening the dough (Hoseney 1985).

Oxidation causes doughs to behave more like a solid than do unoxidized doughs. Conversely, incomplete fermentation causes doughs to act like liquids. In other words, fermentation results in doughs that are more elastic, and oxidation reduces the ability of a dough to flow under the force of gravity (Faubion and Hoseney 1990). Fat added to doughs was found to delay the onset of viscous flow and to attenuate the short-time elastic properties of the gluten fraction (Fu et al. 1997).

Bakers sometime speak of the "mass effect" of dough. By this they refer to the fact that fermentation of dough in bulk proceeds faster than it would in smaller quantities (Suas 2009). Thus, a batch of dough weighing 6 lb or less will need to ferment longer than a larger one, a factor that product developers and researchers should consider when scaling up from home- or bench-size formulations.

A variety of fermentation approaches characterize bakery practices in different parts of the world. Some bakers hold back a portion of one day's dough to seed the next day's batches, while others start each day and each batch with fresh leavening. **Table 6.08** defines many of the words commonly used to describe fermentation methods and styles. Older references often describe bulk fermentation as "panary fermentation," from the Latin word for bread, *panis* (Jago 1895). This usage persisted into the 1950s and is occasionally applied to fermentation processes that involve yeast, are fueled by sugar and produce alcohol and carbon dioxide.

Studying rheological changes in yeasted doughs during fermentation is complicated by the fact that the yeast continues to evolve gases during testing procedures, and scientists are not able to ascertain which properties result from previous fermentation, the parameter of interest or from fermentation during measurement (Faubion and Hoseney 1990). When Hoseney et al. (1979) developed a simple spread test to measure the rheological properties of dough, they documented the effect of yeast on a fermenting dough vs. the flour-water mixture typically used in research testing (**Figure 6.20**). For this reason, most rheological

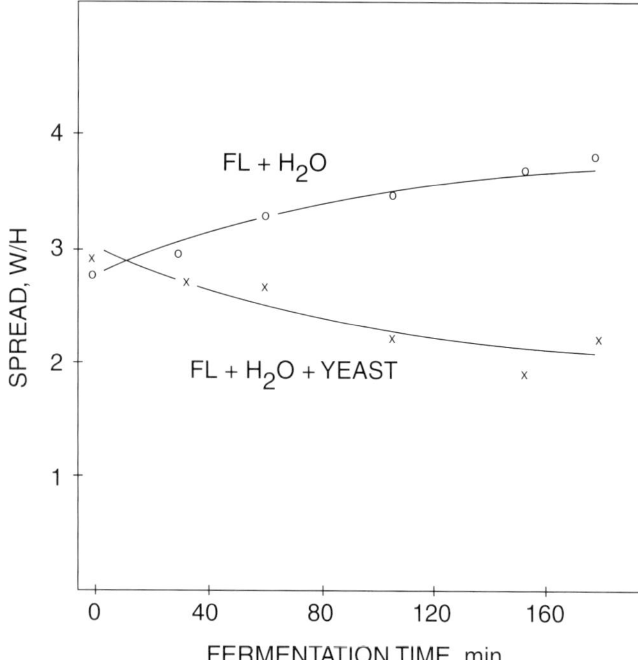

Figure 6.20. Yeast demonstrably changes the rheological properties (spread ratio, W/H) of doughs.
(Hoseney et al. 1979)

studies conducted on doughs use unyeasted formulations; however, yeasted methods have emerged (Newberry et al. 2002). Rheological data generated by these studies are interpreted as evidence of increased cross-linking of dough proteins during fermentation.

6.B.1. Sponge and straight doughs

In normal bakery practice, the mixed sponge or dough is discharged from the mixer into a clean trough whose interior walls previously received a light, even coating of grease or release agent to prevent the dough from sticking to the sides of the trough. The dough is then pulled over and flattened to create a smooth top surface. This so-called "dressing" or facing of the dough is presumed to aid in subsequent gas retention by drawing a smooth skin over the dough mass; however, except for affording the mixer operator an opportunity to manipulate the dough and thereby evaluate its physical condition, no other discernible benefits appear to be derived from this practice (Nicolait 1960).

The amount of dough placed in a trough requires some consideration. With straight doughs, the general practice is to allow 2 ft of length in a standard-sized trough for each 100 lb of flour in the dough. With sponges, which are allowed to rise to a much greater height, the allocated trough space is twice that length, or 4 ft on the same basis. In dough troughs that are too large for a given dough volume, the dough will spread along the bottom rather than rise, thereby altering the surface-to-volume ratio, with adverse effects on fermentation; however, the use of space boards can confine the dough within an appropriate space. Dough troughs that are too small for a given dough volume will be unable to contain the dough on rising and cause obvious difficulties.

The troughs holding the mixed doughs are transferred to a fermentation room where they remain for the required time. This room should be maintained at a temperature of about 27°C (80°F) and a relative humidity of 75% to provide an optimum environment for the doughs. Perceptibly cooler temperatures will retard fermentation, while temperatures higher than 27°C (80°F) will accelerate fermentation and increase the risk of so-called "wild fermentations" by extraneous yeasts, lactic acid and acetic acid bacteria, and by mold and rope organisms.

Proper humidity control is equally important. An atmosphere with a relative humidity of less than 70% will dry the dough surface and produce a dehydrated crust-like outer skin. This dry surface will not only retard the fermentation rate but also cause irregularities in the finished product. A widely accepted rule of thumb is to maintain a relative humidity in the fermentation room that equals, or slightly exceeds, the numerical percentage value of the moisture in the dough. This figure must include both the added dough water and the original flour moisture, which normally ranges between 11 to 13%. Thus, dough made from flour with an original moisture content of 12% and an absorption of 63% has an actual moisture content of 75% and will require a relative humidity of 75% in the fermentation room. Precautions should also be taken to avoid drafts within the room because these create temperature fluctuations in the doughs, thereby leading to irregular fermentations.

Most trough-based fermentation systems follow first-in, first-out protocols, with each trough experiencing the same time, temperature and humidity conditions. Such approaches work best when schedules call for long runs of single varieties, although many bakers are moving to use of common sponges. This practice allows ease of scaling and uniform fermentation as well as forgiveness in scheduling. (Whole-wheat and whole-grain products are the exceptions because their formulations do not use white refined flour.)

New high-rise bulk fermentation rooms use automated storage-and-retrieval systems sequenced by computer. Such methods allow the baker to set multiple dough varieties and accommodate schedules involving frequent changeovers. The details of these systems are discussed in Chapter 9 of this volume.

6.B.1.a. Sponge doughs

In the sponge-and-dough process, sponges are generally set to ferment at temperatures of 23 to 26°C (74 to 78°F), the selected temperature depending on bakery plant conditions. Bakers generally prefer to work with cool sponges and adequate levels of yeast. Using approximately 2% yeast (flour weight basis), fermentation in a properly formulated sponge will normally proceed quite vigorously. Full maturation of the sponge will be reached within 3 to 4.5 hours. Fermentation involves exothermic reactions that result in a temperature increase within the dough mass. In a properly controlled dough room, the rise in temperature should not exceed 5.6 C° (10 F°) over the entire fermentation period.

The aim generally is to return the fermented sponge to the dough mixer at 30 to 30.5°C (86 to 87°F), or 0.5 to 1.1 C° (1 to 2 F°) lower in instances when fungal enzymes are used to reduce the dough mixing time. Because the temperature rise during fermentation is readily measured, it is a simple matter to arrive at the temperature at which the sponge needs to be set to attain the desired remix temperature. While a ±0.5 C° (±1 F°) difference in sponge temperature at the remix stage is of little consequence, an increase of 1.6 C° (3 F°) will cause delays in doughs reaching cleanup and thus extend the total mixing time for optimum results. Holding to a fixed mixing time under such conditions will introduce variations in dough development from batch to batch (Ford 1968).

In practice, sponge fermentation times may range from 2.5 to 6 hours. Variations of relatively wide magnitude have only a nominal effect on final bread quality as long as the minimum fermentation time exceeds 3 hours (Garnatz 1957). Ford (1968) pointed out that sponge times held within 3.5 to 4.5 hours yield bread with better keeping qualities, grain and texture than is the case when fermentation is either greatly reduced or extended. According to Kamman (1970), over-fermented sponges tend to result in an open, uneven grain and a coarse texture in the final bread. Under-fermented, or young, sponges, on the other hand, produce "bucky" doughs that are difficult to machine properly. In the finished bread, they produce a grain structure with large, round, thick-walled cells. Moreover, the crumb color will tend to be dull and gray. The effects of young and old sponges, respectively, on loaf volume and crumb appearance are illustrated in **Figure 6.21**.

Bakers use the word "bucky" to describe a dough in which the elastic component is too dominant. A dough said to be bucky or have the quality of buckiness is characterized by a lack of pliability and by excessive stiffness, resilience and gassiness, resistance to extension and inability to recover and relax from imposed stresses — all factors that contribute to significant handling difficulties during processing.

For determining the optimum length of time required by the sponge to reach proper maturity, the so-called "drop" or "break" represents a useful point of reference. Normally, a sponge will expand to about 4 to 5 times its original size and then recede in volume. Referred to as the drop or break, this decrease in volume is quite noticeable and is taken as the point from which the additional fermentation time is calculated. Depending on whether young or old sponges are desired, the drop represents the completion of 70% or 66% of the total sponge fermentation, respectively, and the sponge is then given the additional fermentation time. Generally, well-matured flours perform better with younger sponges, and in this case, the post-drop time is reduced to 30%. For example, if a sponge made from a fully matured flour required 3 hours to arrive at the break, it would then be permitted to stand for an additional 54 minutes (30% of 3 hours). The total sponge fermentation time would thus be 3 hours and 54 minutes, or about 4 hours.

Figure 6.21. Crumb appearance shows the effects of under-fermentation (left), correct fermentation (center) and over-fermentation (right). (Kamman 1970)

6.B.1.b. Straight doughs

In the straight-dough process, doughs are normally set at slightly higher temperatures than are sponges, within a range of 27 to 29°C (80 to 85°F). The accelerating effect of the higher temperatures is desirable in this case because straight doughs contain all of the dough ingredients, some of which (salt and especially mold inhibitors) have a retarding effect on yeast action. Straight-dough fermentation, as a rule, proceeds at a somewhat slower rate than does sponge fermentation, so straight doughs take longer to reach maturity than do sponges; however, the combined time of the sponge and the final dough fermentations normally exceeds that of straight-dough fermentation alone.

The straight-dough method known as the no-time dough was developed to bypass bulk fermentation altogether, although as some bakers practice it, the method can actually incorporate a short-time fermentation (Reedich 1989).

Straight doughs differ from sponges in not only their fermentation rates but also their handling during fermentation. The general practice is to leave sponges undisturbed until they are ready for the return to the mixer. In contrast, straight doughs receive periodic punching or turning, during which a good portion of the generated carbon dioxide gas is expelled, thereby reducing the dough volume.

While the actual punching or vigorous kneading of the dough is still practiced in many bakeries, the recommended procedure is to more gently turn and fold the sides of the dough well into the center. Automated dough systems employ knock-down bars that descend into the trough to degas the dough. Vigorous kneading, when well-matured flours are used, has a tendency to produce bucky doughs that will subsequently create difficulties in makeup. Folding the dough, on the other hand, avoids this problem.

Moreover, this method of dough manipulation assures a more uniform fermentation by (a) equalizing the temperature throughout the dough, (b) minimizing the possible retarding effect caused by excessive carbon dioxide gas accumulation within the dough, (c) introducing atmospheric oxygen with its stimulating effect on yeast activity and (d) increasing the gas-retaining capacity of the dough by promoting the mechanical development of its gluten through the stretching and folding action involved in this process.

According to Elion (1943), this last effect appears to be of primary significance.

He observed that gas production is not constant during fermentation but rises at first to its maximum rate and then declines. The increase in dough volume corresponds to gas production during the first hour of fermentation only. Thereafter, a marked decline occurs in the rate at which dough volume increases. A dough that goes through fermentation without punching will lose a considerable amount of carbon dioxide; however, if the dough is turned and folded at the right time, its gas retention properties are improved sufficiently to prevent a significant loss of gas. Under practical conditions, the rate of dough expansion is again accelerated by the punch back, and this action leads to the conclusion that there has been a corresponding increase in the fermentation rate. Elion's results indicated that the beneficial effects of punching result essentially from the improvement in the dough's gas retention properties.

Punching affects the size and distribution of gas cells, as noted by Shimiya and Nakamura (1997). The size of gas cells in punched dough became more uniform and better dispersed than in unpunched dough (**Figure 6.22**).

The correct time at which the dough should first be turned, or punched, is usually established manually simply by inserting your hand into the dough, withdrawing it quickly and observing the dough's behavior. If the dough reshapes itself, showing only a very slight recession or indentation, it is ready to be turned and folded. This point is usually taken as the 60% completion mark of the total fermentation time. The dough is then turned again after one-half this initial time, which thus represents another 30% of the total fermentation time. During the remaining 10%, the dough is sent to the divider.

In practice, this procedure can work as follows. A dough is found to be ready for the first punch after a fermentation time of 120 minutes. Because this time period represents the 60% completion mark, the total fermentation time thus amounts to $120 \div 0.60$, or 200 minutes. The second punch, coming in half the time required for the first punch, is given the dough after an additional 60 minutes, which represents 30% of the total fermentation time. During the remaining 20 minutes, or 10% of the total fermentation time, the dough is taken to the divider.

The above procedure merely indicates general practice and must be adapted to different conditions. For example, the quality of the flour plays an important role in determining actual fermentation times. Well-matured flours normally require shorter fermentation and less frequent punching or folding than do so-called "green" or immature flours. The fermentation time may be shortened by timing the first punch at either two-thirds or even three-fourths of the total fermentation and omitting the second punch. This procedure will yield "young" doughs. "Old" doughs, on the other hand, are obtained by scheduling the first punch to represent a lesser proportion of the total fermentation and giving the dough a series of periodic turnings or punches. This practice is normally followed with strong flours of high protein content or with lower grade flours of longer extraction. Such flours may need 4 or 5 punches. There is the risk, however, that this may give rise to bucky doughs. Slightly overmixing the doughs or increasing the absorption somewhat will ameliorate this condition. A small increase in dough temperature will also act to accelerate fer-

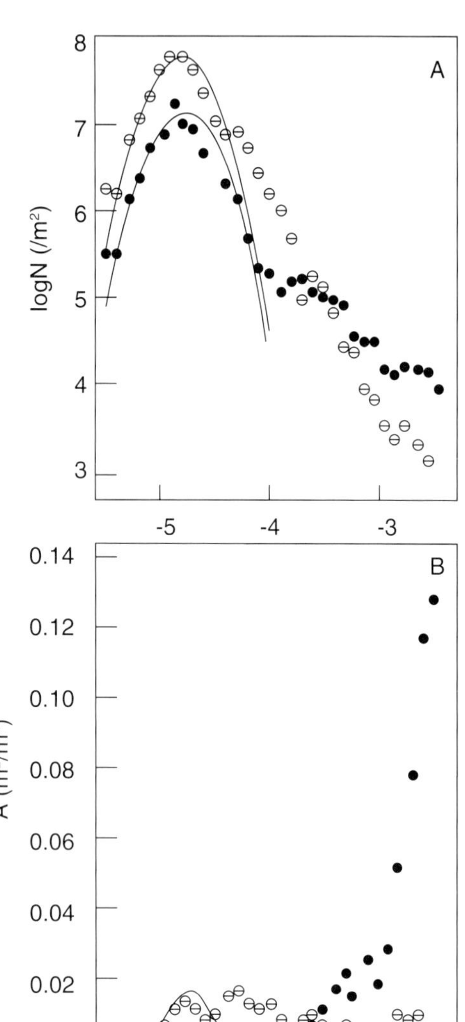

Figure 6.22. After 100 minutes of fermentation, the cell size distribution (A) and sectional area distribution (B) show the effect of punching (open circles) to improve uniformity and distribution compared with results in unpunched dough (solid circles). (Shimiya and Nakamura 1997)

mentation and reduce total time.

"Green," or immature, flours may trigger difficulties by causing the fermenting dough to slacken markedly. In this case, increasing the number of punches will tend to stiffen the dough. Other corrective measures include a slight increase in the amount of yeast food or of both yeast food and yeast. With either of these adjustments, the salts of the yeast food will exert a tightening effect on the gluten and also accelerate the rate of yeast fermentation, thereby shortening the fermentation time.

The practice of punching originated when doughs were mixed by hand, and yeast was expensive and scarce (Doerry 1995a). The manual process also involved folding the dough, thus adding more oxygen to the system for the yeast to use, especially important when bakers used very low yeast levels or depended on wild yeast in their starters. The punching process helped develop the gluten as well.

6.B.1.c. Fermentation time

Optimum fermentation time represents that point at which the effects of interacting factors such as character of flour, yeast level, temperature, formula ingredients, degree of oxidation, etc., are in balance. Practical experience will establish the most suitable procedure for processing a given type of flour, and this result is generally closely adhered to in the interest of uniformity. Occasions may arise, however, when it becomes necessary to either shorten or extend the established fermentation time. To meet such exigencies, certain rules evolved concerning changes in yeast quantity and temperature, and these approaches work reasonably well but should always be regarded only as temporary expedients. Any major deviation from an accepted procedure that has yielded good results will usually result in some loss of quality, so while it is possible to shorten or lengthen the fermentation time by such adjustments, the final product will usually not meet optimum quality standards.

There is an inverse relation between the amount of yeast and fermentation time. Reducing the amount of yeast will result in longer fermentation times, while increasing yeast will shorten them. The actual quantitative relations are expressed by the following equation:

$$(y \times t) \div n = x$$

where y = the percent of yeast normally used, t = the normal fermentation time, n = the new fermentation time desired and x = the percent of yeast needed for new fermentation time.

The following example illustrates how this equation works in practice. Assuming that with 2% yeast a given flour yields best results with a 4-hour fermentation, and the baker wants to reduce the fermentation time to 3 hours. By substitution, we arrive at the following equation:

$$(2 \times 4) \div 3 = 2.66\%$$

Under the above assumptions, the amount of yeast will have to be increased to 2.66% to reduce the fermentation time to 3 hours.

Rules of this nature have their limitations, of course. Again using the above assumptions, if the fermentation time had to be reduced to only 2 hours, then 4% of yeast would be required. Bakers routinely use more than 4% yeast yielding good-quality bread without unpleasant yeast-type off flavors.

Generally speaking, fermentation times may be varied up to a maximum of 30% in either direction by changes in the amount of yeast. If greater changes are required, adjustments in other factors must also be made such as temperature and amount of yeast food.

A generally accepted rule is that a change of 0.56 C° (1 F°) in dough temperature will cause a 15-minute variation in straight-dough fermentation time. Hence, a dough that comes out of the mixer 0.56 C° (1 F°) warmer than normal will require about 15 minutes less fermentation under average conditions and vice versa. Here again, practical considerations impose limits on the extent to which fermentation time may be altered; about 45 minutes appears to be the maximum when no other changes are involved.

Exploring the rheology of cracker sponges, Doescher and Hoseney (1985) found that resistance to extension and extensibility of the sponges decreased with longer fermentation times, as shown in **Figure 6.23**.

6.B.1.d. Floor time

The fermentation stage called "floor time" takes its name from the interval of time between final mixing and dividing of the dough (O'Donnell 1996). In commercial production, batches always experience some delay between the start and end of the dough in the divider hopper. Batches can be run more frequently to minimize the variation caused by such delay, or the baker can add a dough degassing stage between the mixer and the divider. Generally, bakers seek to minimize floor time, but they may deliberately hold a dough for a few minutes before sending it to the depositor, thus allowing it to relax to an optimum point.

When plant practices call for floor time, its duration can run from 10 minutes to more than 3 hours and depends on (a) temperature of the dough, (b) amount of yeast in the dough, (c) amount of flour that has been prefermented, (d) level of chemical dough conditioners in the dough and (e) the further processing that will be given the dough (Doerry 1995a). Warm doughs in the range of 27°C (80°F) or above produce more yeast activity and thus require less floor time, while cool doughs (below 25.5°C, or 75°F) need more. Unless floor time exceeds 45 minutes and doughs are small in size, ambient conditions have little or no effect. The more flour in the preferment, the less time needed on the floor. For example, dough prepared from a plastic sponge containing 80% of the formula flour will be given only about 10 minutes of floor time, while a similar dough made with a 30%-flour preferment may require a floor time of 45 minutes.

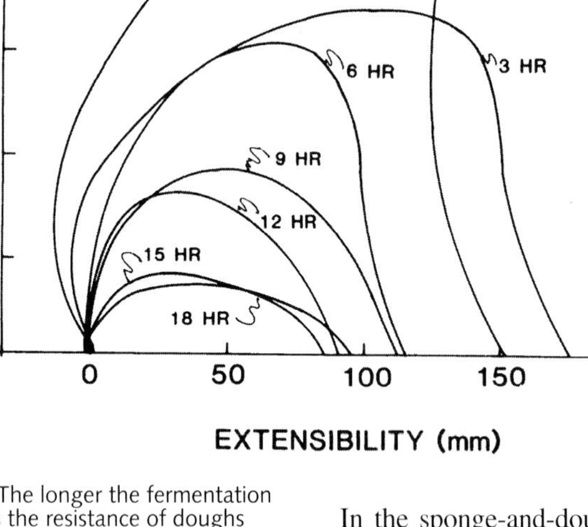

Figure 6.23. The longer the fermentation time, the less the resistance of doughs (BU = Brabender unit). Each sponge described by this Extensigram was adjusted to pH 7.0 with soda. (Doescher and Hoseney 1985).

In the sponge-and-dough process, the fully fermented sponge is returned to the mixer after bulk fermentation is completed and mixed into the final dough, which then receives additional fermentation for a relatively short period of floor time. The dough is considered to be fully matured when it develops shortness to a sharp pull and a rather dry feel to the touch. This stage is normally reached after a floor time of 20 to 45 minutes under average conditions. Warmer ambient temperatures reduce the floor time and may eliminate it altogether, while cooler temperatures tend to lengthen it.

Straight-dough batches are fermented for periods of 2 to 4 hours, with the actual time in practice being generally close to 3 hours. Following fermentation, the dough is taken immediately to dividing to be made up into loaves of proper weight for final proofing and baking. Although no-time doughs are basically straight doughs formulated and mixed to eliminate the bulk fermentation stage, they may receive a short period of floor time, usually 5 to 10 minutes, but not much longer.

6.B.2. Preferments

When the continuous mixing method for preparing doughs was devised, its inventors did their experimental and pilot plant work with fermented sponges. The inconvenience and difficulty of handling plastic sponges at the commercial scale led to development of watery, pumpable liquids containing yeast, described as water preferments (Kulp 1983, Watkins 1985), as well as preferments containing a portion of the formula flour (Fuhrmann 1964). This technique spread among bakers using continuous mixing methods, and it also found use for batch preparation of doughs, particularly those intended for buns and rolls. Adoption of liquid sponge, or preferment, methods proceeded very quickly during the late 1970s and early 1980s, at which time Thompson (1980) reviewed the development of this process and its technology. Most recently, liquid ferments have found successful use in preparation of white bread, variety bread, buns, English muffins, sweet goods, rustic breads, focaccia and other standard and artisan-inspired baked foods.

Preferments go by a variety of names, but their chief purpose is to precondition the yeast to optimize its performance during breadmaking. Operationally, they provide the advantages of lower capital costs, reduced floor space, less labor, clean-in-place sanitation, flexibility to cuts and adds, breakdown protection and automatic operation (Watkins 1991).

As Uhrich (1975) explained, a sponge created with 100% of formula water results in a very soft mass, and its degree of viscosity depends on the amount of flour used. Made with half of the formula flour and all its water, the result becomes even more fluid and is readily metered and pumped. The level of flour used in relation to the 100% level of formula water determines the pumpability of the liquid sponge, which has come to be called a preferment.

Fermentation times decrease markedly when less flour is used in the preferment, cutting this stage of doughmaking from a high of 3 to 5 hours to 2 hours or less. Other process variables change as well, with the need for oxidation and other improvers increasing as the flour component decreases (**Table 6.09**). Mixing time and dough-out temperatures also rise as the amount of flour in the preferment drops (Uhrich 1975).

When baked, the differences between sponge-and-dough breads and those baked from liquid preferments containing flour were not appreciable except for a lower flavor intensity in the preferment-based breads, especially those made with water brews (no-flour ferments), according to Kulp (1986). Reporting from his own bakery experience, Fields (1985) observed that a higher percentage of flour in the preferment yielded better market quality.

6.B.2.a. Water brews
Some bakers developed a 2-stage fermentation process to feed continuous-mixing

Table 6.09. Differences Between Sponges and Preferments

Condition	Sponge-and-dough	Liquid preferment (high flour)	Liquid preferment (low to medium flour)	Liquid preferment (low to no flour)
Flour level	50 to 100%	40 to 70%	15 to 40%	0 to 15%
Sugar in preferment	None required	Up to 0.5%	Up to 2%	2 to 3%
Set temperature	74 to 80°F	76 to 80°F	80 to 86°F	82 to 88°F
Fermentation time	3 to 5 hours	2 to 3 hours	2 hours or less	2 hours or less
Yeast	2.5%	Gradual increase to 3.5%	Gradual increase to 3.5%	Gradual increase to 3.5%
Yeast-nutrient-oxidation	15 ppm	20 to 50 ppm	25 to 60 ppm	35 to 75 ppm
Buffers, enzymes, acidity, additives, mix-time reducers	None required	Gradual increase to high levels\	Gradual increase to high levels	Gradual increase to high levels
Dough mixing time	Normal	Add 10%	Add 40%	Add 60%
Dough temperature	Normal: 80°F	Gradual increase to 95°F	Gradual increase to 95°F	Gradual increase to 95°F
Dough floor time	Normal: 20 minutes	Gradual increase in time	Gradual increase in time	Gradual increase in time

(Uhrich 1975)

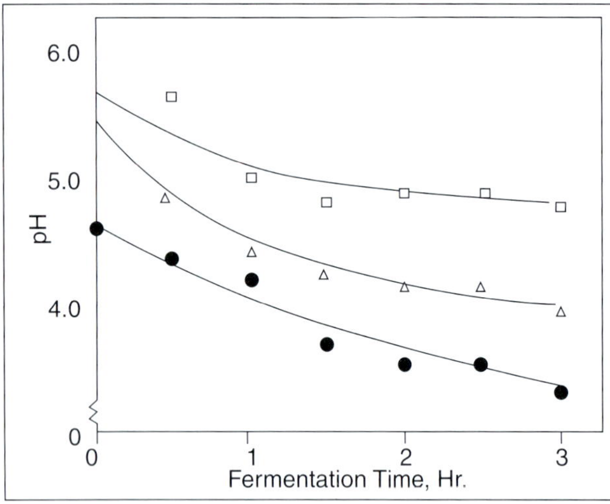

Figure 6.24. Buffers improve the control of pH during fermentation of liquid ferments with 0% flour and no buffer (solid dot), 20% flour with buffer (open triangle) and 50% flour with buffer (open square).
(Kulp 1986)

systems. A primary, or short-term, water preferment was made and then used in preparation of the second state, a flour preferment (Watkins 1985).

As bakers learned more about liquid preferments, they also experimented with yeast slurries augmented with sugar, also termed water brews. As described by Shirley (1977), all of the day's yeast needs would be dissolved in water at a water-to-yeast ratio of 4:1. The water temperature for dissolving the yeast was high enough to produce a slurry temperature of 29 to 31°C (85 to 88°F). After agitating and fermenting the yeast slurry for 1 to 1.5 hours, the temperature was reduced to 7 to 10°C (45 to 50°F) and maintained at that level by the tank's refrigerated jacket. The slurry's pH was in the range of 4.3 to 4.5, depending on the pH of the water and the yeast.

Water preferments can be held longer than those containing flour. Maintained at 4°C (40°F), the chilled preferment can be held overnight without loss of activity. A no-flour ferment with pH of 4.0 to 4.2 and total titratable acid (TTA) content of 13.0 is typically used at 38 to 40 lb per cwt flour (Perrou 2000). The flour chosen for dough preparation when using water brews is an important factor, and Stakley (1985) cautioned, "The process demands a consistent and good quality protein for best results."

The ratio of water to yeast can be varied to suit the baker's needs. A water brew, or no-flour liquid preferment, consists of water, yeast, salt and sugar only. Over the years, bakers have altered the proportions of the ingredients, and Turner (1980) analyzed these differences as moving toward a more concentrated system, using examples from his own bakery plants (**Table 6.10**). He explained that temperature control serves as the buffering factor in the newer formulation mostly because better chilling technology became available for the holding tanks.

Such water brews use no buffers or acid-type yeast foods because these materials will change the system's pH and result in inferior products; however, appropriate levels of ammonium salts can be used to further stimulate the yeast (Glover 1975). Also, Kulp (1986) and Perrou (2000) observed that brew buffers such as calcium carbonate will help control the fermentation rate, pH and TTA. Buffer concentration was optimized at 0.2% (Kulp 1986) (**Figures 6.24** and **6.25**).

In water brews, sugar substitutes for flour as the source of fermentable carbohydrates. Sugars, which can also be provided in the form of high-fructose corn syrup (HFCS), are absolutely essential because yeast will continue to consume sugars throughout the fermentation period. If the system is depleted of sugar, the yeast will begin to cannibalize its cells, a process known as autolysis. A sulfur-like odor, similar to that of rotten eggs, is evidence of autolysis. In such systems, which lack the buffering effect of flour, the total titratable acid (TTA) will drop suddenly, and the yeast will release glutathione, a protein that breaks down the gluten's disulfide bonds and causes a dramatic and erratic reduction of mix time. These reactions result in poor dough strength and gas retention, increased proofing time, poor ovenspring, foxy red crust color, open and harsh grain and poor keeping quality of the finished bread.

6.B.2.b. Liquid ferments flour ferments, the word is best applied to fermentation methods that incorporate some flour in the pumpable ferment. Most use 30 to 50% of formula flour, and a typical 50%-flour ferment may contain optional ingredients such as ammonium sulfate, monocalcium phosphate, soybean oil and powdered emulsifiers (Perrou 2000). Because of the buffering effect of the flour, addition of a separate brew buffer is unnecessary. Neither are sugars required because the flour will supply sufficient stores of glucose, fructose and maltose as its starches hydrolyze.

Fermentation time is longer than the no-flour ferment: 30 minutes to 3 hours, depending on the amount of flour used. Target pH for liquid ferments is between 4.4 and 5.0, with a TTA of 6.0 to 11.0. The optional addition of powdered emulsifiers (mono- and diglycerides, sodium stearoyl lactylate or DATEM) allows liquid ferments to thoroughly hydrate to improve their functionality in later stages of breadmaking.

Table 6.10. Liquid Preferment Formulation Trends

Ingredient	1950s through 1960s (formula %)	1970s forward (formula %)
Water	83.33	80.00
Yeast	8.33	14.00
Sugar solids	5.57	5.00
Salt	2.07	1.00
Buffering agent	0.70	variable
Conditions		
Set temperature	29 to 30°C (85 to 86°F)	28 to 29°C (84 to 85°F)
pH at set	5.8	5.1
Fermentation time	2+ hours	1 hour
Temperature rise	2.8 C° (5 F°)	1.6 to 2.2 C° (3 to 4 F°)
Temperature peak	33°C (91°F)	38°C (89°F)
Foaming action	Mild	Vigorous
pH attained	4.8 to 5.5	3.7 to 4.2
Hold temperature	16°C (60°F)	9°C (48°F)

(Turner 1980)

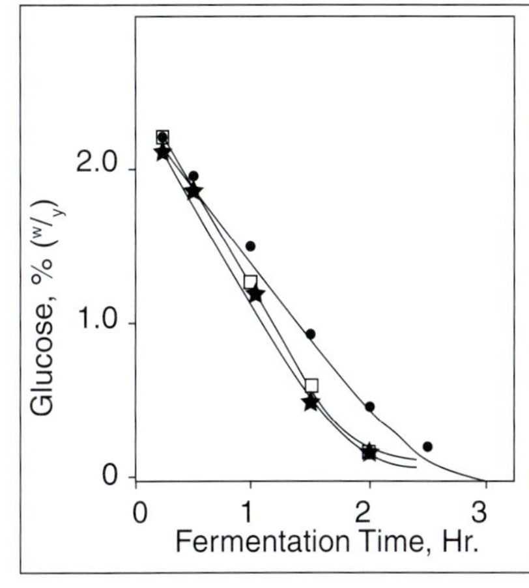

Figure 6.25. The fermentation of glucose in water brews is also affected by the buffer level (solid dot, 0% buffer; solid star, 0.2% buffer; open square, 0.5% buffer). (Kulp 1986)

In liquid ferments containing flour, TTA values reached their maximum after approximately 1.5 hours, and Kulp (1986) attributed this to the exhaustion of rapidly fermentable glucose, while fructose continued to ferment at a somewhat slower rate. The decrease in TTA values was explained by a loss of carbon dioxide, and the secondary increase in TTA in flour ferments was due to maltose fermentation. Water ferments have more ability to dissolve carbon dioxide, and addition of calcium carbonate buffers to these systems reduces the amount of dissolved carbon dioxide.

The fermentation rates for glucose, fructose and maltose in no-flour and liquid ferments was investigated by Kulp (1986), with results confirming the rapid uptake of glucose, followed by fructose and finally by maltose (**Figure 6.26**).

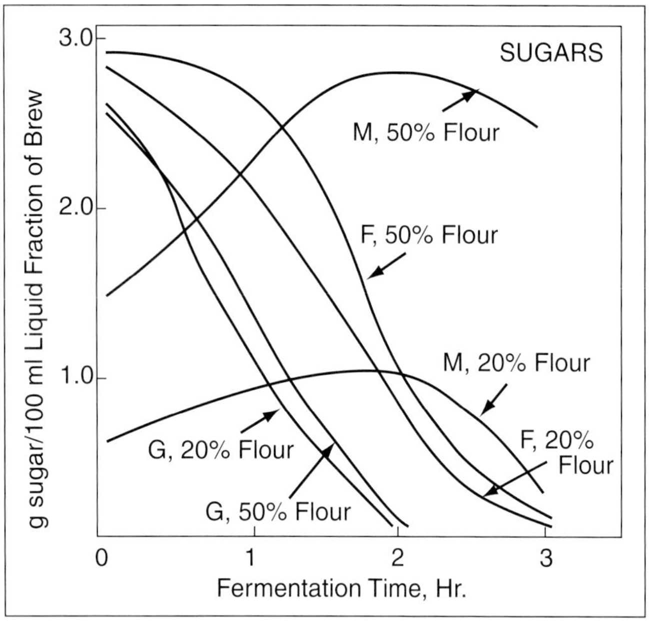

6.B.2.c. High-flour preferments

As Perrou (2000) observed, when more flour is used in the fermentation step and/or the fermentation time is lengthened, the flour hydrates better and the yeast releases more by-products. These benefits result in more fermentation flavor and aroma, softer crumb and slower crumb firming or staling. When using no-flour ferments, production of richer, longer-lived bread can be achieved by adding higher levels of sugar and/or fat.

Shop advantages from high-flour preferments include increased hydration, stronger doughs, good temperature control, cooler doughs, more uniform doughs, reduced mixing time, improved machineability and better slicing, according to Watkins (1991). Obviously, the higher the flour percentage in the preferment, the larger the tanks, the heavier the pumps and the greater the refrigeration required.

Figure 6.26. In liquid ferments containing flour, glucose (G) is used at a faster rate than fructose (F) or maltose (M), regardless of flour level (20% and 50%). (Kulp 1986)

In liquid ferments containing flour, care must be taken to avoid excessive agitation of the slurry in the preparation and holding tanks or else the gluten will separate out. Slow, gentle stirring is required during the aging period. Fermentation proceeds faster in liquid preferments than in sponges because they are wetter and the agitation continually exposes new surfaces to the action. The fully aged ferment then runs through a heat exchanger to bring its temperature down. Such systems can handle ferments with up to 40 to 50% of the formula flour.

Development of the continuous ferment mixer eliminated the mixing damage and gluten separation that could be possible with impeller mixing and agitation systems. As described by Watkins (1991), the continuous ferment mixer combines 70% or more of the formula flour with other ingredients and delivers it immediately into the fermentation tanks for aging. At such high flour levels, preferments approximate sponges, which typically contain 50 to 80% of total formula flour.

6.B.3. Fermentation control

A prerequisite to a controlled fermentation is a fully hydrated, homogeneous dough such as is obtained by correct mixing. As fermentation progresses, the surface appearance of the sponge usually provides a reliable indication of the adequacy of its mixing. A properly mixed sponge will exhibit good gas retention that will make it rise in the dough trough and assume a well-rounded top. The surface of an under-mixed sponge, on the other hand, will remain flat, which indicates incomplete incorporation of the formula ingredients and uneven fermentation (Fuhrmann 1955). In straight doughs, mixing plays a much more critical role because the aim here is to obtain optimal physical dough development.

When a correctly mixed sponge or dough is fermented, two forces come into play: gas production and gas retention. Gas production involves primarily the biological functioning of yeast on available fermentable carbohydrates, and gas retention is largely a measure of the mechanical and physicochemical modifications of the colloidal structure of the dough during mixing and during the course of fermentation.

The principal task of the baker is to control fermentation so that the forces of gas production and gas retention are properly balanced. Thus, if gas production attains its maximum rate before the dough's gas retention capacity is fully developed, then too much gas will be lost to bring about maximum aeration of the dough. On the other hand, if the gas retention capacity peaks before gas production reaches its maximum rate, then again much of the gas is unable to perform its aerating function. Hence, the aim of fermentation control is to get gas production capacity and gas retention capacity to coincide both in rate and time. As Clark (1938) stated, "When both peaks are reached at the same time, there frequently is combined in one loaf the largest volume together with the best grain, texture, crust color and other loaf characteristics which the flour in question will produce."

Most flours possessing adequate baking properties pass through a stage in the course of fermentation during which gas production and gas retention are in optimum balance. The time range over which this is true may properly be designated as the flour's fermentation tolerance. Because fermentation is subject to many influences that affect its course, it is evident that one and the same flour may have rather limited fermentation tolerance under one set of conditions and good tolerance under a different set of conditions.

Swortfiguer (1950) and Fuhrmann (1955) provided comprehensive descriptions of the visual and rheological changes undergone by sponges and doughs in the course of fermentation. **Figures 6.27** through **6.30**, taken from the data of Swortfiguer, illustrate these changes at the designated sponge time intervals and dough development stages. The formation of the so-called "web structure" of the dough is initiated at the outset of fermentation and reaches a recognizable state by the time one-third of the total sponge time, or

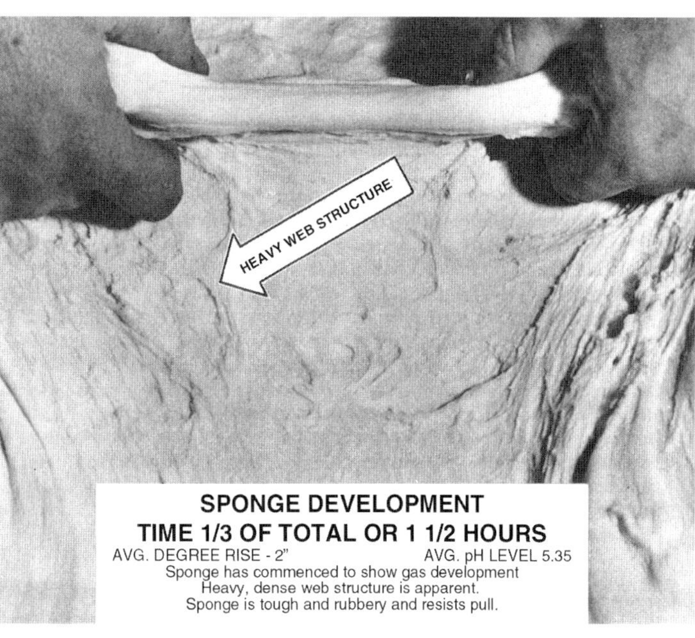

Figure 6.27. After 1.5 hours of fermentation, or one-third of total fermentation time, gas generation has begun, and the sponge character is tough and rubbery. (Swortfiguer 1950)

Figure 6.28. After 3 hours of fermentation, or two-thirds of total fermentation time, the sponge is mellowing, though still marked by wet gluten strands and some dense areas. Its temperature has risen by 4.4 C° (8 F°). (Swortfiguer 1950)

Figure 6.29. In a fully fermented sponge, the web structure, when pulled up, reveals thin-walled gluten strands that are dry and mellow and offer minimum resistance to stretching. (Swortfiguer 1950)

Figure 6.30. An over-fermented sponge develops bucky, over-gassed characteristics and assumes a stringy and inelastic web structure. Its pH has dropped from an initial 5.5 to 4.5. (Swortfiguer 1950)

some 1.5 hours, has elapsed. As **Figure 6.27** illustrates, this web structure is rather heavy and dense at this stage, and the sponge has a rubbery feel when pulled back.

When fermentation has advanced to two-thirds of the total time, the sponge becomes more mellow and less resistant to pulling, and its web structure is now made up of thinner gluten strands, as shown in **Figure 6.28**. By this stage, the sponge temperature has risen by 4.4 C° (8 F°) and its pH has declined from its previous level of 5.35 to 4.9, indicating a rather marked increase in acidity.

The sponge reaches full maturity in 4.5 hours, by which time its temperature has increased by 5.5 C° (10 F°), and its pH has dropped further to 4.5. As illustrated in **Figure 6.29**, the dough has acquired a soft, dry and pliable character, with an extensible web structure that consists of thin-walled gluten strands. If the sponge is permitted to continue its fermentation beyond this stage, it soon degenerates, and its web structure loses its soft, dry appearance and becomes over-gassed, bucky and wet, as shown in **Figure 6.30**.

Following the remix, in which the dough is brought to its optimum physical development after the remaining dough ingredients have been added, the dough gets a much briefer second fermentation, generally referred to as "floor time" and usually lasting no longer than 30 to 90 seconds. The principal purpose of this second fermentation is to bring about a relaxation of the stresses created within the dough by the mixer action. In general, the greater the work input during dough mixing (i.e., the longer the mixing time), the more floor time is required for the dough to recover from its physical working and to develop desirable machining properties.

The modifications of dough properties that occur during the floor time are illustrated in **Figures 6.31** through **6.34**. The freshly-mixed dough, illustrated in **Figure 6.31**, is soft, pliable and highly extensible and, if pulled out sufficiently, will break with a somewhat ragged tear. As floor time progresses, the dough becomes somewhat drier, loses its surface sheen and, when stretched, resists extension and breaks more cleanly. As **Figure 6.32**, it also assumes a more spongy character. The fully matured dough, pictured in **Figure 6.33**, has developed a fine, thin web structure, similar to that observed in the ripe sponge. The matured dough, when pulled, breaks quickly with short, clean fractures. If the floor time is extended much beyond this stage, the dough becomes over-gassed and bucky and acquires the wet and sticky character illustrated in **Figure 6.34**. Such dough will present great, if not insurmountable, problems in the subsequent makeup operations.

Fermentation in a straight dough passes through ripening stages similar to those of sponge fermentation: The dough aerates and develops in its rheological properties until it attains the degree of maturity needed for optimum volume and crumb quality characteristics in the finished loaf.

Using scanning electron microscopy, Khoo et al. (1975) observed the changes brought on by fermentation in dough structure at the microscopic level. **Figure 6.13** (on Page 23) shows a scanning electron micrograph of a freshly mixed dough in which the veil-like protein film covers the starch granules. In **Figure 6.14**, which represents a fully fermented dough, minute gas cells have formed within the protein matrix (at FS). A portion of a large air cell is visible in the upper left-hand corner (at AC). The increase in the size of the air cells as a result of gas generation causes the veil-like protein coating on the surface of the starch granules to stretch and roll up into fibrils. Not apparent in this micrograph, but revealed by transmission electron microscopy, is evidence that some of the starch granules have undergone partial internal enzymatic degradation without distortion. This, it is believed, improves the granules' capacity to stretch and distort during ovenspring.

6.B.3.a. Fermentation loss

Bakeries usually determine the so-called fermentation loss of sponges and doughs either by (a) calculating the total formula weight and comparing it with the determined weight of the fermented sponge or dough or (b) weighing the mixed sponge or dough before and after fermentation. Generally, a slight reduction in the weight of the fermented dough will be found, which may amount to as little as 0.5% or to as much as 3 to 4%. Under general conditions, a weight loss of 1% is commonly considered normal.

This manner of determining fermentation losses, however, deals only with apparent rather than actual losses because it fails to take into account the ultimate disappearance of dry substance that represents a true loss. In actuality, much of the loss of weight by the sponge during fermentation is due to moisture evaporation and can be made up by an adjustment in dough water during remixing. Moreover, this loss in sponge weight will vary with the humidity conditions in the fermentation room. The carbon dioxide gas that evolves from the sponge has too little mass to be of much consequence. Hence, real fermentation loss, or the loss of dry substance, does not become apparent until baking takes place.

During oven baking, the volatile substances (alcohol, carbon dioxide, certain organic acids, esters and similar compounds) formed by yeast from carbohydrates and nitrogenous substances are expelled from the baking dough by the oven heat. Such losses can be significant, as shown by Eisenberg (1948), who investigated the effect of malt addition to sponges made by a commercial formula. The higher the malt increment, the more vigorous was the fermentation and the greater the volume of gas produced. The relationships between malt increments, total gas produced, resultant loaf weight and loaf volume as found by this investigator are shown in **Table 6.11**.

Ethanol, driven off during the baking process, as noted, and exhausted through roof vents, can be involved in formation of smog. With the input of sunlight, it is a precursor to several smog-related environmental issues. Some states have already requested that bakeries install scrubbers on the bakery

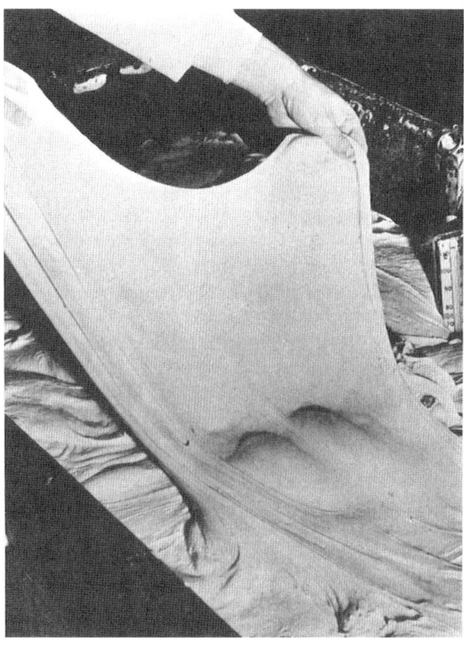

Figure 6.31. Freshly mixed dough is soft and pliable, with a highly extensible character.
(Swortfiguer 1950)

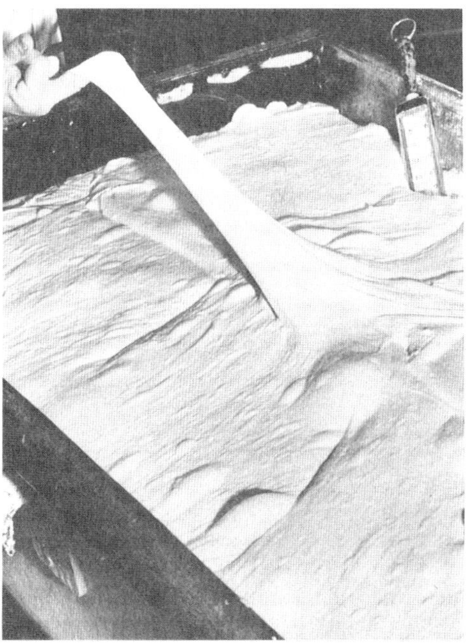

Figure 6.32. A dough that has received about one-fourth of its required floor time will be slightly spongy in appearance and breaks clean when over-stretched.
(Swortfiguer 1950)

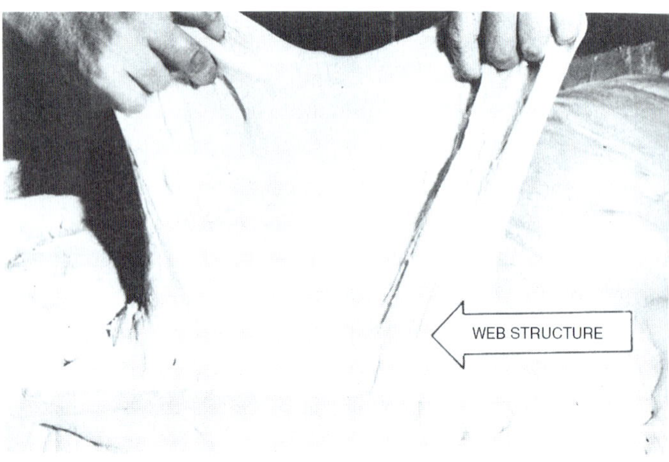

Figure 6.33. A fully matured dough exhibits a dry and mellow character and will break clean and sharp with minimum resistance to pull.
(Swortfiguer 1950)

Table 6.11. Fermentation Loss as a Function of Malt Flour Additions to the Sponge

Malt flour (g)	Total gas (cu cm)	Loaf weight (g)	Loaf volume (cu cm)
0.0	844	134.1	586
0.1	1,180	132.6	581
0.2	1,300	131.6	589
0.3	1,370	130.9	604

All data are calculated to 100 g total flour.
(Eisenberg 1948)

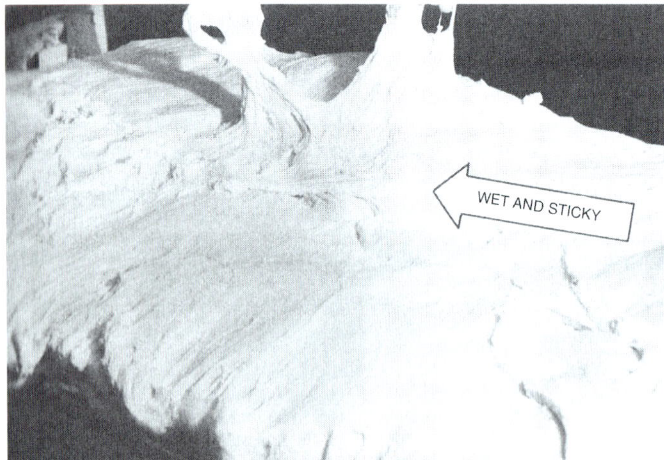

Figure 6.34. An over-fermented dough becomes over-gassed and bucky, with wet and sticky properties.
(Swortfiguer 1950)

oven stacks. Costs can be prohibitive especially if a plant has multiple ovens. Limiting yeast levels and or fermentation time can decrease the ethanol produced. The American Institute of Baking studied the matter (Stitley et al. 1987) and developed a program to estimate ethanol emission based on flour, yeast, fermentation time and oven capacity.

Davis and Stephens (1954) calculated the fermentation loss on a dry-substance-loss basis. Using a standard formula under standard baking conditions, they found a dry matter loss of 5.6 to 6.1% from dough mixing to finished bread with the sponge-dough method and of only 3.2% with the straight-dough method. Among factors that markedly influenced the dry-substance loss were yeast level, sponge percentage, sponge temperature and level of amylolytic activity in the flour.

Fermentation losses can be minimized by controlling sponge ingredients and fermentation conditions to limit the production of volatile fermentation by-products. Thus, reducing sponge time or temperature will decrease the fermentation loss. Low sponge percentages will have the same effect. Using flours of low diastatic activity for sponges and omitting malt supplements in the sponge stage are the most effective means for reducing fermentation losses. Eisenberg (1948) pointed out that bakeries, in changing from high- to low-fermentation loss conditions, can increase bread yield by as much as 4%. This represents a saving of sufficient economic significance to justify a close study of the factors that affect fermentation losses.

Worth noting is the loss of carbon dioxide that occurs when it is processed (**Table 6.12**). The amount of carbon dioxide in a fully proofed dough is only about 40% of the total produced by fermentation (Moore and Hoseney 1985). The balance is lost during punching, moulding and proofing.

6.B.3.b. Auxiliary effects

Yeast fermentation is but one of many reactions of a chemical and biological nature that occur in a dough or liquid preferment. For example, various enzymes, either naturally present in flour or added in the form of dough conditioners, catalyze numerous hydrolytic reactions, bringing about progressive degradation of the starch, proteins and lipids. Inorganic salts, serving as yeast nutrients and oxidants, cause far-reaching modifications to the general character of the dough.

The liquid phase of the dough is a highly complex colloidal sol. Baker (1946) separated the liquid phase of dough by means of super-centrifugation and obtained a very viscous solution that can be whipped to a stiff foam like the whites of egg. Analysis showed this liquid to contain dissolved pentosans and soluble proteins (mostly low-molecular albumins and globulins), carbohydrates, salts, enzymes and gases.

Table 6.12. Carbon Dioxide Balance in Bread Doughs

Source	Moles (CO_2) (x 10^{-2})	Volume (cu cm) (28°C, 750 mm Hg)
CO_2 produced by fermentation of 4 g carbohydrates	4.44	1,097
CO_2 retained by dough (end of proof)		
In gas cells	1.49	370
In aqueous phase	0.22	55
CO_2 lost during fermentation and proofing		
Surface diffusion	0.22	56
During punching and moulding	2.49	616

(Moore and Hoseney 1985)

As fermentation progresses, certain definite changes occur in the physical character of the dough that are collectively termed dough ripening or mellowing. Proper dough maturity or mellowness constitutes that point in fermentation at which dough possesses optimum spring and elasticity and will yield the best quality bread that the particular flour being used is capable of producing. Dough maturity comprises the sum total of all the effects produced by the reactions that take place during fermentation.

The two main by-products of yeast fermentation are alcohol and carbon dioxide, each being generated in about equal amounts on a weight basis. Because alcohol is a liquid at normal dough temperatures, it accumulates in the liquid phase at a significant concentration. Thus, it can be calculated that a dough to which 4 to 6% glucose has been added will, on complete fermentation, produce 2 to 3% alcohol, based on flour. Relating this level to the liquid phase, the concentration becomes 3 to 4.5%, a level that not only exerts a definite inhibitory effect on yeast activity but also will have some influence on the colloidal character of the proteins. Freshly-baked bread, in which most of the alcohol has been volatilized and driven off during baking, still contains some 0.5% ethanol, according to Wiseblatt (1960).

Carbon dioxide is fairly soluble in water, so the gas generated by yeast does not all remain in a gaseous state. According to Reed and Nagodawithana (1991), 100 g of dough will dissolve about 55 mg of carbon dioxide, or about 7.5% of the amount of gas evolved in one hour. Some carbon dioxide combines with water to form carbonic acid, a weak, unstable and only slightly ionized acid. The dissolved gas eventually vaporizes and becomes available for leavening when the dough is heated in the oven during baking.

Enzymatic hydrolysis proceeds from the time the dough is mixed until the oven's heat inactivates the enzymes. The rates of enzymatic action are not constant throughout, being affected by changes in the availability of appropriate substrates, pH of the dough and temperature. The amylases convert available starch and dextrins into maltose and, at the same time, degrade those starch granules that were structurally damaged by milling. Proteolytic enzymes act upon the protein materials of the dough, reducing some of them to lower-molecular-weight products that are then assimilated by the yeast. The overall effect of these enzymatic reactions is a softening of the dough, due in part to a reduction in the absorption capacity of the starch material and in part to a weakening of the gluten system. Other enzymes such as lipases, lipoxidases and pentosanases are also active and are thought to aid amylolysis by attacking, among other reactions, the pentosans and the lipid coatings that cover the starch granules.

Dough fermentation, in addition to generating alcohol and carbon dioxide, also produces small amounts of various acids, including lactic, acetic, succinic, propionic, fumaric and pyruvic acid. The formation of acids is seen in the time-dependent decrease of pH and an increase in titratable acidity in the fermenting medium. Lactic and acetic acids predominate and survive at levels of 50 to 100 mg per lb and 10 to 50 mg per lb, respectively, in the finished bread (Jackel 1969b). The accumulation of lactic acid and acetic acid in fermenting dough is due primarily to the presence of heterofermentative microorganisms of the genus Lactobacillus in both flour and compressed yeast, although homofermentative species of the same genus may also play a significant role in this respect. Of the two acids, acetic acid is normally found in smaller quantities. It is also weaker than lactic acid, with a lesser degree of ionization, and its effect upon the pH of the dough is correspondingly smaller.

6.B.4. Role of yeast

The fermentation stage of doughmaking gives yeast the resources and time these single-celled micro-organisms need to respire and grow. The results are measured in not only leavening power but also flavor and conditioning effects. A variety of chemical reactions occur as the yeast takes advantage of the dough's supportive environment that provides it with factors such as an adequate level of moisture, moderate temperatures, a proper degree of acidity and an ample supply of fermentable carbohydrates and nitrogenous substances, as well as certain essential minerals. These conditions form the basic requisites for proper fermentation.

In dough, when yeast ferments 100 lb of sugar (sucrose, glucose, fructose, maltose or any combination of these sugars), it forms 49 lb of alcohol, 47 lb of carbon dioxide (10.86 l of gas at 25°C, or 77°F) and 4 lb of glycerol, organic acids, aldehydes, fusel oils and other flavor precursors (Sanderson et al. 1983). Each gram of sugar fermented by bakers yeast generates 240 cu cm of gas. In the presence of oxygen (aerobic conditions), yeast will use the sugar to fuel production of more yeast cells; however, it quickly consumes all the oxygen in the dough's air cells, creating an anaerobic environment. Now the yeast turns the available sugars into carbon dioxide and ethanol, with only a small amount of yeast growth. In the course of fermentation, yeast also modifies pH conditions and softens, or mellows, the gluten character. All these effects add up to a highly complex system whose study is rendered more difficult by the introduction of additional variables in the form of different flours, different yeast strains and different formulations.

It is worth noting, as Reed (1975) did, that the bakers yeast strain of *Saccharomyces cerevisiae* performs its job of bread fermentation faster and in substantially different ways than the other strains responsible for beer, wine and whisky (**Table 6.13**). For one thing, in dough fermentation, there is little or no increase in the number of yeast cells, while in all of the other industries, a 10-fold increase in yeast cells occurs. He also stated, "One can make fairly acceptable beer and wine and whisky with a bakers yeast, and conversely, one can bake a fairly acceptable loaf of bread with a wine yeast or with a top-fermenting ale yeast." Indeed, before the commercial availability of bakers yeast, bakers leavened their doughs with the frothy foam that brewers skimmed from their wort tanks.

Table 6.13. Parameters for Commercial Use of Yeast in Industry

Parameter	Bread dough	Lager* beer	Ale beer	Wine	Whiskey
Raw material	Flour, sugar	Wort	Wort	Grape or fruit juice	Cereal mash
Fermentation time	1 to 3 hours	8 to 10 days	2 to 6 days	5 to 10 days	3 days
Fermentation temperature	30 to 35°C	10°C	20°C	15 to 27°C	35°C
pH	5.2 to 4.7	5.2 to 4.2	5.2 to 4.0	3.5	4.9 to 4.0
Final alcohol concentration	2 to 3%	4%	4%	11 to 13%	7 to 9%
No. of yeast cells at start**	275	6 to 10	6 to 10	5 to 10	5 to 10
No. of yeast cells at end**	300	36	24	50 to 150	50 to 150

** For primary fermentation*

*** Expressed in million cells per g or per ml*

(Reed 1975)

6.B.4.a. Growth

The biochemical reactions involved in the transformation of sugars into carbon dioxide and alcohol by yeast and sourdough bacteria are discussed in detail in Volume I, Chapter 2, Part B. Anaerobic environments characterize dough, so one would expect the primary physiological activity of yeast to be that of fermentation; however, evidence indicates that the organism also undergoes some growth and cell multiplication.

Hoffman et al. (1941a) were first to develop an accurate method for counting yeast cells in doughs. They found that in a standard test dough made with 1.67% yeast (flour weight basis) and fermented at 27°C (80°F), no significant increase in yeast-cell count occurs during the first 2 hours of fermentation, with the actual rise in cell numbers being on the order of 0.003%. The most vigorous yeast growth was observed during the period between 2 and 4 hours of fermentation, when the yeast cell count increased by 26%. Between 4 and 6 hours, the rate of yeast multiplication declined again to about 9%, based on the original cell count (Hoffman et al. 1941b).

The effect of yeast level on the rate of cell multiplication was also studied. Findings indicated that the smaller the original quantity of yeast in the dough, the greater the percentage increase in cell numbers during the fermentation, with all other conditions being held constant. Thus a 0.5% yeast addition to the test dough produced an 88% increase in cell count after 6 hours of fermentation, yet with a 2% original yeast level, the corresponding increase in cell numbers was only 29%.

In a later study, Merritt (1960) found 56% yeast growth in a sponge fermented for 4 hours, and only an additional 1% was observed during dough fermentation and until the end of the proof period. The original yeast level of 2.25% was thus increased to 3.55% in the course of the entire fermentation. In a liquid preferment made with 3% yeast, the cell count increased by only 1% in the preferment, but by 15% in the dough, again including the final proof, for a total quantitative increase to 3.48%. This reduced growth rate of yeast in liquid ferments accounts for the general practice of using higher original yeast levels in liquid ferments.

Kosmina (1977) summarized results from studies about yeast growth in sponges, liquid preferments and doughs conducted by researchers in the former Soviet Union. In general, their findings showed increases in yeast cell numbers of 40% in sponges, 32% in doughs made from sponges and 44% in proofed dough pieces. The corresponding increases in yeast cells for liquid preferments were 12%, 46% and 59%.

The quantitative rate of gas production tended to correlate roughly with the increase in yeast cell numbers during fermentation.

In contrast, Carlin (1958), in a study of the microbiological composition of sponges and straight doughs, found no increase in the yeast population during a 4-hour fermentation period. Reed (1975) reported essentially the same observations. He pointed out that although it is rather difficult to determine the actual number of cells in a dough, it is relatively easy to establish the percentage of yeast cells that have buds. Compressed yeast will normally contain about 2 to 5% budding cells, and this number increases to about 30 to 50% by the end of the sponge fermentation, with no additional increase during dough fermentation. This increase in bud formation by the yeast cells is basically a sign of incipient yeast growth. In the case of straight doughs, there is very little budding of yeast cells during the first three rises but a substantial increase to about 40% during the proof period. No increase in the number of yeast cells was observed in liquid flour preferments, while budding was found in only about 18% of the cells after 3.5 hours of fermentation (Thorn and Ross 1960). Aside from budding, yeast also exhibits a perceptible increase in cell size during fermentation in these dough systems. This, of course, is another sign of growth.

The conditions present in preferments affects the growth rates of yeast (Trivedi et al. 1989). For example, liquid sponges, which incorporate a major portion of the flour, resemble plastic sponges and are quite tolerant to variations in fermentation time. With water brews, which contain no flour, the type of yeast is more critical because all the fermentable carbohydrates are provided by added sucrose, dextrose or corn syrup. These sugars ferment very quickly, while the pH of the unbuffered water brew drops to 4.2 or lower because of formation of carbon dioxide and organic acids by the yeast. This change slows the rate of yeast fermentation. Trivedi et al. (1989) recommended that bakers use a fast-fermenting yeast, buffer the water brew, adhere to exact timings of brew fermentation and apply refrigeration if brews are to be held for extended periods. **Table 6.14** summarizes common formulations for liquid sponge, water brew and concentrated water brew forms of preferments.

6.B.4.b. Effects of nutrients

The noticeable spur to the rate of yeast activity given by the addition of yeast nutrients may also be considered evidence that some active growth of yeast takes place during dough fermentation. It is a well-established fact that the ammonium

Table 6.14. Liquid Preferment Formulations

Ingredient	Liquid sponge	Water brew	Concentrated water brew
Water, %	59 to 64	61 to 66	30
Yeast (compressed), %	2.5	3.5	3.0
Sugar (sucrose), %	0.5	2.5	2.0
Salt, %	–	0.25	0.75
Buffering agent, %	0.1	0.19	0.25
Yeast nutrient, %	0.5	0.60	–
Flour, %	40 to 70	–	–

All values are based on flour = 100%

(Trivedi et al. 1989)

salts used in yeast foods (ammonium sulfate, ammonium chloride and ammonium carbonate) all stimulate yeast activity. Ammonium chloride, in particular, is effective at low yeast levels.

Buffers. Ling and Hoseney (1977) prepared a synthetic medium of nutrients and a buffer that gives a yeast fermentation rate equal to that obtained with flour. Maximum carbon dioxide production required the presence of ammonium, phosphate, magnesium, sulfate and potassium ions in the medium. Flour and nonfat dry milk were found to serve as excellent buffering agents.

Salt. In concentrations of more than 1.5% (flour weight basis), salt inhibits yeast activity, either by its osmotic pressure or by a specific chemical effect. For this reason, salt is generally withheld from the sponge in the sponge-and-dough process; however, evidence shows that at lower levels, rather than being detrimental, salt actually exerts a favorable influence on yeast fermentation. In a series of studies, Preston and co-workers (Preston et al. 1984, Kilborn et al. 1981, Preston and Kilborn 1982) demonstrated that use of 0.5 to 1.0% salt in the sponge made according to the sponge-and-dough process reduced fermentation time and bromate levels, while at the same time producing a better quality bread vs. using a sponge with 0.15% or no salt. Working with a hard red spring wheat flour with a protein content of 12.7%, an ash content of 0.39% and a Farinograph absorption of 65.6%, the researchers found that with 1.0% salt in the sponge, bread of good quality could be produced after only 2.25 hours of fermentation with 20 ppm bromate, while with only 0.15% salt in the sponge, a fermentation time of 4.5 hours was required. Good quality bread could be produced without bromate with 3.75 hours of fermentation and 1.0% salt in the sponge, whereas a salt-free sponge required 6 hours of fermentation for comparable bread quality. Optimum bread quality scores resulted with 0.5 to 1.0% salt levels and a total bromate addition of 15 ppm after a 2.5-hour fermentation. Comparable results were obtained with other flours of varying protein content and grade.

Sugars. Yeast exhibits a variable preference for different sugars. It readily assimilates four sugars: (a) sucrose (after hydrolysis to glucose and fructose by the yeast's native invertase or sucrase enzymes), (b) glucose, (c) fructose and (d) maltose (after hydrolysis of glucose by yeast maltase). Koch et al. (1954) and Griffith and Johnson (1955) studied the preferential use of sugars by yeast. Bakers yeast consumes glucose first, then fructose and finally maltose (**Figure 6.35** and **6.36**) (Tang et al. 1972). The fermentation rate of fructose is slower than that of glucose, and it is sensitive to pH, and fermentation of maltose proceeds even more slowly.

Doughs prepared without added sugar (i.e., made only from flour, water, yeast and salt) will initially contain about 0.5% glucose and fructose derived from the flour. This relatively low level is adequate to start fermentation and to activate the yeast's adaptive malto-zymase system responsible for maltose fermentation. Fermentation is sustained by the action of the α- and β-amylases native to flour that convert the susceptible damaged starch granules into maltose. Damaged starch results from milling, and its level is normally much higher in hard wheat flours than in soft wheat flours.

Pelshenke and Koeber (1940) demonstrated a steady increase in the maltose content of sugar-free, un-yeasted doughs, resulting from the hydrolytic action of the flour amylases. In yeasted doughs, this increase in maltose also occurs during the first stages of fermentation, until the initial supply of glucose and fructose is exhausted, after which the maltose content gradually declines.

Koch et al. (1954) studied straight doughs with 3% yeast to which 7.5% sugar has been added and learned that although glucose shows a steady decrease during a 3-hour fermentation, and fructose shows at first a slight increase and then a rather rapid decline during the third hour of fermentation, there is a slight but steady increase of maltose during the entire fermentation period because of starch hydrolysis.

Quantitative calculations show that 1 g of yeast will ferment about 0.32 g of glucose per hour during a normal fermentation. Piekarz (1963) traced the disappearance of sugars in a liquid-preferment dough system to which 8% fermentable solids was added in the form of glucose and maltose. He observed that the maltose content decreased somewhat in the liquid ferment but then increased in the dough stage as a result of amylolysis in the dough. The system used up about 3% of the fermentable carbohydrates, with the remaining 5% forming the residual sugars found in the finished bread.

The quantitative changes in the various sugar concentrations in fermentation systems such as straight-dough, sponge-and-dough and liquid preferment-and-dough methods, with the preferments containing 0, 25, and 50% of flour, respectively, were studied by Tang et al. (1972). Gas production was observed manometrically by measuring the changes in gas pressure, and residual sugars were determined by chromatography. The findings showed that inversion of sucrose during mixing, while rapid, was not completed immediately, and the inversion rate was slowest in flour-free preferments. Gas production rates in liquid ferments correlated positively with their re-

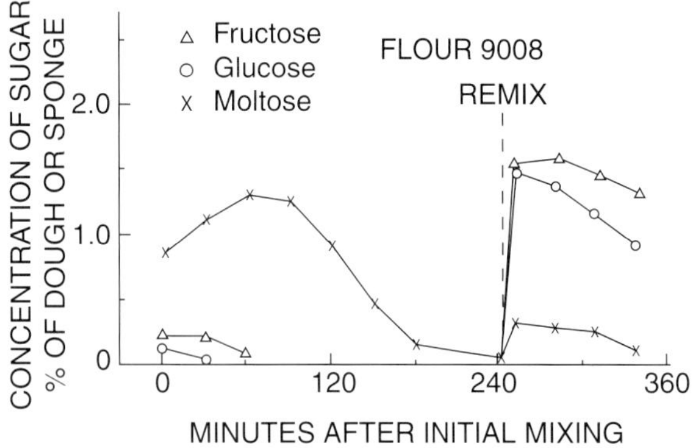

Figure 6.35. Results in sponges (75% flour) and doughs made with two different flours show the changes in concentration of glucose (circle), fructose (triangle) and maltose (cross) as fermentation progresses and after remixing.
(Tang et al. 1972)

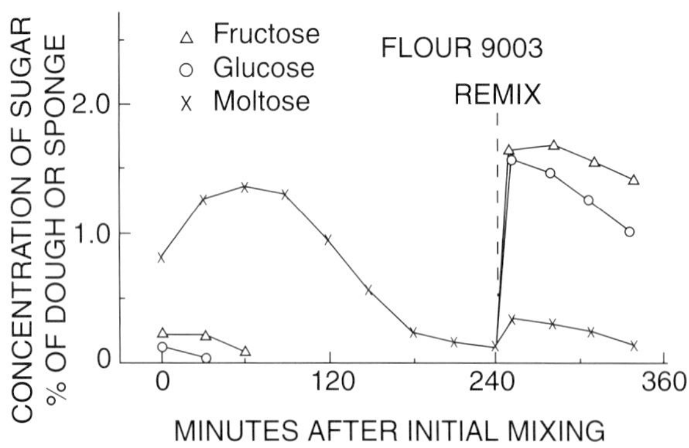

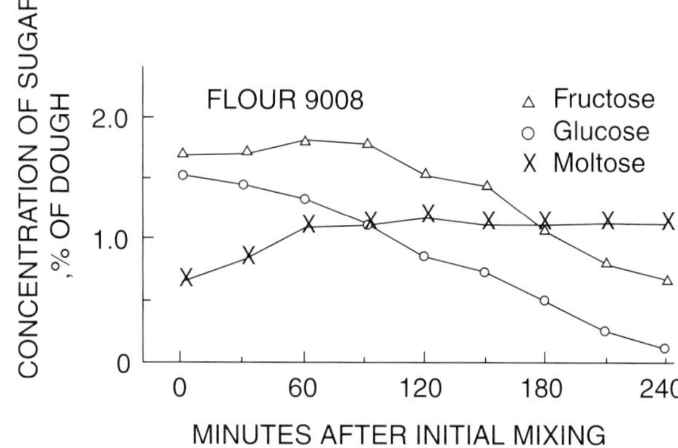

Figure 6.36. Results in straight doughs made with two different flours show the changes in concentration of glucose (circle), fructose (triangle) and maltose (cross) as fermentation progresses.
(Tang et al. 1972)

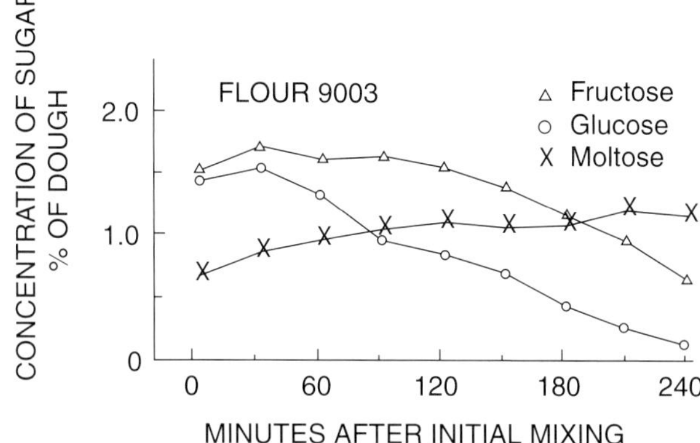

spective flour levels. The breads from the different fermentation systems varied both in their residual sugar contents and sugar compositions. Thus, straight-dough bread had a high maltose content but was lowest in glucose and fructose. On the other hand, sponge-and-dough bread had the lowest maltose content but large amounts of glucose and fructose. Breads made by the preferment-and-dough methods generally contained the highest level of residual sugars.

Different yeast strains vary in their maltase activity. White (1954) cited experimental results in which one yeast strain, with a low maltase activity, needed 21 minutes longer to produce two rises in a dough than did a high-maltase yeast. A single yeast strain may also exhibit variable maltase activity under different test conditions. Thus, Seeley and Ziegler (1962) tested one strain of yeast that yielded satisfactory gas production in a lean dough in which maltose was the primary sugar substrate but failed to ferment pure maltose in an aqueous solution even though it readily assimilated glucose. This observation led these authors to hypothesize that some constituent of flour contributes in some manner to the yeast's ability to ferment maltose. The rate of maltose fermentation by yeast also has been shown to be influenced by pH to a much greater degree than is true of glucose fermentation (1945). Yeast strains incapable of fermenting maltose are a factor in San Francisco-style sourdough systems (Sugihara et al. 1970, 1971).

Vitamins, minerals. In addition to carbohydrates and nitrogenous compounds, yeast requires various vitamin and mineral nutrients to attain maximum activity. Atkin et al. (1945) identified the specific minerals and vitamins essential to yeast growth and fermentative action by the use of synthetic media. While most of the nutrients found to be essential are supplied in adequate amounts by flour, the addition of a readily available nitrogen source significantly promoted gas production. For this reason, many commercial yeast foods contain ammonium salts as a major component.

Yeast foods. Regarding the use of yeast food to manipulate fermentation time, no universally applicable rules can be advanced. Speaking very generally, higher levels of yeast food will promote shorter fermentation times, and with longer fermentation times, the level of yeast food must be reduced. A safe procedure to follow is to introduce such changes gradually, preferably in increments of 20 to 25% of the originally used amount.

6.B.4.c. Effects of dough environment

pH. Yeast tolerates considerable extremes of pH and is able to maintain active fermentation in a 5%-glucose solution in the pH range of 2.4 to 7.4 but ceases activity at pH 2.0 or pH 8.0 (Neish and Blackwood 1951).

The duration of exposure to adverse pH conditions is of significance in this connection. Pomper (1969) found that yeast could actively ferment at a pH 3 for about one hour at 30°C (86°F) with very little effect on final leavening activity. Yet when the fermentation time was extended beyond one hour, subsequent leavening performance was adversely affected. In general, good practice dictates that the pH of the fermenting medium be maintained within the range of about 4.0 to 6.0 for optimum results (Cooper and Reed 1968). Garver et al. (1966), for example, observed that in preferments at pH 3.5, a decided drop of more than 50% occurred in fermentative activity. More gradual declines in yeast activity were encountered at higher pH levels, with measurable effects showing up at pH values over 6.0.

The explanation for the yeast's ability to maintain a relatively constant activity over a 100-fold change in hydrogen ion concentration (as occurs when going from pH 4 to pH 6) is found in the fact that the pH of the cell interior of the yeast remains quite constant at about pH 5.8, regardless of any relatively wide pH variations in the fermenting medium. The enzymes involved in fermentation thus operate in an optimum pH environment within the yeast cell that is largely unaffected by external changes in pH (Cooper and Reed 1968).

Although bakers yeast fermentation itself produces various acids, the dough's pH is more strongly affected by the presence of ammonium salts in yeast foods, especially if the ammonia is present as the salt of a strong acid such as hydrochloric or sulfuric acid. Yeast readily assimilates ammonia as a nitrogen source, thereby liberating the acids as shown by the following, greatly simplified equations:

$$(NH_4)_2SO_4 + \text{yeast assimilation} \rightarrow H_2SO_4$$
$$(\text{ammonium sulfate} + \text{yeast assimilation} \rightarrow \text{sulfuric acid})$$

$$NH_4Cl + \text{yeast assimilation} \rightarrow HCl$$
$$(\text{ammonium chloride} + \text{yeast assimilation} \rightarrow \text{hydrochloric acid})$$

Sulfuric and hydrochloric acids are both very strong acids that ionize completely, and hence, all their hydrogen ions are available to affect the pH of the system.

The acidification of the dough during fermentation is quite marked, even though the amounts of acids produced are relatively small. Thus, the pH of a freshly mixed dough is generally within a range of 5.3 to 5.5. By the end of fermentation, it will have dropped to 4.7 to 4.5. Similarly, there is about a 40% increase in titratable acidity in the fermented dough. This increase in the acidic character of the dough has measurable effects on the hydration and swelling of the gluten, the rate of enzyme action and on various chemical reactions involving organic salt formation and oxidation-reduction processes.

Temperature. The fermenting medium's temperature also exerts a significant effect on the yeast's gassing rate. In general, the fermentation rate increases with a rise in temperature up to a maximum of perhaps 38 to 41°C (100 to 105°F). **Figure 6.37** shows the rates of carbon dioxide generation in a dough without added sugar over a 3-hour period at various temperatures within the range of 27.5 to 35°C (81.5 to 95°F). The initial high rate of fermentative activity is due to the yeast's rapid assimilation of the free sugars available in the flour. The drop-off in the rate that follows marks the exhaustion of the supply of this free sugar and the period of adaptation of the yeast to the fermentation of the maltose that is being produced by the action of amylases on the damaged starch in the flour. The gassing rate of the yeast rises again for about 3 hours, when the maltose supply also becomes depleted. The final decline in the fermentation rate is most pronounced at 35°C (95°F) because here the fermentation is faster and exhausts the maltose supply earlier.

Once the dough or ferment temperature exceeds about 41°C (105°F), inhibition of the yeast enzymes will ultimately make itself felt, resulting in a decrease in the fermentation rate. This decline is shown in **Table 6.15**, taken from Garver et al.

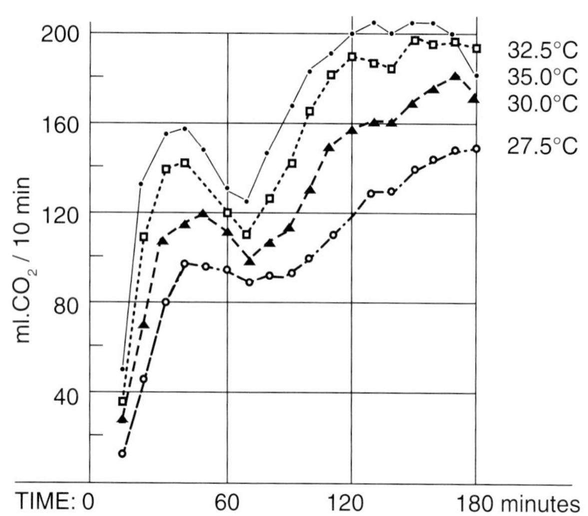

Figure 6.37. Gassing rate curves for doughs show carbon dioxide generation as a function of temperature. (Harbrecht and Kautzmann 1967)

(1966). The tabulated values report that gas production increases as the temperature rises to 38°C (100°F) and then declines at temperatures above that level.

Research into the effect of proofing temperature on pan bread quality by Siffring and Bruinsma (1993) came to similar conclusions for products made by sponge-and-dough methods. Loaf volume (**Figure 6.38**) changed most dramatically with rising proofing temperatures. The cooler the proof, the larger the volume. Also, to keep proof time constant through a range of proof temperatures, varying amounts of yeast were necessary.

Osmotic pressure. High concentrations of sugars, inorganic salts and other solubles inhibit yeast fermentation as a result of the physicochemical effects produced by high osmotic pressures. Basically, all fermentable sugars begin to exert an inhibiting effect on yeast when their concentration exceeds about 5% in the dough, with the degree of inhibition becoming progressively greater as the concentration of the sugar rises beyond the optimum (Schulz 1965). This inhibitory effect is more pronounced with sugars such as sucrose, glucose and fructose than with maltose. The last sugar is a disaccharide that persists as such in the fermenting medium until it is consumed by the yeast and therefore exerts a lower osmotic pressure than the monosaccharides and the readily hydrolyzed sucrose. The sensitivity of yeast to osmotic pressure varies with different strains, so some are better suited than others for fermenting sweet doughs with their high sugar contents.

Salt exerts a similar osmotic effect, except that some fermentation inhibition appears to occur at concentrations below the normal 2.0% level. Seeley and Ziegler (1962) cited experimental data that show a decrease in gas production from 929 mm to 753 mm Hg pressure (4-hour total) when the concentration of sodium chloride was increased from 1.5 to 2.5% in a straight dough. According to White (1954), 1% salt (flour weight basis) exerts an osmotic effect equal to that of 6% glucose.

Mold and rope inhibitors, when used beyond maximum recommended levels, also depress the gassing rate of yeast. In this instance, however, the effect appears to be specifically chemical in nature rather than because of osmotic pressure. Seeley and Ziegler (1962) tested the effects of calcium propionate and sodium diacetate on the proof times of doughs. They found that when calcium propionate is increased from 0.19% based on flour (a level that provides mold protection in bread for 1 week) to 0.32%, the final proof time is extended from 67 minutes to 79 minutes, or by about 18%. In the case of sodium diacetate (where the 0.32% level is needed to provide mold inhibition for 1 week),

Table 6.15. Effect of Temperature on Gas Production of Liquid Ferments

Temperature °C (°F)	Maximum gas production rate in mmoles CO_2 per hour per g dry yeast solids	Time to maximum gas production rate in minutes
29 (84.2)	20.0	150
31 (87.8)	23.0	135
33 (91.4)	24.5	135
35.5 (95.9)	25.0	120
38 (100.4)	26.0	90
40 (104.0)	22.5	75
42 (107.6)	20.0	30

(Garver et al. 1966)

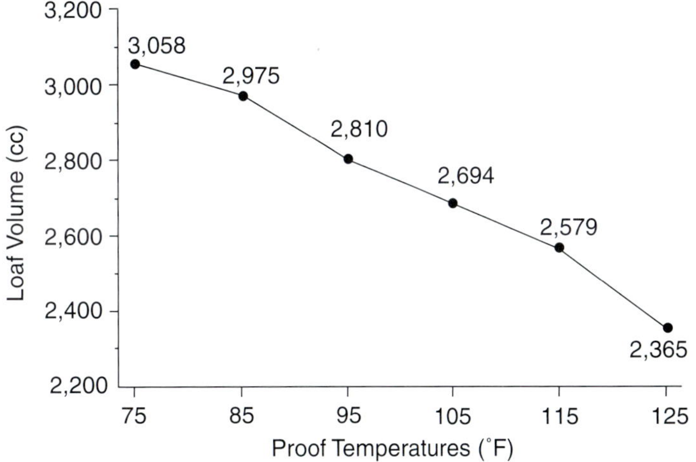

Figure 6.38. Mean bread volumes (cu cm) decreased when doughs were proofed at 75, 85, 95, 105, 115 and 125°F. (Siffring and Bruinsma 1993)

a similar increase from 0.19 to 0.32% caused the proof time to increase from 64 minutes to 70 minutes, or not quite 10%.

6.B.4.d. Fermentative adaptation

When yeast is first added to the sponge or dough, it is still in a relatively dormant state induced by the final stages of its manufacture and refrigeration. According to Jackel (1969a), yeast requires about 45 minutes in a favorable environment to fully adapt to fermentation, although it begins to produce carbon dioxide and ethanol in a much shorter time. During this period of adaptation, yeast is highly sensitive to both favorable and unfavorable environmental influences. It is essential, therefore, in the initial stages of fermentation, to carefully control all factors that are known to affect yeast behavior. This control is somewhat more readily accomplished in sponge-and-dough than in straight-dough systems. In sponges, in which the critical yeast adaptation takes place, yeast-inhibitory ingredients such as salt, mold inhibitors and high sugar levels are normally withheld for the specific purpose of providing an environment that will favor the prompt initiation of the fermentative activity of yeast. No such amelioration of the environment for yeast is possible with straight doughs, so that in this system, the adaptive stage of fermentation represents a more critical phase. The common practice with flour-containing preferments of withholding the salt, mold inhibitors and the bulk of the fermentable carbohydrates for the first 45 minutes, or until after the yeast has fully adapted, is also intended to provide the yeast with an optimum growth-conducive environment.

All other factors being equal, yeast adaptation is promoted perceptibly by a plentiful supply of moisture, as in slack sponges and dilute preferments. Because water serves as the indispensable medium in which the metabolic processes of yeast take place, its relative abundance significantly accelerates the rate at which these processes occur. The lower levels of water in stiff sponges and highly concentrated preferments accounts for the common observation that these systems are usually marked by delays in full yeast adaptation.

In no-time dough processes, the preliminary bulk fermentation is eliminated as a dough conditioning phase because its function is accomplished by appropriate mixing at ultra-high speeds and/or by the use of reducing dough additives such as cysteine and proteases. In doughs made by no-time and high-speed-mixing methods, full yeast activity during the makeup and final proof periods is often difficult to attain. This shortcoming is normally corrected by increasing the amount of yeast in the dough by 50 to 100% greater than the usual level or by the prior activation of the yeast in special slurry systems and flour-free preferments.

The rate of gas production by yeast under normal temperature conditions does not usually reach its maximum until some 2 hours after the yeast has been placed into the fermentation medium. This maximum rate, however, is not wholly comparable to the full yeast adaptation referred to by Jackel (1969a). The actual time interval before the onset of maximum gas production depends markedly on the temperature of the medium (Reed 1966, Garver et al. 1966).

6.B.5. Sour doughs

While breadmaking using wheat flour first developed in Egypt and the Middle

East and spread throughout temperate zones, the agricultural conditions in colder regions with shorter growing periods such as Northern Europe caused its people to turn to faster-growing rye as their chief cereal grain. Rye flours posed special problems during doughmaking, noted by Reed and Nagodawithana (1991) and Doerry (1995a), among others. Rye flour contains high levels of amylase enzymes, and those enzymes cause the crumb of bread made from 100% rye flour to collapse during baking and shrink away from the crust. An acid dough did not exhibit the same problems so bakers learned to acidify, or "sour," their doughs by treating them with yeast and/or bacteria. By so fermenting their rye-based doughs, they created the required acidic environment, thus making rye flours suitable for breadmaking.

Sour dough fermentation is also applied to wheat flour doughs to achieve flavor and texture effects not possible through use of bakers yeast alone.

Acidic doughs also provide optimum conditions for phytase enzymes to break down phytic acid, which is concentrated right below the bran layer. Phytic acid interferes with absorption of metallic ions such as calcium, iron, copper and zinc in the intestinal tract. This problem exists in not only rye products but also whole-grain items because they are made from flour containing all the bran of the original grains. Reducing dough pH from the usual 6 to 4.5 cuts phytic acid to less than 10% of its original concentration (Fretzdorff and Brümmer 1992).

Sour dough fermentation produces bread that is more acidic, with a pH ranging from 3.7 to 4.0, than that made by other breadmaking methods, which posses a pH of 5.0 to 5.5. The sourness is a result of the presence of acetic and lactic acids, although other acids are produced by the bacterial fermentation involved. Acetic acid is the more prevalent, representing 50% or more of the total acid content of the sourdough product (Hoerner and Boge 1997). Lactic and butyric acids give a smooth "buttery" flavor, while acetic and propionic acids are sharper — "vinegary" — in taste. The differences in flavor profiles of sourdough breads reflect the differences in the mix of bacteria in their starters (Anon. 2002).

But first, a word about words. There is "sourdough" the product and "sour dough" the process, but the two are often confused (Anon. 1995). Not only do the two concepts sound alike to the ear, but also they overlap in their meaning during production, thus raising the level of misunderstanding. Sourdough bread is produced through a classic sour dough process. The baker saves a portion of today's dough as the starter for tomorrow's doughs. Even before bakers knew about yeast's role in baking, they used starters to keep their leaven vital, and they termed the method "sour" because starters smelled and tasted like soured milk.

North American bakers tend to apply the word "sourdough" to both the process and the flavor of the finished product, as well as the product itself. For Europeans, the usage is for process only. A linguistic reason also fosters the confusion: Germanic languages favor the use of a single concatenated word to represent a process, in this case, *Sauerteig* (sourdough).

Sour dough refers specifically to letting doughs ferment for long periods, 10 to 24 hours or more. As the micro-organisms — yeast and bacteria — present in the dough grow, they produce many different organic compounds. Some enable leavening. Others act as flavorants, dough conditioners and mold inhibitors. But all count as natural.

Breads leavened with sourdough do not necessarily possess a strong sour or acid flavor, and good sourdough bread has only a slight sour taste and a very pleasant aromatic bread flavor (Doerry 1998). They are generally leavened by a spontaneous fermentation of a flour-water mixture enriched with naturally occurring micro-organisms, mainly wild yeast and bacteria found in wheat flour and/or rye flour. All flours harbor a large population of micro-organisms, but their numbers are larger in whole-grain flours and those with high ash content.

The ratio of flour to water is not critical, but using 1.25 parts of water to 1 part of flour will give a sour ferment with a consistency similar to liquid sponge. Doerry (1998) explained that the first water/flour blend is set at about 28 to 30°C (82 to 86°F) and allowed to rest at 32 to 35°C (90 to 95 °F). During the next 24 hours, the blend develops some acidity and needs to be fed more water and flour at the rate of four times the original amounts. This changes the water-to-flour ratio to 6.25:5.0. A resting period of 6 to 8 hours follows, and the mixture is again replenished at the same multiplier factor, creating a 31.5:25.0 ratio of water and flour. After 10 to 16 more hours, the replenishing step is repeated periodically one to three times a day. After 2 days, the sour is matured for no longer than 6 to 9 hours at 27°C (80°F) before replenishing again. If the sour is replenished only once or twice every day, then it should be refrigerated 9 hours after the last replenishing of the day. It may take six to 10 more replenishing steps to bring a new sour to sufficient development for dough leavening.

Replenished sourdough starters are best set and kept at 24 to 27°C (75 to 80°F). In use, such starters should be kept at cool temperatures and replenished at least daily. Higher temperatures favor the growth of undesirable organisms and may lead to off-flavors in the finished products. Doerry (1998) advised that it is better to start a new spontaneous sour than try to nurse an old starter back to health.

When using a mature sour as a starter, the entire dough becomes a replenish-ment step, and the amount of starter added to the dough determines the overall fermentation time. Typical amounts of flour in the starter account for 3 to 5% of the formula flour but may be as high as 10%. Bulk fermentation is like that of the straight-dough process: It requires troughs and floor space. Sponge methods also work, with the amount of flour prefermented in the mature sour ranging from 10 to 40% of total formula flour.

A small amount of yeast may be added to sour doughs to supplement their gas production and to adjust to schedules for proofing and baking operations. If using long proof times for products made with sour dough, then a yeast spike is not recommended.

Many wild yeasts produce a fermentation similar to that of the commercial bakers yeast. Some tolerate more or less acidity and prefer a softer or firmer ferment. The ferments do differ in pH, with wild yeast at 3.5 to 4 and regular bakers yeast at above 4.8.

The bacteria in spontaneous sour doughs are both homofermentative, producing lactic acid but no carbon dioxide, and heterofermentative, yielding lactic and/or acetic acids plus carbon dioxide. Dry and wet doughs tend to favor different micro-organisms. Dry sour doughs (50 to 60% absorption) that mature at cool temperatures (12 to 15°C, or 53 to 59°F) produce a very strong, sharp taste in bread. The addition of only a small amount of salt will drastically cut sour activity, and some bakers will deliberately add a very small amount of salt to stabilize sours over weekends or days when no production is scheduled.

Prepared sourdough bases are widely available, and their strength varies according to the types and amounts of acids present (Ziemke and Sanders 1988). Some are made by fermenting flour over long periods and then concentrating or drying the preferment, thus inactivating the wild yeasts and bacteria. Others include live micro-organisms. Some bases contain only natural fermentation acids, while others are blends of organic acids (acetic, lactic) and acid salts. Such blends may also contain flour, starch and vegetable shortening.

Doerry (1998) provided a succinct guide to starting and replenishing sours and discussed current commercial practices. Earlier, Lorenz (1981) described multiple-, 2- and 1-stage sour doughs based on the classic Detmold, Monheim and Berlin rye sour doughs of Germany. San Francisco sourdough bread, its process, fermentation and makeup are discussed by Ziemke and Sanders (1988) and Hoerner and Boge (1997). The microbiology of the sour dough process was described in additional detail in Volume I, Chapter 2, Part B, and formulation of sourdough products will be covered in Chapter 8 of this volume.

6.C. Dividing

The basic function of a bakery's makeup department (**Figure 6.39**) is the division of the fermented bulk dough into individual dough pieces of proper weight that, when moulded, proofed and baked, will yield the desired finished product. At one time, this operation was done entirely by hand and involved cutting the bulk dough into pieces of appropriate loaf or roll size, rounding the pieces on a flour-dusted dough bench to seal the surface with a gas-retaining skin and, following a brief rest, degassing and moulding them into the desired shape, ready for panning and proofing. All these operations are now performed by a series of specialized machines, described in Chapter 9 of this volume.

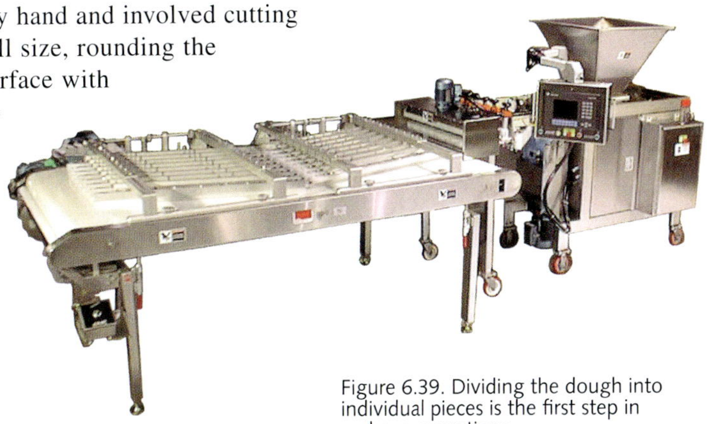

6.C.1. Volumetric vs. gravimetric methods

Accuracy in dividing is so critical that bakers often refer to the divider as the bakery's "cash register." Get the weight right, and you make money. Get it wrong by over-scaling, and you give profits away. Worse still, if you get it wrong by under-scaling, you risk consumer dissatisfaction, as well as legal and regulatory problems.

Figure 6.39. Dividing the dough into individual pieces is the first step in makeup operations.
(AMF Bakery Systems)

The craft baker can "eyeball" the manual division of dough and place the dough piece on a small bench scale to add or pinch off small portions to reach an exact weight, but the automated shop has neither the time nor the talent to manage dough dividing this way. The rheological properties of dough have previously been a nearly insurmountable obstacle to the development of an acceptable gravimetric method of scaling. So, until recently, automated dough dividers have operated on the principle of volumetric measurement, a predictive method that uses density and volume to determine weight.

Volumetric dividing is done by forcing dough by its own weight or externally applied pressure into a compression chamber of fixed size (**Figure 6.40**). The chamber, usually cylindrical in shape, is sized to contain enough dough to meet

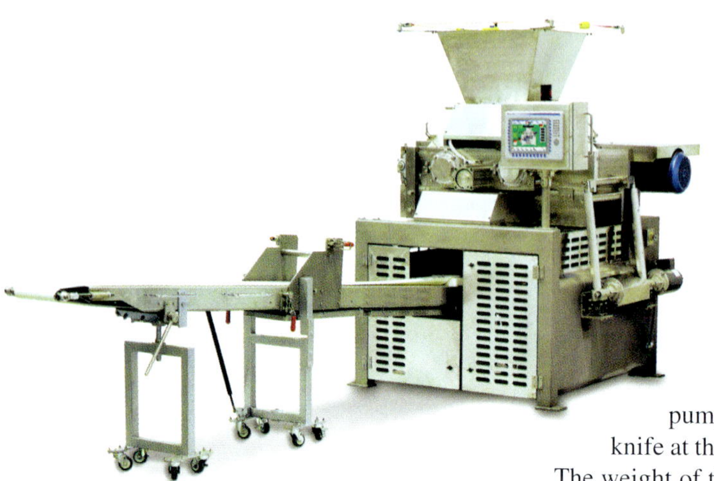

Figure 6.40. Ram-and-knife, pocket and press dividers use volumetric methods to portion dough.
(Turkington USA)

the weight requirements of the individual loaf. The major problem associated with volumetric scaling is that the dough, because of continuing fermentation, undergoes a perceptible change in density during the dividing operation. Borthwick (1973) found that the dough's density may decrease up to 20% during the 20 minutes it normally takes to process a dough batch through the divider. Hence, unless corrective steps are taken, the last dough pieces to emerge from the divider will weigh less than the earlier dough pieces.

Like the ram-and-shear dividers, rotary dividers also use volumetric methods. Here the dough is pumped through tube-like chambers, with a timed cut-off knife at the exit to separate the bulk dough into individual pieces. The weight of the individual piece depends on the tube's dimensions, the knife's timing and the dough's density.

Because the rotary divider can add to the development of the dough as it passes through the system, some bakeries find it possible to reduce time after cleanup in the horizontal mixer by 30 seconds up to 1 minute. Such under-mixed doughs are generally a few degrees cooler than a fully mixed dough. The development action of the divider's transfer pump and the single-pocket divider add back the missing heat.

Because final development occurs just prior to division, rotary dividing methods yield no discernible difference in product quality from the front to the back of a dough. Also, this process requires no divider oil.

Gravimetric methods, which divide based on weight, would be more accurate because they involve neither volume nor density. Dough is sticky and balky, as noted earlier; however, the advent of laminating as a bread makeup technology, a method that handles dough as a continuous sheet, opened the path to true gravimetric dividing. Application of computerized control techniques also proved necessary (Gorton 2001, Whitaker 2008).

As currently practiced, the gravimetric dividing method begins with a chunk of dough dropping by gravity from a dough hopper onto a conveyor (**Figure 6.41**). The weight of the dough is recorded as it passes over a scale under the conveyor. The dough is joined to the chunk in front of it and continues along the conveyor. The computer monitors the dough's weight at several points along the line and feeds back signals to control the hopper doors and conveyor speeds. Because dough is handled as

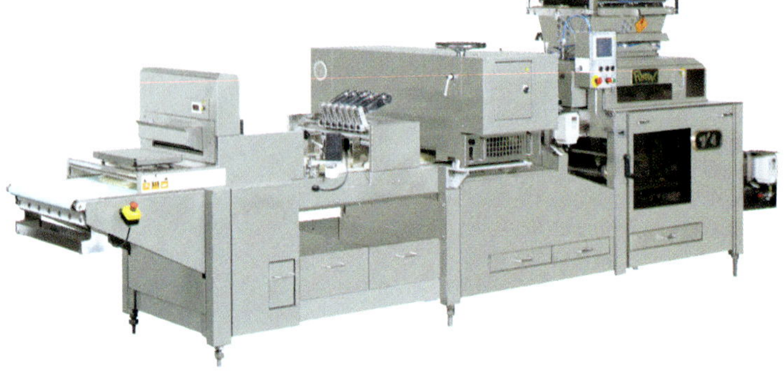

Figure 6.41. Chunks of dough, dropped by gravity onto conveyors monitored by scale use gravimetric methods to portion dough.
(Rheon USA)

a continuous sheet, dividing does not take place until the end of makeup, but control over the line's speed assures accurate scaling despite the volume and density changes that occur during the process.

6.C.2. Control over dividing

For optimum results, batch doughs should be completely scaled within 20 minutes or less. Batch sizes that take longer to run through dividing will show excessive variation in density from beginning to end and thus compromise product uniformity and create problems for downstream operations. Sizing and scheduling of dough batches must match that of makeup, proofing and baking equipment.

Because of unavoidable fermentative and evaporative baking losses that occur subsequent to dividing, the scaled weight of the dough piece must exceed the intended weight of the baked product by a certain margin. Depending on the operating efficiency of a given plant, this extra weight allowance will range from 1.5 to 2.0 oz per lb of finished product so that, for a 1-lb (16-oz) loaf of bread, for example, the individual dough piece is scaled at 17.5 to 18 oz. To ensure that the baked products do not fall short of legal weight requirements, bakers frequently increase the weight allowance by an extra 0.25 to 0.5 oz.

Weight control for volumetrically scaled items is still to a large extent performed by manually checkweighing individual dough pieces at prescribed intervals. For this purpose, a sensitive scale is placed next to the take-away belt conveyor of the divider with which the operator checks the weight of the individual dough pieces. Checkweighing is essential not only to guard against short weights but also to avoid unnecessary losses that result from over-weights. Deviations beyond acceptable tolerances are readily corrected by appropriate adjustments in the volume of the divider's dough measuring pockets.

Frequent regular checks on weights provide a valuable discipline for managing the manufacturing process, whether doughs are divided volumetrically or gravimetrically. Although not yet as widespread in North America as it is in Europe, automated checkweighing can replace manual methods for performing these measurements. The checkweigher is positioned between the divider and rounder. In earlier such systems, the scaled dough pieces had their weight determined while they traveled over a weigh belt at speeds of up to 160 units per minute (Abbot 1958). Dough pieces that fell outside the preset weight range were ejected and returned either to the divider hopper or to the mixer.

Computers have vastly improved the operation of checkweighing systems (Benier 1983). In such systems, the checkweigher is linked electronically to the divider, so whenever a weight deviation is sensed by its computer, the corrective adjustment in the volumetric settings on the divider is performed automatically. Installing the checkweigher after the rounder offers the advantages of higher weighing speeds and greater baked weight accuracy.

The balance of viscoelastic properties affects dough as it is divided and rounded (Spies 1990). In rheological terms, a dough that is too viscous flows too much and will not maintain its shape properly. If the elastic component is too dominant — if the dough is "bucky" — then it will be difficult to round, and the final product will not have the desired shape. Stickiness, another rheological property, affects these processes, too. Doubles often result when rounding doughs that are too sticky, yet if the dough is not sticky enough, it does not round properly, thus altering the crumb texture of the finished product.

6.C.3. Effect on dough

Dough undergoes considerable physical stress during the dividing process, especially in the compression stage when it is forced into the individual pockets.

This compression, followed by the cutting or shearing action, causes an immediate and continuing loss of carbon dioxide gas. As Matz (1972) pointed out, further changes in dough properties are produced by the disorientation of gluten fibrils caused by (a) dough compression and cutting, (b) the increase in dough temperature due to the added working of the dough and (c) the incidental pickup of divider oil by the dough pieces.

The rate at which scaling is carried out exerts a variable effect on dough properties and line performance. In multi-pocket configurations, ram-and-shear dividers can achieve speeds of more than 140 pieces per minute (Stimpson 1993), but because they drop dough pieces as a string onto the discharge belt. Spacing out these pieces uniformly can be difficult, and non-uniform spacing can create doubles at the rounder, intermediate proofer and moulder. The higher the speed of division, the greater the work on the dough.

One major reason for holding to an established dividing time is the practical impossibility of maintaining a uniform temperature within the dough while it resides in the divider hopper. Not only is there a temperature rise that results naturally from the continuing fermentative action within the dough, but the divider is usually located in a warmer section of the bakery that also contributes to a warming effect. As doughs warm, their fermentation rate is perceptibly accelerated. This causes a more rapid rate of carbon dioxide generation, with a corresponding loss in the dough's density, and also increases the dough's acidity and stickiness, as well as its age. Such doughs tend to scale irregularly, with some individual dough pieces exceeding acceptable weight tolerances, and the baked loaves will often exhibit a streaked grain, pale crust color and reduced keeping quality. However, as Doerry (1995a) noted, cooler dough temperatures (23 to 24°C, or 73 to 75°F) alleviate much of the problem of changing weights. And pressure compensators on some dough dividers will allow adjustment for different types of dough (Marsh 1998).

Development of rotary dividing fed by screw-type dough pumps substantially increased the line speeds possible. Campbell (1989) described a system using rotary dividers with double cut-off knives (**Figure 6.42**) capable of producing 100 1.25-lb pieces per minute, and Robinson (2000) observed extrusion bun dividers operating at more than 1,000 pieces per minute.

Figure 6.42. This 3-lane rotary extrusion divider currently runs bread doughs at 170 loaves per minute but can go faster, reaching 300 cuts per minute under the right circumstances.
(Hickory Photography and *Baking & Snack*)

Pumping, shear and pressure do affect doughs divided through extrusion systems. To maintain accurate scaling, uniform pressure has to be maintained to the metering pump, and as the dough changes density during processing, the screw speed will increase to maintain the pre-set pressure, according to Robinson (2000). This phenomenon is most apparent during variety changes and delays, so any dough in the divider during these stoppages must be purged from the system and reworked with fresh dough.

Extrusion doughs do feel softer, but cutting back on water (absorption) yields products that have poor pan flow and symmetry. Such doughs also experience higher heat gain, resulting in accelerated yeast activity and an over-aged dough. Robinson (2000) also recommended reducing yeast levels in doughs that are divided by extrusion, but he said that oxidant and dough strengthener content generally should not be adjusted when adopting extrusion dividing. However, if the product exhibits indications of excessive strength, wild break-and-shred or dark spots, then reduce oxidation. Poor gas retention, weakness and white spots indicate that oxidation or strengthener levels may be too low.

6.C.4. Degassing of dough

Seeking to replace trough hoists with simpler, less costly systems, bakers tried discharging batches into large vats equipped with pumps intended to feed the dough into the hopper above the divider (**Figure 6.43**). Gas in the dough impeded early efforts by binding the pump's action, but when engineers decided to let the gas bleed out of the system, they achieved success. Degassing the dough in this way achieved another benefit: uniformity.

Accuracy of scaling is greatly improved by reducing the changes in dough density during divider operation. Control over dough density is readily accomplished by the use of dough degassers, or dough pumps, that transfer the dough from the mixer or dough trough into the divider hopper at a rate that keeps the dough's dwell time in the hopper at an absolute minimum (Bingeman 1969, Doerry 1995a). These units are essentially dough pumps of various designs that effectively expel most of the carbon dioxide gas from the dough and, in the process, impart to it varying degrees of additional development. According to Tesch (Tesch 1971), the following advantages derive from the use of dough degassers: (a) more uniform scaling weights, the result of a more constant dough density; (b) improved pan flow of doughs, obtained by the elimination of their gassy and bucky characteristics; (c) greater uniformity of grain and texture in the baked product, the result of more constant dough properties from start to finish of the scaling operation; (d) ability to work with larger doughs over longer processing times, thereby facilitating mixing schedules and increasing efficiency; (e) providing a safeguard against losses in case of brief production interruptions by extending dough tolerance; and (f) ease of dough transfer from trough to divider hopper

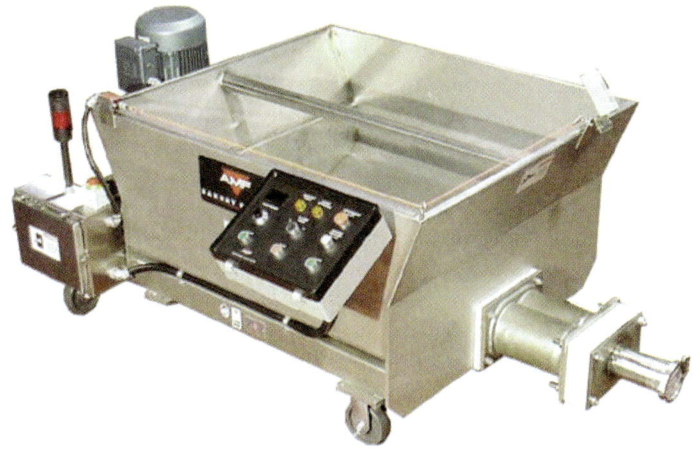

Figure 6.43. Dough pumps not only transfer dough to the divider, they also degas it to assure uniform texture and accurate scaling.
(AMF Bakery Systems)

To obtain optimum benefits from dough pumps, certain requirements must be met. These, according to Pierce (Pierce 1974), include (a) an adequate pump size that should exceed by 70% the actual or projected production poundage; (b) an adjustment in the degree of dough development during mixing to account for any additional dough development imparted by the dough pump; and (c) a reduction in mixed dough temperature to compensate for any temperature rise resulting from the pumping operation. He further suggested that the pump be located within 15 ft of the divider. For longer distances, he recommended depositing unless the dough by the pump onto a conveyor belt that feeds into the divider hopper.

Because the pumps feeding rotary dividers act as degassers, uniform dough density characterizes the results of this process (Robinson 2000).

Degassing produces its best results with doughs prepared from strong flours such as those of North America; it is less successful with softer, lower-protein flours (Marsh 1998).

6.C.5. Rounding

Rounding generally follows dividing and precedes resting or intermediate proofing. This stage manipulates the dough ball to smooth and seal its skin. Dough pieces come out of the divider in irregular shapes, possessing sticky cut surfaces. Moreover, they have lost a good part of their aeration because of the compression, shearing and cutting actions that are part of the dividing operation.

The next task, therefore, is to reconstitute the dough piece by giving it a continuous, nonsticky surface skin that will retain the carbon dioxide gas that continues to be generated by the yeast. Dough that has been partly deaerated is no longer sufficiently pliable for moulding to yield a stable loaf. Hence, the scaled dough piece must be given a chance to recover some of the aeration and structural gluten orientation so it will be suitable for moulding. Rounding initiates this recovery, which is the purpose of the resting or intermediate proofing stage.

The principal function of the rounder is to restore to the dough piece a smooth and continuous surface skin that will retain the carbon dioxide gas being generated within the dough piece. Additional functions include rendering the dough piece nonsticky by the application of a fine coating of dusting flour and bringing about the desired gluten fibril alignment and gas cell distribution that contribute to uniform symmetry and fine texture in the baked loaf.

6.C.5.a. Rounder styles

Rounders generally have grooved surfaces to improve the traction of dough pieces and are available in umbrella or inverted cone, cone or bowl, drum, cup and belt configurations. These descriptions indicate the type of working surfaces because each design features a stationary spiral track positioned against a rotating surface.

In the umbrella-type rounder, the dough track is fixed on the outside surface of a cone whose apex faces upward, whereas in the bowl-type rounder, this track is positioned around the interior of the bowl surface whose apex faces downward.

The drum-type or cylindrical rounder resembles the umbrella rounder in that its dough track is also mounted externally, except that the rounder's sides are vertical rather than sloped. The dough piece receives essentially the same treatment in each of these three types of rounders, but their rate of travel is faster initially and slower at the end of the run in the umbrella-type rounder, the reverse in the bowl-type rounder and relatively uniform with the cylindrical rounder.

A slightly different form of drum rounder is commonly used for rolls. Instead of a spiral track, this rounder uses a cylinder configured with rows of large holes into which the divider drops the dough pieces. The cylinder revolves around a large drum, rolling the dough pieces against the drum's surface to round them. To handle larger or smaller dough pieces, the cylinder can be changed out for another with the correct size holes.

The belt rounder offers another exception in design: Its working surface consists of two parallel belts arranged in an open "V" or "U" shape, usually with another belt running below. This rounder style readily handles heavy hearth bread doughs and is more common in European bakeries than North American plants.

For rounding buns, the divider drops dough pieces onto a moving belt that crosses a table, generally equipped with a refrigerated surface. A series of parallel bars set obliquely across the belt pick up the balls and the action of the belt moving forward rolls the dough pieces against the bars.

In operation, the irregularly shaped dough piece with its sticky raw surface is transformed by rounding into an essentially spherical shape with a compacted dry skin that acts as a barrier to gas diffusion from the dough. Dusting flour may be used in the rounding process and is discussed later in Part E of this chapter. Rounding can be done without dusting flour if an air-skinning system with dehumidified air is provided (Stimpson 1993).

The various configurations of rounders are illustrated and described at greater length in Chapter 9.

6.D. Resting (Intermediate Proofing)

The purpose of intermediate proofing is to ready the dough piece for sheeting and makeup. This step allows the dough's gluten to relax by dissipating energy acquired during dividing and rounding operations. These processes subject the dough to considerable physical abuse, resulting in marked loss of fermentation gases and deterioration of rheological properties such as pliability and elasticity. To repair these physical properties, the rounded dough balls are given a brief period of rest, generally referred to as an intermediate or overhead proof, during which additional fermentation and the structural relaxation of gluten take place and make the dough piece more suitable for final moulding.

6.D.1. Intermediate proofing

The intermediate proof is commonly carried out in so-called overhead proofers that consist of a cabinet raised sufficiently high to provide floor space beneath for other makeup machinery. In cases where no adequate overhead space is available, special floor cabinets are used. In overhead proofers, the rounded dough pieces are deposited into canvas dough pockets, cups or trays carried through the proofer in a series of laps on a continuous conveyor or onto endless belts that are arranged in tiers and traverse the cabinet from one end to the other, transferring dough pieces from the upper to the next lower tier by simply dropping them at the end of the tier to the one below. Other names for the intermediate proofer include dry proofer, first proofer and interproofer.

Although there has been a move away from tray proofing for white pan breads in recent years, some specialty products require longer intermediate proofing times, and for these, the tray proofer is desired (Osborne 1998). Doughs made by no-time, short-time and/or high-speed mixing methods also benefit from intermediate proofing, and intermediate proofing time must be increased when oxidants are not used in these dough-making systems (Kilborn and Tipples 1979). Reduced loaf volume and coarser texture result when such doughs receive inadequate intermediate proofing (Marsh 1998).

Since most formulations include dough conditioners, the actual proof or resting time can last anywhere from 30 seconds to 3 minutes as compared with 40 years ago when intermediate proof times lasted up to 20 minutes (Olmsted 1970). Most processes have moved to belt resting, described below, which eliminates the need for intermediate proofing, increases floor space and reduces flour dust.

The purpose of intermediate proofing is to assure that dough enters the moulding system sufficiently relaxed so that it will not tear during sheeting. The longer the time of this first proof, the more open the bread cell structure becomes, provided that no degassing occurs in final moulding, thus suiting products such as French baguettes (Marsh 1998).

If intermediate proof times extend beyond 10 minutes, transpositors should be used within the proofer to change the position of the dough pieces at about the midpoint of the proofing cycle. The optimum overhead proof time is influenced by factors such as temperature, formulation and previous dough processing and must generally be determined experimentally.

While minor variations in intermediate proof time normally have no perceptible effect on final product properties, excessive deviations from established optimum proof times will adversely affect the grain and texture of the baked product. In the case of insufficient proof time, quality defects include an open, uneven grain with thick cell walls and the appearance of cores in the crumb. In the case of excessive intermediate proof time, the defects show up as thick cell walls and as dense areas, streaks and cores in the crumb (Kamman 1970).

Overhead proofers are not usually equipped with separate temperature and humidity controls, and the cabinets thus largely take on the atmospheric conditions that prevail in the room in which they are located. In most instances, these conditions remain sufficiently constant so they do not present major control problems. Moreover, the dough's tolerance to environmental influences at this point is generally adequate to carry it through the rather brief proof stage without adverse effects from minor atmospheric fluctuations.

In general, suitable proofing conditions include a temperature range of 27 to 29°C (80 to 85°F) and a relative humidity of around 75%. Temperatures much above that range will tend to age the dough excessively and reduce its gas-holding capacity, producing stickiness. If temperatures are too low, fermentation will slow and thus delay the adequate expansion of the dough pieces. Relative humidities much lower than 75% will promote skin formation on the dough pieces and lead to the formation of hard curls and streaks in the crumb of the baked loaf. Excessively high humidity leads to equally undesirable moisture condensation on the dough surface and concomitant stickiness. The practice of opening the doors of the overhead proofer in an attempt to adjust either the humidity or the temperature of the interior is usually ill-advised because it often creates drafts that can only have an adverse effect on the uniformity of the dough pieces.

6.D.2. Belt resting

During the past two decades, high-volume bread bakers have increasingly abandoned conventional overhead proofing methods in favor of open-air "resting" conducted at plant ambient temperatures. This practice reduces overall processing time considerably, something long sought by commercial wholesale bakers, as well as increasing floor space and reducing repair, cleaning and dusting flour needs. Both Campbell (1988) and Osborne (1998) attributed this change to better quality ingredients, new additives, improved mixers, extrusion dividing and the continuing need for competitive advantage. Brixey (1998) reported how use of rotary extrusion dividers eliminated intermediate proofers, allowing use of short-time belt proofing for breads, while completely doing away with this stage for buns.

After rounding, dough balls transfer to a 12- to 18-in.-wide conveyor, constructed of open-mesh plastic, cotton or a slick solid and connected to the sheeting and moulding system. Although bakery practices differ, the dough pieces get about 15 to 30 seconds up to 1 minute of rest time as they travel along the conveyor. Dough pieces do not go directly from the rounder to the moulder because a minimum amount of time is required prior to sheeting to allow the dough piece to hydrate any excess surface moisture and prevent sticking at the moulder.

A certain amount of fermentation does occur during intermediate proofing, so when bypassing this step, the baker may need to lengthen the dough's original fermentation time. On the other hand, less gas forms during the belt resting step than in doughs travelling through an intermediate proofing, so the sheeter has less to expel.

Some other processing changes may be necessary, including reduction of final mix time and an increase in oxidation. Because doughs handled this way tend to be warmer — 31°C (88°F) in an example cited by Campbell (1988) — no increase was needed in final proof time.

Among the benefits attributed to belt resting is that it eliminates the inherent slugging characteristics of conventional tray proofers, so a standard sheeter-moulder-panner can generally handle about 20% more production (Campbell 1983). Rotary timing gates, zig-zag boards, proofer cup transfer mechanisms and dual gate panning mechanisms are also eliminated (Brixey 1998).

6.E. Makeup

The purpose of makeup processes is to give dough pieces their final shape. In this stage, the baker can exert considerable creativity to shape dough pieces to suit customer and consumer preferences. Makeup has been mechanized to a considerable extent, yet the principles remain closely aligned with manual methods. During makeup, dough pieces are degassed, with their gas cells subdivided and made finer, and then formed into their final shape using the techniques of sheeting, curling, twisting and, on occasion, stamping.

Many aspects of makeup involve sheeting — the reduction of dough thickness by rolling under pressure. The dough is not so much compressed as it is deformed by the application of shear, which elongates the dough, thus thinning it. The purpose of sheeting differs for each product. Bread dough is sheeted by the moulder to control gas cell distribution as well as loaf shape. Biscuit dough requires sheeting to form the dough and work the gluten. Corn masa is sheeted to enable the dough to cohere for preparation of tortillas. Dobraszcyk and Morgenstern (2003) reviewed various rheological test methods for studying the effects of makeup and recommended changes in how researchers evaluate the rheology of breadmaking.

(The description that follows covers moulding of pan bread, but the same principles apply to shaping buns, baguettes and most other yeast-raised baked products created from individually divided dough pieces. The lamination and sheeting processes for the makeup of sweet goods, danish, croissants, swirl bread and similar products treat the dough as a continuous band and will be described later in this section.)

6.E.1. Moulding

On leaving the intermediate proofer or resting belt, dough pieces should have a dry surface and a relaxed appearance. They then enter the moulder in which they are given their final shape (be it a cylindrical loaf form for bread, a disk for buns or a long string for baguettes) prior to being deposited in the baking pan or onto peel boards.

This operation involves three distinct steps: sheeting into a uniformly thin layer, rolling the sheeted dough into a cylindrical form, and finally, passing the rolled dough under a pressure board to seal its seams and impart to it the final desired shape.

Two essentials for correct moulding are a suitable dough and appropriate settings on the moulder. The ideal dough for moulding has a dry surface, is soft to the touch and is extensible. In general, over-mixed doughs spread excessively during sheeting, and under-mixed doughs exhibit undesirable bucky characteristics.

Sticky doughs that result either from over-use of malt or wet intermediate proofing conditions usually cause defective moulding. Dough pieces that have been dusted too heavily in the rounding and proofing operations tend to acquire a thick, tough skin that resists the action of the sheeting rolls and will tend to tear while passing through the head rolls. Moreover, such a skin will lack adequate sealing properties, causing the moulded piece to uncurl during final proofing and baking; the result is deformed loaves. Skinning also leads to formation of unsightly streaks in the crumb of the baked product.

6.E.1.a. Sheeting

Sheeting of dough pieces during the makeup of bread and buns has several effects (Levine 1998): (a) Sheeting develops dough, measurable as changes in extensibility and resistance; (b) it aligns protein to texturize the dough and the finished product; (c) it expels gas, while the pressures involved may dissolve carbon dioxide in the dough to feed gas cell growth after sheeting; and (d) it may disrupt the dough's laminated structure.

Dough pieces to be made into loaf bread pass through an initial sheeting operation consisting of 2 or 3 sets of closely spaced head rolls that successively flatten and degas the dough. It is important that the dough piece be fed to the first head rolls with its thin edge so as to prevent its being folded into a double thickness and torn during the initial sheeting action.

The spacing, or gap, between each successive set of rolls is progressively smaller. The first pair of rolls is normally spaced 0.64 cm (0.25 in.) apart and serves the primary purpose of degassing the dough in preparation for final sheeting (Kamman 1970). In a moulder with 3 sets of rolls, the second or center set will generally be spaced 0.32 cm (0.125 in.) apart, while the final sheeting rolls should have a clearance of 0.16 cm (0.06 in.) for optimum crumb grain and texture in the baked loaf.

In nearly all cases, the steel head rolls are enclosed in a sleeve of Teflon which, because of its nonstick character, allows much closer settings of the rolls than are possible with unprotected steel rolls. The optimum setting of the final sheeting rolls is established by progressively reducing the gap between them until the sheeted dough pieces show evidence of tearing or sticking. The clearance between the rolls is then increased just enough to produce a smooth-surfaced dough sheet.

Setting and controlling roll gaps requires considerable skill and knowledge. As the science of rheology progresses in its examination and quantification of dough properties, it may offer an automation answer. A transducer could monitor the force developed when a dough piece passes through a sheeter. By measuring the work thus involved and determining the length of the sheeted dough piece, the relative extensibility (buckiness) of a dough can be determined. This information could be used in an automatic feedback system to control the gap of the sheeting rolls (Spies 1990).

Careful maintenance of the dough sheeter's head rolls is a prerequisite for a consistently uniform grain and texture in the baked loaf, and the rolls should be kept free of any nicks, ridges or accumulations of hardened dough. Toward that end, the guides and scrapers fitted to the rolls must be periodically cleaned and adjusted. The scrapers should be set with a clearance of not more than 6 mils (0.15 mm) from the roll surface. It is good practice to regularly apply small amounts of divider oil to the surface of the rolls and thereby prevent any adhering dough from hardening and damaging the scraper.

The second essential for satisfactory moulder performance is proper settings and operation of the moulder. Normal practice is to set the sheeting rolls as close together as practicable to obtain maximum gas expulsion and redistribution of gas cells because this fosters the formation of a fine, uniform grain in the baked loaf. However, setting the sheeting rolls too close causes the skin of the dough pieces to rupture and expose the sticky interior, with consequent "gumming up" of the machine. Uneven sheeting, with the dough sheet being thicker at the side edges than in the center, will produce a dumbbell shape in the moulded loaf. In such a moulded piece, both the cell distribution and cell size will vary throughout the length of the loaf.

The other extreme (head rolls that are set too loose) fails to achieve both adequate degassing and proper cell dispersion in the dough piece. This results in coarse grain structure and large holes in the finished loaf. Such settings also fail to sheet the dough thin enough to permit a sufficient number of curls to ensure uniformity of the baked bread. Practical experience shows that 2.5 curls represent the optimum extent of curling. The effects of various head roll settings are illustrated in **Figure 6.44** in which the loaf at the left has been sheeted too loose, the one in the center to the correct thickness and the one at the right too thin (Kamman 1970).

Figure 6.44. Moulder head-roll settings alter loaf characteristics: left loaf, loose setting of 0.5 in.; center loaf, normal setting of 0.25 in.; right loaf, tight setting of 0.175 in. (Kamman 1970

Scientific examination of the effects of sheeting, reported by Leong and Campbell (2008), found clear evidence that gas is removed during this process. The extent of degassing increased with decreasing roll gaps. The gas, however, is not redistributed uniformly in the piece: The highest gas content exists in the center of the sheet, while the edges contain the lowest amount.

Also, the surface of the dough sheet tends to be more degassed than the interior, and when curled during moulding, this effect produces a dense spiral in the dough that persists through proofing and after baking, as seen in work by Withworth (2008).

It is good practice to adapt the setting of the head rolls to the requirements of individual dough batches and, of course, to the different sizes of the dough pieces being moulded. Thus, an 18-oz dough piece calls for a closer setting of the head rolls than does a 23-oz dough piece. Slack doughs handle better with more open settings of the sheeting rolls than do stiffer doughs. The same holds true of sponge doughs compared with straight doughs. To determine whether or not the rolls are set too tight for a given dough, examine the surface of the moulded pieces: A noticeable roughness occurs when sheeting rolls are set too close.

How the dough pieces enter the first set of sheeting rolls makes a significant difference. Their thin edge must enter the rolls first. In automatic equipment that feeds the dough pieces directly from the overhead proofer into the moulder by way of a connecting chute, faulty design may cause the dough pieces to roll or tumble, rather than slide, into the head rolls. When this happens, the broad side of the dough piece may contact the rolls first, preventing the latter from taking immediate hold of the piece. This may not only result in two dough pieces being combined into doubles but will also cause a sudden application of excessive pressure on the dough piece as it begins to pass between the rolls and subject it to a more severe punishment than is desirable for good results.

6.E.1.b. Curling

After passing through the head rolls, the sheeted dough piece enters the unit's curling section. In modern moulders, this usually involves a belt conveyor, with a flexible woven metal chain or a mat consisting of thin metal bars positioned over it. As the conveyor carries the dough sheet forward, the upper curling chain engages the lead edge of the sheet and holds it back sufficiently so that the dough is rolled into a cylinder. This curling action can also be performed by a special set of curling rolls within the moulder head or by canvas belts running at different speeds. One aim of this rolling operation is to produce a relatively tight curl with a minimum of air entrapment.

6.E.1.c. Compressing

One principal objective of the moulding process is to expel as much carbon dioxide gas from the dough as possible. That not all the gas can be eliminated derives from the fact that carbon dioxide is relatively soluble in water. When the dough is subjected to pressure as it is sheeted between the rolls, some of the free gas is forced into solution in the dough liquid, only to come out again and migrate into gas cells as the pressure is released. According to Hibberd and Parker (Hibberd and Parker 1976), there will always be a significant volume of gas bubbles in the dough following the sheeting operation.

In the process of moulding, the dough cylinder finally passes under a stationary compression board whose purpose it is to expel any entrapped air (as opposed to degassing the dough, which the sheeter has already done), elongate the dough piece to the desired length and completely seal its seams so that it will retain the gases generated during proofing for loaf expansion. Pressure boards range in length from 34 to 48 in., and their dough contact surfaces are generally lined with sponge rubber, canvas belting or other materials.

The boards are configured to apply somewhat greater pressure in the center of the dough cylinder to facilitate air expulsion from the dough (Olmsted 1970). By slanting the pressure board slightly downward toward its discharge end, the pressure exerted on the dough increases and thus elongates the piece. The actual length of the moulded dough piece is controlled by guides mounted along each side of the pressure board section. These guides should also be set at a slant that narrows toward the discharge end to provide a final seal to the dough cylinder ends.

The pressure boards should be just tight enough to seal the dough seam and to impart a uniform cylindrical shape to the dough piece. A compression plate that is too loosely set tends to produce a dough loaf that bulges in the center and exhibits a tendency to open up during baking, with an open, non-uniform grain. On the other hand, setting the pressure boards too tightly punishes the dough piece excessively, forms it into a dumbbell shape with thick ends and a thin middle, and produces coarse, open-textured cores and dense areas in the crumb of the baked bread.

6.E.1.d. Twisting

In the production of twist bread, two moulded dough cylinders are twisted together prior to being deposited into the pan. The number of twists ranges from three to five and depends on the length of the pan being used (Cackler 1957). Twisting improves the crumb structure by producing small, uniformly elongated cells, a fine regular grain, and a silky texture. The operation may be performed either manually or by special mechanical twisting devices (Miller 1961, Anon. 1958). In manual panning of hand-twisted loaves, it is important to place the two free dough stubs at each loaf end into the pan corners to ensure an even, uniform expansion of the dough during the final proof (Beaverson 1960).

Automatic twisting systems, or the "tender curl" method, require very relaxed and extensible doughs (Doerry 1995a). Typically absorption will be on the high end, with mixing taken to full gluten development. Dough pieces are sheeted thinner than in straight-grain or cross-grain moulding, yielding a very long dough cylinder after curling, about twice as long the loaves produced by the other bread moulding processes. The long dough log moves onto a second table placed at right angles to the first moulder station and passes at a 35 to 45° angle under another curling chain. The result is a twisted dough piece with three to five helical turns and the same length as the pan (Ferrell 1961). This final coiling action is illustrated in **Figure 6.45**. The cells in bread moulded in this fashion will point in many directions, making the crumb grain slightly irregular and giving it an old-fashioned look.

Figure 6.45. Coiling section of the curl-type moulder in which the dough cylinder receives its final curling action. (Ferrell 1961)

6.E.1.e. Reverse, cross-grain, 4-piecing

Several modifications of the conventional bread moulding procedure have been developed over the years and put into practice by bakers in an effort to improve on the crumb and general loaf properties of the baked bread. The principal variations include reverse sheeting and cross-grain moulding, and these have been described in some detail by Mohr (1949) and Hunter (1949). The aim in reverse sheeting is to obtain a more uniform moisture distribution in the final loaf by having the wet end of the sheeted dough folded into the center of the curled dough piece rather than have it form the exterior layer. This is accomplished by reversing the dough piece between the second and third set of rolls and thereby, changing the trailing, or wet, end of the dough sheet into the leading edge as it enters the curling section.

In the cross-grain moulder, the conveyor feeding the curling section travels at a right angle to the sheeting rolls. This configuration causes the sheeted dough piece to enter this section with one of its side edges in the lead, which then becomes the center of the loaf. This method of cross curling produces a desirable elongated cell structure in the baked loaf.

The technique, called 4-piecing or cut-and-turn, divides the moulded cylinder of dough into four equal lengths, each equal to just less than the width of the pan (Marsh 1998). The pieces are turned 90° in the horizontal plane and reassembled side-by-side before they drop as a unit into the pan (**Figure 6.46**). In Japan, one of the end cuts is turned 180° with respect to the direction of the other 3 pieces so the grain on both loaf heels match.

The reasons for manipulating the dough cylinder by 4-piecing are the same as those behind cross-grain moulding. As Cauvain and Young (2001) explained, sheeting will elongate some of the gas cells in the direction of dough movement through the moulder. These cells remain stretched out during curling because the dough's viscoelastic properties prevent the bubbles from returning to spherical shape. When the baked bread is sliced, these long cells, now cut through their short sides, cast a significant shadow, thus giving the crumb a dull, gray color. By turning the dough pieces 90° as both these processes do, such cells are cut through their long axis, and the overall appearance of the crumb is brighter. These techniques eliminate the appearance of swirling in the crumb structure and are said to improve softness and longer shelf life.

6.E.1.f. Dusting flour

Dusting flour is often used to prevent the dough from sticking to the equipment, but this additional material can affect product quality. To promote a dry dough surface, the moisture content of the dusting flour should be as low as possible. Reclaimed or unused dusting flour is preferably incorporated in next day's dough production rather than immediately re-used at the rounder.

As in all stages of rounding and makeup, use of dusting flour should be kept to a minimum consistent with the satisfactory performance of the equipment. As a rule, the application of excessive dusting flour at the head rolls will give rise to streaks and uneven color in the crumb. Some dusting flour is usually required at the pressure board in high-speed operations that run in excess of 70 to 80 dough pieces per minute to minimize occurrence of possible defects in the final loaf. Good practice dictates that under normal operating conditions the amount of dusting flour, starch or any other material used for dusting during makeup not exceed 1.0% of the dough weight out of the divider.

6.E.1.g. Air skinning

To rid makeup operations of the dust and sanitation problems inherent with flour

Figure 6.46. The moulding method known as 4-piecing cuts moulded loaf dough into 4 sections, turns them 90° and places them into a waiting pan. (Baker Perkins UK)

dusting, bakery engineers developed air skinning methods. Essentially dustless, this technique applies drying air at a minimum of 600 cu ft per minute for an average conveyor length of 8 ft (Stimpson 1993). If the plant is air conditioned or humidity is low, ambient air can be used, but high plant humidity or extremely wet dough conditions will require warm air. Under extremely moist conditions, the air may have to be dehumidified as well.

6.E.2. Continuous dough band makeup (sheeting and lamination)

Lamination, or the process of layering, creates the unique dough properties essential to successful makeup and production of danish pastry, sweet goods, croissants and similar products. Layering doughs with shortening is essential to the texture of these items as well as pie crusts and toaster pastries. For yeast-raised crackers (saltines), lamination of the dough alone produces the flakey effects desired in the finished product. (Crackers may also be laminated with a mixture of shortening and flour, rather than shortening alone.) The process also enables addition of fillings to cinnamon rolls and other pastries. Such doughs can be formulated with yeast or not.

The addition of shortening to laminated doughs can be done several ways. The Scotch, or "all in" method, mixes flakes of high-melt-point shortening directly into the dough to create pockets of shortening within the dough sheet. Roll-in methods extrude the shortening layer directly onto the dough sheet after it is first formed; to enclose the shortening during subsequent processing, the dough sheet gets a single or double-lap fold in the direction of travel. Co-extrusion systems create a hollow tube of dough while simultaneously filling it with shortening; the system flattens the tube before subsequent processing.

The sheeted dough is then put through a series of rolling and folding steps to build up its layered structure. Folding, also called lapping, can be accomplished in different ways. The sheet can be cut and stacked onto a moving conveyor, whose speed regulates the stack height of the new continuous sheet; cut-sheet lamination is often used for cracker production. The sheet can be swung back and forth across a conveyor, falling in laps from the paddle that guides its travel. The sheet can also be folded by plows that turn the dough along the direction of travel. Grooved rolls laid at an oblique angle on the conveyor and rotating on their long axis spin against the dough sheet to create a long cylinder with a spiral layer of filling.

Sheeting and lamination may also be applied to blocks of dough, which are reduced in thickness by running through reversible sheeters. The shortening is added as a thick layer on the first pass through the sheeter. After a certain number of passes, the dough is folded into a block, or book, and stored under refrigerated conditions. This process, also called booking, takes place in several stages, each followed by a stay in the refrigerator or retarder.

The act of sheeting, if carried out at too great a reduction ratio, disrupts the layering of laminated doughs. For this reason, ratios for sheeting operations could be no higher than 4:1 at any given set of large-diameter rolls. As explained by Hayashi (1978), the heavy force interferes with the smooth internal relocation of the dough particles. However, repeated "pinnings" by small-diameter rolls will stretch the dough, enabling a 10:1 reduction ratio. This technique mimics manual use of rolling pins. To achieve the short duration time also necessary, the small rolls were mounted in a single roll station, designed to move the rolls around a circular (actually elliptical) track so only one small-diameter roll contacted the dough at any given time. Also, the conveyor belt was divided, allowing the dough to be pulled out of the roll station, leaving it at a higher speed than it entered. In effect, the multiple-roll head stretches the dough more so than sheets it.

Such multiple-roll, stretching systems are also termed "satellite" rolls because the small rolls revolve around a track much like satellites travel around the earth. These roll stations act in the same direction that the conveyor travels. They elongate the dough. In contrast, small-diameter rolls can be set to move across the width of the belt. These cross-rolls stretch the dough in a direction transverse to belt travel, thus widening the dough band.

Gravimetric dividing, also described as relaxed dough processing, is actually a sheeting process. As explained earlier in this chapter at Part C, the first step in this method creates a thick sheet of dough, which is then flattened by rollers. At this point, the dough sheet can be cut and formed as individual pieces, or it can continue along a conveyor to receive fillings and toppings, with individual pieces not cut until the end of the moulding stage. Such systems can handle very wet doughs, some as high as 80 to 90% absorption, which are too sticky for conventional makeup machinery. At such high absorption, these doughs are too delicate to develop in mixers or kneaders and difficult to machine, but they can be brought to optimum performance through sheeting because of the very efficient, low-energy "mixing" that occurs during this process (Levine 1998).

Sheeting changes the rheology of dough sheets. Kilborn and Tipples (1974) established that repeated sheeting of an under-developed dough results in its development because the sheeting process introduces work. They estimated that the amount of energy required is about 15% of that needed when the work is done by mixing. They compared the energy inputs (Watt-hours per lb) to the number of sheeting passes and finished baked loaf volume and found that optimum development occurs at a work input of 0.39 Watt-hours per lb (**Table 6.16**).

When Levine and Drew (1990) plotted that same data as energy input (vertical axis) vs. number of sheeting passes (horizontal axis), they discovered that the curve looked very much like the development curve for a mixer, with the exception that the ordinate (horizontal axis) was the number of passes instead of time (**Figure 6.47**). Thus, from the rheological point of view, the curve indicated the flow resistance (viscosity) of the dough is being reduced after the dough is developed.

Sheeting aligns protein, proven by the findings that (a) sheeted doughs are much stronger and more elastic in the direction of sheeting than in the cross direction and (b) the shrinkage (snap back) of dough after cutting is much greater in the length direction than in the width direction (Levine 1998).

Extrusion of bread doughs has certain negative effects including network disruption and release of water from the network, yet these can be partially restored by the moulding step. The orientation of gluten strands that induces higher rheological stress after extrusion is also counteracted by the moulding step, which Esselink et al (2003) noted during study of extruded and sheeted doughs using nuclear mag-

Table 6.16. Effect of Repeated Sheetings and Energy Input of a Bread Dough

Number of sheetings*	Energy (Watt-hour per lb)	Baked loaf volume (cu cm)
12	0.07	770
22	0.17	875
32	0.25	925
42	0.39	935
62	0.47	910
82	0.61	880

*One sheeting was defined as a pass between a pair of rolls with a 7/32-in. gap followed by a pass through a 5/32-in. gap, followed by a folding of the dough in half and a turn of 90°.

(Kilborn and Tipples 1974)

netic resonance (NMR) and electron microscopy.

Photomicrographs of doughs made with hard wheat and processed by sheeting revealed an organized protein network similar in nearly all respects to that produced by mixer development. Levine and Drew (1990) summarized additional research (Moss 1980, Svenvert et al 1980) verifying that the shear, sheeting and energy input to doughs from repeated sheeting dispels gas, reduces gas cell size and yields fine-grained bread. In rheological terms, the shear and/or stretching that the dough sheet received during rolling controls the specific volume and textural properties of the finished product. Measuring the specific energy input during sheeting may provide a means for automatically controlling the sheeting process.

6.E.3. Panning

Moulded dough pieces, after emerging from the pressure board section of the moulder, are immediately deposited into baking pans. Formerly performed manually — with the operator transferring the moulded dough pieces by hand from the discharge apron of the moulder and placing them into the pans — this panning operation is now carried out mostly by specialized panning units.

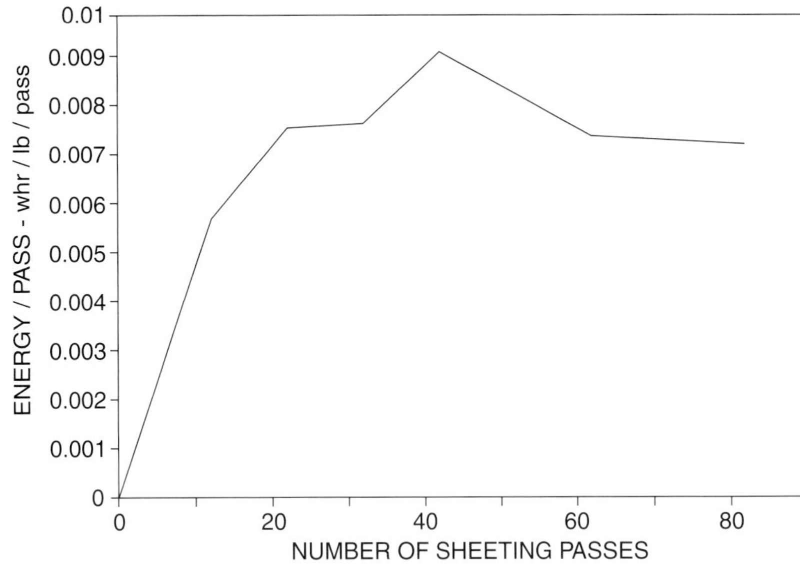

Figure 6.47. Plotting energy input against the number of sheeting passes, the result resembles a typical mixer development curve.
(Levine and Drew 1990)

Panning should be timed and adjusted so it will deposit the dough loaf into the pan with the seam down. This presentation will prevent the seam from opening during final proofing and baking and thereby minimize the appearance of rough and irregular top crust surfaces. Placing an accurate dough scale at the discharge end of the moulder allows the operator to periodically check and record weights as well as test the weight of any dough piece that appears to be non-uniform.

Even under good operating conditions, two dough pieces may occasionally be moulded together to yield a loaf of double weight, or dough sheets may tear into two parts to yield two under-weight loaves. Such off-weight dough pieces are best returned to the mixing room for incorporation into new doughs. As stated earlier in this chapter, it is critical when using rework to follow the practice of "like into like," or else labeling and allergen issues can ensue.

The condition of the pans as they arrive at the panning unit has a major effect on final proofing, baking and depanning operations and on the quality of the baked product. Pans must be tempered to the appropriate panning temperature, and their interior surfaces should be properly coated with pan oil or glazed with silicone resins, or preferably both, to facilitate dough expansion during proofing and ovenspring, and ease release of the baked loaf. Non-stick pan coatings composed of fluoropolymers require little to no use of pan release oils.

Pan return temperatures may be as high as 60°C (140°F), potentially causing a dip in product quality from being panned in hot tins. Also, hot pans returning to the proof box may add extra heat in the proofer and cause difficulty in controlling the system's temperature and humidity.

The generally recommended pan temperature for panning is about 32°C (90°F). Depending on circumstances, this may involve either pre-warming the pans, as would normally be the case at the start of a day's operation or, more commonly, cooling the pans from a depanning temperature of about 127°C (260°F) after the previous bake. Some bakeries have standardized on higher pan temperatures, up to 49°C (120°F), in the interest of somewhat shorter final proof times, without experiencing any adverse effects on either crumb grain or texture of the baked product (Trausch 1954).

When the temperature of the pans going into the proof box falls below the dew point (the temperature at which water vapor becomes supersaturated and changes to tiny water droplets or dew), moisture will condense on the pans. The water may penetrate into the porous glazing and degrade it, thus reducing the ability of the pan to release the baked product. Such cool pans also increase proofing time.

The time required to bring about the necessary temperature reduction may vary from as short as 6 minutes to as long as 2.5 hours. The most rapid method of cooling the pans is by means of a forced air draft within a hood on the conveyor that carries pans from the depanning station to the pan greasing machine or moulder discharge end. The most efficient of such pan conveyor-cooling systems will bring about a temperature reduction to 32°C (90°F) in some 5 minutes.

Many baking plants prefer to cool their pans by placing them on a moving wire-mesh, steel-rod or slat-type conveyor and letting them cool in the open atmosphere. This method will require about 12 to 15 minutes for the pans to reach 32°C (90°F). The most common procedure, and also the most time consuming, is to stack the hot pans on specially designed pan trucks and let them cool at the prevailing room temperature. Here, pan cooling times will range from 1.5 to 2.5 hours, depending on ambient temperatures. Directing an air fan on the pans will shorten the cooling time considerably.

The most obvious advantages of pan conveying and cooling systems include the savings in labor costs made possible by their automatic features and a reduction in pan inventory. The more quickly pans are cooled, the shorter is the idle interval between depanning and their reuse, and consequently, the fewer sets needed for a given production volume.

6.F. Proofing

Dough pieces that undergo sheeting and moulding processes become degassed and small in volume, while also exhibiting bucky (highly elastic) characteristics. They require a period of time for the gluten to regain its extensibility and to replenish the leavening gases to achieve the aeration that yields proper cell structure in the finished product. The purpose of the final proofing stage is to bring about the recovery of those dough properties that are essential to the production of a well-risen loaf.

North American usage is "proofer" and "proofing," while bakers in other parts of the world may refer to this equipment as the "prover" and the processing step as "proving." For commercial bakers, this stage in the dough process refers to final fermentation, the last period of time when the yeast can add leavening gases to the dough, while the home baker would describe the step as "allowing the dough to rise" (Doerry 1995a).

By the end of final proofing, doughs generally expand, or rise, to roughly three to four times the size of the moulded piece. In the past, bakers looked for dough to rise to a constant height or volume, but with automation and today's more uniform doughs, final proofing can be considered a time-regulated process carried out under controlled temperature and humidity conditions.

6.F.1. Final proofing

Pans containing the moulded dough pieces are placed in the proofer, generally configured as a relatively large chamber, fabricated of well-insulated panels of metal or other materials and equipped with an air conditioning system capable of maintaining the interior temperature and humidity at any desired level.

Proofers come in several designs. Rack proofers may be either manually or automatically loaded with mobile racks on a first-in, first-out basis, with fixed floor tracks an option for guiding the racks. Monorail systems carry racks through the humidified environment. Tray proofers accept pans or peels onto fixed trays that carry them along lengthy loops arranged in tiers. Conveyorized proofers transport pans filled with dough through tunnel-type proofers or arranged in spirals as in continuous proof-and-bake systems, that move the pans through the proofing cycle, much in the fashion of bread baking in a conveyorized oven (Gardner 1957, Lanham 1970).

An alternate term for "final proofing" is "pan proofing," particularly as it applies to products baked in some form of permanent pan or a even an aluminum tray. Other terms for the final proofer include "proof box" and "steam box."

The three basic control factors in final proofing are temperature, humidity and time. Former standards called for a temperature of 35°C (95°F), a relative humidity (RH) of 85% and a proofing time of 60 to 65 minutes. These parameters still constitute valid guidelines, although in current practice, temperatures within the range of 32 to 54°C (90 to 130°F) and RH readings of 60 to 90% are encountered (Gardner 1957), with proofing temperatures of 41 to 43°C (105 to 110°F) being most prevalent for bread doughs.

Siffring and Bruinsma (1993) experimented with proofing white pan variety dough at different temperatures (24 to 52°C, or 75 to 125°F), while adding enough yeast to keep proof time constant. Best results were had when keeping the exit temperature of the proofed product at 35 to 38°C (95 to 100°F). Yeast activity will double for each 10 C° (16 F°) and can prompt excess enzyme activity.

Relative humidity describes the amount of water vapor actually in the air compared with the total possible amount that the air could contain. Moore (1988) described the complex relationships involving moisture in the air as it affects proofing, baking, cooling, drying and storage of baked foods, as well as its effect on the comfort of bakery employees. For breads and buns, a temperature of 35 to 37°C (95 to 98°F) at 80 to 90% RH provide optimum conditions for the 50- to 60-minute proof such items require.

If RH drops below 80%, doughs will experience excessive loss of moisture and may crust over early in the oven, affecting the product's ovenspring and expansion. Lighter color and rougher crust conditions will also present themselves. If RH rises above 90%, water will condense on the surface of the dough.

In hearth products, this excess water will cause greater pan flow, resulting in undesirably flat bottoms. The crust will be smoother and slightly darker in color with small blisters, white spots or blotches.

Continuous-mix doughs do well at higher RH, while some products such as doughnuts benefit from conditions of 75 to 78% RH, which help form a dry skin around the product to reduce fat absorption during frying. French bread and other hearth products require a lower RH, in the range of 75 to 80%.

During the initial stages of baking, the dough's continuous gluten-starch matrix acts as a primary support stabilizing the spherical gas cells. Strain hardening proved to be the key rheological property responsible for stabilizing the primary gluten-starch matrix (Sroan et al. 2009). The role of liquid lamellae that line the inner side of the cells becomes significant during late proofing and baking, when gas cells expand to come into contact with each other and discontinuities begin to appear in the gluten-starch matrix (Sroan and MacRitchie 2008, 2009).

These researchers also found that surface-active components (emulsifiers and similar lipid compounds) influence the stability of the lamellae and, thus, improve bread volume.

Although a dough piece will fill the pan as it proofs, it does so through expansion rather than spreading. In rheological terms, a properly oxidized and fermented bread dough does not spread because its elastic forces exceed the force of gravity (Faubion and Hoseney 1990). "Green" or under-oxidized doughs, however, do flow, and the resulting loaf will have sharp corners and edges. In other words, the viscous nature of the dough takes over, while a dough that is too elastic does not expand sufficiently during proofing and baking and will have low volume and a shape that resembles the initial moulded piece, rather than the loaf pan (Spies 1990).

A fully proofed dough piece offers little resistance to the touch but will not sustain a permanent impression. The dough surface should feel moist — neither tacky nor wet (Doerry 1995b).

The spread test developed by Hoseney et al. (1979) calculates a spread ratio that gives insight into the rheological condition of the dough. **Figure 6.48** shows how the spread ratio for doughs changes after being rested after various fermentation times, thus demonstrating that fermentation transforms dough from a highly mobile system to one of little or no spread.

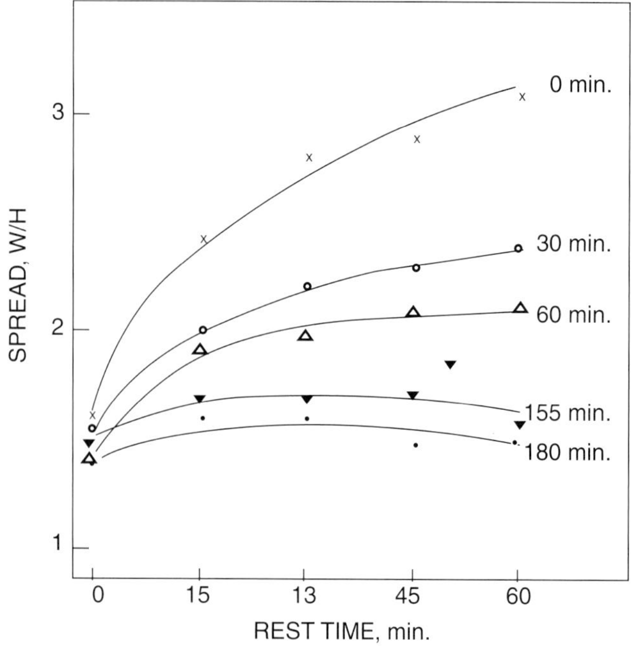

Figure 6.48. Spread ratios, which compare the width (W) to the height (H) of a standardized cylinder of dough, show how fermentation times of 0 to 180 minutes affect the flow of dough during rest time. (Hoseney et al. 1979)

6.F.1.a. Temperature

The temperature of the dough as it reaches the proofer differs between conventionally mixed and continuously mixed styles. Conventional dough mixing results in doughs of 27 to 29 °C (80 to 85°F) when they reach the proofer; continuously mixed doughs at this stage range in temperature from 39 to 43°C (103 to 110°F). Since proof box temperatures should at least equal or, preferably, exceed the dough temperature, continuously-mixed doughs are generally proofed at 41 to 46°C (105 to 115°F), while proof temperatures for conventional doughs are about 5 F° (2.8 C°) lower.

Compared with bulk fermentation, final proofing takes place at higher temperatures. Also, continuously-mixed doughs require somewhat higher RH levels of 80 to 90% — compared with 75 to 85% for the bulk fermentation of sponge doughs — and this humidity level must be held under more constant control (Kamman 1970). Sweet rolls, danish pastries and similar products require the lower range of proofing temperatures (Doerry 1995b).

Yeast is most active at 35 to 40°C (95 to 104°F), so proofing must add some heat to the dough system, raising its temperature by 10 to 15 C° (18 to 27 F°). The moisture in the proofer supplies part of the extra heat as it condenses on the dough piece and pan, thus giving up its latent heat. Wiggins (1998) explained that the temperature gradient so established drives heat by conduction into the interior of the dough piece. After about 20 minutes, the dough will reach a uniform temperature of around 35°C (95°F), ideal for yeast activity. Because the temperature of the dough piece stabilizes at the dew point temperature, additional heat transfer will evaporate moisture from the surface rather than raising dough temperature any further. For this reason, the atmosphere of the proofer will be nearly saturated at the system's exit.

Average proofing conditions for major yeast-raised products are listed in **Table 6.17**. (White 1970). The actual proofing temperature selected is influenced by factors such as flour strength, dough formulation with special regard to the types of oxidant, dough conditioner and shortening used, degree of fermentation, treatment received by the dough during mixing and makeup, and type of product such as rye bread or French sour dough bread. For example,

Table 6.17. Average Proofing Conditions

	Dry bulb		Wet bulb differential		Relative humidity
	°F	°C	F°	C°	RH%
Sponge doughs, bread	105 to 115	40.5 to 46.1	8	4.5	75
Sponge doughs, rolls	100 to 110	37.8 to 43.3	3 to 5	1.7 to 2.8	80 to 90
Continuous process doughs	115 to 120	46.1 to 48.9	3 to 5	1.7 to 2.8	80 to 90
Straight doughs, bread	100 to 110	37.8 to 43.3	5 to 8	2.8 to 4.5	75 to 80
Straight doughs, rolls	100 to 110	37.8 to 43.3	3 to 8	1.7 to 4.5	75 to 80
Sweet goods*					
Basic sweet doughs	98 to 110	36.7 to 43.3	8	4.5	75
Danish doughs (high butter content)	90 to 95	32.2 to 35.0	8 to 13	4.5 to 7.3	60 to 75
Danish doughs (low butter content)	95 to 100	35.0 to 37.8	8 to 10	4.5 to 7.3	60 to 75
Yeast-raised doughnuts*					
Bench-cut doughnuts**	100 to 110	37.8 to 43.3	5 to 10	2.8 to 5.6	70 to 85
Machine-cut doughnuts**	115 to 130	46.1 to 54.4	10 to 20	5.6 to 11.2	45 to 70

When bakery ambient dry bulb temperature is higher than the desired sweet goods proofing temperature, cooling will be required.

**Machine-cut doughnuts, in contrast to other products, require a high horizontal air flow across them to help retard their spread.*

(White 1970)

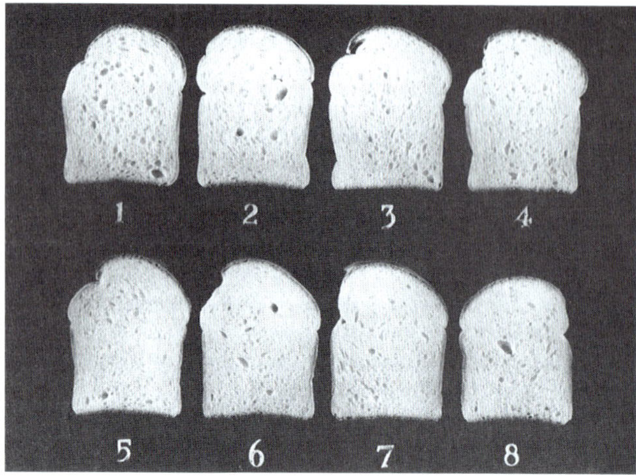

Figure 6.49. Changes in proofing temperatures affect loaf volume and crumb character; the number under each sample corresponds to the loaf number in Table 6.18. (Freilich 1949).

if the proofing temperature exceeds the melting point of the bread shortening's hard fraction, loaf volume will decline. Or if the temperature rises above the optima for enzyme and yeast activities, their activities are variably inhibited, again leading to changes in loaf volume and internal characteristics. Excessive proofing temperatures are often the result of a desire to shorten the proofing time. Thus, an increase temperature from 38°C to 49°C (100°F to 120°F) results in a reduction of 10 minutes in proof time and of as much as 20 minutes when the temperature is raised to 130°F (54°C) (Hildebrand 1952).

The effect of proof temperature was investigated at different levels within the range of 13 to 57°C (56 to 135°F), while proofing to constant volume (Freilich 1949). The results are tabulated in **Table 6.18** and illustrated in **Figure 6.49**. Loaf volume and crumb character were influenced only to minor extents by the different proof temperatures. Thus, the loaf volume of bread proofed at 40°C (104°F) and 57°C (135°F), respectively, differed only by 190 ml. Optimum loaf volumes, as well as bread of normal appearance, texture and grain, were achieved within the temperature span of 30 to 46°C (86 to 115°F). Loaves proofed at the lower temperatures had a slightly more open grain than normal and appeared to have a different cell structure. Doughs proofed at the higher temperatures (52 and 57°C, or 125 and 135°F) yielded bread of nearly normal texture and grain but with smoother sides and sharper corners than normal, indicating some softening at the points of contact with the pan wall caused either by starch gelatinization or proteolysis or both.

Proofing temperatures had their greatest influence on proof times: These ranged from 270 minutes for the lowest temperature (13°C, or 56°F) to only 36 minutes for the highest temperature (57°C, or 135°F). Proof times when the temperature was in the range for normal loaf volume and quality (20 to 46°C, or 86 to 115°F) showed a maximum difference of only 19 minutes.

Table 6.18. Effect of Proofing Temperature on Proof Time and Loaf Volume

Loaf No.	Proof temperature (°F)	Proof temperature (°C)	Proof time (minutes)	Volume per lb of bread (ml)
1	56	13.3	270	2,160
2	76	21.1	120	2,200
3	86	30.0	60	2,280
4	95	35.0	50	2,270
5	104	40.0	47	2,290
6	115	46.1	41	2,260
7	125	51.7	37	2,210
8	135	57.2	36	2,110

(Freilich 1949)

6.F.1.b. Relative humidity

The second major control factor in pan proofing is the moisture content of the proofer atmosphere, which may vary from a low of 75% to a high of 90% RH. Values lower than 75% tend to promote formation of excessively dry skin on the proofing dough pieces that will restrict optimum expansion and interfere with the desired crust coloration during baking. Excessive humidity, on the other hand, may cause moisture condensation on the dough piece that could result in a tough crust and creation of surface blisters in the finished bread. Relevant definitions are offered in **Table 6.19**.

Also, over-aged doughs tend to dextrinize excessively at their surface during baking when exposed to a moist proof box and then yield brittle crusts. As a rule, relative humidities in the range of 75 to 80% are recommended when low proofing temperatures are used.

As Wiggins (1998) explained, wet bulb temperature is relatively easy to measure and can be used to estimate the relative humidity using **Table 6.20** (on Pages 84 to 86). Likewise, at retarding and proofing temperatures, the dew point provides a good indication of whether dough surfaces will experience condensation or evaporation.

The effect of humidity during proof on bread quality was studied by Freilich (1949), who varied this factor from a low of 35% to a high of 90% RH at a proof temperature of 37 to 40°C (100 to 104°F). The results are given in **Table 6.21**. While variations in humidity had no significant effects on loaf volume, crumb texture and grain, they did markedly affect crust color and appearance: The loaves proofed at the lower humidities had crusts that were light in color and spotty and dull in appearance; those proofed at the higher humidities had crusts that were darker in color and more uniform in appearance. Low humidities also increased the proof time and decreased the bread yield. Optimum results were achieved with RH in the range of 80 to 90%, and this finding conforms to generally accepted standard practice.

Table 6.19. Humidity Definitions

Dry bulb temperature	The actual temperature of a gas
Wet bulb temperature	The temperature measured in an airstream by a thermometer when its bulb is kept wet
Dew point	The temperature at which moisture condenses out of a mixture of air and water vapor
Relative humidity	The ratio of the partial pressure of water vapor to its saturation pressure at the same temperature; the RH of fully saturated air is 100%
Specific humidity	The mass of water per unit mass of dry air in a mixture of air and water vapor

Dry bulb readings are always higher than wet bulb until the atmosphere reaches saturation, the point at which the atmosphere's air can no longer absorb any more moisture.

Table 6.21. Effect of Humidity During Proofing on Proof Time, Loaf Volume and Yield

Relative humidity	Proof time	Loss in proofing and baking	Volume per lb of bread
(%)	(minutes)	(g)	(ml)
35	57	74	2,230
50	52	72	2,320
60	54	71	2,230
80	49	64	2,150
90	46	64	2,270

(Freilich 1949)

6.F.1.c. Time

The third controlling factor in proofing is time. In practice, proof times generally fall within a range of 55 to 65 minutes, with 60 minutes being regarded by many bakers as the optimum for conventional doughs. Continuously-mixed doughs, because of their higher initial temperature and more extensive physical development, usually attain their maximum expansion within 55 minutes. In either case, the principal aim of proofing should be to bring about an optimum balance of the gassing rate and gas retention capacity within the panned dough.

For the most part, panned dough is proofed to volume or height rather than for a fixed time. As a result, the actual proof time will vary depending on the dough's character. Factors such as an inadequate yeast content or poor control of time and temperature during fermentation will result in extended proof times. The correct proofing time can be established only by practical experimentation in each particular plant, using as the criterion the time required for the loaf to expand to a predeter-

Table 6.20. Relative Humidity and Dew Point

Wet bulb temperature, °F

		Dry bulb temperature, °F										
		90	92	94	96	98	160	102	104	106	108	110
70	RH	36	32	29	26	23	21	16	16	14	12	11
	DP	61	60	69	66	57.5	57	56	55	54	53	52
72	RH	41	37	33	30	27	24	22	20	17	16	14
	DP	64	63	62	61	60	59	56.5	56	57	56	55.5
74	RH	47	42	38	35	32	28	26	23	21	19	17
	DP	67	66	66	64	63	62	61	60	59	59	58
76	RH	52	48	43	39	36	33	30	27	24	22	20
	DP	70	69	68	67	66	65	65	64	63	62.5	62
78	RH	58	53	49	44	40	37	34	31	28	25	23
	DP	73	73	72	71	70	69	69	68	67	66.5	66
80	RH	65	59	54	50	45	41	38	35	32	29	26
	DP	76	76	75	74	73	72	72	71	71	70	69
82	RH	71	65	60	55	50	46	42	39	36	33	30
	DP	79	79	78	77	76	76	75	75	74	73	72.5
84	RH	78	72	66	61	55	51	47	43	40	37	34
	DP	82	81	81	80	79	79	76	76	77	77	76
86	RH	85	78	72	66	61	56	52	48	44	41	38
	DP	85	84	84	83	82	82	81.5	81	80	80	79
88	RH	92	85	79	73	67	62	57	53	49	45	42
	DP	87	87	86	86	85	85	84.5	84	83.5	83	82
90	RH	100	92	85	79	73	68	62	58	53	49	46
	DP	89.5	89	89	88	88	87	87	86.5	86	85.5	85
92	RH	–	100	93	86	79	73	68	63	58	54	50
	DP	–	92	91.5	91	90	90	89.5	89	88.5	88	88
94	RH	–	–	100	93	86	60	74	69	64	59	55
	DP	–	–	94	93.5	93	93	92	91.5	91	91	90.5
96	RH	–	–	–	100	93	86	80	74	69	64	60
	DP	–	–	–	96	95.5	95	95	94.5	94	93.5	93
98	RH	–	–	–	–	100	93	86	80	75	70	65
	DP	–	–	–	–	98	97.5	97	97	96.5	96	95.5
100	RH	–	–	–	–	–	100	93	87	81	75	70
	DP	–	–	–	–	–	100	99.5	99	99	98.5	98
102	RH	–	–	–	–	–	–	100	93	87	81	75
	DP	–	–	–	–	–	–	102	101.5	101	101	100.5
104	RH	–	–	–	–	–	–	–	100	93	87	81
	DP	–	–	–	–	–	–	–	104	103.5	103.5	103
106	RH	–	–	–	–	–	–	–	–	100	93	87
	DP	–	–	–	–	–	–	–	–	106	106	105.5
108	RH	–	–	–	–	–	–	–	–	–	100	93
	DP	–	–	–	–	–	–	–	–	–	108	108
110	RH	–	–	–	–	–	–	–	–	–	–	100
	DP	–	–	–	–	–	–	–	–	–	–	110

RH = relative humidity; DP = dew point

Dry bulb temperature, °F

112	114	116	118	120	122	124	126	123	130
9	8	–	–	–	–	–	–	–	–
51	50	–	–	–	–	–	–	–	–
12	II	9	8	–	–	–	–	–	–
55	54	53	52	–	–	–	–	–	–
15	13	12	11	9	8	–	–	–	–
57.5	57	56	55	54	53	–	–	–	–
18	16	14	13	12	10	6	8	–	–
61	60	59	66	57	56.5	56	55	–	–
21	19	17	16	14	13	11	10	9	–
65	64	63	62	61	60	59	58	57	–
24	22	20	18	17	15	14	12	11	10
68	67.5	67	66	65	64	63	62	61	60
27	25	23	21	19	18	16	15	13	12
72	71	70	69	68	67.5	67	66	65	64
31	28	26	24	22	20	18	17	16	14
75	74.5	74	73	72	71	70.5	70	69	68
35	32	29	27	25	23	21	19	18	16
78.5	78	77	76.5	76	75	74	73.5	73	72
36	35	33	36	28	26	24	22	20	19
81.5	81	80	79.5	79	78.5	78	77	76.5	76
42	39	36	34	31	29	27	25	23	21
84.5	84	83.5	83	82	81.5	81	80.5	80	79
47	43	46	37	34	32	30	27	25	24
87.5	87	86	85.5	85	84.5	84	83.5	83	82
51	47	44	41	36	35	33	30	28	26
90	89.5	89	88.5	88	87.5	87	86.5	86	85
55	52	48	45	41	39	36	33	31	29
92.5	92	91.5	91	91	90.5	90	89.5	89	88.5
60	56	52	49	45	42	39	37	34	32
95	95	94.5	94	93.5	93	92.5	92	91.5	91
65	61	57	53	49	46	43	40	37	35
98	97.5	97	96.5	$96	96	95.5	95	94.5	94
70	66	61	57	53	50	47	44	41	38
100	100	99.5	99	99	98.5	98	97.5	97	97
76	71	66	62	58	54	50	47	44	41
103	103	102	102	101.5	101	101	100	100	99.5
81	76	71	67	62	58	54	51	48	45
105	105	104.5	104	104	103.5	103	103	102.5	102
87	82	76	72	67	63	59	55	52	48
107.5	107	107	106.5	106	106	105.5	105	105	104.5
94	86	82	77	72	67	63	59	56	52
110	109.5	109	109	108.5	108.5	108	108	107.5	107

Table 6.20. Relative Humidity and Dew Point

		Dry bulb temperature, °F										
		110	112	114	116	118	120	122	124	126	123	130
112	RH	100	94	88	82	77	72	68	64	60	56	
	DP	112	112	111.5	111	111	110.5	110.5	110	110	109.5	
114	RH	–	100	94	88	82	77	73	68	64	60	
	DP	–	114	114	113.5	113	113	112.5	112.5	112	112	
116	RH	–	–	100	94	86	83	78	73	69	64	
	DP	–	–	116	116	115.5	115.5	115	115	114.5	114.5	
118	RH	–	–	–	100	94	86	83	78	73	69	
	DP	–	–	–	118	118	117.5	117	117	117	116.5	
120	RH	–	–	–	–	100	94	88	83	78	73	
	DP	–	–	–	–	120	120	119.51	119.5	119	119	
122	RH	–	–	–	–	–	100	94	88	83	78	
	DP	–	–	–	–	–	122	122	121.5	121	121	
124	RH	–	–	–	–	–	–	100	94	89	78	
	DP	–	–	–	–	–	–	124	124	124	123.5	
126	RH	–	–	–	–	–	–	–	100	94	89	
	DP	–	–	–	–	–	–	–	126	126	126	

(Wet bulb temperature, °F is the row label.)

RH = relative humidity; DP = dew point

(Moore 1998)

mined standard height.

Proofing to height acts to compensate for variations in proof box conditions that are difficult to control. The temperature and humidity levels may not always be uniform throughout the chamber and may also vary from one day to the next, thereby causing non-uniformity in the final product. Proofing to standard height largely neutralizes such variables and results in more uniform bread. In recent years, however, computer-based operating techniques have helped quantify proofing results, building up a history of performance that allows bakers to better predict and control the times required for individual varieties.

Over-proofing results in loaves with pale crust color, coarse grain, poor texture, impaired keeping quality and a flavor with acid overtones. When using a "green" or weak flour, an additional loss in loaf volume occurs, brought on by collapse in the oven. Under-proofing usually yields small loaf volumes, shell tops, a foxy red crust color and occasional bursting at the sides.

Freilich (1949) studied the effects of broad variations in proofing conditions on bread characteristics. The influence of proof time variations on volume were determined by subjecting 1-lb laboratory test loaves to proof periods ranging from 0 to 150 minutes at 40°C (104°F). The results, shown in **Table 6.22**, reveal a range in loaf volume from 1,270 ml for the 0-minute proof time to 4,090 ml for the 150-minute proof time. This volume difference is illustrated visually in **Figure 6.50**.

Equally pronounced differences in grain and texture and in bread quality occurred with different proof periods. Loaves proofed for 0 and 15 minutes were compact and dense. While the 30-minute proof loaf showed considerable improvement, it still exhibited dense crumb characteristics. Normal texture and grain properties were achieved with the 45- and 60-minute proof times, and the 60-minute loaf possessed the greater tenderness. Loaves proofed for 75 and 90 minutes had a rather open grain but were still acceptable. Longer proof times resulted in large cells, a very open grain and poor keeping quality. The pH values declined from 5.49 to 5.13 as the proof time increased, indicating an increasing acid development in the dough. Baking loss also increased with prolonged proofing.

The effects of proof time on visual and physical texture of bread made from sheeted doughs were examined by Zghal et al (2001) using rheological testing methods. Loaf volume improved significantly and bread crumb density decreased (**Figure 6.51**) with increasing proof time.

Using a modern commercial bread formula, Kamman (1970) subjected panned dough to proofing periods of 48, 63 and 72 minutes. As shown in **Figure 6.52** the 48-minute proof yielded an under-proofed compact loaf with an open and uneven grain, the 63-minute proof produced optimum loaf characteristics, while the 72-minute proof resulted in an over-proofed loaf with a coarse grain marked by large round cells.

6.F.2. Retarding

Interruption at specific points in dough processes creates a spectrum of partially prepared bakery products that represent considerable commercial potential. As Sluimer (2005) noted, these stoppages (and their resulting products) take place after rounding (frozen dough), after moulding and before resting (retarded dough, frozen dough), after final proofing (pre-proofed frozen dough) and after the first stages of baking (par-baked or pre-baked products).

Retarding describes the use of low temperatures to slow or halt fermentation. The German word for this stage, *Gärunterbrechung*, literally means "fermentation interruption." This method is vital to the production of many sweet goods, danish and puff pastry products. The simple fact is, doughs containing layers of shortening must remain as cool as possible or else risk melting the fats and destroying the layering and leavening lift these products need. Sheeting and laminating add work and heat, so dough pieces must be cooled periodically during makeup. Sour dough methods also employ retarding as a way to build flavor while reducing the rate of fermentation. Bagel doughs are generally retarded because this process fosters development of the small surface blisters considered desirable.

The practice of retarding bread doughs emerged during the 1970s as a way to reduce the need for night work at bakeries (Sluimer 1981). The European bakers who opted for this method split the doughmaking process into two parts, one from mixing up to and including moulding and the second for baking. Doughs were cooled to 0°C (32°F) and kept overnight. The next morning, an automated process warmed the dough pieces to be baked.

Table 6.22. Effect of Proof Time on Loaf Volume, pH of Bread and Loss of Weight in Baking

Proof time	Volume per lb of bread	pH of bread	Loss in baking
(minutes)	(ml)		(g)
0	1,270	5.49	46
15	1,610	5.46	52
30	1,980	5.41	61
45	2,310	5.40	69
60	2,640	5.34	72
75	2,780	5.31	73
90	3,030	5.26	80
120	3,550	5.16	88
150	4,090	5.13	89

(Freilich 1949)

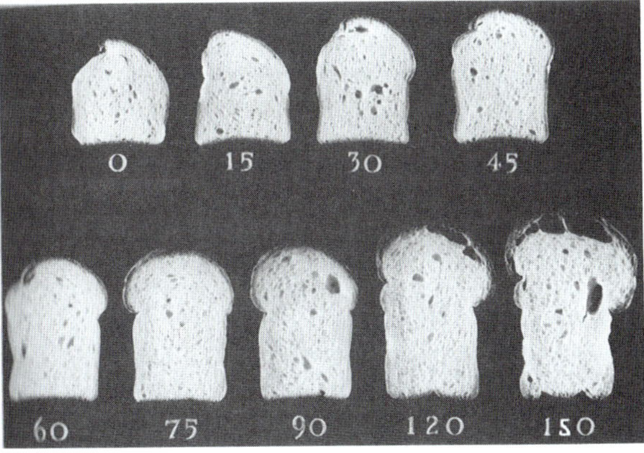

Figure 6.50. Changes in proof times show substantial effects on loaf volume and crumb structure; proof times in minutes are indicated by the number under each sample.
(Freilich 1949)

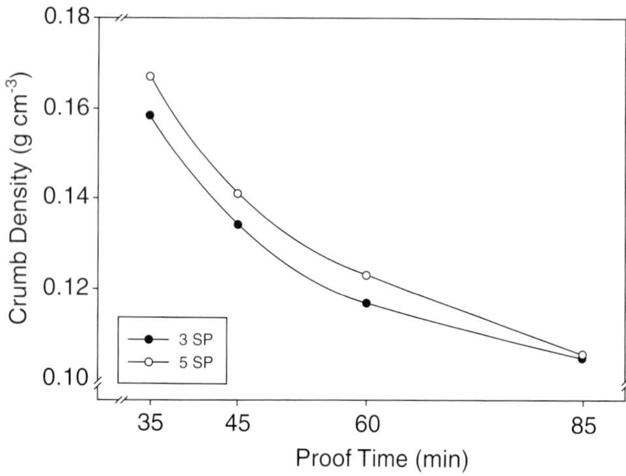

Figure 6.51. Crumb density of bread decreased with longer proof time and increased number of sheeting passes (SP).
(Zghal et al. 2001)

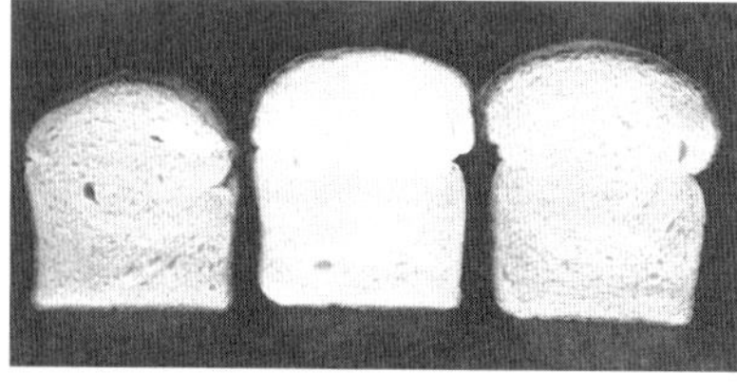

Figure 6.52. Final proof times can alter loaf characteristics: left loaf, short proof of 48 minutes; center loaf, normal proof of 63 minutes; right loaf, excessive proof of 72 minutes.
(Kamman 1970)

Sluimer (1981) noted that the first experiments with retarding bread doughs were conducted in 1926 at Vienna, and he cited French bakers' use of "fermentation dirigee" in which the final proofing of doughs lasted 10 hours at 10°C (50°F). Essential to the modern process are the requirements for full dough development during mixing and restriction of carbon dioxide production during retarding, as well as careful temperature control during retarding, storage and warming before baking.

An additional use of retarding occurs during preparation of frozen dough for bake-off. In this process, an in-store or retail baker pans pieces of frozen dough onto baking sheets, pans or trays and places them in the retarder or, when using a roll-in retarder, onto a mobile rack. The retarder controls the temperature and humidity within the cabinet to optimize thawing and tempering, usually on an overnight schedule. The next morning, the thawed dough pieces are ready for makeup and bake-off.

Humidity is particularly important during this stage of preparation, having effects similar to those it exerts during final proofing. When entering the retarder, the dough's RH (90 to 95%) will be much higher than that of the retarder, which can be as low as 60%. As Cauvain (1998b) explained, dough thus loses moisture from its surface during the early stages of retarding as it tries to achieve equilibrium with the air, running the risk of forming a dry skin on the dough piece, an irreversible process. Because higher yeast levels produce more dough expansion, the dough experiences greater moisture loss.

All types of retarders must be able to hold temperatures within the range of 1.7 to 4.4°C (35 to 40°F) at 85% RH They must provide sufficient air circulation to ensure uniform conditions within the cabinet. Temperature reduction of the doughs is determined by size and thickness of the individual dough pieces being refrigerated. Most retarded doughs retain their full functionality for 48 hours at retarding temperatures of 4 to 7°C (40 to 45°F) and 85% RH (Kulp 1995).

Straight doughs mixed with a dough-out temperature of 21°C (70°F) generally work best for retarding purposes. If bulk doughs need to be retarded, Kulp (1995) recommended they be divided into 5- to 10-lb portions to facilitate cooling.

Suas (2009) reported three basic retarding techniques: (a) delayed first fermentation, (b) slow final proof and (c) retarding-proofing process. A timeline chart for the three processes is shown in **Figure 6.53**. Although the methods differ, a dough-out temperature of 23°C (73°F) is recommended for all three.

Delayed first fermentation. This method uses a dough of medium-soft consistency. Its yeast level should be 1.2%, and use of preferment is recommended because of the gluten conditioning it provides. The baker places the dough in containers in the retarder set at 7 to 9°C (45 to 48°F) for 12 to 18 hours. Then the dough is divided, although it can wait about 1 hour before scaling. It is divided and rounded as normal but will require a longer resting time to allow the dough to warm up and accelerate fermentation. The rest of the makeup, proofing and baking stages proceed as normal. The advantage to delayed first fermentation is that fermentation, though slowed, does not stop completely. Because the dough ferments in bulk before makeup, no blisters form in crusts.

Slow final proof. A stiff, intensively-mixed dough made with 0.8 to 1% yeast and a preferment suits this method. After mixing, the dough ferments for 20 to 30 minutes, and then is divided, rounded and rested for another 20 to 30 minutes before final makeup. The shaped pieces are put into the retarder, set at 10°C (50°F), and held for 12 to 15 hours. At this point, the pieces can be baked directly out of the retarder. At this retarder temperature, yeast fermentation does not stop, but carbon dioxide production is slowed considerably, giving the baker a generous time frame in which to bake the product. The skin of the dough pieces may dehydrate, so use of additional humidity is suggested.

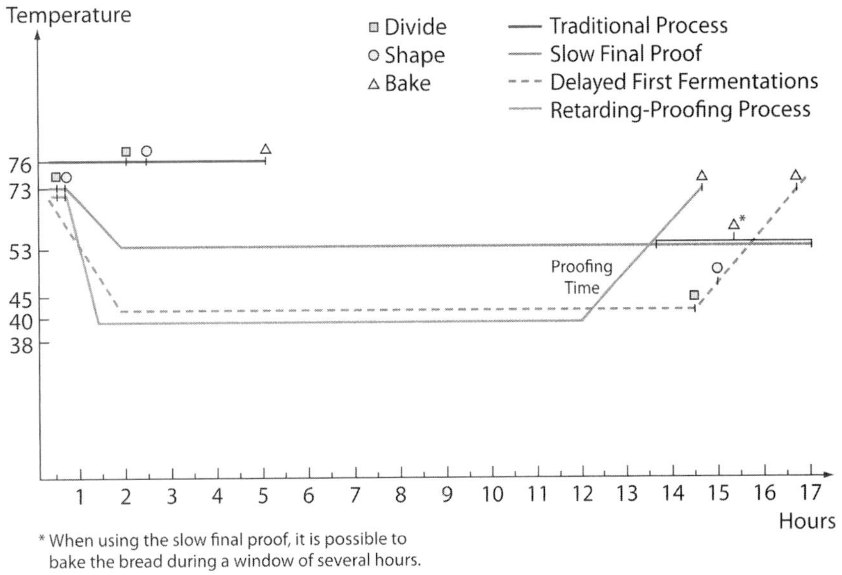

Retarding-proofing process. A relatively stiff dough made with 1.8 to 2.0% yeast and a preferment is recommended. After mixing, the dough is fermented in bulk for 20 to 30 minutes before being divided and rounded. Another 20 to 30 minutes of resting follows. During makeup, the pieces are given a tight curl and placed in the retarder, set at 3 to 4°C (38 to 40°F), for 12 to 48 hours. When brought out of the retarder, the dough can be left at room temperature for final proofing. This process can also take place in a retarder-proofer that automatically raises the cabinet's temperature to 22 to 24°C (72 to 75°F) after the retarding period ends. Care must be taken to provide enough humidity at the lower temperatures to avoid drying the skin of the dough piece. Also, dough strengtheners are necessary in the formula.

When sourdough is used as a preferment, according to Suas (2009), its high level of acidity naturally reinforces the dough characteristics, giving gluten greater tolerance to handle the longer fermentation times. This extra strength benefits formulations containing rye and whole-wheat flours.

Although retarding does slow fermentation, the effects of other ingredient activities must be considered. Flour and malt contains some natural α-amylase enzymes, and this and other carbohydrase and protease enzymes present or added by the baker during formulation will continue to work in the retarder. Excess dextrinization by amylase will result in darker crust color, while over-treatment by protease will weaken the dough structure, resulting in loss of gas retention and too much pan flow.

Figure 6.53. Retarding processes shift the timelines for preparing yeast-raised and sourdough products. (Suas 2009)

6.G. Baking

The final step in breadmaking is the actual baking process in which heat transforms the raw dough piece into a light, porous, readily digestible and flavorful product. The various reactions that underlie this transformation are both basic — they irreversibly

Beginning of Bake

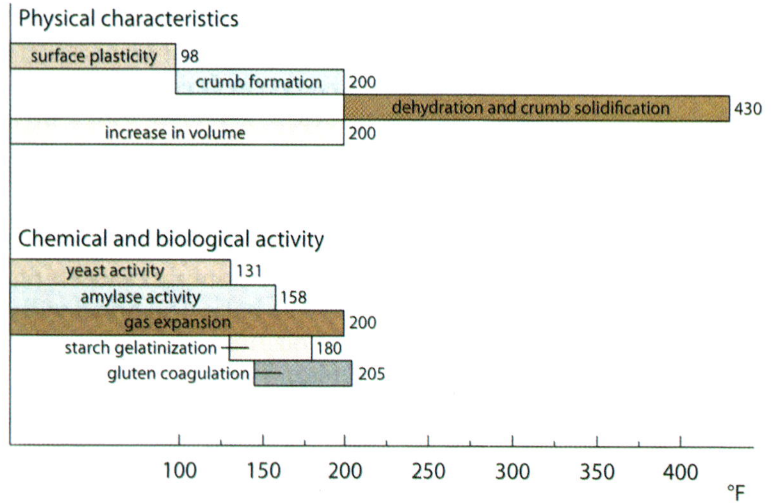

Figure 6.54. The physical, chemical and biological changes that transform dough into bread occur as temperatures increase during baking. (Suas 2009)

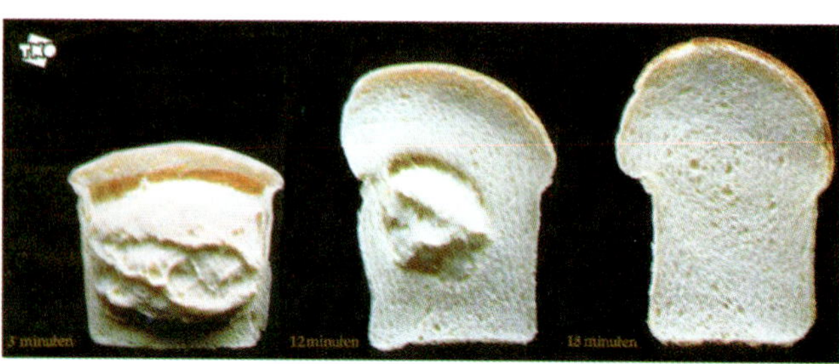

Figure 6.55. Cross sections of dough taken at after (from left) 3, 12 and 18 minutes of baking reveal the dough's transformation from a foam-like material into the sponge-like texture desired. (Sluimer 2005)

alter the structural nature of the major dough constituents — and highly complex because they involve a vast series of physical, chemical and biochemical interactions (**Figure 6.54**).

The most apparent effects produced by oven heat on the dough piece are an expansion of its volume, the formation of an enveloping crust, the inactivation of yeast and enzymatic activities and the coagulation of the dough's protein and partial gelatinization of its starch. Simultaneously, extensive stabilization occurs of the otherwise rather sensitive colloidal dough system. These basic transformations are accompanied by the formation of new flavor substances such as caramelized sugars, pyrodextrins and melanoidins, as well as a broad range of aromatic compounds comprising aldehydes, ketones, various esters, acids and alcohols.

Production of bread meeting desired quality attributes requires a carefully controlled baking process. The rate of heat application and the amount of heat supplied, the humidity level within the baking chamber and the duration of the bake — all exert a vital influence on the final quality of the bread.

Baking involves both heat exchange and mass exchange (Knott 1996). Heat exchange involves the transfer of heat energy by conduction, convection and radiation. Mass exchange is primarily related to the removal of water.

Baking transforms the liquid foam-like dough into a solid sponge, setting the final crumb structure as a consequence of the gelatinization of the starch and the heat-induced setting of the gluten (Sluimer 2005). The crust forms as the dough piece's outer surface dehydrates, and its brown color is contributed by the Maillard reaction between proteins and sugars. Ovenspring occurs because of the gas retained in the dough expands to greatly increase the volume of the dough piece. **Figure 6.55** shows cross sections of dough taken at different times during the baking process.

In their description of digital image analysis as a means to explore bread texture, Scanlon and Andrews (2001) reviewed the many changes involved in breadmaking processes and how they affect the final crumb structure of bread. The heat of the oven prompts a variety of changes within the dough. Polymers such as gluten undergo aggregation and cross-linking; the hydrated starch melts partially, yet individual granules still remain in identifiable fashion; some cell walls rupture, while others set up and limit further expansion. During baking, the heat-set cellular structure of the outer regions is compressed by pressure exerted by ovenspring occurring inside the dough mass, elongating the outer cells. The final structure of bread crumb is a 2-phase system: randomly dispersed gas in a matrix of cells, with walls 20 to 200 μm thick, more open than closed.

The effect of heat on dough and its components was well described by Eliasson and Larsson (1993), who portrayed baking as the most critical point in the bread-making process: "All mistakes made earlier in the process will now be revealed."

6.G.1 Stages of baking

Modern ovens are generally designed to convey the baking loaf either on trays or a traveling hearth through a series of zones in which it is exposed for definite time periods to different temperature and humidity conditions. As Swortfiguer (1968) pointed out, the first stage of baking, at a temperature of about 204°C (400°F), lasts about 6.5 minutes and comprises one-fourth of a total baking time of 26 minutes. During this period, the temperature of the outer crumb layers increases at an average rate of 4.7 C° (8.5 F°) per minute to a level of about 60°C (140°F). The first observable change produced by the oven heat is the almost instantaneous formation of a thin and initially expandable surface skin.

Bakers have long recognized the importance of time to the baking process. The shorter the time required to reach an internal temperature of 70 to 77°C (160 to 170°F), the more elastic the crumb, while the longer the time, the gummier the crumb (Sievers 1976).

At first, the rise in temperature accelerates enzymatic activity and yeast growth. Loaf volume increases noticeably through "oven rise" — a reaction caused by the rapid expansion of carbon dioxide gas that continues to be evolved early in the oven. At about 50 to 60°C (122 to 140°F), most enzymes undergo thermal inactivation, and the yeast and other bacteria are killed. At this temperature, all of the carbon dioxide gas has been released from solution and contributes to loaf expansion. The surface skin thickens, loses its elasticity and begins to acquire the first signs of brown color. "Ovenspring" occurs next — the rather sudden expansion of the dough by about one-third of its original volume (Hlynka 1972).

The second and third phases of baking together last some 13 minutes, or about one-half of the total bake time. During this period, the oven temperature is held constant at around 238°C (460°F). The crumb temperature rises at a rate of 5.4 C° (9.7 F°) per minute during the second stage until it reaches 98 to 99°C (209 to 210°F) by the start of the third stage, and then remains constant.

This temperature level coincides with the maximum rates of moisture evaporation, starch gelatinization and protein coagulation. The dough interior is progressively transformed into a crumb structure from its outer to its inner portions by the penetrating heat. As the crust temperature reaches 150 to 205°C (300 to 400°F), the crust begins to assume its typical brown color. The final, or finishing, oven zone is maintained at a constant temperature of 221 to 238°C (430 to 460°F) and serves to firm up the cell walls and develop the desired crust color. Representing the final one-fourth of the total baking time, this finishing stage is marked by volatilization of certain organic substances that is designated as the "bake-out loss."

While these temperatures and durations of the individual baking phases represent usual baking practice, considerable deviations are encountered. Factors such as oven design, weight or volume of product, crust character and color, level of residual crumb moisture and others all have a bearing on the actual baking tempera-

Table 6.23. Effect of Baking Temperature on Bake-out Loss (% of moisture of white bread)

| Baking time (minutes) | Baking temperature | | Bake-out loss (%) | Moisture in bread (%) |
	Location	°C (°F)		
23	Feed end	217 (420)		
	Zone 2	227 (440)		
	Zone 3	238 (460)		
	Discharge end	232 (450)	9.8	37.0
23	Feed end	227 (440)		
	Zone 2	249 (480)		
	Zone 3	249 (480)		
	Discharge end	239 (460)	10.0	36.5
23	Feed end	210 (410)		
	Zone 2	274 (525)		
	Zone 3	260 (500)		
	Discharge end	271 (520)	11.5	35.7

(Prouty 1965)

ture and time. Product size in particular is important in determining baking time, with smaller loaves of pan bread reaching full bake faster than larger loaves at an appropriately regulated temperature. Thus, if a 16-oz loaf requires 18 to 20 minutes to bake adequately, the time for a 24-oz loaf will normally be 20 to 22 minutes.

With the development of extended shelf life (ESL) formulations that use softening enzyme systems, finished bake temperatures should be between 93 and 94°C (200 and 202°F) as product exits the oven. If the product is much above this temperature, excessive moisture is driven off and the product dries more quickly on the shelf. If the temperature is less than 93°C (200°F), the product is not fully baked, resulting in excess softness, poor slicing, collapse on the shelf, inability to stack product and other faults.

The preference for baking continuously-mixed doughs is to use a rising temperature gradient that starts at a relatively low temperature such as 199 to 227°C (390 to 400°F) and ends at about 221 to 227°C (430 to 440°F). Care must be taken, however, not to let the temperature of an oven zone drop below that of the preceding zone or else loaf sidewalls weaken, resulting in a "keyhole" shape.

The importance of proper oven temperature control for bread quality was demonstrated by Prouty (1965), who investigated the effects of temperature variations, at constant baking time, on bake-out and moisture losses in the finished bread. His results, shown in **Table 6.23**, found differences of up to 1.7% in bake-out loss and 1.3% in moisture loss when the oven-zone temperatures were allowed to vary. All other conditions being equal, bread with an initial moisture content of 37.0% will feel fresher when it reaches the consumer than the bread with only 35.7% initial moisture content.

6.G.2. Baking conditions

Baking temperatures normally encountered in the production of most breads range from 191 to 232°C (375 to 450°F). (A notable exception is pumpernickel, which is baked in closed pans for up to 24 hours at temperatures of 100 to 191°C [212 to 375°F] under saturated steam conditions.) The humidity levels within the various zones of the baking chamber will vary from high in moisture at the front section of the first zone, created by the injection of low-pressure saturated steam, to relatively low moisture content in the subsequent oven zones. The baking time for bread may range anywhere from 18 to 35 minutes, depending on oven temperature, loaf weight and type of product. Thus, the actual baking process, as is true with all the preceding stages of breadmaking, is circumscribed by time, temperature and humidity as the principal control factors.

More specifically, ordinary white pan bread requires a baking time of about 1 minute per oz of dough at a temperature of 218 to 232°C (425 to 450°F), with steam injection for the first 0.5 to 2 minutes of baking. Thus, a 1-lb loaf of bread, scaled at 18 oz of dough, will take about 18 minutes to bake. With larger loaf sizes, the unit bake time needs to be extended by a fraction and the oven temperature lowered by a few degrees to account for the relatively constant heat transmission rate within the loaf.

As a rule, Pullman bread is baked slightly longer than open-top pan bread. Rye breads and hard rolls call for both higher sustained temperatures, from 227 to 238°C (440 to 460°F), and copious amounts of steam at the outset of baking to promote formation of a smooth, glossy crust. Doughs containing high levels of sweeteners should be baked at somewhat lower temperatures to avoid premature and excessive caramelization that leads to dark crusts. The same applies to white bread containing 4 to 5% of dry milk solids or other dairy-type additives, although these ingredients have fallen out of favor in most applications during the past 20 years.

The prevalent practice is to limit steam injection to the very front section of the first baking zone and to rely on moisture evaporation from the baking product to maintain an appropriate atmospheric moisture level in subsequent oven zones. Anderson (1966) calculated that a pound of dough, on baking, will generate about 2.7 cu ft of steam at 100°C (212°F), while the combustion of natural gas in direct-fired ovens supplies 0.9 cu ft of steam per lb of dough. Typical steam injection practice calls for an additional 9.25 cu ft per lb of dough.

Most large bakeries no longer pipe steam to the oven unless breads requiring a hard or glossy crust form part of the product mix. In such latter cases, experience has shown that best steaming results are obtained by injecting low pressure (2 to 5 psi) saturated steam at a rate of 200 to 500 ft per minute over the baking product during the first minute of baking. Excessive steam turbulence around the product will interfere with moisture condensation on the dough surface and thereby negate the purpose of the steam injection.

Baking temperatures and baking times are influenced to a marked degree by product formulation. In general, relatively lean formulations call for higher baking temperatures and a shorter baking time than do richer formulations. The reason is that the sugars and dairy ingredients present in greater amounts in rich formulations enter readily into thermal browning reactions. As a result, an excessively dark crust can form before the crumb has reached its optimum bake. Similar effects can be observed with young doughs that retain an excess of residual sugar. On the other hand, in lean doughs, as well as in old doughs, these thermolabile ingredients are either absent or present in only minimal amounts, so crust coloration must depend to a greater extent on the brown pyrolysis products of starch and dextrins. To compensate for the higher baking temperatures required in such cases, somewhat shorter baking times are needed to avoid excessive bake-out losses.

Because of these variables, as well as others that relate to oven design and operational procedures, it is impossible to establish optimal baking conditions with a high degree of precision. These can be determined only by a practical study of the actual oven performance in individual plants.

A dough piece exposed to oven heat will undergo rapid warming on its surface and progressively slower warming of its interior mass as the distance from the surface increases. Auerman (1977) showed that the temperature of the dough surface reaches 150°C (302°F) during the first third of the baking cycle at a constant temperature. Thereafter, its rate of climb slows perceptibly until it reaches 180°C (356°F) or higher at the end of baking. The temperature of the crumb never exceeds 99°C (210°F), and this level is reached after variable time intervals that depend on the distance between the point of measurement and the crust.

The center of the loaf does not attain the maximum temperature until near the end of the bake. The mechanism that accounts for the temperature of the crumb failing to rise to the boiling point of water is the greater rate of heat loss caused by the evaporation of water as compared with the rate of heat absorption by the dough.

Baker and Mize (1939) charted the temperature rise in a dough that was heated dielectrically. (The dough serves as the resistor in an electric current of constant energy input. This method produces uniform heating throughout the dough mass but results in a finished loaf lacking a brown crust.) They observed that when fermented dough is subjected to a uniform heat input, the temperature rise does not follow a straight line but deviates slightly as different temperature levels are reached, indicating variations in heat absorption. A slight decrease in the rate of temperature rise occurs during the first stage of baking until a temperature of about 49°C (120°F) is reached. The researchers attributed this initial higher heat absorption to the carbon dioxide coming out of solution in the dough. The dough temperature then rises uniformly to about 54 to 58°C (130 to 136°F) when starch swelling sets in and again causes heat absorption to increase. Next, temperature rises uniformly to about 79°C (175°F), when further heat absorption, coinciding with the evaporation of alcohol and water, takes place and becomes progressively greater until heating ends at 100°C (212°F).

Ponte et al. (1963) found that the time required for the crumb to reach any given temperature level is measurably influenced by the oven temperature. As the individual curves show, a small internal temperature rise takes place in the dough mass during the first 8 minutes in the oven. Thereafter, the rise becomes quite sharp, with the higher oven temperatures producing the steeper temperature slopes. Finally, the rate of the internal temperature increase levels off as a maximum temperature of about 94°C (202°F) is approached. Such temperatures set the loaf's structure sufficiently to withstand slicing (Wiggins 1998).

Marston and Wannan (1976) suggested that the pattern of temperature rise in a dough mass involves a 3-phase sequence: (a) a variable initial lag period, (b) a steep rise to approximately 85°C (185°F) and then (c) an asymptotic approach to the boiling point of water. Only at points on the surface or within about 3 mm of the surface does the temperature pattern deviate markedly from this. Finally, the temperature slope of the second, or steep-rise, phase is essentially similar for all points within the dough mass.

Auerman (1977) provided a detailed summary of the temperature changes that occur in a dough piece during the course of baking, covering aspects such as developing temperature gradients within the crumb, moisture translocations and steam formation, effects of oven steam on heat transfer, and the effect of loaf form on rate of heat penetration.

6.G.2.a. Heat transfer

In conventional baking processes, heat is transmitted to the dough piece in three different ways, namely, by radiation, convection and conduction (Matz 1972). While all three modes play significant roles in baking, their relative importance depends largely on the type and design of the oven. Condensation and evaporation, which involve latent heat, are also involved. Heat transfer methods are covered in more detail in Chapter 10, Part B.

Radiant heat consists principally of invisible infrared rays that emanate from the heated internal surfaces of the oven. Its behavior differs from the other types of heat in two distinct ways: (a) It is blocked in its transmission by any intervening opaque object, and (b) it is highly responsive to the absorptive properties of the product that is exposed to it.

Convected heat is that which is transferred by means of inter-mixing fluid media such as air, water vapor or combustion gases. In ovens, convected heat is distributed through the baking chamber by the turbulence of the internal atmosphere and is transferred by conduction to the dough piece when the hot air contacts the dough surface. The hot air enters the oven chamber through perforated pipes or plates, called "coloraiders," located above and below the product. It is recommended that the air is blown onto the product in a defined pattern to provide good color development and maximum heat transfer.

Conducted heat is that which is transmitted by physical contact from one body to another or from one part to another in the same body. Thus, the side and bottom crusts in pan bread result mainly from the heat that is transmitted by the walls of the pan, and the gradual heating of the interior of the dough piece during baking is also largely the result of heat conduction.

According to Matz (1972), conduction and radiation tend to localize heat differentials, with conduction acting to raise the temperature of the loaf bottoms and sidewalls of pan bread, and radiation that of exposed loaf surfaces; convection, on the other hand, tends to create a more uniform heat distribution within the oven.

Sluimer (2005), however, stated that conduction contributes only a small part of the heat transport of baking, and the greater part of the heat required to bake a product originates from condensation of steam within the product. Bakery engineers and bakers alike (Sievers 1978, Lanham 1994) have observed that the cellular structure of dough makes it a poor conductor of heat.

6.G.2.b. Humidity and oven steam

Humidity within the oven plays a key role in the baking process by controlling the rate of heat input to the dough. Water vapor present inside the oven comes from ambient air, from the combustion process (if the oven is direct-fired), from evaporation from previously baked loaves and from steam added to the oven environment. When it condenses on dough pieces as they enter the oven, the water vapor adds its latent heat to the product, a process that continues until the dough piece reaches the dew point of the oven. Humidity also affects the net evaporation rate from the baking foods, altering the surface texture, color and moisture content (Johnson and Walker 2003).

Although the baker has many different names for steam used in the oven (**Table 6.24**), there are only two distinctly different steams produced in boilers (Dersch 1989): dry saturated steam, with a temperature at the boiling point of water, 100°C (212°F) but containing no water in suspension, and super-heated steam, with a temperature above the boiling point, corresponding to the pressure.

Steam performs several necessary functions during the initial stages of baking, including (a) preserving the extensibility

Table 6.24. Steam Types and Terms

Baker's term	Engineer's term
Dry steam	Dry saturated steam
Wet steam	Dry saturated steam with entrained water
Hard steam	Super-heated steam
Soft steam	Super-heated steam with entrained water

(Dersch 1989)

of the surface skin on the dough piece over the critical periods of continued oven rise and ovenspring; (b) imparting a desirable gloss to the crust, particularly of hearth loaves and hard rolls; and (c) promoting heat penetration into the loaf interior. In a dry oven, the dough piece will almost immediately experience rapid evaporation of water from its exposed surface. This evaporation causes premature formation of a dry, inelastic outer shell that restricts loaf expansion or gives rise to unsightly tears in the finished crust, or both. Because of inadequate atmospheric moisture, the surface layer of starch undergoes pyrolysis rather than partial gelatinization, and the crust will not acquire the desired gloss. Finally, the evaporative process absorbs considerable heat from the surface, thereby slowing the rate of heat penetration into the loaf interior. These effects are minimized by proper steam conditions in the oven. When optimum conditions exist, atmospheric moisture will first condense on the dough's surface as it enters the oven. Given the porous nature of the surface, this moisture penetrates into the surface skin and keeps it flexible during the initial baking stage; it further promotes starch gelatinization and the concomitant gloss formation in the crust; and, finally, it facilitates more rapid heat flow into the loaf (Auerman 1977, Marston and Wannan 1976, Dersch 1989).

Low-pressure (2 to 5 lb), high-volume steam (also called "wet steam") in the early zones of the oven prevents dough from "bursting" (Moore 1988). When hearth doughs and French breads enter the oven, their surface temperature is well below the dew point of the oven. Water vapor from the injected steam will condense on the product, delaying crust formation. The upper surface remains flexible during early baking stages, allowing internal pressures to equilibrate with oven conditions, thus preventing the crust from cracking.

High-pressure steam is not recommended for baking and fails to give the proper effects. When steam pressure is greater than the gas line pressure, it can douse the fire by interfering with gas flow in the burner (Doerry 1995a). Additionally, too much steam will corrode the equipment, and when steam is allowed to escape from the oven into the bakery, it will carry with it volatile components that tend to deposit as a smudgy, brown film on surfaces, creating sanitation problems.

Johnson and Walker (2003) provided a comprehensive review of oven humidity in terms of baking performance for breads, cakes, cookies and crackers. Wiggins (1998) described how an evaporation front, located in the region of the crust, determines whether diffused moisture is driven off through evaporation as steam or condenses into the product as interior moisture. Each gas cell acts as a heat pipe, with moisture evaporating from the hot end and condensing at the cool end.

6.G.2.c. Ovenspring

The term "ovenspring" (or "oven rise") describes the extremely sudden expansion of the dough loaf by about one-third of its original volume that occurs during the initial stage of baking. This volume increase, initiated by the penetration of heat into the dough mass, involves the interplay of several basic physical phenomena. According to Charles's Law, heat applied to a gas at constant volume increases the pressure of the gas. If the gas is confined in an elastic or expandable vesicle or cell, one visible effect of this increased pressure is expansion in the volume of the cell.

A dough piece contains millions of minute gas cells confined within elastic gluten walls. The cells contain carbon dioxide, gaseous ethanol, water vapor and air. When heat is applied, the pressure of the gas within the cells increases, and the elastic gluten walls permit the individual cells to expand.

A second effect of heat is to reduce the solubility of gases. A major proportion of the carbon dioxide generated by yeast fermentation is dissolved in the dough's aqueous phase. As the temperature of the dough increases to 49°C (120°F) and beyond, the carbon dioxide held in solution is released and migrates into existing cells, thereby adding to their internal pressure and, concomitantly, to their size.

A third effect of heat is to change the physical state of liquids with low boiling points into gases by volatilization or distillation. Although ethanol is quantitatively the major low-boiling liquid present in dough, other dough constituents that are volatile at temperatures below 79°C (175°F) include many of the organic acids, esters, aldehydes and ketones. They are transformed into vapor early in the baking process, thereby contributing to the gas pressure within the cells and to their expansion.

Studying the contribution of carbon dioxide to loaf expansion during ovenspring, Moore and Hoseney (1985) determined that 57% of this action can be attributed to gas expansion as a result of the rise in temperature, 39% to the release of carbon dioxide from the aqueous phase and only 4% to gas generated by the temperature-dependent increase in yeast activity. Moreover, because this expansion in carbon dioxide volume during ovenspring accounts for only about one-half of the increase in loaf volume, the evaporation of ethanol at elevated temperatures is responsible for the remaining increase, which is roughly equivalent to that produced by the carbon dioxide.

A fourth factor affecting ovenspring is the reciprocal relation between the gas pressure in a cell and the cell's radius. As Hlynka (1970) pointed out, small gas cells require considerably greater pressures to expand than do large cells. So, once the pressure in the minute gas cells of the dough exceeds a certain critical limit, the restrictive forces of the cell walls suddenly give way, and the cells undergo an abrupt expansion. Since the crust has begun to form by the time this stage is reached, one readily observable effect of ovenspring is appearance of the characteristic "break and shred" on the upper sides of the pan loaf.

When the pressure changes within a baking loaf are traced, it is found that the pressure at first increases steadily as a result of the gradual penetration of heat and its accelerating effect on gas generation. This is followed by a sharp drop in pressure — which coincides with the period of the ovenspring — at about the time when the crumb temperature has reached the level at which starch begins to gelatinize. Some of the pressure drop also results from the coalescence of small cells into larger cells and by the transformation of the dough into a more porous, permeable structure brought about by the amylolysis of gelatinized starch and the rupture of cell walls by excessive pressure buildup (Hlynka 1970).

Baker and Mize (1939) found that this pressure drop is greatest in fat-free doughs and in doughs made with 3.0% liquid oil, but it is minimized by including 3.0% semisolid shortening (flour weight basis) in the formula. Doughs made from inadequately oxidized flours possess a relatively weak gluten structure whose gas cells are likely to coalesce more readily, and such doughs exhibit a more pronounced pressure drop. Bread from such doughs tends to have a crumb with an uneven grain marked by large air cells, rather than a crumb with fine, elongated cells and a silky texture such as is obtained with properly oxidized flours.

The effect of fermentation on ovenspring was demonstrated by Baker (1957) who used two yeasted doughs, one of which was fermented for 4 hours and proofed to height, while the other received only proofing to height without prior fermentation. The doughs were heated dielectrically.

The unfermented dough expanded during heating until starch swelling began, after which there was no further volume increase. The fermented dough, on the other hand, continued to increase in volume until about 79°C (175°F), showing twice the expansion of the unfermented dough. Evidently, fermentation improves the baking quality of the dough by increasing the cells' gas retention ability. The bread obtained from the fermented dough had a fine-grained, thin-walled cell structure, whereas the bread from the unfermented dough exhibited a coarse grain and thick cell walls. When, however, suitable oxidants were added to the unfermented dough, its ovenspring and cell structure equaled those of the fermented dough.

Oven rise ends when the cell walls rupture under tensile stress, and the leavening gases escape to the exterior. Bloksma (1994a) debunked the idea that crust formation determines the end of oven rise by preventing further expansion. If this were true, the crust would carry the full strain of the excess gas pressure and there would be no stress in the dough membranes and no cause for the transformation of the foam structure of the dough into the sponge structure of the baked crumb.

Compression phenomena caused by crust formation were observed using magnetic resonance imaging (MRI) at the gas cell scale during study of dough as it baked (Wagner et al. 2008). Another study found that restriction of expansion by the crust caused internal pressures to increase and forced CO_2 to be transported out of the bread (Zhang et al. 2008).

6.G.3. Reactions during baking

Application of heat to dough in the quantities supplied by the oven produces a variety of effects on various components. Studying the rheological properties of dough as it bakes reveals how components change to yield the finished product.

Bushuk (1998) described the important changes during baking as (a) expansion of the loaf by 50% due to the additive effects of carbon dioxide production and evaporation of water, carbon dioxide and ethanol; (b) transformation of the predominantly viscous dough into the predominantly elastic bread crumb and into crisp crust, through the gelatinization of starch (involving mainly noncovalent bonds) and the thermal denaturation of gluten (involving both noncovalent and disulfide bonds); and (c) conversion of dough from a foam structure of self-contained gas cells into a sponge structure of interconnected cells.

6.G.3.a. Starch gelatinization

During baking, the starch granules begin to swell at a temperature of about 40°C (104°F). The viscoelastic properties of dough diminish, supplanted by fluidity by the time the temperature reaches about 50 to 65°C (122 to 150°F). This rheological change is caused principally by enzymatic degradation before swelling becomes significant.

During swelling and gelatinization, starch granules avidly absorb the dough's free water and compete for that held by its protein. But even though their granular structure undergoes considerable deformation, becoming quite flexible at temperatures of 60 to 70°C (140 to 158°F), a large proportion of the granules remains intact because of the limited supply of water (Sandstedt 1961).

Schoch (1965) suggested that during starch swelling and gelatinization a part of the linear fraction of starch dissolves and diffuses out of the granules and into the surrounding aqueous medium. This dissolved starch becomes concentrated as the amount of interstitial water is reduced by continued starch swelling. When the finished product cools, the dissolved linear starch fraction sets up into a gel and appears to play a significant role in bread staling because of its pronounced tendency to retrograde.

The extent of mechanical starch damage sustained by the flour during milling also matters during the baking stage. Flours with relatively high levels of starch damage exhibit increased water absorbing capacity; however, the damaged starch is readily attacked by amylase prior to gelatinization and liberates its absorbed water. This free water then becomes available for more extensive starch swelling and gelatinization during baking (Marston and Wannan 1976).

While the extent of starch gelatinization depends greatly on availability of water, the temperature and duration of water's action on starch also play major roles. Yasunga et al. (1968) observed a greater degree of starch gelatinization in the crumb layers next to the crust, where higher temperatures prevail for more extended periods, than in the center of the loaf with its less extreme temperature conditions.

Audidier (1968) reported that in long French loaves, crumb temperature of 99°C (210°F) is reached in about 8 minutes of baking and is then maintained for an additional 20 minutes. This time-temperature relation results in nearly complete starch gelatinization in this type of loaf. In pan bread, on the other hand, 20 minutes are needed for the crumb temperature to reach 99°C (210°F), leaving only 6 to 10 minutes for a subsequent exposure at that level. Here, the starch granules remain largely intact. In the crust, a very rapid and steep rise in temperature greatly curtails the reaction time in which starch pasting can occur. As a result, the starch granules in the crust, though considerably deformed, undergo only slight modifications in their crystalline structure.

Gelatinization of starch should take place later in the baking cycle, as is true for wheat starch, to prevent early setting of the dough. Kusunose et al. (1999) experimented by substituting potato and tapioca starch for wheat starch in bread doughs. Potato starch gelatinized early in the baking cycle, inhibiting dough expansion, while tapioca starch fused together during gelatinization, forming an impermeable gas membrane. The individual gelatinization of granules, typical of wheat starch, causes a disruption of cell membranes, which prevents shrinkage of the loaf after baking.

6.G.3.b. Protein denaturation

Gluten proteins are present in dough in a hydrated state, binding an estimated 31% of the total dough absorption water. They participate in the formation of the dough structure by providing the matrix in which strings of small starch granules are embedded (Pomeranz et al. 1984).

As the temperature of the crumb reaches about 60 to 70°C (140 to 158°F), the proteins begin to undergo thermal denaturation, which reduces their water-binding capacity to practically zero. Thus, baking causes the transfer of water from the proteins to the starch in the course of gelatinization. In dough, the gluten films provide the main structural element that sustains the loaf volume.

When the dough temperature rises above 74°C (165°F), the denaturation of proteins by heat transforms the gluten films surrounding the individual gas cells into a semi-rigid structure by interaction with the swollen starch. As the gas cells expand, the flexible starch granules within the cell wall are elongated, thereby enabling the gluten film to become thinner and ultimately to rupture, as is shown in **Figure 6.56**. By this time, however, starch swelling has advanced sufficiently to prevent a collapse of the dough structure (Bushuk and Hlynka 1964).

Gas cell coalescence in doughs has been studied by a number of researchers using rheological methods and was modeled mathematically by van Vliet (1999).

6.G.3.c. Enzyme activity

The amylases begin to hydrolyze starch during baking with the onset of swelling, their rate of action approximately doubling for each 10 C° (18 F°) rise in temperature. At the same time, the higher environmental temperatures begin to exert their inactivating effect until ultimately amylolysis is stopped.

Amylase activity during the early stages of baking has a 2-fold effect: (a) It renders the dough more fluid and thereby promotes dough expansion, and (b) it increases the levels of both dextrins and maltose. The latter sugar is partly fermented by the yeast whose activity is also increased at the start of baking.

Inadequate amylase activity, or exclusive reliance on heat-labile fungal amylases, results in reduced loaf volume. Conversely, excessive amylase activity may produce over-expansion of the loaf volume and even cause the loaf to collapse completely (Marston and Wannan 1976).

Walden (1959) found that inactivation of malt α-amylase takes place between 65 and 95°C (149 and 194°F), with the most rapid inactivation occurring between 68 and 83°C (154 and 181°F), a temperature range traversed in about 4 minutes during baking.

β-Amylase is inactivated rapidly at 57 to 72°C (134 to 161°F), a range that lasts less than 2.5 minutes. Fungal α-amylase is most active at about 50°C (122°F) and is largely inactivated at 60°C (140°F).

The activity of the proteolytic enzymes present in dough also increases with the rise in temperature until the inactivation level has been reached. While fungal proteases used in dough conditioners are relatively heat labile, the proteolytic enzymes of cereals such as barley and wheat have been shown to retain most of their activity in the dough at temperatures up to 70°C (158°F), at which level far-reaching protein denaturation occurs (Yasunaga et al. 1968).

6.G.3.d. Water movement

When baking is carried out in a moisture-saturated oven atmosphere, a slight water uptake by the dough happens during the first few minutes as the steam condenses on its surface. However, once the surface temperature exceeds the dew point of the baking chamber atmosphere and crust formation begins, the moisture in the outer loaf layers is transformed into steam.

Part of this steam escapes through the incipient crust, while some migrates into the loaf interior and condenses. As baking proceeds, the moisture content of the crust and outer layers up to 3 to 4 mm is reduced to some 5%, whereas in the interior crumb, it remains relatively constant at 43.5 to 45.1%, similar to that of dough before baking.

As soon as the bread leaves the oven, moisture rapidly migrates toward the dry crust layer. Evaporation from the crust continues during loaf cooling until the water content of the bread as a whole is reduced to the legal limit of 38%. (Actually, the wording of the US Standards of Identity stipulates that standard bread, rolls and buns contain not less than 62% total solids.) According to Marston and Wannan (1976), most of the water in bread is loosely bound, and the crumb's water activity

(a_w) is a rather high 0.95 to 0.98.

Mass flow of the air in the baking process affects the moisture loss of bread, according to Knott (1996). Air's density is proportional to the inverse ratio of its absolute temperature. For example, 50 cu ft per minute of air per sq ft of oven bed at 21°C (70°F) has an equivalent mass of 3.68 lb of air per minute per sq ft, but when the same volume of air is heated to a normal baking temperature of 288°C (550°F), the mass falls to 2.02 lb of air per minute per sq ft, or 55% of the original mass. When velocity is increased, the higher air flow allows lower baking temperatures to be used, leading to a reduction in the amount of moisture lost during the baking process.

6.G.3.e. Cell structure formation

The crumb structure of bread consists of a porous and resilient protein-starch-lipid matrix that encloses, in honeycomb fashion, minute gas cells, which make up most of the loaf volume. The character of the cell structure is influenced primarily by processing conditions that prevail prior to baking, explained earlier in this chapter.

According to Garnatz (1946), under-fermented or "young" doughs tend to produce crumb cells that have thick and coarse walls, are irregular in size and are interspersed with large holes; over-fermented or "old" doughs tend to produce a crumb whose cells are thin-walled, weak or crumbly, round in shape and only moderately open.

A fast fermentation rate in the intermediate proofer makes it difficult for the moulder to effectively degas the dough piece, and this condition may lead to an irregular crumb structure with large holes in the baked loaf. Rapid final proofing tends to produce a cell structure described as "young," whereas slow proofing yields a structure that is designated as "old." Both under- and over-mixing may cause cell structure characteristics that are generally associated with young doughs.

The cellular structure of proofed dough originates from the gas bubbles created during mixing from either occluded or entrapped air and subsequently dispersed by the sheeting action. The proper setting of the moulder to ensure uniform gas bubble dispersion is a significant factor in creating an ideal cell structure. Equally important is the ratio of pan size to the scaled dough weight. The smaller the cubic displacement of the pan in relation to the weight of the dough piece, the easier it is to obtain a fine, uniform cell structure.

With pans that are too large for the scaled dough piece, bakers tend to over-proof in an attempt to achieve adequate loaf height. Such over-proofing results in an open grain with round cells typical of an "old" dough.

Correct baking conditions also have a major influence on the cell structure. For example, if the crust is formed prematurely, it will restrict loaf volume expansion and create thermal stresses within the crumb that disrupt the cells and result in a heavy-walled, coarse, open and irregular crumb structure. Garnatz (1946) defined an ideal crumb structure as one in which the cells are "small, fairly thin-walled, slightly elongated, uniform in size, free from large holes and possess a smooth, soft, velvety feel when touched lightly with the tip of the fingers."

The finished crumb structure of bread involves a continuum of pores exhibiting a minimal surface yet a disordered network. Eliasson and Larsson (1998) compared such a surface to a gyroid, representing an effective close packing of helical pores in three directions in space. The pore surface consists of a monomolecular lipid film with a few patches of polymerized high-molecular-weight storage protein units dispersed in it. The pore wall consists of only one continuous phase: the dried aqueous phase of partially gelatinized starch.

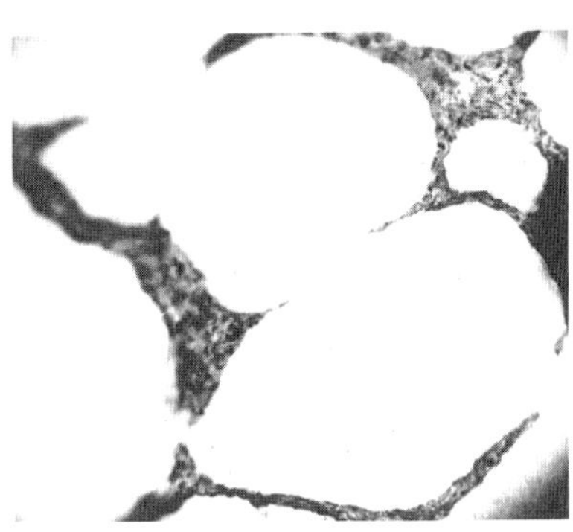

Figure 6.56. Micrograph of bread films shows ruptures of expanded gas cells. (Sandstedt 1961)

6.G.3.f. Flavor development

When dough is baked by means of dielectric or microwave heating, which produces a crustless loaf, little flavor development occurs. The resulting bread has a rather flat, yeasty flavor similar to that of dough. Thus, much of the characteristic bread flavor is formed in the loaf's crust region and diffuses into the crumb portion and retained there by absorption. (What researchers call as a "crustless" loaf is better described as a loaf with a colorless crust. "Crustless" bread is a relatively new style of product made by trimming off the crusts of baked bread prior to slicing and packaging.)

Johnson and Sanchez (1973) defined bread flavor as the psychological reactions to the physiological stimuli produced by a multitude of chemical compounds present in both the crumb and crust of bread, supplemented by such stimuli as crumb softness and resilience and crispness of the crust.

The mildly acid taste of conventional white bread comes from water-soluble organic acids (acetic, lactic, propionic and pyruvic) formed by yeast and bacterial fermentations. The aroma of fresh bread is a composite of volatile alcohols (ethyl, amyl and isoamyl) in addition to organic acids (caproic, isocaproic, lauric, myristic and palmitic) and a variety of ethyl esters (Johnson and Sanchez 1973). The carbonyl compounds, present as aldehydes and ketones, are produced mainly by the Maillard reaction that takes place primarily in the crust region. They are, therefore, concentrated in the crust area, according to data in **Table 6.25**. From the crust, they then migrate into the crumb on cooling.

According to Jackel (1969b), the flavor of white bread is derived from (a) ingredients, (b) yeast and bacterial fermentation products, (c) mechanical and biochemical degradations and (d) thermal reaction products. Major flavor attributes such as sweetness, saltiness, wheaty and starchy characteristics originate largely in the formula ingredients. Mixing, hydration and enzymatic modifications and hydrolysis of proteins and starch alter the original raw starchy and wheaty notes into a smoother and blander flavor. This, in turn, supplements other flavors that are subsequently formed.

Caul and Vaden (1972) analyzed the flavor of white bread by the flavor profile method, which uses descriptive terms to designate specific flavors and aromas that make up the overall flavor system of the baked product. Based on taste panel results, the terms that describe the crumb flavor of fresh bread include sweet, alcoholic, estery, yeasty, doughy and wheaty, while those that designate its top crust flavor include sweet, caramel, browned flour and wheaty.

Most of these terms refer to aromatic qualities. When bread is held at room temperature over a period of time, the integrity of its flavor blend weakens progressively, and only some of the flavor components survive. After 96 hours, the bread has become stale, and its flavor has suffered a loss in amplitude, sweet aromatics and sweet taste, its sour impression has increased, the yeasty character has deteriorated, and its flour-based flavor has changed.

While the significance of yeast and bacterial fermentation products to character and intensity of bread flavor has been questioned in recent years, the fact remains that the typical bread aroma cannot be duplicated without fermentation (Jackel 1962). As the same writer (Jackel 1969b) later pointed out, of the approximately 4 g

Table 6.25. Amounts of Carbonyls in White Bread

Carbonyl	Crust	Crumb
	(mg per g dry matter)	
Acetone	14.0	1.13
Hydroxymethyl furfural	4.6	0.63
Isovaleraldehyde	2.0	0.69
Acetaldehyde	2.0	0.33
Miscellaneous	2.2	0.27
Total	**24.8**	**3.05**

(Jackel 1969b)

of ethanol produced by fermentation per lb of white bread, some 2 to 3 g is retained in the freshly baked bread. Less volatile alcohols (isoamyl alcohol, isobutanol, isopropanol and propanol), though present in trace amounts only, possess highly potent flavor notes and are thought to exert a major influence on the bread's flavor profile.

The volatile organic acids retained in white bread are listed in **Table 6.26**. Lactic and acetic acids predominate. Propionic acid may occur in greater than trace amounts when calcium propionate is included in the formula as a mold inhibitor, and it will exert an unfavorable effect on the over-all bread flavor. Butyric acid, because of its great aromatic potency, may also have a flavoring effect out of proportion to its quantitative presence.

Studying the volatile organic acid content of French bread, Richard-Molard et al. (1979) compared the respective effects of the three fermentation methods most commonly used in France. These methods include the straight-dough method that use 2% yeast, the "sur poolish" method that employs a semi-liquid sponge with 0.5 to 1.0% yeast and resembles the American sponge-and-dough procedure, and the "sur levain" method that relies on the spontaneous fermentation of a sour for about 8.5 hours.

Compared with the bread made by the straight-dough method, the "sur poolish" bread had a stronger, more pleasant flavor, whereas the "levain" bread had a decidedly sour taste that differs markedly in character from the two other types. The qualitative composition of the volatile organic acids was the same in all three types of bread.

Quantitatively, however, the "sur poolish" crumb had twice as much acetic acid as the straight-dough crumb and the "levain" crumb 20 times as much. Whereas in the last type of bread, the high level of acetic acid resulted in a decidedly sour flavor. In the "sur poolish" bread, the moderate increase in acetic acid served to enhance, rather than alter, the over-all bread flavor. **Table 6.27** reports the many flavor compounds found in bread.

One by-product of yeast fermentation is acetylmethyl carbinol, which, by itself, is nearly odorless but when oxidized yields diacetyl, the pleasant flavor factor of butter and freshly baked bread. The amount of the precursor formed in bread is influenced by the method of production. Thus, straight doughs are relatively deficient in acetylmethyl carbinol, yet sponge and liquid ferment doughs contain higher levels when adequate amounts of sugar and oxidants are present.

Wiseblatt and Zournut (1963) showed that the products that result from

Table 6.26. Fermentation Acids in White Bread

Acid	mg per lb
Lactic acid	50 to 100
Acetic acid	10 to 50
Butyric acid	trace
Propionic acid	trace
Pyruvic acid	trace

(Jackel 1969b)

Table 6.27. Flavor Compounds

The extremely complex nature of bread flavor may be gauged by the following summary of the different categories of flavor compounds that have been detected in white bread by various investigators.

Category	Compounds detected
Alcohols	Ethanol, isobutanol, n-propanol, isoamyl alcohol and d-amyl alcohol
Acids	Acetic, propionic, butyric, isobutyric, valeric, lactic, isovaleric, caproic, heptanoic, octanoic, nonanoic, capric, pyruvic, hydrocinnamic, benzilic, itaconic and levulinic
Esters	Ethyl acetate, ethyl lactate, ethyl succinate, ethyl itaconate, ethyl pyruvate, ethyl levulinate and ethyl hydrocinnamate
Aldehydes	Formaldehyde, propionaldehyde, n-valeraldehyde, 2-methylbutanal, 2-ethylhexanal, benzaldehyde, furfural, 2-butanal, acetaldehyde, isobutanaldehyde, isovaleral, n-hexanal, cro-tonaldehyde, pyruvaldehyde and hydroxymethyl furfural
Ketones	Acetone, methyl n-butyl, ethyl n-butyl, diacetyl, acetoin and maltol

(Coffman 1967)

the thermal reaction of proline with dihydroxyacetone, a product of yeast fermentation, have a crusty-type odor commonly associated with bread flavor. Kiely et al. (1960) similarly found that the thermal reaction of dextrose with the amino acids leucine, histidine and arginine resulted in compounds with an aroma simulating that of fresh bread.

The loss of flavor substances during the shelf life of bread was first quantified by Farber (1949) who measured the decrease in the level of volatile reducing substances in a bread sample by aspirating them with a measured volume of air into 10 ml of alkaline 0.1 N potassium permanganate solution. The amount of permanganate reduction caused by the volatile substances was determined iodimetrically and served as an index of the content of volatile reducing substances (VRS) in the sample. He found that the VRS values of 2-g samples of fresh white bread crumb decreased from between 179 to 275 micro-oxidation equivalents to between 4.4 to 6.3 in 24 hours.

Baker et al. (1953) analyzed the condensate from oven vapors for the presence of flavor substances. They also determined the volatile reducing substances by the Farber method. Oven vapors from both normally fermented and over-fermented sponges were analyzed to determine why bread made from over-fermented sponges was less flavorful than normal bread. Their findings revealed that both doughs contain alcohol, acetaldehyde, fusel oil and acids (as acetic) in their condensates, but only normally fermented dough additionally yielded furfural, pyruvic acid, diacetyl and fisoaldehydes. All the latter substances exhibited marked odors that are suggestive of bread aroma.

The aromatics that are believed to be formed by fermentation and baking and that characterize or enhance the flavor of bread are listed in **Table 6.28**. Succinic acid is derived from glutamic acid during fermentation. Lactic acid is produced principally by bacteria but may also be formed by the incorporation of water into pyruvic aldehyde. Acetic acid is also formed by the action of bacteria on alcohol in the presence of oxygen. All these acids may, in turn, give rise to ethyl esters in the dough.

Baker et al. (1953) emphasized the major role played by free amino acids in influencing the character of bread flavor. Thus, when leucine was added to a fermenting dough in amounts exceeding 55 ppm, the resulting bread acquired an aromatic, cheese-like, unappetizing flavor. Leucine and isoleucine are the sources of isoamyl alcohol formed during fermentation.

When valine was added, isobutyl alcohol, which has a mild and less disagreeable flavor than isoamyl alcohol, was produced. Addition of phenylalanine resulted in a flowery aroma. Since most ordinary amino acids occur in their free state in flour and in yeasted dough (El-Dash and Johnson 1970, El-Dash 1971), it is likely that some of the observed differences in the flavor of freshly baked bread may result from variations in the levels of individual amino acids in the dough.

The same authors observed that bread, after 15 minutes out of the oven, contained 440 micro-oxidation equivalents of volatile reducing substances (VRS) per 2-g crumb sample, and that after 1 hour that value was still 420. On the other hand, following storage for 1 day in open air, it had diminished to only 13. Wrapped bread after 1 day retained a value of 411, and after 3 days, declined to a value of 315. These findings underscored the importance of keeping the time interval between baking and packaging to a practical minimum in order to preserve the maximum amount of the aromatic volatiles. Freezing provided the most effective method for retaining volatile reducing substances.

Grosch and Schieberle (1997) reviewed recent studies examining how favor and aroma develops in grain-based foods. They described the identification of volatile compounds causing the characteristic odor notes and the laboratory methods used. Recent progress in instrumental analysis, particularly high-resolution gas chromatography and mass spectrometry, was able to quantify the myriad volatile compounds responsible for the aroma of baked foods, but only a small number of these compounds are of significance in determining flavor.

6.G.3.g. Thermal reactions

The thermal browning reactions that occur in the crust have long been known to be responsible for the development of crust color and flavor and for the ultimate flavor of the crumb. These reactions are of two distinct types: caramelization and carbonyl-amino reactions (specifically, the Maillard reaction), and both occur during baking of grain-based foods.

Caramelization reactions involve sugars, heated in the absence of nitrogen-bearing compounds. The Maillard reaction also involves sugars, plus aldehydes and ketones, reacting with naturally occurring nitrogen-bearing compounds such as amines and proteins. The results are insoluble brown pigments known as melanoidins. The two reactions occur simultaneously; at about 177°C (350°F), the brown color seems and tastes like caramel, and around 246 to 260°C (480 to 500°F), the melanoidins produce a black color and bitter taste.

Both reactions are non-enzymatic and non-oxidative in nature but require the presence of heat, with caramelization being by far the more energy intensive. (Although a form of caramelization, the enzymatic browning that occurs on cut surfaces of fruits does not follow the same chemical path as caramelization of baked foods.)

6.G.3.g.i. Caramelization

Caramelization is the transformation of sugars, under the influence of heat, from colorless sweet substances into compounds varying in color from pale yellow to dark brown and in flavor from mild and pleasant caramel to burnt, bitter and acrid (Hodge 1967). The chemistry of caramelization is complex and difficult to reduce to simple terms. Larger carbohydrate molecules are reduced in size under the influence of acid, heat and pressure. They undergo dehydration. Then a type of condensation or polymerization takes place in which the simple sugars are recombined into larger complex color bodies (Kamuf et al. 2003). The more heating that sucrose undergoes, the darker, larger and more insoluble are the polymers formed.

While caramelization resembles the Maillard reaction in some respects, there are some basic differences with regard to the activation temperature. Typically Maillard reactions take place around the boiling point of water, while caramelization requires much higher temperatures. The two reactions also differ in the nature of the flavor and aroma compounds produced.

Table 6.28. Flavor Substances in Bread Formed by Fermentation and Baking

Volatile	Less volatile	Low volatile
Alcohol	Isoalcohols	Melanoidins* (crust)
Pyruvic aldehyde*	Acetic acid	Dihydroxyacetone
Diacetyl	Pyruvic acid	Ethyl succinate
Isoaldehydes	Furfural*	Lactic acid
	Acetoin	Succinic acid
	Butylene glycol	
	Ethyl lactate	

Formed during baking.

(Baker et al. 1953)

6.G.3.g.ii. Maillard browning

The Maillard reaction, whose end products are melanoidins, involves specifically the interaction of free amino groups of amino acids, peptides or proteins with free reducing sugars. The reaction was first described by Maillard (1912) and has been extensively studied since then.

Hodge and his co-workers (1953, 1955) made major contributions to a fuller understanding of the complex pathways and intermediary compounds that are involved in the transformation of the starting materials into a broad spectrum of complex compounds that play a decisive role in bread flavor.

Pentose sugars react more than hexoses and those more than disaccharide sugars, and different amino acids produce different amounts of browning and flavors. Of all the amino acids, lysine results in the most color, while cysteine gives the least.

Hodge (1953) outlined the broad scheme of reactions that occur during the development of melanoidins (**Table 6.29**).

These three basic phases are illustrated by **Figure 6.57**. The initial reaction consists of the condensation of the carbonyl group of a reducing sugar (aldose) with a free amino group of a protein or amino acid, which loses a molecule of water to form N-substituted glycosylamine (step A). This compound is unstable and undergoes Amadori rearrangement to form 1-amino-1-deoxy-2-ketoses, known as ketosamines (step B). These compounds can react three ways during the second phase: (a) loss of two water molecules through dehydration, creating reductones and dehydro reductions (step C); (b) production of short-chain hydrolytic fission products such as diacetyl, acetol, pyruvaldehyde, etc. (step D); and (c) loss of three water molecules through the Schiff's base/furfural path (step C).

The fission products undergo Strecker degradation with amino acids to form aldehydes (step E) and by condensation to aldols, or in the absence of amino acids, they may give aldols and high-molecular-weight nitrogen-free polymers (step F). The Schiff path products react with amino acids and water. All of these products react further with amino acids in the third phase to form brown nitrogenous polymers and copolymers, known as melanoidins (step G). Step H represents the direct rough to fission products from *N*-substituted glycosylamine without formation of Amadori rearrangement products.

Because water is formed as part of the Maillard reaction, it is added to the substrate, increasing its water activity (aw). The reaction proceeds most slowly in foods with high and low water activities and best at intermediate aw values of 0.5 to 0.8. pH also influences this reaction, with low pH values ($\leq$6) favoring formation of furfurals and higher pH ($\geq$6) favoring reductones and fission products. The intermediate stage of the Maillard reaction takes place along all three pathways, with the system's pH influencing the ratio of resulting compounds (Scaman undated).

The Maillard reaction can also be represented in simplified fashion (**Figure 6.58**).

Table 6.29. Maillard Reaction Stages

Initial stage	Colorless	Sugar-amine condensation
		Amadori rearrangement
Intermediate stage	Colorless or yellow	Sugar dehydration
		Sugar fragmentation
		Amino acid degradation
Final stage	Highly colored	Aldol condensation
		Aldehyde-amine polymerization
		Formation of heterocyclic nitrogen compounds

(Hodge 1953)

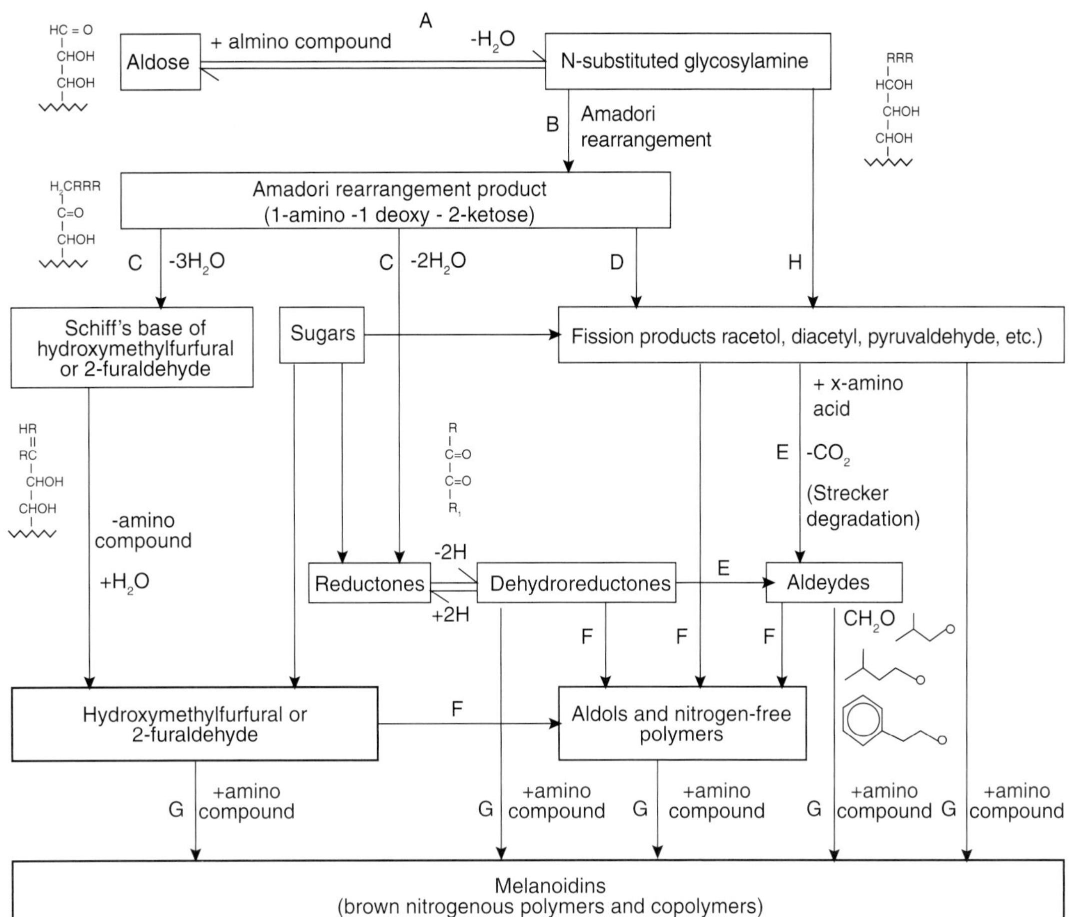

Figure 6.57. The Maillard reaction involves three phases (initial, step A; intermediate, steps B-F; and final, step G) with an alternate path (step H). (Scaman undated)

The Maillard reaction is a major source of the aromatic and flavor compounds that result from heat application to certain food systems such as dough. For example, Lane and Nursten (1983) assessed the odors produced in more than 400 model systems involving mixtures of 21 amino acids and 8 sugars that were heated under different conditions of temperature and humidity. They found that odors reminiscent of bread, crust, biscuit, cakes and toast were produced when glucose was heated with the amino acids arginine, glutamine, histidine, lysine, proline, serine, threonine and tyrosine in a 1:1 ratio at temperatures of 100 to 140°C (212 and 284°F) for periods ranging from 0.5 to 4 minutes. Compounds produced by the Maillard reaction that are of principal importance to bread flavor include (Baker 1957): (a) pyruvic aldehyde obtained from the breakdown of sugar, (b) isoaldehydes from amino acids, (c) furfural from pentosans and (d) the melanoidins themselves. The volatile, highly flavored aldehydes are condensed and retained by the crumb to provide flavor in fresh bread. When bread that has been on the shelf for a few days is heated, these aldehydes are released, and they then impart the aroma and flavor of fresh bread to such reheated bread. All the aldehydes that diffuse from the crust into the interior crumb of the loaf during cooling are thus absorbed.

Schoch (1965) suggested that many of the bread flavor substances may become "locked" within the linear fraction of wheat starch during bread cooling because it is known that amyl and butyl alcohols may enter into the helical structure of the amy-

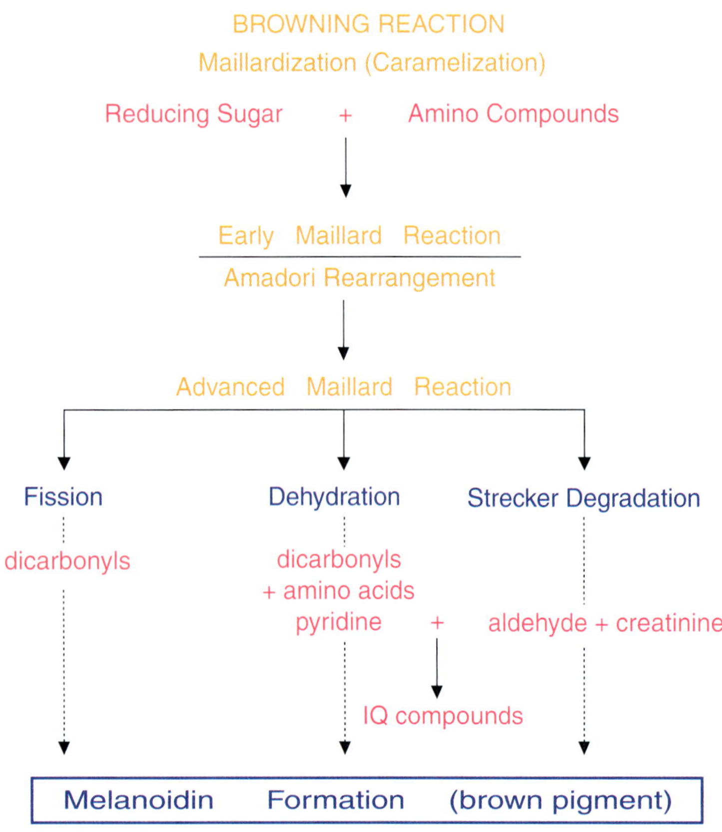

Figure 6.58. Maillard browning proceeds in three steps. (Kitts undated)

lose and that heat can reverse this reaction.

Lactic and acetic acid, organic acids that form during fermentation, act as catalysts for rearranging the condensation products of amines and reducing sugars during the baking process, thereby increasing the production of Maillard-type brown pigments (Johnson et al. 1958). Researchers (El-Dash and Johnson 1970, El-Dash 1971) found that the addition of yeast to dough substantially augmented the dough's free amino acid content, with the greatest increases occurring in lysine, alanine, proline, cystine and dicarboxylic amino acids. Even after fermentation, the free amino acid content of the dough was double that originally present in flour. A marked decrease in free amino acid content occurs in the bread crust as a result of the Maillard reaction.

Although essential for the development of desirable bread flavor, the Maillard reaction adversely affects the nutritive value of bread. For example, feeding tests conducted by Tsen and co-workers (1983) established that oven baking lowered the protein efficiency ratio (PER) of bread by about one-third compared with steamed or microwave-baked bread. Toasting also produced a similar harmful effect on bread's nutritive value by reducing the PER of bread to 0.64, 0.45, and 0.32, respectively, for light-, medium-, and dark-toasted slice samples, compared with 0.90 for the untoasted sample (Tsen and Reddy 1977).

They attributed this reduction in nutritive value of bread primarily to a loss in lysine or to its lessened nutritional availability that resulted from the browning reaction in baking. Lysine has been shown to be especially susceptible to side reactions and cross-linkings that reduce its nutritional availability.

The discovery that acrylamide, a possible human carcinogen, could occur in heat-treated, starch-rich foods, led to recognition of asparagine and reducing sugars as important precursors for acrylamide formation. Because of the involvement of a protein (amino acid) and sugars, scientists explored and reported a link with the Maillard reaction (Mottram et al. 2002; Stadler et al. 2002). Adding asparaginase to dough systems addresses this problem by enzymatically reducing asparagine into aspartic acid, thus eliminating an acrylamide precursor, but so does yeast, although in a different fashion. During fermentation, yeast assimilates free amino acids and metabolizes them as a source of nitrogen for growth. Fredriksson et al. (2004) determined that at least 2 hours of yeast fermentation removes most of the free asparagine from dough.

6.G.3.h. Rheology of baking

The mechanical properties of dough and bread differ significantly. A good deal of rheological study has been applied to the mechanisms of dough and bread (Hamer and Hoseney 1998). For example, the effects of lipids and shortening were found to be related to a change in the expansion rate that occurs at approximately 55°C

(131°F): The expansion rate of doughs made without shortenings decreased at that temperature (Moore and Hoseney 1986).

The oven baking process conducts heat from the dough piece's exterior to its interior of the dough piece, producing internal temperature gradients in the dough. So, as Faubion and Hoseney (1990) observed, any temperature-triggered changes in dough rheology occur at many different times as each points heats to the required temperature. Rapid and irreversible changes take place between 55 and 75°C (113 and 176°F). The researchers suggested that one possible effect of starch gelatinization is to increase hydrogen bonding between starch and gluten molecules.

Dough is both viscous and elastic, and the ratio between these components drops significantly when heated, mostly because of the large increase in the elastic nature of dough. This change led Spies (1990) to speculate that changes in the rheology of gluten, which determines the elastic nature of dough, appear to be responsible for the final setting of the loaf.

Bloksma (1990a) described the changes during baking as starting with an initial decrease in dough viscosity by a factor of five as temperature rises from 26 to 60°C (79 to 140°F). Heat causes water to be transported to the interior of the dough, and at this stage of baking, dough is much more fluid than during fermentation. Polymerization of glutenin molecules also add to the enormous increase in viscosity.

Gelatinization of starch increases the dough's viscosity at temperatures above 80°C (176°F), which causes a marked rise in the tensile strength of dough membranes, noted Bloksma (1990a). The membranes rupture when the tensile stress exceeds the strength of the liquid dough phase. For best baking performance, the dough must remain extensible for a long enough time to avoid premature rupture of membranes between gas cells. The rupture of the gas cells marks the end of oven rise.

Eliasson and Larsson (1993) related changes in rheological properties to the end of ovenspring, noting that the gelatinization of starch puts an end to ovenspring but also inhibits the collapse of the crumb structure. Starch gelatinization causes an enormous change in rheological properties of the dough. When the temperature of the dough starts to rise, its viscosity decreases, but at about 60°C (140°F), the viscosity begins to increase. These changes continue to about 75°C (167°F), when the viscosity value becomes more or less constant.

Looking into the rheological properties of gas cells, Dobraszczyk et al (2003) determined that the stability of the gas cell walls during baking is related to their strain hardening properties. Cell walls in dough with good bread making properties remained stable and retained their strain hardening properties at higher temperatures (60°C, or 140°F), while the cell walls of poor breadmaking doughs became unstable at lower temperatures (45 to 50°C, or 113 to 122°F) and had lower strain hardening. Strain hardening measured at 50°C (113°F) correlated well with baking volume, suggesting that extensional rheological measurements can be used as indicators or baking quality.

Creep recovery, another important rheological property, helped Wang and Sun (2002) rank various flours for their breadmaking quality. Higher recovery ratings favored larger loaf volume. They found creep recovery to also correlate positively with resistance to extension, Mixograph mixing time and Farinograph water absorption.

Knott (1996) observed that during baking, the evaporation of water represents the majority of the weight loss from the product. Thus, the mass exchange, or transfer, function is primarily related to the removal of water. Development of a mathematical model that takes into account heat and mass transfer combined with expansion was noted by Wagner et al. (2008). It has been compared to a broad range of data including temperature and water content profiles, total CO_2 release, total water loss, total height and local porosity.

6.H. Cooling

Bread requires proper cooling prior to slicing and packaging to avoid difficulties during slicing that often result in crippled loaves and undesirable moisture condensation within the package, which occurs when hot bread is wrapped or bagged.

While bakers disagree about what represents optimum bread cooling, the general consensus is that the interior crumb temperature should be reduced to a range of 35 to 41°C (95 to 105°F), and that this should be accomplished in as short a time as possible and without excessive evaporative moisture loss. Another expert recommended cooling temperature of 27 to 29°C (80 to 85°F) and 85% RH for most baked products (Moore 1988). Improper cooling that promotes excessive moisture loss can cause wrinkles in the crust and weakened sidewalls, leading to collapse at the slicer.

The atmospheric and temperature conditions that prevail during bread cooling must ensure that the moisture content of bread reaching the consumer does not exceed the legal limit of 38%, set by US Standard of Identity for bread, rolls and buns (21 CFR 136.110). The evaporative moisture loss that has to take place during cooling is, therefore, related to the magnitude of the bake-out loss that occurred in the oven. In general, an additional moisture loss of 2% on cooling may be regarded as average.

Aside from simple atmospheric cooling, where the bread is exposed to the ambient atmosphere of the bakery either on racks or conveyors for periods of from 3 to 4 hours or longer, other methods, including convection cooling, cooling with air conditioning and vacuum cooling, can accelerate and control the rate of cooling.

6.H.1. Process of cooling

A loaf emerging from the oven possesses a fairly uniform temperature throughout its mass, with the exception, of course, of its crust zone. However, the heat loss by radiation from the crust is so rapid that, for all practical purposes, the temperature may be assumed to have equalized in all parts of the loaf within a few minutes after depanning.

Moisture distribution within the loaf, however, presents a quite different situation. The outer layers of the loaf, because of their longer exposure to the high baking temperatures, experience the greatest evaporative loss of moisture. When the loaf exits the oven, its water migrates from the interior to the crust zone, changing the character of the crust from dry and crispy to soft. The rate at which moisture diffuses into the crust, and then escapes into the atmosphere by evaporation, is governed by the differences in vapor pressure within the respective loaf zones. The vapor pressure, in turn, is a function of temperature: the higher the temperature, the greater is the corresponding vapor pressure and the more rapid the evaporation rate.

These simple facts underscore the importance of lowering the interior crumb temperature of the loaf to about 38°C (100°F) prior to wrapping because such cooling reduces the vapor pressure correspondingly and prevents the subsequent outward migration of moisture that can result in soggy crusts, moisture condensation and deformation of the wrapped loaf of bread.

Interior temperatures higher than 35 to 41°C (95 to 105°F) will cause the loaf to collapse at the slicer. Excessive moisture will be present within the package, causing condensation and risking mold growth.

Cooling also gives time for the starch to set up sufficiently to resist collapse during slicing (Doerry 1995a). Such "set up" is actually initial staling but necessary to allow the bread to be handled and distributed. Adequate cooling time for breads is about 1 hour, while 30 minutes suffices for buns and rolls because of their smaller size and slightly lower moisture content. Under conditions of low humidity or in dry climates, baked foods cool more quickly than in humid environments.

Cooling involves two mechanisms: heat transfer, mainly by convection to the surrounding air, and evaporation, which withdraws energy from the crust. According to Wiggins (1998), an 800-g (28-oz) loaf will lose 20 to 35 g (about 1 oz) during cooling, which along with the weight lost during transfer (about 12 g, or 0.5 oz) represents about half the load required to cool the loaf to 25°C (77°F), a temperature that allows slicing in a reciprocating slicing. (Products with higher fat content can be sliced successfully at higher temperatures.) The process is charted in **Figure 6.59**.

Seasonal differences. In a heated loaf, the movement of water from its interior to its outer zones, and thence into the atmosphere, is quite rapid. As the crust zone cools, the vapor pressure differential between it and the surrounding atmosphere diminishes.

Under these circumstances, the rate of moisture evaporation becomes progressively less affected by the temperature gradient and rather more by the prevailing vapor pressure difference between the crust and the atmosphere. Thus, at the low atmospheric vapor pressures that coincide with the low relative humidities common during winter months, the rate of evaporation from the crust will continue at an accelerated pace, but under the conditions of high vapor pressure that usually prevail during humid summer months, evaporation will be perceptibly slowed.

So, depending on seasonal atmospheric conditions, a loaf of bread may lose either too much or not enough moisture during the time span that is needed to bring the loaf interior to the desired temperature level.

Excessive moisture loss tends to result in a dry, checked crust, and a firm loaf with poor keeping quality. Restricted moisture loss from the crust, on the other hand, causes a soggy and excessively soft loaf to reach the slicer and wrapper. Auerman (1977) reviewed in some detail the reactions that take place during the bread cooling process.

During fall and winter months, precautions should be taken not to expose the warm bread directly to the cold air drawn in from the outside or else the crust will

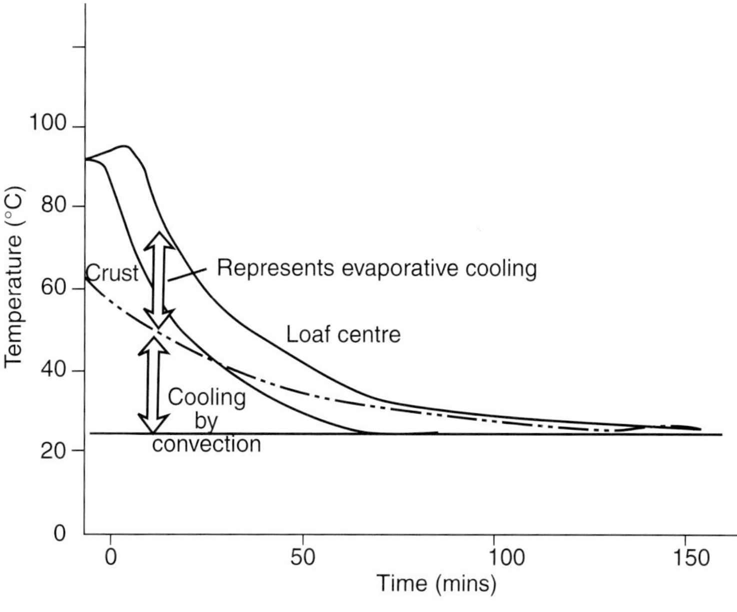

Figure 6.59. The cooling process involves both convection and evaporation. (Wiggins 1998)

cool too rapidly, while the interior crumb remains being warm and humid. Under these conditions, the crust shrinks and forms a vapor barrier causing moisture to condense just under the crust. Ultimately, a thin layer of gummy crumb is formed directly under the crust, leading to slicing difficulties (Gable 1960).

6.H.2.a. Ambient

Convection cooling (also termed ambient cooling) is the simplest method. It takes the form of a rod- or slat-type conveyor configured as a spiral or multitier design, mounted on the plant floor or hung from the bakery ceiling. It may be housed in a box or, more generally, enclosed in an overhead tunnel equipped with an air exhaust system. Bread from the depanner transfers to the conveyor at the top run of the cooler unit and then descends in a series of loops until it reaches the discharge end, ready for slicing and packaging.

An exhaust fan located in the uppermost part of the cooler removes the heat radiated by the bread. Fresh air is drawn in at the discharge end of the cooler, moving slowly upward and past the cooling loaves, thereby creating a dual cooling effect by convection and accelerated evaporation. Average cooling time is reduced to 2 to 2.5 hours by the added air flow. This method is by far the most common way of cooling bread at high-volume bakeries.

While this system does not provide accurate control of moisture loss by the cooling loaf, some regulation of the overall cooling process is possible by appropriate adjustments. Thus, cooling time may be shortened and the rate of moisture loss accelerated by increasing the velocity of the air currents drawn past the loaves. At the same time, higher air velocities will tend to perceptibly reduce the actual moisture loss of the bread by shortening the cooling time.

To enhance cooling speed yet limit evaporation loss, Wiggins (1998) recommended that the air at the entrance to the cooler be as cold as possible without refrigeration, noting air velocities of roughly 1 m per second (about 3 ft per second), air temperatures of 20°C (68°F) and 80% RH. These conditions will cause the crust temperature to drop so quickly that the crust will act as a barrier to further moisture loss.

6.H.2.b. Conditioned air

Air movement capacity for conditioned bread cooling is governed by the physical conditions of the plant ambient and conditioned air as well as the temperature of the bread coming out of the oven. Air has a specific heat of 0.24 Btu per lb (equal to 13.4 cu ft) at a temperature of 22°C (72°F). To raise its temperature by 1 F° (0.56 C°) per cu ft requires 0.24 ÷ 13.4 = 0.0178 Btu, or a total of 0.302 Btu for a temperature rise of 10 C° (17 F°), which represents an average increase in air temperature during bread cooling.

Assuming that a 1-lb loaf of bread requires the removal of 82 Btu to bring its internal temperature from 100°C (212°F) to the projected level of 38°C (100°F), and that some 11 Btu are lost by the evaporation of 2% of the loaf moisture, then there remains a net of 71 Btu to be removed. Calculations show that a volume of 3,990 cu ft of air at 22°C (72°F) is required to achieve this heat removal under optimum air velocity conditions. A bakery operating at a capacity of 5,000 1b per hour (or 83 lb per minute) would thus require a volume of 19,500 cu ft of such air per minute.

Since both the temperature and relative humidity of the cooling medium are held relatively constant in air-conditioned bread cooling, the rate of moisture loss from the cooling loaf is essentially predetermined at the start of the cooling cycle for as long as the relative humidity of the external air remains constant. High humidity in plant ambient air, as can occur during summer months, may impair the efficiency of an air-conditioned bread cooler unless sufficient refrigeration capacity is available to remove the excess moisture from the incoming air.

6.H.2.c. Vacuum

The third method of bread cooling involves the application of a vacuum to the bread. This approach greatly accelerates the vaporization of its free moisture, which, by absorbing energy in the form of the latent heat of vaporization, rapidly reduces the bread's temperature. In other words, vacuum cooling is fundamentally different from conventional cooling. The low pressure evaporates the hot food's moisture at a lower temperature because as pressure falls, water's boiling point also falls. The latent heat of evaporation is extracted more quickly, cooling it to slicing temperature in as little as 3 minutes (**Figure 6.60**).

The process reduces the temperature of the food through the latent heat of evaporation. Evaporation is in the region of 0.9% of product weight for each 10 C° (18 F°) temperature drop, compared with probably 1% per 15 C° (27 F°) for conventional systems. Thus, cooling time reductions of 10:1 are common, and most bakery products can be cooled in less than 15 minutes, some in less than 1 minute (Newbery 1996).

The temperature drop in the products takes place throughout its mass, cooling from the center rather than from the outside. Thus, products can be cooled in their pans, if required, yet the pans remain warm, facilitating depanning.

Early attempts to apply vacuum cooling to bread (Duval 1949) failed to find widespread acceptance, partly because vacuum-cooled bread was prone to mold infections. The so-called modulated vacuum cooling technique was described by Bradshaw (1976), and a newer patented system was detailed by Newbery (1996).

Two different designs are available, one of which constitutes a rack cooler, while the other is in the form of a short tunnel and is capable of continuous operation. Bread intended for vacuum cooling is removed from the oven 5 to 6 minutes before the end of the normal bake period (representing about 20% of the total baking time) and after its crumb structure has stabilized. Because the primary purpose of the final stage of baking is to reduce the bread's moisture content to an acceptable level, bread that is withdrawn earlier will contain more moisture than a fully-baked loaf. This extra moisture offsets the loss in weight brought about by vacuum cooling. The problem of mold infection is averted by maintaining an essentially sterile environment within the cooling chamber by automatic washing and by passing the air through a microbiological filter.

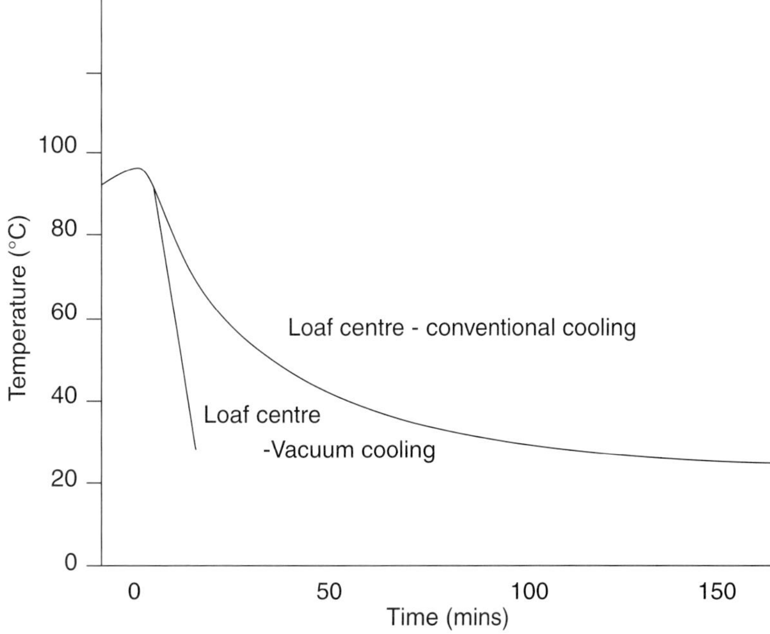

Figure 6.60. Considerable time is saved by vacuum cooling methods. (Wiggins 1998)

Vacuum cooling is an essential aspect of the Milton-Keynes process for producing par-baked, ambient temperature breadstuffs and will be discussed in the next section of this chapter.

6.I. Freezing

Low-temperature processes — refrigeration, retarding and freezing — can be effectively used by bakers to manage the timely production of fresh baked foods.

When freezing any food, its moisture undergoes a change of state, and a relatively large amount of energy, called the latent heat of fusion, must be removed to change liquid water to ice. Although the freezing point of pure water is 0°C (32°F), baked foods contain enough solutes (dissolved gases, liquids and solids) to depress their freezing point to between -6 and -2°C (20 and 28°F). Leaner formulations freeze at the high end of the range, while richer products require lower temperatures.

Consumers commonly think that freezing stops time, but processors know better. Changes, big and small, can take place in frozen foods, changes that will affect how the product looks, tastes and performs once it has been thawed and finished. Free water, for example, can form ice crystals and thus dehydrate the surrounding crumb or dough and collapse gels, while also producing mechanical damage at the microscopic level. Ice crystals are not stable, and water vapor will pass between ice crystals in frozen foods. The result can be seen as white, dry, crumbly regions, familiarly termed "freezer burn." Rapid freezing tends to form small crystals widely dispersed throughout the product, while slow freezing allows free water to collect, thus prompting development of large, damaging crystals.

Consumers also commonly believe that refrigeration prevents staling, but any processed food containing starches goes stale much faster at such temperatures. The staling zone stretches from -6 to 21°C (20 to 70°F), but firmness (staling) proceeds three times as fast at temperatures between 0 and 2°C (32 and 36°F) than at room temperature. The maximum rate for bread occurs at -2°C (28°F). Gelatinized starch retrogrades rapidly, and crumb acquires a harshness. Such staling may not be much of a factor in rich cakes, but it can be very important in bread and similar products (Matz 1989).

6.I.1. Effects of low temperatures

Freezing at low temperatures affords an effective and relatively inexpensive method for temporarily bringing to a halt the chemical and biological reactions in bakery foods, thereby extending the shelf life of both baked and unbaked products. Frozen bread and cake products, as well as their corresponding unbaked forms, are stable for weeks or months at low temperatures in freezer storage or in the frozen food sections of retail outlets. When either defrosted and warmed up, in the case of baked products, or baked off at in-store bakeries or at home in the case of the frozen dough piece, the eating quality of the end product rivals that of freshly made items.

Frozen yet fully baked products have been found in supermarket freezer cases for many years, satisfying consumer desires for attractive foods to serve their family needs. A different kind of need is served by a growing host of frozen fully baked foods produced for commercial customers. Supermarket organizations are in a constant quest to make their bakery operations more efficient and hold down costs. "Thaw and sell" doughnuts, cakes, cookies and pastries answer the call.

6.I.1.a. Dough

The large-scale freezing of formed dough pieces for a wide range of bakery products received a major impetus with the introduction and rapid expansion of bake-off bakeries in the larger food stores and in supermarkets. In such operations, the frozen dough products — ready to be thawed, proofed and baked by personnel without extensive training, and which require only minimal oven facilities — are supplied by central production plants. Another major market for frozen dough is represented by the consumer who prefers to do his or her own baking at home but is disinclined to spend the time and effort required for the entire process. Finally, institutions involved in the feeding of large numbers of people have come to rely to an ever increasing extent on the use of frozen dough products for reasons of economy, uniformity and quality.

Since the advent of bake-off preparation during the 1950s, the idea of frozen, partially prepared dough has been carried forward into new categories: frozen batters, frozen fully proofed doughs and frozen partially baked products. Inspired by such creativity, bakers also developed par-baked products that could be transported and stored at ambient temperatures.

6.I.1.b. Fully baked products

Fully baked products generally pose fewer problems during freezing and frozen storage than do unbaked doughs.

Low-temperature freezing was initially adopted by bakers primarily in an endeavor to stop the staling process in bread products in which the resultant quality deterioration was most evident. The pioneering investigations of Bailey (1932), Cathcart and Luber (1936) and particularly of Pence and co-workers (Pence and Standridg e 1956; Pence 1955; Pence et al. 1955a, 1955b, 1958) not only demonstrated the feasibility of preserving the fresh characteristics of bread by freezing but also established the most suitable parameters for achieving optimum results. Bamford (1975a) described freezing conditions for fully baked foods, taking packaging into consideration (**Table 6.30**).

Whole categories of consumer products evolved through freezing of baked foods. Cheesecakes, dinner rolls, cream pies, iced layer cakes and more acquired thaw-and-eat convenience for consumers. Matz (1989) observed that nearly every variety of baked food has been offered in frozen form at one time or another, with the possible exception of low-moisture items such as crackers. Thompson (1978) charted the freezing rates for large and small dough pieces, buns, brown 'n serve rolls, pies, doughnuts and cupcakes in contact plate and blast freezers.

The primary reason for freezing fully baked foods is to improve their storage stability, but lengthening the distribution reach provides another justification. National markets can be served from single bakeries. For example, freezing allowed Sara Lee cheesecake and Lender's bagels to be sold coast-to-coast through retail grocery freezer cases. Campbell Taggart took a different direction to introduce the Earth Grains brand of variety bread: It centered production of this product line at a highly automated, capital-intensive bakery, which baked, packaged and froze the loaves for distribution throughout the company's bakery and depot network. The frozen loaves arrived at the order assembly point. Enough products to satisfy daily needs were pulled and thawed before being put onto the route trucks. Thus the company was able to leverage a single bakery across wide-flung sales territories, gaining economies of scale in production and maximizing customer and consumer choice at the point of sale.

In the late 1970s, a major food service customer, McDonald's Corp., launched a new supply chain pattern that put delivery of all consumables to its stores into the hands of single local shippers. The "single source" initiative included bakeries, now required to supply their fully baked buns in frozen format to the distributor instead of delivering them fresh on their own trucks to individual shops. Although those bakers were glad to get out of the trucking business, they had to learn how to best freeze their products.

Davis and Rogers (1980) performed a study of the effect of the freezing rate and time on the quality of frozen and defrosted bread, specifically hamburger rolls, compared with fresh bread. Knowing that moisture differences in the crust and crumb are related to sensory perception of staleness, they determined that

Table 6.30. Suggested Freezing Conditions for Bakery Products

Product	Packaging	Freezing method	Freezing time (hours)	Temperature °C (°F)
Baked cakes	Full sealed package, small headspace	Blast* or contact plate	3.00	-40 (-40)
Bread and rolls				
1-lb bread	Bare	Blast or contact	2.75	-6 (-20)
	Single wrapped	Blast or contact	3.25	-6 (-20)
	Double wrapped	Blast or contact	3.50	-6 (-20)
	Double wrapped (bag and wrapped)	Blast or contact	3.50	-6 (-20)
2-lb bread	Bare	Blast or contact	3.00	-6 (-20)
	Single wrapped	Blast or contact	3.50	-6 (-20)
	Double wrapped	Blast or contact	4.00	-6 (-20)
Dinner rolls, rich formula	Plastic bag, foil pan	Blast or contact	1.00	-6 (-20)
Cinnamon rolls, rich formula	Plastic bag, foil pan	Blast or contact	1.50	-6 (-20)
Fruit pies, 1 lb	Foil pan, overlay and box	Blast or contact	4.50	-40 (-40)
Danish pastry, rich formula	Foil pan, sealed or overwrapped box	Blast or contact	2.00	-40 (-40)
Ready to bake products	Foil pan, overlay and box	Blast or contact	2.00	-40 (-40)
Frozen bread dough (1-lb, rich formula)	Plastic bag	Blast or contact	3.00	-6 (-20)
Ready to bake cakes (rich formula, shallow pan)	Foil pan and overlay	Blast or contact	2.00	-6 (-20)
Yeast-raised dough (rich formula, 1-lb package)	Foil lined, fiber-wound can	Blast or contact	2.50	-6 (-20)

Air flow in the blast freezer is 600 ft per minute.

(Bamford 1975a)

the best time to freeze buns was no more than 30 minutes after baking, when crust moisture reaches a peak and begins to decrease until an equilibrium point is reached (**Figure 6.61**).

Compression tests (**Figure 6.62**) showed that the crumb structure of frozen buns, when thawed, firms (stales) at about the same rate as if they had not been frozen. The researchers found a slight advantage to blast freezing over simply placing the bulk-packed products in a freezer with limited air movement, explaining that the blast method takes products much faster through the rapid staling zone around the freezing point of water. By freezing and thawing the buns, the product ages about 12 hours. By the time of service, weeks may have passed but bun quality is what it would have been for a fresh 24-hour-old product.

6.I.2. Partial processes

Freezing and refrigeration technologies enable bakers to halt product processes partway through to finish production at a later time or a remote location. As partial processes, each has its advantages and disadvantages. Although refrigeration and freezing technologies have been available to food processors for many decades, the development of some partial processes awaited the advent of several new methods, notably low-stress sheeting and laminating in the case of pre-proofed doughs and vacuum cooling for ambient par-baked, or preformed, items.

6.I.2.a. Frozen doughs

The most common procedure for the production of frozen dough is to prepare a rather stiff no-time straight dough that is mixed to a temperature not exceeding 22°C (72°F) and transferred immediately to makeup (Boyd 1980, Rosenholtz 1985). Optimum dough mixing, examined by Dubois and Blockcolsky (1986b), favored standard (delayed salt) and all-in methods over delayed yeast methods. The idea is to minimize fermentation prior to moulding and freezing, and no floor time is given to bread products.

Frozen doughs for sweet goods should be slightly undermixed because they will receive additional development during the sheeting process. A dough-out temperature about 3 C° (5 F°) cooler than bread doughs are preferred, and such doughs should not be retarded (Boyd 1980).

In some instances, the rounded dough pieces are given a 3- to 5-minute interme-

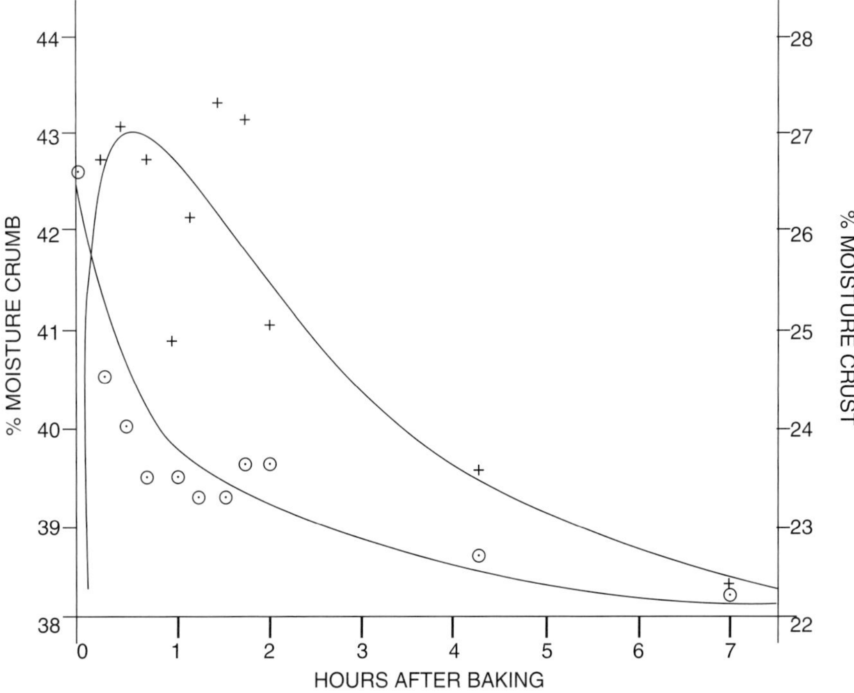

Figure 6.61. Moisture levels in the crust peak 30 minutes after baking (+ = crust, ⊙ = crumb).
(Davis and Rogers 1980)

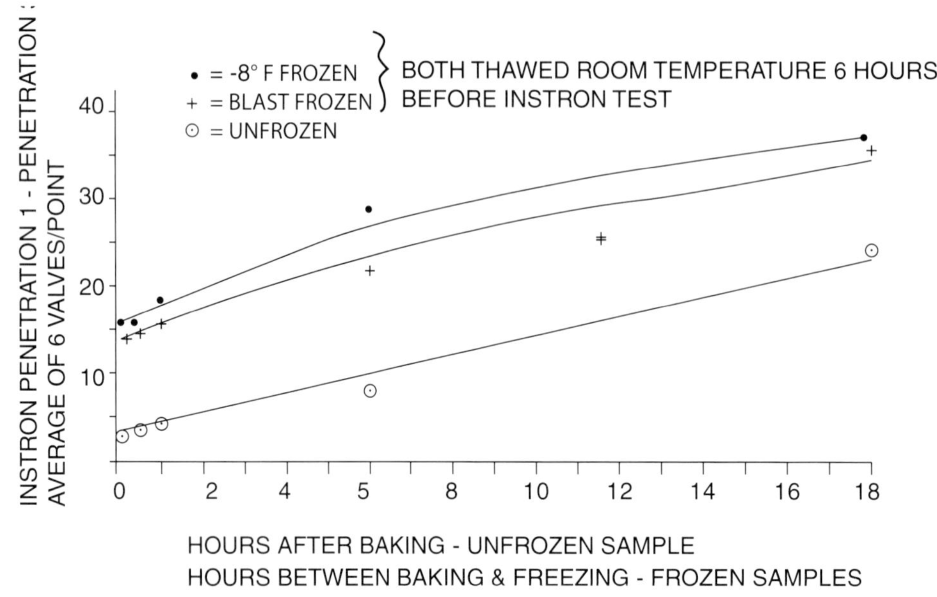

Figure 6.62. Frozen, then thawed, buns show the same rate of change in compressibility as unfrozen buns. The compression force compares first and third penetrations in one spot by Instron, thus measuring the rate of staling. (Davis and Rogers 1980)

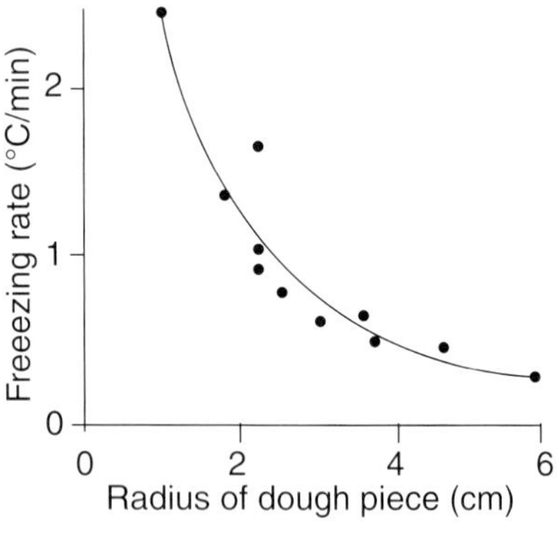

Figure 6.63. The wider the radius of the dough piece, the longer its core takes to freeze. (Cauvain 1998b)

diate proof to allow them to relax. During moulding, the sheeter rolls are open so that the piece is flattened only enough to be able to be curled, and the pressure board is set just high enough to form the loaf. This procedure is done to keep from weakening the structure of the dough. The result when finally baked, as Boyd (1980) observed, is the highly desirable "old fashioned" look with a fat crown and fairly open texture with good flavor.

The moulded or made-up dough pieces are next deposited on trays, which are then loaded on racks or conveyors and either held within a freezer for the required time or are slowly transported through the freezing chamber or tunnel. Dough pieces can also be frozen in spiral blast freezers, a method that requires no additional handling between makeup and freezing. The temperature within the primary freezer area is maintained at -29 to -40°C (-20 to -40°F) (Bamford 1975b), and the product is exposed to strong air currents, generally of 600 ft per minute, while in transit through the chamber for 50 or so minutes. During freezing, pieces must be separated from each other or else they will not freeze properly.

The most important variables to which dough is subjected during freezing are (Lehmann and Dreese 1981): (a) the freezing rate in the first freezer and (b) the temperature in the center of the dough piece (core temperature) at the time of packaging just prior to transfer to the storage freezer. During the first freezing stage, the loaf is crust frozen and still has a soft core in the middle of the loaf about the diameter of a quarter. The second freezing stage is slower and is done at a temperature of -23°C (-10°F) for 24 hours before the product can be shipped.

Freezing proceeds from the exterior to the interior of the dough piece so that the outer portion is frozen solid first. According to Marston (1978), freezing of the outer portion to create a hard, solidly frozen layer some 3 to 4 mm thick should proceed rapidly to minimize moisture loss. Once the interior of the dough piece has attained a temperature of 0°C (32°F) and the crust portion is sufficiently firm, further freezing can take place in an equilibration or holding room maintained at -20 to -23°C (-4 to -10°F). An internal core temperature of -7°C (20°F) is optimum, according to Lorenz and Kulp (1995), and the remaining freezing will take place during equilibration, packaging and frozen storage.

Size matters when freezing dough pieces. Items with large radii take longer to reach a given core temperature than those with small radii. Cauvain (1998b) plotted the freezing rate of dough pieces against their size (**Figure 6.63**) and shape (**Table 6.31**). The center portion takes nearly twice as long as the surface to reach the frozen state. Le-Bail et al. (2008) confirmed the importance of freezing rate, noting that the gassing power of the yeast differed by its location within the dough piece and was highest in the surface region represented by dough in the outer one-third of the piece's radius.

Table 6.31. Effect of Radius on Dough Freezing Rate

Nominal shape	Length (cm)	Radius (cm)	Volume (cu cm)	Freezing rate (C° per minute)
Cylinder	22.0	3.75	884	0.46
Cylinder	55.0	2.50	1,080	0.75
Sphere	—	5.75	797	0.24

(Cauvain 1998c)

Three phases comprise the freezing process of dough: cooling above the freezing point of the product, cooling in the freezing zone and subfreezing cooling. Typical freezing curves (**Figure 6.64**) describe the temperature changes during dough freezing. Hsu et al. (1979) found two eutectic points, the melting/freezing temperatures at which complete ice formation in the system takes place, one at about -12°C (10°F) for freezer temperatures of -10°C (14°F) and the other at about -35°C (-31°F) for freezer temperatures of -40°C (-40°F). Dough's thermal conductivity affects the cooling rate above freezing, when only specific heat can be removed. In the freezing zone, removal of latent heat is necessary for the phase transition, which requires more energy and thus slows down the cooling rate, resulting in the plateau seen in the curve. Application of lower freezer temperatures to increase the difference between product temperature and freezer temperature will shorten the plateau, yielding faster cooling and lower risk of ice crystal formation (Kulp 1995).

To prevent excessive moisture loss, the frozen dough pieces are packaged in polyethylene bags and placed in moisture-resistant corrugated cases prior to transfer to the cold storage room. While cold storage temperatures within the range of -15 to -20°C (15 to -4°F) are quite adequate, the common practice is to maintain a storage temperature of -23°C (-10°F). The barrier qualities of the packaging are important because cold air has a low moisture content and would, therefore, dehydrate any unprotected dough products. Films chosen for this use should provide (a) a good moisture barrier, (b) a good oxygen barrier, (c) physical strength at low temperatures against brittleness and breakage, (d) stiffness for machineability on packaging equipment and (e) good heat sealability.

Despite their frozen condition, frozen doughs have a relatively short shelf life, with most manufacturers striving to move the dough from the central plant freezer within a week and use it at the retail or institutional level within 90 to 120 days (Lorenz and Kulp 1995). A variety of changes can occur during the 4 to 12 weeks of frozen storage typical for frozen doughs. Proofing times can increase, loaf volumes decrease, grain gets coarser and texture worsens (Reed and Nagodawithana 1991). When Varriano-Marsten et al. (1980) examined the viscoelastic properties of frozen doughs, they reported a shift in extensibility (**Figure 6.65**).

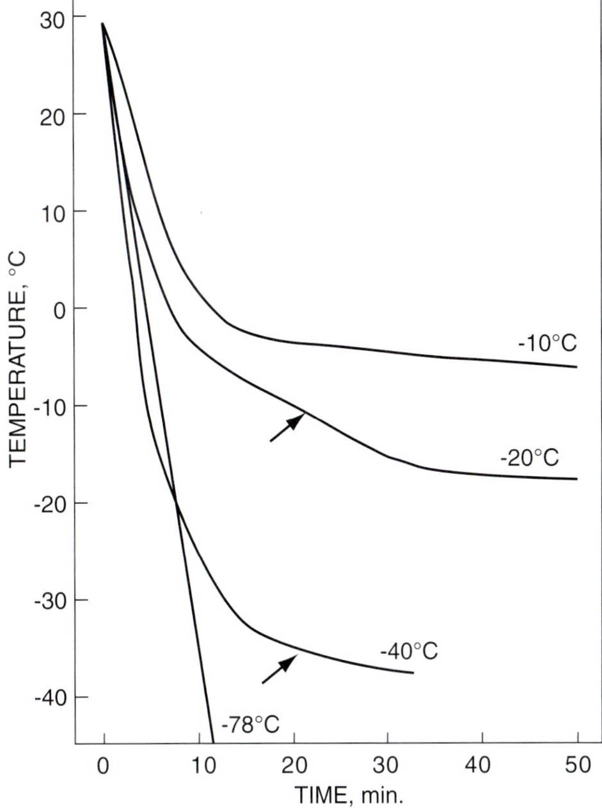

Figure 6.64. Freezing curves for bread dough (submerged in temperature controlled baths at indicated temperatures) reveal eutectic points (arrows) at about -12°C (10°F) and -35°C (-31°F).
(Hsu et al. 1979)

Frozen doughs have received much attention from cereal scientists seeking to understand the differences between breadstuffs produced by "fresh" methods and those baked from frozen doughs. For example, researchers (Varriano-Marston et al. 1980, Wolt and D'Appolonia 1984, Autio and Sinda 1992) suggested that a lack of gluten cross-linking was at fault, not the release of reducing materials, as reported by other researchers. Ice crystals were blamed by Berglund et al. (1991) for disrupting the gluten matrix, separating it from the starch granules. Kulp (1995) provided a comprehensive review of the biochemical and biophysical properties of freezing as they impact frozen doughs.

Extremely low temperatures should be avoided. Boyd (1980) described how his company's marketing department once shipped samples of frozen dough by packing them in dry ice, which has a temperature of -73°C (-100°F). By the time the dough reached its destination and was thawed, it was completely dead.

Workers in the laboratories of the American Institute of Baking studied the effects of variables such as dough mixing methods, freezing temperatures and freezing rates, use of additives of various types, and changes in the level of specific ingredients, among others. They observed that the most consistent quality bread was produced by blast freezing the loaves at temperatures of +21 to -29°C (-5 to -20°F) to a core temperature between -9 to -5°C (15 to 23°F) (Lehmann and Dreese 1981). The substitution of 62 DE corn syrup or a 42% high-fructose corn syrup for sucrose as the sweetener at use levels of 8 and 10% reduced the final proof time of the frozen dough stored over a 26-week period at -24°C (-12°F). However, the corn syrup doughs generally yielded a lower bread volume than did the other sweeteners (Dubois and Dreese 1984).

The effects of additives such as potassium bromate, ascorbic acid, sodium stearoyl lactylate (SSL), glycerol, glutamic acid and xanthan gum on frozen dough stability over a 20-week period was investigated. Both potassium bromate and ascorbic acid brought about a definite improvement in bread quality, whereas the addition of glycerol, glutamic acid or xanathan gum had no perceptible improving effect. SSL, by strengthening the dough, produced a greater oven spring and an improved crumb grain (Dubois and Blockcolsky 1986a).

It should be noted that potassium bromate is banned from use in Canada and heavily regulated in Califormia. Most bakers have switched to bromate-free flour.

The mixing method, or the sequence in which dough ingredients are incorporated during dough making, was found to have a definite effect on the final proof time and on yeast activity, with two of the four procedures employed yielding consistently superior results. While holding the frozen dough in a retarder 16 to 24 hours prior to proofing definitely shortened the final proof time and produced bread with a greater loaf volume, no measurable improvements in other quality characteristics were observed (Dubois and Blockcolsky 1986b).

Trivedi et al. (1989) offered the following recommendations for processing frozen doughs: (a) minimize fermentation prior to freezing by using a short-time straight-

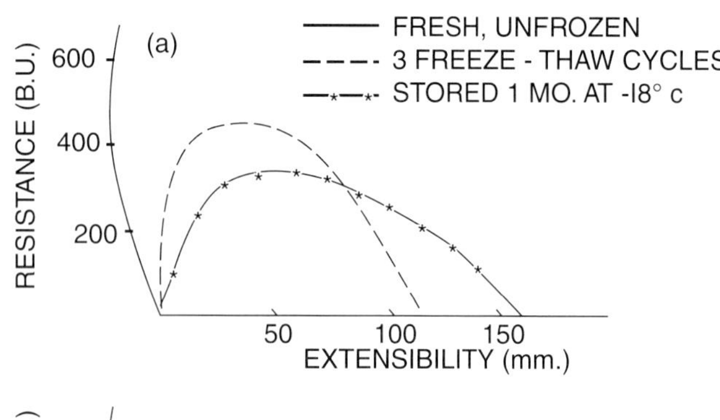

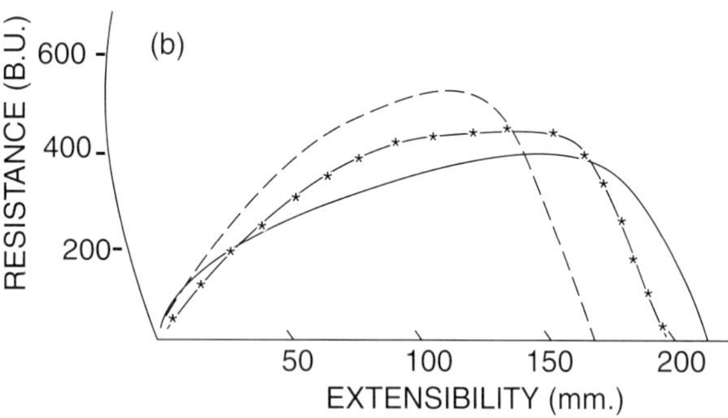

Figure 6.65. Freezing and frozen storage affect the extensibility of doughs, as shown by extensigrams of yeasted (a) and non-yeasted (b) doughs. (Varriano-Marsten et al. 1980)

dough process; (b) bring the dough out of the mixer at 13 to 22°C (56 to 72°F), (c) reduce the time between mixing and freezing; (d) freeze quickly in blast freezers; (e) store between -15 and -21°C (5 and -5°F); (f) avoid freeze/thaw cycles during storage or delivery; and (g) thaw doughs for at least 8 hours in a refrigerator or retarder.

Thawing is also an essential aspect of frozen dough usage. The functional effects involve rehydration of the gluten matrix and yeast cells. A variety of methods are used: (a) retarding the dough piece for 16 to 24 hours before proofing, (b) thawing at room temperature and (c) thawing in a proofing cabinet. Dubois and Blockcolsky (1986b) got the best results from the first method, retarding, observing that the other methods resulted in extremely long proofing times because of the lower internal dough temperatures involved. Flexible retard-and-proof cabinets combine these processes under pre-set timed control so the baker can load frozen dough pieces into the units in the evening and work with fully proofed items the next morning.

6.I.2.b. Frozen pre-proofed

With the advent of low-stress laminating and sheeting technology, pre-proofed doughs became possible. These products go directly from the freezer into the oven without any need for thawing, retarding or additional proofing and save considerable time and manpower for customers in the supermarket and food service industries. Croissants proved to be a good test case for this method (Gorton 2000).

The yeast in these products is fully activated prior to freezing, and shelf life can be a year or more under -18°C (0°F) storage conditions. Pre-proofed requires stronger dough conditions than that of the conventional process in order to withstand the extreme temperature change from 40°C (104°F) at proofing to -40°C (-40°F) at freezing.

Such frozen pre-proofed doughs will generally expand 1.5 times during baking. Good ovenspring seems to depend on maintaining the water in the dough system in a bound state rather than as free water. (Free water will crystallize during freezing and damage the dough.)

Retention of the dough's elasticity is also an essential condition, hence the use of low-stress sheeting methods that use stretchers in place of conventional gauge rolls. Pressures generated by stretching systems are very low, typically in the range of 70 g per cu cm. Gentle vibration also encourages water to be strongly drawn to the molecular structure of the gluten, becoming "bound water." Nakagawa (1991) explained the pre-proof process in detail.

The most successful pre-proofed products are those containing yeast and a laminated structure such as croissants and danish, according to Cauvain (1998b). These products rely primarily on water vapor for leavening, and the fat layering helps keep the water in place during freezing and storage. He observed that yeast cells in proofed dough pieces do not survive well during frozen storage and thus do not contribute any "extra" carbon dioxide during early oven stages. Any expansion of the dough during baking, therefore, comes from the thermal expansion of gases trapped in the dough, supplemented by water vapor.

6.I.2.c. Par-baked (frozen and ambient)

Actually a 2-stage baking process, the par-baked method employs a truncated initial bake with a second short bake at a later time. The first stage bakes the items to achieve final shape and size but with only a minimum of crust formation. The second stage completes the crust formation and coloring to finish the bake. Between times, the product is cooled, packaged and distributed, often in frozen condition. Where North American producers use the term "par-baked" for items made by this partial process, Europeans call such products "pre-baked."

The first par-baked product were brown 'n serve rolls, invented in 1949 by Joe Gregor, a Florida volunteer fireman who took his undercooked rolls out of the oven to go fight a fire. Returning later, he finished the baking and found the results highly satisfactory. General Mills acquired the rights to the idea, developed the concept further and patented the process, making it available to the baking industry without restrictions (Pai and Walker 2004).

Baking should progress to the point at which the dough sets and the yeast and enzymes are inactivated. Two different approaches may be taken to this first stage: (a) bake at a low temperature for the normal baking time, but cut proofing time to allow extra expansion in the oven, or (b) bake at a high temperature to set the dough structure, but remove products from the oven before the onset of crust coloration. The choice depends on the diameter of the product. For example, larger items benefit from the lower temperature process, while high temperature methods suit smaller items such as baguettes. As Pai and Walker (2004) explained, par-baking is most successful with products having a large ratio of surface area to crumb volume, which allows heat to quickly penetrate to the crumb center and set it without browning the crust.

A par-baked item reaches its full volume during the first bake, which does not increase with the second bake. In fact, volume may decrease during the second bake by up to 10%.

The mechanism for structure setting in par-baked bread has yet to be clarified, although Pai and Walker (2004) suggested its relationship to starch gelatinization and/ or protein denaturation. These factors suggest an explanation for why sidewall collapse can sometimes be a problem for par-baked breads. The rigidity of the sidewall, which is related to the degree of starch gelatinization, must be able to withstand the internal contraction force from gluten protein.

Loss of moisture and carbon dioxide occurs during both baking cycles. Higher baking temperatures in the first cycle, however, create higher vapor pressures in the internal crumb, thus promoting faster moisture and vapor loss than at lower baking temperatures. Breads are reported to be more porous with higher first bake temperatures and thus more subject to evaporation of moisture during the second bake.

Par-baked products are less rigid than fully baked items so packaging must provide adequate protection during transportation to prevent crushing. Because of the high moisture levels, gas-flush packaging that replaces oxygen with nitrogen or carbon dioxide within the package will help prevent microbial growth.

The second bake is intended not only to color the product but also to give it the texture of freshly baked bread (**Figure 6.66**). Bread firmness decreases as the internal temperature increased, reaching its softest point at temperatures as low as 55°C (131°F), according to Pai and Walker (2004). Care must be taken not to over-bake the product, which increases baking loss.

Commercial par-baked products are most often distributed in frozen form. They become "thaw and bake" items for customers in the supermarket and food service industries.

In the 1990s, an ambient temperature system of par-baked products was developed and patented by 4 European technology partners: Sainsbury's, a leading UK supermarket chain; Kears Group, Britain's third-largest wholesale baker; APV

Baker (now Baker Perkins), a UK-based bakery equipment manufacturer; and Gist-brocades (now part of DSM), a Dutch ingredient company. They had the following requirements, devised to satisfy consumer expectations: (a) the process must replicate and be indistinguishable from craft products; (b) the products made must embrace the scratch bakery range, especially the 800-g (28 oz) pan-baked loaf; (c) flavor, eating and keeping qualities must be as good as the best; (d) the process must

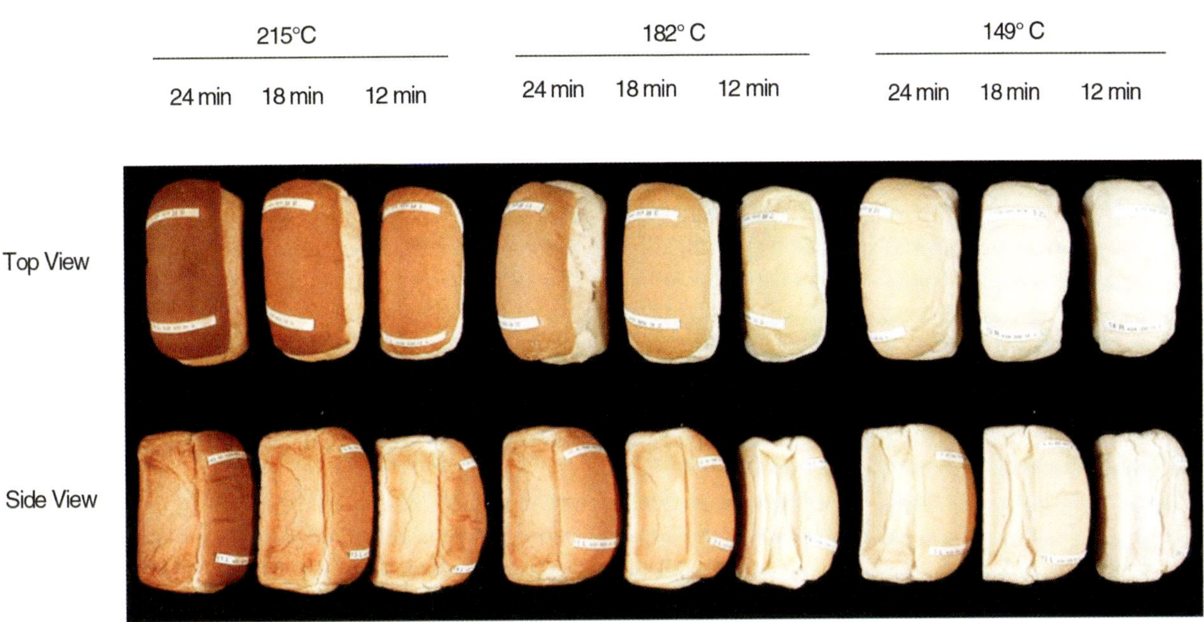

Figure 6.66. During the first baking stage, bake temperature and time affect crust color.
(Pai and Walker 2004)

accommodate the increasing demand for variety; (e) bread must be available for sale freshly baked within 1 hour; and (f) the process must not require freezing or refrigeration at any point in its manufacture or distribution cycle (Roberts 1997). The city that became home to the first bakery using the process, Coolcore Processing at Milton Keynes, Buckinghamshire, England, gave the method its name: the Milton Keynes process (Gorton 1995).

Basically, the Milton Keynes process for ambient par-baked products employs liquid brew and conventional mixing, makeup and proofing technology for bread, baguette and roll products, 65 different items in all at the UK bakery. It halts baking at the point when the product structure has stabilized. The bake tends to be cooler and longer, sufficient to deactivate the yeast, gelatinize the starch but leave the crust incomplete. It can use most forms of bakery ovens. Developers of this process termed its products "preformed" to distinguish them from conventional par-baked items (Roberts 1995).

At this point, the preformed products are comparatively unstable and must be transferred with minimal delay to the reduced pressure, or vacuum, chamber. The products get very little exposure to the atmosphere and its airborne contaminants. This cooling method proceeds rapidly but does not rob the product of its moisture content. The preformed baked foods are then depanned by conventional methods, bulk packaged with a polyethylene overwrap and placed into rigid plastic delivery baskets. As long as it remains in the sealed package, product is stable for 7 days

— the day of production and 6 days of storage at ambient temperature. At the customer's bakery, enough pieces are withdrawn from the packages to satisfy immediate demand and baked.

6.I.2.d. Frozen batters

Frozen cookie, biscuit and muffin doughs find common use by supermarket and food service customers because these product styles extend the range of offerings without the risk of excessive scrap. The doughs are produced in bulk or as individual pre-scaled pieces.

These doughs use chemical leavening acids such as sodium aluminum phosphate that activate only when heated and can thus be frozen, shipped, stored and thawed with no loss in leavening power. Nonetheless, as Lorenz (1995) observed, such batters perform well only if stored for very short periods of time. The standard storage life of frozen batters is 16 weeks.

Cake batters held in frozen storage decrease in baked volume over time, due to loss of air from the batter. The air bubbles provide the nuclii that later collect leavening gases and are entrained in the batter by the fat. As storage time increases, fat tends to pull away from the batter's aqueous phase and form globules. The air bubbles coalesce into larger ones, which escape earlier in the baking process than would the original smaller bubbles. Texture coarsens and volume decreases. For this reason, highly aerated cake batters such as angel, sponge and chiffon styles do not freeze well.

Muffin formulations high in sugar and shortening and mixed as cake batters can be frozen, but those made by the standard muffin method (low shortening, low sugar, short mixing time) deteriorate rapidly.

Although some batters can be successfully thawed before baking, most bakers prefer to put the frozen pieces directly into the oven, skipping the thawing stage and using a slightly lower baking temperature and a bit more baking time.

References

Abbot, J. 1958. Precision dough weight scaling. Proc. Am. Soc. Bakery Engrs. 34: 191.

Alava, J.M., Navarro, E, Nieto, A, and Schäuble, O.W. 2004. COVAD: The continuous vacuum dough process. In: Using Cereal Science and Technology for the Benefit of Consumers: Proceedings of the 12th International ICC Cereal and Bread Congress, May 23-26, 2004, Harrogate, UK. S.P. Cauvain, S.S. Salmon and L.S. Young, eds. CRC Press: Boca Raton, FL.

Anderson, R.C. 1966. Oven temperature and humidity control. Bakers Digest 40 (6): 60.

Andrews, G., Copeland, J., Fairburn, N., French, F., and Zielsdorf, R. 1989. High speed dough mixing and mixers. AIB Tech. Bull. 11 (12).

Anonymous. 1958. Mechanical bread twisting: New automatic twister yields superior uniformity over manual twisting. Bakers Digest 32 (4): 38.

Anonymous. 1995. Sourdough or sour dough? Baking & Snack 17 (8): 86.

Anonymous. 2002. Living leaveners. Baking & Snack 24 (4): 28.

Atkin, L., Schultz, A.S., and Frey, C.N. 1945. Cereal Chem. 22: 321.

Audidier, Y. 1968. Effects of thermal kinetics and weight loss kinetics on biochemical reactions in dough. Bakers Digest 42 (5): 36.

Auerman, L.J. 1977. Technologie der Brotherstellung. VEB Fachbuchverlag: Leipzig, GDR.

Authier, D.K. 1961. Continuous mix bread production: Production problems. Proc. Am. Soc. Bakery Engrs. 37: 177.

Autio, K., and Sinda, E. 1992. Frozen doughs: Rheological changes and yeast viability. Cereal Chem. 69 (4): 409.

Autio, K., Flander, L., Kinnunen, A. and Heinonen, R. 2001. Bread quality relationship with rheological measurements of wheat flour dough. Cereal Chem. 78: 654.

Bailey, L.H. 1932. Cereal Chem. 9: 65.

Baker, C. 1964. Fermentation in bread. Proc. Am. Soc. Bakery Engrs., 40: 73.

Baker, J.C. 1946. Bread as I see it. Bakers Digest 20 (1): 28.

Baker, J.C. 1957. The effects of yeast on bread flavor. Bakers Digest 31 (5): 64.

Baker, J.C., and Mize, M.D. 1937. Mixing doughs in vacuum and in the presence of various gases. Cereal Chem. 14: 721.

Baker, J.C., and Mize, M.D. 1939. Cereal Chem. 16: 517.

Baker, J.C., and Mize, M.D. 1941. The origin of the gas cell in bread dough. Cereal Chem. 18: 19.

Baker, J.C., Parker, H.K., and Fortmann, K.L. 1953. Cereal Chem. 30: 22.

Bamford, R. 1975a. Freezing and thawing of bakery products. Proc. Am. Soc. Bakery Engrs. 51: 118.

Bamford, R. 1975b. Freezing and thawing of bakery products. Bakers Digest 49 (3): 40.

Beaverson, R. 1960. Production procedures necessary for producing twist and large volume bread. Proc. Am. Soc. Bakery Engrs. 36: 67.

Beaverson, R.M. 1968. Combining the batch and continuous mixing process. Proc. Am. Soc. Bakery Engrs. 44: 50.

Bechtel, D.B., Pomeranz, Y., and de Francisco, A. 1978. Breadmaking studied by light and transmission electron microscopy. Cereal Chem. 55: 392.

Benier, J. 1983. Automated checkweighing. Proc. Am. Soc. Bakery Engrs. 59: 113.

Berglund, P. Shelton, D., and Freeman, T. 1991. Frozen bread dough ultra structure as affected by duration of frozen storage and freeze-thaw cycles. Cereal Chem. 68 (1): 105.

Bernardin, J.E., and Kasarda, D.D. 1973. The microstructure of wheat protein fibrils. Cereal Chem. 51 (6): 735.

Bingeman, D. 1969. Degassing equipment for processing bread and bun doughs. Proc. Am. Soc. Bakery Engrs. 45: 106.

Bloksma, A.H. 1971. Rheology and chemistry of dough. In: Wheat Chemistry and Technology, 2nd ed. Y. Pomeranz, ed. American Association of Cereal Chemists: St. Paul, MN.

Bloksma, A.H. 1990a. Rheology of the breadmaking process. Cereal Foods World 35 (2): 228.

Bloksma, A.H. 1990b. Dough structure, dough rheology and baking quality. Cereal Foods World 35 (2): 237.

Bloksma, A.H., and Bushuk, W. 1988. Rheology and chemistry of dough. In: Wheat: Chemistry and Technology, Vol. II. Y. Pomeranz, ed. AACC International: St. Paul, MN.

Borthwick, J.T. 1973. Technology of dough degassing. Bakers Digest 47 (3): 24.

Boyd, W.E. 1980. Manufacture and processing of frozen dough. Proc. Am. Soc. Bakery Engrs. 56: 38.

Bradshaw, W. 1976. Modulated vacuum cooling for bakery products. Bakers Digest 50 (1): 26.

Brixey, R. 1998. New bun makeup systems. Proc. Am. Soc. Bakery Engrs. 74: 121.

Bushuk, W. 1966. Distribution of water in dough and bread. Bakers Digest 40 (5): 38.

Bushuk, W. 1984. Cereal Foods World 29: 162.

Bushuk, W. 1998. Interactions in wheat doughs. In: Interactions: The Keys to Cereal Quality. R.J. Hamer and R.C. Hoseney, eds. AACC: St. Paul, MN.

Bushuk, W., and Hlynka, I. 1964. Water as a constituent of flour, dough and bread. Bakers Digest 38 (6): 43.

Bushuk, W., and Winkler, C.A. 1957. Cereal Chem. 34: 73.

Bushuk, W., Kilborn, R.H., and Irvine, G.N. 1965. Cereal Sci. Today 10: 402.

Bushuk, W., Tsen, C.C., and Hlynka, I. 1968. The function of mixing in breadmaking. Bakers Digest 42 (4): 36.

Cackler, H. 1957. Bread twisting technique. Proc. Am. Soc. Bakery Engrs. 33: 68.

Campbell, G.P. 1988. Bread production without intermediate proofing. Proc. Am. Soc. Bakery Engrs. 64: 129.

Campbell, S.P. 1989. Make-up systems. Proc. Am. Soc. Bakery Engrs. 65: 166.

Carlin, G.T. 1958. The fundamental chemistry of breadmaking. Proc. Am. Soc. Bakery Engrs. 34: 55.

Carpenter, D.H. 1977. Combining continuous mixing and batch-type systems for bread. Proc. Am. Soc. Bakery Engrs. 53: 43.

Cathcart, W.H., and Luber, S.V. 1939. Ind. Eng. Chem. 31: 362.

Caul, J.F., and Vaden, A.G. 1972. Flavor of white bread as it ages. Bakers Digest 46 (1): 39.

Cauvain, S.P. 1998a. Breadmaking processes. In: Technology of Breadmaking. S.P. Cauvain and L.S. Young, eds. Blackie: London, UK.

Cauvain, S.P. 1998b. Dough retarding and freezing. In: Technology of Breadmaking. S.P. Cauvain and L.S. Young, eds. Blackie: London, UK.

Cauvain, S.P., and Young, L.S. 2001. Baking Problems Solved. Woodhead Publishing: Abington, Cambridge, UK.

Cauvain, S.P., and Young, L.S. 2006. The Chorleywood Bread Process. Woodhead Publishing: Abington, Cambridge, UK.

Cauvain, S.P., Whitworth, M.B., and Alava, J.M. 1999. The evolution of bubble structure in bread doughs and its effect on bread structure. In: Bubbles in Food, G.M. Campbell, C. Webb, S.S. Pandiella and K. Niranjan, eds. AACC: St. Paul, MN.

Chamberlain, N. and Collins, T.H. 1979. The Chorleywood bread process: The roles of oxygen and nitrogen. Bakers Digest 53 (1): 18.

Chin, N.L., and Campbell, G.M. 2004. Effects of mixing speed and work input on dough development and aeration. In: Using Cereal Science and Technology for the Benefit of Consumers: Proceedings of the 12th International ICC Cereal and Bread Congress, May 23-26, 2004, Harrogate, UK. S.P. Cauvain, S.S. Salmon and L.S. Young, eds. CRC Press: Boca Raton, FL.

Chin, N.L., and Campbell, G.M. 2005a. Dough aeration and rheology. I. Effects of mixing speed and headspace pressure on mechanical development of bread. J. Sci. Food Agric. 85 (13): 2184 (doi: 10.1002/jsfa.2236).

Chin, N.L., and Campbell, G.M. 2005b. Dough aeration and rheology. II. Effects of flour type, mixing speed and total work input on aeration and rheology of bread dough. J. Sci. Food Agric. 85 (13): 2194 (doi: 10.1002/jsfa.2237).

Clark, C.B. 1985. Sponge-and-dough process. Proc. Am. Soc. Bakery Engrs. 61: 66.

Clark, R.J. 1938. Cereal Chem. 37: 342.

Clark, R.J. 1947. Guideposts in dough mixing. Bakers Digest 21 (2): 26.

Coffman, J.R. 1967. Bread flavor. In: The Chemistry and Physiology of Flavors. W.H. Schultz, E.A. Day, and L.M. Libbey, eds. Avi Publishing Co.: Westport, CT.

Cooper, E.J., and Reed, G. 1968. Yeast fermentation effects of temperature, PH, ethanol, sugars, salt and osmotic pressure. Bakers Digest 42 (6): 22.

Cottle, F.E. 1972. Production of bread by combination of continuous mixing and batch processes. Proc. Am. Soc. Bakery Engrs. 48: 101.

Dalby, G. 1960. The mixing of bread doughs. Bakers Digest 34 (4): 34.

Daley, C. 1955. Mixing and makeup. Proc. Am. Soc. Bakery Engrs., 31: 125.

Davis, A.B., and Rogers, D.E. 1980. Quality preservation in frozen rolls: Effect of rate and time of freezing. Bakers Digest. 54 (2): 10.

Davis, C.F., and Stephens, W.J. 1954. What is fermentation loss? Bakers Digest 28 (1): 25.

Dempster, R.E., Olewnik, M.C., and Smail, V.W. 2004. Development of a controlled dough mixing system. In: Using Cereal Science and Technology for the Benefit of Consumers: Proceedings of the 12th International ICC Cereal and Bread Congress, May 23-26, 2004, Harrogate, UK. S.P. Cauvain, S.S. Salmon and L.S. Young, eds. CRC Press: Boca Raton, FL.

Dersch, J.A. 1989. The use of steam in bread ovens. Am. Soc. Bakery Engrs. Bull. 218.

Dibble, W.E. 1977. Combining continuous mixing and batch-type systems for buns. Proc. Am. Soc. Bakery Engrs. 53: 48.

Dobraszczyk, B. J., and Morgenstern, M. 2003. Rheology and the breadmaking process. J. Cereal Sci. 38 (3): 229.

Dobraszczyk, B.M., Smewing, J., Albertini, M., Maesmans, G., and Schofield, J.D. 2003. Extensional rheology and stability of gas cell walls in bread doughs at elevated temperatures in relation to breadmaking performance. Cereal Chem. 80 (2): 218 (doi: 10.1094/CCHEM.2003.80.2.218).

Doerry, W. 1995a. Baking Technology, Vol. I: Breadmaking. AIB International: Manhattan, KS.

Doerry, W. 1995b. Baking Technology, Vol. II: Controlled Baking. AIB International: Manhattan, KS.

Doerry, W. 1998. Sour doughs and breads. AIB Tech. Bull. 20 (7).

Doescher, L.C., and Hoseney, R.C. 1985. Saltine crackers: Changes in cracker sponge rheology and modification of a cracker sponge procedure. Cereal Chem. 62: 158.

Dubois, D.K. 1981. Cereal Foods World 26: 617.

Dubois, D.K., and Blockcolsky, D. 1986a. Frozen bread dough: effects of additives. AIB Tech. Bull. 8 (4).

Dubois, D.K., and Blockcolsky, D. 1986b. Frozen bread dough: effects of dough mixing and thawing methods. AIB Tech. Bull. 8 (6).

Dubois, D.K., and Dreese, P. 1984. Frozen white bread dough: effects of sweetener type and level. AIB Tech. Bull. 6 (7).

Duval, M.H. 1949. Cooling and conditioning bread by the vacuum processs. Bakers Digest 23 (5): 50.

Eckstedt, H.G. 1949. Fermentation fundamentals in the production of bread. Bakers Digest 23 (4): 23.

Eisenberg, S. 1948. Fermentation losses in sponge-dough bread production. Bakers Digest 22 (2): 25.

El-Dash, A.A. 1971. The precursors of bread flavor: Effect of fermentation and proteolytic activity. Bakers Digest 45 (6): 26.

El-Dash, A.A., and Johnson, J.A. 1970. Influence of yeast fermentation and baking on the content of free amino acids and primary amino groups and their effect on bread aroma stimuli. Cereal Chem. 47: 247.

Eliasson, A.-C., and Larsen, K. 1993. Cereals in Breadmaking: A Molecular-Colloidal Approach. Marcel Decker: New York, NY.

Elion, E. 1943. The effect of punching back on gas production and gas retention in dough. Bakers Digest 17 (6): 16.

Esselink, E., van Aalst, H., Maliepaard, M., Henderson, T.M.H., Hoesktra, N.L.L., and van Duynhoven, J. 2003. Impact of industrial dough processing on structure: A rheology, nuclear magnetic resonance and electron microscopy study. Cereal Chem. 80 (4): 419.

Farber, L. 1949. Food Technol. 3: 300.

Faridi, H. 1985. Rheololgy of Wheat Products. Proc. Rheology of Wheat Products Symposium, held Sept. 24, 1985, at Orlando, FL. AACC: St Paul, MN.

Faridi, H., and Faubion, J.M., eds. 1986. Fundamentals of Dough Rheology. Proc. Fundamentals of Dough Rheology Symposium, held Oct. 7, 1986, at Toronto, Ont., Canada. AACC: St Paul, MN.

Faridi, H., and Faubion, J.M., eds. 1990. Dough Rheology and Baked Product Texture. Van Nostrand Reinhold: New York, NY.

Farrand, E.A. 1972. The influence of particle size and starch damage on the characteristics of bread flours. Bakers Digest 46 (1): 22.

Faubion, J.M., and Hoseney, R.C. 1990. The viscoelastic properties of wheat flour doughs. In: Dough Rheology and Baked Product Texture. H. Faridi and J.M. Faubion, eds. Van Nostrand Reinhold: New York, NY.

Fay, E. 2008. Bread, dough mixing: New science and advancements. Proc. Am. Soc. Baking 84: 76.

Ferrell, C.D. 1961. Curl-type moulding. Bakers Digest 35 (2): 54.

Ferrell, C.D. 1963. Progress report on continuous mix bread. Proc. Am. Soc. Bakery Engrs. 39: 179.

Fields, E.T. 1985. Flour pre-ferments. Proc. Am. Soc. Bakery Engrs. 61: 70.

Fish, A.R. 1982. High speed dough development. Proc. Am. Soc. Bakery Engrs. 58: 130.

Ford, K.W. 1968. The conditioning of bread dough through fermentation. Proc. Am. Soc. Bakery Engrs. 44: 87.

Frazier, P.J., Daniels, N.W.R., and Russell Eggitt, P.W. 1975. Rheology and the continuous breadmaking process. Cereal Chem. 52 (3): 106r.

Frederiksson, H., Tallving, J., Rosén, J., and Åman, P. 2004. Fermentation reduces free asparagine in dough and acrylamide content in bread. Cereal Chem. 81 (5): 650.

Freilich, J. 1949. Time, temperature and humidity factors in dough proofing. Bakers Digest 23 (2): 31.

Fretzdorff, B., and Brümmer, J.-M. 1992. Reduction of phytic acid during breadmaking of whole-meal breads. Cereal Chem. 69 (3): 266.

Fu, J., Mulvaney, S.J., and Cohen, C. 1977. Effect of added fat on the rheological properties of wheat flour doughs. Cereal Chem. 74 (3): 304 (doi: 10.1094/CCHEM.1997.74.3.304).

Fuhrmann, D. 1955. Principles of dough fermentation. Proc. Am. Soc. Bakery Engrs. 31: 118.

Fuhrmann, D. 1964. Progress report on continuous mix bread. Proc. Am. Soc. Bakery Engrs. 40: 50.

Gable, R. 1960. Bread and roll cooling. Proc. Am. Soc. Bakery Engrs. 36: 175.

Gan, Z., Ellis, P.R., Schofield, J.S. 1995. Gas cell stabilization and gas retention in wheat bread dough. J. Cereal Sci. 21 (3): 215 (doi: 10.1006/jcrs.1995.0025).

Gardner, H. 1957. Today's concept for final proofing of bread and rolls. Proc. Am. Soc. Bakery Engrs. 33: 127.

Garnatz, G. 1946. Problems in baking: Cell structure of young and old doughs. Bakers Digest 20 (4): 48.

Garnatz, G. 1957. Relationship of yeast fermentation, ingredients and bread processing methods to finished bread quality. Bakers Digest 31 (6): 73.

Garver, J.C., Navarini, I., and Swanson, A.M. 1966. Cereal Sci. Today 11: 410.

Geigenburger, A.A. 1985. Straight/no-time dough process. Proc. Am. Soc. Bakery Engrs. 61: 64.

Glover, H.L. 1975. No-time dough methods. Proc. Am. Soc. Bakery Engrs. 51: 59.

Gorton, L. 1995. Bread break through. Baking & Snack. 17 (8): 19.

Gorton, L. 2000. Proving oven-ready. Baking & Snack 22 (8): 40.

Gorton, L. 2001. Pan natural. Baking & Snack 23 (3): 31.

Gould, J.T. 1998. Baking around the world. In: Technology of Breadmaking. S.P. Cauvain and L.S. Young, eds. Blackie: London, UK.

Griffith, T., and Johnson, J.A. 1955. Cereal Chem. 31: 130.

Grosch, W., and Schieberle, P. 1997. Flavor of cereal products — A review. Cereal Chem. 74 (2): 91.

Hamer, R.J., and Hoseney, R.C. 1998. Interactions: The Keys to Cereal Quality. AACC: St. Paul, MN.

Harbrecht, A., and Kautzmann, R. 1967. Branntweinwirtschaft 107 (21-23).

Harrel, C.G., and R.J. Thelen. 1959. In: Conversion Factors and Technical Data for the Food Industry, 6th ed. Burgess Publishing Co.: Minneapolis, MN.

Hayashi, T. 1978. Automated puff pastry production. Proc. Am. Soc. Bakery Engrs. 54: 139.

Hayman, D., Sipes, K., Hoseney, R.C., and Faubion, J.M. 1998. Factors controlling gas cell failure in bread dough. Cereal Chem. 75 (5): 585 (doi: 10.1094/CCHEM.1998.75.5.585).

Hibberd, G.E., and Parker, N.S. 1976. Gas pressure-volume-time relationships in fermenting doughs. I. Rate of production and solubility of carbon dioxide in dough. Cereal Chem. 53: 338.

Hildebrand, H.E. Jr. 1952. Proof boxes — their design and operation. Proc. Am. Soc. Bakery Engrs. 28: 83.

Hlynka, I. 1962. Dough structure: Its basis and implication. Bakers Digest 36 (5): 44.

Hlynka, I. 1964. Cereal Chem. 41: 243.

Hlynka, I. 1970. Rheological properties of dough and their significance in the breadmaking process. Bakers Digest 44 (2): 40.

Hlynka, I. 1972. Some rheological aspects of yeast-leavened dough. Bakers Digest 46 (2): 44.

Hodge, J.E. 1953. Agr. Food Chem. 1: 928.

Hodge, J.E. 1955. Adv. Carbohydrate Chem. 10: 169.

Hodge, J.E. 1967. Nonenzymatic browning reactions. In: The Chemistry and Physiology of Flavors. H.W. Schultz, N.A. Day, and L.M. Libbey, eds. Avi Publishing Co.: Westport, CT.

Hoerner, G., and Boge, T. 1997. San Francisco style sourdough bread. AIB Tech. Bull. 19 (8).

Hoffman, C., Schweitzer, T.R., and Dalby, G. 1941a. Cereal Chem. 18: 337.

Hoffman, C., Schweitzer, T.R., and Dalby, G. 1941b. Cereal Chem. 18: 342; Factors affecting the growth of yeast in fermenting doughs. Bakers Digest 14 (1): 23.

Hoseney, R.C. 1984. Mixing and over-mixing of dough. In: International Symposium on Advances in Baking Science and Technology. Dept. of Grain Science, Kansas State University: Manhattan, KS.

Hoseney, R.C. 1985. Rheology of fermenting dough. In: Rheology of Wheat Products. H. Faridi, ed. Proc. Rheology of Wheat Products Symposium, held Sept. 24, 1985, at Orlando, FL. AACC: St Paul, MN.

Hoseney, R.C., and Finney, P.L. 1974. Mixing: A contrary view. Bakers Digest 48 (1): 22.

Hoseney, R.C., and Seib, P.A. 1973. Structural differences in hard and soft wheats. Bakers Digest 47 (6): 26.

Hoseney, R.C., Hsu, K.H., and Junge, R.C. 1979. A simple spread test to measure the rheological properties of fermenting dough. Cereal Chem. 56: 141.

Hsu, K.H., Hoseney, R.C., and Seib, P.A. 1979. Frozen dough. II. Effects of freezing and storage conditions on the stability of yeasted doughs. Cereal Chem. 56 (5): 424.

Hunter, C.L. 1949. Conventional moulding vs. loose-curl cross moulding. Proc. Am. Soc. Bakery Engrs. 25: 91.

Jackel, S.S. 1962. Techniques to determine flavor factors in bread. Proc. Am. Soc. Bakery Engrs. 38: 59.

Jackel, S.S. 1969a. Fermentation — today and tomorrow. Proc. Am. Soc. Bakery Engrs. 45: 91.

Jackel, S.S. 1969b. Fermentation flavors of white bread. Bakers Digest 43 (5): 24.

Jago, W. 1895. A Text-Book of the Science and Art of Bread-Making. Simpkin, Marshall, Hamilton, Kent & Co: London, England.

Johnson, A.M., and Walker, C.E. 2003. Humidity inside ovens. AIB Tech. Bull. 25 (6).

Johnson, J.A., and Sanchez, C.R.S. 1973. The nature of bread flavor. Bakers Digest 47 (5): 48.

Johnson, J.A., Miller, B.S., and Curnutte, B. J. 1958. Agr. Food Chem. 6: 384.

Jones, P.C. 1960. Review of continuous bread mixing. Proc. Am. Soc. Bakery Engrs. 36: 77.

Junge, R.C., Hoseney, R.C., and Varriano-Marston, E. 1981. Effect of surfactants on air incorporation in dough and the crumb grain of bread. Cereal Chem. 58 (4): 338.

Kamman, P. 1967. The case for continuous process bread. Proc. Am. Soc. Bakery Engrs. 43: 82.

Kamman, P.E. 1970. Factors affecting the grain and texture of white bread. Bakers Digest 44 (2): 34.

Kamuf, W., Nixon, A., Parker, O., and Barnum, G.C. Jr. 2003. Overview of caramel colors. Cereal Foods World 48 (2): 64.

Khoo, U., Christianson, D.D., and Inglett, G.E. 1975. Scanning and transmission microscopy of dough and bread. Bakers Digest 49 (4): 24.

Kiely, P.J., Nowlin, A.C., and Moriary, J.H. 1960. Cereal Sci. Today 5: 273.

Kilborn, R.H., and Tipples, K.H. 1972. Factors affecting mechanical dough development. I. Effect of mixing intensity and work input. Cereal Chem. 49: 34.

Kilborn, R.H., and Tipples, K.H. 1979. The effect of oxidation and intermediate proof on work requirements for optimum short-process bread. Cereal Chem. 56 (5): 407.

Kilborn, R.H., Nomura, S., and Preston, K.R. 1981. Sponge-and-dough bread. I. Reduction of fermentation time and bromate requirement by the incorporation of salt in the sponge. Cereal Chem. 58: 508.

Kitts, D.D. undated. Course materials for FNH 301, Food Chemistry, University of British Columbia, Faculty of Land and Food Systems.

Knott, K.G. 1996. Ovens: New technology in mass air handling. Proc. Am. Soc. Bakery Engrs. 72: 73.

Koch, R.B., Smith, F., and Geddes, W.F. 1954. Cereal Chem. 31: 55.

Kosmina, N.P. 1977. Biochemie der Brotherstellung. VEB Fachbuchverlag: Leipzig, GDR.

Kulp, K. 1983. Technology of brew systems in bread production. Bakers Digest 57 (6): 20.

Kulp, K. 1986. Influence of liquid ferments on quality characteristics of white pan bread. AIB Tech. Bull. 8 (9).

Kulp, K. 1995. Biochemical and biophysical principles of freezing. In: Frozen and Refrigerated Doughs and Batters. K. Kulp, K. Lorenz and J. Brümmer, eds. AACC International: St. Paul, MN.

Kusunose, C., Fujii, T., and Matsumoto, H. 1999. Role of starch granules in controlling expansion of dough during baking. Cereal Chem. 76 (6): 920.

Lane, M.J., and Nursten, H.E. 1983. The variety of odors produced in Maillard model systems and how they are influenced by reaction conditions. In: The Maillard Reaction in Foods and Nutrition. G.R. Waller, and M.S. Feather, eds. ACS Symposium Series 215. Am. Chem. Society: Washington, DC.

Lanham, W.E. 1970. A new technology of continuous proofing and baking. Bakers Digest 44 (6): 54.

Lanham, W.E. Jr. 1994. Efficient oven usage. Proc. Am. Soc. Bakery Engrs. 70: 141.

Le-Bail, A., Grenier, A., Hayert, M., Davenel, A., and Lucas, T. 2008. Impact of freezing rate of bread dough and dough expansion during fermentation. Use of MRI to assess local porosity. In: Bubbles in Food 2: Novelty, Health and Luxury. G.M. Campbell, M.G. Scanlon and D.L. Pyle, eds. AACC: St. Paul, MN.

Lehmann, T.A and Dreese, P. 1981. Stability of frozen dough: Effects of freezing temperatures. AIB Tech. Bull. 3 (7).

Leibowitz, J., and Henderson, S. 1945. Adv. Enzymolology 5: 87.

Leong, S.S.J., and Campbell, G.M. 2008. Degassing of dough pieces during sheeting. In: Bubbles in Food 2: Novelty, Health and Luxury. G.M. Campbell, M.G. Scanlon and D.L. Pyle, eds. AACC: St. Paul, MN.

Levine, L. 1998. Principles of sheeting dough. 1998. AIB Tech. Bull. 20 (9).

Levine, L., and Drew, B.A. 1990. Rheological and engineering aspects of the sheeting and laminating of doughs. In: Dough Rheology and Baked Product Texture. H. Faridi and J.M. Faubion, eds. Van Nostrand Reinhold: New York, NY.

Levine. L. 2007. Product damage in mixing and coating drums. Cereal Foods World 52 (2): 81 (doi: 10.1094/CFW-52-6-0328).

Lind, J.M. 1965. Progress report on continuous process bread. Proc. Am. Soc. Bakery Engrs. 41: 59.

Ling, R.S., and Hoseney, R.C. 1977. Effect of certain nutrients on the gas produced in pre-ferments. Cereal Chem. 54: 597.

Lorenz, K. 1995. Freezing and refrigeration of cake and muffin batters in the US. Kulp, K. 1995. Biochemical and biophysical principles of freezing. In: Frozen and Refrigerated Doughs and Batters. K. Kulp, K. Lorenz and J. Brümmer, eds. AACC International: St. Paul, MN.

Lorenz, L. 1981. Sourdough processes — methodology and biochemistry. Bakers Digest 55 (1): 32.

Loudenslager, H.E. Sr. 1974. Combination bread process. 50: 69.

Madson, O.T. 1994. Continuous mixing – a second look. Proc. Am. Soc. Bakery Engrs. 70: 57.

Maillard, L.C. 1912. Compt. rend. 154: 66.

Marsh, D. 1998. Mixing and dough processing. In: Technology of Breadmaking. S.P. Cauvain and L.S. Young, eds. Blackie: London, UK.

Marston, P.E. 1966. Cereal Sci. Today 11: 530.

Marston, P.E. 1971. Chemical activation of dough development under slow mixing conditions. Bakers Digest 45 (6): 16.

Marston, P.E. 1978. Frozen dough for breadmaking. Bakers Digest 52 (2): 18.

Marston, P.E., and Wannan, T.L. 1976. Bread baking: The transformation from dough to bread. Bakers Digest 50 (4): 24.

Martin, P.J., Tassell, A., Wiktorowicz, R., Morrant, C.J., and Campbell, G.M. 2008. Mixing bread doughs under highly soluble gas atmospheres and the effects on bread crumb texture: Experimental results and theoretical interpretation. In: Bubbles in Food 2: Novelty, Health and Luxury. G.M. Campbell, M.G. Scanlon and D.L. Pyle, eds. AACC: St. Paul, MN.

Mattern, P.J., and Sandstedt, R.M. 1957. Cereal Chem. 34: 252.

Matz, S.A. 1972. Bakery Technology and Engineering, 2nd ed. Avi Publishing Co.: Westport, CN.

Matz, S.A. 1989. Freezing preservation of bakery products. In: Bakery Technology: Packaging, Nutrition, Product Development, QA. Pan-Tech International, Inc.: McAllen, TX.

Meredith, P. 1969. Water absorption in wheat flour. Bakers Digest 43 (4): 42.

Merritt, P.P. 1960. Fermentation problems confronting the baker today. Proc. Am. Soc. Bakery Engrs. 36: 54.

Meyer, H.A. 1962. Production of continuous mix bread. Proc. Am. Soc. Bakery Engrs. 38: 115.

Miller, R.A. 1961. The breakthrough in mixing and makeup. Bakers Digest 35 (5): 142.

Mohr, J. 1949. Conventional moulding vs. loose-curl straight moulding. Proc. Am. Soc. Bakery Engrs. 25: 93.

Moore, M. 1988. Humidity — effects on baking quality and human comfort. AIB Tech. Bull. 10 (12).

Moore, W.R., and Hoseney, R.C. 1985. The leavening of bread doughs. Cereal Foods World 30: 791.

Moore, W.R., and Hoseney, R.C. 1986. The effects of flour lipids on the expansion rate and volume of bread baked in a resistance oven. Cereal Chem. 63 (2): 172.

Mottram, D.S., Wedzicha, B.I., and Dodson, A.T. 2002. Acrylamide is formed in the Maillard reaction. Nature 419: 448.

Nakagawa, M. 1991. Pre-proofed frozen dough technology. Proc. Am. Soc. Bakery Engrs. 67: 68.

Neish, A.C., and Blackwood, A.C. 1951. Can. J. Technol. 29: 123.

Newberry, M.P., Phan-Thien, N., Larroque, O.R., Tanner, R.I., and Larsen, N.G. 2002. Dynamic and elongation rheology of yeasted bread doughs. Cereal Chem. 79 (6): 874.

Newbery, D. 1996. Vacuum cooling. Am. Soc. Bakery Engrs. 72: 81.

Newton, J.M. 1961. Problems in baking: Heat of solution for sucrose and dextrose. Bakers Digest 35 (2): 101.

Nicolait, R. 1960. Problems in baking: Dressing of the trough. Bakers Digest 34 (3): 83.

Noll, B. 2002. Presentation of the Rapidojet procedure (Vorstellung des Rapidojet-Verfahrens: schnelle, energiesparende und staubfreie Teigbereitung mittels eines Hochdruckwasserstrahls). Proc. 53rd Tagung für Bäckerei-Technologie, held at Detmold, Germany, Nov. 4-5, 2002. Published online at http://www.rapidojet.de/Rapidojet_english.PDF.

O'Donnell, K. 1996. Methods of bread dough making. AIB Tech. Bull. 18 (12).

Olmsted, J.P. Jr. 1970. Fundamentals of mechanical makeup. Proc. Am. Soc. Bakery Engrs. 46: 54.

Osborne, D. 1998. Advances in bread and bun makeup. Proc. Am. Soc. Bakery Engrs. 74: 129.

Pai, Y., and Walker, C.E. 2004. Par-baking technology. AIB Tech. Bull. 26 (6).

Pelshenke, P., and Koeber, H. 1940. Biochem. Z. 360: 205.

Pence, J.W. 1955. The freezing, storage and defrosting of commercial bread. Proc. Am. Soc. Bakery Engrs. 31: 106.

Pence, J.W., and Standridge, N.N. 1956. Some experiments on bread freezing. Bakers Digest 30 (1): 25.

Pence, J.W., Standridge, N.N., Black, D.R., and Jones, F.T. 1958. Cereal Chem. 35: 15.

Pence, J.W., Standridge, N.N., Lubisich, T.M., Mecham, D.K., and Smith, G.S. 1955a. Food Technol. 9: 342.

Pence, J.W., Standridge, N.N., Mecham, D.K., and Olcott, H.S. 1955b. Food Technol. 9: 494.

Perrou, E. 2000. Liquid ferments vs. sponge and dough. Proc. Am. Soc. Baking 76: 93.

Piekarz, E.R. 1963. Evaluation of sugars in ferment systems. Proc. Am. Soc. Bakery Engrs. 39: 118.

Pierce, W.L. 1974. Pumping of bread and bun dough. Proc. Am. Soc. Bakery Engrs. 50: 92.

Pomeranz, Y. 1980a. Molecular approach to breadmaking: An update and new perspectives. I. Bakers Digest 54 (1): 20.

Pomeranz, Y. 1980b. Molecular approach to breadmaking: An update and new perspectives. II. Bakers Digest 54 (2): 12.

Pomeranz, Y., Meyer, D., and Seibel, W. 1984. Wheat, wheat-rye and rye dough and bread studied by scanning electron microscopy. Cereal Chem. 61: 53.

Pomper, S. 1969. Biochemistry of yeast fermentation. Bakers Digest 42 (2): 32.

Ponte, J.G. Jr. 1971. Bread. In: Wheat Chemistry and Technology. 2nd ed. Y. Pomeranz, ed. American Association of Cereal Chemists: St. Paul, MN.

Ponte, J.G. Jr., Titcomb, S.T., and Cotton, R.H. 1963. Some effects of oven temperature and malted barley level on breadmaking. Bakers Digest 37 (3): 44.

Preston, K.R., and Kilborn, R.H. 1982. J. Food Sci. 47: 1143.

Preston, K.R., Kilborn, R.H., and Tipples, K.H. 1984. Effects of fermentation, sponge salt and oxidation on sponge-and-dough bread quality. In: International Symposium on Advances and Baking Science and Technology. Dept. of Grain Science, Kansas State University: Manhattan, KS.

Prouty, W.W. 1965. Guidelines for a quality control program. II. Process control. Bakers Digest 39 (4): 69.

Reed, G. 1966. Yeast, what it does and how. Proc. Am. Soc. Bakery Engrs. 42: 126.

Reed, G. 1975. Fermentation defined. Proc. Am. Soc. Bakery Engrs. 51: 35.

Reed, G., and Nagodawithana, T.W. 1991. Use of yeast in baking. In: Yeast Technology, 2nd ed. Van Nostrand Reinhold: New York, NY.

Reedich, E.L. 1989. No-time dough product update. Proc. Am. Soc. Bakery Engrs. 65: 238.

Richard-Molard, D., Nago, M.C., and Drapron, R. 1979. Influence of the breadmaking method on French bread flavor. Bakers Digest 53 (3): 34.

Roberts, D. 1997. The Milton Keynes process. Am. Soc. Bakery Engrs. 73: 75.

Robinson, J. 2000. Formulating for extrusion dividing. Am. Soc. Baking 76: 159.

Rosenholtz, S. 1985. Frozen dough manufacturing: The production process. Proc. Am. Soc. Bakery Engrs. 61: 141.

Sadd, P. 2008. Mathematical modeling of crumpet formation. In: Bubbles in Food 2: Novelty, Health and Luxury. G.M. Campbell, M.G. Scanlon and D.L. Pyle, eds. AACC: St. Paul, MN.

Sanderson, G.W., Reed, G., Bruinsma, B., and Cooper, E.J. 1983. Yeast fermentation in breadmaking. AIB Tech. Bull. 5 (12).

Sandstedt, R.M. 1961. The function of starch in the baking of bread. Bakers Digest 35 (3): 36.

Scaman, C.H. undated. Course materials for FNH 401, Food Chemistry II, University of British Columbia, Faculty of Land and Food Systems.

Schiller, G.W. 1968. Continuous mixing production of buns and rolls. Proc. Am. Soc. Bakery Engrs. 44: 58.

Schneeberger, F. 1948. Problems in baking: Remixed straight dough. Bakers Digest 22 (6): 35.

Schoch, T.J. 1965. Starch in bakery products. Bakers Digest 39 (2): 48.

Schulz, A. 1965. Brot u. Gebäck 19 (4): 61.

Seeley, R.D., and Ziegler, H.F. 1962. Yeast: Some aspects of its fermentative behavior. Bakers Digest 36 (4): 48.

Shimiya, Y., and Nakamura, K. 1997. Changes in gas cells in dough and bread during breadmaking and calculation of critical size of gas cells that expand. J. Texture Stud. 28: 273.

Shimiya, Y., and Yano, T. 1987. Measurements of accompanying air, specific surface area and micropore volume of some flour particles. Agric. Biol. Chem. 51: 25.

Shirley, E.H. 1977. The Canadian concept of no-time doughs. Proc. Am. Soc. Bakery Engrs. 53: 36.

Sievers, R.S. 1978. New baking methods. Proc. Am. Soc. Bakery Engrs. 54: 98.

Siffring, K., and Bruinsma, B.L. 1993. Effects of proof temperature on the quality of pan bread. Cereal Chem. 70 (3): 351.

Silva, J. 1941. Pullman bread: Flour, formula, methods, pans. Proc. Am. Soc. Bakery Engrs. 17: 45.

Sluimer, P. 1981. Principles of dough retarding. Bakers Digest 55 (4): 6.

Sluimer, P. 2005. Principles of Breadmaking: Functionality of Raw Materials and Process Steps. AACC International: St. Paul, MN.

Smith, D.E., and Andrews, J.S. 1957. Cereal Chem. 34: 323.

Spies, R. 1990. Application of rheology in the bread industry. In: Dough Rheology and Baked Product Texture. H. Faridi and J.M. Faubion, eds. Van Nostrand Reinhold: New York, NY.

Sroan, B.S., and MacRitchie, F. 2008. Mechanism of gas cell stability in breadmaking. In: Bubbles in Food 2: Novelty, Health and Luxury. G.M. Campbell, M.G. Scanlon and D.L. Pyle, eds. AACC: St. Paul, MN.

Sroan, B.S., and MacRitchie, F. 2009. Mechanism of gas cell stabilization in breadmaking. II. The secondary liquid lamellae. J. Cereal Sci. 49 (1): 41 (doi: 10.1016/j.jcs.2008.07.004).

Sroan, B.S., Bean, S.R., and MacRitchie, F. 2009. Mechanism of gas cell stabilization in breadmaking. I. The primary gluten-starch matrix. J. Cereal Sci. 49 (1): 32 (doi: 10.1016/j.jcs.2008.07.003).

Stadler, R.H., Blank, I., Varga, N., Robert, F., Hau, J., Guy, P.A., Robert M.-C., and Riediker, S. 2002. Acrylamide from Maillard reaction products. Nature 419: 449.

Stakley, D.M. 1985. Water pre-ferments. Proc. Am. Soc. Bakery Engrs. 61: 72.

Stauffer, C.E. 1997. When flour meets water. Baking & Snack 19 (4): 44.

Stauffer, C.E. 1998. Principles of dough formation. In: Technology of Breadmaking. S.P. Cauvain and L.S. Young, eds. Blackie: London, UK.

Sternberg, G. 1968. A new concept in conventional dough mixing. Bakers Digest 42 (1): 60.

Stimpson, D.M. 1993. Bread makeup. Proc. Am. Soc. Bakery Engrs. 69: 135.

Stitley, J.W., Kemp, K.E., Kyle, B.G., and Kulp, K. 1987. Bakery oven ethanol emissions — experimental and plant survey results. AIB Tech. Bull. 9 (12).

Stribling, J.W. 1947. Bakery equipment panel. Proc. Am. Soc. Bakery Engrs., 23: 155.

Suas, M. 2009. Advanced Bread and Pastry: A Professional Approach. Delmar Cengage Learning: Clifton Park, NY.

Sugihara, T.F., Kline, L., and McCready, L.B. 1970. Nature of the San Francisco sour dough French bread process. II. Microbiological aspects. Bakers Digest 44 (2): 48.

Sugihara, T.F., Kline, L., and Miller, M.W. 1971. Microorganisms of the San Francisco sour dough bread process. I. Yeasts responsible for the leavening action. Appl. Microbiol. 21 (3): 456.

Swortfiguer, M.J. 1950. White bread sponge and dough development. Proc. Am. Soc. Bakery Engrs., 26: 94.

Swortfiguer, M.J. 1968. Dough absorption and moisture retention in bread. Bakers Digest 42 (4): 42.

Tang, R.T., Robinson, R.J., and Hurley, W. 1972. Quantitative changes in various sugar concentrations during breadmaking. Bakers Digest 46 (4): 48.

Tesch, J.W. 1971. Degassing of bun doughs — equipment and methods. Proc. Am. Soc. Bakery Engrs. 47: 112.

Thompson, D.R. 1978. Freezing bakery products. Bakers Digest 52 (4): 33.

Thompson, D.R. 1980. State of the art — bakery fermentation. Bakers Digest 54 (3): 28.

Thorn, A.J., and Ross, J.W. 1960. Cereal Chem. 37: 415.

Tipples, K.H., and Kilborn, R.H. 1974. Dough development for shorter breadmaking processes. Bakers Digest 48 (5): 34.

Tipples, K.H., and Kilborn, R.H. 1975. "Unmixing" — The disorientation of developed bread doughs by slow speed mixing. Cereal Chem. 52: 248.

Trausch, A. 1954. Proper handling of pans from oven to moulder. Proc. Am. Soc. Bakery Engrs. 30: 49.

Trivedi, N., Hauser, J., Nagodawithana, T., and Reed, G. 1989. Update on bakers yeast. AIB Tech. Bull. 11 (2).

Trum, G.W. 1971. Bun production by the continuous mixing process. Proc. Am. Soc. Bakery Engrs. 47: 106.

Tsen, C.C. 1970. Chemical dough development. Bakers Digest 44 (4): 28.

Tsen, C.C., and Bushuk, W. 1963. Cereal Chem. 40: 399.

Tsen, C.C., and Hlynka, I. 1963. Cereal Chem. 40, 145.

Tsen, C.C., and Reddy, P.R.K. 1977. J. Food Sci. 42: 1370.

Tsen, C.C., Reddy, P.R.K., El-Samahy, S.K., and Gehrke, C.W. 1983. Effect of the Maillard browning reaction on the nutritive value of breads and pizza crusts. In: The Maillard Reaction in Foods and Nutrition. G.R. Waller, and M.S. Feather, eds. ACS Symposium Series 215. Am. Chem. Society: Washington, DC.

Turner, J.E. Sr. 1980. Liquid pre-ferments. Proc. Am. Soc. Bakery Engrs. 56: 176.

Uhrich, M.G. 1975. Formulation of liquid pre-ferment. Proc. Am. Soc. Bakery Engrs. 51: 42.

Underhill, F. 1966. Production of buns and wheat bread on continuous mixing equipment. Proc. Am. Soc. Bakery Engrs. 42: 89.

Valentyne, P.H. 1959. Practial aspects of heat balance in dough mixing. Bakers Digest 33 (1): 34.

van Vliet, T. 1999. Physical factors determining gas cell stability in a dough during bread making. In: Bubbles in Food, G.M. Campbell, C. Webb, S.S. Pandiella and K. Niranjan, eds. AACC: St. Paul, MN.

Varriano-Marston, E., Hsu, K.H., and Mahdi, J. 1980. Rheological and structural changes in frozen dough. Bakers Digest 54 (1): 32.

Wagner, M., Zhang, L., Quellec, S., Doursat, D., Flick, D., Trystram, G., and Lucas, T. 2008. Role of the crust formation on local expansion during bread baking.

In: Bubbles in Food 2: Novelty, Health and Luxury. G.M. Campbell, M.G. Scanlon and D.L. Pyle, eds. AACC: St. Paul, MN.

Walden, C.C. 1959. The action of flour amylase during oven baking. Bakers Digest 33 (1): 24.

Wang, F.C., and Sun, X.S. 2002. Creep-recovery of wheat flour doughs and relationship to other physical dough tests and breadmaking performance. Cereal Chem. 79 (4): 567.

Warren, J. 1999. Continuous dough mixing and mixers. AIB Tech. Bull. 21 (12).

Watkins, F.H. Jr. 1985. Continuous mixing process. Proc. Am. Soc. Bakery Engrs. 61: 68.

Watkins, F.H. Jr. 1991. High-flour liquid ferments. Proc. Am. Soc. Bakery Engrs. 67: 168.

Weegels, P.L., Groeneweg, F., Esselink, E., Smit, R., Brown, R., and Ferdinando, D. 2003. Large and fast deformations crucial for the rheology of proofing dough. Cereal Chem. 80 (4): 424.

Weipert, D. 1990. The benefits of basic rheometry in studying dough rheology. Cereal Chem. 67 (4): 311.

Whitaker, S. 2008. Artisan solutions. Baking & Snack 30 (6): 99.

White, D. 1970. Fermentation and proofing rooms. Bakers Digest 44 (3): 45.

White, J. 1954. Yeast Technology. John Wiley & Sons, Inc.: New York, NY.

Whitworth, M. 2008. X-ray tomography of structure formation in bread and cakes during baking. In: Bubbles in Food 2: Novelty, Health and Luxury. G.M. Campbell, M.G. Scanlon and D.L. Pyle, eds. AACC: St. Paul, MN.

Wiggins, C. 1998. Proving, baking and cooling. In: Technology of Breadmaking. S.P. Cauvain and L.S. Young, eds. Blackie: London, UK.

Wiseblatt, L. 1960. Cereal Chem. 37: 728.

Wiseblatt, L., and Zournut, H. 1963. Cereal Chem. 40: 116.

Wolfe, J.E., and Dalby, G. 1961. The mixing of Bread doughs by conventional methods. Am. Soc. Bakery Engrs. Bull. 168.

Wolt, M.J., and D'Appolonia, B.L. 1984. Factors involved in the stability of frozen dough. II. The effects of yeast type and dough additives on frozen-dough stability. Cereal Chem. 61 (3): 213.

Yasunaga, T., Bushuk, W., and Irvine, G.N. 1968. Effect of papain on amylograph viscosity of flour. Cereal Chem. 45: 269.

Zhang, L., Lucas, T., Doursat, C., Flick, D. and Le Ray, D. 2008. CO2 release during baking as a response parameter for monitoring the bubble opening. In: Bubbles in Food 2: Novelty, Health and Luxury. G.M. Campbell, M.G. Scanlon and D.L. Pyle, eds. AACC: St. Paul, MN.

Ziemke, W.H., and Sanders, S. 1988. Sourdough bread. AIB Tech. Bull. 10 (10).

CHAPTER 7

Fundamental Bakery Batter Processes

INTRODUCTION

If dough processing resembles biochemistry, then batter preparation is more like organic chemistry — no live micro-organisms like yeast to manage, but still plenty of complex ingredients. Flour and sugar comprise the bulk of batter-based products, and flour can vary season-to-season like any other natural-source, minimally processed ingredient.

Many of the stages of fundamental bakery batter processes are nearly the same as those for dough, discussed in Chapter 6. Mixing is responsible for cell creation; baking changes the labile foam-like batter into solid sponge-like crumb; and cooling

Success with batter-based, chemically leavened baked foods requires careful management of complex ingredients through closely controlled processes.

Batter-based baked foods range from cakes to muffins to cookies, plus many more, with process requirements that facilitate chemical leavening methods. (i-Stock.com)

assures optimum packaging conditions. But one important difference exists: No fermentation is involved. (Yeast-raised doughnuts represent one of the few exceptions.)

Baked products made via batter processes differ considerably from each other. This chapter will examine the basic processes involved in preparation of cake, pie, doughnut and several related products. Cookie and cracker procedures are described here because these items are made with flour milled from soft or low-protein wheat as are cake items. Also, most are leavened chemically or by steam, rather than yeast. Because some products such as muffins, refrigerated biscuits and cheesecakes, among others, employ unique processes, these procedures will be examined in Chapter 8 along with their specific formulating parameters.

A multitude of factors including composition and processing affect the final properties of baked batter foods. Many people have attempted to identify these factors, to explain their effects and to use them to maintain consistency and desirable structural and organoleptic qualities in the end products.

Researchers studying the structure of baked foods have long reported that water-soluble pentosans of wheat flours form a gel at room temperature in the presence of oxidants (Neukom et al. 1968). As scientists looked further into this subject, Neukom and Markwalder (1978) suggested that ferulic acid associated with the pentosan forms the necessary cross-links that increase viscosity, later verified by Ciacco and D'Appolonia (1982).

Chlorination of soft wheat flours (commonly used for cakes), as it turns out, enables enhanced oxidative gelation of solvent-accessible arabinoxylans, which Kweon et al. (2009) demonstrated using a Bostwick trough-style consistometer to measure flow.

The unique structure-building effect caused by oxidative gelation, as Bettge and Morris (2007) determined, contributes to soft wheat batter viscosity. Oxidative gelation, thus, impacts cake volume as well as cookie spread, baking time and checking. Although hard wheats have greater potential for oxidative gelation than the soft wheats used for cookies and cakes, such activity is eclipsed in bread doughs by gluten's powerful structuring capacity (Bettge 2009).

7.A. Mixing and Slurrymaking

The primary purpose of mixing is to bring about a complete and uniform dispersion and homogeneous mutual emulsification of the various ingredients, usually with the entrapment and size reduction of air cells and, in the case of most baked products made from soft wheat flour, minimum development of the gluten.

Formation of air cells, discussed in Chapter 6, Part A, is just as important for batters as it is for doughs. Only mixing can create air cells; leavening gases migrate to existing cells and enlarge them. The greater the number of air cells in a batter, the better the chemical leaveners function, resulting in optimized volume. Evenness of size improves the grain as well. Chemical leavening is explained in Volume I, Chapter 2, Part B.

In mixing batters and soft wheat doughs, not only must ingredients be dispersed but certain ones must also be solublized, principally sugar but also salt and bicarbonates. Because sugar readily goes into solution in these products, it actually functions as a liquid, and the presence of sugar syrup as a continuous phase in cookie doughs is essential for optimum finished results. When cookies cool, the sugar crystallizes, acting as a hardening agent to make the product crisp.

To assure tender eating quality, batters and doughs for cakes, cookies and similar products must be prepared in a way that minimizes gluten development. Therefore, viscosity determines the retention of leavening gases and flow characteristics and finished product quality. According to Bettge and Morris (2007), proper batter viscosity is crucial in preventing settling during holding or loss of leavening gases in higher moisture products such as cake and pancake batters. Effects on lower-moisture items like cookies show up as reduced dough plasticity, increased bake-out time and problems with checking.

7.A.1. Cake mixing

Most often done in a planetary mixer (**Figure 7.01**), cake mixing serves three main functions: hydration of ingredients, dispersion of ingredients and aeration of the batter (Zelch 2001). Depending on the nature of the cake being produced, the mixing procedure will differ in aspects such as the order of ingredient incorporation, the duration and rate of mixing action during the different stages in multistage methods, the temperature of the ingredients and other factors.

Under- and over-mixng have imortant consequences for such baked foods (**Figure 7.02**). Over-mixing causes excessive aeration of the batter, over-extending the structure and making the finished cake extremely tender or fragile with a rather brittle crumb. The over-extended air cells at the bottom can collapse, leading to dense crumb character. The cake's top crust may also peak or crack because of excess internal temperature. Over-mixing a batter using flour with more than 9% protein may lead to tough texture.

Under-mixing can pose problems with ineffective ingredient distribution and insufficient air incorporation. Water in the batter may not properly bind with the dry ingredients and can evaporate readily during baking, leaving behind a sticky sugar deposit on the crust. Without sufficient air and too few air cells, leavening of an under-mixed batter will not be uniform. Air cells will be larger, and the final grain of the cake will contain holes.

Cell collapse in the center of the cake layer can sometimes lead to the dense, moist layer referred to as a "bone." Likewise, large air cells will sometimes coalesce and rise, disrupting the top surface and forming "tunnels."

7.A.1.a. Batter cakes

The ingredients used in batter-type cakes may be combined by three different methods: (a) the "sugar batter" or creaming method, (b) the "flour batter" or blending method and (c) the "single stage" method.

Creaming method. Also called the "sugar batter" method, the creaming method first combines the shortening with the granulated sugar. Frequently, some of the other dry ingredients are included, and mixing takes place at slow or medium speed until the components are thoroughly blended and the mixture is aerated.

Figure 7.01. A dual-ratio 340-qt vertical mixer can perform a wide variety of mixing actions.
(AMF Bakery Systems)

Figure 7.02. Effects of over-mixed (top, 0.70 specific gravity) and under-mixing (bottom, 1.01 specific gravity), compared with the control (middle, 0.80 specific gravity), can be seen in cake cross-sections.
(Zelch 2001)

This stage is followed by incorporation of the eggs, while the creaming action is continued. The subsequent addition of the milk and flour, in alternate small portions, completes mixing.

Major advantages of the creaming method are the incorporation of large volumes of air in the form of minuscule cells in the fat phase of the batter, the coating by fat of the flour and sugar, which delays their respective hydration and solubilization, and the near absence of flour gluten development. (With modern cake flours, the last benefit no longer possesses the significance it had formerly.)

Total mixing time for the creaming method will range from 15 to 20 minutes. The initial creaming stage takes 8 to 10 minutes; the second stage of egg incorporation, 5 minutes; and the final stage of milk and flour addition, 5 to 6 minutes. The method applies to all regular batter-type cakes, except those with high sugar contents.

Bailey and LeClerc (1935) showed that the moisture of the eggs and milk forms an oil-in-water (O/W) emulsion with the shortening when these ingredients are added gradually. The rate of liquid addition is critical because if it is done too rapidly, the emulsion phase may invert into a water-in-oil (W/O) emulsion and impart a curdled appearance to the batter (**Figure 7.03**). Characteristics observed in a cake produced from curdled batter include low volume, coarse crumb, sugary top crust and tender structure (Zelch 2001). However, the batter may again be smoothed out with the addition of the flour without perceptibly impairing the quality of the finished cake.

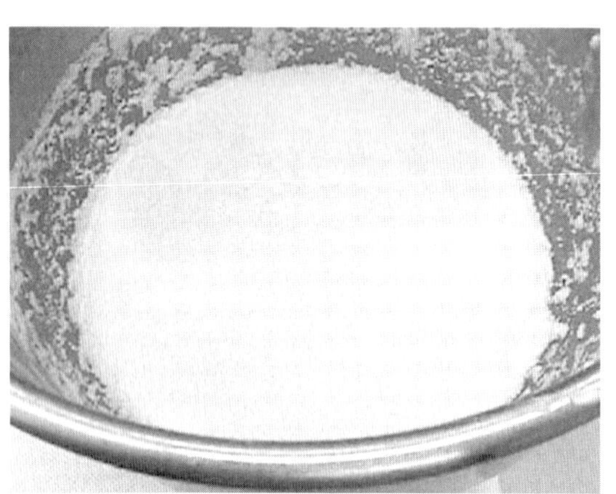

Figure 7.03. A curdled batter can happen when adding too much liquid or adding it too quickly, resulting in a water-in-oil emulsion. (Zelch 2001)

Flour-batter method. In the flour-batter method (a modified creaming method), the shortening and flour are creamed to a fluffy mass in one bowl. At the same time, the eggs and sugar are whipped at medium speed to a semi-firm foam in a second bowl. These separate steps require about 10 minutes. The sugar-egg foam is then combined with the creamed flour-shortening mixture, after which the milk is added gradually in small increments.

This method achieves a very thorough dispersion of the shortening throughout the batter and produces an extremely fine grain and uniform texture in the cake. This method permits use of higher levels of sugar and liquids than is possible with the creaming method. On the other hand, it results in somewhat less air incorporation with subsequent loss in product volume and more pronounced development of gluten, which expresses itself in a perceptible toughness in the cake. Also, the method requires two mixing bowls instead of one.

Single-stage method. In the single-stage procedure, all major ingredients are introduced into the mixing bowl at one time and mixed into a homogeneous mass. The mixing process generally consists of blending the ingredients into a homogeneous mixture with a flat beater at low speed for 1 to 3 minutes, followed by mixing at medium speed for 3 to 5 minutes and finally again at low speed for 2 minutes, for a total mixing time of 8 to 10 minutes. Normal practice is to incorporate the baking powder during the final mixing stage.

Mixing method variations. Several additional mixing procedures are practiced, each claiming to yield superior results. Most recently described by Zelch (2001), the "sugar-and-water method" combines all of the formulation's sugar and about one-half its water in the bowl to be mixed at medium speed for about 30 seconds. Next are added the emulsified shortening, flour, nonfat dry milk solids, baking powder (reduced by 25%) and salt, and mixing continues for 5 minutes at medium speed.

The remaining water, eggs and flavoring are added last and mixed for an additional 1 minute at low speed. Because this procedure promotes good aeration, either the amount of leavening must be reduced by 25% or the liquid (water) increased by 15%. Cakes produced by this method were said to develop a better crust color, a more tender crust with less indication of undissolved sugar and a greater volume than control cakes mixed by conventional methods. The improvement in cake quality was attributed to the initial solution of the sugar, which, in effect, provides the benefits associated with the use of liquid sugar.

Another approach, termed the "emulsion method," is especially suited for large volume cake mixers. Here, the sugar and shortening are creamed together for 2 to 3 minutes into a smooth mass. The milk is then added in several portions, with beating continued at medium speed for about 15 minutes until a light and fluffy mass is obtained that resembles a buttercreme. This stage is followed by the addition of flour during the course of 2 minutes, the subsequent addition of the eggs and mixing for an additional 4 to 5 minutes. The total mixing period of this method thus extends more than 12 to 15 minutes.

High-ratio cakes, so-named because the ratio of sugar is higher than that of flour, are also high in liquid ingredients. They require specialty shortenings with added emulsifiers in order to incorporate the extra liquids. Such cakes are best mixed by a variation of the flour-batter method, in which the flour and shortening are creamed for 4 minutes, followed by addition of the sugar and part of the liquid ingredients and mixing for an additional 4 minutes. The remainder of the liquids are combined with the eggs and added to the batter in stages. Final mixing requires about 5 minutes.

Development of fluid cake shortenings resulted in a perceptible improvement of cake mixing efficiency. Lawson (1965) attributed this beneficial effect partly to the greater ease with which the fluid fat is dispersed in both the dry and liquid batter ingredients and partly to its more effective lubrication of the mixing bowl walls, which reduces the need for their frequent scraping down. Moreover, the inclusion of emulsifiers in the shortening aids more rapid incorporation of air in the batter and permits the ready emulsification of higher levels of liquids. All these factors contribute to a reduction in mixing time compared with use of plastic shortenings.

7.A.1.b. Foam cakes

Foam cakes (for example, angel food and sponge styles) depend for their structure and volume (**Figure 7.04**) on the ability of eggs to occlude air and to form stable foams.

Figure 7.04. Egg proteins provide the structure of foam cakes. (Shutterstock)

Egg white method (angel food cake). In preparation of angel food cakes, beating or whipping egg whites results in incorporation of air, and the air cells become increasingly smaller as beating continues. The color of the whipped mass gradually changes from a light greenish-yellow tint to an opaque white, and the surface loses its sheen and turns dull and dry as the foam reaches its maximum volume and stiffness. The presence of fat in egg yolk and whole egg prevents these materials from producing foams possessing the stiffness that characterizes egg white foam (Palmer 1972). Beating time affects the stability of egg foams, as revealed by the amount of drainage from the foam in a given time, with more stable foams being formed as the time is extended. The beating time, in turn, is influenced by the conditions of beating, including temperature of the eggs, type of beater (wire whip or blade), speed of beating and time of sugar addition (Palmer 1972).

In commercial practice, the general procedure in preparing angel food cake is to first whip the egg whites, to which salt and cream of tartar (or other acidifiers and whipping aids) have been added, at medium speed until the whites begin to form body. At this point, 50 to 60% of the sugar (of fine crystallinity to promote rapid solution) is added in a slow stream, while whipping continues until the meringue retains a wet peak. The flavor materials are added next, followed by the remainder of the sugar and flour, which have been sifted together. At this stage, mixing is carried out at the lowest available speed because the aim here is to obtain a uniform distribution of the ingredients and, at the same time, maintain to a maximum degree the foam structure of the whites.

The importance of the foam structure to angel food quality was extensively studied by Barmore (1936). He observed that maximum cake volume is obtained when the egg whites are whipped to a foam with a specific gravity in the range between 0.15 and 0.17. Foams with specific gravities higher than 0.17 incorporate too little air to yield light cakes, while those with specific gravities lower than 0.15 lack stability and extensibility and, hence, undergo excessive shrinkage during baking. As pointed out by this investigator (Barmore 1936), two opposite factors come into play as the beating of the egg whites proceeds: "One is the tendency to increase the cake volume because of the increasing amount of air incorporated; the second, the tendency to decrease the cake volume because of the decreased foam stability. When the egg white foam specific gravity is between 0.17 and 0.15, these two effects are approximately balanced."

Whole egg, egg yolk method (sponge cake). Foam cakes that use whole eggs or egg yolks depend on the ability of yolk to form a stable foam and thus aerate the batter. Yolk contains high levels of lipids present in an emulsified state. The additional presence of protein and lecithin endows the yolk solids with unusual extensibility conducive to foam formation. When whole eggs are beaten, air is occluded in the form of minute cells surrounded by films of yolk substance.

The mixing of sponge cake batters may be carried out in a variety of ways. In some instances, bakers prefer to separate the whites and yolks of eggs and beat them separately with a portion of the sugar to the desired specific gravity before recombining them — the aim is to attain maximum batter volume. The most common procedure, however, is to beat the eggs, which have been tempered to about 27°C (80°F), with a wire whip or blade beater at medium speed. To counteract the tendency of whites to over-whip, sugar may be added at the outset of mixing or in a slow stream during beating. After the egg foam has reached the proper specific volume, the liquid and the flour are folded in as lightly as possible to avoid a breakdown of the foam structure. Utensils used in the production of sponge cake batters must be free of all traces of fat or else the foaming ability of the eggs will be impaired. In so-called "short" sponge cakes, in which either shortening or butter is incorporated, the fat must be added at the final mixing stage to minimize the loss in volume.

One variation of the foam cake process adds the shortening in the form of melted butter. Another method melts the butter in hot milk and adds the mixture after incorporation of the flour. Some bakers supplement the leavening power of eggs by using whole eggs and yolks in the base batter and then adding whipped egg whites during the final stage of mixing. This separated egg sponge method is noted as particularly beneficial for cakes that will be rolled during finishing (Suas 2009).

7.A.1.c. Continuous cake batter processes

To achieve high-volume production, many wholesale bakers adopted continuous shearing-style mixers. The process used by these systems involves shearing, dispersing, emulsifying and aerating actions.Preparation of the slurry-style batter is a relatively simple process and is usually accomplished in an automatic slurry mixer (**Figure 7.05**) into which all the dry and wet ingredients are automatically metered, followed by the manual addition of the shortening and minor ingredients. The ingredients are blended into a homogeneous fluid mixture with little or no aeration within less than 90 seconds. The finished slurry then transfers to the holding tank that feeds the continuous aerating mixer.

Figure 7.05. Automated slurry mixing saves labor, avoids ingredient loss and enables clean-in-place sanitation. (The Peerless Group)

The slurry can also be supplied by a standard vertical batch mixer. In this process, the shortening, sugar and half of the liquid are placed in the bowl and creamed for 2 minutes at low speed, followed by the addition of the flour and eggs and continued mixing for 3 minutes at medium speed. Slurry preparation is completed by the addition of the remaining liquid and mixing for 1 to 2 minutes, again with a minimum of air occlusion (Bonavia 1967). The homogenous slurry is then transferred by a large-volume pump to the holding tank of the continuous mixer.

The continuous mixer has a self-contained pump that draws the slurry from the holding tank into the mixing chamber at a controlled rate. Batters are subjected to shearing action within the closed mixers by being forced through mixing heads with teeth configured in a stator-and-rotor design. Here, the slurry is homogenized and emulsified by the rotor, revolving at speeds of 145 to 300 rpm, and aerated by the incorporation of purified air compressed up to 135 psi. The pump speed, rotor speed, air flow and back pressure are all under close control that is frequently computerized. The specific gravity of the batter leaving the continuous mixer can be automatically controlled by a densitometer that continuously monitors the degree of aeration and adjusts the air flow accordingly. Batter temperatures, which would normally rise by 1.6 to 5.5 C° (3 to 10 F°) as a result of rotor friction, are controlled either by circulating cold water through a jacket surrounding the mixing chamber or by an appropriate adjustment of the rotor speed. Most continuous mixing units operate automatically once the proper parameters have been established.

Rotor speed affects the size of air cells in batters prepared in a continuous rotor-stator mixer, according to Hanselmann and Windhab (1999), who worked with food foams such as mousses using whey protein isolate as the foaming agent. An increase of the rotor speed from 600 to 2,000 rpm resulted in a decrease of bubble size by a factor of about 4.5 for a low-viscosity liquid. For highly viscous liquids, the decrease of bubble size in the same speed range was only 20%.

Some comparisons of the mixing times required to prepare aerated batters in standard vertical cake mixers and the slurries for continuous processing are shown in **Table 7.1**. Also included are the respective batch weights based on equal volumes and their corresponding specific gravities to point out some of the differences that exist between the continuous and the conventional cake-mixing systems. Continu-

Table 7.1. Comparisons of Conventional Cake Batters and Slurries

Cake variety	Batter weight		Specific gravity		Mixing time	
	Batter (lb)	Slurry (lb)	Batter	Slurry	Batter (minutes)	Slurry (minutes)
Angel food	212	580	0.30	0.82	18	4.5
Sponge	459	670	0.65	0.95	18	4.0
Chiffon	248	670	0.35	0.95	20	5.0
Pound	496	672	0.71	0.98	17	5.0
Chocolate layer	637	700	0.93	0.99	15	4.0
Yellow layer	637	672	0.90	0.98	15	4.0
Devil's food	670	785	0.95	1.11	17	5.0

(Bonavia 1963)

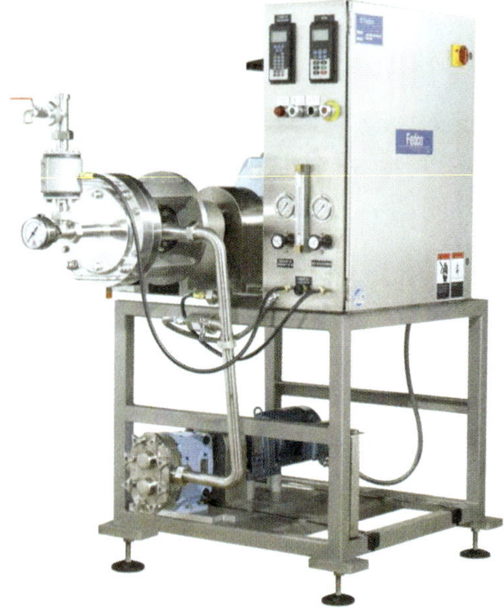

Figure 7.06. Mixers that prepare cake batters by continuous aeration technology use controlled, pressurized direct injection of air to control the batter's specific gravity.
(The Peerless Group, Fedco)

ous aerating mixers of the sort shown in **Figure 7.06** control the specific gravity of batter by direct injection of pressurized air.

Considered rheologically, the viscosity of cake batter controls the final volume of the finished cake. The most important parameters affecting the rheological properties of cake batters are type and concentration of ingredients, level of air incorporation, and temperature according to Sahin (2008), who summarized extensively the influences of these factors.

7.A.1.d. Cake processing conditions
7.A.1.d.i. Batter temperature

The temperature attained during batter mixing has a marked impact on final cake quality. Temperature affects the viscosity of the batter, which, in turn, influences both batter aeration and batter stability. Batters must have a suitable consistency in order to achieve optimum specific gravities and exhibit adequate stability during normal floor or processing time. With shortening-based cakes, high temperatures render the batter excessively fluid by softening the fat phase, while low temperatures have the opposite effect. According to Prouty (1965), the general temperature, specific gravity and pH ranges shown in **Table 7.2** for specific cake types represent good practice.

Batters of high-ratio cakes (also called "high-sugar cakes") tend to be thinner in consistency than low-sugar batters and thus require greater care in arriving at the most effective temperature as established by prior trials. Rees (1971) recommended processing temperatures for high-sugar batters of 18 to 21°C (65 to 70°F) when the batters are mixed in standard vertical mixers and of 16 to 18°C (60 to 65°F) when prepared in continuous mixers because the latter tend to generate more heat during mixing.

Temperatures of batters affect the activity of chemical leaveners. Too warm, and the leaveners will release their gases prematurely, resulting in flat, low-volume cakes. Cold batters delay the leavening activity until late in the baking process, thus prompting undesirable peaks and cracks in the top crust.

7.A.1.d.ii. Specific gravity

Batter specific gravity has long been recognized as a primary determinant of the tenderness, grain, texture and volume of the finished cake. The more air incorporated into the batter, the lower its specific gravity. Because the specific gravity of a batter is essentially the result of the mixing action and its duration, the importance of close control of batter mixing time is readily apparent. For example, Ellinger and Shappeck (1963) showed that when the batters of yellow layer, white layer and devil's food cakes are over-mixed, the resulting cakes are excessively fragile and their crusts tend to develop cracks and fissures. Moreover, over-mixed layer cakes produce dense crumb strata along the bottom as a result of collapsed air cells. The cakes also tend to form peaked top crusts, which makes the preparation of 2-layer cakes difficult.

Whenever changes are made in the character of the flour, shortening type, mixing operation or equipment design, good practice dictates that the batter specific gravity be re-determined to ensure that it remains within the optimum range. Because the viscosities of liquid and plastic shortenings differ, as noted in Volume I, Chapter 2, Part A, they have a marked influence on batter specific gravity, as do emulsifiers. Even in the absence of intentional ingredient or operational changes, the baker should periodically measure the specific gravity of batters.

Table 7.2. Recommended Temperature, Specific Gravity and pH Levels in Various Cake Batters				
Batter type	Temperature		Specific gravity	pH
	°F	°C		
Sponge	92 to 94	33 to 34	0.46 to 0.48	7.3 to 7.6
Yellow layer	70 to 72	21 to 22	0.94 to 0.97	7.2 to 7.8
White layer	70 to 72	21 to 22	0.95 to 0.97	7.2 to 7.8
Devil's food	72 to 74	22 to 23	0.95 to 0.97	8.8 to 9.2
Pound	58 to 60	14 to 16	0.83 to 0.85	6.6 to 7.1

(Prouty 1965)

Specific gravity is the ratio between the weight of a given volume of cake batter and the weight of the same volume of water. The specific gravity of water is 1.0. A properly mixed batter contains air so its specific gravity tends to be less than that of water, even though it may contain a considerable amount of solutes, especially dissolved sugar.

Determination of specific gravity is simple and rapid, requiring only a measuring cup for the batter, a straight-edged spatula and a scale. The two preliminary weighings — of the empty cup (its tare weight) and of the water held by the cup when completely full — need only be done once. The weight of the batter held by the container is determined by carefully filling the cup with batter so it rises slightly above the rim, striking off the excess with the spatula and weighing the container and batter. The weight of the batter itself is then determined by subtracting the weight of the empty cup from the total weight. The batter specific gravity can then be calculated by dividing the weight of the batter by the weight of an equal volume of water, or

Specific gravity = weight (batter) ÷ weight (equal volume of water)

Many continuous cake mixing units are equipped with automatic densitometers (**Figure 7.07**) that continually monitor the specific gravity of the batter and correct for deviations from the norm with appropriate adjustments (Stevens 1962).

European bakers use a slightly different method, termed "batter density." This measurement is determined by weighing a known volume of batter and calculating the grams per milliliter (Suas 2009).

Seelinger (1956) investigated the effect of temperature on the specific gravities of cake batters during the creaming stage of mixing. Three temperature levels were employed: 10, 21 and 29°C (50, 70 and 85°F). Batters for pound cake, yellow layer cake and white layer cake produced the lowest specific gravities in the short-

Figure 7.07. The triangular component (right) automatically measures the specific gravity of batters prepared in this continuous mixer.
(E.T. Oakes)

est mixing time at 21°C (70°F). At 10°C (50°F), batters for only pound cake and white layer cake achieved the same low specific gravities after extended mixing. Batters maintained at 29°C (80°F) failed in all instances to yield satisfactory specific gravities. On baking, the batters mixed at 21°C (70°F) produced the best volume in every instance. Adjustment of the temperature to the optimum level during the final mixing stage did not restore the cake volume to that of the control cake mixed at a constant 21°C (70°F).

7.A.1.d.iii. pH

A cake with an excessively low pH value will exhibit an acidic, biting flavor, but too high a pH level will impart a soda or soapy taste to the cake. Crumb and crust colors, particularly in chocolate and devil's food cakes, are markedly influenced by the cake's pH value, and optimum cake volume, grain and texture are achieved only at appropriate pH levels. As the pH of a cake increases, its grain tends to become coarser, with thicker cell walls, while its volume increases. Conversely, as pH is lowered, cake crumb becomes progressively closer and finer, and the cake volume is reduced (Ash and Colmey 1973).

Cake pH is established by its major ingredients and by its leavening system (**Table 7.3**). While ingredients such as sugar, shortening and properly balanced baking powders are without effect on pH, others either lower it or raise it. The ingredients that tend to lower the pH of cake batters generally include syrups, flour, fruit and fruit juices, milk, buttermilk, certain cake emulsifiers and leavening acids. Among the ingredients that raise the pH of cake batters are cocoa, both natural and dutched, egg products, sodium bicarbonate and possibly water.

In practice, the pH of batters is controlled by varying the amount of leavening agents. Thus, if the pH is on the acidic side, corrective downward adjustments are made in the level of leavening acids, and if alkaline pH values are encountered, the level of sodium bicarbonate is reduced correspondingly. Care must be taken, however, to properly balance the amount of sodium bicarbonate and leavening acid so that no significant amounts of either remain unreacted in the baked cake, and that the crumb pH will fall within the neutral range of 6.5 to 7.5. In general, the flavor of a cake is at its optimum at a neutral or slightly acid pH level. Exceptions to this general rule are angel food cake, which needs a low pH for maximum egg white functionality, and chocolate and devil's food cakes, which require an alkaline pH for maximum flavor and appropriate color (Ash and Colmey 1973).

7.A.2. Cookie mixing

The particular mixing method employed for cookie doughs depends partly on the type of equipment available to the baker and partly on the ultimate nature of the end product. (It is worth noting that what North Americans call "cookies" go by the name "biscuits" in the UK and other parts of the English-speaking world.) The three basic methods are known as single stage, multiple stage and continuous process (Lehmann et al. 1994). Cookie doughs are much more tolerant to mixing than yeast-leavened doughs because the flour proteins, present at 8 to 10% in the grain, form only a minimum amount of gluten.

Single stage. Satisfactory results can be achieved by the single-stage mixing method in which all ingredients are placed in the mixing bowl at one time. Put the

Table 7.3. Typical Cake pH Values

Variety	pH range
Angel food	5.2 to 6.0
Yellow layer	6.7 to 7.5
White layer	7.0 to 7.5
Chocolate	7.5 to 8.0
Devils food	8.0 to 9.0

(Ash and Colmey 1973)

flour in the mixer bowl first and add the minor ingredients on top to assure uniform distribution during mixing. Particulates (chocolate drops, nutmeats, fruit pieces, fabricated bits) should be added only near the end of mixing to ensure they retain their piece integrity. Estimated mixing time in a horizontal mixer is 2 to 4 minutes and 20 to 30% longer in vertical mixers.

Multiple stage. The most commonly used commercial procedure, the multiple-stage method first creams the shortening with the sugar, invert syrup, salt, flavors and other minor ingredients, then adds the eggs and other liquid ingredients while mixing is continued, and finally incorporate the flour and leaveners. Coarser materials such as nutmeats, chocolate chips, raisins and similar particulates are added to the dough at the very end, with just enough additional mixing to ensure their uniform distribution. Multiple-stage mixing incorporates more air into the dough than does the single-stage method. Estimated mixing time in a horizontal mixer is 10 to 18 minutes and 20 to 30% longer in vertical mixers.

According to Velzen (1963), uniform dough temperatures are essential if uniform cookies are to be obtained by these processes. Mixing temperatures are preferably maintained at about 21°C (70°F) and the mixing speed should be held to a slow rate of 25 to 35 rpm to minimize the dangers of over-mixing. The mixing time, which will normally range from 5 to 10 minutes, is affected by factors such as flour type, product variety, dough consistency and temperature, mixing speed and batch size. The temperature rise during single-stage mixing is higher than in multiple-stage methods because the dough mass is larger and mix time longer.

Continuous process. Continuous mixing methods applied to cookie dough preparation were evaluated by Kulp and Olewnik (1984) and described by Lehmann et al. (1994). The twin-shaft system incorporated a variety of flat and helical paddles, with flat styles promoting mixing action and helical designs for throughput. Ports along the length of the mixer allow addition of ingredients at different points in the process. Mixer speeds varied from 65 to 115 rpm. Fixed peg and rotating stator systems have also been used to prepare cookie doughs. Mixing time is 1 to 2 minutes, although residence time will differ according to cookie type (Lehmann et al. 1994).

Aeration of cookie doughs is an important function of mixing because this action nucleates the dough with the air bubbles required for proper leavening. The void fraction governs the mechanical and fracture properties affecting processing, packaging and structural development. Sheeting of biscuit (cookie) dough degasses it somewhat, with gentle sheeting removing more gas than severe sheeting (Brijwani et al. 2008). These same researchers experimented with mixing cookie doughs under different atmospheres and learned that mixing under higher pressure and/or with carbon dioxide in the mixer's headspace gave softer doughs that spread more during baking but lifted more as well, resulting in thicker biscuits (cookies). The larger biscuits had lower densities and softer texture than when doughs were mixed at low pressure under nitrogen.

Some cookie doughs require floor time, but most do not. Such resting periods of 10 to 30 minutes at plant-ambient temperature (24 to 29°C, or 75 to 85°F) allow time for dough ingredients to hydrate, sugar to dissolve and chemical leavening to start evolving gas. Floor time can reduce stickiness in wire-cut products and enhance the release of rotary moulded items. Batter-type cookies made with emulsifiers will also benefit from rest time.

Faridi (1990) examined cookie and cracker processing with a view to the rheological properties involved. He observed that cookie doughs lack the extensibility and elasticity characteristic of bread doughs, but their relatively high quantities of fat and sugar give a plasticity and cohesiveness to the dough without the formation of a gluten network. The lack of elasticity in cookie doughs mean they will spread rather than shrink during baking.

A cookie dough is more of a plastic mass than a bread dough and is held together mainly by the cohesive character of the shortening. During mixing, the aqueous phase and fat compete for the surfaces of the flour particles. When fat coats the flour prior to hydration — as is desirable for cookie doughs — gluten formation is inhibited. Faridi (1990) observed that the rheological properties of cookie doughs reflect those in the solid phase of the shortening in the formulation. The temperature of the dough affects its physical properties, and for best results, it should be kept below the upper limit of the plastic range of the shortening, usually between 21 and 27°C (70 and 80°F) or lower. The rheological methods, equations and interpretations of such measurements involving cookies were extensively summarized by Yener (2008), while Sablani (2008) reviewed the physical and thermal properties of cakes, cookies and other sweet goods.

7.A.3. Pie dough mixing

Pie doughs are normally prepared by a 2-stage procedure and with the use of a vertical double-arm mixer. In the first stage, the flour and shortening are blended together, and in the second stage, the water is added, with mixing continued until the dough holds together. The actual mixing method adopted depends on the crust character desired: mealy, moderately flaky, flaky and long-flaky, the latter being produced by a sheeting method similar to that used for puff pastry. Mixing procedures that will produce each of these various types of crusts have been discussed by Knuepfner (1960) and are summarized here. Zelch et al. (2004) recently reviewed formulation and preparation of pie crusts.

Mealy texture. Mealy crusts are achieved by thoroughly blending the flour and shortening into a paste in which the flour particles are almost completely coated with the fat. Chilled water, equal to about 25% of flour weight and containing the salt, sugar and other additives, is then added and mixed in lightly to yield a dough with a wet, grainy appearance. Resting the dough at 16°C (60°F) for periods ranging from several hours to overnight will (a) ensure complete water absorption, (b) enzymatically modify the dough, (c) reduce shrinkage and toughness in the baked crust and (d) minimize its soaking tendency. Flours intended for use in mealy crusts may be somewhat stronger than those specified for flaky crusts.

Moderately flaky texture. For the production of semi-flaky crusts, a flour-shortening paste is prepared as above, but with only one-half of the flour, creating a paste-like dough. The remainder of the flour is added, and mixing continues until a lumpy consistency results. The water and the minor ingredients are added next, and the dough is mixed until absorption is completed. The same crust character can be had by combining all the flour with the shortening but stopping the blending operation once the shortening has become uniformly dispersed in the form of very small, discrete particles, after which the water is added and mixing continued until the dough holds together. While the dough may be mixed out for immediate use, general preference is to redice the mixing time somewhat and give the dough floor time similar to that of a mealy crust, as outlined above.

Flakey texture. Flaky crusts are obtained when the flour and shortening are combined to a point where the blend resembles "very coarsely ground corn meal mixed with kernels of uncooked rice" (Knuepfner 1960). The fat must be of such consistency that it will not smear into the flour. The temperature of both ingredients should be within the range of 13 to 16°C (55 to 60°F) during the blending operation. After the chilled water has been added, mixing continues until a cohesive dough results.

Long-flake texture. Doughs for the long-flake type crust require a rather firm shortening that is cut into the flour only to an extent that results in the formation of walnut-sized clumps of fat. The water is then added, and the dough mixed just enough to allow it to hold together. The dough is then divided into pieces that can be readily handled, rolled to a thickness of about 2 in., given a 3-fold as in puff pastry production and then rolled out again to a 2-in. thickness. This process is repeated twice. The final dough sheet is then rested in a refrigerator or a cool room for several hours or overnight. This procedure yields a crust with large, tender flakes and excellent color.

These two factors exert a telling effect on the quality of pie dough: the extent of mixing and the control of temperature. Over-mixing should be avoided because it will result in excessive gluten development that ultimately imparts toughness to the crust and causes shrinkage during baking.

The final temperature of pie dough should range from 13 to 16°C (55 to 60°F). Cool ingredient temperatures are essential to prevent softening of the shortening and excessive oiling of the flour particles. Good practice calls for flour and fat temperatures no higher than 16°C (60°F) during the initial blending operation. Chilled water will also help achieve proper temperature ranges. Zelch et al. (2004) cautioned against adding chunks of ice to pie doughs because the short mix times are insufficient to melt the ice. The result would be high-moisture spots that interfere with machining and blisters in the final crust.

It is inadvisable to mix out doughs to a point where they are ready for immediate processing. Better results will generally follow when dough mixing is kept to a minimum, followed by a rest to permit the dough to hydrate and mellow. This resting period can be as long as several hours or overnight. Such chilling also hardens the fat, reducing the chance it could liquefy during subsequent processing.

7.B. Depositing

7.B.1. Cake depositing

Once cake batter has been mixed, it should be deposited into cake pans and conveyed to the oven with a minimum loss of time. The need to process the batter without delay is because the leavening agents, having entered into solution during mixing, have begun to interact and are evolving carbon dioxide gas. In more fluid batters, this gas tends to rise upwards, and the small bubbles coalesce into larger cells that have greater buoyancy. There is an inevitable escape of carbon dioxide gas from the batter as it rests in the open hopper of the depositor, as well as a coarsening of the cell structure with the passage of time.

Such loss of aeration and its associated detrimental effects are avoided when using manifold-type depositors or those that are enclosed and operate under pressure. Both styles avoid exposure of the batter to the open atmosphere. These depositors are normally limited in their application to continuous cake mixers in which the mixing action is carried out in pressurized mixing chambers. In cases where the batters are mixed in open vertical cake mixers, the use of automatic depositors is desirable because such machines can be adjusted to efficiently and accurately deposit predetermined amounts of batter into the cake pans with a minimum of batter handling.

7.B.2. Cookie depositing and forming

Cookies are formed by three general methods: (a) cutting or stamping their shapes from sheeted dough; (b) moulding the dough by means of dies engraved in a cylinder and then extracting the dough pieces and (c) extruding the dough through variously-shaped dies and either cutting or depositing the individual pieces on a baking sheet or oven belt. Each of these methods requires dough that possesses certain physical properties suiting it for the kind of processing entailed with each method.

From a very general standpoint, the doughs or batters intended for extruded deposit or wire-cut cookies are relatively soft so they yield the desired high spread during baking. Doughs destined for rotary moulding are mixed relatively stiff and plastic, have no elasticity and contain high fat and sugar contents to ensure good cohesive properties that will facilitate the release from the die moulds onto the canvas apron. Finally, doughs that are to be cut or stamped out require adequate tensile strength and elasticity so they can be sheeted to a uniform thickness without tearing.

Sheet and cut. The sheeting and laminating process that transforms bulk cookie dough into dough sheets and laminates is similar to the methods that create laminated pastry products, described in Chapter 6, Part E. This technique also is used for preparation of hard biscuits and digestives.

The dough is subjected to a series of reductions, sometimes interspersed with fat application and folding where lamination is employed, until it attains the desired uniform thickness. The dough sheet is then fed on a conveyor belt into the stamping and cutting machine of either the reciprocating or the rotary type.

Rotary moulded. Rotary moulded cookie doughs tend to be stiff due to their low water and low fat content, yet they exhibit little to no stickiness. These characteristics facilitate the rotary moulding process in which cookie dough is pressed into dies engraved in brass, bronze or stainless steel cylinders. The roller turns against the bottom of the feed hopper to pull dough into the dies. After it rotates past the hopper, the dough is extracted by a canvas belt or a rubber-coated roll and transferred to the oven band. The extraction roller may also feature a non-stick surface. If doughs are too soft (too much fat), they will not release properly from the die and will tend to lose their shape and imprint during baking. Likewise, doughs with too much water or the wrong sugar will be sticky and not release well from the moulds. The individual components of the rotary moulder are diagrammed in **Figure 7.08**, while the actual machine is illustrated in **Figure 7.09**.

Deposited. Deposited cookies are made using soft, rich doughs, often having a batter-like consistency. They flow under the influence of feed rollers through so-called die cups directly onto the baking surface, which may be either a cookie sheet or an oven band. These dies or nozzles may oscillate as well as raise and lower with respect to the baking surface, thus creating particular cookie shapes, and they can be configured with ridges and other features to mimic hand-forming methods that use pastry bags.

Wire cut. Wire-cut forming processes require firmer doughs than deposited cookies and softer than those use for rotary moulded products. Wire-cut doughs often contain high levels of particulates such as chocolate drops, nuts, raisins or inclusions. Dough is extruded and cut off by a fast-moving wire that moves against the bottom of the die orifices. The wire-cut process is less sensitive to dough temperatures than the rotary method, but doughs should be kept within reasonable limits to prevent fat melting.

Other methods. Patty-making systems have been adapted to deposit and split "hockey puck" shaped frozen cookie dough pieces. Also, encrusting methods allow creation of internally filled and multicolored patterned doughs — this process enabled development of the dual-textured doughs responsible for "soft and crispy" cookies. Depositors can be configured to extrude continuous bands of doughs. Set up as co-extruders, these systems can handle multiple streams of dough and/or fillings, creating filled bars and multicolored or patterned cookies (**Figure 7.10**).

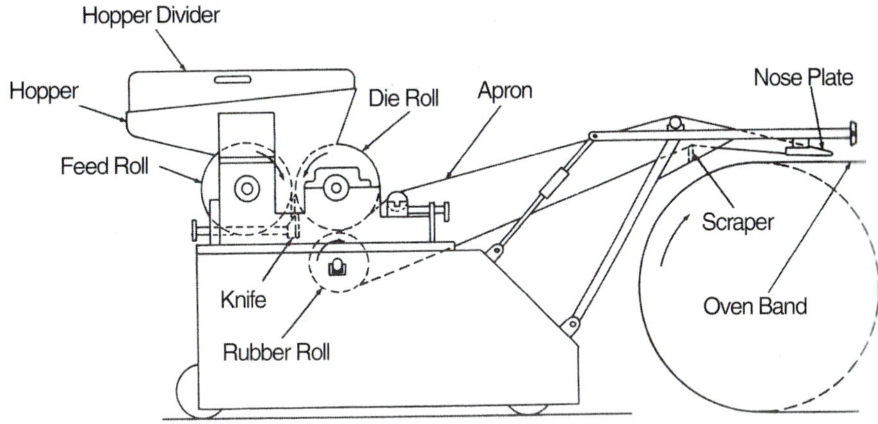

Figure 7.08. Schematic of a rotary cookie moulding machine shows the relationship between the dough hopper, die rolls, apron and the take-off sysem. (Weidenmiller Co.)

Figure 7.09. Example of a rotary cookie moulding machine shows the relatively long extraction apron that feeds cookies to the oven belt. (Weidenmiller Co.)

7.B.3. Pie dough makeup

The simplest procedure for making up pies involves dividing the pie dough into individual, rounded dough pieces and then pressing them by a manually- or mechanically-operated pie press into dough sheets that conform to the pie plate shape for both bottom and top crusts. This procedure is best applied only to small-volume production, and it greatly alters the character of the dough, producing essentially a mealy rather than a flaky crust.

Rotary methods enable high-speed production (**Figure 7.11**) and sheet the pie dough by cross-rolling it. The process creates one or two long strips that can be divided into individual rectangles that drop into forming plates and pie pans (Engstrom 1981).

Dough thickness must remain consistent because variations may result in uneven baking. Likewise, stretching of the dough should be avoided to reduce the risk of shrinkage during baking (Zelch et al. 2004).

For optimum product quality, certain dough handling controls must be observed. In manual or semi-automatic operations, for example, care must be taken in scaling so that individual dough pieces conform as closely as possible to the size of the pie. The idea is to (a) reduce the amount of trim dough produced by over-scaling and (b) avoid the need for stretching the sheeted dough

Figure 7.10. Consumers want affordable cookies with a difference such as these made with sweetened dried cranberrries. (Ocean Spray Cranberries ITG)

Figure 7.11. Straight-line and rotary (shown here) systems enable rapid preparation of filled and topped pies. (Colborne Foodbotics)

in the case of under-scaling. The recovered trim or scrap dough that results from over-scaling may be incorporated as rework back into fresh doughs, but in an excessive amount, it will have an adverse effect on crust quality. Many bakers reincorporate scrap dough only into the bottom crusts because they believe any change in texture would be less noticeable there.

Dusting flour used in pie dough sheeting should be a soft wheat flour, and its application should be held to a minimum. One recommended dusting mixture consists of a 7:1 blend of pastry flour and nonfat dry milk. The milk solids are said to counteract the possible toughening effect of the flour protein. Moreover, they enhance desirable crust browning during baking.

Docking the crust dough should produce vents large enough to persist through the baking stage but not so big that they allow filling to seep through the crust. When baking unfilled shells, a second pie tin may be used to cover the crust as it goes through the oven. The second tin provides a sandwiching effect helping to prevent shrinkage or formation of blisters as well as reducing maintaining a more even thickness (Zelch et al. 2004).

Top crusts are usually washed with an egg wash, a dilute milk-and-egg solution or melted butter to promote a rich golden color on baking. Excessively concentrated wash solutions should be avoided because they tend to impart a heavy, artificial-looking glaze to the crust.

7.C. Heat Treatment

7.C.1. Baking

7.C.1.a. Cake baking

The optimum baking conditions for cake baking are determined by factors such as sweetener level of the formula, amount of milk used in the batter, fluidity of the batter, pan size, etc. As a general rule, batters with high sugar contents require somewhat lower baking temperatures than leaner formulations. Large cakes normally call for lower baking temperatures and longer baking times. The baking time is inversely related to the baking temperature: the higher the oven temperature, the shorter is the oven time, but the relationship is not strictly linear and has limits to how much one can be changed at the expense of the other. Good practice dictates using just enough time to ensure a thorough bake, or else evaporative losses will exceed accepted norms, impairing the product's shelf life.

Trimbo et al. (1966) investigated how cake batters flow when baked in pans. **Figure 7.12** reveals batter flowing up from the bottom and along the outer edge of the pan, when it turned toward the center and across the top of the cake, and then downward again. This batter flow results from the natural convection currents that are caused by differences in batter density produced by lateral and vertical temperature gradients within the heated batter. **Figure 7.13** depicts the lateral flow of batter along the bottom and middle of the pan.

Representative cake baking temperatures and times are shown in **Table 7.4**. The indicated ranges in both temperature and time for individual cake varieties provide the needed margins for adjustments in both factors to conform to the particular scaling weight of the product. In most instances, the maximum internal temperature of the cakes remains at a uniform 98.3 to 98.9°C (209 to 210°F). However, in some cases, the internal temperature can exceed the normal boiling point of water — 100°C (212°F) — because the dissolved sugars have raised the boiling point.

Cakes are generally baked in ovens that use indirect-fired heating methods. The thinking is that the products of combustion generated by direct-fired heating may affect the delicate flavors of cake products.

Cooling is essential before cakes can be depanned because their structure can be quite fragile right out of the oven. If "drop shocked" (dropping the hot cake rather sharply) immediately after baking, the cake's cell walls can crack, permitting air to enter as the crumb cools.

It is important to remove batter and foam cake items from pans 10 to 15 minutes after leaving the oven; angel food cakes can be cooled in their pans for longer periods. If left in sheet pans too long, thin cakes can dry too much. If left in walled pans, the cake may shrink from the pan edges, sweat (release moisture) and re-absorb the water, leaving a too-moist edge.

The rheology of cake baking continues to get extensive study. For example, Yasukawa et al. (1986) examined the viscoelastic properties of batter in a model cake system and noted that the initial structural development, which occurred below 83°C (181°F), was due to starch gelatinization.

Examining the shear modulus of cake batters during baking, Mizukoshi (1986) confirmed the tendency of sugar concentration to retard structural development but to increase finished cake volume (**Figure 7.14**). Flour and fat caused increased shear moduli, but water, sugar and oil decreased them.

7.C.1.b. Cookie baking

Baking temperatures for cookies normally range from 182 to 218°C (360 to 425°F), with actual temperature depending on dough composition and the weight and shape of the dough pieces. Baking times also are variable within a range of 8 to 12 minutes for average weight cookies. Except for the soft varieties, the moisture content of baked conventional wire-cut cookies is generally about 2.5 to 3.0%, where water tends to be bound rather tightly, also the level

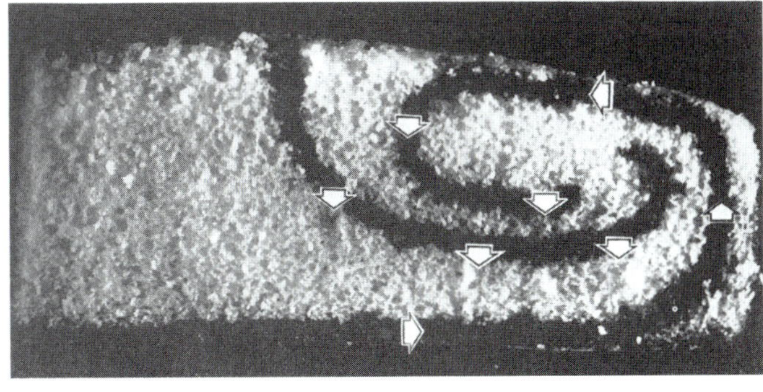

Figure 7.12. Partial cross-section of a white layer cake shows the flow pattern of the batter during the oven stage. (Trimbo et al. 1966)

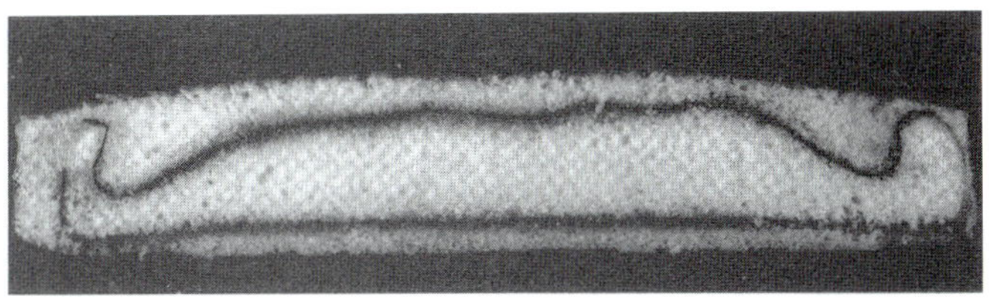

Figure 7.13. In white layer cakes made with normal water content, batter flows laterally across the bottom of the pan, turning up at the pan edges. (Trimbo et al. 1966)

Table 7.4. Baking Temperatures and Times for Cakes

Cake variety	Temperature		Time
	°F	°C	(minutes)
Pound cake	325 to 365	163 to 185	50 to 65
Layer cake	365 to 375	185 to 190	20 to 25
Loaf cake	350 to 360	177 to 182	35 to 50
Sponge cake	390 to 420	199 to 216	10 to 20
Angel food	350 to 400	177 to 204	30 to 45
Chiffon cake	350 to 375	177 to 190	30 to 45
Cup cake	375 to 400	190 to 204	15 to 20

(Harrel and Thelen 1959)

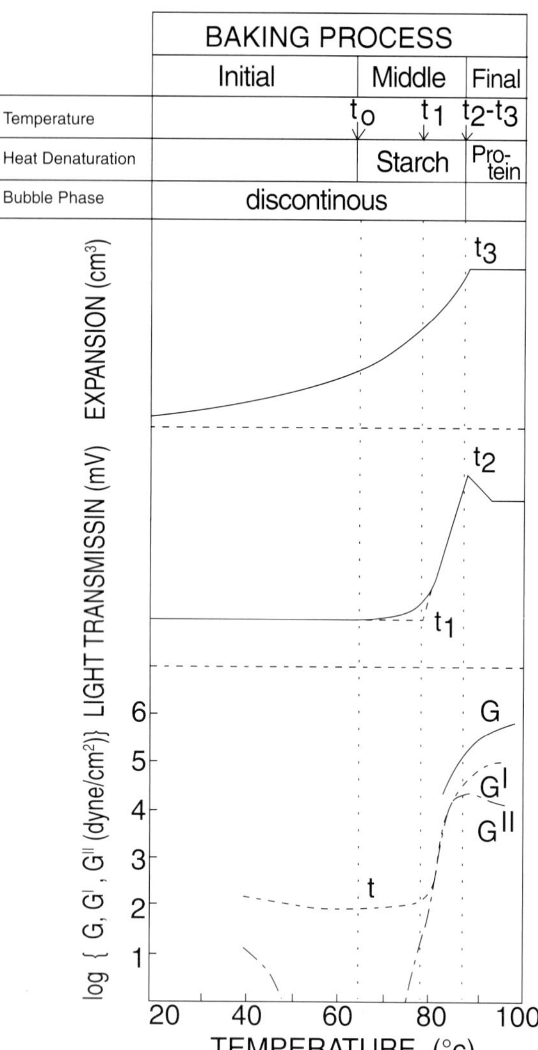

Figure 7.14. Cake batters reveal rheological transitions during baking, including changes in expansion, light transmission and storage (G') and loss (G") moduli measurements. (Mizukoshi 1986)

typical for rotary moulded cookies.

As with cake products, ovens configured for cookie baking normally use indirect-fired heating methods. Temperature profiling of cookie ovens according to cookie variety was extensively discussed by Lehmann et al. (1994).

The baking properties of cookie doughs are influenced by their large quantities of fats and sugars. Cookie baking involves crust formation, melting of shortening in the dough, conversion of water to steam, gas expansion and the escape of carbon dioxide, other gases and steam, according to Tireki (2008), who succinctly summarized the effects of baking on cookie doughs.

Crust formation begins at 28°C (82°F) and proceeds quickly at 38°C (97°F). During the first 2 zones of a 4-zone oven, the moisture content of the dough and the humidity within the oven determine the crust's thickness and elasticity. If the crust thickens excessively and/or loses its elasticity, the cookie will burst during baking and leavening action is suppressed, affecting texture formation. Shortening melts along the range of temperatures represented by its solid fat index. Low-melting components seep into the cookie's structure, but most shortening pockets remain at their original position in the dough, contributing to the structure of the finished product.

The gelatinization process for wheat starch generally takes place in the presence of water at 50 to 55°C (122 to 131°F), but in cookie doughs, free water is limited and most is bound, either to insoluble flour components or by the sugar. These factors delay the gelatinization of starch until a higher temperature is reached, about 90 to 95°C (194 to 203°F) (Hoseney 1980). In low-moisture products such as cookies, the gelatinization and irreversible swelling do not take place or are severely restricted.

Fully developed gluten is not present in optimally mixed cookie doughs due to limitations of water and competition for that water by the sugar and starch, but Kulp (1994) argued that the hydration of both sugars and flour proteins are involved in controlling cookie spread.

Gluten and other proteins derived from milk and eggs begin to coagulate at 63°C (145°F), which adds strength to the cookie structure, and as heat denatures the proteins, they become less extensible, fixing the cell walls in place. Water contributes steam, which expands the piece. As Tireki (2008) noted, expansion due to steam formation is much greater than expansion due to carbon dioxide or ammonia, even though carbon dioxide is generated much earlier in the baking process. Chemical leavening proceeds to open up the mass, developing the crumb texture. Some of these leavening gases escape during baking and may cause the structure to collapse. The gases retained help stabilize structure through the final stages of baking and cooling.

The caramelization of sugar takes place around 149°C (300°F), which, along with the Maillard reaction, gives cookies their brown crust color.

Cookie spread. Among the effects of baking cookie dough is the increase in size known as spread, caused by the viscous flow of the dough under the influence of heat. Spread is affected by factors such as formulation, nature of ingredients, processing methods and conditions of baking.

As the dough temperature increases in the oven, the shortening melts, allowing the dough to flow until stopped by starch gelatinization. During mixing, part of the water in the dough, contributed by eggs and other liquid ingredients (including the water naturally present in butter), is bound by flour components such as damaged starch, pentosans and proteins. The rest dissolves the sugar and forms a syrup. Cookie spread is positively related to the amount of sugar syrup in the dough. The higher the level of syrup, the slacker the dough and the greater the spread.

Uniformity in cookie size has major significance for packaging because cookies that spread excessively during baking will present problems in filling standard packages. On the other hand, cookies with restricted spread will exhibit increased cookie heights and yield either slack package fills or not fit into the package at all.

Because of these potential packaging problems, the factors that influence cookie spread have undergone extensive investigation, often with variable results. According to Fuhr (1962), the ratios of free moisture and sugar in the dough constitute the principal factors that control the spread. Any ingredient or processing condition that reduces the dough moisture that would otherwise be available for dissolving the sugar will restrict the spread. Among the former, abnormally high levels of damaged starch (Yamazaki 1962) or soluble pentosans (Sollars 1959) have been shown to limit spread. When flour is extracted with water-saturated n-butanol to remove its lipids, it will yield cookies with greatly reduced spread as a result of its increased water-binding capacity (Cole et al. 1960). Yamazaki (1953) used the water-retention capacity of flour as the basis of a test to predict the flour's cookie spread factor.

Other factors that influence spread include the flour's protein content and protein quality, granulation, viscosity, extent of chlorination, the level of sugar in the dough, extent of mixing, dough and oven temperatures, leavening and the pH level. Speaking rather generally, ingredients that function as structure builders will usually act to reduce cookie spread, whereas tenderizing ingredients tend to have the opposite effect. Lorenz et al. (1972) observed a significant correlation between atmospheric pressure at different altitudes and cookie spread.

Cookies generally come out of the oven with a crust temperature of 116°C (240°F) and a crumb temperature of about 99°C (210°F). They are still rather plastic in physical state, with the flour starch still somewhat paste-like, the sugars still in partial solution and the shortening present as oils rather than more solid fats. The protein is firmer and, during cooling, draws water to it and away from the sugars and starches. The sugars will crystallize out, and the cookie becomes rigid, or "set" (Tireki 2008).

The baking process changes the moisture content of cookies, with the result that crusts will be dryer than interiors. This moisture difference must be eliminated before packaging, but if cookies cool too rapidly, they may crack ("check") because of internal stresses due to delayed moisture movement. Checking leads to breakage during packaging, shipping and storage. Dielectric drying, applied to cookies hot out of the oven, helps equilibrate moisture content rapidly throughout the cookie, practically eliminating checking. Most cookies and crackers will have an optimum moisture content and will be subject to checking after packaging if they are very much above or below the target level.

7.C.1.c. Pie baking

The time required to properly bake the crust depends on a number of variables, including the levels of sugar, milk and shortening used in formulating the dough, thickness of the crust, type of fruit filling, kind of wash mixture, oven temperature and others (**Figure 7.15**). Hence, it is difficult to designate specific baking times. Harder and Jabush (1946) suggested the following representative temperatures and baking times for various types of pies, depending upon pan size and shape and oven heat transfer coefficient: pies with raw fillings, 227 to 232°C (440 to 450°F) for 35 minutes; pies with cooked fillings, 232°C (450°F) for 30 minutes; empty crust shells, 260°C (500°F) for 12 minutes; and crust shells with custard fillings, 163°C (325°F) for 30 minutes. Unfilled shells should cool before being filled to reduce moisture migration into the crust.

When baking a filled pie, two factors of critical importance must be balanced, namely, properly baking the crust and avoiding boil-over of the fruit filling. A satisfactory bake will generally be achieved with oven conditions that provide a solid bottom heat and a medium top heat. Commonly recommended oven temperatures for 2-crust pies fall within the range of 219 to 260°C (435 to 500°F). For so-called oven-filled pies, such as custard, pumpkin, etc., lower temperatures are in order: 193 to 204°C (380 to 400°F). Sufficient bottom heat is important to complete baking of a pie's bottom crust, especially for filled pies.

A hotter oven will obviously cause a filling to boil sooner than will a cooler oven, but it will also bake the crust more quickly. Normally, crust browning in a hot oven proceeds at a more rapid pace than does the increase of the temperature of the filling. So boiling over of the filling before the crust is properly baked is a relatively rare occurrence with hot ovens. Cool ovens, on the other hand, necessitate extended baking time to achieve proper crust color development. The filling is thus exposed to elevated temperatures for a longer period and is more apt to reach the boiling point.

Other causes exist for the tendency of fruit fillings to boil over or stew in the oven besides a cool oven or inadequate tempering of the filling. Chief among these is insufficient solids content, whether of fruit or sweetener, which tends to cause the filling to boil over before the crust has been properly baked. Fillings should be formulated so that their minimum solids content, exclusive of the fruit, is not less than 30 to 40% (Denton 1950).

Figure 7.15. Direct-fired impingement technology bakes pies evenly and quickly. (*Baking & Snack*)

7.C.2. Frying

While baking heats doughs and batters through radiation, convection and conduction methods, frying is a matter of straight conduction: The liquid, hot fat surrounds the dough piece and conducts the oil's heat energy directly onto the submerged dough's surface. This process also incorporates a portion of the cooking medium, the hot oil, into the finished product. Hence, the ultimate character of fried products is established not only by the quality of their formula ingredients and the method of their processing but also to a substantial degree by the quality of the frying medium.

In addition to chemically leavened doughnut batters, frying is applied to doughs leavened by yeast, air or steam, principally yeast-leavened doughnut dough. A few regional specialties are also fried, notably the "French" doughnuts prepared from choux paste and the Polish paczkis, both found in the upper Midwest states, plus the deep-fried Danish pastries local to lower Michigan, the funnel cakes so popular at state fairs across the country and the hush puppies that accompany so many meals in the Southeast.

Frying as a process is covered in detail later in this volume at Chapter 10, Part D.

7.D. Related Product Processes

7.D.1. Doughnuts

7.D.1.a. Chemically leavened

Most chemically leavened doughnuts are made from commercially formulated, proprietary mixes that require only the addition of water. They can also be produced by weighing out the formula's individual requirements. The use of prepared mixes offers the advantages of uniformity of composition, a predetermined degree of richness, a largely predictable production performance and major economies in labor by eliminating numerous scaling operations in the bakery.

Production begins with mixing the dry ingredients with water into a uniform batter with a temperature in the range of 24 to 27°C (75 to 80°F). Drastic deviations in batter temperature must be avoided to prevent undesirable quality variations in the final product. The mixing time normally required is 1 to 3 minutes (Owen 1975). Close control of the mixing time is important to the ultimate product quality because over-mixing results in doughnuts with excessive toughness and inadequate fat absorption; under-mixed batters produce fragile products with high fat absorption (Goodsell 1984).

A floor time of 10 to 15 minutes will generally condition the batter properly by bringing about adequate hydration and activation of the leavening system (Willyard 2002). Here again, lack of control of the floor time, terminating it either too early or too late, produces such specific defects in the finished product as reduced volume, poor product symmetry, high fat absorption and split crusts (Goodsell 1984).

The batter is next transferred into a hopper from which it is deposited in predetermined amounts and sizes into the frying medium by means of a depositor of either the gravity-feed type, the air-pressure type or the vacuum-mechanical type (Fischer 1976, Belshaw 1976, Dixon 1983).

The batter ring is deposited directly into the frying medium where it remains for 1 to 2.5 minutes. Dwell time is determined by the size and variety of the doughnut and by the temperature of the frying fat, which usually is within the range of 182 to 193 °C (360 to 380°F). Most large fryers have separate temperature controls for the front and discharge ends. This allows the front frying temperature to be set about 10 F° (5.5 C°) higher to equalize the frying time for both product sides. Because of its initially lower temperature, the frying rate of the raw product side that enters the hot fat first is comparatively slower than that of the upper side, which is heated up by the time the product is turned midway through the frying cycle.

When doughnuts are first deposited into the frying fat, they sink below the surface, often striking a drop plate, only to rise again to the surface. This "rise time" can serve as a control factor because it is affected by the leavening level and the conditioning of the batter (Owen 1975). Rise time varies by doughnut size, with 3 to 4 seconds for smaller items and 5 to 6.5 seconds for larger varieties.

Soon after the doughnut resurfaces, a break near the fat level begins to form on the inside of the hole. Because the outer edge of the piece is comparatively rigid, the batter flows toward the center, imparting a star shape to the center hole by the time the products reach the turner (**Figure 7.16**). If the break occurs on the top of the doughnut, or the outer crust is weak, the batter will flow out rather than in. Willyard (2002) explained that batter sticking to the cutter during depositing can cause this fault. The break line is determined by where the batter is pinched together by the cutter. When batter sticks to the depositor, the break line moves up to the top of the batter ring.

Because batter continues to expand and flow to the center, it develops maximum volume by the time it reaches the turner. The partially cooked doughnut will be slightly gassy and glossy in appearance. A surface that appears too glossy and/or gassy indicates problems with batter viscosity that is too low or frying time that is too long. Although volume will expand for a few seconds after turning, the chemical leavening system must be balanced so that it is exhausted by the time the doughnut reaches the turner, otherwise the crust will break, creating cracks on the bottom side and excessive oil absorption.

7.D.1.b. Yeast leavened

Yeast-raised doughnuts differ from cake doughnuts by being made from a yeast-fermented dough rather than a chemically leavened batter and by receiving a final proof before they are deposited into the fryer. As a result, their formulation and processing requirements differ from those of cake doughnuts. A review of yeast-leavened doughnut processes was offered by Smith (1996).

Either the sponge-and-dough method or the straight-dough method may be used. In instances where the sponge-and-dough method is not feasible, Wise (1971) recommended the preparation of a straight dough some 2 hours before the first doughnut dough is scheduled. This straight dough then serves as a starter dough to be added to each subsequent fresh dough in amounts equivalent to some 25% of the total dough. This procedure results in doughs that perform like sponge doughs, with end products that benefit from the more extended fermentation.

Doughnut production methods range from partly automated to fully automated (**Figure 7.17**). In one of the simpler systems, the dough is sheeted, and the doughnuts are cut in the conventional manner on the bench or makeup table. The individual dough pieces are then placed on a proofing cloth, screen or proofing board for proofing for 25 to 35 minutes in a proof box that is maintained at 35 to 46°C (95 to 115°F) and at 61 to 66% relative humidity. The proofed pieces are then automatically transferred to the infeed conveyor that passes them into a conveyor-type fryer.

Yeast-raised doughnuts may also be produced by extrusion methods, either air-pressure or vacuum extrusion systems. Extrusion has the advantage of being highly automated and, hence, requires a minimum of labor. As Wise (1971) pointed out, doughs age rapidly when placed under air pressure, so their floor time must be carefully controlled. While young doughs cut better because they are less extensively aerated and possess good flow characteristics, they tend to yield smaller product volumes because of insufficient expansion during frying. In contrast, old doughs

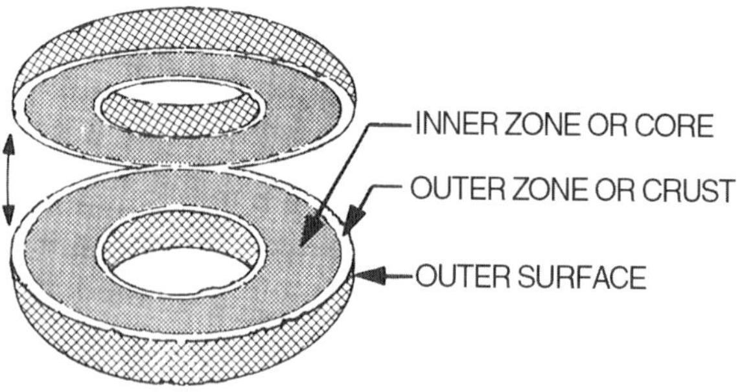

Figure 7.16. Cross-section of a cake doughnut shows its major structural zones. (Robertson 1966)

Figure 7.17. Like chemically leavened doughnuts, yeast-raised styles also require flipping half-way through the frying process.
(Belshaw Adamatic Bakery Group)

require less air pressure but yield non-uniform dough pieces.

Sponge doughs allowed to ferment at 27°C (80°F) for 2 to 2.5 hours appear to be best adapted to the extrusion process. The dough is mixed for 15 to 20 minutes to full development, with an absorption that favors optimum extensibility. Floor time should be limited to less than 5 minutes, and the dough should be processed within 15 to 20 minutes.

Yeast-raised doughnut dough pieces require relatively dry and warm proofing conditions, within a temperature range of 35 to 46°C (95 to 115°F) and a relative humidity of 35 to 45% to promote skin formation. Proof time will normally run 20 to 35 minutes. High humidity proofing tends to cause excessive product expansion and to produce blister formation and high fat absorption in the fried product. The general practice calls for a moist zone at the outset of proofing to promote the spread of the doughnuts and a dry zone toward the discharge end to favor product rise and volume increase, as well as to facilitate product release off the trays (Braden 1976).

The temperature of the frying medium should be maintained within a range of 204 to 213°C (400 to 415°F). Frying time will normally run from 45 to 60 seconds per side, depending on doughnut size, for a total of 1.5 to 2 minutes.

7.D.1.c. Fried pie process

Using pie dough prepared as reported earlier in this section, the process for making fried pies uses specialized forming equipment. The dough, sheeted into a

Figure 7.18. Fried pies must be fully cool before packaging. (The Bama Companies)

continuous ribbon, receives a measured amount of filling on one-half of the dough strip, which is then covered as the other half folds over the filling. This is followed by automatic crimping, trimming and sealing (Stephens 1972). In another method, two continuous sheeted dough strips form the top and bottom crusts, with the fruit deposited between them. The filled dough strip is then cut, crimped and sealed into individual pies.

A twin conveyor, with the top and bottom chain belts spaced about 1 in. apart, transports the pies fully submersed through the fryer. Except for the constraints imposed by the conveyor belts, the pies float freely in the hot shortening and will absorb some 5 to 8 oz of the fat per dozen fried pies. The frying temperature is held at about 188°C (370°F) and the frying time, for the regular 4- to 5-oz pies, will approximate 4 to 5 minutes. These frying conditions will ensure a thoroughly fried crust, without bringing the filling to a boil and causing the pies to burst.

Following the discharge from the fryer, the hot pies receive a starch or sugar glaze and are then transferred to an atmospheric cooler. It requires about 90 to 100 minutes for the filling center of fried pies to reach near ambient temperatures. Proper cooling is important because pies that are packaged (**Figure 7.18**) before their centers have cooled adequately will sweat, thereby causing the crust to lose its desirable crispness and the glaze to flake.

7.D.2. Crackers

Soda cracker production normally involves prolonged fermentations (up to 24 hours) and lamination of the dough into seven or more layers without an intervening filling.

According to Faridi (1980), fermentation is normally carried out by the sponge-and-dough process, with the sponge containing 60 to 70% of the total flour, the yeast, a small amount of old dough and the water, all mixed for 1 to 4 minutes. The sponge ferments for about 16 to 18 hours at 26 to 29°C (78 to 84°F) and 70 to 78% relative humidity. This is followed by gentle dough mixing for 3 to 7 minutes in which the remaining flour and other ingredients (shortening, salt and sodium and ammonium bicarbonates) are incorporated. The dough is then fermented for an additional 4 to 6 hours.

Full gluten development is not expected or even desired for cracker doughs, according to Strouts (2008). Typically lower protein flours are used, which means less gluten is present than in bread doughs. Full development of cracker doughs takes place during sheeting, rather than in the mixer.

The fermented dough then passes through a laminating machine that transforms it into a continuous sheet by a series of rolls that reduce its thickness to about 0.25 in. This reduced dough sheet is then folded into five to seven layers by lapping or cut-sheet methods (**Figure 7.19**) and again reduced in thickness by passage through a set of rollers. The final rolling is set down to a 3- to 4-mm gap in order to produce the desired final thickness in the finished cracker. Faridi (1990) stated that the reduction in thickness should be about 2:1 for each pass through a roll pair, although ratios of up to 4:1 are used.

Because of the dough's elastic properties, it emerges from a gauge roll slightly thicker than the roll gap. The sheet is allowed to relax and shrink before it reaches the cutter. Relaxation is promoted by over-feeding the emerging sheet onto the conveyor, thus forming ripples across the band of dough. When the sheet reaches the cutting station, the conveyor increases in speed just enough to take up the ripplesThe laminated sheet is then cut, docked and stamped, and receives a sprinkling of salt prior to entering the oven. Docking uses pins with blunt ends, and the purpose of this process is to pin the dough together so it will not separate into layers on baking.

Baking is done on wire mesh or steel bands for a very brief time, e.g., 2.5 to 3.5 minutes, at temperatures that typically are 570°F (300°C) in the first zone and decline to 480°F (250°C) at the end of the oven. Dielectric drying is sometimes used to establish a uniform moisture profile. The baked crackers are then broken across sheets into rows and lengthwise, permitted to cool (when their moisture equalizes at about 2.5%), stacked and packaged in moisture-proof bags.

Yeast, at the low level at which it is used, appears to play a subordinate role in cracker dough fermentation, with the major changes that occur being attributed to bacterial fermentation, as might be expected because of the long fermentation time. Micka (1955) appeared to be the first to thoroughly investigate the bacterial aspects of cracker dough fermentation. He observed that the major sources of bacteria were the yeast, flour, remnants from the previous doughs in the fermentation trough and the addition of ferments held over from preceding doughs. Faridi (1980) pointed out that the major portion of carbon dioxide generated during fermentation originates with the bacteria, principally Lactobacillus plantarum, L. delbrueckii and L. leichmanii. Similarly, the increase in acidity with progressing fermentation is due to the bacteria. Faridi and Johnson (1978), in tracing the formation of organic acids in cracker sponges and doughs, found increases of 8.4 times and 6.4 times in acetic acid and lactic acid levels, respectively, during a 20-hour sponge time, with additional increases at the dough stage.

Fields et al. (1982), in a study of the microbiology of cracker sponge fermentation, found that lactic acid bacteria were the dominant species in doughs and appeared to be primarily responsible for the rapid lowering of the pH of the sponge (**Figure 7.20**). The number of yeast cells was observed to decline as fermentation progressed, possibly because of the competition among the organisms for fermentable carbohydrates.

In practice, sodium bicarbonate is normally added to the dough stage to neutralize the acids formed during sponge fermentation, to generate additional carbon dioxide and to establish the pH of the finished cracker. The neutralizing effect of the soda addition is clearly apparent from the rather steep rise in pH from a value of about 4 to above 7 (Manley 1983). When soda is omitted, the color of the baked cracker will be too light, and if too much soda is added, the final color will be too dark. Soda

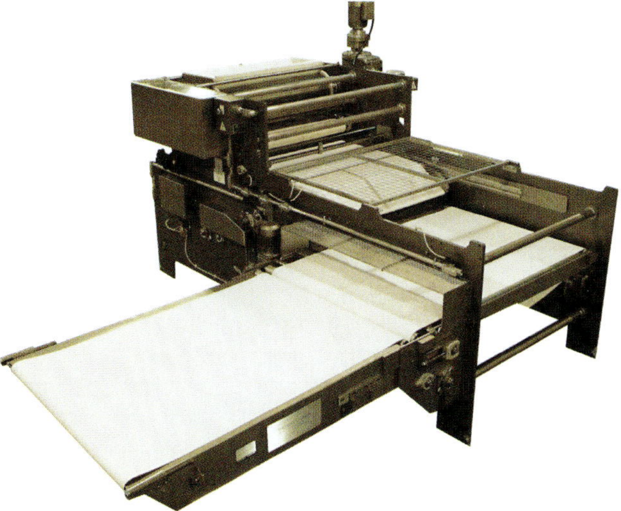

Figure 7.19. Used in cracker lamination, this servo-driven cut-sheet system divides a continuous dough band into individual sheets and layers the lengths with a reciprocating conveyor. (Reading Bakery Systems)

crackers should be slightly on the alkaline side, within a pH range of 7.5 to 8.5.

The rheological changes that occur during cracker sponge fermentation have been studied by Pizzinatto and Hoseney (1980) by means of the Extensigraph. They found that adding the shortening to either the sponge or the dough had no perceptible influence on fermentation or the pH of the sponge. The amount of mixing applied to the dough did, however, affect dough properties. Over-mixing resulted in sticky doughs that were difficult to handle. Optimum mixing times were 3 minutes for the sponge and 5 minutes for the dough, for a total time of 8 minutes. As fermentation progressed, the sponges became less resistant to extension and lost some extensibility, probably because of the increase in acidity as indicated by the decline of the pH from 5.35 to 4.15 in the course of fermentation. Addition of soda increased the dough's extensibility, whereas salt addition strengthened the dough as exemplified by an increase in its resistance to extension.

Looking at the effect of fermentation time on the extensibility of cracker doughs, Doescher and Hoseney (1985) showed that resistance to extension decreased with time. This lower resistance is important because cracker doughs do not become fully developed during mixing but when they are sheeted. Doughs made with stronger flours, thus, will require more rigorous sheeting to become fully developed.

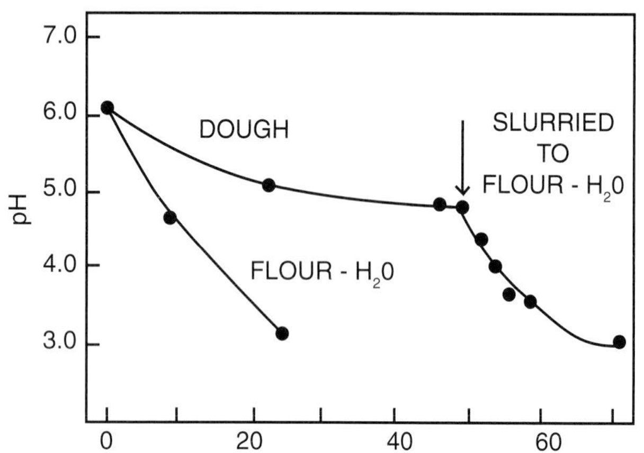

Figure 7.20. pH decreases as a function of fermentation time for dough, flour-water slurry and dough slurried to flour-water.
(Fields et al. 1982)

Although soda, or saltine, crackers and many snack crackers employ yeast as their leavening source, other varieties depend on chemical leavening. Obviously, fermentation is not a process used for the latter form of cracker, but floor time (also described as resting or lay time) is usually given to these doughs to allow the gluten structure developed in the mixer to relax. A proteolytic enzyme is frequently added to chemically leavened snack cracker dough to improve dough relaxation in a shorter time. Processing of chemically leavened crackers follows the same stages as for yeasted doughs. Lamination is what gives all crackers their open, flaky texture, while sheeting assures consistent thickness.

Trimmed scrap, or rework, is often integrated back into cracker doughs, either at the mixer or at the dough hopper. Strouts (2008) recommended that no more than 5% by total weight is a reasonable guideline. To maintain proper dough consistency, adjustment may also be needed in total formula water.

During baking of crackers, oven humidity plays an important role, summarized by Johnson and Walker (2003). Crackers must be baked to below 3 to 4% moisture content. Stack height is effectively set in the first zone of the oven. If oven humidity is too low in the early stages, products such as cookies and crackers will case-harden on the outside, thus reducing stack height. Case hardening also impedes moisture loss from the interior, resulting in checking, or cracking, of the finished product. Stress cracking, the result of uneven expansion and contraction during and after cooling, is caused by differences in moisture between the interior and the surface.

Low oven humidity may also cause excessive blistering of cracker surfaces. Blisters burn easily, causing undesirable dark spots, and they break readily during filling operations for sandwich crackers and during packaging. A fine water mist applied to the top of the cracker dough just as it enters the oven can reduce blister formation and control stack height.

Faridi (1990) examined cracker processing and the rheological properties involved. Saltine cracker doughs, he noted, are mixed just long enough to wet the flour, limiting gluten development during this stage. Major rheological changes take place during fermentation, and gluten development takes place primarily during sheeting processes.

References

Ash, D.J., and Colmey, J.C. 1973. The role of pH in cake baking. Bakers Digest 47 (1): 36.

Bailey, L.H., and LeClerc, J.A. 1935. Cereal Chem. 12: 175.

Barmore, M.A. 1936. The influence of various factors, including altitude, in the production of angel food cake. Colo. Expt. Sta. Tech. Bull. 15. The station: Fort Collins, CO.

Belshaw, T.E. 1976. Cutting and frying equipment. Proc. Am. Soc. Bakery Engrs. 52: 112.

Bettge, A.D. 2009. Enhancing end product quality through testing (white wheat). Halversen Award Lecture delivered at the 2009 Spring Technical Conference of the Milling & Baking Division of AACC International, May 14, 2006, Albuquerque, NM.

Bettge, A.D., and Morris, C.F. 2007. Oxidative gelation measurement and influence on soft wheat batter viscosity and end-use quality. Cereal Chem. 84 (3): 237.

Bonavia, W. 1963. Practical aspects of continuous cake batter mixing. Bakers Digest 37 (3): 72.

Bonavia, W. 1967. Techniques, operation and engineering aspects of continuous production of cake batter. Proc. Am. Soc. Bakery Engrs. 43: 301.

Braden, B.W. 1976. Yeast-raised doughnuts. Proc. Am. Soc. Bakery Engrs. 52: 127.

Brijwani, K., Campbell, G.M., and Cicerelli, L. 2008. Aeration of biscuit doughs during mixing. In: Bubbles in Food 2. G.M. Campbell, M.G. Scanlon and D.L. Pyle, eds. AACC International: St. Paul, MN.

Ciacco, C.F., and D'Appolonia, B.L. 1982. Characterization of pentosans from different wheat flour classes and of their gelling capacity. Cereal Chem. 59: 96.

Cole, E.W., Mecham, D.K., and Pence, J.W. 1960. Effect of flour lipids and some lipid derivatives on cookie-baking characteristics of lipid-free flours. Cereal Chem. 37: 109.

Denton, C. 1950. Pie filling faults. Proc. Am. Soc. Bakery Engrs. 26: 312.

Dixon, J. 1983. Cake donut production: A controlled process. Bakers Digest 57 (5): 26.

Doescher, L.C., and Hoseney, R.C. 1985. Saltine crackers: Changes in cracker sponge rheology and modification of a cracker-baking procedure. Cereal Chem. 62 (3): 158.

Ellinger, R.H., and Shappeck, F.J. 1963. The relation of batter specific gravity to cake quality. Bakers Digest 37 (6): 52.

Engstrom, L.E. 1981. Update on automatic pie production methods. Bakers Digest 55 (5): 92.

Faridi, H. 1990. Application of rheology in the cookie and cracker industry. In: Dough Rheology and Baked Product Texture. H. Faridi and J.M. Faubion, eds. Van Nostrand Reinhold: New York, NY.

Faridi, H.A. 1980. Short-time saltine cracker. Bakers Digest 54 (3): 16.

Faridi, H.A., and Johnson, J.A. 1978. Saltine cracker flavor. I. Changes in organic acids and soluble nitrogen constituents of cracker sponge and dough. Cereal Chem. 55 (1): 7.

Fields, M.L., Hoseney, R.C., and Varriano-Marston, E. 1982. Microbiology of cracker sponge fermentation. Cereal Chem. 59 (1): 23.

Fischer, L.G. 1976. Cake doughnuts. Proc. Am. Soc. Bakery Engrs. 52: 121.

Fuhr, R.R. 1962. Cookie spread: Its effects on production and quality. Bakers Digest 36 (4): 56.

Goodsell, G.R. 1984. Cake doughnut production. Proc. Am. Soc. Bakery Engrs. 60: 118.

Hanselmann, W., and Windhab, E. 1999. Foam generation in a continuous rotor-stator mixer. In: Bubbles in Food. G.M. Campbell, C. Webb, S.S. Pandiella and K. Niranjan, eds. AACC: St. Paul, MN.

Harder, M.J., and Jabusch, H.W. 1946. Points to watch in pie production. Bakers Digest 20 (5): 23.

Harrel, C.G., and Thelen, R.J. 1959. Conversion Factors and Technical Data for the Food Industry, 6th ed. Burgess Publishing Co.: Minneapolis, MN.

Hoseney, R.C. 1980. Cookie flours and the function of flour components and other ingredients in cookies. Presented at Cookie Fundamentals seminar of the Biscuit and Cracker Manufacturers' Association, held May 21-22, 1980, at Manhattan, KS.

Johnson, A.M., and Walker, C.E. 2003. Humidity inside ovens. AIB Tech. Bull. 25 (6).

Knuepfner, W.H. 1960. Pie crust and fillings. Proc. Am. Soc. Bakery Engrs. 36: 292.

Kulp, K., and Olewnik, M. 1984. Continuous mix in cookie dough production — an alternative to batch mixing. AIB Tech. Bull. 6 (12).

Kulp, K. 1994. Functionality of ingredients in cookie systems. In: Cookie Chemistry and Technology. K. Kulp, ed. American Institute of Baking: Manhattan, KS.

Kweon, M., Slade, L., and Levine, H. 2009. Oxidative gelation of solvent-accessible arabinoxylans is the predominant consequence of extensive chlorination of soft wheat flour. Cereal Chem. 86 (4): 421.

Lawson, H.W. 1965. Cake formula balance. Proc. Am. Soc. Bakery Engrs. 41: 251.

Lehmann, T.A., Zeak, J.A., and Strouts, B.L. 1994. Technological processes and problems in cookie production. In: Cookie Chemistry and Technology. K. Kulp, ed. American Institute of Baking: Manhattan, KS.

Lorenz, K., Maga, J., and Dilsaver, W. 1972. Cookie spread: Effects of baking under varying atmospheric pressures. Bakers Digest 46 (3): 22.

Manley, D.J.R. 1983. Technology of Biscuits, Crackers and Cookies. Ellis Horwood Ltd.: Chichester, West Susex, UK.

Micka, J. 1955. Cereal Chem. 32: 125.

Mizukoshi, M. 1986. Rheological studies of cake volume. In: In: Fundamentals of Dough Rheology. Proc. Fundamentals of Dough Rheology Symposium, Oct. 7, 1986, Toronto, Ont., Canada.

H. Faridi and J.M. Faubion, eds. AACC: St Paul, MN.

Neukom, H., Geissmann, T., and Painter, T.J. 1967. New aspects of the functions and properties of the soluble wheat-flour pentosans. Bakers Digest 41 (5): 52.

Owen, J.A. 1975. Cake doughnut production. Proc. Am. Soc. Bakery Engrs. 51: 142.

Palmer, H.H. 1972. Eggs. In: Food Theory and Applications. P.C. Paul and H.H. Palmer, eds. John Wiley & Sons, Inc.: New York, NY.

Pizzinatto, A., and Hoseney, R.C. 1980. Rheological changes in cracker sponges during fermentation. Cereal Chem. 57 (3): 185.

Prouty, W.W. 1965. Guidelines for a quality control program. II. Process control. Bakers Digest 39 (4): 69.

Rees, R.F. 1971. Baking Ind. J. 4 (6): 71.

Robertson, C.J. 1966. The principles of deep fat frying for the bakery. Bakers Digest 40 (5): 54.

Sablani, S.S. 2008. Physical and thermal properties of sweet goods. In: Food Engineering Aspects of Baking Sweet Goods. S.G. Sumnu and S. Sahin, eds. CRC Press: Boca Raton, FL.

Sahin, S. 2008. Cake batter rheology. In: Food Engineering Aspects of Baking Sweet Goods. S.G. Sumnu and S. Sahin, eds. CRC Press: Boca Raton, FL.

Seelinger, F. 1956. Controlled cake quality, pound and layer cake. Proc. Am. Soc. Bakery Engrs. 32: 284.

Smith, R. 1996. Technology of yeast-raised doughnuts. AIB Tech. Bull. 18 (2).

Sollars, W.F. 1959. Cereal Chem. 36: 498.

Stephens, C. 1972. Automation in modern pie making operations. Bakers Digest 46 (4): 56.

Stevens, T.R. 1962. U-Tube density meter: A system for the automatic control of cake batter density. Bakers Digest 34 (1): 71.

Strouts, B. 2008. Basic cracker technology. II. Processing. AIB Tech. Bull. 30 (6).

Suas, M. 2009. Advanced Bread and Pastry: A Professional Approach. Delmar Cengage Learning: Clifton Park, NY.

Tireki, S. 2008. Technology of cookie production. In: Food Engineering Aspects of Baking Sweet Goods. S.G. Sumnu and S. Sahin, eds. CRC Press: Boca Raton, FL.

Trimbo, H.B., Ma, S.-M., and Miller, B.S. 1966. Batter flow and ring formation in cake baking. Bakers Digest 40 (1): 40.

Velzen, B.H. 1963. Production of wire-cut cookies. Proc. Am. Soc. Bakery Engrs. 39: 243.

Willyard, M. 2002. Formulation of cake doughnuts (an update). AIB Tech. Bull. 24 (9).

Wise, C.E. 1971. Production quality control of extruded yeast-raised doughnuts. Bakers Digest 45 (6): 32.

Yamazaki, W.T. 1953. An alkaline water retention capacity test for the evaluation of cookie baking potentialities of soft winter wheat flours. Cereal Chem. 30: 242.

Yamazaki, W.T. 1962. Cereal Sci. Today 7: 98.

Yasukawa, T., Mizukoshi, M., and Aigami, K. 1986. Dynamic viscoelastic properties of cake batter during expansion and heat setting. In: Fundamentals of Dough Rheology. Proc. Fundamentals of Dough Rheology Symposium, Oct. 7, 1986, Toronto, Ont., Canada. H. Faridi and J.M. Faubion, eds. AACC: St Paul, MN.

Yener, M.E. 2008. Cookie dough rheology. In: Food Engineering Aspects of Baking Sweet Goods. S.G. Sumnu and S. Sahin, eds. CRC Press: Boca Raton, FL.

Zelch, R. 2001. Batter cakes. II. Mixing. AIB Tech. Bull. 23 (10).

Zelch, R., Sieloff, T., and Lehmann, T. 2004. Production of pie crusts. AIB Tech. Bull. 26 (9).

CHAPTER 8

Formulating

By L.A. Gorton (Parts A-E, G-K, O, P and R),
Michael Bakhoum (Part F)
and Hans van der Maarel (Parts L-N and Q)

Michael Bakhoum, MS
Bakery R&D Consulting, Inc.
1396 Huntington Dr., Mundelein, IL 60060. Phone (847) 680-1072;
e-mail mbakhoum1@aol.com

Hans van der Maarel
International Bakery Consulting, Ltd.
1070 Beech Hollow Rd., Ambler, PA 19002. Phone (215) 591-3821;
mobile (267) 252-2465; e-mail hvdm@comcast.net

Different products require different approaches when formulating.

Careful measurements, repeated throughout testing and into production, will keep product development projects on track.
(*Baking & Snack*, ©2005 David Hills)

INTRODUCTION

Where do bakery formulations come from? Anywhere and everywhere.

Over the years, enterprising individuals founded a good number of commercial bakeries by using their family recipes, and many bakers got their start — and continue to take inspiration — from Old World bread, cake and pastry formulations that immigrated with them and their families. New World concepts such the corn tortillas of the Mesoamericans figure in the rich heritage of bakery formulations, too. Flatbreads from the Middle East, steamed breads from Asia — baked foods are common to every region where cereal grains dominate agriculture. Others such as the meringue-based pavlovas so popular in Australia resulted from the pure artistry of their inventors.

War and politics inspired some baked foods, and food historians credit the origin of both the croissant and the bagel to celebrations of heroism, respectively by Viennese bakers and by the city's Polish allies led by King Jan Sobieski, in the defense of Vienna from attack by the Ottoman Turk army in the 17th century (Balinska 2008). For those interested in baking through the ages, Jacob's extremely readable history of bread, originally published in 1944, has recently been updated and reissued (Jacob and Reinhart 2007).

8.A. Starting Formulations
By L.A. Gorton

Whether working on new products or re-inventing current ones, the formulator needs a starting point, which is the function of starting formulations and the subject of this chapter. Starting formulations are just that: a starting point. Often they give measurements of ingredients in ranges rather than absolute quantities, with the intent of guiding the formulator, but not restricting creativity.

All starting formulations require fine-tuning to meet the exact conditions of the bakery and its equipment platform. Also, ingredients derived from nature vary in the real world from harvest to harvest. Careful specification of purchased ingredients can reduce such variability to a certain extent, but not always. Additionally, marketing imperatives (and corporate financial needs) can impact formula percentages.

8.A.1. Sources

Discussion of formulating necessarily involves reporting of actual formulations, and the reader will find a number offered here; however, these will be of a general nature. A myriad of sources can be tapped for starting formulations.

Of course, the best source for a starting formula is another baker, but many companies consider their formulations to be trade secrets and will not release them to outsiders. Patents protect some formulations, while registered trademarks cover others. Even when a formula can be shared, it often will not work exactly the same way in every bakery or even at other plants operated by the same company.

Many excellent professional textbooks provide commercial formulations and commentary about production techniques. Most recently, Suas (2009) compiled a comprehensive presentation of bread and pastry formulations offered in bakers percent, metric, English and test formats along with comments on processing technology. Gisslin (2008) also updated his classic textbook about commercial baking, which encompassed formulations and methods. When variety breads began making an impact in wholesale baking, Miller (1981) included many starting formulations. Tressler and Sultan (1975) assembled a comprehensive formulary from commercial sources, including ingredient suppliers and equipment manufacturers. Many issues of the *AIB Technical Bulletin* carry formulations, particularly those covering specific baked foods as well as ingredients such as nuts and fruits.

Because the popularity of home baking resurged greatly during recent years, hundreds of cookbooks written around this topic now fill library and bookstore shelves. Although nearly any good consumer cookbook that offers recipes for baked foods can serve as a starting point for bench development, among the more useful books written for consumers about baking are those by Corriher (1997, 2008) and Brown (2004). Companies such as Bob's Red Mill and King Arthur Flour, which have connections in both the industrial and consumer flour markets, have produced useful cookbooks with plenty of bakery recipes.

8.A.2. Home flours vs. commercial flours

Millers prepare flour to exacting needs and offer a myriad of choices for commercial bakery use. They work in close collaboration with their customers to produce the protein profile and starch qualities preferred.

Among the problems of adapting home recipes for commercial use is flour style. Home bakers have a much more limited palette of flours than do commercial bakers, although the number of different flour types has grown with the advent of the home bread machine. Still, the formulator seeking inspiration from home recipes will need to "translate" the home kitchen's flour into commercial styles.

8.A.2.a. All-purpose flour

Home baking recipes typically call for "all-purpose flour" (**Figure 8.001**). Millers blend such flours, also called "family flour," to allow successful home preparation of a wide range of baked foods — from bread to pies to cakes to tarts and cookies — with the same bag of flour. The flour is made from a combination of hard and soft wheat, with hard winter wheat the primary component, milled to a short patent grade. All-purpose flour is blended to be slightly weaker than bread flour, ranging from 9 to 12% protein, and offered in bleached, unbleached and organic versions. In the US, no single standard exists for all-purpose flour, other than the general Standard of Identity for flour published in the Code of Federal Regulations (21 CFR 137.105).

Hensperger (2004) observed that all-purpose flour is blended from an approxi-

Figure 8.001. All-purpose flour is milled and blended to produce a wide range of products in the home kitchen. (Wheat Foods Council)

mate composition of 80% hard wheat and 20% soft. Brands of all-purpose flour vary in different regions, with that sold in Southern states containing a higher percentage of soft wheat, while in the Northern, Midwestern and Western states, a higher percentage of hard wheat is used (Hoseney et al. 1988).

To substitute for all-purpose flour, Figoni (2008) recommended a 60:40 blend of bread and cake flours; however, she noted that commercial flours specifically milled for bread, cake, pastry and cookie applications perform better in such uses than any all-purpose flour.

Infrequently, a home recipe will refer to "brownie flour." This term lacks specific definition but appears to be another name for all-purpose flour.

8.A.2.b. Self-rising and phosphated flour

Self-rising flour contains baking powder (sodium bicarbonate and a phosphate leavening acid) and, usually, salt. Matz (1991) described the manufacture of self-rising flour through both batch and continuous processes. Self-rising flour has long been popular for making biscuits and has remained a staple in the kitchen cupboards of Southern homes (Ensminger 1994). Because the moisture naturally present in flour can activate the baking powder component, self-rising flour can lose its leavening power over time.

In the US, the federal government established Standards of Identity for many types of flour (21 CFR 137). Included are phosphated and self-rising flours, both milled from wheat and used primarily by consumers rather than commercial bakers. Phosphated flour contains monocalcium phosphate, while self-rising flour is defined in 21 CFR 137.180 as made with "sodium bicarbonate and one or more of the acid-reacting substances monocalcium phosphate, sodium acid pyrophosphate and sodium aluminum phosphate. It is seasoned with salt." The standard limits chemical leavening components to 4.5 parts per 100 parts of flour. Self-rising white cornmeal is also identified (21 CFR 137.270) with the same limits on leavening components as self-rising flour.

When testing formulations that call for self-rising or phosphated flour, it is always better to begin with bread flour and add the chemical leavening ingredients separately. The 4.5-parts-per-cwt level of the Standard of Identity provides a good starting point for such additions.

Little attention is paid to all-purpose and family flours in the classic milling texts for a simple reason: The vast majority of flour is milled for commercial use. At the present time, family flour accounts for less than 10% of all flour sold in the US and self-rising flour, 1%.

8.A.3. Units of measure

With many new product concepts originating from home and food service sources, these recipes must be translated into formulations for use in commercial production and thus written in terms of weight, not volume. Quantities of ingredients will be expressed in percentages, usually based on flour weight.

8.A.3.a. Weight vs. volume

Bakery formulations measure ingredients by weight, even the liquids, and mathematical conversions (**Tables 8.001, 8.002a and 8.002b**) can be made. While the scal-

Table 8.001. Dry Material Densities

Material	Density (weight per volume)	
	kg per cu m	lb per cu ft
Air	1.2238	0.0764
Ammonium bicarbonate	768	48
Baking powder	656 to 737	41 to 46
Barley, grain	576 to 688	36 to 43
Barley, flake	192	12
Barley, meal	400 to 448	25 to 28
Barley, rolled	336 to 384	21 to 24
Bicarbonate of soda	720 to 880	45 to 55
Bran, wheat	160 to 256	10 to 16
Bread crumbs	320 to 400	20 to 25
Buttermilk, dried	480 to 560	30 to 35
Chocolate powder	400 to 480	25 to 30
Cocoa beans, whole	416 to 672	26 to 42
Cocoa beans, roasted	320 to 480	20 to 30
Cocoa beans, ground	480 to 560	30 to 35
Coconut	464	29
Corn, whole	720 to 768	45 to 48
Corn, cracked	720	45
Corn, flakes	192	12
Corn, flour	512	32
Corn, germ	363 to 480	21 to 30
Corn, grits	672 to 688	42 to 43
Corn, ground	480 to 576	30 to 36
Dicalcium phosphate	640	40
Flaxseed, whole	720	45
Flaxseed, ground	448	28
Flour, wheat	480 to 560	30 to 35
Germ, wheat	384	24
Ginger, ground	336	21
Ice, block	913	57
Lentils, whole	784	49
Locust beans, whole	512	32
Locust beans, kibbled	384 to 480	24 to 30
Malt	576 to 640	36 to 40
Milk powder	400	25
Millet, whole	608 to 372	38 to 42
Oatmeal	640	40
Oats, whole	416 to 480	26 to 30
Oats, flaked	240	15
Oats, rolled	288 to 352	18 to 22
Palm kernel, meal	284 to 448	24 to 28
Peanuts, in shell	240 to 320	15 to 20
Peanuts, shelled	560 to 640	35 to 40
Peas, dried	720 to 800	45 to 50
Popcorn, popped	96 to 160	6 to 10
Potato starch	640	40
Rapeseed (canola), whole	720 to 768	45 to 48
Rapeseed (canola), meal	672	42
Riboflavin	592	37
Rice, bran	320	20
Rice, grits	672 to 720	42 to 45
Rice, hulled	720 to 784	45 to 49
Rice, meal	384	24
Rye, whole	688 to 720	43 to 45
Rye, bran	240 to 320	15 to 20
Rye, flour	480	30
Salt, dry, fine	1,121 to 1,201	70 th 75
Semolina	448 to 544	28 to 34
Sorghum, whole	512 to 560	32 to 35
Sorghum, meal	496	31
Soy beans, whole	720 to 800	45 to 50
Soy, flour	480 to 560	30 to 35
Sugar	800 to 1,041	50 to 65
Water	999	62.3
Wheat, whole	720 to 768	45 to 48
Wheat, germ	450	28
Whey powder	544	34
Yeast, dried	656	41

(Stoate 1981)

ing of dry materials is a straight-forward concept, liquids can be trickier. For example, eggs in their natural state vary in size. The conversion that formulators should use is for "large eggs" because this size is the general standard for home and food service recipes. The standard weight for a large egg is 45 g. Stauffer (1998) detailed how to convert a home recipe to commercial standards and scale up for the plant floor.

Flowmeters are frequently employed to determine mass flow of liquids and, hence, the amount delivered to a mixer or other processing system. Based on the Coriolis effect produced by liquids in motion, such meters sense the fluid's velocity electromagnetically. Thermocouples gather temperature information. Together, data about the motion and temperature allow calculation of mass and, hence, weight. Vortex flowmeters allow volumetric determination of flowing liquids. Magnetic, ultrasonic and laser Doppler measurement methods can also control the dispensing of liquids. Coriolis systems are commonly used to manage the delivery of liquid bulk ingredients (water, fats, sweeteners and cream yeast) to mixers in today's automated commercial bakeries. Such measuring systems are explained in Chapter 9, Part A.

Table 8.002a. Weights and Measures for Common Ingredients

Ingredient	Weight per cup*	
	g	oz
Eggs		
Eggs, white, 8 large	225	8
Eggs, whole, 5 large	225	8
Eggs, yolks, 12 large	225	8
Flours and cereals		
Bran, dry	50	1.75
Cornmeal, uncooked	165	5.75
Corn starch, unsifted	150	5.33
Crumbs, bread, dry	100	3.50
Crumbs, cake, dry	100	3.50
Crumbs, bread or cake, moist	45	1.50
Flour, all-purpose, unsifted	135	4.75
Flour, all-purpose, sifted once	115	4.00
Flour, bread, unsifted	140	5.00
Flour, bread, sifted once	120	4.25
Flour, cake, unsifted	125	4.38
Flour, cake, sifted once	95	3.38
Flour, whole-wheat, unsifted	130	4.50
Oats, rolled	85	3.00
Rice, uncooked	190	6.75
Fruits, nuts and peels		
Apple, medium (1 whole)	170	6.00
Apricots, dried, cooked, no juice	150	5.33
Banana, fresh, medium peeled (1 whole)	100	3.50
Banana, fresh, crushed	200	7.00
Banana, dried	100	3.60
Blueberries, fresh	150	5.24
Cherries, whole, candied	200	7.00
Citron, cubed, dry	185	6.50
Citron, thin sliced or cubed, in syrup	200	7.00
Coconut, long thread	80	2.75
Coconut, macaroon	90	3.00
Cranberries, uncooked	85	3.20
Currants	150	5.33
Dates, whole, pitted	170	6.00
Figs	200	7.00
Nuts, chopped	130	4.50
Orange, ground, with juice	225	8.00
Peaches, dried	160	5.60

Ingredient	g	oz
Peels, candied	115	4.00
Pineapple, canned, crushed	250	8.75
Prunes, pitted, cooked, drained	225	8.00
Prunes, pitted, uncooked	175	6.25
Raisins	150	5.25
Rhubarb, cooked	240	8.50
Liquids		
Cream	240	8.50
Fruit juice	250	8.75
Milk, evaporated	250	8.75
Milk, liquid	245	8.63
Milk, sweetened condensed	305	10.75
Vinegar	235	8.33
Water	235	8.33
Shortenings		
Butter	225	8.00
Lard	205	7.25
Oil\	215	7.50
Vegetable shortening, hydrogenated	190	6.75
Sugars and syrups		
Brown sugar	220	7.75
Fruit (fructose)	180	6.33
Granulated sugar	200	7.00
Honey	340	12.00
Molasses	340	12.00
Powdered sugar, 6X, sifted once	100	3.50
Syrup	340	12.00
Miscellaneous		
Apple sauce	245	8.63
Cheese, Pamesan, grated	100	3.50
Cheese, semi-soft, grated	113	4.00
Chocolate liquor (1 square)	28.4	1.00
Chocolate liquor, melted	240	8.50
Chocolate liquor, scraped	113	4.00
Cocoa	85	3.00
Coffee, ground	70	2.50
Cottage cheese	220	7.75
Cream cheese	235	8.25
Gelatin (1 packet)	10.5	0.38
Jam, jelly, marmalade (1 tablespoon)	19	0.67
Milk, dry, full or skim	100	3.50
Potato, raw, grated	225	8.00

Table 8.002b. Weights and Measures for Common Ingredients.

Ingredient	Weight per teaspoon*	
	g	oz
Leavening		
Ammonium carbonate	3.8	0.13
Baking powder, cream of tartar type	3.4	0.13
Baking powder, phosphate SAS type	4.4	0.17
Baking soda	5.3	0.20
Cream of tartar	3.4	0.18
Monocalcium phosphate	4.5	0.17
Yeast, compressed (1 cake)	14.2	0.50
Spices and flavors		
Caraway seed, ground	3.3	0.18
Cardamon seed, ground	2	0.06
Cinnamon, ground	2.7	0.10
Cloves, ground	2.7	0.10
Flavoring extracts	5.4	0.20
Ginger, ground	1.9	0.06
Lemon rind, grated	2.7	0.10
Lemon (1 oz)	28.35	1.00
Mace, ground	2.3	0.08
Nutmeg, ground	2.3	0.08
Orange rind, grated	2.7	0.10
Orange (1 half, 1 oz)	28.35	1.00
Poppy seed, whole	3.3	0.18
Salt, table	6	0.20
Salt (1 dash, 0.04 oz)		0.04

* If unit measure is different from cup or teaspoon, it is given in parentheses.

(Gorton 1994)

Density, or mass per unit volume, is calculated as mass divided by volume. Measuring by weight avoids density variations to which some ingredients, like flour, are subject. Unsifted flour is always denser than sifted flour, and until recently, recipe writers generally counted on home bakers to know this fact and to sift their flour without being prompted. Today, the need to sift flour is usually included in home recipes, but cookbooks published before the 1980s tend to leave out this step.

In commercial use, sifting is an established stage in flour's journey from silo to mixer. In-line sifting, described in Chapter 9, Part A, not only aerates flour and removes oversize clumps and agglomerations but also acts as a check point in food safety programs.

8.A.3.b. Bakers percent vs. formula percent

Bakers use a special sort of math to balance formulations: bakers percent. Basically, this method uses the weight of all the flour (and any gluten added separately) in the formula as its basis and calculates the proportion of other ingredients as a

Table 8.003. Elevation of Cities and Towns

State	City	Elevation (ft above sea level)
Arizona	Tucson	2,680
	Flagstaff	6,831
Colorado	Boulder	5,276
	Colorado Springs	6,325
	Denver	5,470
	Fort Collins	4,997
	Leadville	10,108
	Pueblo	4,665
	Trinidad	6,017
Idaho	Boise	2,743
	Idaho Falls	4,711
Montana	Billings	3,215
	Bozeman	4,806
	Helena	4,003
Nebraska	North Platte	2,802
	Scotts Bluff	3,891
Nevada	Reno	5,039
New Mexico	Albuquerque	4,967
	Gallup	6,653
	Las Vegas	6,463
	Santa Fe	6,919
North Carolina	Boone	3,195
South Dakota	Rapid City	3,281
Texas	Amarillo	3,652
	El Paso	3,898
Utah	Ogden	4,334
	Salt Lake City	4,222
Wyoming	Casper	5,161
	Cheyenne	6,076
	Laramie	7,146

(National Elevation Dataset, US Geological Survey)

percentage of the weight of flour. For example, if the formula contains 85 lb of flour and 54 lb of water, then the bakers percents will be 100% flour and 63% water. By the way, when bakers refer to the absorption of a particular flour or formulation, it will be the percentage of water measured by bakers percent.

Most other food processors use formula percent to write their formulations. In this method, the total weight of the formula becomes the basis. Thus, in the example above, if the total formula weighs 154 lb of which 85 lb is flour and 54 lb is water, then the formula percent for flour is 55% and water 35%.

Infrequently, formulations high in sugar will use the sugar as the basis, or they may be reported in formula percent. Fillings and other bakery components that contain little or no flour are normally reported in formula percent.

A detailed explanation of bakers percent vs. formula percent is offered in Appendix 2.

8.A.3.c. Formula vs. recipe

In the baking industry, and throughout the food processing and manufacturing industries, the word "formula" (or "formulation," with the plural being "formulations" for both) is preferred to "recipe," which is common to the food service, retail and home sectors. The term "recipe," however, finds frequent use in computer-operated systems where it refers to a group of program settings that govern the processing conditions for a specific application.

8.A.4. At elevation

Cakes may overflow pans and/or fall, cookies often spread excessively and breads get fluffier when baked at geographical locations higher than 2,500 ft above sea level. The higher the elevation, the more pronounced the effect. Because bakery formulations tend to be developed and tested in labs and plants sited at lower elevations, they will need some adjustment to perform properly when baked at facilities above this height.

(Although common usage terms this practice "high altitude" baking, the accurate reference is "high elevation." Altitude describes the spatial distances between the earth and things in the sky such as airplanes, clouds, planets and stars. Elevation measures a place's distance above or below sea level.)

Nearly 21% of the US population lives at elevations of 3,000 ft or more, mostly in the western one-third of the country, plus a few areas high in the Appalachian Mountains (**Table 8.003**). Denver earned its nickname as the Mile-High City at 5,470 ft (5,280 ft equal 1 mile), and its 2.7 million inhabitants make it the country's largest "high altitude" city. At 10,108 ft, Leadville, CO, is home to more than 3,000 individuals plus several retail bakeries and bakery cafes and is the highest-elevation incorporated location in America.

Many major cities around the world are also known for their high elevations:

Mexico City, Mexico, at 7,350 ft is the largest with a population of 8.8 million, but other sizeable, high-elevation cities include Bogota, Columbia, at 8,660 ft and 7.8 million people and La Paz, Bolivia, at 11,913 ft with its 2.1 million inhabitants.

When it comes to baking, three aspects of the physical environment change as elevation increases: (a) gases expand at greater speeds, (b) water boils at lower temperatures and (c) moisture evaporates at faster rates. The effects of these changes on baked foods are not seen in any practical way when processing takes place at elevations lower than 2,500 ft above sea level.

The expansion of gases follows an inverse relationship between pressure and volume, described by Boyle's Law ($P_1V_1 = P_2V_2$, where P refers to pressure and V to volume). Fermentation, when measured by gas cell size, proceeds faster at the lower atmospheric pressure at elevation. During baking, leavening gases tend to over-expand doughs and batters, pushing them up and over pan walls. Gas cells rupture, and structures collapse.

Water boils at 100°C (212°F) at sea level, or when the saturated vapor pressure is equal to the surrounding atmospheric pressure (**Table 8.004**). Because there is less air per cubic volume at higher elevations, the vapor pressure of liquids decreases. This physical condition means that water boils at lower temperatures relative to sea level. Thus, the maximum internal temperature, which for most baked products is the same as the boiling point of water, is lower at higher elevations so baking time must be extended (**Figure 8.002**). Increasing the baking temperature causes the interior to reach its maximum temperature earlier and minimizes the reduction in crust temperature due to evaporation.

Lower vapor pressure also means that moisture evaporates more quickly as elevation increases. In a room with a relative humidity of 38% (± 2%), water evaporation increases by 15% at 5,000 ft and 29% at 8,000 ft, compared with sea level (Lorenz 1979). The faster speed of evaporation causes crust browning problems. The amount of water in the formula makes a difference because evaporation cools the crust surface. Low-moisture systems such as cookies tend to over-brown, while high-moisture systems such as cakes may not brown enough.

Higher elevations also tend to be lower in relative humidity: The ambient air is not able to hold as much moisture. Storage conditions for dry ingredients, particularly for flour, must be environmentally controlled if baking performance is to be maintained.

The operation of laboratory instruments is also affected by elevation, according to Lorenz (1979). Amylograph readings at 2,500 ft found a 3.5% increase in

Table 8.004. Boiling Temperatures of Water at Various Elevations

Elevation, altitude (ft)	Atmospheric pressure (mm Hg)	Boiling point of water (°C)	(°F)
Sea level	760.0	100.0	212.0
2,000	700.6	98.4	208.4
5,000	632.4	95.0	203.0
7,500	571.0	92.4	198.4
10,000	529.0	90.0	194.0

(Lorenz 1979)

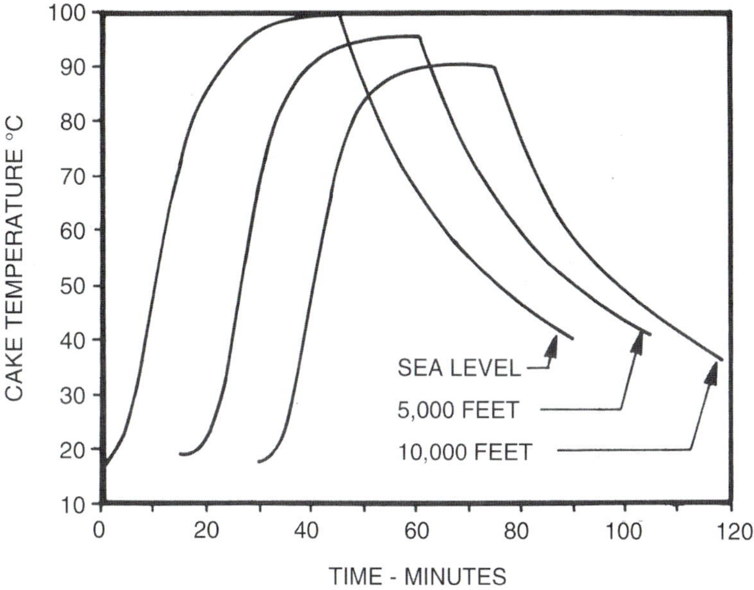

Figure 8.002. Elevation influences the internal temperature of cakes throughout the baking and cooling periods. (Lorenz 1971)

Brabender unit (BU) readings, rising to a 9.5% increase at 5,000 ft and 11.3% at 10,000 ft. The higher the BU reading of a given flour at sea level, the greater it increased at elevation. Mixogram readings also increased with rising elevation, and the rate of increase depended on the kind of flour. Mixograph data taken indicated a lower absorption and a higher protein content than the flour actually had at lower elevations. Farinograph values were similarly affected.

"High altitude" flour can be found in the marketplace. The description, however, refers to it being milled at elevation. It offers no specific advantages for baking at elevation than flour milled closer to sea level.

8.A.4.a. Formula modification: bread

When judged by expansion, bread doughs ferment faster and proof quicker at elevation. Lorenz (1979) reported that white bread dough containing 2% compressed yeast showed a 16% decrease in fermentation time and a 19% reduction in proof time at 7,500 ft. At 10,000 ft, fermentation time shrank 25%, with proof time 26% less. Ovenspring increased slightly at greater elevation as did compressibility: The bread was softer than that baked at sea level.

Formula and processing changes recommended by Lorenz (1979) included: (a) adjustment upward in absorption to compensate for the extra moisture lost to evaporation, (b) a slight decrease (0.25%) in yeast to reduce carbon dioxide generation, (c) proofing to height rather than time, (d) packaging the bread as soon as possible to avoid further evaporation losses and, for formulations in which yeast content has not been changed, (e) reduction in fermentation time and (f) reduction in proofing time.

8.A.4.b. Formula modification: cake

Elevation makes even more difference to cake performance than it does with bread. For one thing, specific gravity, an important variable in controlling batter performance, increases as elevation increases (**Figure 8.003**). (Specific gravity is the ratio, at constant temperature, of the density of the batter to the density of an equal amount of water. It is common to use the density of water at 4°C, or 39°F, the point at which water is heaviest, weighing 1,000 kg per cu m, or 62.4 lb per cu ft.) This change makes the batter less stable, and when baked, cakes are prone to collapse.

In practice, however, batter density cannot always be predicted and seems to be chiefly a function of the batter's strength, which depends on the kind of cake being made. If the batter is capable of holding more air and leavening gases, its density will decrease, but density will increase if the air incorporated during mixing is not held by the batter. Lower density results in greater leavening action and larger finished volume, while higher density yields less leavening and smaller volume.

To maintain batter stability at high elevation, flour needs to be increased in the formula by 2.5% at 3,500 ft and up to 10% at elevations of 8,000 ft and higher. For the same reason, the egg content, in the form of either liquid whole eggs or egg whites, must similarly be increased. Normally, the first increase by some 2.5% in the egg level is required when the elevation reaches 2,500 ft, and this increase becomes progressively greater, reaching a maximum of 15% at an elevation of 7,500 ft.

Another way to approach this problem is by dividing ingredients according to their strengthening or weakening functions. Strengtheners include flour, eggs and cocoa. Weakeners are sugar, corn syrup, fat and water. At elevation, an unadjusted

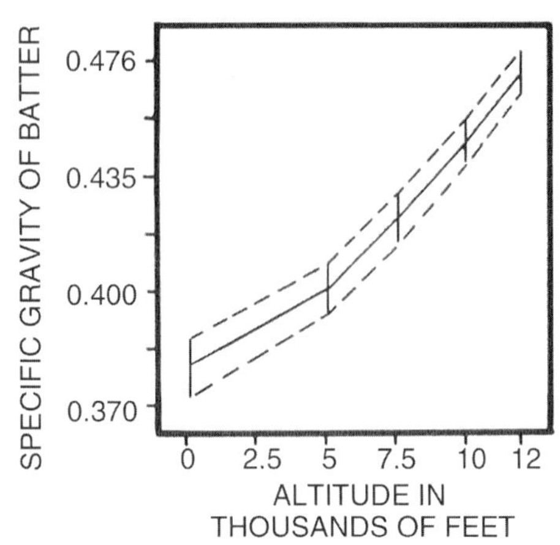

Figure 8.003. The specific gravity of cake batter increases with elevation.

formula will have too much weakness and not enough strength; it will need to be rebalanced (Foehse 2009).

The level of baking powder or other leavening material is critical at higher elevations. Thus, the baking powder must be reduced by 15% at an elevation of only 2,000 ft. At increasingly higher elevations, proportionately greater amounts of leavening material must be withheld, up to a maximum of 60% at an elevation of 8,000 ft.

Fats, as noted, tend to weaken doughs and batters, allowing excessive leavening expansion. Solid shortenings give better results than liquid fats because the emulsifier content of the shortening enables the dough or batter to tolerate larger amounts of liquid (Archuleta 2005).

Other factors that deserve consideration in cake baking at higher elevations include the following:

(a) Both batter- and foam-type cakes should be mixed to somewhat higher specific gravities than are usual at sea level (Lorenz et al. 1971). In other words, less air should be incorporated during mixing.

(b) The cake pans must receive a heavier coating of an appropriate release agent to prevent sticking during product depanning. The use of silicone-glazed and nonstick-coated pans should minimize the problem of product sticking.

(c) Whole eggs or egg whites, rather than egg yolk, should be used to adjust the amount of eggs to the required level. Egg yolk lacks sufficient moisture and protein to provide the necessary batter stabilizing effect.

(d) Cakes baked at elevations of 7,500 to 10,000 ft fail to acquire the degree of crust coloration of those made at sea level at the same oven temperature. The cooling effect of the rapid evaporation rates that prevail at high elevations makes it difficult for the crust to reach caramelization temperature.

To counteract this problem, Barmore (1936a) recommended that either the oven temperature be increased by 14 C° (25 F°) or that the bake time be extended proportionately to compensate for the lower crust temperature, taking care, however, to avoid excessive drying of the top crust. Although cakes baked at high elevations tend to have reduced volume, they exhibit greater crumb tenderness; this accounts for the need for more extensive pan greasing. The cakes should be depanned with minimum delay after emerging from the oven and cooled in an area free of drafts to minimize evaporative losses that would shorten their shelf life. For the same reason, they should be iced as soon as they have cooled adequately.

8.A.4.c. Formula modification: cookies and other baked foods

Formulations for biscuits, muffins, scones, quick breads and other chemically leavened items will also need adjustment, or else they will bake out lighter and fluffier or even collapse from the weight of fruit and nut particulates. To produce results corresponding to those made at elevations below 2,500 ft, the amount of baking powder and fat should be slightly decreased. A small reduction in sugar may also be required.

Atmospheric pressure affects cookie spread, and changes multiply at higher elevations. Spread increases by a factor of 10% when going from sea level to 5,000 ft and rises to 30% when going from 5,000 to 7,500 ft. The cookies get larger and their thickness decreases. Additional flour and less sugar may be required to "tighten" spread behavior (Lorenz 1978).

The choux paste method for preparation of cream puffs, eclairs and similar items yields doughs with well-developed gluten structures. These formulations are also comparatively low in weakening ingredients (sugar, fat, etc.). As a result, the change in atmospheric pressure at elevation has little effect on such products.

Pie crust is also not much affected by changes in elevation, other than the faster rate of evaporation of water. A bit more liquid may be required. Care in baking is required, however, because the crusts are often under-done in the middle. Lower atmosphere pressure means air in the oven holds less heat energy, slowing its penetration during baking.

Deep-fat frying, however, poses some challenges. As Lorenz (1979) observed, doughnuts frequently show cracked surfaces and high fat absorption when made at high elevation. They are often too deeply browned. Leavening expands the dough faster, creating a porous surface before the crust can seal itself. To remedy this, (a) reduce the leavening and fat in the formulation, (b) add a small portion of hard wheat flour, (c) reduce sugar in particularly rich formulations, and (d) lower the frying temperature to 182 to 185°C (360 to 365°F) from the 191°C (375°F) normally recommended.

Baking at elevation has been well studied by food scientists at Colorado State University and New Mexico State University, among other locations. Recent extension service publications and books describing their results include Archuleta (2005) and Kendall (2005). For those looking to home formulations for inspiration, a classic text is Norton (1903), now available online via Google Books, and Purdy (2005) is also recommended.

8.B. Bread

Updated by L.A. Gorton

The breadmaking process demands a lot of its ingredients, and the final result must meet the expectations of consumer and baker alike. In the US market, white bread was king for many years, and by 1997, white bread represented half of all bread sales, according to the Economic Census of Manufacturers, conducted every 5 years by the US Census Bureau of the Department of Commerce. The general category of variety breads, however, overtook white styles in sales after that, with the 2007 census reporting white pan bread as accounting for 44% of sales.

In recent years, bakers supplemented white bread (**Figure 8.004**) formulations with added fiber, vitamin D, calcium and other ingredients to build up choices in this category. Premium and super premium categories emerged in the past decade, commanding prices 2 to 3 times that of conventional white bread (Hotze 2004). Bakeries typically market such breads under their own brands and formulate them with brown sugar, molasses, honey and other "rich" ingredients. Scaling weight also increases, from the typical 24 oz to the premium 29 oz.

Although the following discussion concerns primarily the formulation of white pan bread, the fundamentals of ingredient usage apply to many other styles of baked foods. The processes of doughmaking are described in Chapter 6, while the ingredients are covered in Volume I, Chapter 2.

Figure 8.004. White pan bread, split down the top with a drizzle of butter before baking, has been a standard product for years. Application of sesame seeds provides a premium touch.

8.B.1. Batch doughs

Whether prepared as straight doughs, no-time doughs or sponges and final doughs, bread is primarily a mixture of flour, water, yeast and salt that is allowed to ferment before being baked. Supplementary ingredients include shortening and sugar and functional additives such as oxidants, reducing agents, buffers, emulsifiers, dough conditioners, crumb softeners and antimicrobials, all intended to improve the dough's machining, baking and keeping qualities.

The different production times required by each of the different breadmaking methods in current use are summarized by Tipples (1967) in **Figure 8.005**, with the time range of each individual processing step indicated separately. Short-duration operations such as dividing, rounding, moulding and panning are identified by the colored bands. A wide disparity exists between the various procedures. Thus, the sponge-and-dough process requires on an average 6.5 hours of production time, yet the mechanical and chemical dough development methods require 2 and 3 hours, respectively. At present, the sponge-and-dough method is the one

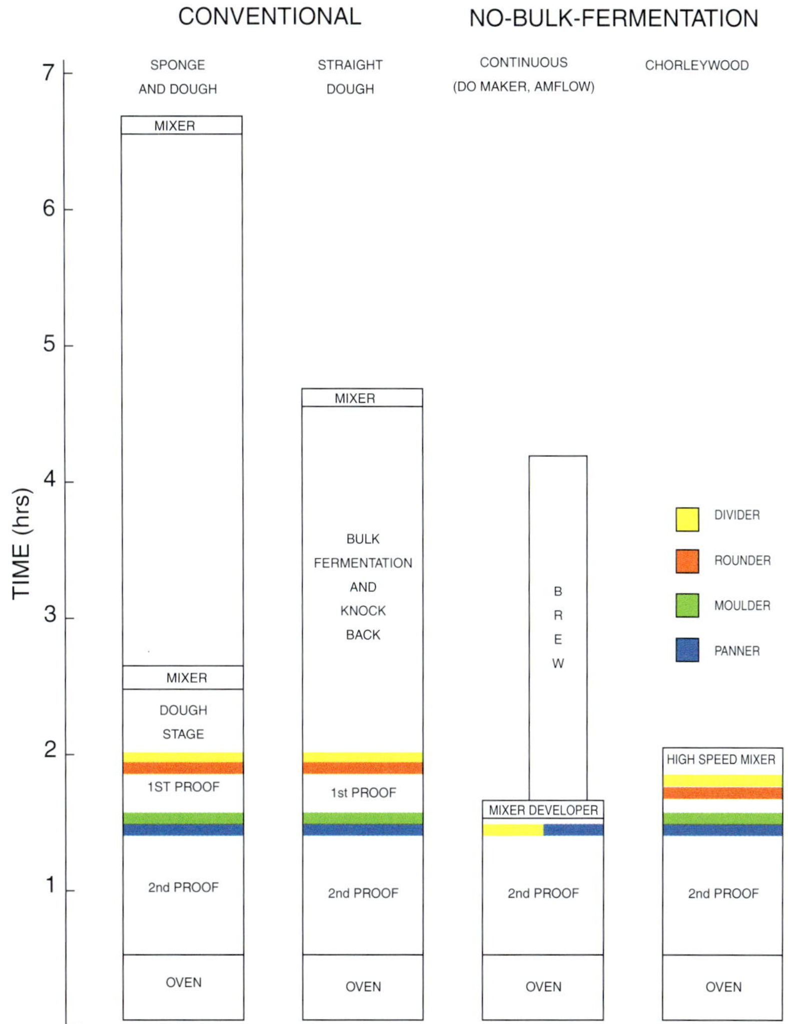

Figure 8.005. Batch (conventional) and liquid ferment (no-bulk-fermentation) methods of breadmaking vary widely in time requirements. (Tipples 1967)

most used by commercial wholesale bakers.

The differences in the various doughmaking processes are explained in Chapter 6, with ingredients figuring into the discussion. What follows here is a review of ingredient functionality with an eye toward formulating. The longer discussion of liquid ferments that follows illuminates many of the functions of these ingredients as well.

8.B.1.a. Flour

First of all, bread contains flour as its dominant ingredient. (The data in **Table 8.005** represents summary information from an American Institute of Baking survey covering 28 companies operating 210 plants. **Table 8.006** further defines the variables for the sponge-and-dough process among these same plants.) Flour is the single most important and basic ingredient in breadmaking, and it contributes to the volume, crust color, crumb color, grain, texture and taste of the finished bread.

Flour provides the structure, or framework, for baked foods because it forms gluten from the water-insoluble proteins unique to wheat, gliadin and gluten, which together represent 85% of the protein in flour. The gluten hydrates and binds water to become a viscoelastic material capable of retaining leavening gases. As the heat of the oven exceeds 85°C (185°F), the protein network changes, becoming relatively rigid and stable.

Flour's starch adds to that structure, being suspended in the gluten network. In the oven, starch granules rupture at a temperature range of 60 to 82°C (140 to 180°F), releasing the amylose and amylopectin molecules that gelatinize under the influence of heat and moisture.

The individual components of flour — gluten and starch, in particular — can be supplemented into formulations as needed. For example, modified wheat starches increase bread yield because they improve the water absorption by as much as 6%, thus raising the usual 66% absorption to 72% (Miller et al. 2008). Vital wheat gluten may be added to supplement the natural gluten in years of low protein flours and to improve "hinge strength" for buns and similar items.

Bread flours are typically milled from hard wheats, both red and white, delivered with a protein content of 11 to 18%. Protein quality is measured by the ability of the glu-

Table 8.005. Enriched White Bread Formula

Levels of major ingredients used

Ingredient	Range (bakers %)	Typical (bakers %)
Flour	100	100.0
Water*	52.7 to 72.6	63.5
Yeast, compressed	1.10 to 4.71	3.0
Salt	1.75 to 2.28	2.0
Sweetener solids	5.0 to 11.4	8.5
Shortening	1.5 to 8.8	3.0
Dairy product	0 to 4	2.0

Includes water from sweetener syrups
(Dubois and Vetter 1987)

Table 8.006. White Bread, Sponge-and-Dough Process

Variable	Range	Typical
Total flour in sponge	65.0 to 75.0%	70%
Sponge set temperature	23 to 29°C (74 to 84°F)	26°C (78°F)
Sponge fermentation	3 to 5 hours	4 hours
Sponge temperature rise	3 to 6 C° (5 to 11 F°)	4 to 5 C° (8 to 9 F°)
Dough mix	8 to 13 minutes	10 to 11 minutes
Delayed salt method used?	Variable	Yes
Dough temperature	26 to 28°C (78 to 82°F)	26 to 27°C (79 to 80°F)
Floor time	7 to 30 minutes	15 to 20 minutes
Scaling weight*	1.13 to 1.25	1.17
Intermediate proof	6 to 8 minutes	8 minutes
Proof time	50 to 65 minutes	55 to 60 minutes
Proof temperature, dry bulb	43 to 48°C (110 to 118°F)	46°C (115°F)
Proof temperature, wet bulb	38 to 43°C (100 to 110°F)	42°C (107°F)
Bake time	17 to 24 minutes	18 minutes
Oven temperature	188 to 238°C (370 to 460°F)	221 to 238°C (430 to 460°F)

Scaling weight = dough weight divided by baked product weight
(Dubois and Vetter 1987)

ten to expand properly and retain gas to produce a satisfactory product. Uniform particle size and adequate flow properties are required of flour to ensure its passage through the pneumatic flour handling and feeder systems of the bakery.

8.B.1.b. Water

Hydration of dry ingredients is the primary function of water in breadmaking. Water combines with wheat proteins, and it acts as a solvent to dissolve salt, sugar, milk powders and similar ingredients. It makes possible the actions of enzymes because they are active only in liquid systems. By wetting and swelling starch during baking, water contributes to gelatinization.

The proportion of water in relation to the flour (also called its "absorption") contributes to the rheological properties of the dough — its mobility, plasticity, extensibility and stickiness. In free and bound forms, water affects the quality of the finished product. Bound water delays staling, while free water accelerates it and can cause microbial problems.

As the second highest percentage inclusion in bread formulations, water assists in controlling dough temperature. Bakers are able to mix heated and chilled water sources with ambient tap water to achieve exact temperatures. Depending on local conditions, ingredient water may require conditioning or buffering to achieve optimum pH, which determines fermentation and enzyme activity rates.

8.B.1.c. Yeast

Bakers yeast (*Saccharomyces cerevisiae*) leavens bread by consuming (fermenting) simple sugars to produce carbon dioxide (CO_2) and ethanol (C_2H_5OH) gases. Other by-products of yeast fermentation include acids and heat, which biochemically condition the gluten and lower the dough pH. The fermentation of yeast results in the distinctive and appetizing flavor and aroma unique to yeast-raised products.

The most common forms of bakers yeast used by US wholesale bakers are compressed and cream, while retail bakers prefer compressed and instant active dry forms. Bakers yeast in its many forms is described in Volume I, Chapter 2, Part B.

In the sponge-and-dough process, the best results come from hydrating compressed or dry yeasts before they are added to the mixer. Instant active dry yeast can be incorporated into doughs directly with the other dry ingredients without any need for preliminary hydration.

8.B.1.d. Salt

Much of the natural taste of bread is brought out by the enhancing effect of salt, which is said to "round out" the flavor. Typical usage level for salt is 2% (flour weight basis), but current interest in sodium reduction is taking that down to 1.5%. Going much lower risks a marked diminishment in flavor, according to Dubois et al. (1984), who tested salt levels ranging from 0 to 2.1%.

Salt is present in bread for two technical reasons (Vetter 1979): (a) It plays a major role in controlling the rate of yeast fermentation by lessening yeast activity and by preventing the development of objectionable "wild" bacterial action, and (b) it strengthens gluten to ensure good dough handling properties on high-speed processing equipment and thus assures superior grain and texture in the finished product (**Figure 8.006**). As a drawback, salt reduces water absorption, but this activity can be a benefit when correcting soft, sticky doughs. Because salt strengthens gluten, it also lengthens mixing time so bakers often delay salt addition to the last stages of mixing.

Figure 8.006. Bread requires salt to control yeast activity and strengthen gluten as well as enhance flavor.

Particle size has major effect with salt. A medium granulation that dissolves with fair to rapid solubility is best for dough and batter systems because a minimum of time is available for this action.

Salt's functions and use in bread were reviewed by Gelroth and Strouts (2008).

8.B.1.e. Fats

Bakery shortenings are defined as a fat or oil that shortens the protein strand, reducing its tendency to knit together or complex with carbohydrates in wheat flour. In bread, shortening acts as a lubricant, assisting cell expansion in the dough and aiding the passage of slicer blades through the finished bread. Shortening also contributes in a minor way to moisture retention, which improves shelf life and helps tenderize the crumb. Shortening contributes to the nutritional value of bread, providing energy to the consumer.

8.B.1.f. Mineral yeast foods

The term "mineral yeast foods," as used by the American Institute of Baking, covers ingredients that adjust the performance of water, yeast and dough. Water conditioners include calcium carbonate, calcium sulfate, magnesium phosphate and magnesium chloride, which control the mineral content of locally sourced ingredient water, plus acid salts such as monocalcium phosphate for pH control. Ammonium salts, which provide a nitrogen source, are considered yeast conditioners, or yeast foods. And the dough conditioners that encompass materials such as oxidizing and reducing agents are discussed below.

Mineral yeast foods are specifically not the enrichment package.

8.B.1.g. Sugar

Bread formulations often include sugar to fuel the yeast fermentation process. The starch component in flour provides the bulk of the sugar needed by yeast and released as enzymes split the starch molecules into their glucose, fructose and maltose components. Even the disaccharides sucrose and maltose must first be separated into dextrose and fructose components before yeast can metabolize them.

Sugar is usually added to dough in the form of high-fructose corn syrup in the 42%-fructose format (42 HFCS), which replaced sucrose (cane or beet sugar) during the 1980s. Liquid sucrose and invert syrup have also been used, but these materials require heated storage and heat-traced piping, which 42 HFCS does not. High-DE corn syrups have been used as well, but these too must be heated to achieve the best flow properties. When formulating bread with a syrup form of sugar, the baker must account for its water when balancing formulations. For example, a syrup with 71% solids content carries 29% water.

A small amount of sugar remains in the dough after the oven deactivates the yeast, and these residual reducing sugars participate in the Maillard reaction that produces the attractive brown color of the crust. Because sugar is very hygroscopic, it improves the shelf life of baked products.

8.B.1.h. Milk, whey, soy

Milk products possess more of a reducing character than does flour, and they weaken the crumb structure of the baked bread as their relative proportion increases (Swortfiguer 1962). This defect can be largely overcome by boosting the oxidant level in proportion with the level of milk products (Doty and McCurrie 1964), preferably by adding such fast-acting oxidants as potassium iodate or azodicarbonamide.

The primary reason for including milk products in bread is the nutrition they provide. Nonfat dry milk is 36% protein (casein) and 51% carbohydrates (lactose) and also contributes calcium. Milk's proteins also participate in the Maillard browning reaction.

For economic reasons, however, today's bread formulations tend to use whey- or soy-based ingredients to replace milk. Potato flour is sometimes used for its ability to bind moisture. Soy flour is well known for its improving aspects, whitening the crumb of the finished product and adding its protein. Its water-binding capabilities enable higher absorption and thus higher yield (**Figure 8.007**).

It is recommended that the dairy ingredients, like other protein-bearing ingredients, be added at the initial stage of the mixing process to ensure complete incorporation into the dough and thus reducing brown spotting and lumping.

8.B.1.i. Enzymes

As they do in nature, enzymes act as catalysts to speed up chemical reactions. The enzymes chosen for bread applications are present in the formulation to modify specific wheat flour fractions to enhance their functionality in breadmaking, thus improving final bread quality. Enzymes are proteins and act under specific physical conditions. The heat of baking denatures, or deactivates, enzymes so they qualify as production aids, not subject to label declaration. Enzymes augment loaf volume, crumb structure, dough stability, tolerance, taste and flavor, and crumb softness (**Figure 8.008**).

Figure 8.007. Soy flour enhances moisture retention in bread, thus increasing yield for bakers and shelf life for consumers. (Cargill)

Enzyme-based dough conditioners address such needs as bromate replacement, shelf life extension, dough machineability and reduction of emulsifiers and gluten. Enzymes as bakery ingredients are described in Volume I, Chapter 1, Part D.

8.B.1.j. Oxidizers and reducing agents

Chemical dough development results from the action of reducing agents such as L-cysteine and oxidants such as potassium bromate or ascorbic acid, used either singly or in combination. The principal function of the reducing agents is to disaggregate the flour proteins, breaking the disulfide bonds and thereby cutting the dough's mixing time, while also making it more pliable and extensible. On the other hand, oxidants act to strengthen the mixed dough's gluten structure and thereby ensure adequate gas retention capacity (Tsen 1973). The role of oxidants and reducing agents is to

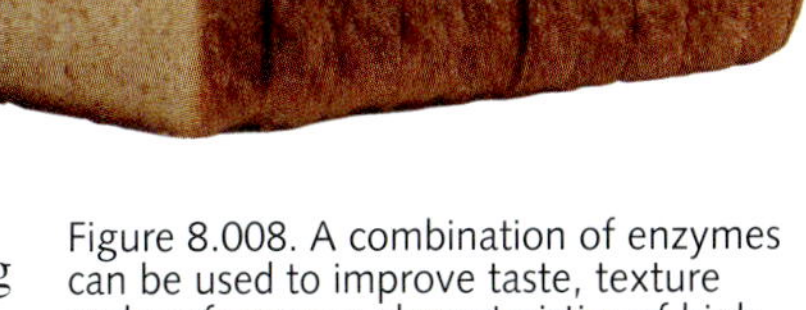

Figure 8.008. A combination of enzymes can be used to improve taste, texture and performance characteristics of high-fiber and/or whole-grain breads.

improve the rheological properties of the dough and finished product attributes.

Potassium bromate remains a highly effective oxidizer for bread production, although its use has been scrutinized closely and is currently being monitored by the Food and Drug Administration in the US. The American Bakers Association issued an industry guide to its use, available through its Web site, www.americanbakers.org. Use of this ingredient was analyzed by Gelroth et al. (2009), who reiterated restricting bromate to 30 ppm, which with proper processing will hold residues to below the critical 30 ppb limit. The advantages and disadvantages of bromates are covered in Volume I, Chapter 2, Part C, along with the other oxidants and reducing agents that benefit bread applications.

A number of commercial practices have evolved to implement chemical dough development, ranging from simple formula adjustments to the use of ferments, from variable mixing speeds to the inclusion of special additives in the form of yeast foods, enzymes and dough acidulants (Powell 1977). The various active reagents that find use in such doughs (cysteine, ascorbic acid, potassium bromate, proteolytic enzymes, monocalcium phosphate, ammonium salts, etc.) are available as commercial dry blends in various combinations that are designed to satisfy different production requirements. The basic formula adjustments for short-time and no-time doughs are essentially similar to those found desirable in mechanical dough development, namely, a reduction by 1% in the sweetener level, an increase in yeast by 0.5 to 1.0%, and an increase in absorption of up to 3.0% (Smerak 1973).

Two preconditions that must be met for chemical dough development are (a) a mixing rate that is above a minimum critical speed and (b) a work or energy input that exceeds a minimum "critical energy" level (Tipples and Kilborn 1974). Both of these requirements are greatly influenced by mixer design. While reducing agents act to lower both the critical mixing speed and the energy requirements needed to achieve peak dough development, they are unable to eliminate either of them entirely. When used at the optimum level, however, cysteine will reduce the energy requirements in mixing to about one-fifth of that expended in mechanical dough development (Ewart 1968). It also simultaneously shortens the mixing time by about one-third, regardless of the original mixing time required by any given flour (Finney et al. 1971). Hence, the level of cysteine needed to achieve a specific mixing time or work input varies with the strength of flour. While the general recommendation is to keep the dough temperature within the range of 28 to 30°C (83 to 86°F), slightly higher temperatures will accelerate the fermentation rate with satisfactory results (Glover 1975).

Table 8.007. Enrichment Levels in the US

Nutrient	Flour (mg per lb)	Bread (mg per lb)	Corn meal (mg per lg)	Corn grits (mg per lg)	Corn masa (mg per lb)
Vitamins					
Thiamine (vitamin B₁)	2.9	1.8	2.0 to 3.0	2.0 to 3.0	2.0
Riboflavin (vitamin B₂)	1.8	1.1	1.2 to 1.8	1.2 to 1.8	1.2
Niacin (vitamin B₃)	24.0	15.0	16 to 245	16 to 245	16.0
Folic acid, folate (vitamin B₉)	0.7	0.4	0.7 to 1.0	0.7 to 1.0	0.7 to 1.0
Minerals					
Iron	20.0	12.5	13 to 26	21 to 26	13 to 26
Calcium - optional	960.0	600.0	960.0	960.0	960.0

8.B.1.k. Dough conditioners

Compounds such as calcium stearoyl lactylate (CSL), sodium stearyl fumarate and succinylated monoglyceride (SMG) find extensive use in conventional as well as continuous bread production. They act variously to strengthen the gluten in continuously-mixed dough and improve its extensibility, thereby increasing the dough's mixing tolerance, stability during scaling and gas retention capacity during proofing.

Emulsifiers are fat-based ingredients that function both as dough stabilizers when they interact with the gluten protein in the dough and crumb softeners when they complex with gelatinizing starch during baking. The emulsifiers with the best dough stabilizing effect — diacetyl tartaric acid esters of mono- and diglyerides (DATEM) and ethoxylated mono- and diglycerides (EMG) — are usually the worst crumb softeners, while those with the best crumb softening effects (monoglycerides) are usually inferior dough stabilizers.

Sodium stearoyl lactylate (SSL) is the most commonly used emulsifier in white pan bread, having both fair dough stabilizing and crumb softening action. The monoglycerides can be added to further improve crumb softness, while DATEM can be added to shore up dough stability.

8.B.1.l. Enrichment

US law mandates the enrichment of white bread with certain nutrients to specified levels of fortification (**Table 8.007**). In US practice, enrichment is generally done by the miller before the flour leaves the mill. Bakers wishing to manage this ingredient on their own can use enrichment mixtures packaged as soluble sachets, sized one packet per batch of dough, or as tablets, calibrated one tablet per 100 lb flour. The reasons for enriching cereal grain products are explained in Volume I, Chapter 2, Part C.

8.B.1.m. Other ingredients

Bread formulations may also include a variety of other ingredients. These materials include, but are not limited to, malt and malt flour, for its flavor and enzyme content; mold inhibitors such as calcium or sodium propionate or vinegar; and particulates such as seeds, spices, dried fruits, nuts and raisins.

8.B.2. Liquid ferments

When bakers adopted continuous mixing processes during the 1960s, they launched themselves into the future's technologies of automatic process control while tapping the past's application of liquid ferments. Many of the advantages of lengthy bulk fermentation could now be obtained through the use of prefermented brews and liquid sponges. To understand formulating of liquid ferments, it is necessary to first understand formulating of continuous mix doughs. Modern day applications of liquid ferments grew directly out of continuous mix techniques. Entringer (1975) provided an interesting discussion of how his central-plant bakery used a common preferment to produce not only bread but also French rolls, hamburger buns, sweet goods, cinnamon rolls and yeast-raised doughnuts.

8.B.2.a. Continuous mix doughs

The methods of dough manipulation in continuous mixing differ from those of conventional batch methods and require adjustments in both formulation and in the functional properties of the dough ingredients. Early experience with continuous mixing systems pointed very clearly to different requirements in the areas of dairy-based products, oxidant levels, enzyme supplementation, shortening characteristics and flour properties compared with the sponge-and-dough and straight methods. **Table 8.008** summarizes the variables of the continuous-mix process as currently practiced.

Table 8.008 White Bread, Continuous Mix, Typical Process

Variable	Range
Total flour in brew	0 to 50%
Brew set temperature	24 to 33°C
	(76 to 92°F)
Fermentation time, 0% flour	2 to 2.5 hours
Fermentation time, 50% flour	2 to 3 hours
Temperature rise to	31 to 37°C
	(88 to 98°F)
Cooled to	8 to 14°C
	(46 to 58°F)
Dough temperature	39 to 40°C
	(102 to 104°F)
Proof time	44 to 60 minutes
Proof temperature, dry bulb	42 to 49°C
	(108 to 120°F)
Proof temperature, wet bulb	40 to 44°C
	(104 to 112°F)
Bake time	14 to 18 minutes
Oven temperature	205 to 254°C
	(400 to 490°F)

** Scaling weight = dough weight divided by baked product weight*

(Dubois and Vetter 1987)

8.B.2.a.i. Flour

Protein quality, rather than protein quantity, determines a flour's suitability for continuous mixing. Strong flours either need longer mixing or faster mixing speeds, while weak protein flours, although developing more rapidly, tend to be deficient in mixing tolerance.

The flour must exhibit a rapid hydration rate, or else adequate dough development may not be attained, even with increased mixing speeds. Although the flour may have received oxidation and enzyme supplementation at the mill, corrective adjustments of these factors will likely be necessary at the bakery to meet production needs.

In general, spring wheat flours, because of their higher protein content and stronger gluten character, compared with winter wheat flours, will require higher absorption and greater developer speeds to yield bread of acceptable quality. In most commercial production, a blend of spring and winter wheat flours is used in continuous processing.

8.B.2.a.ii. Bakery shortenings

Because regular plastic shortenings will melt at the higher mixing and proofing temperatures that prevail in continuous processing, their function resembles more that of ordinary oils than of plastic fats. The addition of hard flakes, with a melting point of about 60°C (140°F), or monoglycerides raises the softening point above the normally encountered operating temperatures and brings about an improvement in the gas retention and stability of the dough.

The basic amount of flakes required in continuous dough processing appears to be independent of the total fat in the formula (Baldwin et al. 1965). When the flake level was held constant at 0.18% based on flour, no differences in bread quality were detected as the total fat content was varied from 1.5 to 6.0%. Monoglycerides with melting points of 55 to 58°C (131 to 136°F) are available in flaked or granular form. With these melting points, they not only show greater effectiveness in retarding the firming rate of the bread crumb (Baeuerlen 1966) but also offer the added advantage of augmenting the function of hard flakes as they become part of the fat solids at the operating temperatures of the mixer.

A major advantage of fluid shortenings is, no surprise, their pumpability over a relatively broad temperature range; however, storage under gentle agitation is recommended in the range of 15 to 32°C (60 to 90°F), according to Paulicka (1990). A number of fluid shortening suppliers narrow that range to 10 to 21°C (50 to 70°F).

8.B.2.a.iii. Sugar

Sugar is added in doughmaking to provide readily fermentable carbohydrates for yeast to initiate and sustain its fermentative activity. In flour-free ferments, the added sugars constitute the sole source of carbohydrates. In flour-containing ferments, the flour may serve as an adequate source of fermentables to sustain fermentation. Depending on the amount of flour used in the ferment, the required sugar additions may range from 0.75% (based on flour) in ferments with flour contents that exceed 30 to 40%, to about 2% in ferments with lower flour levels. While the addition of some sugar to flour ferments will hasten the onset of yeast fermentation, this addition should be held to the minimum level required to achieve the intended purpose.

8.B.2.a.iv. Dairy products

Today, soy flour and soy protein products have taken over the role of dairy ingredients in baked foods. Knowing what dairy can accomplish, however, enables the baker to be flexible in the choice of such ingredients. During the early days of continuous mixing, nonfat dry milk levels beyond 1% had a deleterious effect on bread quality. Swortfiguer (1960, 1962) found the strong buffering action of milk to be a critical factor in preventing a normal decrease in the pH of the ferment. This adverse effect was ameliorated by the use of acidifying salts or of lactic acid.

8.B.2.a.v. Oxidants and reducing agents

The mixing action of the continuous process takes place in a closed system with the virtual exclusion of atmospheric oxygen and thus requires the use of an oxidizing agent. Because the actual development time in the continuous mix process is limited to about 1 minute or less, fast-acting oxidants such as azodicarbonamide (ADA) or ascorbic acid are generally employed to bring about the rapid gluten tightening effect needed for adequate gas retention (Trum and Rose 1964). Potassium bromate is normally added with the faster oxidants to strengthen the gluten structure during the proofing and initial baking stages. As a rule, total oxidant levels range from 60 to 75 ppm, and use of potassium bromate is recommended at levels of <30 ppm (Gelroth et al. 2009).

A suitable alternative is azodicarbonamide (ADA). Its special suitability for use in continuous dough mixing derives from the fact that, while it is a fast-acting oxidant, its activity rate is less intense than that of bromate and extends over a longer period of time.

In continuous mixing systems, ascorbic acid retains its reducing function because it is not exposed to atmospheric oxygen in the developer head. Under these conditions, ascorbic acid reduces the mixing requirements of the dough and increases the output of the mixing unit (Mauseth and Johnston 1967). An essentially similar effect is produced by L-cysteine when it is added to dough in the form of the hydrochloride monohydrate with sweet dry whey and potassium bromate during continuous mixing. Used at levels of 25 to 100 ppm of flour, it will bring about reductions of up to 40% in dough mixing requirements (Henika 1965).

Table 8.009. White Bread, Brew (Liquid Sponge) Process

Variable	Range	Typical
Total flour in brew	0 to 55%	0% or 40 to 50%
Brew set temperature	21 to 30°C	26 to 27°C
	(70 to 86°F)	(78 to 80°F)
Fermentation, 0% flour	1 to 1.5 hours	1 to 1.5 hours
Fermentation, 40 to 50% flour	1.5 to 2 hours	2 hours
Temperature rise to	27 to 33°C)	30 to 31°C
	(80 to 92°F)	(86 to 88°F)
Brew cooled to	2 to 10°C	4 to 7°C
	(36 to 50°F)	(40 to 45°F)
Dough mix time	11 to 15 minutes	13 to 14 minutes
Delayed salt method used?	Variable	Majority, no
Dough temperature	26 to 29°C	26°C
	(78 to 85°F)	(78°F)
Floor time	0 to 35 minutes	10 to 20
Scaling weight*	1.12 to 1.25	1.15 to 1.17
Intermediate proof	2.75 to 9 minutes	6 to 9 minutes
Proof time	42 to 64 minutes	55 minutes
Proof temperature, dry bulb	41 to 49°C	43 to 46°C
	(105 to 120°F)	(110 to 114°F)
Proof temperature, wet bulb	39 to 43°C	42°C
	(102 to 110°F)	(108°F)
Bake time	14 to 28 minutes	18 to 20 minutes
Oven temperature	205 to 238°C	210 to 221°C
	(400 to 460°F)	(410 to 430°F)

Scaling weight = dough weight divided by baked product weight
(Dubois and Vetter 1987)

Table 8.010. ADMI Stable Ferment Formula

Ingredient	% (flour basis)
Water	70.0
Yeast	2.0
Yeast food	0.5
Malt	0.4
Sugar	3.0
Nonfat dry milk	6.0
Salt	2.0

(McLaren 1954)

8.B.2.a.vi. Yeast activation

In the absence of bulk fermentation, a rapid onset of yeast activity is of critical importance for maintaining established proof times. One common procedure for achieving this goal is to suspend the yeast in a dilute sugar solution tempered to about 32 to 38°C (90 to 100°F) for the purpose of bringing the yeast out of its lag phase. After a fermentation of about 30 minutes, the yeast slurry is cooled to 10°C (50°F) and held at this temperature until required for dough mixing. Other additives that may be used to stimulate yeast activity include yeast foods, buffer salts, and varying amounts of flour.

8.B.2.b. Liquid ferments

Liquid ferments developed as part of the continuous mixing process, but with time, bakers began to add flour to the preferment. When many of these bakers switched back to sponge-and-dough methods, they kept their "liquid brew" and preferment systems, adapting these technologies to batch methods. Thus it was that various components of the continuous mixing systems were modified to efficiently handle preferments containing 50 to 70% of flour. **Table 8.009** summarizes the variables of the liquid sponge, or brew, process as currently practiced.

The use of liquid ferments in breadmaking actually has a long and varied history. Nearly a century ago, Jago and Jago (1911) ago gave detailed instructions for the preparation of various types of barms (liquid or semi-liquid ferments) that were in common use in France and Great Britain during the 1800s.

8.B.2.b.i. Stable ferment process

American bakers were initiated into the technology of liquid ferments through introduction of the "ADMI stable ferment process" by the American Dry Milk Institute in 1954 (McLaren 1954) and by the simultaneous development of continuous dough mixing processes.

The purpose of the original stable ferment process was to simplify the sponge-and-dough method of breadmaking by replacing the plastic sponge with a liquid, flour-free ferment. The basic formula of the ferment, based on 100 parts of flour, is shown in **Table 8.010**. In practice, the required volume of water, at a temperature of 35 to 38°C (95 to 100°F), was metered into a tank and the solid ingredients dispersed in it. The suspension was fermented at a constant temperature for 6 hours under gentle agitation. The mature ferment was then either used immediately for doughmaking, or it could be stored in a stable condition by cooling to 10°C (50°F). At this temperature, it retained its fermentative vitality for some 48 hours. For doughmaking, a portion of the ferment, sufficient to satisfy the absorption needs of the flour, was introduced into a standard mixer, together with the flour and the balance of the dough ingredients, and mixed into a dough.

The primary role of nonfat dry milk was to control the pH of the ferment, its effect being essentially proportional to its amount in the ferment. Thus, the pH levels obtained in the mature ferments were 2.3 when no milk was used, 4.4 with 2% milk, and 5.2 when 5 to 6% of milk was added.

For the ferment to yield acceptable bread, it had to undergo a specified period of fermentation and conditioning. Within the recommended temperature range of 35 to 43°C (95 to 110°F), a suitable ferment was obtained in 6 hours, even though active fermentation may have ceased well before then as a result of sugar depletion.

At the time that the stable ferment concept was introduced, average levels of milk in bread production had declined to 4%, thus making a method requiring 6% nonfat dry milk not generally accepted by bakers. In the years since, use of milk ingredients has been under continuing pressure in terms of their costs, leading many bakers to substitute whey and soy ingredients for nonfat dry milk.

8.B.2.b.ii. Variants of liquid ferments

Shortly after its introduction, the stable ferment process went through several modifications, now referred to as liquid sponges, liquid ferments, preferments, brews or broths. Scarborough (1955) described three such variants. In one of these, the nonfat dry milk content of the ferment was reduced to 2%, with an additional 2% introduced at the dough-mixing stage. The yeast level was increased to 2.5% in the ferment, with a further 1% added to the dough. Total formula sugar was increased to 10%, of which about 3.5% was used in the ferment. Potassium bromate and potassium iodate were the oxidants added in dough mixing. Fermentation of the liquid required 5 to 6 hours at 32°C (90°F). (Potassium iodate has since disappeared as a common bakery oxidant.)

A second proposed variant eliminated all milk from the ferment and used buffer salts for pH control. Moreover, the sugar normally used in the ferment was replaced by 5% of the total formula flour to serve as a source of fermentable carbohydrates and as a buffer for pH control. Fermentation was conducted at 29°C (85°F) for 8 to 24 hours under constant agitation.

A third ferment process offered greater simplicity by limiting the solid ingredients of the ferment to yeast, sugar, salt and buffer salts, with a fermentation time of 3 to 4 hours at 29°C (85°F). In succeeding years, so-called concentrated yeast ferments were developed that, except for the salt and flour, contained the full complement of the dough ingredients but used only about one-half of the total dough water (Cavalier 1963). This approach not only increased the practical capacity of existing fermenting tanks but also enabled the baker to control the dough temperature by tempering the remaining dough water as required to obtain the desired dough temperature.

8.B.2.b.iii. Liquid ferments in practice

A liquid ferment process that found extensive application in the baking plants of a major grocery chain was described by Ziemke (1956). It used the ferment formula shown in **Table 8.011**, based on 100 lb of flour. The initial set temperature of 27°C

Table 8.011. Water Ferment Formula

Ingredient	lb
Water	30.0
Yeast	1.5
Salt	1.0
Sugar	3.0
Buffer and yeast nutrients*	0.5

** Blend of $CaCO_3$ plus $Ca(H_2PO_4)_2$ and either $(NH_4)_2SO_4$ or NH_4Cl in a flour carrier*

(Cavalier 1963)

Table 8.012. Water Ferment

(based on 3.5% yeast per 100 lb flour)

Ingredient	lb
Water	21.0
Yeast	3.5
Salt	0.5
Sugar (solids)	1 to 2

Set ferment at 84 to 85°F (29 to 29.5°C)
Adjust pH to 3.8 by adding sugar
Ferment to a 7 F° temperature rise (30 to 40 minutes)
Chill to 50 to 54°F (10 to 12.2°C) for holding

(Glover 1975)

Table 8.013. Representative Water Ferment

Ingredient	%
Water	82.35
Sweeteners (solids)	7.75
Yeast	8.00
Salt	1.40
Buffer	0.50
	100.00

Set ferment at 28°C (82°F)
Ferment for 1 to 1.5 hours
Temperature rise to 33°C (92°F) and hold there

(Dubois 1984)

(80°F) rose to 35°C (95°F) during fermentation, which was completed in 3.5 hours. The finished ferment, its pH stabilized at about 4.9, was cooled to 16°C (60°F) at which temperature it could be held for 48 hours without loss in activity. This formula produced a concentrated ferment — 33.5 lb of the finished ferment being used per 100 lb of flour. The balance of the dough water and remaining ingredients, as well as 1 lb of additional yeast, were added at the dough-mixing stage.

Another flour-free liquid ferment that found successful application was described by Glover (1975) and is summarized in **Table 8.012**. Its composition is such that 7 lb of the ferment contains 1 lb of yeast.

The pH of the ferment is readily controlled at 3.8 by adjusting the sugar addition within the range of 1 to 2 lb because an increase in the sugar level results in lowering of the pH. With a set temperature of 29 to 29.5°C (84 to 85°F), fermentation terminates when the temperature has risen by 4°C (7 F°) to 32.8 to 33.3°C (91 to 92°F), which usually occurs within 30 to 40 minutes. By cooling the ferment to 4°C (40°F), its vitality remains undiminished when held overnight.

A major advantage of this flour-free ferment is that it suits production of all yeast-raised products because the yeast level in the final dough is controlled by varying the amount of ferment used, with a compensating change in the added dough water.

According to Dubois (1984), the formula shown in **Table 8.013** is typical of the flour-free ferments in current use. These ferments undergo fermentation for 1 to 1.5 hours while being mildly agitated. The temperature is allowed to rise by 5 C° (9 F°), that is, from 28 to 33°C (82 to 91°F), at which level it is stabilized by applying refrigeration to the fermentation tank. When fermentation is complete, the ferment is cooled to below 10°C (50°F) and held at that temperature until needed. At a use level of 35%, based on flour, this ferment contributes 31.1% of water, 3.0% yeast, 0.5% salt and 0.4% residual sweeteners to the final dough formula.

In general, the time required for proper fermentation of liquid ferments depends primarily on the level of flour in the ferment. Flour-free ferments, given an appropriate set temperature, require about 1 hour of fermentation, whereas ferments containing 40% flour need 2 to 2.5 hours to reach the end-point (Dubois 1984).

Additional reviews of the practical aspects of various systems of liquid ferment have been provided by Alesch (1970), Hallberg (1974), Uhrich (1975) and Turner (1980).

The current technology of liquid ferment systems in bread production was reviewed by Kulp (1983). On the basis of typical formulations for liquid ferments, concentrated yeast ferment and the traditional plastic sponge, as shown in **Table 8.014**, he listed the following differences between the various ferments:

(a) Flour levels vary from 0% for water ferments up to a maximum of 70% for a ferment that can still be pumped. Plastic sponges contain from 60 to 100% of the formula flour. To facilitate mechanical transfer by pumps, liquid ferments have higher water levels than do plastic sponges.

(b) All systems use ammonium salts as yeast food in rather comparable amounts, although flour ferments tend toward the lower levels of the range shown.

(c) Buffers such as calcium carbonate are generally added to the liquid ferments and especially to the water ferments to keep the pH within the desirable range for yeast activity. Monocalcium phosphate is also used to adjust acidity.

(d) Sugar is used in water ferments to support yeast fermentation. In flour ferments, its use is optional.

(e) Salt is used optionally in liquid ferments to control fermentation and release carbon dioxide from the fermenting broth.

In a subsequent summary of the influence of liquid ferments on the quality characteristics of white pan bread, Kulp (1986) concluded that the liquid ferment process will produce bread comparable in quality to that made by the sponge-and-dough method when not less than 50% of flour is used in the ferments. Breads from water brews, which have no flour in the preferment, were found to have a shorter shelf life in terms of softness retention and retained flavor intensity.

Table 8.014. Typical Ferment Compositions

Ingredient	Plastic sponge	Ferments	Concentrated yeast ferment
Flour (%)	60 to 100	0 to 70	0
Water (%)	33 to 55	61 to 66	15 to 30
Yeast (%)	0.75 to 2.5	3.5 to 2.5	3.5 to 0.5
Ammonium salts (%)	0.09 to 0.03	0.09 to 0.03	0.09 to 0.06
Buffers (%)	None	0.3 to 0	0.25 to 0.2
Sugars (%)	None	3.0 to 0	3.0
Salt (%)	None	0.5 to 0	0.5 to 0
Set temperature (°F)	74 to 75	80 to 76	80 to 86
Ferment time (hours)	3 to 6	1 to 3	1

(Kulp 1983)

8.B.2.b.iv. Yeast and bacteria

Liquid ferments are normally made with compressed yeast. Thorn (1963) pointed out that if dry yeast is used for this purpose and is rehydrated directly in the ferment, the latter should have a temperature of at least 32°C (90°F). A better procedure is to hydrate the dry yeast separately, as is the practice in the sponge-and-dough process. No perceptible loss of fermentative activity occurs when liquid ferments are held for periods of 19 to 24 hours at 8°C (46°F). Holding at 12°C (54°F) for that period will lead to an increase in proof time of 5 to 6 minutes.

Adding salt at a level of 0.5% to the ferment was found by Bayfield and Young (1964b) to stimulate yeast activity, whereas the normal 2.0% salt level had a deleterious effect on final bread quality.

A systematic investigation of the microbiological population that develops in liquid ferments was undertaken by Robinson et al. (1958a) to evaluate the influence of the metabolic by-products of the individual bacterial species on the final bread flavor. The bacterial population in all ferments increased slightly through the second hour of fermentation and then declined by some 75 to 95% during the next 4 hours, except for Kohman's salt-rising ferment in which it remained relatively constant.

The decline in the bacterial population in ferments and doughs has long been attributed to either the effects of alcohol or acids, representing a depletion of nutrients, or a lack of oxygen. Robinson et al. (1958b), however, found that yeast elaborates antibiotic substances during fermentation that exert an inhibitory action on the microorganisms of liquid ferment cultures.

The production of organic acids, carbonyls and alcohol was studied by Cole et al. (1962) in a series of 3 ferments containing progressively higher levels of sugar, yeast and salt, and fermented for 6 hours at 35°C (95°F) and then held for 17 hours at 4°C (39°F). Alcohol and acid production, which were proportional to the initial sugar concentration, reached their maximum rates within 2 to 5 hours of fermentation, whereas the volatile carbonyls continued to increase during the entire fermentation period. Nonvolatile carbonyls, with pyruvic acid as the major representative, reached a peak within 2 to 4 hours and then declined substantially. Fermentation at lower temperatures reduced total carbonyl production but caused no significant change in the quantities of alcohol and total organic acids.

8.B.2.b.v. Buffering and pH

Martinez-Anaya and Kulp (1984) studied the changes in various liquid ferments during fermentation. They compared ferments without flour (both unbuffered and buffered) with those containing 20% and 50% flour. A sharp drop in pH occurred during the first hour of fermentation in all ferments, with a lesser subsequent decline in pH in the flour ferments. Either flour or a proper level of buffer is needed in the ferment to maintain the required pH range of 4 to 5 after 3 hours of fermentation.

The current technology of liquid ferments evolved largely from earlier studies of the effects of such factors as carbohydrate sources, pH, temperature, fermentation time, etc. Thus, Bayfield and Lannuier (1962), comparing the influence of different sources of carbohydrates in the ferment on final bread quality, observed that while ferments with 8% glucose had the greatest gassing power, 10% flour ferments, with much less gas production, yielded bread with a significantly better loaf score. They concluded that a vigorous fermentation in the ferment was not needed for optimum bread quality if the proper pH is obtained by other means such as acidification.

Maselli (1955) was among the first to establish the importance of pH to yeast activity in a ferment by showing that the maximum rate of gas production is obtained within a pH range of 4 to 5.4. If the pH of the ferment is allowed to drop below 4, yeast activity is retarded, with some of the inhibition becoming irreversible, especially on extended storage of the ferment.

Bayfield et al. (1963) studied the effects of ferment pH over a range of 3 to 8.3. At pH levels lower than 3, the ferment failed to yield workable doughs. Optimal loaf volumes and bread scores were obtained with ferments at pH 4.5. The type of acid (citric, lactic, phosphoric or hydrochloric) used to obtain the required ferment acidity had no significant effect on bread quality, indicating that pH is the primary factor affecting loaf properties.

The proteins of milk, wheat flour and soy flour are effective buffers. When calcium carbonate is used as the principal buffer, the addition of yeast nutrients in the form of so-called brew improvers is generally required. Typical of such products is a formulation made up of some 62% dibasic ammonium phosphate, 15% potassium sulfate, 8% magnesium sulfate and 15% calcium carbonate. Ferments buffered with mineral salts show a lesser foaming tendency than do those that are protein-buffered.

Calcium propionate, a commonly used mold inhibitor, is a salt of a strong base and a weak acid and, therefore, has a marked buffering capacity. It is, for this reason, generally added to the liquid ferment. Gross et al. (1967) showed that the addition of 0.1% calcium propionate, along with 0.33% nonfat dry milk, effectively keeps the pH in flour-free ferments above 4.0 with fermentation times as long as 3.5 hours. This addition results in a shorter proof time and a greater loaf volume.

Bayfield and his co-workers (1961 through 1965) subjected flour ferments to an extensive investigation in which the effects of various treatments and additives were studied. In ferments containing 10% flour as the only source of fermentable carbohydrates, acidification with salts such as sodium aluminum phosphate, monocalcium phosphate and mono-potassium phosphate yielded a bread quality either superior, or at least comparable, to that obtained with a control that contained glucose as the sole fermentable carbohydrate (Lannuier and Bayfield 1961).

A progressive rise occurs in the gassing rate as the amount of flour in a sugarless ferment is increased to 50% (Bayfield and Young 1964b). Acidification of the flour ferments with lactic acid further increases the fermentation rate. Salt above the 1.0% level in the ferment has a depressing effect on yeast activity. Flour ferments are improved by the addition of about 0.5% sugar as a fermentation stimulator.

8.B.2.b.vi. Enzymes

Enzyme supplementation with diastatic malt syrup (**Figure 8.009**) or fungal preparations is effective with flour-containing ferments (Bayfield and Young 1964c). The addition of 0.5% malt syrup perceptibly improved bread flavor. This improvement is directly attributable to the syrup and is independent of its enzymatic activity. When fungal preparations are used, all salt should be withheld from the ferment because salt greatly inhibits protease activity (Johnson and Miller 1957).

Enzyme activity in the ferment is markedly affected by pH. Carroll et al. (1956) found that in buffered ferments the activities of both malted wheat flour and fungal α-amylase and protease remained essentially constant for 24 hours of fermentation, but in unbuffered water ferments, no α-amylase activity from either source survived 2.5 hours of fermentation, and a drastic drop in pH occured. Loss of protease activity was 25% for wheat malt and 50% for the fungal preparation in the same ferment after 6 hours of fermentation.

Figure 8.009. Diastatic malt extracts act as both enzyme sources and sweeteners in baked foods.
(Malt Products)

8.B.2.b.vii. Fermentation time

Over time, bakers gradually reduced fermentation time from the 6 hours specified for the original stable ferment process to an average of 2 to 2.5 hours for liquid flour ferments and 1 hour for water ferments.

Aside from the production of carbon dioxide, alcohol, organic acids and other by-products, a critical function of fermentation is the reduction of the pH to a range that will produce optimum bread baking results. Means other than fermentation are available for the control of pH such as the addition of acidifying and buffer salts. Bayfield and Young (1964a) found that bread quality improved with a fermentation time up to 45 minutes and that, thereafter, no further improvements were obtained. They concluded that the fermentation time of the ferment can be reduced to 45 minutes without effect on bread quality as long as the pH is properly adjusted. The yeast is assumed to need this minimum time to become fully activated.

The same authors investigated the effect of temperature on fermentation time (Bayfield and Young 1965). Three temperature levels, 30, 40 and 49°C (86, 104 and 120°F) and three fermentation times, namely, 15, 30 and 45 minutes, were compared to a control of 135 minutes. While fermentation at 30°C (86°F) yielded the largest loaf volume with each of the fermentation times, best overall bread scores were obtained with fermentation at 40°C (104°F) for 30 minutes.

Table 8.015. Hearth Bread Formula

Ingredient	Amount (g)
Sponge	
Flour, spring wheat	600
Water	348
Compressed yeast	25
Mineral yeast food	5
Dough	
Flour, spring wheat	400
Water	230
Compressed yeast	5
Salt	20
Sugar (sucrose)	25
Dry malt powder	10
Ascorbic acid solution*	22 ml

* One tablet (30 ppm ascorbic acid) dissolved in 500 ml water

(O'Donnell 1993)

Table 8.016. French Bread Formula, Sponge and Dough Method

Ingredient	Sponge (%)	Dough (%)
Flour	60	40
Water	33	22
Yeast	2	–
Yeast food	0.375	–
Salt	–	2
Sugar	–	2
Shortening	–	2
Malt	–	1

(Feinberg 1975)

Table 8.017. French Bread Formula, "Improved" French Method

Ingredient	Amount (bakers %)
Flour	100
Water	64
Fresh yeast	1.5
Salt	2

(Forestier 1996)

8.C. Variety Bread

Updated by L.A. Gorton

In the US, variety breads represent approximately 54% of all bread products shipped by commercial bakeries, according to the 2007 Economic Census of Manufactures issued by the US Census Bureau of the Department of Commerce. Among the varieties, whole-wheat, cracked wheat, multigrain and other "dark" breads accounted for 18% of volume; French, Italian and Vienna hearth-type breads made up 15%; and other varieties such as rye, English muffins, bagels and croissants, 21%. Variety breads differ to varying degrees from white pan bread in their flavor, taste, crust character and crumb texture. The expansion in the market share of variety breads in recent decades points to a growing acceptance of these products among consumers.

The macro- and micronutrient profiles of many variety breads were reported by Ranhotra et al. (1984, 1986). Breads made from less refined flours tended to have slightly higher levels of vitamin and mineral nutrients than those made from more refined styles, but the difference was not great, a percentage point or two on average. The researchers singled out the B vitamins (B_6, folic acid and pantothenic acid) as being considerably diminished when wheat flour is refined, but this analysis was done before mandatory folic acid enrichment went into effect in 1998.

Depending on the specific type of product being made, the technology involved in variety bread production may be nearly identical to that used for conventional white bread, or it may deviate considerably (Ponte 1981). Thus, hearth varieties usually require drier doughs (lower absorptions) to maintain their shape on the oven hearth; the fermentation procedure for many of the sourdough products is often lengthy and complex; and steam in the oven frequently plays a more crucial role than with white pan bread.

8.C.1. White hearth breads

French bread is a variety of white hearth bread that shares many similarities with Italian and Vienna bread types. They all are baked on the hearth with steam to produce a rather thin, crisp and glossy crust and a characteristic flavor. They are generally produced from relatively lean formulations that accentuate their inherent wheaty and fermentation-derived flavors, their grain is rather open and irregular, and their texture rather chewy.

These hearth-baked varieties often use lean formulations, being high in complex carbohydrates and low in fat. O'Donnell (1993) analyzed the formulation, fermentation and baking conditions for such lean-formula products using the control formula in **Table 8.015**. Data from tests of many formula alterations revealed malt to be an effective addition, providing flavor and color and providing more tolerance than sugar alone. Nonfat milk solids lessened quality while egg whites slightly improved it. Higher protein flours were more effective than lower protein styles, although vital wheat gluten could adjust their performance. Minimum bulk fermentation and maximum proofing times worked best, yet over-proofing should be avoided.

Oven conditions favoring high temperatures, around 249°C (480°F), were preferred. Oxidizers, enzymes and other dough conditioners in hearth bread applications and formula modifications were reviewed by Jackson (1998). Hearth bread characteristics were also analyzed scientifically by Aamodt et al. (2005).

8.C.1.a. French bread

A representative formula for French hearth bread is given in **Table 8.016**, and **Table 8.017** offers the formula for French bread typical of European production. The flour generally specified for this type of bread is a strong unbleached patent or first clear flour with a protein content of 11.5 to 13.0% and an ash content of about 0.45%. (The French designation for such flour is Type 55.) Bleached flour is not suitable, and high-protein flour should be avoided because it yields excessively thin crusts and tough crumb.

Absorption is in the range or 60 to 65 parts water to 100 parts flour (Forestier 1996). Excessively soft water will produce sticky soft doughs that are difficult to ferment, while hard water may retard fermentation. Although French bread is often made via the sour dough process, the leavening for all formulations comes from bakers yeast (*Sacharomyces cerevisiae*). Salt, added at 1.8 to 2.2% (flour weight basis) is another critical ingredient, which functions as a flavor balancer and enhancer, while regulating fermentation. It contributes to shelf life by slowing the softening of the crust in humid environments and slowing the drying of the crumb in dry climates. Fats and sugars are never added to French bread.

Various methods of fermentation may be used for French bread, including fermented cultures such as poolish and levain-levure (sour dough methods), preferments and the bulk fermentation of sponge-and-dough and straight dough methods.

The sponge should be mixed just enough to ensure the homogeneous dispersion of the sponge ingredients, a condition generally achieved by blending for 1 minute at low speed and mixing for 3 to 4 minutes at high speed (72 rpm). The sponge is fermented for 4 to 5 hours at the relatively cool temperatures of 23 to 24°C (74 to 76°F). Dough mixing time is generally limited to 2 minutes at low speed and 6 to 9 minutes at high speed to yield a pliable dough. A floor time of 5 minutes is often found adequate, although 10 to 15 minutes is a more normal practice. The dough temperature requires close control within a range of 25 to 28°C (75 to 80°F).

In the "improved" French method described by Forestier (1966), the process mixes (*frasage*) ingredients at low speed for 3 minutes, which are left to rest and hydrate (*autolyse*) in the mixer bowl for 15 to 30 minutes. The dough is then kneaded (*petrissage*) for an additional 10 minutes, with a dough-out temperature of 24 to 25°C (75 to 77°F). Bulk fermentation (*pointage*) proceeds for 2.5 hours with a turn given to the dough after 1 hour. Dividing (*pesage*), rounding (*boulage*) and moulding (*façonnage*) take place during a 30-minute window, and the dough pieces receive a final proof (*apprêt*) of 1.25 hours. Loaves are slashed (*coupe*) and set to bake (*caisson*) for 30 minutes at 234°C (470°F). A short period of cooling (*ressuage*) for 20 minutes at 24°C (75°F) is necessary to dissipate excess leavening gases and steam.

Special bases designed specifically for French hearth bread production have become available to bakers in recent years. These bases contain all the essential active ingredients, as well as appropriate levels of salt, sweeteners, shortening and emulsifiers, dough conditioners, oxidizing agents and fungal proteases. They require, in

Figure 8.010. The dough for making baguettes must accept sheeting and elongation without distortion.

fact, only the addition of flour, yeast and water, and mixing for some 10 minutes to produce uniform no-time doughs (Loeb 1981). Bases are generally used at a level of 4%, flour weight basis, and are available in plastic and liquid formats.

French bread is generally produced in elongated loaves, ranging from oval shapes to thin, long loaves, or baguettes, some 28 to 30 in. long (**Figure 8.010**). The crumb is a translucent cream, pale yellow color, having the tint of the natural color of the wheat grain and lacking any hint of gray. The structure is open, with many sizes of irregularly shaped, thin-walled alveoli (holes).

The moulding process is frequently carried out stepwise with special equipment. The dough piece, having received both a preliminary moulding to a length of 12 to 14 in. and an intermediate proof of 9 minutes, is elongated to the desired final length by pressure boards acting along with moving belts, with an additional intermediate proof of 15 minutes. The resulting dough string may then pass through a roll cutter mechanism to produce club rolls or may be left intact to yield a long loaf. The narrow ends of the loaf can be given sharply pointed ends to enhance the bread's authenticity.

The moulded loaf is given a final proof of 45 to 60 minutes at a temperature of 29 to 32°C (85 to 90°F) and a relative humidity of 75 to 80%. Before entering the oven, the loaf receives a series of diagonal cuts on its top surface with a sharp thin blade to impart to it an attractive appearance and prevent its sides from bursting in the oven. The oven chamber atmosphere should be provided with copious volumes of low-pressure moist steam for the first 2 minutes of baking. Oven temperature will range from 221 to 249°C (430 to 480°F) with baking times of 25 to 40 minutes (Tweed 1983).

So important to French culture is the baguette that, in September 1993, the French government legally defined it. This legislation also applied to the different methods of baguette breadmaking, and specified permitted additives such as fava bean flour (a crumb whitener), soy flour, malt, wheat gluten, fungal amylase, lecithin, ascorbic acid, mono- and diglycerides and sodium acid pyrophosphate (Forestier 1996).

8.C.1.b. Italian breads

Italian-type hearth bread closely resembles French bread in many of its characteristics, as well as in its method of production. Its shape, however, is shorter and wider, and the lengthwise scoring gives the loaf a distinctive top break (**Figure 8.011**).

A representative formula is shown in **Table 8.018**. The product requires strong flour, with a protein content of 13 to 15%. If 15 to 25% of this flour is replaced with a short patent flour, the bread will have a closer crumb grain, while a similar replacement with an unbleached high protein flour will produce a more open grain. Sponge mixing time should be limited to 5 minutes, and the sponge fermented for 4 to 5 hours. The dough is mixed for about 6 minutes, or until it is smooth and pliable. The scaled dough pieces are generally moulded into stubby loaf forms with narrow but rounded ends. Final proofing is for 45 minutes at 35°C (95°F) and 85% relative humidity. The bread is baked at 227°C (440°F) for 18 to 20 minutes in

Figure 8.011. Scoring gives Italian loaves their distinctive top breaks. (*Baking & Snack*)

Table 8.018. Italian-Type Hearth Bread Formula

Ingredient	Sponge (%)	Dough (%)
Flour	70	30
Water	39	20
Yeast	2	–
Yeast food	0.375	–
Malt	0.5	–
Sugar	–	1
Shortening	–	3
Salt	–	2.125

(Pyler 1988)

Table 8.019 White Hearth Bread Formulas
(Ingredients based on 100 parts of flour)

Ingredient	White hearth*			Sour French**		
	Total (%)	Sponge (%)	Dough (%)	Total (%)	Sponge (%)	Dough (%)
Flour	100	60	40	100	60	40
Water (variable)	55	33	22	59	35	24
White sour	–	–	–	4	4	–
Yeast	2	2	–	1.75	1.75	–
Yeast food	0.375	0.375	–	0.5	0.5	–
Salt	2	–	2	1.5	–	1.5
Sugar	2	–	2	2	–	2
Shortening	2	–	2	1.5	–	1.5
Malt (nondiastatic)	1	–	1	–	–	–
Vital wheat gluten	–	–	–	2	2	–

Sponge temperature, 24°C (76°F); ferment 4.5 hours; dough temperature, 27°C (80°F); floor time, 15 to 20 minutes; bake, 204 to 221°C (400 to 430°F)

** *Sponge temperature, 24°C (76°F); ferment 4 hours; dough temperature, 27°C (80°F); floor time, 20 minutes; bake, 204 to 221°C (400 to 430°F)*

(Ponte 1981)

a steam-saturated oven, directly on the hearth. These conditions produce a relatively light, amber-colored, thin and crisp crust.

Ciabatta and focaccia are exceptions to the rule that hearth breads require low-absorption doughs. Their wet, sticky doughs often use as much water as flour in the formula, counting both poolish (preferment) and dough, and processing techniques look to low-stress sheeting for proper development and handling.

Two excellent papers by Bastetti (2001a, 2001b) opened up the subject of Italian breads in the widest way possible. He examined the use of sours, preferements and starters in formulating products as diverse as ciabatta, pugliese, rosetta, maggiolino, sicilia and como breads, as well as baguettes, milk breads and breakfast buns. He followed up with another report (Bastetti 2002) about Italy's fermented cakes, which are actually more bread-like in character. Earlier, Lugon (1992) examined preparation of panettone bread, a soft, cake-like bread containing raisins and candied fruits.

8.C.2. Sourdough bread

Sourdough hearth breads closely resemble white hearth bread in formulation and overall physical characteristics, except that their flavor is modified toward an acid character by natural bacterial sour reactions or by addition of small amounts of commercial white sour containing a balance of lactic and acetic acids. **Table 8.019** shows representative formulations for both types of bread.

Among American sour hearth breads made with natural sours, the best known is San Francisco sourdough French bread (Sugihara et al. 1970a, 1970b), which is characterized by a distinctive acid flavor, a rather thick, hard crust, an open, un-

Figure 8.012. The distinctive flavor and texture of San Francisco sourdough French bread are created by its leavening system.

even grain and a chewy crumb texture (**Figure 8.012**). Its production process uses a starter that not only provides the source of the requisite leavening and souring activities but also serves as the key to perpetuating the process (Sugihara 1977). A new sour starter can be developed by boiling peeled potatoes and mixing a high-protein flour into the potato water to form a fluid barm. This mixture is allowed to ferment spontaneously until gas formation ceases, when additional flour is mixed in to form a stiff dough. After this dough has doubled in size, it is ready for use in the regular dough in which it should comprise about 15% by weight (Paul 1970).

In commercial practice, the sourdough starter sponge is rebuilt about every 8 hours, or 3 times a day, 7 days a week. When making a new starter sponge, 25 to 40% of the previous ripe starter sponge is used to ensure an adequate inoculum of the essential microorganisms and to create the required acidic environment for the acid-producing bacteria. Kline (1970) recommended a starter sponge formula containing 40% previous starter, 40% high-protein flour and 20% water, and holding the sponge for 8 hours at a temperature of 27°C (80°F) for full development. At the end of that period, the initial pH value of 4.4 will have dropped to 3.9, making it an extremely acidic system.

The first researchers to characterize the bacteria involved (Sugihara et al. 1971, Kline and Sugihara 1971) identified the sourdough yeast as *Saccharomyces exiguus*. (*S. exiguus* has since been reclassified as *Candida milleri* sp. nov.) They further isolated a new heterofermentative bacterial species that they named *Lactobacillus sanfranciscensis*. These two organisms coexist in a pH range of 3.8 to 4.5, with the bacterium preferentially using maltose as its source of carbon. The microbiology and the micro-organisms involved in sourdough fermentation are discussed in detail at Volume I, Chapter 2, Part B, covering both San Francisco sourdough and pain au levain sourdough.

The dough is made up of 20% starter sponge (flour weight basis), representing 11% of the final dough mass, 100% regular patent flour, 60% water and 2% salt. The dough is mixed to 27°C (80°F) and given a floor time of about 1 hour at 24°C (75°F). It is then scaled and rounded, given a 20-minute intermediate proof at 32°C (90°F), moulded and placed on canvas dusted with rice flour or corn meal. The dough pieces are given an extended final proof of 6 to 8 hours at 29 to 32°C (85 to 90°F), during which time their pH drops from about 5.3 to 3.9.

Just prior to entering the oven, the dough pieces receive razor-like cuts or are docked to ensure appropriate crust development. The bread is baked directly on the hearth for a period of 45 to 50 minutes at a relatively low temperature of 190 to 199°C (375 to 390°F), with introduction of low-pressure steam during approximately the first half of the baking cycle or until the crust begins to develop color.

Shenkenberg et al. (1972) proposed a shortened method for sourdough French bread that eliminates the need for the lengthy fermentation of the starter sponge. Essentially, it calls for adding lactic and acetic acids to a French bread formula,

Table 8.20. Sourdough Bread Formula

Ingredient	Amount (lb)
Dough starter	
High gluten flour	100
Water, approximate	50
Starter	25
Dough	
High gluten flour	300
Water, approximate	180
Sourdough starter, from above	54 to 72
Salt	6.75
Yeast	0.375

(Ziemke and Sanders 1988)

using acid whey, either in powder or in condensed form, as the source of lactic acid and 50-grain vinegar as the source of acetic acid. With this process, the normal production time of 20 to 22 hours of the traditional procedure is reduced to 6 hours for the sponge-and-dough method and to only 3 hours for the straight-dough method.

Shorter processing time was also the goal of a sourdough method developed by a bakers yeast manufacturer based in Canada (Gorton 2006). The company prepared dried cultures that combine bacteria and yeast and yield ready-to-use sour (*levain tout point*) within 18 to 20 hours at temperatures between 20 to 34°C (70 to 90°F). For example, a Parisian style bread is made with a combination of *Pediococcus acidilacti* bacteria and *Saccharomyces cerevisiae* yeast that produces a very mild, low-acid sour with strong "fruitiness" and yeast aroma. Descriptions of finished flavors range from sweet-and-fresh to cheesy to sour-and-spicy to sour-and-pungent notes.

Ziemke and Sanders (1988) reviewed sour dough processing, commenting specifically on use of prepared bases. They provided a typical formula (**Table 8.020**) as a control. Dry, free-flowing instant bases were found useful in cutting processing time. The authors also remarked on regional market differences in sourdough breads, noting that consumers in the Midwest and South preferred a milder flavor and softer crust. Easterners liked a mild flavor but wanted a thicker crust. Most Westerners, however, favored both extra-sour flavor and a heavy, crisp crust.

Updates on San Francisco style sourdough bread by Hoerner (1996) and Hoerner and Boge (1997) reviewed current methods of formulating and processing this product, including adapting it to par-baked methods.

Figure 8.013. The Food Guide Pyramid interprets the Dietary Guidelines for Americans 2005, noting "make half your grains whole" to encourage consumption of whole-grain foods. (USDA, FDA)

8.C.3. Wheat and grain breads

The Dietary Guidelines for Americans, issued every 5 years jointly by the US Department of Agriculture (USDA) and the Food and Drug Administration (FDA) of the Department of Health and Human Services (**Figure 8.013**), launched the era of whole-grain eating in 2000 by including whole grains in the recommendation that a variety of grains be eaten as part of the 6 daily servings. The next set of guidelines, announced in 2005, added that at least half of those 6 daily servings of grains be whole grains. At the time, most Americans ate less than 1 serving (1-oz equivalents) of whole grains daily, and on any given day, 40% of Americans ate none at all.

Figure 8.014. Bread and buns "made with whole grains" help push whole-grain consumption in a way that suits American tastes.
(Sara Lee Food & Beverage)

Figure 8.015. Sandwich buns made with whole-grain white wheat flour entered the market.
(Hostess Brands)

The baking industry, it appeared, had a great opportunity because its most basic ingredient, flour, is a cereal grain. Yet Americans currently eat their whole grains most commonly in the form of breakfast cereal (primarily oats) and corn and tortilla chips, according to the USDA's Economic Research Service. Even this consumption is way under the 50% of cereal grains recommended in the 2005 guidelines. In 2004, whole-grain breakfast cereals accounted for 3% of grain foods intake; crackers and salty snacks, 5%; bread and rolls, 2%; and pasta, cooked cereals and rice, 2% (Anon. 2004).

Whole-wheat bread, long a fixture on supermarket shelves, has always lagged far behind enriched white and most variety breads, and whole-wheat flour currently accounts for 5% or less of flour supplies purchased by commercial bakers (Gorton 2004). However, commercial bakers offer a good number of "wheat breads" made with a blend of whole-wheat and enriched white flours. Multigrain breads have also been part of bakers' offerings. Also, the push to increase whole grains in the American diet prompted a number of bakers to develop breads "made with whole grains" to address this market need (**Figures 8.014** and **8.015**).

It is important to note that wheat bread, multigrain bread (**Figure 8.016**) and made-with-whole-grains breads do not qualify as whole-grain products under current government guidelines and accepted definitions of whole grains. The subject of whole grains is examined in Volume I, Chapter 2, Part A.

8.C.3.a. Whole-grain breads

Whole grains mentioned by the Dietary Guidelines Committee included brown rice, bulgur (cracked wheat), graham flour (coarsely ground whole-wheat flour), oatmeal, pearl barley, popcorn, whole-grain corn, whole oats, whole rye and whole wheat. The Whole Grains Council expanded further on this group, listing amaranth, barley, buckwheat, corn (including whole cornmeal and popcorn), millet, oats (including oatmeal), quinoa, rice (both brown and colored rice), rye, sorghum (also called milo), teff, triticale, wheat (including spelt, emmer, farro, einkorn, Kamut, durum, bulgur, cracked wheat and wheatberries) and wild rice as "whole grains familiar to consumers." Many of these are described in Volume I, Chapter 3.

Learning that whole grains would appear in the 2000 Dietary Guidelines for Americans, AACC International developed the following definition for whole grains: "Whole grains shall consist of the intact, ground, cracked or flaked caryopsis, whose principal anatomical components — the starchy endosperm, germ and bran — are present in the same relative proportions as they exist in the intact caryopsis." ("Caryopsis" is the technical term for a small one-seeded dry indehiscent fruit, as of Indian corn or wheat, and "indehiscent" means that the fruit remains closed at maturity.)

In February 2006, FDA released its first guidance document on the topic. The intent is to clarify the labeling of whole-grains products, and its definition of whole grains came very close to the AACC's effort.

In the document, the agency said it considered whole grain to include cereal grains that consist, either intact, ground, cracked or flaked, "of the fruit of the grains whose principal components — the starch endosperm, germ and bran — are present in the same relative proportions as they exist in the intact grain." As examples, the agency cited barley, buckwheat, bulgur, corn, millet, rice, rye, oats, sorghum, wheat and wild rice.

Under US regulations, if a product claims to be "whole grain," it must be made with at least 51% whole grain by weight. This requirement, known as "the 51% rule," is the principle problem in formulating whole-grain breads. Although making 100% of the formula flour whole-grain will be the usual solution, other ingredients can contribute. Malted whole-grain barley and pregelatinized (soaked) whole kernel and flaked forms of the kernel also count toward the 51% threshold. To get a better grip on formula balance, Freedman (2007) recommended that bakers should consider writing formulations for whole-grain products using true percent (formula percent) rather than bakers percent.

Preparation of whole-grain baked foods (**Figure 8.017**) requires a baker to think differently about formulation and processing matters, according to Meyer (2005). Specifically, he recommended (a) consider flakes, grits, cuts, whole kernels and soaked grains for inclusion as well as whole-wheat flour; (b) increase dough strength by using ingredients such as vital wheat gluten; (c) add mix-time adjustment agents; (d) use compatible sweeteners such as brown sugar, honey, molasses, raisin juice and nondiastatic malt; (e) be aware that dough development for such doughs will differ from conventional doughs; (f) adjust for the additional friction in the mixer with additional bowl refrigeration; (g) monitor and maintain absorption to account for the greater uptake of water by the fiber component of whole grains; and (h) do not over-sheet whole-grain doughs. Increases in usage levels for vital wheat gluten, enzymes and emulsifiers were among the formulating factors identified by Gorton (2005) and Freedman (2007), discussing the practical aspects of formulating and processing whole-grain baked foods.

Moon (2006) also took a practical approach to formulating with whole grains. He observed that the type of grain selected has the biggest influence on the taste and texture of the finished product, noting the emergence of whole-wheat hard white wheat flour, which "quiets down" taste problems consumers have associated with whole-wheat breads. The flour's particle size is also

Figure 8.016. Because current US labeling rules requires separate listings for each grain in multigrain bread, the formulation does not meet whole-grain labeling guidelines. A recommendation from AACC International's Whole Grain Task Force offered an alternative listing format that could remove such exclusion.

Figure 8.017. Dense, hearty loaves made with whole wheat, barley and other whole grains are capturing consumer attention around the world.

Figure 8.018. Toppings help bakers differentiate premium breads from standard products. (Burford Corp.)

Figure 8.019. To tempt the growing appetite for whole-grain breads, bakers introduced many new varieties, including this style offering 24 g of whole grains per serving and made with organic flour. (Flowers Foods)

Table 8.021. Whole Wheat Bread Formula

Levels of major ingredients used

Ingredient	Range (bakers %)	Typical (bakers %)
Whole-wheat flour	100	100.0
Water*	61.7 to 87.6	73.5
Yeast, compressed	1.25 to 4.74	3.0
Salt	1.75 to 2.37	2.1
Sweetener solids	4.5 to 11.4	8.5
Shortening	1.97 to 8.0	3.0
Vital wheat gluten	0 to 9.0	4.0
Dairy product	0 to 5.0	2.0

** Includes water from sweetener syrups*

(Dubois and Vetter 1987)

critical to texture and mouthfeel. And he discussed the potential for addition of natural flavors, as well as honey and molasses, to offset flavor problems. Whole-grain toppings provide a way not only to improve eye appeal but also increase the whole-grain content of the bread without affecting the crumb (**Figure 8.018**).

Recent commentary by Beaven (2007) indicated synergies can be developed between gluten and some wheat, soy and dairy protein isolates to produce a naturally emulsified system to support the heavy fiber content of whole-grain breads. He offered a variety of formulating tips, including the use of organic acids (specifically acetic acid in whole-grain sourdough) to cover the flavor of bran. In sweet rolls, for example, he recommended masking bran's characteristic bitter flavor by incorporating it in a cinnamon sugar swirl.

8.C.3.b. Whole-wheat breads

Whole-wheat bread is a whole-grain product, whose formula is closely defined by the US Standards of Identity for whole-wheat bread (21 CFR 136.180). The flour component of whole-wheat bread must be 100% whole wheat, which can be in the form of finely milled flour and other forms of whole wheat ingredients such as cracked wheat, coarse ground (graham) or crushed wheat, rolled wheat or wheat bran. Such bread normally exhibits a compact loaf, has a dark dense crumb and a characteristic wheaty flavor (**Figure 8.019**). **Table 8.021** shows the ranges of ingredients used for whole-wheat bread during a study done in 1987.

Processing concerns described above for whole-grain breads apply equally to whole-wheat breads. **Table 8.022** details the times and temperatures that bakers use to prepare whole-wheat bread by the sponge-and-dough method, while **Table 8.023** reports these variables as they apply to whole-wheat bread made by the straight and no-time methods. When making whole-wheat bread with a preferment, the practice is to use a no-flour brew.

When bakers began to explore opportunities to provide whole-grain products, they ran up against a taste problem caused by the bran present in whole-wheat flour. The bran of hard red wheat (**Figure 8.020**) contains a bitter-tasting red pigment, and its sharp, strong flavor carries over into whole-wheat products. Formulators found a solution to the taste problem in hard white wheat (**Figure 8.021**), which lacks the red pigment and its accompanying bitterness.

At the same time, millers developed new "ultra fine milling" technologies that minimized the appearance of the brown flecks contributed by bran to the flour. The flour's creamy ivory appearance yielded a very light crumb, almost indistinguishable from bread made from white flour without whitening ingredients (**Figure 8.022**).

8.C.3.c. Wheat breads

In wheat bread, on the other hand, whole-wheat flour constitutes the lesser proportion, generally 20 to 40%, of the total flour, the actual ratio depending on the loaf

Table 8.022. Whole-Wheat Bread, Sponge-and-Dough Process

Variable	Range	Typical
Total flour in sponge	53.0 to 70.0%	60.0%
Sponge set temperature	23 to 26°C	24°C
	(74 to 78°F)	(76°F)
Sponge fermentation	2 to 5 hours	4 hours
Sponge temperature rise	2 to 6 C°	4.5 to 5 C°
	(4 to 11 F°)	(8 to 9 F°)
Dough mix	6.5 to 12.0 minutes	8 minutes
Delayed salt method used?	Some	Generally no
Dough temperature	24 to 28°C	27°C
	(76 to 82°F)	(80 to 81°F)
Floor time	5 to 20 minutes	15 to 20 minutes
Scaling weight*	1.14 to 1.31	1.18
Proof time	45 to 60 minutes	55 to 60 minutes
Proof temperature, dry bulb	38 to 49°C	46°C
	(100 to 120°F)	(115°F)
Proof temperature, wet bulb	33 to 43°C	42°C
	(92 to 110°F)	(107°F)
Bake time	18 to 28 minutes	20 to 23 minutes
Oven temperature	205 to 232°C	210 to 227°C
	(400 to 450°F)	(410 to 440°F)

* Scaling weight = dough weight divided by baked product weight

(Dubois and Vetter 1987)

Table 8.023. Whole-Wheat Bread, Straight and No-Time Processes

Variable	Straight dough		No-time dough	
	Range	Typical	Range	Typical
Dough mixing time	8 to 15 minutes	12 to 13 minutes	7 to 17 minutes	12 minutes
Dough temperature	26 to 28°C	26°C	26°C	26°C
	(78 to 82°F)	(79 to 80°F)	(78 to 80°F)	(79°F)
Fermentation time	30 to 105 minutes		5 to 10 minutes	
Scaling weight*	1.14 to 1.25	1.18	1.12 to 1.30	1.20
Intermediate proof time	6 to 10 minutes	7 minutes	5 to 8 minutes	7 minutes
Final proof time	45 to 60 minutes	58 minutes	42 to 65 minutes	
Proof temperature, dry bulb	42 to 44°C		42 to 44°C	
	(108 to 112°F)		(108 to 112°F)	
Proof temperature, wet bub	39 to 41°C		39 to 42°C	
	(102 to 105°F)		(102 to 108°F)	
Bake time	17 to 36 minutes		19 to 24 minutes	
Oven temperature	205 to 221°C		205 to 232°C	
	(400 to 430°F)		(400 to 450°F)	

* Scaling weight = dough weight divided by baked product weight

(Dubois and Vetter 1987)

Figure 8.020. Hard red wheat has dark-colored bran.
(Wheat Foods Council)

Figure 8.021. Hard white wheat has light-colored bran.
(Wheat Foods Council)

volume and crumb characteristics that the baker desires in the final product (**Table 8.024**). Wheat breads, in general, resemble regular white bread rather closely, except when coarsely ground, cracked or rolled wheat flour is added at meaningful levels to produce desired textural effects.

The bran component of whole-wheat flour tends to dilute the gluten proteins, thus diminishing dough strength, and bran absorbs water, thus limiting its availability to the protein and starch. Lai et al. (1989) found that bran's interaction with water could be overcome by a combination of increased absorption, addition of shortening and sodium stearoyl lactylate and by fine grinding of the bran itself.

In wheat breads, white flour comprises 40 to 80% of the formula flour. Because of bran's effect, the white flour used for these wheat breads is usually a strong protein flour or is supplemented with a small amount of vital gluten.

Toppings of cracked or flaked grains, often supplemented with seeds, are frequently provided to wheat breads to enhance their visual appeal.

Brown bread is the name usually given to such wheat breads baked in the UK.

"Made with whole grains." The "ultra milled" whole-wheat white wheat flours inspired a new class of bread products, which proclaimed "made with whole-grains" on their labels. The proportion of whole-wheat white wheat flour to white flour varied from company to company. Bakers also altered the proportions of the flours to create a spectrum of products with varying degrees of whole-wheat content.

The validity of the "made with whole grain" formulating concept was supported by Rosen et al. (2008). Researchers learned that elementary school students will eat more whole grains when healthier bread products are gradually introduced into their school lunches. Current consumption of whole grains by children is about one-third of the recommended level. At two schools in Hopkins, MN, the bread and rolls fed to kindergartners through sixth graders over the course of a year included increasing proportions of whole red wheat and whole white flour content, starting at 0% and reaching 91% of the formula flour. As measured by plate waste methods, the students did not throw away more bread products until the percentage of whole-grain flour reached about 70%. Researchers concluded that whole-grain bread products for school meals may be more acceptable with a total whole-grain flour content approaching 75% than to serve bread products made with 100% whole-wheat flour.

8.C.3.d. Oat-based breads

While many varieties of oats are cultivated, the most widely grown species is *Avena sativa* L., or common white oats. Used principally as animal feed, oats also find extensive use as a food in various prepared forms and as an ingredient in a wide range of food products. In baking, various milled oat products are used principally in certain varieties of cookies, snack items, rolls and specialty breads.

Oat products available to the baker include rolled oats produced by flattening dehulled whole grain oats, or groats as the dehulled product is commonly referred to, quick oats that represent groats that have been steelcut into smaller fragments and then flattened between steel rolls, steelcut oats (fragmented oat kernels that have not been flattened), finely granulated oat flour, as well as variants of the above products. Depending on the type of bread being produced, oat levels incorporated in the formulations will vary from 5 to 15% in the case of multi-grain breads, to as high as 20 to 30% in oatmeal-based breads. The specific processing requirements imposed by high levels of oat products in the production of specialty breads have been discussed by McKechnie (1984).

Figure 8.022. New developments in milling technology allow preparation of whole-wheat flour from white wheat that includes the bran yet strongly resembles white flour.
(ConAgra Mills)

8.C.3.e. Multigrain bread

Multiple-grain or mixed-grain breads have been popular in the US and Canada since the 1950s, and their consumption has remained fairly constant (Bruinsma 1993). These products contain, in addition to white flour, various other cereal flours, grits or meals, such as barley, oats, corn, rye, soybean, triticale, buckwheat, and rice, and such other vegetable foods as potato, alfalfa and even sauerkraut. The resulting breads and rolls can range from very light, airy and only slightly different from white pan varieties in color to very dense, dark and nearly black-colored loaves, with every type in between.

What may perhaps be considered a typical formula for mixed-grain bread is shown in **Table 8.025**. This formula calls for a soaker stage in which the various dry ingredients are blended for 5 minutes at low speed with sufficient water to form a mash that is then allowed to soak for 8 hours. The dough combines the mash with the balance of the dough ingredients by mixing 4 minutes at low speed and 4 minutes at high speed, at a temperature of 27°C (80°F). Over-mixing should be avoided because it will yield bread with flat tops and lack of ovenspring.

The dough is given a floor time of 30 minutes, scaled at 18.4 oz and baked at 205°C (400°F) for 30 minutes. Internal temperature out of the oven should be 64 to 96°C (201 to 204°F). Under-baked loaves will be gummy and may exhibit collapsed sidewalls upon cooling. This variety retains high levels of moisture after cooling, which can be a problem to slicers unless they are well maintained with routine blade honing, functional

Table 8.024. Wheat Bread Formula
Levels of major ingredients used

Ingredient	Range (bakers %)	Typical (bakers %)
Flour	40 to 82	70
Whole wheat flour	18 to 60	30
Other grain-based flour	2.0 to 4.16	2.0
Water*	52.8 to 85.5	63.5
Yeast, compressed	1.5 to 5.25	3.0
Salt	1.25 to 2.63	2.0
Sweetener solids	1.95 to 11.4	8.5
Shortening	1.67 to 6.6	3.0
Vital wheat gluten	0 to 5.26	2.5
Dairy product	0 to 4.16	2.0

Includes water from sweetener syrups

(Dubois and Vetter 1987)

Table 8.025. Multiple-Grain Bread

Soaker stage*	Amount (bakers %)	Dough stage*	Amount (bakers %)
Whole wheat kernels	14	Mash (from soaker stage)	
Coarse rye meal	14	Water	13
Buckwheat flour	12	Clear flour (16% protein)	36
Ground barley	3	Salt	2.5
Ground millet	7	Soy flour, defatted	4
Ground oats	7	Blackstrap molasses	4
Ground alfalfa	1	Buckwheat honey	4
Toasted wheat germ	3	Potato flour	3
Wheat gluten	3	Margarine	3
Water	55	Yeast	3
		Lecithin	0.375

Mix well together, 5 minutes at low speed; soak 8 hours

Mix 4 minutes low and 4 minutes high speed; temperature, 80°F (26.6°C); floor time, 30 minutes; bake, 30 minutes at 400°F (204.4°C)

** Based on bakers percent, with 64% grains in soaker stage and 36% flour in dough stage*

(Vellone 1972)

oilers and scheduled blade changes.

With some adjustments, multigrain breads can be made by the major dough-making methods in common use today: sponge-and-dough, straight dough and brew systems. Grain blends are almost always added to the sponge side because fermentation's 3 to 4 hours allows the coarser grains to fully absorb the moisture necessary to soften them for further processing. In straight dough and brew systems, the grains are added directly to the mixer, which may lead to excessively long mixing times. Adequate water must be provided or else doughs will become dry and difficult to machine.

As a general rule, multigrain breads require addition of vital wheat gluten. If the amount of grain mix is very high (20 to 40%, flour weight basis), an additional 9 to 15% gluten will be needed. Higher levels of oxidation, sweeteners, emulsifiers and strengtheners are generally required, compared with conventional white breads. Also, an additional 1 to 2% yeast will help these doughs proof in the same time as white doughs.

Many of the various multiple grain breads are produced with commercially prepared proprietary bases or mixes that contain balanced mixtures of the different grains. They are designed to yield baked products with specific flavor and eating qualities, as well as supply some added nutritional benefits to the consumer. As a general group, they are characterized by a rather dense grain, a dark crumb and a coarse texture.

8.C.4. Special dietary breads

The intense interest today in gluten-free baked foods is the latest stage in the baking industry's work to develop foods intended to meet special dietary needs. The subject of gluten-free baking will be covered later in this chapter along with other contemporary issues in bakery formulating.

Dietary breads include products that have been enriched with higher levels of ingredients such as wheat germ and protein derived from soybean, cottonseed and peanut flours, wheat gluten, dairy products and other sources. Also belonging to this category are low-sodium breads, breads made with modified fats such as those consisting of medium-chain triglycerides (Lorenz et al. 1971), breads with high dietary fiber contents, as well as products with other added ingredients that meet the dietary needs of consumers who have certain alimentary or metabolic problems.

8.C.4.a. High-fiber breads

Interest in the dietary fiber content of processed cereal foods developed in the early 1970s when clinical evidence suggested that certain diseases of western civilization are caused by a failure to consume adequate amounts of fiber or roughage, particularly wheat bran (Saunders 1980). Dietary fiber is that fraction of a food that is not enzymatically broken down in the human digestive tract. While its principal components are cellulose and lignin, it also includes hemicelluloses, pectins, gums and other carbohydrates not normally digested by man (Leveille 1975).

Fiber as a component of baked foods is discussed in Volume I, Chapter 1, Part C, with Volume I, Chapter 2, Part B, reporting the specifics on the many fiber-bearing ingredients now available.

Major fiber sources that are commonly used in bread production are wheat bran, corn bran, soy bran, oat hulls, rice bran and powdered cellulose. These ingredients range in dietary fiber content from 45% for rice bran to 99.5% for cellulose (Pomeranz 1977b, Dubois 1978). Other fiber sources that have been investigated for use in bread products include triticale bran (Lorenz 1976) and brewer's spent grains (Pomeranz et al. 1976).

Dubois (1978) suggested the following processing adaptations in the production of bread containing in excess of 10% added fiber material. Strong, high-protein flour is recommended to ensure adequate gluten structure and satisfactory loaf volume, with 60 to 70% of the flour to be used in the sponge stage. In cases where fiber additions of 20% or more are used, a corresponding increase in total absorption to about 120% is required to provide sufficient water to ensure complete hydration of the gluten proteins and the fiber material. In such instances, the inclusion of about 10% vital wheat gluten will be required to produce satisfactory cell structure. With the sponge-and-dough method, 3 to 5% of the vital wheat gluten should be added to the sponge and the remainder to the dough. Yeast level should be increased to 3 to 5%, with 1 to 2% being added at the dough stage. Salt is also increased somewhat, the normal range for high-fiber breads being 2.5 to 3.0%. The total sugar content ranges between 8 to 12%. In wheat-type fiber breads, part of the sugar may be replaced by equal amounts of honey or molasses. Shortening is frequently excluded from the formula to reduce the caloric content of the finished bread. Dough conditioners such as sodium stearoyl lactylate (SSL) or ethoxylated monoglycerides (EMG) at levels of 0.5% and 0.25%, respectively, will markedly increase the loaf volume, particularly in the absence of shortening (Shogren et al. 1981). Because the finished bread will have a somewhat higher moisture content, the use of mold inhibitors is essential.

Reviewing the subject of formulating fiber bread (**Table 8.026**), Sutherland (1990) summarized needs to include (a) increasing vital wheat gluten from 8% to 12% (flour weight basis), (b) using higher levels of dough conditioners such as SSL and EMG, with both used in combination and (c) adding vegetable gums at 0.25 to

Table 8.026. High-Fiber, Low-Calorie Bread Formula

Ingredient	Amount (bakers %)
Basic ingredients	
White flour	88 to 92
Vital wheat gluten	8 to 12
Fiber	15 to 22
Water	108 to 120
Yeast	6
Salt	2.8 to 3
Sugar solids	11
Shortening	1
Additives	
Vegetable gums	0.25 to 0.625
Sodium stearoyl lactylate	0.5 to 0.75
Ethoxylated mono- and diglycerides	0.5 to 0.75
Hydrate emulsifier	0.5
Bromate	60 to 75 ppm
ADA	10 to 20 ppm
Ascorbic acid	100 to 300 ppm

(Sutherland 1990)

0.625% (flour weight basis) to improve water-holding capabilities. He noted that the gums could be eliminated if the fiber ingredient has high water-holding capabilities and cautioned that fibers have a wide range of pH and TTA, from a low pH of 4.0 and a TTA of 21.3 for apple fiber to a high pH of 7.0 and a TTA of 0 for white oat fiber. In processing high-fiber doughs, fewer holes will appear in the finished product if the dough piece is cross-grained and twisted during final makeup.

The sponge is mixed for 1 minute at low speed, 4 minutes at high speed and is set at a temperature of 22 to 24°C (72 to 75°F). It is fermented for 2.5 to 3.5 hours, with a temperature rise of 3 to 4 C° (6 to 8 F°). Total dough mixing time is 18 to 22 minutes, with 1 minute at low speed and 17 to 21 minutes at high speed, and the salt is added at about the midpoint. Dough temperature is 26 to 27°C (78 to 80°F). The dough is given a floor time of not more than 15 minutes prior to scaling. The scaled dough pieces receive an intermediate proof of 7 to 10 minutes, are sheeted with the head rolls being set slightly less tight than for white bread doughs and are moulded with the pressure board set to exert a light pressure only. Final proof is for 50 to 55 minutes at a temperature of 43°C (110°F). Baking is done at a temperature of 221 to 232°C (430 to 450°F) for 18 to 20 minutes.

8.C.4.b. High-protein breads

Among the dietary breads, those with higher-than-normal protein contents have historically represented the largest group (Shellenberger 1974). Pomeranz (1970) provided an extensive review of these breads. In the years since, enhancing the protein content provided a way to cut carbohydrate levels in foods. The development of so-called "low carb" breadstuffs is described later in this section.

Because soy protein constitutes the least expensive source of high-quality dietary protein for bread fortification, its use for this purpose has received greatest attention. Tsen and Hoover (1973) and Ranhotra et al. (1974), in investigating wheat flour fortification with different levels of defatted, full-fat and high-fat soy flours and protein concentrates and isolates, observed that full-fat and high-fat soy flours produced breads of acceptable volume, flavor and over-all quality up to fortification levels of 15 to 20%, whereas defatted soy flour produced inferior results. It appeared that the presence of such natural emulsifiers as lecithin and glycolipids in the unextracted soy flours had a favorable influence on bread quality. The glycolipids, in particular, were found by Pomeranz et al. (1969a, 1969b) to effectively improve breadmaking properties at low use levels, thereby permitting the addition of up to 16% of soy flour or other protein supplements.

Researchers at Kansas State University (Tsen and Tang 1971, Tsen et al. 1971) developed the K-State Process for making high-protein bread with soy flour or other protein-rich adjuncts. The process can be summarized as follows. The formula, on a flour basis, calls for 100% flour, 12% (variable) soy flour or other protein-rich foodstuffs, 3% yeast, 5% sugar, 2% salt, variable water, variable bromate and 0.5% sodium stearoyl lactylate (SSL). All the ingredients are mixed together at low speed for 1 minute and at medium speed to optimum dough development. The dough is scaled into 1-lb pieces, rounded and rested for 40 minutes at 30°C (86°F) and 85% relative humidity (RH). The doughs are then moulded, panned and proofed at 36°C (96°F) and 92% RH to height. Baking is at 218°C (425°F) for 25 minutes. Inclusion of SSL as a dough conditioner appeared to be essential for producing bread with good volume and satisfactory grain.

Later, Kulp et al. (1980) demonstrated that acceptable bread fortified with 12%

soy flour can be produced with a low-protein wheat flour (less than 11% protein) provided that some of the production steps are optimized. These recommendations included use of appropriate oxidizing agents and selected surfactants, and the late addition of the soy flour. In the optimized procedure, the dough is first fully developed, the soy flour is added, and the dough is then brought to full extensibility by additional mixing.

8.C.4.c. Calorie-reduced breads

According to Bruinsma (1993), calorie-reduced breads have become popular since the 1980s.

Under US regulations that carry out the Nutrition Labeling and Education Act (NLEA) of 1990, only foods that achieve at least a 25% reduction in caloric content, compared with its counterpart reference food, can be labeled as a "reduced calorie" product. The term "light" applies when the reduction is at least one-third. Whole grains, whole-grain flours and bran fractions are high in fiber and thus lower in calories than refined flours; however, substitution for refined flours alone will not achieve caloric reductions sufficient to allow reduced calorie claims. Only highly refined fiber sources, containing around 70% fiber, would do the job, but other formulation changes will be necessary.

When developing reduced-calorie products, the formulator should take advantage of some special circumstances involving insoluble fiber. NLEA regulations permit insoluble fiber to be subtracted from total carbohydrates when calculating calories.

To produce reduced-calorie bread, Bruinsma (1993) recommended using fiber sources that contain 70% or more fiber and using them to replace 20 to 30% of the formula's flour. Other steps include reducing or eliminating fat and adding 10 to 15% (flour weight basis) vital wheat gluten. The addition of fiber and reduction of fat will complicate the processing of reduced-calorie bread doughs. Fiber absorbs and binds water, making the dough stiffer, and loss of fat will affect machining and slicing characteristics. Sanders (1990) recommended use of xylanase enzymes to solve problems in producing reduced-calorie, high-fiber, whole-wheat and multigrain breads.

Bakers have the choice to slice breads thinner, thus cutting calories, too. Thin-

Table 8.027. High-Protein, High-Fiber Bread Formulations

Using white or whole-wheat flours

Ingredient	White flour (bakers %)	Whole-wheat red flour (bakers %)	Whole-wheat white flour (bakers %)
Flour, bread	32	–	–
Flour, fine whole-wheat, red	–	32	–
Flour, fine whole-wheat, white	–	–	32
Vital wheat gluten	20	20	20
Resistant wheat starch, type RS 4*	23	23	23
Wheat protein isolate**	12	12	12
Soy fiber***	13	13	13
Salt	1.9	1.9	1.9
Soybean oil	5	5	5
Sodium stearoyl lactylate	0.35	0.35	0.35
Ethoxylated monoglycerides	0.35	0.35	0.35
Calcium propionate	0.375	0.375	0.375
Sugar, granulated	1.5	1	1
Data esters (DATEM)	0.35	0.35	0.35
Ascorbic acid	0.015	0.015	0.015
Yeast, compressed	8	8	8
Sucralose	0.008	0.008	0.008
Water	77	78	80

*Fibersym 70 (MGP Ingredients), ** Arise 5000 (MGP Ingredients), *** FI-1 (The Fibred Group)*

(Maningat et al. 2005)

sliced bread is quite acceptable to the dieter, but achieving such cuts requires careful maintenance of slicers and their blade lattices.

8.C.4.d. Low-carbohydrate breads

The "low carb" or Atkins Diet, first popularized during the 1970s and revived in the 1990s and early 2000s, stipulated a low-carbohydrate, high-protein eating pattern. The quick rise in its popularity challenged bakers to respond with formulations suitable for this diet. Carbohydrate claims were not defined by NLEA, and standards do not currently exist. The low-carb diet introduced the concept of "net carbohydrates," which the consumer calculated by subtracting fiber and sugar alcohols from total carbohydrates, but FDA refused to define this term. A simple factual statement of the amount of carbohydrates present in the product is the sole permissible type of carbohydrate label claim.

Ingredients suitable for such formulations include proteins, fibers, alternative sweeteners and resistant starches, analyzed in detail by Maningat et al. (2005), who developed the starting formulations in **Table 8.027**. Product development in this category concentrated on removing easily digestible carbohydrates (flour, starch, oligosaccharides and sugars) and replacing them with proteins, non-digestible carbohydrates (resistant starch, inulin and other fructo-oligosaccharides), alternative sweeteners or water. Besides the taste and texture issues posed, removal of the lower molecular weight materials often resulted in moisture retention and control issues, including water activity (a_w) problems that led to rapid development of mold in the finished products.

Although a number of tasty products were developed, common criticisms of low-carb baked foods were that they were pricey and compared unfavorably in taste and texture with conventional baked items. By 2005 and almost as soon as low-carb dieting hit its peak, it declined in popularity. Low-carb baked foods have largely disappeared from supermarket shelves, but a knowledge of the formulating requirements should help product developers the next time this diet fad surfaces. Maningat et al. (2005) reviewed the many high-protein, high-fiber, high-fat, low-carb diets popular with consumers. For example, the South Beach Diet, which focuses on the glycemic index (how a particular food raises the blood sugar level), is still popular with consumers today. The authors also advised about labeling rules and restrictions for restricted-carbohydrate products.

8.C.5. Raisin bread

What makes raisin bread different from white pan bread is the addition of a minimum of 50% raisins (flour weight basis) at the dough stage. This level of raisin use is required by the US Standard of Identity for raisin bread (21 CFR 136.160). A representative formula for raisin bread is presented in **Table 8.028**.

Bergholz (1957) outlined the following guidelines for the production of raisin bread. The flour should be a high-quality first clear or high-protein flour. The sponge, containing 70% of the total flour, is held to an absorption of about 60%,

Table 8.028. Formula for Raisin Bread

Ingredient	Sponge (%)	Dough (%)
Flour	70	30
Water (variable)	60 to 62	64 to 72 (total)
Yeast	3.5 to 4.0	0.25 to 0.5
Yeast food	0.25 to 0.5	–
Malt (optional)	0.5	–
Shortening	3 to 5	–
Salt	–	2
Dairy products	–	3
Sugar	–	7 to 10
Raisins	–	72

(Bergholz 1957)

yielding relatively stiff consistency. It is fermented with 3.5 to 4.0% yeast for about 4 hours at a temperature of 24 to 26°C (76 to 78°F). The dough receives an additional 0.25 to 0.5% yeast and is mixed to the pickup stage, at which point the raisins are added. Mixing is continued for 1 minute at low speed and 2 minutes at high speed to uniformly disperse the raisins. Floor time is limited to 10 to 20 minutes because the additional yeast promotes rapid recovery.

The length of the intermediate proof should be sufficient to ensure adequate recovery of the scaled dough pieces. In makeup, the sheeting rolls of the cross-grain moulder or reverse sheeting moulder need to be set somewhat loose to prevent excessive mashing of the raisins; in straight-away moulders, the pressure board setting also should be looser than for regular white bread.

During final proof, raisin doughs reach their maximum height in about 60 to 70 minutes because the increased yeast level counteracts the inhibiting effect of the tartaric acid introduced with the raisins. The baking temperature should be held to 190 to 205°C (375 to 400°F), or about 28 C° (50 F°) lower than for white bread to prevent excessive browning of the crust. Raisins release reducing sugars that readily enter into the Maillard reaction. Low-pressure steam should be introduced during the initial oven stage to promote adequate loaf expansion during ovenspring. The loaves should be baked thoroughly to prevent the sidewalls of the loaves from caving in (keyholing) during depanning and cooling.

Raisins require appropriate conditioning prior to their use. As received at the bakery, raisins normally have a moisture content of 15 to 17%. The raisins must therefore be brought to a moisture content equal to that of the dough so they will not rob moisture from it. This rehydration is best accomplished by soaking the raisins for 10 to 15 minutes in water and then draining thoroughly. This relatively short time avoids the loss of soluble solids induced by prolonged soaking yet adequately conditions the dried fruits.

Raisins that have become hard and flinty as a result of prolonged storage under dry conditions are best reconditioned by first covering them with water for 10 minutes, followed by thorough draining, and then holding for at least 4 hours in a covered container.

8.C.6. Salt-rising bread

Salt-rising bread differs from white pan bread chiefly by having a dense crumb, unusual texture, dark smooth crust, a pungent aroma and a flavor suggestive of a mild cheese. Its texture is quite short, and it disintegrates readily on chewing. These properties are imparted by the combined fermentative action of yeast and selected bacterial cultures. Consumer acceptance of this specialty product is largely a matter of personal taste preference. While this bread was formerly produced by a natural sourdough process, present practice is to use a commercial dry yeast and bacterial preparation.

According to Kohman (1944), the originator of the commercial ferment, the procedure for making salt-rising bread is quite simple. A pre-weighed amount of the ferment is mixed with nonfat dry milk, the mixture stirred into boiling water, and the suspension held at 38°C (100°F) for several hours to permit the culture to rehydrate. When gas begins to evolve, the mixture is ready for setting the sponge with about one-third of the total flour and one-half of the absorption water. Fermentation normally requires about 1.5 to 2 hours, after which the dough is mixed at low speed until smooth and taken directly to makeup. The dough loaves, placed in small pans, are proofed for about 1 hour at 38 to 46°C (100 to 115°F), or until the loaves have doubled in volume, and baked at the usual temperature.

8.C.7. Canned breads and cakes

The highly specialized category of tinned breads and cakes was examined in detail by Matz (1989). These products were developed to serve the Armed Forces, but this style of preparation and packaging is also provided for gourmet cakes, campers' rations, emergency reserves and other uses requiring a long shelf storage life. The key problem in formulating these products is maintaining a suitable water activity (a_w) and pH in the finished product. Although developed as a canned product (the famous C Ration of World War II), such baked foods are now packaged in flexible retort pouches, which provide a better configuration for carrying in clothing pockets. The packets are processed at 121°C (250°F) under steam pressure in a retort, which both cooks and sterilizes the product.

A starting formula for military canned bread is provided in **Table 8.029**. The sorbitol and lactic acid are present to increase acidity and improve the keeping properties of the canned bread, while the inactive dry yeast adds vitamin fortification. Also, the shortening is specified with a stability of 100 hours or more. The reasons for the comparatively high shortening level are (a) to provide a high caloric content and (b) to soften the crumb to make the effects of staling less evident.

The military standard for a Meal, Ready-to-Eat, or MRE, sets an average of 1,250 Cal per packet, with 13% of energy from protein, 36% from fat and 61% from carbohydrates (Deuster 2009). Packets include a variety of foods and condiments that comprise a meal and can be supplemented by shelf-stable sliced bread provided in single-portion, 200-Cal servings.

As consumer products, canned breads and cakes are rare; however, a New England specialty, B&M brown bread, plain or with raisins, can be found in regional markets, and at least one bakery in Japan makes canned bread in chocolate chip, raisin and nut, strawberry, green tea and other flavors for the vending market. Canned tea cakes, with a texture resembling pound cakes, are offered in the US as gourmet foods and as camping items.

Table 8.029. Military Canned Bread Formula	
Ingredient	**Parts by weight**
Hard wheat flour, enriched	100.00
Water, not more than	50.00
Compressed yeast	2.00
Salt	1.75
Sugar	0.50
Shortening	20.00
D-sorbitol	7.00
Edible lactic acid (80%)	0.30
Inactive dry yeast	1.50

(Matz 1989)

8.C.8. Rye breads

Rye bread is produced by commercial bakers in many different formulations to satisfy ethnic and regional consumer preferences and demands. Thus, rye bread styles have proliferated under descriptive designations such as American, Jewish, German, Bohemian, Russian, Polish and Swedish rye bread, all purporting to identify distinctive product variations. Rye breads may vary in crumb color from practically white to deep brown, in shape from pan-baked to round and elongated hearth-baked loaves, in taste from mildly acidic to a tangy, distinctly sour taste, sometimes supplemented with caraway seeds, onion bits and other flavoring materials.

The ingredients of rye bread may be a simple mixture of wheat and rye flours, water, yeast and salt, or they may include shortening, molasses, caramel color, buttermilk, nondiastatic malt, rye sour or sourdough, dairy products, etc., all meant to endow the finished product with a special character or to enhance its flavor, color and keeping quality. It is thus seen that among the traditional bread products, rye bread offers wide latitude for modification of form, color, taste and texture. The baker thus has an opportunity to adapt his rye products, within broad limits, to the special taste preferences of consumers in his locality.

The production of rye bread for the most part closely resembles that of conventional white bread. The differences that do exist are more of degree than of kind, with the possible exception of sourdough fermentation.

8.C.8.a. Rye flour

The general composition and properties of rye and the various grades of flour that are milled from it are discussed in some detail in Volume I, Chapter 2, Part A. Depending on their degree of extraction, rye flours are generally differentiated into three major groups, namely, white rye, medium rye and dark rye, with rye meal forming a special category. **White rye flour** represents the patent flour obtained from the endosperm portion of the grain. It is light in color, low in protein content, smooth in texture and most suitable for use in mildly flavored, light colored rye breads. **Medium rye flour** is a straight-grade flour with an ash content of 0.85 to 1.0% and a light gray color. It develops a more pronounced rye flavor on fermentation and is used primarily in medium to dark rye breads. **Dark rye flour** is a low-grade flour, with an ash content of 1.0 to 2.0% and a rather high protein content, which, however, is of minor qualitative importance. It is dark in color, rather coarse in texture and develops a strong rye flavor. Its use is limited to the production of heavy dark rye breads. **Rye meal** is whole rye flour available as a flaky, variously coarse or steel-cut product. Because of its dark color, its use is limited mainly to the production of pumpernickel, snack rye, rye crisps and similar products (Rozsa 1976).

Because no federal Standards of Identity for rye flours have been promulgated, a wide range of blends, representing various combinations of the three basic types, is available to American bakers. A representative formula for a standard American rye bread is given in **Table 8.030**.

Because rye proteins do not produce a gluten structure when rye flour is mixed with water, as is true of wheat flour proteins, rye doughs with few exceptions contain a major proportion of wheat flour to provide the necessary structural support for a desirable loaf volume. Breads made entirely from rye flour have dense crumb and compact loaf volume since their doughs lack elasticity and gas retention properties.

The amount of rye flour used in the formulation of a given product is governed largely by the physical characteristics and the nature and intensity of flavor sought for the baked product. Nonetheless, the limiting ratio of rye flour to wheat flour that can advantageously be employed depends, to a major extent, on the quality of both flour types. In general, a strong first clear wheat flour is preferred for most rye bread production because it can carry higher percentages of rye flour and still yield satisfactory loaf volume. In many types of rye bread, strong patent and second clear wheat flours also perform with good results.

Concerning rye flours, white rye flour exhibits the lowest volume-depressing ef-

Table 8.030. Rye and Pumpernickel Bread Formulas

(Ingredients based on 100 parts flour)

Ingredient	Standard rye bread*			Pumpernickel**		
	Total	Sponge	Dough	Total	Sponge	Dough
Flour, clear	60 to 80	60 to 80	–	24	24	–
Medium rye flour	24 to 40	–	20 to 40	–	–	–
Dark rye flour	–	–	–	38	38	–
Rye meal	–	–	–	38	–	38
Water (variable)	64	34	30	71	32	39
Yeast	2	2	–	2	2	–
Salt	2	–	2	2.5	–	2.5
Rye sour, commercial	0 to 5	–	0.5	–	–	–
Sour dough	–	–	–	10	–	10
Malt, nondiastatic or other sweetener	0 to 4	–	0 to 4	1	–	1
Shortening	2	–	2	1	–	1

*Sponge temperature, 24°C (76°F); ferment 3.5 to 4 hours; dough temperature, 26 to 27°C (78 to 80°F); floor time, 20 minutes; bake approximately 221°C (430°F) with steam

**Sponge temperature, 24°C (76°F); ferment 3 hours; dough temperature, 27°C (80°F); scale, round, rest 15 minutes, mould; bake approximately 221°C (430°F) with steam

(Ponte 1980)

fect and may constitute up to 50% of the total formula flour without causing an appreciable loss in loaf volume. Medium rye flour exerts a more adverse effect on loaf volume, and its quantitative limit is about 35% of total flour. Dark rye flour is generally limited to 20% or less of the total formula flour to avoid excessive loaf volume reductions. Part of its adverse effect comes from its relatively high content of bran particles that tend to puncture the gluten film of the dough and thereby reduce its gas retention capacity.

Rye flour offers a more favorable acid environment for yeast than does wheat flour. Moreover, its levels of sugars and dextrins are also somewhat higher. In contrast to wheat flour, sound rye flour exhibits a certain amount of α-amylase activity that attacks its starch, which not only gelatinizes at lower temperatures but is also more susceptible to enzyme attack in its native state. All these factors combine to support more active fermentation in rye doughs. For this reason, salt assumes greater significance as a fermentation control factor than in wheat flour doughs and is normally added at the somewhat higher levels of 2.5 to 3.5%. The additional salt also serves to accentuate the final flavor.

Another approach to controlling the fermentation rate is to adjust the yeast addition in accordance with the amount of rye flour used in the formula. For example, if a dough with 20% rye flour is fermented with 2% yeast, an increase in the rye flour portion to 30 or 35% would entail a reduction in the yeast level to 1.5%. This reduction, with a corresponding compensatory adjustment in fermentation time, will result in a loaf with a moister crumb and improved keeping qualities. The factors that affect either favorably or adversely the baking quality and functionality of different types of rye flour have been reviewed by Drews and Seibel (1976) and Auerman (1977).

8.C.8.b. Rye sourdough fermentation

There are two ways whereby the characteristic acid flavor can be imparted to rye bread: (a) The baker may use commercially prepared proprietary sours that consist of blends of lactic and acetic acids in various ratios, often combined with dried yeast and appropriate bacterial cultures, with flour serving as a carrier; or (b) he may prepare his own sourdoughs on a perpetual basis and in amounts to meet his daily requirements. Prepared sours are available in a broad range of acid concentrations as well as acid ratios (**Figure 8.023**). In production, they are generally used at levels of 5 to 10% based on total flour, with the lower amounts being more common in sponge-and-dough processes. In these systems, which are said to promote a fuller flavor and greater loaf volume, the prepared sours are added at the sponge stage. To promote the maximum development of the acidic taste and tangy flavor in the baked loaf, reduced yeast levels of 1.5 to 2.0% are recommended (Johnson 1978).

Sourdoughs are essentially rye sponges that are fermented under special conditions that favor the formation of acids by hetero- and homofermentative Lactobacilli. Their use predates by far the introduction of compressed yeast, and they still find wide acceptance by bakers of traditional rye breads. There are several procedures for the preparation and perpetuation of sourdoughs that the baker can use in the production of rye breads.

Rye sourdoughs are prepared by the sour dough process described in Chapter 6, Part B, and the equipment in Chapter 9, Part C.

Figure 8.023. Liquid and dry sours enable consistent flavor and finished results batch after batch because they have been standardized by the ingredient manufacturer. (Puratos)

8.C.8.c. Dough aeration

The aeration — and thus the leavening — of sour rye doughs results from three general sources that supply additional gases to the air cells occluded in the flour or incorporated during mixing: (a) heterofermentative lactic acid bacteria, (b) wild yeasts and (c) the compressed yeast that is normally added to the dough. The most important of the heterofermentative Lactobacilli species found in sourdough is *L. brevis* because it produces, aside from lactic and acetic acid and traces of various alcohols, relatively large amounts of carbon dioxide. It is also largely responsible for producing the typical fermentation flavor of rye bread (Rohrlich 1961). The various species of wild yeast that occur naturally in rye flour constitute the second important source of aeration in sourdough. Knischewsky (1910) identified two morphologically distinct varieties of yeasts in sours that possess different fermentation activities: one variety that ferments sucrose, dextrose and raffinose but not maltose and lactose, and another variety that is able to ferment sucrose, dextrose and maltose, but not lactose and raffinose.

The final source of aeration in sourdough bread production is regular bakers yeast, added at levels of 0.5 to 2.5% when the ripe sour is incorporated into the final sponge or dough. The actual amount of yeast required is governed by factors such as the ratio of rye flour to wheat flour in the formula, the amount and nature of the sourdough, and the level of salt used either in the sourdough or in the final dough.

8.C.8.d. Dough acidification

The rate at which acidification proceeds in sourdough is influenced by several factors, including temperature, absorption and ripening time. Schulz (1966) showed that maximum acid formation occurs at a temperature of 35°C (95°F) over a period of some 4 hours, when the pH of the sourdough reaches about 3.8, at which level bacterial growth essentially stops. To reach the same pH level at a temperature of 25°C (77°F) requires a ripening time of 8 hours. Thus, the stability of sourdough is considerably greater at the lower temperature.

The rate of acidification is also greatly influenced by the absorption level. Soft doughs, with absorptions of 80 to 90%, show maximum rates of acid production, whereas stiff doughs, with 60% absorption, are relatively slow to acidify. With absorptions that exceed 100%, however, acidification rate again declines. Acid production tends to be proportional to ripening time up to the point where the medium's pH value has reached the critical level. The addition of salt to sourdough also acts to depress the rate of acid formation, a fact often used to stabilize sours for extended holding periods.

The two principal acids formed in rye sourdoughs are lactic acid and acetic acid. Their combined acidity is usually determined by titrating an aqueous suspension of 10 g of the sour with 0.1 N NaOH against a color indicator. This method, however, does not differentiate between the acids, nor does it indicate their relative ratios. For this, additional analytical procedures are needed. Rohrlich and Essner (1951) designated the ratio of lactic acid to acetic acid, in which both acids are expressed in ml equivalents of 0.1 N NaOH per 100 g of sourdough, as the fermentation quotient. This procedure allows the accurate determination of the effect of any change in the conduct of the sourdough fermentation on the relative ratios of the two acids. It was found, for example, that an increase in either the temperature or the absorption also increased the proportion of lactic acid, whereas lower temperatures and reduced absorptions favored acetic acid formation. The same authors (Rohrlich and Essner 1950-51) analyzed various types of rye bread for their lactic and acetic acid contents (**Table 8.031**).

Table 8.031. Rye Sourdough Acids

Bread type	Lactic acid (mg per 100 g bread)	Acetic acid (mg per 100 g bread)
Light rye bread	447	131
Dark rye bread	602	195
Whole rye bread	672	193

(Rohrlich and Essner 1950-51)

It is thus possible to influence the flavor of rye bread by appropriate control of temperature and absorption. To obtain the milder taste and more delicate aroma that lactic acid imparts to the bread, higher temperatures and absorptions should be selected. Acetic acid, in such a situation, provides the more subtle acidic note required for optimum bread flavor.

8.C.8.e. Production

The production of consistently uniform natural sours requires considerable skill and accurate control because even relatively minor variations in parameters such as flour type, temperature, absorption, etc., will produce marked changes in the character of the sour. Unless good control facilities are available to the baker, he may find it preferable to use commercially prepared rye sours and cultures in his production. When manufactured by reliable suppliers, these products are consistently uniform and capable of materially improving the flavor of the final product.

While both sponge-and-dough and straight-dough methods find use in rye bread production, the former method is more widely practiced because it has been shown to yield improved grain and texture, better keeping qualities, greater uniformity, greater fermentation tolerance, improved loaf volume and better machinability of the dough. The straight-dough method will also produce good results but is judged to require more careful supervision.

Opinions differ regarding the efficacy of adding part of the rye flour to the sponge, with the majority of bakers opting for the exclusive use of wheat flour at this stage. In general, a more intense sour rye flavor is produced with sponges that contain part or all of the rye flour. In such instances, absorption should be high enough to produce a relatively soft sponge with a minimum of mixing. If rye flour is used in the sponge, it will accelerate the rate of fermentation. Dark rye flours, because of their greater acidity and possibly higher diastatic activity, tend to cause a noticeably faster maturing of the sponge than do light rye or wheat flours.

Rye doughs differ significantly from wheat flour doughs in their mixing requirements, basically because rye flour is nearly devoid of gluten forming proteins. Denk (1965) suggested that the dough-mixing time of rye doughs containing 15 to 20% of rye flour be held to about one-half that of wheat flour doughs. Doughs made with young sponges tend to have a greater mixing tolerance than those with old sponges. While mixing at low speed reduces the likelihood of over-developing the dough and causing it to become sticky and produce poor quality bread, mixing at regular high speeds is the general rule wherever accurate controls are practiced. Lower mixing speeds and shorter mixing times are advisable with higher levels of rye flour in the dough or with the use of dark rye flours.

Tesch (1950) recommended that rye doughs with more than 35% of medium rye flour be mixed at low speed, whereas those with 20 to 30% may be mixed at high speed. However, in the latter case, bread with improved moisture retention is obtained if the doughs are mixed initially at low speed and are then finished off at high speed. In practice, however, low speed mixing of rye doughs is the general rule, if only as a safeguard against undesirable over-development.

Rye sponges and doughs are usually held at somewhat lower temperatures than white flour doughs, within a range of 23 to 26°C (73 to 78°F), to promote more rapid formation of acetic acid because this acid contributes to a tangier flavor in the baked loaf.

Properly fermented rye doughs do not present any special problems during mechanical makeup and will pass through the scaling and rounding operations with the same ease as comparably developed wheat flour doughs. After a brief intermediate proof time (8 minutes or less), the dough pieces are sheeted and moulded with conventional equipment. The head rolls of the sheeter should be corrugated so that they immediately engage the dough piece, which tends to develop a dry surface during overhead proofing. This roll design will help avert doubles. The sheeting rolls are spaced somewhat farther apart than in white bread production. Also, the pressure board should be adjusted so that excessive compression of the curled dough piece is avoided to prevent breaks in the baked loaf.

Recommended conditions for the final proofing of rye doughs are essentially the same as those for white bread: a temperature of 35 to 43°C (95 to 110°F) and a relative humidity of 85%. Proof times will range from 35 to 60 minutes. As a general rule, dark rye doughs and doughs with a high proportion of rye flour require less proofing than do the lighter varieties. Also, high yeast levels of 2%, and low salt contents (1 to 1.5% vs. the more usual 2 to 3%) will shorten the proof time appreciably.

Heavy rye doughs that will be baked free-standing on the hearth or in basket-type pans frequently are cut or docked on achieving full proof and just before they enter the oven. The cuts may be a single longitudinal one down the middle of the top crust or several transverse or diagonal ones, while docking or stippling involves punching a series of small holes into the top surface. The purpose of these operations is to produce a symmetrical loaf and prevent its cracking or bursting during baking.

The practice of washing the dough loaves with water or applying a thin gelatinized starch solution or a light egg wash to the top surface of the dough loaf just prior to baking is widely followed. Its aim is to impart crust characteristics such as a high gloss or a superior bloom to the finished loaf. The application of the wash, which must be done before the loaves are cut or docked, also minimizes the appearance of surface cracks during baking.

8.C.8.f. Baking

Rye breads are baked either in pans, in wire baskets or directly on the hearth. They require a stable, solid heat of 218 to 237°C (425 to 450°F), with liberal amounts of low-pressure steam to produce a glazed crust. Doughs designed for free-standing hearth baking should be turned out sufficiently stiff to yield well-shaped loaves with round bottoms. Baking times will range from 23 to 40 minutes, depending on oven temperatures and loaf volumes. Higher temperatures are needed with lean doughs whose formulations do not include dairy products and sweeteners, and those made with lighter rye flours. Dark rye doughs, because of their higher amylolytic activity, tend to color more rapidly and hence are more properly baked at lower temperatures. The liberal use of saturated steam, at a pressure of 2 to 3 psi, during the first one-third of the baking time, is essential.

Table 8.032. Pumpernickel Formula

Ingredient	Amount (g)
Sour*	
Basic sour	500
Whole rye meal	1,000
Water	700
Residue bread**	
Pumpernickel residue, ground, roasted	1,500
Water, 70 to 100°C	3,000
Dough	
Sour (above)	2,200
Residue bread (above)	4,500
Whole rye meal	9,000
Water	2,000
Salt	150
Bakers yeast	50

** Temperature, 28°C; ripening time, 2 to 3 hours*

*** Keep in 35°C proofbox for 8 hours*

Procedure

Mix on low speed for 20 to 25 minutes.
Rest for 15 minutes.
Remix for additional 15 minutes.
Dough temperature, 28°C.
Makeup immediately.
Final proof, 50 to 60 minutes.
Bake with steam at 110°C for 20 hours.
Let bread cool in pans.
Slice after 1 or 2 days.

(Lorenz 1980)

Not all ovens are equally suited to rye bread baking. In general, ovens with low crowns are considered superior to those with high crowns because both steam conditions and top heat, which represent critical factors in rye bread baking, are more readily controlled in a shallow baking chamber. With the restricted overhead space in a low-crown oven, both steam moisture and evaporated moisture remain in more intimate contact with the loaves for longer periods. During the early stages of baking, this moisture condenses on the loaf surface to produce conditions conducive to good ovenspring and the formation of an appealing crust. Rye breads can, of course, be successfully baked in nearly all types of modern ovens as long as they permit proper steam conditions and appropriate top and bottom heats to be maintained.

A defect occasionally observed in rye bread is the so-called "water ring," a circular crumb zone about an inch beneath the crust that exhibits a firmer, denser and somewhat darker cell structure. According to Hoepfner (1964), it is caused by a collapse of the cell structure as the crumb shrinks during cooling. The defect is found only in hearth loaves of rye bread that are formulated with admixtures of white wheat flour. Preventive measures include fuller acidification of the dough, use of stronger clear wheat flours, correct dough fermentation and more thorough baking to strengthen the crumb structure.

8.C.8.g. Pumpernickel

In its traditional form, pumpernickel rye bread is a whole rye meal bread with a very dark and dense crumb and a highly aromatic, either mildly sweet or sweet-sour flavor, depending on its method of production. It originated in Germany and is now produced in various forms and according to a wide range of formulations. Lorenz (1980) listed the basic ingredients of pumpernickel to include medium coarse-ground whole rye meal, salt (0.5 to 1.5%, flour weight basis) and a properly prepared sour to which is added residual pumpernickel bread that has been roasted and soaked overnight in warm water (**Table 8.032**). Optional ingredients include yeast at levels of 0.3 to 0.5%, sweeteners up to 3% and a preferment or *Brühstück* obtained by soaking up to 10% of the rye-meal in water at 50 to 60°C (122 to 144°F) for some 3 hours to produce thorough hydration and some saccharification. The sour for pumpernickel may be produced by any of the procedures used in rye bread production.

Because rye meal hydrates at a slower rate than do other flours, a 2-stage mixing procedure is normally used with pumpernickel doughs. In the first stage, the dough is mixed at low speed for 20 to 25 minutes at 28°C (82°F), given a 15-minute rest and then remixed for an additional 10 minutes, again at low speed. A typical old-fashioned pumpernickel dough will contain approximately 12% sour and 20% residue bread, with the balance consisting of whole rye meal, water, salt and yeast.

Steam is essential to optimum baking of pumpernickel bread. Specially designed oven chambers are preferred,

Table 8.033. Conchas Formula	
Ingredient	**Amount (bakers %)**
Sponge (40%)	
Bread flour	100
Water	60
Yeast, instant active dry	0.1
Dough (60%)	
Bread flour	100
Water	40
Eggs	25
Yeast, instant active dry	1.98
Salt	1.8
Sugar	30
Butter	11
Milk powder	11
Vanilla	1
Sugar paste topping	
Bread flour	100
Shortening	66.66
Powdered sugar	66.66
Food color	Sufficient quantity to produce desired color

(Suas 2009)

Figure 8.024. The Hispanic baking heritage includes colorful conchas and many other baked foods, from sweet cakes to cinnamon rolls. (*Baking & Snack*)

but regular ovens may be used if they can create the requisite steam-saturated atmosphere. The process is carried out in fully closed, rectangular, covered baking pans, after a full proof for a period of some 50 to 60 minutes. Baking temperatures are held rather low, within a range of 100 to 170°C (212 to 338° F), and baking times range from 10 to 24 hours, with 16 hours being considered average (Schünemann and Treu 1988).

The slightly sweet-sour taste of pumpernickel has its origin in the acids that form in the sour as it ripens and in the amylolysis of the starch during ripening, proofing and baking that produces glucose, maltose and dextrins. Temperatures at which amylases are inactivated are not reached for some 12 hours after start of baking. According to Lorenz (1980), the residual sugar content of pumpernickel lies within the range of 11 to 26%, compared with about 7% for regular rye bread made without sugar in the formula. Moreover, the oven conditions that prevail in pumpernickel baking favor the caramelization of sugar and the Maillard browning reaction whose end products contribute to both the color and overall flavor of the baked bread.

8.C.9. Hispanic breads

Bread and buns associated with Hispanic consumers present unique characteristics in shape and even color but are quite similar in formulation to other products on the US market (Savelli 2004). For example, *pan de auga* is a traditional lean bread with a chewy crust and soft interior, and *bolillos* are rolls made using the sponge-and-dough method but including a small amount of cinnamon added at the dough stage. Hispanic cuisine has a rich baking heritage, described by Sieloff (2006), consisting of items from 22 different nationalities.

When most consumers think of Hispanic breads, they usually have *conchas* in mind (**Table 8.033** and **Figure 8.024**). These soft, slightly sweet rolls have a distinct tropical flavor provided by honey and chopped almonds or cocoa. The addition of a highly colored sugary topping gives this product its name: In Spanish, concha means shell, and the topping cracks resemble the striations of seashells.

Another item unique to this culture is *pan de los muertos*, a traditional bread made in the shape of a skull and cross bones and produced to celebrate the Day of the Dead, observed on Nov. 2. The sponge ferments for up to 12 hours. Orange and anise infuse the water added at the dough stage, along with eggs, supplemented with additional yolks, sugar, butter and vanilla for a very rich product (Suas 2009).

Savelli (2004) provided formulations and procedures for *empanandas*, half-moon shaped sweets made of a cookie or pie crust with a fruit filling, and *pastel de tres leches*, a traditional dessert cake made with 3 milks.

8.D. Buns and Rolls

Updated by L.A. Gorton

While a great variety of both soft and hard crust buns and rolls are produced by commercial bakers, the two principal categories are hamburger buns and hot dog rolls. The current king of hard rolls, the bagel, is also described here along with bialys, a variation of the bagel.

8.D.1. Soft buns and rolls

Hamburger and hot dog (weiner) buns (**Figure 8.025**) are made from formulations that resemble those of conventional white bread, except for some quantitative enhancement with enriching ingredients such as sweeteners and shortening. A typical formula is shown in **Table 8.034** in which only the major ingredients are listed. The sweetener level ranges from 10 to 12%, compared with 7% for conventional white bread, and the shortening content is about double the 2 to 3% generally found in white pan bread. Such minor ingredients as dough strengtheners, crumb softeners, oxidants, yeast foods and mold inhibitors are used at levels consistent with good manufacturing practice.

The properties sought in buns include uniformity of size and form, an attractive bloom on the top crust, which should be reasonably flat and smooth and without blemishes, and a soft crumb with enough strength and resilience to resist permanent deformation during depanning, slicing and packaging (Farmer 1973).

Figure 8.025 Soft buns and rolls feature slightly richer formulations than pan breads.

Bun doughs may be prepared by any of the conventional procedures, although for large volume production, liquid ferment systems appear to be generally preferred. In these systems, 50% or more of the total flour is recommended for incorporation into the preferment so it receives the benefits of full fermentation (Trum 1971). This procedure will yield increased bun volume, stronger crumb body and improved retention of crumb resilience. This method also reduces the necessary work input during mixing, which results in lower dough temperature and savings in sweeteners during the fermentation stage.

The flour used for bun and roll production should have a protein content of 12% or higher and should have a fair proportion of spring wheat flour blended into it to promote optimum bloom and color in the baked bun. The type of sweetener used (sucrose, dextrose or corn syrups) appears to have little or no effect on ultimate dough behavior and product quality as long as appropriate quantitative adjustments are made to arrive at equivalent sweetener solids levels (Morgan 1980).

With horizontal mixers, the dough is generally ejected into a stationary trough that features a dough pump for transferring the dough to the divider hopper either through a pipe or, where longer distances are involved, preferably by means of a belt. As a rule, the consistency of bun doughs is markedly softer than that of bread doughs because of the higher levels of sugar solids and shortening in the former. Bent (1998) commented on these differences, noting that the reduced water in hamburger bun formulations (55% vs. 60% for white bread doughs) takes into

Table 8.034. Typical Soft Roll Formula	
Ingredient	% flour basis
Flour	100
Water (variable)	58 to 60
Sugar	10 to 12
Yeast	3 to 3.5
Shortening	5 to 6.5
Nonfat dry milk	1 to 2
Salt	2 to 2.25

(Trum 1971, Morgan 1980)

Figure 8.026. These buns get their braided appearance from passing under a patterned roller.

account the dough softening caused by the addition of higher levels of fat (3 to 5% vs. 1%) and sugar (5 to 10% vs. 0%).

Although stamping to mimic hand-knotting is a technique used more with hard rolls, some soft buns receive such treatment (**Figure 8.026**). As dough pieces leave the intermediate proofer and are sheeted, they also run under a roller engraved with a wide herringbone pattern, which simulates a braided pattern for the bun.

8.D.2. Hard rolls

Despite the many styles of hard rolls in the market (**Figure 8.027**), very little has been written about the formulation of such products, probably because their doughs are so similar, if not identical, to hearth and sourdough breads. For example, French dinner rolls (petit pain) are commercially produced on stringline systems by elongating the dough and then cutting it into individual pieces. In Europe, the popular square roll is made by processing a white hearth-style dough on a sheeting line with a reciprocating cutter configured with a lattice of knives. (This method automates the craft baker's quick approach of cutting a batch of dough on lever-style hydraulic divider and then placing the cut but unrounded dough pieces on peels to proof.)

Long (1993) reported that hard rolls can be formulated as straight doughs, no-time doughs and sponge-and-dough products. Traditionally, hard roll doughs are of low absorption with tight, stiff characteristics, but the advent of ciabatta styles and other such rustic products bring with them high absorption and soft, slack dough characteristics.

Commercial formulations for several hard roll styles were provided by Suas (2009), including dinner rolls and pretzel rolls, as well as *filoncini burro y nocci*, an Italian roll made with ground walnuts. Hitz (2008) explains stamped rolls from an artisan viewpoint.

Figure 8.027. Hard rolls come in many forms, flavors and toppings.

8.D.3. Bagels

Although bagels are shaped like doughnuts, their formulations and processing methods are quite different, but they do share the hole (**Figure 8.028**). Bakers originally made bagels in the shape of a stirrup (*Bügel* in German), but simplicity prevailed, and the stirrup became a ring. The bagel's shiny, chewy crust and dense crumb structure set it apart from other hard rolls, and the crust accounts for most of the product's overall flavor (Meloan and Doerry 1988).

As a hard bread roll, the bagel ranges in size from mini-bagels at ¾ to 1 oz (20 to 28 g) up to "bull" bagels at 4 to 7 oz (110 to 200 g), the most common sizes are in the range of 2.5 to 3.5 oz (70 to 100 g).

Bagel formulation varies from very lean (or tough) to very rich (or tender), and the basic formula consists of high-gluten flour, water, sugar or malt, salt, yeast and topping ingredients. To make a richer, or more tender bagel, the baker can add more sweetening and/or softening agents, which Petrofsky (1986a) identified as sugar, fat, eggs, malt, honey, molasses, soy flour and so forth. He noted that the minimal amounts of these more expensive ingredients do not radically raise production costs but do allow greater merchandising latitude with respect to food value as perceived by the customer. And bakers have taken great latitude with formulating, offering these rolls now made with ingredients as diverse as raisins, dried cranberries or blueberries, corn, rye, pumpernickel, jalapeño peppers, cheese, pumpkin puree, spinach, onion bits, garlic, apple bits, nutmeats and even chocolate chips. Toppings also run the gamut from caraway, dill, poppy and sesame seeds, garlic bits, salt, grated cheese to cinnamon sugar. Considerable regional variation characterizes the bagel market (Eberts 1998), with Easterners preferring traditional hard, chewy styles, while their Midwestern and Western cousins liked softer styles, yet Montreal customers opted for very dense, very sweet, very thin, bracelet-like bagels.

Figure 8.028. The bagel has become a popular American food. (Harlan Bakeries)

The flour chosen for bagels (**Table 8.035**) should be a good clear spring wheat, treated with potassium bromate and with a protein content averaging 13.5 to 14%. Lower protein flours, however, can be used as long as the baker supplements the formula with vital wheat gluten. Salt is present at 1.5 to 2.2% to retard fermentation, especially after boiling, to enhance flavor and to toughen the gluten. The sugar addition is relatively low (0 to 4%, flour weight basis) and can be in the form of sucrose, dextrose, corn syrup or high-fructose corn syrup. Sugar's function here is to provide fermentable sugars for the yeast and to contribute to crust browning. Honey or molasses may also be used as sugars and for addition of natural flavors. Meloan and Doerry (1988) evaluated the contribution of each ingredient, along with alternate oxidizers (azodiacaronamide, ascorbic acid), crumb softeners and dough strengtheners, to bagel quality.

Table 8.035. Plain Bagel Formula

Ingredient	Lean formula (bakers %)	Rich formula (bakers %)
High-gluten flour	100.00	100.00
Sugar	0.62	2.92
Salt	1.98	1.98
Vegetable oil	–	2.92
Water	53.33	50.00
Yeast	0.73	0.83

(Petrofsky 1986b)

Supplementary ingredients include defatted soy flour, 0 to 3% (flour weight basis), to increase dough absorption and improve the crumb body and resilience of the bagel. Vegetable oil, 0 to 5%, lubricates the dough and increases crumb tenderness. When making egg bagels, whole eggs are added at up to 12% provide both flavor and natural color. Use of dried egg ingredients for this variety was investigated by Doerry (1994). He determined that whole egg solids, used at levels up to 3.7% (flour weight basis) contributed little to bagel quality and seemed to aggravate "shelling" of the crust near the center hole; however, egg yolk solids reduced that effect and, because of the relatively high fat content of the yolk, tended to improve the taste and eating quality of the bagels.

Because this dough is very stiff, dough sizes should be kept to a minimum and should not exceed 60% of the mixer capacity. Using a straight, no-time dough method, all ingredients are placed into the mixer, which runs at low speed for 2 to 3 minutes to combine the materials and then at second speed for 8 to 10 minutes, or until the dough is extensible. Dough temperatures will be in the range of 24 to 27°C (76 to 80°F).

If bagels are to be made by hand, the dough is rested for about 5 to 10 minutes.

Figure 8.029. After a short period of cooking, the surface starch of the raw bagel gelatinizes.
(*Baking & Snack*)

Figure 8.030. The shiny crust of bagels is a result of the boiling process.
(Gemini Bakery Equipment)

After being shaped, bagels are generally retarded for 12 to 18 hours at 2 to 6°C (35 to 42°F) to build flavor. Meloan and Doerry (1988) suggested that such low temperatures favor the fermentation by lactic acid bacteria, rather than yeast, an activity that produces desirable flavor components. Extended low-temperature retarding can produce the small surface blisters, called "fish eyes," that some bakers prefer for bagel crusts.

Continuously produced (non-retarded) bagels are proofed at 40 to 43°C (104 to 110°F) under relatively low humidity (65 to 75% RH) to avoid skin formation, but bagels held overnight in a retarder are usually allowed to proof at lower temperatures, 30 to 32°C (86 to 90°F). (Producers of bagels containing chocolate chips report problems during proofing at temperatures that melt the chocolate bits. If retarding, with its cooler proofing temperatures, is not an option, then chocolate-flavored chips made with higher-melting fats such as those of compound coatings should be considered.)

After proofing, bagels cook briefly in simmering water (about 93 to 100°C, or 200 to 212°F). Bagels float so they must be turned halfway through cooking allowing each side to get about 30 seconds of cooking. Some bakers add molasses or malt to the water at about a 2.5% level (4 oz to every 10 lb of water) to give the bagels a better surface shine (**Figure 8.029**). Boiling not only gelatinizes the starch on the outside of the bagel to give the hard crusty feel and high shine but also sets the outside structure of the role so it retains its shape. Baking takes place at about 205 to 232°C (400 to 450°F) for around 17 minutes (**Figure 8.030**).

Another reason existed for boiling of proofed bagels, according to Eberts (1998). When bagels were formed by hand, it took considerable time to complete the makeup of a batch, thus bakers kept yeast levels low, 0.125 to 0.25% (flour weight basis). Consequently, proofing took a long time, 2 to 3 hours so bagels were tested for proof by dropping them into a container of room-temperature water. If they floated, then they had adequate proof; if they sank, additional proofing was required. The verification of proof carried over to the boiling process. Bagels had to float in the hot water bath, and they had to swell or expand slightly, which was a sign that the core temperature of the bagel had exceeded 60 to 65°C (140 to 150°F), thereby activating the yeast.

Because bagels are produced by what amounts to a straight, no-time method, the only fermentation time given to the yeast is during proofing plus the short period of cooking and transfer to the oven.

In the past 20 years, bagel preparation has been simplified for use at retail outlets. Retarded or frozen bagels supplied to these locations are generally baked off in rack ovens. To replace the cooking step, bakers flood these ovens with steam during the early stages of baking. Egg wash may also be used. The result is a softer bagel but one that still has a surface shine. Described as "Americanized bagels" by Petrofsky (1986b), such bagels suit sandwich uses. Bakers still using the traditional cooking method often call their products "water bagels" to differentiate them from the steam-baked style.

Bagels not scalded with hot water or abundant wet steam will expand excessively in the oven and will look more like regular hard rolls. Over-proofing will also cause bagels to expand markedly during cooking and collapse during the drying period ahead of baking.

The bialy is very similar to the bagel, but it is not boiled, and instead of a hole, it has a slight depression on top filled with diced onions or other savory ingredients. As Hitz (2008) explained, bialys are made from bagel dough shaped into rounded disks. The same retarding stage is employed, after which the baker forms a hollow in the top of the dough piece. A filling of cooked onions, poppy seeds, garlic or similar ingredients is deposited into the hollow. Baking at 215 to 227°C (420 to 440°F) for 15 to 20 minutes follows.

8.E. Flatbreads

Increasingly, consumers are adding flatbreads to their bakery choices. The pizza, which came to North American shores with Italian immigrants, exploded in popularity during the baby boom years after World War II and shows no signs of slowing down. Similarly, the tortilla (**Figure 8.031**), the common breadstuff of Central and South America, followed these populations on their northward journey. So it was with pita. The equipment and processing systems for these products, as well as cracker breads, are detailed in Chapter 12, Part E.

8.E.1. Tortillas
Updated by L.A. Gorton

Figure 8.031. Women making tortillas in early 19th century Mexico.

In the marketplace, a variety of terms describe tortillas. As Steinberg (1994) explained, tortillas are often called "soft tortillas" because the tortilla chip and taco, both hard-textured items, appeared first on US store shelves. Tortillas are beginning to find their way into international markets, particularly Europe, but the Chinese have eaten such products for centuries. The Chinese variety of flour tortilla is very white, thin, flexible and free of brown spots and blisters, in contrast to Mexican-style flour tortillas where such features are highly desirable.

The term "flour tortilla" is commonly used to describe tortillas made of wheat flour (**Figure 8.032**) instead of corn, the traditional tortilla base. At the time tortillas were first made from wheat flour, shortly after the Spanish introduced wheat to the

Figure 8.032. Made from wheat flour, tortillas have been popular in the Americas since the introduction of wheat by the Spanish. They are also eaten widely in China.

Figure 8.033. Corn tortillas, tortilla chips, taco shells and corn chips contain the whole content of the corn kernel, thus fitting the definition of a whole-grain food.
(Minsa Corp.)

New World, no other type of flour existed, certainly not corn flour. So the difference then was clear. Today, however, the milling industry produces flours from a wide variety of grains. The Tortilla Industry Association recommends that tortillas made with wheat flour be termed "wheat tortillas," thus differentiating them from corn tortillas.

Corn tortillas (**Figure 8.033**) fit the definition of whole-grain foods and contain the whole content of the corn kernel. When made with whole-wheat flour, so do wheat tortillas. Now as whole-grain products become more popular, "flour" tortillas made from grains other than wheat are entering the marketplace. Also, the traditional tortillas of other Latin American regions commonly use sorghum flour as their base (Rooney et al. 1986), as do gluten-free formulations now gaining popularity in the US.

Tortillas are thin, round flatcakes that were formerly made exclusively from corn that had been steeped in a dilute lime ($Ca[OH]_2$) solution and then ground into a soft mass but are now also produced in a significant amount from wheat flour. They are indigenous to Central American countries, chiefly Mexico (Steinberg 1994), and are normally consumed as a table bread or with various types of meat and/or vegetable filling that form the basis for such related ethnic foods as burritos, tacos, tamales and enchiladas. A variety of styles for corn tortillas exist: hot rack, shelf stable, thin for frying, thick for table use.

Cultural preferences normally determine the type of corn selected for preparation of corn tortillas. White corn, for example, is generally preferred by traditional Hispanic consumers, while yellow corn is the choice of non-ethnic populations. The color difference can even be regional, and Riley (1991) noted that white corn tortillas are preferred in Southern California, while consumers in many locations in New Mexico and Texas do not know white tortillas. Recently, "blue corn" tortillas and tortilla chips have come to be favored by trendy restaurateurs.

Soft tortillas get primary use as table breads or entree components, but corn tortilla doughs find additional uses as the basis for snacks such as corn chips and tortilla chips. Corn chips are basically a cooked corn dough that is fried, not baked, while tortilla chips are made from baked corn tortillas that are then fried. The big difference is that the dough for corn chips carries 52 to 56% moisture, which results in higher oil absorption and a different texture and flavor than a standard tortilla chip, which contains 38% moisture as it enters the fryer (Riley 1991).

In addition to corn and wheat, tortillas can be successfully made for a variety of other cereal grains, including triticale (Serna-Saldivar et al. 2004), a drought-resistant crop, and sorghum (Fernholz 2008), a gluten-free grain safe for celiac patients.

8.E.1.a. Corn and maize tortillas

In the original nixtamal process of making tortillas, which is still followed in some instances, the basic raw material is whole corn heated in a 1-to-2% lime solution (pH 11) to about 93°C (200°F) for 1 to 1.5 hours. The alkali assists corn starch to gelatinize, and the usual target for cooking and steeping is to hydrate roughly half the starch in the corn kernels. Treatment of corn by lime (calcium hydroxide) is essential, not only to the flavor, color and texture of the finished corn tortilla but more importantly to its nutritional quality. Specifically, it enhances niacin and calcium content (Stauffer 2004, 2006).

This treatment, termed nixtamalization, developed in pre-Columbian times when Central American natives found that by preprocessing maize, they could make baked foods that were preferable to the simple ground corn-and-water product. They leached wood ash to make an alkaline solution or used slaked calcium hydroxide, obtained from caves and called *cal* or *tequesquite* (Trevino and Norton 2006). Cooking maize in this water loosened the bran and germ, which were then removed by washing. Cooking also partially gelatinized the starchy endosperm.

The mixture is then allowed to soak or steep at room temperature for about 14 hours. After this steep period, the lime liquor is drained off, and the corn is washed two or three times with fresh water to remove the lime. Following the final wash, the corn is ground into a fine dough-like mass, referred to as *masa*, which has a moisture content of about 50% and constitutes the processed starting material from which the individual tortillas are formed (Parades-López and Saharópulos-Parades 1983).

Flint corn, the typical Central American maize, is preferred for corn tortillas because it has a small kernel and a very small husk. Conventional field corn, or "dent" corn, can be used, but masa yield is reduced by 10 to 20% (Schmidt 1985).

Production of corn tortillas in the US is for the most part based on the use of masa flour, or dehydrated nixtamal. The flour is produced either by first drying the alkaline-cooked and steeped maize in a drum dryer and then reducing it in a hammer mill or by preparing the masa in the traditional manner and then subjecting it to drum drying.

Improvements in the nixtamalization process have included use of enzymes to aide digestion of grain components in the absence of lime (Jackson and Sahai 2000).

Whole-corn meal can be pregelatinized by other means, but the calcium contributed by lye used in nixtamalization will be absent (Stauffer 2006). The properties of the resulting masa are somewhat different from those of traditional masa (nixtamal), different enough that some of these non-traditional masas are finding applications in dairy and other areas of the food industry. Pregelatinized whole-corn meal shows enhanced ability to bind moisture in the finished food, contributing to better shelf stability in a variety of products.

Recent work to nixtamalize corn meal (Cuevas-Rodríguez et al. 2009) treated corn endosperm fractions with an alkali solution to produce masa or instant masa flour. The researchers sought to reduce the long soaking times and high levels of alkaline liquid-waste discharges of the traditional process. They found that their process was optimized with a nixtamalization time of 15 minutes and cooking temperature of 83°C (181°F).

In selecting a dry masa, granulation is of paramount importance (Riley 1991). Tortillas for table use (at home or in a restaurant) require a fine granulation to help retain steam during baking, giving a desirable puffing effect. The resulting tortilla is soft, with a bread-like interior and good pliability. Tortilla chips and taco shells, on the other hand, need a coarser dry masa. Steam escapes readily during baking, giving a

Table 8.036. Typical Corn Masa Flour Specification

Proximate analysis

Moisture	9 to 12%
Protein, dry basis	8 to 11%
Fat, dry basis	3.5 to 5.5%
Ash, dry basis	1 to 2.5%

Sieve analysis (Ro-Tap 20-minute test)

On US Standard Sieve No. 18	0%
On US Standard Sieve No. 45	4% maximum
Through US Standard Sieve No. 100	40% minimum

Microbiological

Standard plate count	Meet reasonable customer requests
Yeast and mold	Meet reasonable customer requests
Coliforms and E. coli	Meet reasonable customer requests
Extraneous material	Meet reasonable customer requests

Process characteristics

Water absorption	115 to 120 lb water per 100 lb corn masa flour (water at 21 to 32°C, or 70 to 90°F)
Mixing time	4 to 6 minutes (low speed @ 20 rpm using sigma blade mixer)
pH (10% solution)	6.0 to 7.0
Color	White
Storage	

Store in a cool, dry location using GMP (proper pest control, etc.)
(Trevino and Norton 2006)

Figure 8.034. Dry corn flour speeds production of corn tortillas and aids uniformity.
(Azteca Milling)

smoother surface without undesirable bubbles and air pockets.

Corn masa flour specifications, discussed by Trevino and Norton (2006) and noted in **Table 8.036**, reflect the variability in water absorption capacity.

Table tortillas require elasticity, and rollability is a very important characteristic. If tortillas are being manufactured and packaged for supermarket retail sale, staling must be considered. Stale tortillas lose their flexibility and tend to break when wrapped around fillings. Studies addressing this problem are still under way, but the best current suggestion is to incorporate 5% defatted soy flour into the masa. According to Suhendro et al. (1999), the tortillas showed improved flexibility and rollability during storage.

Critical specifications for corn tortillas, as well as corn chips and tortilla chips (**Figure 8.034**), are (a) consistency of color, (b) pH, (c) consistent and predictable particle stratification resulting in texture control, (d) water demand or viscosity, with masa flour, and (e) dough moisture, with cooked corn (Riley 1991).

The quality of corn tortillas and end user demands differ among markets. Some areas desire a high-pH, highly-alkaline-flavored tortilla; others prefer a brightly white, low-pH tortilla lacking in alkaline taste. Color is associated with pH.

The ingredient list for corn tortillas is generally quite simple and short, consisting of corn and water, but other ingredients are frequently used. For example, preservatives are added to retard microbial growth, and hydrocolloids, stabilizers and/or emulsifiers (dough conditioners) will help maintain the tortilla's flexibility. In Mexico, the corn tortilla industry voluntarily enriches its products with vitamins. Burton et al. (2008) recently verified the survival of micronutrient fortification in nixtamal tortillas and found it to be satisfactory although some losses during processing were noted. A Mexican regulatory proposal mandated iron fortification of corn flour and nixtamalized corn flour, and the initial choice was ferrous sulfate or ferrous fumarate, but color and stability problems were associated with these more reactive iron sources. The proposal was then modified to allow use of other iron sources. Comparing iron fortification sources, Richins et al. (2008) recommended use of electrolytic iron because it had a minimal effect on color and was significantly lower in cost than other iron sources evaluated.

Table 8.037. Representative Formula for Wheat Flour Tortillas	
Ingredient	% (flour weight basis)
Wheat flour (high protein)	100
Water (tempered to 100°F)	46
Shortening	8
Salt	1.5
Baking powder	0.375
Dough conditioner	0.5
Mold inhibitor	0.75
(Schmidt 1985)	

8.E.1.b. Wheat flour tortillas

Tortillas made from wheat flour are processed in a manner that differs from that used for corn flour tortillas. In contrast to corn tortillas, whose formula consists essentially only of corn flour and water, wheat flour tortilla doughs contain, in addition to a high-protein flour and water, preferably tempered to 100°F (38°C), variable amounts of shortening, salt, soy flour, baking powder, dough conditioner and minor amounts of other optional ingredients as may be dictated by special processing and market conditions. A representative formula for a wheat flour tortilla is shown in **Table 8.037**. The use of relatively low water content (absorption), in conjunction with high-protein flour, yields rather stiff doughs. In their finished form, wheat tortillas have a moisture content of 30 to 32% and a pH of 5 to 6 (Gelroth et al. 2005). Wheat tortillas also take well to additional flavors such as sun-dried tomato, spinach and other vegetables (**Figure 8.035**).

The rapidly expanding popularity of tortilla-based foods and their growing impact on the diet of an ever increasing number of consumers has prompted a series of studies concerning their nutritional value. Ranhotra (1985), in reviewing the recently developed nutritional information relating to both corn and wheat tortillas,

Figure 8.035. Addition of specialty wheat proteins help these flavored wheat tortillas maintain flexibility for 20 to 40 days. (MGP Ingredients)

concluded that both types are a significant source of nutrients. Wheat flour tortillas, when compared to corn tortillas, are found to contain higher levels of protein, fat, carbohydrates and the three enrichment vitamins thiamine, riboflavin and niacin. Corn tortillas, in contrast, tend to be higher in their phosphorus, calcium and potassium levels, but lower in sodium.

8.E.1.b.i. Production styles

The three methods for making wheat (flour) tortillas — hand-stretched, heat-pressed and die-cut — yield different results (Janson 1990, Kraut 2006, Gorton 2008). Pressed tortillas are smooth and slightly shiny in appearance. They tend to be pliable and slightly elastic and can be easily rolled or folded without tearing. Their texture and crumb are light and fluffy, with pronounced layering and flake. Hand-stretched tortillas generally have a dull appearance and dry, powdery feel caused by residual dusting flour from the manufacturing process. They have a tender bite and are dense with little layering or flake. Die-cut tortillas have a dry, powdery feel from the dusting flour and are generally tough, chewy and very dense, with no flake or layers.

Pressed tortillas generally find use as table tortillas and for preparation of fajitas, soft tacos and burritos. Hand-stretched tortillas are also eaten as table tortillas and used in burritos and some fried products such as sopaipillas and chimichangas. Die-cut tortillas are used to make fried salad bowls, chimichangas, bunuelos and sopaipillas, as well as frozen entrees including tightly rolled flautas.

8.E.1.b.ii. Ingredients

Flour characteristics in terms of absorption and Farinograph dough consistency for wheat tortillas were summarized by Qarooni (1993), who used a water absorption of 53% and the 680 Farinograph consistency line as standards for his research. He found the best results for heat-pressed tortillas with a 75%-extraction hard wheat flour of moderate protein (11.6%).

The wheat tortilla dough system is not the same as that of bread because it involves chemical leavening, and any yeast in the formula is present primarily for flavoring purposes. When the dough is formed, it is rested to allow the gluten to relax so that thin tortillas of large diameter can be formed.

Pressed tortillas. The ranges for ingredients of pressed wheat flour tortillas are noted in **Table 8.038**, while **Table 8.039** summarizes the functions of minor ingredients. The preferred flour is usually a winter wheat style that is bleached and enriched, having a protein content of 9.5 to 11%. The bleaching is not for strength but for whiteness of the finished product. Lower protein flours produce a less tenacious dough, as Janson (1990) observed in his discussion of wheat flour tortilla formulating, which is advantageous for the pressed flour process, minimizing the heat and pressure needed. The amount of water depends on the flour's absorption capabilities and on the quantity of shortening and reducing agents present. High percentages of shortening and use of reducing agents dictate less water and vice versa. Dough pH should be kept in the range of 5.5 to 6.5.

The shortening lubricates the gluten, tenderizes the finished product and helps with separation of the tortillas as they are removed from the package. It also helps lubricate the heated pressing plates and conveyor belt. The most popular shortening for wheat tortillas was lard, which also imparted a distinctive flavor still favored by many consumers. Tortilla manufacturers have, however, moved away from ani-

Table 8.038. Wheat Tortilla Formulations			
Ingredient	Pressed (bakers %)	Hand-stretched (bakers %)	Die-cut (bakers %)
Basic ingredients			
Flour	100	100	100
Water	47 to 55	45 to 50	40 to 50
Shortening	5 to 15	4 to 8	5 to 8
Salt	1 to 2	1 to 1.5	1.5 to 2
Optional ingredients			
Baking powder	1 to 3	0 to 2 (optional)	0 to 2 (optional)
Acidulants	variable	optional/variable	optional/variable
Mono- and diglycerides	0.5 to 1.0	0 to 1.5 (optional)	–
SSL or CSL	–	–	0.25 to 0.5
Mold inhibitors (preservatives)	variable	optional/variable	optional/variable
Reducing agents	variable	variable	optional
Oxidizing agents	optional	optional	required/variable
Yeast	optional	optional	optional
Flavoring agents	optional	optional/variable	optional/variable

(Janson 1990)

mal shortenings, replacing them with vegetable oils and shortenings. Bejosano et al. (2006) determined that replacement of partially hydrogenated fats with solid-fat zero-trans-fat compounds such as palm oil-based and interesterified oil shortenings did not significantly affect quality characteristics such as opacity, diameter and texture. Fats with a low melting index such as oils required some minor adjustments in processing procedures.

Mono- and diglycerides perform the same functions in wheat tortillas as they do in conventional breads and buns. They improve machinability, shelf life and tenderness. They also reduce stickiness and tearing when tortillas are removed from packages.

The salt is used for flavor and to strengthen the gluten. Higher levels of salt are used in formulating die-cut tortillas because a stronger dough is desirable.

Leavening of wheat tortillas is accomplished with baking powder and yeast as well as the steam generated by the dough's moisture. The leavening gases produced by the baking powder expand the dough piece to create a layered effect responsible for the light, flakey texture of the finished tortilla. Baking powder also tenderizes and whitens the finished tortilla.

Most consumers prefer fluffy, thick, opaque tortillas so finding the right leavening system is critical. While sodium bicarbonate is most often chosen as the leavening base, Bejosano and Waniska (2003) found ammonium bicarbonate to also be acceptable and poses fewer storage stability concerns.

Leavening acids had an influence on all wheat-flour tortilla properties measured — weight, diameter, stack height, pH, moisture and texture (Book et al. 2002). Sodium aluminum phosphate (SALP) produced tortillas with the largest diameter, whereas monocalcium phosphate (MCP) used alone produced the thinnest tortillas. SALP and sodium acid pyrophosphate (SAPP) produced tortillas with the greatest stack height. MCP used in combination with the other acids tested did not significantly affect stack height. Although fumeric acid was added to lower pH, the leav-

Table 8.039. Minor Ingredients Used in Flour Tortillas

Ingredient	Use level	Effects	Method of tortilla production
Emulsifiers			
Sodium stearoyl lactylate (SSL)	0.1 to 0.4%	Dough conditioning	Hot press
Monoglyceride	up to 1%	Improve dough machineability	Hand stretch
Diglyceride	up to 1%	Reduce shortening level	Die cut
		Improve tearing quality	
		Help in eliminating sticking after packaging	
Gums			
Guar, carboxymethyl cellulose, xanthan gum, gum arabic	0.25 to 0.5%	Improve dough machineability	Hot press
		Decrease dugh and product stickiness	Hand stretch
		Delay staling	Die cut
		Improve rolling and folding properties	
		Bind large amount of water	
		Improve freeze-thawing properties	
		Decrease moisture loss	
Preservatives and acidulants			
Sodium and calcium propionate	0.3%*	Mold inhibitor	Hot press
Potassium sorbate	0.4%*	Catalyst for some preservatives	Hand stretch
Sorbic acid	0.2%	pH adjustment	Die cut
Fumeric acid	0.1 to 0.2%		
Phosphoric acid	to lower pH to 5.5		
Citric acid	80 g per 100 kg flour		
Monocalcium phosphate	0.15 to 0.4%		
Reducing agents			
L-cysteine	Depends on flour quality	Improve dough machineability	Hot press
Sodium bisulfite		Improve extensibility	Hand stretch
Sodium metabisulfite		Decrease elasticity	Die cut
Oxidizing agents			
Ascorbic acid	Depends on flour quality	Improve mixing tolerance	Die cut
		Improve dough machineability	
Potassium bromate			

* Optimum pH 5.5
(Qarooni 1993)

ening acid system used determined the final pH. All pH values were low enough to provide shelf life stability. With regard to texture, tortillas made with SALP required the least force to break (which can be interpreted as being the most tender), whereas tortillas made with sodium aluminum sulfate (SAS) required the most force to break.

As is common practice in the tortilla industry, dough temperatures for wheat tortillas tend to be higher than those for bread doughs, which serves to increase mixer throughput and decrease dough resting time, but such temperatures have an effect on the action of chemical leaveners, releasing the leavening gases earlier in the process than may be desired. Cepeda et al. (2000) studied this aspect and determined that at 38°C (100°F), the dough required more leavening acid and base to compensate for some of the loss of carbon dioxide incurred during mixing and resting. These researchers also observed that, contrary to the perception in the tortilla industry, increasing the amount of baking powder to increase the thickness and opacity of tortillas instead produced only small or insignificant improvements.

Yeast in several forms — active dry, instant, compressed and inactive dry — is used more as a flavor and a source of glutathione than for leavening gases. The glutathione helps mellow and relax the gluten during intermediate proofing.

Acidulants help adjust the pH of the dough, and fumeric acid, used at 0.1 to 0.2%, is generally sufficient to accomplish this task, as will monocalcium phosphate at 0.15 to 0.4%. Other acids include citric acid. Dough pH in the range of 5.5 to 6.5 optimizes the action of mold inhibitors, or preservatives, and enhance the flavor of the finished products. Gelroth et al. (2005) observed that fumeric acid is generally the preferred acidulent for wheat tortillas. In its uncoated form, it reacts very rapidly, so encapsulation or coatings will help extend its functionality to reduce product pH over time and thus extend the shelf life of the tortilla. Interaction between acidulants and baking powder can cause undesirable opaque spots on wheat tortillas; however, encapsulation of the fumaric acid can solve this problem.

The reducing agents most often used for wheat tortillas are sodium bisulfite, sodium metabisulfite, L-cysteine and sorbic acid. They condition the gluten to improve machineability.

Sugar, milk powder and, again, yeast, are the most common flavoring agents used in wheat tortillas. Vegetable powders and concentrates such as spinach, sun-dried tomato and beet give unique colors and flavors to new styles of wheat tortillas, often used as sandwich wraps.

Shelf life also affects formulating concerns when making tortillas, specifically the use of preservatives such as potassium sorbate, calcium propionate and sodium propionate. In locations where only short distances separate processing plant and store shelf, no preservative may be needed. In Hispanic neighborhoods, shoppers are accustomed to buying table tortillas daily, and they often judge the freshness of corn tortillas by the warmth of the product.

Where longer distances prevail, a preservative system may be needed to prevent surface molding of corn and wheat tortillas because they have relatively high water activity (a_w) ratings, 0.88 for flour and 0.98 for corn. This additive can be added to the dough or applied as a surface spray. Rolow (2002) described the use of preservatives for both wheat and corn tortillas. The most commonly anti-microbial agents are calcium or sodium propionate (propionic acid), potassium sorbate (sorbic acid), sodium diacetate (acetic acid), sodium benzoate (benzoic acid) and methyl or propyl paraben, with calcium propionate and potassium sorbate the most popular.

Modified atmosphere packaging is another way to protect tortillas during distribution. Such packaging also allows marketing of tortillas on bread shelves instead of refrigerated cases.

Hand-stretched tortillas. A leaner formula characterizes hand-stretched tortillas, compared with pressed tortillas. Water, shortening and salt are lower, and baking powder is optional.

Water temperature can be a controversial topic, according to Schmidt (1985), who observed that in cold climates water should be tempered to 38°C (100°F) for best results.

Die-cut tortillas. This method punishes the dough more than the pressing and hand-stretching processes, hence the use of dough conditioners and oxidizing agents in the formula.

Gurkin (2002) reviewed the functions of hydrocolloids in wheat tortilla processing and found that these ingredients — alginates, carboxy methyl cellulose (CMC), carageenan, guar and locust bean gum, konjac flour and xanthan gum — when used at relatively low levels (0.1 to 0.3%) enhanced flexibility and strength, reduced stickiness during processing and packaging, increased post-bake moisture levels, slowed the staling process and extended shelf life. This report followed up on an earlier study by Friend et al. (1993) that employed the natural gums at 0.2 to 0.5%, with cellulose and commercial blends studied at a somewhat higher level, 0.3 to 1.0%.

Because of its growing importance in the diet, tortillas are a continuing subject for scientific research seeking to improve their quality characteristics. In many ways, the wheat tortilla is similar to bread baked from wheat flour. For example, Alviola and Waniska (2008) determined that the flexibility of tortillas (a measure of their freshness) results from the combined functionalities of the amylose gel and amylopectin solidifying the starch granules during storage.

8.E.2. Pizza crust
Updated by Hans van der Maarel

Pizzas may be described as flat bread products topped by a sauce based chiefly on tomato paste but generally containing additions of various cheeses, spices, flavors, meats and other garnishes to provide variety. The topping will normally represent some 45% of the finished pizza weight, with the bread-like crust or shell making up the remaining 55% (Lehmann and Dubois 1980).

Pizza crusts may be differentiated into three categories according to whether they are formed by pressing, by sheeting and cutting to produce a thick, or so-called deep-dish crust that is more bread-like in character, or by hand shaping or tossing into a retail type pizza as sold by pizza chains. Because all these crusts are quite different in their properties and eating quality, their formulations vary accordingly. The ranges in ingredient levels encountered in pizza crust formulations are shown in **Table 8.040**.

Pizza styles are also differentiated by their crust character, according to Lehmann (1986a). Cracker-type crusts are relatively thin with an open porous crumb structure offering many large holes or blisters. This style is typical of smaller pizzerias yet has been automated. The crispy-type crust, a variant of the thin crust, has a close internal cell structure and a high oil content and is generally typical of frozen pizzas (**Figure 8.036**). The chewy, or New York style, pizza crust is made with high-protein flour and reduced oil content to yield a pronounced tough, chewy eating experience. Many people refer to the

Table 8.040. Pizza Crust Formulations

Ingredient	% (flour weight basis)
Basic	
Flour	100
Water	55.0 to 70.0
Salt	1.0 to 2.0
Sugar	1.0 to 5.0
Shortening	3.0 to 14.0
Yeast	0.5 to 5.0
Baking powder (in place of yeast)	0.5 to 4.0
Calcium propionate	0.1 to 0.3
Optional	
Proteolytic enzyme	As recommended
L-cysteine or NaHSO3	45.0 to 90.0 ppm
Corn meal	10.0 to 20.0
Flavoring	As desired
Sours	1.0 to 3.0
Vinegar (200 grain)	0.5 to 1.0
Sodium stearoyl lactylate (SSL)	0.25 to 0.50
Vital wheat gluten	1.0 to 2.0

(Lehmann and Dubois 1980)

latter as a bread-type crust.

Recent innovations have brought rising-crust and filled-crust pizzas to the market. The latter involves deposition of a ring of cheese or sauce during the pizza crust formation process, while the former represents a formulation innovation: addition of chemical leavening to the crust's yeasted dough. Par-baked and take-and-bake varieties have also emerged. Crust sizes run from round styles with diameters of 3.5 to 16.5 in., as well as squares and rectangles. Lipped styles include deep-dish, pan-style or crown-style (Valentino 1994, Lehmann 1997, Lehmann 2002).

A significant part of the fresh pizza market uses dough balls either in frozen or retarded state that are produced in commissary style facilities in a process similar to breadmaking with mixers, dividers and rounders and shipped either frozen or refrigerated at below 3°C (38°F). The dough balls are then shaped into pies by either a simple cross-grain sheeter and hand finished or completely hand shaped or tossed. A comprehensive description of commissary methods for processing refrigerated and frozen pizza doughs was provided by Lehmann (1986b).

Figure 8.036. Thin, cracker-like crusts support a multitude of sauces and toppings to create an attractive pizza.

Gourmet, or signature, pizzas have become very popular. Their preparation, described by Rowe and Lehmann (2000), may involve traditional or unique ingredients as toppings. These pizzas are built on crusts that complement the toppings, with characteristics of thin or thick, light and tender or somewhat chewy and bread-like. Flour high in protein (13.5 to 14.5%) is required for the thin styles, while lower protein (10.5 to 12.0%) flour is best for thicker crusts. Companies wishing to bring whole grains appeal to pizza crusts have turned to wholewheat flour as a formulating option (**Figure 8.037**).

8.E.2.a. Ingredient essentials

A relatively strong spring wheat flour, with a protein content of 12 to 14%, is recommended. Thin pizza crusts call for higher protein flours to minimize sauce soaking into the crust

Figure 8.037. All-natural toppings complement this whole-grain pizza crust. (Pizza Hut)

and to preserve its desirable crispness. The protein content of flour may be augmented by the addition of 1 to 2% vital wheat gluten. For thick pizza crusts, flours of lower protein content will be found more suitable because they minimize dough shrinkage and impart a more desirable chewiness to the finished crust.

Water absorptions will range from 55 to 70%. The thin crusts generally take less water, 45 to 52%, while absorptions of 55 to 60% are normally used for thick crusts (Lehmann 1986a). The correct absorption for each type of crust is essential to avoid sticky doughs with poor machining properties that result from excessive absorption and fragile doughs that produce rather leathery crusts in the case of under-absorption. Salt is added primarily for its flavor-enhancing action, which is more significant in thick crusts than in thin crusts.

The level of sugar in pizza doughs is relatively low. Its main purpose is to provide readily-fermentable carbohydrates to support the rather limited fermentative action assigned to the yeast. In chemically-leavened doughs, sweeteners are either omitted or held to a minimum.

Shortening levels of 3.0 to 14.0% are relatively high, particularly in thin crusts and in those formed by pressing or stamping in which the fat creates a more tender texture and a greater resistance to soakage of the sauce. Liquid or plastic shortenings are equally suitable.

Fine ground yellow cornmeal can be used in both thin and thick crusts to impart chewiness and improve the "bite" without developing toughness. In thin crusts, the amount of corn meal is generally limited to 10%, while in thick crusts up to 20% may be used.

For yeast-leavened pizza doughs that are to be frozen, the generally recommended yeast level is increased to 5% to compensate for the loss in yeast viability brought about by the freezing process. Yeasted doughs are normally mixed to a temperature of 32 to 38°C (90 to 100°F) and given a floor time of 10 to 15 minutes. With chemically-leavened doughs, on the other hand, the finished dough temperature is held to 24 to 27°C (75 to 80°F), and the floor time is omitted. Frozen pizza shells often formulated with calcium propionate (0.2 to 0.3%) to combat mold development during the periods before freezing and should freeze/thaw cycles occur during distribution.

Development of rising-crust pizza (**Figure 8.038**) marked a revolution in frozen pizza formulating. Use of heat-activated chemical leaveners provided additional aeration to crusts, thus allowing consumers to better duplicate the pizzeria experience at home. Lehmann (1997) described the development and formulation of this style of pizza (**Table 8.041**). Typically, such crusts use yeast leavening for the bulk fermentation stage, with the yeast's action supplemented by sodium acid pyrophosphate (SAPP) and sodium aluminum phosphate (SALP) plus sodium bicarbonate. Coated leavening acids will extend the frozen storage life of such crusts for 5 to 6 months. When using heat-activated acids, care must be taken when processing such doughs on heated stamping systems. Both the temperature of the hot press and the dwell time will need adjust-

Figure 8.038. Chemical leavening supplements the yeast in rising-crust pizza to recreate the pizzeria experience in the home kitchen.
(ICL Performance Products)

ment. Generally a top die temperature of 190 to 218°C (375 to 425°F) and a bottom or base temperature of 177 to 205°C (350 to 400°F) works well with a dwell time of 4 to 6 seconds. Many manufacturers add fine-grind yellow cornmeal to the bottom of the crust to assist with removal of the crust from the forming belt and to add crackle to the eating characteristics.

Take-and-bake pizza, too, represents a new category for this popular product. This style involves preparation of the pizza and its toppings at a supermarket deli or a food service outlet, with the final baking done at home by the consumer. Crust styles include both par-baked and fresh preparation on a raw dough "skin." Lehmann (2002) described the formulation, preparation and service parameters for such doughs and crusts.

8.E.2.b. Processing parameters

Pizza doughs are generally mixed in conventional horizontal or vertical tool mixers in batch sizes that can be processed within a 15-minute period. The judicious use of proteolytic enzymes or of reducing agents will aid in reducing the mixing time: 60 to 75 ppm L-cysteine for sheeted crusts or 75 to 90 ppm for stamped crusts. Yeast-leavened doughs are given a brief floor time to allow them to relax, while chemically-leavened doughs are taken directly to makeup. Under-mixing is preferred because the dough's gluten gets additional work during the stamping or sheeting processes. An over-mixed dough will have a fine, cake-like structure, while under-mixing fosters a more desirable open crumb.

A dough-out temperature of 23 to 24°C (74 to 76°F) allows the dough to begin fermenting slightly after it is divided, rounded and placed into trays for retarding, a period that can last from 12 to 96 hours. If doughs are retarded, which is a common practice at manual and pizzeria operations, then they must be given floor time of 30 to 60 minutes before final shaping and proofing, a 15- to 45-minute process.

In automated production of stamped crusts, dough is mixed sufficiently to achieve a smooth consistency, which takes 3 to 5 minutes at high speed in a conventional horizontal bread mixer. The high (38°C, or 100°F) dough temperature yields a soft, relaxed dough that will flow and exhibit minimum shrinkage at the stamping station. The divided dough balls receive a light oil spray and enter the intermediate proofer for 10 to 15 minutes of rest. They drop out onto pans and proceed to the stamping station to be pressed out to a specified size. Some lines employ a second stamping station, 45 seconds to 2 minutes after the first station. Thin crusts go directly to the oven, but thicker crusts are often given 5 to 10 minutes of final proofing at 32°C (90°F) (Lehmann 1979).

The dough for sheeted-and-cut crusts is mixed using no-time dough methods, taking 8 to 10 minutes at high speed. The target dough temperature is 22 to 28°C (78 to 82°F). The dough gets 5 to 10 minutes of floor time before going to the sheeting line. Reduction rolls create sheets with a thickness of $^{1}/_{8}$ to $^{3}/_{16}$ in. for thin crusts or $^{1}/_{4}$ to $^{5}/_{16}$ in. for thick crusts. The dough is docked (**Figure 8.039**) and cut to the desired size, with the scrap web returned to the extruder. Final proofing is done under conditions of 32 to 35°C (90 to 95°F) and 80 to 90% RH for 8 to 10 minutes for thin crusts or 20 to 40 minutes for thick crusts (Lehmann 1986a).

Pizza crusts, because of their relative thinness, require baking times of only 3 to 5 minutes at temperatures that normally range between 205 to 316°C (400 to 600°F).

Table 8.041. Self-Rising Pizza Crust Formula

Ingredient	Amount (bakers %)
Flour	100
Salt	1.75
Sugar	2
Oil	5
Leavening acid (SALP)	0.75
Sodium bicarbonate	0.75
Yeast, compressed	0.25
Water	50
Hard fat flakes (opt.)	8
Reducing agent	As required

(Lehmann 1997)

Figure 8.039. Fat reduction in pizza crusts can be accomplished with hydrocolloids and emulsfiers. Note that the crust has been docked.
(Cargill Texturizing Solutions)

They must be cooled thoroughly to the ambient temperature before the topping is applied because they will otherwise collapse.

A departure from this process involves the hot press pizza crust. After the press cycle, these crusts may run first through a short tunnel oven for 30 to 40 seconds and be topped with most ingredients, including sauce and cheeses. In a continuous flow, these crusts are then partially baked in a tunnel oven followed by a blast freezer.

Some bakeries temper fresh baked shells for 24 to 96 hours to allow them to equilibrate and firm slightly before proceeding to the topping line for finishing. Such shells should be protected against mold with antimicrobial ingredients such as calcium propionate. If shells are marketed without sauce and refrigerated, they will also benefit from antimicrobials and/or an external spray of potassium sorbate.

Par-baked pizza, detailed by Valentino (1994), follows the production methods for pressed or sheeted crusts, but interrupts baking at the point where yeast is deactivated and the size is stabilized. The crust has a firm surface, facilitating packaging and, later on, topping with cheese, sauce and other ingredients. Most par-baked pizza is either frozen or refrigerated and should be protected against microbial damage with either calcium propionate or potassium sorbate. These products benefit from modified atmosphere packaging in film with good moisture and oxygen barriers. Some processors shrink-wrap or vacuum-form the film around the crust.

8.E.2.c. Toppings

Major developments have taken place in the marketplace for topping of pizza crusts. The standard tomato sauce and cheese topping finished with pepperoni or crumbled cooked sausage is still popular, but many toppings have been added. Where uncommon or exotic toppings were the domain of individual pizza stores or restaurants, unique toppings have become mainstream for mass-produced pizzas. The standard application of toppings is the waterfall system, a relatively simple process but expensive to operate because of cleaning requirements. Spot depositing of tomato sauce is now most preferred, and new technologies also allow a variety of cheeses to be spot deposited, saving ingredients and making a more distinct pizza crust.

After the topping is applied, the pizzas are frozen in blast freezers, individually packaged and bulk packed in cartons for storage at freezer temperatures until required for shipment. The practical aspects of commercial pizza crust production have recently been described by Fischer (1981) and Lehmann (1979, 1986a). Ranhotra (1984) examined the nutritional value of pizza products.

8.E.3. Pita
Updated by L.A. Gorton

Pita breads are flat, circular, 2-layered loaves that have their origin in the Middle East, and Arabic bread, balady, shamy, Syrian bread and pocket bread are only a few of their many names. Although they are similar in shape and appearance, they do vary in some specific aspects such as level of water absorption, type of flour used, thickness of the loaf and others. Doerry (1983), for example, pointed out that in Egypt, where pita breads are indigenous, the highly popular balady bread is made with 82% extraction flour, 70 to 75% absorption, 0.5% salt and 20% sour dough held over from a previous batch; shamy bread, on the other hand, is made from 72% extraction flour, 58% absorption, 0.5% salt, and 1.5% yeast. It is evident that these and related types of bread have very simple formulations, with examples shown in **Table 8.042**, and that their distinctive character is largely derived from the leavening action of steam (Dalby 1963).

An even simpler formula was quoted by Cooper (1986): 100 parts high-protein flour, 50 parts water and 3 parts yeast. He noted that some wheat gluten may be added to strengthen the dough, and an oxidizing agent such as bromate or ascorbic acid may facilitate the process. Faridi and Finney (1980) documented the flat breads of Iran, giving formulations that used date syrup as the sweetener, a good portion of sour dough ferment and some with the addition of baking soda.

Fats and oils are not common in flatbread doughs, and when used, account for 0.5 to 1.0%. Only vegetable source oils should be allowed to ensure the finished bread meets halal and kosher requirements. The fat will soften the crumb by thinning crumb cell walls, which can make the bread more fragile. Quail (1996) comprehensively analyzed supplemental ingredient additions of bran, fats and oils, emulsifiers, gluten, sugar, milk powder, pre-gelatinized starch and enzymes.

Mixed by the straight dough method, this dough is generally given 30 minutes of bulk fermentation in the trough before being divided and rounded. Because the dough surface undergoes considerable stress during baking, rounding should produce a dough piece that is as round and smooth as possible. Ten to 20 minutes of intermediate proofing follow, and then the dough pieces are flattened in a sheeter to no thicker than $1/16$ in. A final proof of about 15 minutes at 29°C (85°F) and 65% RH readies the pieces for baking. The pieces traverse a multi-tiered proofer, turning over at each turn to prevent case hardening. Optimum proofing supplies the extra leavening gases that inflate the dough piece in the oven, where the temperature can reach as high as 538°C (1,000°F) for the very short bake. Dough pieces puff within 5 seconds of entering the oven and complete their expansion within 30 seconds (**Figure 8.040**). A small blow hole forms, reducing the size of the dough piece, reducing its silhouette from that of a basketball to more like a football. Products cool within 10 minutes, and the loaf collapses.

Formation of the pocket characterizes double-layered flatbreads (**Figure 8.041**), but single-layered flatbreads remain flat during baking. According to Qarooni (1990), the only processing difference between the two styles is that the double-layered product gets a second proof (final proof), while a delay of only a few seconds between makeup

Table 8.042. Pita Bread Formula

Ingredient	% (flour weight basis)
Flour	100
Water	57
Yeast	1
Salt	1.5
Malted barley	0.3
Ascorbic acid	50 ppm

(Faridi and Rubenthaler 1984)

a

c

b

d

Figure 8.040. Pita bread dough pieces inflate quickly in a 500°C (932°F) oven. The pocket begins to form after about (a) 12 seconds, inflating rapidly after (b) 15 seconds and (c) 22 seconds. When pocketing is complete after about (d) 26 seconds, the steam usually escapes through a crack at the bottom. (Quail 1996)

Figure 8.041. The pocket that forms in pita makes it an attractive choice for sandwich meals. (Kangaroo Brands)

and oven characterizes single-layered products. Additionally, puffing of single-layered flatbreads is prevented by docking the dough sheet prior to baking. Docking thus performs both functional and decorative purposes.

Faridi and Rubenthaler (1984) investigated the effects of changes in flour extraction, baking temperatures, water absorption and shortening levels on the physical quality and shelf life of pita bread after various storage periods. Their findings led them to conclude that optimum pita bread quality is obtained with high water absorptions (67%), high baking temperatures of 482°C (900°F) for 90 seconds and an absence of shortening. Breads baked at the high temperatures and absorption levels were softer initially and retained their softness longer during storage, but omitting the shortening rendered them more resistant to tears as the time of storage became extended. In contrast, Qarooni (1990) observed that Middle Eastern types of flatbreads have low water absorption, often 50 to 52%. Quail (1996) quoted Farinograph values ranging from 58 to 65% as best for Arabic bread production. Higher absorptions make the dough difficult to handle, yielding loaves that are fragile and lack the characteristic chewiness.

In the Middle East, the preferred flour is milled from

hard white wheat and has a protein content of 9 to 12%. Higher protein levels make doughs that are too strong and difficult to sheet, with rough crusts. Bakers working with white, low-extraction flours may add 1 to 2% of fine bran to increase water absorption and improve dough handling, especially sheeting. In some countries such as Yemen, a slightly granular or "sharp" high-extraction flour known as atta is preferred, which Quail (1996) explained is essentially a meal from which the coarse bran has been removed.

8.F. Griddle Products

By Michael T. Bakhoum, MS

Although diverse in appearance and formulation, English muffins, pancakes and sugar wafers have in common their baking process, which takes place not in an oven but on heated griddle plates.

8.F.1. English muffins

English muffins are a round yeast-leavened form of quick-baking bread. They measure roughly 4 in. in diameter and 1 in. in height, weighing between 2 and 3.5 oz each. They are grilled rather than baked, which imparts a brown color to their top and bottom sides, while their sidewalls remain pale. They typically possess a coarse grain, with a chewy texture, and are either toasted or grilled prior to their consumption. Muffins are usually split, toasted, buttered (**Figure 8.042**) and then used with savory or sweet fillings and has become the base of a popular food service morning sandwich meal. The general description of a good eating English muffin is: "relatively tough, chewy, and honeycombed with medium to large size holes ($^1/_8$ to ¼ in. diameter). Flavor is bland and somewhat sour. Side walls are straight and light colored."

English muffin formulations (**Table 8.043**) are dictated by the processing conditions necessary to produce an acceptable muffin. The dough is basically lean, very cold and slack and has a very short fermentation time. It is proofed in a hot, semi-humid atmosphere and baked in a griddle oven. The low temperature dough provides firmness with little stickiness. The high absorption provides for good dough flow and abundant crumb porosity in the grilled muffin.

Noel (1971) and Jackel (1984) provided English muffin formulations based on straight dough and no-time methods (**Table 8.044**).

8.F.1.a. Basic ingredients

Flour and vital wheat gluten. Flour having a protein content of 12 to 13% is recommended, in the form of a spring wheat or spring/winter patent or straight grade flour. This level of protein strength is needed to carry the high level of water (79 to 85% absorption) and to produce a gluten network that retains the carbon dioxide (CO_2) and water vapor during fermentation, in the proof box and on the griddle.

Also, the higher protein is essential for the characteristic chewy texture of the muffin. Vital wheat gluten at 1 to 2% may be used to supplement and strengthen

Figure 8.042. A sliced and buttered English muffin shows the "nooks and crannied" for which this griddle-cooked item is famous.
(Fresh Start Bakeries)

Table 8.043. English Muffin Formula

Ingredient	Amount (% flour basis)
Flour	100
Water	83 to 87
Vital wheat gluten	0 to 2.0
Yeast	5.0 to 8.0
Sugar	0 to 2.0
Salt	1.0 to 1.5
Shortening	0 to 1.0
Calcium propionate	0.5 to 0.7
Supplementary	
Protease enzymes	0 to 3.0
Baking powder	0 to 0.5
Vinegar, 100-grain	0.5 to 1.0
Sour	1.0 to 4.0

Table 8.044. English Muffin Formulations

Ingredient	Straight dough* (% flour basis)	No-time dough**
Flour (13% protein)	100	100.0
Water	80	76
Vinegar	–	4
Yeast	1	6.5
Salt	1.75	1.75
Sugar	2.25	2
Shortening	1	1
Calcium propionate	0.625	0.5
Fungal protease	1	1

* (Noel 1971)
** (Jackel 1984)

the natural flour protein. The function of the vital wheat gluten is the same as the protein in the flour, to improve gas retention and provide chewiness. One to 2% gluten on a flour weight basis is the usual level of usage. Some gluten products are coated with surfactants or emulsifiers to make them functional at a lower level than standard vital wheat gluten (Pfefer 1976).

Water. Dough water is either bound to the dough ingredients or free in the system. In English muffin dough, the free water is the key to leavening during baking on the griddle. It is the free water that is most easily vaporized into steam and produces the open porous structure. The recommended range of water is much higher than for bread dough, 83 to 87% (flour weight basis) being common (Juers 1982).

Dough water that is chilled to 1°C (33°F) will help with dough incorporation and yield a dough that can be handled in the automatic divider and rounder. The dough must be very cold 20°C (68 to 69°F) when discharged from the mixer. If the dough is too warm, it will be sticky and will not process through the divider and rounder satisfactorily. Such doughs become soft and sticky in the proof box and will adhere to the cups, resulting in an uneven depositing of the dough pieces in the griddle cups.

Some bakers greatly under-mix their muffin doughs to achieve the desired coarse crumb texture; however, over-mixing produces optimum dough flow and the desired coarse crumb structure as well (Pfefer 1976). For a normal fermentation time, the temperature of the mixed dough should not exceed 21°C (70°F) to minimize stickiness and prevent subsequent problems during makeup and proofing. Higher mixer dough temperatures, for example, 24 to 28°C (75 to 82°F), are needed with accelerated fermentations of 1 hour or less.

If the entire amount of water is added at the beginning of the mixing cycle, complete water incorporation is difficult to attain, and mixing time becomes excessively long. The preferred method is to add the water in two stages, followed by the salt addition. If this procedure is not followed, the dough may be very soft and sticky (Dubois 1979).

The addition of ice to replace all or part of the ingredient water is the least favorable method of keeping the dough cool. The reason is that ice requires a certain length of time to melt and therefore a varying amount of water is available for flour hydration during the course of mixing (Pfefer 1976).

Leavening. Leavening action in English muffins is a combination of expansion of the fermentation gases from yeast activity and from steam produced by water vaporization in the griddle. The function of the yeast is to provide fermentation gasses during proofing and early stages of baking and to contribute flavor to the finished product. The yeast fermentation gases produce the initial expansion in the proof box and during the initial stage of baking on the griddle. Then, as the temperature of the dough rises to near the boiling point of water, the water vaporizes and expands rapidly, forming the large holes and tunnels characteristic to the product. Because of the short fermentation time and the cold dough, a high level of yeast is used, normal levels being 5 to 8%.

Chemical leavening agents alone, or in combination with yeast, do not seem to improve the porosity of the muffin. In fact, they usually do more harm than good to the product (Pfefer 1976).

Sugar. English muffins are not considered sweet products. To produce lean dough, sweeteners (in the form of sucrose, dextrose, corn syrup or high-fructose corn syrup) are low and should not exceed the equivalent of 2% dextrose. The upper level provides fermentable carbohydrates for yeast fermentation, and a small amount of residual sugar contributes to browning of the crust.

Salt. English muffins have a bland flavor, and salt does not contribute materially to this flavor. A low salt level (1 to 1.5%) produces a minimum toughening effect on the gluten, and this weak cell structure contributes to improved porosity.

Shortening. Inclusion of shortenings should be kept to a minimum — enough to aid in achieving the goal of optimum eating characteristics. Excessive shortening — greater than 2% — contributes to dough lubricity, decreased porosity and greater crumb tenderness. Any and all of these characteristics in English muffins defeat the goal of a tough, chewy texture. Many formulations contain no shortening.

Mold inhibitors. English muffins have higher moisture content than bread yet are expected to have a longer shelf life. These conditions raise the risk of mold growth and necessitate the use of high levels of mold inhibitors, the major one being calcium propionate. Normal usage level is 0.5 to 0.7% and sufficiently prevents mold growth during normal muffin shelf life, which is 8 to 10 days. In addition to its mold inhibiting function, the calcium propionate contributes to the tart flavor typical for most English muffins.

Dry mold inhibitors used in the dough are sometimes blended with the dusting compound to provide external protection from mold. An effective way to control external or surface mold is the use of liquid potassium sorbate as a surface spray. Equipment is available for spraying the finished English muffins with a fine mist of potassium sorbate solution just prior to packaging (Dubois 1979).

8.F.1.b. Supplementary ingredients

Sours. Some markets prefer muffins with a distinctly sour taste. Inclusion of a high level of calcium propionate in the formula to prevent mold contributes to this flavor. In addition, the formula is sometimes supplemented with one of the commercially available sours. These sours may be based on mixtures of lactic acid, acid whey, vinegar and other acidulants or may be groups of cultures made from fermentation products of a variety of microbiological agents. The sours are used at a level of 1 to 4%, flour basis. Vinegar also is used as an acidulant at between 0.5 and 1% of 100- to 200-grain vinegar. These sours enhance the mold inhibiting performance of calcium propionate, which is more effective in an acid medium.

Dairy products. A small amount of nonfat dry milk is sometimes incorporated into the muffin formula to provide crust color and to round out the flavor profile of the product. Usually, no more than 1 to 1.5% is used. Other dairy ingredients such as acid whey, sweet whey or specially blended dairy products are used to meet individual requirements.

Enzymes. In general, protease enzymes mellow the gluten to produce soft pliable dough, and in English muffins, they improve the "flow" or spread in the griddle cup during the early stage of baking. Protease enzyme functionality depends on time and temperature conditions, and the short fermentation time and cold dough of English muffins will require higher than normal use levels.

Typical enzyme levels in English muffins are 2 to 3% of standard commercial preparations. Another enzyme used successfully to improve the porosity of muffins is fungal α-amylase, which helps digest damaged starch granules in the flour. This action not only alters the physical characteristics of the dough but also provides additional fermentable carbohydrates for the yeast (Pfefer 1976, Dubois 1979).

Fumeric acid and rice flour. A patent (Rucker et al. 1978) established that a combination of fumaric acid and rice flour produces a muffin having improved internal structure, including increased and more uniform porosity and elimination of bread-like fine grain and cell structure. Usage levels cited in the patent are 0.1 to 0.5% fumaric acid and 0.25 to 3% rice flour.

8.F.1.c. Processing considerations

English muffins are produced by automatic equipment capable of producing up to 2,300 doz per hour. The dough is scaled by piston or extrusion dividers into dough balls weighing between 2.25 and 3.8 oz. They receive a dusting of flour (a mixture of corn flour and fine corn meal with or without rice flour) and are loaded into a final proofer on trays covered with a thin layer of coarse meal (cornmeal, farina). The meal adheres to the bottom side of the dough pieces as they travel through the passer. Proofing conditions conform to those used with buns and proof time ordinarily extends to 25 to 35 minutes, although in some instances it may be as long as 1 hour.

The specialized equipment for preparation of English muffins is described in Chapter 12, Part H.

English muffins, their formulations and general method of production have been reviewed by Noel (1963, 1971), Thompson (1981), Juers (1982) and Jackel (1984).

8.F.2. Pancakes

Pancakes — also called hotcakes, flapjacks, fried cakes and griddlecakes — come in a wide range of sweet and savory flavors. They often incorporate a variety of particulates such as blueberries or pecans, even chocolate chips. Pancakes are produced by depositing a fluid batter directly onto a very hot surface, and their baking and final shaping of the product are finished within a very short time (approximately 2 minutes). Consequently, characteristics of the final product are determined by the formula, the consistency of ingredient qualities and the effectiveness of process controls.

This section discusses formula ingredients, while Chapter 12, Part H, provides descriptions of the equipment and its operating considerations.

8.F.2.a. Pancake formula and batter characteristics

A pancake formulation (**Table 8.045**) with improved shelf life, freeze/thaw stability and acceptable microwave reheating is a necessary requirement for large-scale wholesale operations.

Pancake batter is a complex colloidal dispersion, a formed fat-in-water emulsion containing suspended flour particles, dissolved sugars and proteins in aqueous phase. The finished pancake is a heat-set foam having a light aerated structure consisting of air cells. The function and description of the main ingredients are reviewed with relation to the formation of satisfactory structure as follows.

8.F.2.b. Ingredients

Flour. Flour serves as a structure builder in almost every bakery product. Starch is the major constituent of wheat flour and would, therefore, expect to play a major role in finished product quality. The role of starch is to act as a water-sink and to set structures in the baking process. The protein or the gluten is the second largest constituent of the flour. It has limited water absorption capability in comparison with the starch but still contributes to the structure by cross linking and denaturing of the proteins during baking.

Both the water absorption properties and the degree of gelatinization of the starch during baking are important characteristics in pancake flour. When batter changes from a fluid, aerated emulsion to a solid porous structure, the gelatinization properties of the starch become important in the control of the physical properties of the finished product. The type of the flour or blend of flours used depends on the characteristics of the desired end product and the processing conditions.

As with almost every chemically leavened bakery products, soft wheat flour can be used to make up pancake batter manually at home and small food service stores; however, in automated large operations, stronger flour is recommended so the batter can stand the mechanical abuse. Hard wheat flour can be used to impart chewiness to the finished pancake and reduce mushy texture when the sugar syrup is added to the finished product. Usually, the flour is unbleached and unmalted (Pyler 1952).

Fats. Shortening and oils serve a variety of functions in the processing and the finished product. Their main function is that of tenderizers by providing lubrication and a softening effect. Also, they trap air and foster leavening action by incorporating air cells during mixing, which later collect carbon dioxide produced by the chemical leavening system.

These gases and water vapor are ultimately responsible for the grain and texture of the finished pancake. A number of different fats are available for use in pancake formulations, with soybean oil the most commonly used. However, if any other fats are used, some adjustments in formulation are required to compensate for the differences in melting point and degree of fluidity to control batter viscosity.

Sugar. Sugar is another basic ingredient in pancake formulations, and it serves many functions. The most obvious is sweetness. Also, sugar tenderizes the pancake by delaying starch gelatinization, aids moisture retention and improves shelf life. Different types of sugars are available for pancake formulations, the most common of which is high-fructose corn syrup (HFCS), which acts as a reducing sugar. It affects the crust color through the Millard browning reaction.

Emulsifiers. Emulsifiers in general are surface-active agents that possess both hydrophilic and lipophilic properties. Therefore, emulsifiers orient themselves at the interface between oil and water phases, contributing to the stability of the batter. A stable emulsion improves crumb structure, volume and eating quality.

Table 8.045. Typical Pancake Formula	
Ingredient	Amount (% flour basis)
Wheat flour	100
Water	130 to150
Sugar	10 to 15
Soybean oil	10 to 15
Liquid egg	10 to 15
Sodium bicarbonate	2 to 3
Acid phosphates	1.5 to 3
Emulsifiers	1 to 2
Salt	0.8 to 1.0
Gum	0.1 to .15

Flavors and colors can be added as desired.

Figure 8.043. Because it has the same neutralizing value as sodium acid pyrophosphate (SAPP), a calcium-based, slow-acting leavening acid can replace SAPP on a 1:1 basis in the chemical leavening system of pancakes, thus reducing overall sodium content. (Innophos)

Figure 8.044. The grid-like indentations on the two halves of a waffle iron give these products their characteristic shape and form.

A blend of more than one emulsifier is usually more effective and may give preferable results in final pancake products (Kamel 1993). Also, emulsifiers may improve the microwave re-heating of the finished product (Schiffmann 1998).

Chemical leavening. Light palatable baked pancakes are achieved by first forming many finely divided gas bubbles in the batter and by then timing the desired expansion of these bubbles during baking to coincide with the thermal setting of the structure. Fast action is critical because griddle time is very short — approximately 2 minutes (**Figure 8.043**).

The initial or nucleating gas comes from the air incorporated. The air cells collect the carbon dioxide (CO_2) from leavening agents after the liquid is saturated with CO_2. The greater the dispersion of the gas and its stability, the finer will be the grain and the thinner the cell walls.

Emulsifiers and, to some extent, the mixing process play important roles in producing stable gas emulsions. Therefore, emulsifiers and chemical leavenings work together to impart the desired cell structure and crumb into the finished product. During baking, most of the available CO_2 must be released before the product reaches its setting temperature.

If the leavening proceeds too quickly, a coarse or even collapsed structure tends to form because gas release will be completed before the structure sets. If the rate is too slow, a smaller volume can result or the structure may rupture, with doming and cracks occuring. All the above explain the reasons behind selecting different acids with different release rates to neutralize the soda (Dubois 1981).

Eggs. During the initial stage of baking, when the loss of batter liquidity takes place, proteins from egg denature and contribute to the batter viscosity increase, thus stabilizing the air bubbles and strengthening the crumb and structure. The fat portion of the egg (lecithin) acts as an emulsifier.

Gums. Gums dramatically increase water absorption and moisture retention, therefore, improving the shelf life and freeze/thaw stability of the finished product.

8.F.2.c. Final preparation and microwave re-heating

Many frozen bakery products go through a number of partial freeze/thaw cycles during distribution. When reheated in the microwave, the result is in poor organoleptic properties. These products tend to be excessively tough, chewy and dry. A patent (Bakhoum 1996) established and described a mixture of ingredients that, when added into the pancake batter before baking, improves the product's eating quality and makes it comparable to a fresh product off the griddle.

8.F.3. Waffles and wafers

Waffles and wafers have many similarities. They are made of fluid batters and baked on griddle ovens. They are baked as large sheets that are later cut into individual units. The main ingredients in both formulations are the same, and both are leavened by chemical agents except for special thick waffles such as Belgian waffles, which may be leavened with yeast.

Waffles are soft but crispy with deep indentations on both sides imparted to it by the grid-like design on the two hinged halves of the waffle iron used for baking (**Figure 8.044**). The most common waffle types are thin waffles and the thick Belgian waffles.

Wafers are crisp, often sweet, very thin, flat and dry — essentially foamed and dehydrated starch gels (Gorton 1996). They usually further processed into moulded coated bars with variations in shapes (**Figure 8.045**). The wafer types include flat wafers and hollow wafers. Flat wafers are manufactured with fine, medium and deep reeding in a wide variety of designs and may even include company logos or special engraving. They are filled with cream, caramel, chocolate or jam in one or several layers. Hollow wafers consist of two filled and joined wafer halves. A particularly interesting version is the insertion of an additional whole hazelnut. Also hollow wafers are sometimes sprinkled with chopped nuts and coated with chocolate.

Figure 8.045. Layers of crisp wafers alternate with flavored fillings. (Franz Haas Waffelmaschinen)

Typical starting formulations (**Table 8.046**) include 100 parts of flour, 140 parts water, 1 part coconut oil, 0.5 part sodium bicarbonate, 0.5 part salts, and 0.1 part lecithin. Other ingredients may be added to optimize the formula and obtain the desired finish product. These ingredients may include flavors, colors, cocoa, nonfat dry milk, ammonium carbonate, corn starch and egg yolks. A slightly different formulation for sugar wafers is provided in **Table 8.047**.

As with most batters and chemical leavening products, soft wheat flour is recommended. A short extraction flour with good gluten quality is preferred, but if the gluten is excessively weak, wafers will be very dense, close in texture and very fragile. If the gluten is overly strong, wafers will be hard and flinty. The batter viscosity should be low enough so it spreads rapidly over the baking plates. The high water content of these formulations is explained in the fact that steam is the primary leavener of wafers. The use of chemical leavening agents boosts nucleation to increase the number of gas cells in the wafer batter.

Table 8.046. Waffle/Wafer Formula

Ingredient	Amount (% flour weight basis)
Flour	100
Water	125 to 140
Coconut oil	0.5 to 1
Sodium bicarbonate	0 to 0.5
Ammonium bicarbonate	0.4 to 0.8
Nonfat dry milk	0 to 5
Dried whole milk	0 to 3
Cornstarch	0 to 5
Dried egg yolk	1.25 to 2.5
Salt	0.2 to 0.5
Lecithin	0 to 0.05

Table 8.047. Sugar Wafer Formulation

Ingredient	Amount (flour weight basis)
Flour	100
Water	125 to 150
Sodium bicarbonate	0.2 to 0.75
Ammonium bicarbonate	0.5
Non-fat dry milk	0 to 5
Dried whole milk	0 to 3
Corn starch	0 to 5
Dried egg yolk	0 to 2.5
Salt	0.75
Lecithin	0.4
Coconut oil	0 to 2.5

(Gorton 1996a)

Flavorants are usually not added to wafer batters because they tend to be lost through steam distillation during baking. The fillings perform the flavor functions. Likewise, selection of coloring agents — yellow and pink are the usual choices — must take into account the high heat of the process. Cream of tartar is sometimes added to bring batter pH to slightly below 7.0, which improves the color of white wafers. Dark color and chocolate taste can be developed in the waffle and wafer products by adding 10% cocoa, but this change may require an increase of the water by up to 15%.

Corn starch promotes a more tender texture in wafers. Other optional ingredients include heat-treated, defatted cottonseed flour and degerminated white corn flour, both of which add viscosity to the batter without risking gluten separation during mixing.

Old-style "enriched" formulations contain milk (up to 5%), eggs (up to 2.5%) or sometimes sugar (up to 3.5%). These materials, however, lead to carbon buildup on oven plates, causing release difficulties and brown or black specs on the wafers. To solve such problems, shortening (coconut oil or lecithin) is added to the formula at very low percentages.

Cone wafers have substantial amounts of sugars in the formula, so the sheets are flexible when hot and get rigid upon cooling to form the cone shape. Cream of tarter showed to be effective to improve the color of the product, when the PH is reduced slightly below 7.0.

When preparing and holding batters, bakers must avoid over-mixing, or else gluten can form into strings and separate from the batter. Starch can also settle out. Some agitation of the batter is needed if it is held before depositing. Oscillating screens and stirrers in the holding tank prevent precipitation of solids and stop batter sticking to the tank's side walls. High-volume wafer systems usually configure mixing to prepare new batches every 6 to 10 minutes, and holding batter for longer than 30 minutes is not recommended (Gorton 1996).

Figure 8.046. Stroopwaffles, or syrup waffles, consist of two wafers layered with syrup.
(Franz Haas Waffelmaschinen)

Syrup waffles (**Figure 8.046**) were originally a Dutch product and recently started to be known to the rest of the world. Its typical bite and taste makes this sandwich-style product unique. After the product is baked by the traditional way by a wafer oven, syrup is deposed onto the bottom wafer and the top wafer capped on. A light press to assure adherence finishes the product.

Clyma (2007) predicted the expansion of the functional foods trend into the wafers industry in the near future. There are already some products on the market that incorporate proteins, probiotics and other fortification ingredients. Combined with variety of fillings, new products can be made that are better tasting and lighter in texture compared to traditional nutritional bars.

8.G. Pre-proofed, Par-baked, Frozen and Refrigerated Doughs
By L.A. Gorton

Baked foods, whether in raw dough or partially or fully baked format, deserve some care in formulation. The role of various ingredients — and the survival of the leavening agents — will have a major impact on the quality of the product that reaches the consumer.

8.G.1. Frozen doughs

When working with any style of frozen dough and partially baked products, the researcher and processor must keep in mind that the freezing point of water in dough is not 0°C (32°F). **Table 8.048** reports how ingredients depress freezing in doughs. To keep dough cores frozen solid, storage temperatures in the range of -10 to -15°C (14 to 5°F) are recommended. Because frozen dough is quite sensitive to fluctuating temperatures, control methods must not allow changes of more than ± 5 C° (± 9 F°) (Brümmer 1995).

Frozen doughs typically get no floor time, intermediate or final proofing; instead, they proceed directly from dividing and rounding into the blast freezer (**Figure 8.047**). Frozen pre-proofed items, however, get full proofing treatment, and frozen par-baked products follow conventional processes until the point that their structure is stabilized in the oven.

Formulation advice from Fuhrmann (1985) included: (a) use a flour with good quality protein at 13.5 to 14.% levels and good tolerance, (b) chill water to 3 to 4°C (38 to 40°F) and (c) increase slightly the levels of sugar, above 4% (flour weight basis). He also recommended reducing water absorption to eliminate free water in the product and thus avoid water crystallization, which is detrimental to product stability. He warned about use of ice in the mixer: When added in large amounts, ice will be still in the process of melting by the time the dough mass has already hydrated and cannot properly absorb the remaining water from the melted ice. Also, direct-expansion jackets on mixers can be a problem for straight no-time doughs because the liquid ingredients may freeze to the jacket before the dough has developed. Flour chilling systems can be advantageous in holding down dough temperatures, and liquid carbon dioxide injected directly into the mixing chamber to displace oxygen not only cools the dough but improves the reducing action of ascorbic acid to cut mixing time.

As noted in **Table 8.049**, hearth doughs show reduced absorption and higher yeast levels, compared with the standard formula for hearth bread. Soft roll doughs (**Table 8.050**) may include vital wheat gluten and somewhat reduced absorption. Sweet doughs, such as the cinnamon rolls reported in **Table 8.051**, will be somewhat richer and may require additional oxidation and conditioning agents to compensate for machining.

Table 8.048. Freezing Point Depression in Frozen Doughs		
Composition	°C	°F
Water only	0	32
Flour and water only	-4	25
Flour, water, fat, sugar, salt, yeast	-7 to -9	18 to 16

(Adapted from Brümmer 1995)

Figure 8.047. Frozen doughs get no floor time and are not allowed to proof. They go directly from dividing and rounding into the blast freezer. (ADM)

Table 8.049. Frozen Hearth-Style Dough Formula

Ingredient	Frozen (bakers %)	Standard (bakers %)
Flour	100	100
Water	55 to 56	58 to 59
Salt	1.75 to 2.0	1.75 to 2.0
Yeast	5 to 6	3.25 to 3.75
Sugar solids	(optional) 1 to 2	(optional) 1 to 2
Shortening	0.5 to 1.0	(optional)
Yeast nutrient	0.125 to 0.5	0.125 to 0.5
Dough conditioners	(optional)	(optional)
Diastatic malt	1.0 to 1.5	1.0 to 1.5
Fungal enzyme	(optional)	(optional)
Vital wheat gluten	(optional)	(optional)
Mold inhibitor	none	variable

(Fuhrmann 1985)

Table 8.050. Frozen Soft Roll Dough Formula

Ingredient	Frozen (bakers %)	Standard (bakers %)
Flour	100	100
Water	54	60
Salt	2	2
Yeast	7.5 to 8.5	4.5 to 5.5
Sugar solids	11 to 12	11 to 12
Shortening	6 to 7	8 to 9
Dry whole eggs	(optional)	(optional)
Yeast nutrient	0.125 to 0.5	0.125 to 0.5
Dough conditioners	variable	variable
Nonfat dry milk solids	(optional)	(optional)
Fungal enzyme	(optional)	(optional)
Vital wheat gluten	(optional)	(optional)
Mold inhibitor	none	variable

(Fuhrmann 1985)

8.G.1.a. Leavening agents

Yeast survival and gas retention are major problems in frozen dough manufacture (Hino et al. 1987). The search for yeast strains best suited for frozen doughs was summarized by Trivedi et al. (1989), who noted a preference for yeasts that have developed a protective mechanism against cell disruption by ice crystal formation. They observed that such yeast strains are found among those tolerant of very high concentrations of sugars and salt, the so-called "osmotolerant" yeasts. Reed and Nagodawithana (1991) discussed cryoresistance in selected yeast strains with higher concentrations of trehalose than in conventional commercial bakers yeasts. They also reported that these yeast strains performed exceptionally well in sweet doughs (30% sugar) but poorly in low sugar doughs (5% sugar), compared with unfrozen controls.

The rate of freezing influences the survival rate of yeast cells, with rapidly frozen cells sustaining greater damage than slowly frozen cells (**Figure 8.048**). When yeast cells are cooled rapidly to -30°C (-22°F) or below, the survival rate is less than 0.01%, yet when cooling proceeds slowly to the same temperature, up to 65% of the cells may remain viable (Mazur and Miller 1967). The destruction of yeast cells by rapid cooling is explained by the formation of intracellular ice crystals that disrupt the structure of the cellular protoplasm sufficiently to kill the cell. With slow cooling rates, it is believed that the yeast cells are able to transfer a sufficient portion of their intracellular water to the external ice to prevent ice crystal formation within the cell.

Freezing at excessively low temperatures also has a pronounced adverse effect on yeast viability. In a dough medium, yeast cells freeze at about -35°C (-31°F). Hsu et al. (1979) observed proof times of 72 and 132 minutes for doughs frozen at -10°C (14°F) and -40°C (-40°F), respectively. Doughs frozen at -78°C (-108°F) exhibited very little yeast activity after thawing. Lorenz (1974) suggested that for improved frozen dough stability: (a) the dough be frozen to a temperature of only -10°C (14°F), (b) freezing be conducted slowly and (c) defrosting take place rapidly.

Studying the effects of various factors on the shelf life of frozen dough, Wolt and D'Appolonia (1984b) obtained the following results: (a) fresh compressed yeast performed slightly better than active dry yeast and instant active dry yeast over a storage period of 20 weeks; (b) while the addition of the surfactants sodium stearoyl lactylate (SSL) and diacetyl tartaric acid esters of mono- and diglycerides (DATEM) had no effect on the proof time of frozen doughs, these dough conditioners did improve the dough's rheological properties to varying degrees and resulted in greater loaf volume after baking; and (c) flour type is an important variable in the proof-time stability of frozen doughs, but a flour's protein content is not a reliable indicator of its performance in frozen dough.

Four to 12 weeks of frozen storage are the norm for frozen doughs, placing stress on the yeast and decreasing its fermenting activity. As Reed and Nagodawithana (1991) emphasized, the loss of such activity occurs during frozen storage, not during freezing of the dough. Thus, storage conditions are of prime importance.

Bruinsma and Giesenschlag (1984) examined the effects of 12 weeks of storage and daily freeze-thaw cycles on the viability of dry yeast and regular compressed yeast. Contrary to Wolt and D'Appolonia (1984b), they found that the level of dry yeast was the greatest variable in determining proof time: Higher levels of active dry yeast gave consistently shorter proof times than the compressed yeast. Neither proof time nor gas production changed appreciably over 7 consecutive freeze-thaw cycles for either type of yeast, but crumb structure deteriorated rapidly and drastically over the 7 cycles. Also, each successive freeze-thaw cycle caused the dough to become weaker, more fragile and more difficult to handle and to assume a wet appearance.

Because of the reduced viability of yeast in frozen doughs after thawing, Holmes and Hoseney (1987) explored combinations of yeast and chemical leavening in these products but failed to find any benefits in the system they tested.

Recently, Ribotta et al. (2003) took another look at the effect of freezing on yeast in frozen dough systems. The researchers froze and stored compressed yeast at -18°C (0°F) and used it to make frozen dough and compared their results with frozen doughs made from fresh yeast. In doughs, the frozen compressed yeast performed better in baking quality than did doughs made with fresh yeast, although the frozen yeast's production of carbon dioxide decreased overall. Additionally, substances leached from the frozen yeast increased as storage time lengthened and caused an increase in the solubility of some gluten proteins.

8.G.1.b. Fermentation factors

Wolt and D'Appolonia (1984a) defined frozen dough stability as the "ability of a thawed dough to proof in an acceptable period of time and to bake into a loaf with normal volume and bread characteristics." This ability is related to factors such as

Table 8.051. Frozen Sweet Yeast-Raised Dough Formula

Ingredient	Frozen (bakers %)	Standard (bakers %)
Flour	100	100
Water	50 to 52	50 to 54
Salt	1.75	2
Yeast	9 to 10	6 to 7
Sugar solids	9 to 11	8 to 10
Shortening	5 to 6	5 to 6
Dry egg yolks	2 to 3	1 to 2
Yeast nutrient	0.125 to 0.5	0.125 to 0.5
Dough conditioners	(optional)	(optional)
Nonfat dry milk solids	(optional)	(optional)
Fungal enzyme	(optional)	(optional)
Mold inhibitor	none	variable
Flavor	none	variable

(Fuhrmann 1985)

Figure 8.048. Frozen dough poses a formulation challenge because yeast cells do not retain their original leavening ability after freezing and thawing.

dough formulation, yeast type and quality, fermentation prior to freezing, duration of storage and freeze-thaw rates. It is generally agreed that frozen doughs perform best when their fermentation is greatly restricted or eliminated entirely.

Much evidence has been developed to show that fermentation prior to freezing is detrimental to yeast viability (Sugihara and Kline 1968). The greater stability of yeast in frozen unfermented dough has been attributed to its dormant state at mixing (Merritt 1960). Hsu et al. (1979), working with a liquid ferment system, found that fermented frozen doughs gave poorer quality bread than did doughs that were frozen without fermentation. They attributed the quality-depressing effect primarily to the accumulation of the highly volatile fermentation products. Release of glutathione, a reducing agent, by the yeast during frozen storage and thawing was also a problem because this substance negatively affects gluten strength. They also observed that the quality of the yeast employed greatly affected the stability of the frozen dough. Yeasts with protein contents higher than 57% performed better.

8.G.1.c. Other ingredients

To minimize the adverse effects produced by freezing on the proof time of thawed doughs and on the volume, grain and texture of the baked products, certain changes in dough formulation are required. According to Lorenz (1974), who provided a useful summary of the factors involved in frozen dough, these alterations included: (a) an increase in the yeast level to 4 to 6%, (b) an increase in shortening to 5% and (c) a slight decrease in absorption. Maintaining an average sugar level of 6% and keeping nonfat dry milk at 4% will contribute to the development of a desirable crust color.

Tirvedi et al. (1989) offered the following recommendations for formulating frozen doughs: (a) increase yeast level by 2 to 3 percentage points above the level normally used; (b) use adequate oxidation (30 ppm potassium bromate plus 100 ppm ascorbic acid) and dough conditioners (sodium stearoyl lactylate); (c) increase shortening to 4% (flour weight basis); and (d) use a fairly strong bread flour.

Oxidation. According to Marston (1978), dough destined for freezing should receive full development in the mixer, but its yeast activity and gas generation should be kept at a minimum. Adequate oxidation is essential for such doughs to assure full dough maturity, and at the same time, the reducing agents that are ordinarily used in conventional breadmaking should be omitted. Varriano-Marston et al. (1980) found when potassium bromate is supplemented with ascorbic acid, the proof time of frozen dough stored for 2 months was shortened by 23 minutes at final bake-off.

DeStefanis et al. (1986), in an investigation of the factors that contribute to quality deterioration during freezing as evidenced by loss of loaf volume and unsatisfactory grain, found that the prevailing practice of mixing the dough at lower than ambient temperatures results in poor ovenspring, which, in turn, leads to a loss in loaf volume. This deleterious effect of low-temperature mixing can be effectively overcome by an increase in oxidation. The optimum oxidation level was observed to be inversely related to the dough mixing temperature, that is, the lower the mixing temperature, the more oxidation is required to achieve full restoration of product quality.

The effect of dough temperature on frozen dough performance was reported earlier by Boyd (1980), who described formulating and processing practices at the bakery he managed. The company's target was dough-out temperatures of 21 to 22°C (70 to 72°F). Temperatures lower than 21°C (70°F) tended to weaken the dough in its initial stages, while doughs even slightly above 22°C (72°F) started producing gas rapidly, causing considerable rupturing of the dough piece.

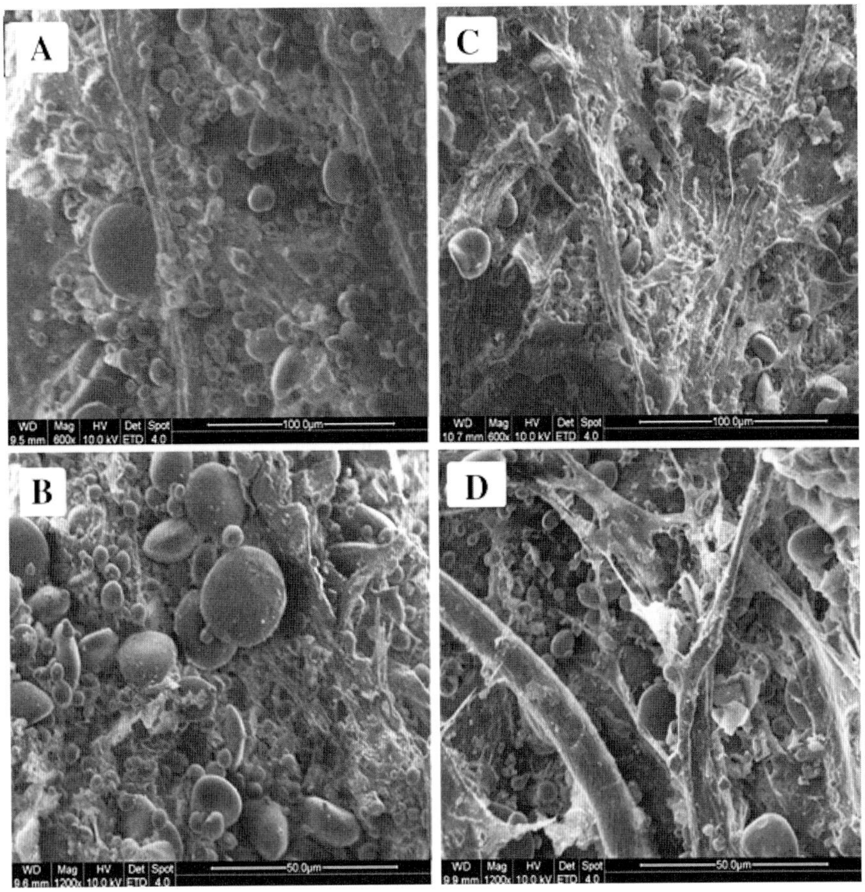

In a later review, DeStefanis (1995) summarized favorable formulating conditions for processing frozen doughs as (a) reduced water absorption, (b) reduced dough mixing temperature, (c) high level of shortening, (d) high level of yeast, (e) high level of surfactant, (f) straight-dough no-time baking method, (g) freezing of dough immediately after mixing, (h) suitable packaging having moisture and oxygen barriers and (i) freezer temperature of -23°C (-9°F). He also detailed the functions of micro-ingredients in frozen bread doughs, giving special attention to oxidants.

Surfactants. Davis (1981) evaluated the effects of 3 widely-used surfactants on frozen dough stability after 1 to 3 freeze-thaw cycles. The surfactants tested were the dough conditioners sodium stearoyl lactylate (SSL), ethoxylated mono- and diglycerides (EOM) and the crumb softener mono- and diglycerides (MDG). The dough conditioners produced a significant improvement in baked volume, with SSL being the more effective. Best crumb softness in the bread prepared from frozen dough having gone through 3 freeze-thaw cycles was obtained with SSL. The superior improving action of SSL in frozen dough was attributed to its ability to complex with both the protein and the starch fractions of the flour.

Figure 8.049. After 5 weeks of frozen storage, scanning electron micrographs show the survival of well-developed gluten structures in test doughs containing 0.5% transglutaminase (C and D) vs. control doughs (A and B). (A and C are at 600x magnification, while B and D are at 1,200x.)
(Huang et al. 2008)

Enzymes. Formulations for frozen doughs employ enzymes for the usual technical doughmaking reasons, but recently Huang et al. (2008) experimented with transglutaminase, a protein-linking enzyme not usually employed in breadmaking. They found that the enzyme's presence resulted in less disruption or fracturing of the gluten network (**Figure 8.049**), yielding baked products that were greater in volume and softer than those made from control doughs without transglutaminase.

Flavorings. When making frozen yeast-raised sweet doughs flavored with cinnamon, formulators should consider using an encapsulated form of the spice. Cinnamon contains cinnamic acid and cinnamaldehyde, chemical compounds that can be metabolized by yeast and that lead to appearance of off flavors (López-García 2008). Research is being done to establish bakers yeast strains that resist these effects.

8.G.1.d. Doughmaking methods

For frozen dough operations, short-time or no-time dough methods are the best system from the standpoint of product quality and freezer stability (Reedich 1989). The doughmaking process for frozen doughs, pre-proofed and par-baked items are generally similar to that of conventional yeast-raised doughs, with a few important exceptions. Kulp (1995) comprehensively reviewed the formulation, makeup and processing of frozen doughs, including recent rheological studies of these doughs and the effects on them of freezing. Ingredients, formulating, processing and reconstitution conditions specific to frozen dough usage in the US were examined in equal detail by Lorenz and Kulp (1995). Brümmer (1995) described frozen dough preparation methods as practiced in Europe.

Interestingly enough, the original developers of the pre-proofed method first tried changing formulations in the usual ways (higher gluten flour, more dough conditioners and/or dough strengtheners, etc.). After considerable testing without achieving the desired results, they chose to solve the problem not with changes in formulation or new ingredients but by changes in the production process (Nakagawa 1991).

8.G.1.e. Frozen batters

Freezing of cake batters was widely researched in the 1940s and 1950s, when many retail bakeries typically froze products at one or more stages of processing. A decade later, however, the practice of freezing such batters had waned, partly because baked cakes freeze so well, observed Lorenz (1995), who summarized formulating and processing of frozen cake batter. Freezing of muffin batters, which emerged during the 1980s, proved much more useful to in-store and food service customers.

Muffin batters are typically packed in buckets, which the end user thaws and portions into prepared or lined muffin tins. Development of frozen muffin dough in pre-scooped or pre-deposited format was a considerable improvement: The end user simply popped the frozen dough piece into a pan and baked it. The chemical leavening systems that aerate such doughs are even more critical when the dough is frozen. Batters held in frozen storage show a progressive decrease in baked volume as the storage period lengthens because of the loss of air from the batter. Formulators sought chemical leavening systems that would release gases only slowly during storage or completely delay release until heated.

Batters made with phosphate leavening acids proved to release carbon dioxide at a slower rate than similar batters with either tartrate or sulfate-phosphate leavening agents (**Table 8.052**). Sodium aluminum phosphate (SALP) performs well in frozen batters because its action is delayed until the oven.

Although emulsified shortenings are critical in the production of high-ratio frozen cake batters, frozen muffin batters are more tolerant to variations in shortening types and levels.

8.G.2. Par-baked doughs

In recent years, pre-proofed and par-baked products have been introduced that take the doughmaking process through proofing in the case of the former process and into the oven until set but not colored in the case of the latter (**Figure 8.050**). Both use freezing to stabilize the partially processed items. An alternate term for "par-baked" is "pre-baked," which is widely used in Europe, while the former is

Table 8.052. Leavening Acids in Frozen Batters

Baking acid	Comparative rate of reaction
Anhydrous monocalcium phosphate	Delayed
Dicalcium phosphate	Very slow
Sodium acid pyrophosphate	Slow
Sodium aluminum phosphate	
Hydrous	Slow
Anhydrous	Very slow
Sodium aluminum sulfate	Very slow
Glucono delta lactone	Delayed
Monocalcium phosphate	Fast

(Lorenz 1995)

preferred in North American markets.

A commercial definition of par-bake, according to Stoecklein (1995), is a product baked at 205 to 215°C (400 to 420°F) to within 90 to 95% completion of starch gelatinization and then given a final preparatory stage of 205°C (400°F) for 10 minutes prior to use, with this second bake being more in the nature of reheating.

8.G.2.a. Brown 'n serve

The original par-baked product was the brown 'n serve roll, introduced to consumers in 1949 by General Mills. The product line came to include partially baked rolls, breads and pastries, fully formed and prebaked to exact shape and size, except for crust browning and full baked-flavor development. The purpose of this process was to make available to the consumer bakery products of extended keeping quality that could be baked off in the kitchen oven, thereby placing oven-hot bakery foods into the home.

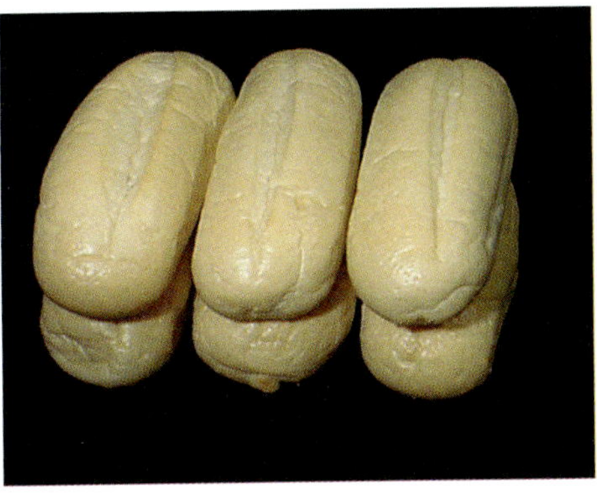

Figure 8.050. Hoagie buns are set but not colored during the par-baking process. (Turano Baking)

The partial baking process requires some modifications in the formula, the fermentation process and baking conditions (Roth 1950). The objective is to bake yeast-raised products to a point of stability and full volume without any crust coloration. This is achieved by reducing the oven temperature to a level of 121 to 149°C (250 to 300°F), and by conditioning the dough so that the ovenspring that normally occurs at the lower oven temperatures is held to an acceptable level. Dough absorption should be reduced to yield stiffer doughs that will have the desired rigidity out of the oven. Straight doughs require higher mixing temperatures, in the range of 32 to 35°C (90 to 95°F), while sponge-doughs may be mixed at normal temperatures. Both the yeast and the yeast food levels should be reduced slightly to prevent excessive ovenspring.

Generally, rich formulations, especially with regard to shortening and eggs, are preferable because they contribute to the flavor, aroma and eating quality of the finished, home-baked product. Fermentation should be conducted at warm temperatures. Proofing at 38 to 41°C (100 to 105°F) is desirable because it promotes a fast proof.

At the bakery, the products must bake for as long as possible without causing crust color to form. One recommendation calls for a temperature of 121°C (250°F) and a baking time of 30 minutes (Turner 1970). However, a solid heat at 141°C (285°F) will impart adequate rigidity to the products in 10 to 15 minutes. The interior temperature of the products as they come from the oven must exceed 77°C (170°F) and preferably reach 82°C (180°F), otherwise their volume will shrink excessively during cooling. This temperature is readily attainable, without exterior coloration, with the aid of high final proofing temperatures. Cooling and packaging of the partially-baked products must be carried out under strict sanitary conditions to reduce the chances of mold infection and to preserve the unique appearance of the products.

8.G.2.b. Commercial par-baked

Modern par-baked doughs differ from brown 'n serve in that they were developed for the food service and in-store markets (**Figure 8.051**). Such products allow service of warm, freshly baked breads and rolls throughout the day, without requiring the labor of a trained baker. The use of par-baked products in the retail setting can shorten the freezer-to-customer cycle to 30 minutes, compared with 3 to 4 hours for raw frozen doughs and 6 to 12 hours for scratch operations.

Figure 8.051. Offered in white, wheat and multigrain, frozen loaves are formulated to go directly into the oven at the in-store bakery, without thawing or proofing.
(Maple Leaf Bakery)

The production process is explained in Chapter 6, Part I, and because of their importance in commerce, par-baked products have received considerable scientific attention.

Unlike the formulation changes necessary for frozen dough, par-baked bread may be produced with little modification of conventional bakery formulations, as Stoecklein (1995) reported. Flours for typical par-baked white breads, hearth breads or rolls usually contain 11 to 13% protein, and absorptions range from 55 to 60%. Vital wheat gluten may be added to provide additional volume and strength. Yeast levels are in the normal 3% (flour weight basis) range for conventionally prepared breadstuffs. Use of oxidants, emulsifiers and shortenings also follow conventional formulations.

Pai and Walker (2004) reported slight differences in formulations to compensate for the second baking stage. For example, rich formulations are preferred because they improve the flavor, aroma and eating quality of the rebaked product. The greater richness, however, required that baking temperatures and times be carefully monitored because such products brown more rapidly than do leaner doughs. Higher absorptions result in less rigid par-baked products with a tendency for the upper surface to shrivel. Gums such as guar, locust bean, xanthan and blends have been successfully used to control moisture migration. The time of the first bake, however, is critical (**Figure 8.052**).

Moisture content of par-baked bread decreases and crumb firmness increases as the freezer storage time increases, according to several researchers. When finishing the baking of par-baked bread, thawing and baking conditions influence quality. Working with par-baked French bread, Park and Baik (2007) prepared the loaves by par-baking them at 218°C (424°F) for ≥6 minutes to reach a crumb temperature to 97°C (207°F). Freezing to -30°C (-22°F), thawing (180 minutes at ≈20°C, or 68°F) and a second baking (12 minutes at the same temperature as the first bake) decreased loaf volume by ≥100 ml and produced a darker color crust than controls. If given no thawing time, the required baking time increased to 16 minutes, yet the crumb moisture was higher than for breads thawed before baking. They also worked with loaves given a first bake at a lower temperature of 163°C (325°F) and times of 4 to 12 minutes. The result was decreased crumb firmness, measured at 3 and 48 hours after baking.

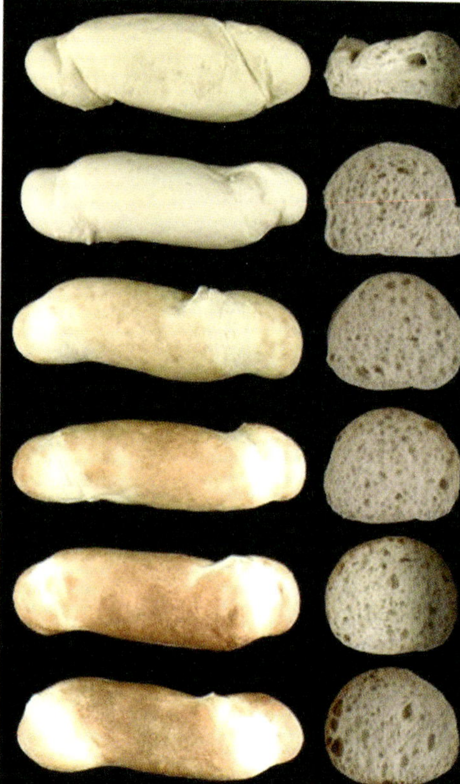

Figure 8.052. French bread made from hard red spring wheat flour show variation in crust color and crumb structure as baking time increased from 3 minutes (top) to 6, 9, 12, 15 and 20 minutes (bottom), leading researchers to select 6 minutes for the first bake in a par-baked process.
(Park and Baik 2007)

8.G.3. Refrigerated doughs

Chemically leavened biscuit dough, introduced in 1937, was the first refrigerated dough commercially produced, but it has since been joined in the supermarket refrigerator case by dinner rolls, sweet goods (danish and cinnamon rolls), breads and pizza crusts. Allenson (1982) provided a comprehensive overview of the refrigerated dough process.

The formulation for commercially made refrigerated biscuits is quite different from the home-style product (**Table 8.053**), being far less rich in shortening and sugar. The flour chosen for commercial use will be milled from soft wheat, exhibiting low protein, low enzymatic activity, low water absorption (about 56%) and a pH range of 5.6 to 6.0.

After water and shortening is added to the flour, the refrigerated biscuit dough is mixed to full development to ensure that the gluten network will retain the gas matrix for the entire shelf life. The dough is extruded and cut into long ribbons and sheeted, producing a wide dough band, ¾ in. thick. Dough pieces in the shape of circular disks are stamped out of the band, vacuum-lifted from the belt and placed in cans made of a triple-ply, spiral-wound composite of foil, fiberboard and paper. Scrap is returned to the beginning of the belt for recycling. Cans are sealed, placed in cartons and loaded onto pallets. The loaded pallet is proofed at room temperature for 1 to 3 hours to allow the dough to expand to fill the canister. The full pallet is then placed in a refrigerated warehouse and chilled to 0.5°C (33°F) in preparation for distribution. Refrigerated biscuits made by this process have a shelf life of approximately 10 weeks.

The leavener system is key to successful manufacturing of refrigerated biscuits. It contains bicarbonate as the carbon dioxide source, but the leavening acid must be slowest-acting available. Even so, the leavening system must be active during processing, and in the proofing stage, it expands the dough about 20% to fill all the space available in the can. Because the carbon dioxide generated replaces the oxygen in the can, an anaerobic environment is created. During baking, no additional carbon dioxide is generated; instead, the gas in the existing cell network expands to increase the volume in the product (**Figure 8.053**).

Table 8.053. Biscuit Formulations		
Ingredient	Refrigerated commercial (bakers %)	Homemade (bakers %)
Flour	100	100
Leavener	5	15
Sugar	2	10
Salt	1	3
Shortening	5	50
Milk, liquid	60	70

(Allenson 1982)

Figure 8.053. Refrigerated canned biscuit dough is leavened by the gases present at the time of packaging.

8.H. Pastries and Sweet Goods

Updated by Hans van der Maarel

Sweet dough products, as their name implies, are made from doughs with relatively high sugar content, in addition to high levels of enriching ingredients such as shorten-

Table 8.054. Comparitive Bread, Danish Dough Formulations

Ingredient	Bread dough (%)	Danish dough (%)
Patent flour	100	75
Pastry flour	–	25
Water	63	43
Sugar	4	18
Shortening	3	15
Salt	2	2
Nonfat dry milk solids	–	6
Whey solids	4	–
Whole eggs	–	12
Yeast	3	10
Yeast food	1	–

(Goodsell 1985)

Figure 8.054. Danish pastry features laminated dough, fruit or creme fillings and a sugary glaze. (ConAgra)

ing, milk solids and whole eggs. This difference becomes evident when representative formulations for white bread dough and danish type sweet dough are compared, as in **Table 8.054**. The higher levels of sugar, shortening and milk, and the inclusion of eggs, all contribute extra flavor and tenderness, improved texture and extended keeping quality to the baked product. The addition of roll-in fat, at levels of 3 to 4 oz per lb of dough, serves to enhance the flaky, airy texture of danish-type products.

Moreover, in their finished form, sweet dough products normally contain generous amounts of fillings and toppings in the form of icings, glazes, fruit jams or jellies, nuts, streusels and sundry other flavored mixtures. Products belonging to this category include cinnamon buns, sweet rolls and coffee cakes of diverse size, shape and variety that are normally produced from regular sweet doughs, and danish pastry (**Figure 8.054**) and puff pastry items in a virtually infinite assortment, whose flaky structure is derived from a roll-in or laminating process that is applied to the dough (**Figure 8.055**).

In Germany, bakers classify sweet goods as confectionery products, according to their formulations. Basically, confectionery items contain more than 10 parts of fat and sugar ingredients per 90 parts of cereals and/ or starches. They are further classified into doughs (yeasted and unyeasted) and batters (whipped and unwhipped).

In the retail trade, sweet goods such as croissants, danish pastries, brioche and similar products are often described as Viennoiserie, a type type of bread that originated in Vienna and was first made exclusively for the monarchy. The butter, sugar and eggs transformed lean doughs into sweet pastries tht could only be afforded by the powerful (Suas 2009).

8.H.1. Sweet goods

Dough preparation for sweet goods may be either by straight-dough, sponge-and-dough, liquid ferment or no-time dough procedures, and the baker's selection of method depends on considerations such as type of product involved, desired product character, available production facilities and so forth. Opinions vary as to the relative benefits of the different methods of dough production. Traditionally, these products were based on straight doughs and sponge-and-dough methods, but more recently, the use of no-time doughs and preferments has gained wide acceptance in the production of sweet doughs (O'Reilly 1976, Shaffer 1977).

General details of the formulation, functions of the ingredients, dough processing steps, makeup procedures and finishing operations of sweet dough products were outlined by Meigs (1968), Poehlman (1979), Rijkaart (1984), Doerry and Meloan (1986), Vey (1986), Doerry (1997, 1998) and Bent (1998), among others.

8.H.1.a. Ingredient requirements

Regular sweet doughs for the production of sweet rolls, coffee cakes and similar products will generally contain from 15 to 25% each of shortening, sugar and whole eggs, 8% compressed yeast, 5 to 6% nonfat dry milk, 1% salt and 42 to 45% water, all based on flour weight. For danish pastry and puff pastry, in which 15 to 25% of roll-in fat in the form of butter, margarine or special roll-in shortening is additionally used, the amount of the dough shortening is generally reduced somewhat to perhaps 8 to 10%. Roll-in fat levels can be as much as 33% of the dough weight.

The flour used in sweet doughs must possess good gluten quality if it is to carry the high levels of sugar, shortening and eggs and still yield a satisfactory product volume. For the extrusion process, in which extra physical stresses are imposed on the dough, a strong spring wheat flour of 12 to 13.5% protein is generally recommended, while for conventional make-up procedures, a winter wheat flour with about 12% protein will normally be found satisfactory.

Sugar provides tenderness, sweet flavor and crust color, and corn sugars may be used if a darker crust color is desired. Whole eggs should be in proportion to the tenderizing ingredients (Poehlman 1979). If higher levels of sugar and shortening are used, then the eggs should also be added at higher levels to carry that weight. Eggs perform a structural function in danish and may be fortified with whites for added strength or yolks for added tenderness.

Figure 8.055. Alternating layers of sweet dough and shortening gives these miniature puff pastries their flaky texture and rich eating quality.

Sugar affects the dough water absorption, and rich doughs (high sugar content) tend to absorb less water than lean doughs, but yeast activity is also slowed down. To offset this effect, yeast is normally increased as more sugar is added to the dough. Doerry (1997) observed that generally, the amount of compressed yeast added to sweet doughs is about one-third the amount of sugar solids in the formula.

Salt controls fermentation rates and enhances flavor. Nonfat dry milk helps buffer the fermentation aids and aids crust color. Doughs for danish and coffee cakes benefit from yeast fermentation, which can be provided by the addition of yeast to doughs or through yeast slurries and preferments.

Although the main flavor of danish pastries comes from the filling, topping and icing, with the roll-in fat providing a secondary level, bakers occasionally add flavorings to these doughs. Lean doughs, in particular, benefit from use of vanilla and/or citrus flavorings. Color additives such as Yellow No. 5, Yellow No. 6, beta carotene or the blend known as "egg shade" bolster the richness of the crumb's appearance.

While cake margarines and cake shortenings will perform satisfactorily as the shortening components in sweet dough, the roll-in or layering fats used in the production of danish and puff pastries do require certain specific functional characteristics (McGill 1975). Above all, they must possess a suitable plasticity and toughness because it is their ability to form thin, continuous layers during the roll-in or laminating process that accounts for the creation of a flaky structure in the baked pastry.

Pastry fats should retain adequate plasticity at temperatures of 10 to 13°C (50 to 55°F) to be spreadable and sheetable. Their melting points should be in the range of

40 to 44°C (104 to 111°F) so that they will not impart a waxy aftertaste to the baked products as higher-melting fats tend to do (McGill 1975). While most roll-in fats are specially-formulated margarines in which water may constitute a significant component, some bakers prefer pastry shortenings that consist entirely of fat because they yield a crisper and shorter flakiness in the baked product.

The past few decades have witnessed a marked expansion in the use of commercial sweet dough bases. In a concentrated form, these products combine all the enriching and flavoring ingredients that are normally found in a high-quality sweet dough formula. These plastic bases thus contain the shortening, sweeteners, salt, milk solids, eggs, emulsifiers and flavor systems and require the addition only of the flour, water and yeast (Weber 1963). Their consistency resembles that of plastic shortenings, and their usage levels generally average about 30 to 35% based on the flour weight.

Doerry (1997) observed that two types of danish pastries are commonly made in the US. The original European-style pastry is a relatively lean product, deriving its taste from the roll-in fat and the fillings, toppings and icings, but also having a relatively short shelf life. The second, or American, style is prepared from a richer dough and has better shelf life, although it is not as flaky as the European variation. Ingredient usage that characterize the American version is shown in **Table 8.055**. Vey (1986) divided danish styles into three categories based on the amount of roll-in fat used per pound of dough: lean (2.0 to 2.75 oz), medium (3.0 to 4.5 oz) and rich (4.75 to 5.5 oz).

8.H.1.b. Dough preparation

In the traditional procedure of sweet goods production, the sponges are normally mixed in conventional horizontal or vertical mixers for some 4 to 5 minutes, after which they are fermented for 3 to 4 hours. More yeast is usually added at the dough stage with the remaining dough ingredients. Dough mixing generally requires some 12 to 15 minutes until the pickup stage is reached and is followed by 15 to 30 minutes of floor time, after which the dough is ready for processing.

Doughs intended for extrusion require some adjustments to counteract the adverse effects of the greater physical abuse that is inherent in this process. These changes include: (a) using up to 75% of the flour in the sponge, (b) increasing the absorption by 1 to 3%, (c) extending the fermentation time by 30 minutes, (d) maintaining a yeast level of 5% in the sponge, with a supplemental addition of 3% at the dough stage, and (e) a corresponding increase of 0.75 to 1.0% in the yeast food. Floor time for the dough should be extended to 30 to 45 minutes, while a dough temperature of 29 to 30°C (83 to 85°F) will ensure a more rapid recovery during makeup and the proof (Stiles 1958).

The introduction of no-stress dough band systems has largely eliminated the need for these additional steps, and it has allowed the operator to increase the moisture absorption.

For straight sweet doughs, the common procedure is to cream the sugar, shortening, salt, flavoring materials and dry milk solids at slow speed in a vertical mixer into a smooth, slightly aerated paste. This process requires about 5 minutes. With creaming continued at medium speed, the eggs are gradually added during the next 5 minutes. The addition of yeast, dissolved in part of the dough water, follows, along

Table 8.055. Danish Pastry Formula

Ingredient	Amount (bakers %)
Primary	
Flour	100
Sugar	8 to 20
Roll-in fat	10 to 33
Yeast	3 to 8
Salt	1.5 to 2.0
Water	51 to 59
Optional	
Dairy solids	4 to 8
Egg solids	5 to 8
Dough fat	8 to 20
Flavors	variable
Food coloring	variable
Dough conditioners	variable
Crumb softeners	variable

(Doerry 1998)

with the balance of the total water. Finally, the flour is incorporated and the dough mixed at medium speed for another 8 to 10 minutes to the cleanup stage. Dough temperature at this point should be about 27°C (80°F).

The dough may also be fully developed in a much shorter time in high-speed mixers, in which case the mixed straight dough will go directly to the makeup table without a lengthy fermentation. Chemically-developed doughs also are frequently used in the interest of reducing the production time.

For ordinary sweet yeast-raised dough products, the finished dough is scaled into relatively large pieces of 10 to 15 lb, given a rest of 20 to 25 minutes and transferred to the pastry table for sheeting, makeup and finishing. In more highly mechanized operations, the dough is normally passed through an extruder that feeds it in the form of a continuous dough ribbon onto the pastry table for final makeup. Here, too, the development of no- or low-stress dough delivery systems has allowed the baker to increase the floor proof time and eliminate the rest time between the initial and final sheeting rollers.

The number of layers present in danish have changed over the years in an effort to reduce labor. In 1979, Poehlman observed that the previous industry average had been 81 layers of dough and 54 layers of shortening but had decreased to as few as 54 of dough and 36 of shortening. He recommended that if less than 4 oz of shortening is rolled-in per pound of dough, then the number of folds should be reduced further. "Every additional fold given the piece reduces the thickness of the shortening film on a direct ratio to the number of folds," he stated. "Too many folds with too little roll-in shortening results in a sweet dough mixed the hard way."

The ultimate quality and taste appeal of the sweet dough and danish pastry product are established by a combination of factors, which include the final shape and structure given the product, the nature of the flavors incorporated either into the dough or the icing and the kind and amount of icing, filling or topping applied to them. Formulation and processing of these components are discussed later in this chapter.

8.H.2. Puff pastry and croissants

Although puff pastry and croissant doughs may include chemical leavening and yeast, respectively, in their formulations, steam is what primarily leavens these items. (**Table 8.056**) The puffing action that creates puff pastry depends solely on the significant increase in volume of moisture, trapped between dough layers separated by thin films of fat resulting from the laminating process, as it turns into steam and inflates the structure (Doerry 1998).

Akin to puff pastry, croissants are small, rich, crescent-shaped rolls with a flaky, tender crumb that are produced either with or without fillings (**Figure 8.056**). Their origin is said to date back some three centuries to Vienna (Calvel 1952), from whence their popularity slowly spread throughout Europe. Although croissants have long been made by many French pastry shops in the US, their popularity blossomed during the 1980s, and they have become a mainstay for food service sandwiches and are widely available as a consumer product.

8.H.2.a. Ingredient considerations
Puff pastry (**Figure 8.057**) requires the ingredients described in Table 8.056. The

Figure 8.056. Crescent-shaped croissants get their texture and appeal from multiple layers of dough interleaved with shortening.

Figure 8.057. Prepared puff pastry sheets allow food service operators to unleash their creativity with picture-perfect results.
(Pennant Foods)

flour should be capable of forming a gluten structure strong enough to maintain the dough films that entrap the leavening water vapor, and a good long patent bread flour with a protein content of 11.5 to 12.5% is uses. Higher protein levels tolerate slightly more lamination but may not produce a better pastry, according to Doerry (1998). Absorption of 52 to 57% will produce a stiff consistency, like that of bread dough and similar to the roll-in fat. When calculating water and absorption, the liquid portion of any eggs must be counted as well. Soft doughs are difficult to process and tend to slide over the roll-in fat during sheeting, and the fat will eventually break into lumps rather than forming a continuous film.

Some fat may be added directly to the dough itself and serves to lubricate the gluten during laminating. The style of fat is important. If butter is used as the roll-in fat, then butter should also be the choice for use in the dough and for fillings. If using a special puff-paste shortening, then regular shortening or margarine can be put into the dough and/or filling.

Butter is an excellent roll-in fat, but it requires a relatively narrow temperature range during processing, 15 to 20°C (59 to 68°F). When butter warms to 21° (79°F) or more, it softens and is absorbed into the dough during lamination. Shortenings and margarines formulated specifically for roll-in use, called "puff pastes," tolerate wider operating ranges because they have a relatively high melting point. Puff pastes often include some moisture, 9 to 18%, with added dairy flavors and salt, 1.8 to 2.6%.

The optional ingredients include liquid whole eggs, which add moisture to the dough, as well as strength and crust color to the finished product. The egg protein participates in the Maillard browning reaction, and the bright color that results will mask the graying effect caused by fat bloom as the pastry ages.

Salt is present not only as a flavor enhancer but also to delay gluten development during mixing and to reduce dough extensibility during lamination. The addition of an "acid salt" such as cream of tartar or acid creme helps relax the dough between lamination stages. Lemon juice may be substituted for the acid salt. Dough conditioners are seldom used; however, addition of 30 to 60 ppm ascorbic acid improves the dough's tolerance to floor time.

Croissant ingredients (**Table 8.057**) are similar to those of puff pastry, with the exception of yeast. Yeast assists with flavor and dough conditioning and will affect proofing time, but given sufficient proofing time, croissant volume is independent of the level of yeast used (Doerry and Meloan (1986). The flour recommended for croissant is that milled from hard red winter wheat with a protein content of 11.0 ± 0.5% for best results. They observed that many bakers of French training will blend a high-protein spring wheat flour with a low-protein soft wheat flour, which more nearly reproduces the Alveograph curves given by typical French flours. Often these blends consist of up to 50% soft wheat flour, but when the protein content is calculated, it generally falls into the range of an average winter wheat flour, and the performance is similar.

Sugar can be granulated sucrose or high-fructose corn syrup, as long as the sweetener solids levels are consistent. Higher sugar levels not only retard the yeast activity, but they also increase the tolerance of the croissants to over-proofing.

Salt improves the general quality of croissants and can be added to the dough, the roll-in fat or both. Doerry and Meloan (1986) found the best results when using an unsalted roll-in and incorporating the salt into the dough.

Although many European formulations for croissants do not call for fat to be added to the dough, it can help lubricate the gluten structure during the laminating process. At 4% (flour weight basis) addition to the dough, shortening assists during sheeting and laminating.

Like puff pastry doughs, croissant doughs are stiff, with dough absorption running 58 ± 2% (flour weight basis). Doughs with too much water in them will be soft and sticky, requiring excessive dusting flour. Also, dough layers will tear easily when manually handled, and resulting croissants tend to flatten out during the final proofing phase.

Milk, a part of the French croissant formula, is actually an optional ingredient. If used in it liquid form, the milk should be heat treated to inactivate its sulfhydryl groups, which have an adverse effect on wheat gluten proteins. Milk aids crust color, a useful function in low-sugar doughs.

Roll-in fat functionality mirrors that of roll-ins for puff pastry. The fat provides a barrier between adjacent dough layers, preventing them from fusing together during reduction and lamination. It must remain a continuous film throughout processing. The amount of roll-in fat varies according to bakery practice, ranging from 17 to 35% of the dough weight. Higher levels of roll-in fat will require more folds than lower levels.

Proofing must be done at a temperature that does not exceed the melting point of the roll-in fat, or else the fat will bleed into the dough, destroying the layering effect so important to proper texture and appearance. Relative humidity (RH) should be in the range of 75 to 85% to prevent formation of skins on the dough pieces. Higher RH will cause the crust to lose its flaky appearance, turning it light and blotchy. Proofing should proceed to the point where the croissants expand 2.5 times their original size, taking 1 to 3 hours. If under-proofed, the internal structure will collapse, the coiled form may separate at its curls, and the crumb becomes chewy and tough.

Bakers who proof croissants under open conditions often apply a mild egg wash to the surface beforehand. The wash provides the baked croissants with appealing color and crust.

8.H.2.b. Dough preparation

Puff paste and croissant doughs are mixed only to partial development; the sheeting process will assure full development. The baker has a choice of methods for adding the fat: the English method, the French method, the Scottish method and the blitz method, followed by batch or continuous lamination (Doerry 1998).

In the English method, the dough is sheeted into a rectangular shape, and the roll-in fat is spread over two-thirds of the dough area. The uncovered dough portion is folded over half of the covered portion, and the remaining covered half is folded over the doubled-up dough to form 3 dough layers separated by 2 fat layers.

In the French method, the dough is sheeted into squares, and the roll-in fat applied as another square with corners at the mid-points of the sides of the dough square. The uncovered corners of the dough square are folded toward the center to form an envelope of dough with a single layer of fat between 2 dough layers.

Table 8.056. Puff Pastry Formula

Ingredient	Amount (bakers %)
Primary	
Flour	100
Water	52 to 57
Roll-in fat	50 to 100
Dough fat	0 to 20
Optional	
Liquid eggs	10
Salt	variable
Acid salt	0.75
Lemon juice	optional
Dough conditioners	optional

(Doerry 1998)

Table 8.057. Basic Croissant Formula

Ingredient	Amount (bakers %)
Flour	100
Sugar	10
Salt	1
Mineral yeast food	0.5
Margarine or butter	4
Instant dry yeast	3
Water	58
Total dough weight	176.5
Roll-in margarine or butter*	45.5

** 25.72% of dough weight*

(Doerry and Meloan 1986)

The Scottish method is similar to making pie dough. The roll-in fat is cut into small chunks about 2 in. on each side. These chunks are dispersed in the flour before the liquids are added. After combining all ingredients, they are blended without permitting gluten development, and the dough is rested for 30 minutes to allow hydration.

The blitz method is a variation of the Scottish method. The roll-in fat is cut into small chunks, but its addition is delayed until the dough is mixed and the gluten partially developed. The fat is dispersed in the dough.

All the above methods allow batch lamination, but the Scottish and blitz methods must be put through a significantly lower number of reduction and folding operations. These methods generally produce smaller, less flakey pastries than the others, and Doerry (1998) recommended that butter not be used for blitz doughs. Continuous lamination allows dough and roll-in fat to be coextruded or layered and then gradually reduced and folded. Stress-free methods prove well adapted to preparation of such doughs. Rijkaart (1984) described a curling method in which the roll-in fat is laid down on a sheet of dough that is then coiled into a continuous cylinder by a curling roller. This method creates an initial structure with 6 layers of fat and 7 of dough at the first reduction.

Puff pastry doughs accept scrap dough well for rework, provided that the baker is careful to add "like to like" and not combine doughs of different formulations or those carrying traces of fillings.

8.H.2.c. Laminating and texture

Like puff pastry, the croissant's overall texture results both from the leavening produced by yeast fermentation plus steam and from the flakiness created by repeated folding and rolling of the dough-and-fat laminate. Representative formulations for croissants of different degrees of richness are given in **Table 8.058**. The roll-in fat, which most often is butter, may range from a low of 16% to a high of 35%, with the higher levels yielding final products that are flakier, with improved volume and an open, somewhat lacy grain. Margarine is also successfully used in producing "value" croissants.

Croissant texture is markedly affected by the number of layers given the dough during lamination. According to Rowe (1985), croissants with 16 layers will exhibit the optimum volume and flakiness and an open and lacy grain. Increasing the number of layers much beyond this level, for example, to 48, will result in loss in flakiness and volume and produce a close and bread-like grain. Rijkaaart (1984) states that 36 layers of roll-in fat is more than enough for croissants and that in Europe the number of layers varies from 16 to 48. Sheeting thickness also affects the texture and volume of the croissant. Dough sheets that have been rolled excessively thin, down to 3 mm ($^1/_8$ in.), yield croissants of lower volume, less pronounced flakiness and a denser grain structure than do dough sheets twice as thick.

However, when properly laminated, individual dough layers in puff pastries measure about 0.0005 in. (0.013 mm). At this thickness, the gluten structure in

Table 8.058. Representative Croissant Formulations

Ingredient	Formula I (%)	Formula II (%)	Formula III (%)
Bread flour	100	80	100
Cake flour	–	20	–
Sugar	10	8	7
Yeast	7	7	7
Yeast food	0.5	0.4	0.4
Margarine	2	10	–
Butter	–	–	4.5
Eggs	–	10	–
Nonfat dry milk	3	3	–
Milk	–	–	20
Salt	1.5	2	2
Water	50 to 55	50 to 55	40 to 45

(Rowe 1985)

the dough assumes a 2-dimensional orientation, rather than the 3-dimensional cell structure of most other doughs and batters. This flat structure resembles a film and is able to trap steam during baking to produce the flaky texture characteristic of puff pastry and croissants.

8.I. Cheesecakes
Updated by L.A. Gorton

Cheesecakes, nearly unique among bakery products, require no flour at all or limit its use to a very low level and that mostly in preformed crusts. Plain cheesecake styles remain popular, but bakers have supplemented these with varieties flavored with chocolate, coffee, caramel and containing nuts, fruits and fruit purees of all sorts (**Figure 8.058**). Toppings of whipped cream or chocolate ganache are also popular. The only limit seems to be the baker's creativity.

As noted in **Table 8.059**, the main ingredients of cheesecake are bakers cheese or cream cheese, sugar, eggs and shortening. The first three ingredients account for 95% of the batch weight, according to Abboud (1998). Voorhees (1958) classified cheesecakes into two broad categories: (a) the light type, exemplified chiefly by French cheesecake to which varying amounts of egg white meringue are added to produce maximum lightness and volume in the baked product, and (b) the more solid type that is made without beaten egg whites. This classification, however, is rather imprecise because the types overlap considerably in both formulation and ultimate eating properties. In practice, the formulations given here merely provide basic guidelines that leave much room for improvisation. Abboud (1998) further differentiated the light cheesecake category by adding a California variation that is somewhat sweeter than the French and provided formulations for chocolate and low-fat cheesecake variations.

Although the variety of cheeses that can suitably be used in cheesecake production is quite diverse, the two types most commonly used by American bakers are bakers cheese and cream cheese, which are described in Chapter 2, Part B. An accounting of cheese in baked foods was provided by Willey (1988), who noted the differences in cheese composition (**Table 8.060**) between bakers, Neufchâtel and cream cheeses. Quechatel, a pasteurized process Neufchâtel cheese product, and fat-free cream cheese may also be used (Abboud 1998).

To review, bakers cheese is made

Figure 8.058. A swirl mechanism duplicates hand motions for marbling raspberry puree into cheesecake batter. (Colborne Foodbotics)

Table 8.059. Cheesecake Formulations

Ingredient	Solid type lb	Solid type % (batch weight basis)	French type lb	French type % (batch weight basis)
Bakers cheese	100	41.5	100	34.5
Sugar	41	17.25	36	12.4
Salt	1	0.5	1	0.35
Starch	3.75	1.5	–	–
Bread flour	–	–	7.25	2.4
Cake flour	–	–	7.25	2.4
Whole eggs	30	12.5	23.5	8
Egg yolks	10	4	–	–
Egg whites	–	–	21.25	7.25
Nonfat dry milk	1.25	0.5	6.75	2.3
Emuslifier shortening	40	16.5	–	–
Butter	–	–	9	3
Powdered lemon juice	0.625	0.25	1	0.35
Vanilla extract	0.625	0.25	1	0.35
Water	12.5	5.25	77.5	26.5

(Voorhees 1955)

Table 8.060. Cheese Composition

	Bakers cheese (%)	Neufchâtel cheese (%)	Cream cheese (%)
Moisture	74.00	64.00	54.00
Fat	0.02	20.50	33.50
Protein	19.00	12.00	9.80
Salt	0.00	0.75	0.75
Stabilizer	0.00	0.35	0.30
pH	4.50	4.60	4.60

(Willey 1988)

from casein curd that has been precipitated from cultured skim milk either by rennin or lactic acid, or by both. It has a pleasant, bland, slightly yogurt-like flavor. Its curds are soft, dry and pliable and should be free of granulation so that they can be kneaded and blended into a smooth batter. It has good moisture-absorbing character and produces a cheesecake that is light and cake-like. Bakers cheese contains no fat so bakers must add fat in the form of butter, margarine or shortening.

Bakers cheese contains about 75% moisture, with the remainder representing cheese solids chiefly in the form of milk proteins. It will perform optimally at a pH of 4.5. This form of cheese has a relatively short shelf life but can be frozen without affecting end use to a large degree.

Cream cheese, as its name implies, is derived from dairy cream, with or without additions of milk or nonfat milk solids. The cream or cream mixture is treated with lactic acid bacteria and/or rennin, to bring about coagulation. The coagulated mass is then drained, followed by mixing and kneading to obtain the desired consistency and uniformity. Cream cheese contains no less than 33% butterfat, about 15% casein curds and not more than 55% moisture.

Most cream cheese today is hot packed, thereby giving it excellent shelf life. It comes in 30-lb tin cans or in polyethylene-lined 50-lb cartons. Willey (1988) recommended that cream cheese not be frozen. The cheese is also available in a dehydrated powder form with a moisture content of only 3% and a practically unlimited storage stability.

Cream cheese requires less sweeteners than bakers cheese and does not have the rough texture that often characterizes bakers cheese; however, it absorbs less moisture and thus does not have the yield advantages of bakers cheese. Because it is high in fat, cheesecake formulations made with cream cheese require little if any additional fat.

Neufchâtel cheese is similar to cream cheese but has a lower fat content. It is made in a manner almost identical to cream cheese; however, the finished product lacks the smoothness of body and positive cream flavor of cream cheese. In use, it is typically combined with bakers cheese or cream cheese to achieve the desired body and flavor qualities.

Additional dairy ingredients such as sour cream, heavy cream and/or yogurt are used by various bakers to improve texture and taste. Flour or starch, when used, serve primarily as structure builders and stabilizers, as are pectin and gelatin. Salt acts mostly as a flavor enhancer. Abboud (1998) observed that it is now common to replace some of the sucrose with honey and corn sweeteners.

Cheesecake, really a form of baked custard, is set by the coagulation of egg protein within the batter (Suas 2009). Bringing all ingredients to room temperature will optimize mixing, and the mixer should be scraped down frequently to ensure uniform mixing.

In the production of the solid-type cheesecake, the cheese, sugar, salt and starch are placed in the mixing bowl and creamed into a smooth mass at low speed. Next are added the whole eggs, yolks and shortening, with continued slow mixing until the batter has become homogenous. Finally, the liquid ingredients (water or diluted cream) are added and the batter mixed to complete smoothness.

In the production of French-type cheesecake, in which a meringue made of egg whites and hot syrup is employed, the handling of this stage of production is critical to the ultimate quality of the cake. The meringue is prepared by boiling about one-third of the formula sugar in sufficient water to produce a syrup, incorporating the hot syrup into the egg foam when it has reached the wet peak and whipping the mixture to a new wet peak. In a separate bowl, the cheese, remaining sugar, salt and starch, shortening and liquids are creamed and mixed into a smooth batter by the same procedure as employed for the solid-type cheesecake. The meringue is then folded into the batter.

While some bakers deposit the cheesecake batter into greased pans, others prefer to first line the bottom of the pan with mixtures of cracker meal or cake crumbs, or a sweet dough or cookie dough, or ordinary pie dough. Often this base will have been baked beforehand.

Different types of cheese cake require somewhat different baking conditions. The heavier types are preferably baked at 163 to 188°C (325 to 370°F) for about 35 to 45 minutes until the cake is firm to the touch, indicating that the interior of the cake has properly set, and has developed an attractive, slightly brown color. Lighter types of cheesecake should be baked at more moderate temperatures of 149 to 177°C (300 to 350°F), with low-pressure steam in the oven to prevent cracks and fissures from developing. Abboud (1998) recommended baking cheesecakes in a moderate oven of 149 to 163°C (300 to 325°F) for about an hour.

Normally, the batters of light cheesecakes rise in the pan somewhat beyond the rim during baking but settle back again during cooling to their original scaling level. Cheesecakes should not be allowed to over-bake.

Voorhees (1958) recommended that if two ovens are available, the lighter cheesecakes be prebaked in a very hot oven at 260°C (500°F) for just long enough (15 minutes) to obtain the desired crust color. Then the cake is transferred to a cooler oven at about 93°C (200°F) to complete the baking without generating any steam in the cake interior that would cause the crust to split.

Cooling is critical if cracking, a major defect, is to be avoided. Slow, steady, draft-free conditions are required.

A traditional finish for cheesecake is a thin layer of lightly sweetened sour cream, applied after baking.

8.J. Cakes
Updated by L.A. Gorton

Cakes made by bakers have changed greatly from the original "pound" cake that combined a pound each of sugar, flour, eggs and butter (**Figure 8.059**). As simple as that formulation was (and still is), it provided the base on which most of today's cakes have been built. Cakes contain soft wheat flour, water (also supplied by liquid eggs and milk), sugar, shortening, flavors and chemical leavening systems. They are sweet, with a short, tender crumb and a pleasing aroma or taste. They are made from batters, which are not only far more liquid in nature than doughs but also contain far more sugar. The sugar content will equal or, in most cases, exceed that of flour. Mixing is a matter of wetting and hydrating, distinctly avoiding gluten formation.

Additionally, cake density and crumb texture depends on what gives the system its

Figure 8.059. Classic pound cake contains a pound each of sugar, flour, eggs and butter.
(American Egg Board)

structure. Light, foam-type cakes (angel, sponge, chiffon) rely on the egg content for their structure, while heavier cakes (layer cake, pound, fruit) support their structure with a fat-and-water emulsion (Anon. 1999a, 1999b).

Cake products are difficult to define precisely because of their wide variety and the broad range of their formulations. Essentially, they are products that are leavened mainly by baking powder but also by air incorporation, as in the case of foam-type cakes and, ever so occasionally, by yeast. They usually contain relatively high levels of such enriching ingredients as sugar, shortening, eggs, milk and flavorings, in addition to soft wheat flour, and are consequently characterized by a sweet taste, a short and tender texture, and pleasing flavors and aromas. They may be classed into two broad categories: (a) shortening-based cakes whose crumb structure is derived from the fat-liquid emulsion that is created during batter processing and (b) foam-type cakes that depend for their structure and volume primarily on the foaming and aerating properties of eggs.

Three major parameters govern the quality of cakes in all instances, namely, (a) the special suitability of the ingredients for the type of cake being made, (b) an appropriate and properly balanced formula and (c) the adherence to optimal mixing and baking procedures.

8.J.1. Functional roles of ingredients

The major ingredients used in cake baking are for the most part the same as those that find application in the production of bread-type products or differ from them at best only in degree. Materials such as eggs, milk products, sweeteners, shortenings, emulsifiers, salt and even flour are either identical to those used in yeast-raised products or vary from them only in functional rather than basic properties.

A balanced cake formula is one in which the essential ingredients are present in such proportions as to yield a good quality cake. The unique characteristics of each type of cake demand adjustment in the levels of individual ingredients. Also, because each ingredient differs to a greater or lesser degree in its functionality from the others, a significant change in the level of one basic ingredient necessarily entails compensating changes in the other formula components. Zelch (2001a, 2001b) provided a current review of ingredient roles and their technical considerations, as well as mixing procedures.

The basic cake ingredients may be grouped into five general categories according to their functional roles: (a) tougheners, or structure builders; (b) tenderizers; (c) moisteners; (d) driers; and (e) flavorings (**Table 8.061**). Many of the ingredients that are commonly used in cakemaking perform more than one of these roles. In general, the major cake ingredients may be designated according to their functions as follows:

Flour is preeminently a toughener because it is intimately involved in establishing the crumb structure of most types of cake. Because its principal components (starch and protein) have pronounced moisture-absorbing properties, at some stage

Table 8.061. Functions of Basic Cake Ingredients

Category	Ingredient
Tougheners	Flour, milk solids, egg whites
Tenderizers	Sugar, fats (shortening, oil, butter), egg yolks, chocolate, other fat-containing ingredients, chemical leaveners, emulsifiers, starches, gums
Moisteners	Water, liquid milk, eggs, syrups, liquid sugars
Driers	Flour, milk solids, instant starch, gums
Flavorers	Salt, sugar, cocoa, chocolate, butter, vanilla, other flavor-providing ingredients

(Zelch 2001a)

of cake baking, flour also functions as a drier.

Sugar is the major flavoring, and its primary function is to impart a desirable sweet taste to the finished product. It acts as well as a moistener if it used as a liquid sugar or syrup or as a drier when added in its crystalline form. It also functions as a tenderizer by diluting the flour proteins.

Shortening is the primary tenderizer of cake baking. Fats also contribute moist eating qualities to the final product and extend its shelf life by inhibiting the premature loss of moisture and volatile flavor materials. Modern cake shortenings contain selected blends of surfactants that greatly improve their moisture-carrying capacity and contribute to the dispersion of fat throughout the batter. The surfactants thus improve the shortening's ability to produce a uniform dispersion of minute fat particles that then serve as the foci for the air cells that determine grain and texture in the baked cake.

Dry milk solids and similar soy- and whey-based proteins provide support to the cake's crumb structure and also function as driers. Liquid milk, on the other hand, is an obvious contributor of moisture. Milk also enhances flavor, both directly and by participating in the Maillard reaction.

Eggs have many functions in cake baking, depending on the specific nature of the egg material involved, as well as on the type of cake. Fresh egg whites, with a moisture content of approximately 85%, frequently serve as a principal moistener, while their albumen content contributes to structure formation. Egg yolks, on the other hand, contain only some 49% moisture, in addition to 32% lipids and 16% protein. Their function in cake baking encompass the roles of moistener, structure builder and tenderizer. Whole liquid eggs contain about 74% moisture, 13% protein and 11% lipids so hat their effects resemble more closely those produced by egg yolks than by egg whites. Finally, dried egg products act primarily as driers and as structure formers.

Chocolate serves principally as a flavoring but, because of its relatively high cocoa butter content, also exerts a marked tenderizing effect. Cocoa powder, on the other hand, with its greatly reduced fat content, is used primarily as a flavor. It also functions as a drier and additionally plays a minor role as a tenderizer.

Leaveners, by imparting volume and lightness to the final cake, are classified as tenderizers.

Salt serves primarily as a flavor-enhancing ingredient. Unlike in bread and roll systems, salt in cakes is not used to toughen the gluten.

Formulating cake batters requires the baker to balance toughening ingredients (flour, egg white, milk solids and salt) and tenderizing ingredients (sugar, fat and egg yolk).

8.J.1.a. Eggs

The whipping properties of egg whites vary with their viscosity: Thinner whites foam up more rapidly and to a greater volume than more viscous thick whites. The latter, however, yield foams of greater stability. According to Almquist and Lorenz (1932), thick whites comprise a fine fiber network of pure ovomucin in which are dispersed the thin whites. The loss of carbon dioxide during the first days after laying results in an increase in alkalinity and a concomitant hydrolysis of the disulfide bonds of the ovomucin, leading to a thinning of the whites. According to these workers, the difference between thick and thin whites is one of structure rather than of moisture content.

In a study comparing frozen and fresh egg whites in angel food production (**Figure 8.060**), Miller and Vail (1943) found that fresh whites, and frozen thick and thin whites, whipped best at a temperature of 21°C (70°F) and yielded stable foams. The resulting cakes in all instances were more tender and possessed a better texture than did those from whites whipped at other temperatures. The frozen thin whites foamed up more rapidly than the frozen thick whites, and both whipped more quickly than the fresh whites. Fresh whites and frozen thin whites produced cakes of comparable high quality, while the cakes from frozen thick whites were less desirable.

In separating whites from yolks in fresh shell eggs, utmost care is required to obtain a clean separation because any contamination of the whites with yolk will substantially reduce their foaming capacity. This adverse action results from the relatively high lipid content of the yolks. Similar foam-depressing effects may be experienced with bowls and utensils that are not absolutely free of all traces or films of fat. Hence, all equipment and utensils coming into contact with the whites during whipping must be thoroughly washed beforehand with a hot, mild detergent solution, followed by liberal rinsing.

Figure 8.060. The distinctive crumb texture of angel food cake depends on egg whites.
(American Egg Board)

8.J.1.b. Shortening

Shortening performs three basic functions in cake production: (a) It entraps air during the creaming process to aid in the proper aeration or leavening of the batter and the finished cake; (b) it emulsifies large amounts of liquid that contribute to greater crumb moisture and, concomitantly, to the softness of the cake product; and (c) it coats the protein and starch particles, thereby disrupting the continuity of the gluten and starch structure that makes up the cake crumb and, in the process, tenderizes it. A satisfactory cell structure can be produced without added fat in yeast-leavened products and foam-type cakes. However, most types of cake require fairly high levels of shortening for the development of their characteristic crumb structure.

8.J.1.b.i. Air cells entrapment

Fat solids also exhibit crystallinity, taking several forms, as explained in Volume I, Chapter 2, Part A. Compared according to melting points, the alpha form (α) has the lowest, the beta-prime form (β') is somewhat higher, and the beta (β) has the highest. Evaluating the cake baking performance of shortenings in which a single type of crystal predominated, Hoerr et al. (1966) found that shortenings with β' crystals were superior to all others. This finding reflects the difference in crystal shape because β′ forms consist of small, needle-shaped, rosettelike crystals that readily absorb oil and produce a smooth, creamy shortening, whereas the β crystals are larger and more granular and impart a detectable "graininess" to the shortening.

During mixing, the dry materials (sugar, salt and baking powder) dissolve in the liquid ingredients, and the resulting solution mixes freely with the flour. The fat is not absorbed but is, rather, dispersed. Microscopic examination of cake batters made with plastic fats reveals that the fat is dispersed throughout the batter in the form of small, irregularly-shaped discrete particles, whose degree of dispersion depends in large measure on the amount and intensity of mixing received by the batter.

When the fat particles are closely examined, they reveal numerous minute air bubbles or cells that have been created during mixing. At the same time, the external or aqueous phase is essentially free of air bubbles. Hence, in batters that contain an effective level of shortening, aeration during the mixing process is essentially a function of the fat.

Development of effective emulsifiers has enabled bakers to use fluid shortenings, not just plastic styles, to make cases.

8.J.1.b.ii. Emulsification

Cake batter can be considered a complex oil-in-water (O/W) emulsion with a continuous aqueous phase containing dissolved or suspended dry ingredients (sugar, flour, salt and baking powder). The oil phase is dispersed in clumps throughout the continuous liquid phase. Sahi (2008) examined cake emulsions in comprehensive detail, with particular attention to interactions involving fats, water-soluble proteins and flour.

Emulsifiers promote the incorporation of air in the form of fine bubbles and disperse the shortening in small-sized particles, thereby increasing to a maximum the number of effective nucleating sites. The aerating action of emulsifiers can be attributed to their unique interfacial behavior at the oil-water boundaries, and these surface effects give them their alternate name, surfactants. When the concentration of surfactants exceeds the solubility limit, they form an interfacial membrane whose hydrophilic portions extend into the aqueous phase. This membrane, in effect, encapsulates the droplets of dispersed oil or liquid shortening within a protective coating, thereby preventing their migration into the aqueous phase where they would reduce the foaming properties of the soluble proteins and lessen their air-incorporating capacity (Wootten et al. 1967).

Handelmann et al. (1961) studied the role of emulsifiers in cake batters by a mathematical analysis of the pertinent bubble mechanics. They concluded that the volume and the grain of the cake are primarily affected by the number and size of the individual air bubbles. The greater the number of bubbles and the smaller their individual size, the more numerous the sites receiving leavening gas and the fewer bubbles that reach the critical buoyant size and rise out of the batter (**Figure 8.061**).

According to Ellinger (1962), hydrophilic emulsifiers, which have a hydrophilic-lipophilic balance (HLB) higher than 13, promote the uniform dispersion of minute fat particles and their entrapped air cells in a cake batter, thereby creating a large number of sites where the water vapor can expand during the baking stage. This emulsifier effect is illustrated in the micrographs of **Figure 8.062**, which depict cake batters with low and optimum levels, respectively, of a suitable surfactant. Expansion of water vapor, which accounts for some 90% of the increase in cake volume over the batter volume, occurs only within the fat-entrapped air cells. Excessively large and buoyant air bubbles tend to rise out of the batter; this results in a coarse-

Figure 8.061. Without the proper emulsifier, cakes do not achieve their soft crumb structure, characterized by uniform small cells.

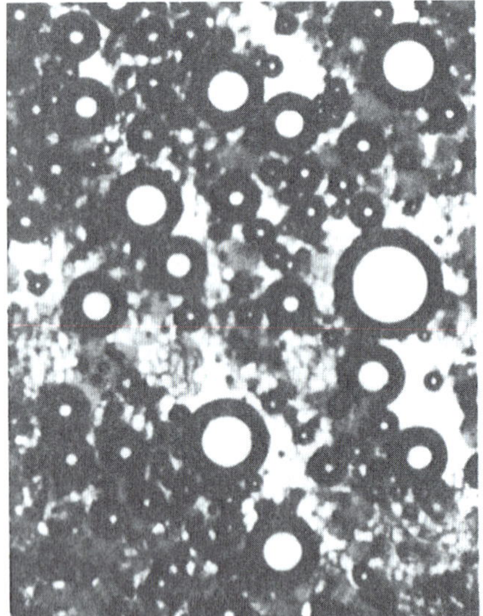
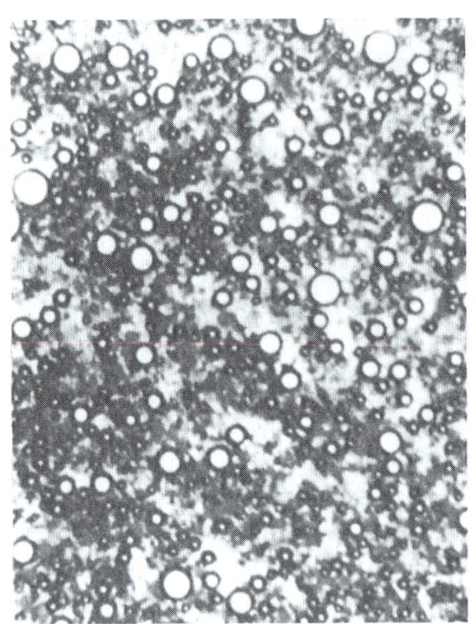

Figure 8.062. Photomicrographs of cake batter show the effect of low (left) and optimum (right) levels of monoglyceride on size and dispersion of air cells in the batter's fat phase. (Moncrieff 1970)

grained cake of low volume. Contrariwise, the smaller the individual air cells are, the larger will be the cake volume and the finer its grain. Moreover, as the surface area within the bubble is decreased, its moisture-retention capacity during cake cooling is increased. The result is a cake with a greater volume and improved eating quality because of its increased moistness and more rapid flavor release. Hydrophilic emulsifiers, in general, are functionally more effective in cake shortening than are lipophilic emulsifiers, which have an HLB of 5 or less.

In cake batters, the presence of an emulsifier aids the dispersion of the fat in the batter and prevents the oil and water separating into layers. During baking, the fat melts, and trapped air bubbles are released into the aqueous phase. The fluid batter increases in viscosity as the starch gelatinizes, and the viscous foam structure changes into a sponge.

8.J.1.b.iii. Shortening effect

The third major function of shortening in cake baking is to render the cake crumb short and tender — in other words, "the shortening effect." Shortening accomplishes this tenderizing effect by coating the starch and gluten particles with a film of fat, thereby preventing formation of a continuous gluten matrix with its inherent toughness. In this manner, fat creates, in effect, numerous weak points in the structural framework of the crumb. The effective tenderizing action of a shortening depends in part on its amount in the formula and in part on its degree of dispersion throughout the batter.

The tenderness of cake crumb increases progressively with the fat content up to an optimum level, after which additional fat causes lesser improvements in cake tenderness, until the practical limit of fat addition is reached. Also, fats that disperse readily in a fine pattern produce a greater shortening effect than do fats that emulsify less completely. The presence of mono- and diglycerides and other emulsifying agents in shortening greatly improves the dispersion of the fat in the batter.

8.J.1.c. Flour

Cake flours are normally milled from soft red winter wheat and soft white winter wheat. In general, soft red winter wheats tend to be preferred for milling high quality cake flour, whereas soft white winter wheats are frequently specified for use in cookie, pie and cracker production. According to Loving and Brenneis (1981), the baking performance of these soft wheat varieties is essentially the same whether they are used for cake, cookie, cracker or pie baking, although they do exhibit certain minor analytical differences.

A soft wheat flour intended for use in high-sugar layer cakes usually consists of a blend of those mill streams that have the lowest protein and ash contents. It has an extraction rate in the range of 45 to 65%. Such a flour, even though it has a finer average particle size than the remaining streams, is normally further reduced in average particle size by passage through a pin mill or by other means and is subsequently treated with chlorine gas (Yamazaki and Donelson 1972). Chlorine treatment makes a noticeable improvement in the flour's cake-baking performance, which is attributed, in part, to hydrolytic depolymerization of the starch molecule that increases its hydration capacity (Whistler and Pyler 1978).

As a general rule, fancy or short patent flours milled from soft wheat varieties offer a better potential for superior crumb tenderness and softness of texture in cakes than do lower grades of flour. A typical cake flour will have the following range of specifications: protein content, 8.5 ± 0.5%; ash content, 0.36 ± 0.04%; pH, 4.7 ± 0.2; and particle size, 10 ± 0.5 μm (Johnson and Hoseney 1979b). Different types of cakes require somewhat different flour specifications, summarized in **Table 8.062**.

According to Cathcart (1951), cake flours intended for use in high-sugar cakes should have 7.5 to 8.5% protein, those intended for heavier cakes, 8.5 to 9.5%, and cookie flours, 8.0 to 9.0%.

The milling preparation and baking performance of cake flours are discussed in Volume I, Chapter 2, Part A.

Table 8.062. Cake Flour Types and Their Uses

Flour	Protein (14% moisture basis)	Ash (14% moisture basis)	Uses
A	4.70	0.23	Angel food
B	7.35	0.29	Chiffon, angel food, white and yellow layer cakes
C	8.30	0.32	Sponge, chocolate, pound, other heavier cakes
D	9.10	0.42	Pound, chocolate and lower-grade cakes

(Dubois 1961)

8.J.1.d. Sugar

The sugar level in a cake formula can vary over a rather wide range. Today, few formulations will contain less than 100% sugar based on flour. For regular white or yellow cakes, the upper limit for sugar is considered to be 140%. The majority of cake formulations call for an average of 125% sugar. Cakes made with substantial levels of cocoa or chocolate will tolerate higher sugar ratios, with the upper limit approaching 180%.

The practical amount of sugar that can be used is governed by other factors such as the amount of liquid in the formula. The level of liquids derived from milk, eggs or added water must be sufficiently high to bring the sugar into solution without depriving the starch component of flour of adequate moisture for gelatinization (Woodruff and Nicoli 1931). Hence, the amount of sugar should not exceed 90 to

95% of the combined liquids. Once the desired flour-to-sugar ratio has been established, the remaining ingredients must generally be quantitatively adjusted to the sugar moiety.

When sucrose is replaced completely with a high-fructose corn syrup (HFCS) of 42% fructose content, the resulting layer cake will exhibit a darker crumb, reduced volume, excessive tenderness, thicker crusts, a "sandy and grainy" appearance on staling and a limited shelf life compared with all-sucrose cakes (Strickler 1981). These adverse effects are largely alleviated when less than 50% of the sucrose is replaced with HFCS.

With a total substitution of HFCS for sucrose, several formula modifications are required. Thus, Beery (1982) found the following adjustments to be effective for producing layer cake of a quality that is comparable to that of all-sucrose cake: (a) reduce the shortening to 10%, based on flour; (b) substitute oil such as liquid soybean oil for plastic fat; (c) use 7.5% of a composite emulsifier (a hydrated mixture of sorbitan monostearate, α-mono-glycerides, polysorbate 60 and propylene glycol, augmented with 1% sodium stearoyl lactylate, proved most effective); and (d) select slow-acting sodium aluminum phosphate (SALP) as the leavening salt at a level of 1.88% (flour basis). The more rapid staling rate of all-HFCS cakes can be slowed by blending one-third of 62 DE corn syrup with two-thirds HFCS as the sweetener. This blend, however, reduces the sweetness of the resultant cakes somewhat when compared with all-sucrose cakes.

Moreover, with all-HFCS cakes, powdered emulsifiers, which are highly effective in cakes made with sucrose, will not yield satisfactory results. Suggs (1982) attributed this failure to the acidic character of HFCS that tends to precipitate the powdered emulsifier and render it ineffective. Even so, neutralizing the acidity with baking soda does not eliminate the problem completely.

8.J.1.e. Chemical leavening

Chemical leaveners in the form of baking powder (a blend of bicarbonate carbon dioxide source and a leavening acid) provide the gases that expand the air cells in cake batters, thus creating their light texture. Chemical leaveners and their myriad applications are explained in Volume I, Chapter 2, Part B, but a short discussion of their effects in cakes is offered here.

In addition to their basic function of providing optimum aeration to the product prior to and during the baking process, chemical leaveners affect the internal structure of the baked products by their positive (cation) and negative (anion) ions. Among the cations of phosphate leaveners, calcium and aluminum ions have been shown to improve crumb structure by (a) promoting the formation of fine grain and thin cell walls, (b) imparting a desirable resilience to the crumb and (c) strengthening the protein phase of the batter. On the other hand, high levels of the sulfate ion tend to weaken the batter's protein structure. Of the ortho- and pyrophosphate anions present in phosphate leaveners, the latter will occasionally react with the proteins and increase their moisture absorption and retention capacities, thereby producing moister crumb in finished product (Kichline and Conn 1970).

The crumb color of cake is often significantly affected by its pH. Thus, in the case of white cake with a given fineness of grain, lowering the pH by 0.2 units will perceptibly improve crumb whiteness. This pH effect can be produced by an appropriate leavener-bicarbonate balance as well as by leavener choice. Sodium acid pyrophosphate tends to buffer doughs and batters at a pH of about 7.3 to 7.5, and aluminum phosphate by 0.1 to 0.2 units lower. Calcium phosphate, on the other hand, exhibits a lesser buffering tendency and, hence, produces lower pH levels. If a pH of 7.0 or lower is desired in a baked product, combinations of calcium phosphate with either the sodium or aluminum leavening acids should be considered. Higher pH levels of around 9.0 are required for chocolate and devil's food type products to achieve optimum color and taste and can also be obtained by appropriate leavener-bicarbonate balances. The slightly bitter aftertaste ("pyro" taste) occasionally created by the residual salts of sodium pyrophosphate can be alleviated by providing a calcium ion source and is further masked by the sugar and flavoring normally added to the product formula.

8.J.1.f. Other ingredients

Chocolate, cocoa. The popular flavor of chocolate or cocoa (**Figure 8.063**) may be added to cake batter in one of several ways. In the case of chocolate, the material must first be fully melted, carried out in jacketed kettles — never over a direct fire — at moderate temperatures to avoid the development of burnt flavors. The hot melted chocolate should be brought down in temperature before addition to the cake batter to avoid curdling the proteins.

In the case of cocoa, the method of incorporation should be adapted to the type of batter being produced. The following procedures are recommended:

(a) For pound cakes and batter cakes made by the creaming method, the cocoa should be creamed with the sugar and shortening.

(b) For cakes made by the blending method with high-absorption shortenings, the cocoa should be blended with the shortening, flour and part of the sugar.

(c) For foam cakes, the cocoa should be blended with the flour and part of the sugar by sifting.

Humectants and water activity. Moist eating quality is highly desirable in cakes, but high water activity can prompt mold growth during shelf life. Cooper et al. (1966) studied the relationship between the mold-free shelf life of cakes and their equilibrium relative humidity (ERH), now better known as water activity (a_w). The a_w is the ratio of the vapor pressure of the moisture in the cake product to the vapor pressure of pure water. Each type of cake exhibits a specific relation between its moisture content and its a_w value, which is markedly affected by formula ingredients that reduce vapor pressure. It is possible, therefore, to modify the a_w of a cake by appropriate changes in its formulation on the basis of the known sucrose equivalents of individual ingredients. Humectant materials such as invert sugar, dextrose, sorbitol and glycerol are all more effective than sucrose on an equivalent weight basis in reducing the cake's a_w without a corresponding reduction of actual moisture content. Because most microorganisms require relatively high humidity conditions for growth, even a small reduction in a cake's a_w can become an important control factor in extending the products mold-free shelf life.

Zelch (2001a) observed that antimicrobial agents such as sodium propionate

Figure 8.063. Dutched cocoa alters the pH of cake batters, requiring changes in leavening choices.

or potassium sorbate can be added to cake formulations to extend mold-free shelf life, but that such preservatives should be used in conjunction with, not replacement of, other procedures to inhibit mold growth. These procedures include following appropriate sanitation practices and controlling temperature, product pH and water activity.

Modified starches, gums. Batter characteristics and final cake quality are both often improved by the use of hydrophilic materials such as chemically modified or pregelatinized starches and certain vegetable gums. Starches with relatively low gelatinization temperatures, which include potato starch and modified corn, tapioca and waxy maize starches, when added to the batter in amounts of 1 to 5%, will increase batter viscosity and improve the volume, symmetry, grain and texture of the resultant cakes. Similarly, pregelatinized modified waxy maize starch (Schiek 1966) and tapioca and wheat starches (Hahn 1969), when used at levels of 1 to 3%, facilitate control of batter properties and increase volume, improve crumb softness and extend shelf life of the cake product.

Boettger (1963) investigated the effects of pregelatinized starches on cake quality, using a modified waxy maize starch as the test ingredient. He observed that the addition of 3.0 to 3.5% of the pregelatinized starch effectively increased moisture absorption and yielded batters with higher viscosities and lower specific gravities. This, in turn, resulted in improved cake scores, higher moisture contents, and better moisture retention in the finished cake. Dubois (1961) found a marked improvement in cake quality when a poor-quality cake flour was replaced by as much as 50% of wheat starch in a cake formula.

Cellulose gum (carboxymethylcellulose, or CMC) is a highly hydrophilic material that is used in cake batters as a viscosity stabilizer and moisture absorbent. Average use levels are between 0.25 to 0.375%, based on flour, and generally, the liquid in the batter must be increased at a rate of 30 to 50 oz for each ounce of CMC added (Dubois 1966).

Young and Bayfield (1963) compared the effects of different hydrophilic colloids in white layer cakes. They found that the addition of 0.1% of CMC produced the highest cake scores both in the freshly baked cake and after storage (unwrapped) for 48 hours. Of the other hydrocolloids tested, 0.2% gum tragacanth, 0.2% gum arabic and 0.1% carrageenan all produced better cakes than the controls, whereas agar at 0.1% produced no measurable improvement after 48 hours of storage.

Hydrophilic gums may prove useful in overcoming certain cake defects, such as the one described by Trimbo et al. (1966) in white and yellow layer cakes made from mixes. The defect assumed the form of a surface ring that appeared at the periphery of the pan about 2 minutes after the start of baking and migrated toward the center, while shrinking in diameter, until it became stationary after about 7 minutes of baking. The ring exhibited a rough surface above a weak structure and craters that earlier had surrounded large gas bubbles. The surface ring was produced by an upward movement of the cake batter from the bottom and along the outer edge of the pan, when it turned toward the center and across the top of the cake, and then downward again. This batter flow resulted from the natural convection currents that are caused by differences in batter density produced by lateral and vertical temperature gradients within the heated batter. Ring formation could be prevented by adding 0.5% (based on flour) guar or cellulose gums that bind the water, increase batter viscosity and prevent lateral batter flow.

Yeast. Yes, some cake-like baked foods are made with yeast as the leavener. These products include baba, a brioche soaked in rum, and many Italian specialties such as panetone, discussed in this chapter along with variety breads.

8.J.2. Formula balance

The rules of formula balance for cakes take into consideration the ratios, first, of sugar to flour; second, of shortening to eggs; and third, of liquids to solids. These rules pertain to the heavier, shortening based cakes. Foam cakes use somewhat different ratios that relate sugar to eggs and liquids to solids but tend to count sugar among the liquids (**Table 8.063**).

Table 8.063. Formula Balance for Cakes

(Based on weight)

Modernized "pound" cake

Sugar	equals	flour.
Shortening or butter	equals	eggs.
Liquids (milk + eggs)	equals	flour or sugar.

High-ratio cake

Sugar	more than	flour.
Eggs	more than	shortening.
Liquids (milk + eggs)	slightly more than	sugar.

Low-ratio cake*

Sugar	less than or equal to	flour.
Eggs	equals	shortening.
Total liquids	equals	liquid eggs + liquid milk
Total liquids	greater than or equal to	sugar.

Foam cake

Sugar	equals	egg whites.
Flour	about 33% of	sugar.

Sponge cake

Sugar	equals or slightly exceeds	whole eggs.
Liquids (milk + eggs)	exceed by 25%	sugar.
Either sugar or whole eggs	more than	flour.
Eggs + flour	more than	sugar + liquids (except eggs).

** Adapted from Zelch (2001a)*

8.J.2.a. Shortening emulsion cakes

Among the earliest examples of an aerated batter cake with an acceptable quality is the original pound cake whose household recipe called for equal amounts of flour, butter, sugar and eggs. In adapting this cake to commercial baking, bakers found that not only were the cake's volume, grain and texture improved by modifying the mixing method and by reducing the levels of eggs and butter or shortening but also the cost was cut as well. The following rules of formula balance evolved at this stage for the **modernized "pound" cake**:

(a) The weight of sugar should equal the weight of the flour.

(b) The weight of butter or shortening should equal the weight of the eggs.

(c) The liquid ingredients (milk and eggs) should equal the weight of the flour or sugar.

While these early rules established definite quantitative ratios between sugar and flour, shortening and eggs, and the liquid ingredients and flour or sugar, they did not relate the sugar to eggs, on the one hand, and the shortening to sugar, on the other. As a result, pound cakes were marketed that varied considerably in composition. Brooke (1934), for example, in examining 6 commercial pound cake formulations, found the ingredient levels to range, on a flour-weight basis, from 79 to 120% for sugar, 45 to 68% for shortening, 46 to 120% for eggs and 22.5 to 70% for milk.

By the mid-1930s, several flour mills introduced special cake flours milled from selected soft wheats and incorporating only the best patent streams. These flours ranged in protein content from 7 to 9%, with an ash content of 0.3%, and were chlorinated and also bleached with benzoyl peroxide for optimal whiteness (Loving and Brenneis 1981). Such flours tolerated higher levels of liquids than did earlier cake flours and yielded cakes of superior eating quality. Shortening manufacturers developed improved cake shortenings that, at first, contained mono- and diglycerides as emulsifiers and, subsequently, other surfactants as well. The newer shortenings permitted incorporation of higher liquid levels and produced more stable batters with a finer and more uniform dispersion of the fat and air phases than was possible with non-emulsifier shortenings. This style of bakery shortening enabled bakers to make richer cakes, with higher moisture contents and extended shelf life. These cakes were commonly referred to as high-ratio or high-absorption cakes.

The first rule of formula balance relates sugar to flour. To exploit the potential offered by these improved ingredients, the rules of formula balance were modified as follows for the **high-ratio cake**:

(a) The weight of the sugar should exceed that of the flour.

(b) The weight of the eggs should exceed that of the shortening.

(c) The weight of liquids (in eggs, milk or added water) should exceed slightly the weight of the sugar.

The term "low-ratio cake" refers to a formulation in which total sugars are less than or equal to flour in weight, as explained by Zelch (2001a). These cakes are typical of traditional or old-fashioned products. They tend to be less sweet and have a firmer, less tender texture and a low finished moisture content.

The second rule of formula balance specifies that the weight of the shortening not exceed that of the eggs. In regular cakes, the toughening effect of egg proteins must be counterbalanced by the tenderizing action of an appropriate amount of fat. With non-emulsifier hydrogenated shortening, it was a common practice to hold to a ratio of 1:1 for the shortening and eggs to attain the desired degree of crumb tenderness. However, as modern emulsifier shortenings show more effective tenderizing action, their level is usually reduced by 15 to 20% below that of the eggs.

The above considerations are valid when whole eggs are used. With either egg whites or egg yolks, appropriate adjustments are required. Egg whites average 13% higher in moisture and 1.7% lower in protein, compared with whole eggs. Hence, for best results, either the shortening level must be reduced somewhat, or the amount of egg whites has to be increased proportionally. Yolks, on the other hand, contain some 20% more lipids and some 24% less moisture than whole eggs. Where yolks constitute the main egg product in a cake formula, this difference in composition must be taken into account in establishing the proper fat-to-egg ratio. In regular yellow and white cakes, the shortening content will range from 35 to 50% based on flour. On this basis, and in order to maintain the desired ratio, the amount of eggs should exceed the shortening level. However, because eggs generally constitute the costliest ingredient, the usual practice is to keep their proportion in the formula to the minimum level imposed by the shortening content.

The third rule of formula balance specifies that the weight of the combined liquid eggs and milk, or any added water, be equal to or exceed slightly the weight of the sugar. Liquids, in the sense used here, comprise the actual liquid ingredients rather than their moisture contents only. In cakes made with non-emulsifier shortening, the milk and eggs are used in a ratio of 1:1, and their combined weight about equals that of the flour. In cakes made with emulsifier shortenings, the amount of milk is often double that of eggs, and their combined weights may reach a ratio to flour as high as 1.65:1. This ability to carry increased levels of liquids distinguishes modern cake flours and emulsifier-type shortenings from their earlier versions.

The incorporation of an optimum amount of liquid is essential to good cake quality. Cakes in which an insufficient amount of liquids has been used are characterized by a harsh texture, a dry crumb and impaired palatability. On the other hand, excessive amounts of liquids will weaken the crumb structure and produce cakes of low volume caused either by a failure of the batter to rise adequately in the oven or by a collapse subsequent to a satisfactory rise.

Fluid shortenings normally contain a highly efficient emulsifier system so their use in cake baking generally requires some minor adjustments in the formulations. Lawson (1970) found that white, yellow and devil's food cakes are all improved when the fluid shortening level is reduced by 10% compared with plastic shortening, the liquids increased to 1.5 times the weight of flour and the amount of baking powder decreased by 25%. He further found that white cake quality is improved by replacing 10% of the egg whites with whole eggs.

Urban (1975) observed that the excessive tenderness that develops in cakes when plastic shortening is replaced by fluid shortening in commercial practice can be corrected by reducing the shortening and baking powder levels by 5% and 20%, respectively, and by increasing the amount of water by 6%. Increasing the level of eggs will generally accomplish the same purpose. The batter should be mixed, to a specific gravity of 0.90, and the addition of 5% pregelatinized starch to the formula further adds firmness to the crumb.

8.J.2.b. Egg foam cakes

The discussion thus far has centered on balancing the formulations of the more complex shortening-based cakes. The need for adhering to a proper balancing of the formula is no less great for foam-type cakes such as angel food and sponge cakes. The general rules that apply to **angel food cake** may be stated as follows:

(a) The weight of the sugar should equal the weight of the egg whites.

(b) The weight of the flour should approximate one-third the weight of the sugar.

Angel food cake is thus seen to be based essentially on the rather simple formula of one part flour to three parts each of egg whites and sugar.

Sponge cakes differ from angel food cakes mainly in their use of whole eggs rather than just of egg whites. In balancing their formulations, one of the aims is to dilute the toughening effect of the whole eggs by incorporating an amount of sugar that will adequately serve that purpose, with an appropriate amount of liquids. The applicable rules for **sponge cakes** may be summarized as follows:

(a) The amount of sugar should either equal or slightly exceed the amount of whole eggs.

(b) The combined weights of the liquid in whole eggs and milk, or water, should exceed the weight of the sugar by a ratio of 1.25:1.

(c) The weight of either the sugar or the whole eggs should exceed that of the flour.

(d) The combined weights of the eggs and flour should exceed the combined weights of the sugar and liquids other than whole eggs (milk or water).

8.J.2.c. Adaptations

While the formula balance rules are based both on broad empirical data and exacting experimental studies, they are by no means inflexible and do, therefore, permit adaptations to changing requirements. It is advisable, however, to avoid drastic modifications if cakes of good volume and symmetry, eating quality and shelf life are to result.

Davies (1937) studied the effects of gross variations in ingredient ratios, with the following results: When the sugar level was increased by 25%, the crumb grain became courser and less uniform, the cake volume increased slightly, and the texture became more tender than in the control; decreasing the sugar content by 25%, on the other hand, yielded a finer grain, a smaller cake volume and a slightly tougher and tighter texture. A 25% increase in the shortening level over the control resulted in no perceptible change in the grain of the cake but caused a slight reduction in its volume and imparted a greasy mouthfeel; a decrease of 25% in the shortening level produced the same or slightly coarser grain than the control, an increase in cake volume, and a tight, harsh texture. An increase in the liquids of 25% over the control cake resulted in a finer grain, a smaller volume and a more moist and tender crumb; when the liquids were reduced by 25%, the grain became coarse and less uniform, the cake volume increased, and the texture turned tight and dry. When baking powder was increased by 50%, the results were a somewhat coarser but uniform grain, a larger volume and a harsh and dry texture; with a 50% reduction in baking powder, the resultant cake possessed a fine, close grain, a smaller volume, and a tight and slightly soggy texture. These results are summarized in **Table 8.064**.

More recently, Ngo and Taranto (1986) measured the effects of different sucrose levels on the rheological properties of cakes. They observed that a reduction in sucrose by 30% below the standard sugar level yielded final cakes that were less tender, more elastic and had a smaller volume than the control cakes. They further concluded that the proteins in the batter — derived from flour, the milk and eggs — function as plasticizers and contribute to the tenderness and reduced elasticity in the final cake.

8.J.3. Formulating specifics

8.J.3.a. Conventional and high-ratio cakes

Cakes based on the structuring effect of shortenings are often termed "batter" cakes to differentiate them from "foam" cakes. Zelch (2001a) divided the batter cake category into "layer" cakes, which are chemically leavened, and pound cakes, which leavened only by the air entrapped in the batter during mixing.

Representative formulations for **yellow and white cakes** are given in **Table 8.065** and **Table 8.066**. These basic formulations can be readily modified by the use of

Table 8.064. Effects in Ingredient Level Changes in Cakes

Ingredient	Change	Effect on crumb	Effect on volume	Effect on texture
Sugar	Increase 25%	Coarser, less uniform	Increased slightly	More tender
Sugar	Decrease 25%	Finer grain	Smaller volume	Slightly tougher, tighter
Shortening	Increase 25%	No perceptible change	Decreased slightly	Greasy mouthfeel
Shortening	Decrease 25%	Same or slighly coarser	Increased	Tight, harsh
Liquids	Increase 25%	Finer grain	Smaller volume	More tender, moist
Liquids	Decrease 25%	Coarser, less uniform	Increased	Tight, dry
Baking powder	Increase 50%	Coarser but uniform	Increased	Harsh, dry
Baking powder	Decrease 50%	Fine, close	Smaller volume	Tight, slightly soggy

(Davies 1937)

Table 8.065. Representative Formulations for Various Types of Yellow Cake

Ingredient*	Ordinary yellow cake**	High-absorption loaf cake***	High-absorption layer cake***	Fluid shortening layer cake†
Sugar	25.5	29.6	29.8	25.1
Flour	29.8	22.5	21.2	21.4
Shortening	13.4	11.4	11.6	12.8
Whole eggs	14.8	11.4	12.6	19.5
Milk	14.8	22.5	22.2	18.8
Baking powder	0.7	1.3	1.3	1.1
Salt	0.6	0.8	0.8	0.8
Flavor	0.4	0.5	0.5	0.5
TOTAL	100.0	100.0	100.0	100.0

** Ingredients expressed as % of total batter weight*

*** Made with regular hydrogenated shortening*

**** Made with emulsifier shortening*

† Adapted from Urban (1975)

optional ingredients such as fruits, nuts, spices, cocoa, flavorings and so forth. The minor variations in the formulations for yellow layer cake and loaf cake, both made with high-absorption shortening, take into account the fact that layer cakes require less structural strength than loaf cakes and, for this reason, can tolerate somewhat higher levels of both liquids and sugar. The formula for the layer cake made with fluid shortening, on the other hand, deviates considerably from the other formulations in several respects, reflecting the difference in functionality of fluid shortening, compared with plastic shortening. The composition of white cake is quite similar to that of yellow cake, except that the whole eggs or egg yolks are replaced by 25% to 35% higher levels of egg whites.

Bar or block cakes, a conventional product popular internationally, is a form of low-ratio cake that balances sugar at 75% of flour weight. During mixing, shortening is withheld until the last stages (Anon. 1999b).

Madeira cakes, more commonly found in international markets, are fairly heavy cakes with lots of egg, 65% or more (flour weight basis). The formula is rich in shortening (61%) and high in sugar (105%). It uses milk powder and water instead of liquid milk, and a special emulsifier system has been developed

Table 8.066. Representative Formulations for Different Types of White Cake

Ingredient*	Ordinary white cake**	High-absorption white cake***
Sugar	25.8	29.3
Flour	25.8	20.3
Shortening	13.0	11.5
Egg whites	17.8	15.7
Milk	15.4	20.0
Baking powder	0.9	1.3
Salt	0.5	0.8
Flavor	0.5	0.5
TOTAL	100.0	100.0

Ingredients expressed as % of total batter weight

**Made with regular hydrogenated shortening*

***Made with emulsifier shortening*

Table 8.067. Categories of Cocoa and Chocolate Cakes

Ingredient	Devil's food cake	Fudge cake	Chocolate cake	Milk chocolate cake
Flour weight basis (bakers %)				
Flour	100	100	100	100
Sugar	170	193	160	160
Shortening	75	65	48	55
Eggs, whole	90	80	60	60
Cocoa, natural	48	48	–	–
Chocolate liquor	–	–	48	25
Nonfat dry milk solids	20	20	17	50
Water	150	152	128	130
Salt	3.75	3.75	3.75	3.75
Soda	3.75	1.25	0.75	0.75
Baking powder	–	3	3.75	3.75
Formula % basis				
Flour	15.1	15.0	17.6	17.0
Sugar	25.8	29.0	28.1	27.2
Shortening	11.4	9.8	8.4	9.4
Eggs, whole	13.6	12.0	10.5	10.2
Cocoa, natural	7.3	7.2	–	–
Chocolate liquor	–	–	8.4	4.2
Nonfat dry milk solids	3.0	3.0	3.0	8.4
Water	22.7	22.8	22.5	22.2
Salt	0.55	0.56	0.68	0.64
Soda	0.55	0.19	0.16	0.12
Baking powder	–	0.45	0.68	0.64

(Schaal and Montminy 1946)

to help blend the water and margarine in the first mixing stage (Anon. 1999b).

Chocolate cakes were classified by Schaal and Montminy (1946) into the basic categories of devil's food cake, fudge cake, chocolate cake, and milk chocolate cake. Representative formulations for these basic types are given in **Table 8.067**, offered in both bakers and formula percent style. The same authors also provided details of the procedures to be followed in combining and mixing the various ingredients.

When choosing cocoa for the formulation of devil's food or fudge cakes, either Dutched or natural cocoa may be used. Because natural cocoa does not receive the alkali treatment that Dutched cocoa does, minor adjustments are required in leavening to reach the correct pH level. Zelch (2001a) explained that when using natural cocoa, baking soda (sodium bicarbonate) is added, and the amount required can be estimated by multiplying the percentage of natural cocoa by a factor of about 0.07. Because the soda provided leavening action, the amount of baking powder can be reduced.

If substituting cocoa for chocolate, or vice versa, an adjustment in shortening will be required because cocoa contains considerably less fat than chocolate, with average figures being 20% fat for cocoa and 50 to 55% fat for chocolate. Also to be taken into account is the fact that cocoa butter possesses only half the shortening power of partially hydrogenated shortening. Hence, the addition of 3 oz of hydrogenated shortening, which is equivalent to one-half the difference between the respective fat contents, to 10 oz of cocoa powder will convert the latter into a chocolate substitute that is equal in shortening and flavor value to true chocolate.

Table 8.068 provides

guidance for making the substitution of cocoa for chocolate and vice versa. These figures are based on 1 lb of chocolate liquor (54% fat content) equaling 8.25 oz cocoa powder (10% to 12% fat content) and 7.75 oz cocoa butter. On the basis of equal functionality in a cookie or cake, the weight of cocoa plus plastic shortening is 75% of the weight of chocolate liquor. Thus the rules of substitution are:

To substitute cocoa for chocolate liquor. Multiply the weight of the chocolate liquor to be replaced by 10 ÷ 16 (or 0.625) and add shortening equal to one-half the weight difference. On a per-pound basis, this means that each pound of chocolate liquor is replaced by 10 oz of cocoa and 3 oz of shortening.

To substitute chocolate liquor for cocoa. Multiply the weight of the cocoa to be replaced by 16 ÷ 10 (or 1.6) and reduce the formula shortening by an amount that is equal to one-half the weight difference. Hence, on a per pound basis, cocoa is replaced by 26 oz of chocolate liquor, and 15 oz of shortening (one-half of 10-oz weight difference) is withheld from the batch for each pound of cocoa being replaced.

In the US, federal Standards of Identity strictly define chocolate and differentiate it from cocoa. These differences must be kept in mind when labeling the finished product because it is not legal to designate a cake as chocolate cake if, in fact, cocoa instead has been used in its production.

Cocoa extenders. The relatively high cost of chocolate and cocoa products and the often severe price fluctuations associated with them have led to periodic efforts to develop so-called "extenders" of various types. Their chief aim is to bring about meaningful cost savings without perceptibly altering the properties and flavor characteristics normally associated with cocoa and chocolate. Materials used in varying amounts for this purpose include powdered forms of caramel color, black malt and various other materials (Sterk 2009), plus dark molasses solids and roasted defatted wheat germ.

Among the most widely-used chocolate extenders is carob powder. It is the ground product obtained from the dried pod of an evergreen tree, *Ceratonia siliqua*, native to the Mediterranean region. The bean-like pod, which grows to a length of 4 to 12 in., is also known as St. John's Bread or locust bean, and its flinty brown seeds are the source of locust bean gum. By harvest time in the fall, the pods become quite dry, with a deep brown color and a pleasant sweet flavor. On roasting and grinding, they acquire a color and flavor that are markedly similar to cocoa. Commercial carob powder, processed from carefully roasted carob pods from which the seeds have been removed, is available, in various color grades that range from a light brown to very dark brown. It is free of theobromine, the stimulant of chocolate, its fat content is quiet low at about 1.5%, and it contains

Table 8.068. Chocolate and Cocoa Conversion Values

For chocolate weighing:	To replace chocolate with cocoa, use cocoa (10 to 12% fat) weighing:	And increase shortening by:
8 oz	4 oz	2 oz
1 lb	8 oz	4 oz
2 lb	1 lb	8 oz
4 lb	2 lb 1 oz	15 oz
10 lb	5 lb 3 oz	2 lb 7 oz

For cocoa (10 to 12% fat) weighing:	To replace cocoa with chocolate, use chocolate weighing:	And decrease shortening by:
8 oz	1 lb	4 oz
1 lb	1 lb 15 oz	7 oz
2 lb	3 lb 14 oz	14 oz
4 lb	7 lb 12 oz	1 lb 13 oz
10 lb	19 lb 6 oz	4 lb 8 oz

some 40% natural sugars. It is used normally to replace 20% of cocoa, although its use level may reach as high as 50% in certain applications.

8.J.3.b. Low-calorie cakes

Formulation of reduced- or low-calorie cakes takes advantage of the sugar replacement ability of fructose, in the form of high-fructose corn syrup (HFCS), and the fact that surfactants and emulsifiers can replace a major portion, if not all, of the shortening in cakes. Fructose, with a generally accepted sweetness rating 1.7 times that of sucrose, may replace 2 times its weight of sucrose in cake without a perceptible loss of sweetness in the finished product and thereby cut the cake's sucrose level in half.

According to Jackel (1980), sugar in a typical white cake formula contributes about 32.3% of the total calories, shortening about 37.7%, flour about 25% and the remaining ingredients about 5%. By cutting the sugar level in half, the caloric value of the cake would thus be reduced by about 16% — not enough to justify a claim for a low-calorie cake. To achieve that goal, the level of shortening would also need to be reduced considerably. Experimental studies with surfactants have demonstrated their ability to assume the functional role formerly attributed exclusively to shortening. Jackel (1980) went on to report that the caloric content of a typical white cake could be cut by 34% by (a) replacing 90% of the shortening with 4% of surfactant, (b) increasing the moisture content by approximately 50%, (c) adding α-cellulose and xanthan gum to stabilize the extra water and (d) increasing the level of egg whites to 12%.

Working with a high-ratio yellow layer cake, Kamel and Washnuik (1983) reduced the caloric value by (a) replacing the shortening with 3.8% emulsifier, (b) lowering the egg content by 50% and (c) cutting the sugar level by 20%. The quality of the resulting cake remained equal to, or even surpassed, that of the control cakes. The specific emulsifiers used for these tests were a textured water dispersion of 32% sorbitan monostearate and 8% polysorbate 60, and a textured hydrated blend of mono- and diglycerides, polysorbate 60 and sodium stearoyl lactylate.

8.J.3.c. Angel food

Angel food cake, a foam cake, has one of the simplest formulations because it calls for only 3 basic ingredients: egg whites, sugar and flour, with their respective approximate ratios being 42:42:15. Also included are minor amounts of salt, cream of tartar (an acidifier) and flavoring. As a rule, soft wheat patent flours of 40 to 50% extraction are most suitable for foam-type cakes. It is well known that bleached flour increases the volume of angel food cakes, and Ngo et al. (1985) demonstrated this increase using rheological properties.

A representative angel food formula is shown in **Table 8.069**. In addition to the conventional angel cake, a number of variations have gained popular acceptance, including cakes that contain ground orange rind, minced nut meats, spice mixtures with molasses or cocoa.

Egg whites are naturally alkaline, and bakers need to add a small amount of acidifying materials to the whites to increase their foaming capacity, improve their foam stability and brighten the whiteness of the foam. The most common choice of acidifier is potassium acid tartrate, or tartaric acid. Grewe and Child (1930), in their pioneering study on the effects of tartaric acid on angel food quality, found that its addition resulted in fine-grained white cakes, while its omission produced cakes with a yellowish color, coarse grain, thick cell walls and a tough texture. They observed similar improvements in grain and color with citric and acetic acids and concluded that these effects were due largely to a reduction of the pH to an optimum range of 5.0 to 6.6. This range is normally attained by adding 1.5 to 1.75% tartaric acid, based on the weight of the egg whites.

Acid addition to angel food cakes, according to Barmore (1936b), accomplishes dual functions: (a) to stabilize the foam sufficiently so it will not collapse in the oven before the temperature of coagulation is reached, and (b) to prevent the drastic shrinkage of the foam during the last stage of baking and during subsequent cooling. The first function ensures a fine, even grain, while the second promotes maximum cake volume.

Egg whites subjected to extended storage undergo an increase in pH that may reach as high as 9.6. Under such conditions, the level of added tartaric acid will have to be increased incrementally to arrive at the optimum pH in the egg foam. The functional properties of egg whites are impaired by prolonged storage. This adverse effect happens because egg proteins hydrolyze occurs on aging, resulting in some liquefaction of the whites. Kahlenberg (1948) compared the performance of whites separated from eggs held at the summer temperature of 30°C (86°F) for periods of 0, 4 and 9 hours, and 3 to 6 days after gathering, respectively, and then stored at the refrigerator temperature of 7°C (44°F). Baking tests showed that the whites from eggs held at 30°C (86°F) for 3 to 6 days produced cakes with an objectionably coarse and heavy cell structure, compared with the fine, feathery light textures obtained with whites from eggs that were placed under refrigeration the same day they were gathered.

The ultimate quality of angel food cake is affected significantly by the care with which the operator attends to seemingly minor, but nonetheless important, details of ingredient handling and processing. Some of these have been discussed at length by Hurley (1967) and Borders (1968). While it is true that egg whites of comparable quality will whip into a foam of nearly the same volume over a temperature range of 7 to 24°C (45 to 75°F), maximum specific volume will be more rapidly attained at the lower temperatures. Angel food batters with final temperatures of 21 to 24°C (70 to 75°F) will be found to yield best results. To arrive at these optimum temperatures, the initial temperature of the egg white should be within the range of 17 to 22°C (62 to 72°F).

The air incorporated into the angel food batter serves as the sole leavening agent so the role of the developing vapor pressure is critical to the cake's volume and texture. When batters with too low temperatures (below 18°C, or 65°F) reach the oven, adequate vapor pressure may not develop in their interior until after the crust has formed. This results in cakes with a very tight grain and reduced volume. On the other hand, batter temperatures above 27°C (80°F) produce cakes with an open grain, large air pockets and cracks in the top crust. These defects are the result of excessive volume expansion before the cake has set in the oven. The effects of egg white temperatures on whipping time, batter temperature and finished cake volume are given in **Table 8.070**.

Different investigators have at various times recommended temperatures and oven times for the baking of angel food cake that differ over a broad range. In practice, however, the most general advice for obtaining optimum cake quality is to combine the highest temperature consistent with the size and shape of the cake with the shortest oven time. While the majority of angel cakes are baked in tube pans, which provide a more efficient heat distribution within the batter as well as additional inter-

Table 8.069. Angel Food Cake Formula	
Ingredient	Amount (formula %)
Flour	15.000
Sugar	41.500
Egg white	41.500
Salt	0.575
Cream of tartar	0.626
Vanilla	0.800

nal support that promotes cake volume expansion, excellent cakes are also obtained with many other types of baking pans.

Recommended temperatures are 177 to 182°C (350 to 360°F) for larger cakes (22 to 26 oz) and 191 to 204°C (375 to 400°F) for smaller cakes (10 to 14 oz). Temperatures of 204 to 219°C (400 to 425°F) are best for maximum moisture retention, but they may cause a premature setting of the crust that can result in reduced cake volume or splits in the final crust. Barmore (1936b) subjected a series of cakes to baking temperatures of 138 to 180°C (280 to 356°F) and showed that the higher temperature range produced cakes of greater volume and improved tenderness. The relationships that exist between the baking temperature, baking time, cake volume and moisture retention of angel food cake are shown in **Table 8.071**.

Properly processed dried egg white solids are successful as the sole egg ingredient in angel food cake. Prior to use, the egg white solids are often reconstituted into liquid whites by mixing them with 6 to 7 parts by weight of water and letting the mixture stand for about 3 hours to ensure complete hydration.

A more effective procedure, according to Robertson and Haney (1963), is to dry-blend the egg white solids with other dry ingredients (half of the formula sugar and the cream of tartar) and then combine this blend with one-third of the total water in the mixing bowl. The remaining water is added in portions, and whipping is continued at high speed until a stiff peak results. The balance of the sugar is then incorporated into the meringue with the flour. The addition of small amounts of whipping aids such as sodium lauryl sulfate will prove helpful in obtaining maximum foam volumes. Aside from a small reduction in the level of the cream of tartar, no other formula adjustments are required when using dried egg white solids.

Egg white solids perform equally satisfactorily with continuous batter mixing systems. In such applications, best results are obtained when the specific gravities are held to 0.86 to 0.90 in the slurry stage, and to 0.28 to 0.32 in the final batter. The temperature of the slurry should preferably be held at 10°C (50°F) or lower.

A more moist and close-grained crumb is obtained with incremental addition of water to the egg whites during the whipping stage. The maximum amount of

Table 8.070. Effects of Egg White Temperature on Whipping Time, Batter Temperature and Cake Volume

Egg white temperature		Whipping time	Batter temperature		Cake volume
°F	°C	(minutes)	°F	°C	(cu cm)
32	0	8	50	10	1,920
42	8	7	67	19	2,110
52	11	6	69	21	2,230
62	17	5.5	71	22	2,490
72	22	5.5	74	23	2,450
82	28	6	78	26	2,360

(Borders 1968)

Table 8.071. Effect of Baking Temperature on Angel Food Cake Quality

Egg white temperature		Baking time	Cake volume	Cake moisture
°F	°C	(minutes)	(cu cm)	(%)
325	163	45	2,440	28.8
350	177	40	2,520	29.7
375	190	35	2,600	30.6
400	204	30	2,690	31.4
425	219	25	2,760	32.3
450	232	21	2,790	32.9

(Borders 1968)

water that can be added is limited to 2 oz per lb of whites. While this practice reduces the cake volume slightly, it does yield cakes with a closer grain and a more moist crumb. The uniformity of the cake's cell structure may be improved by slightly tapping the filled pans before they enter the oven. This procedure, while it causes a slight, and generally acceptable, loss of volume, will eliminate any large air pockets within the batter that often survive baking to appear as unsightly holes in the crumb of the baked cake.

Excessive browning of the cake crust can either be avoided or ameliorated by wetting the interior surface of the pans prior to filling them with batter. The application of moisture to the pans sufficiently delays the rise of the surface temperature to the caramelization level to bring about a lighter crust color.

A frequent problem encountered in angel food cake production is the formation of indentations in the top crust of the cake, a condition referred to as "cupping." This condition is thought to arise from excessive richness of the formula (Robertson and Haney 1963) and can be essentially eliminated by a moderate increase in the flour level. Hurley (1967) further showed that the flour protein content should not be diluted below the 5.3% level and that the total batter protein content should not decline below 4.7%, if the problem of cupping is to be effectively avoided.

Dubois (1959) observed improvements in angel cake quality when up to 30% of the formula flour is replaced by wheat starch. Such substitution results in an increase in cake volume, enhanced grain, texture and eating properties, and an improved freshness retention.

Because egg white performance is so critical to angel food cakes, mixing equipment and utensils must be completely free of any fats or oils, which are detrimental to the egg foam.

8.J.3.d. Sponge

A second type of foam cake is important in commercial baking: the sponge cake, which forms the basis for many small snack cakes (**Figure 8.064**). Also using the protein of eggs as their structural component, sponge cakes are made with whole eggs and often supplemented with egg yolks. Sometimes fats are blended into the batter after initial mixing to further enrich the product.

8.J.3.e. Chiffon cakes

Cakes made with fluid shortenings or liquid oils are sometimes called "chiffon cakes," the name given them by their inventor, who baked them for a famous restaurant in Hollywood, CA, according to Corriher (2008). He achieved the cake's unique texture by substituting vegetable oil for the solid shortening normally used.

Figure 8.064. Many snack cakes are made from sponge cake batters.

Chiffon cakes, in common with angel food cake, depend for their aeration or leavening on the foaming properties of egg whites. Both contain egg whites, flour and sugar as their basic ingredients, but unlike angel cakes, chiffon cakes also contain both egg yolks and fat. The latter normally is a liquid vegetable oil. A representative formula for chiffon cake is given in **Table 8.072**.

Table 8.072. Chiffon Cake Formula

Ingredient	% (batch weight)
Egg yolk	10.750
Oil	10.750
Egg whites	32.000
Salt	0.375
Granulated sugar	16.000
Cake flour	14.000
Powdered sugar	16.000
Cream of tartar	0.125

(Borders 1968)

Both the sequence and method of combining and mixing the ingredients are critical in the production of chiffon cake. First, the egg whites and salt are whipped into a soft foam, followed by the addition of the cream of tartar and the granulated sugar, with continued beating until a soft peak is obtained. In a second bowl, the yolks are whipped, with the slow addition of the oil, into a uniform, well-aerated mixture. The yolk and oil mixture is then carefully folded into the meringue with a minimum of mixing. The sifted blend of the powdered sugar and flour is then folded into the egg mixture.

8.J.3.f. Fruit cakes

Most fruit cakes employ their batters as a glue to hold together the overwhelming weight of candied and/or dried fruits and nutmeats. The use of bread flour strengthens the weaker cake flour by adding gluten to the structure. **Table 8.073** offers the formulations for both the traditional dark, rich style and a lighter version.

8.J.4. Batter specific gravity

Control over the specific gravity of a cake batter provides essential control over the finished results. Specific gravity is defined as the ratio of the weight of a known volume of a substance at a given temperature to the weight of an equal volume of a standard substance, usually water at the same temperature, when systems comprising liquids, solids, and gases are involved. It is expressed by the equation:

$$S = W_s \div W_w$$

where S = specific gravity; W_s = weight of the substance; and W_w = weight of an equal volume of water. The equation can also be expressed in terms of density (weight per unit volume) as:

$$S = D_s \div D_w$$

where S = specific gravity; D_s = density of the substance; and D_w = density of water. The density of water is 1 g per cu cm (62.4 lb per cu ft) at 4°C (39°F), making the specific gravity of water equal to 1. (Ice floats in water because its specific gravity is 0.915, lower than that of water.)

Batter specific gravity indicates the degree of its aeration and has a direct relation to the volume, tenderness, and quality of grain and texture in the finished cake. To attain the optimum quality potential of any given cake product, the optimum specific gravity for its batter system needs first to be established. Burns (1970) recommended the following specific gravity and batter temperature ranges, respectively: devil's food cake, 0.950 to 1.00 and 21 to 22°C (70 to 72°F); sponge cake, 0.800 to 0.825 and 14 to 15.5°C (58 to 60°F); and yellow cake, 0.850 to 0.875 and 18 to 19°C (65 to 67°F).

In general, optimum specific gravities of batters prepared with plastic shortenings tend to be noticeably higher than those of batters with fluid shortening. The greater degree of crystallization in plastic and solid shortenings, compared with fluid shortenings, as well as the presence of emulsifiers enhances the fat's aeration ability.

Table 8.073. Fruit Cake Formulations

Ingredient	Amount (bakers %)	Procedure
Rich fruit cake		
Brown sugar	73.0	Cream on second speed until
Bakers flour	30.0	moderately light
Cake margarine	73.0	
Glycerine	6.0	
Parisian essence	4.0	
Eggs, whole	77.0	Gradually add on low speed.
Bakers flour	70.0	Add sifted ingredients; mix until clear.
Baking powder	0.7	Scrape during mixing.
Nutmeg	0.7	
Mixed spice	2.1	
Ginger, ground	1.4	
Sultanas (raisins)	310.0	Add slowly and blend on low until
Chopped almonds	30.0	evenly dispersed.
Mixed dried fruit	267.0	

Scale 2,100 g (74 oz) in 200 x 75 mm (8 x 3 in.) pan and bake approximately 3 hours at 150°C (302°F).

Ingredient	Amount (bakers %)	Procedure
Light fruit cake		
Bread flour	100.0	Mix to a crumble.
Sugar, superfine granulated (castor sugar)	108.0	Do not mix to a paste.
Milk powder	8.4	
Salt	4.4	
Starch, pregelatinized	8.4	
Cake margarine	92.0	
Eggs, whole	100.0	Add gradually. Scrape down.
Egg color	0.2	Mix on medium speed for 7 minutes.
Vanilla extract	0.5	
Water	51.0	Mix on low speed while adding. Blend thoroughly.
Cake flour	50.0	Sift together and add.
Baking powder	1.5	Blend until smooth on low speed. Add on low speed.
Sultanas (raisins)	175.0	Mix only until evenly dispersed.

Scale 1,500 g (53 oz) in a 200 x 75 mm (8 x 3 in.) pan and bake 2 hours at 150°C (302°F).

(Anon. 1999b)

Table 8.074. Comparisons of Conventional Cake Batters and Slurries						
Cake variety	Batter weight		Specific gravity		Mixing time	
	Batter (lb)	Slurry (lb)	Batter	Slurry	Batter (minutes)	Slurry (minutes)
Angel food	212	580	0.30	0.82	18	4.5
Sponge	459	670	0.65	0.95	18	4.0
Chiffon	248	670	0.35	0.95	20	5.0
Pound	496	672	0.71	0.98	17	5.0
Chocolate layer	637	700	0.93	0.99	15	4.0
Yellow layer	637	672	0.90	0.98	15	4.0
Devil's food	670	785	0.95	1.11	17	5.0

(Bonavia 1963)

These specific gravity values are noted in (**Table 8.074**).

Specific gravities that exceed the optimum range usually result in cakes that have reduced volumes, dense grain and tough eating qualities, whereas those below the optimum range tend to produce cakes with dips on the surface and with very fragile and crumbly crumbs.

The lower specific gravities normally found in batters that are formulated with fluid shortenings usually yield greater cake volumes. Thus, there appears to exist a general inverse relationship between specific gravity and cake volume. Taking into account all cake quality characteristics as a whole, the optimum final specific gravities for cakes produced with fluid shortenings range between 0.750 and 0.775, while those for cakes prepared with plastic shortenings fall within the range of 0.800 to 0.850 (Ellinger and Shappeck 1963).

A product's optimum specific gravity depends on the formula used and is influenced by any changes in the relative ratios of the ingredients. Thus, each time changes in either amount or kind of ingredients are introduced into a formula, the optimum specific gravity required to produce the desired cake quality must be reestablished. Similarly, changes in processing conditions (mixing time, mixing speed, mixing method and so forth) need to be followed by new estimations of the optimum specific gravity. Because the major portion of air incorporation in the batter takes place during the second stage of mixing, control of specific gravity must occur during that processing stage.

8.K. Muffins and Biscuits

By L.A. Gorton

Generally tender and crumbly, cake-like muffins and baking powder biscuits comprise a class of baked foods all their own. While biscuits tend to be plain, muffins exhibit wide variety in flavors and particulate inclusions: nuts, bran, blueberries, apple bits, cranberries, raisins, chocolate chips, poppy seeds, even chopped vegetables, peppers mild and spicy, onion pieces, sun-dried tomatoes and shredded bacon or other meats (**Figure 8.065**).

Made from scratch or a mix or produced fully baked and frozen for thaw-and-sell use, muffins can be found in restaurant, in-store bakery, deli and salad bar settings.

Figure 8.065. Blueberry muffins, the consumer's favorite, have been joined by other flavors, styles and sizes.

Baking powder biscuits are more often encountered by consumers in food service locations or as frozen prepared breakfast sandwiches.

8.K.1. Muffin styles

The earliest muffins, hawked on the streets of 19th century London, were round, spongy, unsweetened cakes, while American muffins were first offered as a type of bread or scone made from a batter, poured into a well-greased tin and baked in a hot oven (Benson 1988a). Today, hundreds of formulations and several sizes of muffins are marketed, most commonly weighing 2 to 2.5 oz and made in a standard cupcake tin measuring 2.75 in. at the top, 2 in. at the base and 1.5 in. deep (**Figure 8.066**). Gourmet muffins weighing 6 to 8 oz and made in pans with larger cups are also produced commercially, as are petite or "mini" muffins of 0.5 to 1.5 oz each.

Figure 8.066. A universal depositor equipped with a standard nozzle deposits muffin batter.
(Unifiller)

Basic styles include (a) peak top, with straight sides, no overhang and a cracked peak, with a slightly tough or bread-like texture (**Figure 8.067**); (b) bell top, with a ¼-in. overhang and rounded, smooth top or with only slight cracking, tender with a cake-like texture (**Figure 8.068**); and (c) flat top, with sides rising above the pan and rolling to the center, generally made with corn or bran, having coarse texture, very open and bready (**Figure 8.069**). The recently introduced "muffin top" is made by baking bell-top muffin batters in very shallow cups (often a hamburger bun pan), resulting in the characteristic overhang but very little bottom.

Muffin batter can also be deposited in small loaf pans to make quick breads, classified as chemically leavened tea breads and scaled from 4 oz to 1 lb per loaf.

Although much like cake in ingredients, muffin formulations (**Table 8.075**) fall between high-ratio cakes and baking powder biscuits in richness. They have less sugar and generally less shortening, eggs and milk than cakes, with the exception of the creme cake muffin. The grain of muffins is denser than cake's grain but with larger holes and tunnels, and muffins tend to be slightly chewier, with less tender eating characteristics (Willyard 2000). A relatively new addition to the muffin menu, creme cake styles are based on creme cake formulations with high levels of vegetable oil and whole eggs. The oil is added at two different stages of mixing, as noted by the table.

Figure 8.067. Straight sides, no overhang and a cracked peak characterize peak-top muffins.

8.K.2. Biscuit varieties

Consumers in the US understand biscuits to be small, bread-like rolls leavened with baking powder or baking soda and having a crumbly or flaky texture. Anywhere else in the English-speaking world, this baked product is likely to be called a scone. Sweeter formulations often take the name "shortcake" or "tea biscuit."

Baking powder biscuits are a familiar specialty of Southern US cuisine and are often made with buttermilk and "self rising" flour. They are generally a breakfast food or a side offering at other meals, and when smothered with country gravy, they even become the main course. Commercially prepared biscuits are a staple of

Figure 8.068. A rounded bell top on muffins typically shows a smooth appearance.
(MGP Ingredients)

Figure 8.069. These corn muffins show more of a flat top appearance. (OmegaPure)

fast food breakfast sandwiches, and they also compose the base for frozen breakfast sandwiches stocked in supermarket freezer cases (**Figure 8.070**).

Biscuits of this sort have a firm brown crust and a soft interior. Crust texture varies from smooth to extremely lumpy. Several varieties of baking powder biscuits exist. For example, cheese biscuits can be made by adding grated Cheddar or American cheese to the basic formula. Prepared without baking powder, "beaten" biscuits resemble hardtack and are kneaded (beaten with rolling pin) for 15 to 45 minutes to incorporate sufficient air to leaven them during baking. "Angel" biscuits, which get a leavening boost from bakers yeast in addition to baking powder, closely resemble dinner rolls with a relatively undeveloped gluten structure.

Table 8.075. Muffin Formulations

Ingredient	Basic muffin (bakers %)	Corn muffin (bakers %)	Bran muffin (bakers %)	Creme cake muffin* (bakers %)
Flour component				
Flour**	100	76	50	–
Corn meal	–	24	–	–
Cake flour	–	–	18.75	100
Bran	–	–	31.25	–
Sugar	60	32	31.25	120 to 140
Pregelatinized starch	–	–	–	12 to 18
Baking soda	–	–	2.2	–
Baking powder	5	4.5	1.5	–
Sodium bicarbonate	–	–	–	1.5 to 2.0
Sodium aluminum sulfate	–	–	–	1.5 to 2.0
Vital wheat gluten	–	–	–	2 to 5
Salt	1.25	1.5	1.5	3
Milk powder	7.5	7.9	12.5	3 to 6 ***
Molasses	–	–	37.5	–
Honey	–	–	19	–
Corn syrup	–	6	–	–
Shortening	40	24	18.75	–
Soy oil	–	–	–	1st stage: 10 to 20 3rd stage: 75 to 85
Whole eggs, liquid	30	24	12.5	90 to 105
Raisins	–	–	25	–
Water	60	72	100	60 to 70

Adapted from Willyard (2000)

** *Can be a blend of bread flour and up to 50% cake flour*

*** *Whey*
(Benson 1988b)

8.K.3. Role of ingredients

Flour. Representing 30 to 40% of the total formula's weight, flour provides structure to muffins and holds the other ingredients together. Flour choice ranges from soft wheat and cake flour to patent bread flour and whole-wheat varieties. Bran, corn flour and corn meal are also used as the flour component. Willyard (2000) observed that most muffin formulations contain a blend of cake or pastry flour with higher protein hard wheat or bread flour (11 to 12% protein) or even all bread flour. The addition of the stronger flour yields a product with a slightly chewier, resilient character and helps better define the dome or bell shape.

Corn meal, counted as flour for formula balance purposes, requires sufficient hydration during mixing, a property influenced by its granulation, which also determines the textural properties of the finished muffin. Coarser meal yields a more crunchy character, while very fine meal or corn flour gives a smoother or slighty gummy texture.

Figure 8.070. Cooled biscuits will be packaged and frozen to become a base for frozen breakfast sandwiches. (*Baking & Snack*)

Bran, another ingredient counted as flour, contains cellulose and pentosans that absorb large amounts of water. Bran's bitter flavor tends to limit its usage level so formulators may add caramel colors to give bran muffins a more "branny" appearance.

The original home recipe for baking powder biscuits called for self-rising flour, which contains salt, sodium bicarbonate and leavening acid (Conn and Jelinek 1982). The biscuits could, thus, be prepared by adding only shortening and liquid milk to the self-rising flour.

Commercial preparation of such biscuits adds the leavening system separately to bleached soft wheat patent flour (8.5 to 9.5% protein). The low-protein flour does not require as much shortening as a hard wheat flour to yield a tender, light biscuit with a friable crust.

Sweeteners. Tenderness, sweet flavor, crust color and keeping quality are provided to muffins by sweeteners. The formulator can choose among granulated sugar, corn syrup, molasses and honey. The total sugars in muffins range from 50 to 70% (flour weight basis). Sugar influences the timing of starch gelatinization. Sucrose, the most commonly used sweetener for muffins, does not enter into the Maillard reaction (unless split by bakers yeast or other enzymes into dextrose and fructose components) so reducing sugars such as dextrose, corn syrup or high-fructose corn syrup are added at 1 to 3% to assist with crust coloring. Humectant sugars (corn syrup, honey, molasses) provide moisture retention properties.

Sweeteners are generally not used in Southern-style biscuits, but 1 to 4% dextrose is sometimes added to commercial formulations to increase crust browning and to tenderize the biscuits. Sweet biscuits will contain 2 to 4% sucrose, and about 10% sucrose is suggested for shortcake-type, dessert-style biscuits.

Shortening. Another tenderizing ingredient, shortening also helps retain moisture to improve the eating and keeping qualities. Both plastic shortenings and fluid oils are suitable and range in usage level from 18 to 40% (flour weight basis), with corn and bran muffins containing the least amounts.

Emulsifiers tend not to be as critical in muffins as in high-ratio cakes but are often added to extend shelf life. When eggs are reduced to save costs, the emulsifying function of their lecithin must be replaced by emulsifiers or emulsifier shortenings.

Milk powder. Providing a binding effect on flour proteins, milk powders give muffins strength and body as well as flavor and crust color. This ingredient also retains moisture and aids in keeping qualities. Milk powder is used in the range of 5 to 12% (flour weight basis). Traditionally, baking powder biscuits are made with liquid milk in sweet, sour and buttermilk styles.

Whole eggs. Eggs provide structure, volume, body and eating quality to muffins, as well as crumb color. Either liquid or dry eggs may be used, with appropriate adjustments in water levels. Liquid eggs are added at 10 to 30% (flour weight basis). The natural fats and lecithin in egg yolks contribute to tenderness and eating quality. By increasing the yolk content, tenderness is enhanced in the finished product. By adding more egg whites, structure and resilience increases, thus reducing damage or breakage during packaging and distribution.

Salt. This ingredient acts primarily as a flavor enhancer, added at 1.5 to 2% (flour weight basis).

Leavening. Muffins employ chemical leavening to generate carbon dioxide that inflates the air cells in the batter. Standard baking powder is the usual choice, and usage level runs 2 to 6% (flour weight basis). Lower ranges characterize bran muffins, and addition of 2 to 3% bicarbonate is needed in such formulations because of the natural acidity of molasses and honey.

The leavening system for muffins (baking powder) contains both sodium bicarbonate (baking soda) and a leavening acid, with monocalcium phosphate (MCP) chosen for its fast action during mixing and early baking. Intermediate leavening acids (for example, sodium acid pyrophosphate) and slower-acting acids (for example, sodium aluminum phosphate) also provide benefits. The leavening system influences specific gravity or density and thus the ability of the batter to maintain proper suspension of particulates during baking. A fine granular form of bicarbonate is recommended to blend uniformly with other dry materials when mixed.

The leavening system for commercially produced biscuits functions best with slower-acting leaving acids that prevent excessive loss of carbon dioxide during processing because it can take 15 to 40 minutes to process large batches (Conn and Jelinek 1982). The authors recommended a blend of sodium acid pyrophosphate and slow-type sodium aluminum phosphate.

When Conn and Jelinek (1982) evaluated different leavening systems for baking powder biscuits, they used the formula shown in **Table 8.076**.

Water. The percentage of water has an effect on the appearance of muffins, according to Benson (1988a). Less water, as low as 40%, achieves a round- or bell-top muffin, while peak-top styles use higher percentages, up to 55%. Water is also related to the fill level for the pan cavities: the fuller the cavity, the more water is used. For example,

Table 8.076. Baking Powder Biscuits, Laboratory Formula

Ingredient	Amount (bakers %)
Flour, semi-hard wheat, general purpose*	100.00
Soy oil, partially hydrogenated	10.00
Salt	2.00
Sodium bicarbonate	1.80
Sodium acid pyrophosphate**	1.24
Sodium aluminum phosphate***	0.90
Milk, fresh whole homogenized	67.00

The authors recommended that soft wheat patent flour be used instead for commercial production.

** *SAPP-28,* *** *Levn-Lite (ICL Performance Products)*

(Conn and Jelinek 1982)

when baking bell-top muffins and filling the tins to the top of the pan, water would be 45%. But when filling tins below the top, water would be 40%. If making a peaked muffin and filling the batter to the top, water would be 50%, but if filling to below the top, use less water, 45%.

Other ingredients. Pregelatinized starches and gums can assist shelf life, and they increase viscosity to influence product symmetry. Only small amounts are needed, 0.1 to 0.4%.

8.K.4. Methods

Baking powder biscuits and muffins share a common approach to mixing: just enough to wet down the ingredients but not enough to develop the gluten. Mixing takes about 7 to 8 minutes, done in 2 or 3 stages in planetary bowl mixers. Horizontal, sigma-blade and bar-arm mixers may also be used. Over-mixing causes toughness, resulting in poor eating quality and misshaped products.

Dry ingredients are mixed with eggs, shortening and part of the water in the first stage, with the remainder of the water added in the final stages. Particulates (fruits, nuts, chocolate chips, vegetables, meats) are withheld until the end of the mixing cycle to avoid damage. Especially delicate materials may be added after the dough is deposited using target toppers.

For doughs high in particulates, care must be taken during depositing. Hand depositing with scoops is quite gentle to these materials, but at commercial wholesale speeds, piston depositors are required. Systems that draw batter positively without the need for separate valves tend to be gentler on viscous, particulate-laden formulations. The action should prevent, or at least hold to a minimum, any cutting of the particulates, especially bright-colored berries that can bleed into doughs, causing unattractive streaks.

In the meantime, paper cup denesters, configured as rotary arms with suction cups, can automatically place liners into pans at speeds of 22 rows per minute (Gorchow 1992). A final topping of streussel or other dry materials (bran, oats, decorative sugar) is provided as required.

When baking muffins, good flow of heat into the bottom of the pan improves the bake. Oven temperature ranges from 182 to 232°C (360 to 450°F), with convection ovens set somewhat lower at 160 to 205°C (320 to 400°F).

Preparation of baking powder biscuits involves quick mixing of the batter, followed by sheeting and cutting. The work provided by sheeting develops the gluten sufficiently for it to maintain structure of the cut biscuit through baking, which follows immediately, and freezing. Final dough thickness of 0.25 in. produces short, crusty biscuits in the Southern style.

Conn and Jelinek (1982) recommended refrigerating the plastic shortening and cooling the flour to obtain a flaky biscuit texture. Before liquids are added, the dough should be mixed to the point where it is still flowable and meal-like; it should not be over-mixed to become a sticky plastic mass. A minimum of mixing after adding the liquids is all that is required. Recommended dough temperature will be 18°C (65°F) or lower.

Scones (**Figure 8.071**), which require a highly viscous batter, are formed without pans, dropped by measured amounts onto flat baking trays. The batter can also be formed into a rough sheet and cut into triangles, the characteristic scone shape,

Figure 8.071. The rough, lumpy appearance of scones belies their tender eating quality.
(American Egg Board)

before baking.

Quick breads, which are formulated along the same lines as muffins, can be produced by three different techniques, according to Sokol (2006): the biscuit method, the muffin method and the creaming method.

In the biscuit method, dry ingredients are blended first and the cold fat is cut into the mixture. Liquids are combined separately and added to the drys, with mixing only to combine the materials.

In the muffin method, dry and wet ingredients are blended separately. The liquids are poured into the drys, and the mass is mixed until just combined.

In the creaming method, the fat and sugar are creamed until light and fluffy, with the eggs added gradually. In the meantime, the dry and wet ingredients are blended separately and added alternately to the creamed mixture. Mixing proceeds until the ingredients are just combined.

Formulating and processing of refrigerated biscuits, which requires full development of the gluten so it retains the carbon dioxide through long storage periods, is quite different from preparation of fresh or frozen biscuits, as explained earlier in this chapter at Part G.

8.L. Doughnuts
Updated by Hans van der Maarel

Oil cakes, made by frying pieces of rich dough in hot cooking fat, were one of mankind's first luxury foods. They celebrated special occasions and were often served as one last indulgence before starting a fast. Indeed, the day before Ash Wednesday is called Fat Tuesday ("Mardi Gras") because of all the oil-rich foods consumed on the last day before Lent begins. Their formulations reflected the need to use up household fat, sugar, egg and fruit supplies, which would otherwise spoil before they could be eaten again after the fasting period concluded 40 days later.

Ash (1979a) found cake doughnuts, or fried cakes, noted in history as early as the fifth century BCE, and Willyard (2002) reported that archeologists discovered foods similar in shape to doughnuts to have been eaten by Pueblo Indians. Others point to Dutch fried cakes, called "olykoeks," made during America's Colonial period, while still other sources credit a New England ship's captain with inventing the hole in the doughnut. These items remained a seasonal treat until after World War I. When the first automatic doughnut machines and accompanying doughnut mixes were introduced in the 1920s, the popularity of these foods grew exponentially.

8.L.1. Doughnut styles

Doughnuts are not baked but deep-fried in fat without a container or pan to control their shape. The frying medium becomes part of the product, and of the cake doughnut's finished fat content, which accounts for 20 to 25% of its weight, some 80 to 85% of that is absorbed frying fat (Ash 1979a).

8.L.1.a. Cake

Cake doughnuts (**Figure 8.72**) are produced from batters that, in many essentials, resemble layer-cake batters. They are scaled or cut into small ring-shaped forms, each weighing from 0.5 to 2 oz, deposited into shortening or oil heated to 182 to 193°C (360 to 380°F) and cooked for 1 to 2.5 minutes.

When correctly formulated and properly fried, cake doughnuts are characterized by (a) a rich, golden-brown exterior color, conveying an image of quality; (b) a crisp crust, formed by the dehydration of the outer portion of the doughnut; and (c) an inner core, comprising the major quantitative portion and resembling a baked product more than a fried food. The 25 to 30% moisture retained by the core during frying will ultimately migrate outward during storage and alter the crispy character of the freshly-fried crust.

Doughnuts may be formulated in several ways, for example, (a) by weighing out the formula's individual ingredients, (b) by the use of proprietary bases to which are added flour and water and possibly a few optional ingredients or (c) by the use of commercially-formulated proprietary mixes that require only the addition of water. Most doughnuts produced commercially are made from some form of prepared mixes because these offer the advantages of uniformity of composition, a predetermined degree of richness, a largely predictable production performance and major economies in labor by eliminating numerous scaling operations in the bakery (Fischer 1976, Ash 1979b). Bakers also view mixes as a way to avoid stocking and scaling the many expensive spices and flavorings required.

The formula of a representative cake doughnut mix is given in **Table 8.077**. This mix is based on a blend of cake (pastry) and bread flours with the appropriate flour strength in terms of protein content. In addition, it contains finely granulated sugar as the principal sweetener, nonfat dry milk, shortening, egg yolk solids and defatted soy flour. Aeration of the doughnut batter during frying is derived largely from chemical leavening agents.

Cake doughnut batters, like cakes, take well to flavoring, with lemon, orange, cherry, strawberry, apple cider, chocolate and spice among the varieties noted by Treadwell (1980). Pumpkin-flavored doughnuts have become a Halloween and Thanksgiving specialty. Shape, too, can be varied, and popular forms include balls, sticks, twirls and crescents, each shaped by a different cutter configuration. Preparation of old-fashioned doughnuts takes adjustment of the formulation: 2 to 3 percentage points more sugar, lower leavening content (to create a more acid pH) and lower water absorption (Moyer 1986). This style is dense, lacks the star at the doughnut hole and will have a single crack or cracks on both sides.

Some years ago, introduction of filled ring cake doughnuts made news. The jelly filling was based on a formula with 60% solids, rather than the 65% solids for standard bakery jellies.

Figure 8.072. Attractive cake doughnuts appeal to consumers through flavor and toppings.
(MGP Ingredients)

Table 8.077. Representative Cake Doughnut Mix Formula

Ingredient	Amount (bakers %)
Cake flour	65.00
Bread flour	35.00
Finely granulated sugar	40.00
Dextrose	3.50
Nonfat dry milk	10.00
Egg yolk solids	7.00
Defatted soy flour	7.00
Shortening	5.75
Salt	1.50
Mace	0.75
Sodium bicarbonate	1.70
Sodium acid phosphate	2.30
Vanilla	to suit

(Wheeler and Stingley 1963)

Figure 8.073. Long, thin churros are made from a cooked dough extruded into a frying kettle.

Churros, long thin sticks of deep-fried sweet-flavored doughs, are a Spanish dessert adopted into the Mexican market and provide the Hispanic "take" on cake doughnuts (**Figure 8.073**). As Sieloff (2006) explained, churros are cooked first in a manner similar to choux paste to gelatinize the starch and incorporate the high percentage of eggs (**Table 8.078**). The cooked dough is then extruded through a fluted die into hot oil, and the finished churro is rolled in granulated or powdered sugar or a mixture of cinnamon and sugar. Often, churros will be filled with chocolate or fruit jams and pastes.

The typical cake doughnut exhibits 3 distinct zones. The crust or outer surface is the fried zone and is usually a crisp, medium brown in color. It has been exposed directly to the hot fat and contains a relatively high amount of absorbed frying fat. The second zone makes up the bulk of the doughnut and is called the baked zone. It is very cake-like with little absorbed fat. The inner zone, or core, is a dense, semi-firm area that has been exposed to insufficient heat to complete the batter's leavening. The high level of moisture in this zone eventually migrates outward, softening the crust and accelerating the breakdown of the doughnut coating sugar.

Ash (1979a) observed an appreciable difference between the first and second fried sides of the doughnut. The first side has a relatively smooth surface with minimal porosity, while the second side has a rough irregular surface and, in some cases, may even crack. He explained that at initial deposition, the batter surface encountering the hot oil has a smooth character that is rapidly sealed by the frying medium. As frying progresses the second side, exposed to the air, becomes warmer, softer and more porous, and moisture escapes from its surface. Leavening expansion also occurs. When flipped, the second side presents a rougher surface to the oil and does not seal like the original wet batter. The second fried side will have a higher fat content, by as much as 5%, and lower moisture than the first side. Because of these initial differences, doughnut coating sugars and glazes will be more stable when applied to the second side.

Table 8.078. Churros Formula

Ingredient	Amount (bakers %)
Flour, all-purpose	100
Water	125 to 170
Fat (oil, butter)	5 to 35
Sugar, granulated	5 to 15
Whole eggs	60 to 80
Egg yolks	7.4
Baking powder	1.4
Vegetable oil	5 to 16
Salt	1.5 to 2.5
Vanilla	1 to 2
Lemon peel	To taste
Orange peel	To taste

(Sieloff 2006)

8.L.1.b. Yeast-raised

Yeast-raised doughnuts differ from cake doughnuts by being made from a yeast-fermented dough rather than a chemically-leavened batter and by receiving a final proof before they are deposited into the fryer. As a result, their requirements with respect to formulation, ingredient functions, method of processing and type of equipment also differ from those of cake doughnuts. Yeast-raised doughnuts take a variety of forms: rings (**Figure 8.074**), twists, sticks and filled shells (called "bismarks" as shown in (**Figure 8.075**) and rectangles (called "long johns"). Whole-wheat styles are possible, as are yeast-raised doughnuts made with chocolate or cocoa in the dough.

Figure 8.074. Yeast-raised doughnuts go through full fermentation before frying. (Cargill)

A basic formula for yeast-raised doughnuts is given in **Table 8.079**. As Smith (1996) observed, it resembles that of a white bread with the exception of flour type (a blend of bread and pastry styles) and level of shortening (10%, flour weight basis, which is 4 to 5 times that of standard white bread). The formula may, of course, be augmented by the addition of functional ingredients such as yeast food, dough conditioners, emulsifiers, flavors, etc.

Mix manufacturers produce many types of doughnut formulations designed for specific production processes such as hand makeup, air-pressure cutting, vacuum extruding and automatic stamping (Smith 1996).

Two special styles of yeast-raised doughnuts add interesting diversity to this category: honey buns and paczki.

Honey buns, a form of cinnamon roll sometimes called "pershings," were first made with potatoes and up to 20% honey, but the formulation has changed considerably since then (**Table 8.080**). While salt helps controls fermentation, soy flour adjusts water absorption and contributes to crust color. The rich eating characteristics are seen in the inclusion of eggs, milk and honey. A small amount of baking power ensures full expansion in the fryer.

During makeup, the fermented dough is sheeted into a continuous band. Excess dusting flour is removed and a light coating of oil applied across the width of the band, except for a 2-in. wide strip on the edge opposite to the curling arm. The oil ensures retention of the cinnamon-sugar blend applied to the dough before being coiled. The long, thick cylinder is compressed slightly to give the dough an oblong cross section, and a guillotine blade cuts off individual pieces. The honey buns proof and are then fried like any other yeast-raised doughnut (**Figure 8.076**).

Paczki, or Polish-style yeast-raised doughnuts, are served during the Carnival period ahead of Lent. The name means "little package" and is pronounced "ponch'-eck" for singular usage and "ponch'-key" for plural, and although the Polish spelling stays the same for both usages, some Americans have adopted "paczkis" as the plural form.

The round yeast-raised shell-style doughnuts are somewhat larger than bismarks and richer than conventional styles (**Table 8.081**). After frying, they are filled and topped with granulated or powdered sugar or iced with white or chocolate fondant. Traditional fillings include lemon, prune, apricot, raspberry, custard, Bavarian cream and rose petal jam. Other fillings often used are peach, apple, cherry, blueberry and strawberry.

Whether the odd name or the tasty quality is responsible, paczkis have become quite a draw for retail and in-store bakers in recent years. Krumrei (2001) reported that the modern popularity of this doughnut in the US can be traced to Ohio retail bakers who started merchandising them during the mid-1980s.

Figure 8.075. The filling for bismarks stabilizes its fruit or creme ingredients with starch.
(National Starch Food Innovation)

Table 8.079. Basic Formula for Yeast-Raised Doughnuts

Ingredient	Amount (bakers %)
Flour	100
Water	54 to 62
Sweetener, sucrose and/or dextrose	6 to 12
Shortening	8 to 15
Salt	1 to 2
Nonfat dry milk	2 to 5
Egg yolk	0 to 5
Yeast	4 to 6

(Wise 1971)

Table 8.080. Honey Bun Formula

Ingredient	Amount (bakers %)
Flour	100
Sugar	7 to 15
Shortening	10 to 18
Yeast	4 to 9
Honey	0.75 to 8
Milk or milk product	2.5 to 6.5
Salt	1.25 to 3.1
Soy flour	0 to 6
Eggs, yolks and/or whites	0 to 3
Dough conditioners	0.25 to 1.5
Baking powder	0 to 4.5
Flavor	as desired
Total liquid	38 to 45

(Hildebrand 1980)

Figure 8.076. Honey buns fry for 2 minutes, automatically flipped halfway through the process. (*Baking & Snack*)

Table 8.081. Paczki Formula

Ingredient	Amount (bakers %)
Bread flour	50
Cake flour	50
Water	50
Yeast, compressed	4
Butter	18.75
Egg yolks	25
Sugar, granulated	12.5
Nonfat dry milk	6.25
Salt	1.5
Lemon emulsion	1.5
Vanilla	1.5

(*Krumrei 2001*)

Figure 8.077. Profiteroles (small cream puffs) can be filled and covered with chocolate or compound coatings.

8.L.1.c. Choux paste

Doughnuts may also be prepared from choux paste (*pâte à choux*), a cooked batter more commonly used to make eclairs and cream puffs (profiteroles), as shown in **Figure 8.077**.

The process differs from that of other baked and fried products in that the batter is prepared by boiling a mixture of shortening, water and salt (and sometimes sugar) in a heated kettle. After turning off the heat, flour is added to the hot liquid, and the mass is again worked over low heat until it clears the side of the kettle. Taken off the heat, the batter is supplemented with whole eggs, added gradually until the batter becomes smooth. The finished choux paste is put into a doughnut depositor equipped with a fluted cutter and portioned into the frying oil (**Figure 8.078**). Automated cook-chill systems (**Figure 8.079**) are a recent development for preparation of choux paste doughs.

Table 8.082 reports ingredient ratios for products based on choux paste. Careful heating during dough preparation is required because the gluten must not be allowed to denature or else it will not be able to incorporate the eggs, and volume will suffer. Steam generated from the water and the moisture content of the eggs leavens choux paste products. Egg whites and sometimes ammonium carbonate may be added to help make the puffs dry and crispy (Sokol 2006). The more whole eggs added, the lighter the finished product will be because the egg holds some air, which also contributes to leavening, but too many eggs makes the batter too thin.

8.L.2. Role of ingredients

Flour. A blend of soft and hard wheat flours, ranging from 50:50 to 75:25 (soft to hard), is the choice for cake doughnuts, although some bakers use 100% soft wheat flour. Flour comprises 55 to 65% of the total batch weight and provides structure to the product. The protein content influences batter viscosity and flow at lower temperatures, while the gelatinization of the starch impacts batter flow at higher temperatures (Willyard 2002).

Flour provides structure to yeast-raised doughnuts as well, but a hard wheat patent flour with a protein content of 11 to 13.5% is preferred (Smith 1996). Soft pastry flour can be blended with the hard wheat flour to increase machineability during processing and tenderness in the finished product. Higher protein flours will increase volume and extend shelf life, while lower protein flours yield a more tender bite but reduce volume and shorten shelf life.

Soy flour. Water absorption and water binding increase appreciably when defatted soy flour is added to cake doughnut formulations at 1.5 to 3.0% (flour weight basis). Soy flour also inhibits fat absorption and provides early crust strength. An optimum protein dispersability index (PDI) for soy flour in doughnut applications is 70.

In yeast-raised doughnuts, defatted soy flour also helps increase water absorption.

Too much, however, will weaken the dough, causing an open grain, lower volume and darker crust color.

Sweeteners. Total sweetener levels for cake doughnuts range from 22 to 26% (flour weight basis) and take the form of sucrose, dextrose and/or corn syrup. These ingredients provide sweetness and act as tenderizing agents, accelerating crust browning and assisting in binding water to extend shelf life. Dextrose, at levels as low as 1 to 2% (flour weight basis), contribute to rapid crust browning. When granular sugar is used, particle size becomes critical. If too small, the sugar dissolves faster than other ingredients and will slow hydration of the flour. Coarse granulation will retard sugar solution but can cause excessive wear on cutters.

Sweeteners for yeast-raised doughnuts include the full range: sucrose, dextrose, corn syrup and high-fructose corn syrup. They contribute tenderness, flavor and crust color, while also serving as fuel for yeast fermentation. Because dextrose caramelizes at a lower temperature, 154°C (310°F), than sucrose, 136°C (325°F), it contributes to darker crust color in the finished product.

Figure 8.078. "French doughnuts," also called "French crullers," are made from a cooked dough deposited by a fluted cutter.
(MGP Ingredients)

Nonfat dry milk. Used at up to 4% (flour weight basis), NFDM provides binding and structure to cake doughnuts. It helps buffer the batter and contributes to formation of the protein seal that prevents excessive fat absorption. The milk's protein content contributes structure as well. Dry milks provide similar benefits to yeast-raised doughnuts

Eggs. Dried egg yolk provides richness and tenderness to cake doughnuts, making a marked improvement to volume and shelf life. The dried yolks must be fully hydrated for them to be completely functional. Typical usage is 0.5 to 2.0% (flour weight basis), but an upper limit of 3% was noted by Ash (1979a). Today, egg yolk usage is 0.5 to 1.0%, with emulsifiers making up for some of the egg functionality. Egg whites and whole eggs tend to give an undesired toughness, and fat absorption can be overly restricted by use of egg whites; however Willyard (2002) said that egg whites at very low levels will increase resilience to solve problems with breakage occurring while processing cake doughnuts.

Figure 8.079. Heating and cooling capability is combined in this mixing system, which can be used to produce choux paste, as well as custards and cremes.
(Tonelli Group)

In yeast-raised doughnuts, whole eggs tend to strengthen the dough, and their albumin content helps reduce the tendency of the desirable white ring to collapse (Smith 1996). They improve the eating quality, crust color and shelf life of these products. The water portion of the eggs must be counted with other liquids in the formula for proper balance.

Leavening. Cake doughnut batters require double-acting leavening systems, using sodium bicarbonate as the carbon dioxide source. The leavening acids most often employed are the fast-acting sodium acid pyrophosphate (SAPP) in combination with slower-acting glucono delta-lactone (GLD), sodium aluminum phosphate (SALP) and monocalcium phosphate (MCP). Some cake doughnut formulations use as many as 3 leavening acids to control and balance carbon dioxide release during processing.

Yeast-raised doughnuts are, no surprise, leavened by bakers yeast. The usage level, around 6.5% (flour weight basis), should be adjusted to obtain 30 to 45 min-

Table 8.082. Choux Paste Formula	
Ingredient	**Amount (bakers %)**
Whole milk	89
Water	89
Salt	3
Sugar	4
Butter	79
Pastry flour	100
Eggs	143

(Suas 2009)

utes of proofing time. Also, as the level of yeast increases, fermentation time accelerates, causing gassiness, reducing tolerance to over-proofing and increasing the susceptibility to collapse when removed from the fryer or during glazing operations. The richer the formula (more sugar), the higher the percentage of yeast required.

Fats. Cake doughnut formulations require addition of some fat, typically 7 to 9% (flour weight basis), to the batter. This fat, plus that absorbed during frying, contributes to the richness of the finished product.

Lecithin, added at 0.25 to 0.5% (flour weight basis), not only functions as an emulsifier to stabilize the batter but also aids in control of batter flow, symmetry and fat absorption. Other emulsifiers may also be added to promote better shelf life and to give the doughnut a desirable short bite.

Shortening in the dough of yeast-raised doughnuts provides lubrication to the system to improve sheeting and handling during makeup. The fat also contributes tenderness and mouthfeel to the finished product, reducing toughness and chewiness. Shortening helps reduce moisture migration.

Salt. In cake doughnuts, salt performs a flavor enhancement function and is added at 1 to 1.5% (flour weight basis). In yeast-raised doughnuts, however, salt also helps regulate fermentation, preventing a rapid start and slowing the finish of yeast activity. It thus improves bench tolerance and helps control the age of the dough.

Other ingredients. Potato starch can be used at up to 1.25% (flour weight basis) in cake doughnuts or 2 to 10% in yeast-raised formulations. It is an effective water-binding agent that slows staling and will inhibit fat absorption. Formulations may also include milk replacers (casein, whey, sodium caseinate), moisture binders (gums and other hydrocolloids, even rye flour) and coloring agents. Pregelatinized starches may be added at 0.5 to 1.0% to increase moisture retention and improve shelf life. Numerous spices and flavors find use in cake doughnuts, the most common being nutmeg, mace, lemon and vanilla. Yeast-raised doughnut doughs will benefit from use of oxidants and reducing agents in ways similar to other yeasted baked foods.

Frying oil. Fat absorption should be about 16 to 20% for standard cake doughnut varieties, 24 to 26% for old-fashioned doughnuts and 28 to 32% for crullers (Goodsell 1984). The fat absorption by doughnuts was found by McComber and Miller (1976) to increase by some 6% when lecithin was included in the formulation. The substitution of tartrate baking powder for sulfate-phosphate baking powder had a similar effect. Frying temperatures of 188 to 193°C (370 to 380°F) are optimum. Ash (1980) provided a thorough examination of frying fats.

8.L.3. Methods

The specialized process of frying is explained in Chapter 7, Part C, with the equipment involved described in Chapter 10, Part D, and Chapter 12, Part E.

8.L.3.a. Cake
Production of cake doughnuts starts by mixing the dry ingredients with water into a uniform batter with a temperature in the range of 24 to 27°C (75 to 80°F). Drastic deviations in batter temperature must be avoided to prevent undesirable quality variations in the final product. The mixing time normally required is 1 to 3 minutes (Owen 1975).

Close control of the mixing time is significant to ultimate product quality because over-mixing results in doughnuts with excessive toughness and inadequate fat absorption, whereas under-mixed batters produce fragile products with high fat absorption (Goodsell 1984).

Water temperature represents another critical variable because batter temperature affects the rate of hydration of dry ingredients, the viscosity of the batter and the rate of leavening. If the water is too cold, below 7°C (45°F), some ingredients may not go into solution and hydration of all ingredients will be retarded. Yet if water temperature exceeds 32°C (90°F), the leavening system may be activated prematurely, resulting in a gassy batter. Ash (1979b) gave the following formula for calculating the temperature of water to be added cake doughnut doughs:

$$T_w = 3 \times T_d - (T_m + T_r + F)$$

where T_w = calculated water temperature; T_d = desired dough temperature; T_m = mix temperature; T_r = room temperature; and F = friction factor of the mixer. For example, if desired dough temperature is 24°C (76°F); mix temperature, 19°C (67°F); room temperature, 21°C (70°F); and friction input factor is 3, then the water temperature is calculated to be 31°C (88°F).

Hard water conditions, with mineral content above 150 ppm, will require adjustment of the chemical leavening system.

Because cake doughnuts employ a chemical leavening system, floor time for these batters should be considered as bowl time plus hopper time. Because the hopper (**Figure 8.080**) is usually located above the frying fat, it will expose batter to warmer temperatures, which accelerate the leaving reactions. Doughnut batters do require hydration to achieve uniform symmetry during frying, and 10 to 20 minutes provides ample stability. Mixing should be scheduled to keep floor times as uniform as possible. If floor time is too short, volume will be reduced, crusts will crack and too much oil will be absorbed. If too long, volume will decrease and little to no star formation occurs.

When doughnut batter is deposited into the hot fat, it remains submerged for 3 to 7 seconds. A break point forms inside the doughnut hole at or slightly below the fat level. Formation of a central "star" marks a well-made cake doughnut. As Goodsell (1984) explained, the star develops when extensions from the break point move toward the center of the hole. Just after the star forms and prior to the doughnut being flipped, a uniform wet area forms, extending from the break point to the center of the doughnut. The doughnut should be turned just before gas starts bubbling from this wet area. After turning, the wet surface and the balance of the dough are fried.

Figure 8.080. Batter for cake doughnuts, held in the depositor hopper, will be released by cutter mechanisms into hot frying fat.
(Belshaw Adamatic Bakery Group)

In the meantime, the outer edge of the doughnut should be rigid enough to prevent any significant spread to the outside. Such rigidity causes the plump appearance expected of cake doughnuts. If the break line forms high on top of the doughnut or the outer edge is weak, the batter will spread out rather than in (Willyard 2002).

Cake doughnuts generally receive a glaze or coating after frying. The "powdered sugar" topping is actually powdered dextrose, which complements the flavor of the doughnut with a cooling sensation in the mouth during eating. Additionally, powdered dextrose does not dissolve as quickly as powdered sucrose and thus gives longer stability. Doughnuts should be cooled sufficiently so that sugar application takes place at surface temperatures between 31 and 33°C (88 and 92°F) (Fischer 1976), although Goodsell (1984) reported the temperature range to be 32 to 35°C (90 to 95°F), with no more than a difference between external and internal temperatures of 1 to 2 C° (2 to 4 F°). Other finishes include coconut and crumb mixtures as well as sugar glazes and icings.

8.L.3.b. Yeast-raised

Either the sponge-and-dough method or the straight-dough method may be used. In instances where the sponge-and-dough method is not feasible, Wise (1971) recommended preparation of a straight dough some 2 hours before the first doughnut dough is scheduled. This straight dough then serves as a starter dough added to each subsequent fresh dough in amounts of about 25% of the total dough weight. This procedure results in doughs that perform like sponge doughs, with end products that benefit from the more extended fermentation.

Well-developed doughs are necessary for best results with yeast-raised doughnuts and cause less sticking and hang-up on cutters. Dough temperature should be between 26 and 28°C (78 and 82°F) (Roth 1975). If scrap is used, the dough should be slightly cooler, according to Smith (1996), who also said that many bakers incorporate scrap into new doughs at 15 to 20%. He cautioned that scrap should be weighed so that equal amounts go into each dough, thus allowing uniform fermentation and proofing cycles. As always, the principle of "like into like" applies. Doughs should ferment 45 to 90 minutes under conditions of 27 to 29°C (80 to 85°F) and enough humidity to prevent crusting.

After makeup, using equipment and techniques explained in Chapter 12, Part E, yeast-raised doughnut dough pieces (**Figure 8.081**) require relatively dry and warm proofing conditions, within a temperature range of 35 to 46°C (95 to 115°F) and a relative humidity of 35 to 45% to promote skin formation. Proof time will normally run 20 to 35 minutes. High humidity proofing tends to cause excessive product expansion and to produce blister formation and high fat absorption in the fried product. Some of the newer automatic proofers feature zone control that permits adjustment of proofing conditions in different sections of the box. The general practice calls for a moist zone at the outset of proofing to promote the spread of the doughnuts and a dry zone toward the discharge end to favor product rise and volume increase, as well as to facilitate product release off the trays (Braden 1976).

Most yeast-raised doughnuts receive a glaze during the final finishing operation. Top icing, crumbing and sugaring (with granulated sugar) are also provided to yeast-raised doughnuts.

Figure 8.081. After extrusion, yeast-raised doughnuts will be proofed for 20 to 35 minutes.
(Belshaw Adamatic Bakery Group)

8.M. Icings, Glazes, Fillings

Updated by Hans van der Maarel

Icing on a baked food is not merely a sweet covering, it is also a means of merchandising and affects the consumer's ultimate decision to buy, according to Smith (1989).

Icings and glazes are essentially 2-phase systems consisting of small sugar crystals dispersed in a sugar syrup (saturated sugar solution). The suspended sugar crystals give these mixtures their white color. Water solubilizes about twice its weight of sugar, and the key to manufacturing a successful icing is developing a product that contains the minimum amount of dissolved sugar (syrup) and has satisfactory spreading and drying characteristics. The challenge of maintaining control over this sugar-water system is accomplished through use of supplementary ingredients that stabilize the icing during changes in temperature and humidity and maintain pliability, gloss, body and good eating characteristics (Dubois 1980a).

8.M.1. Icings and glazes

Cake icings have been characterized by Lipman (1972) as "modified sugar-water systems in which hydrocolloids and other ingredients are used to control the balance between the dissolved sugar and the suspended sugar, modifying the solubility and crystallizing characteristics of the sugar in the aqueous medium, and thereby stabilizing the size of the sugar crystals." Icing stability refers to the ability of an icing to retain its aerated cellular structure and smooth nongranular texture yet resist liquid separation during storage, use and subsequent shelf life. To ensure such stability, various hydrocolloids with suitable gelling, suspending, emulsifying, film-forming and hydrating properties are commonly used in the preparation of most icings. Additional quality features sought in an icing include (a) ease of spreading and of handling at normal working temperatures; (b) good adherence to the baked product without thinning and running off; (c) firm setting within the desired time limit; (d) retention of a uniform moisture content without either drying out too rapidly or absorbing extraneous moisture to cause melting or stickiness; (e) maintenance of its glossy appearance and true color during the anticipated shelf life; and (f) absence of possible grittiness development during storage (Lachmann and Voll 1969).

The development and formulation of fillings and toppings, in practically limitless varieties, have been discussed in some detail by Burny (1956), Ogilvy (1960) and Kavanagh (1969), Dubois (1980a, 1980b, 1980c), Smith (1989) and Zelch et al. (2008)

8.M.1.a. Varieties

Icings are generally classified according to their fat content into three general types: (a) flat icings that normally do not contain fat and are used primarily for sweet dough products, (b) cupcake icings that contain 3 to 5% fat and (c) cake and creme icings with fat contents ranging from 10 to 25%. Smith (1989) further divided the category into non-aerated (water icings, confectionery coatings, fudges, fondants), partially aerated (high- and low-density buttercreme) and aerated (nondairy whipped toppings, marshmallow) icings (**Table 8.083**). (Chocolate and confectionary coatings are examined in Volume I, Chapter 2, Part D.)

Flat icings. Often referred to as water icings, flat icings (**Figure 8.082**) are non-aerated icings that consist primarily of water and sugar in the approximate pro-

Table 8.083. Icing Formulations

Ingredient	Water icing (formula %)	Buttercreme icing (formula %)	Marshmallow (formula %)
Water	16	10	10 to 20
Stabilizer	6	–	–
Sugar, granulated	16	–	0 to 60
Sugar, powdered	62	70	–
Salt	0.2	–	–
Shortening	–	20	–
Corn syrup	–	–	20 to 83
Invert sugar	–	–	0 to 85
Gelatin, 200 bloom	–	–	1.25 to 2.25

(Smith 1989)

Figure 8.082. This bakery applies flat icings to danish pastries at an icing station within the cooler. (Gold Standard Baking)

Figure 8.083. Cupcakes sport brightly colored icings to attract shopper's attention. (Uncle Wally's Muffin Co.)

portions of 12 to 15% of water and 85 to 88% of sugar and that are stabilized with an icing base whose primary stabilizer is agar (Levine 1980). Increased opaqueness and improved gloss are obtained by including suitable mono- and diglycerides in the icing base (Birnbaum 1960). Flat icings may be prepared either by the cold process in which all ingredients are worked in special mixers at room temperature or by the boiling process in which a sugar syrup is brought to a boil prior to the incorporation of the powdered sugar. Flat icings are frequently modified by the addition of selected ingredients. Thus starch, added to the boiling syrup, will upon gelatinization increase both the icing's opaqueness and moisture retention capacity. Egg whites or gelatin are occasionally included to impart more body and improved setting properties to the icings, while low levels of invert sugar tend to reduce their brittleness and enhance their gloss.

Cupcake icings. As a rule, cupcake icings (**Figure 8.083**) contain 5 to 10% of emulsifier-shortening, which, because of its aerating capacity, causes air to be incorporated during the icings' preparation. This type of icing, therefore, tends to acquire a fudge-like consistency and qualifies as a high-density buttercreme. This type of icing will not draw moisture from the cake because it forms a water-in-oil emulsion.

Cake icings. Because they contain the relatively high levels 10 to 25% of fat, cake or creme icings are worked until a light, aerated structure with low specific gravities are obtained. Such low-density buttercremes can be used not only to cover cakes but also to fill them or as sponge roll and snack cake fillings (**Figure 8.084**). The lightness will be determined by the level and type of fat used, which can range up to 100% (sugar weight basis) in some cases.

Frequently, the degree of aeration is further enhanced by including in their formulation whipping aids such as soy proteins, egg whites and gelatin (Birnbaum 1960). The grain, texture and stability of cake icings are materially improved, as Knightly and Lynch (1966) pointed out, by surfactant blends that include mono- and diglycerides, sorbitan monostearate and polyoxyethelene (20) sorbitan monostearate (an ethoxylated monoglyceride). Mono- and diglycerides alone tend to depress icing volume; on the other hand, they also reduce the tendency of icings toward syneresis, or "weeping."

In the preparation of creme icings, fats such as butter or shortening are creamed with powdered sugar. They are frequently augmented with whole eggs, yolks or egg whites to impart body and smoothness, as well as improved stability, to the icing. For fluffy or foam-type icings, egg whites provide the basic structure-forming ingredient. They are first whipped into a foam and then combined either with powdered sugar for cold process icings or with hot syrups for boiled icings.

Finished icings in ready-to-use form, packed in pails, provide time savings to bakery operations.

Colored icings. These icings can be flavored and colored with chocolate and/or cocoa, and they can be tinted with all the colors of the rainbow for decorating purposes. Powdered color additives tend to produce the most stable color results in buttercreme icings. Colors can bleed from one icing to another when the icings exhibit different moisture levels. In other words, if the base icing is still wet when the colored icing is applied, the color of the latter may bleed into the former. Livingston (1963) suggested that use of a hydrocolloid in a gel colored by lake-style pigments will stop such leaching by forming a stable complex between the color and the hydrocolloid.

Fondants. Consisting of a grained chewy confection, fondant is made from a supersaturated sugar solution and has a low moisture content (about 15%). Smith (1989) described commercial preparation of fondant. The first step mixes 70 to 80 parts sucrose with 20 to 30 parts corn syrup to yield a solution of 60 to 75% solids, by weight. Heating to 114 to 117°C (237 to 243°F) evaporates some of the water, bringing solids content to 85%. The heated syrup is cooled to 55 to 70°C (131 to 160°F), causing the sucrose to crystallize out of solution and form a fondant. The pliable fondant can be used on its own to ice baked foods or combined with additional shortening and milk to create a spreadable icing.

Marshmallow. These aerated icings and sandwich cookie fillings contain a high percentage of sugar syrup (approximately 80%) and use gelatin as the whipping and stabilizing agent. Marshmallow icings are commonly used as fillings and as bases on which to apply coconut, chopped nuts, sugar decorettes and so forth. It is made by preparing a syrup of sucrose, corn syrup and/or invert syrup, heating it to boiling and then reducing the temperature to 60°C (140°F). The gelatin, wetted in at least 4 parts of cold water and soaked for at least 30 minutes, is then blended into the warm syrup and whipped to incorporate the maximum amount of air, also called "overrun." Because any fatty substance will interfere with the whipping capability of the mixture, flavor choice is restricted. Even when coated, marshmallow tends to dehydrate over time through moisture loss, usually to the base cookie or cake. Matz (1968) detailed marshmallow's reactions to seasonal and geographical variations.

Ganache. The traditional chocolate icing for tortes, ganache is a simple emulsion of chocolate and heavy cream (35% fat content). The cream is scalded by heating to 88°C (190°F) and poured over chopped chocolate, with the mixture stirred gently until the chocolate melts and the mass becomes smooth. The classic ratio for this oil-in-water emulsion is equal parts of heavy cream and chocolate; the fats from the cocoa butter and cream are dispersed in the water of the cream (Corriher 2008). Some formulations add a small percentage of corn syrup, which contributes gloss to the surface, and/or butter, which extends the fat system of the chocolate. Suas (2009) noted that fruit purees may be used in place of the cream. Ganache can be poured

Figure 8.084. Snack cake fillings are made from low-density buttercremes. (Caravan Ingredients)

Table 8.084. Pastry Creme Formula (Crème St. Honoré)

Ingredient	Amount (% milk weight basis)
Milk	100
Sugar	13
Egg yolks	8
Whole eggs	11
Cornstarch	8
Sugar	12.5
Butter	6
Vanilla	1.5
Gelatin	1.5
Cold water	12.5
Egg whites	38

(Busscher 2003)

Figure 8.085. Creme fillings, essentially 2 parts sugar to 1 part fat, complement the flavors of the sandwich cookie's base cakes.
(Tate & Lyle)

directly over cakes and petit fours for a thin coating but will need to be cooled to achieve thicker icing patterns. While the shelf life of these products is relatively short, it can be increased by adding humectants such as corn syrup or gelling agents such as gelatin (Hofberger 1999).

Glazes. One of the chief differences between opaque icings and transparent glazes is their water content, with glazes having a 4 to 6% higher level of water (Zelch et al. 2008). Most yeast-raised doughnuts receive a glaze during the final finishing operation. In general, glaze formulations will call for 100 parts of powdered sugar, 20 to 22 parts of hot water, 1 to 1.5 parts of gelatin, up to 10 parts of corn syrup or honey and up to 2 parts of glycerin (Flick 1971). Some 35 % of the powdered sugar may be replaced with granular sugar. The incorporation of 1 to 2% hard fat flakes with a melting point of 54 to 60°C (130 to 140°F) will minimize weeping of the glaze coating subsequent to packaging (Braden 1976). During application, the glaze temperature should be maintained at 38 to 43°C (110 to 120°F).

Bakeable jams and jellies. The jams and jellies that top some cookie styles require specific functional attributes (ASBE 1978). They should have a high solids content of approximately 72 to 75%, and modified starches, rather than pectin or other gums, should be the jelling agent. Partial substitution of invert syrup for sugar will help retain moisture in the jelly instead of allowing it to migrate to the cookie crumb. A hot, but short, baking time is often recommended for the cookie: 232 to 260°C (450 to 500°F).

Pastry cremes. Often used as fillings for cakes, pastries and creme pies, pastry cremes (**Table 8.084**) are stabilized by gelatin. The gelatin is allowed to soak in cold water until wetted. The milk and sugar are combined and scalded, and egg yolks and whole eggs added, with mixing proceeding until the mass is smooth. Returned to heat, the mixture is brought to a boil until thickened. The butter, flavor and hydrated gelatin are added. Egg whites, whipped separately, are added immediately after the softened gelatin is put in.

Sandwich cremes. The creme fillings for sandwich cookies (**Figure 8.085**) are a relatively simple blend of 2 parts sugar to 1 part fat, plus relatively low levels of flavor and color additives (**Table 8.085**). The type of sugar and filler fat are critical to this application. Particle size is the most important characteristic of the sugar, while the solid fat index is most important for the filler fat. Powdered sucrose is the most frequently used sugar because of its very small particle size. Matz (1968) reported that the small amount of starch routinely added to powdered sugar to prevent lumping has little to no effect on sandwich cremes other than a slight increase in density.

Dextrose can be added to decrease the cloying sweetness of the creme and to provide a cool sensation in the mouth. Milk powders are occasionally employed to also cut the sweetness. Cocoa (10%, sugar weight basis) or chocolate liquor will make chocolate-flavored filling cremes, but the overall moisture content of the finished filling must be kept below 4%. Because much more chocolate liquor is required to produce equivalent color, a combination of cocoa and chocolate is favored. Colors should be oil-soluble compounds or finely milled lakes of the water-soluble compounds.

Some cremes are aerated, others are not. In some cases, melted fat is added directly to the creme mixer, while other bakers will plasticize the melted fat prior to addition. Vetter (1984) examined the effects of these processing

Table 8.085. Sandwich Creme Filling Formulations

Ingredient	Low-cost vanilla (%, sugar basis)	Deluxe vanilla (%, sugar basis)	Chocolate (%, sugar basis)	Fudge (%, sugar basis)	Coconut (%, sugar basis)	Peanut (%, sugar basis)
Powdered sugar	100	100	100	100	100	100
Fat	34	52	40	50	70	50
Milled coconut	–	–	–	–	25	–
Lecithin	0.2	0.2	0.2	0.2	0.2	0.4
Dextrose, anhydrous	–	–	–	–	50	–
Salt	0.75	0.4	0.6	0.6	0.6	0.5
Vanillin	0.02	0.04	0.04	0.04	–	–
Dried buttermilk	–	11	5	8	–	–
Cocoa, dutched	–	–	10	8	–	–
Chocolate, natural	–	–	–	6	–	–
Nonfat dry milk	–	–	–	–	–	12.5
Peanut butter	–	–	–	–	–	37.2

(Matz 1969)

styles. Lecithin has been recommended for use in sandwich cremes at 0.375% to lower the viscosity when traces of moisture are present, and it is said to contribute to cleaner stenciling of the creme onto the basecakes.

8.M.1.b. Role of ingredients

Sweeteners. While the principal sweetener used in icings and glazes is sugar (sucrose), other sweeteners such as dextrose, invert sugar and corn syrup also find application for their specific effects on the stability and appearance of the finished icing. For boiled icings, granulated sugar will be found both satisfactory and economical. For flat icings made by the cold process, on the other hand, confectioners' or 4X powdered sugar will be satisfactory for most requirements. Where superior smoothness in the icing is desired, more finely ground sugars such as 6X or 10X pulverized sugar, or fondant sugar are required. The latter is a specially processed sweetener mixture consisting of some 80 to 85% granulated sugar, 10 to 15% dextrose and 5% invert sugar that has been boiled with 20 to 25% water. On cooling, the fondant is worked to hold crystal formation to a microscopically small scale. The use of dextrose, corn syrup and invert sugar at relatively low levels is intended mainly to impart a gloss to the final product. Because of their humectant properties, these sweeteners form a microscopic film of syrup on the surface, thereby producing a shiny effect (Dubois 1980c).

Humectants. Such ingredients help the icing retain or absorb water and include corn syrup, dextrose, honey and invert sugar (**Figure 8.086**). Used at low levels, they improve the gloss or shine of the icing or glaze and also produce a more pliable icing. Used in excess, they can retard drying, causing sticky icings and leading to melting of the icing or glaze during storage.

Shortening. The amount of shortening or fat used in icings is governed by the type of icing: buttercream icings may contain 20 to 25% fat; plain creme icings, 10 to 15%; cupcake icings, 2.5 to 5%; and flat icings, 0 to 1%. When butter is used in icings, it should possess a mild, clean flavor, and its salt content must be included when calculating the total salt in the icing formulation. Chocolate, with its high fat

Figure 8.086. Glazes and icings retain their character when humectants are included in formulations. (Cargill Texturizing Solutions)

content, should also be considered as contributing significantly to the fat content of icings. Low levels of fully hydrogenated hard flakes, with a melting point range of 46 to 54°C (115 to 135°F), are occasionally used in conjunction with plastic shortening to accelerate the drying rate and assist in stabilizing the icing at room temperature. Plastic shortening is used when softer icings are desired or when the iced product is to be frozen. For creme-type icings, special icing shortenings containing an appropriate blend of surfactants have proven highly effective in imparting improved volume, stability, grain and texture, and palatability to icings (Knightly and Lynch 1966).

The ability of a shortening to absorb and retain water is of considerable importance for the production of certain types of creme fillings. This property can be readily evaluated by slowly adding water to a measured amount of the shortening while it is being creamed in a laboratory mixer until the point is reached where the fat will no longer take up any water. Different fats possess different water-absorbing capacities, with hydrogenated shortenings being superior to lard, and high-emulsifier shortenings being able to absorb several times their weight of water. In general, the shortenings with high water-absorption capacities will yield light and fluffy creme fillings and icings.

It is worth noting that the term "buttercream" should be used only for icings made with butter. If the formula calls for a shortening other than butter, the result is termed a "buttercreme" or "creme" icing. As Smith (1989) noted, butter and margarine can be used in such icings, but their major function will be to impart a delicate flavor; the creaming properties of emulsified shortening will always be superior.

Milk products. While milk may be used in any of its available forms, dry milk is commonly recommended because it supplies flavor and color without adding extra water. In icings that can carry the extra moisture, sweetened condensed milk will enhance the product's richness and flavor. Fresh fluid milk, because of its tendency to become sour, is rarely used in icings.

Water. The primary function of water in icings is to serve as a solvent for the sugar to produce a saturated syrup that aids in stabilizing the icing during its shelf life. Water further acts to establish the desired spreadability of the product and to bring about the optimum hydration and activation of the hydrocolloids that are used as stabilizing agents. In general, it is good practice to use the minimum amount of water necessary to produce the desired consistency in icings. Dubois (1980c) cited the data in **Table 8.086** to demonstrate how the relatively small increase of 5% in the formula water of an icing can alter the ratio of its syrup phase to undissolved sugar from 1:2.2 to 1:1.3. This change is sufficient to markedly affect the icing's resistance toward excessive weeping and melting.

When reducing the consistency of fat-containing icings, the use of plain water should be avoided because it often leads to a breakdown of the creme structure as a result of a separation of the fat. The cause for this is the removal by solution of part of the sugar from the creme structure. To thin out icings, it is better, therefore, to use a simple syrup that consists of 2 parts of sugar and 1 part of water because this mixture can no longer dissolve additional sugar at ordinary temperatures. In the case of flat icings, merely raising their temperature to 38 to 43°C (100 to 110°F) will decrease their consistency.

Eggs. Eggs in the form of whole eggs, yolks or whites find use in the preparation of some icings. Fresh whites intended for icing use should be rather firm so they will whip into a foam with good volume and strength and thus reduce the tendency of the icings to bleed or water out.

Flavorings. Flavors in icings may be natural, that is, derived from the normal formula ingredients or may arise from processing procedures or represent added flavors. Processing flavors are produced by the heat-induced interaction of various ingredients. Thus, a mixture of milk and brown sugar, when heated, will produce the flavor of caramel, whereas when butter replaces the milk, a butterscotch flavor results under the same conditions. Among added flavors, the most popular ones include butter, citrus and vanilla, as well as chocolate and some fruit-based flavors. Correct flavor balance is of great practical importance in icings for assuring their consumer appeal.

Table 8.086. Effect of Water on Syrup/Sugar Solids Ratios		
Ingredient	Sugar-to-water ratio in icing	
(g per 100 g of icing)	90:10	80:20
Syrup		
Water	10	15
Dissolved sugar	21	32
Total (g)	31	47
Undissolved sugar (g)	69	53
Ratio (syrup/sugar solids)	1:2.22	1:1.13
(Dubois 1980a)		

Whiteners. The whiteness in an icing, highly valued by consumers in some sections of the country, can be augmented and brightened by the use of whitening agents at low levels. These whiteners include titanium oxide, calcium carbonate and calcium sulfate. They are generally incorporated directly in icing stabilizer bases.

Icing stabilizers. A stable icing is one that retains its integral character unchanged during its use and over its projected shelf life. A stable icing's aeration, texture and consistency will resist the deleterious effects of syneresis, sugar crystallization, hardening and moisture loss. This kind of icing stability is normally attained by the use of stabilizing agents, either individually or in the form of commercially developed blends or bases.

Bakers of cake and sweet dough products to which icings are applied generally use commercially formulated icing bases that contain a balanced blend of gums and other additives. They are available either as pastes or, more commonly, as dry, free-flowing powders and are supplied in various strengths: single strength for use at a level of about 10% based on powdered sugar; double strength, used at a level of 4 to 6% sugar basis; and concentrate, whose usage level generally is 1 to 3% (Dubois 1980c).

A representative dry base for a boiled flat icing, typically applied to sweet dough products, may contain the following ingredients: sugar as the diluent; calcium carbonate and calcium sulfate as buffer salts; agar, locust bean gum and cellulose gum as the hydrocolloids and gelling agents; mono- and diglycerides as emulsifiers for whatever shortening will be used in the finished icing; and titanium oxide for increased whiteness (Guckenberger 1981).

Drabbe (1998) summarized the composition of prepared icing stabilizer blends to include sugars, hydrophilic gums and other ingredients. It can be used at 8 to 10% as a single-strength stabilizer, 4 to 6% as a double-strength stabilizer or 1 to 3% as a concentrated icing stabilizer (all percentages are based on the weight of powdered sugar in the formula).

Stabilizers are either natural vegetable gums such as agar, algin, gum arabic, locust bean gum, guar gum, carrageenan and pectin; proteins of animal origin, of which gelatin is practically the sole example; various plant starches, either chemically modified or pregelatinized; and modified cellulose-derived gums such as carboxymethylcellulose, among others. Of these, agar is the basic ingredient in practically all icing stabilizer bases, the others being used in varying amounts as supplements for their special attributes.

Before introduction of stabilizers, icings had a tendency to break down over time, particularly inside packaging. They would dry out and chip or become soggy by absorbing moisture from the product.

For more detailed discussions of the composition and functional characteristics of plant gums, the reader is referred to Svolos (1971) Klose and Glicksman (1972) and the monograph of Smith and Montgomery (1959), as well as Volume I, Chapter 2, Part C.

8.M.1.c. Methods

Bakers most often used boiled icings that owe their popularity to the improved stability resulting from full activation and hydration of the stabilizing agents during the boiling process. In carrying out the process, the icing stabilizer system, with a preliminary addition of granular sugar, is first suspended in cold water and then brought to a rolling boil for 2 to 3 minutes in a covered steam-jacketed kettle. Thereupon, the rest of the granulated sugar and fat are added, and the mixture is again brought to a boil. The final step consists of placing the powdered sugar and remaining ingredients into a jacketed bowl equipped with a mixing paddle and gradually combining them with the hot syrup under constant low-speed agitation until the icing acquires a smooth appearance. In modern plant installations, the mixing bowl is generally equipped with a sanitary pump that transfers the finished icing via a flexible hose or other type of line to the icing depositor head (**Figure 8.087**), which then applies it in the desired amount and manner on the baked product. By integrating mixing and transfer systems, an uninterrupted flow of icing to the point of application can be maintained.

Figure 8.087. Rosettes of icing are automatically applied to cake tops. (Unifiller)

It is good practice to prepare icings as close as possible to the time of their intended use to avoid extensive holding periods that may entail evaporative moisture losses and cause changes in the icings' character. Maintaining a constant temperature during the holding period is an important quality control factor.

The method of icing application will differ somewhat with the type of the baked product being iced (sweet rolls, cupcakes, doughnuts, danish, coffee cakes and so forth) and with the kind of icing being applied. Thus, on products such as sweet rolls, danish and coffee cakes, the icing is generally applied at a temperature of 49°C (120°F) in either strings, thin films or continuous or intermittent sheets. Depositing is accomplished by means of heads with adjustable orifices that permit accurate control of the amount of icing being deposited on the product being conveyed beneath them, or the icing can be imprinted on the product passing beneath a rotating heated cylinder to which the icing has been applied for transfer to the product. Another method, used mainly for doughnuts and honey buns, is to carry the product through a pool of icing on a conveyor so its lower side is iced; the product is then inverted for the cooling cycle.

The time required by icings to set and attain a sufficient degree of dryness to permit packaging of the iced product is of considerable importance because it establishes the rate of production flow in instances where no product accumulation is practiced. Normally, drying times of 4 to 7 minutes will meet most production requirements. Where necessary, the drying time may be shortened to 1 to 2 minutes by appropriate increases in the granulated sugar and icing base levels during cook-up and by the selection of suitable stabilizers in the formulation of the icing base.

Some bakers will reclaim icing for use in subsequent batches, and industry standards suggest no more than 20 lb of reclaimed icing or glaze should be added per 100 lb powdered sugar. The reclaimed materials should be added during the boiling phase and brought to a boil to reactivate the stabilizer gums (Drabbe 1998).

If the finished product will be frozen for distribution, then the icing must be made in a way that prevents moisture migration. Any free water will break down the icing when the product encounters a freeze-thaw cycle. Drabbe (1998) recommended that flat icings and doughnut glaze formulations be changed by reducing water content by 2%, granulated sugar by 5% and elimination of hard fat flakes, along with increases of non-emulsified shortening by 4% and corn syrup by 3%. Zelch et al. (2008) examined the problem of freeze-thaw stability, noting similar changes but also stressing that the stabilizer be capable of holding a large amount of water.

Topping, icing and decorating equipment is also discussed in Chapter 11, Part A.

8.M.2. Fillings

Pie fillings (**Figure 8.088**) are conveniently classified into two general types: (a) fruit-based fillings, and (b) cream-style or soft fillings.

8.M.2.a. Fruit fillings

The quality of fruit pies is in large measure determined by the treatment given to the raw fruit and the precooked fillings prior to their use (**Figure 8.089**). Fresh fruit should be stored in a cool, well-ventilated room to prevent mold growth. Musty or moldy fruit pieces must never be incorporated in fillings because they will invariably spoil the end product with their highly objectionable flavor. If the fruit requires washing, this should be done just prior to its processing, rather than before it enters storage because wet fruit is prone to fermentation and accelerated spoilage.

Quick-frozen fruits, harvested and processed at their peak of ripeness, have largely replaced fresh fruit for pie making because they offer practical advantages such as product uniformity, absence of waste, excellent keeping quality and significant labor savings. Normally, frozen fruits are supplied in standard weight containers such as 30-lb tins, which facilitates their handling in the plant.

The thawing of frozen fruit may be accomplished in one of three ways: (a) holding the containers at room temperature for the required period; (b) placing the containers into tanks of circulating cold water, which greatly shortens the thawing time; and (c) thawing the containers just enough to loosen their contents and then heating the fruit with a little

Figure 8.088. Pie fillings include cream, or soft, styles and fruit-based compositions. (Colborne Foodbotics)

Figure 8.089. High-quality pies require high-quality fillings. (Cargill)

water to about 84 to 91°C (185 to 195°F). The last procedure tends to preserve the form and flavor of the fruit better than the other two thawing methods.

8.M.2.b. Soft fillings

The so-called soft pie fillings, which include puddings and custard creams, are generally stabilized by the use of modified starchs. In milk- or plain water-based fillings, the starch level is normally held to 8 oz per gal of liquid. In fillings that contain eggs, the starch addition should be reduced by 4 oz per lb of eggs because the latter act as thickening agents. If soft fillings of the pudding or custard-cream type are to be beaten or stirred after cooling, or if butter, cream or high levels of sugar are to be incorporated, the usage level of starch should be increased to 10 oz per gal of liquid or more. Lemon fillings require higher starch thickener levels still, on the order of 12 oz per gal.

In the preparation of these types of filling the recommended procedure is to first carry out starch gelatinization in dilute sugar solutions and then incorporate the remaining ingredients such as the balance of the sugar, eggs, flavorings, etc.

Bisno (1951) provided a useful discussion of the viscous properties of different starch gels and of the effects produced on them by diverse electrolytes, pH values, sugar concentrations, lipids, etc.

Doerry (1996) studied preparation of shelf-stable pumpkin pies, seeking a formula that would remain fresh for up to 8 days at room temperature. Results showed that a shelf stable pie with good eating qualities could be produced within the following parameters: (a) added moisture (water, liquid eggs) in the filling to not exceed 100% of pumpkin weight, (b) using 0.15% sorbic acid or 0.2% potassium sorbate (based on total filling weight) as chemical preservatives in the filling and (c) adding sufficient food acids to the filling to lower the pH to 4.75 or less.

Chiffon pie fillings and Bavarian creams are discussed by Busscher (2003). Chiffon fillings are created by adding beaten egg whites and sometimes whipped cream to a creme or fruit base stabilized with gelatin, slightly thickened but not fully set. Bavarian creams consist of custard sauce or sweetened fruit puree to which is added gelatin and whipped cream.

8.M.2.c. Role of ingredients

Nearly all types of fillings use gelling or stabilizing agents to give them the desired consistency and texture, on the one hand, and to reduce the rate of liquid soaking into the crust, on the other. Modified corn and waxy maize starches are most commonly used for this purpose, although tapioca, potato or rice starches also yield good results. Supplemental hydrocolloids that also find extensive use as pie filling stabilizers include alginates, carrageenans, guar, locust bean, karaya, xanthan gums and sodium carboxymethyl cellulose, or cellulose gum.

Starches. To be suitable as a thickening agent, starch should possess the following properties: (a) gelatinize readily; (b) yield good gloss and transparency; (c) resist the action of fruit acids; (d) have no effect on fruit flavor and color; and (e) on cooling, form a semisolid gel that has shortness, a syrupy consistency and is free of cereal taste (Trempel 1946). Special modified cross-linked corn starches are normally used for stabilizing pie fillings.

The amount of starch commonly used for thickening ranges from 3.0 to 3.25 oz per qt of liquid, or about 10% on a weight basis. While a starch-water slurry of such concentration would yield an excessively stiff gel, the fruit acids, sweeteners and fruit pulp present in pie fillings act to soften and tenderize the final gel. The higher the fruit or pulp content of a filling, the lower the level of starch needed to impart to it the desirable consistency and body. Thus, fruit fillings containing 50 to 60% fruit will normally require 2 to 4% starch to attain a desirable consistency. As the fruit content of the filling is decreased, the use level of starch as the thickening agent must be increased correspondingly to produce a final filling of the proper consistency, stability and shelf life.

Hydrocolloids. Various forms of alginates find wide use as auxiliary stabilizers, including sodium alginate, propylene glycol alginate, and ammonium/calcium alginate (Dermott 1963, Edlin 1967). These substances all possess distinctly different properties. Thus, sodium alginate yields clear gels that exhibit good freeze-thaw stability and flavor release and finds its use primarily in fruit fillings. In contrast, propylene glycol alginate exhibits both hydrophilic and lipophilic functions and thus acts as a true emulsifier; it is most commonly used in cream, custard and whipped fillings and in high-acidity fruit fillings. Ammonium/calcium alginate is heat resistant, with excellent freeze-thaw stability, and possesses superior thickening properties.

The carrageenans produce high viscosities in aqueous solutions, and their gels are stable over a pH range of 3.5 to 6.0. They generally are used in fruit fillings in combination with sufficient amounts of trisodium citrate to bring the pH to about 3.7 for added stability. Locust bean gum does not enter into complete solution and acts primarily as a swelling agent. It is used mainly to augment the gelling action of the carrageenans. Guar gum swells rapidly in warm water, and its gels are relatively heat-stable and acid-resistant to a pH of 13.2. Cellulose gum yields gels that are thermally reversible as the solution is heated and cooled. It is compatible with most other hydrocolloids and is effective in minimizing syneresis of fillings thickened with corn starch (Bisno 1960a, 1960b).

Xanthan gum, a fermentation product of the microorganism *Xanthomonas campestris*, is made up of a glucose chain in which alternating glucose units possess side chains consisting of two mannose and one glucuronic acid residues. It reacts synergistically with guar and locust bean gums to increase their gel viscosities at either high or low temperatures and is used primarily for this gel-forming reaction in pie fillings, bakery jellies and flavor emulsions (Kelco 1975). Up to 25% of the starch used in stabilizing pie fillings may be replaced by hydrocolloids or gums, which, by their presence, tend to result in a general improvement in the body, syneresis, texture and clarity of the filling (Meer et al. 1973).

Sweeteners. Food starches, when heated in an excess of water, undergo gelatinization within a temperature range of 62 to 78°C (144 to 172°F) (Osman 1972). When sugar is added to the starch slurry, the gelatinization temperature rises with increasing sweetener concentration until eventually no gel formation happens. The amount of sugar present in pie fillings during the boiling stage thus represents an important control factor for the ultimate character of the filling. If the sugar level is too high, the starch will not gelatinize adequately and will yield a gel that lacks luster and body and retains a perceptible cereal taste. With too little sugar present, the gel will set up too firmly and cause

Figure 8.090. For best results, fruit fillings, like this apple filling, are cooked prior to depositing into crusts. (The Schwann Food Co.)

difficulties in subsequent processing.

Normally, the starch-sugar ratio during the gelatinization stage is maintained at 1:3 to 1:3.5 so for each pound of starch used in a batch of boiling fruit, juice and water, a sugar addition of 3.0 to 3.5 lb is required. With frozen fruits that contain variable amounts of sugar, it is generally preferable to defer the incorporation of any additional sugar until full gelatinization has been achieved.

8.M.2.d. Filling preparation

Fruit fillings are normally precooked prior to being deposited into pie crusts (**Figure 8.090**). Depending on the type of fruit involved, the entire fruit mixture may be cooked or only the drained juice to which the various minor ingredients have been added.

In either case, the usual procedure is to place the fruit or the drained juice into the cooking kettle, add the necessary water and part of the sugar, and bring the mixture to a temperature of at least 88°C (190°F), or to a boil. The starch thickener, with any additional hydrocolloids, is added incrementally as a slurry to the hot mixture so as not to lower the temperature of the batch too much. The entire mixture requires slow but thorough stirring until the starch has gelatinized and the mass assumes a clear appearance. The balance of the sweetener is then added, together with any flavoring and color substances required by the formula, and heating is continued only for as long as it is necessary to completely dissolve the sugar.

If the batch has been cooked with the fruit included, then it merely needs cooling to be ready for depositing in the pie shells. If, however, only the juice is cooked, then the fruit must be added and stirred in gently. With some fruits, it may be desirable to bring the combined batch to near boiling temperature to tenderize the fruit, to prevent its "bleeding" and to prevent possible subsequent fermentation. Once the starch has been incorporated and has formed a gel, further processing must be carried out expeditiously to avoid any heat- or acid-induced breakdown of the gel.

Rapid cooling of the cooked fillings, preferably in specially designed cooling tables, offers the best means for preserving their flavor, color and body. Uneven cooling, in which the center of the batch remains at high temperatures much longer than the perimeter and which occurs when the batch is permitted to stand at room temperature or even in a refrigerator, is a major cause of such common faults as bleeding of the fruit and loss of gel stability. Fruit fillings thickened with ordinary (unmodified) starch should not be stored at low temperatures, except for short periods, because chilling results in a loss of gel clarity and stability. With the proper use of approved preservatives, precooked fillings may be held for 3 to 4 days without loss of quality at temperatures of 10 to 16°C (50 to 60°F).

Fruit fillings should be at room temperature when deposited into pie shells. Warm fillings tend to melt the discrete shortening particles dispersed in the pie crust, thereby causing their premature absorption by the dough and, as a consequence, largely destroying the flakiness of the final crust. Also, warm fillings are prone to reach the boiling point too early during the oven stage and hence produce underbaked, soggy bottom crusts. On the other hand, cold fillings, with temperatures of 4 to 10°C (40 to 50°F), also create problems in baking. As Carlson (1942) reported, cool fillings produce partially baked crusts if regular baking times are adhered to, with the crust exterior exhibiting normal coloration, while the crust interior is still in a raw, unbaked state.

Factors that may be responsible for the breakdown of the filling gel include hydrolysis of the starch by fruit acids, which may occur when the filling is held for extended periods at room temperature, and enzymatic starch hydrolysis, which may result when the heat treatment given the fruit is insufficient to inactive its amylolytic enzymes. Imbalances in formulations such as inadequate levels of sweetener, an excess of thickener or an improper stabilizer will result in fillings that exhibit excessive shrinkage, tend to dry out or are otherwise deficient in shelf life. Waxy maize starch, with its high content of the amylopectin fraction and a resultant greater moisture retention capacity, will frequently impart superior shelf life stability to fruit pie fillings.

A common fault of fillings is improper consistency: too thin or too firm. Thin fillings generally indicate an inadequate level of stabilizer or incomplete gelling during the boiling stage. The latter problem can usually be corrected by withholding part of the sugar during the boiling process until complete starch gelatinization is achieved, after which the balance of the sweetener is added. An excessively high sugar level in the filling may cause a subsequent breakdown of the starch gel and result in a fluid, stringy mass. Conversely, if insufficient sugar is used and the deficiency is made up by an increase in starch, the filling tends to become excessively thick and firm.

8.N. Pies and Fried Pies
Updated by Hans van der Maarel

Understanding pastry and pie equipment requires some knowledge of the specific ingredients used for such production. A brief description is provided here. Additional information on ingredients and processing can be found in Chapters 7 and 12.

Pies are pastries that consist of two distinct components: a flour-and-shortening-based thin crust and a filling that is usually made up of either fruits or some type of custard with or without an aerated cream topping. While the filling that comprises the predominant portion of the finished product also normally establishes the specific character of the pie, the overall quality of the pie is influenced in large measure by the structural and eating properties of the crust. Pies may have only a bottom crust, as is usual with the custard and cream varieties, or both bottom and top crusts, as is generally the case with fruit-filled pies. In discussing the technology of pie making, it is convenient to deal separately with the production of the crust and of the filling, discussed in the previous section.

8.N.1. Pie crusts

The crust for pies serves to contain the fillings and toppings. While a good number of refrigerated and frozen creme pies feature crusts made of compressed cookie or graham cracker crumbs, the focus of this segment will be the baked flour-and-shortening pastes that comprise the majority of commercially made pies. (Zelch et al. [2004] offered formulations and procedures for cookie and graham crusts.)

8.N.1.a. Role of ingredients

The character of the pie crust is established to an essentially equal degree by the quality of the ingredients and by the manner in which the dough is mixed and processed. Miller and Trimbo (1970), in reviewing the factors that affect pie crust quality, arrived at the following conclusions: (a) Crust tenderness increases as the level of shortening is increased up to 80%, based on flour, after which the crusts become excessively mealy and fragile; (b) soft shortenings produce more tender crusts than do hard shortenings; (c) crust tenderness is inversely related to the protein level of the flour; (d) crust flakiness is affected by shortening hardness, with soft shortenings tending to produce crusts with shorter flakes; (e) flours with high protein contents will yield very flaky crusts which, however, lack tenderness; and (f) high dough water levels tend toward over-mixing that results in mealy crusts. The range of ingredients in pie crusts is shown in **Table 8.087**.

Flour. Pie doughs are normally made from unbleached pastry flours. Typical analyses of representative pie flours are given in **Table 8.088**. They are generally milled from soft white winter wheat, although soft red winter wheat also finds use for this purpose. The flours are normally unbleached to preserve their mellow character that contributes to a desirable tenderness in the finished crust. The protein content of such pastry flour is usually less than 10%.

Occasionally, excess chlorine treatment is employed to weaken the protein of flours that possess strong gluten properties. Such treatment results in a lowering of the flour's pH from its normal level of about 6.0 to one approaching 5.0; however, over-chlorinated flours tend to yield excessively sticky doughs that are difficult to process.

When suitable pastry flours are not available, bread flour may be used after an appropriate dilution of its high protein content by replacing up to 20% of the bread flour with a cereal starch such as wheat, corn or rice starch to bring its protein to the desired level. The same end may be achieved by blending bread flour with cake flour in a ratio of about 3:2. Such modified flours usually require slight upward adjustments in absorption and shortening to counteract the greater strength of the gluten proteins (Harder and Jabusch 1946).

Shortening. Fat exerts a significant effect on the final structure, texture, tenderness and appearance of the baked crust. The layering effect in pie dough comes from the shortening, present in flat pockets within the dough. It ranges in amount from 20 to 100% (flour weight basis) depending on the type of crust required by the final product. Zelch et al. (2004) noted that 2-crust pies generally have a fat content of

Table 8.087. Pie Dough Formulations for Eating Characteristics

Ingredient	Amount (bakers %)			
	Chewy	←	→	Tender
Flour	100	100	100	100
Fat	50	60	70	80
Water	35	30	25	20
Salt	to taste	to taste	to taste	to taste

(Zelch et al. 2004)

Table 8.088. Typical Analysis of Pie Flours

Component	
Protein, %	8.0 to 8.5
Ash, %	0.40 to 0.44
Moisture, %	13.0 to 13.5
pH	5.95 to 6.05
Viscosity, °MacMichael	45 to 55
Farinograph values	
Peak time, minutes	1.0 to 1.75
Mixing tolerance, minutes	1.5 to 2.5
MTI, BU	80 to 90
Absorption, %	52

(Preonis et al. 1968)

65%; prebaked and unbaked shells, 50 to 60% fat; and fried pies, 20 to 45%.

The kind of fat selected for pie doughs is largely a matter of personal preference. Historically, lard was preferred due to its excellent shortening action and distinctive flavor. However, consumer tastes have changed, and plastic all-vegetable shortenings have taken over. The selection of the most suitable type of pie fat is governed by factors such as prevailing ambient temperatures, method of processing and kind of crust desired. Thus, the specifications of the shortening will differ depending on whether a mealy or flaky crust is to be produced. Pronounced seasonal variations in ambient temperatures may require several adaptations in the functional properties of the pie shortening in the course of a year.

Plasticity is important, as is melting point, but use of a shortening with too low a melting point will result in excessive oiling or soaking of the fat into the flour. The result is a diminishing of the flakiness of the crust. Too high a melting point may lead to a waxy eating texture.

Salt. Flavor enhancement is salt's primary function in pie crusts, and its omission results in an insipid, flat-tasting crust. Levels range from 1.5 to 3%. It is preferably dissolved in the dough water to ensure its uniform distribution and to minimize any toughening effect on the flour proteins.

Water. For optimum results in pie dough mixing, water should be chilled to maintain the low temperatures that yield best results. When available, ice water is preferable for its hardening effect on the dispersed shortening particles. By resisting homogenization during dough mixing, such hard fat particles aid in creating the desired flakiness in the crust. Flakiness is established during the initial flour-shortening blending stage; when chilled or ice water is subsequently added, the discrete fat particles harden sufficiently to survive the mixing process in the form of small individual lumps that eventually produce extended interfaces with the dough.

Other ingredients. Milk enhances crust color and adds to the product's nutritive value. Normally, optimal results are obtained by the addition of 1 to 3% of nonfat dry milk, based on flour. The milk should be properly heat-treated, otherwise it will tend to promote soaking of the bottom crust under warm shelf conditions (Bisno 1950). Crust coloration during baking may also be improved by the use of low levels of dextrose, soy flour, corn syrup or corn syrup solids and/or sodium bicarbonate in the dough formula.

Mold inhibitors, specifically calcium propionate at 0.1 to 0.3% (flour weight basis), are necessary for dough that will be refrigerated. Vinegar may be used to reduce dough pH as a means to retard mold. Reducing agents are sometimes used at the rate of 10 to 100 ppm to decrease shrinkage that may occur on baking.

8.N.1.b. Methods

Preparation of pie doughs is described in Chapter 7, with makeup equipment detailed in Chapter 12. Baking will be discussed here. After mixing, the final dough temperature should range from 13 to 16°C (55 to 60°F). Cool temperatures assist in maintaining the flakiness of the crust. Large-scale pie plants typically keep the mixing and makeup room at a constant 16 to 18°C (60 to 65°F). A rest period of several hours to overnight under refrigeration is typically given to pie doughs before makeup. This cool rest not only keeps the shortening hard but also mellows the gluten for proper hydration.

When baking the filled pie, dual conditions must balance: (a) proper baking of the crust and (b) avoidance of boiling over of the fruit filling. A satisfactory bake will generally be achieved with oven conditions that provide a solid bottom heat and a medium top heat. Commonly recommended oven temperatures for 2-crust pies fall within the range of 219 to 260°C (435 to 500°F). For so-called oven-filled pies such as custard or pumpkin, lower temperatures are in order, for example, 193 to 204°C (380 to 400°F).

A hot oven will obviously cause a filling to boil sooner than will a cool oven, but it will also bake the crust more quickly. Normally, crust browning in a hot oven proceeds at a more rapid pace than does the increase of the temperature of the filling. Hence, boiling over of the filling before the crust is properly baked is a relatively rare occurrence with hot ovens. Cool ovens, on the other hand, need an extended baking time to achieve proper crust color development. The filling is thus exposed to elevated temperatures for a longer period and is more apt to reach the boiling point.

Other conditions add to the tendency of fruit fillings to boil over or stew in the oven. Chief among these problems is an insufficient solids content, whether of fruit or sweetener, which tends to cause the filling to boil over before the crust has been properly baked. Fillings should be formulated so that their minimum solids content, exclusive of the fruit, is not less than 30 to 40% (Denton 1950). To prevent this, the addition of apple powder or apple flakes will help bind moisture and raise the solids level (Deuel 1986).

The time required to properly bake the crust depends on a number of variables, including the levels of sugar, milk and shortening used in formulating the dough, thickness of the crust, type of fruit filling, kind of wash mixture, oven temperature and others. Hence, it is difficult to designate specific baking times. Pies can be baked in basically any oven, but high-volume bakeries typically employ tunnel ovens, either direct or indirectly heated. The temperature of direct gas-fired ovens above the product is usually more difficult to control as heat rises, and the overhead radiation provides an increased bake intensity.

Recent development and use of air impingement ovens has proven beneficial to pie bakers because the only medium of baking is the hot air from heat exchangers, not from any radiation heat. Harder and Jabush (1946) suggested the following representative temperatures and baking times for various types of pies: pies with raw fillings, 227 to 232°C (440 to 450°F) for 35 minutes; pies with cooked fillings, 232°C (450°F) for 30 minutes; empty crust shells, 260°C (500°F) for 12 minutes; and crust shells with custard fillings, 163°C (325°F) for 30 minutes.

8.N.2. Fried pies

Fried pies are distinguished from conventional pies by being fried, like doughnuts, rather than oven-baked. They consist of a golden brown crust, usually covered with a light glaze that envelops a fruit filling of relatively firm consistency. The weight of the filling in fried pies normally exceeds that of the crust, with a ratio of 3 oz of filling to 2 oz of crust being the norm. Individual pies weigh from 4 to 6 oz, comprising a single serving, which is generally eaten out of hand. Much of the taste appeal of fried pies is derived from the fried character of the crust. While the original shape of fried pies was that of a half-moon, obtained by folding over a circular sheet of dough, one-half of which contained the filling, their prevailing current form is that of a rectangle, about 2.5 in. wide by 5 in. long and 1 in. thick (**Figure 8.091**).

Downs (1971) stipulated that the dough for fried pies should possess an adequate degree of toughness but should become short and mealy upon frying. Because the product is intended to be hand-held during consumption, a flaky crust would be too fragile to serve this purpose (Burris 1979). A representative formula for a fried pie dough is given in **Table 8.089**. It specifies soft wheat flour and a good grade of hydrogenated vegetable shortening to yield a dough with good sheeting properties and one that will not shrink during makeup and frying. Dough with a mealy texture tends to work best for fried pie production. Inclusion of low levels of soy flour, sugar, nonfat dry milk and salt serves to improve the dough's handling properties, crust tenderness and crust color and flavor. The dough ingredients are combined with 18 to 20% chilled water and mixed for 5 to 7 minutes at low speed in a vertical double-arm mixer to produce an extensible dough that when pulled apart stretches slightly before parting. The dough temperature should be kept low — 18°C (65°F) or lower (Burris 1979) — to facilitate trouble-free handling on the production line. The dough should have a rest period, or floor time, of about 15 minutes to permit more uniform distribution of the limited water present.

The dough is sheeted into a long, continuous ribbon, free from pin holes and requiring only a minimum of dusting flour. Some bakers include reducing agents such as L-cysteine or sodium bisulfite to aid sheeting.

Either fresh or frozen fruit may be used for fried pies, with the most popular varieties being apple, peach, cherry, pineapple and berry (**Figure 8.092**). Lemon and chocolate are also favorites. The filling, on a total batch basis, contains about 40% fruit solids, 25% sugar, 31% liquids that include drained juice and added water and 5 to 6% modified corn starch as the stabilizer. Cooking of the filling is performed in a jacketed steam kettle under continuous stirring. The fruit is first boiled until tender, the starch is then added and cooking continued until complete gelatinization is achieved, when the sugar addition is made. The cooked filling is then transferred to a jacketed cooling table where circulating cold water or refrigerant is used to bring about rapid cooling to room temperature.

Figure 8.091. Fried fruit pies receive a syrup glaze almost immediately after exiting the fryer.
(Heat and Control)

Table 8.089. Pie Crust Mix for Fried Pies

Ingredient	% (flour weight basis)
Soft wheat flour	100.0
Soy flour	6.0
Nonfat dry milk solids	2.0
Sugar	6.0
Salt	2.5
Sodium propionate	0.5
Hydrogenated shortening	30.0

(Downs 1971)

8.O. Cookies

Updated by L.A. Gorton

Cookies are small, slightly raised, hard, crisp sweetened items made from chemically leavened, cake-like batters, which can often be quite stiff. That description defines "cookie" to American and Canadian consumers, but the British would term this item a "biscuit." On the other hand, Americans describe biscuits as shortened quick bread leavened with baking powder or soda, and American bakers would note that formulation and production of biscuits are much like those of muffins. The word "biscuit" comes from Old French (and Latin before that) meaning "twice baked," while "cookie" developed from the Dutch word "koekje," the diminutive of "koek" (cake).

So is there a difference between biscuits and cakes? Here, a legal definition intervenes, at least in the UK. In 1991, the British baker McVitie's challenged imposition of the country's value added tax (VAT) on its Jaffa Cakes. Under UK law, no VAT is charged on biscuits and cakes, but chocolate-covered biscuits are subject to a 15% VAT.

Jaffa Cakes measure 54 mm (2.175 in.) and consist of a sponge cake base, a layer of orange-flavored jelly and a coating of dark chocolate (**Figure 8.093**). McVitie's claimed that these products were miniature cakes, not biscuits, and produced a 30-cm (12-in.) diameter sample to prove it to the court. The bakery argued that the difference between cakes and biscuits is that biscuits would normally be expected to go soft when stale, whereas cakes go hard. The company also pointed to the manufacturing process (a sponge cake batter deposited onto a baking band) as another proof of the cake nature of the product.

Her Majesty's Customs and Excise court ruled that the Jaffa Cake is a cake and thus no VAT is due.

Figure 8.092. A bubbly crust and rectangular shape characterize fried pies prepared for fast food operations. (Fresh Start Bakeries)

8.O.1. Styles

Cookies may be defined as small cakes made from a dough that is sufficiently viscous to permit the dough pieces to be baked on a flat surface (Pieper 1968). This definition is broad enough to encompass the almost infinite diversity in shape, size, composition, texture, tenderness, color, flavor and taste that marks the products that fall under the general designation of a cookie in the US. Despite the apparently seamless transition of one cookie type into the next, there are certain fundamental distinctions that permit them to be classified into several basic categories. Thus, Pieper (1968) proposed that they be grouped according to the basic forming machine employed in their production into: (a) cutting machine cookies, (b) rotary moulded cookies (**Figure 8.094**), (c) bar machine cookies, (d) wire-cut cookies (**Figure 8.095**) and (e) deposited cookies.

The differences in cookie formulation largely follow the requirements of the particular method employed in their production. The rheological properties of the cookie dough must conform closely to the needs of the forming and shaping machines being used. Thus, extremes in dough consistency are encountered among doughs intended for processing by the deposit machine, on the one hand, and by the rotary machine, on the other. In the former instance, the dough requires a nearly batter-like fluidity, whereas in the latter case, the dough needs to be rather firm and dry. According to Velzen (1963), the most appropriate ratios of flour, shortening and sugar for the different cookie types are the following: wire-cut cookies, 100:50:50; rotary machine cookies, 100:30:30; and cutting machine cookies, 100:50:variable. In practice, considerable variations can be found in these ratios, but excessive deviations will result either in machining difficulties or in the impairment of the ultimate quality of the finished product. Ratios are summarized in **Table 8.090**.

The nearly limitless diversity of commercially produced cookies precludes a de-

Figure 8.093. Cut in half, a McVitie's Jaffa Cake shows its cake base, orange jelly filling and chocolate coating.

tailed consideration, in a general work on baking such as this, of their individual formulations and specific technologies. For more extensive discussions of this subject, the reader should consult specialized texts and monographs such as those by Bohn (1957), Matz (1968), Whitley (1971), Smith (1972), Manley (1983) and Lehmann et al. (1994). A series of studies at the American Institute of Baking examined the specific effects on cookie performance of fats (Vetter 1984), continuous mixing (Kulp and Olewnik 1984), chlorinated flour (Kulp et al. 1985), sweetener syrups (Vetter et al. 1986) and chemical leavening (Vetter and Zeak 1989). Kulp (1994) provided chapters concerning flour, carbohydrates, fats and oils, chemical leavening, eggs and minor ingredients involved in cookie formulating, along with numerous cookie formulations. Yener (2008) summarized the rheology of cookie doughs, providing the relational equations for evaluating stress, viscosity and other aspects affected by ingredient variations.

Figure 8.094. Rotary moulded cookies feature embossed images and designs on their tops.

8.O.1.a. Deposit

Deposit or drop cookies require a dough that approaches layer cake batters in fluidity. Their formulations will typically contain 35 to 40% sugar, 65 to 75% shortening and 15 to 25% liquid whole eggs, based on flour weight (Matz 1968). The category is the machine-made counterpart of hand-bagged cookies such as spritz styles.

8.O.1.b. Wire-cut

Wire-cut cookies vary widely in both their formulations and final shapes. They are the machine-made counterpart to hand-scooped, hand-dropped or rolled-and-cut cookies, and their doughs range in consistency from soft cake batters to quite stiff doughs similar to those used in rotary cookie production. They tend to be more open in texture and somewhat less uniform than deposited or rotary-cut cookies.

The basic prerequisites for the doughs are that they possess adequate cohesiveness to hold together yet yield clean separations of the individual dough pieces as they are cut by the wire. In the case of special, high-quality cookies, dough formulations may contain well over 100% sugar, up to 100% shortening and up to 25% liquid whole eggs, all based on flour. Representative formulations for the highly popular chocolate chip and oatmeal wire-cut cookies are shown in **Tables 8.091** and **8.092**.

Figure 8.095. Wire-cut cookies tend to include particulates such as chocolate chips or nuts and offer a homemade appearance.

8.O.1.c. Bar cookies

Bar-type cookies are processed in a fashion similar to that of wire-cut cookies, except that here the rather soft dough is extruded from the hopper through narrow slit dies onto a conveyor belt or an oven band (**Figure 8.096**) and then cut into desired length by a guillotine cutter either before or after baking. The jacket dough comprises about 40% of the finished cookie, the jam 60%. Eggs keep the dough jacket soft and tender after baking. Although fig jam is the most common filling, other fruits such as apples, strawberries, blueberries and raspberries are finding more frequent use.

Table 8.090. Major Ingredients of Cookie Doughs by Type			
Type	Water (bakers %)	Shortening (bakers %)	Sugars (bakers %)
Rotary moulded	5 to 15	10 to 40	20 to 45
Cutting machine	10 to 25	5 to 20	15 to 50
Wire-cut	10 to 40	10 to 50	30 to 85
(Matz 1968)			

8.O.1.d. Rotary moulded

As their name implies, rotary moulded cookies are shaped and moulded by a cylinder in whose surface are embossed variously designed dies. Dough from the hopper

Table 8.091. Representative Formula for Chocolate Chip Cookies

Ingredient	Amount (bakers %)
Flour	100
Sugar	75
Shortening	60
Egg solids	7
Water	17
Salt	1.25
Sodium bicarbonate	0.6
Flavor	1
Chocolate chips	55

(Reget 1966)

Table 8.092. Representative Formula for Oatmeal Cookies

Ingredient	Amount (bakers %)
Oatmeal and flour (50:50)	100
Shortening	50
Sugar	60
Sodium bicargonate	1
Salt	2
Nonfat dry milk solids	2
Egg solids	2
Flavor	1
Cinnamon	0.25
Water	15
Invert sugar	2
Chocolate chips (or ground raisins or ground dates)	30

(Reget 1966)

is forced into these dies by a pair of serrated feed rolls. The excess dough is trimmed off the die cylinder by a closely fitted knife or scraper blade. The moulded dough pieces are then extracted from the die cavities by an extraction belt of special weave for transfer onto the oven band.

Doughs designed for the production of rotary moulded cookies should be well mixed, with a relatively firm consistency. Their formulation should yield a plasticity that will ensure good moulding properties. In other words, they should readily fill the die cavities under appropriate pressure from the feed rolls, and they should possess sufficient cohesiveness so the dough pieces will retain their shape on extraction. During baking, there should be just enough flow to obliterate and soften any imperfections or irregularities in the surface design of the cookie. A representative formula for rotary moulded cookies is given in **Table 8.093**.

8.O.1.e. Cutting machine

Cutting-machine cookies (**Figure 8.097**) differ in their production in one basic aspect from the other categories: They require a preliminary dough sheeting and/or laminating process, rather than a simple extrusion process. The individual cookies are then cut or stamped out from the resulting continuous sheet by either reciprocating or rotary cutters. For this operation to be more or less trouble-free, the dough must have sufficient cohesiveness to produce a uniformly thin, continuous sheet yet also exhibit enough shortness to ensure a clean separation of the cut or stamped dough pieces from the remaining scrap dough. This style of cookie includes the hard biscuits known as "digestives."

8.O.1.f. Biscotti and more

Biscotti. This style of cookie originated in the Tuscany region of Italy, and the name is a literal translation of "twice baked," which describes the process for making biscotti (**Figure 8.098**). Lewis (1997) detailed their formulation and manufacturer. A typical formula comprises 25 to 36% flour (pastry, bread or whole-wheat),

Figure 8.096. A coextrusion system lays down filled cookie dough logs to be baked and then cut into individual bar cookies. *(Baking & Snack)*

22 to 28% sweeteners (granulated sugar, brown sugar, dextrose, corn syrup, honey, molasses), 10 to 16% eggs (whole, yolks, whites), 6 to 12% shortening (butter, vegetable shortening, lard, tallow), 0.5 to 1.25% leavening (baking powder), all measured in formula percent, along with various flavorings and particulates (nuts, chocolate chips). They may be topped, dipped or completely coated in chocolate or compound coatings, often flavored.

The process involves mixing the dough using methods similar to other cookies, with particulates added last. The dough is chilled and the formed into slightly flattened logs. An egg wash and top coating of granulated sugar is sometimes applied. The logs under go a first bake at 163 to 177°C (325 to 350°F) for 30 to 40 minutes. Allowed to cool for 30 minute to 1 hour, the logs are then sliced transversely into pieces 0.75 to 1 in. wide. Placed cut-side up on pans or the oven belt, the pieces bake a second time at 163°C (325°F) for 10 to 15 minutes. The second bake is actually a drying process that removes moisture and adds very little color. When cooled again, the biscotti receive coatings or toppings, and a period of tempering sets the coating to allow packaging.

Brownies. A chocolate-flavored bar cookie, brownies have more in common with cakes than cookies, when it comes to their formulations (**Table 8.094**). They are produced by mixing the soft batter and then depositing it onto sheet pans or directly onto a solid oven band. Cutting by guillotine, water-jet or sonic systems creates the individual bars. A regional difference in brownie styles exists among some consumers, with fudgy textures generally favored in the South and more cake-like products preferred in the North. And the bar type is the richest of them all.

While cocoa powder is the most commonly used form of chocolate flavoring for brownies, chocolate liquor may also be used (Smith 2001). Blond, or butterscotch, brownies are made without cocoa but often include chocolate chips as well as nuts.

Cake brownies exhibit the greatest volume, fudge brownies the least. When mixing cake brownies, aeration of the batter is desired so mixing times can be relative long. Fudge and brownies should be dense so mixing must be done without much air incorporation. Because the high sugar-to-flour ratio of fudge and bar types increases their tendency to collapse, Smith (2001) recommended use of smaller baking pans.

Brownies may be iced with any of several toppings, including chocolate and compound coating as well as high-density buttercreme.

Sometimes a thin, light-colored shiny crust will form on the surface of baked brownies and cakes. At its most exaggerated, it puffs up and can separate from the rest of the item. According to Corriher (2008), this happens when over-mixing the dough after eggs are added. The egg white and sugar components form a meringue that collects at the top of the batter and creates this crust.

Dual-textured cookies. Described as "crisp on the outside, soft in the middle,"

Table 8.093. Representative Formula for Rotary Moulded Cookies	
Ingredient	Amount (bakers %)
Flour	100
Sugar	40 to 50
Shortening	35 to 40
Salt	1.5
Nonfat dry milk solids	2
Invert sugar	2
Sodium bicarbonate	0.5
Egg solids	2
Water	8
Flavor	1.5

(Reget 1966)

Figure 8.097. Biscuits of this European style are made from laminated doughs and cut by stamping.

Figure 8.098. Biscotti are baked twice to produce their unique hard texture. (American Egg Board)

dual-textured cookies are made by co-extruding two different doughs. Use of different sweetening systems creates the gradient in texture that characterizes these cookies. The same extrusion technology can be used to create filled cookies as well as those with different colored doughs (**Figure 8.099**).

Table 8.094. Brownie Formulations

Ingredient	Fudge type (bakers %)	Cake type (bakers %)	Bar type (bakers %)
Flour, pastry	100	100	100
Sugar, granulated	166	133	300
Cocoa	25	28	38
Shortening	67	88	88
Salt	4	4	4
Corn syrup	25	–	–
Vanilla	4	4	4
Whole eggs	50	45	45
Liquid milk	25	24	55
Leavening	1	1	1
Nuts	75	75	75

(Smith 2001)

Figure 8.099. Multiple doughs and fillings can be co-extruded to create interesting new cookie styles. (DFE Meincke)

Lady fingers. Another deposited style item, lady fingers are often found on the cookie shelves of supermarkets, but they are actually cake products based on the pound cake formula.

Macaroons. More a candy than a cookie, macaroons (**Figure 8.100**) are deposited cookies made with little or no flour but large proportions of sugar and, of course, shredded coconut kept moist by glycerin and/or corn syrup. They are held together by egg white. Some bakers use leaveners (sodium bicarbonate and tartaric acid) to spread the deposit slightly.

Shortbread cookies. Made by wire-cut or rotary methods, shortbread cookies contain shortening in amounts of one-half to three-quarters of the weight of flour. Butter or margarine is preferred for these cookies because of the flavor provided.

Soft cookies. In recent years, several types of cookies characterized by soft textures and relatively high moisture contents have achieved a considerable degree of consumer acceptance. Their formulation usually combines relatively high levels of invert syrup and eggs with the regular use of vanilla, spices, honey and other flavor and enriching materials. Popularly referred to as "soft" or "home-style" cookies, they may be grouped into three general types, namely, drop cookies, folded cookies and bar cookies. The drop cookies are essentially high-moisture versions of conventional wire-cut cookies with a more cake-like eating quality. In folded cookies, a fruit jam or jelly filling is deposited onto the flat dough piece before it is folded and baked. Smith (1970) described in some detail the formulation, ingredient requirements, production procedures and general characteristics of soft cookies.

Trolley cakes. A form of deposited or wire-cut cookie, trolley cakes are enrobed by dipping into marshmallow and chocolate coatings and then finished with a shiny transparent sugar coating much like a water icing (**Figure 8.101**). Matz (1968) noted that the basecakes for this cookie can also be made from doughs flavored with honey, vanilla, coconut, raisins and other materials as long as they have sufficient structural integrity to hang on the trolley hooks during the dipping and transfer stages of the process. The method does not accommodate excessively tender basecakes so formulations cannot use high levels of shortening.

8.O.2. Role of ingredients

The ultimate texture of the cookie is established by the balance of both toughening and tenderizing ingredients, with flour providing the basic framework. Ingredients that contribute to structure formation include water, whole eggs and egg whites, milk solids, cocoa and leavening acids. On the other hand, product tenderness is imparted by sugars and syrups, egg yolk, shortening, leavening agents, starch and by non-reactive substances in general.

As Faridi (1990) observed, cookie doughs are cohesive but to a large degree lack the extensibility and elasticity characteristic of bread doughs. The relatively high quantities of fat and sugar in the dough allow dough plasticity without the formation of a gluten network (Hoseney 1986).

While the type and overall character of cookies are largely the result of the kind of machine processing they receive (**Table 8.095**), their intrinsic quality depends mainly on the suitability of the ingredients employed in their production and by their formulation. Not only must the functional performance of ingredients conform to the special needs of cookie processing, but the formulations must also be properly balanced if costly production problems and serious quality impairment are to be avoided.

Figure 8.100. Coconut macaroons are a cookie made with little or no flour but lots of coconut and sugar, held together by egg white.
(Richard Lanenga)

Flour. While acceptable cookies can be made from hard wheat flours — with appropriate increases in the formula levels of sugar and shortening — cookie flours are generally milled from soft white winter and soft red winter wheat varieties. Flours of low starch damage are preferred.

Cookie flours are normally long patent or straight-grade flours that may be, but generally are not, chlorinated, depending on the spread factor required by the baker. The spread factor is obtained by dividing the width in mm by the thickness in mm of a baked round cookie whose raw dough dimensions are standardized to 7 mm in thickness and 60 mm in diameter. Typically, these flours fall within the following range of specifications: protein content 9.0 to 10.0%, ash content, 0.40 ± 0.05%, pH, 4.0 to 6.0; and spread factor 5.5 to 9.5 (Mansour 1982).

The changes in flour proteins that result from chlorination tend to interfere with cookie spread. Heavily chlorinated flours produce cookies with reduced spread and correspondingly greater thickness (Brenneis 1965) so chlorination of cookie flours is normally omitted. Exceptions are flours intended for the production of soft cookies in which greater strength is required to carry the higher levels of tenderizing and enriching ingredients.

Figure 8.101. Cake-like cookies coated with marshmallow and chocolate are actually low in fat.
(Kraft Foods)

Kulp et al. (1985) revisited the subject of chlorination's affect on cookie quality and determined that the functional changes in flours due to chlorination were most likely to be caused by changes in proteins and possibly lipids, and while they cast doubt on the contribution of starch changes, they noted that chlorination degraded pentosans, which normally inhibit spread.

The flour most commonly used for deposit cookies is a soft white winter wheat flour with a protein content of 7.5 to 8.5%, an ash content of 0.38 to 0.42%, a viscosity of 30 to 50°MacMichael, a spread factor of 90 to 100 and pH of 5.8 to 6.0.

Table 8.095. Typical Percentages of Various Cookie Types (United States)

Ingredient	Wire-cut (butter cookie)	Rotary-moulded (vanilla basecake)	Extruded (vanilla spritz)	Deposited (spongette)
Butter	30.00	–	5.00	22.00
Shortening	30.00	25.00	40.00	22.00
Sugar	40.00	30.00	55.00	75.00
Salt	0.62	0.60	0.75	–
Whole eggs	10.00	–	12.00	42.00
Flour	100.00	100.00	100.00	100.00
Sodium bicarbonate	0.40	0.60	–	1.00
Water	18.50	12.80	20.70	30.90
Nonfat dry milk	–	2.00	3.00	–
Vanilla	–	0.50	–	–
Ammonium bicarbonate	–	0.50	–	–
Flavor	–	–	0.66	–
Dough-out temperature	21 to 23°C (70 to 75°F)	21 to 23°C (70 to 75°F)	21 to 23°C (70 to 75°F)	16 to 18°C (60 to 65°F)

All percentages are based on flour equal to 100%.
(Lehmann et al. 1994)

When stronger flours are used to prevent excessive cookie spread during baking and to preserve any top design imparted by the extrusion, the levels of shortening and sugar need to be increased to retain optimum tenderness.

Standardized cookie formulations for wire-cut and sugar snap styles are used by AACC International Approved Methods for testing to study the effects of flour quality on cookie properties. The sugar snap is the most widely used procedure (Hoseney 2007).

Shortening. Bakery shortenings play a critical functional role in biscuit processing. They aid in machinability, control shelf life and define the finished product texture. The shortening typically provides the structure of the biscuit. It also shortens the protein strands from knitting or matrixing together and reduces the interaction between gluten proteins and carbohydrates in wheat flour. It also affects flavor release in the finished cookie. In the brittle cookie matrix, fat acts as a filler at low concentrations (16% by weight), resulting in a fat-dispersed system, or forms a partly continuous phase at high concentrations (28% by weight), a fat-continuous system.

Shortenings are made up of three basic components: the base fat of either animal or vegetable origin, the hard fats or flakes and the emulsifier, which is normally a monoglyceride or one of its esters. Most vegetable hydrogenated shortenings are currently manufactured from blends of cottonseed, soybean and palm oils.

In sandwich cremes, fats have dual functions: They carry the sugar and other ingredients, and they establish finished product eating quality by controlling the consistency and body of cremes (Vetter 1984). The filler fat forms the continuous phase in the creme by coating the sugar particles and other materials present. As particle size decreases, its surface area increases, requiring higher levels of fat for complete coverage. Large particle size and too little fat will give a gritty, dry mouthfeel to the creme. These negative aspects also occur when the fat selected is too high in solids at temperatures of 21 to 27°C (70 to 80°F), yet if the fat is too low in solids at these temperatures, the creme will be soft and may smear out of the sandwich. Excess solids at temperatures of 33°C (92°F) and above will produce a creme that does not melt properly when consumed, resulting in a waxy sensation on eating.

Dairy products. In cookies, dairy ingredients improve the color, texture, taste, shelf life and nutritional value of the products. It is recommended that the dairy ingredients be added at the initial stage of the mixing process to ensure complete incorporation into the dough and thus reduce brown spotting and lumping. In biscuit processing, milk products affect the flavor, taste, color, texture and nutritional levels.

Eggs. Both liquid whole eggs, either in their frozen or fresh state, and dried whole eggs may be used almost interchangeably in cookie production. Many bakers continue to prefer liquid eggs, either fresh or frozen, to dried eggs, perceiving that the former make a greater contribution to the structure, volume and texture of the final cookie product than do dried eggs.

Sweeteners. While sugar over a wide range of granulations is used in cookie production, most bakers prefer finely granulated sugar for its rapid solution during dough mixing, even though coarser granulations yield cookies with a more tender texture and greater spread. Sucrose acts as a hardening agent by crystallizing as the cookie cools, which makes the product crisp, yet large amounts of sugar tend to make cookie dough sticky and hinder release from dies and wires (Hoseney 1986).

Although powdered sugar dissolves still more rapidly, it tends to decrease cookie spread and cookie tenderness. In high-sugar cookies, replacing sucrose with corn sweeteners up to 20% not only reduces the intense sweetness of the finished product but also contributes to the tenderness, open texture and eye appeal of the finished product (Hickenbottom 1977).

In recent years, the greater availability of high-fructose corn syrup has led to its increasing use as a supplemental sweetener in many cookie formulations. However, the formulator must make sure that the amount of water in the syrup does not exceed the total water in the formula.

Soft cookies tend to lose moisture during storage, and the physical state of the sugar (sucrose) in these products can change, often spontaneously, resulting in a loss of soft texture. As long as the sugar is present in a dissolved or supersaturated syrup state, the texture will remain soft. If the sugar crystallizes from the syrup, the texture becomes hard and brittle. Vetter et al. (1986) examined the effect of sweetener syrups (full invert syrup and high-fructose corn syrup) on the hygroscopicity of soft cookies, their ability to hold water in the finished product. They found that the use of these syrups had the following effects: (a) higher initial and equilibrium moisture content, (b) slower rate of moisture loss during storage, (c) reduction in cookie spread and height, (d) reduction in top surface cracks, (e) increased initial softness of texture and (f) increased tendency to maintain softness during storage when 50% or more of the sugar is replaced with invert syrup or HFCS. A reduction in bake time resulted from a higher initial moisture content, but an increased rate of moisture loss occurred in cookies during storage.

The different humectant qualities of sweeteners permit creation of dual-textured cookies composed of 2 doughs, one resulting in soft texture and the other crisp. One dough contains sucrose, and the other adds a crystallization inhibitor such as corn syrup or invert sugar (**Table 8.096**). Packaging with superior barriers against vapor and gas transmission is a must for such products.

Malt, in the form of flour, extract or syrup, is widely used as a flavor-enhancing ingredient and as a humectant in cookie production. Invert syrup, when properly used, produces a tenderizing effect on the cookie texture that is particularly desirable with soft cookie types, improves the product's moisture retention and also accelerates crust coloration.

Leavening. Vetter and Zeak (1989) explained the use of chemical leavening in

Table 8.096. Dual-Textured Cookies Formula

Ingredient	Amount (bakers %)
Outer dough	
Pulverized sugar	90
Hydrogenated shortening	37
Vanilla flavor	variable
Sodium bicarbonate (soda)	0.8
Salt	0.8
Molasses	6
Unbleached cookie flour	100
Water	19 (variable)
Inner dough	
Pulverized sugar	37
Margarine (or hydrogenated shortening and butter flavor)	54
Vanilla flavor	variable
Sodium bicarbonate (soda)	1.5
Salt	1.5
Invert syrup	95
Whole powdered eggs (predissolved in water*)	2
Invertase enzyme	0.2
Pre-gelatinized corn starch	8
Pastry flour	100
Pure chocolate chips	120

** Water comprises 10%, flour weight basis*
(Moreth 1994)

cookies and crackers, studying the effects of sodium (soda) and ammonium bicarbonate (ABC) as the carbon dioxide sources, alone and in combination with the leavening acids monocalcium phosphate (MCP) and sodium acid pyrophosphate (SAPP). Leaveners primarily affect the grain and texture of cookies. With no leavening, very dense grain and brittle, hard texture are the result. Soda by itself can provide some gas because many ingredients in the cookie dough are slightly acidic. The fast-acting acid MCP works in the mixer to improve overall grain.

In general, rich products with relatively high levels of shortening and sugar require lower levels of leavening to achieve the desired volume and tenderness. Conversely, lean doughs such as those used for rotary moulding are improved by leavening.

Use of leaveners affects spread and height, but to a limited extent. According to Vetter and Zeak (1989), spread is better controlled by reducing the chlorination of the flour, using a harder flour and/or adjusting sugar and shortening levels.

Surface cracks, or checking, form when leavening gases are released from a still plastic internal dough after the top exterior of the cookie sets. Delayed release leavening from soda or ABC will result in such cracks so adjusting their levels will be most effective in controlling surface cracks.

The choice of leavening also influences pH of the dough and finished product and, hence, its color. Browning, for example, is accelerated at alkaline pH and retarded at acidic pH. The formulator should work to achieve a neutral pH in the finished cookie for optimum color and flavor. Many chocolate products, however, benefit from an alkaline pH, achieved by adding excess soda.

Minor ingredients. Additional materials that are commonly used in cookie production include (a) salt, at levels of 0.75% to 1.25%, whose principal role is that of a flavor enhancer; (b) various types of surfactants to assist in the homogeneous dispersion of fat; and (c) different flavors and colors, whose uses are dictated by the demands of the market for traditional and special flavors and colors in different cookie varieties.

8.O.3. Processing effects

Chapter 12, Part D, describes the equipment for preparing and baking cookie doughs, while their doughmaking processes are reported in Chapter 7, Parts A and B. The discussion here looks at some of the processing variables involved. Hoseney (2007) also described the technology of cookie and cracker production, giving special attention to the role that flour quality plays in the process. Tireki (2008) summarized cookie processing principles, with particular attention to the oven's effects on products.

Horizontal mixers and, recently, continuous mixers produce the stiff, tight doughs required for cookie manufacturing. Because the water content of cookie doughs is so low (about 10 to 20%), the high content of sugar and shortening results in a dough in which gluten does not develop; the hydration of this protein is insufficient to form a gluten network. Although cookie mixing procedures do not allow gluten to develop, cookie doughs are often left to relax for 30 to 45 minutes before makeup.

The creaming of sugar and shortening during cookie dough preparation not only coats the sugar particles with shortening but also incorporates air, which serves to nucleate the air cells that leaven the cookie during baking. Chemical leaveners act during the processing of cookies to inflate those cells.

Cookie dough's void fraction — the air cells — governs the mechanical and fracture properties of cookies. Aeration thus influences final cookie size and texture, and its importance to producing biscuit (cookie) doughs was studied by Brijwani et al. (2008) by varying the atmosphere present in the headspace of the mixer, using normal air, 100% carbon dioxide (CO_2) and 100% nitrogen (N_2) at various pressures, including partial vacuum. The resulting doughs were sheeted, cut and baked, and the cookies showed a variety of different textures. The gas content of cookie doughs mixed under partial vacuum and 100% CO_2 was lower than that of the dough mixed under 100% N_2 and partial vacuum. Doughs mixed at higher pressures showed more gas loss during sheeting but still retained significantly greater amounts of gas than those mixed at normal pressures. These results demonstrated that varying the headspace gas compositions and pressures affects cookie characteristics, with the potential for making products with novel textures and enhanced consumer appeal.

Cookie doughs are generally soft with little to no cohesive properties, often termed a "short dough." They are processed by compression into dies (rotary moulded) or by extrusion to be cut off by a wire (wire cut) or a guillotine (bar style). "Hard dough" describes a different type of cookie dough. These stiff doughs produce cookies with a firmer bite than do short doughs. They contain more water (20 to 30%, flour weight basis) and less sugar than short doughs and thus allow some gluten development during mixing and processing. Hard doughs are typically processed by sheeting and cutting machines; the gluten development stops spreading baking of this type of cookie.

In the production of deposit cookies, the dough, mixed by the conventional creaming and mixing method, is placed into the hopper of the depositing machine. These doughs are more fluid than rotary moulded or wire-cut styles, although pressure is still needed to force them through nozzles that deposit the individual dough pieces either on cookie sheets or, in larger operations, on a belt for subsequent transfer to the oven band or directly on the oven band.

At large wholesale bakeries, cookie baking takes place in band ovens, varying in length from 30 to 150 m, with a solid steel or woven wire mesh band up to 1.2 m wide. These ovens employ direct and indirect heating methods, and newer hybrid ovens may combine these methods. Baking temperatures vary from about 200 to 240°C (392 to 464°F), and completion is judged by the products color and moisture content.

Steam is also a significant leavener of cookies. To prevent the steam from escaping the oven during baking's early stages, exhaust dampers are closed. They are opened later to facilitate the moisture removal necessary to bring the product to optimum moisture content.

Study of cookie baking using the AACC formulations reveals three successive but overlapping stages, described by Hoseney (2007). In the first, the dough piece increases in thickness due to the leavening action of air and carbon dioxide, and moisture loss starts. In the second, the product sets as spread stops and moisture loss reaches its maximum. In the third, coloring occurs.

During these stages, the fat melts, causing the dough to flow under the force of gravity. Because cookie doughs are so low in water, only half the sugar dissolves during mixing, the remainder stays in a crystalline state until the dough is heated. This action increases the volume of solution because 1 g of sugar, dissolved in 1 g of water produces about 1.6 cu cm of solution. The sugar actually has an anti-plasticizing effect in cookie doughs.

Cookie expansion is related to the viscosity of the system. The low water and high sugar content allows only a minimal, if any, amount of starch gelatinization. Some other factor must be involved, and it turns out to be the protein quality of the flour that has the most effect on viscosity during baking. Although gluten is generally not developed during mixing and makeup, the component proteins (glutenin and gliadin) undergo their glass transition during baking, gaining mobility, which allows them to interact and form a continuous gluten phase. The viscosity of this phase is sufficient to stop the flow of cookie dough.

Checking. The air volume within the cookie and how it is distributed determines the product's finished texture. Large air cells are a size defect that causes fracture, or checking, and such crack initiation is followed by crack propagation.

Moisture is lost from the surface at a rapid rate during baking, to be replaced by water diffusing from the interior, thus concentrating the sugar syrup to a greater extent. When sugar crystallizes at the surface of the cookie, it releases its water and keeps the surface moist and flexible. However, the surface continues to dry, and if the leavening system releases more gas, it will expand any cracks to result in the surface breaking characteristic of many types of cookies. Small levels of high-fructose corn syrup or other humectants will interfere with sugar crystallization and inhibit cracking.

8.P. Crackers
Updated by L.A. Gorton

Products marketed under the generic designation of crackers range widely, with some closely similar to semisweet, machine-cut cookies, while others have a fermented, crisp, nonsweet, laminated nature all their own. The former, which are nearly all chemically leavened, include the categories of the semisweet graham crackers and the highly flavored snack crackers with predominant onion, garlic, caraway, smoke, bacon, chicken or cheese flavors, among others. In the category of fermented products, the soda or saltine cracker is the most representative type, although the cream cracker also belongs to this group.

These baked foods reportedly got their name, cracker, from the crackling sounds they made during baking.

The first crackers to be produced commercially in the American colonies were a form of pilot bread or hardtack, a very hard, flinty product made for sailors and travelers (Krubert 1990). Such products had to be low in moisture and free of fats that could go rancid to achieve the extended shelf life needed for long journeys. Strouts (2008a) traced the evolution of hardtack into today's flaky, rich snack crackers and saltines. Hardtack was usually broken up into coffee, soup or stews, and it supplied the needs of armies as late as World War I. Application of fermentation and addition of shortening considerably improved the eating quality and appeal of crackers.

Pilot bread, by the way, remains an essential ingredient in old-fashioned New England clam chowder and is widely consumed by Alaskans and Civil War re-enactors. It is also a mainstay in parts of Canada, particularly the Maritime Provinces.

8.P.1. Styles

In the US, the term "cracker" is applied to products made from flour and fat with levels of sugar varying from 0 to about 40% (flour weight basis), with saltines representing one extreme and graham crackers the other. In the UK, the term is given to products made from flour and fat but with little, if any, added sugars. The British-style products include cream crackers and water biscuits. Semisweet biscuits, which contain 20 to 30% sugar (flour weight basis), include rich tea, morning coffee, thin arrowroot and similar styles, but they bear no resemblance to American crackers (Hoseney 2007).

General formulations for US-style crackers are offered in **Table 8.097**.

8.P.1.a. Chemically leavened

Graham crackers. When properly formulated and processed, graham crackers possess a slightly sweet, nutty, caramel-like flavor. This typical graham flavor is derived in part from the bran portion of whole-wheat flour and in part from various sweeteners, generally molasses, brown sugar, malt and honey (Smith 1972). Typically, formulations for high-quality graham crackers will include the following ingredient levels: flour, 100%; whole-wheat or graham flour, 25%; granulated sugar, 25%; brown sugar, 10%; honey, 11%; malt syrup, 1%; shortening, 18%; whey solids 4%; sodium bicarbonate, 1.25%; leavening acid, 1.0%; ammonium bicarbonate, 0.75%; lecithin, 0.5%; and water (variable), 34%. Cinnamon is a common flavoring.

While the typical shape for a graham cracker is a perforated (docked) square or rectangle, styles also feature small animal shapes. A chocolate-flavored variety is particularly popular with small children and their parents. When the Rev. Sylvester Graham invented the crackers in 1929 that now bear his name, he offered them as a health food because they contained whole-wheat flour and honey.

Snack crackers. Flavored with cheese, onions, garlic, sun-dried tomatoes, plus herbs and spices, snack crackers provide consumers with a wide variety from which to choose. Typically small in size, snack crackers are produced in squares, circles, rectangles, ovals, triangles, random-edged oblongs and even animal shapes. A woven texture, produced in a fashion similar to that of popular ready-to-eat breakfast cereals, characterizes several lines of snack crackers. Their formulations are typically savory, rather than sweet, and they are often finished with an oil spray followed by an application of cheese powder or other seasonings (**Figure 8.102**).

Sandwich crackers, made with shelf-stable cheese or peanut butter fillings, are an important product in the snack food and baking industry. The "basecakes" consist of saltine or snack crackers, while the filling is typical of sandwich cremes made for cookies but without the high levels of sugar.

8.P.1.b. Fermented

Soda (saltine) crackers. The yeast-leavened dough of soda crackers (**Figure 8.103**) normally requires prolonged fermentations (up to 24 hours) and lam-

Table 8.097. General Cracker Formulations

Ingredient	Saltines (bakers %)	Snack crackers (bakers %)	Graham crackers (bakers %)
Flour, white	100	100	80
Flour, whole wheat	–	–	20
Sugar	–	6	25
Malt syrup	1.5	2	–
Invert sugar	–	3	–
Honey/molasses	–	–	5
Shortening	10	12	12
Yeast	0.125	–	–
Salt	1.5	1	1
Water	30	40	20
Sodium bicarbonate	0.625	1.125	1
Ammonium bicarbonate	–	–	0.5
Monocalcium phosphate	–	1.25	–

(Vetter and Zeak 1989)

Figure 8.102. Round crackers often receive a light spray of oil to improve their eye and taste appeal.

ination of the dough into seven or more layers without an intervening filling. A representative soda cracker or saltine formula is given in **Table 8.098**. Saltines are leavened both by yeast and steam, although some baking soda is added at the dough stage to neutralize the pH for flavor and color purposes. Saltines dominate cracker markets and are offered in an increasing number of varieties, including no-salt, whole-wheat and peppered.

Oyster crackers. Also known as soup crackers, this style (**Figure 8.104**) is made from the same dough used for saltines. Matz (1968) suggested some modification in absorption because stiffer doughs will create fewer problems in cutting and baking.

Cream crackers. Occupying roughly the same place in the UK market as saltines do in the US, cream crackers are made from yeast-fermented dough with the simplest of formulations, namely, flour, water, yeast and salt. At the start of lamination, a layer of shortening blended with flour is applied and enclosed by the dough through folding, creating a single band. According to Manley (1983), the filling for the lamination is prepared by mixing 33 parts of plastic shortening into 100 parts of flour and 1 part of salt until a fine, uniform, powdery mixture is formed. To prevent the shortening from melting and thus cause lumps to develop in the mixture, it is kept at refrigerator temperatures until needed.

The flaky and blistered character of cream crackers forms during baking when the laminations lift apart and create irregular surface blisters. Baking requires 4.5 to 5 minutes at a temperature of 310°C (590°F) in the first zone and of 210°C (410°F) in the final zone to reduce the moisture content of the product to 2.5 to 3.0%.

Water biscuits are made using only flour and water, without shortening or other fats. These fermented crackers are thin, hard and brittle and very bland in flavor.

Cheese crackers. Many popular snack crackers incorporate cheese, and the additional moisture and protein contributed by this ingredient will require changes in product formulation (**Table 8.099**). Cheese crackers are usually made from fermented doughs because fermentation not only complements the cheese flavor but enhances it as well. The cheese itself does not add enough color to the dough, hence the use of Yellow No. 6, a certified color additive. Paprika at about 0.25% (flour weight basis) may be used to intensify the color, and a small amount of cayenne (red pepper) is included in some formulations. Matz (1968) reported that caraway and poppy seeds and/or spices such as sage add to the character of blue-cheese crackers.

When using natural cheese, the rind and any large areas of mold should be removed beforehand, with the cheese ground as fine as possible immediately before placing it in the mixer. If the ground cheese dries to any extent, it will not incorporate smoothly into the dough. Some bakers make a pre-mix of the ground cheese and the shortening, using a spindle mixer, and keep it in the fermentation room for

24 hours. This method is said to develop more flavor and lead to better dispersion of cheese in the dough.

8.P.1.c. Enzyme crackers

Strouts (2008a) added a third category, enzyme crackers, to differentiate the way cracker doughs develop during mixing and forming stages. This style requires addition of a protease enzyme to reduce the length of the protein strands, which can then be more easily aligned into a continuous sheet for processing. Enzyme activity depends on pH, temperature and time. Because dough pH is relatively fixed, the selection of the best proteolytic enzyme for the formula will depend on matching the pH optimum of the enzyme with the dough pH. Dough temperatures affect the rate of enzyme activity, and oven temperatures typically deactivate this catalyst. A great deal of work with protease enzymes in recent years has made their performance quite predictable. Generally a 3-hour floor time or resting period will be needed for enzymatically developed doughs.

8.P.2. Role of ingredients

As a rule, crackers contain little or no sugar but moderate levels of fat, typically 10 to 20% (flour weight basis). Doughs are generally low in water at 20 to 30% or no more than 45%. Strouts (2008a) summarized the effects of cracker ingredients and formulation. The most important aspects of cracker production are pH, temperature, concentration and time.

Flour. Cracker flours, which are long patent or straight-grade flours made from soft red or white winter wheat, normally have somewhat higher protein content than do cookie flours and, as a result, may be characterized as strong flours. The quality of their protein is usually determined by a viscosity test. Because they are subjected to extensive fermentation during cracker production, their diastatic activity represents an important quality factor.

The flour designed for cracker production is generally of two types: (a) a stronger soft wheat flour of 8.5 to 10% protein and 0.39 to 0.42% ash for use in the sponge and (b) a medium-strength flour of 8 to 9% protein and 0.40% ash for the dough stage. Compared with bread flours, cracker flours typically have lower absorption capacity, finer granulation, less starch damage and mellower gluten (Faridi 1980).

Leaveners: yeast and bacteria. At the low level at which yeast is used, it appears to play a subordinate role in cracker dough fermentation, with the major changes that occur being attributed to bacterial fermen-

Figure 8.103. Soda crackers, also called saltines, undergo full fermentation before being made up.

Table 8.098. Representative Soda Cracker Formula

Ingredient	Sponge (bakers %)	Dough (bakers %)
Flour (strong)	70	30.00
Malt (diastatic)	0.02	–
Ferment	0.5	–
Yeast	0.2	–
Shortening	–	8
Sodium bicarbonate	–	0.7
Ammonium bicarbonate	–	0.25
Salt	–	1.0
Fermentation time	16 to 20 hours	4 to 5 hours
Temperature	18 to 29°C (65 to 85°F)	27 to 32°C (80 to 90°F)

(Hickenbottom 1977)

Figure 8.104. Oyster crackers will be dried to reach a moisture content of less than 10%. Here, an oscillating feed conveyor and revolving metal tines evenly distribute the crackers on the dryer belt.
(Baking & Snack)

Table 8.099. Cheese Cracker Formula

Ingredient	Amount (bakers %)
Flour, soft wheat	100.00
Shortening, all vegetable	16.00
Water	25.00
Lecithin	0.19
Liquid malt syrup	2.25
Yellow No. 6 color additive	0.02
Cheese powder	5.00
Cheese flavor	0.82
Shredded fresh cheese	5.00
Sodium bicarbonate	0.56
Fresh yeast, compressed	0.25
Enzyme (protease)*	0.02
Ammonium bicarbonate*	1.00
Salt, granulated	1.13
Red pepper	0.19

Dissolve separately in water before adding
(Strouts 2008a)

tation. Micka (1955) appeared to be the first to subject the bacterial aspects of cracker dough fermentation to a thorough investigation. He observed that the major sources of bacteria were the yeast, flour, remnants from the previous doughs in the fermentation trough and the addition of ferments held over from preceding doughs. Faridi (1980) pointed out that the major portion of carbon dioxide generated during fermentation originates with the bacteria, of which the principal species are *Lactobacillus plantarum, L. delbrueckii* and *L. leichmanii.* Similarly, the increase in acidity with progressing fermentation is attributed to the bacteria. Faridi and Johnson (1978) traced the formation of organic acids in cracker sponges and doughs and found increases of 8.4 times and 6.4 times in acetic acid and lactic acid levels, respectively, during a 20-hour sponge dime, with only additional increases at the dough stage.

Fields et al. (1982) studied the microbiology of cracker sponge fermentation and determined that lactic acid bacteria were the dominant species in doughs and appeared to be primarily responsible for the rapid lowering of the pH of the sponge. The number of yeast cells was observed to decline as fermentation progressed, possibly because of the competition among the organisms for fermentable carbohydrates or the accumulation of toxic waste products.

Leaveners: chemical. In practice, sodium bicarbonate is normally added to the dough stage of fermented crackers, including saltines (hence their synonymous name "soda" crackers) to neutralize the acids formed during sponge fermentation, to generate additional carbon dioxide and to establish the pH of the finished cracker. The neutralizing effect of the soda addition is clearly apparent from the rather steep rise in pH from a value of about 4 to above 7 (Manley 1983). When soda is omitted, the color of the baked cracker will be too light, and if too much soda is added, the final color will be too dark. Soda crackers should be slightly on the alkaline side, within a pH range of 7.5 to 8.5.

Vetter and Zeak (1989) analyzed the role of chemical leavening in cookies and crackers. They observed that the use of baking soda (sodium bicarbonate) in saltines was not so much for its leavening action but for its ability to adjust pH for flavor and color development. Snack crackers, however, employ chemical leavening (soda combined with monocalcium phosphate) for to lower the system's pH and enhance flavor. The leavening system provides some lift, although most comes from steam generated within the laminated dough structure. Graham crackers use a combination of steam, soda and ammonium bicarbonate for lift during baking.

Shortenings. The main function of shortening in crackers, unlike cookies, is to lubricate the dough during lamination and create layers of flakiness in the finished product. Lard was the traditional favorite for cracker formulation because of its good shortening value and flavor, but it has been left behind for more healthy vegetable fats. Krubert (1990) recommended use of fats with shortening values between 90 and 100 for crackers because these softer fats improve dough consistency and eating characteristics. Also, liquid oils are sprayed on after baking for flavoring purposes. Spray oils should have a low melting point and a clean or bland flavor profile. **Table 8.100** compares the shortening content of various cracker and cookie styles.

Salt. When added to the dough, salt provides both flavor enhancement and fermentation control. It is also applied topically. Finely particulated salt, also known as "flour salt," is usually the choice for cracker doughs, while a flaked style will be used for toppings. The larger size and rough edges of the flake salt help it adhere to the cracker surface.

Sweeteners. Granulated sugar is the primary sweetening ingredient for crackers, but 42- and 63-DE corn syrup, high-fructose corn syrup, malt, molasses and honey are also used. Because sugar imparts hardness to the finished product, it is not used in very high levels except for graham crackers. Fructose and dextrose tend not to be used because they so actively take part in the Maillard browning reaction and may cause premature and excessive browning.

Other ingredients. Most cracker doughs use dome type of dough conditioner, usually sodium sulfite and/or proteolytic enzymes. These functional additives act on gluten strands to help them form a network better capable of carrying the starch granules. Although they weaken the cohesive and elastic properties of gluten and thus assist machining, this activity has only a small effect on finished product structure.

Chemically leavened crackers depend also on the reducing action of sodium bisulfate or metabisulfite to relax the protein structure of the dough. These functional ingredients interact at the linkages between and within the gluten strands. The process is very rapid and requires no floor time, but it does not continue over time so there is little change in dough rheology if floor time is extended.

Bakers employ oxidants and reducing agents in fermented doughs for the same reasons these ingredients are present in bread doughs: They condition the protein bonds to make the dough more pliable and extensible.

Emulsifiers may also be used to improve the rheological properties (ease of machining and resistance to shrinkage) of the dough and the texture of the finished products.

Various grains (oats, rye, corn and cracked and steamed wheat), cheeses and other dairy ingredients, plus sesame, poppy and caraway seeds are often used in crackers. Spices, flavors and colors also find application (**Figure 8.105**).

8.P.3. Processing effects

Full gluten development is not expected, or desired, in cracker dough. Blending and dispersion, with sufficient physical work to transform the mixture into a cohesive mass, are the prime requirements. Ingredients such as sugar, salt, sodium and ammonium bicarbonate must solubilize during mixing, yet cracker doughs tend to be low absorption systems, with water added at 43 to 45% (flour weight basis). Mixing operations for all styles of crackers tend to function more to wet ingredients and blend them into a uniform mass than to develop the protein. Most hydration occurs not in the mixer but during floor time.

Table 8.100. Shortening in Cookies and Crackers

Product	Fat per 100 lb flour
Ship's biscuit, "hard tack"	None
Captains biscuit	None to 1.5 lb
Army ration biscuit, World War II	10 lb
Hard, semi-sweet	18 to 20 lb
Shortcake types, rotary moulded	25 to 30 lb
Wire-cut types	40 to 50 lb
Scotch shortbread	45 to 55 lb
Sugar wafers	None

(Smith 1969)

Figure 8.105. Freshly baked "garden veggie" varety crackers transfer to the dryer.
(Baking & Snack)

Strouts (2008b) recently summarized the effects of processing on crackers. His analysis provided a valuable troubleshooting guide.

Fermented crackers. The dough for saltines is generally made in a spindle mixer. The blades of spindle mixers are designed to cut and tear the dough rather than knead or stretch it. Using this type of mixer gives a prolonged, intensive mix without the toughening effect from formation of an extensible dough (Krubert 1990).

According to Faridi (1980), fermentation is normally carried out by the sponge-and-dough process, with the sponge containing 60 to 70% of the total flour, the yeast, a small amount of old dough and the water, all mixed for 1 to 4 minutes. Cracker sponges are mixed just long enough to wet the flour so gluten development is quite limited until the final dough is mixed and laminated. The consistency of the sponge changes greatly during fermentation, becoming less and less elastic. The sponge is fermented for about 16 to 18 hours at 26 to 29°C (78 to 84°F) and 70 to 87% relative humidity. Then follows gentle dough mixing for 3 to 7 minutes during which the remaining flour and other ingredients (shortening, salt and sodium and ammonium bicarbonates) are incorporated. The dough is then fermented for an additional 4 to 6 hours.

The rheological changes that occur during cracker sponge fermentation were studied by Pizzinatto and Hoseney (1980) by means of the Extensigraph. They found that adding the shortening to either the sponge or the dough had no perceptible influence on fermentation or the pH. The amount of mixing applied to the dough did, however, affect dough properties. Over-mixing resulted in sticky doughs that were difficult to handle. Optimum mixing times were 3 minutes for the sponge and 5 minutes for the dough, for a total time of 8 minutes. As fermentation progressed, the sponges became less resistant to extension, and lost some extensibility, probably because of the increase in acidity as indicated by the decline of the pH from 5.35 to 4.15 in the course of fermentation. Addition of soda increased the dough's extensibility, whereas salt addition strengthened the dough as exemplified by an increase in its resistance to extension.

Wanting to shorten the fermentation time required for saltines, bakers have begun to work with liquid ferments that would maintain the quality advantages of the conventional sponge-and-dough process. Lactic acid bacteria and yeast cultures will shorten the time to less than 4 hours while also improving process control, reducing floor space and cutting capital investment.

The fermented dough then passes through a laminating machine that transforms it into a continuous sheet by a series of rolls that reduce its thickness to about 0.25 in. This reduced dough sheet is then folded into 5 to 7 layers and again reduced in thickness by passage through a set of rollers. The final rolling is set down to a 3- to 4-mm gap in order to produce the desired final thickness in the finished cracker. As Faridi (1990) observed, dough enters the sheeter as a dry mass that just barely hangs together and exits as a continuous cohesive sheet. Gluten development takes place during sheeting, and the layering provides tenderness to the finished product.

Describing the dough sheet's surface as it emerges from the sheeter, Faridi (1990) said that the appearance of the sheet will predict the final appearance of the baked cracker and the degree of lift obtained in the oven. A rough, rippled or holey sheet surface cannot be satisfactorily "repaired" during subsequent gauge rolling.

The laminated sheet is then cut, docked and/or stamped, and receives a sprinkling of salt prior to entering the oven. Baking is done on wire mesh (the preferred style) or steel bands for a very brief time, 2.5 to 3.5 minutes, at relatively hot temperatures, typically 300°C (570°F) in the first zone and declining to 250°C (480°F) at the end of the oven. Dielectric dryers are used after the oven when the moisture profile must be exact.

The baked crackers are then broken across sheets into rows and lengthwise, permitted to cool (when their moisture equalizes at about 2.5%), stacked and packaged in moisture-proof bags.

Snack crackers. Other than saltine and graham crackers, all cracker doughs employ horizontal mixers for their preparation. Such mixers are equipped with a single shaft carrying a sigma-style mixing blade. Double-arm mixers can be used for softer doughs, but most cracker dough mixers do not require such intensive action. A 2- or 3-stage process is followed, with the first stage combining fat, sugar and miscellaneous ingredients in a creaming stage and the second stage adding the dry ingredients and water. Doughs are mixed between 4 and 7 minutes and brought out at 32 to 38°C (90 to 100°F).

Graham crackers. The following procedure for the production of graham crackers was outlined by Matz (1968): The sweeteners are first combined with nearly all the water and heated to 74 to 77°C (165 to 170°F) to form a syrup. This liquid is then added to the flour, shortening, whey and lecithin and mixed for 5 minutes in a 3-spindle mixer. After that, the remaining ingredients are added, including the ammonium bicarbonate that has been dissolved in the withheld water. Total mixing time will need to be adjusted to the flour strength but will range from 25 minutes to 1 hour. Finished dough temperature should be about 48°C (118°F). The dough then receives preliminary sheeting, followed by several foldings and reductions, producing a thin dough sheet that is then ready for the cutting or stamping process.

If graham cracker dough is made in a horizontal mixer, its dough-out temperature should be around 49 to 54°C (120 to 130°F) so that dough stickiness from sugars does not affect machining.

A somewhat simpler method was suggested by Smith (1972): The sweeteners, shortening, salt, lecithin and flavors are creamed for 7 minutes at high speed, followed by the addition of the flour and other dry ingredients and further mixing at slow speed for an additional 14 or more minutes. Mixing is facilitated by the addition of dissolved sodium sulfite at a rate of 0.5 oz per 100 lb of flour at the outset of mixing. This procedure is said to yield dough with good machinability that can go directly to the sheeting rolls of the cutting machine.

Matz (1968) reported some graham crackers were previously made with sponges but that this procedure was rarely if ever used today. The flavors added by fermentation tended to be overwhelmed by the stronger flavors of other ingredients.

Oil spraying. Many cracker varieties are sprayed with oil shortly after baking to improve their taste and eating quality. Refined coconut oil or peanut oil is used to make this change in appearance, bite and taste. The oil should be about 60°C (140°F) in temperature, with the coverage adjusted to average 13% of the cracker weight (Dubois 1987). Recently, bakers have reduced their use of spray oils to give a "healthier" profile to these products, and BCMA (2002) stated that a typical spray oil application ranges between 1 and 2%.

To avoid checking or other problems, the crackers should be allowed to equilibrate for a few minutes before spraying.

Additionally, oil is commonly sprayed onto baked snack crackers to enable dry seasonings to adhere to the crackers. Slurries made of oils combined with seasonings are also used.

Checking. Crackers, like cookies, can suffer from checking during cooling. Krubert (1990) cautioned against forced cold air or cold drafts in the cooling area. Hairline cracks can appear within the product and on its surface from 6 to 24 hours after packaging and cause excessive breakage during distribution.

8.Q. Pretzels
Updated by Hans van der Maarel

While pretzels have been a popular snack food in central Europe for many centuries, it was not until 1861 that the first American pretzel bakery was established in Lititz, PA (Modanna 1983). These products, traditionally low in fat, have become very popular snack foods. Actually, pretzels provide dieters with an excellent snacking option: low in calories, no cholesterol, generally fat free and about 1 kcal per thin pretzel stick.

Reportedly invented in a monastery in Southern France or Northern Italy, pretzels were originally named *pretiola*, a Latin word meaning "little reward." The pretzel made its way north over the Alps into Austria, Germany and Central Europe where it became the *brezel*, the old German translation of little reward, and finally, the pretzel (Groff 1999).

8.Q.1. Varieties

8.Q.1.a. Hard pretzels
Originally, pretzels were soft, with a texture that resembled that of soft rolls and a high moisture content that greatly limited their shelf life. In contrast, the currently far more popular hard pretzels have their moisture content reduced to a level of 2 to 3%, which gives them a crisp, crunchy character and greatly extends their shelf life to 6 months in good packaging.

Thin twists (**Figure 8.106**) are the most popular shape for hard pretzels today, but pretzel bakers can offer consumers a broad variety from sticks to knots and almost everything in between, limited only by the imagination of the baker and the craft of the die maker. Generally, the body of hard pretzels is quite thin, but thicker, crunchier versions include the Dutch or Bavarian pretzel knots and pretzel rods up to 7 in. long. Plain pretzels with no topping salt not only satisfy low-sodium dietary restrictions but are also frequently given to teething toddlers.

Figure 8.106. Hard pretzels shaped in thin twists like these are the most popular shape today.

8.Q.1.b. Soft pretzels
Soft pretzels occupy their own distinct category yet were the original style of pretzel offered to consumers in fresh baked form. Today, soft pretzels come as frozen 3.5-oz dough pieces, often partially processed, and sold through the freezer case at grocery stores and supermarkets. The consumer salts and bakes them at home before eating. In a large 6-oz size (**Figure 8.107**), they are also popular with street vendors in certain geographic areas and can be found at many sporting events as well as in airport kiosks and food courts. A 2-oz size is used by some school lunch programs

as a bread substitute.

The largest difference between a soft pretzel compared to a hard pretzel lies in its final moisture. It can range from 15 to 25% compared with the 2 to 5.0% of the hard pretzel. This attribute give the pretzel its bread-like texture, but shelf life is limited to only a few days. As Groff (1996) rightly observed, products with moisture contents between the two extremes are known as stale pretzels.

8.Q.1.c. Filled pretzels

These pretzels exhibit the outer shell of a standard hard pretzel, but have a soft filling inside. This form is a pretzel nugget, filled most commonly with peanut butter, cheese or chocolate. A soft pretzel version is also produced through coextrusion of the dough around the filling.

8.Q.1.d. Pretzel rolls

Called *Laugenbrotchen* or *Laugenbrezel* in Germany, pretzel rolls are essentially soft bread rolls that receive a caustic bath (an unheated 6% solution of sodium hydroxide) right before the oven. They may be formed in the classic pretzel knot or as short club rolls, and some are shaped by braiding or stamping.

8.Q.2. Role of ingredients

Figure 8.107. Sharing the shape of hard pretzels, the soft variety cones in larger sizes and is a popular snack and street food.
(J & J Snack Foods Corp.)

Most pretzel doughs consist primarily of low-protein flour, a sweetener such as corn syrup or malt syrup, oil or vegetable shortening and leavening agents such as yeast and/or sodium bicarbonate. A typical formula is shown in **Table 8.101**. The resulting dough is very stiff. Hoseney (1986) described the formula for pretzel dough as essentially flour and water, and the addition of minor ingredients such as 0.25% yeast, 1.25% shortening, 1.25% malt and 0.04% ammonium bicarbonate, with all quantities based on flour weight. Two formulations for soft pretzels are provided in **Table 8.102**.

Flour. Both spring and winter wheats can be used for pretzels, but the most often selected style is an enriched soft red winter wheat with 8 to 10% protein and 10 to 13% moisture. The flour chosen determines water absorption, development of the dough and the texture of the finished pretzel.

Additional protein sources can be used, according to Kazemzadeh (1999), including soy isolates, wheat gluten, casein and whey protein.

Fats. Lubrication is the primary function of fats when used in pretzels. Typically fats are added as hardened palm kernel oil or hydrogenated vegetable oil, although formulators are working with low-saturated and non-trans fats, too. Liquid oils reduce the viscosity of the dough, making it more difficult to process. Many pretzel formulations contain no fat.

Sweeteners. The typical pretzel formula calls for sweeteners, usu-

Table 8.101. Hard Pretzel Formula

Ingredient	Amount (formula %)
Flour	70
Water	25
Sweetener	2 to 3
Fat	2
Salt*	0.1 to 0.2
Compressed yeast	0.3

Other than that applied on the pretzels
(Kazemzadeh 1999)

Table 8.102. Soft Pretzel Formulations

Ingredient	Hand/machine twisted (bakers %)	Extruded (bakers %)
Flour, hard spring wheat (14.5% protein)	100	33.3
Flour, soft red winter (9.5% protein)	–	66.7
Malt, diastatic	2	2
Yeast, fresh compressed	1.5	1.5
Water	35 to 45	35 to 45

(Groff 1996)

ally granulated sucrose but sometimes liquid sugar, brown sugar, glucose syrups and invert syrups. These sugars provide a substrate for yeast growth.

Yeast. Bakers yeast provides the leavening effect to pretzels, although some products are chemically leavened as well, with the yeast present for flavor.

Salt. The dough for pretzels uses a very small amount of salt as a flavor enhancer. The bulk of the salt in finished pretzels is present as topping salt in the form of large crystals evenly distributed on the surface. Salt application rate for pretzels ranges from the salt-free variety to as high as 15%, but typical rates are 5 to 8 %.

A slightly clear crystal called rock pretzel salt is used on most hard pretzels on the market. The most popular topping salt is predominantly 14 to 20 mesh with a particle thickness of 0.03 in. Rock salt particles are harder than flake salt and much less friable, an important quality because topping salt that misses its target during depositing is generally recycled using automatic reclamation equipment. Salt smaller than 40 mesh tends to cloud the golden brown surface of pretzels, an undesirable characteristic. While salt adheres well to the wet surface of cooked pretzel dough, the crust is quite thin after baking, and salt will abrade off the pretzel during packaging and handling. As much as half the salt is lost before consumption (Strietelmeier 1988).

Manufacturers of soft pretzels prefer topping salts with an opaque white appearance, selecting thickly flaked compacted vacuum granulated salts. Because these salts can melt and disappear if the frozen soft pretzels are subjected to multiple freeze-thaw cycles, manufacturers generally package the salt separately for the consumer to apply before baking.

Water. The dissolved minerals and pH of water make an impact on pretzel doughs in the same way as with any yeast-raised dough. For example, the higher the water's pH, the more relaxed the dough. The result is a lower gelatinization temperature and faster cooking in the lye bath.

While pretzel formulations call for 35 to 45% water (flour weight basis), the range allows great latitude, and practical experience tends to favor a mid-range value. Lower amounts of water tend to increase product breakage, a condition well known within the pretzel industry and verified by Seetharaman et al. (2004). The researchers found that gluten development in pizza doughs was significantly influenced by water content, as it is in bread doughs. Also, low water content (37.5%) resulted in far more ungelatinized starch in the finished pretzel, resulting in breakage from events involving far lower energy than with control doughs made with 42.5% water.

For soft pretzels, absorption levels are lower, in the range of 30 to 35% (flour weight basis).

Other ingredients. Diastatic malt may be added for its dough conditioning enzymes and flavor, while nondiastatic malt provides flavor alone. A variety of flavoring materials have been added to pretzel doughs, including extracts and herbs, according to Kazemzadeh (1999). The formulator must evaluate such materials to assure their survival in the relatively rigorous cooking and baking process.

Caustic. The characteristic gloss and golden brown color of pretzels results from treatment of the dough with an alkaline solution, usually 0.5% sodium or potassium hydroxide or 2% sodium carbonate (Kazemzadeh 1999). Sodium hydroxide (lye) is usually the choice for commercial production because it provides superior color, flavor and surface texture; however, sodium carbonate provides some advantages in a gas-fired oven or for home use. The strength of the lye solution can vary according to baker preference. For example, Suas (2009) recommended a 3.3% lye solution, while Schünemann and Treu (1988) noted a maximum of 4%. The Grain Science and Industry Department at Kansas State University conducts its baking science course's lab work with a 5% solution.

The dough pieces are immersed in such solutions, held close to the boiling point, for 10 to 25 seconds. This process cooks the dough piece's surface, gelatinizing the starch present there. Larger pieces may be treated with caustic by running them through a waterfall (**Figure 8.108**). Contact between the alkaline solution and the relatively neutral dough surface drops the pH of the solution that adheres to the product, giving the finished product its characteristic flavor: slightly alkaline, but not unpleasantly so. As explained in Chapter 12, Part H, the cooking stage slightly puffs the pretzel and provides a barrier to moisture loss during baking, resulting in a light, crisp pretzel.

Figure 8.108. After proofing, large soft pretzels travel through a waterfall of hot caustic solution that produces the rich brown color and crunchy outer crust when the rolls are baked.
(*Baking & Snack*)

8.Q.3. Methods

8.Q.3.a. Hard pretzels

The production steps involved in pretzel production are basically mixing, product formation, proofing, cooking, baking, drying and packaging.

All of the dry ingredients are blended in the mixer or a pre-blender prior to adding any liquid ingredients. This process of pre-blending the dry ingredients will help ensure the dough ends up in a homogeneous mass, which is critical for consistent pretzel quality.

With an absorption of 38 to 42%, the dough is very stiff and requires a heavy-duty mixer to achieve homogeneous ingredient incorporation. A horizontal mixer equipped with double sigma arms is most generally used (Weaver 1978). Such doughs generally receive 30 minute of floor time for fermentation, but many pretzel bakers take a no-time approach and send the dough immediately to makeup.

Increasingly, pretzel dough is produced by continuous mixer-kneader systems that discharge dough automatically into the extruder or forming system that shapes it into the final pretzel configuration either by twisting or extrusion. In the twisting machine (**Figure 8.109**), an extruded dough string is rolled to a prescribed thickness between two belts and is then twisted into the traditional pretzel shape by a special device and deposited on the proofing belt that has the same width as the oven hearth. In extruding machines, the dough is pressed through pretzel-shaped dies to be wire-cut for deposit on the proofing belt (**Figure 8.110**).

To make filled pretzel sticks, the dough runs through a low-pressure extruder equipped with a special compression head and die. The dough forms a continuous tube as it exits the die onto the proofer belt. Simultaneously, filling is pumped continually into an inner nozzle thereby filling the inside of the tube. The filled "rope" is then cut on the proofer belt to the desired length and follows the same process as the hard pretzel. These ropes can be as small as 2 to 3 mm in diameter (filled stick)

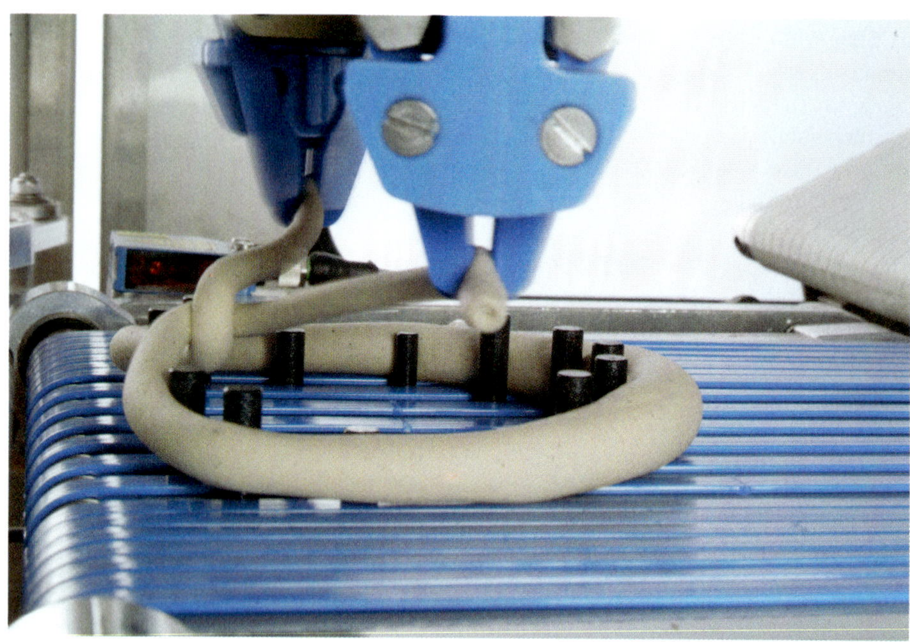

Figure 8.109. A twisting machine forms the traditional pretzel shape. (Fritsch)

Figure 8.110. Pretzels extruded from dies can be made in many shapes such as this holiday assortment. (Reading Bakery Systems)

or as large as 20 mm in diameter (filled nugget).

The raw pretzels receive a proof ranging from 3 to 8 minutes, after which they are transferred onto a stainless steel wire mesh belt for immersion in a solution of sodium hydroxide heated to 88 to 93°C (190 to 200°F) and controlled at a pH of 13. Immersion time is about 10 to 25 seconds, during which some starch gelatinization takes place on the outer surface of the dough. This caustic treatment may also be applied by conveying the raw pretzels through a cascade of the hot caustic solution.

On emerging from the caustic bath, the pretzels pass under a curtain of salt that is dispensed from a hopper by means of a grooved roller. From the salter, the pretzels enter the oven on a wire-mesh hearth belt. Baking temperatures range from 205 to 260°C (400 to 500°F), with the higher temperatures being applied at the start of baking. Baking times normally range from 3.5 to 8 minutes, during which the moisture content of the product is reduced to 12 to 18%.

To impart the distinctive crunchy, crisp character to the pretzels, and to ensure an adequate shelf life for them, the pretzels emerging from the oven are next subjected to drying in a kiln or dryer maintained at about 107°C (225°F). These dryers may be either free-standing heated enclosures or form a substructure underneath the oven chamber from which they are separated by an insulating divider. Drying for 20 to 90 minutes will reduce the moisture content of the pretzels to 2 to 3%. They are then ready for packaging.

8.Q.3.b. Soft pretzels

The soft pretzel process is quite similar to hard pretzels. Final dough temperatures are typically 28 to 30°C (83 to 86°F) to retard yeast action during the lay time.

Twisting machines can generally produce 35 to 40 pretzels per minute, with an error rate of 3 to 5%. Mis-twisted pretzels are either removed from the proofing conveyor apron or corrected by hand. Changes in dough viscosity, room temperature or humidity and even old vs. new crop flour can drive error rates above 15% (Groff 1996).

Today, a growing number of soft pretzels are being extruded rather than tied by machine. The amount of gluten in the dough can cause shear or tear marks to form along the edges of extruded products. Also, extruded products tend to be denser than tied styles. To run on such systems, the formula must be altered by replacing one-third of the high-protein flour with a low-protein variety.

Soft pretzels, like hard pretzels, must receive a caustic bath to produce the characteristic crust color. This process was a troublesome extra step for food service and vending customers who baked off the frozen soft pretzels. Thus, pretzel bakers experimented with frozen raw dough shapes that had been pre-treated by running them through a waterfall of cold sodium hydroxide solution prior to freezing. The coating tended to react negatively with cryogenic gases in the freezer, and when the coating broke down, it created a gummy surface and reduced shelf life. Today, most frozen soft pretzels are cooked and parbaked before reaching the freezer. The topping salt is packaged separately. To prepare the soft pretzels, the operator pulls the product from the freezer and lets it thaw until the surface becomes tacky. Salt is then sprinkled on the surface, and the pretzel is baked in a toaster oven, pizza oven or tunnel oven and served to the consumer in hot, fresh condition.

8.R. Contemporary Issues in Formulating
By L.A. Gorton

A broad range of themes characterize product development efforts today. The following discussion touches on a few of these currents. For additional insight, the reader is urged to turn to the scientific journals and industry business magazines — and their Web sites — that cover grain foods for up-to-the-minute discussion of influences that shape these products.

By paying attention to marketing trends, bakery formulators can get ahead of the curve in their product development efforts. The plain truth is, however, that most new products tend to be reactive rather than proactive, following the path the consumers take rather than breaking trail for them. Consumer products research organizations such as Nielsen and Information Resources Inc. (IRI) collect and report information about nearly every demographic possible. The International Food Information Council Federation monitors dietary trends and provides information about the nutritional aspects involved.

8.R.1. Control of staling

No subject has vexed more cereal scientists, bakery formulators, bakers and their marketing personnel than staling. From the moment a baked food leaves the oven, it starts to go stale. The staling process involves many variables, with starch retrogradation and water activity chief among them. But transport and storage conditions play a part, too. Staling affects not only bread but nearly every other type of baked food, from cakes to crackers and beyond.

To get at this problem, bakers commonly use crumb softeners, emulsifiers, preservatives and antioxidants, as well as gas-flush packaging and high-barrier films, to gain additional shelf life for their products. For example, emulsifiers help keep breads soft by complexing with starches so starch granules swell less, thus decreasing the rate of retrogradation. Preservatives hold back microbial degradation, and antioxidants combat rancidity.

Hoseney and Miller (1998) analyzed staling from the standpoint of current knowledge as well as where scientists are looking for breakthroughs. They found evidence that the starch retrogradation theory does not fully explain bread firming and suggested that interactions between protein and starch be studied further.

8.R.1.a. Extended shelf life

Recently, the role of water and how it interacts within baked foods at ambient, refrigerator and freezer temperatures has come into play.

Water activity. When food scientists developed the concept of water activity (a_w), they found immediate application in explaining the linkage between free water and microbial spoilage. Ash (1984) was among the first to describe to bakers the significance of water activity in controlling microbial contamination during ambient temperature storage of baked foods.

Water activity measures the energy levels of water molecules. The higher the activity, the more likely the possibility of microbial contamination. Public health authorities agree that common food pathogens will not multiply when water activity is below 0.85. (Pure water has an a_w of 1.) Reducing water activity is a matter of tying up free water by increasing the system's soluble solids content (salt, corn syrup, sugar). Another tactic is to cut the total moisture from all sources. Bakers use both approaches.

A more detailed examination of water activity can be found in Volume I, Chapter 2, Part C.

Enzymatic combinations. The formulating technique today known as "extended shelf life" (ESL) had its origins in the practical knowledge among bakers that bacterial α-amylase enzymes could slow the pace of bread firming. But it did so at a cost, not only in monetary terms but also in product quality. Often, too much bacterial α-amylase survived the oven, turning crumb from desirably soft and springy to overly soft, gummy and sticky.

Starch retrogradation, principally through amylopectin recrystallation within the starch granules, drives the firming of the crumb structure of baked foods. As scientists studied the problem, they determined that small size dextrins exerted an antifirming effect (Martin and Hoseney 1991). They used amylase enzymes to generate these dextrins by partially hydrolyzing starch molecules, which disrupted the continuity of the starch network and reduced its rigidity (firmness). Different sources of amylase produced dextrin fragments of different sizes.

While such mechanisms extended bread shelf life out to 5 days, bakers continued to seek longer periods for limiting firmness, up to and exceeding 15 days. Knowing that enzymes have highly specific activities and that many variables are involved in staling, the idea of blending enzymes to extend shelf life took hold.

What pushed the concept closer to commercial application was development of bacterial maltogenic α-amylase with lower thermostability than traditional bacterial enzymes (Forman 2003). Such enzymes survive starch gelatinization and are active when most of the substrate is available, but they are functionally inactivated by the time bread exits the oven. These enzymes act in a different manner: Instead of shattering the starch, they make a few selective cuts in the starch backbone, generating oligosaccharides from the ends of the starch molecule. The net effect is starch that recrystallizes (retrogrades) at a much slower rate.

Other enzymes involved in ESL applications include pentosanase and lipase. Pentosanase, more specifically xylanase, works on the flour's pentosans, which tend to interfere with the gluten's ability to form an extensible and elastic network. Pentosans steal water in the dough, limiting its availability to the proteins that need it. By altering the pentosans, this enzyme allows gluten proteins to become more functional, yielding loaves with better volume, finer grain, thinner cell walls and silkier texture. Bakers need to avoid over-dosing with this enzyme because it can break down the overall water-holding capacity of the dough, making it sticky.

Lipases act on flour's lipid components, which tend to aggregate with the protein, thus limiting gluten's ability to form an optimum network. The enzyme reduces this interference to yield loaves with smoother grain, better volume and silkier texture. Among the newer lipases now in bakery use is one that modifies flour lipids to help them stabilize the film surrounding the air cells responsible for leavening, preventing their coalescence and yielding a finer crumb with desirably thinner cell walls. Over-dosing with lipases leads to overly strong doughs, resulting in loaves with low volume and dense texture.

Manufacturing aspects of ESL with enzymes strongly recommend that bread not be under-baked. Such conditions do not allow the amylose starch to fully cross-link with the gluten protein, thus weakening the structure of the bread. Higher levels of mold inhibitor will also be necessary because ESL bread stays moist for longer periods than conventional products.

The optimum temperature range for maltogenic α-amylase is 65 to 74°C (150 to 165°F). The oven profile should be adjusted to keep the loaf's interior temperature in this range for as long as possible without drying out the crumb.

In 2001, led by Interstate Bakeries Corp. (now Hostess Brands), the baking industry started to adopt enzyme blends intended for ESL purposes, but bakers soon learned that the enzymes alone could not do the full job. As Bruinsma (2003) observed, the baker must also implement fermentation control, pH control and mold control through plant sanitation. Success also requires process control and accurate temperature profiling of oven conditions, discussed in detail by Swymeler (2003). Extensive trials will be necessary before the exact blend can be established. Although enzyme isolation has improved by quantum leaps in recent years, side activities for some enzymes must still be considered.

Some baked products must be refrigerated such as prepared sandwiches made with sliced bread and sold through convenience stores and vending machines. These distribution channels hold items at peak staling temperatures (explained in the next section) so use of an enzyme shelf life extender allows major improvement in quality, demonstrated by Sargent (2008) through a 4-week period.

8.R.1.b. Lower temperatures

Contrary to a widely-held belief among consumers that storing bakery products at refrigerator temperatures retards staling, many objective observations have shown exactly the opposite: Crumb firming accelerates progressively as the storage temperature approaches the freezing point. For this reason, temperatures between 0 and

2°C (32 and 36°F) are known as the staling zone. (Consumers also typically refrigerate baked foods to retard mold growth.)

Elton (1969) and Cornford et al. (1964), in a definitive investigation of the relationship between the elastic modulus of bread crumb and time and temperature, found that loaves of bread stored at different temperatures within the range of -1 to 32°C (30 to 90°F) ultimately attained the same value of crumb firmness, but the rate at which this value was reached varied with the storage temperature. They further found that the firming rate of bread crumb could be quantified by the following Avrami equation that expresses the rate of crystallization of a supercooled system:

$$\theta = \exp(-kt^n)$$

where θ = the fraction of uncrystallized material that remains after time t; k = a rate constant designating crystal growth; and n = the characteristic mode of nucleation, expressed by an integer varying from 1 to 4.

Working on the assumptions that the starch in bread immediately out of the oven is (a) totally amorphous, (b) entirely crystallized when the limiting modulus is reached and (c) the elastic modulus is directly proportional to the amount of crystallized starch present, Cornford and co-workers (1964) were able to demonstrate experimentally that the nucleation process is instantaneous and that the form of crystalline growth is rodlike.

X-ray studies showed that stale crumb exhibited diffraction patterns characteristic of crystalline starch. When such crumb is heated under moist conditions, it gives mainly amorphous diffraction patterns. In other words, starch crystals melt and revert to the fresh state (Axford and Colwell 1967). Kim and D'Appolonia (1977a, 1977b), in their study of the effect of the storage temperature on crumb firming, calculated that starch crystallization accounted for about 90, 50 and 20% of the total crumb firmness when the bread was stored for 5 days at temperatures of 21, 30 and 35°C (70, 86 and 95°F), respectively. The authors estimated the rate of starch retrogradation at 21°C (70°F) to be nearly twice that at 30°C (86°F) and four times that at 35°C (95°F).

Cornford and co-workers (1964) pointed out that in high-polymer systems, as represented by the starch phase in bread, the rate of crystallization is generally slow at temperatures near the melting point of the crystals and becomes progressively more rapid as the temperature is reduced. Following a peak, the rate again slows with continued decreasing temperatures until it reaches zero at a temperature at which molecular mobility is inadequate to permit crystallization to occur. Such findings account for the practical observation that bread does not stale perceptibly when stored either at elevated temperatures (above 43°C, or 110°F) or well below freezing.

The practical significance of the temperature dependence of bread staling was reviewed by Meisner (1953). He found that bread held at -1°C (30°F) for 20 hours resulted in a loss of compressibility equal to that caused by storage for 75 hours at 24°C (75°F). The staling rate was most rapid during the first 24 hours of storage at all temperatures, accounting for 50% of the ultimate increase in crumb firmness. The author recommended that bread delivery trucks be heated during severe winter weather to prevent the bread from cooling to 4 to 10°C (40 to 50°F), the zone where the staling rate is more rapid.

8.R.1.c. Freezing and staling control

Although Meisner (1953) found that when bread is frozen, it undergoes rapid firming during the first 24 hours, it then remains stable for the next 76 hours. Bread held at -14°C (5°F) for 100 hours and allowed to thaw at 24°C (75°F) was as soft as bread held at room temperature for 24 hours.

Low temperature freezing represents an effective practical means for either inhibiting or greatly retarding the staling process in bread products. Such freezing opened up distribution of bread over longer distances, a fact exploited by Campbell Taggart (now part of Sara Lee) when it introduced the Earth Grains line of bread. The company baked the variety breads in one highly automated plant, packaged and froze them for distribution to its network of depots, where the breads were thawed and sold as fresh, as explained in Chapter 6.

Over the years, numerous researchers reported on the experimental and commercial freezing of bread. Among the earlier investigators, Bailey (1932) found that bread stored for 3 days at -9°C (16°F) and then thawed had retained the characteristics of fresh bread. Cathcart (1941) and Cathcart and Luber (1939), using experimental and commercial freezers in a series of tests on conventional white bread, found that bread retained its fresh flavor and aroma for 30 days when held at -34°C (-30°F) and remained in good condition and saleable for up to 345 days. Occurrence of an off-odor over time became the limiting factor.

Pence and his co-workers (Pence and Standridge 1955, 1956; Pence 1955, 1961a, 1961b; Pence et al. 1955a, 1955b) carried out a series of fundamental studies on the practical aspect of bread freezing. They arrived at the following basic guidelines for the freezing of bread that have been widely adopted by the baking industry:

(a) To stabilize bread, its temperature must be lowered below its freezing point, about -7°C (20°F).

(b) With freezer temperatures maintained at -23 to -29°C (-10 to -20°F) and with air movements at velocities between 200 to 500 linear ft per minute, bread will reach its freezing point in about 2 hours.

(c) Thereafter, a storage temperature of -18°C (0°F) will provide satisfactory holding conditions.

Pence (1961a) found that properly frozen and thawed conventional white bread, 48 hours after thawing, will be equivalent in crumb firmness to 2-day old unfrozen bread and perhaps superior in flavor. Although freezing causes an increase in crumb firmness during the first 24 hours, the practical shelf life of thawed bread is equal to, or slightly better than, that of fresh unfrozen bread.

Bakery products are generally frozen when already wrapped or packaged even though packaging greatly reduces the cooling rate of the product. For example, Pence (1961b) found the freezing time, defined as the period needed for the temperature at the loaf center to decrease from 21°C (70°F) to -7°C (20°F), for wrapped bread exposed to an air current of 1,300 ft per minute at -29°C (-20°F) to be 104 minutes, compared with 46 minutes for the unwrapped loaf under the same conditions. When the wrapped loaves were further packed in delivery cartons prior to freezing, the freezing time, even under the best of conditions, was increased to about 5.5 hours. Moreover, differences of some 3 hours in freezing times were observed among loaves occupying different positions within the carton.

Bread and other bakery products are wrapped and packaged prior to entering cold storage for the principal purpose of minimizing moisture losses. At the low relative humidity conditions that normally prevail in storage freezers, unwrapped bread and similar yeast-raised products will dry out excessively in 1 or 2 weeks.

Freezer storage temperatures have a marked effect on the rate of bread staling. Bread held at -9 to -7°C (15 to 20°F), just at or slightly below its freezing point, will experience a perceptible loss in softness and flavor within a week. At a storage temperature of -18°C (0°F), crumb softness remains relatively stable for a month.

Care must be taken to avoid exposure of frozen bread to extraneous odors because it will absorb them quite readily and then release them on thawing. Storage for periods beyond a month, even at -18°C (0°F), will eventually adversely affect the bread's quality.

Storage temperatures should be maintained at a constant level of -18°C (0°F) or below. If the temperature is allowed to rise to -12°C (10°F), still well below the freezing point of bread, then crumb firming will become detectable within a few days. Temperature fluctuations, particularly above -7°C (20°F), must be avoided to minimize moisture migration within the frozen bread. Pence et al. (1958) demonstrated that the white rings that begin to appear beneath the crust within 2 weeks' storage at -9°C (15°F) are caused by a transfer of moisture by sublimation and diffusion from the high-moisture center of the crumb to the low-moisture crust region.

8.R.2. Health and wellness

Measured by their purchasing behavior, consumers select foods in contradictory patterns: They want indulgent products, yet they also demand good-for-you foods. This dichotomy may be dramatic, but it gives plenty of latitude to formulators. Strouts (2009) provided an excellent review of the product development opportunities afforded by whole grains, antioxidant-rich foods, trans fat reduction, omega-3 fatty acids, sodium reduction and gluten-free formulating.

Health and wellness, as a consumer trend, has been around for a long time and will continue to influence food product development. Here are a few of its more important aspects.

Sodium. Serious nutritional concerns about the micronutrient content of foods continue to surface. Current attention to sodium content is one of these, arising first in the late 1970s. The Institute of Medicine of the National Institute of Health, the body that sets the standards for nutrients described by the Nutrition Facts panel on food labels, established an adequate intake (AI) of sodium to be 1,500 mg (equal to 3,800 mg salt) as the minimum amount needed by most healthy people and set the maximum at 2,300 mg. The daily reference value (DRV) for sodium was established by the Nutrition Labeling and Education Act of 19990 (NLEA) to be 2,400 mg per day, based on a 2,000-Cal daily diet. The problem is that current sodium consumption in the US is much higher: an estimated 4,000 mg per day (IFIC 2005).

In most foods, salt serves only as flavor enhancement, but yeast-raised baked products needed it also for its ability to control the rate of yeast fermentation and to strengthen gluten. Bread can be successfully baked without salt, but the flavor of such formulations is uniformly described as flat and insipid.

Cereal scientists looked into reduction of sodium in various foods. Bread, for example, had commonly been made with up to 3% salt (flour weight basis), although 2% was closer to the average. Vetter (1979) analyzed the many sodium sources in baked foods. Vetter et al. (1983) studied sodium reduction in pizzas. Dubois et al. (1984) examined the effects on white bread of salt levels ranging from 0 to 2.1% and determined that a minimum of 1.0 to 1.5% salt appeared to be required for optimum bread production and quality. Gelroth and Strouts (2008) summarized the sodium situation in regard to baked foods, examining its technical functions, alternative ingredients and regulatory status.

Low-fat, low-carb. Weigh-control dieting brought the introduction of reduced-calorie breads during the 1950s. The 1970s saw the first coming of the Atkins low-carbohydrate diet. Alarmed that bread was being cast as a diet villain, the American Bakers Association prepared a public relations campaign based on a university study that showed eating up to 12 slices of bread a day actually helped participants lose weight. Today's "Bread for Life" diet offers much the same benefit. The Weight Watchers diet, developed in the mid-1960s, offers basically a high-fiber, low-fat eating plan, relatively friendly to baked foods when modestly consumed.

When the Atkins diet resurfaced at the turn of the 21st century, its demand that dieters give up carbohydrate-rich foods altogether threw the baking industry for a loop. Low-fat, high-fiber formulations could be achieved by many categories of baked foods, but low-carb products were more difficult. Nonetheless, several bakeries achieved some success with these items.

The low-carb diet has since waned in popularity, but it added the concept of glycemic index (GI) to the public forum. GI has specific meaning to diets intended to control the effects of diabetes. It measures the impact of a particular food on the glucose level in the blood of the person consuming that food. Formulators can select ingredients and processes that reduce the GI of baked foods. GI and the accompanying concept of glycemic load are discussed in Volume I, Chapter 1, Part A.

Whole grains. Representing one of the most positive aspects of the health-and-wellness trend, whole grains are a "natural" for bakery product development. With the release of the 2000 Dietary Guidelines for Americans and the subsequent 2005 guidelines, consumers are strongly urged to include whole-grain foods in their daily diets. The current recommendation is that we eat 6 "ounce equivalent" servings of grains daily and that at least half of those be whole grain products. Research, however, has shown that Americans barely consume a half-serving a day, and on any given day, 40% of the population eats no whole grains at all.

Whole-wheat bread certainly qualifies as a whole-grain food, but flavor issues with the bitter bran had limited its appeal. The bran of hard white wheat, however, lacks the bitter pigment and has opened the door to a spectrum of new whole-wheat and "made with whole grains" products. Bakers have begun to offer whole-grain cakes and cookies. Dough stickiness seems to be the biggest processing problem to overcome with cookies (**Figure 8.111**).

Figure 8.111. A breakfast cookie flavored with cinnamon and made with whole-wheat flour represents a new market opportunity based on increasing the consumption of whole grains. (Cargill)

The Whole Grains Council, formed to foster whole-grain consumption, makes available a great deal of information at its Web site, www.wholegrains.org, about the use of whole grains in foods. Whole grains as ingredients are discussed in Volume I, Chapter 2, Part A, and Chapter 3.

8.R.3. Organic foods

Does organic flour make better bread (**Figure 8.112**)? It depends on who defines "better."

The organic food movement has been around since the 1930s, initially formed as a reaction to the agricultural industry's heavy reliance on chemical fertilizers. The movement built its philosophy on English, American and German agricultural reformers of the period. For years, however, the organic foods sector remained tiny, only gaining popular attention in the late 1980s. No formal rules defined what organic farming and organic foods were. As consumer attention grew, the nascent industry opted for regulation to assure the purity of its category.

The Organic Foods Production Act of 1990, part of that year's Farm Bill, created the National Organic Program (NOP) within the US Department of Agriculture (USDA). NOP regulates organic foods with rules that define certification, production, processing and labeling requirements. In Canada, organic foods regulations are even stricter than those governing American goods.

Three Canadian researchers explored the sensory values of bread containing 60% of its flour milled from organic wheat vs. 60% whole-wheat bread made from conventionally grown grain (Annett 2007). The organic grain contained more protein, but both were greater than 14% protein. Mixograph analysis found that the conventional flour produced a stronger dough, and visual observation reported larger loaf volume as well. When sensory qualities were evaluated, no differences were observed for flavor, aroma or color attributes, although the panel perceived the organic bread to be denser in texture with smaller air cells in the appearance of the crumb than conventional bread.

8.R.4. Clean label

Trends involving health-and-wellness and organic foods represent consumers' desires for more control over the foods they eat. So, too, does the "clean label" issue. Observers of the food industry find nothing new in this trend: Many in the public forum have long voiced a dislike of the "chemical sounding" names found among the ingredients listed on food packages. Yet the naming protocols set forth by rules governing food labeling require such identification, and the regulatory debate over the required use of such terminology ended in the US with implementation of the Nutritional Labeling and Education Act of 1990.

In Europe, regulators chose a numbering system, the so-called "E numbers," to represent the dough conditioners, emulsifiers, colorings and other additive ingredients listed on food packages. Yet E numbers get just as much heat from European consumers as chemical names do in the US.

While food manufacturers know that such additives must establish their safety with rigorous proof accepted and approved by government food regulatory agencies before they can ever be used in foods, this fact generally does not enter the public debate. Without sufficient background, consumers can easily be led to believe that chemical-sounding names and E-numbered additives are "bad for you," if not downright harmful.

A "clean label" product is one that does not contain any artificial additives, thus catering to the consumers' desire for healthy and natural products (van Benschop

2007). Using the example of bread, she categorized its ingredients as follows:

(a) "Real" bread ingredients — wheat flour, gluten, water, corn syrup, salt, yeast, fat/oil.

(b) "Natural" additives — molasses, malted barley, ammonium salts (yeast nutrients).

(c) "Artificial" (chemical) additives — oxidizing agents, emulsifiers, preservatives.

So, when working with bread, reaching clean label status means evaluating and eliminating oxidizing agents, emulsifiers and preservatives. The problem of replacement represents the next hurdle.

Enzymes have great potential because, according to current US regulations, they are classified as processing aids and thus exempt from inclusion in the ingredient list printed on food packaging. Replacement of emulsifiers with lipase enzymes (**Figure 8.113**) is an increasing practice among bakeries today, as is use of xylanase to adjust pentosans and "age" the flour in place of oxidants and reducing agents.

Vinegar and raisin juice concentrate, for example, are effective natural mold inhibitors. Deodorized rosemary extract, which also qualifies as a natural ingredient, functions as an antioxidant to protect fats and oils against rancidity. Formulators wishing to pursue clean label approaches should strive to match the technical performance of the ingredients being replaced with those that seem more "real" or "natural" to consumers. Costs must also be considered.

Figure 8.112. Bakeries have begun to add organic varieties to their bread styles, using organic flour and following formulation rules that assure product authenticity.
(La Brea Bakery)

8.R.5. Allergens and gluten-free

The number of individuals suffering from true food allergies and celiac disease continues to increase and thus represents a population segment worthy of consideration by formulators. For example, gluten-free products have been available for many years, but consumers have long complained about their quality, especially the flavor and texture (**Figure 8.114**). Much improvement has taken place in the past few years, but much remains to be done.

Because baked foods commonly contain ingredients that prompt allergic reactions in certain individuals, formulation of allergen-free products can be difficult. The Big 8 allergenic foods — milk, eggs, peanuts, tree nuts, fish, shellfish, soy and wheat — are widely prevalent in the diet. All true food allergens known to science are proteins, and ingestion of an allergen causes anaphylaxis, an immediately life-threatening condition. Although there is no cure, as such, for food allergies, some contemporary research suggested that allergies may diminish in severity as an individual grows older, and recent success with desensitizing regimes for peanut allergies may prove beneficial.

Finding alternatives to allergens present in formulations is difficult enough, but the chief problem in formulating around allergens is proper labeling. When aller-

Figure 8.113. A lipolytic enzyme hydrolyzes both phospholipids and galactolipics so they function act as bioemulsifiers.
(DSM)

Figure 8.114. When developing a gluten-free double chocolate cookies, formulators learned that cocoa masks the less-familiar flavors of gluten-free flours.
(Arico Natural Foods)

gens are in the formula, their presence must be disclosed on the product label. The US Food and Drug Administration (FDA) publishes more notices about food recalls based on mislabeling than for any other reason. Most of the mislabeling incidents involve undisclosed ingredients that qualify as allergens. This fact leads to the other concern with allergens: careful cleaning and sanitizing at the end of runs involving allergens.

Gluten poses serious risks to individuals susceptible to celiac disease (CD), also called celiac sprue, an inherited condition in which gluten proteins prompt autoimmune reactions that damage the small intestine. Although not life-threatening in the immediate sense, CD can result in digestive problems and malnutrition. If gluten is eliminated from the diets of CD sufferers, the intestines can repair themselves, but there is no cure other than life-long avoidance of gluten-bearing foods.

CD is very hard to diagnose, yet epidemiologists estimate that 1 in 113 Americans are at risk for this condition. This high potential has prompted much interest in gluten-free foods, particularly baked foods, and several bakers have started producing such products. The natural foods supermarket chain, Whole Foods, now operates a completely gluten-free wholesale bakery to supply its stores. Much progress is being made. For example, Bellar (2009) reported preparation of "nonflour" baked foods made with egg and soy proteins, stabilized by a hydrocolloid component. Also, the top winners at the 2009 AACC International annual meeting's student product development competition were both gluten-free foods: rice-flour-based waffle cones for ice cream and pea-based pancake-like breakfast items. Gluten-free couscous was also entered in the contest.

The chief problem in formulating gluten-free baked foods is that the main culprit is also the products' principle structuring agent: gluten. The proteins involved in CD are commonly called gluten but are actually prolamin proteins: gliaden and glutenin (wheat), secalin (rye) and hordein (barley). Related proteins are also found in triticale, spelt and Kamut. The avedin of oats, however, has been ruled out. Kasarda (1991) provided an excellent review of grains and how they relate to CD.

Allergens and celiac disease are also discussed in Volume I, Chapter 2, Part C.

References

Aamodt, A., Magnus, E.M., and Færgestad, E.M. 2005. Hearth bread characteristics: Effect of protein quality protein content, whole meal flour, DATEM, proving time and their interactions. Cereal Chem. 82 (3): 290.

Abboud, A. 1998. Technology of producing cheesecakes. AIB Tech. Bull. 20 (4).

Alesch, E. 1970. Alternate methods of batch processing. Proc. Am. Soc. Bakery Engrs. 46: 69.

Allenson, A. 1982. The refrigerated dough process — An overview. AIB Tech. Bull. 4 (7).

Alviola, J.N., and Waniska, R.D. 2008. Determining the role of starch in flour tortilla staling using alpha-amylase. Cereal Chem. 85 (3): 391.

American Society of Bakery Engineers (ASBE). 1978. Bakeable jellies and jams. Am. Soc. Bakery Engrs. Bull. 60.

Annett, L.E., Spaner, D., and Wismer, W.V. 2007. Sensory profiles of bread made from paired samples of organic and conventionally grown wheat grain. J. Food Sci. 72 (4): S254.

Anonymous. 1999a. Cakes and the roll of specific gravity. I. Lighter types. BRI Bakers Tech. Bull. No. 99/01.

Anonymous. 1999b. Cakes and the need for balanced formulas. II. Heavier type cakes. BRI Bakers Tech. Bull. No. 99/02.

Anonymous. 2004. Examination of grain foods intake shift brings whole grains to fore. Milling & Baking News 83 (35): 1 (Oct. 26, 2004).

Archuleta, M. 2005. High altitude cooking. New Mexico State University Extension Service Guide No. E-215. The university: La Cruces, NM. Published online at http://aces.nmsu.edu/pubs/_e/E-215.pdf.

Ash, D.J. 1979a. Cake doughnuts. I. Formulation. AIB Tech. Bull. 1 (6).

Ash, D.J. 1979b. Cake doughnuts. II. Mix preparation, scaling, mixing and frying. AIB Tech. Bull. 1 (7).

Ash, D.J. 1980. Cake doughnuts. III. Frying fat. AIB Tech. Bull. 2 (7).

Ash, D.J. 1984. Shelf life improvement of bakery products. Proc. Am. Soc. Bakery Engrs. 60: 66.

Auerman, L.J. 1977. Technologie der Brotherstellung. VEB Nachbuchverlag: Leipzig, GDR.

Axford, D.W.E., and Colwell, K.H. 1967. Chem. Ind. (London), 467.

Baeuerlen, R.J. 1966. Shortening as a component of continuous process bread. Bakers Digest 40 (6): 56.

Bailey, L.H. 1932. Cereal Chem. 9: 65.

Bakhoum, M.T. 1996. Additive for the Preparation of Microwaveable Products, US Patent WO/1996/003885 (Feb. 15, 1996).

Baldwin, R.R., Johansen, R.G., Keogh, W.J., Titcomb, S.T., and Koedding, D. 1965. Cereal Sci. Today 10: 452.

Balinska, M. 2008. The Bagel: The Surprising History of a Modest Bread. Yale University Press: New Haven, CT.

Barmore, M.A. 1936a. Cereal Chem. 13: 71.

Barmore, M.A. 1936b. The influence of various factors, including altitude, in the production of angel food cake. Colo. Expt. Sta. Tech. Bull. 15. The station: Fort Collins, CO.

Bastetti, G. 2001a. Breads produced in Italy. I. Sours, preferments and starters. AIB Tech. Bull. 23 (5).

Bastetti, G. 2001b. Breads produced in Italy. II. Bread formulas and production. AIB Tech. Bull. 23 (9).

Bastietti, G. 2002. Fermented cakes produced in Italy. AIB Tech. Bull. 24 (7).

Bayfield, E.G., and Lannuier, G.L. 1962. Flour brew studies. III. The role of fermentable carbohydrates. Bakers Digest 36 (6): 57.

Bayfield, E.G., and Young, W.E. 1964a. Flour brew studies. V. Effect of brew fermentation times. Bakers Digest 38 (1): 69.

Bayfield, E.G., and Young, W.E. 1964b. Flour brew studies. VI. Varying the proportions of total flour, salt or "starter" dextrose in the brew. Bakers Digest 38 (4): 58.

Bayfield, E.G., and Young, W.E. 1964c. Flour brew studies. VII. The use of malt syrup and enzymes. Bakers Digest 38 (6): 52.

Bayfield, E.G., and Young, W.E. 1965. Flour brew studies. X. Short time brews. Bakers Digest 39 (3): 50.

Bayfield, E.G., Lannuir, G.L., and Young, W.E. 1963. Flour brew studies. IV. The importance of correct pH. Bakers Digest 37 (2): 55.

Beaven, M. 2007. Reconstitution strategy for whole grains. Proc. Am. Soc. Baking 83: 150.

Beery, K.E. 1982. 100-Percent corn sweeteners in small cake items. Proc. Am. Soc. Bakery Engrs. 58: 118.

Bejosano, F.P., and Waniska, R.D. 2003. Functionality of bicarbonate leaveners in wheat flour tortillas. Cereal Chem. 81 (1): 77.

Bellar, W.F. 2009. Non-flour containing baked and related food compositions. US Patent No. 7,595,081.

Benson, R.C. 1988a. Muffins. Proc. Am. Soc. Bakery Engrs. 64: 92.

Benson. R.C. 1988b. Muffin technology. AIB Tech. Bull. 10 (6).

Bent, A.J. 1998. Specialty fermented goods. In: Technology of Breadmaking. S.P. Cauvain and L.S. Young, eds. Blackie: London, UK.

Bergholz, B. Jr. 1957. Elements of raisin bread production. Proc. Am. Soc. Bakery Engrs. 33: 77.

Birnbaum, H. 1960. The functional characteristics of icing stabilizers. Bakers Digest 34 (2): 62.

Biscuit and Cracker Manufacturers' Association (BCMA). 2002. Cookie and Cracker Manufacturing, Vol. I. The association: Silver Spring, MD.

Bisno, L. 1950. Some considerations in commercial pie baking. Bakers Digest 24 (2): 31.

Bisno, L. 1951. Thickeners used in pie fillings. Bakers Digest 25 (1): 26.

Bisno, L. 1960a. Some newer thickeners and stabilizers for pie bakers. I. Bakers Digest 34 (4): 44.

Bisno, L. 1960b. Some newer thickeners and stabilizers for pie bakers. II. Bakers Digest 34 (5): 70.

Boettger, R.M. 1963. Cereal Sci. Today 8: 106.

Bohn, R.M. 1957. Biscuit and Cracker Production. American Trade Publishing Co.: New York, NY.

Bonavia, W. 1963. Practical aspects of continuous cake batter mixing. Bakers Digest 37 (3): 72.

Book, S.L., Brill, R.V., and Heidolph, B. 2002. Effects of leavening acids on characteristics of fresh and 30-day-old tortillas. Cereal Foods World 47 (8): 390.

Borders, J.H. 1968. A look at foam cakes. Bakers Digest 42 (4): 53.

Boyd, W.E. 1980. Manufacture and processing of frozen doughs. Proc. Am. Soc. Bakery Engrs. 56: 38.

Braden, B.W. 1976. Yeast-raised doughnuts. Proc. Am. Soc. Bakery Engrs. 52: 127.

Brenneis, L.S. 1965. Qualitative factors in the evaluation of cookie flours. Bakers Digest 39 (1): 66.

Brijwani, K., Campbell, G.M., and Cicerelli, L. 2008. Aeration of biscuit doughs during mixing. In: Bubbles in Food 2. G.M. Campbell, M.G. Scanlon and D.L. Pyle, eds. AACC International: St. Paul, MN.

Brooke, M. 1934. Pound cake. Proc. Am. Soc. Bakery Engrs. 10: 152.

Brown, A. 2004. I'm Just Here for More Food: Food ´ Mixing + Heat = Baking. Harry N. Abrams: New York, NY.

Bruinsma, B. 1993. Multigrain and calorie-reduced breads. AIB Tech. Bull. 15 (8).

Bruinsma, B. 2003. The science [of extended shelf life]. Proc. Am. Soc. Baking 79: 156.

Bruinsma, B.L., and Giesenschlag, J. 1984. Frozen dough performance — compressed yeast-instant dry yeast. Bakers Digest 58 (6): 6.

Brümmer, J.-M. 1995. Bread and rolls from frozen dough in Europe. In: Frozen and Refrigerated Doughs and Batters. K. Kulp, K. Lorenz, and J. Brümmer, eds. American Association of Cereal Chemists: St. Paul, MN.

Burns, W.B. 1970. Small cake items. Proc. Am. Soc. Bakery Engrs. 46: 106.

Burny, J. 1956. Quality fillings and toppings for sweet goods production. Proc. Am. Soc. Bakery Engrs. 32: 151.

Burris, J.B. 1979. Fried pies. Proc. Am. Soc. Bakery Engrs. 55: 111.

Burton, K.E., Steele, F.M., Jefferies, L., Pike, O.A., and Dunn, M.L. 2008. Effect of micronutrient fortification on nutritional and other properties of nixtamal tortillas. Cereal Chem. 85 (1): 70.

Busken, D. 2009. Formulating strategies. Cereal Foods World 54 (2): 90.

Busscher, R.K. 2003. Gelatin and its uses in the baking industry. AIB Tech. Bull. 25 (5).

Calvel, R. 1952. La Boulangerie Moderne. Editions Eyrolles: Paris, France.

Carlson, F.W. 1942. Quick cooling of pie fillings. Proc. Am. Soc. Bakery Engrs. 18: 214.

Carroll, L.P., Miller, B.S., and Johnson, J.A. 1956. Cereal Chem. 33: 303.

Cathcart, W.H. 1941. Cereal Chem. 18: 771.

Cathcart, W.H. 1951. Baking and bakery products. In: Chemistry and Technology of Food and Food Products. 2nd ed. M.B. Jacobs, ed. Interscience: New York, NY.

Cathcart, W.H., and Luber, S.V. 1939. Ind. Eng. Chem. 31: 362.

Cavalier, G. 1963. Liquid ferment systems for the productiio of yeast-raised products. Bakers Digest 37 (5): 76.

Cepeda, M., Waniska, R.D., Rooney, L.W., and Bejosano, F.P. 2000. Effects of leavening acids and dough temperature in wheat flour tortillas. Cereal Chem. 77 (4): 489.

Clyma, K. 2007. Ensuring efficiency. Baking & Snack 29 (7): 60.

Cole, E.W., Hale, W.S., and Pence, J.W. 1962. The effect of processing variations on the alcohol, carbonyl and organic acid contents of pre-ferments for nread baking. Cereal Chem. 39 (2): 114.

Conn. J.F., and Jelinek, D.R. 1982. Commercial production of baking powder biscuits. AIB Tech. Bull. 4 (11).

Cooper, I. 1986. Pita/pocket bread. Am. Soc. Bakery Engrs. 62: 151.

Cooper, R.H., Knight, R.A., Robb, J., and Seiler, D.A.L. 1966. Food Trade Rev.: 40.

Cornford, S.J., Axford, D.W.E., and Elton, G.A.H. 1964. The elastic modulus of bread crumb in linear compression in relation to staling. Cereal Chem. 41 (4): 216.

Corriher, S.O. 1997. CookWise: The Secrets of Cooking Revealed. William Morrow Cookbooks (Harper Collins): New York, NY.

Corriher, S.O. 2008. BakeWise: The Hows and Whys of Successful Baking. Scribner: New York, NY.

Cuevas-Rodríguez, E.O., Reyes-Moreno, C., Eckhoff, S.R., and Milán-Carrillo, J. 2009. Nixtamalized instant flour from corn (Zea mays L.) meal: Optimization of nixtamalization conditions. Cereal Chem. 86 (1): 7.

Dalby, G. 1963. The baking industry in Egypt. Bakers Digest 37 (6): 74.

Davies, J.R. 1937. Cereal Chem. 14: 819.

Davis, E.W. 1981. Shelf-life studies on frozen doughs. Bakers Digest 55 (3): 12.

Denk, H.G. 1965. Production of rye bread. Proc. Am. Soc. Bakery Engrs. 41: 66.

Denton, C. 1950. Pie filling faults. Proc. Am. Soc. Bakery Engrs. 26: 312.

Dermott, F.X. 1963. Alginates: Improvers of flavor quality in pie fillings. Bakers Digest 37 (6): 66.

DeStefanis, V.A. 1995. Functional role of microingredients in frozen doughs. In: Frozen and Refrigerated Doughs and Batters. K. Kulp, K. Lorenz, and J. Brümmer, eds. American Association of Cereal Chemists: St. Paul, MN.

DeStefanis, V.A., Erickson, R.W., and Ranum, P.M. 1986. Oxidation requirements for the preparation of frozen dough. Paper No. 19. Presented at the 71st annual meeting of the American Association of Cereal Chemists, held Oct. 5-8, 1986, at Toronto, Canada.

Deuel, C.L. 1986. Dehydrated apples for the baking industry. AIB Tech. Bull. 8 (8).

Deuster, P.A., Kemmer, T., Tubbs, L., Zeno, S., Minnick, C. 2009. Combat rations. In: The Warfighter Nutrition Guide. Published online at www.usuhs.mil/mem/warfighterguide.html.

Doerry, W. 1983. Cereal Foods World 28: 677.

Doerry, W. 1994. Egg bagels. AIB Tech. Bull. 16 (11).

Doerry, W. 1996. Shelf-stable pumpkin pies. AIB Tech. Bull. 18 (10).

Doerry, W. 1997. Technology of producing Danish pastries (sweet rolls and coffee cakes). AIB Tech. Bull. 19 (10).

Doerry, W. 1998. Formulation and production of puff pastries. AIB Tech. Bull. 20 (2).

Doerry, W.T., and Meloan, E. 1986. Croissant technology. AIB Tech. Bull. 8 (10).

Doty, M.J., and McCurrie, R.N. 1964. The use of nonfat dry milk in baking, with special reference to continuous dough mixing. Bakers Digest 38 (1): 62.

Downs, D.E. 1971. Basic aspects of fried pie production. Bakers Digest 45 (3): 62.

Drews, E., and Seibel, W. 1976. Bread-baking and other uses around the world. In: Rye: Production, Chemistry and Technology. W. Bushuk, ed. American Association of Cereal Chemists: St. Paul, MN.

Dubois, D.K. 1959. Wheat starch: A key to better cakes. Bakers Digest 33 (6): 38.

Dubois, D.K. 1961. Automation in variety cake production. Proc. Am. Soc. Bakery Engrs. 37: 274.

Dubois, D.K. 1966. Problems in baking. Bakers Digest 40 (5): 73.

Dubois, D.K. 1978. The practical application of fiber materials in bread production. Proc. Am. Soc. Bakery Engrs. 54: 48.

Dubois, D.K. 1979. English muffins, production technology. AIB Tech. Bull. 1 (1).

Dubois, D.K. 1980a. Icings and glazes for sweet yeast raised bakery foods. I. Ingredient functions. AIB Tech. Bull. 2 (5).

Dubois, D.K. 1980b. Icings and glazes for sweet yeast raised bakery foods. II. Formulation and processing. AIB Tech. Bull. 2 (6).

Dubois, D.K. 1980c. Cereal Foods World 25: 391.

Dubois, D.K. 1981. Chemical leavening. AIB Tech. Bull. 3 (9).

Dubois, D.K. 1984. Processing and ingredient trends in US breadmaking. In: International Symposium on Advances in Baking Science and Technology. Kansas State University: Manhattan, KS.

Dubois, D.K. 1987. Technical assistance. AIB Tech. Bull. 9 (1).

Dubois, D.K., and Vetter, J.L. 1987. White, whole wheat, wheat and multigrain bread — a survey of formulas and processes. AIB Tech. Bull. 9 (2).

Dubois, D.K., Blockcolsky, D., and Dreese, P. 1984. Effect of salt level on processing and flavor of white pan bread. AIB Tech. Bull. 6 (8).

Eberts, J. 1998. Bagels: formulation and regional differences. Proc. Am. Soc. Bakery Engrs. 74: 99.

Edlin, R.L. 1967. Algin products in bakery foods. Bakers Digest 41 (6): 49.

Ellinger, R.H. 1962. The development and uses of fluid shortenings. Bakers Digest 36 (6): 65.

Ellinger, R.H., and Shappeck, F.J. 1963. The relation of batter specific gravity to cake quality. Bakers Digest 37 (6): 52.

Elton, G.A.H. 1969. Some quantitative aspects of bread staling. Bakers Digest 43 (3): 24.

Ensminger, A. 1994. Foods & Nutrition Encyclopedia, 2nd ed. CRC Press: Boca Raton, FL.

Etringer, D.D. Jr. 1975. Variety production from single pre-ferments. Proc. Am. Soc. Bakery Engrs. 51: 52.

Ewart, J.A.D. 1968. J. Sci. Food Agric. 19: 617.

Ewart, M.H., and Chapman, R.A. 1952. Anal. Chem. 24: 1460.

Faridi, H.A. 1980. Short-time saltine cracker. Bakers Digest 54 (3); 16.

Faridi, H.A. 1990. Application of rheology in the cookie and cracker industry. In: Dough Rheology and Baked Product Texture. H. Faridi and J.M. Faubion, eds. Van Nostrand Reinhold: New York, NY.

Faridi, H.A., and Finney, P.L. 1980. Technical and nutritional aspects of Iranian breads. Bakers Digest 54 (5): 14.

Faridi, H.A., and Johnson, J.A. 1978. Saltine cracker flavor. I. Changes in organic acids and soluble nitrogen constituents of cracker sponge and dough. Cereal Chem. 55 (1): 7.

Farmer, W.W. 1973. Production of buns to meet specific requirements. Proc. Am. Soc. Bakery Engrs. 49: 101.

Feinberg, A.J. 1975. Hearth and modified hearth-type products. Proc. Am. Soc. Bakery Engrs. 51: 98.

Fernholz, M.C. 2008. Evaluation of four sorghum hybrids through the development of sorghum flour tortillas. MS thesis. Kansas State University, Manhattan, KS.

Fields, M.L., Hoseney, R.C., and Varriano-Marston, E. 1982. Microbiology of cracker sponge fermentation. Cereal Chem. 59 (1): 23.

Figoni, P. 2008. How Baking Works, 2nd ed. Wiley: Hobeken, NJ.

Finney, K.F., Tsen, C.C., and Shogren, M.D. 1971. Cysteine's effect on mixing time, water absorption, oxidation requirement and loaf volume of Red River 68. Cereal Chem. 48 (5): 540.

Fischer, H.A. 1981. Pizza crust production. Am. Soc. Bakery Engrs. 57: 170.

Fischer, L.G. 1975. Cake doughnuts. Proc. Am. Soc. Bakery Engrs. 52: 121.

Flick, O.B. 1971. Production of yeast-raised doughnuts. Proc. Am. Soc. Bakery Engrs. 47: 174.

Foehse, K.B. 2009. Managing food preparation at high altitude. Presented at the AACC International Milling and Baking Division 2009 Spring Technical Conference, held May 15, 2009, at Albuquerque, NM.

Forestier, D. 1996. Technology of producing French breads (in France and North America). AIB Tech. Bull. 18 (7).

Forman, T. 2003. ESL — Where enzyme chemistry meets manufacturing. Proc. Am. Soc. Baking 79: 166.

Freedman, J. 2007. Whole grain flour strategies. Proc. Am. Soc. Baking 83: 155.

Friend, C.P., Waniska, R.D., and Rooney, L.W. 1993. Effects of hydrocolloids on processing and qualities of wheat tortillas. Cereal Chem. 70 (3): 252.

Fuhrmann, D.F. 1985. Frozen dough manufacturing — ingredients and formulation. Proc. Am. Soc. Bakery Engrs. 61: 149.

Gelroth, J., and Strouts, B. 2008. Sodium and salt: Health concerns, use in the baking industry and regulatory status. AIB Tech. Bull. 30 (3).

Gelroth, J., Glaser, B., Lehmann, T., Moore, T., O'Donnell, K., Pickering, D., Rootrinig, J., and Sieloff, T. 2005. Technical assistance. AIB Tech. Bull. 27: 1.

Gelroth, J., Sanders, L., Cogswell, T., and Zvaners, R. 2009. The use of potassium bromate by the commercial baking industry. Cereal Foods World 54 (5): 205.

Gisslen, W. 2008. Professional Baking. Wiley: Hoboken, NJ.

Glover, H.L. 1975. No-time dough methods. Proc. Am. Soc. Bakery Engrs. 51: 59.

Goodsell, G.R. 1984. Cake doughnut production. Proc. Am. Soc. Bakery Engrs. 60: 118.

Goodsell, G.R. 1985. Making danish: Basics that determine quality results. Bakers Digest 59 (1): 16.

Gorchow, J.J. 1992. Cake muffin production. Proc. Am. Soc. Bakery Engrs. 68: 145.

Gorton, L. 1994. Reference Source. Sosland Publishing Co.: Kansas City, MO.

Gorton, L. 1996. More on wafers. Baking & Snack 18 (10): 74.

Gorton, L. 2004. The whole grains story. Baking & Snack 26 (9): 61.

Gorton, L. 2005. Working with whole grains. Baking & Snack 27 (9): 87.

Gorton, L. 2006. Bioleavening for bakers. Baking & Snack 28 (11): 83.

Gorton, L. 2008. Smooth operations. Baking & Snack 30 (9): 91.

Grewe, E., and Child, A.M. 1930. Cereal Chem. 7: 245.

Groff, E.T. 1996. Soft and chewy pretzels. Proc. Am. Soc. Bakery Engrs. 72: 151.

Gross, H., Bell, R.L., Fischer, F., and Redfern, S. 1967. Cereal Sci. Today 12: 394.

Guckenberger, J.D. 1981. Bakery icings. Bakers Digest 55 (1): 12.

Hahn, R.R. 1969. Tailoring starches for the baking industry. Bakers Digest 43 (4): 48.

Hallberg, L.F. 1974. Pre-ferments. Proc. Am. Soc. Bakery Engrs. 50: 61.

Harder, M.J., and Jabusch, H.W. 1946. Points to watch in pie production. Bakers Digest 20 (5): 23.

Henika, R.G., and Rodgers, N.E. 1965. Reactions of cysteine, bromate and whey in a rapid breadmaking process. Cereal Chem. 42 (4): 397.

Hensperger, B. 2004. The Bread Bible. Chronicle Books: San Francisco, CA.

Hickenbottom, J.W. 1977. Sweeteners in biscuits and crackers. Bakers Digest 51 (6): 18.

Hildebrand, W.G. 1980. Honey buns. Proc. Am. Soc. Bakery Engrs. 56: 85.

Hino, A., Takano, H., and Tanaka, Y. 1987. New freeze-tolerant yeast for frozen dough preparations. Cereal Chem. 64 (4): 269.

Hitz, C. 2008. Baking Artisan Bread. Quarry Books: Beverly, MA.

Hoepfner, J. 1964. Brot u. Gebäck 18: 15.

Hoerner, G., and Boge, T. 1997. San Francisco style sourdough bread. AIB Tech. Bull. 19 (8).

Hoerner, G.P. 1996. San Francisco style sourdough. Proc. Am. Soc. Bakery Engrs. 72: 65.

Hoerr, C.W., Moncrieff, J., and Paulika, F.R. 1966. Crystallography of shortenings. Bakers Digest 40 (2): 38.

Hofberger, R. 1999. Processing and food uses of chocolate. AIB Tech. Bull. 21 (7).

Holmes, J.T., and Hoseney, R.C. 1987. Frozen doughs: Freezing and thawing rates and the potential of using a combination of yeast and chemical leavening. Cereal Chem. 64 (5): 348.

Hoseney, C., and Miller, R. 1998. Current understanding of staling of bread. AIB Tech. Bull. 20 (6).

Hoseney, R.C. 1986. Principles of Cereal Science and Technology. American Association of Cereal Chemists: St. Paul, MN.

Hoseney, R.C. 2007. Flour quality for cookies and crackers. Presented at the Biscuit and Cracker Manfuacturers' Association 82nd annual technical conference, held Sept. 23-26, 2007, at Niagara Falls, NY.

Hoseney, R.C., Wade, P., and Finley, J.W. 1988. Soft wheat products. In: Wheat: Chemistry and Technology, Vol. II. Y. Pomeranz, ed. AACC: St. Paul, MN.

Hotze, M. 2004. Super premium bread production. Proc. Am. Soc. Baking 80: 148.

Hsu, K.H., Hoseney, R.C., and Seib, P.A. 1979. Frozen dough I. Factors affecting stability of yeasted doughs. Cereal Chem. 56 (5): 419.

Huang, W.N., Yuan, Y.L., Kim, Y.S., and Chung, O.K. 2008. Effects of transglutaminase on rheology, microstructure and baking properties of frozen dough. Cereal Chem. 85 (3): 301.

Hurley, W.C. 1967. Advances in angel food production. Bakers Digest 41 (5): 130.

International Food Information Council Foundation (IFIC). 2005. Sodium in Food and Health. Published online at www.foodinsight.org.

Jackel, S.S. 1980. New research makes "reduced calorie" cakes possible. Bakery Production & Marketing 15 (7): 91.

Jackel, S.S. 1984. You've come a long way in 30 years, English muffin. Bakery Prod. Marktg. 18 (1): 115.

Jackson, D.S., and Sahai, D. 2000. Enzymatic process for nixtamalization of cereal grains. U.S. Patent No. 6,428,828.

Jackson, R.B. 1998. Dough conditioning systems — applied formulations. Proc. Am. Soc. Bakery Engrs. 74: 87.

Jacob, H.E., and Reinhart, P. 2007. Six Thousand Years of Bread. Skyhorse Publishing, Inc.: New York, NY.

Jago, W., and Jago, Wm. 1911. The Technology of Breadmaking. Bakers Helper Co.: Chicago, IL.

Janson, J.J. 1990. Tortilla manufacturing. Proc. Am. Soc. Bakery Engrs. 66: 110.

Johnson, A.C., and Hoseney, R.C. 1979b. Chlorine treatment of cake flours. III. Fractionation and reconstitution techniques for C12-treated and untreated flours. Cereal Chem. 56 (5): 443.

Johnson, F.E. 1978. Sourdough products. Proc. Am. Soc. Bakery Engrs. 54: 42.

Johnson, J.A., and Miller, B.S. 1957. Pre-ferments: Their role in breadmaking. Bakers Digest 31 (3): 29.

Juers, A.A. 1982. English muffins. Proc. Am. Soc. Bakery Engrs. 58: 46.

Kahlenberg, O.J. 1948. Preliminary studies on factors affecting egg white quality. Bakers Digest 22 (6): 26.

Kamel, B.S. 1993. Surfactants in bakery foods. AIB Tech. Bull. 15 (7).

Kamel, B.S., and Washnuik, S. 1983. Cereal Foods World 28: 731.

Kasarda, D.G. 1991, updated in 2000. Grains in relation to celiac disease. AACC International: St. Paul, MN. Published online at www.aaccnet.org/grainbin/kasarda.asp.

Kavanagh, J.A. 1969. Fillings for sweet yeast-raised products. Proc. Am. Soc. Bakery Engrs. 45: 189.

Kazemzadeh, M. 1999. Technology of producing hard pretzels. AIB Tech. Bull. 21 (9).

Kelco. 1975. Xanthan gum, 2nd ed. Kelco Div., Merck & Co., Inc.: San Diego, CA.

Kendall, P.A. 2005. High Altitude Baking. 3D Press, Inc.: Boulder, CO.

Kichline, T.P., and Conn, J.F. 1970. Some fundamental aspects of leavening agents. Bakers Digest 45 (4): 36.

Kim, S.K., and D'Appolonia, B.L. 1977a. Bread staling studies. I. Effect of protein content on staling rate and bread crumb pasting properties. Cereal Chem. 54 (2): 207.

Kim, S.K., and D'Appolonia, B.L. 1977b. Bread staling studies. II. Effect of protein content and storage temperature on the role of starch. Cereal Chem. 54 (2): 216.

Kline, L. 1970. Nature of San Francisco sour dough French bread process. Proc. Am. Soc. Bakery Engrs. 46: 83.

Kline, L., and Sugihara, T.N. 1971. Microorganisms of the San Francisco sour dough bread process. II. Isolation and characterization of undescribed bacterial species responsible for the souring activity. Appl. Microbiol. 21 (3): 459.

Klose, R.E., and Glicksman, M. 1972. Gums. In: Handbook of Food Additives, 2nd ed. T.E. Furia, ed. CRC Press: Cleveland, OH.

Knightly, W.H., and Lynch, M.J. 1966. The role of surfactants in baked foods. Bakers Digest 40 (1): 28.

Knischewsky, O. 1910. Z. ges. Getreidewes. 2: 272.

Kohman, H.A. 1944. The production and characteristics of salt rising bread. Bakers Digest 18 (1): 15.

Kraut, C. 2006. Die cut or pressed production for tortillas, pizza and pita. Proc. Am. Soc. Baking 82: 145.

Krubert, G.J. 1990. Cracker production. Proc. Am. Soc. Bakery Engrs. 66: 90.

Krumrei, D. 2001. Fat Tuesday and beyond. Baking Buyer 13 (4): 13.

Kulp, K. 1983. Technology of brew systems in bread production. Bakers Digest 57 (6): 20.

Kulp, K. 1986. Influence of liquid ferments on quality characteristics of white pan bread. AIB Tech. Bull. 8 (9).

Kulp, K. 1995. Biochemical and biophysical principles of freezing. In: Frozen and Refrigerated Doughs and Batters. K. Kulp, K. Lorenz and J. Brümmer, eds. AACC International: St. Paul, MN.

Kulp, K., and Olewnik, M. 1984. Continuous mix in cookie dough production — an alternative to batch mixing. AIB Tech. Bull. 6 (12).

Kulp, K., ed. 1994. Cookie Chemistry and Technology. American Institute of Baking: Manhattan, KS.

Kulp, K., Olewnik, M., and Bachofer, C. 1985. Functional effects of chlorinated flour on cookie spread and quality of sugar snap cookies. AIB Tech. Bull. 7 (5).

Kulp, K., Volpe, T., Barrett, F., and Jonsson, K. 1980. Cereal Foods World 25 (9): 609.

Lachmann, A., and Voll, H. 1969. Structure and behavior of icings. Bakers Digest 43 (2): 40.

Lai, C.S., Hoseney, R.C., and Davis, A.B. 1989. Effects of wheat bran in breadmaking. Cereal Chem. 66 (3): 217.

Lannuier, G.L., and Bayfield, E.G. 1961. Flour brew studies. I. The effect of certain salts upon fermentation of brews and brew breads. Bakers Digest 35 (6): 34.

Lawson, H.W. 1970. Functions and applications of ingredients for cake. Bakers Digest 44 (6): 36.

Lehmann, T.A. 1979. Guide to pizza crust production. AIB Tech. Bull. 1 (11).

Lehmann, T.A. 1986a. Pizza crust. Am. Soc. Bakery Engrs. 65: 167.

Lehmann, T.A. 1986b. Commissary methods of processing pizza dough. AIB Tech. Bull. 8 (12).

Lehmann, T.A. 1997. Chemically-leavened pizza crusts. AIB Tech. Bull. 19 (11).

Lehmann, T.A. 2002. Take and bake pizza. AIB Tech. Bull. 24 (10).

Lehmann, T.A., and Dubois, D.K. 1980. Cereal Foods World 25: 589.

Lehmann, T.A., Zeak, J.A., and Strouts, B.L. 1994. Technological processes and problems in cookie production. In: Cookie Chemistry and Technology. K. Kulp, ed. American Institute of Baking: Manhattan, KS.

Leveille, G.A. 1975. The importance of dietary fiber in food. Bakers Digest 49 (2): 34.

Levine, L.W. 1980. Icing stabilizers. Proc. Am. Soc. Bakery Engrs. 56: 96.

Lewis, T. 1997. Biscotti. Proc. Am. Soc. Bakery Engrs. 73: 123.

Lipman, H.J. 1972. Advances in icing technology. Bakers Digest 46 (1): 47.

Livingston, G.E. 1963. Method of forming decorative particles for incorporation into food and process of manufacturing thereof. US Patent No. 3,111,411.

Loeb, R.V. 1981. Modern production of hearth breads. Bakers Digest 55 (5): 56.

Long, J.W. 1993. Hard roll makeup. Proc. Am. Soc. Bakery Engrs. 69: 145.

López-García, R. 2008. Yeast makeover. Baking & Snack 30 (4): 85.

Lorenz, K. 1974. Frozen dough — present trend and future outlook. Bakers Digest 48 (2): 14.

Lorenz, K. 1976. Triticale bran in fiber breads. Bakers Digest 50 (6): 27.

Lorenz, K. 1979. Baking at high altitude. AIB Tech. Bull. 1 (9).

Lorenz, K. 1980. Pumpernickel production and quality characteristics. Bakers Digest 54 (6): 14.

Lorenz, K. 1995. Freezing and refrigeration of cake and muffin batters in the United States. In: Frozen and Refrigerated Doughs and Batters. K. Kulp, K. Lorenz, and J. Brümmer, eds. American Association of Cereal Chemists: St. Paul, MN.

Lorenz, K., and Kulp, K. 1995. Freezing of doughs for the production of breads and rolls in the United States. In: Frozen and Refrigerated Doughs and Batters. K. Kulp, K. Lorenz, and J. Brümmer, eds. American Association of Cereal Chemists: St. Paul, MN.

Lorenz, K., Bowman, F., and Maga, J. 1971. High altitude baking. Bakers Digest 45 (2): 39.

Lorenz, K., Bowman, F., and Maga, J. 1971. Special dietary breads. Bakers Digest 45 (5): 34.

Loving, H.J., and Brenneis, L.J. 1981. Soft wheat uses in the United States. In: Soft Wheat: Production, Breeding, Milling and Uses. W.T. Yamazaki and C.T. Greenwood, eds. American Association of Cereal Chemists: St. Paul, MN.

Lugon, R.B. 1992. Panettone bread. AIB Tech. Bull. 14 (8).

Maningat, C., Bassi, S., Woo, K., Dohl, C., Gaul, J., Stempien, G., and Moore, T. 2005. Formulation of high-protein, high-fiber (low-carbohydrate), reduced calorie breads. AIB Tech. Bull. 27 (4).

Manley, D.J.R. 1983. Technology of Biscuits, Crackers and Cookies. Ellis Horwood Ltd.: Chichester, West Sussex, UK.

Mansour, K.H. 1982. Quality control in soft flour. Cereal Foods World 27 (7): 315.

Marston, P.E. 1978. Frozen dough for breadmaking. Bakers Digest 52 (2): 18.

Martin, M.L., and Hoseney, R.C. 1991. A mechanism of bread firming. II. Role of starch hydrolyzing enzymes. Cereal Chem. 68 (5): 503.

Martinez-Anaya, M.A., and Kulp, K. 1984. Fermentation of liquid ferments and bread quality. In: International Symposium on Advances in Baking Science and Technology. Kansas State University: Manhattan, KS.

Maselli, J.A. 1955. Bakers Weekly 168 (6): 30.

Matz, S.A. 1968. Cookie and Cracker Technology. AVI Publishing Co.: Westport, CT.

Matz, S.A. 1991. The Chemistry and Technology of Cereals as Food and Feed, 2nd ed. Van Nostrand Reinhold: McAllen, TX.

Mauseth, R.E., and Johnston, W.R. 1967. Oxidizing and reducing effects in the continuous dough process. Cereal Sci. Today 12: 390.

Mazur, P., and Miller, R.H. 1967. Cryobiology 3: 365.

McComber, D., and Miller, E.M. 1976. Differences in total lipid and fatty acid composition of doughnuts as influenced by lecithin, leavening agent and use of frying fat. Cereal Chem. 53 (1): 101.

McGill, E.A. 1975. Puff pastry production. Bakers Digest 49 (1): 28.

McKechnie, R.W. 1984. Oat products in variety breads. Proc. Am. Soc. Bakery Engrs. 60: 56.

McLaren, L.H. 1954. Bakers Digest 28 (3): 23.

Meer, W.A., Meer, G., and Gerard, T. 1973. Natural plant hydrocolloids in bakery applications. Bakers Digest 47 (3): 45.

Meigs, H.T. 1968. Sweet doughs. Am. Soc. Bakery Engrs. Bull. 186.

Meisner, D.F. 1953. Importance of temperature and humidity in the transportation and storage of bread. Bakers Digest 27 (6): 17.

Meloan, E., and Doerry, W.T. 1988. Update on bagel technology. AIB Tech. Bull. 10 (4).

Merritt, P.P. 1960. The effect of preparation on the stability and performance of frozen, unbaked, yeast-leavened doughs. Bakers Digest 34 (4): 57.

Meyer, B. 2005. Managing for whole grain production. Proc. Am. Soc. Baking 81: 95.

Micka, J. 1955. Cereal Chem. 32: 125.

Miller, B.S., and Timbo, H.B. 1970. Factors affecting the quality of pie dough and pie crust. Bakers Digest 44 (1): 46.

Miller, B.S., ed. 1981. Variety Breads in the United States. Proceedings of a symposium presented at the AACC 65th annual meeting, Sept. 21-25, 1980. AACC: St. Paul, MN.

Miller, R.A., Maningat, C.C., and Hoseney, R.C. 2008. Modified wheat starched increase bread yield. Cereal Chem. 85 (6): 713.

Modanna, M.D. 1983. Pretzels as low calorie snacks. Cereal Foods World 28 (5): 297.

Moncrieff, J. 1970. Shortenings and emulsifiers for cakes and icings. Bakers Digest 44 (5): 60.

Moon, C. 2006. Formulating whole grains for taste. Proc. Am. Soc. Baking 83: 130.

Morgan, B.A. 1980. Sweeteners in bun production. Proc. Am. Soc. Bakery Engrs. 56: 43.

Moyer, J.H. 1986. Doughnuts. Proc. Am. Soc. Bakery Engrs. 62: 120.

Nakagawa, M. 1991. Pre-proofed frozen dough technology. Proc. Am. Soc. Bakery Engrs. 67: 68.

Ngo, W., Hoseney, R.C., and Moore, W.R. 1985. Dynamic rheological properties of cake batters made from chlorine-treated and untreated flours. J. Food Sci. 50 (5): 1338.

Ngo, W.H., and Taranto, M.V. 1986. Cereal Foods World 31: 317.

Noel, E.M. Sr. 1963. Production of English muffins. Proc. Am. Soc. Bakery Engrs. 39: 252.

Noel, E.M. Sr. 1971. English muffin production. Proc. Am. Soc. Bakery Engrs. 47: 128.

Norton, C.T. 1903. The Rocky Mountain Cookbook: For High Altitude Cooking, 3rd ed. Robinson Printing: Denver, CO.

O'Reilly, M.J. 1976. The practical production of sweet yeast-raised varieties. Proc. Am. Soc. Bakery Engrs. 52: 72.

Ogilvy, W. 1960. Latest ideas for coffee cake and sweet roll varieties, fillings and toppings. Proc. Am. Soc. Bakery Engrs. 36: 202.

Osman, E. 1972. Starch and other polysaccharides. In: Food Theory and Applications. P.C. Paul and H.H. Palmer, eds. John Wiley & Sons, Inc.: New York, NY.

Owen, J.A. 1975. Cake doughnut production. Proc. Am. Soc. Bakery Engrs. 51: 142.

Pai, Y., and Walker, C.E. 2004. Par-baking technology. AIB Tech. Bull. 26 (6).

Parades-López, O., and Saharópulos-Parades, M.E. 1983. Maize: A review of tortilla production technology. Bakers Digest 57 (5): 16.

Park, C.S., and Baik, B.-K. 2007. Influences of baking and thawing conditions on quality of par-baked French bread. Cereal Chem. 84 (1): 38.

Paul, H.E. Sr. 1970. Sour dough French bread: Production. Proc. Am. Soc. Bakery Engrs. 46: 91.

Paulicka, F. 1990. Shortening products. In: Edible Fats and Oils Processing: Basic Principles and Modern Practices. D.R. Erickson, ed. American Oil Chemists Society: Urbana, IL.

Pence, J.W. 1955. The freezing, storage and defrosting of commercial bread. Proc. Am. Soc. Bakery Engrs. 31: 106.

Pence, J.W. 1961a. Research on freezing of bakery products. Bakers Digest 35 (5): 64.

Pence, J.W. 1961b. Freezing and thawing baked products. Proc. Am. Soc. Bakery Engrs. 37: 192.

Pence, J.W., and Standridge, N.N. 1955. Cereal Chem. 32: 519.

Pence, J.W., and Standridge, N.N. 1956. Some experiments on bread freezing. Bakers Digest 30 (1): 25.

Pence, J.W., Standridge, N.N., Black, D.R., and Jones, F.T. 1958. Cereal Chem. 35: 15.

Pence, J.W., Standridge, N.N., Lubisich, T.M., Mecham, D.K., and Smith, G.S. 1955a. Food Technol. 9: 342.

Pence, J.W., Standridge, N.N., Mecham, D.K., and Olcott, H.S. 1955b. Food Technol. 9: 494.

Petrofsky, R. 1986a. Bagels. Proc. Am. Soc. Bakery Engrs. 62: 143.

Petrofsky, R. 1986b. Bagel production and technology. AIB Tech. Bull. 8 (11).

Pfefer, D. 1976. English muffins. Am. Soc. Bakery Engrs. 52: 51.

Pieper, W.E. 1968. The role of ingredients in wire-cut and deposited cookies. Proc. Am. Soc. Bakery Engrs. 44: 265.

Pizzinatto, A., and Hoseney, R.C. 1980. Rheological changes in cracker sponges during fermentation. Cereal Chem. 57 (3): 185.

Poehlman, R.W. 1979. Premium Danish production. Proc. Am. Soc. Bakery Engrs. 55: 91.

Pomeranz, Y. 1970. CRC Crit. Rev. Food Technol. 1 (3): 453.

Pomeranz, Y. 1977b. Fiber in breadmaking: A review of recent studies. Bakers Digest 51 (5): 94.

Pomeranz, Y., Shogren, M., and Finney, K.F. 1969a. Improving breadmaking properties with glycolipids. I. Improving soy products with sucroesters. Cereal Chem. 46 (5): 503.

Pomeranz, Y., Shogren, M., and Finney, K.F. 1969b. Improving breadmaking properties with glycolipids. II. Improving various protein-enriched products. Cereal Chem. 46 (5): 512.

Pomeranz, Y., Shogren, M.D., and Finney, K F. 1976. White wheat bran and brewer's spent grains in high-fiber bread. Bakers Digest 50 (6): 35.

Ponte, J.G. Jr. 1981. Production technology of variety breads. In: Variety Breads in the United States. B.S. Miller, ed. American Association of Cereal Chemists: St. Paul, MN.

Powell, A.G. 1977. Agents to reduce mixing time. Proc. Am. Soc. Bakery Engrs. 53: 99.

Preonas, D.L., Nelson, A.I., and Steinberg, M.P. 1967. Continuous production of pie dough. Bakers Digest 41 (6): 34.

Purdy, S.G. 2005. Pie in the Sky: Successful Baking at High Altitudes. William Morrow Cookbooks, Harpercollins: New York, NY.

Pyler, E.J. 1952. Baking Science and Technology, 1st ed. Siebel Publishing Co.: Chicago, IL.

Pyler, E.J. 1988. Baking Science & Technology, 3rd ed. Sosland Publishing Co.: Kansas City, MO.

Qarooni, J. 1990. Flat breads. AIB Tech. Bull. 12 (12).

Qarooni, J. 1993. Wheat flour tortillas. AIB Tech. Bull. 15 (5).

Quail, K.J. 1996. Arabic Bread Production. AACC International: St. Paul, MN.

Randleman, A.R., Conn, J.F., and Lyons, J.W. 1961. Bubble mechanics in thick foams and their effects on cake quality. Cereal Chem. 38 (3): 294.

Ranhotra, G. 1984. Nutritional value of pizza products. AIB Tech. Bull. 6 (11).

Ranhotra, G. 1985. Cereal Foods World 30: 703.

Ranhotra, G., Gelroth, J., and Novak, F. 1986. Nutrient profile of variety breads. AIB Tech. Bull. 8 (5).

Ranhotra, G., Gelroth, J., Novak, E., and Bohannon, F. 1984. Macronutrients in selected variety breads. AIB Tech. Bull. 6 (2).

Ranhotra, G.S., Loewe, R.J., and Lehmann, T.A. 1974. Breadmaking characteristics of wheat flour fortified with various commercial soy protein products. Cereal Chem. 51 (5): 629.

Reed, G., and Nagodawithana, T.W. 1991. Use of yeast in baking. In: Yeast Technology, 2nd ed. Van Nostrand Reinhold: New York, NY.

Reedich, E.L. 1989. No-time dough product update. Proc. Am. Soc. Bakery Engrs. 65: 238.

Reget, G. 1966. Wire-cut cookie manufacture. Proc. Am. Soc. Bakery Engrs. 42: 263.

Ribotta, P.D., León, and Añon, M.C. 2003. Effects of yeast freezing in frozen dough. Cereal Chem. 80 (4): 454.

Richins, A.T., Burton, K.E., Pahulu, H.F., Jefferies, L., and Dunn, M.L. 2008. Effect of iron source on color and appearance of micronutrient-fortified corn flour tortillas. Cereal Chem. 85 (4): 561.

Rijkaart, C. 1984. Croissant production. Proc. Am. Soc. Bakery Engrs. 60: 137.

Riley, J.P. 1991. Corn tortillas, corn chips and tortilla chips. Proc. Am. Soc. Bakery Engrs. 67: 142.

Robertson, R.G., and Haney, H.N. 1963. The functional and baking characteristics of egg white solids. Bakers Digest 37 (5): 64.

Robinson, R.J., Lord, T.H., Johnson, J.A., and Miller, B.S. 1958a. Cereal Chem. 35: 295.

Robinson, R.J., Lord, T.H., Johnson, J.A., and Miller, B.S. 1958b. Cereal Chem. 35: 306.

Rohrlich, M. 1961. The biochemistry of rye bread production. Bakers Digest 35 (1): 44.

Rohrlich, M., and Essner, W. 1950-51. Jahresber. Versuchanst. F. Getreidevertung, Berlin, Germany, p.71.

Rohrlich, M., and Essner, W. 1951. Brot u. Gebäck 5: 85.

Rolow, A.M. 2002. Preservatives and their applications in flour and corn tortillas. AIB Tech. Bull. 24 (8).

Rooney, L.W., Kirleis, A.W., and Murty, D.S. 1985. Traditional foods from sorghum: their production, evaluation and nutritional value. In: Advances in Cereal Science and Technology, Vol. III. Y. Pomeranz, ed. AACC: St. Paul, MN.

Rosen, R.A., Sadeghi, L., Schroeder, N., Reicks, M.M., and Marquart, L. 2008. Gradual incorporation of whole wheat flour into bread products for elementary school children improves whole grain intake. J. Child Nutr. Mgmt. 32 (2). Published online at www.schoolnutrition.org.

Roth, R.L. 1975. Fried yeast-raised production. Proc. Am. Soc. Bakery Engrs. 51: 149.

Roth, W.C. 1950. Production of partially baked products. Proc. Am. Soc. Bakery Engrs. 26: 138.

Rowe, C. 1985. Croissants. Proc. Am. Soc. Bakery Engrs. 61: 154.

Rowe, T., and Lehmann, T. 2000. Designing gourmet pizzas. AIB Tech. Bull. 22 (6).

Rozsa, T.A. 1976. Rye Milling. In: Rye: Production, Chemistry and Technology. W. Bushuk, ed. American Association of Cereal Chemists: St. Paul, MN.

Rucker, D.A., Wollerman, L.A., and Krum, J.K. 1978. Porous yeast-leavened dough products. US Patent 4,109,023.

Sahi, S.S. 2008. Cake emulsions. In: Food Engineering Aspects of Baking Sweet Goods. S.G. Sumnu and S. Sahin, eds. CRC Press: Boca Raton, FL.

Sanders, S.W. 1990. Non-starch carbohydrate enzymes — bakery applications. Proc. Am. Soc. Bakery Engrs. 66: 203.

Sargent, K. 2008. A "softer" approach to improving the quality of refrigerated bakery products. Cereal Foods World 53 (6): 301.

Saunders, R.M. 1980. Wheat bran as a dietary fiber. In: Cereals for Food and Beverages. G.E. Inglett, and L. Munck, eds. Academic Press: New York, NY.

Savelli, R. 2004. Formulation and production of Hispanic breads and sweet goods. Proc. Am. Soc. Baking 80: 96.

Scarborough, C. 1955. Brew fermentation: Bread and variety products. Proc. Am. Soc. Bakery Engrs. 31: 52.

Schaal, A.A., and Montminy, H.P. 1946. A real opportunity in cocoa and chocolate cakes. Bakers Digest 20 (5): 26.

Schiek, K.A. 1966. Corn starches: Some of their applications in the baking industry. Bakers Digest 40 (3): 50.

Schiffmann, R.F. 1988. Microwave product development. Presented at the International Conference on Formulating Food for the Microwave Oven held in March 1988.

Schmidt, C.O. 1985. Tortilla production. Proc. Am. Soc. Bakery Engrs. 61: 114.

Schulz, A. 1966. Fundamentals of rye bread production. Bakers Digest 40 (4): 77.

Schünemann, C., and Treu, G., 1988. Baking: The Art and Science. Baker Tech, Inc.: Calgary, AB.

Seetharaman, K., Yao, N., and Rout, M.K. 2004. Role of water in pretzel dough development and final product quality. Cereal Chem. 81 (3): 336.

Serna-Saldivar, S.O., Guajardo-Flores, S., and Viesca-Rios, R. 2004. Potential of triticale as a substitute for wheat in flour tortilla production. Cereal Chem. 81 (2): 220.

Shaffer, T. 1977. Automated sweet yeast-raised production. Proc. Am. Soc. Bakery Engrs. 53: 117

Shellenberger, J.A. 1974. The status of high-protein bread. Bakers Digest 48 (2): 32.

Shenkenberg, D.R., Barnes, F.G., and Guy, E.J. 1972. Food Prod. Dev. 6 (1): 29.

Shogren, M.D., Pomeranz, Y., and Finney, K.F. 1981. Counteracting the deleterious effects of fiber in breadmaking. Cereal Chem. 58 (2): 142.

Sieloff, T. 2006. Formulation of Hispanic sweet goods. Proc. Am. Soc. Baking 82: 176.

Smerak, L. 1973. Effective commercial no-time dough processing for bread and rolls. Bakers Digest 47 (4): 12.

Smith, A. 1970. Soft cookies. Proc. Am. Soc. Bakery Engrs. 46: 114.

Smith, F., and Montgomery, R. 1959. The Chemistry of Plant Gums and Mucilages. Reinhold: New York, NY.

Smith, R. 1989. Update on icings. AIB Tech. Bull. 11 (3).

Smith, R. 1996. Technology of yeast-raised doughnuts. AIB Tech. Bull. 18 (2).

Smith, R. 2001. Formulation and production of brownies. AIB Tech. Bull. 23 (11).

Smith, W.H. 1969. Mixing: An art or a science? Presented at the 44th Annual Technical Conference of The Biscuit Bakers Institute, division of the Biscuit and Cracker Manufacturers' Association, held March 16, 1969, at Chicago, IL.

Smith, W.H. 1972. Biscuit, Crackers and Cookies, 2 vols. Applied Science Publishers: Barking, Essex, UK.

Sokol, G. 2006. About Professional Baking, The Essentials. Thompson Delmar Learning: Clifton Park, NY.

Stauffer, C.E. 1998. The recipe for success. Baking & Snack. 20 (1): 40.

Stauffer, C.E. 2004. Maize to masa. Baking & Snack 26 (4): 45.

Stauffer, C.E. 2006. Native grain. Baking & Snack 28 (2): 98.

Steinberg, I.I. 1994. Trends in the tortilla industry. Proc. Am. Soc. Bakery Engrs. 70: 35.

Sterk, R. 2009. Color alternatives exist for cocoa powder. Food Business News 5 (17): 26 (Oct. 13, 2009).

Stiles, L. 1958. Mechanized coffee cakes, Danish and sweet roll types. Proc. Am. Soc. Bakery Engrs. 34: 200.

Stoate, D. 1981. The Millers Manual. Printing & Graphic Services Ltd.: Bristol, UK.

Stoecklein, R.C. 1995. Frozen par-baked products. Proc. Am. Soc. Bakery Engrs. 71: 49.

Strickler, A.J. 1981. High-fructose corn syrup in cakes. Proc. Am. Soc. Bakery Engrs. 57: 107.

Strietelmeier, D.M. 1988. Salt grade selection for baking application. AIB Tech. Bull. 10 (2).

Strouts, B. 2008a. Basic cracker technology. I. Ingredients and formulation. AIB Tech. Bull. 30 (4).

Strouts, B. 2008b. Basic cracker technology. II. Processing. AIB Tech. Bull. 30 (6).

Strouts, B. 2009. Concepts for healthy baking. AIB Tech. Bull. 31 (3).

Suas, M. 2009. Advanced Bread and Pastry: A Professional Approach. Delmar Cengage Learning: Clifton Park, NY.

Suggs, J.L. 1982. Powdered cake emulsifiers. Proc. Am. Soc. Bakery Engrs. 58: 110.

Sugihara, T.F. 1977. Non-traditional fermentations in the production of baked goods. Bakers Digest 51 (5): 76.

Sugihara, T.F., and Kline, L. 1968. Factors affecting the stability of frozen bread doughs. II. Prepared by the sponge and dough method. Bakers Digest 42 (5): 51.

Sugihara, T.F., Kline, L., and McCready, L.B. 1970a. Nature of San Francisco sour dough French bread process. II. Microbiological aspects. Bakers Digest 44 (2): 48.

Sugihara, T.F., Kline, L., and McCready, L.B. 1970b. Nature of the San Francisco sour dough French bread process. II. Microbiological aspects. Bakers Digest 44 (2): 51.

Sugihara, T.F., Kline, L., and Miller, M.W. 1971. Microorganisms of the San Francisco sour dough bread process. I. Yeasts responsible for leavening action. Appl. Microbiol. 21 (3): 456.

Suhendro, E.L., McDonough, C.M., and Rooney, L.W. 1999. The effect of soy products on corn tortilla quality. Presented at the 84th annual meeting of the American Association of Cereal Chemists, held Oct. 21 to Nov. 3 at Seattle, WA.

Sutherland, W.R. 1990. Fiber breads. Proc. Am. Soc. Bakery Engrs. 66: 192.

Svolos, T. 1971. Hydrocolloids as icing stabilizers. Bakers Digest 45 (3): 57.

Swortfiguer, M.J. 1960. Practical production problems of continuous doughmaking. Bakers Digest 34 (3): 56.

Swortfiguer, M.J. 1962. Nonfat dry milk in the continuous mix process. Bakers Digest 36 (2): 39.

Swymeler, G. 2003. ELS and your oven. Proc. Am. Soc. Baking 79: 162.

Tesch, J.W. 1950. Rye bread production. Proc. Am. Soc. Bakery Engrs. 26: 146.

Thompson, J.B. 1981. English muffins. Proc. Am. Soc. Bakery Engrs. 57: 141.

Thorn, J.A. 1963. Yeast performance in liquid ferments. Bakers Digest 37 (3): 49.

Tipples, K.H. 1967. Recent advances in baking technology. Bakers Digest 41 (3): 18.

Tipples, K.H., and Kilborn, R.H. 1974. Dough development for shorter breadmaking processes. Bakers Digest 48 (5): 34.

Tireki, S. 2008. Technology of cookie production. In: Food Engineering Aspects of Baking Sweet Goods. S.G. Sumnu and S. Sahin, eds. CRC Press: Boca Raton, FL.

Treadwell, J.H. 1980. Variety doughnuts. Proc. Am. Soc. Bakery Engrs. 56: 103.

Trempel, L. 1946. The use of starch in pie fillings. Bakers Digest 20 (6): 23.

Tressler, D.K., and Sultan, W.J. 1975. Food Products Formulary. Vol. 2. Cereals, Baked Goods, Dairy and Egg Products. AVI Publishing Co.: Westport, CT.

Trevino, E., and Norton, R.C. 2006. Nixtamalized corn tortillas. AIB Tech. Bull. 28 (2).

Trimbo, H.B., Ma, S.-M., and Miller, B.S. 1966. Batter flow and ring formation in cake baking. Bakers Digest 40 (1): 40.

Trivedi, N., Hauser, J., Nogodawithana, T., and Reed, G. 1989. Update on bakers' yeast. AIB Tech. Bull. 11 (2).

Trum, G.W. 1971. Bun production by the continuous mixing process. Proc. Am. Soc. Bakery Engrs. 47: 106.

Trum, G.W., and Rose, L.C. 1964. Cereal Sci. Today 9: 156.

Tsen, C.C. 1973. Chemical dough development. Bakers Digest 47 (5): 44.

Tsen, C.C., and Hoover, W.J. 1973. High-protein bread from wheat flour fortified with full-fat soy flour. Cereal Chem. 50 (1): 7.

Tsen, C.C., and Tang, R.T. 1971. K-State process for making high-protein breads. I. Soy flour bread. Bakers Digest 45 (5): 26.

Tsen, C.C., Hoover, W.J., and Phillips, D. 1971. High-protein breads: Use of sodium stearoyl-2 lactylate and calcium stearoyl-2 lactylate in their production. Bakers Digest 45 (2): 20.

Turner, J.E. 1970. Partially baked foods. Proc. Am. Soc. Bakery Engrs. 46: 74.

Turner, J.E. Sr. 1980. Liquid pre-ferments. Proc. Am. Soc. Bakery Engrs. 56: 176.

Tweed, A.R. 1983. Cereal Foods World 28: 397.

Uhrich, M.G. 1975. Formulation of liquid pre-ferment. Proc. Am. Soc. Bakery Engrs. 51: 42.

Urban, C.J. 1975. Cake production with fluid shortening. Proc. Am. Soc. Bakery Engrs. 51: 128.

Valentino, F. 1994. Par-baked pizza. Am. Soc. Bakery Engrs. 70: 153.

van Benschop, C. 2007. Cleaning up your label. Proc. Am. Soc. Baking 84: 44.

Varriano-Marston, E., Hsu, K.H., and Mahdi, J. 1980. Rheological and structural changes in frozen dough. Bakers Digest 54 (1): 32.

Vellone, L.A. 1972. Production and profitability of variety breads. Proc. Am. Soc. Bakery Engrs. 48: 136.

Velzen, B.H. 1963. Production of wire-cut cookies. Proc. Am. Soc. Bakery Engrs. 39: 243.

Vetter, J., Ranhotra, G., Gelroth, J., and Novak, F. 1983. Sodium in frozen pizzas and opportunities for sodium reduction. AIB Tech. Bull. 5 (5).

Vetter, J.L. 1979. Technology of sodium in bakery products. AIB Tech. Bull. 1 (3).

Vetter, J.L. 1984. Selection of fats and control of fat quality for cookies. AIB Tech. Bull. 6 (5).

Vetter, J.L., and Zeak, J. 1989. Chemical leavening of cookies and crackers. AIB Tech. Bull. 11 (7).

Vetter, J.L., Sutton, T., and Blockcolsky, D. 1986. Effect of sweetener syrups on quality characteristics of soft cookies. AIB Tech. Bull. 8 (7).

Vey, J.E. 1986. Danish. Proc. Am. Soc. Bakery Engrs. 62: 111.

Voorhees, E.M. 1955. Cheese cake production. Proc. Am. Soc. Bakery Engrs. 31: 304.

Voorhees, E.M. 1958. The quality factors in cheese cake production. Bakers Digest 32 (2): 58.

Weaver, J.A. 1978. Automation in the pretzel industry. Bakers Digest 52 (5): 30.

Weber, A. 1963. Plastic sweet dough bases: Their formulation and uses. Bakers Digest 37 (1): 66.

Wheeler, F.G., and Stingley, D.V. 1963. Cereal Sci. Today 8: 120.

Whistler, R.L., and Pyler, R.E. 1968. Action of chlorine on wheat flour polysaccharides. Cereal Chem. 45 (2): 183.

Whiteley, P.R. 1971. Biscuit Manufacture. Elsevier Publishing Co.: London, UK.

Willey, L.E. 1988. Cheese in bakery foods. Proc. Am. Soc. Bakery Engrs. 64: 102.

Willyard, M. 2000. Muffin technology (update). AIB Tech. Bull. 22 (10).

Willyard, M. 2002. Formulation of cake doughnuts (an update). AIB Tech. Bull. 24 (9).

Wise, C.E. 1971. Production quality control of extruded yeast-raised doughnuts. Bakers Digest 45 (6): 32.

Wolt, M.J., and D'Appolonia, B.L. 1984a. Factors involved in the stability of frozen dough. I. The influence of yeast reducing compounds on frozen-dough stability. Cereal Chem. 61 (3): 209.

Wolt, M.J., and D'Appolonia, B.L. 1984b. Factors involved in the stability of frozen dough. II. The effects of yeast type and dough additives on frozen-dough stability. Cereal Chem. 61 (3): 213.

Woodruff, S., and Nicoli, L. 1931. Cereal Chem. 8: 243.

Wootton, J.C., Howard, N.B., Marin, J.B., McOsker, D.E., and Holme, J. 1967. The role of emulsifiers in the incorporation of air into layer cake batter systems. Cereal Chem. 44 (3): 333.

Yamazaki, W.T., and Donelson, D.H. 1972. The relationship between flour particle size and cake-volume potential among Eastern soft wheats. Cereal Chem. 49 (6): 649.

Yener, M.E. 2008. Cookie dough rheology. In: Food Engineering Aspects of Baking Sweet Goods. S.G. Sumnu and S. Sahin, eds. CRC Press: Boca Raton, FL.

Young, L. 2000. Formulation balance for sweet goods. Proc. Am. Soc. Baking 76: 85.

Young, W., and Bayfield, E.G. 1963. Hydrophilic colloids as additives in white layer cakes. Cereal Chem. 40 (3):195.

Zelch, R. 2001a. Batter cakes. I. Ingredients and formulations. AIB Tech. Bull. 23 (3).

Zelch, R. 2001b. Batter cakes. II. Mixing. AIB Tech. Bull. 23 (10).

Zelch, R., Lacado, A., and Kutner J. 2008. Icings and glazes, a panel discussion. Proc. Am. Soc. Baking 84: 171.

Zelch, R., Sieloff, T., and Lehmann, T. 2004. Production of pie crusts. AIB Tech. Bull. 26 (9).

Ziemke, W. 1956. Liquid ferment process for bread production. Proc. Am. Soc. Bakery Engrs. 32: 53.

Ziemke, W.H., and Sanders, S. 1988. Sourdough bread. AIB Tech. Bull. 10 (10).

CHAPTER 9

Mixing and Forming Equipment

Updated by Mihaelos N. Mihalos (Parts A-C and F)
and Sigismondo De Tora (Parts D and E)

Mihaelos (Michael) N. Mihalos
Kraft Foods, Inc., 200 DeForest Ave., East Hanover, NJ 07936.
Phone (973) 503-2168; e-mail Mihaelos.Mihalos@Kraft.com.

Sigismondo De Tora
314 Blauvelt Rd., Pearl River, NY 10965. Phone (845) 620-9139.
e-mail sigisdetora@verizon.net.

INTRODUCTION

This section discusses the machinery and equipment involved in the first stages of dough and batter processing, from ingredient handling and the initial combination or blending of ingredients specified in the formula through fermentation, dividing,

Best doughs and batters depend on accurate ingredient handling and mixing as well as optimized forming. Equipment choice makes all the difference.

Fully automated ingredient handling interfaces with the company's SCADA system and reduces labor in raw material receiving at this bakery to one person. (Flowers Foods)

makeup and panning. Most concerns bread, buns and other yeast-raised products, but also includes here is the equipment necessary for the ingredient handling and mixing of baked foods made by batter and chemical leavening methods. Added to this discussion is examination of the extrusion, sheeting, lamination and encrusting equipment responsible for a growing amount of bakery output.

Readers will also find coverage of an older technology, that of continuous mixing and the equipment that feeds such systems. Although many commercial bakeries have replaced this technology, it is "alive and well" and operating every day in the plants of at least one major multiple-unit US baker. The legacy of this technology continues to influence the design and operation of today's preferment and sponge systems.

As purchasers, owners and users of processing equipment, bakers should be aware that the design and construction of these machines affects not only the production of the desired doughs and finished products but also the overall sanitary condition of those doughs and products. In 1949, the baking industry decided to get ahead of sanitation regulations with voluntary standards and formed the Baking Industry Sanitation Standards Committee (BISSC). The cooperative effort between wholesale and retail bakers, bakery equipment manufacturers and public health authorities resulted in publication of voluntary standards for the design and construction of bakery equipment.

BISSC established its office of certification in 1966, which controls the use of the BISSC Certified and BISSC Verified symbols on bakery equipment (**Figure 9.001**). To display these symbols, the manufacturer must warrant that equipment conforms to the group's standard (BISSC Certified) and successfully pass a third-party inspection by a BISSC-appointed independent testing agency (BISSC Verified).

During the late 1990s, the group worked with the American Society of Baking's Z50 Committee to develop an American National Standards Institute (ANSI) standard for the design of bakery equipment. The ANSI/BISSC/Z50.2-2003 standard provides guidance for a variety of manufacturing equipment regarding proper design for sanitation and food safety. BISSC, a not-for-profit corporation, became a wholly-owned subsidiary of AIB International in 2007. The standards can be downloaded from the group's Web site, www.bissc.org.

Figure 9.001. Use of BISSC symbols tells bakery equipment buyers that the manufacturer has followed rigorous, industry-established standards for design and construction.

9.A. Ingredient Storage and Handling Equipment
Updated by Mihaelos N. Mihalos

Management of ingredients during storage and transfer to processing operations calls for a variety of equipment solutions involving silos, tanks, bins, totes and transfer conveyors as well as weighing and dispensing machines of many different designs. The baker's inventory of ingredients represents a considerable — and perishable — investment. Equipment for storing and handling bakery ingredients should be capable of containing and maintaining these raw materials in safe wholesome condition. The dosing, weighing and transfer equipment must be configured to deliver ingredients in accurate amounts, no more or no less than required. The equipment must also be sized to fit production needs, neither flooding nor starving downstream processes. An effective ingredient handling system must keep up with demand for ingredients at each usage point. No system operator should wait needlessly for the ingredient system to finish delivering to another station before receiving his station's needed ingredients.

Bakery formulations contain many ingredients, but bakers tend to group them by their level of usage: bulk, minor or micro. Bulk, also termed "major," ingredients make up the majority of the formula. Flour, typically the most important major ingredient, constitutes 55 to 60% of bread formulations, based on total formula weight, while sugar occupies the top of the ingredient list for most cakes, outweighing flour. Minor ingredients will range from 5 to 10% (formula weight), and micro ingredients are added at 5% or less.

Figure 9.002. Bulk tanker trucks fill exterior silos, each capable of holding 110,000 lb or more of flour. (©2003 Dan Pearce Photography)

Ingredient handling systems generally follow this pattern, too. Tall exterior silos hold the bulk ingredients and contain 110,000 lb or more of flour each (**Figure 9.002**). Inside the bakery, large tanks contain liquid oils and syrups. Medium-size tanks manage dry ingredients such as milk powder or specialty starches. Tote bins made of metal, reinforced corrugated cardboard or nylon and polyethylene sacking manage the delivery and dispensing of other minor ingredients, for example, spray oils, eggs and chocolate chips (**Figure 9.003**). Many minor and micro ingredients, ranging from nutmeats to dough conditioners, enter the bakery delivered in bags and boxes and are held on elevated racks until called for use. Most bakery ingredients are dry materials, but a good number are liquid so physical state enters into the equipment choice. Particulated characterizing ingredients present additional concerns when being stored and transferred.

Most commercial bakeries operate computer-sequenced bulk systems, but automated systems for storing and dispensing minor and micro ingredients are less common. The return-on-investment (ROI) for automating "small" ingredients frequently runs longer than the 3 years average for most bakery equipment, yet savings earned through avoiding batching errors can be significant.

Specifying the capacity of any component of the ingredient handling system depends on the quantity of materials required for production. Whitt (1994) offered a good rule of thumb: Size the system to hold a full day's supply of ingredients. Moore (1988) recommended that the capacity of the flour delivery system, in particular, be sufficient to satisfy the demands of all flour use points. Of course, the layout and scale of ingredient storage and handling systems also depend on space available for placement of the equipment and best access to it for cleaning.

The Statistical Process Control (SPC) functions of automated ingredient handling systems dovetail nicely with today's management disciplines involving Enterprise Resource Planning (ERP) and Supervisory Control And Data Acquisition (SCADA) programs (**Figure 9.004**). By gathering, sorting, collating and analyzing information, these methods measure internal operations against guidelines and benchmarks, portraying information through charts and graphs. They give managers actionable data needed for continuous improvement of bakery operations.

Figure 9.003. A fork-lift places pallet-mounted totes filled with liquid ingredients onto the tote stand, equipped with a transfer pump. (Shick USA)

Bakery engineers make decisions about equipment based not only on production needs but also on regulatory concerns. For example, European authorities consider air-born dust to be a health hazard and require bakeries use dust collection and

Figure 9.004. Networked supervisory control and data acquisition (SCADA) terminals throughout the bakery not only allow operators to run equipment at that station but also to review up- and downstream system status. (©2002 Joe A. Clark)

abatement systems. In the US, California's Department of Industrial Relations Division of Occupational Safety and Health (Cal/OHSA) is considering regulations to classify flour dust as a "respiratory sensitizer" compound subject to Permissible Exposure Levels (PELs) for airborne contaminants. Just about any finely particulated material lightweight enough to mix readily with air can explode under the right conditions, and legislation has been considered by the US Congress to regulate "combustible dust" as a fire prevention measure. Flour and sugar dust would qualify under proposed rules.

Efforts to control allergens in the food manufacturing plant start with ingredient storage and handling technologies. All too many food recalls involve errors in handling ingredients. Although automated ingredient handling can reduce the risk of such errors, it must also be accompanied by the discipline of proper receiving, record-keeping, sanitation and maintenance methods. The same care in handling allergenic materials also applies when working with certified-organic ingredients. Isolation of bins, tanks and supply lines is often the only solution to maintaining the certified-organic status of such ingredients in a plant making both organic and conventional product styles.

Additionally, a well-controlled ingredient system is an essential part of post 9-11 food security measures. Tracking and validation methods, already in use by the pharmaceutical industry, are likely in the future of the food industry, too (Gorton 1993). Traceability predates bio-terrorism concerns and figures in supply chain management programs. In fact, bar code scanners are now used by some plants to track ingredients by lot, following them through formula/batch management software as they enter on-site raw materials inventory and move through silos and bag dump stations into use bins and out to batching and mixing operations.

9.A.1. Bulk flour systems

Flour is normally delivered to the bakery in bulk containers — flour tank trucks of 50,000-lb capacity or rail tank cars that hold up to 190,000 lb — or multi-walled kraft bags of 100-lb capacity, delivered by the pallet load. A common question in designing a bulk ingredient system is "What usage level justifies the move from bagged flour to bulk?" Bakeries can generally start to account for the cost of a bulk ingredient system if they use that ingredient at the rate of one truckload (40,000 to 45,000 lb) or more per week (Gorton and Whitaker 2004).

Typically, all bakeries are equipped with internal or external silos to meet the bakery capacity requirements for a certain time period. Whether the flour in such cases is delivered by flour tank truck or tank railcar is governed by the volume of flour being processed and on whether the bakery has access to a railroad siding. Bulk storage has advantages in terms of improved sanitation and hygienic storage conditions, less labor and storage space, reduced ingredient costs, better homogeneity, easy conveyance within the facility and quicker batch mixer cycles. The disadvantages are that these systems require installation of silos, which is a capital cost and requires continuing emptying and handling; deliveries cannot be delayed for detailed quality control checks; and mechanical breakdowns, cleaning and maintenance of equipment requires special training and techniques support by good management.

9.A.1.a. Delivery methods

Bulk flour is typically delivered in either bulk rail cars or tanker trucks. The rail cars and the flour delivery trucks are configured for unloading by either pressure differential (PD) methods shown in **Figure 9.005** or by air-slide systems.

The pressure differential system is easier to operate than the air-slide system because (a) no electric power is necessary; (b) unloading time is reduced approximately 50%; and (c) sanitation is improved because the rail car or truck does not need to be opened to the outside environment, which reduces the potential for outside contamination and results in the improved hygienic quality of flour

Figure 9.005. This modern pressure differential (PD) tank flour truck, fabricated of aluminum, has a capacity of 1,525 cu ft that will accommodate a payload in excess of 535 cwt of flour. Tank trucks for carrying bulk sugar are of similar size and design. (Fruehauf Corp.)

Earlier designs of these tank trucks, some of which are still in use, came in various configurations, with cone bottoms and rotary feeder outlets, air-slide bottoms with rotary feeder outlets and screw bottoms. Their normal payloads were 400 hundredweights (cwt) of flour, and they required 2 to 3 hours to unload. Modern PD trucks not only accommodate greater loads but also unload at more rapid rates.

Bulk tank trucks usually carry their own powered conveying blower. To unload a truck, its discharge port is connected to the feeder tube of the storage silo or bulk storage bin by means of a flexible hose. The operator activates the conveying system, which runs until either the truck is empty or the storage bin is full. The latter condition is indicated by a high-level control that either sounds an alarm or automatically shuts down the loading operation. Most trucks can carry between 45,000 to 55,000 lb of flour and can unload between 700 and 1,200 lb per minute. It is important to sample flour from each delivery to determine whether the flour meets the specifications established as well as the grade of flour. Attempts to rapidly monitor moisture of the flour inline have been unsuccessful to date because the temperature and the humidity of the conveying air have an effect on the overall flour moisture content. Typical flour moisture content is between 13 and 15%.

To an ever-increasing extent, flour shipments are currently being made in special railway tank cars, a modern version of which is shown in **Figure 9.006**. Their capacities have gradually increased from an initial 2,000 cu ft to more than 5,000 cu ft. Their loading capability improved from 94 to 97%, and their maximum load capacities are now in excess of 1,930 cwt or nearly 100 tons of flour. Available in various sizes to meet the different flour storage facilities of bakeries, the railcars are divided into a series of compartments with sloping bottoms that feed into a single discharge line.

Flour tank cars with air slides are unloaded pneumatically, using special portable

Figure 9.006. Covered rail tank cars have a capacity of 5,650 cu ft and are capable of carrying nearly 100 tons (1,930 cwt) of flour.
(American Railcar Industries)

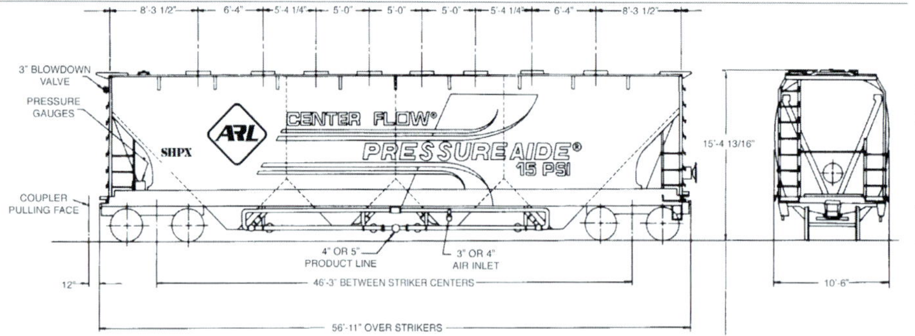

Figure 9.007. A portable unloader slides under the pressurized bulk flour railcar to unload its contents.
(Shick USA)

Figure 9.008. Relief hatches keep silo operations safe by protecting systems from excess pressure. Combination vacuum/pressure hatches are available.
(American Railcar Leasing)

unloaders of the type illustrated in **Figure 9.007**. The unloader is positioned under the car and pulled up manually against the flanges of its discharge gate to form a tight seal. Two positive displacement air blowers facilitate unloading. The first transfers the flour from the car to storage. The other fluidizes the flour by introducing low-pressure air to aerate the flour within the car and thereby enhance its flow properties. The fluidizing blower is preferably started up some 10 minutes prior to unloading the flour to eliminate bridging of flour within the car.

With PD rail tank cars, unloading is somewhat simpler. In this case, air from a single blower is piped into the car until a maximum internal pressure of 14.7 psi is established. Aeration of the flour takes place in the course of this initial stage. Like all methods that pressurize delivery of ingredients or filling of silos, the PD system requires a bin vent and pressure relief valve. Combination vacuum/pressure relief hatches are shown in **Figure 9.008** on the top side manway.

Opening an air control valve to the unloading line creates a pressure differential of 1 to 2 psi between the tank car and the discharge line, and the difference in pressure causes the flour to move through the line. The individual hoppers of the tank care are all connected to a single discharge line and empty in sequential order by opening the appropriate control valves. Because both the unloading system and the bakery's pneumatic conveying and storage systems are usually integrated under one central control, the high-level indicator of the receiving storage bin or silo is generally assigned the role of shutting down the unloading operation and of purging the conveying line when the bin has been filled to capacity.

Most flour storage installations consist of several bins or silos. A common method of loading multiple bins is to manifold the pneumatic lines at or near the unloading site (Morris 1971). Each bin's individual conveying line terminates at the manifold and can be connected directly to the flexible hose of the unloading device, as shown in the flowchart of **Figure 9.009**. Limit switches on the manifold automatically interlock with the level switch of the receiving bin. In instances where the silos are situated at some distance from the unloading site, it may be better to use a single conveyor line to the storage site and depend on diverting valves to channel the flour into the individual bins.

9.A.1.b. Storage bins

Flour storage bins come in various configurations and sizes. Where outdoor flour storage is dictated by a lack of floor space in the baking plant, the most commonly selected container is the cylindrical silo, mounted vertically on its long axis. On rare occasions when plant layout dictates, bulk flour silos may be installed horizontally. Silos and large bins can be equipped with explosion-relief systems and should be accessible via ladder and catwalks so maintenance and sanitation staff can reach all sides, tops and bottoms.

For in-plant storage, round, square or rectangular bulk containers of suitable size called "use bins" are frequently employed. Typically, they are installed when a large number of use points place enormous demands on the delivery line from the bulk storage bins. Their capacities will range from 400 to 1,000 cwt of flour. Most bulk flour systems are augmented with smaller holding and use bins of various designs that serve variously as surge, holding, batching or weighing stations for flour and other dry ingredients during their transit from bulk storage to processing.

Ideally, an outdoor storage silo should be sized so that it can accept the load of a single delivery vehicle (truck or rail car) whose nominal cubic capacity may range from 3,000 to 5,000 cu ft and which delivers payloads of 1,200 to 2,000 cwt. Silos that accommodate full loads of flour will not only reduce shipping costs, but they will also avoid the mixing of separate flour shipments that may differ in their baking characteristics.

Silos of this capacity are typically 9 to 12 ft in diameter and 54 to 60 ft in height and are generally provided with skirted bottoms (**Figure 9.010**) that may provide shelter for the auxiliary blowers and control panels (White 1981). Silos usually hold only one style of flour, but to save space, some can be configured as two separate bins within a single structure, each capable of storing a different style of flour. At the bakery level, silos made of steel, fiberglass and treated canvas are most common. Flexible fabric silos for in-plant installation are now capable of storing as much as 110,000 lb of flour or other dry ingredients (**Figure 9.011**). Concrete and rubber are almost never used as construction materials for silos. Grain mills and sugar refineries may use silos made of slip-form concrete, but not a bakery.

While bolted silos are available, the most practical design uses all-welded construction — the manufacturing method that conforms to BISSC sanitation standards. Welded silos use either carbon steel, with an FDA-approved epoxy-coated interior and a painted enamel exterior, or aluminum construction. According to Moore (1988), steel silos are a bit less expensive initially; however, they do require more maintenance, while aluminum silos offer the advantage of requiring no painting, inside or out, and are generally maintenance-free.

The interior surface may be either polished steel or a synthetic coating that is smooth, nontoxic, suitable for food contact, non-abrasive and free of odor and taste. It is essential that all internal welds be ground smooth and the tank interior sand-

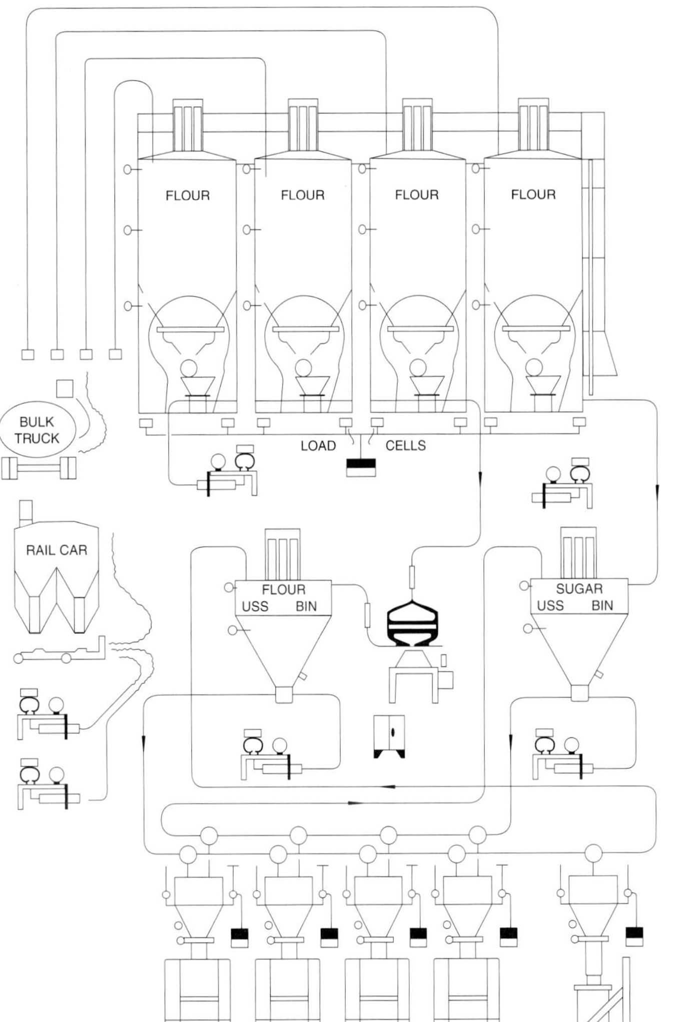

Figure 9.009. Flowchart illustrates an integrated bulk flour storage and pneumatic in-plant conveying system. (Fred D. Pfening Co.)

Figure 9.010. Six 150,000-lb flour silos, safeguarded by locked delivery ports, automatically supply both white enriched and whole-wheat flours to 1,500-lb hoppers above this bakery's mixers. (Fred D. Pfening Co.)

Figure 9.011. Indoor silos, made of flexible fabrics, provide secure storage for dry ingredients. (Contemar Silo Systems)

blasted prior to being coated to ensure the permanent bonding of the coating (Hailey 1973). The key design feature is to provide smooth and easy-to-clean surfaces because flour is not a highly flowable material. In regions of extreme seasonal temperature fluctuations, outdoor silos must be housed in some type of protective structure to minimize problems with interior moisture condensation. To avoid moisture condensation, temperature and humidity controls should be installed. As a rule of thumb, under normal circumstances and to prevent flour infestation by insects, no flour should be stored in any one bin or silo for more than 28 days.

9.A.1.b.i. Dust collection

Because flour is conveyed by air into storage bins and storage silos, these structures must be equipped with dust collectors that separate the flour dust from the conveying air before the latter is vented to the atmosphere. Almost all dust collectors are reverse pulse jet designs, although the occasional automated shaker-style system is seen. A number of static "puff" bags are still in use on use bins; they are a cheap way to vent, but they are falling out of favor with inspectors.

Dust collectors or bin vents in inaccessible locations — on top of flour silos or on bins with inadequate headroom — are generally of the automatic, self-purging type. Frequently, these collectors are made up of a number of long bags, arranged in 3 or more rows to provide an adequate filtration area. Periodically, an adjustable timer activates its mechanical shakers or reverse jets to dislodge the accumulated flour and restore the fabric's optimum venting rate. The most common way to describe venting is in terms of air-to-cloth ratio. Ideally, the ratio is no more than 4:1 and should be around 3:1 if possible.

Introduction of quick-change filters (**Figure 9.012**) marked a major improvement in dust collection. Designed as side- and top-insertable models, the filter uses elements made of spun-bonded polyester and PTFE membranes that can be replaced in minutes, compared with hours required by traditional bags and cages. The side-insertable system suits dust collection areas with height restrictions.

9.A.1.b.ii. Fluidizing methods

Flour silos and storage bins rely on various means of unloading, nearly all of which involve some type of aerating or "fluidizing" action. Historically, the sloped bottoms of the smaller, rectangular bins were equipped with screw conveyors, which proved adequate as long as the cubic capacity of the bin did not exceed a limiting volume and some knocking device was used to prevent bridging of the flour. Bridging of the flour results in the flow of powder being halted and the particles compressed into a solid mass. The silo design should provide ample entry points to permit access by employees for frequent cleaning and maintenance.

With the introduction of pneumatic conveying systems, the screw conveyors were replaced by fluidizing bottom slopes or aeration disks (**Figure 9.013**). These are equipped with a shallow air plenum covered by heavy canvas.

and into which air, pressurized to 3 to 5 psi, is introduced. As the air penetrates through the fabric and into the surrounding flour mass, it produces a fluidizing effect that causes the flour to move by gravity along the sloped bottom toward the discharge gate. In some instances, the fluidizing system has to be supplemented with vibrators and air-pulsing cones affixed to the bin bottoms to aid in maintaining flour movement.

High silos with large capacities tend to create an excessive head load at the discharge point, which makes unloading difficult. Such silos may require a vibrating bin bottom. This vibrating device, which normally occupies half the diameter of the sloping bin bottom, has proven to be highly efficient in expediting the unloading of large silos at a uniform rate.

To an increasing extent, silos rest on electronic load cells that facilitate inventory control. Load cells are sensitive electronic devices that, by means of a wire resistance strain gauge, measure the strain created by an applied weight and translate the reading into electrical signals transmitted to a central control panel. This technology provides the means for checkweighing each flour load received and each volume of flour withdrawn to production and for maintaining a perpetual inventory. Typically, weight and date are recorded for all such activities.

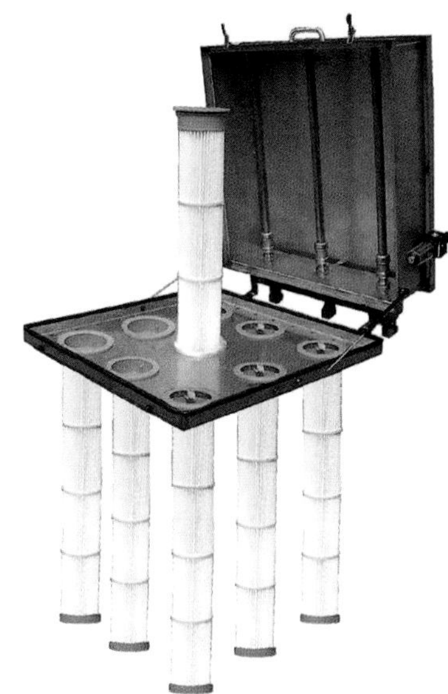

Figure 9.012. Designed to vent air from hoppers or silos, this top-loading bin vent dust collector uses filters that can be snapped in and out without tools and cleaned by an air wand.
(Fred D. Pfening Co.)

9.A.1.c. Pneumatic conveying

Movement of flour and other dry ingredients from storage silos and bins is generally done pneumatically, inducing transfer by creating a pressure differential between two points, either by increasing the air pressure at one end or by decreasing it to produce a partial vacuum at the other. Although bakery engineers commonly describe systems that blow or push ingredients with air or other gases at pressures above plant ambient as "pneumatic" or, more commonly, "pressure" and those that suck or pull materials at pressures below ambient as "vacuum," both approaches are variations of pneumatic technologies, differently applied. In practice, a combination of both is frequently encountered to exploit the inherent advantages of both (Irvin 1976).

Besides pressure and vacuum, two additional categories characterize pneumatic conveying systems: dilute and dense phase. Dilute phase is most common in bakeries and moves raw materials by suspending them in air along the entire length of the pipeline with a product-to-air ratio of 1:10. The dilute phase systems, which operate at air pressures between 6 to 12 psi and convey at speeds of 3,500 to 5,000 ft per second, use positive displacement air pumps, either singly or in series, as the source of the moving air, rotary valves for air seals and fabric dust collectors. Abrasive materials may require special handling (**Figure 9.014**).

Figure 9.013. This aeration disk features a 20° slope that aids discharge.
(Shick USA)

Dense-phase conveying suits transportation of friable materials, with granular sugar being a main application. This method enables composite ingredients such as mixed grains for whole-grain bread or muesli to be transported without separation. Compared with dilute phase systems, conveying speeds are slower, for example, low-velocity slug flow proceeds at 50 to 800 ft per minute; however, because of the high volumetric concentration of product within the pipeline, reasonable

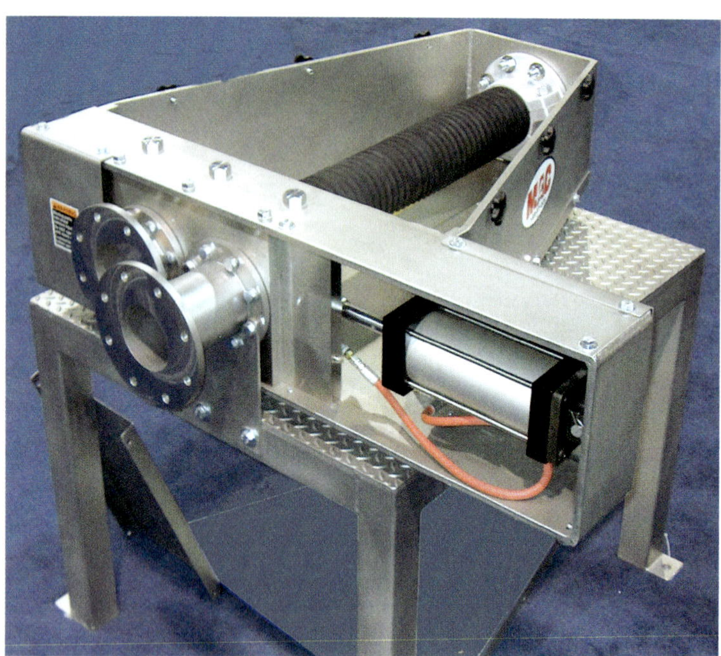

Figure 9.014. A hose switch diverter valve enables transport of cornmeal and other highly abrasive materials in dilute phase transfer systems. (MAC Equipment)

Figure 9.015. A twin-pot installation manages railcar unloading using dense-phase, semi-dense, low-pressure and/or pressure differential conveying. (ALL-CON)

conveying rates are still achieved.

A relatively new idea, low-pressure continuous dense phase (CDP) conveying applies a gentle touch to moving low-density friable materials such as particulates and ready-to-eat cereals. As in conventional dense-phase conveying, CDP conveying speeds are relatively low, ranging from 800 to 1,500 ft per second, while internal pressure is 15 psi. Vacuum dense phase (VDP) manages product flow at velocities of less than 1,000 ft per minute, with material-to-air ratios up to 50:1. VDP minimizes product segregation and line wear and does not allow build-up when handling high-fat products. These systems are self-cleaning and add no heat to the product stream.

A unique vacuum-pressure system manages dense-phase, semi-dense, low-pressure and pressure differential conveying. The manufacturer described the effect on the product as similar to toothpaste being squeezed from its tube. A twin "pot" system readily manages railcar unloading (**Figure 9.015**).

In essence, all pneumatic systems involve the movement of a predetermined volume of air through a conveyor line and a means for introducing into the air stream the material to be conveyed and for separating it out at the designated destination. Dry ingredient conveying systems consist of five basic elements: (a) blowers that create either air pressure or a vacuum for moving flour or sugar through the lines; (b) the lines themselves, with diameters that normally range from 3 to 5 in.; (c) rotary feeders or valves for introducing the material into the air stream; (d) diverting valves that permit the selective diversion of the material from a single line to multiple destinations; and (e) dust collectors or vacuum receivers to separate the material from the air before the latter is vented to the atmosphere.

Correct sizing of the blower is an important aspect of pneumatic conveying. As described by Slattery (1962), the first step requires establishing the required air volume and the best product-to-air ratios. Excessive air velocities waste energy, and relatively inefficient, yet inadequate, velocities can plug the lines because the material settles out of the air stream. Also, it is vital when installing or using a pneumatic system that it be grounded to earth to minimize the potential for static electricity.

Several factors affect the ability of pneumatic systems to move a given volume of flour within a unit time interval. These aspects include the capacity of the blower equipment, the diameter of the conveying lines, the air volume and velocity, the solids-to-air ratio and the operating pressure of the system.

The heart of the pneumatic system is the positive displacement blower, which should be capable of generating high enough air velocities to convey flour at velocities of 3,000 to 4,500 ft per minute through conveying lines with a diameter of 3 to 5 in. To ensure the most trouble-free operation of pneumatic systems, it is essential that they not be subjected to conditions of excessive pressure or operating speeds. Thus, intermediary surge bins need to be used when the distance from the storage silos to the mixer is excessively long or when several production lines are supplied from a single storage facility. It is usually desirable to employ a number of conveyor lines from storage to production because this layout will permit several operations to be carried out simultaneously without undue stress on the system.

A vital element in any pressure conveying system is the rotary airlock valve, which meters the product into the conveyor line at a predetermined rate and, at the same time, minimizes or prevents the loss of pressurized air. Such valves separate spaces of different pressures and are designed to handle the material's flow properties. It is recommended that manufacturer's tables be consulted when selecting and sizing an air lock.

Rotary airlock valves come in two basic designs: (a) the drop-through type in which the product enters the device by gravity and is expelled through the bottom opening by rotating blades and (b) the blow-through type, which connects the product source to the pressurized conveying line. The valve consists of a housing that contains a rotary vane with very close tolerances between the vane tips and the housing. Other auxiliary components of pneumatic systems include diverting valves, which permit selective change in the direction of product movement.

In-plant vacuum conveying systems are used primarily where relatively small volumes of material are to be transferred over short distances, although in some new plants they represent the exclusive method of internal flour conveyance. Their selection for this purpose is based mainly on their dust-free operation as well as their avoidance of conveying air temperature rises. However, vacuum systems do require larger blowers, higher capacity motors and bigger dust collectors to handle the greater air volumes needed to produce an adequate negative pressure within the vacuum system.

Moreover, there is a practical limit to the negative pressure that can be produced by such blowers. As Morris (1971) pointed out, such units can reduce the negative pressure to only about one-half of the theoretical vacuum, or about 7.5 psi. Since the normal operating vacuum is about 4 to 5 psi (8 to 10-in. Hg), this level leaves a reserve of only 3 psi for purging any obstruction in the lines. In contrast, pressure systems, which normally also operate at about 6 psi positive pressure, can readily increase this pressure to 15 psi should an obstruction in the conveying line occur.

As air is compressed, its temperature increases correspondingly; however, the resulting temperature increase in conveyor air has only a moderate effect on the temperature of the material being conveyed (Morris 1971). For example, if intake air at 21°C (70°F) is pressurized by the blower to 10 psi — as might be required to move granulated sugar at a rate of 200 lb per minute through a 3-in. line — then the air temperature at the blower exit will be about 88°C (190°F). If the sugar being fed into the hot conveyor air is also at 21°C (70°F), the resulting air-sugar mixture will have a temperature of 27°C (80°F), or only 6 C° (10 F°) higher than at the outset. Heat exchangers are often used when pressure conveying sugar. Product temperature must be kept below 38°C (100°F) to prevent any potential browning or caramelization of the sugar.

With the lower operating pressures that prevail in flour conveying, the rise in temperature of the pressurized conveying air will be correspondingly smaller and the temperature in the flour only marginally higher. The use of pneumatic handling, however, does increase the oxidation process in flours. The system causes minimal flour drying under normal moisture content of up to 2% (depending on the region). Controlling the temperature and humidity of the conveying air ensures minimal drying of the flour.

9.A.1.d. Mechanical flour conveying

Although pneumatic systems are the prevalent mode of conveying flour from one point to another in larger bakeries, in-plant mechanical transfer systems also find application, not only in smaller bakeries but also in the batching systems of larger plants. Thus, single- or twin-screw conveyors are frequently used to discharge flour from storage tanks into the in-plant pneumatic conveying system (Willhoft 1967).

At present, both vertical and horizontal mechanical transport of flour is most commonly achieved by means of spiral or helical screw conveyors within a steel housing. The use of bucket elevators for vertical flour movement was formerly quite common, but this method has now been almost completely abandoned, mainly because of the system's inherent sanitation problems.

Screw conveyors consist of a motor-driven central shaft to which is affixed an endless spiral or helical metal ribbon (**Figure 9.016**). As the shaft revolves, the traveling effect imparted by that motion to the spiral ribbon pushes the flour in the direction of travel. Depending on whether they are of the overhead- or floor-type, screw conveyors are usually provided either with removable top lids or drop-bottom sections to facilitate their cleaning and sanitizing. Screw conveyors of either the single or twin-screw type are available in several standard sizes, with spiral-flight diameters of 6 to 9 in. and rated capacities ranging from 100 to 600 lb per minute.

Figure 9.016. Screw conveyors, attached to the bottom of the storage silo, transport flour or other dry materials to use hoppers.
(Kaak Group North America, Spiromatic)

9.A.1.e. In-line flour cooling

Mixing to a constant final temperature is necessary for uniform production of doughs. Considered on the basis of weight alone, flour is the biggest single contributor to batch temperature. If flour comes into the mixer cool enough, then the temperatures of ingredients other than water almost do not matter.

As configured today, flour cooling takes place by injection of the cold gas or dry ice snow at various process sites. It can be injected into the pneumatic pipe, or enclosed auger conveyor, that transfers flour from silo to receiving hopper or batching vessel. It can be introduced at a batching vessel such as a pneumatic blender. And it can be injected at the mixer. Safe venting of the spent gas must be part of the final system design.

Ice, chilled water, or injection of carbon dioxide (CO_2) in the mixer bowl accomplishes somewhat inefficient and imprecise compensation for winter to summer differences in ingredient temperatures. Conditioning of flour temperature through injection of CO_2 during pneumatic conveying is a substantial improvement over current temperature reduction methods.

Reduction of flour temperature occurs through injection of liquid CO_2 directly into the flour conveying system at a point or points before the mixer. When the liquid CO_2 passes through an injection nozzle into the flour line, it instantly flashes into fine particles of CO_2 "snow." The fine particles mix with the fluidized flour as they sublime into CO_2 gas. At the operating temperature of -78°C (-109°F), the CO_2 causes an immediate temperature reduction of the flour and any air conveyed with the flour.

Most vendors differ only in the method of CO_2 injection. Some provide a series of nozzles, located at multiple sites through control valves in the horizontal flour lines, while others handle coolant injection with multiple nozzles at a single location on the vertical flour line immediately ahead of the flour use bin. Chief consideration must be given to the length of time (a function of the length of the pipe in horizontal lines) and fluidization of the flour within the blend of cryogenic gas and conveying air. The vertical system is reported to be more efficient in fluidization to ensure uniform mixing of the CO_2 and flour.

The vertically installed flour temperature reduction system consists of five parts (**Figure 9.017**): (a) CO_2 piping, (b) electronic control panel, (c) mechanical control panel, (d) CO_2 injector and (e) flour temperature thermocouple. At the system's control panel, the operator sets the desired temperature for flour as it enters mixing. The inline cooling system automatically activates when the flour valve at the silo is opened. Thermocouples located in the flour line detect the temperature of the flour and send a signal to the temperature control system. Based on the difference between the flour temperature and the set point, the control system determines the flow rate of CO_2 through the injector valves needed to reach the set point. Liquid CO_2 flows through the nozzles mounted around the circumference of the injector until the temperature of the flour reaches the set point. This action results in achievement of the desired flour temperature at the weigh hopper or mixer.

A similar system adds a phase separator to ensure that the cryogen (liquid nitrogen) is always present at the injector (**Figure 9.018**), and there is not loss of cooling when the nitrogen sublimates, turns to gas, in the manifold. This system controls flour temperature to ± 0.5°C (± 1 F°). Liquid nitrogen's boiling point temperature, -195.8°C (-320.4°F), is much lower than that of carbon dioxide, -78.6°C (-109.5°F). The length of this vertical injection system varies from 16 to 50 in., depending on the diameter of the flour line.

Another design injects the cold CO_2 into flour scale hoppers above mixers, which means it works with both pressure and vacuum conveying systems. A thermocouple measures the temperature of incoming flour and dry ingredients, reporting this data to the control system, which calculates the amount of cryogen required and opens the valve sending the cold gas into the scale hopper. The hopper's fluidizing bed assures distribution of CO_2 throughout the dry ingredients. All these activities take place during the normal time delay between delivery of dry ingredients to the scale hopper and the end of mixing for the previous batch.

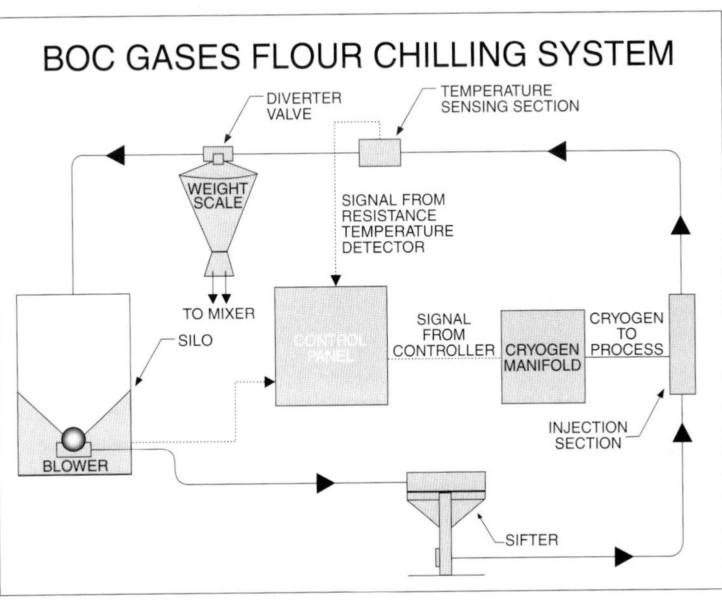

Figure 9.017. A system that injects a cryogenic gas (carbon dioxide or nitrogen) and regulates its action provides accurate control over flour temperature.
(Shick USA, BOC Group)

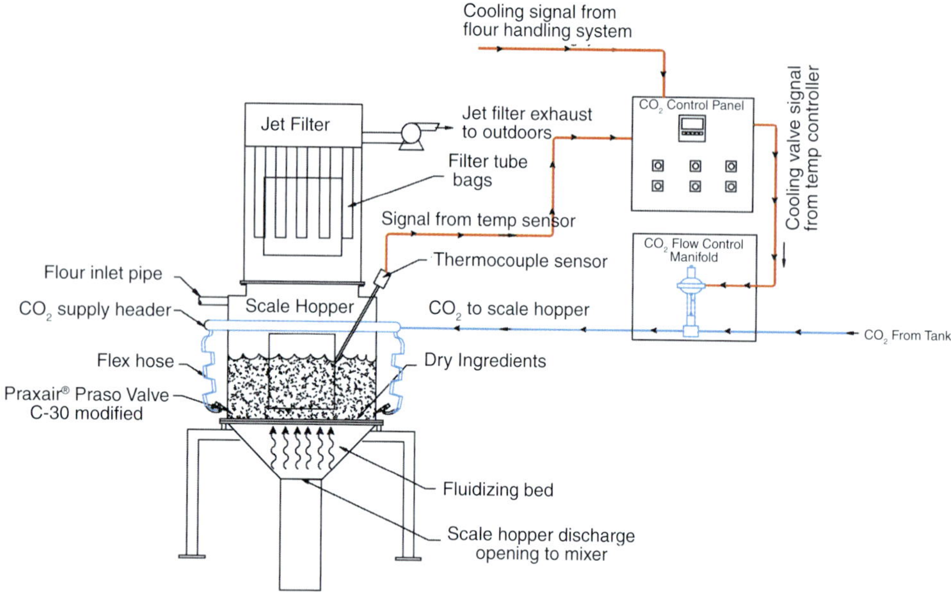

Figure 9.018. The fluidizing bed of the scale hopper distributes cold gases throughout the dry ingredients before the control system releases them into the mixer. (Praxair)

Figure 9.019. As flour is unloaded, it passed first through a metal detector before it reaches the inline sifter and silos. (Mettler-Toledo Safeline)

Mechanical conveyors can also be fitted with flour cooling systems. Configured as heat exchangers, the cooler circulates cold water or glycol in a double-walled jacket around the stainless-steel tubes carrying the flour.

9.A.1.f. Flour sifters

While the sifter at the flour mill is one of a number of pieces of processing equipment that separate or classify in-process material by size, the sifter at the bakery serves a quality control function, occupying an important role in any Hazard Analysis Critical Control Point (HACCP) program. By sifting flour at delivery, suspect material can be kept out of inventory altogether. Magnets and metal detection (**Figure 9.019**) provide additional protection against tramp metal. Weekly inspection of sifters is mandated under AIB International inspection protocols. Preventative maintenance involves regular lubrication of bearings every 30 to 60 days (Whitaker 2007b).

The design of a bakery's flour sifter is different from a mill sifter: It is smaller in size, and the screens for its sieve frames all use the same mesh size, 30-mesh with 50 to 60% open space. All the "overs" — the material that will not pass through the screen — go into a single tailings pot. A sifter in a flour mill employs multiple screen sizes and moves its overs into several different streams for further processing.

Sifters are defined as the means for separating a ground material into various particle sizes. Posner and Hibbs (2005) listed six principles for designing the proper sifting system: (a) screen acceleration, (b) rate of movement (velocity) of the particles, (c) size of mesh openings, (d) amount of sieve surface available area, (e) amount of material on sieve surface and (f) granulation and shape of the particles. Designs encompass gravity (centrifugal, gyratory, gyratory-reciprocal and vibratory) and pressure methods.

All flour handling systems are provided with one or more flour sifters of some type. Sifters vary in complexity from simple tubular sieves made from metal and inserted at the discharge end of the screw conveyor, to elaborate gyratory systems containing up to 30 sieves each, which are the primary sifters used in the industry (**Figure 9.020**).

The two principal functions of sifters are (a) to remove extraneous material (lint, string, insect fragments) from the flour and (b) to thoroughly aerate the flour and thereby bring about its more uniform blending. The sifters used in bakeries include gravity sifters (flat- or sloped-screen, centrifugal or rotary-drum type) and pressure sifters (**Figure 9.021**).

Formerly, gyrating screen type sifters were most prevalent. These consist basically of a rectangular base frame that supports a sieve box that, in turn, holds a combination sieve and cleaning-ball retainer frame and an actuating mechanism. The sieve box, with its multiple screens, is put into a rapid vibrating and gyrating motion by the actuating mechanism. This action not only acts to cause the flour to pass through the screen, but it also agitates the cleaning balls, retained in compartments under each screen, so they bounce against its underside and prevent the screen from binding. The tailings that fail to pass through the screens are removed through a special tailings port.

If such a gravity sifter is installed as a stand-alone system, it requires a cyclone, airlock and dust control mechanisms. But if made part of an ingredient delivery system, these extra pieces of equipment can be eliminated.

In the rotary drum sifter, it is the revolving motion of the drum that causes the flour to pass through the screen. In some designs, rotating paddles cause flour to pass through the screen. The paddles, also called blades, should not contact the sieve cloth, and there should be no rubbing friction between the blades and cloth. Instead, the rotary mechanism should carry the flour forward and create the air movement that conveys the flour onto and through the screen.

Inline pressure sifters (**Figure 9.022**) are directly inserted into pneumatic conveying lines and need no separate hoppers, blowers or dust control system. Recent improvements include adaptation of the nested frame design of gravity sifters to pressure sifter applications (**Figure 9.023**). Made of stainless steel, ring-like frames are fitted with O-ring gaskets and tie-rod assemblies to keep the system tightly sealed,

Figure 9.020. Gyratory sifters, this one constructed of stainless steel for washdown cleaning, can be installed directly into pneumatic lines. (Great Western Manufacturing Co.)

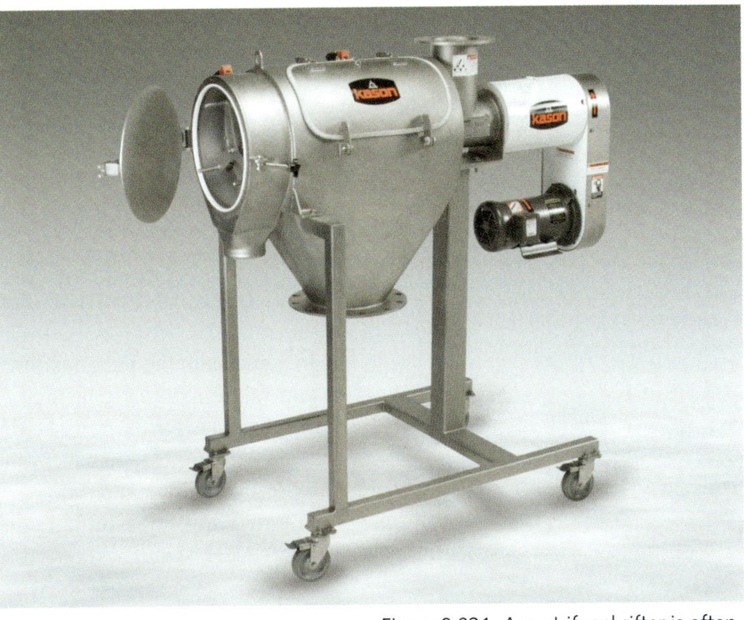

Figure 9.021. A centrifugal sifter is often placed between the flour silo and the mixer. (Kason)

Figure 9.022. This circular vibratory screener uses multiplane, inertial vibration to cause particles to pass through the screens. (Kason)

Figure 9.023. In-line pressure sifters feature modular nested frame design, keeping the system tight but allowing ready disassembly for inspection and maintenance. (Kason)

yet they disassemble quickly for inspection and maintenance.

Today's larger-sized pressure sifters allow their use at the receiving dock as a first-line quality defense. They can accept flour directly from the delivery truck or rail car, screening the flour before it enters the bakery's storage silos.

In addition to the high-capacity flour sifters fully integrated into the bakery's basic flour handling system, auxiliary sifters may be needed specifically to deal with smaller flour volumes. These sifters are available as portable floor types and bench-mounted types and are used wherever small batches of flour require sifting immediately before introduction into the production process.

Recent advances in flat frame-style sieve screens have improved their sanitary performance, making them easy to service (**Figure 9.024**). Stapling, as a means to attach screens to sieve frames, is being replaced by mechanical stretch-and-glue methods. The nylon cloth is stretched and tensioned by machine, then glued to the frame surfaces. The glue fills in the mesh, leaving no harborages for pests.

Screen breaks do occur because of normal wear-and-tear. Sharp edges on impurities will cause damage to screen materials, allowing coarse materials and impurities to slip through. Bakers expect flour to contain little to no tailings so it is not unusual for the sifter's tailings bucket to contain very little material. Periodic inspection of tailings, however, may reveal breaks.

A new screen monitoring system was introduced for rotary sifters. It takes advantage of screen construction that uses coated metal rods in one direction of the weave and PE or PA rods in the cross direction. Stainless steel rings tension the screen, and breaks generate electrical signals and set off alarms.

The action of entrained air and screen vibration provide whatever de-lumping action flour requires; however, opinions differ about the use of sifters as delumping devices. For some bakery ingredients, delumping can be an important process, and sifters with beater mechanisms can be dedicated to such applications.

Special centrifugal impact machines of the Entoleter type find extensive use in mills for the control of live insect infestation and are also found to some extent in bakeries. These devices, which consist of a high-speed rotor with impact disks housed in a steel casing, destroy insect life in all its stages by subjecting the flour to powerful centrifugal and impact forces as it passes through them.

9.A.2. Bulk and minor ingredient systems

In addition to the bulk handling of flour, bakeries now resort to an ever increasing extent to the automatic handling of other dry ingredients such as powdered sugar, milk powders, cocoa powder, dextrose, specialty starches and similar ingredients that are delivered to the bakery in non-bulk lots. These are unloaded either mechanically or manually and fed into appropriately sized intermediate holding bins. These bins form part of a small ingredient handling system, also comprised of conveyors, weighfeeders, scales and micro-scales (Baumann 1984, Long 1984, Whitt 1994).

9.A.2.a. Drums, totes and super sacks

Food plants receive a variety of dry ingredients in portable, semi-bulk containers, notably 55-gal drums, tote containers and large flexible bags, sometimes termed "super sacks" or "big bags." Drums and totes typically manage the delivery of liquid materials, but totes have also been used to transport flour or prepared mixes to bakeries. When they contain liquid ingredients, these delivery containers can be hooked up directly with the in-plant ingredient delivery system, using dedicated piping that leads to liquid supply hoppers above mixers or use points. They can also be unloaded into intermediate storage tanks. Some feature integrated metering screws.

Flexible super sacks, 30 cu ft in size and containing up to 3,000 lb of ingredients each, feature a variety of configurations, lined and unlined, in reusable or disposable formats. Spouts located at the bottom of the bag enable unloading, but the bags are best handled in the bakery using specialized unloading equipment (**Figure 9.025**). A fork lift is generally required to bring the large bag into position, although some bulk bag unloading systems offer the option of an integrated hoist, thus allowing one bag to be unloaded while a second is moved into position. Designs are available to accommodate installation in low headroom situations. Because compaction of materials can result during shipping, these unloaders can be supplied with different discharge devices. Vibratory feed, for example, assists gravity in unloading the sacks, while a paddle-style mechanism is available to massage the bag to facilitate release of materials, a job that can also be done by a ram-base agitation system. The unloaders can be configured with a material cut-off device to allow tying off of bag spouts when a partially unloaded bag is removed.

9.A.2.b. Dry sweetener handling

Bulk quantities of sugar and other sweeteners in their dry granular form are handled in a manner similar to that used for bulk flour and can be delivered either by rail car or truck. Sucrose is the basic dry sweetener for the baking industry and therefore of extreme importance in its handling.

Sugar grades range from extra fine to coarse granulation and are controlled during the crystallization process by using sieves for separation into the proper particle size. Therefore, the handling and conveyance of the sweetener is of paramount importance because alteration of the physical composition, particularly the particle size, will have a profound effect on many formulations, especially cookies. If significant particle degradation occurs, the result may be stratification in the supply bin and delivery of incorrect particle size, thus altering the final product quality of the cookies.

Both mechanical and pneumatic systems are applicable to the in-plant movement of dry sweeteners. The mechanical transport of granular sweeteners, typically using a screw conveyor or vibratory feeder, has the advantage of subjecting the individual particles to less attrition and dust formation than does pneumatic conveyance. Also, to overcome sugar's high bulk density, the pneumatic system intended for dry sweeteners requires larger capacity blowers than needed in flour conveying systems, which handle comparatively lighter ingredient. In this case, the bins are fluidized and contents discharged using rotary air lock valves. For either of the two scenarios, a bullet magnet or metal detection device is installed in the line to detect and remove any metal contaminants.

Sugar exhibits definite hygroscopic properties: It is prone to absorb moisture from the atmosphere. This characteristic, in turn, increases its tendency to cake and bridge

Figure 9.024. A pneumatic sieve compression system speeds access for inspection and maintenance of the lift-out screen frames.
(Great Western Manufacturing Co.)

Figure 9.025. Bulk bags, also called super sacks, transfer their contents into the ingredient system using gravity.
(Fred D. Pfening Co.)

in the storage bin. Because the sucrose has a low moisture content, temperature variation can cause surface crystallization, allowing it to stick to other sucrose particles and cake. The standard practice is to circulate air at 20°C (68°F). Dehumidification systems that employ a combination of mechanical and desiccant methods, along with cooling of the air that comes into contact with sucrose, are strongly recommended for the storage and handling of granular sugar.

To further minimize this problem, Hagedorn (Hagedorn 1965) recommended that sugar, as delivered to the bakery, not exceed a moisture content of 0.2%, nor that its temperature be above 35°C (95°F).

Moreover, according to the same authority, it is good practice to (a) limit the size of the storage bins for sugar to the smallest practical capacity consistent with delivery loads, (b) recirculate the sugar during plant shutdown periods or humid weather conditions, (c) select conveying equipment that minimizes attrition or particle reduction and (d) use multiple screw conveyors at bin bottoms to assist in the discharge of sugar lumps.

Sugar dust, like flour dust, can be explosive so dust must be controlled and minimized inside the bakery. Dust collection equipment, along with the collection bins and motors powering ingredient handling systems, must feature explosion-proof design. Sugar dust should not be recycled back to use bins or silos; its fine size can promote caking and lumping.

As in the case of granulated sucrose, a combination of mechanical and desiccant drying also provides the best solution for conveying powdered sugar. The cooling and drying action not only helps remove the mechanical heat generated by the pulverizer when powdered sugar is produced in-plant but also aids in reduction of the product's moisture content, allowing more accurate conveying.

9.A.2c. Liquid sweetener handling

To an ever-increasing extent, bakeries have converted from the use of dry sugars to liquid sweeteners because the latter are available in a variety of blends with various proportions of sucrose, invert sugar, dextrose and corn syrup. These liquids are more conveniently handled and are more efficiently weighed or metered; however, during 2009, a trend of reverting back to dry sucrose seemed to be emerging, driven by consumer marketing demands.

Liquid all-sugar blends comprise concentrated sucrose/invert solutions with a solids content of about 67%, whereas the solids content of corn syrups is nearly 80%, and that of different sucrose/corn syrup blends ranges from 69.6% to 79.1%, depending on the sucrose-to-corn-syrup ratios (Hoynak and Bollenback 1966). At these concentrations, the liquid sweeteners are biologically stable, unless they are inadvertently diluted with water from cleaning operations or from possible condensation formed inside delivery and storage tanks.

Liquid sweeteners, for the most part, are delivered to the bakery in tank trucks with capacities of 3,000 to 4,500 gal. The tanks are frequently divided into compartments with independent loading and unloading facilities so that more than one type of sweetener can be delivered. Rail tank cars are able to carry several times the loads of tank tracks, for example 100,000 lb, which accounts for the former's greater economy of delivery.

Bulk systems for liquid sweeteners usually consist of several stationary storage tanks of suitable size, complete with permanent piping for both receiving the sweeteners from the delivery vehicle and for pumping them to in-plant use points. The basic elements of a simple liquid sugar bulk handling system are indicated in **Figure 9.026**.

Tanks are normally cylindrical in shape, of all-welded construction and may be mounted vertically or horizontally. Their heads are provided with ultraviolet sterilization lamps, blowers and air filters to ensure sterile conditions in the headspace.

Ventilation is provided either using a blower system or by two openings in the tank heads near the periphery to prevent condensation due to high humidity levels at the top of the tank, which could initiate microbial growth by yeast bacteria or mold. A calibrated sight glass, gauge or level sensor provides a ready indication of the tank's content level. Tanks intended for the storage of corn syrup are usually equipped with heating coils to maintain the product at a temperature of 32 to 38°C (90 to 100°F) to promote its flow properties and to control viscosity or rate of crystallization. (Corn Industries Research Foundation 1965). Such heating is not required for tanks inside the bakery that store high-fructose corn syrup.

According to Schuettinger (1966), liquid sweetener bulk systems should consist of at least two storage tanks to permit alternate emptying and filling. The size of each should be sufficient to receive either a full truck tank or rail tank load. The best tank design is a vertical cylinder of welded construction with dished bottom and top heads,

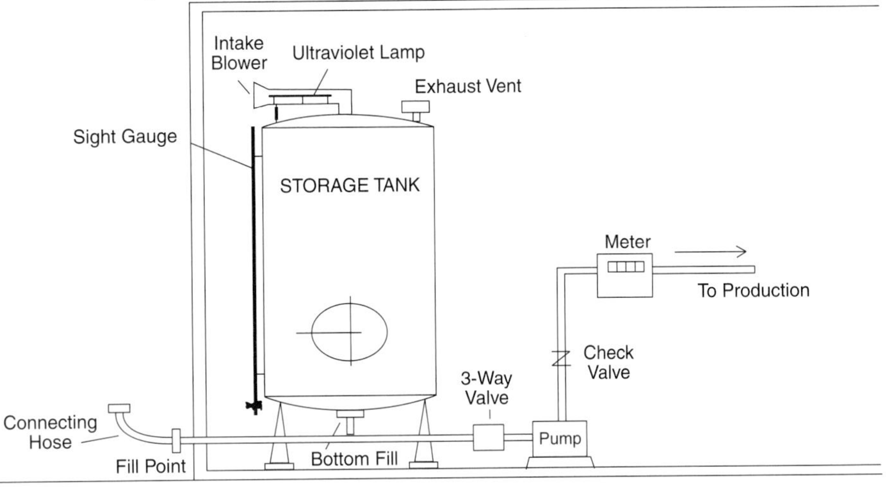

Figure 9.026. Schematic diagram shows the basic components of a liquid sugar handling system. (Corn Industries Research Foundation 1965).

either mounted on legs or hung in the building. Where the headroom is limited or the load-carrying capacity of the floor is inadequate, horizontal cylindrical tanks will prove equally satisfactory as long as they are slightly tilted toward the discharge side for proper drainage.

Stainless steel is the ideal material for fabricating such tanks. Because of its high cost, however, it is often replaced by mild steel of proper gauge and suitably reinforced, which, in contrast to stainless steel, requires sandblasting and lining on the product side. Several types of FDA-approved tank lining materials are available; these coatings are typically non-absorbent, although baked-on linings provide superior durability and ease of maintenance.

Nearly all metals that find common use in food plants are suitable for the distribution piping, although, again, stainless steel is the preferred material. Piping must be pitched to permit complete draining of all lines. All valves should be of the sanitary plug types that are readily disassembled for cleaning. Materials of construction include iron or iron body with bronze trim construction. Liquid sweeteners are generally measured by automatic or manual flowmeters, although volumetric, gravimetric and proportioning pump methods are also used. Flowmeters may express the amount of liquid sweetener either in pounds or in gallons, and they must be calibrated for the density of the sweetener being handled.

Because the viscosity of liquid sugar is largely unaffected by even broad temperature variations, many bakeries make use of liquid sugar coolers as an aid in the control of batter and dough temperatures. The coolers are basically heat exchangers with cooling capacities ranging from 3 to 10 tons and capable, depending on their size, of cooling 1,000 to 4,000 lb of product from 32 to 10°C (90 to 50°F) in one hour. High-DE corn syrups, in contrast, become increasingly viscous at below-ambient temperatures, so that their flow characteristics are impaired. Hence, to maintain their flow rates, they are generally stored at 32 to 38°C (90 to 100°F) in tanks that are equipped with heating coils. Distribution pipes may also require some form of heating. High-fructose corn syrup (HFCS) does not encounter these flow problems and can be kept at bakery ambient conditions.

9.A.2.d. Liquid shortening handling

Except for fats whose plastic character is essential to their proper functioning — shortenings used in some cakes, in icings and pie crusts and as roll-in fat, as well as water-fat emulsions such as margarine — all shortenings are suitable for bulk handling as long as their use volume is sufficiently high to justify the necessary capital investment for the required handling equipment. These would include the frying fats, bread shortenings and all fluid shortenings.

Bulk fat or oil deliveries are made either in tank trucks of 30,000- to 45,000-lb (4,000- to 6,000-gal) capacity or in rail tank cars that can carry from about 60,000 to 150,000 lb (8,000 to 20,000 gal), as shown in **Figure 9.027**. The delivery tanks are generally unloaded through either 3- or 4-in. flexible hoses provided with quick couplers and some straining or filtering device. A positive displacement pump is normally used for unloading and should have a rated capacity of 100 gal per minute so that it will empty a 60,000-lb tank car in about 2 hours. A 100-mesh screen should be installed ahead of the pump to remove any foreign debris.

In-plant holding tanks for bulk shortening can be manufactured from any of several materials such as stainless steel or stainless-clad steel, carbon steel, aluminum or reinforced polyester fiberglass. Their configuration is generally dictated by the available storage area: Low ceilings call for horizontal tanks, whereas vertical tanks are in order where the floor space is limited. Bronze, copper, brass should never be considered because they act as a catalyst for oxidation, which creates rancidity in the fats and oils.

Figure 9.027. Bulk tank trucks deliver liquid sweeteners, oils and other bulk liquid ingredients. (ADM)

The tanks should be cylindrical in shape using welded construction, with dished heads to ensure complete draining of the fat and be provided with the appropriate openings: 2 manholes, one each near the top and bottom of the tank, inlet and outlet openings, and openings for venting and for the heating coil, agitator and thermostat installations. Horizontal tanks may have either dished or flat ends and they should be sloped at a rate of 1 in. per 10 ft toward the discharge end to ensure adequate draining. Rectangular tanks are inadvisable because their corners present cleaning problems.

Tank capacities should be large enough so each will hold at least one full truck tank load and 2 storage tanks accommodate a full rail tank load. The inlet line should extend to within a few inches of the tank bottom to minimize aeration of the liquid fat during filling and recirculation. Inventory control is provided either by an electronic load cell or some kind of level indicating device such as a sight gauge made from clear plastic tubing or a float gauge that calibrates the depth of the tank in terms of weight or volume of its contents. Of these, the load cell is not only the most reliable but also provides a perpetual inventory of the tank contents.

In order to keep shortening, other than the fluid type, in a melted or liquid state, its temperature must be maintained at least 6 C° (10 F°) above its melting point to maintain stability but allow the material to be pumped. Various means may be employed to achieve this purpose. For example, heating coils may be installed in the tank through which hot water or low-pressure steam is circulated, or electric immersion heaters may be used. When such internal heating methods are applied, it is advisable to insulate the tanks to minimize heat loss and prevent localized chilling. The heating coils are preferably situated about 4 in. above the tank bottom so that they will always be immersed in the liquid fat and will also promote maximum circulation by convection. Localized overheating must be guarded against because it will lead to quality deterioration of the fat.

Other approaches include equipping the tanks with external heating jackets or locating the tanks in so-called hot rooms, with the heat in both instances being applied externally to the shortening. Fats that solidify at ambient temperature require heating be provided for the lines leading from the storage tank to the pump and subsequent use points by tracing them with either a steam line or an electrical heating tape and by insulating them. With fluid shortenings, narrow temperature control is far less critical because these products retain their fluid state at temperatures as low as 10°C (50°F) and remain unaffected in their functional properties at temperature levels up to 43°C (110°F). It should be noted that even under the best storage conditions there will be fat deterioration; therefore, a regular schedule of sample collection is recommended to determine the peroxide value and the level of free fatty acids.

9.A.2.e. Liquid egg handling

Most bakeries that require eggs in their production use them in their frozen state, either in 30-lb metal cans or buckets, or as frozen blocks packaged in some type of corrugated container. However, if the requirements for eggs are sufficiently large, definite economic advantages can accrue from the use of liquid eggs in bulk. Eggs are among the most biologically unstable food products so their handling in an unfrozen state is circumscribed by rather stringent sanitary controls.

The principal requirement, aside from exemplary housekeeping, is unfailing temperature control. Liquid eggs are most stable at temperatures of 1.6 to 3.3°C (35 to 38°F). When their temperature rises above 4.4°C (40°F), bacterial growth accelerates rapidly, and their holding period becomes correspondingly shorter. According to Grant (1972), the temperature of liquid egg products at the outset of shipping should be about 1.6°C (35°F) for yolks and 4.4°C (40°F) for egg whites. Because many tank trucks lack refrigeration capacity beyond that required for temperature maintenance, deliveries must be completed within 24 to 33 hours if temperature increases greater than 1 to 2 C° (2 to 3 F°) are to be avoided. The dairy-type tank trucks used for liquid egg transport have maximum capacities of up to 40,000 lb. For smaller shipments, self-refrigerated portable tanks can be used. These tanks hold about 1,800 lb and are handled by fork lifts.

To justify economically a liquid egg handling system, a bakery's minimum use of eggs should be no less than 40,000 lb every 20 days. This level of use will require two 5,000-gal tanks, one for holding and the other for receiving, and refrigeration capacity sufficient to maintain both tanks at temperatures no higher than 4.4°C (40°F). The same considerations regarding tank design and tank fabricating materials that govern liquid shortening tanks also pertain to liquid egg storage tanks.

Based on the above discussion, it is quite difficult to store liquid eggs because of the high potential for micro-organism growth. Such concern especially affects the cookie manufacturing environment where all equipment needs to be sterilized because eggs are classified as an allergen.

Eggs contribute to the tenderness and fine texture of cookies by stabilizing the gluten matrix and the emulsifying the dough mix. They also contribute to the structure, moisture retention, flavor and a brown color to the baked product (BCMA 2002b). Eggs are normally added to the creamed sugar and shortening in the beginning mixing stage to insure complete incorporation and avoid lumping and brown spotting.

In recent years, egg substitutes have gained popularity when eggs are required in a formulation but plants do not want to deal with storage and handling of real eggs. They are either purchased in frozen or spray dried form. Using eggs in the cookie manufacturing process is typically expensive, and their emulsifying effect on fats can be obtained from other more stable sources. Pasteurization of egg products is required to destroy pathogenic organisms, particularly Salmonella, which poses a serious health hazard.

9.A.2.f. Cream yeast systems

Because of its vacuum-packed format, instant active dry yeast requires little more of its storage area than clean, dry conditions, but compressed yeast must be kept refrigerated at 2 to 7°C (36 to 45°F) until use. It has a high level of moisture (68 to 71%), and its activity diminishes over time. Compressed yeast, as well as its crumbled form, is delivered to the bakery in 50-lb, multiple-walled, poly-lined bags, stacked 50 bags to the pallet. Because this form of bakers yeast is short-lived, deliveries are generally scheduled two to three times a week.

Cream yeast systems (**Figure 9.028**) consist of a minimum of 2 large insulated storage tanks, ranging in size from 2,600 to 6,000 gal and equipped with refrigerated jackets and clean-in-place (CIP) capacity, plus insulated, stainless-steel, ringmain-style piping that constantly circulates the yeast between the holding tanks and the air-actuated, sanitary dispensing valves at each mixer (Boge 1994). Glycol cooling of the storage tanks is typical because many bakeries also use glycol to cool mixer jackets and refrigerated and freezer storage areas. Two centrifugal pumps move the yeast through the ringmain, and the size of the pump motors depends on the number of dispensing points and the length of the ringmain. Sanitary design of cream yeast equipment is essential and should follow standards such as 3A, BISSC, NEMA or Z50 for all components.

Flow meters regulate the delivery of cream yeast to use points, and two strategies

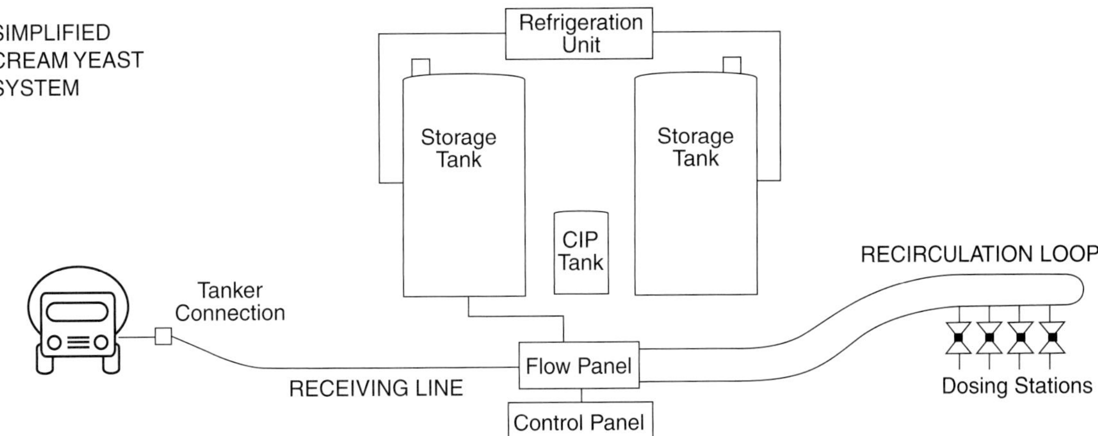

Figure 9.028. Two tanks, a recirculating loop with dispensing valves, CIP capability and refrigeration, plus a receiving line and controls, make up the basics of a cream yeast system. (Lallemand)

can be employed. One is to put a single meter in the yeast loop (ringmain). When yeast is required at a given drop point, the control system locks out all the other drop points. It closes a valve on the return side of the recirculating loop downstream of the drop points and dead-heads the entire system. When the required drop point opens, the single flow meter measures the movement of yeast and thus controls dispensing. A second strategy is to install a flow meter at each drop point, dedicated to that mixer or use point. Although requiring a greater capital investment, this second method avoids compression errors due to gas generation by the yeast in the ringmain. It also prevents system shut-down should a flow meter fail.

Like all liquid ingredient storage tanks, the cream yeast system must be equipped with a means of drainage that complies with environmental regulatory standards. Tanks can be installed either in vertical or horizontal position, depending on the space available. In suitable climates, the tanks can be installed outside under cover, but most bakeries prefer to locate them inside the plant to best control hygiene as well as security.

Computers or PLCs govern the operation of cream yeast systems, displaying status and operating conditions such as amounts in tanks and pipelines, usage rates, alarms, transfers, deliveries, product temperatures, CIP functions and so forth. The hardware and software must provide failsafe operation of the system to prevent contamination or loss of yeast. The bakery's electronic batch controllers interface with the cream yeast system to govern the sequence in which the yeast reaches the mixers.

For more than a decade now, bulk cream yeast systems have been included in the layout of every new large wholesale bakery built in the US (**Figure 9.029**). Many bakeries in Europe use cream yeast, delivered in bulk, 100-l drums and even 20-l bag-in-box packages.

Cream yeast comes into the plant at 78 to 80% moisture and 5.6 to 5.8 pH. Yeast shipping temperature should be between 0.5 and 7°C (33 and 45°F), and storage temperature in the bakery should not exceed 7°C (45°F). Frequency of delivery can be held to once a week, although a bakery should not let its cream yeast supply age beyond 10 days. As Boge (1994) noted, bulk delivery of cream yeast qualifies as environmentally friendly because it does not require disposal of packaging materials.

Because of the sensitive biological nature of cream yeast, the baker should insist on the manufacturer's assurance of a uniform, consistent product with a clean mi-

Figure 9.029. A cream yeast system consists of refrigerated holding tanks, lines that constantly circulate cream yeast to use points in the bakery and a clean-in-place system.
(Shick USA)

crobiological profile. For each shipment, the yeast manufacturer should provide the baker with a tank truck inspection form (**Figure 9.030**). Thermally insulated tanker trucks can maintain the temperature of their contents ± 1 C° (± 2 F°) and should be inspected by the shipper before loading. A list of the three prior hauls should also be presented at the loading site and reviewed by the loading personnel to make certain that previous contents were food-grade only.

Yeast manufacturers can also be asked to provide a certificate of analysis (**Figure 9.031**) for each load. According to Zimmerman (1999), the three most important items on the certificate are the batch or lot code, the loading temperature of the yeast and the gassing activity test results. Although Risograph testing is typical, other measurements of gassing power are used, and the baker must be familiar with the method chosen. The baker should request that the certificate arrive before the delivery of the yeast, being faxed or e-mailed ahead of time. Zimmerman (1999) strongly urged use of a certified thermometer when testing yeast both at delivery and in the bakery. He also stressed that delivery meters be standardized and calibrated to assure accuracy.

Because cream yeast can be vulnerable to bacterial spoilage, the equipment that stores and handles it must be kept in peak sanitary condition. A clean-in-place (CIP) system is an absolute requirement, and it must encompass the receiving line into the plant, both tanks and the ringmain piping. If tanks are cleaned immediately after they empty, they will be ready to receive new supplies in hygienic fashion. The ringmain should be cleaned at least once a week or whenever yeast circulation stops. Zimmerman (1999) recommended thorough sanitation of the whole system every 6 months.

A separate 200-gal CIP tank allows the sanitizing chemicals to be measured and mixed before cleaning operations start. The 1 to 1.5 hours necessary to sanitize the ringmain is usually scheduled for a down day, but the receiving line and the idle stor-

---

TANK TRUCK CLEANING: INSPECTION CERTIFICATE

SANITARY WASH

SANITARY ORDER
No.
Work Order

Date/ Time	Tractor No.	Trailer No.	Requested By	Written By	Starting Time	Begin Time End Time
Customer Name			Phone No		Authorized By	
Address (For Invoicing)			Customer No.		PO No.	
City/State/Zip			Other Billing Information			
Previous Product Information (Complete Names(s) of Last Product Hauled)						B/L No.
Compartment No. 1		MSDS Provided _Y _N	Compartment No. 3		MSDS Provided _Y _N	
Compartment No. 2		MSDS Provided _Y _N	Compartment No. 4		MSDS Provided _Y _N	

TANK TRUCK CLEANING: INSPECTION CERTIFICATE

SANITARY WASH
(Continued)

SANITARY ORDER
No.
Work Order

Work Order By ____________________   Date ________

(Signature of Driver Agent)   Time ________

WASH METHOD
Hot Water
(> 170 degrees)

Emp# ____   Bay# ____   Time ____   Steam

Emp# ____   Bay# ____   Time ____   Detergent

Emp# ____   Bay# ____   Time ____

Time In ________
Time Out ________

Other ____________________

PROCEDURE
Wash Cycle Temp: ________   Proc: ________
Final Rinse Temp: ________   Bay: ________
Elapsed Time: ________   Time: ________
Start Time: ________   Emp#: ________
Finish Time: ________

Figure 9.030. Tank truck inspection forms must accompany the delivery of each lot of cream yeast.
(Zimmerman 1999)

age tank can be cleaned while the plant is in full operation, with at least 20 minutes of wash time allowed. Good Manufacturing Practices (GMPs) for sanitation of this system must be followed. Automation of this sanitation activity allows repeatable uniformity and collects data that document its operations for the plant sanitarian.

The cleaning cycle should use a pre-rinse caustic, wash water of at least 60°C (140°F) and a wash time of no less than 20 minutes. Avoid using any compounds containing chlorine. Zimmerman (1999) noted that these same standards are followed by yeast manufacturers to clean their systems.

The production, handling and use of cream yeast are also discussed in Volume I, Chapter 2, Part B.

9.A.2.g. Water blending

Because water temperature and chemistry can have so much effect on doughs and batters, water supplies must be controlled. Water blending systems combine fixed water streams to maintain a set-point temperature, typically in 2- or 3-stream configuration (**Figure 9.032**). Such streams consist of city water and water treated in-plant, with either or both at chilled or heated temperatures. These blending systems can be operated as stand-alone units or integrated with automated ingredient delivery systems.

<table>
<tr><td colspan="3" align="center">CERTIFICATE OF ANALYSIS</td></tr>
<tr><td>Shipped To: ______</td><td></td><td>Batch / Lot Code: ______</td></tr>
<tr><td>Customer Location: ______</td><td></td><td>Amount Shipped: ______</td></tr>
<tr><td>Date Shipped: ______</td><td></td><td>Product Code: ______</td></tr>
<tr><td></td><td></td><td>Loading Temp: ______</td></tr>
</table>

Yeast Performance

ACTIVITY TEST	ACCEPTABLE RANGE	TEST RESULT
7% Sugar @ 2 Hours	260 -290	______

Microbial

TEST	ACCEPTABLE RANGE	TEST RESULT
Salmonella	Not Detected	Pass Test
Coliform	1000 / gram	Pass Test

Technical Director

Figure 9.031. A certificate of analysis must be provided for each shipment of cream yeast before it can be received into bakery storage. (Zimmerman 1999)

9.A.3. Micro ingredient systems

Most formulations call for some ingredients in such small quantities that hand-adds are a fact of life at bakeries. These materials arrive in bags and boxes to be stored in the raw materials warehouse until needed. Mixer operators or prep room staff draw these ingredients from stores and unload them into bins. Scoops and scales assist in batching hand-adds, and the prep room will make up individual buckets containing the required materials for each batch, usually setting out enough to supply a whole day's needs.

Manual scaling is labor intensive, and scaling errors, no matter how infrequent, are a continual concern. Automated micro ingredient systems developed to address these problems, but cost and complexity of such equipment prompted many bakers to take a wait-and-see attitude. As the need for customized software to run early computer control systems yielded to the more open architecture of PCs and PLCs, micro ingredient handling systems have become more feasible and fundable. The increasing need for traceability also drives adoption of automated micro ingredient systems (Whitaker 2008).

In many cases, it is not necessary to automate every minor or micro ingredient. A bakery's formulations may call for 100 or more different ingredients, but not all

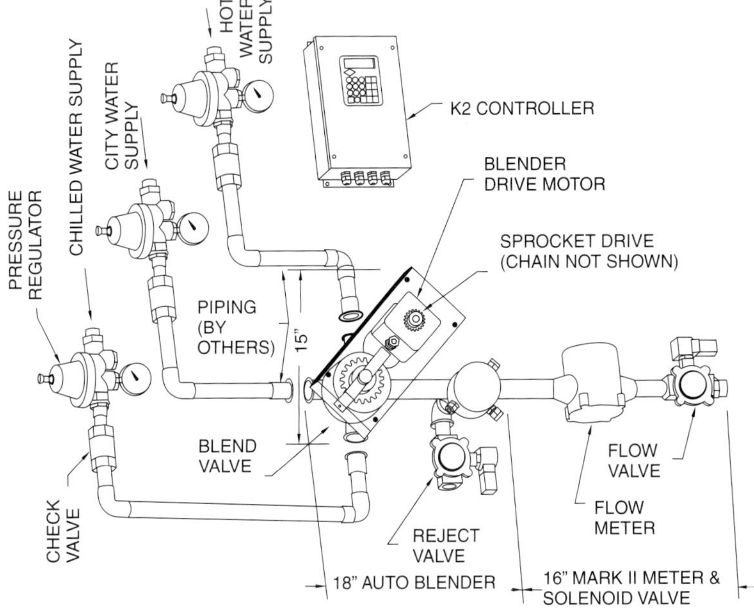

Figure 9.032. With three inlets to mix hot, chilled and city water, an automatic temperature water blender delivers specified outlet temperatures. (Fred D. Pfening Co.)

Figure 9.033. A bank of modular bins hold micro ingredients, scaled and collected according to computer-controlled "recipes." (AZO)

100 need to be automatically delivered. The 20:80 rule usually applies: 20 ingredients will be required for the majority of products, while 80 are needed for only a few items each. The equipment and programming for a 20-module system are far less involved than for a 100-module set-up.

Design and configuration of micro ingredient systems varies among the different OEM vendors of such equipment. One design (**Figure 9.033**) configures its holding capacity as a bank of bins set above a track along which containers travel to accept delivery of ingredients via screw conveyors and mini-scales according to a computer-sequenced recipe. Circular arrangement of the bins is also possible. Another design uses the holding bin as an integrated scaling device, dispensing materials into a mobile scale that travels around the system, collecting ingredients according to individual batch needs (**Figure 9.034**). At least one manufacturer offers removable modular bins to facilitate formulation changes. Individual storage bins range in capacity from 1 to 100 lb. Taking a different approach, another design uses larger ingredient containers not only to collect the raw materials but also to serve as mixing vessels. Instead of transferring the ingredients to a mixer, mixing tools are introduced into the container to mix the dough.

Micro ingredient systems show a high degree of variation in their dispensing methods. Discharge augers, for example, manage many types of dry materials including pre-blended products; a vibratory bottom will benefit crystalline products; and a fluidizing system will be needed for materials that tend to pack and clog (Spooner 1993).

9.A.4. Weighing and batching equipment

Batch weighing can be accomplished by four approaches: (a) transferring ingredients from silos or bins to individual batch weigh stations above the mixer, (b) transferring ingredients from silos and bins to a central weigh station above the mixer, (c) weighing out ingredients using the loss-in weight method and (d) using weigh stations in which the mixer is on load cells and the ingredients are sequentially weighed directly into the mixer. Manley (1991) provided an excellent discussion of this topic as it related to biscuits, crackers and cookies but also applied to most other baked foods. Whitt (1994) detailed the augers, load cells, bag jostlers, discharge chutes, pneumatic separators, pumps, liquid scaling methods and valves involved.

The accurate quantitative measurement of ingredients in product formulation is possibly the most critical operation in maintaining the desired quality of the finished product. For this reason, the techniques of weighing and batching ingredients have seen of extensive study that has resulted in systems that are increasingly more complex but, in general, also offer a markedly higher degree of accuracy.

The traditional method of weighing both major and minor ingredients by beam scales or dial balances, augmented over the years by various control devices such as mercury or micro-switches and photoelectric cells for actuating the required sequencing, has been supplanted by more advanced and more accurate electronic load cells.

Weighing accuracy is a matter of electronic accuracy and feeding accuracy, according to Moore (1988). Electronic accuracy is determined by putting a certified test weight on the scale and comparing its known weight with the data displayed by the scale. Electronic accuracy for scales today is typically ± 0.1%. Feeding accuracy is the difference between the amount of ingredient requested and the amount actually delivered. Industry standard has been ± 0.5%, and today's flour systems can easily attain feeding accuracy of ± 0.1%.

The advent of pushbutton controls, digital readouts, solid-state circuitry and microprocessors (PLC) and computers has made it possible to completely automate most weighing and batching operations located above the mixer or remotely (Schraps 1982). A typical operator interface for a ingredient management and batching system is shown in **Figure 9.035**. Current equipment and methods for ingredient feed systems were well described by Long (1984), Slater (1989) and Whitt (1994).

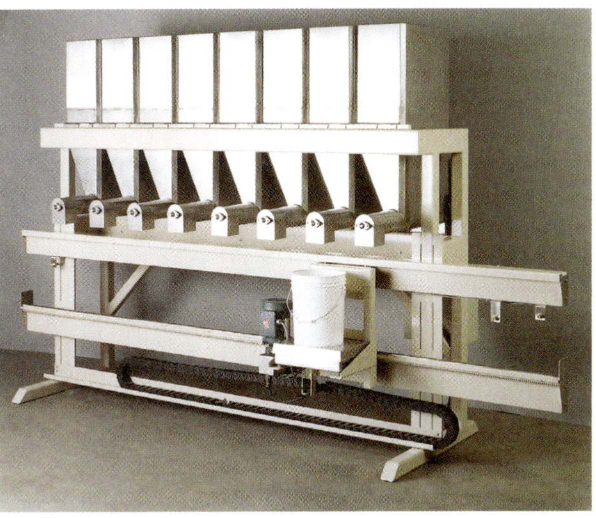

Figure 9.034. Racks of bins hold micro ingredients, which will be collected in a bucket that travels along a track. (ALL-CON)

9.A.4.a. Hopper scales

The most common scales for weighing and batching are hopper scales of either the mechanical or the electronic type. They should be selected based on the capacity, accuracy, durability and ease of operation. Scales need to be calibrated on a daily or weekly basis, based on the manufacturer's recommendation to maintain accuracy and precision.

Hopper scales are mounted either on a platform, on 4-point suspension bearings of knife-edge steel pivots or on 3-point suspensions with 3 or more electronic strain gauge load cells, respectively. After the scale beam or dial pointer of the mechanical scale is set for the desired amount of flour or other dry ingredient, or the formula is entered into the control panel in the case of electronic scales, the actual delivery of the material into the hopper is completely automatic and cuts off when the preset weight has been reached.

The hoppers are generally cylindrical in shape and must possess a volumetric capacity that will meet the maximum charge they are expected to carry, which is generally in the range of 200 to 2,000 lb. They usually feature steeply sloping bottoms to facilitate total emptying and avoid bridging. Both loading and discharge operations are dustless, ensured by a sliding sleeve that fits tightly over the top mixer inlet during flour discharge. A typical flour hopper scale system is shown in **Figure 9.036**.

Figure 9.035. A flexible ingredient management and batch execution software system can be seamlessly integrated into existing systems. (Shick USA)

Mechanical scales are comparatively low in cost, simple to maintain and calibrate, and they permit the exclusion of the tare weight so that their full scale range is accessible to the ingredient weight. On the other hand, their accuracy depends on their resolution — on their smallest readable scale divisions, which generally number from 500 to 1,200 units (Phillips 1965). For example, the smallest readable weight unit on a 2,000-lb dial scale is 2 lb.

The scale's accuracy, which is based on the entire scale range, thus becomes in-

Figure 9.036. The large hoppers above the mixers assemble measured quantities of flour and other dry bulk and minor ingredients, holding them ready for the next batch. Other lines feed liquids, and delivery of all ingredients are managed by a recipe control system.
(Shick USA)

creasingly less, in terms of actual weight, as the amount of material being weighed becomes smaller. Mechanical dial scales are available that can be preset to weigh automatically and additively 6 to 8 ingredients on a consecutive basis.

Hopper scales are either of the stationary or mobile type. Stationary hoppers are permanently fixed over a single mixer, whereas a mobile hopper scale is suspended from an overhead track and services several mixers. In bakeries, however, the latter arrangement is the exception rather than the rule.

9.A.4.b. Load cells

The introduction of electronic and hydraulic load cells or strain gauges as the sensing elements in weight measurement revolutionized instrumental weighing, particularly with regard to automatic weight control in batching and formulating operations. Whether the load cell monitors a single weigh hopper or a full weigh tank installation, the installation normally consists of a special support frame, 3 or more load cells of either the hydraulic or electronic type, proper connections to the control panel containing the weight indicator and microprocessor and various pieces of auxiliary equipment.

The hydraulic load cell consists of a tension cell that converts the force acting on it into pressure on a hydraulic fluid by means of a steel diaphragm. This pressure, in turn, is converted into an electrical signal measured in millivolts. The signal provides the data to control the electrical drives that actuate the conveying mechanisms, and it provides a digital readout of the individual ingredients being weighed, along with recording the information on a data table in a computer. In the case of a suspension-type load cell, the force acting on it is converted into a mechanical strain instead of a tension, and this strain, in turn, induces an electronic signal that controls the associated electric equipment. A major advantage of hydraulic load cells is that they are unaffected by the moisture, electric fields and temperature variations normally encountered in bakeries.

The electronic load cell, which may be of the compression, tension or deflection rod type, has as its basis a Wheatstone bridge enclosed in a steel cylinder. Such cells measure the changes in electrical resistance induced by forces applied to the cylinder. The resultant change in voltage is detected as an analog signal, which, when suitably amplified, may be converted to a digital signal and used as the control element (Schraps 1982). The electronic load cell is normally used in association with a microprocessor into which the data and programs required for automatic and sequential batching operations are fed. Electric load cell systems are sensitive to electrical line noise and subject to interference from other electric equipment and, hence, require adequate shielding. **Figure 9.037** shows a scale mount that incorporates a load cell and is designed to manage 10 to 250,000 lb.

9.A.4.c. Inventory indicators

The contents of storage bins may be determined in two general ways: (a) by mounting the bins on electronic load cells, which then provide an instant and continuous inventory of their contents, or (b) by the use of product level indicators. The latter devices, originally used principally during bin loading and emptying operations to signal full and empty conditions, come in several designs and with different dependabilities.

Indicators range in complexity from slowly rotating paddles mounted at the top of the storage bin or silo that, when their movement is interrupted by the presence of material, generate a signal on a control panel; to capacitance probes; pressure-sensitive diaphragm-type sensors and various photoelectric cells; as well as radar and sonic devices that react to the presence of material between their transmitting; and receiving elements. Although manufacturers claim accuracies within a range of ± 1.0 to 3.0%, real world usage accuracy is more like ± 10 to 15%. Sensors are reliable only when the silo is at rest. Dusting and equipment noise render them inaccurate during system operation. Bear this in mind before refilling silos, and take into account the fact visual inspection is always more accurate.

Unless perpetual inventory control is provided by load-cell mounting of the storage containers or the use of some other suitable electronic device, perhaps the simplest system of inventory control consists of a level-checking device installed at the top of a bin or silo, with its control panel mounted at any convenient site at floor level.

The bin contents are checked by a descending bobber that retracts when its downward motion is arrested by the material's surface. The distance traveled by the bobber is transmitted to the control panel, which converts it into the weight of the material still remaining in the bin or silo. Inaccuracies in level detection are introduced by the phenomenon of cone formation by solid ingredients, with the cones pointing upward during filling and downward during emptying.

9.A.4.d. Dump bins and blenders

Bakeries that receive flour in bags are generally equipped with dump bins and blenders through which the flour enters storage or production. In its simplest design, the dump bin is a rectangular metal cabinet, whose bottom slopes toward a rotary discharge valve or a spiral screw conveyor located at the base. A grid placed above the discharge prevents the sack from getting entangled in the flour transfer mechanism. An air-assist system using compressed air (80 to 90 psi) assures complete transfer of bag contents into the ingredient system.

Capacities of conventional dump bins range from 200 to 7,000 lb of material. For bakeries that must cope with deliveries of relatively large volumes of non-bulk dry ingredients, automated systems for bag opening and dumping have been developed that will also sift the incoming material before conveying it to intermediate storage (Baumann 1984).

Dump bins are frequently equipped with a vacuum-type dust collector in the form of a suction nozzle. In practice, the emptied bag is placed over the nozzle, which turns it inside out and imparts to it a whipping action to dislodge any adhering flour. The recovered flour is drawn into a depositing hopper where it is separated from the conveying air by an air filter. Bag dump design should avoid dead spaces or corners, with a door that closes to prevent possible contamination of materials or leakage into the bakery (**Figure 9.038**).

Basic dump bins do not normally incorporate provisions for blending different flours into a uniform mix. This process is accomplished with special blending bins that consist of two or more blending compartments. Each compartment is equipped with a variable-speed screw conveyor at its base for discharging flour into a common line at a predetermined rate. By properly adjusting the speed of the respective con-

Figure 9.037. A scale mount contains the load cell that monitors the contents of a silo or bin. (Shick USA)

Figure 9.038. When bags of ingredients are unloaded into this bag dump station, their contents are screened and then moved along pneumatically to storage bins by the rotary feeder mounted at the bottom of the unit. (Fred D. Pfening Co.)

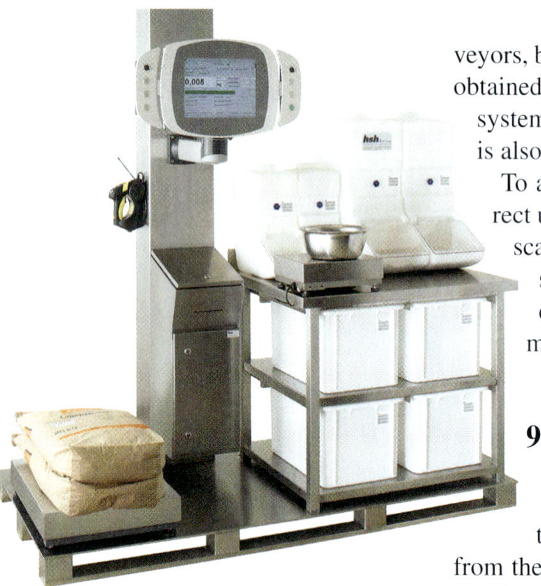

Figure 9.039. Micro ingredients can be weighed manually and then transferred to mixers using the dump station at center.
(AZO)

veyors, blends containing the desired proportions of two or more different flours are obtained. For blending a multiplicity of dry ingredients into ready mixes, pneumatic systems that incorporate accurate weighing devices are normally used. Blending is also discussed in Volume I, Chapter 2, Part E.

To assist in tracing of ingredient lots and to assure proper routing to the correct use bin, dump stations can be equipped with bar code readers. The operator scans the bar code on the ingredient bag. This code then triggers the pre-set sequencing for delivery of the bag's contents and also records the ingredient's movement into use. Dump stations can also be used to move batched minor ingredients to use hoppers above mixers (**Figure 9.039**).

9.A.5. Batching systems

Automatic batching systems are available in three basic types: (a) simultaneous weighing systems in which the several formula ingredients, drawn from their bulk bins or tanks, are weighed by separate scales at the same time and are then discharged into a mixer; (b) accumulative and additive systems in which preset weights of the various ingredients are fed into a single scale hopper in sequence, with the finished batch then being discharged into a mixer; and (c) combination systems that comprise elements of both the simultaneous and additive types (Phillips 1965). A recent improvement in this technology is a system that measures ingredients into a tote that doubles as a blender (**Figure 9.040**).

Modern weighing and batching control systems are comprised of two major functional segments — formula entry and execution of the weighing operation. Formula entry, or the presetting of the required weights, is accomplished by various means: sliding weights in the case of beam scales; setting the pointer on dial scales; or in the case of electronic scales, through load cells, numeric weight-setting plugs and templates with movable markers. The second function is to compare the preset value with the actual delivered weight and to perform the necessary switching actions that will shut down the feed mechanism once the preset value has been reached.

Probably the most common weighing and batching system used in automated ingredient handling systems is the accumulative method, as explained by Spooner (1993). Using a single scale to manage all materials, its scale is tared to zero after each ingredient is added. Additive weighing systems, in contrast, do not tare the scale after each ingredient, and ingredients are added in sequence. Simultaneous weighing uses separate scales for each ingredient and tends to be used when rapid, accurate weighing is required and intermixing of ingredients must be avoided. These methods can work in combination, and computer sequencing is available.

Because the scale capacity in these systems must be based on the total weight of the batch, and given a system accuracy of ± 0.1%, tolerances may be undesirably high when small ingredient are involved. For example, with an accepted tolerance of ± 1 one dial graduation, a 2,000-lb-capacity scale will have a deviation of 2 lb, regardless of whether the amount weighed is 1,000 lb or 100 lb. When such a deviation is unacceptable, a smaller capacity scale, with a smaller range, and, hence, greater accuracy, must be used for the separate weighing of the minor ingredients.

Small weighments require highly accurate methods. Micro-scales and loss-in-weight feeders enable accurate dispensing by automated minor and micro ingredient systems. Micro-scales are engineered to manage very small weighments. The loss-in-weight method continually monitors the weight of the entire holding bin and meters out materials by recording the loss in weight of the container. When extreme accuracy is required, a 2-stage weighing system can be used. Its first stage transfers most of the dose quickly, but in the second stage, the auger or transfer mechanism slows down to trickle the rest of the material into the receiving container.

The portioning of particularly viscous liquids such as honey or molasses involves a different technique. Because these liquids cling to the sides of scale hoppers, they may not all reach the mixer when using gravity feeding alone. So a "washing" method was developed that stages delivery of low-viscosity liquids to the liquid scale hopper after dispensing the high-viscosity materials. Compressed air can also be used to speed discharge. Another choice would be to employ a negative weighing system (Baumann 1984). This loss-in-weight method keeps the liquid scale hopper that handles the high-viscosity ingredient at a constant level 25 to 50% above the maximum weighment required by the formula. On demand from the batching system, the scale hopper's port opens to release the ingredient into the mixer and closes when the hopper's load cell records a loss in weight equal to the required amount.

The washing method also works well for moving liquid ingredients required at low usage levels. The system should be laid out and delivery activities programmed to release low-volume ingredients into supply hoppers first, followed by high-volume liquids, which thus "wash" the materials forward and into the mixer.

For particularly delicate particulates, low-velocity vacuum and pressure systems are available to move products through pipes at rates one-half to one-tenth the normal conveying speed. Because of the high fat content of chocolate chips, they smear easily when transported through pipes. So at least one cookie manufacturer devised a bucket elevator system to move chips from a bulk bag unloader to its mixers (Gorton 1992).

Figure 9.040. Totes, carried by automated guided vehicles, serve as collection hoppers and travel around the system to collect ingredients; then a mixing tool is introduced, and the materials are mixed in the same container before moving to the next processing stage. (Reimelt)

9.A.5.a. Automatic dosing

The most expensive of the batching systems is the one that involves simultaneous weighing because it requires a series of individual scales. Not only is the capital investment involved quite high, but the system itself occupies considerable space and congestion above the mixer. It is, however, the most accurate of all the systems. Least expensive are the accumulative and additive systems in which only one weigh hopper is used into which the centrally located feeders discharge the ingredients.

Complete automation of batching operations is currently done with central control panels, programmable logic controllers (PLC) and computers that permit data input for ingredients, weight settings, water temperatures, sequencing, order of addition and other processing instructions as well as storing such information. All of these new technologies provide a more scientific approach along with increased ingredient accuracy, improved mixing and allow for easier trouble shooting when necessary.

Such systems, once properly programmed, can generally remain unattended and allow the ingredients to be fed directly into the mixer with increased precision, improved mixing cycles and reduced possibility of operator ingredient omissions. One particular automated system is defined as the central weighing approach in which the ingredients are transported from silos/bins and then loaded onto a series of conveyors which takes this material either to holding tanks above the mixers or to the mixers themselves. The main disadvantage is that if the system faults, all the mixers on that line will be affected.

Separate fill lines, storage, gain-in-weight scaling and conveying systems (**Figure**

Figure 9.041. A multitude of use bins may be required to keep allergens separate prior to batching. (MAC Equipment)

9.041) may be required when handling allergens. This approach provides an extra degree of product and process protection.

Various systems for relaying the desired formula information into the control panel are in use. These include, among others, the following: (a) weight selectors that permit dialing of a multiplicity of ingredient weights called for by any given formula; (b) formula capsules that can control more than a score of ingredients in a formula at one time, with the weight of each ingredient preset; and (c) computers that not only can be programmed for any number of product formulations and stored but will additionally control the functions of all essential ingredient handling systems and record the ingredient delivery levels.

Many bakers prefer to measure liquid ingredients by volume, but this approach is changing. Depending on their nature, liquids such as water, syrups, liquid preferments, fluid shortenings and so forth differ in density so the ratio of volume to weight is not constant under varying environmental and processing conditions. For this reason, the scaling of liquids, with the exception of water and cream yeast, is being increasingly converted from volumetric metering to weighing in the interest of greater accuracy.

Metering of liquids has greatly improved with development of positive displacement volumetric meters, mass coriolis meters and electromagnet metering (**Figure 9.042**). Positive displacement methods record volume changes. The mass coriolis meter measures weight directly, and electromagnetic sensors work for electrically conductive ingredients.

Special weigh tank assemblies, complete with support frame, load cells and weight indicator mounted on a control panel, are available for this purpose (Thompson 1981).

9.A.5.b. Pre-blending

Commercially prepared bakery mixes, bases and pre-mixes provide needed efficiency for formulating operations. In addition, some large bakeries have adopted pre-blending to further increase productivity. This technique is relatively new, although some plants have used it for a decade or more. If a bakery operates an automated ingredient delivery system for bulk and minor ingredients, it could gain extra efficiency by upgrading for pneumatic pre-blending.

This method, shown by the flow diagram in **Figure 9.043**, takes advantage of central batch weighing to bring together the ingredient streams for all dry materials required by a formula. The materials are scaled and routed into a pneumatic blending vessel. Micro ingredients can be added to the batch either by an optional automated scaling system or by dumping manually scaled materials into a delivery hopper on the pneumatic system.

Pneumatic vessels accept raw materials, blend them homogeneously using advanced air-mixing and send the batch to the proper mixer (Spooner 1993, Stauffer 1996). The pneumatic blender, an enclosed aluminum or stainless-steel vessel, receives the scaled ingredients. After materials enter the vessel, they are subjected to intense air mixing to combine the ingredients into a homogeneous mass. Blending cycles can run as short as 30 seconds or as long as 3.5 minutes for batch sizes that vary from 10 to 10,000 lb. Incorporation of a maximum of 10% shortening and other liquids is possible with addition of one or more dual-fluid nozzles in the mixer (Sussann 2008).

With ingredients now uniformly dispersed within the mass, the ingredient delivery system pneumatically sends the pre-blended batch to the hopper above the proper mixer. The only "hold" time involved is the cycle time at the mixer. If the bakery uses high-speed mixers, which typically process a dough in 3 minutes or less, pre-blending can make a critical difference in the uniformity of doughs. Pre-blending is also very successful for supplying horizontal mixers.

When designing or retrofitting an ingredient delivery system for pneumatic pre-blending, be sure to allow a bypass option. The bypass set-up requires a series of pneumatic conveyors and holding bin, used for system purge and to remove batch misfeeds.

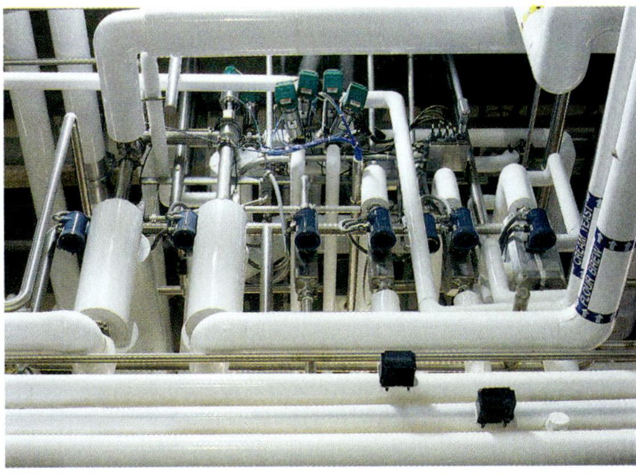

Figure 9.042. Flow meters (small blue units) monitor the mass of liquids flowing through lines. (Shick USA)

9.B. Mixers

Updated by Mihaelos N. Mihalos

When it comes to dough, if you mix it right, all else can follow in good order. But get it wrong, and you'll be changing settings and chasing quality at every point down the line. As the first stage in converting raw materials into finished products, the mixing step sets the foundation on which everything else is built.

Mixers transform a mass of unrelated ingredients into the dough or batter that eventually becomes the baked foods or snacks that attracts millions of consumers to supermarkets and specialty stores worldwide. But what may seem to be a simple procedure requires bakers to make many decisions regarding the mixing system and equipment most beneficial for their products.

A variety of factors enter into the baker's choice of mixer. Mixing time and dough temperature affect plant schedules and influence dough handling properties. The fat, sugar and protein content of ingredients put particular demands on mixing equipment, while hydration of the water in doughs and batters begins in the mixer. Use of various grains and whole-wheat flours also affect mixer drive motor size and agitator speeds. Selection of one mixing technology over another will materially affect the quality of the finished product.

Mixing comprises a complex of physical actions that include the blending of dry materials, the uniform dispersion of dry and wet ingredients, the creation of air cells within doughs and batters and the homogenization and aeration of cake batters. Also, mixing triggers the physical and chemical reactions that affect the final product attributes by developing the desired characteristics for optimum performance and quality. In the case of bread, buns and some sweet goods, an additional vital aspect is the modification of the flour proteins and their development into a suitable gluten structure. To optimally carry out these different actions requires the use of mixers of different design and operating principles.

Two basic styles characterize mixers for bakery applications: batch and continuous. Batch mixers were developed first and are today the style most commonly used

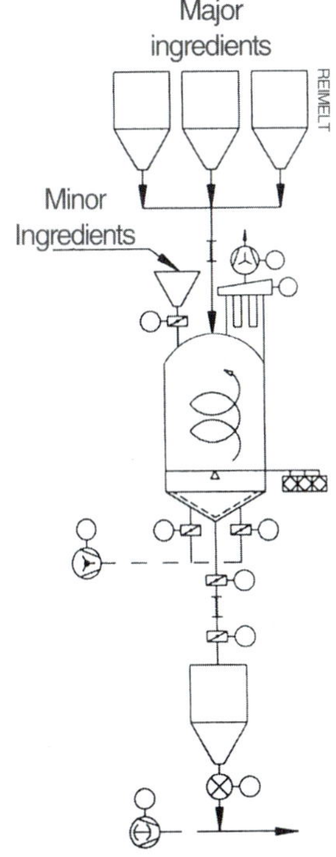

Figure 9.043. A flow diagram shows the stages and systems involved in pre-blending of ingredients in-plant. (Reimelt)

by producers of nearly every variety of baked food; however, continuous mixers earned a place in preparation of white pan breads during the 1960s in the US. Although this trend ebbed by the late 1980s, a number of bakeries still use continuous mix methods, and the liquid handling equipment that developed to serve this type of mixing equipment is hard at work today managing the preparation of liquid ferments, water brews, slurries and other such bakery intermediates.

Bloom (2000) provided a good analysis of current mixing technologies used by bakers, while Meyer (1997) examined the use of automation for this critical processing step. Dough mixing efficiency continues to interest scientists, and studies that explored the mixing efficiency of batch and continuous dough mixers done at Rutgers University received the 2002 Marcel Loncin Research Prize from the Institute of Food Technologists (Mermelstein 2006).

9.B.1. Batch mixers

Batch mixers fall into two basic types: vertical and horizontal, named for the orientation of the main agitator drive shaft. Within the category of batch mixers are machines characterized by high mixing speeds and engineered to act as mechanical dough developers. Slurry mixers, also called ingrediators, fit the batch mixer type as well.

A problem common to all batch mixers is discharging the dough completely after finishing the mix cycle. Often full extraction requires significant manual assistance. Dough residues left behind in the mixer can affect the quality and development of the next mixed dough. Current mixer designs offer bowl tilt angles much greater than 90°, which significantly minimizes this disadvantage (**Figure 9.044**). Tilting bowls and scraper bars assist dough discharge for individual batches, but particularly at changeover time, the bowl must be cleared of any remaining dough.

9.B.1.a. Horizontal mixers

Horizontal mixers, employed chiefly for doughmaking in bread production and for biscuit manufacturing when gluten development is required, are normally configured for 2-speed operation. In the slow-speed mode, the mixing arms rotate at half the rated maximum speed, for example, at 35 rpm in a mixer whose maximum speed is 70 rpm. The purpose of the dual speed is to incorporate or blend the ingredients, including water, into a homogeneous batch. If this blending was done in the high-speed mode, ingredients would become airborne and splash throughout the mixing bowl, taking significantly more time to achieve incorporation.

The majority of new mixers are now supplied with variable-speed AC drives that allow a much greater range of agitator speeds. This feature makes it simple to optimize the ingredient incorporation as well as the development of the dough.

At slow speed, dough development takes more time, producing gluten of limited development, which can be beneficial for laminated products. Nonetheless, special purpose horizontal mixers are available with single-speed drives, operating no faster than 30 rpm, and are used for applications involving relatively stiff dough. Also available are horizontal mixers with agitator speeds of 15 to 120 rpm.

Figure 9.044. The modified frame and housing of this offset tilt-bowl mixer allows the dough trough to be positioned directly under the bowl, which aids automation.
(AMF Bakery Systems)

The batch capacities of horizontal mixers range from about 100 lb for small units to as much as 2,800 and 3,200 lb for large mixers. Corresponding power requirements range from about as little as 15 hp to as high as 200 to 250 hp.

Further differentiating horizontal batch mixers is the design of arms that accomplish the mixing action. Three general types exist: roller bar, single sigma and double sigma. Roller bar mixers are used mostly in the production of pan breads and buns. While single-sigma and double-sigma mixers can and are used to prepare yeast-raised doughs, their shear action in mixing is more often applied to biscuit (cookie), cracker, batter and specialty applications.

9.B.1.a.i. Horizontal mixer action

The actual mixing and development of doughs in a horizontal mixer are performed by the rolling, kneading and stretching actions imparted to the dough by cylindrical mixer bars. These bars are mounted across the bowl width on 2, 3, or 4 opposite arms of a cradle attached to the agitator shaft. The triple-arm cradle usually assumes a Y configuration, whereas that with 4 arms is in the form of a cross.

In some instances, the bars are attached by bearings so they can rotate and roll through the dough, while in others, they are affixed rigidly to produce a more forceful working of the dough. The bars may be straight and smooth or possess various configurations (for example, sigma or curved), be in parallel alignment or at opposing angles, and be equidistant from the shaft or at varying distances.

The selection of any particular pattern and agitator bar configuration is dictated largely by the type of dough to be processed and by the degree of physical development to be achieved. Mixing in these systems is a rather violent process, requiring high torque and very high mechanical strength.

All mixer arms physically work the dough to develop it. The pickup bar carries the dough mass overhead to the back of the bowl, while the remaining kneading bars roll the dough forward, pressing and stretching it in the process. With 3-arm agitators, the mixing bowl frequently is equipped with a so-called "breaker" bar located at its top rear, which serves as a shock absorber and folds the dough mass as it is tossed against the backside of the bowl. The sequence of dough manipulation during a single revolution of the mixer arms of a conventional horizontal mixer is shown in **Figure 9.045**.

9.B.1.a.ii. Horizontal roller-bar mixers

Design of horizontal roller-bar mixers offer two choices: tilting bowl (**Figure 9.046**) and the stationary bowl machines. With a tilting bowl mixer, a gear motor or hydraulic mechanism tilts the bowl forward through a 90° to 120° angle or, as in one recently introduced "over tilt" mixer, through 140 to 160° angles, thus ejecting the finished dough. Two-way tilt systems are also available so sponges can be accepted on one side of the mixer and final doughs discharged from the other.

In the stationary bowl mixer (**Figure 9.047**), the bowl is anchored solidly to the mixer frame, and removal of the finished dough is accomplished by lowering the bowl door (dropping the whole front wall) and slowly revolving the mixer arm in the opposite di-

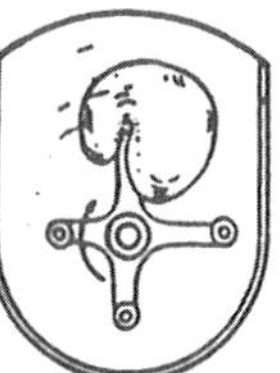
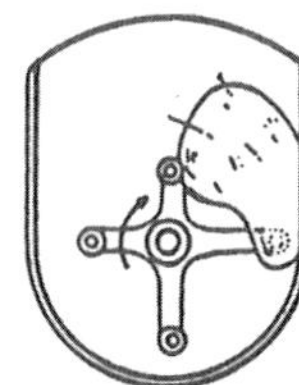
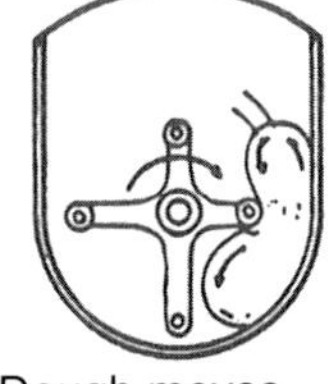

Pick-up bar carries dough up and over to rear of bowl.

First kneading roller engages and rolls gently into the dough.

Dough moves forward while first kneading roller rolls over it.

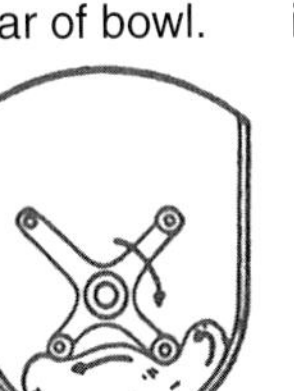
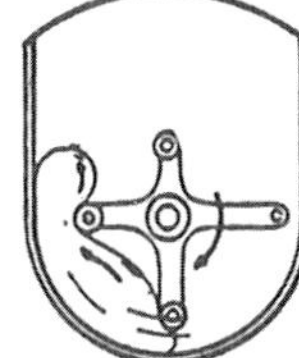
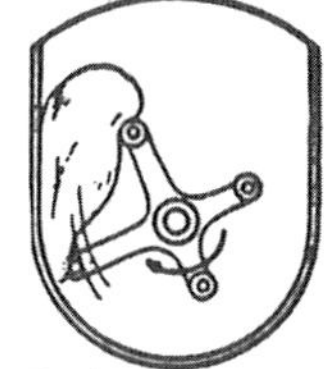

Second roller engages and kneads dough into different shape.

Third roller engages and kneads dough in another position.

Pick-up bar again engages dough, and the cycle is repeated.

Figure 9.045. The arms in a horizontal mixer manipulate dough as they revolve through the chamber. (Food Engineering)

Figure 9.046. A modern, fully automatic tilting-bowl mixer, with roller-bar arms is built with in capacitities ranging from 400 to 3,200 lb (180 to 1,450 kg). (The Peerless Group)

Figure 9.047 . This stationary-bowl high-speed horizontal dough mixer comes in a rated capacities of 1,600, 2,000 and 2,400 lb of dough. (AMF Bakery Systems)

rection, thus "kicking out" the dough into a dough pump or trough waiting in position in front of the mixer.

9.B.1.a.iii. Horizontal sigma-arm mixers

As with horizontal bar mixers for yeasted doughs, the sigma-arm mixers (**Figure 9.048**) employed for cookie and cracker products use rotors and paddle designs that vary considerably depending on the equipment vendor. An important factor in the design of the paddle is that there should be no dead center; meaning that no unmixed material will cling to any part of the paddle. A properly designed paddle provides excellent side to side mixing along the mixing bowl and in the direction of the paddle rotation (BCMA 2002a). Describing the mixing of biscuit doughs in a horizontal mixer, Wade (1988) advised that the paddle should pick up the dough in the lower right hand corner at the front of the mixer and push it over to the left-hand back corner.

Horizontal mixers with double arms (**Figure 9.049**) were originally called creamers because they were primarily used for preparing cake batters. This design does not incorporate much air into the dough, and such mixers have been adapted to mixing doughs for rotary moulded cookies, wire-cut doughs, stiff fillings and danish pastry doughs. Also found in cookie plants are horizontal mixers with arms in the form of a figure 8, which are used to prepare doughs ranging from soft high-fat formulations to very hard, almost dry doughs.

9.B.1.a.iv. Horizontal mixer construction

The majority of today's horizontal mixers operate with variable-speed AC drives, although older designs may be dual speed, with high-to-low speed ratios of 2:1. Basically, these heavy-duty systems consist of a sturdy frame of tubular steel, channel-steel welded construction or plate steel, whose upper portion houses the mixing bowl. Mixers are offered fully clad or with open-frame design (**Figure 9.050**).

Normally, the stainless-steel bowl is traversed by a single agitator shaft carrying three or more mixer bars, either straight or of various configurations (**Figure 9.051**). Some mixers, intended for processing exceptionally stiff doughs, are equipped with dual agitator shafts, also known as a double arm. In all cases on horizontal mixers, power is provided by a high-torque motor located at the side or base of the mixer frame.

Depending on the size of the mixer, the motor will range in its horsepower rating from as low as 15 hp to as high as 250 hp or higher for units that are capable of processing upwards of 3,000 lb of dough. Double-arm mixers of 6,000 lb capacity have been built for cookie doughs, but the limit for bread doughs is 3,200 lb. Although bakery design had been leaning toward larger and larger bowl capacities, a contrary trend was noted by Fay (2008). He observed that the real goal for mixer engineers is to continue to drive efficiency by using smaller mixers (2,000-lb mixers with 12-hp motors vs. 3,200-lb mixers with 200-hp motors) and mixing more batches per hour (6 to 7 vs. 4).

The motors of horizontal mixers are of the variable speed type. Power transmission to the agitator shaft is by means of self-lubricating multi-strand roller chains or synthetic drive belts (**Figure 9.052**). Direct drive, where a gear motor is mounted directly on the agitator shaft, fits into one of the following dual ranges: 35/70, 40/80 or 50/100 rpm — with 35/70 and 40/80 being the most common (Zielsdorf 1977). Recently, mixer manufacturers have adopted variable frequency drives (VFDs) to better control operating speeds of the mixing arms. Direct-drive motors, also a recent innovation in horizontal mixer design, eliminate the belts and chains of older models, making the system more energy efficient and safer.

While speed ratings are standard, the practical speeds of the mixing bars are not the same for any given rating because the agitator radius affects the actual bar speeds. Thus, an agitator bar in a 500-1b mixer will travel 220 ft per minute at an agitator speed of 80 rpm. In contrast, the corresponding travel speed in a 2,000-1b mixer will be 346 ft per minute, or 36.4% faster, because the radial distance of the bar from the center of the agitator shaft is greater in the larger mixer. Without doubt, differences in agitator bar speed of this magnitude exert variable effects on dough development.

The conventional mixing bowl has a trough-like shape, with a curved bottom and flat ends and sides. A rule of thumb is that the bowl should be 1 to 1.5 times as deep as the diameter of the paddle. Another design uses a cylindrically curved front and a flat back. This design forces the dough into a small mass as it rotates through the narrow portion of the cycle at the back of the bowl yet stretches the dough as it rolls against the curved bottom and front walls. Asymmetrical bowl shapes are said to minimize dough "slamming" in the mixer, allowing the agitator to control the dough for the majority of its rotation. Material of construction typically consists of stainless steel bowl sheet, ends, cover, stainless steel agitators and shafts, mechanical power lift, and percent load ammeter. All joints and corners are rounded to facilitate cleaning.

Manufacturers of mixers continue to explore bowl design alternatives. Fay (2008) suggested that amplifying the initial turbulent interaction between flour and water would increase aeration characteristics. This action would reduce the extra time needed in the subsequent pickup and cleanup stages, bringing total mixing time down to 7.5 to 10 minutes.

The entire assembly is enclosed in a stainless steel housing provided with hinged or removable access doors and panels to protect the operator from the drive components. To allow greater access for cleaning, some manufacturers offer an open, tubular frame design. Auxiliary equipment includes a remote refrigeration unit, time and temperature controls, start and stop buttons, various safety devices. Almost all mixers now have microprocessor and video control panels to monitor and control all major mixer functions. Mixer controls can be integrated with the plant's automatic batching system.

9.B.1.a.v. Bowl refrigeration

In larger mixers, the bowls are provided with refrigeration jackets made of the same metal as the bowl. In most designs, jacketing runs from the front to the backside of the bowl. For more effective dough cooling, some mixers jacket their two end sides as well, and in one design, the cooling surface within the bowl is further expanded by a fixed, hollow breaker bar that connects the two jacketed end sides (**Figure 9.053**). Because dough stays in contact with cold surfaces longer, the enhanced bowl refrigeration system can turn out dough as much as 0.5 to 1 C° (1 to 2 F°) cooler than standard cooling methods. At least two mixer manufacturers

Figure 9.048. Single-sigma mixers are ideal for rotary moulded cookies, crackers, biscuits, corn tortillas, muffins, sweet doughs, granola bars and stiff fillings. Capacities range from 900 to 4,000 lb (408 to 1,814 kg). (The Peerless Group)

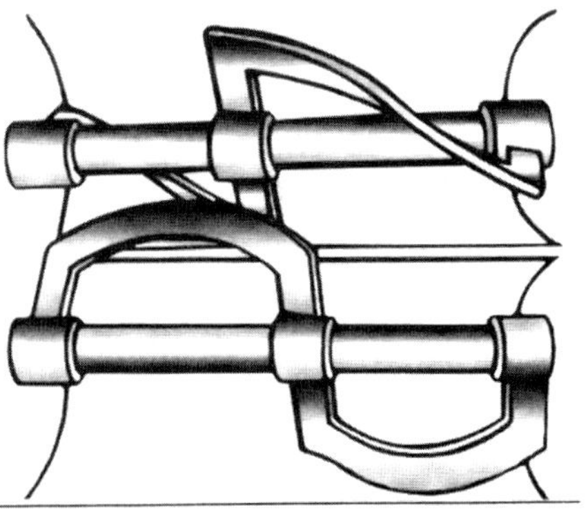

Figure 9.049. The double-sigma arm design provides more intense mixing — more shear — than single-sigma configurations. (Shaffer, a Bundy Baking Solution)

Figure 9.050. Open-frame design for this horizontal mixer allow easy access for sanitation and maintenance. (Shaffer, a Bundy Baking Solution)

offer refrigeration packages where the agitator bars themselves are cooled. This system is commonly known at a refrigerated agitator. With a refrigerated agitator, final dough temperatures can be 3 to 4 C° (5 to 7 F°) colder than without.

In recent years, jacket designs have been modified to facilitate internal coolant flow and expansion and thereby increase their cooling efficiency. The jackets have external insulation to minimize the loss of refrigeration and to prevent undesirable moisture condensation. Another option is a manifold to introduce CO_2 cooling into the bowl when mixing sweet doughs, which require a lower dough temperature during certain stages of the mixing cycle.

The act of wetting 1 lb of flour generates 6.2 Btu in latent heat, but the main source of heat generation in doughs is the energy input by the motor during the mixing process. Because large-capacity mixers generate great amounts of heat, the compressors of the auxiliary refrigeration systems must be of corresponding size. The actual compressor size will further depend on the system of cooling that is employed. In indirect cooling, a low-temperature coolant such as propylene glycol, brine or chilled water circulates through the bowl jacket to absorb heat from the dough. In direct-expansion cooling systems, on the other hand, the coolant is a highly volatile liquid such as ammonia or fluorinated hydrocarbons (Freon) that vaporize directly in the jacket, absorbing heat in the process. Indirect cooling systems generally require smaller compressors because the cyclical demand on them permits the buildup of a reservoir of coolant. The major advantage of direct-expansion systems is their quicker response to cooling needs. The bowl jackets are designed to withstand working pressures upward of 100 psi.

Bakery engineers are cautioned that use of fluorinated hydrocarbons falls under strict environmental regulation, exposing the business to penalties should these coolants be released into the atmosphere. Ammonia systems, too, must be carefully monitored because leaks present serious safety hazards to plant personnel.

9.B.1.a.vi. Sizing horizontal mixers

The numerical designation often applied to horizontal mixers indicates maximum bowl capacities, but only in a general fashion. For example, mixers numbered as 1,000, 2,000 or 2,500 (or 10, 20 and 25, respectively) are presumed to have corresponding capacities of 1,000, 2,000 or 2,500 lb of dough. Even though mixers normally provide for some excess capacity, the rated nameplate capacities represent maxima and should not be consistently exceeded for the purpose of increasing the production rate. Practical experience, in fact, shows that a reduction of dough loads by 10% or more of the rated capacity results in superior mixer performance.

It is critical to understand that when increasing the size of a mixer, the design engineer cannot just lengthen the bowl to achieve more volume and get the mixing action right. This change is more a logarithmic matter, not a simple arithmetic increase (Fay 2006).

In bakeries that employ the sponge-and-dough process of breadmaking, it is common practice to prepare sponges and doughs in separate mixers. Because sponges are normally smaller in volume than doughs, mixers used for them generally have lower-rated capacities than do the dough mixers. Dough mixers, also called "final mixers," are often equipped with a special sponge chute for transferring the fermented sponge into the mixer bowl and by possessing a greater refrigeration capacity.

Representative specifications for horizontal stationary bowl mixers are summarized in **Table 9.1** and for horizontal tilt-bowl mixers in **Table 9.2**. For each designated maximum dough weight, the corresponding sponge weight is reduced to some 60% of the rated mixer capacity. This reduction reflects the generally lower absorptions normally required for sponges, which result in stiffer sponge consistencies that impose greater power demands on mixers. It should further be noted that for any rated mixer capacity, the minimum practical dough load should not fall below half of the maximum if dough mixing problems are to be avoided. Over-loading or under-loading a batch mixer will cause batch-to-batch variations due to under- or over-mixing, which affects the final properties of the dough.

Figure 9.051. Agitator and breaker bars inside the bowls of horizontal mixers can be designed to provide different mixing actions.
(AMF Bakery Systems)

9.B.1.a.vii. Mixer controls

Mixer controls normally include devices such as start and stop switches, thermometers, timers and electrical load meters. Some mixers are provided with 2 temperature probes: one to sense the dough temperature and the other to check the interior bowl surface temperature to prevent liquid ingredients from freezing to the surface during the initial phase of mixing (Broaddus 1978).

In most modern mixers, nearly all operational conditions and functions are monitored and controlled by programmable controllers and frequently are completely integrated into the bakery's automatic batching systems. With such mixers, dough mixing reaches a high degree of automation, constancy and uniformity, and produces successive batches that conform closely to the desired, preset dough property standards.

Dough development and monitoring systems have been developed for use in controlling mixer action, especially that of large horizontal batch mixers (**Figure 9.054**). These PLC-based sensors and monitors (described in detail in Volume I, Chapter 4) record motor data, which allows insight into the nature of the mixed product. This data, when recorded over time, can allow better control and achievement of product character and uniformity. Most recently, near infra-red (NIR) technologies are being developed to allow a direct reading of the dough to achieve better control systems for product character, quality and consistency.

These integrated control systems can also record data for Hazard Analysis and Critical Control Point (HACCP) programs. Such detailed and controlled capture of ingredient usage information not only permits accurate accounting of costs but also enables tracing of ingredients by batch, lot, package, shipping container, warehouse and eventual point of sale. These control functions are critical to maintaining the integrity of the nation's food supply and limit the costs of potential product recalls.

Figure 9.052. Belt-driven horizontal mixers run quietly and are easy to maintain, compared with traditional chain-driven designs.
(The Peerless Group)

9.B.1.b. Vertical mixers

Vertical mixers are specifically designed to either produce bread and roll dough (spiral) or cake and muffin batters (planetary.) The main characteristic of the spiral

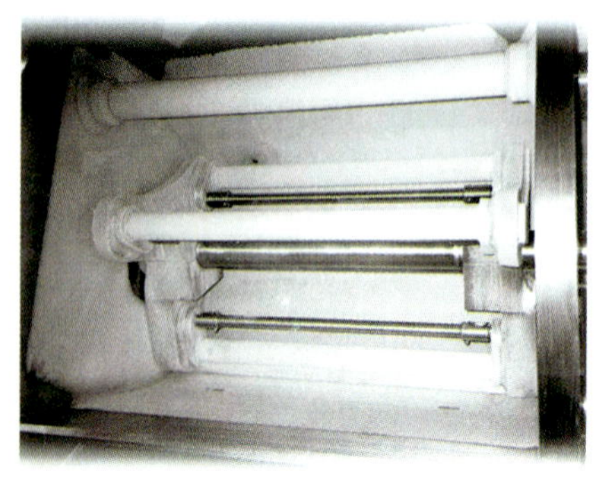

Figure 9.053. Refrigeration jackets the bowl sides and ends plus the agitator and beater bars so dough is always in contact with a refrigerated surface. (The Peerless Group)

vertical dough mixers is that the bowl rotates while the mixing tool or tools are mounted in stationary fashion in relation to the center of the bowl. Cake and muffin batter mixers are of the planetary, vertical style in which the bowl is stationary and the tools rotate in a planetary fashion within the mixing bowl. Although vertical cake batter mixers with a few fixed speeds are available, most of them feature variable speed drives that permit agitator speeds ranging from 40 to 370 rpm. Such mixers, when equipped with appropriate agitators (**Figure 9.055**), are able to perform such varied tasks as dough development, batter homogenization and foaming and whipping, among others, which endows them with great versatility.

Despite the wide range of vertical mixer styles, their basic design is quite similar. They consist essentially of a vertical frame of variable height with a horizontally-extended head housing the drive mechanism that actuates the vertical shaft with the beater attachments. The mixer head may be either stationary, in which case the bowl is elevated into mixing position, or it may be equipped with a motor drive for raising and lowering as required. In some cases, the head may tilt so the beater can be moved free of the bowl (**Figure 9.056**). A recently introduced twin-arm spiral mixer synchronizes its arms and is said to consume less energy yet improve hydration and absorption by 3 to 10%.

Table 9.1. Representative Specifications for Horizontal Stationary Bowl Mixers

Rated mixer capacity (lb)	800	1,000	1,300	1,600	2,000
Maximum - sponge (lb)	480	600	780	960	1,200
Maximum - final dough (lb)	800	1,000	1,300	1,600	2,000
Minimum - all doughs (lb)	400	500	650	800	1,000
Total bowl volume (cu ft)	38.8	41.2	50.6	61.5	79.0
Usable bowl volume (cu ft)	25.5	30.7	38.6	47.2	59.6
Power units					
Agitator (hp)	20 / 40	25 / 50	30 / 60	37.5 / 75	50 / 100
Door (hp)	0.75	1	1	1.5	1.5
Bowl tilt (hp)	1.5	1.5	2	2	2
Compressor (hp)	7.5	20	25	30	40

Table 9.2. Horizontal Tilt-Bowl Mixer Specifications

Mixer size	Maximum dough capacity (lb)	Standard HP	Drive Motor HP Sizes		ASBE volume (cu ft)
			HD1 (standard HP +1)	HD2 (standard HP +2)	
HS6	600	30	40	50	20.6
HS8	800	40	50	60	23.18
HS10	1,000	50	60	75	33.38
HS13	1,300	60	75	100	43.72
HS16	1,600	75	100	125	48.2
HS20	2,000	100	125	150	55.21
HS25	2,500	125	150	200	72.11
HS28	2,800	150	200	225	77.83
HS32	3,200	200	225	250	84.45

(Bartsch 2009)

Vertical mixer bowl capacities normally range from 20 to 340 qt, with drive motors having power ratings within the 2-to-10-hp range. The motor itself, which may use either geared-transmission or variable-speed design, is enclosed in the base of the frame. Some form of cradle is provided at the base below the mixer head to receive and firmly position the mixing bowl.

The capacity of vertical mixers is established by bowl sizes and is usually expressed in quarts and liters or, in the case of dough mixers, in pounds or kilograms signifying maximum dough weight. Numerical designations of mixer models generally provide some key to their capacities. Bowl sizes range anywhere from 50 to 900 lb of dough in the case of spiral dough kneaders and from about 40 to 340 qt for planetary mixers, as shown in **Table 9.3**, which lists representative specifications for the latter type of mixers. Some spiral mixers that are designed specifically for dough kneading are limited to a fixed 2-speed cycle, with the bowl capable of rotating in either direction. Generally, however, the agitator speeds of vertical mixers are continuously variable from 45 to about 330 rpm. Depending on their size, the mixers are powered by motors with ratings that range from about 5 to 25 hp.

Figure 9.054. Mixing curves, describing power usage by the motor, can be displayed via operator interface screens mounted on the mixer housing. (The Peerless Group)

Bowls for vertical mixers are normally fabricated from stainless steel. They are circular in shape, with round bottoms, and are usually provided with exterior handles and lugs, the latter serving to firmly position the bowl in the mixer cradle so that it may be safely raised and held in the mixing position. In the larger mixers, the raising and lowering of the bowl is powered by a separate motor that may range from 0.25 to 2 hp. In high-volume operations, bowls are moved by bowl trucks or dollies and are emptied by special bowl unloaders that lift them to the appropriate height for emptying into divider hoppers. The mixing blades have a triple action purpose to mix, cut and tear to insure rapid incorporation of the ingredients into a homogeneous mixture. Different pitches of blades and blade angles are available to suit the particular mixing dynamics of given sponge or dough processes.

9.B.1.b.i. Spiral mixers

Spiral mixers generally include some provisions for bidirectional bowl rotation. Most vertical mixers feature removable or portable bowls (**Figure 9.057**), but models with fixed bowls are also quite common. Fixed-bowl mixers generally employ a dough discharge mechanism such as a scraper arm that revolves around the side of the bowl and a bottom discharge port (**Figure 9.058**).

The agitator design for spiral mixers takes the shape of a tapering spiral arm. Some designs use a fixed central shaft around which the spiral works the dough. At least one manufacturer offers a hollow spiral arm through which carbon dioxide can be injected to cool doughs. The Wendel arm, which resembles a squared-off figure 8, is used in pairs to manage stiffer doughs. Scraper arms, another option, can installed along the inner side of the mixing bowl to

Figure 9.055. This vertical mixer features dual-implement mixing, which cuts processing times in half. (Topos Mondial)

Figure 9.056. The spiral mixing tool rises with the head of the mixer to allow removal of the bowl.
(*Baking & Snack*)

periodically scraped down accumulated doughs or batters and also to facilitate unloading of fixed bowls. Such discharge tools increase the degree of automation possible with spiral mixers (**Figure 9.059**).

9.B.1.b.ii. Planetary mixers

Planetary mixers feature rapidly rotating agitator shaft that can often be put through opposing circular motions at a slower speed by a planetary gear in the mixer head. In standard machines, the ratio of beater revolutions to the planetary revolution is normally about 3.7:1. With dual-ratio machines, the respective ratios become 2:1 and 4:1. The 2:1 ratio is most suitable for mixing and creaming, while the 4:1 ratio provides superior whipping and aerating actions. This type of agitator action ensures that the entire bowl content receives the same processing. The combination of planetary mixer action with the large assortment of available beater configurations gives practically limitless versatility to such vertical mixers (**Figure 9.060**).

A rather wide variety of agitator types is available. These include batter beaters with two, four and six wings and shaped to fit the bowl interior; deflector and spiral wire whip assemblies shaped to ensure maximum air incorporation and air cell re-

Table 9.3. Representative Specifications for Vertical Mixers						
	120 Size			160 Size			340 Size
Bowl capacities (qt)	40.0	80.0	120.0	40.0	80.0	160.0	340.0
Bowl capacities (l)	37.8	75.6	113.4	37.8	75.6	151.2	312.3
Bowl capacities (cu ft)	1.3	2.7	4	1.3	2.7	5.3	11.3
Mixing speed range (rpm)	70 to 370			40 to 320			45 to 325
Agitator motor (hp)	2			5			10
Bowl lift motor (hp)	0.25			0.33			2

duction, and dough hooks of curved or spiral and helical configurations designed to fold, knead and stretch the doughs being mixed. Some of the beaters are provided with rubber edges for automatic wiping down of the bowl interior during the mixing or creaming operation, or the mixer can be configured with a continuous scraper that revolves around the sides and bottom of the bowl to constant reincorporate dough from those areas back into the batch.

Addition of a second tool in the planetary head gives additional versatility: A wire whip for foaming, for example, can be combined with a cross-beater for development. These mixers (**Figure 9.061**), termed complex planetary batch mixers, offer production rates up to 10,000 lb per hour, with bowl capacities of 250 gal (1,000 qt). Mixer designs that seal and pressurize the bowl enable development of texture, and when the pressure is released before delivering the batter to the depositor, the air bubbles in the batter expand. The flexibility of vertical mixers with interchangeable tools is enhanced by computer controls to sequence ingredients and tools in proper order, thus enabling automatic repeat-batch mixing (Wilkinson 1987).

Specifically designed for mixing batters, complex planetary batch mixers can han-

Figure 9.057. Removable bowls make spiral mixers very flexible in operating style. This 350-l bowl has the capacity for 150 kg flour (240 kg dough).
(Kemper Bakery Systems)

dle any variety of cake, cremes, fillings, doughs for wire-cut and rotary moulded cookies and light pastry doughs.

9.B.1.b.iii. Multiple-bowl mixers

For bakers seeking the benefits of small-batch mixing for high-volume production, spiral mixer manufacturers developed multiple-bowl systems know as "carousel" mixers. Rotating along a circular path like a county fair's sideshow carousel, the system's bowls stop at separate stations that dispense dry and liquid ingredients, engage a spiral mixing head, rest the dough briefly and then discharge the contents to the divider hopper. A carousel mixer with 1,000-lb-capacity bowls can easily match the output of mid-size horizontal mixers, delivering a batch of fresh dough every 12 to 15 minutes. If a re-mix stage or late salt addition is needed, the designer adds another bowl position and mixing head. When longer floor times are desired, spiral mixing systems (**Figure 9.062**, **9.063** and **9.064**) can be configured to move the bowls along tracks that automatically lead them into and out of processing and holding stations. Automated storage-and-retrieval or robotic systems have also been used to move bowls through processing stations. These inline and carousel mixers depend on PLC sequencing to accomplish their actions in correct order.

A vertical continuous-batch mixer uses multiple spiral mixing tools to pick up and mix small batches of dough, outputting 1,000 to 10,000 kg (2,200 to 22,000 lb) of dough per hour. A pre-mixer blends water and flour to supply a hydrated mass to the kneading chamber, containing the spiral mixing tools attached to a planetary head. The backplate of each tool cuts off a discrete portion of dough as it comes out of the pre-mixer to create a series of mini-batches as the planetary head rotates. The spiral tools work the dough against the backplates and the inside of the mixer's chamber wall. Each mini-batch is worked by its own spiral tool and exits the chamber through an opening in the bottom onto a conveyor belt feeding the makeup line. Tool speed is variably controlled, thus controlling the intensity of the mixing (Berne 2007).

9.B.1.b.iv. Spindle mixers

Although the vertical mixers known as spindle mixers (**Figure 9.065**) are available with a few fixed speeds, most of them feature variable speed drives that permit agitator speeds ranging from 15 to 370 rpm. Such mixers, when equipped with appropriate agitators, are able to perform such varied tasks as dough development, batter homogenization and foaming and whipping, among others, which endows them with great versatility. They ensure the incorporation of all the ingredients and a minimum toughening affect on the dough. Typically used for fermented crackers, they are capable of mixing and remixing doughs held in troughs without the need to empty or refill the troughs each time. Typical mix times are 4 to 5 min-

Figure 9.058. The fixed bowl design of this pair of spiral mixers features a bottom discharge port and bowl scraper arm to extract dough after mixing. (Kaak)

Figure 9.059. By elevating the bowl and adding a discharge tool to the design, this double-spiral mixer can automatically transfer dough into a mobile trough waiting below. (Gemini Bakery Equipment)

Figure 9.060. Planetary mixers not only rotate their mixing tools at relatively high speeds but they also carry them in counter-rotation within the bowl to assure complete mixing. (AMF Bakery Systems)

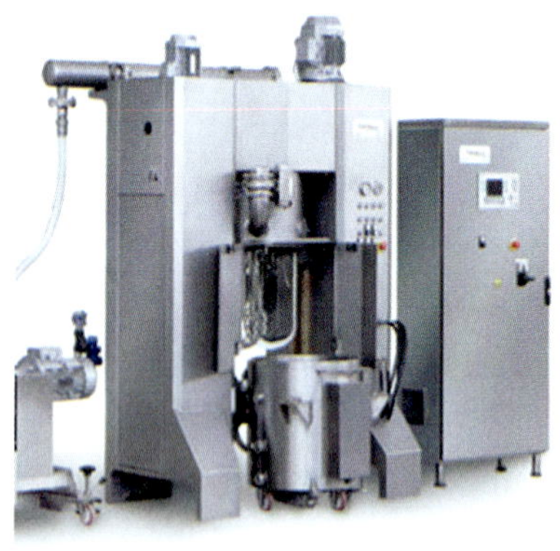

Figure 9.061. Computer-sequencing governs actions by this planetary mixer with an interchangeable tool system. (Tonelli)

utes, which equate to 80 to 100 rpm. Batch sizes range from 272 to 950 kg (600 to 2,000 lb).

9.B.1.b.v. Twin-arm mixers

The vertical twin-arm reciprocating mixer (**Figure 9.066**) simulates most closely the mixing action as it was done manually prior to the introduction of the mechanical process. In these mixers, two agitator arms are mounted vertically on circular planes. As these planes rotate at a moderate speed, the agitators traverse intersecting elliptical paths in a shallow, slowly revolving bowl. As they do so, they impart a gentle kneading, stretching, lifting and folding action to the dough.

Since the rate of energy input corresponds to the relatively slow speed of the mixing arms, there is generally little or no increase in the dough temperature during the mixing process, eliminating the need for refrigeration for this type of mixer. Because of their gentle mixing action, reciprocating arm mixers are particularly suitable for temperature-sensitive doughs such as those for pies and pastries in which the preservation of discrete shortening particles is important and for doughs containing nuts and fruits whose excessive breakdown such as might occur in high-speed mixing would be undesirable.

9.B.1.b.vi. Slurry mixers (ingrediators)

Blending of liquid and dry ingredients to feed preferment and fermentation systems and holding of prepared liquid brews and sponges are often done with conventional slurry mixers, common to other food industry applications such as diary and beverage processing. These mixers typically use impellers or small immersion mixers to agitate their contents and keep ingredients uniformly suspended.

The baking industry adopted a blending mixer (**Figure 9.067**) originally introduced for dairy plant use. These high-speed blending systems liquefy, dissolve and disperse solids or semisolids in less than 5 minutes. Some designs incorporate a built-in scraped surface feature that allows rapid heat transfer without burn-on, a useful characteristic that allows such systems to mix and cook icings.

9.B.1.b.vii. McDuffee bowl mixers

Because 100-lb capacity is the smallest size available for conventionally configured 2-speed horizontal mixers, laboratory and experimental test baking is generally done in a 12- or 20-qt 3-speed vertical mixer equipped with a McDuffee bowl and a 2-tined mixing fork (Doerry 1995a). The movement of the slightly curved pins of the mixing fork around the fixed vertical pin in the center of the flat-bottomed bowl approximates the action of a horizontal mixer (**Figure 9.068**). Three-pronged mixing arms and water-jacketed bowls for additional temperature control are also available.

9.B.1.c. High-intensity mixers

Mixing requires a significant amount of time to bring doughs to optimal development, and cutting that time has challenged generations of engineers working on mixer design. This theme also marks efforts by formulators seeking to reduce mixing time through their choice of ingredients.

Two different directions characterize attempts to make a meaningful reduction in the time required to impart to yeast-raised doughs the necessary physical development prior to the final proof period: (a) mechanical dough development obtained by intensive high-speed mixing of the dough for a short time and (b) chemical dough development in which the dough is treated with appropriate reducing agents and mixed at conventional speeds. Both approaches, in effect, eliminate the bulk fermentation stage, that represents about 60% of the total time in the traditional breadmaking process. Chemical dough development techniques are discussed in Chapter 8.

9.B.1.c.i. Mechanical dough development

Mechanical dough development had its genesis in the continuous mixing process, discussed later in this chapter. Whereas continuous dough processes make use of a liquid ferment and thus involve a separate fermentation stage, the procedures of mechanical batch dough development eliminate bulk fermentation as a distinct phase of doughmaking. Mechanical batch dough development evolved nearly 50 years ago, principally as the result of research carried out in the laboratories of the British Flour and Baking Research Association at Chorleywood, UK (Hall 1965), now a part of The Campden BRI Group, Chipping Campden, UK. This work led to the commercial introduction of the Chorleywood Bread Process (CBP) that had, as its major equipment unit, the high-speed bowl-type Tweedy mixer.

The Chorleywood team of investigators established that optimum dough development occurred at work levels of 40 joules per g (5 Watt-hours, or 0.4 hp-minutes) per lb of dough, expended within a time span not exceeding 5 minutes (Chamberlain et al. 1962). This amount of energy is some 5 to 8 times as high as that required to mix a dough for bulk fermentation and indicates the actual level of energy generated by yeast in a fermenting dough. Recently, CPB mixers have been adapted to work sequentially at pressures above and below atmospheric to allow optimum control over gas cell size (Cauvain 1998a).

(Formulation research and processing parameters for CPB doughs are discussed in Chapter 6.)

Mechanical dough development is said to offer the following advantages: (a) the production time from the start of mixing to the end of baking is reduced to less than 2 hours; (b) the dough fermentation room, with its controlled temperature and humidity conditions, is eliminated; (c) product yield is increased by some 4.0% as a result of higher absorption, reduction in fermentation losses and more accurate scaling because dough reaches the divider more uniform and denser; (d) precise automatic control of dough development results in greater product uniformity; and (e) relatively low-protein flours may be used because the proteolytic breakdown of flour proteins that normally occurs during bulk fermentation is avoided. On the other hand, the process requires higher yeast levels, and its electric power usage is relatively high (French and Fish 1981).

9.B.1.c.ii. CPB mixers

The recognition that bulk dough fermentation may be substituted by appropriate mechanical dough development led to the introduction of several types of ultra-high-speed batch mixers, available in horizontal and vertical configurations. These

Figure 9.062. A carousel mixer employs four or more bowls that rotate through separate dosing/metering, mixing and resting/discharge stations. (Sancassiano)

Figure 9.063. An inline mixing system moves bowls along tracks to processing and resting stations. (Sancassiano)

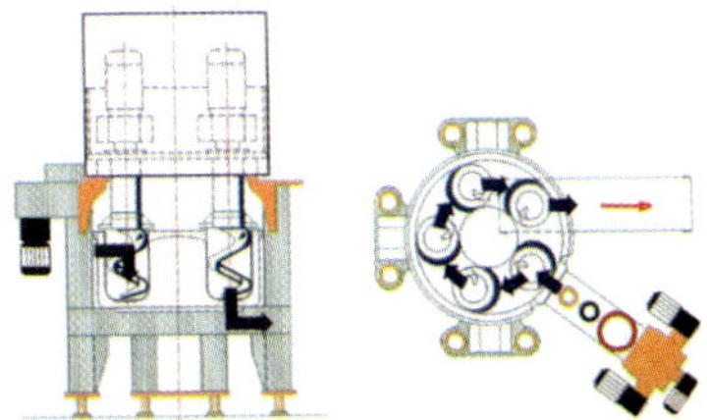

Figure 9.064. Computer-sequencing governs actions by this planetary mixer with an interchangeable tool system. (Sancassiano)

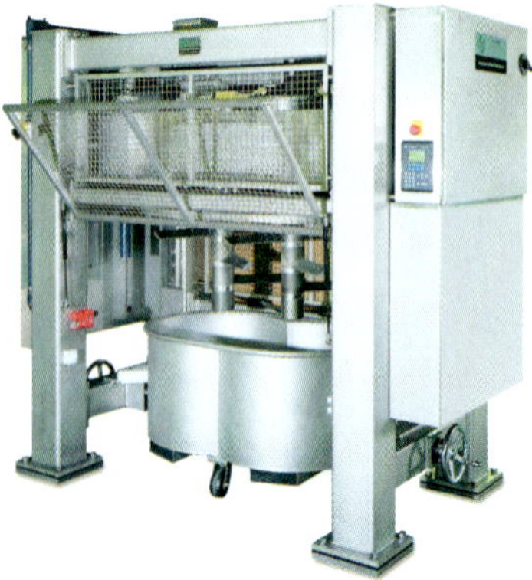

Figure 9.065. The mixing blades on a spindle mixer are mounted horizontally, and the whole mixing head descends into the trough.
(Reading Bakery Equipment)

Figure 9.066. Reciprocating dual-arm dough mixer operates by lifting and stretching dough. A transparent bowl shield, not shown, provides operator protection.
(Excellent Bakery Equipment)

Figure 9.067. A high-speed blender uses a bottom-mounted impeller to mix and disperse ingredients.
(Caravan Ingredients, Breddo)

are capable of fully developing doughs in batch weights up to 1,000 lb in 5 minutes or less by an energy input of 5 Watt-hours per lb within that time span. In those systems that are currently in operation in bakeries, the mixing bowl or drum is cylindrical in shape, and mixing is done by an impact plate or an impeller rotating at speeds of from 280 to 350 rpm.

The mixer developed to carryout the Chorleywood Bread Process consists essentially of a jacketed cylindrical bowl with an impact mixer plate at the bottom that is driven by a suitably sized motor. As shown in **Figure 9.069**, three baffles are attached to the sidewalls of the mixing chamber to deflect the dough toward the mixing plate. The bowl is mounted on a horizontal axis so it can be tilted for dough ejection. Dough production capacities of the larger units range upwards of 7,500 lb per hour. In the newest installations, an overhead frame supports a flour hopper and a liquid ingredient tank on load cells, a shortening feed line, and a vacuum pump. The mixer's computer control system exercises complete monitoring and control functions over practically all the parameters that can affect the ultimate dough character, including mixing time, dough temperatures, absorption levels, energy input, proportioning of ingredients, acceptance of and adaptation to formula changes and even controlled atmospheres (**Figure 9.070**).

The evolution of the mixer developed for the Chorleywood process and subsequently adapted to American production conditions was described by Chamberlain (1983). Fish (1982) offered a plant-by-plant analysis to describe the specifics of the system. Additional details were provided by and French and Fish (1981), French and Kemp (1985) and most recently by Woolley (1996).

9.B.1.c.iii. High-speed, high-intensity mixers

The mixing chamber of the high-speed, high-intensity mixer (**Figure 9.071**) features a trapeze-shaped mixing element, with a baffle arm on the open cover lid. Examining the mixer more closely, the system consists of a horizontally mounted drum-shaped mixing chamber jacketed for temperature control. Ingredients enter through the top opening, and the mixed dough is ejected into the dough trough through a bottom gate. According to the manufacturer, this mixing method allows up to 10% more absorption.

Flour and shortening blocks are automatically fed via the loading slide/gate at the top of the mixer. Water and liquids are weighed or metered and the minor ingredients can be hand added. The ingredients are mixed at between 150 to 1,200 rpm, for 1 to 2 minutes at the high speed, depending on the blade configuration, using a 50-hp motor. The knives or mixing elements are mounted directly to the motor shaft. It is this high-speed mixer action that imparts the requisite energy to the dough for full development within a time span of about 2 minutes.

Forcing materials into the mixer's vortex action allows them to be finely cut, mixed and emulsified. The key is that such high speeds permit the dough to hydrate at a fast rate. The other end of the chamber, which also serves as its lid, features an extended baffle arm, driven by a separate motor, sweeping the chamber's perimeter in a counterclockwise rotation at 24 rpm. The scraper turns inside the mixing chamber to wipe the chamber walls for incorporation of all the ingredients, maintaining the heat transfer rate, as well as directing the viscous material into the center of the mixing blades. After the dough is mixed, it discharges through a bottom slide/gate in 30- to 50-lb chunks onto a conveyor. In the high-speed batch mixing system illustrated here, full automation is achieved by using programmable process controllers

(PLCs) to integrate all dry and liquid ingredient scaling, batching and feeding operations with the mixing process and dough transfer.

Andrews et al. (1989) reviewed specific high-speed mixer technologies, comparing applications, automation, dough size capacities, heat generation and mixing activity.

9.B.2. Continuous mixers

Many manufacturing industries practice continuous mixing, but such techniques came to the US baking industry only in the early 1950s (Baker 1954, McLaren 1954, Geddes 1959, Trum 1967). By adopting this technology, bakers hoped to shorten processing time while also assuring uniform results in fine-textured pan bread. Bakery acceptance of continuous dough mixing crested by the mid-1970s, when some 60% of all commercial bread production in the US was based on this process. Changes in the market for baked foods favored goods made by more conventional methods. Installations of new continuous dough mixing systems for bread production came to a halt for various reasons.

Yet this mixing method is "alive and well" at many plants belonging to publicly held and independent wholesale baking companies in the US. Also, some presently operating continuous mixing systems have been adapted to production of soft buns and rolls.

In addition, the continuous mix experience with breadmaking opened the door to numerous technologies now in common use throughout the baking industry. For example, to be successful with continuous mixing of bread doughs required the baker and bakery engineer to master control over extensive "tank farms" that contained the preferments and liquid sponges required by this technology. Even though wholesale bakers returned to previous batch-based equipment, they retained use of preferments and similar doughmaking processes to enhance their control over the finished product. Continuous aeration methods enable production of cake and wafer products.

Recently, the bread baker's interest in continuous methods has turned to preparation of dough intermediaries such as pre-hydrated flour-and-water mixtures, as well as pretzel doughs, or for dough kneading ahead of sheeting and lamination systems. In the meantime, biscuit and cookie bakers developed and adopted continuous mixing methods for preparation of cookie, biscuit and cracker doughs.

Pyler (1988) discussed in detail the development of the continuous mix process for bread doughs, covering both its science and equipment requirements. The process is also described in Chapter 6 of this volume.

9.B.2.a. Continuous bread dough mixers

The two most widely used continuous dough mixing systems in American baking practice were the Do-Maker process (Baker 1954), better known as the Wallace & Tiernan (W&T) system, and the Amflow process (Trum 1967). Although neither technology is currently being manufactured commercially, one

Figure 9.068. Two- and 3-tined forks work around the fixed pins in a McDuffee bowl, thus simulating the mixing action of horizontal mixers for laboratory test purposes.
(National Manufacturing Co.)

Figure 9.069. The interior of the Tweedy mixing bowl, developed to make CBP doughs, reveals the mixing plate and wall baffles.
(Baker Perkins UK)

Figure 9.070. CBP batch mixers can now mix under controlled atmosphere. (Baker Perkins UK)

Figure 9.071. Ultra-high speed mixing characterizes this high-intensity mixer. (Advanced Food Systems)

major American baking company acquired the rights, patents, blueprints and castings for W&T continuous mixers to support such systems in its plants.

Manufacturers of continuous bread dough mixers designed their systems with several components (**Figure 9.072**), starting with the liquid preferment system, which activates the yeast. A pre-mixer or incorporator blends a homogenous preliminary dough by combining the preferment with the remaining dough ingredients. A kneader — the primary dough developer and the essential component of the continuous mixer — consisting of two counter-rotating impellers or paddles, operates at 50 to 290 rpm to rapidly knead, fold, stretch, shear, compress and degass the dough, thus bringing it to full development. The dough proceeds under pressure (20 to 60 psi) at a controlled rate through a relatively small development chamber. Finally, a scaling depositor dispenses the developed dough directly into baking pans. Production capacity for continuous bread doughmaking systems varied from 2,500 to 7,000 lb of dough per hour, or 42 to 100 lb per minute, outputting up to 85 loaves per minute.

The energy input of 0.3 to 0.4 hp per minute for each pound of dough causes a temperature rise of 10 to 13 C° (18 to 24 F°) in the finished dough. The amount of energy required to develop a unit weight of dough is essentially the same regardless of the processing method employed, except that greater efficiency is achieved when smaller dough masses are processed. The impeller speeds may vary from a low of about 110 rpm to a high of about 220 rpm, depending on flour strength, dough formulation, rate of throughput, and other factors.

The continuously mixed dough is forced into the lower portion of the developer whose exit point is shaped into a narrow orifice leading to the extruder-divider (**Figure 9.073**). This action imparts an elongated form to the dough, which when cut off by opposed, horizontally moving knives, assumes a cylindrical form as it drops into a pan. The desired dough weight is controlled by adjustments in the timing of the pan conveyor and the knife strokes.

9.B.2.b. Continuous kneaders

Continuous mixers for bread doughs developed differently in Europe. Their designs generally separate ingredient incorporation from dough kneading and use different tools for each process. These systems employ slower mixing action than their American counterparts and have stayed in bakery use to this day, with continuing innovation. Recent innovations enable modular design of such systems with modules for liquid dosing, shortening input, mixing, resting and clean-in-place capacity (Madsen 1994).

The mixer's automation system meters dough ingredients into a horizontal cylindrical chamber at one end and conveys them to the other end using auger (single or twin), ribbon or spiral blade mixing elements. The finished dough is thoroughly blended but not necessarily fully developed.

Such continuous mixing/kneading systems (**Figure 9.074**) can be supplied by liquid ferment, brew, sour dough and pre-mix processes. Its helical mixing tools, arranged in an intermeshing double spiral, assure gentle handling of the product, and double jacketed construction allows precise temperature control, with a differential from start to finish of less than 3 C° (5 F°). The system achieves dough-out temperatures of 20°C (68°F). Inclusions such as fruits, nuts, chocolate and candy pieces are easily incorporated into the continual flow of dough by automatic metering of such particulates into the mixer during its final stages.

The equipment actually makes a large number of small batches, pushing the dough forward to knead it in small quantities, rather than handling dough as a large mass as do horizontal mixers. Because mixing activity is separated from kneading action, engineers estimate a 30% savings in energy input for doughmaking using continuous kneading technology. And because the flour hydrates fully ahead of kneading, water absorption can be increased 1 to 2%. The dough is output to a resting belt that conveys it to the divider hopper (**Figure 9.075**). The system has been successfully applied to such diverse products as baguettes, hearth doughs, hamburger buns, pretzels and tortillas.

American manufacturers are also innovating in this direction, and the bakery equipment now offered bears little resemblance to the systems of the past. For example, at least one manufacturer now produces continuous mixers (**Figure 9.076**), computer-controlled to automatically supply dry and liquid ingredients in proper sequence at accuracies greater than 99.5% (Warren 1999) (**Figure 9.077**). The mixing shaft may contain any number of pins and paddles, depending on production requirements. The system can output dough at the rate of 500 to 20,000 lb per hour. A proven technology for pretzel, breadstick and bagel dough processing, this continuous mixer system is designed for wheat-based doughs, including bread, rolls, puns, pizza and pie crusts, cakes and doughnuts, biscuits, corn chips, tortillas and pasta.

Another style of continuous mixer took advantage of thin film technology to mix doughs (Madsen 1994). This method minimized the exposure to waste caused by "out of spec" conditions because only small quantities were continuously mixed at a time, thus just a small amount of material must be discarded

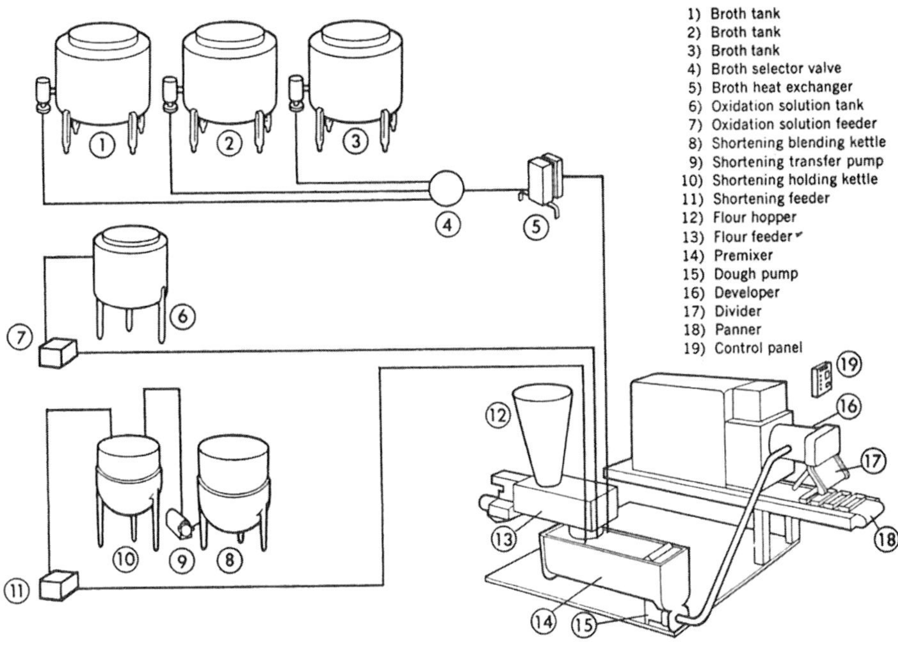

Figure 9.072. Flow chart identifies the individual system components of a continuous mixing system. (Baker 1954)

Figure 9.073. Ingredient incorporation tanks (at left) feed the continuous mixer, and finished dough pieces emerge from the developer-panner head (at right). (Pyler 1988)

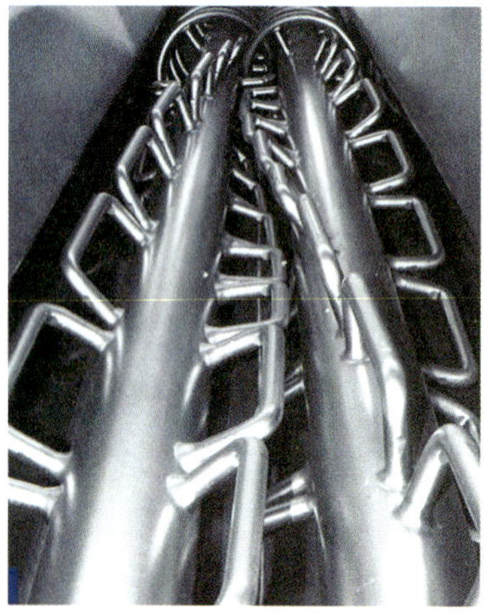

Figure 9.074. The mixing tools for this continuous dough mixing system use spiral shafts (top) in the first stage to thoroughly mix the raw materials, followed by helical kneading tools (bottom) to develop the dough. (Reimelt)

Figure 9.075. Hydrated dough from the continuous mixer rests for about 2 minutes before proceeding to the next processing step, dividing. (Reimelt)

if problems occur. (Other continuous mixers would require the entire mixer barrel to be emptied.)

A stator-and-impeller continuous mixer (a modern type is shown in **Figure 9.078**) found use in Great Britain for bread dough preparation (Elias and Wragg 1963, Eggit and Coppock 1965). This mixer can also be used to prepare short paste or pie doughs (Tireki 2008a). Modern systems have also been used in Europe to make doughs for soft rolls, rusks, bread and biscuits.

The unit consists of a horizontal mixing cylinder divided into some 20 segments and equipped with a central rotating shaft powered by a 35-hp motor, which provides a throughput of up to 4,600 pounds per hour. Segments with open stators and coarse-pitch impellers premix the dough, with subsequent segments with static plates have holes of diminishing size and finely pitched impellers that serve to condition the dough. Several of the final restrictor plates permit adjustment of the size of their apertures to establish the desired finished product texture, either conventional or fine. By reducing the stator-plate openings, pressures approaching 30 psi can be developed within the mixing cylinder. At such pressures, the occluded air in the dough is forced into solution and creates the preconditions for the formation of a finely-textured crumb.

Additional control over the work input and working pressure is obtained by varying the speed of the mixer shaft. The actual work input is continuously recorded on a wattmeter. The normal operating speed of the mixing shaft is about 160 rpm, although it can be varied from 22 to 190 rpm, depending on the throughput rate. The work levels applied are 15 Watt-hours per lb (Wh per lb) for finely-textured bread (equivalent to 0.4 hp per minute per lb of dough) and 3.75 Wh per lb for conventionally-textured bread.

A twin-shaft continuous dough mixer features variously shaped mixing elements

housed cylindrical chamber (Mueller 1971). Depending on the diameter of the mixing chamber, production capacities range from 300 to 5,400 lb of dough per hour. By combining a small unit with a large one into a dual system, hourly production capacities of about 8,500 lb of dough are obtainable. The important characteristic of this system is the automatic scaling section in which the dry and wet ingredients are metered accurately into the mixer hopper. In operation, the automatically scaled dough ingredients are fed into the mixer hopper from whence they are drawn into the mixing chamber by the auger-type fins that are attached to the initial section of the revolving mixer shafts. These fins act to bring about a rapid blending of the dough ingredients into a homogeneous mass and to propel this mass into the developer section. Here, the dough is kneaded under a controlled back pressure that ensures the required energy input for full physical dough development. The developed dough is extruded through an adjustable orifice onto a conveyor belt that carries it to the makeup department. Dough consistency is controlled by a recording wattmeter that will automatically correct any fluctuations in the amount of water being metered to the mixer.

9.B.2.c. Continuous biscuit and cracker dough mixers

Continuous mixers for cookie and cracker mixing are increasingly being used in biscuit operations as well as for preparation of muffins, doughnuts, pretzels, pasta and pizza, to name a few. In use now for the past 25 years, such systems have been found to minimize the batch-to-batch variations inherit with typical batch mixing, and they reduce manpower requirements.

Four considerations govern application of this type of system to biscuit operations: (a) mixing of the ingredients, (b) dissolving the sugar, (c) hydration of the flour and (d) kneading or working the dough to form the gluten matrix. Sugar dissolution and flour hydration depend on the residence time within the mixer, while mixing and kneading are determined by the design of the mixer (especially the mixing screws) and the speed or rpm of the mixer itself.

Figure 9.076. Computerized sequencing assures the accuracy of ingredient dispensing for this modern continuous dough mixer.
(Reading Bakery Systems, ExACT Mixing)

9.B.2.d. Continuous batter mixers

Other uses of continuous mixers are to aerate products such as wafers, marshmallows, icings, fillings, cake batters and whipped toppings. The success to continuous mixing is to implement the correct feeder metering system and limit the amount of metered streams to the mixer, the consideration of pre-blending several steams together prior to metering and the mixer design. Companies like all have various designs of continuous mixers based on the commercial and technical objectives required to meet the consumer demand for products.

Because continuous batter mixers are so specialized to the production of cake and wafer products, they are discussed in Chapter 12, Parts B and H.

9.C. Fermentation and Dough Handling Equipment
Updated by Mihaelos N. Mihalos

The equipment for accomplishing fermentation encompasses both bulk and continuous methods and employs a wide variety of tanks, troughs and transfer mechanisms. Raw materials, mixed or slurried, are fed into these systems or deposited into troughs, where their yeast and bacterial leavens are allowed to ferment and their flour to hydrate. While tanks represent the principal style of fermentation equipment for preferments and liquid brews, bulk fermentation of sponges and floor time of final-mixed doughs take place primarily in troughs.

As explained in Chapter 6, bulk fermentation of preferments, sponges and final doughs and the floor time given to straight doughs perform three major functions that have long been held essential to bread production: (a) the generation of carbon dioxide gas to aerate the loaf, (b) the formation of fermentation by-products to contribute to the ultimate bread flavor and (c) the development of the viscoelastic

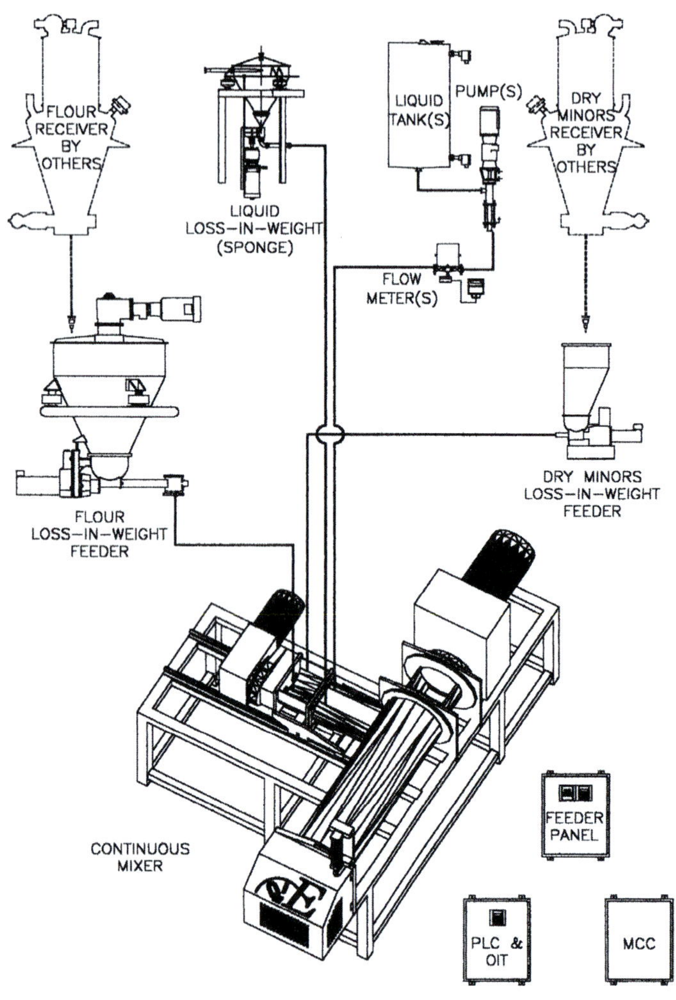

Figure 9.077. Flow chart for a modern continuous dough mixer shows inputs to the system.
(Warren 1999)

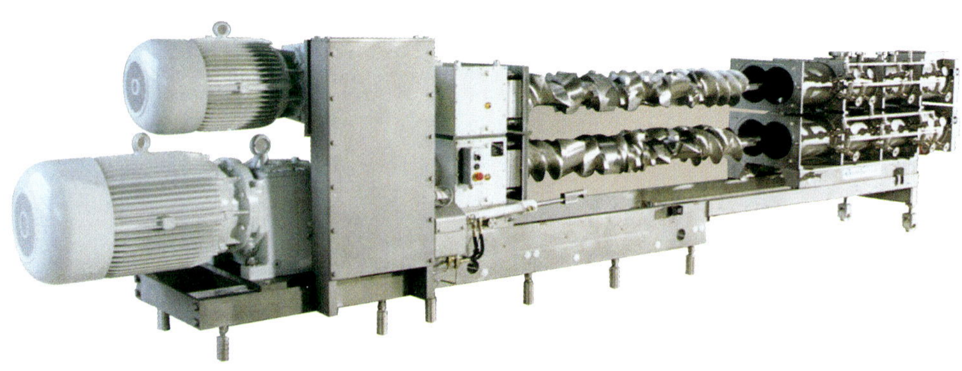

Figure 9.078. The configuration of the stator and impeller mixing elements (shown here with the outer housing drawn back for cleaning) of a high-volume continuous mixer/kneader can be configured for exact formulation requirements. This system can output 1,500 to 7,000 kg of dough per hour.
(Werner & Pfleiderer Industrial Bakery Technologies)

properties of the dough that improve its gas retention ability during baking.

9.C.1. Fermentation systems

A number of systems that combine different elements of liquid ferments with continuous mixing and conventional makeup have been improvised in practice, particularly in the US. Thus, Dibble (1981) described in some detail one such system for the large-scale production of white pan bread in which a rather concentrated flour-free ferment, having first been fermented for 1 hour, is combined with additional water and 60% flour to yield a pumpable liquid sponge. This sponge is fed into a continuous fermentation tank that is equipped with an internal, upright funnel. As fermentation proceeds and fresh sponge continues to be added, the sponge level rises until, after 30 minutes, it begins to overflow the top rim of the funnel. After being pumped through a heat exchanger for cooling, the liquid sponge enters a tank for temporary storage at 7°C (45°F) at which temperature it remains stable for 12 hours.

Although the preferment described by Dibble (1981) was intended to feed a continuous mixing unit, the technique suits preparation of liquid sponges used for batch mixing methods, too.

9.C.1.a. Tank fermentation

The widespread adoption of liquid ferments by commercial bakers led to development of special blending, fermenting, cooling and transferring equipment of different sizes and complexity. In general, they include various sizes of vertical tanks, either with or without refrigeration capabilities, which serve purposes such as small ingredient mixing, blending of flour and water with the other ferment ingredients, fermentation and storing of the fermented liquid ferment. These tanks are normally supplemented by control panels, metering and transfer pumps, flow control valves and heat exchangers.

9.C.1.a.i. Flourless systems

A flourless preferment, variously called a brew or broth, is prepared by metering and scaling the appropriate amounts of water, salt, sugar, dairy type solids, yeast, yeast food, enrichment tablets and other optional ingredients into a tank (**Figure 9.079**). The mixture gets a brief but vigorous agitation by means of a squirrel cage mixer, propeller-style vertical mixers or specially designed agitators in a confined chamber to obtain thorough dispersion. The mixed preferment is then pumped into the selected fermentation tank, where it is gently stirred during fermentation to maintain constant density, temperature and dispersion.

Such mixtures typically ferment under gentle agitation for 2.5 hours. The capacity of a single tank should be sufficient for maintaining production for about one-half hour. The individual ferments must, therefore, be set successively every 30 minutes to ensure a continuity of supply. The mature ferment is then transferred to a final holding tank.

Figure 9.079. Liquid brew systems at modern bakeries operate according to principles derived from use of preferments for continuous mixed doughs.
(Shick USA)

With flour-free water ferments, the same tank often serves for both ferment make-up and fermentation. The tanks are frequently equipped with special agitators that ensure a homogeneous suspension during fermentation, and they generally are jacketed to permit rapid cooling of the ferment to the proper holding temperature on completion of fermentation.

The water ferment is generally set at a temperature of 27 to 32°C (80 to 90°F) and is fermented for 1 to 2 hours, either to a specified pH or until a predetermined temperature rise is attained. On completion of fermentation, the ferment is cooled rapidly to 4 to 10°C (40 to 50°F) to arrest further yeast activity and render the ferment stable for extended storage.

9.C.1.a.ii. Preferments with flour

Preferments made with 60% or more of the formula's flour are quite comparable to traditional sponges, except that they contain nearly all of the dough water. Their formulation, therefore, is also quite similar insofar as most of the salt, as well as the sugar, milk, oxidants, etc., are withheld. These dough ingredients are subsequently added in a separate slurry at the dough premix stage.

Preferment temperatures normally range from 28 to 29°C (82 to 84°F) for those containing up to 10% of the formula's flour, down to 26 to 27°C (78 to 80°F) for those with 50% or more of the flour. During fermentation, that temperature can rise by 5 to 6 C° (10 to 12 F°). Refrigeration-jacketed tanks will control this temperature increase, or the preferment can be run through a heat exchanger before going to a cooled holding tank. Lower temperatures minimize foaming and fluctuations in the ferment's density that may cause erratic metering. Moreover, they improve fermentation tolerance and reduce the risk of the formation of potentially deleterious fermentation by-products. On the other hand, they tend to extend the fermentation time to about 3 hours, thereby imposing the need for larger fermentation tank capacities.

The flour feeder delivers from 25 to 60 lb of flour per minute to the premixer at an accurate, predetermined rate. This pre-mixer is in the form of a horizontal cylinder with a cone-shaped, end that feeds into a dough metering pump. The pump is equipped with a variable pitch screw conveyor that mixes the liquid ferment and added dough ingredients into a homogeneous mass under pressures of 3 to 5 psi before it feeds the mixture into the continuous mixer or liquid batch hopper.

The circular stainless steel tanks involved in preparing preferments have capacities ranging from 15 gal for the constant level tank, to about 60 gal for both the oxidant and shortening tanks. The first of these, if used, holds a sufficient supply of oxidant solution for about 8 hours of production, while the capacity of the liquid, shortening tank is adequate for about 4 hours of production.

Sizes for the preferment system's holding tanks are governed by the desired production capacity, which may range from a low of 3,000 lb to as high as 18,000 lb of dough per hour. To correctly size a liquid flour ferment system, the engineer must take into consideration two requirements: (a) each 1,000 lb of mixed dough will need 60 gal of gas-free liquid ferment, and (b) the maximum loading limit of the fermentation tank must not exceed 50% of its cubic content (Euverard 1967). For example, a production line with an hourly capacity of 7,000 lb of dough requires a 1,000-gal blending tank, two 800-gal fermentation tanks and a 460-gal refrigerated or cold holding tank.

The tanks for batch makeup and fermentation of high-flour ferments normally use a dome-topped, cone-bottomed design, with a relatively large bottom discharge opening to ensure adequate flow rates for the viscous ferment. The fermented liquid sponge is transferred through a plate heat exchanger into a jacketed holding tank and from there to a weighing system that feeds precise batches of the ferment into the dough mixers.

The makeup tanks in such a system normally are equipped with a squirrel cage agitator to facilitate the rapid blending of the flour into the water, with the flour fed into the tank by a scale hopper above the tank. The duration of the agitator action requires close control to avoid undesirable gluten washout.

The fresh ferment is usually transferred into a special fermentation tank equipped with a slow-speed sweeping agitator to maintain uniform temperature and density conditions throughout the ferment. When the fermentation period ends, the ferment is passed through a plate heat exchanger to lower its temperature to 10 to 18°C (50 to 65°F). Ferments at the lower temperature are more stable in the cold holding tank and facilitate temperature control of the doughs during mixing, but they also prolong mixing time. Ferments at the upper temperature level reduce mixing time, but they cannot generally be held overnight in the cold tank (Thompson 1980). Yeast is nearly dormant at 10°C (50°F) and causes very little change in pH or titratable acidity, but at 18°C (65°F), acidity slowly increases during prolonged holding. A com-

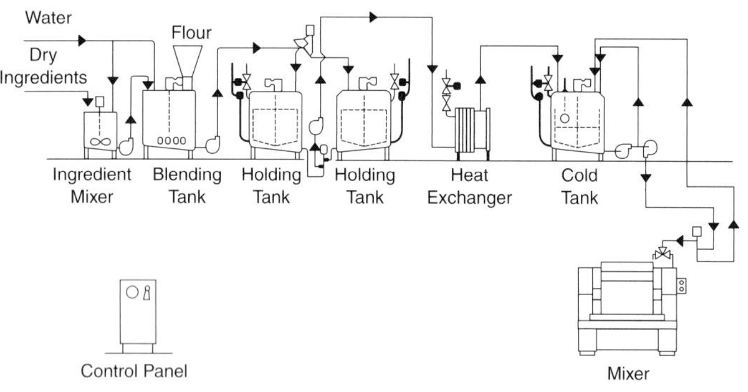

Figure 9.080. A liquid ferment system blends ingredients, allows them to ferment and holds the resulting intermediate product until called by the mixer for use. (Pyler 1988)

monly followed sequence of operations for the production of liquid flour ferments is depicted schematically in **Figure 9.080** (Euverard 1967).

9.C.1.b. Continuous fermentors

The ferment requirements of a continuous mixing unit call for a relatively large-sized makeup tank. The need for rapidly and uniformly dispersing as much as 2,000 lb of flour in 500 gal of dough water by means of a high-shear agitator without causing gluten separation or other undesirable effects in the flour slurry often presents difficulties. These can be circumvented by the use of a system for ferment preparation that, in effect, is a continuous sponge mixer. Two different types of such equipment are shown in **Figures 9.081** and **9.082**. These units consist essentially of a small flow-through type mixer into which the required ingredients (flour, water, yeast slurry, etc.) are introduced by accurate metering feeders (Fortmann 1967b, Watkins 1965).

Automatic spongemakers were developed to handle preferment makeup for high-volume production. These units continuously combine the yeast suspension, the various slurries of yeast food, sweeteners and remaining minor ingredients with the flour and additional water into a relatively viscous ferment and transfer the latter to a fermentation tank. When that tank becomes filled, the flow of ferment is automatically switched to the next empty tank.

The next step up in capacity for automatic preparation of liquid sponges is the flow-through continuous fermentor. A representative installation of a continuous system of liquid sponge making and fermentation is shown in **Figure 9.083**. According to Thompson (1980), liquid ferment systems may be used to advantage for single product lines with hourly capacities as low as 3,000 lb of dough.

One of the drawbacks of most tank fermentation systems is the difficulty of achieving complete homogeneity of the ferments reaching the dough mixer because of inevitable variations in the age of the individual ferments. A major step toward solution of this problem came with the introduction, in 1971, of a continuous method of fermentation (Hancock 1971). The heart of the system is a large, rectangular tank (**Figure 9.084**), divided into two compartments by a slanting baffle and whose bottom slopes gently toward a discharge well (**Figure 9.085**). The practical operation of the continuous fermentor depends on the fact that a liquid ferment made with 65 to 70% of flour, when left undisturbed, undergoes well-defined changes in its density. Thus, a ferment will show a steady, measurable decline in its density during the first hour of fermentation, only to have its density increase again and reach a maximum 2 hours later. Thereafter, the density of the ferment remains constant over a period of several hours.

In practice, fresh liquid ferment from a continuous spongemaker is introduced by a standpipe at a constant rate into the

Figure 9.081. A flow-through mixer supplies a continual stream of liquid sponge to the preferment system. (Pyler 1988)

Figure 9.082. This continuous liquid sponge maker features a fully automated metering system. (Pyler 1988)

Figure 9.083. This liquid sponge fermenting system uses an automatic sponge maker (left foreground) and a continuous fermentor (center background). (Pyler 1988)

Figure 9.084. This installation of a continuous liquid fermentor uses an automatic liquid sponge mixer (foreground). (Hancock 1971)

Figure 9.085. Cross-section diagram shows movement of the sponge within a continuous liquid sponge fermentor. (Hancock 1971)

first compartment of the continuous fermentor (**Figure 9.086**). As the liquid begins to ferment, its density decreases from about 10 lb per gal to less than 5 lb per gal after 1 hour. The lower-density ferment is gradually forced upward by the continual infeed of fresh ferment until it reaches the upper rim of the adjustable baffle and begins to overflow into the second compartment. Here, the change in its density reverses, increasing as fermentation continues. This change causes older, more fully fermented liquid sponge to settle to the bottom and to gravitate toward the lower discharge end of the tank. A pump draws off the mature ferment for transfer to the dough mixer, degassing it in the process. The temperature of the ferment is controlled by the temperature of the fresh material, and the throughput of the system can be adjusted to meet the requirements of the dough mixers. The system is said to improve bread quality and to be more economical to operate because a single tank replaces a series of tanks that would otherwise be required.

The design of another commercial continuous liquid sponge fermentor uses mechanical means to move the sponge through the system in a way that ensures uniform age for all portions of the ferment reaching the dough mixer (Alwes and Jolly 1974). As shown in **Figure 9.087**, the fermentor is a large, horizontally-positioned cylindrical tank that houses a so-called transfer reel.

Shown in schematic illustration by **Figure 9.088**, the reel's central shaft supports both a series of perpendicular disks, whose diameter corresponds closely to the inside diameter of the tank, and flat horizontal partitions that divide each of the smaller circular compartments into two semicircular sections. This arrangement, in effect, provides the vessel with a number of individual compartments that control the flow of the ferment.

The disks have openings alternately located at the periphery and at the central shaft. The discs with central openings also have gates at their periphery that may be opened and closed. The gates are closed during the filling and operating periods to force the ferment to follow a predetermined path through the vessel. During the emptying phase, the gates open to allow direct passage of the ferment when it is at a low level. The gates are adjacent to the partitions that are offset successively to a slight degree, thereby providing a gentle slope that assists the ferment to flow out of the fermentor.

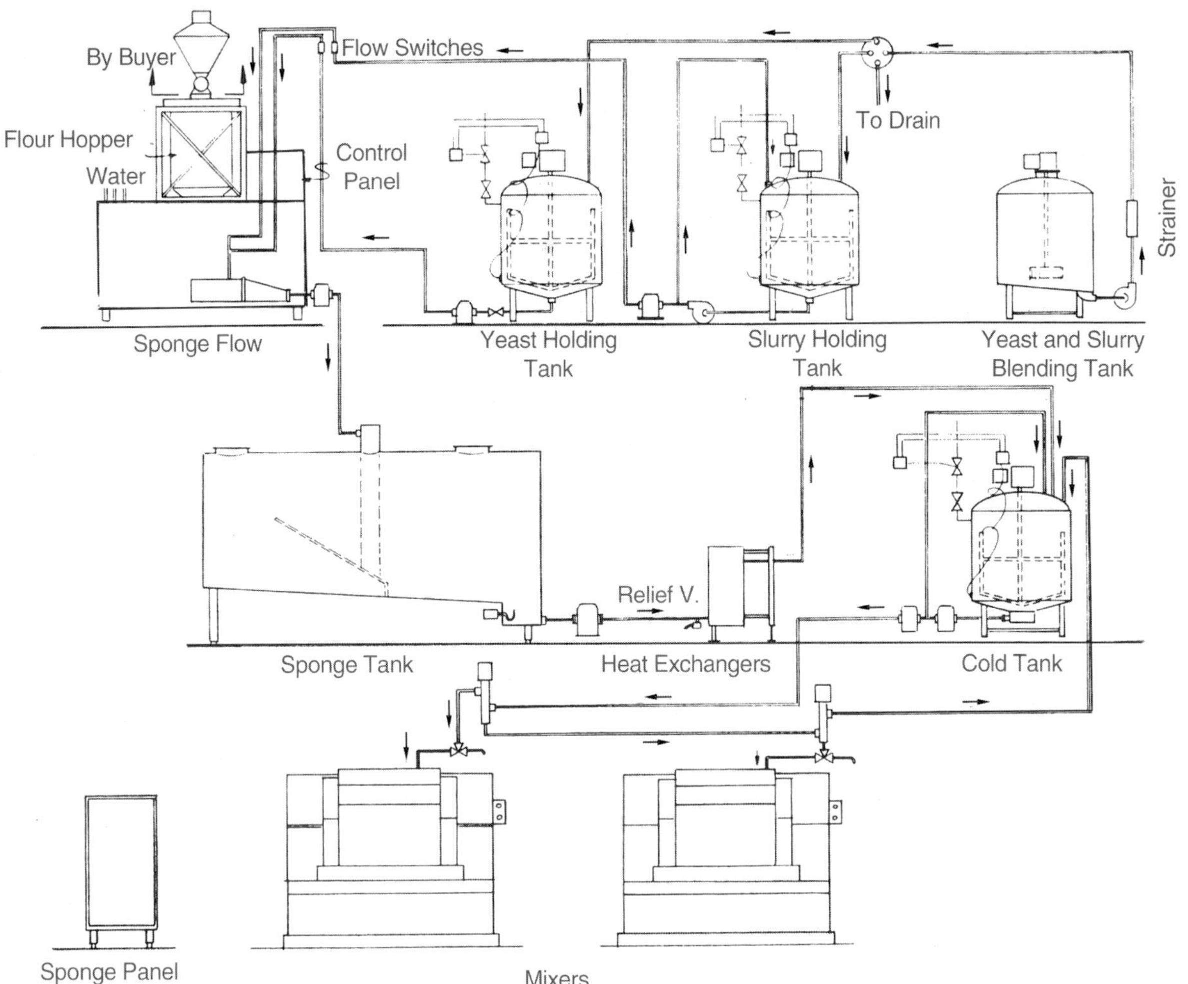

Figure 9.086. From the continuous spongemaker (top left), materials flow into the sponge tank (center left) for bulk fermentation, then to the cold tank (center right) and finally the mixers (bottom).
(Hancock 1971)

In operation, the fresh ferment enters the vessel at the bottom of one end. As the reel rotates slowly, the ferment is progressively advanced from compartment to compartment. After the desired fermentation time has elapsed and the ferment level has reached the rated capacity, the discharge pump withdraws mature ferment at a rate that equals that of the inlet pump so that a constant ferment level and fermentation time are maintained. At the end of the production run, the supply pump stops, while the ferment continues to be drawn from the vessel until the latter is completely empty.

9.C.1.c. Sour dough systems

New technology that transforms sour dough fermentation into a continuous process has received strong acceptance in Europe. This system grew out of a research project conducted at the Technical University of Berlin with the equipment-building assistance of a major German bakery equipment manufacturer (Anon. 1993). Installations of this technology are now in everyday use at several German, Austrian and Danish bakeries. Tests have been conducted at Italian and American plants, too. Most of these locations produce rye-based sourdough products, although wheat-flour sour doughs are also being made on these systems. Installa-

Figure 9.087. An interior transfer reel operated by a variable-speed drive transfers sponge through this continuous liquid sponge fermentor. (Pyler 1988)

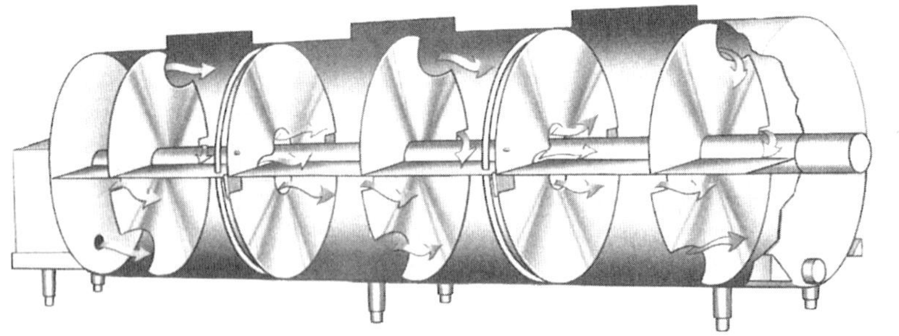

Figure 9.088. The transfer reel of the positive-flow continuous fermentor features circular and horizontal partitions that compartmentalize the tank's interior. (Pyler 1988)

tions range in size from 250 to 5,000 kg per hour (550 to 11,000 lb per hour).

The commercial sour dough fermentation systems are configured as 1- or 2-stage processes, depending on volume desired and product range. Continuous mixers feed raw materials into both systems. This equipment is run by computer and can be integrated with automated ingredient delivery systems and CIM systems.

The 2-stage system, with its separate fermentation tube and fermentation tank, is more flexible than a single-stage unit because the tube and the tank can be fed independently. The fermentation tube provides a high ratio of surface-to-dough contact and is, essentially, a first-in, first-out system. Should downstream operations be halted, the temperature of the fermentation tube can be reduced to slow fermentation down. In the second stage (the fermentation tank), the baker can vary the dough by adding rye or wheat flours and by changing the acidity of the sourdough. From the tank, the mature sour is metered into dough mixers according to formula needs.

In the 1-stage system (**Figure 9.089**), the fermentation tube is linked to a storage tank. The mature dough is conveyed from the fermentation tube to a hopper where the dough is divided. Half returns to the continuous mixer, and the rest is cooled to 10 to 15°C (50 to 59°F) and pumped to the storage tank. To mix batches of the final dough, operators draw sourdough supplies from the storage tank.

Over weekend breaks or when operations are interrupted, the tube is cooled to arrest fermentation. Activity can be restored within a couple of hours in contrast to the usual long "set" time for re-starting batch sourdoughs.

9.C.2. Dough troughs

The purpose of dough troughs is to transfer mixed doughs from a mixer to the next processing operation. They most often are rectangular in shape and mounted on 4 casters to allow easy movement around the facility floor. They are generally fabricated of stainless steel or standard steel, with such design features as rolled top rims (sealed to prevent microbial growth), sanitary caster shoes and smoothly ground welded interior seams and corners, with polished seams, all of which serve to facilitate sanitary maintenance. (In the baker's parlance, the word "trough" is pronounced "tro," with a long "o.")

Troughs serve as the primary vessel for bulk fermentation. For some products, notably crackers, they often help inoculate the dough with the micro-organisms that provide a characteristic flavor and texture. They are available in a wide selection of cubic capacities to accommodate different sponge and dough volumes. In general, dough troughs will vary in width from 26 to 31.5 in., in height from 21 to nearly 34 in. and in length from 4 to more than 12 ft. Their cubic capacities range from 31.5 to 84 cu ft, or the equivalent of 175 to 1,090 lb of sponge and 400 to 3,360 lb of finished dough. The disparity in the respective weights of sponges and doughs that a given trough can accommodate is due to their different degrees of aeration; thus, a finished sponge will weigh about 13 lb per cu ft, whereas a finished dough generally weighs about 60 lb per cu ft.

Dough troughs come in many styles, but their primary design features must facilitate unloading of dough from the mixer to the trough. The styles include (a) standard troughs (**Figure 9.090**), in which all 4 sides are permanently secured and which at present constitute the most prevalent trough; (b) drop-side troughs of increased capacities, made possible by higher sides, to accommodate the output of large mixers, in which one-third of one longitudinal section was hinged at standard trough height so the upper part could be dropped outward to adjust to the height of the mixer bowl during unloading; (c) slide-end troughs in which one of the end walls could be removed for dough discharge; (d) end-gate troughs that feature one end with a hinged lower section that can be opened for trough emptying; (e) rack-end or controlled-flow end troughs (**Figure 9.091**) in which one end wall can be raised for the controlled discharge of dough into the divider hopper; (f) chute-end troughs in which approximately one-third of the lower section of an end wall opens outwardly to form an abbreviated chute for dough discharge; (g) slide-bottom troughs that were equipped with a movable bottom panel for emptying; and (h) sloping-bottom troughs with a gate at the lower end. All the latter styles were designed to facilitate the feeding of divider hoppers from an elevated position.

Bakery experts recommend that dough troughs be individually numbered so that they can be easily tracked especially during the fermentation, proofing or laytime cycle. In this way, doughs are sequentially controlled during the process and experience an equal time frame for the reactions to be completed prior to the forming stage. Additionally, troughs used for doughs may also be labeled with their tare weights, thus simplifying the job of reporting dough quantities when the entire trough is weighed by a floor-mounted scale.

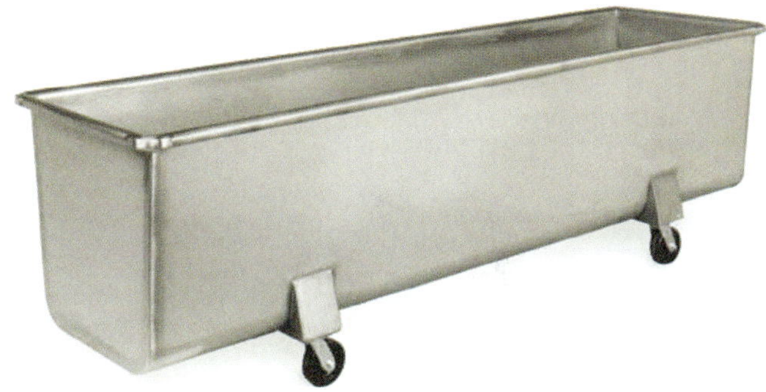

Figure 9.089. By pumping a slurry mixture of starter, flour, water and other ingredients into one end of the fermentation tube of this continuous sour dough system, bakers can draw a fully fermented sourdough from the storage tank at the other end. (Reimelt)

Figure 9.090. A standard medium-sized bakery trough features wheeled castors. (AMF Bakery Systems).

9.C.3. Hoists and elevators

Transfer of the sponge from the dough trough into the dough mixer or of the finished dough into the divider hopper can be done in three ways: (a) by cutting

Figure 9.091. Controlled flow end gates raise to enable dough discharge. (AMF Bakery Systems).

manually the dough mass into smaller portions and tossing these into the mixer or divider hopper; (b) by using a dough pump immediately in front of the tilting bowl mixer or affixed to the trough and connected directly to the divider hopper; and (c) by elevating the trough to a level above the infeed point of either the dough mixer or the divider hopper and letting the sponge or dough flow by gravity into the respective inlets. Bartsch (1999) and Schmidt (2002) summarized these methods.

(Dough pumps, conveyors and chunkers will be described in Part D of this chapter.)

Bakeries in which the mixing and fermentation rooms are located above the makeup department generally can make use of end-gated sloping-bottom troughs that permit the dough to be delivered by gravity into a through-the-floor chute that feeds into the divider hopper below. In bakeries where the production department occupies a single floor, various types of hoists may be used to transfer the dough. Hoists available for this purpose include overhead hoists, hydraulic floor lifts, elevator hoists and cradle-type hoists.

Overhead hoists make use of motor-powered steel cables or chains for elevating the troughs. With the hoist assembly mounted on overhead tracks, these devices are able to move the troughs laterally and can thus serve several mixers and dividers. Either chute-end or rack-end troughs are normally used with these overhead hoists.

The pneumatic floor lift is a single-ram hoist operated by compressed air or hydraulic fluid. It is most frequently encountered in baking plants with limited headroom. Because it occupies a fixed position, it can serve only one mixer or divider.

Most common, however, are elevator hoists (**Figure 9.092**). They consist of 2 upright, vertical or slightly inclined legs, equipped with a powered lifting mechanism that engages the dough trough and raises it in a level position until it reaches the dumping height when the trough is tilted to discharge the dough by gravity into a wide chute that feeds into the mixer or the divider hopper. Here again, the hoist is permanently fixed in one position to serve a single mixer or divider. Trough discharge height can be 6 to 20 ft or more above floor level. At least one manufacturer developed a safety chain approach with 2 lift chains on each end. One chain lifts the trough, while the second can carry the load if the main chain breaks.

The cradle hoist resembles the elevator hoist in that it also features two parallel columns equipped with a drive shaft that powers the lifting arms that support the trough cradle. Once the trough is rolled into position on the cradle, the cradle traverses an arched path as it moves upward. This motion tilts the trough as it reaches the discharge point and the sponge or dough is released into the chute of the receiving unit.

Figure 9.092. Trough hoists come with safety latches to prevent the cradle and trough from falling in the unlikely event that the drive chain breaks. (Shaffer, a Bundy Bakery Solution)

9.C.4. Trough fermentation rooms

Bulk fermentation of bread and bun doughs using troughs also requires a heat-and-humidity controlled area, generally configured as a low-ceilinged room right next to the mixers. Control over the environment in this area critically affects product quality. For example, rising temperatures accelerate yeast activity, while low temperatures retard it. Low humidity prompts formation of crusts on sponges, denser areas that do not reincorporate well during final mixing and form spots or lumps in the baked product.

Fermentation rooms, as defined by Pfening (1955), come in a variety of designs and constructions, but most of their essential features are standard among different manufacturers. The insulated rooms are usually configured with separate entrance and exit doors for troughs, as well as personnel access doors, and bumper guards at trough rim height protect the interior walls. It is essential that the room floor be perfectly level. An air conditioning unit, located outside the room, provides heat, humidity and cooling through ducting into the room.

Capacity is determined by multiplying the required batches per hour by the number of mixers and by the amount of fermentation time. Thus, with 1 sponge mixer producing 4 batches per hour each with 4 hours of fermentation for the sponge dough, a baker would need capacity for 16 troughs (**Figure 9.093**).

These first-in, first-out rooms (**Figure 9.094**) operate in semi-automatic and automatic fashion, with cycle times that match dough schedules. In semi-automatic mode, the mixer operator moves the trough from the sponge mixer to the inlet door and into the room. With the trough's casters engaged by stainless steel runways bolted to the floor, the room's system of transport cradles move the trough though its journey. Heavy, pneumatically powered knock-down bars, positioned at one or more locations within the room, degass the dough. Hydraulically powered cradles facilitate trough movement. When the sponge trough is emptied into the final dough mixer, it is pushed into place at the sponge mixer to receive another batch. A trough oiling station is provided to prepare for the next batch of dough.

Automatic systems differ in that room loading, trough movement and even transfer to the hoist cradle are sequenced automatically, thus the sponge and dough mixers as well as the hoist must be installed in close proximity to the fermentation room.

Recommended conditions for the fermentation of sponges call for a temperature of 27°C (80°F) and a relative humidity (RH) of 75 to 80%. The relative humidity is controlled by the wet bulb control or humidistat. This instrument should preferably be fully automatic in operation and sufficiently precise to maintain the preset dry bulb temperature within a variance no greater than 0.6 C° (1 F°) and the relative humidity within 0.5% of the designated level. This degree of accuracy is attainable by a control system that incorporates highly sensitive thermostats which, in response to changes in the temperature, will activate the appropriate solenoid valves that initiate the heating, cooling and humidification functions of the air-conditioning system.

The fermentation room's air distribution system should be able to make at least 6 changes of air per hour. It should be equipped with efficient impingement

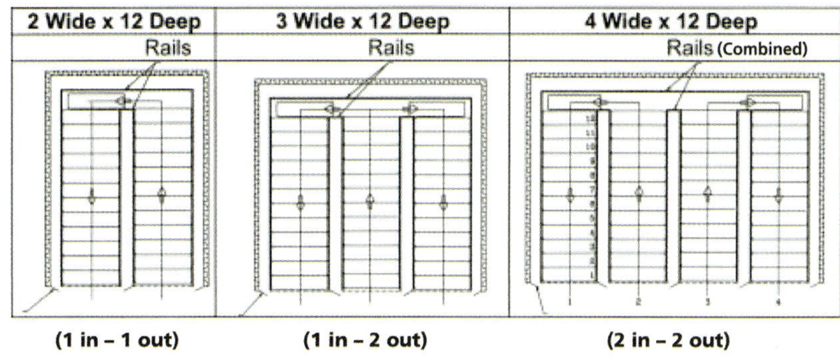

Figure 9.093. Different configurations for fermentation rooms permit increasing numbers of troughs. (Turkington USA)

Figure 9.094. This fermentation room moves dough troughs through bulk fermentation and returns them for final mixing. (Turkington USA)

Figure 9.095. Storage-and-retrieval technology, applied to dough trough management, allows flexibility in fermentation times and production schedules.
(Weldon Solutions)

filters to purify the circulating air and be provided with air diffusers of a design that will ensure a uniform air distribution within the enclosed space without creating drafts or air stratification (White 1970).

Cracker doughs are typically also assigned a separate room for bulk fermentation, but because of the longer time required for this process (12 to 24 hours vs. 4 hours for bread or bun doughs), the room must be considerably larger.

9.C.5. Automatic trough handling systems

In recent years, automatic trough systems have been developed that further automate the fermentation room function. Using the principles of automatic-storage-and-retrieval systems (ASRS), these systems manage each batch of dough separately, doing away with the need for first-in, first-out sequencing. Troughs of fermenting doughs are inventoried into random-access storage racks to be retrieved in any sequence desired by the computer-integrated-manufacturing (CIM) system (**Figure 9.095**). Although these systems require significant capital investment, they allow considerable flexibility in both dough fermentation time and production schedules. The optimum fermentation time can be achieved for each dough variety, and a single system can be used to feed different doughs into each separate production line, thus maximizing production flexibility (Anon. 1993).

Such flexibility pays off by enhancing the freshness performance of the bakery. To get the freshest product to the market often requires that production schedules cycle through items more than once a day. A given product might be baked early for transport to remote depots and again later in the day for distribution on local routes. The "random access" aspect to automated storage and handling techniques adjusts well to such needs, whether handling fermenting doughs or multiple pan styles (Gorton 1994).

The troughs used by the multi-level storage and retrieval system have no casters. This design eliminates expensive floor damage, simplifies cleaning and removes a common maintenance problem. No human handling is required — a big asset in these times when skilled help is hard to find and insurance rates, especially for workers' compensation, are rising rapidly. Instead, a transfer vehicle equipped with a shuttle car runs through the open core of the racks. The car rises and descends to pick up and set down the troughs. The transfer vehicle can include a degassing device.

When a dough is ready for bulk fermentation, the system sends the transfer vehicle to the correct mixer, moving its shuttle car to the mixer discharge station where a trough is waiting. When filled with dough, the trough and car return to the transfer vehicle, and the whole assembly moves through the rack structure, bringing the shuttle car up to the level of an open storage slot. After placing the trough in the slot, the car returns to the transfer vehicle for the start of another cycle.

The location of each trough is tracked by computer so the control system knows where each batch of dough is stored and how long it has been in the fermentation system. At the point of optimum fermentation or as called by the CIM system, the trough is released by the system for further processing.

The transfer vehicle travels to the designated trough slot, and the shuttle cart removes the filled trough. The transfer vehicle moves to the discharge slot, and the cart takes the filled trough to the dump station. A separate mechanism tips the trough to release its contents into the final mixer, divider hopper or other processing equipment, as needed. The empty trough is recycled, returned to the mixer discharge station or put back into the rack empty at the close of production.

9.D. Makeup Equipment
Updated by Sigismondo De Tora

Following its proper development, either by bulk fermentation or appropriate mechanical or chemical treatment, dough enters the next stage of the production process in which it is divided into individual product units of specific weight and shape. The standard equipment involved in these operations include, in sequential order: (a) the divider, which scales the bulk dough into units of predetermined weight; (b) the rounder, which imparts a spherical form to the unsymmetrical dough pieces emerging from the divider and simultaneously seals their raw cut surfaces with a fine skin to prevent excessive loss of the evolving carbon dioxide gas; (c) the intermediate or overhead proofer, which briefly rests the rounded dough pieces to recover from the physical abuse they have sustained during dividing and rounding; and (d) the sheeter/moulder/panner, which sheets and moulds the dough pieces into their final loaf form, expelling most of its gas in the process, then places the pieces into the pans after they leave the moulder.

The made-up dough pieces, placed into pans or on peel boards or baking sheets, next pass into the final proofer in which they undergo a vigorous final fermentation under near-optimum environmental conditions until they have attained the appropriate height or volume. From the final proofer, they are then conveyed directly into the oven for baking. The modifications in physical properties that doughs undergo during this sequence of treatments are detailed in Chapter 6.

9.D.1. Dough transfer systems

Dough troughs and trough hoists represent one way to transfer dough from mixing and fermentation operations to makeup lines. Dough pumps are another method, one that eliminates troughs and hoists. Typically configured as a wide bin with an auger set into its bottom, the pump accepts the final mixer's full batch and then creates a steady stream of dough flowing onto narrow divider-feed conveyors or directly into the divider hopper itself. The open auger causes some release of entrapped gasses, and degassing is an established function of dough pumping. Chunkers are also used on more sensitive doughs to move them from the discharge of a final roller-bar mixer to the divider hopper. Like pumps, chunkers accept the final mixer's full batch and then use rotating "star" wheels to separate dough in segments from the mass, sending these segments via conveyor to the hopper.

9.D.1.a. Dough pumps and degassers
Yeasted doughs require degassing for several reasons (Harris 1985). The first, and perhaps most important, is to improve scaling accuracy. Savings in dough piece weight of a fraction of an ounce per piece can result in thousands of dollars saved over the long-term life of a degassing machine. Second is to increase the run time of the dough or to run larger batches. A degasser improves the final product quality by providing greater uniformity of dough, which translates into improved downstream operations.

During the developmental or fermentation process, dough gradually reduces in density as a result of continuing carbon dioxide gas generation by yeast. Borthwick (1973) reported practical tests in which the weight of 62 lb per cu ft of a dough fresh out of the mixer decreased to only 52 lb per cu ft after a floor time of 20 minutes — and 20 minutes is the average time required to divide a dough.

This change in dough density of nearly 20% within a relatively short time span accounts for the fact that dough pieces of the same volumetric size are measurably heavier at the start of the dividing run than at the end, that is if no corrective volumetric adjustments in the dough pockets of the divider are made. In practice, regular adjustments in the size of the divided dough pieces are required if they are to remain at a constant weight.

Historically, an acceptable accuracy tolerance for ram-and-knife style dividers was approximately 2 to 3%. To avoid the possibility of short weight in the finished baked product, scaling weights were generally set above the minimum or exact weight by amounts proportional to the scaling variation. If the dough can be kept at constant density, then dividers can be set for much less deviance in scaling weight.

Seeking improved ways to transfer doughs from mixers and troughs into divider hoppers, bakery engineers experimented with pumping. In the process, they also invented the dough degasser. Being pumped releases a portion of the gas from yeasted doughs, and some pumps do a better job of it than others. Selecting the best available dough pump and degasser will allow the baker to ensure that dough of proper density and viscoelastic properties is delivered to the divider. By doing so, not only will the divider tolerance to be held within much narrower limits, but also these units greatly reduce the need for the wasteful practice of over-scaling as a safeguard against short weight.

Additional benefits derived from using dough pumps and degassers include improved pan flow, the ability to process larger dough batches over more extended period of time, enhanced dough tolerance during short production interruptions and greater convenience in conveying the dough from the trough to the divider hopper (Tesch 1971).

Dough pumps and degassers are available in two basic designs: a rotary pump type and an auger screw type (Pierce 1974, Harris 1985). The rotary dough pump, represented schematically in **Figure 9.096**, features 2 lobed rotors, turning outwardly in opposite directions, which shear small amounts of dough from the bulk and force them against the pump casing and toward the outlet port. In the process, the dough is subjected to both high and low pressure conditions that cause it to eject the entrapped gas, which is then vented through grooves or special openings in the pump cover.

According to Borthwick (1973), the rotary dough pump contributes very little if any additional dough development as judged by the absence of any increase in the dough temperature at the exit port of the pump. The usually observed temperature rise of 0.6 to 2 C° (1 to 3 F°) in the dough as delivered to the divider hopper is generally attributed to the frictional effect of the feed pipe. The rotary dough pump may form part either of an upright dough hopper of appropriate cubic capacity or

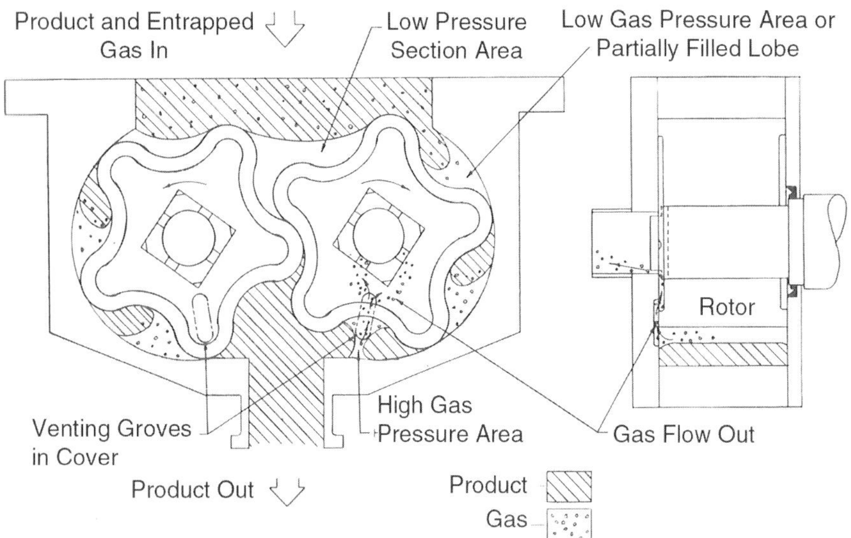

Figure 9.096. The operation of a rotary dough degasser involves subjecting dough to both high and low pressure. (Thompson 1977)

of a special portable trough. It may also, in the case of bun dividers, be mounted above the divider hopper.

In degassers and dough pumps of the auger type, the dough at the bottom of the hopper is drawn into the moving flights of the rotating auger and forced toward the discharge port. This action effectively de-aerates the dough, and the liberated carbon dioxide gas is released to the atmosphere through a vent hole in the auger housing (**Figure 9.097**). The initial degassing is frequently augmented by further conditioning of the dough, performed by a smaller auger that forces the dough through a restricted fluted cylindrical chamber, thus imparting additional development or texturing to the dough (Pierce 1974).

The simplest arrangement uses a single screw to transport dough to the metering pump. The advantage is mechanical simplicity — less maintenance is needed. It is also very gentle and does not increase dough development so the dough delivered to the screw hopper should be fully developed. Some single-auger pumps use vacuum to urge dough into the auger flights, removing excess gas and trapped air out the rear of the auger.

High-speed bun lines are more likely to have a single- or twin-screw pump extruder, in which the counter-rotating screws are interlocked like in simple cooking extruder designs. The advantage of this design is a more positive delivery of dough to the pump; however, the increased work will produce some additional gluten development so the dough should be slightly under-mixed. The baker will need to do some experimentation to determine the proper degree of under-mixing for his specific product. Typically on pumped or extruded doughs, the dough must be fully developed, or else the extra work in the process may produce a weak grain structure. Thus, it is imperative to make sure the protein strands in the mixed dough are fully developed, which may require extended mix time, additional water or both.

Bread lines are more likely to employ a chunker, where counter-rotating "star wheel" rotors act to separate "logs" of dough from the mass and place them onto a conveyor. No additional work is imparted to the dough by a chunker and no temperature rise, suiting this method to dough that would otherwise be damaged by the shear imparted by pumping.

A third variation uses a single screw plus a texturizing paddle in front of the metering pump. This arrangement produces the most dough development of the three types. Typically located above the hopper of the divider, this developer adds a flexible degree of development to the dough just prior to dividing. This provides the optimum dough condition for accurate scaling and consistent grain quality.

Again the baker needs to determine the level of mixing required to compensate for the extra work. Another design employs an open, large-pitch spiral, without the usual central shaft. It can handle up to 20,000 lb of dough per hour, moving it without raising its temperature. Power needs are low, less than 2 hp compared with the 10-hp and 15-hp motors required by conventional dough pumps.

In addition to dough pumps and degassers per se, other dough processing units are designed principally to develop or texturize the dough, particularly in the production of buns (Harris 1985, Campbell 1979, Campbell 2009). These "texturizing"

Figure 9.097. In an auger-style degasser, the twin-screw auger and open hopper eliminate the need for vacuum systems. (AMF Bakery Systems)

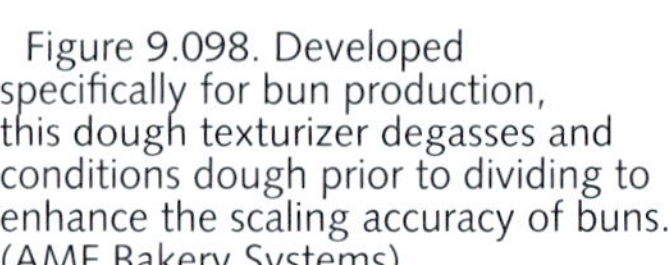

systems come in several variations, with either single- or dual-shaft augers or rotors equipped with vanes or paddles powered by variable-speed drives and which may be positioned either above the divider hopper (**Figure 9.098**) or be of the free-standing kind. To handle stiff doughs, the texturizer can be equipped with a 4-paddle blade instead of the usual 2-paddle design. These systems have throughput ranges of up to 10,000 lb per hour. They are particularly effective for soft hamburger and wiener bun doughs, but less so for hearth bread and hard roll items. New versions of the developers can handle up to 15,000 lb per hour of bun or bread dough.

Because dough texturizers, sometimes called "kneaders," increase the dough temperature by an average of 1.6 to 2.7 C° (3 to 5 F°) because of their mechanical action, doughs intended for post-mixing development should leave the dough mixer at a temperature that is lower by the same margin. Since the friction in the conveying line from the pump to the divider hopper also acts to raise dough temperature, the pump must be located no farther than 15 ft from the divider, unless the dough transfer is by means of a belt. Otherwise, doughs with excessively high final temperatures, and concomitant sticky properties, will reach the divider (Farmer 1973).

Figure 9.098. Developed specifically for bun production, this dough texturizer degasses and conditions dough prior to dividing to enhance the scaling accuracy of buns. (AMF Bakery Systems)

9.D.1.b. Dough conveyors

Additional automation of dough transfer can be accomplished by installing a vertical dough conveyor at the dough pump's discharge port. This transport method carries dough between 2 closely spaced, parallel belts, mounted at steeply inclined angles up to 90° (**Figure 9.099**). Single-belt conveyors can manage dough at inclines up to 30°. The concave belt system keeps the dough centered, while the FDA-approved polystick belts and a belt scraper prevent dough from sticking. The vertical belts move in tandem to draw dough, now sandwiched between them, up to horizontal distribution belts that supply one or more divider hoppers.

The horizontal distribution belt that accepts dough from the vertical conveyor can be configured to serve multiple divider hoppers by using reversible motion. The flow direction changes according to feedback from sensors monitoring the level of dough in the hoppers. Cut-off knives at the ends of these conveyors prevent dough from being pulled back out the hopper when the belt's direction changes.

Use of dough conveyors to replace intermediate proofers is discussed in Chapter 10.

9.D.1.c. Dough chunkers

Although biscuit lines frequently use chunking techniques to move stiff doughs from mixers to the supply hoppers that feed rotary cookie lines, this method is a relatively new approach to dough transfer for bread and bun products (Gorton 2001b). Some spiral mixers discharge doughs from bowl ports in pieces, each chunk weighing a few pounds. Now, a chunking system, also termed a rotary dough feeder, accepts batches directly from horizontal mixers, transforming the large batch into smaller sized chunks.

The chunker's hopper narrows to send dough into a set of elongated star wheels or rotors (**Figure 9.100**). The counter-rotating wheels carve out a log-shaped "slug" of dough from the bottom of the mass and release it to a conveyor belt below. The diameter and length of the cutting wheels determine the quantity of dough per chunk. Falling onto the take-away conveyor, the slugs transfer piece by piece into divider

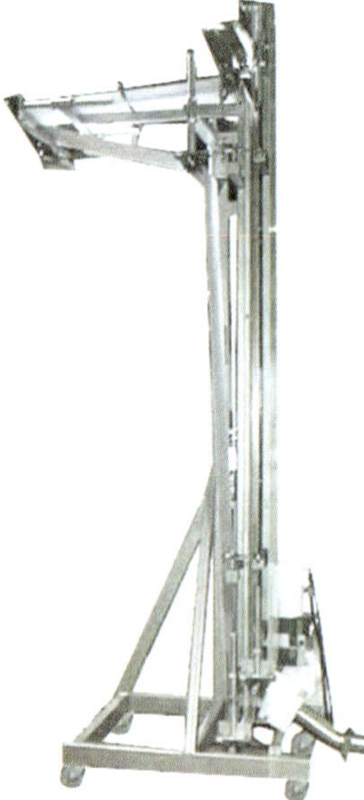

Figure 9.099. Two closely spaced belts carry dough between them, moving it from the dough pump's discharge port up to horizontal distribution belts that lead to dough dividers. (AMF Bakery Systems)

hoppers, thus improving scaling and forming accuracy.

This method imparts less energy or temperature rise to the doughs it handles and thus is particularly well suited to transfer of many low-absorption doughs and most doughs that will be made into frozen dough products (Bartsch 1999). Rotary dough transfer systems have been designed to handle more than 12,000 lb of dough per hour from one mixer or 24,000 lb from a 2-mixer arrangement.

9.D.2. Dough dividers

Dividing technology continues to be a crucial component in almost every bakery operation. Regardless of the end product, bakers need to understand the options available in dough portioning systems to select the equipment that will best fit their needs now and into the future. Dividing dough into manageable portions is a fundamental step in the breadmaking process. The original manual method was simple, easy to control, flexible and gentle on the dough; however, this hand approach would not be able to keep up with today's dividing needs.

Today, bakers are still looking for dividers that are simple to operate, provide better weight control, are more flexible and gentle on the dough. The equipment manufacturers have responded by providing systems that are PLC-controlled, use servo-drive motors and include inline checkweighers. These control technologies have significantly improved the ability of bakers to operate at lower weight tolerances and to improve profitability.

Figure 9.100. This rotary dough feeding system delivers blocks, or "slugs," of dough to downstream operations. (The Peerless Group)

This interaction between bakers and equipment has created many different variations in dividers that are better suited for the new type of doughs being processed. Today, bakers can choose from three basic types of dividers: the volumetric ram-and-shear divider, the rotary drum-and-piston divider and the extrusion-type divider (Osborne 1998). Accuracy, flexibility and gentle handling are all important; however, the equipment must also have the capability for handling a wide range of dough types; high-water absorption; rapid, long-development and sensitive doughs; aged doughs; and different bread types. Additionally, dividers should use little to no oil and be easy to clean and maintain.

9.D.2.a. Volumetric ram-and-shear dividers

Although baked products are sold by weight, dough dividers or dough scalers are generally volumetric proportioning devices. They are designed to turn large portions of dough into individual dough pieces that conform as closely as possible to a preset weight. Because this operation is based on volume rather than weight, it is important that external factors such as time, temperature, rate of yeast activity and others be controlled to ensure dough reaches the divider at optimum density to minimize variability in the scaling process.

Doughs should be scaled in as short a time as possible to avoid excessive fluctuations in dough temperature and dough density. Bread and volumetric roll dividers have the capability of operating at maximum speeds of 20 to 50 strokes per minute, or one stroke every 2 to 3 seconds, with doughs that possess optimum viscosity. Extrusion bread dividers can run at 300 loaves per minute, and extrusion bun dividers can produce more than 1,100 buns per minute. Not all doughs, however, are suitable for dividing at such maximum rated speeds, and many bakers consider it better practice to run the machines at more moderate rates to ensure they get filled dough pockets and handle the dough more gently.

Overly extended divider runs are best avoided by a reduction in the batch size of the dough sent to the divider. In cases where an increase in production is needed, a wiser course of action would be to use dividers with a greater number of pockets.

Conventional bread dividing machines may feature from 2 to 8 dough pockets in their division box, thus each stroke of the ram or plunger will scale off 2 to 8 individual pieces of dough of a preset size. Hence, at an operating speed of 20 strokes per minute, an 8-pocket divider will produce 9,600 dough pieces per hour. The range in size to which the individual dough pieces may be scaled is limited by the number of pockets in the machine, with units having the greater number of pockets also having the more limited size range. Thus, a 4-pocket divider will normally have a scaling range of 12 to 48 oz per dough piece, whereas an 8-pocket divider may have a unit range of 6 to 27 oz.

A conventional dough divider (**Figure 9.101**) consists essentially of a sturdy frame, in which the power drive and auxiliary working parts occupy the lower base, while the head houses the dough chamber and division box and supports the dough hopper. A cam-operated dough knife separates the hopper from the dough chamber immediately below it.

The bulk dough, deposited into the hopper by the dough trough, dough conveying belt or dough pump, flows by gravity into the compression chamber. At the outset of the scaling cycle, the knife situated directly under the hopper cuts off the dough in the chamber with a horizontal reciprocal motion and seals the chamber from the hopper. A reciprocating ram or plunger within the dough chamber then forces the dough into a series of individual measuring pockets in the rotary cylindrical division box. The dough chamber is refilled with fresh dough on the ram's return stroke, during which the knife is also drawn back.

At the end of the ram stroke, the cylindrical division box rotates and cuts off the dough pieces as the filled pockets pass the shear edge of the dough chamber. The individual dough pieces are then ejected from the pockets by pistons activated by a regulator-ejector arm and drop onto a conveyor belt immediately below the division box to be transferred to the rounder.

In earlier models of the divider, when the pockets of the reciprocating division box were filled with dough, the whole head passed the shear edge of the dough chamber on its downward stroke to cut off the dough pieces. Volumetric adjustments were made by changing the piston depth in each of the dough pockets.

The divider deposits dough pieces onto a variable-speed conveyor mounted beneath the division box. This conveyor feeds the pieces to a take-away conveyor that operates at a somewhat higher speed to create even spacing between the dough pieces as they reach the rounder. Each of these belt conveyors has a flour dusting box to prevent sticking of the dough pieces.

Design improvements to the traditional ram-and-shear divider include: the use of servo motors and PLC control, and the substitution of hydraulic drives for the cam and lever systems. The hydraulic cylinder uses a linear transducer to determine the position

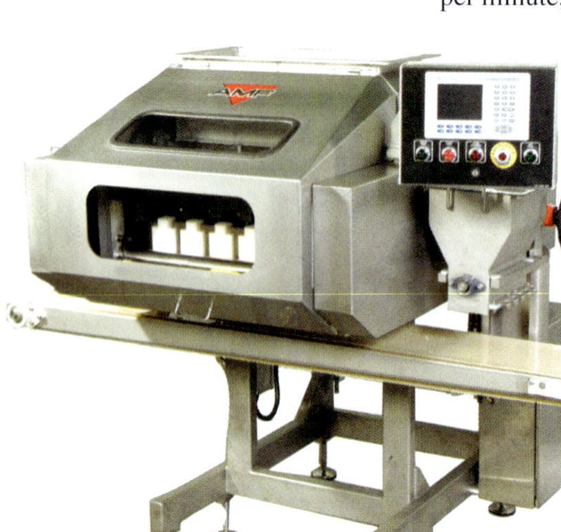

Figure 9.101. This divider combines the technology of ram-and-knife dividing with the precise scaling of the latest servo controls.
(AMF Bakery Systems)

of the ram, and when the ram is slowing down, the system creates a stall signal, which notifies the PLC that enough dough is in the pistons. This feedback significantly improves the scaling accuracy. The addition of inline checkweighing systems, which automatically reject out-of-spec pieces and adjust the scaling hydraulic cylinder, gives the baker the ability to maximize his productivity and virtually eliminate over scaling.

High-absorption doughs require somewhat different dividers (**Figure 9.102**). To make this process as dough friendly as possible, the knife, the volume piston and the slide mechanism movements are all independently powered by servo drives and controlled by dough related software (DRS). Pressure on the volume piston, a preset variable based on dough type, is adjusted by means of the servo drives. Any dough from stiff pizza dough to soft variety bread to artisan-style products can be run on this machine. All movements are independent: The knife closes first, and the dough does not get pushed back into the hopper. The only dough in the hopper is what is being portioned at that time. Because this method imparts less stress on the dough and results in less sticky dough because it is not overworked, higher hydration doughs can be processed on the divider.

Figure 9.102. This divider uses servo drives to independently activate the knife, volume piston and slide mechanism. (Kaak Group North America)

9.D.2.b. Divider lubrication

The lubricating system of ram-and-shear and piston dividers represents an important feature because it has a major bearing on the efficiency of their operation. Freshly-cut dough surfaces exhibit such an extreme stickiness toward metal surfaces that dividing is rendered practically impossible unless the surfaces in contact with the dough are properly coated with thin films of oil.

The lubricant used for this purpose is usually a clear, tasteless and odorless mineral oil of approved specifications. The lubrication system may be either of the gravity type, in which the oil is fed from an elevated reservoir to all critical areas by tubes, with the surplus being drained to a lower receptacle; or it may be of the positive type in which the oil is pumped to the various parts of the dividing mechanism at a controlled rate.

Some dividers use flour instead of oil to aid in the transfer of dough to the dividing and moulding process. In addition to removing the expense and mess factor of oil, the cleaning and sanitation process is also speeded up. According to several manufacturers, an oil-free machine can extend the equipment's work life because, over time, oil can break down the machine's electronic and hardware components. A flour duster is used after the dough is cut to keep the dough from sticking to the discharge belt.

Extrusion type dividers have virtually eliminated the need for oil. The continuous flow principle of the system has no need for lubrication. Another system that uses no lubricating oil are the stuffer-style machines that some food equipment manufacturers have adapted from the meat processing industry.

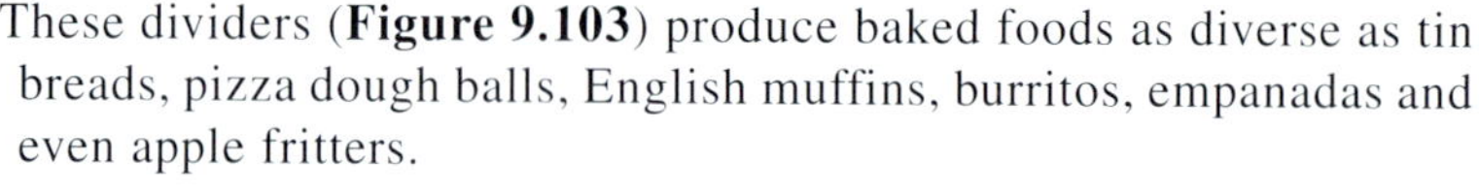

These dividers (**Figure 9.103**) produce baked foods as diverse as tin breads, pizza dough balls, English muffins, burritos, empanadas and even apple fritters.

9.D.2.c. Divider maintenance and sanitation

Aside from purely sanitary considerations, cleaning of dividers deserves great care to prevent the buildup of potentially damaging hard dough films within the scaling mechanism. If the ram-and-shear or piston-style machine is to stand idle for only a brief period, the recommended procedure is to remove all excess dough and pour 0.5 pint of divider oil into the hopper. The machine is then set in motion until the oil has been thoroughly distributed over all the critical surfaces and will thereby prevent the formation of hard dough films.

If the machine is to be cleaned at the end of a day's run, the dough knife, ram and pistons should be removed and washed thoroughly in a sodium carbonate solution, rinsed, dried and wiped with a soft cloth that has been dipped in divider oil. At the same time, the hopper, dough chamber and the dough pockets of the division box should receive equally thorough cleaning. After the completion of cleaning, the scaling head is reassembled, 0.5 pint of divider oil is poured around the inside walls of the hopper and the machine is operated through 2 or 3 cycles to obtain thorough oil distribution. Only wooden or plastic scrapers should be used in dough removal to avoid scoring the metal surfaces.

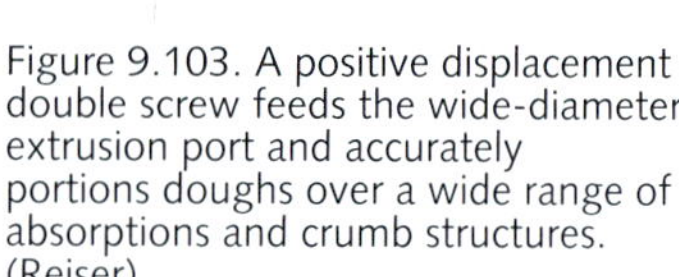

Figure 9.103. A positive displacement double screw feeds the wide-diameter extrusion port and accurately portions doughs over a wide range of absorptions and crumb structures. (Reiser)

The ANSI/BISSC/Z50.2-2003 Sanitary Standards for the Design of Bakery Equipment has developed standards for bakery equipment. In addition to the "basic criteria," "definitions" and "general principles of design, construction and cleaning," such machines should also conform to specific standards for ingredient storage and handling systems, mixers, dough forming equipment, proofers, conveyors, ovens, kettles and coolers, among others. The Baking Industry Sanitation Standards Committee's Web site, www.bissc.org, provides downloadable text for these standards, and it maintains a directory of BISSC-registered equipment vendors.

9.D.2.d. Rotary dividers

Rotary dividers, also known as extrusion dividers, were first described by Campbell (1983). In this system (**Figure 9.104**), the dough is delivered from the mixer by a transfer pump to the hopper of the unit. The hopper bottom is equipped with a pressure-sensitive interfering-type screw pump, augmented by a vacuum system that aids in drawing the dough uniformly into the pump and also assists in degassing it. The screw conveyor then delivers the degassed dough now possessing a constant density to an electronically controlled metering system. This meter, in turn, feeds the dough into an extrusion nozzle, where a rotating knife positioned at the exit port cuts it into individual pieces.

The general scaling range of the divider is 6 to 52 oz, although both smaller and larger dough pieces can be produced, and its scaling accuracy is a reported accurate well within 1%. With all functional components operating on a rotational basis, scaling speeds are readily adapted to prevailing production demands. Maximum scaling rates are in excess of 180 pieces per minute and even higher in double cut-off knife configuration. Recent configurations have multiple metering pumps, each dedicated to a single lane of dough balls going to each moulder. By having 2, 3 or 4 dedicated pumps, the scaling accuracy is very tight, and the lanes can easily be controlled and interlocked to the moulder.

Because the dough pump of the unit adds measurably to the development of the dough, doughs that are 0.6 to 2 C° (1 to 3 F°) cooler than fully mixed doughs are required for processing by this type of divider. The operation of the unit is under computer control, with its operational status constantly displayed on an operator interface screen.

With rotary bread dividers now capable of delivering as many as 315 pieces per minute and scaling ranges of 6 to 60 oz, computer control over sequencing is essential for ease of operation. A color touchscreen panel, provided as the operator interface for these systems (**Figure 9.105**), not only displays machine diagnostics and status but also allows the divider operator to meet changing dough conditions. These systems currently accommodate preset "recipes" for up to 45 different products including white breads, variety breads, ethnic breads and frozen doughs.

Use of the rotary divider, in most cases, eliminates the requirement for intermediate proofing, and when some rest time is needed, an ambient belt-type proofer can be used. Divided dough pieces easily round on belt-style system consisting of a conveyor-topped refrigerated-bed table and tunnel-like rounding bars (Campbell 1989). Robinson (2000) observed that extrusion bun dividers are less complex, with more than 50% fewer parts than a drum-and-piston bun divider.

Rotary dividing is making headway in flour tortilla production. The dual-auger design handles dough gently, and the patented ultra-high molecular weight (UHMW) plastic free-flow manifold evenly distributes dough for 4-, 6-, 8- and 9-across output. Servo motors control the action of the UHMW rotary cut-off mechanism, which operates at 110 to 200 cuts per minute. Divider pressure is set deliberately low at 15 psi to be gentle to the dough, and dough temperature varies less than 0.6 C° (1 F°) from hopper to discharge so no cooling is required for the rounding bed.

9.D.2.e. Extrusion technology

Rotary dividers are extruders, and the basic principles of extrusion technology as applied to bakery processing are simple to understand. Dough is introduced into a hopper, which acts as a reservoir (Steward 1990). The hopper maintains a constant supply of dough to the augers, which maintain a constant pressure to the metering pump. Vacuum is commonly employed to ensure that product fills the auger helix cavities. The rotational movement of the augers provides natural dough degassing, an important element for good scaling accuracy.

To maintain accurate scaling, uniform pressure must be maintained to the metering pump. A pressure sensing devise constantly reads the pressure and causes the feed screw augers to speed up or slow down to maintain uniform pressure. As the dough changes density during processing, the screw speed will increase to maintain the preset pressure (Robinson 2000).

Combining the electronic servo-controlled auger feeding screws, metering pump and cutoff knife provides the baker a very accurate dividing system. They can be configured for multiple lanes feeding multiple rounders (**Figure 9.106**).

Extrusion dividers have an additional benefit of not needing divider oil. The elimi-

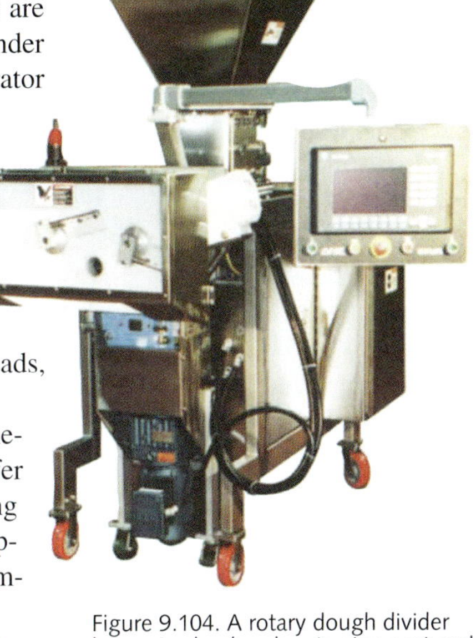

Figure 9.104. A rotary dough divider has a circular dough extrusion port and rotating knife (left), with operations run from an electronic control panel (right). (AMF Bakery Systems)

Figure 9.105. Color touchscreen controls allow operators to monitor and adjust conditions to meet exact dough requirements for this rotary bread divider. (The Peerless Group)

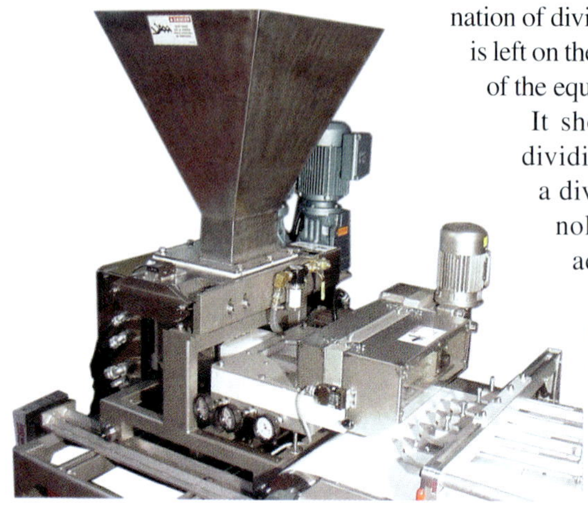

Figure 9.106. This extrusion divider degasses and homogenizes the dough prior to dividing, which gives all the dough a consistent density.
(AMF Bakery Systems)

nation of divider oil helps control product variations in color and taste if too much oil is left on the dough. In addition, excess oil on the machinery can lead to breakdowns of the equipments' electronic and hardware components over time.

It should be noted that converting from conventional knife-and-ram dividing or drum-and-piston dividing to extrusion dividing is not just a divider change out (Robinson 2000). While it may not be new technology, it is certainly different. Bakers have to learn the effects of additional pumping, shear and pressure on the finished product.

To maintain accurate scaling, uniform pressure must be maintained to the metering pump. A pressure sensing devise constantly reads the pressure and causes the feed screw to speed up or slow down to maintain uniform pressure. As the dough changes density during processing, the screw speed will increase to maintain the preset pressure, a change that usually occurs at the end of the dough. At this stage, the dough has more age and is less tolerant to the increased shear and pressure imparted by the higher speed of the screw. This phenomenon is most apparent during variety changes and delays. Dough that has been latent in the divider and exposed to higher screw speeds should be purged from the system and reworked with fresh dough.

9.D.2.f. No-stress dividing

Many doughs do not run well through ram-and-shear, piston or even rotary dividers: They may be too soft, too sticky or too wet or their protein structure too delicate. Bakery engineers sought a different means of moving dough through the dividing process and settled on the force of gravity. In doing so, engineers developed machines that minimize shear forces and eliminate pistons, doing away with suction and ejection methods.

A Japanese bakery equipment manufacturer was the first to patent "stress free" gravimetric dividing. The company's newest such divider (**Figure 9.107**) is supplied with dough through an elevated hopper, which releases dough through the force of gravity plus a gentle massaging motion. The divider deposits the dough in long, rectangular billets onto a belt under continual weight management. Through feedback, the weight determines the speed at which the dough piece is moved forward in the system to be sheeted to a preset thickness and width. As the dough proceeds down the line, it encounters revolving cutters that establish up to 6 lanes and guillotine cutters that slice cut off individual dough pieces. Because the dough remains "stress free" during the dividing process, the baker can minimize or eliminate chemical additives and intermediate proofing.

This gravimetric system also eliminates the need for rest periods or intermediate proofing. It can output 4,400 lb (2 tonnes) per hour, and the technology is scalable to 13,000 lb (6 tonnes) per hour. It handles doughs with absorptions as high as 75 to 80%, compared with the 64% limit of conventional technology. The 2-lane system has a weight range of 7 to 26 oz (200 to 700 g) per piece, and in one-lane configuration, it can output pan-ready dough pieces weighing 14 to 42 oz (400 to 1,200 g) (Gorton 2001a).

Another approach was taken by a European equipment manufacturer that also applies the force of gravity to dividing yeasted doughs. A batch of dough is delivered to this system, which resembles a large drum tilted at an angle (**Figure 9.108**). The cylinder's bottom surface slides out of the way, creating a crescent-shaped port.

The dough then moves through the gap as a continuous string of dough onto a floured weighing belt. When the desired weight is reached, a guillotine mechanism cuts off the dough piece (Clyma 2007). The dough remaining in the hopper experiences no suction or pressure. Scaling accuracy of ± 2% is reported for dough pieces ranging 250 to 1,800 g (9 to 63.5 oz) at 300 to 1,500 pieces per hour.

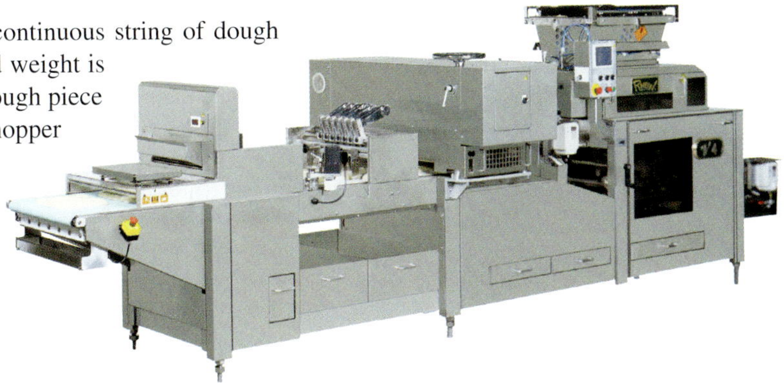

9.D.3. Checkweighing

Equipment manufacturers devote a great deal of time and effort to produce dividers that have better weight control tolerances; however, the only sure way to verify that the divider is producing the right piece weight is to measure it. The method, whether manual or automatic, and the frequency of checking the piece weight depend on the baker's preference and the type of equipment being used.

In manual checkweighing, the operator will weigh individual dough pieces at frequent intervals on a special divider scale that indicates over- and under-weight. He will then manually make the appropriate volumetric adjustments on the divider. Automatic checkweighers, on the other hand, will verify the weight of each scaled dough piece, ensure that it conforms to the preset values and eject any dough piece that is outside the established weight tolerances (Abbott 1958). Such control could give the baker important savings and may also help meet legal requirements with regard to the weights of baked products.

Automatic checkweighers are normally placed directly after the divider and before the rounder; thus providing quick feedback to the divider for in-process changes. They can, however, also be placed after the rounder (Benier 1983). Although you lose some of the quick feedback to the divider, it is easier to establish the proper distance between pieces that assures their individual weighing. The checkweigher verifies the weight of each dough piece coming out of the divider and "informs" the divider of any weight deviations.

The adjustment to the divider can then be made manually, or in more sophisticated checkweigher usage, the volume adjustment is controlled by a computer that will automatically change the divider settings whenever dough weights deviate from the established norm. The checkweighers will detect any sustained tendency of the divider to deviate from the preset weight and activate the synchronous motor that controls the machine's weight adjustment mechanism (Benier 1983).

9.D.4. Dough rounders

After dough is divided, it is common for the dough piece to be rounded into a ball shape for initial proofing. Dough rounders should impart a spherical form to the

Figure 9.107. This "stress free" dough divider forms bread using the force of gravity and sheeting methods. (Rheon Corp.)

Figure 9.108. Charged with a batch of dough, the divider releases it to a weighbelt as a continuous string and cuts it off when the required weight is achieved. (König)

unsymmetrical dough pieces that emerge from the divider and simultaneously seal their raw cut surfaces with a fine skin to prevent excessive loss of the evolving carbon dioxide gas. Large stand-alone rounders accept the dough at the base of a cone or cylinder that rotates. The dough piece travels up the cone against a spiral rounding bar, or track, and is discharged at the top of the cone. Large rounders for 1.5-kg (3.3-lb) pieces can handle up to 8,000 pieces per hour and have working lengths of the spiral approximately 5 to 8 m (16 to 26 ft).

There are basically two types of rounders in current use: the cone-type rounder and the belt rounder. The traditional cone rounder has a very small footprint, does a good job of rounding and sealing the dough ball and handles stiffer doughs quite well.

9.D.4.a. Cone rounders

The traditional cone-type rounding machines consist of an external or internal revolving surface against which the freshly scaled dough piece is held by a spiral track or trough. As the surface revolves, it carries the irregularly-shaped dough piece upward in the spiral rounding track, imparting to the dough a rolling motion. This motion results in a uniformly rounded dough ball with a thin, smooth and dense skin that not only eliminates the stickiness of the cut dough surface but also serves as a membrane that retains the leavening carbon dioxide gas.

The revolving surface may have the form of a conical bowl, an umbrella or a drum. While each design at one time or another had its proponents, the umbrella-shaped rounder with an external surface is the one most commonly encountered in American baking plants.

The cone-type rounder (**Figure 9.109**) is essentially a revolving bowl against whose interior surface a stationary spiral trough, or track, forms the rounding device. The spiral track, which is normally Teflon-coated, extends from the lower section of the bowl to its upper rim where it ends at a discharge chute that leads to a take-away conveyor. In operation, the dough pieces are fed to the rounder by means of a special intake hopper from which they drop to the lower end of the spiral. Here they are immediately engaged by the revolving cone surface, which forces them up the spiral trough in a tumbling and rolling motion that converts them into uniformly shaped dough balls before they are finally discharged charged onto a conveyor that takes them to the intermediate proofer.

The umbrella or inverted cone-type rounder consists of a spindle-supported revolving cone table whose outer surface supplies the rounding action. A stationary dough track, supported against this outer surface, spirals upward from the cone's outer edge toward its central apex where it ends at the discharge chute. The dough pieces enter the rounder at the lower perimeter, which is also its largest diameter, and travel upward toward the discharge chute.

Figure 9.109. Conical or bowl-type heavy duty rounder starts the rounding action from the base, carrying the dough piece up and out. (Turkington USA)

The drum or cylindrical rounder (**Figure 9.110**) differs from the two other types in that its revolving bowl has essentially vertical sides against which the spiraling Teflon-coated dough track is supported. Its principal advantage is its economy of floor space so that it can be positioned in closer proximity to the divider than the other two types.

A 2-stage rounding system (**Figure 9.111**) enables precise sphere shaping: The cylindrical stage initiates the round shape, and the conical stage finishes the dough piece into a precise round shape. The roundness of the dough piece is critical to proper sheeting and moulding. It also helps seal the fermentation gases inside the dough ball. The rounder is designed to provide precise dough rounding for a wide range of bread doughs. Special nonstick coating and plastic materials for dough-contact surfaces improve product quality and minimize dusting flour. Independent, adjustable trough sections allow adjustment of the rounding track's width to suite a wide range of product sizes.

Rounders differ not only in their general configuration but also in certain operational features. Thus, the initial rate at which the dough pieces are taken up differs with each type. In the conical rounder, the dough pieces start out slowly and increase their rate of travel progressively as they approach the top of the spiral. In the inverted or umbrella rounder, the reverse is true because the dough pieces enter the rounder at its larger diameter and travel upward toward its narrower apex. In the cylindrical rounder, the rate of travel of the dough ball is the most uniform of all. While the relative merits of the respective modes may be subject to debate, they all yield good results.

Rounders of different design and manufacture differ in how they achieve certain objectives such as keeping the revolving surface clean, preventing the formation of dough pills, maintaining a positive rounding force on the dough pieces, producing a controlled kneading action and regulating the rate of dusting flour application.

The revolving surface in rounders is normally finely grooved to improve traction and the rolling effect on the dough pieces. The dough tracks are generally lined with Teflon or other suitable nonstick coating to reduce the need for dusting flour.

Most rounders are provided with a flour dusting mechanism that dispenses controlled amounts of dusting flour to prevent the doughs from sticking. In some instances, pneumatic starch dusting has been adopted to achieve the same purpose. In still others, flour dusters have been replaced by air blowers to promote the formation of a dry skin on the dough during rounding.

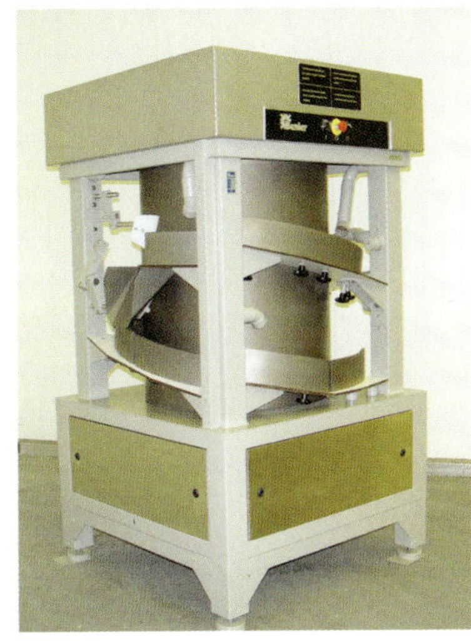

Figure 9.110. The drum or cylindrical rounder has vertical revolving sides against which the dough pieces are held by a stationary track. (Kaak Group, Benier)

9.D.4.b. Belt rounders

In roll plants, the dividing process has been integrated with the rounders and proofing into one system. The divider is typically configured with die heads or rotary dividers producing 4 to 8 pieces across the belt, and some 10-across systems are in use. One manufacturer of a range of integrated bun plant systems using an extruder divider and belt rounder claims a production rate in excess of 30,000 buns per hour. The output of an integrated plant, however, depends on the scaling range available (typically 30 to 130 g, or 1 to 4.5 oz), the number of cutting strokes of the divider (typically 90 ± 40 per minute) and the type of dough so the numbers can vary widely. Traditionally, rounder capacities range up to 200 pieces per minute for dough pieces that do not exceed 27 oz in weight. As the weight of individual dough balls increases, the rated throughput of a given rounder tends to decline. Thus, with dough pieces weighing 36 oz each, the maximum capacity of rounders is normally reduced to 130 pieces per minute.

The adjustment of the dough track against the rotating surface is significant because it affects the tendency to form dough pills. The closer the track is to the moving surface without creating friction, the more effective is the

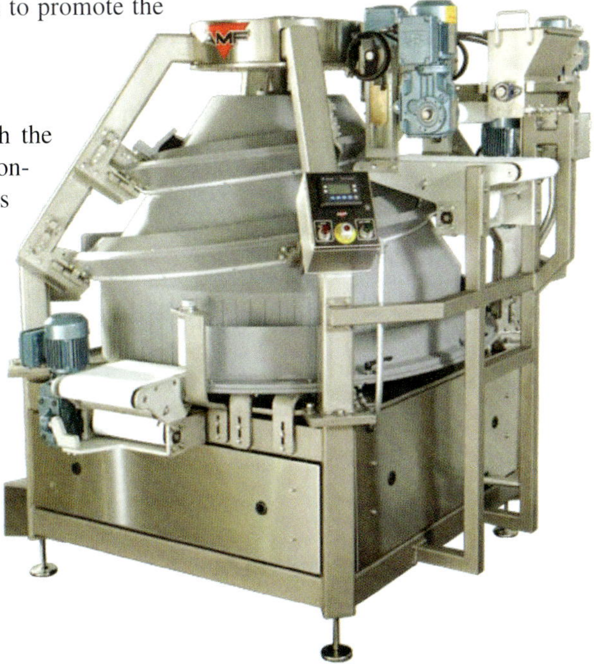

Figure 9.111. This umbrella rounder offers 2-stage rounding action for precise sphere shaping. (AMF Bakery Systems)

control over undesirable dough pill formation. Dough tends to build up a film on the rounder surface, thereby gradually reducing the clearance that separates it from the dough track and necessitating periodic readjustments.

Maintenance of the rounder is chiefly a matter of daily cleaning of the rounding surface and of the dough channel, and of scheduled lubrication of the drive mechanism. It is important to remove all traces of dough at the end of each day's run to prevent their hardening. Should the need for scraping dried dough from the rotating surface or dough race arise, only wooden or plastic scrapers should be used for this purpose to avoid damaging the equipment.

Belt rounders require more floor space than cone or drum rounders and are primarily used with extrusion dividers, both for bun and bread applications (Osborne 1998). They are configured in single, dual and triple lanes (**Figure 9.112**). They do a good job of rounding and sealing the dough ball. They can operate at high speeds and, when used with extrusion dividers, produce a round dough ball without contamination from oil or dusting flour. Some rounders are equipped with bed cooling to prevent sticking of the dough in warm environments.

Belt rounders consist for the most part of a broad canvas belt, coated with a suitable high-release finish, over which are positioned adjustable rounding tunnels or bars (**Figure 9.113**). The scaled dough pieces enter the tunnels at one end and are carried forward by the moving belt. In the process, the dough pieces are transformed into smooth balls of uniform size at capacities as high as 200 pieces per minute per lane.

Belt rounders are also used for certain products to produce a more gentle rounding action such as breads proofed in couches or where a true round shape is not required. Some rye breads also use this process. Belt rounding can be found more often in small or mid-sized bakeries where more time is taken to produce higher quality products or where stickier doughs must be handled. The V-belt rounder (**Figure 9.114**), made specifically for artisan-style products such as boules, does not squeeze water out and degasses the doughs because of way it adjusts the tracks and its track guiding system.

Some bakers skip the rounding process, opting for equipment that divides dough pieces in a way that delivers the gluten structure in a lengthwise position. This technology allows the piece of dough to be elongated more easily after the first proofing and then processed in pans or on a hearth. This technology only works for certain types of bread products and is particularly effective for highly hydrated doughs such as those required for sub rolls and baguette-type products (**Figure 9.115**).

A trend for rounders today is to be more adjustable. Bakers want machines that provide the ability to adjust the pitch and the chamber of the rounding tunnel or maybe even switch in and out different rounder bars to handle the wide variety of products being made on that line.

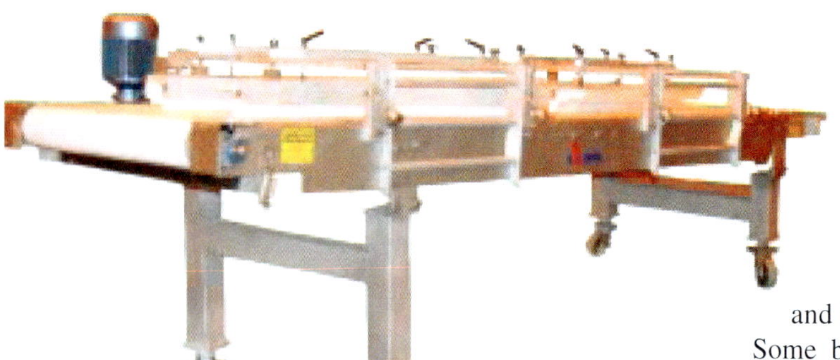

Figure 9.112. A 2-lane rounding table carries dough balls forward on a belt, forcing the dough against rounding bars to turn and seal the pieces smoothly. (Turkington USA)

9.D.5. Moulders

The function of moulders in a bread bakery is to sheet, curl and seal the rounded dough pieces received from the intermediate proofer into a cylindrical form that ultimately assumes the shape of a loaf during final proofing. A moulder has three basic sections. The first is the sheeter section where the dough piece is degassed and sheeted out to a uniform thickness. Second is the moulder section where the dough piece is moulded into the bread form that is required, and third is the sealing and panning section where the product is sealed and put into pans.

During this process, the dough is subjected to manipulative forces that create the desired grain and texture in the baked bread. By correctly moulding the dough piece, the baker avoids defects in the bread such as crumb streaks, hard cores, coarse and uneven grain, and rough texture (Kamman 1970).

Moulders are available in several basic configurations (**Figure 9.116**); however, their essential design consists of a series of roller pairs with successively closer settings that transform the dough ball into a thin sheet. This sheet is then rolled into a cylindrical shape by a pair of curling rolls or a curling mat and sealed by a pressure board (Boston 1953).

9.D.5.a. Sheeting

In conventional moulders (**Figure 9.117**), the sheeting operation is performed by 2 or more, and generally 3, consecutive sets of rolls (**Figure 9.118**). These include a pair of pre-sheeting rolls and two separate pairs of top and bottom rolls, all with progressively narrower settings between the rolls. Often, a preliminary flattening roll set is interposed between the infeed belt and the presheeting roll set to give the dough ball a slight initial flattening so it will engage more readily with the first pair of rolls. The setting of the rolls in terms of speed and gap is related to the strength properties of the dough. Different systems may be specified such as progressive narrowing of roll gaps.

Before the advent of Teflon sleeves, each roll was equipped with a scraper blade to keep the roll surfaces clean of adhering dough. The setting of these blades was quite critical: If the blades were set too close, over-heating of the rolls resulted, and if they were set too loose, the intended purpose was not achieved. Encasing the sheeting rolls in Teflon sleeves has largely eliminated the need for scraper blades because Teflon exhibits excellent non-adhesive properties. At the same time, the amount of dusting flour required to minimize the sticking of dough in the roller sets is also reduced.

In straight-line moulders, the dough piece passes through the consecutive sheeting and curling operations without a change in direction, thus causing the moisture within the dough to be squeezed toward the tail end of the dough sheet. Because the lead edge of the dough sheet is placed at the core of the dough cylinder by the curling action, uneven moisture distribution results within the formed dough loaf, with the low-moisture part forming the center portion. This difference in moisture content between the core and the outer regions leads to a variable crumb grain in the baked loaf.

To correct this undesirable condition, the so-called reverse sheeting moulder was developed. Here, after the dough sheet passes through the first two pairs of sheet-

Figure 9.113. Dough pieces for buns are rounded against bars set at an angle over a moving conveyor belt. This bakery set up its twin bun lines in mirror image fashion.

Figure 9.114. A V-belt rounder runs dough balls through a trough formed by two separate conveyor belts. (Kaak Group North America)

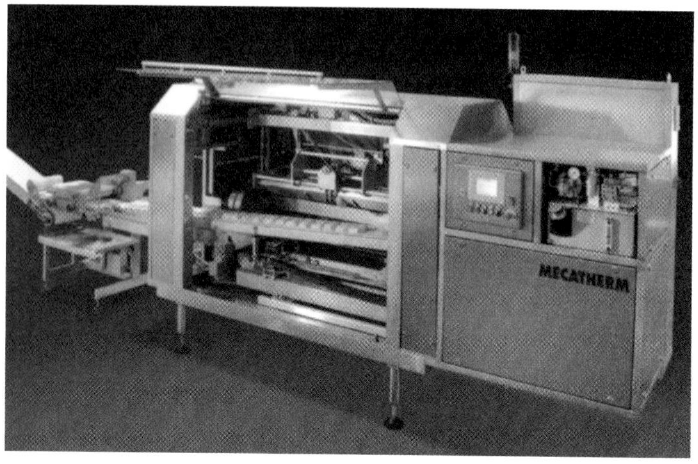

Figure 9.115. This divider handles highly hydrated dough, cutting it into pieces of accurate weight, while also eliminating degassing or tearing of the sticky dough. (Mecatherm)

ing rolls, it is automatically turned end-over-end so that its tail end becomes the lead edge as it enters the final set of rolls, resulting in a more uniform moisture distribution throughout the dough loaf.

This improved moisture distribution should exert a favorable effect on loaf volume. Hibberd and Parker (1976) found that a significant amount of carbon dioxide gas is forced into solution by the high pressures developed during sheeting. As the dough's temperature rises during proofing and baking, the solubility of the gas is reduced, causing the gas to come out of solution and to contribute importantly to the loaf volume. A more uniform moisture distribution in the proofing and baking loaf results in a more even loaf volume expansion and a more pleasing final loaf shape.

Some manufacturers recommend using a greater quantity of smaller diameter rolls for the sheeting section. Such a moulder features four pairs of sheeting rollers with adjustable speed and gap control. Reducing the sheet thickness in four steps can achieve more uniform piecing and tighter dough curling than moulders with fewer sheeting rollers. Dough piece length can be adjusted for a variety of tin lengths, and the sheeting head can handle 200- to 2,100-g (7- to 74-oz) dough pieces.

9.D.5.b. Curling

Following its passage through the sheeting rolls, the dough piece enters the moulder's curling section in which it is rolled into a loose cylinder. Curling of the tensioned dough sheet enables a uniform structure to develop through the even expansion of gas cells during the final proofing.

Curling is done by controlling the tension between the transfer belt, the last reduction or sheeting rolls and the curling restraint mechanism, usually a sheet of chain mesh on top of the dough roll. As the stretched dough emerges from the sheeting rolls, it is contract-

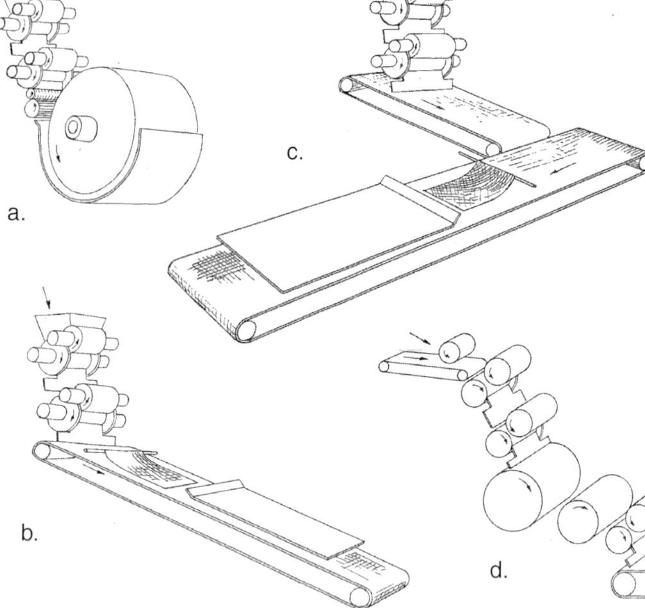

Figure 9.116. Bread moulding follows several sheeting schemes: (a) drum, (b) straight, (c) cross-grain and (d) reverse. (Boston 1953)

ing; therefore, to maintain the correct tension at the curl, the transfer belt travels slightly slower than the roll speed.

In earlier models, the curling operation was performed by a pair of curling rolls that gave the dough piece about 3.5 turns, following which the resulting dough cylinder passed between the surfaces of a revolving drum and a stationary pressure plate. In a subsequent curling device, a pair of canvas belts is mounted in superimposed fashion and move in opposite directions. The lower conveyor belt moves the sheeted dough piece forward until its lead edge is engaged by the upper curling belt or mat, is lifted and the dough piece rolled into a cylinder.

In the latest moulder design, the curling mat consists of a short length of metal mesh or thin linked steel rods whose front end is attached to a bar above the lower conveyor belt, with the remaining length resting on the belt. When the sheeted dough piece reaches the curling mat, its lead edge is engaged by the metal mesh and the dough given a loose curl as it passes beneath the mat.

In straight-line moulders, the lead edge of the sheeted dough piece is rolled into the center of the loaf. In cross-grain moulders (**Figures 9.119 and 9.120**), on the other hand, the curling section is positioned at a right angle to the sheeting rolls so that the dough sheet curls with its side edge forming the center of the loaf. This method of cross moulding yields an elongated cell structure in the baked crumb.

Most high-volume moulders are provided with an automatic panning device. Empty pans are indexed beneath and just beyond the end of the compression board where a pneumatic mechanism deposits a dough loaf into each pan. The accuracy of automatic panning has reached a level where no deformation of the dough piece occurs and each loaf is centered in the pan with its seam facing down. The indexing mechanism that times the strapped pan forward to accept dough pieces can be a physical stop, usually made of UHMW plastic to prevent marring of the pan, or an electronic stop that holds the pan in place magnetically.

A cut-and-turn panning system has found use primarily in the British and Asian bread market, where the curled piece of dough is run through a W-shaped cutting station that cuts the dough into 3 or 4 sections (**Figure 9.121**). The pieces are then turned at right angles and deposited into the pan 4-up for final proofing and baking. The effect is to orient the tension in the dough along the axis of the pan. The four pieces fuse during final proofing and baking to make the one loaf. Operating rates fit a weight range of 200 to 2,100 g (7 to 74 oz) at up to 6,000 pieces per hour, depending on weight. This technology gives the bread a different final grain and appearance and is typically used for sandwich or sliced loaf bread

9.D.5.c. Coiling (twisting)

Many bakers twist bread dough during moulding to improve internal loaf characteristics. Twisting is generally perceived to impart a finer grain, a more elongated cell structure and a silkier texture to the bread crumb and to minimize the occurrence of holes (Cackler 1957). It involves the twisting of 2 half-weight dough cylinders into a single loaf, an operation that is still widely performed manually but which can also be done mechanically by modified moulders equipped with a twisting head (Anon. 1958).

In one such unit, the dough cylinders emerging from the pressure board drop into dough traps which release them in pairs into a first set of U-shaped twisting cups that then rotate 180° in opposite directions and thus apply the first two twists. The partly twisted loaf is then released into a second set of cups that repeat the twisting action, thereby applying the third and fourth twists. If only three twists are desired, one of the cups of the second set is replaced by a stationary plate. The fully twisted loaf is then deposited automatically into pans.

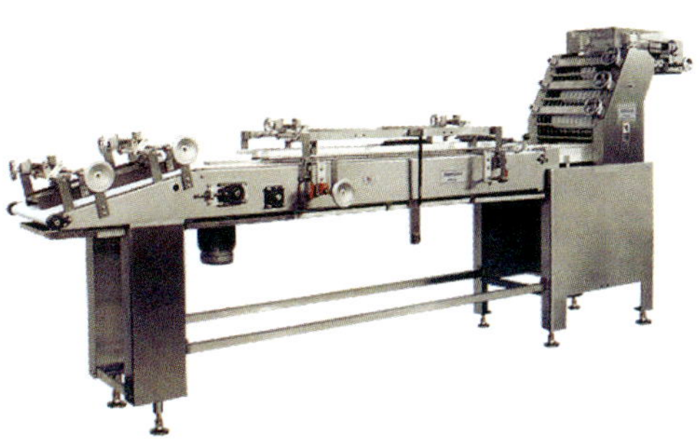

Figure 9.117. Three sets of rolls, plus a presheeting roller assembly, sheets dough pieces gradually to retain leavening gases and enable finer crumb texture.
(The Peerless Group)

Figure 9.118. The sheeting head contains 3 sets of rolls that flatten dough pieces before they are curled into loaves.
(The Peerless Group)

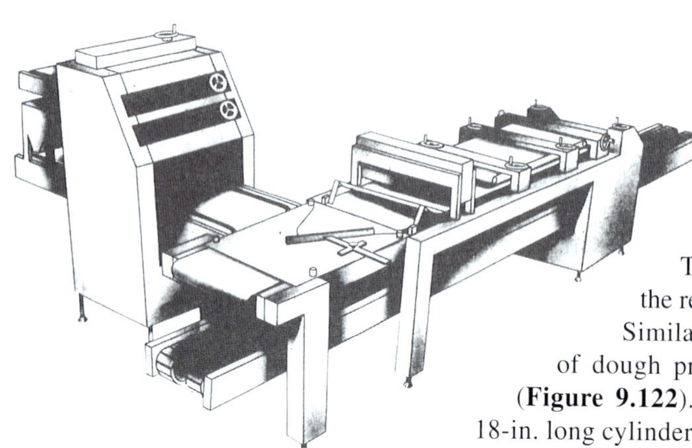

Figure 9.119. Schematic drawing of a cross-grain moulder/panner shows the curling section set at right angle to the sheeting rolls.
(Pyler 1988)

Figure 9.120. Dough pieces sheeted on 3 sets of rollers turn 90° to enter the curling section of this cross-grain moulder.
(The Peerless Group)

In a second twisting device, two dough cylinders, positioned side-by-side by the moulder discharge are brought under a flexible retaining chain mat by a 180° turn conveyor. The chain mat imparts a rolling or twisting action to the two dough pieces, rolling them individually as well as twisting them together into a single loaf (Miller 1961). The required number of twists is controlled by adjusting the retaining chain.

Similar twisting effects can be achieved with a single piece of dough processed through so-called "kurl" or coil moulders (**Figure 9.122**). The sheeted dough piece is first moulded into an 18-in. long cylinder by a special reversing system of pressure boards that discharge the dough piece onto a turn conveyor traveling at a 35° angle to the discharge direction. The turn conveyor then deposits the dough cylinder on the belt that feeds the coiling mechanism. This transfer is accomplished in such manner that the dough piece is stretched an additional 3 to 5 in. The dough piece enters the coiling mechanism at a slight angle, which permits it to be coiled 3.5 to 5.5 turns, depending on its size, to yield a loaf length that will fit into the appropriate pan size.

Coiling occurs when the dough passes under a stationary wire-rod chain after the process has been initiated by a small section of flexible mesh belt. Correct dough conditioning is a critical prerequisite for the successful use of this type of moulder (Ferrell 1961).

9.D.5.d. Belt moulder

The production of certain types of hearth breads and rolls, including varieties such as French baguettes and flutes and long Italian bread, involves moulding the raw dough pieces into relatively long strings (Loeb 1981), using a moulder as shown in **Figure 9.123**. This process of dough elongation is normally carried out in stages, with brief intervening proof periods that permit the dough to recover from the mechanical working it receives. The final moulder consists of two moving canvas or felt belts that travel in opposite directions at different speeds. This difference in belt speeds moves the dough through the compression zone relatively slowly and gently.

In contrast to conventional moulding, the aim in moulding baguettes or Italian loaves is to expose the dough to only a minimum of degassing (Tweed 1983). The dough piece is kept centered during the elongation process by a special device to ensure uniformity of form throughout its length. In practice, the dough pieces receive their first moulding to a length of 12 to 14 in., following by an intermediate proof. They then enter the first extending moulder that stretches them to about 24 in. and returns them to the proofer for an additional 15 minutes. Dough pieces then encounter a second belt moulder (**Figure 9.124**) that elongates them to their final length of 28 to 30 in. The dough strings elongated in this manner are sufficiently stable to retain their length without subsequent shrinkage.

9.D.5.e. Combination systems

There is a growing trend to integrated or combine all the make-up equipment into one system. The unit shown in (**Figure 9.125**) combines dividing, resting, moulding and automatic depositing of dough pieces onto flat surfaces or into channel-shaped trays. This system, designed for baguettes and other similar products, includes a volumetric divider, which portions the dough into pieces from 200 to 900 g (7 to 32 oz). The divider can output between 1,800 and 3,750 pieces per hour.

After exiting the divider, the dough pieces are lifted in a system of elevator belts, and from there, they are transferred to an upper resting belt in the pre-proofing chamber. Here the dough rests as the belts slowly descend. The dough pieces then move into the moulding unit where the dough is laminated and rolled before being moulded. Then, at the moulder exit, the dough enters a cassette in which the dough pieces are stretched to their final size. The cassettes are individually adjustable, either to stretch the baguette to its desired size or to stretch and separate the portioned dough pieces, creating as many cassette groups as there are dough pieces. At the stretcher exit, the baguettes are deposited on trays and transported under the machine.

9.D.6. Bun and roll equipment

The continued expansion and variety of the food service industry as well as the equally dramatic growth in so-called convenience foods has led to an unprecedented demand for buns and rolls of all types. This increase in the market has resulted in far-reaching developments and changes in the processing procedures and in the equipment used by bakers for the production of these items.

In high-volume bakeries, the operations of dough dividing, rounding, proofing, moulding and panning are normally integrated into fully automatic systems that incorporate all equipment sections required to produce the panned dough pieces. A typical bun and roll makeup system that performs all the required actions in one continuous operation is shown in **Figure 9.126**.

Total automation of roll production may be achieved by providing a continuous stream of dough to the divider hopper. The simplest way to do so is to employ a continuous dough mixing process that supplies a steady stream of fully developed dough to the divider hopper via a pipe (Euverard 1970). Continuous mixing systems were discussed in Chapter 9, Part B.

Where dough mixing is performed by the batch method, automation is made possible by installing a suitable dough pump that will provide a continuous supply of dough to the divider hopper (Spooner 1984). One such unit mounts directly over the divider hopper and controls both the rate of dough transfer by means of a variable-speed screw conveyor as well as the dough's final development by an independently operating impeller.

Basically, dough scaling by the divider follows the same principles that apply in regular bread dough dividers. The dough is drawn from the hopper into pockets, which normally number 4 to 8, of the horizontal scaling cylinder by retract-

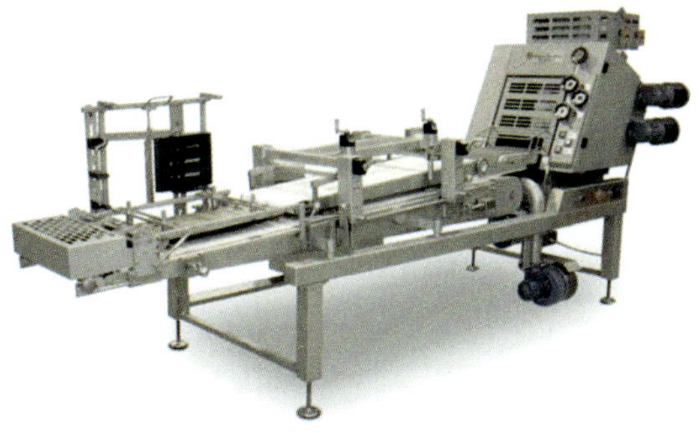

Figure 9.121. The 4-piecing method first cuts the loaf, then turns the pieces before loading all into the same pan. (Baker Perkins UK)

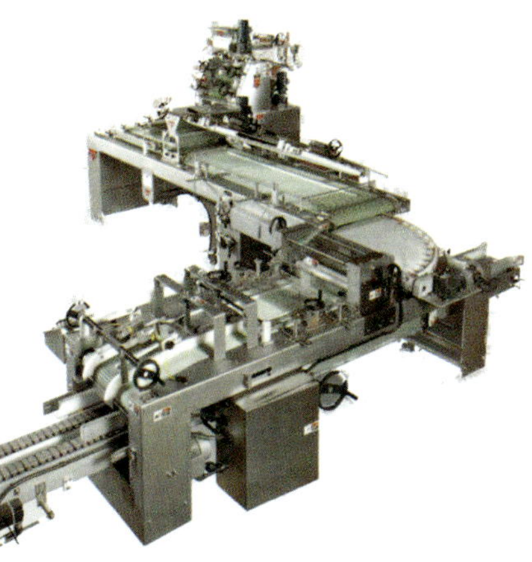

Figure 9.122. Curl, or coil, moulders subject the dough cylinder to an additional coiling action to produce the effects of twisting. (AMF Bakery Systems)

Figure 9.123. Dough pieces, elongated in two or more stages, produces long strings for production of baguettes, French rolls and similar products. (Kaak Group, Benier)

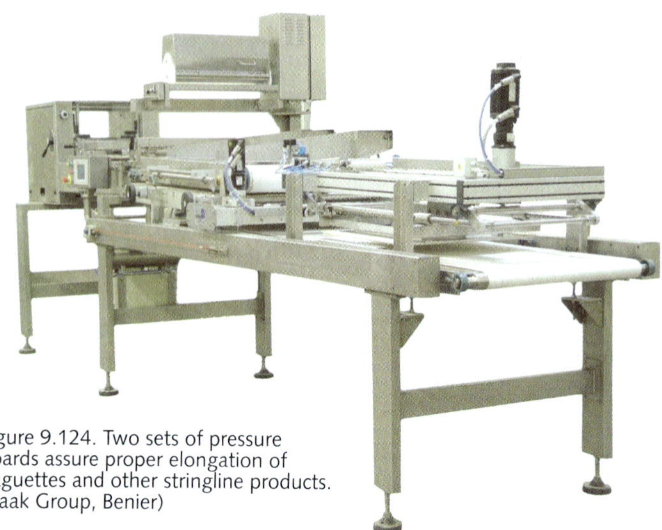

Figure 9.124. Two sets of pressure boards assure proper elongation of baguettes and other stringline products. (Kaak Group, Benier)

ing pistons. The revolving cylinder shears off the dough pieces within the cups and ejects them onto a continuous rounding belt. Cut-off wires improve the accuracy of scaling and aid ejection of the individual dough pieces. Scaling weights are adjustable within a range of 0.75 to 5 oz.; with scaling rates in the range of 600 to 800 pieces per minute.

The deposited dough pieces are conveyed by the rounder belt toward the discharge chutes that feed into the intermediate proofer. During this travel, the pieces kneaded and rounded by Teflon-lined adjustable concave metal or UHMW plastic bars (**Figure 9.127**). As noted earlier, the bars are positioned diagonally to the direction of belt travel to thus induce rounding action.

The rounded dough pieces are next deposited by either a zig-zag dough chute or a rotary timing gate onto the trays of the overhead intermediate proofer. Dusting flour is normally applied at this transfer point, and some systems employ a special vacuum collector for reclaiming excess dusting flour. The proofer trays may be manufactured either of metal or plastic, with the latter material gaining increasing acceptance. The dough pieces are carried through the proofing cycle and fed into the adjustable moulder section.

In the production of hamburger buns, the dough pieces are formed and dropped on the moulder belt that deposits them into the pockets of baking pans, automatically indexed into position and waiting below on a conveyor. In roll production, the proofed dough pieces first enter a set of sheeting rolls and then the moulding and pressure board section where they are shaped into the desired final form before being deposited on the baking pans. The filled pans are then conveyed through the final proofer and ultimately into the oven.

New high-speed bun production systems use extrusion dividing with up to 8 rows across and can provide a scaling range of 0.75 to 6 oz. The rounder is designed to handle up to 1,080 pieces per minute and is equipped with hinged rounder bars for improved rounding symmetry. A gas spring-assisted mechanism allows the rounder bar assembly to be tilted out of the way for cleaning. A servo rotary gate precisely times the transfer between the rounder and the zig-zag dough chute.

Magnetic pan indexing provides the non-stop precision required for high-speed production. This entire system is designed for high capacity: The 8-across divider can process up to 15,000 lb per hour and produce up to 60,000 buns per hour. The system is fully automatic. The computer's recipe management system controls each piece of equipment to sequence the flow of dough and dough pieces from the divider to the oven. It is also designed to meet BISSC standards, which require easy access for sanitation and maintenance.

Figure 9.125. This system integrates dividing, resting, moulding and automatic depositing of dough pieces onto flat surfaces or into channel-style pans. (Mecatherm S.A.)

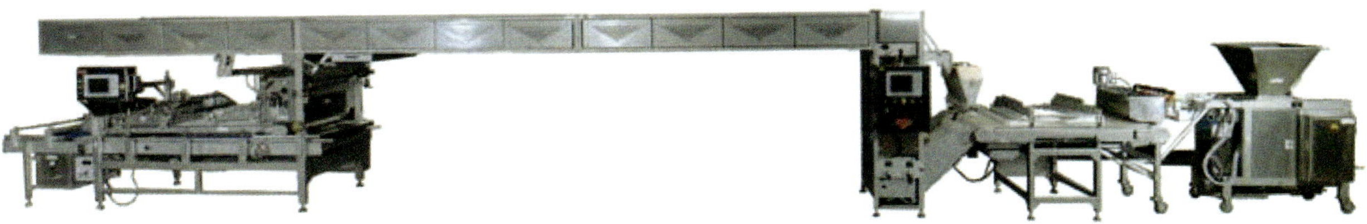

Brixey (1998) described the practical aspects and productivity improvements possible when converting bun systems to newer technology. Goley (1977) examined running bread and bun makeup systems with an eye to increasing production capacity and, thus, reducing costs. The ability to run such systems at truly high speeds, up to 1,000 buns per minute, was studied by Stevens (1991).

Figure 9.126. As dough pieces move from right to left through this high-speed bun line, they are rounded and placed in the overhead intermediate resting proofer, then moulded and dropped into pans.
(AMF Bakery Systems)

9.D.7. Hard roll equipment

Today, the products called "hard rolls" are produced from straight doughs, no-time doughs and sponge doughs. Some of these doughs are characterized by low absorption with tight, stiff characteristics and others are high absorption, being soft and slack; some hard, some soft, some hearth baked and some baked on a pan (Long 1993).

The changes in appearance and character to the hard rolls produced today have, of course, impacted the design and manufacture of hard roll makeup equipment. Machines had to be redesigned to accommodate the increased variety of products, the range of water absorption in doughs and the ever-increasing demand for higher production speeds, higher accuracy and more user-friendly controls.

During the 1970s and 1980s, the equipment used for hard roll production was generally single purpose, that is, it was designed to produce product from low absorption, tight, stiff doughs, with a limited product line that included a few shapes and weights. Production rates on most roll lines were around 800 doz rolls per hour. Today, hard roll production equipment has advanced and is so versatile that hard roll products, which can weigh as little as ¾ oz or as much as 10 oz, can be produced from any type of dough the baker chooses to mix. For the most part, reciprocating and gyrating motions in dividing and rounding have given way to short stroke, hydraulic motion for dividing and rotary motion for rounding. Today's hard roll lines operate comfortably at speeds up to 50 rows per minute on a typical 8-pocket line, which equates to 400 rolls per

Figure 9.127. Teflon-coated rounder bars work the dough ball against the moving belt, kneading and shaping the extruded dough pieces.
(AMF Bakery Systems)

minute or 2,000 doz rolls per hour. Each piece of the makeup equipment line had to be redesigned to attain higher speeds and greater accuracy (Long 1993).

Changes in equipment for making stamped rolls (**Figure 9.128**) exemplify the diversity now possible when producing hard rolls. Before mechanization of Kaiser, Parker House or other shaped rolls, the baker divided and rounded multiple small dough pieces, combining them into a single cup to proof. Stamping a pattern into a single piece of dough considerably simplified this process and allowed for higher production rates.

Rolls are stamped using an air or mechanical system that exerts pressure on the rolls after they come out of the first proofing stage in the process. Different head designs are used depending on what the bakery is making and what the marketplace wants. On smaller systems, the stamping occurs via a separate machine that takes the rolls out of the first proofer early and directs them into the stamping machine via a chute or conveyor.

Today's stamper for the production of Kaiser, split, star and other shapes is redesigned to complement the higher speeds and versatility of the modern hard roll line. With speeds that reach 50 rows per minute, a stamper is required that can maintain such rates and still produce a smooth and fluid-like motion without undue vibration. Vibration in itself is one of the most destructive forces in machine operation. New stampers are balanced in a way so that operation at 50 rows per minute is as smooth as operation at 25 rows per minute.

Other changes have been made in these systems. For example, lines now allow roll dough pieces to be held in the intermediate proofer cups in seam up position, giving the seam a chance to disappear, and then are stamped seam down — providing a finished product with consistent shape and high eye appeal.

The moulded rolls are discharged from the proofer 8, 6 or 4 at a time, depending upon their lengths and the requirements of the downstream automatic boarding or panning devices.

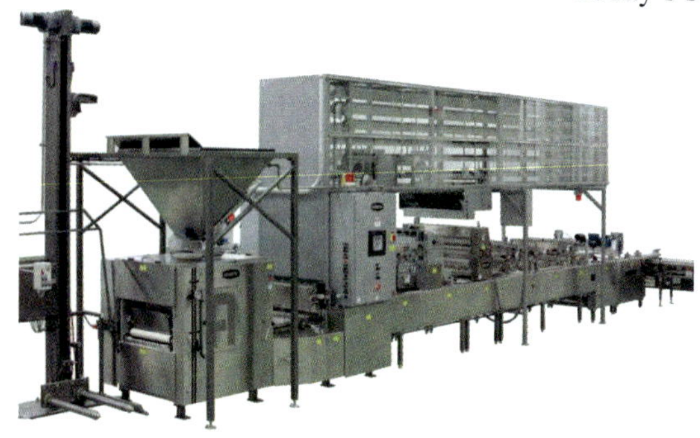

Figure 9.128. Hard roll production now allows automatic stamping to create eye-appealing Kaiser, star and split rolls, among others. (Belshaw Adamatic Bakery Group)

9.E. Pans, Depanners and Pan Management Systems
Updated by Sigismondo De Tora

In addition to the basic mixing and forming production equipment discussed in the preceding sections, bakeries require additional equipment for their operation. Some categories of equipment are essential to production, while others are optional in nature. The presence or use in a bakery of the latter provides marginal, albeit important, benefits in areas of product quality, labor savings and economy, operating efficiency, etc. The diversity of auxiliary equipment found in a given bakery will be further explored in Chapter 11. In the following discussion, only equipment and materials relating to permanent pans, peels, pan handling and depanners are considered. Because pans made of foil and release-coated paper accompany finished products to the end user, they will be examined in Chapter 11 along with packaging materials.

Design of bakery pans is covered by Baking Industry Sanitation Standards Committee (BISSC) requirements at Section 4.34. The specific design requirements stipulate:

(a) All baking surfaces shall be of a corrosion-resistant material that is cleanable and coatable with release coatings.

(b) All individual components of baking pans shall not have sharp edges.

(c) Top rim edges shall be smooth, and the bead shall be curled, cleanable and self draining.

(d) The corners of the reinforcing members attached to nonproduct zone of pans or assemblies shall be required to have a radius.

(e) Top rim edges constructed with a reinforcing member in the rim should be sealed or provided with a minimum of $^1/_8$ in. (3 mm) space between the pans and the reinforcing member.

(f) The exterior pan assembly shall not have protruding wires or metal appendages.

(g) All welding shall be free of burrs, slag or sharp edges.

(h) Exposed welds from wire welding must be of corrosion-resistant materials.

(i) Reinforcing members should be wrapped with a maximum opening of $^1/_{16}$ in. (1.5 mm) and maximum space (gap) of $^1/_{64}$ in. (0.4 mm) between two materials.

(j) Areas of baking pans that tend to trap contaminants shall allow for efficient cleaning and drainage.

(k) When notching is required to form corners and the sheet metal is wrapped over noncorrosive-resistant materials, the noncorrosive-resistant materials shall be totally concealed.

(l) All exposed fasteners shall be of corrosion-resistant materials.

9.E.1. Baking pans

Except for fried products, crackers and some cookies, nearly all bakery foods require the use of pans, baking sheets or peel boards. Baking pans are among the baker's most important assets and, over the years, could be the bakery's largest investment. The original simple folded-end pan has become very complex and requires many operations to manufacture. They are available in a variety of forms, shapes and sizes to meet the requirements of a wide range of different bakery products. Their baking performance is influenced by such factors as the material of construction, design features, surface conditioning and maintenance. Morris (1982) provided a detailed examination of bread and bun pan materials, design and maintenance.

The pan requirements of an average bakery are based on the pan capacity of its ovens (**Table 9.4**). The following assumptions serve as a general basis for estimating this requirement: for each pan set that is in an oven, 2 sets are needed for use in the final proofer and 3 to 5 sets to go through the cooling cycle. By shortening the cooling period, the required pan inventory can be reduced substantially. Moreover, cooling conveyors subject the pans to less rigorous handling and thereby prolong their useful life.

9.E.1.a. Metal pans

The materials used in manufacturing baking pans include, but are not limited to, blue steel or black iron, aluminum, stainless steel, aluminized steel and tinplate, with the latter two finding the widest application. Over the years, the materials used have changed primarily because of the requirements in the baking process and also because of the changes in the steel mill process, availability of raw materials and costs. The tinplate used for bakery pan construction is low-carbon steel of suitable ductility and strength. It is rolled into a uniformly thin sheet and coated with pure tin to a maximum thickness of 2.3 μm. The hot-dipping method originally used to apply the tin coating to the base metal has been largely superseded by an electroplating procedure that results in a more uniform coating. While pans made of tinplate are sturdy and durable, the tin coating has the relatively low melting point of 232°C (449.5°F), a temperature that is frequently exceeded in modern bakery operations. When higher temperatures are encountered, melting of the tin can occur under some circumstances and result in a loss of uniformity in the coating's thickness. Moreover, it is difficult to avoid the occurrence of micro pores in tin coatings through which moisture can penetrate to the base metal and eventually bring about corrosion.

Both of these potential problems are avoided by substituting aluminized or aluminum-coated steel for the tinplate in pan manufacture. The aluminum-steel laminate can withstand the forming, seaming and drawing operations involved in the pan fabricating process without damage to its aluminum coating. The coating, at 25 μm, is more than 10 times that of tin in tinplate and imparts to the pan an improved corrosion resistance (Ehli 1985). Aluminum as such is used on occasion as pan material, particularly for pie plates and cake pans. The metal has excellent heat conducting properties, light weight and superior corrosion resistance but is more expensive and, because of its relative softness, is also more readily deformed. The latter drawback is effectively overcome by aluminized steel. Stainless steel has also found limited application as a pan material. Its advantages of greater strength and corrosion resistance are, however, largely offset by its relatively low heat transmission properties and high cost.

Table 9.4. Calculating Required Number of Pans

Variables	Example
Production rate	12,000 loaves per hour
Proof time	60 minutes
Bake time	15 minutes
Number of pans per strap	5
Length of pan strap	28 in.
Length of conveyors connecting stacker, unstacker, proofer and oven	300 ft
Number of straps required in proofer	12,000 ÷ 5 = 2,400
Number of straps required in oven	(12,000 x 15 ÷ 60) ÷ 5 = 600
Number of straps required on interconnecting conveyors	300 ÷ (28 ÷ 12) = 128.6, round to 130
TOTAL number of active straps required	**2,400 + 600 + 130 = 3,130**

(Spooner 1993)

As a general rule, the best thickness for folded-end bread and Pullman sets is 25 gauge (0.021 in.) and for most bun and roll pans, it is 22 gauge (0.029 in.).

Formerly, new baking pans had to be conditioned prior to being placed into production by a "burning in" treatment that required extensive heating of the pans at 204 to 215°C (400 to 420°F) to produce an oxidized tin surface. The current practice is for the pan manufacturers to deliver new pans with their tin and aluminum surfaces already oxidized or chemically etched, respectively (Blum 1972).

9.E.1.b. Pan coatings

Moreover, most new pans today are coated. The two most acceptable coatings available are silicone glaze and SBS-Teflon coating.

Silicone glaze is a compound that belongs to a group of high-molecular-weight polymers composed of silicon compounded with hydrocarbons and possesses outstanding chemical and thermal stabilities. It does not conduct electricity and is water repellant. Silicone glaze is a semi-permanent coating that creates a smooth, impervious and non-adhesive surface, which protects pans from moisture penetration and facilitates product release during depanning thus either markedly reducing or eliminating the need for pan release oils or agents (**Figure 9.129**). When it is professionally applied, it can provide up to 600 baking cycles before the pans need to be reglazed.

The SBS-Teflon coating systems are specially formulated fluoropolymers designed to withstand the unique environment of the commercial bakery, with its stacking, cleaning and constant thermal cycling. It can provide up to 6,000 releases before the pans need to be recoated. SBS-Teflon coating systems have excellent release characteristics; have extremely high temperature operating range; and are virtually inert chemically, which makes this coating ideal for parts exposed to corrosive environments such as salt, acid and alcohol. The exceptional release property of SBS-Teflon allows the baker to virtually eliminate the use of oil. Reducing or eliminating oil helps keep the bakery environment, electrical components and ovens cleaner.

Like silicone glazes, SBS-Teflon will also fail because of thermal breakdown, abrasion and other damages that expose the bare metal. Thermal breakdown takes place each time a pan is heated and cooled, microscopic cracks begin to form in the coating. Eventually these cracks will grow large enough to allow the accumulation of baking residue, causing the coating to lose its nonstick properties. Excessive heating, uneven heating and abrasion will all contribute to reducing the usable life of the coating pans.

Figure 9.129. Silicone-glazed pans require little if any pan release oils and go up to 600 baking cycles before they need to be reglazed.
(Pan-Glo, A Bundy Co.)

The pans should be brushed and vacuumed before being taken off the line for storage. All residues should be removed from the pan prior to storage. Ideally, the pans should be hand-wiped with a damp cloth as needed — usually between 500 and 1,000 bakes. Such cleaning will insure that the pans will provide the maximum number of releases before recoating (**Figure 9.130**).

Proper use of release sprays can reduce the need to reglaze pans to once per 1,000 bakes or longer (Berne 2006). At least one manufacturer uses a hydroplate system: Under high pressure and atomization of the oil particles, an electric charge is given to the oil, thus enhancing adherence to the metal bread pan's cavities.

In most high-volume bakeries, the pans will go through the baking process between 5 and 10 times a day, depending on the number of pans and production requirements. Such frequencies mean pans coated with a silicone glaze will need to be reglazed every 2 to 4 months, while SBS-Teflon coatings will need to be replaced every 1 to 3 years.

Both silicone glaze and SBS-Teflon are widely used throughout the world. In Europe, about 70% of bakers use fluoropolymer coatings. Large bakeries in other parts of the world use more fluoropolymer coatings than silicone glaze. The US market, however, uses mostly silicone glaze (Obal 2002).

Both silicone glaze and SBS-Teflon coating have certain negative environmental impacts (Schneeman 1995, Mallet 2000). Various levels of volatile organic compounds (VOCs) are released during the stripping and re-coating process. The coating companies are presently addressing these issues. They use thermal incineration, catalytic converters or different methods of removing the old coating and preparing the surface prior to re-coating.

Pan maintenance involves inspection for abrasion and bare spots where the product is sticking to the pan. With silicone glaze, the baker can look for other signs such as using more air pressure to remove buns from pans or requiring a greater amount of release agent, both signifying it is time to get their pans reglazed. Bakers would be wise to establish a cycle average and get the pans recoated and or reglazed on scheduled time frame. The reglazing and the recoating process require that the pans be removed and sent out to the application shop. The relationship and coordination between coater and baker is essential to minimize the number of pans the baker needs to keep on hand to maintain production and keep the pans in optimum working shape.

9.E.1.c. Plastic pans

The pan of the future may very well be made of plastic (Stumpf 1989). Pans constructed of liquid crystal polymers (LCPs) have been used to bake bread at temperatures of 240°C (465°F). The material is lightweight, does not need to be glazed or coated, needs no oil and can withstand the rigors of pan handling.

Flexible pans (**Figure 9.131**) constructed of woven fiberglass covered with FDA-approved flexible food-grade silicone are already in use at European bakeries. The flexible pan is stable at baking temperatures up to 248°C (480°F) and facilitates depanning.

9.E.1.d. Peel boards

Peel boards are to bagels and hearth breads as straps are to pan bread, right up to the oven. These large permanent-use boards (**Figure 9.132**) transport moulded buns, rolls and breads through retarding and the final proofing process. In the past, peel boards were often constructed from wood, but the choice today is hard plastic, an FDA-approved polypropylene.

Different manufacturers offer several designs for peels, whose sizes range from 18 to 30 in. wide and 26 to 40 in. long, as well as custom configurations. Tops and bottoms come with smooth and/or texturized surfaces, and at least one manufacturer offers a hollow center with welded design for a high strength-to-weight ratio. Unlike earlier wooden peel boards, the plastic style will not splinter or absorb moisture, and they resist deflection. The boards suit temperature conditions common to proofing and retarding, 4 to 49°C (10 to 120°F).

9.E.2. Bread pan design

Pan design aims to achieve two basic purposes: (a) to promote product quality by providing the most suitable conditions that will yield optimum volume, crust coloration, flavor development and product uniformity, and (b) to impart to pans sufficient stability so they will withstand, with minimum damage, their handling by mechanized conveying systems.

9.E.2.a. Effect on bread quality

Pans that feature large-radius bottom and side edges and balled corners not only release the bread loaves more readily during depanning, but they also nest with greater facility and with a minimum of scoring, scratching or other damage to the inner pan surface. Slit wrappers or plastic bags are less likely to occur during the packaging of bread loaves that do not have sharp bottom and side edges. The large-

Figure 9.130. SBF-Teflon coated pans can provide up to 6,000 releases before they need to be recoated.
(American Pan, A Bundy Baking Solution)

Figure 9.131. Flexible pans facilitate depanning.
(SASA Demarle)

radius bottoms and side edges also make it easier to clean the pans.

Cupping and tunneling of loaf bottoms, which resulted from steam or air pockets trapped below the loaf, were problems that formerly occurred with some frequency. They have been effectively eliminated by providing the pan with a series of small venting holes (0.0625 in.) on all sides, spaced 1 in. apart and about 0.25 in. above the bottom. The same beneficial effect is achieved by placing 3 to 4 venting holes in the pan bottom. Loaf symmetry can often be improved with pans that feature sidewalls and ends with a slightly convex outward dimension. As the loaf cools, it undergoes some shrinkage that results in straight side crusts conducive to smooth slicing and trouble-free packaging.

The problem of scorched loaf bottoms by localized over-heating is alleviated by pans that feature so-called button bottoms that, in effect, are little more than outward depressions about 0.0625 in. deep. Their purpose is to slightly elevate the pan bottom above the oven hearth. This gap promotes heat circulation under the pan and avoids localized hot spots, thereby producing a more uniform bake and coloration of the bottom crust. This feature is particularly effective with older pans whose bottoms are no longer absolutely flat as a result of extended usage and handling by mechanical systems. It is ineffective, however, with ovens that have grid-type trays.

The sandwich bread and Pullman sets (**Figure 9.133**) use the folded-end design; it permits fractional variation in any dimension for the desired size and shape. The laps formed by the folding provide a good base for the welding of the pans to the strap.

Pans are particularly vulnerable to abrasive wear at their bottom edges and to impact damage at their rims. Several design modifications have been adopted to counteract these problems. Thus, pan wear is reduced by the application of ribbing and corrugation patterns at 45 or 90° angles around the bottom edges of the pan or over the entire bottom surface and about 0.5 in. up the sidewalls.

Impact damage to rims is reduced by spot welding the supporting wire to the rim on all sides of the pan to prevent their possible separation and also by welding the band that unites several pans into a single set in such a position as to provide a permanent cover for the wire rim. The strapping bands also protect the corners of the pan sets against direct damage-causing contact with conveyor rails and serve as guides for pan covers during lidding and delidding operations. The added rigidity they impart to pans will extend the useful life of the pans and preserve their true shape for longer periods (Hardin 1967).

9.E.2.b. Multiple-pan designs

"Straps" or "strap pans" consist of individual loaf pans joined by a reinforced metal band into sets of 3 or more pans. The distance between the pans within the set is permanently fixed by spacer wires attached at intervals to the parallel longitudinal pan rims. The minimum distance between the individual pan sets is determined by spacer lugs or offsets on the exterior strapping bands. These are designed to maintain the same distance between abutting pan sets during oven loading as exists between the pans within the set, and thereby promote uniform baking.

Figure 9.132. Today's bakery peel boards are made of lightweight, durable plastic. (Rehrig Pacific)

Figure 9.133. Sandwich bread is baked in Pullman sets of pans and lids. (American Pan, A Bundy Baking Solution)

Figure 9.134. Conventional open-top bread pans are grouped as a 5-strap set. (American Pan, A Bundy Baking Solution)

Figure 9.135. Flat perforated screen pans allow baking of hearth-style breads in rack ovens. (American Pan, A Bundy Baking Solution)

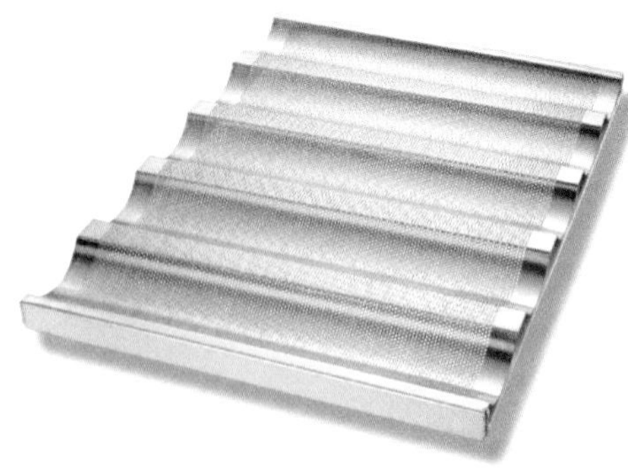

Figure 9.136. Wire and mesh pans configured as a series of channels carry baguettes and French rolls through proofing and baking. (American Pan, A Bundy Baking Solution)

Ten to 18 or more pans per strap are possible, but the most popular number is 3 to 6 (**Figure 9.134**). Maximizing the number of trays reduces the handling of the pans and the motions of the line. Running 12,000 pieces per hour in a 6-pan strap means many motions and movements of the straps. Running 12,000 pieces per hour in a 12- or 18-pan strap means the line motions are reduced 50% or more. These configurations create less wear and tear on the conveyors, final proofers and ovens but do require use of an automatic pan loading and unloading system because individual pan weight exceeds the reasonable limits of manual handling. Overall, line life span is increased and maintenance costs are reduced. The maximum size of the strap sets is dictated first by the oven size and second by the makeup equipment requirements.

Bakers always try to get more capacity out of the same line to improve efficiency and lower costs. Use of wide conveyors allows pans to be sent "the wide way," thus achieving greater throughput on the same system. Additionally, by orienting pans to travel this way, operators can slow the line, increase capacity and experience less wear and tear on the system, which translates to less maintenance. Running the wide way requires that the bread be aligned on the pans or boards so that the short side of the bread becomes the leading end entering the oven. This method is primarily used to maximize oven efficiency. Short-side leading is also used when baking free-standing breads proofed on peels. This orientation enables the peel board unloader to deliver loaves to the oven in a way that prevents damage to the product.

9.E.2.c. Specialty designs

Perforated screen pans are often used for hearth breads baked in rack ovens; in deck, tunnel or traveling hearth ovens, such varieties would bake directly on the oven deck or hearth. These pans (**Figure 9.135**) normally consist of an open frame that supports a perforated insert, which serves as the actual dough mould. The shape of this mould can vary considerably, ranging from a design with flat slanting sides and a flat bottom, to one with curved slanting sides and a minimal flat bottom, or to one with a curved, half-rounded bottom (also called channel pans). The supporting frame may be either completely-open or flanged at the bottom, in which case reinforcing bars are required, or it may feature a perforated bottom platform (Inzerillo 1979).

Channel-style pans (**Figure 9.136**) have long been popular for baguettes. With their curved sides, they support the dough through proofing and baking. The perforated metal mesh has holes roughly 1.8 mm in diameter that produce a characteristic knobby pattern on bottom crusts of goods baked in such pans. The holes enable steam to escape the loaf as it bakes, thus fostering a desirable crispy crust.

To accommodate the dough handling needs of serpentine and vertical baking systems, pan manufacturers have recently begun making pans that can be easily inserted and removed (**Figure 9.137**). These systems typically carry pans on lugs attached to chains and will require an automatic or robotic pan loader during changeovers. Previously, these systems used fixed pans.

9.E.3. Bun and roll pans

Soft buns and rolls are baked on flat pans embossed with moulds of appropriate size and form, for example, round, square or oblong. The spacing of the moulds are arranged to yield either individual buns or clusters of 2 to 12 buns (**Figure 9.138**).

The individual moulds, or cups, in turn, may differ in depth from 0.375 in. to 0.75 in., with the greater depths yielding improved product uniformity. They may feature either convex bottoms to minimize product cupping, or their bottoms may be provided with centered indentations to aid in more accurate dough depositing.

Venting holes are often placed between cups to promote heat circulation and assure a more uniform bake (**Figure 9.139**). The number of moulds or cups in bun pans may range from 12 to 32, depending on the type and size of the product. Special perforated sheet pans are available for baking hearth-type roll products.

Introduction of highly conveyorized pan handling systems in bakeries specializing in soft bun and roll production has imposed the need for certain modifications in the construction and design of pans to adapt them more efficiently to such operations. Here again, spot welding of the rim wire to the pan, particularly at the corners as the points of greatest abuse, will add to the pan's overall strength.

Pan rigidity and ruggedness can be improved by embossing reinforcing ribs in the pan's flat surface between some or all of the mould rows. Because of the low profile of bun pans, they have a tendency to shingle on conveyors whenever their flow is stopped by obstructions while the conveyor continues to run. This problem is largely eliminated by either welding an extra wire below the pan rim or by increasing the vertical width of the rim.

Cake pans are available in a great variety of shapes and forms, ranging from flat sheet pans to cupcake moulds to form-cake pans of various configurations. Pans for larger product sizes are generally fabricated as individual units, whereas pans for snack cake items are normally strapped into sets or consist of frames containing rows of individual cups or moulds.

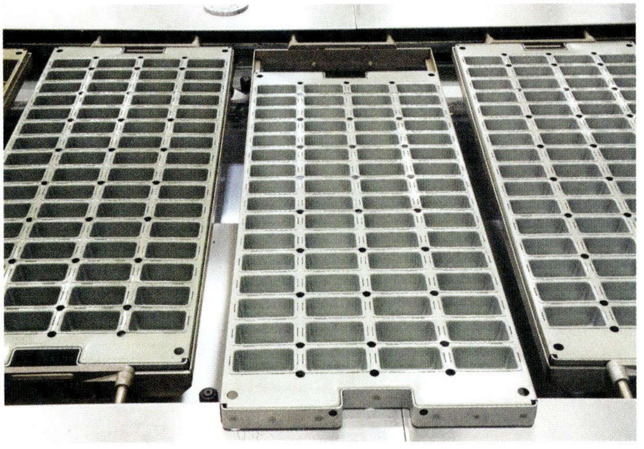

Figure 9.137. Interchangeable pans improve the flexibility of serpentine and vertical baking lines.
(Auto-Bake)

Figure 9.138. The spacing of moulds, or cups, on this pan will result in production of cluster buns.
(American Pan, A Bundy Baking Solution)

9.E.4. Depanners

All pan bread coming from the oven is immediately removed from the pans and allowed to cool prior to slicing and packaging. Soft buns and rolls, by contrast, are sometimes allowed to cool on the baking pans or sheets in those plants where the depanning unit forms an integral component of the roll packaging operation. However, it is generally preferable that buns and rolls also be depanned immediately after emerging from the oven and transferred to the conveyor cooler.

Initially, depanning of bread was performed manually and required the efforts of several workers. While some picked up the pans from the discharge apron of the oven, inverted and struck them against a bumping bar mounted over an accumulating table, others placed the loose hot loaves on rack shelves for cooling. This operation had to be carried out quite rapidly in order to keep pace with the oven's unloading rate, and this haste resulted in frequent burn injuries through contact with the hot pans.

The first mechanical bread depanners were developed more than 70 years ago and ultimately evolved into units capable of depanning 20 to 25 pan straps per minute (Stadelman 1974). The basic mode of operation of these early designs was relatively

Figure 9.139. The deep cups of this pan require use of venting holes to promote heat circulation and a uniform bake.
(American Pan, A Bundy Baking Solution)

simple. Pans were fed into by a metering conveyor into the depanner's throw-over arm. This arm then swung forward and dropped the inverted pan with an abrupt stop on adjustable bars that loosened and freed the loaves. The spacing of the bars was such that they held back the pan strap but cleared the freed loaves, which dropped into a contoured dump chute. As the bar frame moved forward to deposit the pan set onto the pan discharge conveyor, the dump chute assumed a vertical position, thereby sending the loaves by gravity in an upright position to the conveyor leading to the cooler.

Turn-over depanners are still used today for some products, and modern designs for this unit will hold of a number of bread pans, turning them up-side-down. During this motion, breads are prevented from falling out. The empty straps are rotated back to the strap conveyor. The baked products will leave the depanner on the cooling belt conveyor.

9.E.4.a. Vacuum depanners

For the most part, however, the operating speed of mechanical depanners proved inadequate for modern production rates; moreover, they were noisy, shortened the life of pan sets and caused frequent damage to the product. Because of these shortcomings, mechanical depanners soon became obsolete and were eventually replaced by vacuum depanners.

For depanning pans with lids, a delidding device consisting either of a magnetic lifter or stub rollers is positioned immediately before the depanner or incorporated directly into the front of the depanner unit.

Vacuum depanners, as their name implies, use vacuum to lift the baked product from the pans, with minimum damage to both product and the pans. Their basic mode of operation is depicted schematically in **Figure 9.140**. In this particular design, which features a magnetic delidder, the set of lidded pans enters the depanner and first contacts a lid conveyor equipped with powerful permanent magnets. These lift and hold the lid for transfer to a discharge conveyor.

The uncovered pans continue on a flat-top conveyor, which is usually provided with a magnetic rail to hold them down and proceed toward the suction belt which is equipped with numerous vacuum cups made of flexible silicone rubber. Just before the pans reach this vacuum belt, strong air jets are directed between the pan walls and the bread loaves to loosen and separate the loaves from the pan and raise them to the suction cups. These cups then lift the loaves from the pans and transfer them onto the conveyor leading to the cooler. An example of a conventional vacuum bread depanner is shown in **Figure 9.141**.

Depanners are designed specifically for bread, buns and rolls, or for both. Depanning rates may exceed 260 loaves per minute for bread and 35 pans per minute for buns. Efficient depanning, aside from requiring correct equipment adjustment, presupposes that the pans receive appropriate treatment with an effective pan release agent.

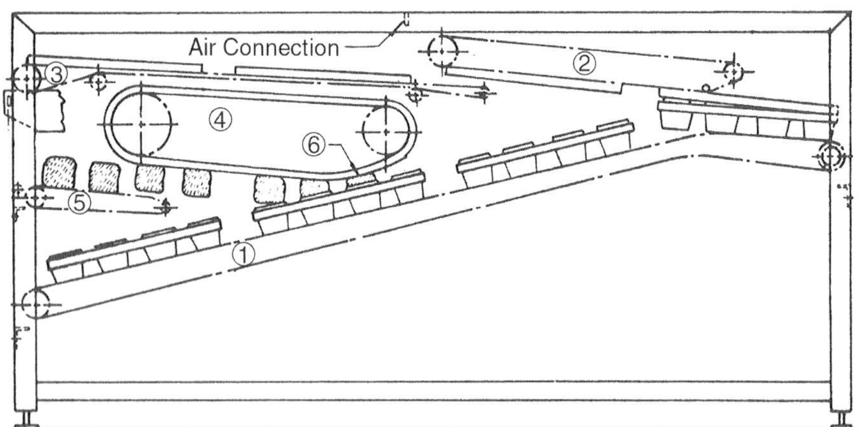

Figure 9.140. The components of a vacuum bread depanner include (1) pan conveyor, (2) magnetic lid conveyor, (3) lid take-out conveyor, (4) suction head, (5) product take-out conveyor and (6) air jets. (Stadelman 1974)

Pans are removed from the depanner by a conveyor that either returns them to the moulder-panner for immediate reuse or to a pan storage area. Adequate time for pan transport from the depanner and the moulder-panner should be provided to permit the pans to cool from their initial temperature of about 149°C (300°F) to about 35°C (95°F) at which temperature they are ready for immediate reuse at the moulder.

9.E.4.b. Alternative designs

Several new and slightly different types of depanners are available today. For example, the needle depanner is designed to take delicate baked products from the baking trays where a suction depanner is not useful. Employing a pick-and-place principle, the depanner positions its head with extending needles above the baking trays. The needles are pushed angularly into the product (**Figure 9.142**). Then they rise to lift products out of the trays and transferred them to the cooling conveyor where the products are released. The holes made by the needles in the warm product mend and disappear during cooling.

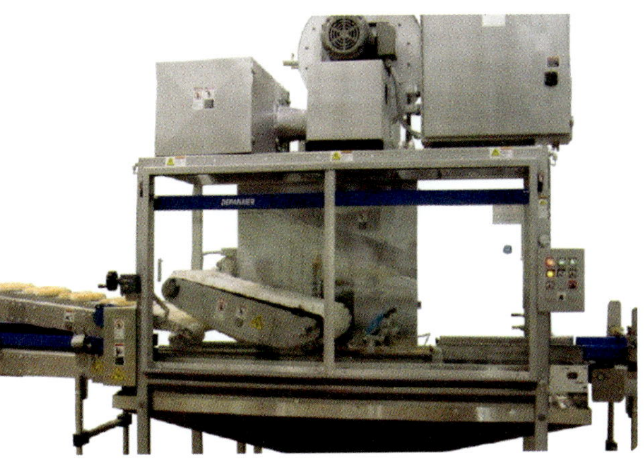

Figure 9.141. Vacuum depanners pull loaves out of their pans, sending the bread to the cooling conveyor while routing the pan back to the moulder-panner.
(Stewart Systems)

The scrabbler depanner can be used to take small bread items from flat baking trays. (The pan rim poses no problem to this method.) The scrabbler's main component is a short belt conveyor with a small-radius nose. Often, a driven soft round brush is installed above the scrabbler to prevent products from rolling back.

Pick-and-place methods are also used by a variation of the suction or vacuum depanner (**Figure 9.143**) designed to take baked products from the baking pan or tray. A vacuum head is positioned above the bread pans to pick up products. The whole head shifts over to above the transfer conveyor and descends to release the baked products for cooling. Vacuum heads come in various configurations and can be readily changed to accommodate different product styles.

Special bun and roll depanner-packers are available that combine depanning and packing operations. Here, the suction cups on the vacuum mechanism are arranged in patterns that align with those of the pan cups holding the rolls. The unit is provided with a conveyor that feeds in the pans containing the rolls and also the cartons or trays that will receive the rolls.

Figure 9.142. A needle depanner manages delicate products that would otherwise experience damage if depanned by vacuum methods.
(The Kaak Group)

Figure 9.144 shows a heavy duty pick-and-place depanner-packer equipped with 2 triple package pick-up heads that can rotate 180° to remove rolls from the pan and deposit them into the carton box. Pick-up heads and vacuum cups can be changed to accommodate different products. **Figure 9.145** shows the suction cups of the pick-and-place depanner-packer.

9.E.4.c. Robotic applications

Robots have found expanded application outside of depanning in so-called robotic pattern loading systems for transport baskets and trays (**Figure 9.146**). In this system, the robot's end effector consists of vacuum actuated pick-up cups that transfer bagged loaves from the packaging machine's outfeed conveyor to a rotating

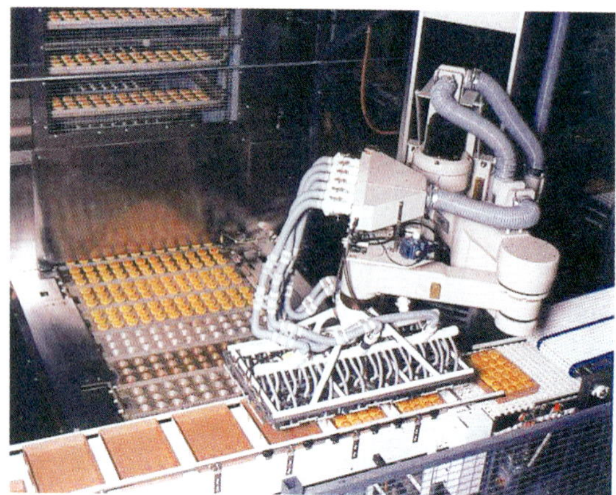

Figure 9.143. This pick-and-place vacuum depanner features interchangeable heads.
(Dunbar Systems)

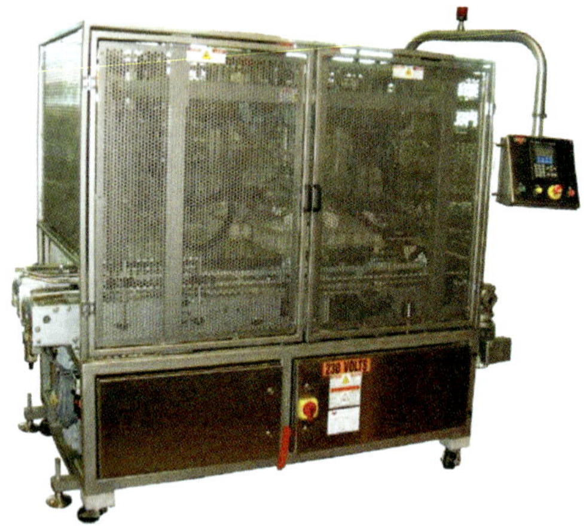

Figure 9.144. A pneumatic bun handling unit performs the dual functions of depanning and carton packing of buns and rolls. It is designed and manufactured in accordance with BISSC standards to ensure that the system is easy to clean.
(AMF Bakery Systems)

Figure 9.145. The vacuum depanning head of the pick-and-place system removes buns from pans and transfers them to the cooling conveyor.
(AMF Bakery Systems)

pattern-forming table. When the proper number and configuration are reached, the head's loading paddles gently compress the pattern on 4 sides to fit loaves snugly in the basket without damaging the bread. This entire operation of repetitive basket or tray loading is completely automatic, under the control of a PLC. A wide range of different patterns can be programmed into the system to permit instant adaptation to various basket dimensions, with the selection of the appropriate pattern being activated by push-button.

The baking industry now uses robots to pack even the most delicate bakery products. A fully automatic robotic loading system offers a flexible, reliable, high-speed solution for wrapped bakery products, including bread, buns, rolls and English muffins. The computer maintains control of the product 100% of the time and assures proper product placement in the tray. Robots are also very effective in organizing products leading to the packing equipment. **Figure 9.147** shows a spider-like delta robot system that rapidly picks up randomly oriented products and positions them for feeding into a carton.

A robot can be a simple machine, consisting of servo motors and gear boxes, operating in two or more axes. The packaging robot shown in **Figure 9.148** uses 5 axes of motion and incorporates a vision system. They are typically self-sealed and self-lubricated and require no more attention than any other servo controlled machine. The end effector — the robot's hand —does the fine-detailed work of picking up and moving objects.

Robots, including automated guided vehicles (AGVs), are finding common employment in the pan handling area of the bakery (Livesay 1992, Hyman 1995). Pick-and-place robots, for example, can remove lids and then pick up the pans and stack them for storage or return them to the moulding section for reuse (**Figure 9.149**).

The latest trend is to include vision systems that bring "sight" to robots, thus providing greater flexibility to the production line. System efficiency, fast changeovers, placement speed, system reliability, small footprint and flexibility are important considerations when choosing a robotic system for your plant.

9.E.5. Pan management systems

The handling of bread and bun pans in the bakery was formerly carried out on a

strictly manual basis. Because this task is highly labor-intensive, its mechanization and automation are being actively pursued, especially in bakeries producing a variety of products. In such plants, large numbers of different types of pans must be frequently cycled in and out of production, stacked and unstacked, and placed into and drawn out of storage. Modern pan handling systems will automatically convey pans to stackers and unstackers, divert them into storage or withdraw them, and shunt them into different production lines (Anderson 1974a, Anderson 1974b, Dobie 1977).

Conveyors form the essential base of any pan handling system. The types appropriate for specific applications include flat-top steel chains for straight sections, gravity-roller and powered-roller conveyors for pan accumulation, and material belting with a magnetic rail beneath it to negotiate steep inclines and declines. Metal rollers in these systems are preferably covered with durable plastic to reduce their noise level.

Most pan stacking and unstacking units use magnetic technologies. Their principle of operation is illustrated in **Figure 9.150**. Pans entering the stacker on an elevated conveyor are carried through the unit by an overhead magnetic rail conveyor. If the pan is merely being recycled to the next production phase, it passes unimpeded to the take-up pan conveyor. If the pan is to be stacked, however, a retractable pan-stop brings it to a halt in the stacking position. Next, a pneumatic vertical plunger pushes the pan down into the forming pan stack supported by a double-flight elevator that automatically lowers as each pan is deposited. Stacking continues until the preset stack height in the range of 40 to 60 in. is reached, and the whole stack is lowered onto a conveyor, pan truck or electric lift truck. A typical pan stacker/unstacker system is shown in **Figure 9.151**.

The magnetic pan unstacker is of similar design. Here, however, the pans from storage are introduced into the unit's elevator in stacks. As the stack is automatically raised, the plunger, in this case equipped with permanent magnets, lifts the individual pans from the stack against the overhead magnetic discharge belt, which deposits them on the conveyor leading to production.

In a traditional bakery, the pans supplied to unstacker would be wheeled in manually using loaded pan trucks held in a storage area. Today, some bakeries use AGVs to transport the stacked pans to and from storage. The system is completely automatic and computer controlled. Only the computer will know where they are.

The latest advances in automated pan management systems include both conventional and robotic pan stacking and unstacking equipment, as well as lasers used for positioning of pan transfer vehicles on automated storage and retrieval systems (AS/RS), as shown in **Figure 9.152**. Also, equipment manufacturers have focused on minimizing wear and tear on pans, and PLCs and laser systems have become much more robust and faster. Many bakeries use multiple-tier storage in these systems to save space (**Figure 9.153**).

A complete system will include robotic lid handling and robotic pan handling. These robots are specifically designed for the baking industry. They both use pedestal-mounted 4-axis robots (**Figure 9.154**) (Whitaker 2009b). The custom-designed magnetic gripper (end effector or end-of-arm tool-

Figure 9.146. A robotic basket loader gently compresses the pattern on 4 sides to fit loaves snugly in the basket without damaging the bread. (Colborne Foodbotics Corp.)

Figure 9.147. Randomly oriented products can be picked and placed rapidly by a delta robot. (Blueprint Automation)

Figure 9.148. An integrated vision system allows this robot to operate with 5 axes of motion for loading trays from a belt carrying randomly oriented products. (Weldon Solutions)

Figure 9.149. A robotic pick-and-place system manages storage and retrieval of multiple pan sets. (Capway Systems)

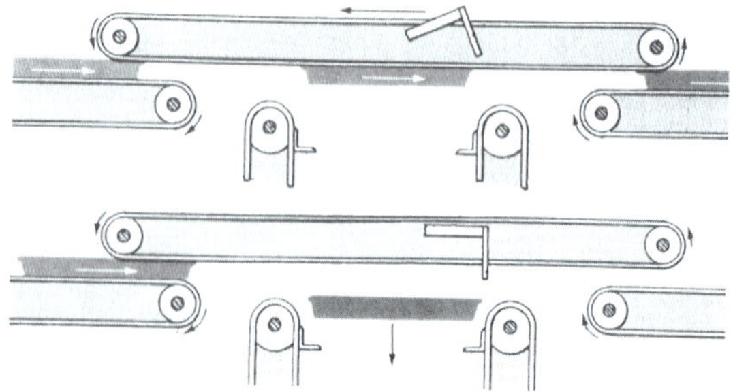

Figure 9.150. With the pan stop of a magnetic pan stacker retracted (upper portion), pans pass unimpeded through the stacker. With the pan stop lowered (lower portion), pan stacking is initiated. (Anderson 1974b)

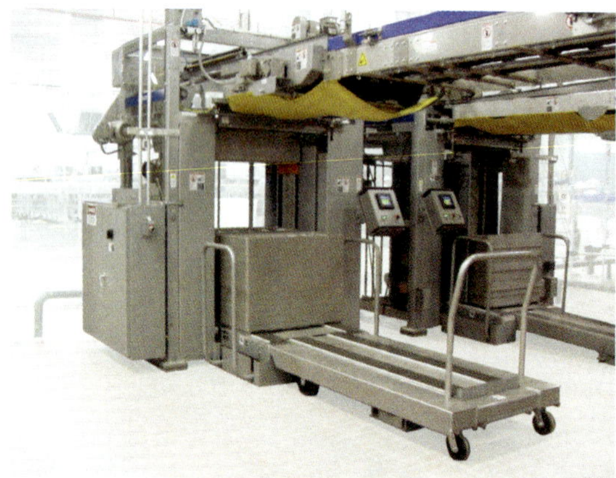

Figure 9.151. An automatic pan stacker/unstacker system ensures the controlled pan flow in and out of production. (Stewart Systems)

Figure 9.152. The transfer vehicle picks up pans stacks to carry them to the processing line and returns with pans stacked as they leave the line. (Weldon Solutions)

ing) is able to pick up multiple lids or pans at a time to gently move items from conveyor to stack and back again after use. The smooth, precise robotic motion minimizes equipment jams and damage to lids or pans. These pick-and-place robots offer many benefits compared with mechanical systems. Robotic pan handling is much gentler on pans, and robots can typically run at much higher speeds than mechanical systems. The robots also make a more stable stack of pans and lids.

Modern pan handling systems include several other features that control the flow of pans. Among these are switches of various designs that divert pans from a single conveyor to 2 or more receiving conveyors or, conversely, can combine pans from 2 or more conveyors into a single conveyor. Pan switches are of 3 basic types: (a) vertical switches with a hinged belt conveyor that may be raised or lowered to feed the pans to receiving conveyors operating at different levels; (b) vertical magnetic switches in which the vertical transfer is achieved by a magnetic belt conveyor; and (c) horizontal switches (Baron 1983). In the latter (**Figure 9.155**), high-strength plastic pallets slide on steel rods supported between roller chains. Each pallet is guided by tracks beneath the carrying surface.

Another feature often included in pan handling systems, particularly involving bun pans, is the pan turn-over device. Its use permits the stacking of pans to greater heights, and hence greater weights, by having the stack weight rest on the pan rims rather than on the nesting pockets or moulds. The device automatically inverts the pans by means of a special rotating cylinder or by a set of belts warped into an appropriate configuration. The entire pan handling operation is controlled by a central control panel and by photoelectric sensors or proximity switches placed at critical points in the system.

Pan inverter-cleaners (**Figure 9.156**) combine 2 technologies into a single machine. It provides a high-efficiency pan cleaning method for each production cycle but also has the ability to discharge pans upright for recirculation back to makeup or to invert them for pan stacking in a clean and stable manner.

All pan-handling equipment should be designed to minimize pan damage so reglazing can be scheduled based on the number of passes a pan makes through the oven and not damage. A formal inventory control plan for pans in storage will ensure that all pans are used evenly. Manual systems could keep using the same pan trucks over and over and actually send out pans for reglazing that have not been used very much.

9.F. Extrusion and Laminating Equipment

Updated by Mihaelos N. Mihalos

Automation has come to the previously manual preparation of sweet dough products such as sweet rolls, coffee cakes and danish and puff pastries. This change in manufacture appreciably reduces processing time by eliminating the roll-in steps, cutting the intervals between fold-ins and either omitting or greatly curtailing retarder dwell time. While many variations in procedures exist in sweet goods production, they all involve the basic functions of sheeting, depositing, laminating and scaling or cutting. By incorporating individual machine units into integrated and synchronized production lines, products ranging from simple sweet rolls to the most complex and delicate puff pastry items can be made on a continuous basis.

Extrusion and the related technology of co-extrusion added considerable flexibility to preparation of sweet goods, including cookies. Changes in lamination systems, as well, improved the baker's ability to handle soft, high-absorption doughs, thus opening the door to commercial-scale production of these popular and profitable items. Additionally, sheeting technologies have recently been applied to processing of white and variety pan bread as well as hearth breads, enabling automated makeup of artisan-style doughs, which are normally difficult to machine.

9.F.1. Extrusion

In the conventional production of sweet dough products, the initial step is to transform the bulk dough into a flat sheet. This stage is most generally done by means of a dough pump that forces the dough either through a large round orifice or a flat extruder nozzle and deposits it on a conveyor belt. This initial operation may also be performed by manually feeding 10- to 15-1b dough pieces, which have first been rolled into 15- to 20-in. wide "stringers" and given a 20- to 25-minute rest, through a dough brake or pre-sheeter and then sealing them together on the conveyor belt (Poehlman 1979). Or an automatic dough scaling unit may be used that will accept an entire dough charge from the mixer in its hopper and divide it into 10- to 12-1b dough strips of the desired width. These are then fed into the hopper of an extruder that produces a continuous dough sheet. Depending on the type of end product, the dough ribbon may pass through several additional sheeting roller sets, each adjusted to a narrower gap between the rolls, until a dough sheet of the desired thickness is obtained (**Figure 9.157**).

A recent development in depositing this first layer of dough employs low-stress sheeting methods, which depend on gravity with a roller assist. Even though such extruders create a fairly shallow sheet, approximately 15 mm vs. 40 to 55 mm from conventional extruders, the sheet can be more irregular in depth. A cross-roll station right after the extruder, however, will bring the dough to uniform dimensions (Gorton 2009).

Dough band formers independently regulate roll speeds and gap settings. The rolls can be linked to drive the top two together, with the bottom indepen-

Figure 9.153. By placing pan stacks on multiple tiers, considerable floor space can be saved with automated storage and retrieval methods. (Workhorse Automation)

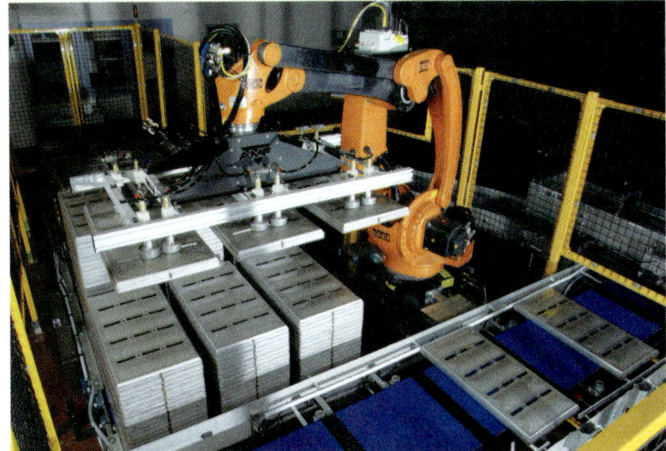

Figure 9.154. Magnetic end effectors manage pan stacking and unstacking. (AMF Bakery Systems)

Figure 9.155. Horizontal conveyor switch diverts pan flow from one conveyor to another. (Stewart Systems)

Figure 9.156. This pan inverter-cleaner can either discharge pans upright for recirculation back into the line or inverted for stacking. (Workhorse Automation)

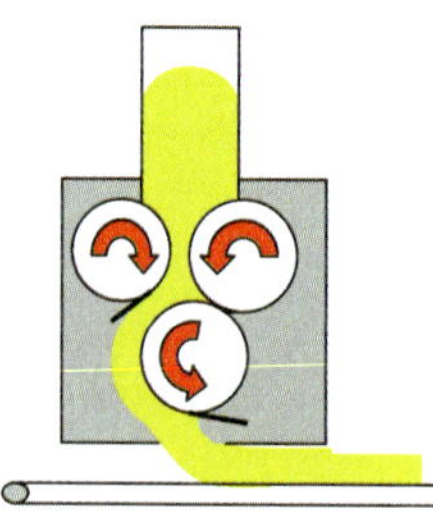

Figure 9.157. Extrusion of yeasted doughs can be done with low-stress sheeters and 3-roll extruders. (Rademaker)

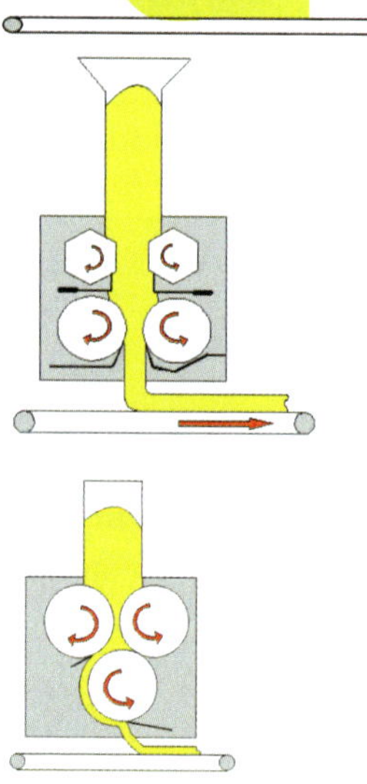

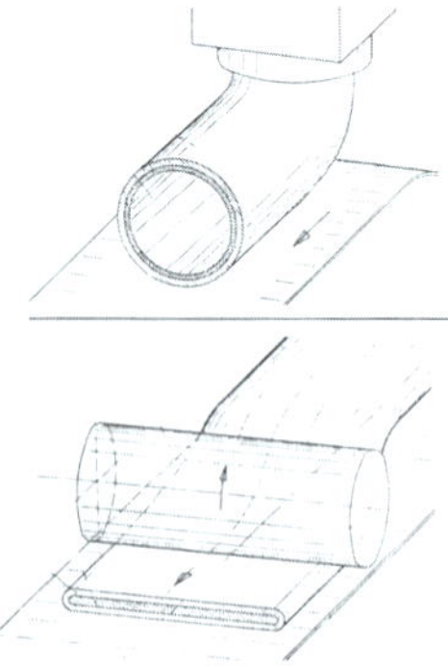

Figure 9.158. This co-extruder produces a hollow dough cylinder with an interior lining of fat as the first step in creating a laminated dough band. (Cleven and Weber 1977)

dent or to run the top and bottom rolls together, with the top roll independent. Also, the rolls can be made with different levels of corrugation to manage dough movement.

Co-extrusion methods enable simultaneous delivery of both dough and shortening. The ring extruder continually co-extrudes dough and fat from two separate hoppers through a wide ring orifice. This action forms a hollow dough cylinder with an internal lining of fat (**Figure 9.158**) (Cleven and Weber 1977, Haarsgaard 1980). Because the thickness of both the dough and the fat can be controlled with great precision, the ratio of the roll-in shortening to the dough is readily adjustable. The cylinder is deposited on a conveyor belt that carries it through the initial flattening roll. One basic benefit derived from this method of lamination is the absolute uniformity throughout the dough and fat layers because no overlapping of either layer occurs.

As bakers moved away from hydrogenated fats, changes were required in the fat pumps that feed dough extrusion machines. Some bakers are going back to butter, a fat that contains 16% water. Excess pressure during pumping will drive out some of this water, making the dough soggy and diminishing the steam generation responsible for leavening laminated baked foods.

All components of fat-handling systems should minimize frictional heat development by using conveyors and auger feeds to progressive cavity-type pumps delivering fat to the application manifold. Volpe (2006) observed that butter or fat ingredients should be tempered to between 13 and 18°C (55 and 65°F). If the butter, margarine or blended fat ingredients are too cold when extruded, large amounts of water will be pressed out of the fat and will not be available for steam leavening. Butter is 16% water; margarine is about the same, although bakers margarine and roll-in or puff paste fats are lower in moisture content. Fat temperature should not increase more than 0.25 C° (0.5 F°) during transfer through the fat pump system.

It is important to note that the extruders used in bakeries operate as cold systems, not like the extruder-cookers employed by snack food, breakfast cereal and pasta manufacturing operations.

9.F.2. Sheeting

Pastry makeup tables normally feature one or more rollers mounted over the conveyor belt. Stand-alone reversible sheeters (**Figure 9.159**) consist basically of a set of rolls and a conveyor that travels along a supporting table and is capable of reversing direction. Working with individual "books" of dough, the operator controls the size of the gap between the rolls, which results in progressive reduction of the dough sheet's depth.

Automation allows more complex sheeting lines (**Figure 9.160**), with multiple gauge rolls and cross rolls. Cross-rolling, in which the roll moves back and forth across the width of the belt, further reduces the sheet's thickness. In general, cross rolling accounts for about 25% of the total sheeting effect. The lateral pressure exerted on the dough ribbon acts to spread it to the desired width and to produce a cross-grain effect within the dough. Finally, its gentle pressure also relaxes the dough sufficiently to relieve the stresses and strains that are imparted in the upstream processing so that dough shrinkage subsequent to cutting and forming is reduced to a minimum. The unitwill uniformly cross-roll about 30 ft of dough sheet per minute.

Dusting flour boxes are usually associated with sheeting roll sets and cross-roller assemblies to apply small amounts of dusting flour to the conveyor belt and to the dough sheet to minimize sticking. More recently, the use of a skinning fan system dries the top surface of the dough sheet as it passes along the conveyor, thus eliminating flour dusters and minimizing sanitation concerns. Any excess dusting flour is subsequently removed by special flour brush mechanisms, usually following the cross rolling and prior to the folding and laminating operations.

Sweet dough products with a distinct flaky character require the incorporation of discrete particles or layers of shortening. In the all-in, or Scotch, method, the fat is cut into the dough during mixing in such manner that the finished dough will contain relatively large particles of fat. When the dough is extruded and passed repeatedly through sheeting rolls, the fat particles are flattened into thin laminae within the dough and ultimately establish its flakiness.

During sheeting, care must be taken not to disrupt the layered structure of the dough. Large-diameter gauging rolls generally should not operate at ratios higher than 2:1, or a 50% reduction, at each station (Seiffer 2002). Some doughs will tolerate a 4:1 reduction.

The principles of sheeting dough were reviewed by Levine (1998), who examined the fluid mechanics of dough sheeting, describing it as an elongation process, not one of compression. He also discussed scaling up procedures and documented the effect of roll diameter, speed and reduction ratios on work and pressure (**Table 9.5**). These figures reveal (a) larger rolls put more work into doughs, (b) faster speeds also increase work imparted to dough and (c) the lower the reduction ratio, the less the stress on doughs. Also, the total force exerted by doughs on rolls increases proportionally with their width.

A innovative change in the method of reducing dough sheet thickness was introduced by a Japanese inventor in 1974 when he substituted a stretcher system, consisting of an endless chain of small cylinders (**Figure 9.161**), for the conventional large-diameter, single or double sheeting rolls in an automatic pastry line (Hayashi 1978). In operation, the small rollers revolve on their supporting chain in a continuous orbital loop, while each roller rotates on its own axis. As the dough sheet is exposed to the action of the stretcher mechanism for a distance of about 20 in., the

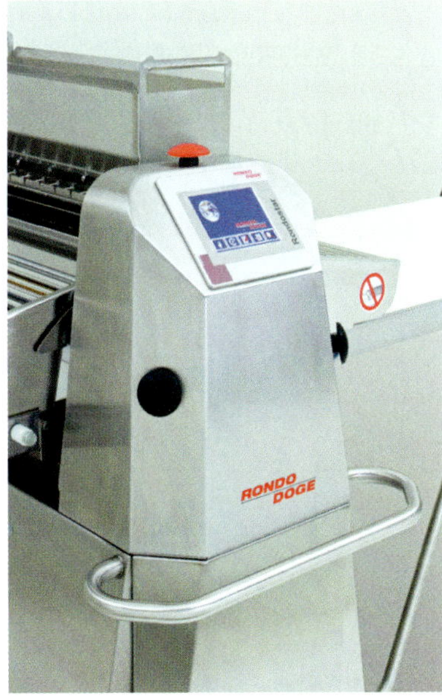

Figure 9.159. Stand-alone reversible sheeters handle books of dough and operate in semi-automatic fashion or can be fully programmed by computer with more than 100 "recipes." (RONDO)

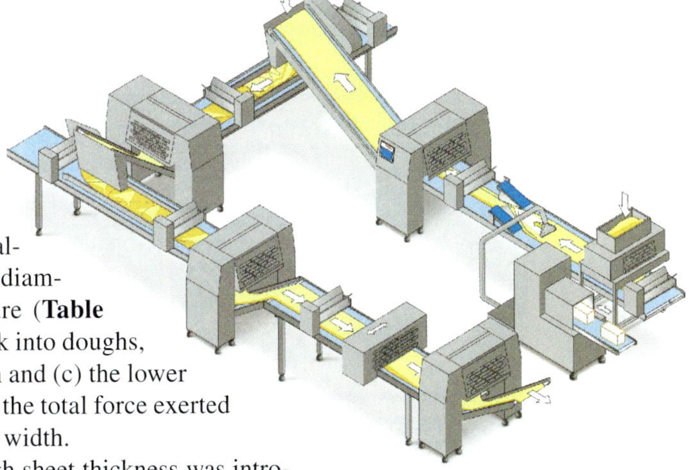

Figure 9.160. Automated pastry makeup lines run dough in a continuous sheet through gauging and cross-rolling stations. (RONDO)

Table 9.5. Effect of Roll Diameter, Roll Speed and Reduction Ratios on Work and Pressure

Roll diameter effect		Roll speed effect		Reduction ratio effect		
Roll diameter	Relative work and pressure	Roll speed	Relative work and pressure	Reduction ratio	Work	Pressure
2	1.0	10	1.0	10	1.00	1.00
4	1.4	20	1.4	5	0.61	0.89
6	1.7	50	2.2	3	0.32	0.71
8	2.0	100	3.2	2	0.13	0.48
12	2.5			1.8	0.09	0.40
				1.4	0.03	0.21
				1.2	0.01	0.10

(Levine 1998)

rollers impact on it some 500 times (**Figure 9.162**). While three belts with increasing speeds stretch the dough sheet from its bottom side (**Figure 9.163**), the stretcher mechanism exerts a constant pressure of some 17 oz per sq in. on the top side. The combined action produces a uniform linear flow that results in a 10:1 reduction of the dough sheet to 4 mm (0.16 in.) with a minimum of stress and without subsequent shrinkage. Stretching does not alter the layering of dough and fat. The company trademarked the term "stress free" for this style of equipment.

These stress-free systems accomplish dough reductions of as much as 10:1 in the course of a single sheeting operation rather than the 2- or 3-roll stands required with large-diameter rolls. Thus, they substantially shorten the overall length of the processing line and save space in the bakery (Seiffer 2002). Some sheet formers in this category can work with doughs of more than 70% absorption, and others use non-stick coatings on dough-contact surfaces in hoppers and on blades (Whitaker 2007a).

Similar technology has since been adopted by a number of equipment manufacturers, and the multiple-roll stations are sometimes termed "satellite rollers" because they travel along a path much like satellite moons revolve around planets. Reduction ratios using stretcher and satellite roll stations of up to 10:1 are possible. Some equipment designs use satellite rollers in pairs, one above and the other below the dough band. By substantially reducing the stress put on doughs, these systems are often able to eliminate the need for resting the dough before the next processing step.

A new technology (**Figure 9.164**) uses high-speed patting instead of gauge rollers to form dough into an appropriately sized band.

Figure 9.161. With guard panels removed, the configuration of the small-diameter rolls in a satellite head is revealed.
(Rheon)

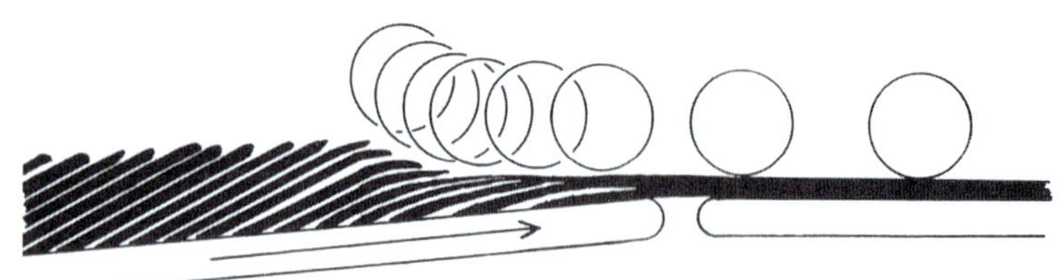

Figure 9.162. This drawing illustrated the action of many small-diameter rolls impacting on dough layers.
(Cleven and Weber 1977)

9.F.3. Lamination

Laminating is about creating texture, and laminating equipment is most often employed to make pastry items comprised of multiple layers of dough and fat, but this method is also used to prepare hard biscuits and crackers in which the physical layering of the dough alone creates the desired textural effects. Doughs suitable for lamination can be yeasted or non-yeasted, but the fundamentals are the same for both. Croissants and danish are examples of yeasted doughs, while puff pastry is the most familiar form of non-yeasted styles (Yankellow 2005).

A more common practice of fat incorporation into pastry doughs is by lamination, also referred to as the French method. This procedure can be carried out in various ways and yields a uniformly layered final structure. In the most prevalent method, the dough is extruded in two continuous ribbons by two successive extruders that are separated by a fat extruder, which deposits a sheet of shortening or butter between the two dough ribbons. In one modified system, the dough sheet is split lengthwise into two strips (**Figure 9.165**), with one strip moving on an upper belt and the other strip on a lower belt. A fat pump then deposits a layer of shortening on the lower dough strip, which is then recombined with the upper strip to form a 3-layer, dough-shortening-dough band. Another method is to lay down the fat in a wide strip along the center of the dough and fold the edges over it (**Figure 9.166**).

No matter which method the baker chooses to introduce shortening into doughs — extrusion, all-in or lamination — the desired degree of flakiness is controlled by the number of folds given the dough sheet. When folding is performed mechanically, the dough sheet, reduced to the appropriate thickness and cut into a suitable length, enters the folding mechanism of the makeup table and is given a book fold. The folded dough sheet is then turned 90° or dropped onto a perpendicular-traveling conveyor by use of a retracting mechanism and passed through sheeting rolls. This process is repeated for the number of times that is required to achieve the desired degree of flakiness.

Further lamination is carried out by folding of the dough sheet, followed by further reductions in dough thickness. Such folding may be accomplished by a variety of procedures. Thus, in one method, the dough sheet is first reduced in thickness by rolling or sheeting. It is then cut transversely into 18-in. long strips that are transferred in shingle fashion onto a belt running at a 90° angle. The shingled dough band is again reduced to a 1-in. thick laminar structure of 6 to 7 layers. By repeating the process, a highly laminated dough sheet is obtained. In continuous systems, the dough sheet is generally transferred by a reciprocating or retracting belt onto a lower belt running at right angle to produce a folding action.

The number of layers considerably affect rise and texture (**Figure 9.167**). But as Yankellow (2005) observed, "Keep in mind that more is not better when it comes to folding dough." If the dough and fat layers get too thin, the fat will practically be absorbed into the dough, and the result is texture more like bread than the honeycomb-like structure desired.

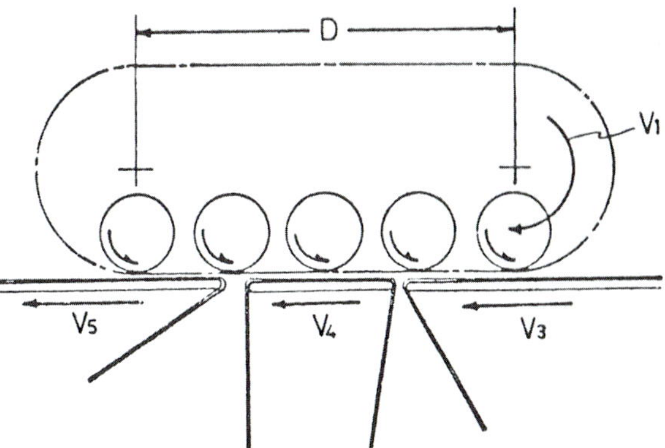

Figure 9.163. This schematic shows how the action of small-diameter rolls above the dough sheet and conveyor belts below stretch doughs without impacting the layering of dough and fat. (Cleven and Weber 1977)

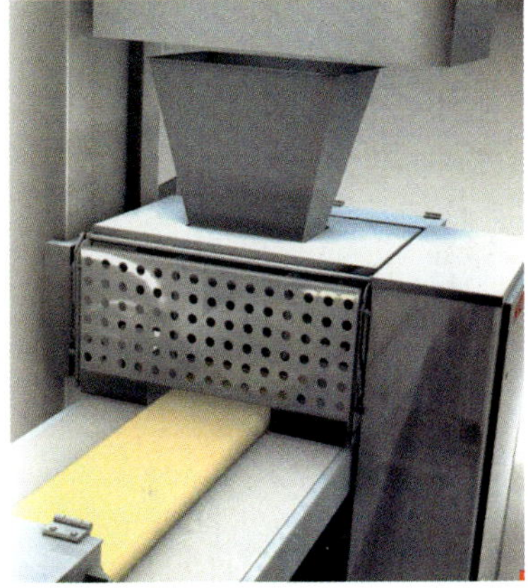

Figure 9.164. High-speed patting forms dough into a band ready for processing. (König)

Figure 9.165. One method of layering butter or shortening is to lift and position half the original dough sheet on top of the other half on which the fat has been deposited. (Fritsch)

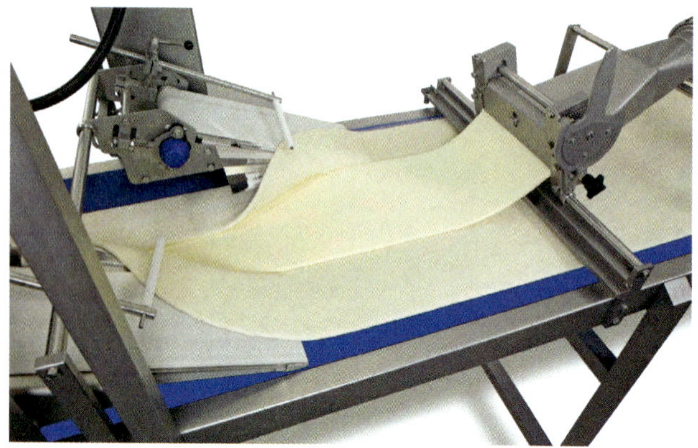

Figure 9.166. Consistency of the extruded fat sheet is controlled by sensors, and the two sides of the dough band are lapped over the fat. (Rademaker)

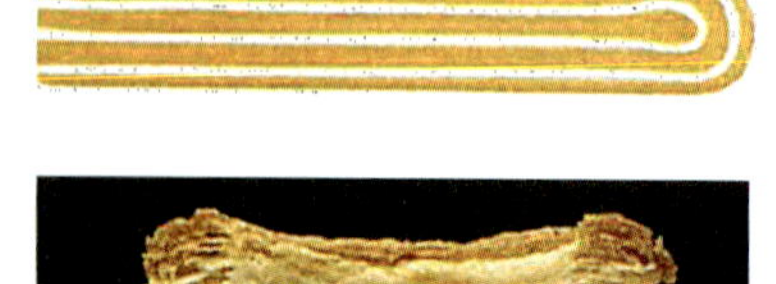

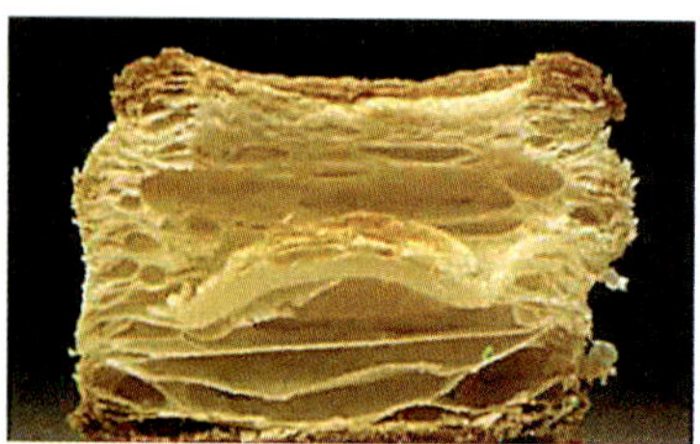

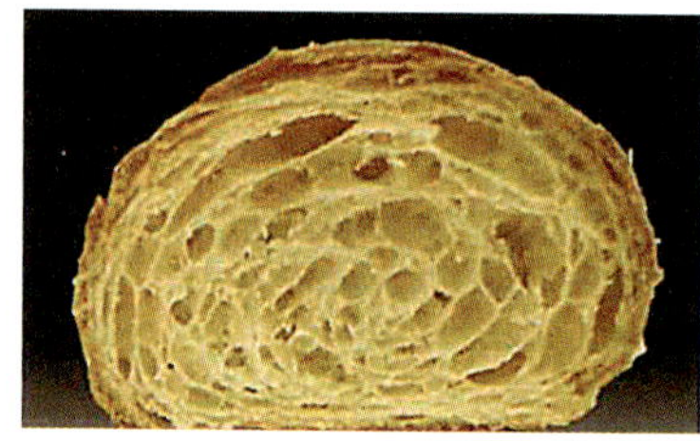

Figure 9.167. Different products call for different numbers of layers in laminated products. (RONDO)

Figure 9.168. A servo-driven cut-sheet laminator divides a continuous sheet of dough into individual sheets and layers the individual lengths with a reciprocating conveyor. (Reading Bakery Systems)

Specialty items such as puff pastry or filo may have up to 144 layers, and croissant or danish pastry may have up to 64 layers of alternating dough and fat. The number of layers also affect line layout in that more layers requires more folds, more reduction rolls and longer conveyor runs. Volpe (2006) observed that turning the dough in the lamination process has a major impact on line layout and floor space requirements. Dual lamination, required to deliver the high number of layers in puff pastry, can have a complex footprint. Such layouts usually fall into one of three designs depending on product type, number of layers and capital available. An "L" layout contains a single lamination step while "C" or "Z" layouts offer two lamination steps.

To lap dough, cut-sheet laminators (**Figure 9.168**) work with a continuous band of dough and cut it into measured lengths. A retracting conveyor drops the sheet onto a slowly moving conveyor to stack up on previous sheets, now traveling at right angles to the feed conveyor. The advantage of this method is that the dough's layers along the new edge of the dough band run straight, not folded, which takes the tension off the dough band's sides.

Another way to accomplish lamination is to reduce the dough to its required thickness, extrude a layer of shortening to cover the dough and then curl the sheet into roll of approximately five layers of fat by using a curling arm, also called a "roll winder" or "torpedo roll," positioned diagonally across the conveyor belt (**Figure 9.169**). The dough roll is then passed through several sets of sheeting rollers that reduce it to the desired thickness.

The dough sheet that emerges from the stretcher or laminating mechanisms next enters the production line's first folding section where an oscillating arm — essentially a swinging gate or retracting conveyor (**Figure 9.170**) — folds, or laps, the dough, piling it onto a conveyor belt traveling at a right angle. The deflection of the folding arm, as well as the speed of the conveyor belt located beneath it, can be varied so that both the width of the lapped dough sheet and the number of layers in the pile can be adjusted. The folded dough ribbon then passes through a second stretcher unit, which again stretches it to the desired thickness and width. If required, this process of folding and stretching is repeated to yield a final dough sheet consisting of more than 220 layers of fat.

Automated laminating systems (**Figure 9.171**) take a continuous band of dough layered with fat and put it through successive lapping and reduction sheeting, followed by a 90° turns and a resting period. Some doughs only require a foot or two of conveyor length to rest, but others such as croissant doughs need 1 to 2 hours. Automated lines now include resting tunnels, generally installed above the sheeting and forming line.

Lamination often requires strict temperature management. The entire makeup room may need to be air conditioned to maintain ambient temperatures of 15 to 21°C (60 to 70°F).

9.F.4. Forming, filling, cutting

Once the desired degree of lamination has been attained, the dough sheet is fed onto the makeup table with its various cutting, depositing and shaping attachments (**Figure 9.172**). These auxiliary devices are available in a wide range of different designs. Thus, the cutters include such varied types as the reciprocating guillotine, circular knife, stamping form cutters, rotating cutting units and others. Depositors may be of the continuous extrusion or the intermittent type and are capable of applying all sorts of fillings in any width and amount. Final shaping attachments will perform such functions as rolling, folding, winding, moulding, stamping, etc., to produce a nearly unlimited variety of product forms and sizes.

Curling rolls also serve to incorporate various types of fillings into sheeted dough to yield alternating layers of filling and dough for production of honey buns, cinnamon rolls and even swirl-style bread.

An interesting recent installation for making dinner rolls uses a guillotine cutter set to cut 5 minutely different sizes. The sizes vary at random to duplicate hand cutting, but when 16 roll pieces are placed in a pan, the total weight reaches the proper target setting.

9.F.5. Encrusting

Encrusting machines can combine 2 or more different materials in a way that the inner filling is completely enclosed by the outer dough. The ratio of interior to exterior materials is completely controllable by machine settings. The properties or rheology of the exterior dough must be such that it is extensible enough to encapsulate and enclose the filler completely.

An ingenious dough moulding-and-filling machine, first developed in Japan in the early 1960s, has found wide application in some areas of the world for the production of a broad range of specialty products containing various types of fillings (Swortfiguer 1968). The inventor of this technology sought a way to make traditional filled buns, a product that was disappearing from the culture because manual preparation was difficult and costly.

The unit (**Figure 9.173**) operates essentially as an enrober. It envelops a measured amount of filling with dough to form dough balls that can range in weight from 1 to 4.5 oz. The machine is capable of a maximum production rate of 2,400 units per hour.

The encrusting process is initiated by pumping the dough from a side hopper into a compound nozzle assembly by an auger-type conveyor of special design. The re-

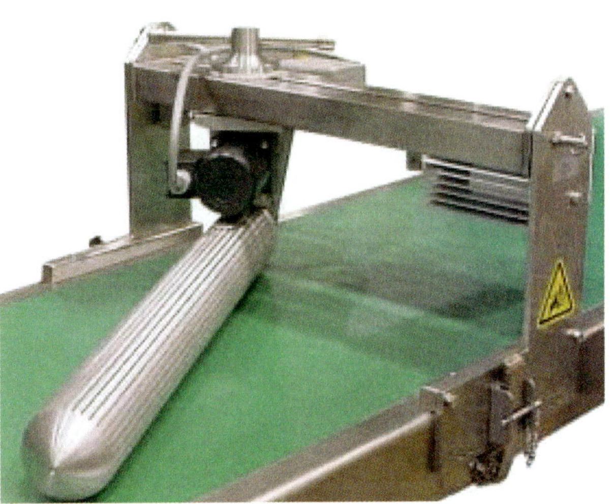

Figure 9.169. A curling arm or roll winder will coil a flat dough sheet into a continuous laminated roll.
(Moline Machinery)

Figure 9.170. A retracting conveyor moves back and forth to stack layers of dough onto one another, thus laminating the dough sheet.
(Tromp)

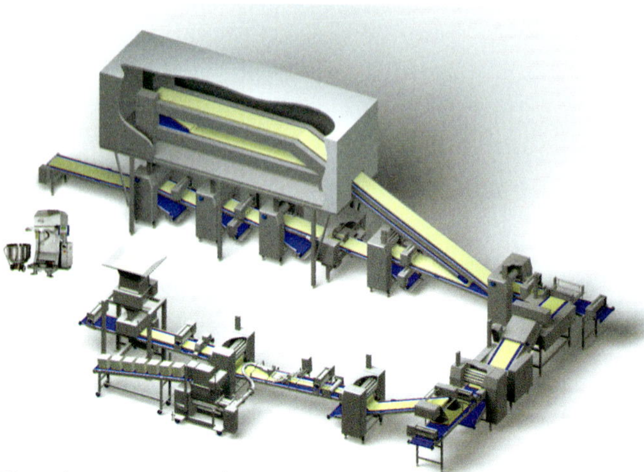

Figure 9.171. Automated laminating lines enable high-volume production of croissants, danish and other layered pastries. (Rademaker)

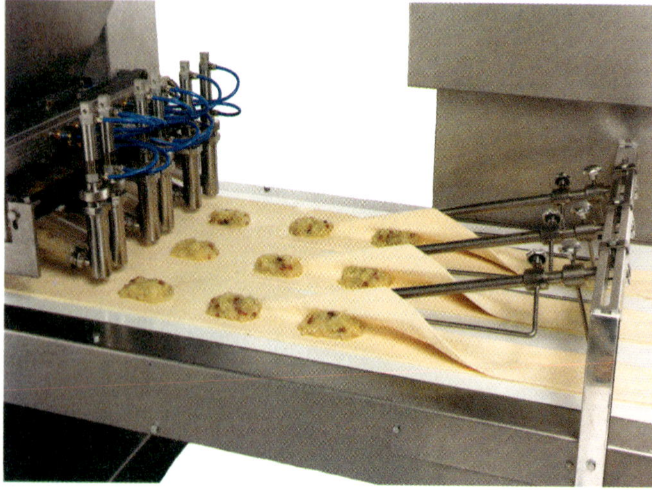

Figure 9.172. A series of cutting, folding and depositing units can be engaged to produce an infinite variety of sweet goods. (Rademaker)

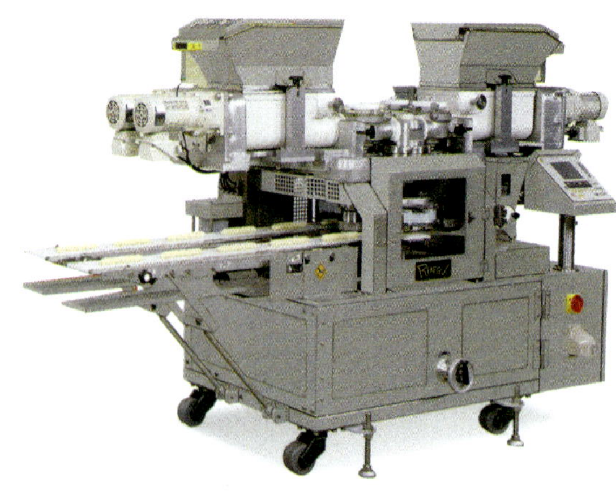

Figure 9.173. An encrusting machine, shown in double-lane configuration, enrobes one dough around another, sealing the top and bottom to completely enclose the second material, which can be a dough, filling or other food matrix. (Rheon USA)

volving nozzle reduces the dough into small spherical pieces at a rate of 180 to 200 units per minute. The dough spheres, which are limited in diameter only by the size of the ring-style sealing assembly, enter the ring assembly where the outside dough strip is sealed and pinched off to completely enfold the filling.

The filling mechanism consists of special applicators instead of a pump to gently move the filling into the guides of the central feed nozzle. As the filling emerges from the nozzle, it is enveloped by the continuous dough strip. The machine then cuts off the spherical, filled dough products and by reforming them into any desired shape by means of suitable forming attachments. Because the filler extruder will accommodate any type of filling from fruits, nuts, jams and various pastes to vegetable and meat combinations, a practically infinite variety of filled and unfilled individual portion bakery products can be produced by this machine. Such systems also accommodate two or more doughs and are commonly used to produce dual-textured cookies. With appropriately shaped extrusion orifices, the encruster can also create tubes of solid dough that when cut into cross-section slices revealing special patterns or designs.

References

Abbott, J.A. 1958. Precision dough weight scaling. Proc. Am. Soc. Bakery Engrs. 34: 191.

Alwes, M., and Jolly, M.J. 1974. Continuous fermentation with a positive flow design sponge fermentor. Bakers Digest 48 (4): 28.

Anderson, R.C. 1974a. Automatic pan handling. Proc. Am. Soc. Bakery Engrs. 50: 85.

Anderson, R.C. 1974b. Modern pan handling techniques. Bakers Digest 48 (6): 36.

Andrews, G., Copeland, J., Fairburn, N., French, F., and Zielsdorf, R. 1989. High speed dough mixing and mixers. AIB Tech. Bull. 11 (12).

Anonymous. 1958. Mechanical bread twisting: New automatic twister yields superior uniformity over manual twisting. Bakers Digest 32 (4): 38.

Anonymous. 1993. Stirring the pot. Baking & Snack 16 (1): 24.

Baker, J.C. 1954. Continuous processing of bread. Proc. Am. Soc. Bakery Engrs. 30: 65.

Baron, D.L. 1983. Dough temperature control systems. Proc. Am. Soc. Bakery Engrs. 59: 100.

Bartsch, T. 1999. Dough transfer systems. Proc. Am. Soc. Baking 75: 83.

Baumann, R. 1984. How to automate delivery of non-bulk ingredients. Baking Equipment 6 (5): BE-55.

Benier, J. 1983. Automated checkweighing. Proc. Am. Soc. Bakery Engrs. 59: 113.

Berne, S. 2006. On target. Baking & Snack 28 (3): 45.

Berne, S. 2007. Keeping it mixing. Baking & Snack 29 (1): 85.

Biscuit and Cracker Manufacturers' Association (BCMA). 2002a. Cookie and Cracker Manufacturing, Vol. I. The association: Silver Spring, MD.

Biscuit and Cracker Manufacturers' Association (BCMA). 2002b. Cookie and Cracker Manufacturing, Vol. II. The association: Silver Spring, MD.

Bloom, S. 2000. Your mixing room in the 21st century. Proc. Am. Soc. Baking 76: 151.

Blum, J.R. 1972. New developments and specifications for bread pans and covers. Proc. Am. Soc. Bakery Engrs. 48: 112.

Boge, T.C. 1994. Cream yeast. Proc. Am. Soc. Bakery Engrs. 70: 123.

Borthwick, J.T. 1973. Technology of dough degassing. Bakers Digest 47 (3): 24.

Boston, J.A. 1953. Theoretical and practical considerations of moulder designs. Bakers Digest 27 (2): 29.

Brixey, R. 1998. New bun makeup systems. Proc. Am. Soc. Bakery Engrs. 74: 121.

Broaddus, M.R. Jr. 1978. Soft roll equipment. Proc. Am. Soc. Bakery Engrs. 54: 122.

Cackler, H. 1957. Bread twisting techniques. Proc. Am. Soc. Bakery Engrs. 33: 68.

Campbell, B. 2009. Dividing technology. Proc. Am. Soc. Baking 85: 109.

Campbell, G. 1983. Dough dividing. Proc. Am. Soc. Bakery Engrs. 59: 106.

Campbell, S.P. 1979. Mechanical dough conditioning — new systems. Proc. Am. Soc. Bakery Engrs. 55: 175.

Campbell, S.P. 1989. Make-up systems. Proc. Am. Soc. Bakery Engrs. 65: 166.

Cauvain, S.P. 1998a. Breadmaking processes. In: Technology of Breadmaking. S.P. Cauvain and L.S. Young, eds. Blackie: London, UK.

Chamberlain, N. 1983. U.K. researcher describes evolution of Chorleywood process, Tweedy mixers. Baking Equipment 5 (1): BE-26.

Chamberlain, N., Collins, T.H., and Elton, G.A.H. 1962. The Chorleywood bread process. Bakers Digest 36 (5): 52.

Cleven, F., and Weber, L. 1977. A new method for the continuous production of puff and danish pastry doughs. Bakers Digest 51 (5): 138.

Clyma, K. 2007. Piece by piece. Baking & Snack International 3 (3): 38.

Corn Industries Research Foundation. 1965. Corn Syrups and Sugars, 3rd ed. The association: Washington, DC.

Dibble, W.E. 1981. Continuous mixing. Bakers Digest 55 (4): 12.

Dobie, M.J. 1977. Automatic pan equipment for efficient pan systems. Bakers Digest 51 (5): 125.

Doerry, W. 1995a. Baking Technology, Vol. I: Breadmaking. AIB International: Manhattan, KS.

Eggit, P.W.R., and Coppock, J.B.M. 1965. Cereal Sci. Today 10: 406.

Ehli, B. 1985. Proper pan selection and maintenance keep baking production costs in line. Baking Equipment 7 (3): BE-22.

Elias, D.G., and Wragg, B.H. 1963. Cereal Sci. Today 8: 271.

Euverard, M.R. 1967. Liquid ferment systems for conventional dough processing. Bakers Digest 41 (5): 124.

Euverard, M.R. 1970. Evolution of bun production systems. Bakers Digest 44 (1): 74.

Farmer, W.W. 1973. Production of buns to meet specific requirements. Proc. Am. Soc. Bakery Engrs. 49: 101.

Fay, E. 2006. Personal communication.

Fay, E. 2008. Bread, dough mixing: New science and advancements. Proc. Am. Soc. Baking 84: 76.

Ferrell, C.D. 1961. Curl-type moulding. Bakers Digest 35 (2): 54.

Fish, A.R. 1982. High speed dough development. Proc. Am. Soc. Bakery Engrs. 58: 130.

Fortmann, K.L. 1967b. Trends and practical hints for continuous mixing of bread and rolls. Am. Soc. Bakery Engrs. Bull. No. 184.

French, F.D., and Fish, A.R. 1981. High speed mechanical dough development. Bakers Digest 55 (5): 80.

French, F.D., and Kemp, D.R. 1985. Cereal Foods World 30: 345.

Geddes, W.F. 1959. Recent developments in foods from cereals. J. Agr. Food Chem. 7 (9): 605.

Goley, F.R. 1977. Increasing production capacity. Proc. Am. Soc. Bakery Engrs. 53: 124.

Gorton, L. 1992. Going east. Baking & Snack 14 (2): 6.

Gorton, L. 1994. Rethinking fermentation. Baking & Snack 17 (8): 38.

Gorton, L. 2001a. Pan natural. Baking & Snack 23 (3): 31.

Gorton, L. 2001b. Managing mixing. Baking & Snack 23 (3): 71.

Gorton, L. 2009. Theory and practice. Baking & Snack 31 (1): 101.

Gorton, L., and Whitaker, S. 2004. Measuring success. Baking & Snack 26 (10): 73.

Grant, F.R. 1972. Recent developments in eggs. Proc. Am. Soc. Bakery Engrs. 48: 150.

Haarsgaard, E.E. 1980. Automatic production of puff pastry. Bakers Digest 54 (1): 16.

Hagedorn, H.G. 1965. New practices in bulk handling of materials with special emphasis on instrumentation controls. Proc. Am. Soc. Bakery Engrs. 41: 148.

Hailey, F. 1973. Bulk material handling equipment. Proc. Am. Soc. Bakery Engrs. 49: 178.

Hall, C.H. 1965. Accelerating batch process bread production. Proc. Am. Soc. Bakery Engrs. 41: 51.

Hancock, M.B. 1971. Continuous sponge fermentation. Bakers Digest 45 (4): 46.

Hardin, O.W. 1967. Pan features as factors in performance efficiency. Bakers Digest 41 (5): 166.

Harris, C. 1985. Degassing and texturizing doughs. Proc. Am. Soc. Bakery Engrs. 61: 57.

Hayashi, T. 1978. Automated puff pastry production. Proc. Am. Soc. Bakery Engrs. 54: 139.

Hibberd, G.E., and Parker, N.S. 1976. Gas pressure-volume-time relationships in fermenting doughs. I. Rate of production and solubility of carbon dioxide in dough. Cereal Chem. 53 (3): 338.

Hoynak, P.X., and Bollenback, G.N. 1966. This Is Liquid Sugar, 2nd ed. CPC International, Inc.: Yonkers, NY.

Hyman, W.R. 1995. Guided vehicles in the baking industry. Proc. Am. Soc. Bakery Engrs. 71: 113.

Inzerillo, A.N. 1979. Pan design. Proc. Am. Soc. Bakery Engrs. 55: 64.

Irvin, J.G. 1976. Basic principles of pneumatic conveying. Bakers Digest 50 (5): 31.

Kamman, P.W. 1970. Factors affecting the grain and texture of white bread. Bakers Digest 44 (2): 34.

Levine, L. 1998. Principles of sheeting dough. AIB Tech. Bull. 20 (9).

Livesay, M.F. 1992. Automatic storage and retrieval systems. Proc. Am. Soc. Bakery Engrs. 68: 153.

Loeb, R.V. 1981. Modern production of hearth breads. Bakers Digest 55 (5): 56.

Long, J.W. 1984. Minor ingredient systems. Proc. Am. Soc. Bakery Engrs. 60: 92.

Long, J.W. 1993. Hard roll makeup. Proc. Am. Soc. Bakery Engrs. 69: 145.

Madson, O.T. 1994. Continuous mixing — a second look. Proc. Am. Soc. Bakery Engrs. 70: 57.

Mallet, R. 2000. Decision time for pan coatings. Proc. Am. Soc. Baking 75: 265.

Manley, D. 1991. Technology of Biscuits, Crackers and Cookies, 2nd ed. Woodhead Publishing Ltd. (CRC): Boca Raton, FL.

McLaren, L.H. 1954. The practical aspects of the stable ferment baking process. Bakers Digest 28 (3): 23.

Mermelstein, N.H. 2006. The Loncin Prize: funding food science research. Food Tech. 60 (12): 22.

Meyer, K.C. 1997. Mixing room automation for sponge and dough. Proc. Am. Soc. Bakery Engrs. 73: 103.

Miller, R.A. 1961. The "breakthrough" in mixing and make-up. Bakers Digest 35 (5): 142.

Moore, R.E. 1988. Flour: handling your most important ingredient. Proc. Am. Soc. Bakery Engrs. 64: 85.

Morris, G. 1971. Pneumatic bulk handling systems in the bakery. Bakers Digest 45 (4): 49.

Morris, J. 1983. Pan selection and care is important! AIB Tech. Bull. 4 (2).

Mueller, G. 1971. Continuous dough mixing system offers maximum flexibility. Bakers Digest 45 (6): 42.

Obal, W.D. 2002. Chemistry of pan coatings. Proc. Am. Soc. Baking 78: 166.

Osborne, D. 1998. Advances in bread and bun makeup. Proc. Am. Soc. Bakery Engrs. 74: 129.

Pfening, F.D. 1955. The fermentation room. Bakers Digest 29 (5): 84.

Phillips, R. 1965. Automatic batching systems for bakeries. Bakers Digest 39 (5): 58.

Pierce, W.L. 1974. Pumping of bread and bun dough. Proc. Am. Soc. Bakery Engrs. 50: 92.

Poehlman, R.W. 1979. Premium Danish production. Proc. Am. Soc. Bakery Engrs. 55: 91.

Posner, E.S., and Hibbs, A.N. 2005. Wheat Flour Milling, 2nd ed. AACC International: St. Paul. MN.

Pyler. E.J. 1988. New technologies of dough making. In: Baking Science and Technology, 3rd ed. Sosland Publishing Co.: Kansas City, MO. *Editors note: For readers interested in more detail about the subject of continuous mixing, this chapter has been posted on the Web at http://www.bakingbusiness.com/ resources.*

Robinson, J. 2000. Formulating for extrusion dividing. Proc. Am. Soc. Baking 77: 159.

Schmidt, H. 2002. Update on dough transfer systems. Proc. Am. Soc. Baking 78: 175.

Schneeman, H.L. 1995. Non-stick coatings for pans. Proc. Am. Soc. Bakery Engrs. 71: 65.

Schraps, S. 1982. Automatic batching of major and minor ingredients in the baking industry. Bakers Digest 56 (3): 12.

Schuettinger, J.C. 1966. Essential elements of liquid sugar systems. Bakers Digest 40 (2): 46.

Seiffer, G. 2002. Stress-free dough technology. AIB Tech. Bull. 24 (3).

Slater, G.B. 1989. Ingredient feed systems. Proc. Am. Soc. Bakery Engrs. 65: 158.

Slattery, J.P. 1962. Factors in determining pneumatic system capacities. Bakers Digest 36 (6): 70.

Spooner, T.F. 1984. Roll production — an equipment update. Baking Equipment 6 (1): BE-31.

Spooner, T.F. 1993. Moving ingredients from here to there. Baking & Snack 15 (2): 19.

Stadelman, F. 1974. The development of the vacuum depanner. Bakers Digest 48 (3): 48.

Stauffer, C.E. 1996. Turning to dry mixes and pre-mixes. Baking & Snack 18 (10): 42.

Sternberg, G. 1968. A new concept in conventional dough mixing. Bakers Digest 42 (1): 60.

Stevens, E. 1991. 1,000-per-minute bun line. Proc. Am. Soc. Bakery Engrs. 67: 125.

Steward, C.D. 1990. The latest in bun dividers. Proc. Am. Soc. Bakery Engrs. 66: 100.

Stumpf, S.O. 1989. New high heat materials for bakery use. Proc. Am. Soc. Bakery Engrs. 65: 230.

Sussann, H.-J. 2008. Mixing technology is decisive for product quality. Food Mktg. & Tech. 2008 (2): 28.

Swortfiguer, M.J. 1968. The Rheon-204 encrusting machine. Bakers Digest 42 (6): 58.

Tesch, J. 1971. Degassing of bun doughs — equipment and methods. Proc. Am. Soc. Bakery Engrs. 47: 112.

Thompson, D.R. 1977. Update on dough transfer and degassing. Bakers Digest 51 (5): 121.

Thompson, D.R. 1980. State of the art — bakery fermentation. Bakers Digest 54 (3): 28.

Thompson, D.R. 1981. Liquid sponge weighing systems for the bakery. Bakers Digest 55 (3): 24.

Tireki, S. 2008a. Technology of cake production. In: Food Engineering Aspects of Baking Sweet Goods. S.G. Sumnu and S. Sahin, eds. CRC Press: Boca Raton, FL.

Tireki, S. 2008b. Technology of cookie production. In: Food Engineering Aspects of Baking Sweet Goods. S.G. Sumnu and S. Sahin, eds. CRC Press: Boca Raton, FL.

Trum, G.W. 1967. High lievel flour ferment systems for continuous dough production. Bakers Digest 41 (5): 120.

Tweed, A.R. 1983. Cereal Foods World 28: 397.

Volpe, T. 2006. Layered design. Baking & Snack 28 (11): 69.

Wade, P. 1988. Biscuit, Cookies and Crackers, Vol. I. Elsevier Applied Science: London, UK, and New York, NY.

Warren, J. 1999. Continuous dough mixing and mixers. AIB Tech. Bull. 21 (12).

Watkins, F.H. Jr. 1965. Novel advancements in the control and technology of continuous mixing. Bakers Digest 39 (6): 50.

Whitaker, S. 2007a. Stress relief. Baking & Snack 29 (10): 59.

Whitaker, S. 2007b. First defense. Baking & Snack 29 (11): 71.

Whitaker, S. 2008. Handle with care. Baking & Snack 30 (2): 85.

Whitaker, S. 2009b. Automation advances. Baking & Snack 31 (4): 113.

White, D.W. 1970. Fermentation and proofing rooms. Bakers Digest 44 (3): 45.

White, D.W. 1981. Bulk pneumatic handling of flour and other bakery ingredients. Bakers Digest 55 (5): 62.

Whitt, D.L. 1994. Ingredient handling systems. Proc. Am. Soc. Bakery Engrs. 70: 39.

Wilkinson, G. 1987. Cake mixing technology. Proc. Am. Soc. Bakery Engrs. 63: 99.

Willhoft, W.H. 1967. Automatic conveying of sugar and flour in a modern bakery. Bakers Digest 41 (1): 66.

Woolley, B. 1996. Pressure vacuum mixing. British Soc. Baking. Paper No. 402.

Yankellow, J. 2005. Lamination: layers beyond imagination. San Francisco Baking Institute Newsletter. Spring edition.

Zielsdorf, R.L. 1977. Developments in high speed dough mixing. Bakers Digest 51 (5): 111.

Zimmerman, B. 1999. Cream yeast standards. Proc. Am. Soc. Baking 75: 147.

Heating and Cooling Equipment

Contributed by Stephen St. Clair-Thompson (Parts A and B)
and updated by L.A. Gorton (Part C),
Richard F. Stier (Part D)
and J. Peter Clark (Parts E-H)

Stephen St. Clair-Thompson, MA, CE, MiMech E
Chief Engineer (retired), Baker Perkins Ltd., Peterborough, UK
21 Crocket Lane, Empingham, Oakham LE15 8PW, UK.
Phone (mobile) +44 7963 973991; e-mail stclairthompson@msn.com

Richard F. Stier, Consulting Food Scientist
627 Cherry Ave., Sonoma, CA 95467. Phone (707) 935-2829; e-mail rickstier4@aol.com

J. Peter Clark, Consultant to the Process Industries
644 Linden Ave., Oak Park, IL 60302. Phone (708) 848-2205; e-mail jpc3@att.net

From proofer to cooler, dough pieces turn into finished foods with the help of varied systems and technologies.

INTRODUCTION

With dough portioned into individual pieces, made up and panned, the baker moves it into the next stages, proofing and baking, followed by cooling. The variety of automated and semi-automated machines involved in these processes allows a wide spectrum of choices. This chapter examines the systems and their technolo-

Loaf after perfect loaf proceeds from oven to cooler to packaging room. (Gardenia Bakeries)

gies, including that of another spectrum: the electromagnetic kind.

Proofers, ovens, coolers and freezers represent "big ticket" items in terms of capital investment. When receiving requests for equipment purchases, company managers will usually ask the bakery engineer to estimate payback for the investment. Although the general industry view was to consider 5 years as a common payback period, recent practice shortened this to 3 years and even 1 year or less, depending on the project.

Accountants generally use the following methods to evaluate capital investments: return on investment (ROI), discounted cash flow (DCF) and cash pay back (CPB). In the ROI method, the original investment is divided into the annual return and the result expressed as a percentage. Under DCF, which is the most complicated technique, the evaluation takes into consideration the value of the dollar over an extended period of time, a consideration especially important when evaluating projects encompassing a long period of time. The CPB method is the most practical in that it clearly shows the improved cash flow resulting from investment in new plant and/or machinery.

Tax laws impact return-on-investment calculations because these rules determine the rate at which the cash value of equipment can be depreciated or expensed. For example, a change in US law in 1986 lengthened the depreciation schedule from 5 years to 8. In the years since, the federal government altered its tax rules many times. The latest, the 2009 American Recovery and Reinvestment Act, added a depreciation "bonus" that allows an additional 50% first-year depreciation of the cost for new equipment purchased and put into service in 2009. Depreciation ratios change with nearly every new tax law enacted, and often they reclassify the type of capital investments covered.

10.A. Proofers and Retarders
Contributed by Stephen St. Clair-Thompson

Between the mixer and the oven stand a variety of machines and equipment systems that accommodate the processing stages of intermediate proofing, final proofing and retarding. Each applies time, temperature and humidity to bring out the desired characteristics required for a high-quality finished product.

With regard to the design and use of this equipment, differentiation should be made between proofing and resting functions. Like the relatively short floor time given to doughs held in troughs, intermediate proofing of scaled dough pieces provides rest time that benefits the gluten protein structure of the dough. While taking as long if not longer than bulk fermentation, retarding inhibits, but does not entirely halt, yeast activity and thus supplies both rest for the protein and time for the yeast to develop its flavor compounds and dough conditioning actions. Final proofing functions not only to rest and condition protein but also to foster generation of leavening gases.

The equipment designed and engineered to accomplish these processing stages varies in configuration and size as well as how it employs heat, humidity and time. The chemical and physical processes involved in proofing and retarding are examined in Chapter 6, Parts B and F.

10.A.1. Proofing requirements

Bakers use intermediate proofers or a period of rest time to help yeast-raised doughs recover from the rigors of dividing and rounding, but the final proofer is what enables the leavening to bring bread and rolls to their optimum volume before baking. Intermediate proofers usually operate at the plant's ambient temperature and humidity, with care taken to avoid drafts that could dry dough surfaces, while final proofers apply controlled heat and moisture to the dough's environment.

The function of the final proofer is to enable the yeast to contribute leavening gases to the air cells that already exist within the dough's protein structure, thus enlarging the size of the moulded dough piece by a factor of about 3 or 4. Such yeast activity is best promoted by a temperature of 35 to 40°C (95 to 104°F). So it follows that the environment in which final proofing takes place must be at a temperature of 35 to 49°C (95 to 120°F), with the actual temperature depending on product variety.

Also, the surface of the dough piece must not be allowed to dry out, or the dough piece will lose weight, and its surface will split. Thus, the environment in which proofing takes place needs to have as high humidity as possible. The achievable humidity is discussed below.

Dough pieces will be going into the proofer at a temperature of 28 to 30°C (82 to 86°F) on peel boards or in pans. It would be helpful if the dough pieces could be at a higher temperature, but if they were any warmer, they would be too sticky for the moulder.

The yeast requires about 50 to 65 minutes to inflate dough's air cells and develop the protein structure, so the proofer must be large enough to contain this amount of product.

Finally, dough pieces at this stage are extremely delicate. Any jarring during final proofing can literally knock it back; thus, the mechanical operation of the proofer and the proofer-to-oven transition needs to be smooth.

10.A.2. Retarding parameters

The fact that the proof time is so long presents a problem to the craft or artisan baker, who wants to have a batch of bread available for the oven first thing in the morning. The solution is the retarder-proofer, a cabinet provided with a controlled temperature and humidity cycle (**Figure 10.001**). Normally, it operates as a simple proof box, with a controlled proof cycle; however, for the last batch of the day, it becomes a chiller that retards the fermentation process overnight until the proofer automatically warms up in the early hours of the following morning and starts its proof cycle (**Figure 10.002**).

Dough retarding is defined as placing a partially fermented dough under refrigeration at temperatures in the range of 1.7 to 4.4°C (35 to 40°F) and a relative humidity of 85%. Such conditions are not intended to freeze the dough but slow down its fermentation rate so the dough can remain stable for either several hours or several days. While quite useful for preparation of bread and rolls, dough retarding has become an integral step in many sweet dough and puff pastry operations. By subjecting a dough that usually contains high levels of shortening to periodic cooling during its early processing stages, bakers preserve its optimum machining properties through somewhat lengthy and intricate handling operations.

Figure 10.001. Retarder-proofer cabinets operate during the day as proofers and overnight as retarders. (MIWE)

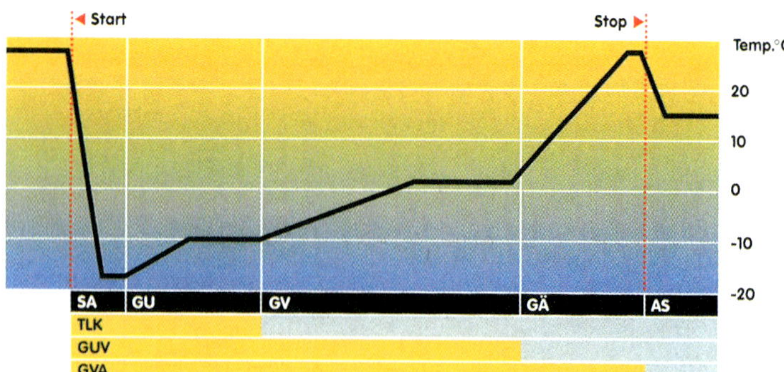

Figure 10.002. Temperature and humidity differ according to processing stage: SA, fast cooling; GU, proofing interruption; GV, proofing retardation; GÄ, proofing; and AS, hardening phase. (MIWE)

Two refinements are worth mentioning: First, retarding can be set for the period of a weekend or holiday when necessary. Yeasted doughs remain essentially stable for periods up to 48 hours. Second, in the event that the proof cycle is complete but the rack has not been removed, the proofer will cool down, delaying any further development.

Versions are available that will freeze retard; these styles are particularly relevant to larger loaves of 800 g (28 oz) or more.

10.A.3. Principles of air conditioning

To better understand what happens in the proofer, it is necessary to recall some basic principles of air conditioning.

When discussing the moisture content of air, the term relative humidity (RH) is often used, and we are aware of its relevance to daily life. It measures the ease with which moisture can evaporate from a surface at any given temperature. In an environment at 10% RH, moisture will evaporate far more readily than it will in an environment at 90% RH. The actual definition of relative humidity is the ratio of the vapor pressure of water at that moment to the saturation vapor pressure of water at the same temperature. This concept is, perhaps, a bit academic for normal working practice so the looser concept of "ease with which the moisture can evaporate" is used when considering proofers.

Another way to think of humidity is in terms of the "dew point." The dew point is the temperature at which the water in the proofer atmosphere would just condense. If the proofer is less humid, the dew point will be lower; if it is more humid, the dew point will be higher. Fortunately, we can gain an understanding of the relationship between relative humidity and dew point by using a humidity calculator. Any of a number of humidity calculators can be found through an Internet search of "humidity calculator."

A few values of humidity of interest to someone working with proofers are provided in **Table 10.01**, for any altitude above sea level.

Using the table, let us review the statement above that "the proofer needs to have as high a humidity as possible" first from the process point of view and then from a practical point of view. In both cases, start with a typical example of dough at 28°C (82°F) coming into a proofer at 40°C (104°F) and 90% RH.

Table 10.01. Humidity Values

	28°C	30°C	35°C	40°C	45°C
Relative humidity %	80	80	80	80	80
Dew point, °C	24.2	26.2	31	35.9	40.7
Relative humidity %	90	90	90	90	90
Dew point, °C	26.2	28.2	33.1	38	43
Relative humidity %	95	95	95	95	95
Dew point, °C	27.1	29.1	34.1	39	44
Relative humidity %	99	99	99	99	99
Dew point, °C	27.8	29.8	34.8	39.8	44.8
	80°F	**90°F**	**95°F**	**105°F**	**115°F**
Relative humidity %	80	80	80	80	80
Dew point, °F	73.3	83	87.8	97.5	107.2
Relative humidity %	90	90	90	90	90
Dew point, °F	77	86.7	91.6	101.5	111.3
Relative humidity %	95	95	95	95	95
Dew point, °F	78.4	88.4	93.3	103.3	113.2
Relative humidity %	99	99	99	99	99
Dew point, °F	79.7	89.7	94.7	104.7	114.6

First, consider the situation from a process point of view. The dew point temperature for a relative humidity of 90% will be 38°C (100°F) so the water vapor in the proofer atmosphere will condense on the dough surface, keeping it moist, which is required. But after about 20 minutes, the surface of the dough piece will have reached about 38°C (100°F) and begin to dry out. Thus, from a process point of view, it would be better to have 95% RH, with a dew point of 39°C (102°F). This level will maintain the surface of the dough piece moist for longer and be even better from a process point of view.

Now, consider the situation from a practical point of view. With 90% RH, the dew point at 38°C (100°F) is only 2 C° lower than the air temperature, and since the air temperature is bound to drop as the air goes through the proofer, the possibility will be high that condensation will form on the metal surfaces. The situation is even worse at 95% RH, because the dew point is only 1 C° lower than the circulated air temperature. Any proofer surfaces on which water condenses will be permanently wet, promoting mold growth.

So it is important not to expect too much of the proofer by just inputting a higher set humidity, since the additional humidity will only condense out on the proofer body. But on the other hand, the need for a well designed and maintained air conditioning circuit becomes obvious. The need for corrosion-resistant materials of construction and good access for cleaning are also evident.

10.A.4. Engineering air conditioning

The various requirements placed on the proofer can be explained by referring to **Figure 10.003**. The diagram is not intended to depict an actual air conditioning unit but rather a compendium of all the possible elements of an air conditioning unit. Some of these components will be required in various areas of the world, but not all. Remember, also, that the demands on a proofer vary throughout the day so sometimes one of the following elements is required to operate for only part of the day.

Clearly, the system depicted is a recirculating system. Referring to the drawing here, start at the "return air" duct. The "temperature and humidity sensor" controls the other devices in the system. Available probes are much better than they used to be, but their outputs do have a tendency to drift so the probes need to be recalibrated regularly.

The "mixing chamber" is required because filtered fresh air is usually required in a proofer to slightly pressurize the proof box. Otherwise, uncontrolled airflows could come in at the loading and unloading stations, compromising conditions within the proof box. The mixing chamber is especially useful for bakeries located in temperate climates where the proofer may over-heat; the fresh inlet air will cool the proofer down.

In addition to their normal operation, the exhaust ("hot air to atmosphere") and "fresh air inlet" have another function: In the event of a downstream production problem, the proofer will need to stop, but the yeast activity will carry on at a rate dependent on the dough temperature. Dumping the proofer air enables the temperature to be brought down, possibly saving the bread in the proofer.

The "water wash system" was provided in hot countries to cool down the returning air, to wash out any dust and spores and to provide a degree of humidification. The water runs down into a sump and is recycled. Water wash systems are less frequent nowadays because of concerns about legionellosis (Legionnaire's disease, a severe form of pneumonia, caused by breathing in vapors containing Legionella bacteria) and because of their high maintenance requirements.

An "atomized water system" is sometimes used to provide humidification and a certain amount of cooling. The water is blasted out of jets using compressed air. Condensation on surrounding surfaces is difficult to avoid, leading (unless checked) to microbial growth and, again, a concern about legionellosis.

"Refrigerant coils" are provided where the air supplies returning from the proofer and makeup air from outside the bakery are too hot. Since the refrigerant coils cool

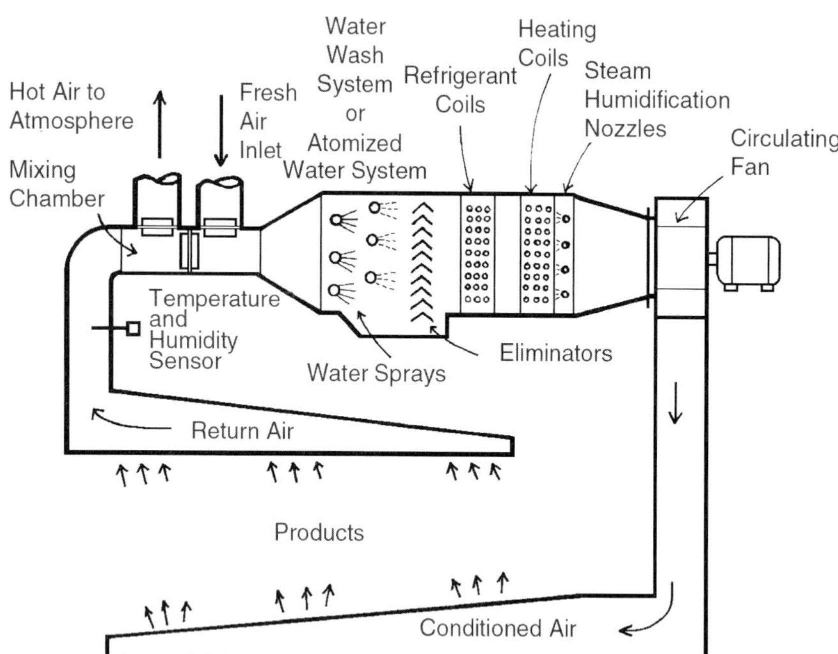

Figure 10.003. Diagram of a hypothetical air conditioning unit shows how air moves through a proofer.

the air, they increase its relative humidity. They should only be considered where forced cooling of the returning pans is already being used.

Refrigerant coils can also be used to lower the humidity ratio of the air when the air condenses below the dew point temperature on the colder coils. Water drops out of the air, and the air becomes cooler. A set of heating coils after the refrigerant coils raises the temperature back to the desired temperature. This is a common application for an air conditioning system where precise temperature and humidity control is necessary.

"Heating coils" will bring the returning air temperature up to that required for the proofing process. The coils have traditionally been steam heated but can be heated by electricity or thermal fluid. Alternatively, a gas-fired heat exchanger can be fitted instead. Note that, even if the refrigerant coils are used, a heating system is needed to bring the humidity back down to the required level.

"Steam humidification nozzles" are provided to bring the returning air humidity up to the humidity required for the proofing process. Steam has the advantage that, when properly treated, it is clean and does not condense on surrounding steelwork.

The "circulating fan" is provided to force the recirculated air around the proofer.

The feed and return ducting must be sized and situated so that the recirculated air reaches all the required parts of the proofer.

10.A.5. Proofer construction

Today, just about all proofer enclosures are built using high-density polyurethane foam slabs held tightly together with camlocks. The slabs are self-supporting blocks covered on both sides with stainless steel sheet. Care is taken to get a good seal between them. They are usually 100 to 150 mm (4 to 6 in.) thick. The polyurethane foam provides good insulation, and no through-metal exists to provide thermal conduction and give rise to condensation spots. The slabs, their associated doors and door fittings, etc., are made in large quantities for the freezer industry and so are available at reasonable cost. If the proofer is to be installed over the oven, it is worth considering an alternative to polyurethane because of the fire risk. The steelwork within the proofer must be made from a material that does not corrode. Proof boxes also are being built with aluminum frames (**Figure 10.004**).

10.A.6. Intermediate proofer equipment

When the makeup process calls for intermediate proofing lasting 6 minutes or more, the baker's choice will always be a conventional tray-style system because as many as 1,000 dough pieces must be stored while making their way to the sheeters. Switching to a belt-style resting system cuts the time involved to a minimum of 15 to 30 seconds but generally no more than 1 minute.

10.A.6.a. Intermediate proofers
Intermediate proofers — also described as dry proofers, first proofers and interproofers — are commonly configured as "overhead" systems that consist of a cabinet installed above other dividing, rounding and/or makeup equipment

(**Figure 10.005**). A rotary feeder or a board equipped with zig-zag channels directs rounded dough pieces into the intermediate proofer's dough pockets, cups or trays. These devices carry dough pieces through a series of laps or tiers that traverse the cabinet from end to end.

The actual proof or resting time can last anywhere from 30 seconds to 20 minutes and generally falls within a range of 4 to 12 minutes, with 6 to 9 minutes being average. If intermediate proof times extend beyond 10 minutes, transpositors should be provided within the proofer to change the position of the dough pieces at around the midpoint of the proofing cycle.

Intermediate proofers are not usually equipped with separate temperature and humidity controls. Instead, they operate at plant ambient conditions, typically 27 to 29°C (80 to 85°F) and around 75% RH. Operators sometimes open the doors of overhead proofers, thinking to adjust either the humidity and/or temperature within, but this action only creates drafts that negatively affect dough piece uniformity.

10.A.6.b. Belt resting

The resting-belt conveyor systems (**Figure 10.006**) now being adopted by many large wholesale bakeries require far less maintenance and sanitation than conventional intermediate proofers and need no dusting flour. The design of these systems is relatively simple, consisting of a few short lengths of conveyor using easily-cleaned plastic-link belting. Other process improvements include a more consistent feed rate to the sheeter, thus preventing slugging and doubles.

Elimination of the intermediate proofer reduces losses caused by downstream stoppages because there is less "product in motion" on a resting-belt system (Campbell 1988). Some bakers report a 20% increase in throughput to makeup by use of such systems in contrast to conventional intermediate proofing. Rotary timing gates, zig-zag boards, proofer cup transfer devices and dual gate panning mechanisms are also eliminated (Brixey 1998).

10.A.7. Retarder equipment

The refrigerated boxes that retard doughs are usually of conventional construction, although they may vary in design to suit different requirements. Thus, some units consist of multiple compartments, each with its own access door (**Figure 10.007**), whereas in others there is but a single enclosed room that can accommodate a series of loaded pan racks, while in still others some features of both types are combined. The rate of initial temperature reduction in doughs in properly maintained retarder boxes is related largely to the size and thickness of the individual dough pieces being refrigerated.

When selecting retarder equipment, four factors should be considered: (a)

Figure 10.004. An aluminum frame provides this proof box with a rigid, rust-free environment.
(Fred D. Pfening Co.)

Figure 10.005. Overhead intermediate proofers give dough pieces 30 seconds to 20 minutes of rest time under plant ambient conditions.
(The Kaak Group, Benier)

Formula: rich doughs can be retarded longer than lean doughs. (b) Dough temperature after mixing: cooler doughs have not reached maturity, and warmer doughs age too quickly. (c) Size and thickness of the dough piece: product cooling rates are slower for thicker pieces, while thin pieces cool more quickly. (d) Cooling capacity of the refrigerated box: higher capacity systems will remove Btus faster from dough pieces, a rate also affected by their size and shape.

While most retarders used in bakeries are configured as large roll-in, roll-out refrigerated rooms, some automated pastry lines include continuous in-line retarders (**Figure 10.008**).

10.A.8. Final proofer equipment

Over the years, bakery equipment manufacturers developed several distinct styles of final proofers. Most designs were inspired by the particular needs of one bakery or another.

10.A.8.a. Rack proofer

A rack proofer is an air-conditioned box with a door on one side. Mobile racks, full of trays of product, are wheeled into the proofer. The door is closed, and proofing begins. Heating for the warm air and humidity generation is by electricity or gas.

Multiple rack proofers are usually several single-rack proofers side by side, each with its own door; however, versions are available with an inlet door at one end, a deep enclosure capable of holding up to four racks and a door at the far end (**Figure 10.004**). This style is generally referred to as a manual flow-through proofer and allows true first-in, first-out sequencing of dough pieces. Automatic loading of rack proofers has also been developed (**Figure 10.009**).

The rack proofer is the only type of proofer that is suitable for a batch process. Versions of the rack proofer are available with retarder and freezer options.

10.A.8.b. Rack tunnel proofer

The rack tunnel proofer is an evolution of the rack proofer. As its name suggests, the racks are loaded into the proofer at one end of the tunnel and unloaded at the other. They are carried through the tunnel on a floor-conveyor. They have largely been superseded by the travelling rack proofer.

10.A.8.c. Travelling rack proofer

A variation of the rack proofer is the travelling rack proofer (**Figure 10.010**) where the racks are hung from a monorail. Automatic doors are provided, and there is the option of automatic loading and unloading of the racks from the monorail. The system does not work as a continuous system, despite it having a monorail. It works as a load – pause for proofing – unload system. The proof and retard times are controllable. The system is suitable for large craft and small industrial bakeries.

Figure 10.006. Open conveyors give dough balls a short period of rest as them move from the divider to makeup lines.
(Intralox)

Figure 10.007. Retarders allow the baker to slow the fermentation rate of dough pieces for periods ranging from a few hours to overnight and weekends.
(Belshaw Adamatic Bakery Group)

Figure 10.008. An overhead retarder provides a period of inline rest for croissant doughs made on an automated line.
(Rademaker and Gold Standard Baking)

Figure 10.009. An automatic loading system supplies racks filled with pans or peels to retarders or proofers.
(Gemini Bakery Equipment, ABI Ltd.)

Figure 10.010. Monorail rack proofers can carry both pan and peel board products and are efficiently served by automatic loading and unloading of the trays.
(Gemini Bakery Equipment Co.)

10.A.8.d. Tunnel proofer

Some processes, such as bread crumb manufacture, require the product to be proofed as a large sheet or as a set of continuous longitudinal slabs. Such a process does not require any batching. So a tunnel proofer, the same width as the oven, is situated immediately before the oven. The proofer would normally be heated by steam or thermal fluid. The proofer is, of course, a continuous one for industrial production.

10.A.8.e. Multi-deck tunnel proofer

The multi-deck tunnel proofer (**Figure 10.011**) consists of a number of "mini proofers," set above one another, each with its own conveyor. The conveyors can either be textile for dough lying directly on the belt or wire mesh for peel boards. This type of proofer is particularly relevant to hearth or artisan breads baked in a variety of styles by small industrial bakeries. Typically, this type of proofer is used in conjunction with a multiple-deck oven. The proofer can be heated by steam, thermal oil or electricity.

10.A.8.f. Multi-step proofer

The multi-step proofer (**Figure 10.012**) is suitable for dough pieces carried by pans, trays or peel boards, as long as they all have the same width. The pans, trays or peel boards are fed into the inline proofer without touching each other by means of an indexing chain. When a tier is full, the proofer indexes it upward by a set of chains, stepping up it up again each time a tier is full. At the top of the proofer, the row moves horizontally to enter another set of tiers. There it is indexed downwards until it is discharged. There are two possible configurations: an inline style and a U-shaped pattern. Heating is by steam or thermal oil.

10.A.8.g. Tray proofer

The tray proofer (**Figure 10.013**) is the companion of the tunnel oven. The proofer is generally the width of the oven, 3 or 4 m (10 to 13 ft) wide, so the bread can be transferred directly from one to the other. The design suits bread baked in pans or on trays. A group of pans is loaded onto a shelf of a carrier, which confusingly is also called a "tray." These trays are transported around the proofer by a pair of continuous chains, with the trays hanging from the chains. The chains are pulled around the proofer by a pair of sprockets, one on either side of the proofer. There may be one, two or three shelves on each tray. The trays on older models were allowed to swing and were known as "swing trays." Current models stabilize the individual trays and are known as "stabilized trays."

The proofers come in two main configurations: box and overhead. In the box type, trays are carried up to a pair of sprockets at the top, then down to a pair of sprockets at the bottom, back up and down repeatedly around more pairs of sprockets until they are unloaded at the far end of the box.

The overhead-type proofer is situated above the oven and thus uses less floor space. In this configuration, the trays are transported up the leg section, along the overhead section, back along the overhead section, down the leg section and unloaded opposite the oven.

With some designs, the loading and unloading can be done with the chain circuit running, but some designs require the chain circuit to be paused.

Tray proofers enable continuous industrial production. They can be heated by electricity or gas.

10.A.8.h. Rack-type proofer

The rack-type proofer (not to be confused with the rack proofer) has a large number of racks built into it (**Figure 10.014**). Each rack has a number of shelves that are loaded in turn by the loading mechanism with a group of pans or trays. The rack is indexed upwards after the loading of each shelf. When the rack is full, it is indexed up to the top section of the proofer by an elevator, pushing forward all the racks ahead of it. At the far end of the proofer, it is picked up and taken to the lower section of the proofer by a lowerator. There it travels back until it reaches the front of the proofer again, and each shelf is unloaded just before it is loaded again for the next circuit. This type of proofer makes efficient use of floor space but suffers from being difficult to clean.

10.A.8.i. Continuous proofers

Continuous proofers move pans or trays through the proofer inline on a conveyor. This design offers a number of advantages. First, trays or pans do not need to be grouped, as required for tray or rack type proofers. Second, the entry and exit ports of the proofer enclosure are small, which keeps temperature and humidity losses to a minimum at these points. Third, every pan or tray receives the same heat and humidity profile.

In general terms, for bread, the proofer will need 3 times the conveying capacity of the oven because their dwell times are about 60 minutes and 20 minutes, respectively. However, the proofer and the oven are driven independently, allowing the proof-to-bake time ratio to be adjusted within limits, as long as the throughput of the system is limited to the throughput of the slower of the two machines. The faster machine will just have bigger gaps between products.

Continuous proofers generally have a narrow, flexible conveyor, and equipment manufacturers provide considerable flexibility in the size and shape of the proofer and the position of the conveyor inlet and outlet openings.

Continuous proofers have space within them for the air-conditioning equipment and ample access for cleaning and maintenance. Since the conveyor is narrow and well spaced from the floor, access to the conveyor is excellent for both cleaning and maintenance.

It is possible to provide multiple input conveyors to some types of continuous proofers so that proof time can be widely altered without greatly affecting the speed of the conveyor.

A wide variety of conveyor types are available depending on the product to be baked and the minimum radius of curvature that can be accepted. The number and

Figure 10.011. Each of the decks of this proofer can be independently controlled for temperature and humidity. (The Kaak Group)

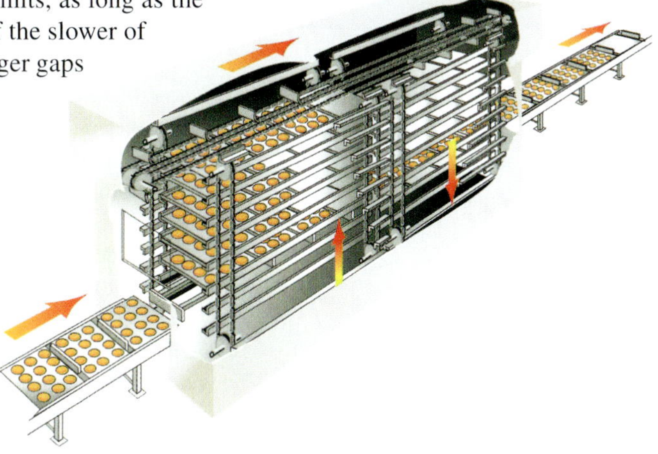

Figure 10.012. When pans, trays or peels fill a tier, the whole tier is indexed up, over and then down again within this inline multi-step proofer. (The Kaak Group)

Figure 10.013. Long tray-like shelves carry loaves as they proof in an overhead proofer. This line includes a break halfway trough the proof to allow manual scoring (slashing) of the crusts to assure proper shape after baking. (MCS)

Figure 10.014. Rack-type proofers load pans or trays onto fixed shelves, which are routed within the proofer until they reach the unloading station. (Turkington)

types of drives are supplied to suit the conveyor type and the length of the conveyor.

There are three particular types of continuous proofers that are distinct enough to merit additional descriptions, as below.

10.A.8.i.i. Serpentine proofer

The principle of the serpentine system (**Figure 10.015**) is that the products are carried on trays that pass through the whole process in single file. The product trays, which may be "free" or "contained," are located on carriers, supported on either side by chains that run through the whole system as products encounter moulding, proofing, oven, cooling, etc., processes as required. As far as the proofer is concerned, the system of chains, carriers, trays and products enter the first proofer at a low level. They are taken on a circuit up to the top, around a pair of small sprockets, travelling a distance horizontally, then down around another pair of small sprockets, back along a horizontal distance, down again, and so on for a number of horizontal laps until they reach the height a which they entered the proofer.

The process is then either repeated or they are carried to the exit, leaving to go into the oven. The carriers are continually stabilized by a series of cams and levelling wheels. The serpentine proofer is suitable for large craft bakers or small industrial bakers. The proofer has the same advantages as described in the generic description of continuous proofers, above.

10.A.8.i.ii. Spiral proofer

A spiral proofer (**Figure 10.016**) operates in the same manner as a spiral cooler. The conveyor belt is spirally wrapped around a driven rotating drum. As the drum rotates, the friction between drum and conveyor pulls the conveyor around. The system can operate with a single drum or, better still, a pair of drums (double spiral) so that the conveyor winds around one on the way up and around the other on the way down.

The benefits of the system are that (a) the drive tension is low all the way around the system, (b) the air conditioning equipment is contained within the proofer enclosure, and (c) clean-in-place systems can be supplied.

The spiral proofer is suitable for industrial bakers, and it has the same advantages as described in the generic description of continuous proofers, above.

10.A.8.i.iii. Conveyorized proofer

The conveyorized proofer (**Figure 10.017**) is one element of the integrated "proof and bake" or "Lanham" system. For a further description of the system refer to Part B of this chapter, which describes conveyorized ovens.

The basis of the proofer system is a single continuous chain, pulled around the proofer in a track. The chain supports carriers, called "grids," which in turn support the pans or trays.

First engineered as a single racetrack-style conveyor that traveled in a single vertical direction, either up or down, conveyorized proofers have since entered "second generation" design, which configures the track as a double oval. Products ride the grid chain up one oval and come down the other. This design allows location of entry and exit conveyors at the same level (**Figure 10.018**).

Outside the proofer, the track forms a simple loop, which accommodates the product unloading station, the grid cleaner, chain oiling station and product loading station. It is usually necessary to have a double loop within the proofer because the proofer conveyor needs to be much longer than the oven, which has a single loop. However, single loop and figure-8 arrangements are also available.

The conveyorized proofer is suitable for industrial bakers, and it has the same advantages as described in the generic description of continuous proofers, above.

10.B. Ovens
Contributed by Stephen St. Clair-Thompson

Industrial baking ovens, although developed decades ago, continue to evolve thanks to new heating technologies, design and engineering innovations, emerging knowledge about dough rheology and, of course, industry demand. Unfortunately for today's baker, this change has lead to much confusion in the use of some basic terms. The following explanations are provided to help the reader better understand the terms used in this chapter.

Convection. In a convection oven, air is withdrawn from the bake chamber, heated and blown back into the bake chamber through orifices, producing peak air velocities at the baking product of about 2 to 5 m per second (400 to 985 ft per minute). If baking a very heavy dense product, air velocities can reach as high as 6 to 8 m per second; however, in most convection ovens baking crackers, biscuits and snacks, the air velocities at the product are closer to 2 to 5 m per second and generally closer to 3 m per second as an average.

Convective. This term is used generically to cover the aspects of fan assist, turbulence, convection and impingement.

Cyclotherm. This term describes a particular type of indirect-fired oven.

Direct fired. In a direct-fired oven, the products of combustion are entrained with the oven's hot air to pass over or under the baking foods as they are conveyed.

Direct gas-fired (DGF). This term is used for a particular type of direct-fired oven with a large number of linear ribbon gas burners located above and below the baking product.

Fan assist. A fan is provided inside the oven bake chamber to air. With this method, typical peak air velocities over the baking product are 0.5 m per second (100 ft per minute).

Figure 10.015. Serpentine systems move pans or trays carrying dough pieces through long horizontal runs to make a full circuit of the temperature and humidity controlled proofer.
(Auto-Bake)

Figure 10.016. Spiral proofers use the same technology as spiral coolers but are housed in temperature- and humidity-controlled enclosures. The ductwork in this proofer is deliberately stationed so it is not flush to the wall, thus making the system easier to clean.
(I.J. White)

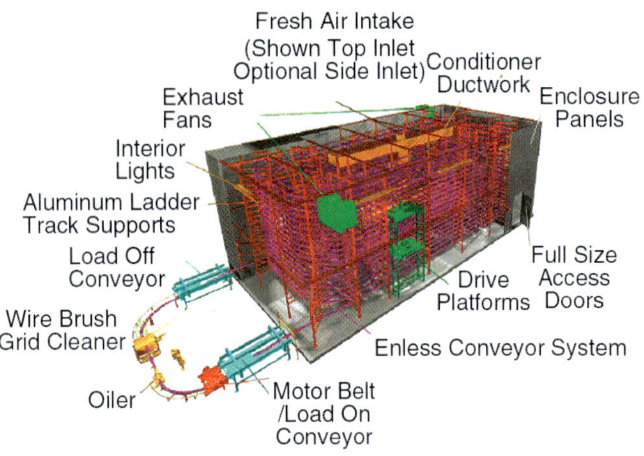

Figure 10.017. Conveyorized proofers, the first stage of integrated proof-and-bake systems, expose every pan to the same heat and humidity conditions. (Stewart Systems)

Figure 10.018. A conveyorized proofer carries pans through a heat-and-humidity-controlled chamber in single file so all products encounter the same conditions. (Baking Technology Systems)

Heat flux. This concept refers to the heat transfer rate per unit area.

Heat transfer. In this chapter, heat transfer implies heat transfer rate, i.e., the transfer of heat per unit time

Heat. Here, this term is used in the same way as commonly used. So it is sometimes used instead of enthalpy, the more correct scientific term.

Impingement. In an impingement oven, air is withdrawn from the bake chamber, heated and blown back into the bake chamber through orifices, producing peak air velocities at the baking product of up to 9 m per second (1,772 ft per minute). At the nozzle of the jet, the air velocity may be 30 m per second, but 3 to 4 in. below the nozzles, those velocities drop significantly to 10 m per second or less. (Some coolers, dryers and freezers also employ impingement methods.)

Indirect fired. In an indirect-fired oven (**Figure 10.019**), the products of combustion do not pass over the baking foods. Instead, a heat exchanger transfers of the heat energy to the oven's air supply.

Mass exchange. Baking drives moisture out of dough pieces. The term mass exchange refers to the transfer of such moisture from the dough into the oven's atmosphere.

Moisture level. The moisture level of a product is described using the wet weight basis. Thus, the product's moisture level is determined by dividing the mass of water in the product by the mass of the product and expressing the result as a percentage.

Turbulence. In a turbulence oven, air is withdrawn from the bake chamber and blown back, without additional heating, into the bake chamber through orifices, producing peak air velocities at the baking product of about 1.5 m per second (300 ft per minute).

10.B.1. Heat transfer mechanisms

The baking oven has two main physical functions to perform on the article it processes: heat exchange and mass exchange. Heat exchange relates to the transfer of heat, and mass exchange, particularly in the case of baked foods, involves removal of water. The two processes are closely related because heat transfer facilitates moisture removal, which accounts for the majority of weight lost from the product.

There are five principal methods of energy transfer between the oven and baking products. Radiation, conduction and convection transfer energy via heat where a temperature difference exists (**Figure 10.020**). The evaporation and condensation process transfers energy when a material such as water changes state from a gas to liquid. A brief explanation of each is given below.

10.B.1.a. Conduction

Conduction is the transfer of heat from one body to another by contact between them. Any baker misfortunate enough to have touched the hearth surface at the oven's exit will be well aware of this effect. For ovens, conduction is mainly important in transferring heat from the hearth of the oven to the product and, where relevant, from the product's pan to the product. Conduction is an important mode of heat transfer to flat products such as pizzas, crackers, tortillas, etc., which are baked principally by contact with a hot surface.

Conduction is a surface effect, in that the heat applied by the external body only heats up the surface of the product. For the inside of the baking product to benefit from the rise in surface temperature, the heat must make its way (by a number of complex mechanisms) into the product.

10.B.1.b. Convection

Convective heat transfer is the transfer of heat from a moving fluid (gas or liquid) to a body. The principle of convective heat transfer will be clear to anyone who has used a hand dryer in a washroom. In the context of a baking oven, convective transfer involves fan assist, turbulence, convection and/or impingement systems.

Convection gives high rates of heat transfer from modest oven operating temperatures and, in general, gives good thermal efficiencies to an oven. Any of the convective techniques will tend to provide uniform heating around the product. This action will usually be an advantage, but sometimes it poses drawbacks. For example, English scones require a white, relatively unbaked "collar" around their sides. To bake this type of product properly, the more directional radiant form of heating from above and below must be used. Also, consider cookies and crackers that have pronounced impressions created by stamping or rotary moulding. Any of the convective techniques will tend to color the valley of the impression as much as the plateau. But a radiant form of heating will not penetrate the valley of the impression as much as the plateau, leaving it slightly paler. This effect gives a slightly more visually pleasing effect, called "highlights."

The higher the air velocity over the baking product, the higher the heat transfer rate per unit area (i.e., heat flux) between the air and the surface of the baking product. **Table 10.02** offers typical figures of heat flux per degree.

With reasonably thin dough pieces, the heat flux within the product can keep pace with the heat flux onto the product. So, providing higher air velocities around the dough piece will produce higher thermal efficiencies and reduced baking times. This speed is normally an advantage but, if taken to excess, will result in reduced flavor development because the complex chemical changes required for flavor development will not have time to take place.

Like conduction, heat transfer to a baking product by any of the convective systems is only a surface effect. Additionally, the air velocity over the product must not

Figure 10.019. Bakers can test run products on this indirect-fired oven that features both a stone and steel hearth. It also features air impingement as well as radiant heat.
(C.H. Babb)

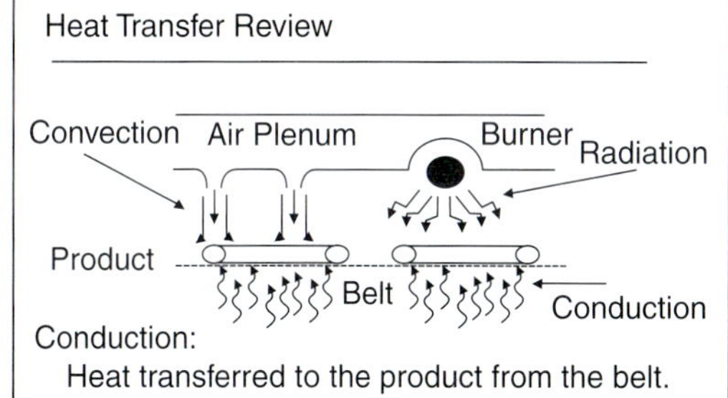

Figure 10.020. Heat transfers through the processes of convection, radiation and conduction.
(Zaleski 1999)

Table 10.02. Heat Flux

	BTU per hr per sq ft per F°	W per sq m per C°
Natural convection	1 to 2	5.7 to 11.4
Forced convection	2.4 to 6	13.6 to 34
Impingement ovens	12 to 20	68.1 to 114

(Walker 1987)

be high enough to blow away any light topping such as sugar, salt or pizza topping.

10.B.1.c. Radiation

Radiation is the transfer of heat from a hotter body to a cooler one by electromagnetic radiation, in the same way as the sun provides Earth with heat.

Any surface, whether the sun or the inside of a hot baking oven, emits the complete range of electromagnetic wavelengths from the far infrared, through the near infrared, through red, yellow, blue and violet to the ultraviolet, microwave and beyond (**Figure 10.021**). But the intensity of the radiation at the various wavelengths is far from uniform. At short wavelengths, the intensity is low, peaking at a wavelength that depends on the temperature of the surface and decaying at longer wavelengths.

Various peak wavelengths, together with the emitting temperatures, are reported in **Table 10.03**.

At the radiating temperatures of a Cyclotherm oven's tubes or a DGF oven's radiating plate, the relevant radiation is unable to penetrate the dough piece's surface. So at these temperatures, radiant heat transfer is a surface effect, much as conduction and convective heat transfer are.

However, if the temperature of the emitting surface is increased to 2,100°C (3,810°F), then the radiation will penetrate into the baking products slightly so that thin items bake throughout their depth. Cookies can be baked this way in approximately half the time required in a conventional oven (**Figure 10.022**), as reported by Wade (1987). The necessary temperature can be achieved by electric elements inside quartz tubes. The process is known as NIR (near-infrared) baking.

Microwave radiation is a well-known example of radiation that can penetrate foods to transfer heating energy. For the practical purposes of heating foods industrially and domestically, microwave radiation is generated using a magnetron, and the heating action is caused by friction as polar molecules resonate in the microwave field. Part H of this

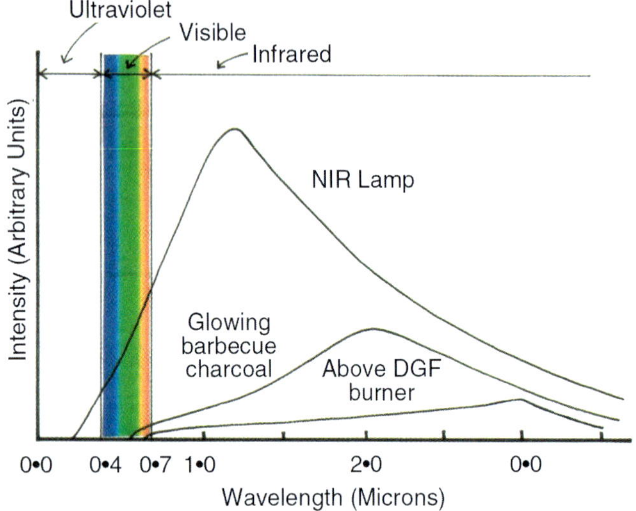

Figure 10.021. Radiation intensity depends on its wavelength.

Table 10.03. Wavelength Temperatures

	Temperature (°C)	Peak wavelength (µ*)	Temperature (°F)	Wavelength (x 10⁻³ in.)
Convection oven plenum	200	6.1	390	2.4
Cyclotherm radiant tubes	400	4.3	750	1.7
Above DGF burner	700	3.0	1,290	1.2
Glowing barbecue charcoal	1,000	2.3	1,830	0.9
NIR element	2,100	1.2	3,810	0.5
Sunlight	5,600	0.5	10,110	0.2

$1\mu = 1 \times 10^{-6}$ m

chapter explains microwave technologies related to baking.

Radiation provides heat "along the line of sight." So radiant baking, by itself, is poor at providing side color to closely spaced bread loaves and similar tall products.

10.B.1.d. Condensation

Every baker who has opened an oven door, peered inside and been scalded by the water vapor coming out of the oven knows just how effective condensation is at transferring heat. Typical dough pieces go into an oven at a temperature similar to that of the human body and will experience the same burst of heat. In addition to this transfer of heat, the condensation on the dough surface has several effects, described in the next section this chapter.

10.B.1.e. Evaporation

Soon after a dough piece enters the oven, its surface reaches a sufficient temperature (the dew point temperature) that causes water on its surface to evaporate. This action applies not only to the water that has just condensed on the crust but also any water that makes its way to the surface from within the product. Evaporation is encouraged by any of the convective systems (fan assist, turbulence, convection or impingement).

10.B.2. Bake chamber parameters

It is important to think of the oven as a device for producing heat flux and not in terms of temperature. An instrument that helps with understanding flux is the oven data logger. These small devices have one or more sensing heads and a recorder in a well-insulated box. It is placed among the dough pieces at the infeed of the oven and retrieved from the baked products after the oven. Both temperature loggers and heat flux loggers (**Figures 10.023** and **10.024**) are commercially available, and some loggers can distinguish between convective heat flux and radiant heat flux.

A glance at the data logs from a 3-zone convection oven (**Figure 10.025**) shows why it is important to think in terms of heat flux and not temperature. In this case, the convection dampers on zone No. 2 were closed, producing a markedly different heat flux than during the other two zones, although the temperatures were generally the same. What would have happened if the process had to be moved to another oven and only the temperatures had been replicated? Clearly, to obtain consistent products, we need to provide consistent heat fluxes.

Providing consistent temperatures is only one, and an insufficient, way of achieving uniform results. We know this fact in our daily lives. Those of us lucky enough to go skiing will know it better than most. Consider a skier standing at the top of a mountain on a still, bright day. He may be pleasantly warm because he gets a warming dose of sunlight and is not subject to any convective effects. But as he sets off downhill, skiing fast through a belt of trees at the same air temperature, he will

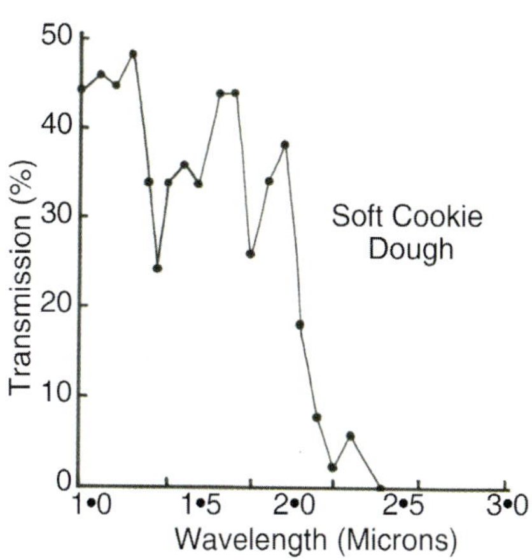

Figure 10.022. Lower near-infrared wavelengths transmit into cookie dough more effectively than higher ones. (Wade 1987)

Figure 10.023. A heat flux data logger sits between rows of cookies to measure the heat conditions within the oven during baking. (Digitron Ltd.)

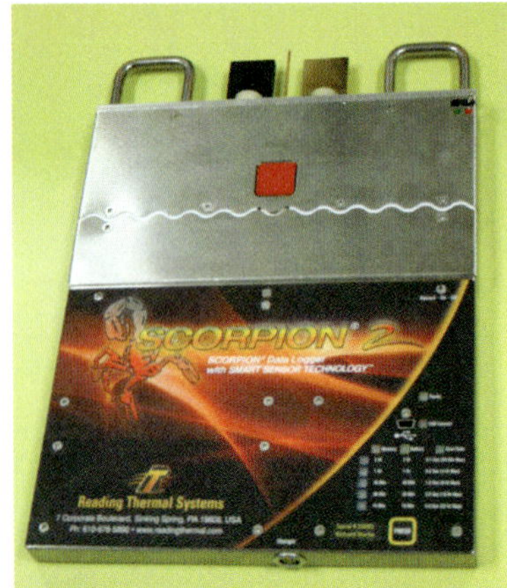

Figure 10.024. This sensor records data on temperature, air velocity, heat flux and humidity inside commercial ovens, dryers and cooling tunnels. (Reading Thermal Systems)

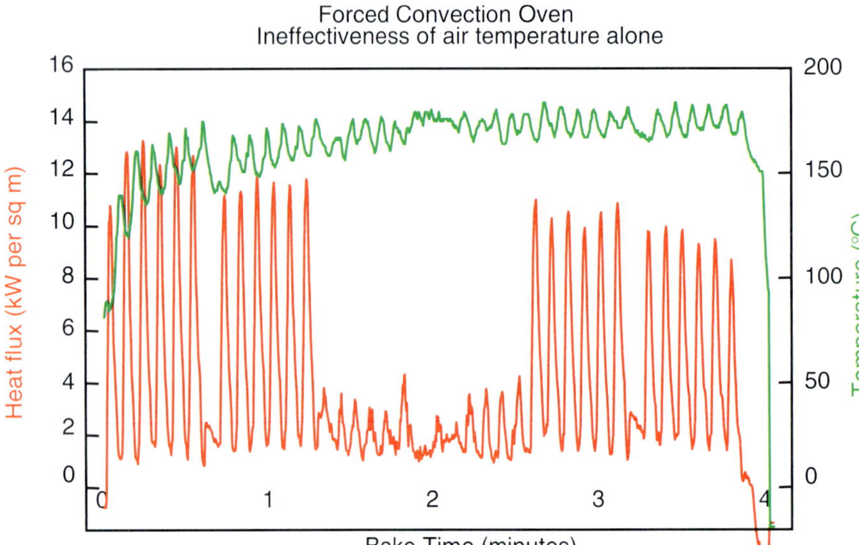

Figure 10.025. Air temperature alone does not fully account for heat flux. (Digitron Ltd.)

rapidly feel cold because the sun's radiation is denied him, and his velocity relative to the air provides him with a substantial (negative) heat flux. Thus, the heat flux in a convective oven is a function of both the air temperature and the velocity of the air as it passes over the dough pieces.

Table 10.04 describes the terms used to measure heat transfer and heat flux. (The unit "kW per hr," frequently seen in magazine articles, is meaningless. The correct unit is "kW" alone or "kWhr" in the usages noted by the table.)

10.B.2.a. Temperature and heat flux

Although heat flux loggers are available to enable understanding of variations of heat flux within an oven, fixed heat transfer sensors to monitor the surface of products during baking are not commercially available. Until they become so, we will have to continue to think in terms of temperature for the baking product.

The diagram in **Figure 10.026** can help visualize the various physical and chemical changes that take place during cookie baking; however, it must be used with caution because the changes are time-dependent as well as temperature-dependent.

One of the most important chemical changes during baking is the Maillard reaction, which gives the baked product its flavor and much of its color. This reaction combines certain amino acids from the proteins with sugars from the carbohydrates (Moreth 1987a, 1987b). In the context of baking, the Maillard reaction produces its attractive reddish-brown hues at about 150 to 160°C (300 to 320°F) (Manley 2000). Taken to excess, however, the Maillard reaction can lead to the development of acrylamides, reported to be carcinogenic (Mottram et al. 2002). Prudence dictates that the heat flux to the product surface should be limited, allowing the Maillard reaction to take place slowly and avoid over-browning.

10.B.2.b. Humidity and the use of steam

In addition to the roles of heat flux and temperature, the other important parameter during baking is bake chamber humidity. The presence of water vapor, or humidity, in the oven's atmosphere comes mainly from the liberation of water from products as they bake. The

Table 10.04. Heat Measures

	Imperial	Metric
Heat (energy)	British thermal unit (Btu)	kilowatt hour (kWhr)
Heat transfer (power)	Btu per hr	kilowatt (kW)*
Heat flux (rate of transfer of heat per unit area)	Btu per hr per sq ft	kW per sq m

* "Kw" is also acceptable for kW.

humidity in existing ovens is usually controlled by fixed-speed extraction fans and extraction dampers; the humidity on new ovens is usually controlled by variable-speed extraction fans.

When considering humidity in the context of baking ovens, it is best to think in terms of the "dew point." —the temperature at which water in the oven atmosphere would condense. If the oven is less humid, the dew point is lower; if it is more humid, the dew point is higher. A dew point temperature of 100°C (212°F) would correspond to an oven atmosphere that is all water vapor. The Internet offers numerous humidity calculators.

When dough pieces enter the oven, they are soft, elastic and moist. Usually, dough pieces must retain their elasticity so they can develop into the required shape. The best way to keep them elastic is to keep them moist. Maintaining high humidity in the oven is the best way to keep dough surfaces moist. So a high humidity is necessary until the final shape of the product is set. In other words, a high humidity is important in the early part of the baking process.

A lack of humidity in the early part of a cookie or cracker oven will cause the product to "case harden," which stops the ability of a cracker to rise, thus limiting its stack height, an important parameter that affects the weight of product in a package of a fixed length. For cookies, case-hardening inhibits the proper escape of internal moisture, leading to differential moisture levels within the cookie. This difference, in turn, causes "checking," the spontaneous cracking of the cookie (Johnson and Walker 2003).

Lack of humidity in a cracker oven causes development of excessive blisters, which burn easily, causing undesirable dark spots. The blisters are also easily broken (Johnson and Walker 2003).

Once the surface temperature of the dough piece exceeds the dew point temperature relevant to the oven humidity, it will start to dry out. After that point, the humidity in the bake chamber is of little importance to the baking. This point is currently not understood by bakers who are keen to reduce baking times. During the second half of the baking process, bakers will often open the extraction dampers excessively in the mistaken belief that having a drier oven will improve the drying process and reduce the bake time. It does not: The only effect is to increase the baker's fuel bill.

Humidity in a bread oven is a special case. Here, the development of the product has already taken place in the proofer. Well-established crusts are important to these products, unlike cookies or crackers. In particular, if the baker is seeking a glossy crust, then bake chamber humidity early in the bake will be vital. The glossy crust is caused by gelatinization of the starch on the dough surface, promoted by a reaction between the water and starch. The higher the dew point temperature, the shorter the time the high dew point must be maintained. For example, optimum gloss formation can be achieved with a dew point temperature of

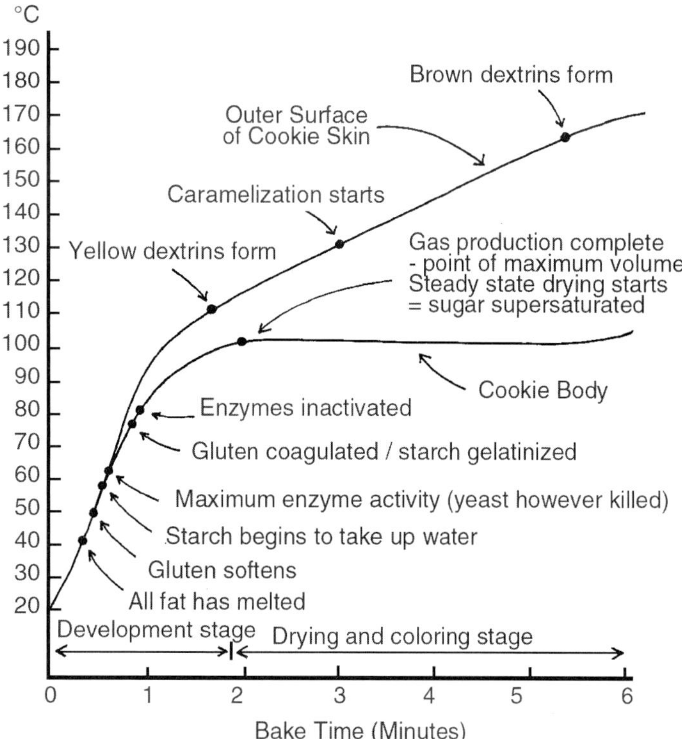

Figure 10.026. Many physical and chemical changes take place during cookie baking.
(Mowbray 1981)

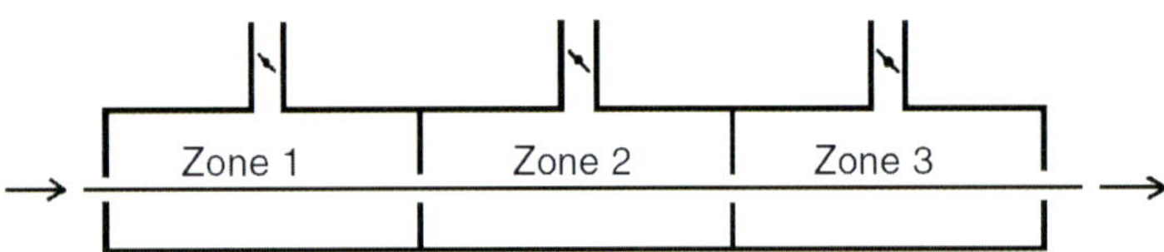

Figure 10.027. Heat and airflow patterns within an oven can be established by zones.

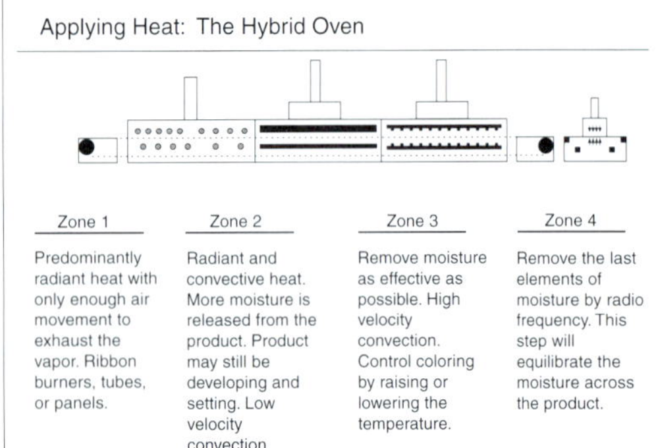

Figure 10.028. Hybrid ovens consist of modules that employ different methods of heat transfer.
(Zaleski 1999)

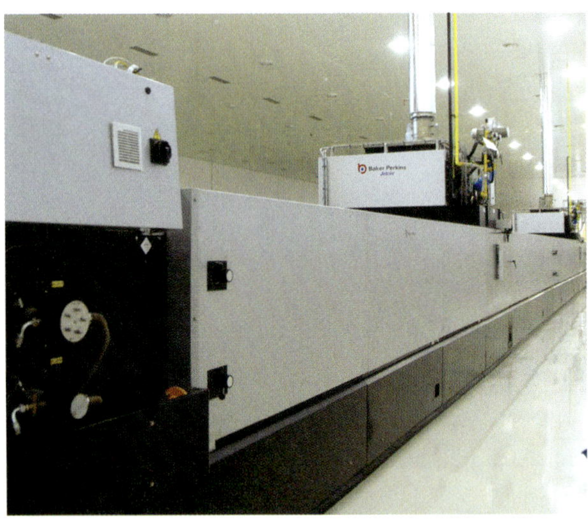

Figure 10.029. Hybrid ovens can offer non-turbulent DGF heating in one zone, convection in another, impingement in a third and so forth to suit the exact baking profile required.
(Baker Perkins Ltd.)

93°C (200°F) for 40 seconds, or 82°C (180°F) for 3 minutes (Dersch 1989).

An extreme case could be in an oven baking ginger snaps. This style and similar cookies have high sugar content. Keeping the humidity high in the early part of the oven promotes extensive cracking in the surface, which is a desirable feature for these items.

Fortunately for those who need to keep track of the humidity within ovens, humidity loggers (similar in concept to the heat flux loggers described above) are now available and can be used to good effect.

10.B.3. Heating systems

In this section, the principal modes of heat transfer are explained. The following section details the way in which the various modes of heating are used in conventional production ovens.

Before describing the various heating modes, a few terms in common usage need to be explained.

Zone. The term zone refers to an area of the oven with its own heating and extraction control system, baffled off, as far as possible, from other zones (**Figure 10.027**).

Overlay. To overlay heating systems is to use two heating sources within one zone. For example, it is possible to have DGF burners in a Cyclotherm zone.

Hybrid. Ovens that have several zones, one or more of which have different heating modes, are described as hybrid systems (**Figure 10.028**). For example, many cookie ovens employ non-turbulent DGF heating for the earlier baking zones and convection for the later baking zones (**Figure 10.029**).

10.B.3.a. Cyclotherm systems

Ovens with Cyclotherm systems are heated by radiator tubes (or radiator ducts) through which the hot combustion gases circulate. These hot gases are generated in combustion chambers separated from the baking chamber. Arranged in banks within the baking chamber (**Figure 10.030**), the radiator tubes give up their heat chiefly by radiation. The products of combustion are thus kept from entering the baking chamber and have no direct contact with the dough pieces so Cyclotherm ovens are considered indirect-fired systems. While natural gas is normally used as the fuel, Cyclotherm systems are capable of burning oil. Very occasionally electricity is used as the fuel.

Cyclotherm zones require two extraction points: one in the bake chamber, the same as a DGF system, and a second from the heating circuit. Since the useful heat from a Cyclotherm system has to be driven through the tube walls, such systems tend to be less efficient than DGF methods. In addition, Cyclotherm systems contain more metal than DGF systems. The presence of all this metal serves to slow the response of these ovens. In the past, this fact meant they were more susceptible to "flash heat," the phenomenon where the first products of a production run were more heavily baked than later products. Newer ovens with improved instrumentation have reduced this problem to negligible levels.

Finally, the heat flux produced by a Cyclotherm oven is limited by the tube temperatures. In general terms, a Cyclotherm oven can provide less than half the heat flux of a DGF oven.

In the absence of turbulence, the primary mode of heat transfer for a Cyclotherm oven is radiation. So care should be exercised if a stainless steel hearth is being considered. Stainless steel can have low emissivity, i.e., low ability to absorb radiant heat.

The heat transfer and temperature received by the baking products as they travel through a Cyclotherm oven are smooth because they do not vary with time.

Turbulence is frequently added as an overlay to most zones in Cyclotherm ovens to improve efficiency and reduce bake time.

Convection ovens are generally replacing Cyclotherm styles because of their lower fuel costs and shorter bake times.

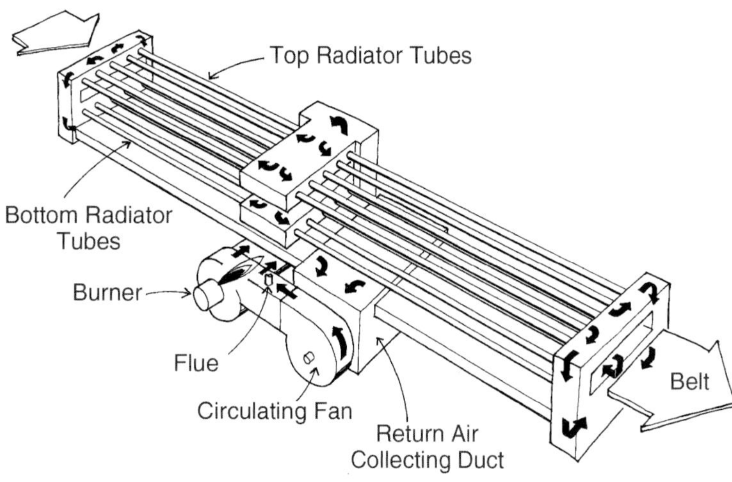

Figure 10.030. The oven belt travels between top and bottom heat-radiating tubes. Arrows indicate the flow of hot gases through a Cyclotherm system. (Baker Perkins Ltd.)

10.B.3.b. DGF systems

In direct gas-fired (DGF) ovens, large numbers of burners are positioned within the baking chamber, set transverse to the direction in which the pans and/or hearth travel. These burners are normally located both above and below the baking surface to provide controllable top and bottom heat. The burners can be of two distinctly different types: ribbon and radiant.

Most of the burners fitted to ovens are ribbon type, so the following explanation refers to this type. Below the belt, the plumes of heat rising from the flames provide the heat transfer to the base of the baking product. Depending on the product, it may be important to ensure that many low-powered burners are fitted, so that each plume is not too powerful.

The heat transfer from the top burners is entirely different. Only a negligible amount of heat transfers directly down from the flames either by radiation or convective heat. In fact, you can safely place your hand immediately under an operating DGF burner that has been removed from an oven. Instead, the top burners are used to heat the crown of the oven or a plate immediately above the top burner. The hot crown or plate radiates heat downward to provide the top heat to the product.

Detailed explanation of the heat transfer mechanism from radiant burners follows later in this chapter.

DGF ovens are, of course, direct-fired systems. In the absence of turbulence, the primary mode of heat transfer is radiation from above and the very powerful natural convection from the plumes of hot gases coming from the burners below the belt. The heat flux and temperature received by the baking products as they travel through a DGF oven are very spiky; that is, they vary sharply with time. Turbulence is frequently added as an overlay to most of a DGF oven (**Figure 10.031**) also to improve efficiency and reduce bake time.

DGF ovens have more flexibility than other oven types. In other ovens, the baker has the ability to control heat transfer rates and humidity on a zone by zone basis, but DGF ovens go one stage further than this. Each burner can (at least in principle) operate independently. Thus, the heat flux to the baking product can be controlled with a much higher precision than any other oven type.

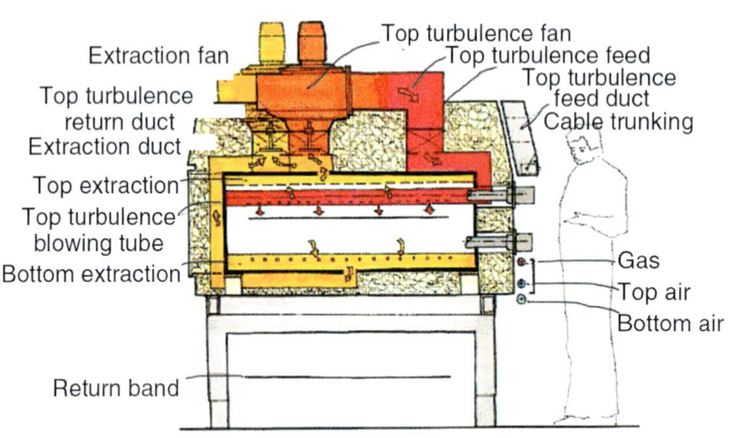

Figure 10.031. Turbulence added as an overlay to a direct gas-fired oven (shown in transverse section here) improves the efficiency of heat transmission and reduced bake time.
(Baker Perkins Ltd.)

10.B.3.c. Electric multi-element systems

The principle of many burners above and below the product is not confined to DGF burners. Their place can be taken by radiating electric elements. Each element usually consists of a nickel-chrome wire, carrying a high current, encased in electrically insulating material running the full length of a U-shaped tube. The tube runs transverse to the product flow direction. The U configuration enables both electrical terminations to be placed at one side of the oven. Electric multi-element systems are only sold in markets where electricity is an economical energy option.

10.B.3.d. Near-infrared systems

A variation of the electric multi-element type of system is the near-infrared (NIR) quartz tube system. The quartz tubes are situated above and below the product and transverse to the direction of the baking belt. Each tube contains a nickel-chrome wire formed formed in a U shape so that both electrical terminations can be at one side of the oven. The wire glows with an intense near-infrared radiation, which passes through the tube and penetrates the dough. As described in the earlier section on radiant heating, cookies can be baked by NIR in approximately half the time required in a conventional oven (Wade 1987).

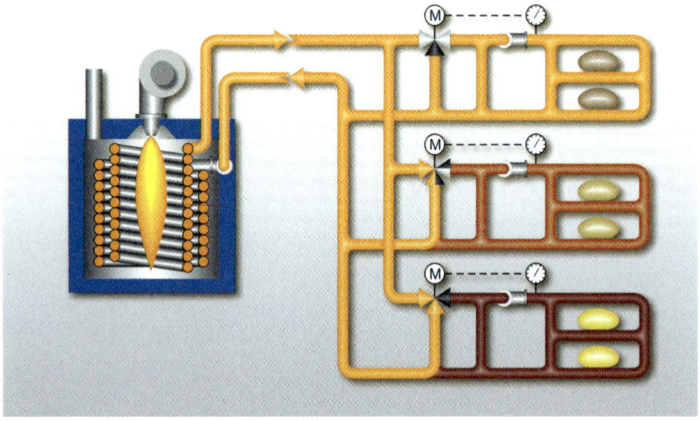

10.B.3.e. Thermal fluid (thermal oil) systems

All oven types other than DGF, electric multi-element and near-infrared types have a source of heat kept remote from the baking product. This fact means there must be some fluid that carries the heat to the proximity of the baking product. On a Cyclotherm or convection oven, the fluid is air.

An alternative fluid is food-grade, noncombustible oil that has a maximum service temperature of about 326°C (619°F) and carries more than 1,000 times the heat content of an equal volume of air. By transferring its heat to the oven belt or deck, it heats by conduction, convection and radiation. In practice, this temperature is a little low for products that need high heat fluxes so thermal fluid systems are limited to smaller baking operations (**Figure 10.032**). However, some equipment suppliers disagree with this statement, particularly where this

Figure 10.032. Thermal oil, heated in a remote system, flows through insulated pipes to circulate in the decks and walls of ovens. Valves control the amount and speed of oil circulation, thus determining the amount of heat transfer.
(The Kaak Group, Daub)

heating method is used to bake snack cakes quite successfully.

The thermal fluid circulates through a sealed system of flat radiators (**Figure 10.033**) lining the decks and walls and thus needs little space in the oven, making it an advantageous heating medium for some types of ovens such as multi-deck (**Figure 10.034**) and serpentine ovens. The oil never comes into contact with baking product. This technology also proves economical when used to supply heat to several ovens.

The high heat capacity of thermal oil allows rapid heat recovery. In fact, the temperature differential between the heating medium and the oven chamber is usually less than 50 C° (90 F°), about half that of standard ovens. Flash heat conditions do not occur. Changing oven temperature is a matter of throttling up or down on the flow of the thermal oil, which also allows heat to be controlled in different baking zones using only one heat exchanger.

The system that heats the oil is typically installed in a remote location, with the oil piped to ovens in insulated lines. Thermal fluid heaters are currently fired by natural gas, oil, biomass or electricity. The thermal oil should be replaced every 5 to 10 years (Diver 2006).

10.B.3.f. Convection systems

In convection ovens, a fan sucks large quantities of air from the bake chamber and blows it through a heating system. The heated air is then propelled along plenums (ducts) above and below the baking products and out of the plenums through orifices directed at the baking products. These orifices, set transverse across the flow of product, can be configured as long slots or rows of circular holes. On contact with the dough piece, the air gives up some of its heat and picks up moisture from the baking product. It recirculates back to the heating system. A small portion of the bake chamber air is taken to extraction.

The heating system may be fired either directly or indirectly. If the heating system is direct-fired, natural gas must be used as a heating fuel because the products of combustion circulate round the baking foods. Note that when natural gas is burned in air (which is principally oxygen and nitrogen), it produces heat, water vapor and carbon dioxide, together with the original nitrogen. Thus, in a direct-fired oven, the humidity in the bake chamber cannot be reduced much below about 0.2 kg of water per kg of air because that is about the humidity produced by burning natural gas without any excess air.

Also, it is not possible to produce very high levels of humidity in direct-fired ovens. Any effort to build up humidity inside the oven (by not exhausting the water vapor driven off the baking products) will be frustrated by the burner diluting the bake chamber atmosphere with more carbon dioxide and nitrogen.

If the heating system is indirect-fired, then there will be a heat exchanger between the primary (combustion) and secondary (bake chamber) systems (**Figure 10.035**). This design limits the heat flux within the zone, but it does allow total control of humidity within the bake chamber between very low (not normally required) to very high. This ability to operate with a high humidity improves the efficiency of indirect-fired convection ovens. So as a general rule, the efficiencies of direct-fired and indirect-fired convection ovens are about the same.

The heat for a direct-fired convection system is generally provided by a gas burner or electricity. The heat for an indirect-fired convection system is generally provided by a gas or oil burner.

Figure 10.033. Flat radiator plates carry the hot thermal fluid so it never comes into contact with product or oven atmosphere.
(Diver 2006)

Figure 10.034. Thermal oil heating technology provides consistent temperature control to multi-deck ovens.
(MIWE)

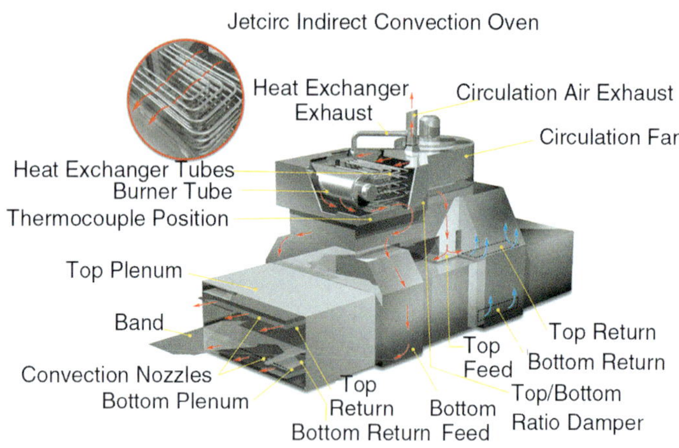

Figure 10.035. In an indirect-fired oven, the combustion system supplies heat to the oven through heat exchangers. (Baker Perkins Ltd.)

10.B.3.g. Recirculating systems

Some convection systems, called recirculating (or recirc) systems, have an additional set of dampers and ducts that allow the oven to be operated in either convection or radiant mode (**Figure 10.036**).

With dampers set in convection mode, the recirculated air is forced out of the orifices and over dough pieces as described above. Thus, most of the heat transfer is by convection, and only a small proportion comes from radiation from the plenums. With dampers in radiant mode, most of the air continues within the plenums and returns to the heating system without blowing over the baking product. Radiation from the heated metal of the plenums performs the baking. Of course, in radiant mode, the temperature of the circulated air must be increased to obtain sufficient heat transfer by radiation. Thus, in radiant mode, most of the heat transfer is by radiation, and only a small proportion comes from convection. The heat for a recirc system is generally provided by a gas burner.

10.B.3.h. Impingement systems

Impingement systems are broadly similar to convection systems; however, at the point of contact with the product being baked, they use much higher air velocities

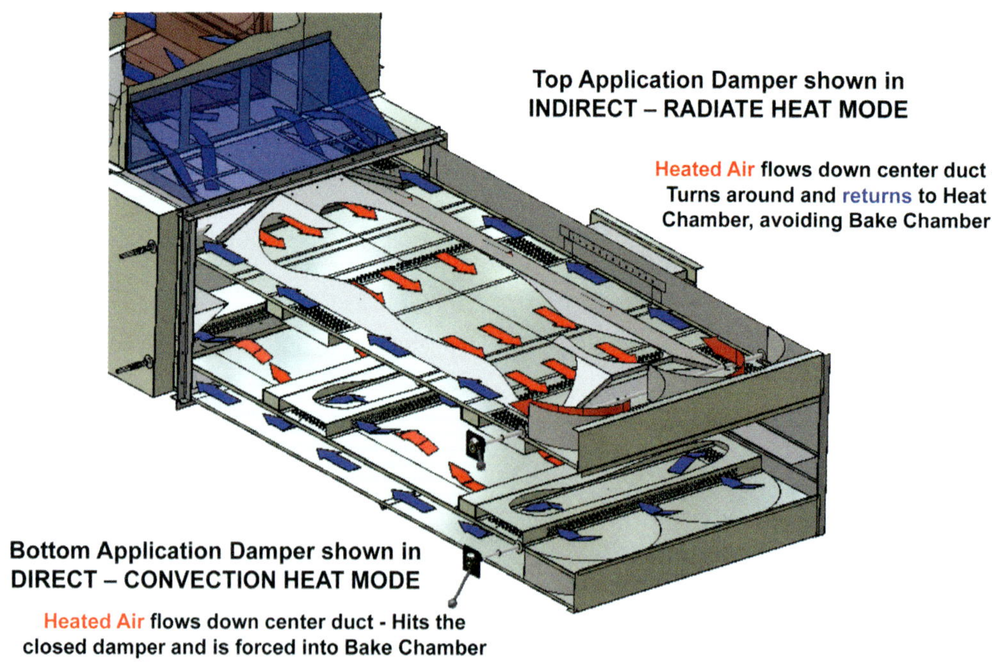

Figure 10.036. The recirculation principle for oven heating employs dampers and ducts that control the direction of air flow. (Baker Perkins Ltd.)

that produce shorter bake times. Impingement systems employ larger volumes of air and shorter zones than convection systems. Orifices in the ducts direct high-speed air to impinge on the dough pieces, stripping away the stagnant layer of moist air eddying around them and transferring heat to the dough surfaces (**Figures 10.037** and **10.038**). **Figure 10.039** charts the air velocity by zone of an impingement oven, showing how these speeds can be controlled to achieve the desired bake profile.

A major benefit of this type of oven is good access for cleaning because the ducting does not restrict cleaning access. With the short length of each zone, necessary access doors can be economically provided (**Figure 10.040**). The heat for an impingement system is provided by a gas burner or electricity. Impingement methods can also be applied to cool and freeze foods and are discussed in more detail in Part G of this chapter.

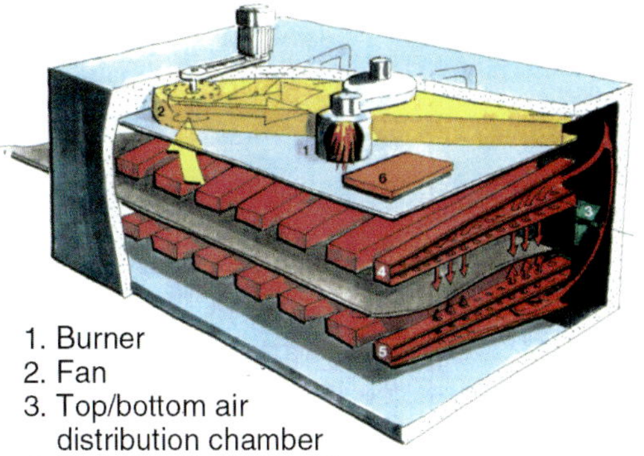

10.B.3.i. Radio-frequency systems

Radio-frequency, or dielectric, systems use radio waves, part of the electromagnetic spectrum, to penetrate the baking products and heat them throughout. The most extensive use of dielectric heating (27.12 or 40.68 MHz) in the baking industry is for the final reduction of moisture in cookies and crackers (**Figure 10.041**). Its effectiveness is based on the fact that heat generation in the product does not depend on any temperature differential between the product and the energy source but is proportional to the former's moisture content. Hence, the higher the moisture content of the product, the more heat is generated to drive off the moisture.

As Spooner (1984) pointed out, an increase in the production capacity of a cookie or cracker tunnel oven normally entails a reduction in the bake time, which, in turn, results in a corresponding increase in the internal moisture content of the baked product. By inserting a dielectric oven (also called a dielectric dryer) immediately following the tunnel oven, the moisture content of the emerging cookies or crackers can be reduced economically to the desired low level. Additional benefits that accrue from the use of dielectric heating immediately after regular baking include the elimination of checking (breaking) of the product and more accurate control over final moisture content. Metallic belts cannot be used in a radio-frequency unit; textile belts are used instead.

Like microwave ovens, radio-frequency systems do not color the crust of baked foods; thermal radiation is required. Experimental work found it possible to combine 13.36 MHz radio-frequency heating with convection heating as in the air radio frequency assisted (ARFA) oven (Kent and Evers 1994), shown in **Figure 10.042**. This method has been applied to production of breadcrumbs and baked snacks.

1. Burner
2. Fan
3. Top/bottom air distribution chamber
4. Top air columnating fingers
5. Bottom air columnating fingers
6. Explosion relief

Figure 10.037. Impingement ovens transfer heat by directing hot air at high velocity through plenums to reach the surface of dough pieces. (Baker Perkins Ltd.)

Figure 10.038 Above and below the oven belt, the columnating holes of the impingement system supply heated air, while the belt's dark surface provides good thermal conductivity. (Berndorf Belt Technology USA)

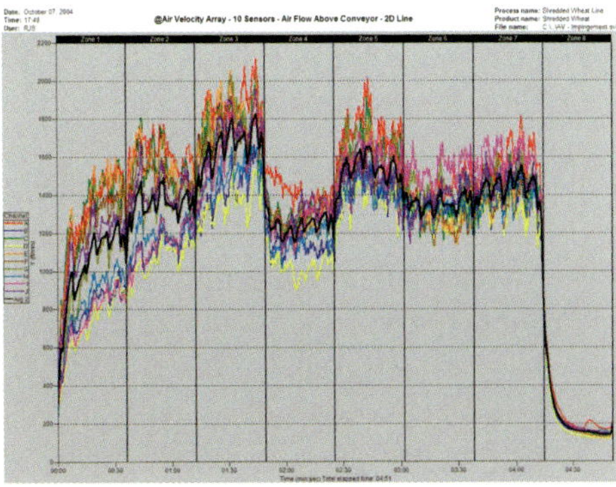

Figure 10.039. A multi-channel data recorder measured the air velocity in an impingement oven, showing zone-by-zone results. (Reading Thermal Systems)

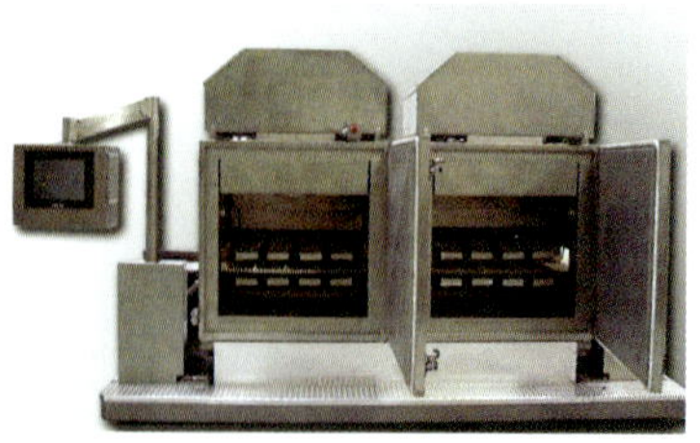

Figure 10.040. Cleaning of impingement ovens is simplified by large access doors and ducting that does not restrict access. (Baker Perkins Ltd.)

Figure 10.041. The rapid reversal of polarity that takes place in a dielectric field causes polar molecules (water in particular) to vibrate quickly, generating heat through friction. (Strayfield Ltd.)

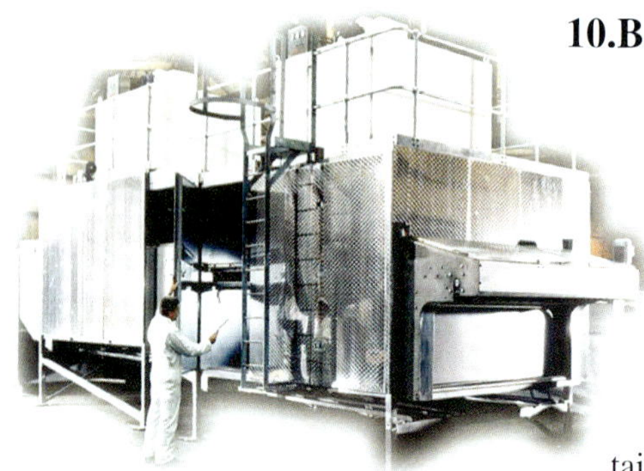

Figure 10.042. Convected hot air bakes the product's surface and is assisted by microwave radiation that bakes the product's interior in an air radio frequency assisted (ARFA) oven. (Petrie Technologies)

Radio frequency methods, also called dielectric drying, are explained in detail later in Part C of this chapter.

10.B.3.j. Heating system comparisons

Each heating system provides benefits and poses drawbacks, and **Table 10.05** summarizes the pros and cons. A brief review of the table shows why convection ovens are replacing Cyclotherm styles and why DGF ovens continue to be popular.

Different baked foods put different requirements on oven technologies. Consider cookies, an example of a product that develops during baking. During the development phase, the dough piece needs to remain elastic. This characteristic could be inhibited by the drying action of air movement so turbulence is not normally fitted to the first part of a Cyclotherm or DGF oven. This need also figures in the popularity of DGF-convection hybrid ovens, where DGF heating is used for the early part of the bake and convection heating for the latter part. Yet there are many successful cookie ovens that are convective throughout their full length. Slightly more care needs to be taken with these ovens to ensure high humidity levels in the early stages of the bake — keeping the dew point high will avoid stripping off the surface moisture.

Thermal fluid is omitted from the accompanying table because the tabulation relates to the point of use for the heating system. A thermal fluid provides the carrying medium of heat up to the point of use. The heat transfer away from the thermal fluid may be radiant (oven chamber surfaces), conductive (hearth surfaces) or convective (air flow).

10.B.4. Oven types

The oven is frequently, and justifiably, referred to as the "heart" of the bakery because it is the means by which heat transforms raw dough or batter into a wide variety of baked products. The origins and evolution of modern ovens were traced and described in varying detail by Varilek and Walker (1983, 1984) and Blümel and Boog (1977), among others.

Massive chambers constructed of brick or stone, with thick soles and crowns, comprised the first commercial ovens. They were heated by building a wood fire within the baking chamber directly on the hearth and maintaining it until the oven had accumulated a sufficient amount of heat to complete a baking run. The oven operator then pulled the fire from the oven and cleaned the hearth of ashes as best as possible. Then the oven was loaded with product. Bakers used long-handled peels to load and unload these ovens, thus accounting for their designation as peel brick ovens.

The first major improvement in these primitive ovens came with the provision of a separate fire box or furnace. Heat was conveyed to the baking hearth by a series of flues located both beneath and above the chamber through which the hot combustion gases passed on their way to the chimney stack. This method of heating removed the limitations on the periods during which baking could be done. By providing a separate and continuous supply of heat at baking temperatures, this improvement freed the baker from the necessity of having to reheat the oven intermittently.

Because of their massive construction, these ovens stored and delivered the kind

Table 10.05. Oven Characteristics

	Heat transfer mode	Flexibility in mode change	Speed of response (ability to deal with production gap)	Ability to form a particular heat curve
Cyclotherm without turbulence	Radiant	Poor	Poor	Moderate
Cyclotherm with turbulence	Radiant and convective	Moderate	Poor	Moderate
DGF without turbulence	Radiant top, convective base	Poor	Good	Very good
DGF with turbulence	Radiant and convective	Moderate	Good	Very good
Radiant electric without turbulence	Radiant	Poor	Good	Very good
Radiant electric with turbulence	Radiant and convective	Moderate	Good	Very good
NIR	Radiant	Poor	Very good	Very good
Convection direct or indirect	Convective	Poor	Very good	Moderate
Convection – electrically heated	Convective	Poor	Very good	Moderate
Recirc	Radiant and/or convection	Good	Very good	Moderate
Impingement	Convective	Poor	Very good	Good
Radiofrequency	Radiofrequency	Poor	Very good	Moderate

of solid bottom heat and proportional radiant top heat considered best for good baking performance. However, these brick peel ovens had some major inherent disadvantages, including their massive weight, variable baking times for individual product units imposed by the peel loading and unloading sequence, lack of uniform heat distribution and high labor costs, among others. They did, however, perform quite satisfactorily when tended by skilled oven men, and many of these ovens survived well into the early decades of the 1900s.

Invention of the Perkins steam tube enabled heat from the fire box to be brought into the baking chamber and did away with the massive brickwork. The tube would nowadays be known as a "heat pipe" — a device that allows very high heat fluxes with little temperature differences. As used in a baking oven, the tubes are hermetically sealed, with a small quantity of water inside. The lower ends project down into the firebox and the upper ends into the baking chamber. The water inside the end of the tube located in the firebox vaporizes into steam. This steam rises within the tube into the section located in the baking chamber. There the steam gives up its latent heat to the baking product and trickles back down inside the tube towards the firebox, to be reheated and repeat the cycle. At normal atmospheric pressure, water boils and steam is generated at 100°C (212°F), but the steam tube needs to reach about 326°C (619°F) if it is to be effective as a thermal fluid system.

Mechanization of ovens made its first appearance when the stationary hearth of the earlier peel oven was replaced by a rotating hearth in the so-called rotary peel oven. This hearth was circular in form and revolved in a horizontal plane, supported on a central, motor-driven vertical axis. This innovation represented a marked improvement over the original peel oven because it simplified oven loading and unloading and thereby helped to establish more regular baking schedules. More importantly, it subjected all products equally to the temperature variations that might develop in different areas of the baking chamber.

Eventually, the massive brick construction of the peel oven gave way to steel frames and sheet metal for interior and outer wall construction, with various types of insulating material for confining the heat within the oven chamber. Because these steel ovens still operated as peel-loaded systems, their inherently limited production capacity in relation to its size prevented widespread acceptance in wholesale baking. Such ovens, however, have survived in the food service industry and are occasionally found in-store bakeries, primarily for their theatrical appeal.

Efforts to facilitate loading and unloading operations, and especially to eliminate the long peels that required rather extensive floor areas for their manipulation, resulted in several modifications of the traditional peel oven. Thus were developed draw-plate ovens, multi-deck ovens and rack ovens. In early draw-plate ovens, the hearth consisted of a large steel plate mounted on tracks and supported at its front end on runners. This design permitted the oven operator to pull the hearth out of the oven chamber for loading and unloading. The relatively large working area needed to accommodate the draw plate during loading and unloading, as well as the heat loss associated with this operation, tended to limit the acceptance of this type of oven.

10.B.4.a. Reel ovens

Reel ovens, essentially an American development, were the first truly mechanical ovens to appear on the scene (**Figure 10.043**) and the first that we can accurately term modern ovens. As their name implies, reel ovens (**Figure 10.044**) employ a reel structure that revolves vertically around a horizontal axis within the baking chamber and supports the baking trays rather like a carnival's Ferris wheel. The reel requires a relatively high baking chamber, and the oven's fuel consumption is thought to be disproportionately high in relation to its production capacity, compared with most other types of oven.

The proportional dimensions imposed on the baking chamber by the reel make it somewhat difficult to attain even, uniform heat distribution throughout the enclosure and to accurately control the temperature. Moreover, the several passes made by the baking product through the upper zone, which frequently has high moisture content, tend to impart a crust character to the product that differs somewhat items baked in tray or tunnel ovens.

Reel ovens are normally heated by direct firing, using either electricity or gas as the energy source. The heating elements are positioned centrally across the floor of the baking chamber. A baffle above the gas burners converts part of the convective heat into radiant heat and thereby provides a proper balance of these two forms of heat. In the past, when coal and oil were the primary fuels, such

Figure 10.043. Reel ovens, loaded and unloaded by operators using long peel boards, were an important innovation in commercial baking technology.
(Reading Bakery Systems archives)

ovens required indirect firing. In indirect-fired ovens, heat was generated in a separate box, located beneath the baking chamber. The hot gases were then conducted through radiators placed across the oven floor and upward at the back between the oven chamber and an insulated back wall to be exhausted to the atmosphere through the flue.

The reel oven continues to be used today and suits batch processing. They are typically found in food service operations and some in-store bakeries. The reel oven has been adapted to pilot plant and lab use as well. They are usually direct gas or electrically heated.

10.B.4.b. Rack ovens

Rack ovens were first introduced in 1958 (Blümel and Boog 1977). They consist of a vertical baking chamber into which the oven operator wheels a special rack carrying as many as 100 trays of product. Usually, the rack is placed on a floor-mounted turntable, which turns around a vertical axis. The oven bakes by using jets of heated air that blow horizontally onto different faces of the dough pieces (**Figure 10.045**).

Some rack ovens incorporate two or more adjacent baking chambers. Alternatively, some suppliers arrange for one or more racks to be put on the turntable.

Rack ovens are heated by gas, oil, electricity or thermal fluid. If heated by gas or oil, they are indirectly fired. When products require steam, it is injected during the relevant part of the baking cycle. The steam is generated within the oven at atmospheric pressure, usually by trickling water down through a heated cast-iron labyrinth.

Because opening the door to remove the rack risks loss of heated air, the air flow patterns of rack ovens are controlled to rapidly transport hot air from the bake chamber into the system's large overhead plenums. Only when the door closes and the baking cycle started again does the control system allow the heated air to return to the bake chamber.

Rack ovens are used by craft bakers and by small industrial bakers (**Figure 10.046**). They provide a batch processing method, useful for small production runs. One version comes with stone shelves fixed within the oven. The product can be loaded from a specialized rack onto the shelves and unloaded after baking.

10.B.4.c. Multi-deck peel ovens

Modern peel ovens can be made very compact so several can be stacked on top of each other. One of their major advantages is that the individual baking compartments are independent of each other and can be maintained at different temperatures. This configuration allows simultaneous baking of several products with different time and temperature requirements. This type of oven is used for batch processes. Loading and unloading are manual. Typically, multi-deck peel ovens are used in the food service industry, for example, for pizzas. They are usually direct gas or electrically heated.

10.B.4.d. Multi-deck draw plate ovens

Modern deck ovens also can be made very compact, permitting stacked design. As with the multi-deck peel ovens, the individual baking compartments are independent of each other and can bake at different temperatures. This capability allows the simultaneous processing of several products with different time and temperature requirements. This type of oven is used for batch processes. Loading and

Figure 10.044. Reel ovens bake products on a revolving system of trays. (Reading Bakery Systems archives)

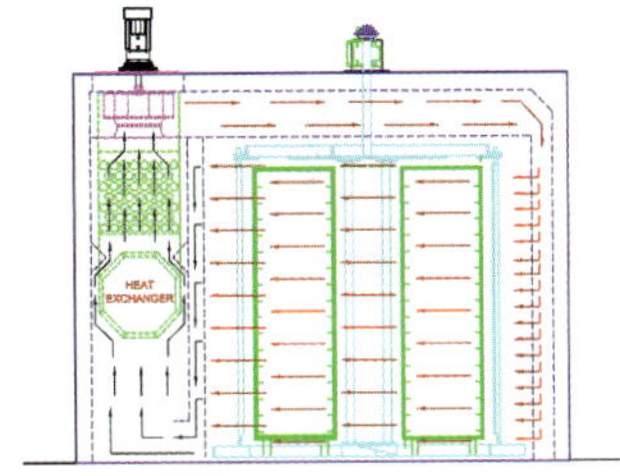

Figure 10.045. Airflow in a rack oven is directed horizontally at products. (Double D Food Engineering, a division of JBT FoodTech)

Figure 10.046. A bank of rack ovens provides the flexibility to efficiently manage multiple products and/or small production runs.
(MIWE)

unloading are semi-automatic or automatic. Typically they are used for craft bakeries. They are usually heated by thermal fluid.

10.B.4.e. Multi-deck conveyor ovens

Modern multi-deck ovens (**Figure 10.047**) can be made with internal conveyors. The various decks are loaded and unloaded from one end of the oven by a load/unload conveyor. This conveyor loads one deck at a time with several batches, with the internal oven conveyor moving forward one "step" at a time. The door of that deck is closed, and its bread is retained for the bake time. Meanwhile the load/unload mechanism shuttles to the other levels. When the bread is baked, the oven's internal conveyor is reversed, and product is unloaded at the same end from which it was loaded. Loading and unloading are semi-automatic or automatic. As with the multi-deck draw plate oven, the independent compartments can operate at different temperatures with different bake times. Heat transfer is by thermal fluid.

This type of oven is very flexible and can be used by both large craft bakers and small industrial bakers.

10.B.4.f. Tunnel ovens

A tunnel oven, as its name implies, features a long, low baking chamber, through which the baking hearth, loaded with baking product, is driven. It has very good zonal independence because each zone can be independently heated and provide independent moisture control. The only space in which zones can interact is the "letter box" that the conveyor and products pass through between zones.

The full range of heating systems can be used: DGF, electric, NIR, thermal fluid, Cyclotherm, direct convection, indirect convection, recirc, impingement, radio-frequency and microwave heating. Overlay heating is particularly appropriate for tunnel ovens because of the simple conveyor circuit. Many ovens are hybrid, having different heating modes in different zones.

The tunnel oven makes poor use of floor space; however, the space above it can frequently be used. For example, final proofers can be installed above bread ovens. The ovens can either be small and loaded by hand for the artisan trade or large, automatic machines for continuous industrial production.

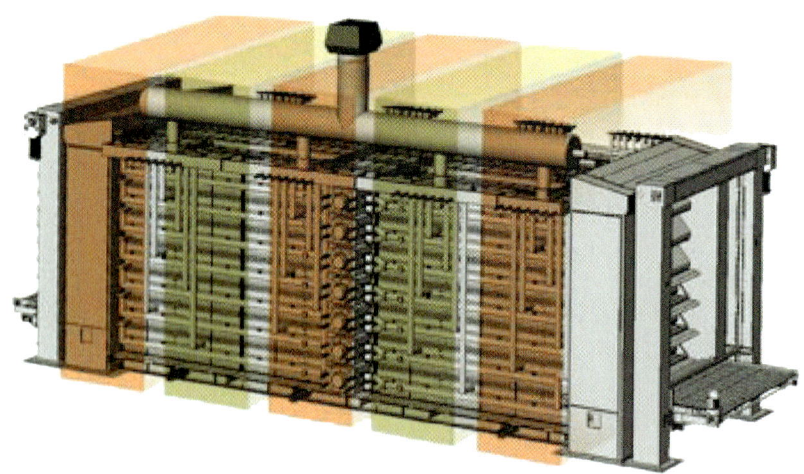

Figure 10.047. Each deck is capable of independent temperature conditions, facilitating the preparation of multiple product varieties.
(Werner & Pfleiderer)

Recent developments have been larger doors for access to clean inside the oven. Some ovens, particularly for baked products with meat or dairy products in them, are now supplied with clean-in-place (CIP) sanitizing equipment.

10.B.4.g. Multi-deck tunnel ovens

The multi-deck tunnel oven (**Figure 10.048**) is very similar to the multi-deck conveyor oven, except that the multi-deck tunnel oven locates its unloader at the opposite end to the loader. Thus, product flows through the oven from one end to the other instead of returning to the front for unloading. The various decks are each loaded and unloaded by external conveyors that automatically shuttle from one level to another. Like the multi-deck conveyor oven, the multi-deck tunnel oven consists of independent compartments capable of supplying different temperatures and different bake times.

This type of oven can be operated in a variety of modes: batchwise, stepwise continuous and fully continuous. The appropriate mode will depend on the throughput of products, product variety and bakery layout.

Batchwise baking. In the batchwise mode, one deck is loaded until it is full. Each time a batch is loaded, the oven conveyor is indexed forward one batch length until the deck is full. The deck is then paused for the bake time. During this pause, the loading mechanism shuttles to the other decks. After each batch has been in the oven for its allotted time, it is unloaded at the far end.

Stepwise continuous. In the stepwise continuous mode, each deck is loaded with a batch of product in turn. As soon as a deck is loaded, the conveyor of that deck moves forward by one "step." The oven conveyor then pauses for a time equal to the bake time divided by the number of steps. While paused, the loading mechanism shuttles to the other decks. After each batch has been in the oven for the programmed bake time, it is unloaded at the far end.

Fully continuous. For fully continuous mode, the decks are loaded with a batch of product in turn. The conveyor of each deck runs continuously, so that any particular deck will move steadily forward while the other decks are being loaded. After each batch has been in the oven for its proper bake time, it is unloaded at the far end.

Multi-deck tunnel ovens can be used by both large craft bakers and small industrial bakers. Heat transfer is by thermal fluid or Cyclotherm.

10.B.4.h. Multi-step (vertical) ovens

Sometimes described as a vertical oven, a multi-step oven handles products baked on trays (**Figure 10.049**). Each tray is indexed into a tier within the oven until the tier is full. The tier is repeatedly indexed vertically up within the first zone. At the top, the top tier-load of trays is cycled forward into the second zone where a similar stepping device brings it down. The process is repeated until the trays leave the oven. These ovens generally employ modular design, with the number of baking (proofing or

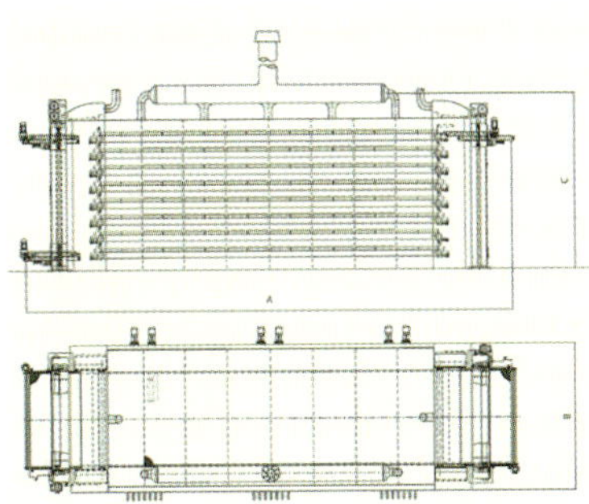

Figure 10.048. In a multi-deck tunnel oven, products enter one end and leave the other. Each independently-controlled tier can provide different temperature and baking time requirements. (Werner & Pfleiderer)

Figure 10.049. The multi-step oven sequences trays up and down through the baking zones. (The Kaak Group, Benier)

freezing) modules depending on the products being made. The heating mode is indirect gas-fired convection.

10.B.4.i. Serpentine oven

The principle of the serpentine system (**Figure 10.050**) is that the dough pieces are carried on trays that pass through the whole process from forming to cooling in single file, following a horizontal serpentine path as they travel through the system (Marino 1998, Trate 2001).

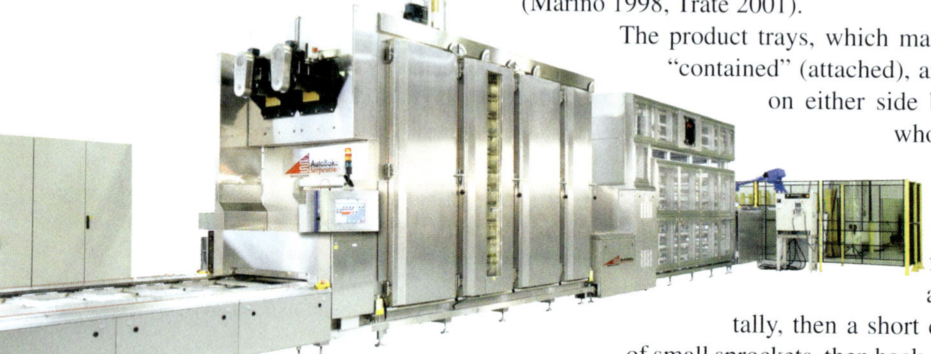

The product trays, which may be "free" (**Figure 10.051**) or "contained" (attached), are located on carriers supported on either side by chains that run through the whole system: make-up, proofing, oven, cooling, etc, as required. The system of chains, carriers, trays and products enter the first zone at a low level. They are taken on a circuit horizontally, then a short distance upwards around a pair of small sprockets, then back again horizontally, again around another pair of small sprockets, and so on for a number of horizontal laps, typically 11 but configurable for different product needs. The laden pans then come down to the exit, set at the same height as the entry, and leave to be cooled or further processed. The travel can also be designed to convey product trays to the top tier first, then serpentine back down, depending on product type. The carriers are continually stabilized by a series of cams and levelling wheels.

Figure 10.050. In a serpentine system, products carried on pans travel in single file through successive tiers of horizontal laps at each processing stage: proofing, baking, cooling and freezing. (Auto-Bake)

The ovens are suitable for large craft bakers and industrial bakers. They have been widely adopted for cake products and are also suitable for bread.

The ovens have a number of advantages. First, since the equipment operates one tray wide (more recently two), each tray receives the same heat profile. Second, the system makes excellent use of floor space. Third, grouping and transfers between the various machines are eliminated. And finally, the ovens can be heated by electricity, thermal fluid or direct convection.

10.B.4.j. Tray ovens

Tray ovens comprise a large number of carriers that are hung from a pair of chains. A third chain acts to stabilize the carriers. The products to be baked must be on trays or within pans. The trays or pans are loaded onto the carriers. The chains take the carriers around a circuitous journey within the oven. A single lap circuit consists of the carriers conveyed vertically up, horizontally to the far end of the oven, back again to the loading end (**Figure 10.052**). The trays or tins are loaded and unloaded at the same end.

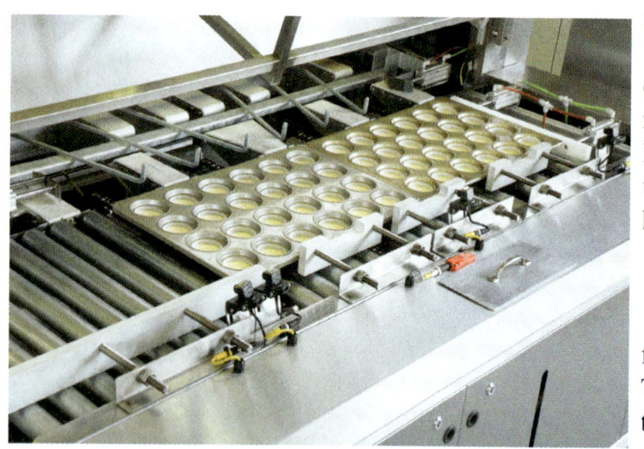

Figure 10.051. The "free" pan loader interface for serpentine ovens allows use of existing pan sets, and a new oven design accommodates 2-pan-wide baking. (Auto-Bake)

It is difficult to get effective zonal control within a tray oven because it is impossible to baffle off one area of the oven from another. Also, the air patterns within the oven alter with the number of trays or tins within the oven.

Single lap tray ovens use less floor space than a tunnel oven. Such ovens can also be configured with a double lap (**Figure 10.053**). An oven with a double lap occupies less floor space than a single lap, but it has increased mechanical complication and even less zonal control than a single lap oven.

Heat transfer systems for either style oven can be DGF, gas-fired direct convection or gas- or oil-fired indirect convection. The ovens are large automatic machines for continuous industrial production.

10.B.4.k. Conveyorized ovens (Lanham ovens)

In the mid-1960s, Lanham (1970) invented an integrated continuous proofing and baking system. Since then, several modifications of the original concept have evolved that differ in the details of their conveyor systems rather than in their basic principles (Grogan 1980, Wells 1983).

A distinctive feature of both proofer and oven is a continuous, grid-type pan conveyor pulled by an endless chain. Each conveyor carries the panned dough product through the final proofer and the oven for the required periods of time with a transfer between them. Typical dwell times of bread in the proofer and oven are about 60 and 20 minutes, respectively. Because of the dwell time difference, there is a corresponding difference in the size of the two units (**Figure 10.054**). Each unit, however, has a separate drive, and as long as the throughput is limited to the slower unit, the proof time/bake time ratio can be changed. The oven body consists of an enclosure formed by insulated panels supported by a steel frame that houses the endless conveyor.

The conveyor circuit can typically be one of two designs. In the older design, the conveyor enters the oven at a low (or high) level, spirals up (or down) in an oval pattern and leaves at a high (or low) level. This single-oval configuration suffers from the fact that the inlet and outlet are at different levels, which sets up the tendency for natural convection to cause hot air to escape at the higher port.

In the newer configuration, known as the "figure 8" or "second generation" design, (**Figure 10.055**) the conveyor enters at a low level, spirals up, crosses over itself in a figure-8 pattern at the top and spirals back down in the opposite direction. At the top of the system, the chain runs across the oval's diagonal, which has the effect of turning the pan's outside edge to the inside, thus exposing both pan ends to heat radiating from the walls for a high degree of uniformity of bake. The pans themselves do not move and stay firmly seated on the grid. At the bottom, the conveyor does a reverse figure-8 before exiting. Outside the oven, it does a simple loop to be unloaded and reloaded. Also located on this exterior loop are the grid cleaner and chain oiling station.

Most conveyorized ovens are DGF fired, with the burners arranged in banks immediately below the grids. The burners are not directly transverse to the conveyor, as on a tunnel oven. Instead, the relatively long burners run along the conveyor, but at a slight angle, so that the heat covers the whole conveyor width. The heat flux and temperature received by the baking products is very spiky, as in a DGF-fired oven. A

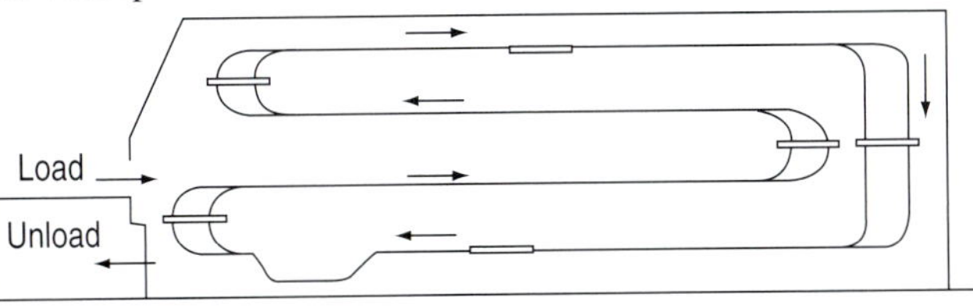

Figure 10.052. A single-lap tray oven carries products through a full back and forth circuit, with loading and unloading taking place at one end.

Figure 10.053. A double-lap tray oven provides two complete back and forth circuits, with loading and unloading at one end.

Figure 10.054. This "second generation" conveyorized oven places its entry and exit ports at the same level, unlike earlier designs.
(Turkington USA)

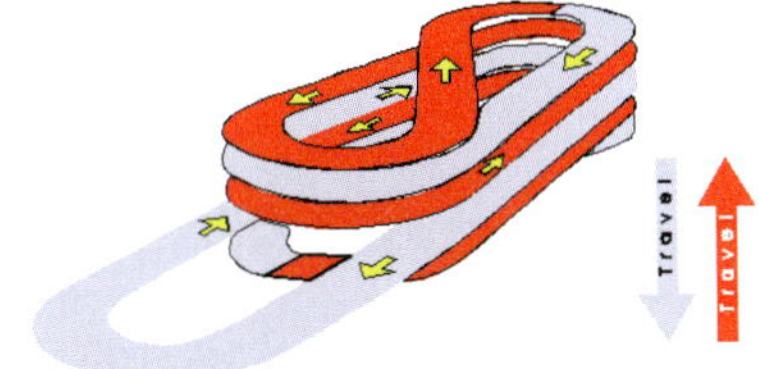

Figure 10.055. In the figure-8 design, the conveyor travels up, across the top and down the other side. The cross-over enables each pan to receive the same exposure to heat radiating from the walls.
(Turkington USA)

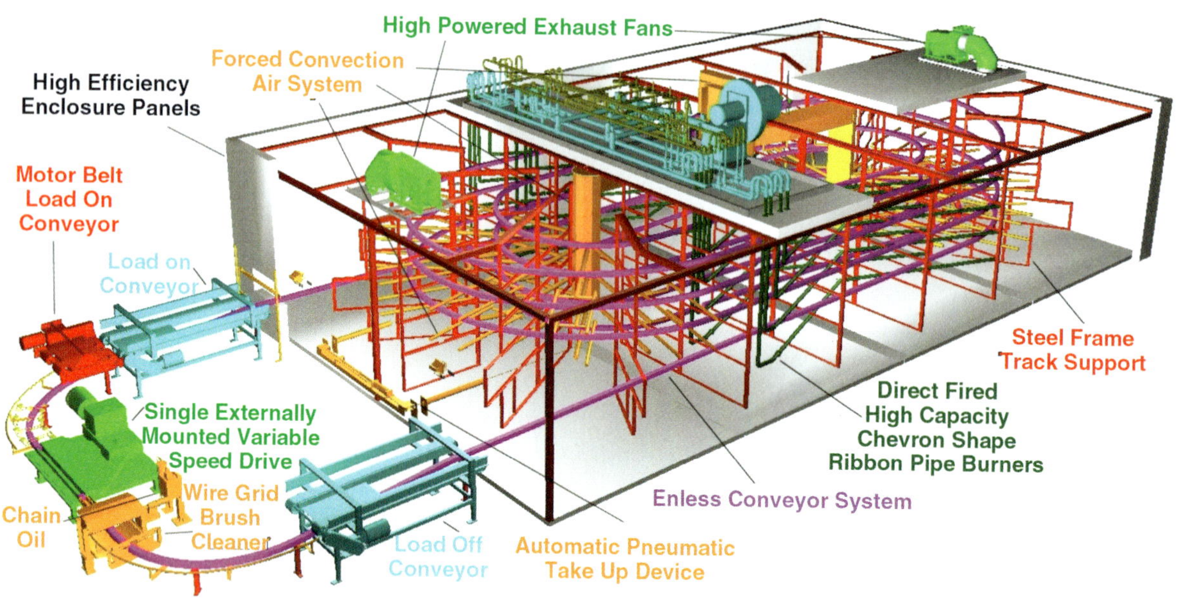

Figure 10.056. The conveyor of a conveyorized oven extends in a loop outside the oven for loading, unloading, cleaning and lubrication. (Stewart Systems)

few conveyorized ovens use convection heating and some employ indirect methods.

Speed of response is good on a conveyorized oven. The heat systems are arranged in zones, with separate control for each zone. Because conveyorized ovens are essentially one big box through which oven air drifts, it is difficult to get true zonal control. To provide steam to products as needed, the oven will be configured with an enclosed length of the conveyor at its entry into the oven (or even before the oven). Steam is injected into this tunnel-like structure.

Conveyorized ovens are only suitable for industrial bakeries and are best for long runs of similar products such as hamburger buns. The capacities of some of the larger systems are 12,000 800-g (1¾-lb) loaves per hour, and 90,000 units per hour for buns and rolls. The oven of a continuous proofing and baking system is shown diagrammatically in **Figure 10.056**.

The compact design of a conveyorized oven uses less floor space than tunnel ovens, providing a significant benefit in bakery layout. Also, the need for grouping and ungrouping activities for the proofer and loading and unloading at the oven is eliminated. Finally, access for maintenance is exceptional, with large doors being provided and space inside the oven to walk around.

10.B.4.l. Oven type comparisons

Table 10.06 compares the various oven types. In the table, "use of floor space" includes racks and grouping. Comparison of the heating systems is considered in Part B of this chapter.

10.B.5. Oven loaders and unloaders

Rack ovens are usually loaded and unloaded manually by the baker pushing the loaded rack in and out; however, mechanical handling systems are available that pick up, load and unload the racks from the oven, under the baker's control.

Table 10.06. Oven Type Comparisons

	Production run length	Use of floor space	Zonal control	Mechanical simplicity
Reel ovens	Short	Poor	Poor	High
Rack ovens	Short	Poor	Poor	High
Multi-deck peel ovens	Short	Poor	Poor	High
Multi-deck conveyor ovens	Medium	Good	Poor	Moderate
Tunnel ovens	Medium and long	Poor	Good	High
Multi-deck Tunnel ovens	Medium and long	Good	Good	Moderate
Multi-step ovens	Medium and long	Good	Reasonable	Low
Tray ovens	Medium and long	Good	Poor	Low
Serpentine oven	Medium and long	Very good	Reasonable	Low
Conveyorized ovens	Long	Good	Poor	Low

Multi-deck peel ovens are loaded and unloaded manually, using peels.

Tunnel ovens with a width less than 2 m are loaded manually or have forming equipment that loads them in-line.

Tray ovens and tunnel ovens wider than 2 m such as bread ovens require the product to be grouped and baked in the following manner. The unbaked product arrives from the side of the oven on a narrow in-line conveyor, until a group of products, matching the width of the oven, is positioned in front of the oven. The group is then accelerated onto a full-width loading conveyor into the oven. A sweep-style pusher bar moves the pans from the loading conveyor onto the oven tray or hearth. Single- and dual-lane systems are available. A similar process is performed for unloading.

Multi-deck conveyor ovens and multi-deck tunnel ovens, when baking panned bread, can be operated in-line or with grouping systems as described above for a tunnel oven (**Figure 10.057**). For oven-bottom bread the process is similar, except that it is necessary for the loaves to be "scrabbled off" the peel boards that they had been proofed on, onto a full width wire belt conveyor. Such crawler-style loaders are usually configured as long platforms, also called wings, as wide as the oven hearth and with curved tops over which a wire-link pick-up belt runs. When the loader's nose reaches the proofed dough, the loosely tensioned wire belt activates to pick dough pieces up off the peels and carry them forward over the wing, depositing them on the oven belt. Such loaders come in fixed and moving wing designs (**Figure 10.058**).

The moulding systems associated with vertical and serpentine systems drop dough pieces or deposit batters directly into the lines' fixed or free trays. The products stay with this tray throughout processing, including proofing, cooling and/or freezing stages, so no separate loading systems are required when they reach the oven. At the end of the line, the finished items are removed from trays by any of several methods. For example, a specially configured sweep arm gently pushes baguettes out of channel-style trays. Robots equipped with vacuum pick-and-place end effectors remove cupcakes from pans. Needle-style pick-up arms are also used for some products.

Conveyorized ovens are linked with their corresponding proofers using conveyors

Figure 10.057. An automatic system unloads a multi-deck tunnel oven. (The Kaak Group, Daub)

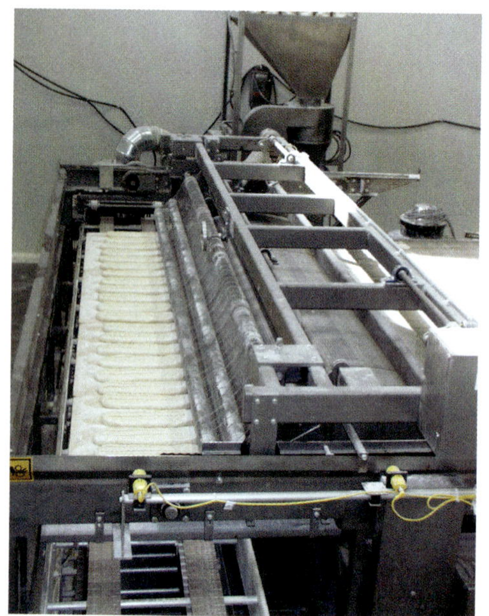

Figure 10.058. A peel board unloader picks up proofed dough pieces with the help of a wire mesh belt and shuttles them forward as the wing simultaneously moves into position to deposit them on the oven hearth. (Gemini Bakery Systems)

that unload pans of proofed products from the proofer's grids and move them along to the grids that will carry the pans through the oven. These links operate in a continuous fashion.

10.B.6. Oven hearths and belts

Stone and metal compose oven hearths. **Table 10.07** reviews the respective benefits of these materials.

Granite has a very much lower thermal conductivity and a higher specific heat than either of the steels. The lower thermal conductivity means that the heat flux provided by the stone to the dough piece will be similar to the heat flux through the baking product so granite is unlikely to overheat the product surface. Bakers describe this condition as a "soft heat." In addition, the higher specific heat enables stone to act as a thermal store.

Such capabilities are the reasons most often given for selecting granite as a hearth material. In fact, the principal reason is marketing, thus allowing finished products to be merchandised as "stone-hearth baked." Such ovens have long been made with metal hearths, which are actually more thermally efficient than stone, as reported in the accompanying table. The conductivity of stainless steel is worse than carbon steel. Nevertheless, there are some occasions where stainless steel is needed because of its corrosion-resistant characteristics.

The process and product type determines the style of hearth or oven band selected. If the product requires moisture removal through its base, as do many hard sweet cookies, then a permeable surface is needed. Such surfaces must, nevertheless, restrict the ability of dough to flow through or sink into the belt, so woven wire-mesh or perforated steel belts are appropriate. Other products will usually be baked on a solid surface, perhaps a tray, solid steel belt or slat. When products bake on trays or in pans, these containers must be supported by a surface (grid, belt, etc.) that is as open as possible to allow heat transfer to the underside of the tray or pan.

Dense, compound balanced weave mesh belts (**Figure 10.059**) are most often used in baking ovens because they retain and conduct significant heat to products, although a myriad of other weaves are available with specific uses (Strouts 2008b). Wire-mesh or perforated belts assure flat bottoms for cookies and crackers, an absolute requirement for sandwich-style items. The mesh or perforations allow cooking gases to escape preventing "steam cavities" from forming on the bottoms of the products.

Table 10.07. Thermal Conductivity and Specific Heat of Oven Hearths

	Thermal conductivity (W per m °C)	Specific heat (W hr per kg °C)	Thermal conductivity (BTU ft per ft 2 hr °F)	Specific heat (BTU per lb °F)
Carbon steel (0.1% carbon)	50 at 300°C	0.122 between 30 and 250°C	28.9 at 572°F	0.105 between 86 and 482°F
Stainless steel (10% nickel)	25.6 at 30°C	0.138 between 30 and 250°C	14.8 at 86°F	0.119 between 86 and 482°F
Granite	1.28 to 2.6 at 49°C	0.291 between 20 and 400°C	0.74 to 1.5 at 120°F	0.250 between 68 and 752°F

(Schack 1965)

Belt selection must consider not only the product but also the length of the oven, process conditions and belt supports. The belt must be strong enough to withstand the high tension under which it will operate. Belt strength depends on the density of the mesh, the diameter of the wire used in the construction and the material. Common oven temperatures allow the use standard carbon steel and stainless steel materials. Should higher temperatures be required, materials with higher nickel content may be required to provide the strength needed at the elevated temperatures. With thousands of available weaves and multiple choices for each application, product marking or the imprint of the weave into the product can be a deciding factor in belt choice.

Not only must an oven belt be strong and properly matched to the product, it must also run straight with minimum waver. Common baking belts are manufactured with joining spirals having alternating weaves: that is, one leans left, and the next leans right. This matched or balanced construction of the spirals is crucial for true straight tracking belts. A mis-match will result in the belt wavering or traveling to one side of the oven. Often, guides are built into the belt conveyor to control minor waver. Rollers to support the belting along its path can be used to "steer" the belt on those occasions when the belt wavers through the center of the oven.

Product build-up within the band can affect both process performance and belt life. A rotating bristle brush located in the return path is used to continuously remove minor product debris from the belt surface. A plow resting directly on the belt surface in the return path will guide any fallen debris off the belt edges, preventing the debris from getting on the idle drum, which would distort or damage the woven belt. When baking products containing high sugar or fat content, product debris can build up within the belt. Should the debris bake hard, it can affect heat transfer into the product and, in the worse case, result in wire breakage of the woven belt. Monitoring the belt for this condition is important. Periodically heating the belt to around 425 to 480°C (800 to 900°F) will carbonize the product debris, which then is removed with the rotating bristle brush.

The proper operation of the baking belt in a conveyor oven is critical to the process. As such, proper maintenance of the belt and system is mandatory. Scheduled inspection of the belt and supporting structure must be performed regularly to avoid belting failures or oven damage.

To compensate for changes in belt length due to thermal expansion/contraction, a tensioning system will be required (**Figure 10.060**). Typical ovens will have the take-up located at the in feed terminal of the conveyor. The take-up must be free to move its entire length to maintain even tension on the belt through all temperature ranges. Commonly, the take-up is activated by a pneumatic system; however, free hanging weights are still found on older ovens, and a tensioning system will be required.

10.B.7. Thermal aspects

In general terms, the thermal efficiency of an oven is governed by the heating system rather than by the physical configuration of the oven. Various definitions of oven thermal efficiency esist. The following one is frequently used (Duffin 1981):

$$E = (H_p + H_w) \div H_f$$

CB5 Dense-Mesh Baking Band

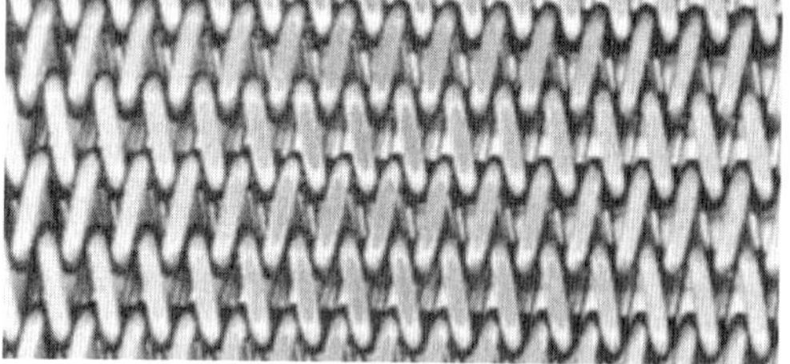

B60 Open-Mesh Baking Band Used for
Indirect-Fired Ovens

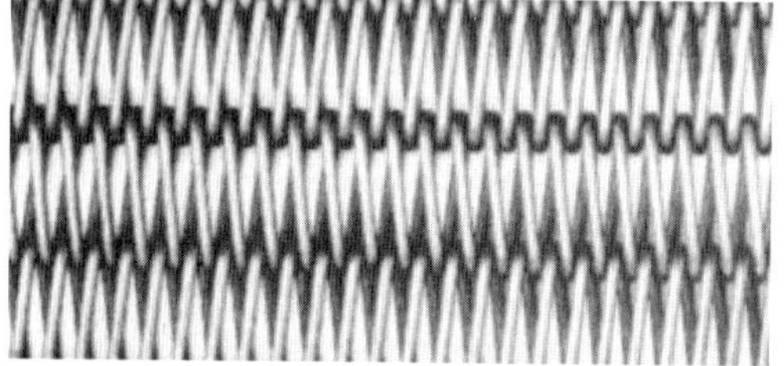

B84 Open-Mesh Baking Band used For
Hearth Ovens

Figure 10.059. Typical meshes for baking bands include dense mesh in a compound balanced weave (top), open mesh for indirect-fired ovens (top center), open mesh for hearth ovens (bottom). (Ashworth Bros.)

where E = the efficiency of fuel usage; H_p = the sensible heat required to raise the product from dough temperature to final temperature as it exits the oven; H_w = the total heat required to raise the water in the dough to its boiling point, vaporize the steam and superheat the steam to flue temperature; and H_f = the net heat value of fuel consumed. (To express E in percent, multiply the result by 100.) In forced convection and indirect ovens, the energy consumed by the oven circulation fans should be added to the H_f factor to give a true measure of total energy usage. Note that the benefit of this definition is that it is independent of the product being baked. It assumes steady state conditions, with a continually full oven.

Typical thermal efficiencies are tabulated in **Table 10.08** for the main oven heating systems.

Thermal oil is deliberately missing from the table because the data describe thermal efficiency at the point where heat is delivered to the product. However, the reasoning that calculates thermal efficiency can also be applied to thermal fluids. For example, assume a convection oven, which the table reports to have a thermal efficiency (E_t) of 55%, uses thermal fluid as the transport medium, and also assume the efficiency of the thermal fluid heater (E_h) to be 80%. Then the overall efficiency of the system (E_s) will be:

$$E_h \times E_t = E_s, \text{ or } 80\% \times 55\% = 44\%.$$

It should also be noted that the difference in fuel usage between the various ovens is greater than first appears from the table. For example, the increased fuel usage in operating a Cyclotherm oven without turbulence, compared with the cost of operating a DGF oven without turbulence, is $40 \div 35$, which equals 14%, not 5%.

The table also does not include the electrical cost of running the fans, which would need to be included in making a thorough analysis.

The importance of the table lies in the following points: (a) It provides a useful first-cut comparison of thermal efficiency of the different heating modes, and (b) it highlights the fact that oven efficiency is strongly influenced by the heating mode and only slightly affected by the size of oven, insulation, etc.

Lastly, it should be noted that the data in table is not only laid out in order of increasing efficiency but also in order of decreasing flue temperature. In other words, the thermal efficiency of an oven depends heavily on the flue temperature. Heat recovery from the oven will change the situation because the final temperature of any rejected heat will be lower. Therefore, the formula can be rewritten to say:

$$F_c = (H_p + H_w) \div C \times E_t$$

where F_c = the fuel consumption; H_p and H_w are as noted above; C = the net calorific value of the fuel; and E_t = the thermal efficiency. (To express F_c in percent, multiply the result by 100.) In other words, the fuel consumption depends heavily on the amount of water liberated from the product (the difference between the initial and final moisture contents of the product).

The above discussion about thermal efficiency and fuel consumption may seem academic. Hopefully, though, it will provide a frame of reference with which to judge the many conflicting claims on efficiency made by oven manufacturers.

Fortunately, an even better way exists for judging the thermal efficiency of ovens, and this method bears in mind the factors important to the bakery manager: How much product he is making, and how much fuel he is using? The following is useful for any given product:

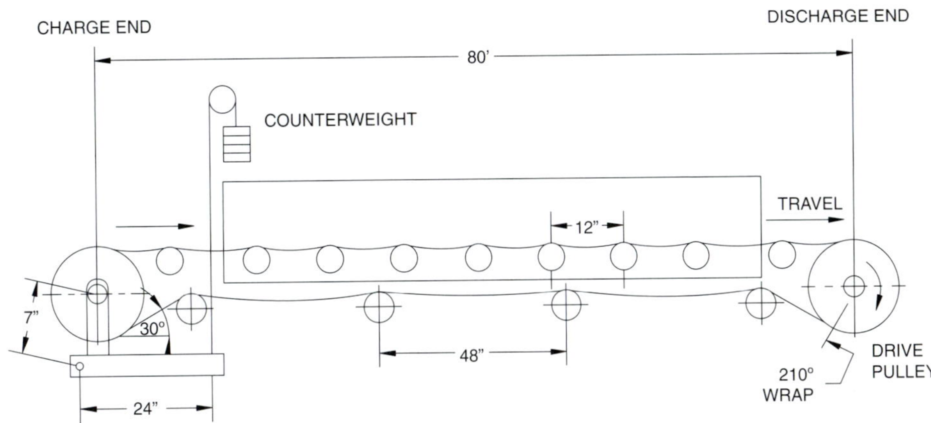

Figure 10.060. The drive pulley for the belt running through a typical bakery oven will be located at the product exit end. (Ashworth Bros., Inc.)

$$\text{Specific fuel consumption} = H_g \div M_p$$

where H_g = the gross heat in the fuel used in a given time, measured in kWhr, and M_p = the mass of product produced in the same time, measured in kilograms. The equation is the same when using imperial measures, with H_g = the gross heat in the fuel used in a given time, measured in Btu, and M_p = the mass of product produced in the same time, measured in pounds.

It should be noted that for any given product, with any given heating system, this equation will define the specific fuel consumption. It therefore provides useful targets for the fuel consumption of existing and future ovens. **Table 10.09** shows fuel consumption for typical bakery products.

Note that no figure is given for crackers and non-turbulent Cyclotherm ovens because this oven style does not have sufficient heat flux to properly bake crackers.

To improve the efficiency of an existing oven, the baker should take the following simple steps:

(a) Install a fuel meter, and monitor it without taking any further action for a month. Monitor the production output for the same period of time. Divide one figure by the other, giving the specific fuel consumption in kWhr of fuel required per kg of product out. You can also calculate this usage figure in Btu per lb.

(b) Reduce the idle periods of the oven. Switch on later, switch off sooner. Monitor the fuel consumption and production output, and again calculate the specific fuel consumption. Give yourself a bonus!

(c) With the involvement of the oven operator, observe the amount of fresh air going into the oven feed and delivery ends. There should only ever be a slight drift of fresh air going into the oven. Any air required for combustion should be introduced at the burner. Reduce the extraction settings to minimize fresh air going in.

Table 10.08. Thermal Efficiencies

	Thermal efficiency
Cyclotherm without turbulence	35%
Cyclotherm with turbulence	40%
DGF without turbulence	40%
DGF with turbulence	45%
Radiant electric without turbulence	45%
Radiant electric with turbulence	50%
Convection — direct fired or indirect fired, but not electrically heated	55%
Convection — electrically heated	60%
Impingement — direct gas fired	60%
Impingement — electrically heated	65%

Table 10.09. Specific Fuel Consumption for Various Heating Systems and Products

	Change in product and humidity during baking	Nonturbulent cyclotherm oven		Turbulent DGF oven		Convection oven, direct or indirect	
		kWhr per tonne	Btu per lb	kWhr per tonne	Btu per lb	kWhr per tonne	Btu per lb
Bread	46% to 42%	340	520	260	400	210	330
Pizza	35% to 28%	420	650	330	510	270	420
Cake	35% to 25%	530	830	420	640	340	530
Cookies	17% to 2%	610	940	470	730	390	600
Crackers	31% to 2%	-	-	1010	1560	830	1280

This action will likely have secondary effects so it needs to be done under controlled conditions. Again calculate the specific fuel consumption. Give the oven operator a bonus!

(d) Reduce the amount of water in the recipe. Again calculate the specific fuel consumption. Give yourself a bonus!

If further improvements are required, then a specialist should be involved.

10.B.7.a. Heat recovery

Let us assume that an existing oven is being well run, according to the principles outlined in the section on thermal efficiency. Also let us assume that it is impractical to replace the oven with a more efficient one, and yet improvements in thermal efficiency must be made. Then heat recovery must be considered. Almost certainly, this approach will mean heat recovery from the flues of the oven. Thus, the "source" side of the equation is likely "heat will come from the flues." But what about the "sink" part of the equation? What use can be made of the heat? Often the answer is that the heat can be used for warming van sheds or other parts of the building. But there is a much more accessible sink that requires heat at precisely the same time as the heat is available — and that is the oven itself.

Sometimes, the waste heat from the earlier zones can be used as the only heating system for the last zone(s) of the oven, where little more than tempering the product needs to take place. More usually, the heat from the flues can preheat the burner intake air on a direct-fired oven or to heat the zonal fresh air intake into an indirect-fired oven. Such usage can typically improve the specific fuel consumption by 5 to 10%.

Generally, applying the oven's waste heat to heat the proofer is not effective. A proofer needs most of its heat at the very start of a production run, when the oven is not even baking. Thereafter, the proofer is usually hot enough (or even too hot) because of the returning hot pans.

The specific heat of the flue gases — in effect, the volume of flue gases multiplied by their temperature — is not the only source of excess but still useful heat from oven. For most bakery processes, much of the heat in the flue gases is carried in the form of the latent (hidden) heat of boiling of the water vapor in the flue gases — in effect, the volume of flue gases times their humidity. For this latent heat to be used, however, the flue gases must be cooled to below their dew point, which may require cooling to about 65°C (149°F). Almost certainly, the only use for this low grade, but perhaps plentiful, heat available in the flue gases below 100°C (212°F) is for heating water.

A word of caution, however: Most bakery flues contain oils to some extent. These oils may condense out in the heat recovery equipment and downstream flues. There, they will cause a fire hazard unless the system is properly maintained and cleaned.

10.B.7.b. Emission control

Ethanol is one of the by-products of yeast activity in bread dough. Typically, this ethanol evaporates and leaves the oven via the flue. In fact, experts estimate that ethanol comprises 98% of the volatile organic compounds (VOCs) in bakery flue gases. In the presence of sunlight, the ethanol and other VOCs react with nitrogen oxides in the atmosphere to form ground-level ozone, which is harmful to human health and the environment (Anon. 2003). Together with more nitrogen oxides and other chemicals, ozone forms smog, the brown haze that can hang over cities on hot, still days.

The American Institute of Baking studied ethanol emissions and how they varied according to product and process (Stitley et al. 1987). Specifically, total fermentation time and yeast content were found to be the most important variables, and study results associated higher rates of ethanol emission with production of white bread than with some variety bread and buns.

Air quality regulations in most areas of the US require control over ethanol emitted from bakery ovens. Various techniques provide such control. Dorfman (1986, 1996) and Stier (1989) reviewed the various US regulations, and Lescure (1992) listed abatement technologies. One involves heating the exhaust gases to 815°C (1,500°F). Clearly, this technique is extremely wasteful of fuel (Kudronowicz 1996). A more common approach employs catalytic oxidizers (**Figure 10.061**). This technique involves heating the flue gases to 260°C (500°F). While catalytic oxidizers require fuel, the consumption rate can be reduced by heat recovery techniques (Kudronowicz 1996).

Unheated methods include the use of a water wash. This technique produces a mixed condensate of water and ethanol that can be economically disposed of using standard wastewater treatment facilities (Coffin 1996). Biofilters and biotrickling filters for eliminating ethanol emissions were discussed by Davies (2000).

10.B.7.c. Cogeneration and other power strategies

Combined heat and power is also known as cogeneration. In bakery or other food plant applications, gas would be burned in an onsite gas turbine, with the principal output being electricity. This power is used within the bakery. Other substances have been used as fuel, most notably by a California nut processor burning walnut hulls.

A significant by-product of cogeneration is hot exhaust gas. The exhaust heat is hot enough to be used as a heating mechanism for a bakery oven. At the present time, the economics of combined heat and power are marginal; however, by using the waste gas to heat a thermal fluid or by slightly different designs of oven, the balance may tip in its favor.

At least one bakery in the Northeast employs two 20-kW fuel cells to make its electrical requirements less vulnerable to utility cost spikes and surge charges. A partnership with the Connecticut Clean Energy Fund covered the cost of these expensive systems with grants. The cells provide baseline power to the plant, with the remainder of its power coming from the utility (Gorton 2003).

Figure 10.061. By integrating a catalytic oxidizer, a bakery can use latent heat energy of the ethanol oxidation process from the oven and reduce fuel consumption by 13 to 20%. (The Henry Group)

On-site generation of electrical power allowed another bakery to place itself on an "interruptible" basis with its utility. The original reason for installing this system was to assure a redundant supply of power in case of weather-related outages, but on-site generation also enabled the bakery to shave costs during peak usage periods (Gorton 2007b).

Yet another bakery installed its own electrical substation so it could buy power directly from the state hydroelectric authority at a lower cost than conditioned, secondary power from the local utility. An engineering analysis that showed a 2-year return-on-investment (ROI) justified the cost of the equipment (Gorton 1996).

10.B.7.d. Fuels

The fuel that should be used for a bakery will depend largely on its availability and price. Natural gas has been widely available and reasonably inexpensive. Because ovens have a long life, during the lifetime of new ovens, the fuel situation may change so it worth considering which heating systems have the most flexibility in terms of fuel usage.

For the sake of discussion, the term "dirty" fuel is used here (**Table 10.10**) to designate a fuel that generates combustion products that cannot be circulated around dough pieces as they bake.

Only Cyclotherm and indirect-fired convection ovens are capable of being heated by more than one fuel. This ability is exploited by some bakers who are able to use an inexpensive gas tariff since they are prepared to switch to oil at short notice. Actually, some gas ovens have the same flexibility and can be switched at short notice from natural gas supplied by the utility company to stored propane or a propane-air mixture.

Because thermal fluid systems locate their combustion activity in areas remote from the ovens they serve, they have even more flexibility in their fuel choices. In the future, with less availability of oil and gas, such heaters could be fired by biomass or even coal.

10.B.8. Burner types

Before considering the different burners available, a review of the concept of "turndown ratio" is appropriate. Simply put:

$$\text{Turndown ratio} = H_{max} \div H_{min}$$

where H_{max} = the maximum heat the burner can supply and H_{min} = the burner's minimum heat. (An alternate expression for this relationship is $H_{max}:H_{min}$). A modern oven, because of its efficiency, requires burners that have a turndown ratio of about 10:1. Otherwise, the burners must be able to switch off automatically should a break in production occur.

There are fundamentally two types of burner used in bakery ovens: burners suitable for DGF ovens and burners suitable for Cyclotherm, convection and impingement ovens.

First, let us consider the burners used in Cyclotherm, convection and impingement ovens. These types of ovens have one burner per zone so there will usually be less than 10 burners in an oven. These burners are usually "nozzle mix" burners. Bakery air is drawn into the burner by a combustion air fan. It is mixed at the burner nozzle with the incoming gas.

A single large flame is produced at the nozzle and projects into the combustion chamber. Its heat is then circulated around the oven zone affiliated with the combustion chamber. Some ovens have burners with very poor turndowns so the burners must operate intermittently on-off or, possibly, high-low-off. These ovens suffer a corresponding reduction in process control. Other ovens use "process burners." These burners have a very good turndown ratio of at least 20:1 so it is rare that they need to turn off automatically because of exceeding the desired zonal temperature.

Second, consider the burners used in DGF ovens. There are many — often more than a hundred — DGF burners fitted to a DGF oven. They are of two types: ribbon burners and radiant burners. Most are ribbon burners, but radiant burners are becoming popular.

A DGF ribbon burner comprises a tube located transverse to the dough piece's direction of travel (**Figure 10.062**). The tube has a matrix of corrugated steel strips along its length, called a "ribbon," which provides the platform for the flame. The ribbon is supplied with a gas/air mixture from within the tube. The gas/air mixture moves up through the ribbon to burn on the outside of the corrugated steel strips, but the flame cannot light back through the ribbon because the strips' structure exerts a quenching effect. Since the gas/air mixture forms prior to the combustion point, these burners are called "pre-mix burners."

There are three systems for supplying the tube with the correct gas/air mixture. The first, now obsolete, is to distribute high-pressure gas down the oven. At each burner position, the gas comes out of a jet just outside the oven pointing into the burner tube and forming a venturi at that point. As the gas goes into the tube at high pressure, it entrains bakery air so a reasonable gas/air mixture is formed. This system had a very poor turndown ratio of about 2:1.

The high-pressure gas system was replaced by the "zero gas" system where the roles of gas and air were reversed. The oven is supplied with high-pressure combustion air fans, each of which blows air through tubes to a bank or zone of burners. At each burner, the air entrains gas at a venturi called a "mixer." This system typically has a turndown ratio of about 5:1, although better can be achieved.

The third system stations a local combustion air fan at each burner. The advantage of this method is that the burners can be controlled individually, rather than in banks.

Table 10.10. Fuel Capability for Various Oven Designs

	Fuels	Able to use "dirty" fuels
Cyclotherm without turbulence	Gas, oil, thermal fluid	Yes
Cyclotherm with turbulence	Gas, oil, thermal fluid	Yes
DGF without turbulence	Gas	No
DGF with turbulence	Gas	No
Radiant electric, no turbulence	Electricity	No
Radiant electric with turbulence	Electricity	No
NIR	Electricity	No
Convection - direct	Gas	No
Convection - indirect	Gas, oil, thermal fluid	Yes
Convection – electrically heated	Electricity	No
Recirc	Gas	No
Impingement	Gas, electricity	No
Radiofrequency	Electricity	No

Each burner has a turndown ratio of about 5:1.

As noted earlier, modern ovens require a turndown ratio of 10:1, yet the DGF burners are only able to offer 5:1. Thus, without further control, the oven would over-heat. Over-heating is avoided by "gap detection," a feed-forward control system. When a break in production is detected at the oven entry, some burners are automatically switched off, following the gap as it goes through the oven, and switched back on again when production resumes.

A more precise method of temperature control monitors the zone combustion air header pressure and schedules the number of zone burners required to match the zone heat demand regardless if the zone is full, empty or partially loaded. With this method, an effective zone turndown ratio of 12:1 is achieved, and zone temperatures are typically held to within ± 1.1°C (2°F).

Also, most DGF burners suffer from the drawback that their combustion air is not isolated when the burner is off. Thus, when a particular burner is not being used, cold air is blown into the oven at that burner position. This temperature change has a negative effect on the efficiency of the oven. It is possible, however, to isolate the air supply for each burner as well as the gas supply.

Figure 10.062. Flame height of this DGF burner offers five distinct "lanes." (Baker Perkins Ltd.)

A DGF radiant burner is fed with an air/gas mixture in the same way as a ribbon burner; however, the mixture, instead of combusting at a ribbon, is burned on a membrane much wider than a ribbon, perhaps 100 mm wide, and which points directly at the baking product. The density of the membrane and the power rating are chosen so that the membrane glows intensely. This glow radiates heat onto the product. Radiant burners have the advantage of higher power than an equivalent ribbon burner. Also, radiant burners heat up and cool down very rapidly, but they have the disadvantage of very poor turndown. The turndown ratio of a radiant burner is limited to about 2:1 while still remaining radiant.

Today, bakery ovens can be fitted with on direct spark ignitions systems that operate in conjunction with burner management programs for fully automated oven control via PLC (Day 2001, 2008). Individual ignition modules, located in close proximity to their associated burners, include a solenoid shut-off valves that replace the previously used constant spark igniter transformers (**Figure 10.063**). The basis of the direct spark igniter system is that once the sensor recognized the flame, the spark shuts off, and the igniter becomes a flame monitor. An automated gas train with an oven gas meter is another key component of automated burner control systems (**Figure 10.064**). The train includes a lockable shut-off and various features that facilitate OSHA inspection and testing. The automatic oven control systems also afford the opportunity for an oven power interruption protection system. The gas meter records usage data, sending this information to the PLC for use in managing energy costs and oven efficiencies.

10.B.9. Safety controls

Oven safety controls are prescribed by national legislation. Furthermore, the bakery's insurers may insist on conformity to additional regulations. Obviously, the bakery must meet relevant legislation and regulations.

These national and insurance regulations define a number of key issues. Such concerns include, but are not limited to, the following: (a) When the oven is started up, it must be automatically purged of any gas that may have leaked into it while the oven was idle. (b) If a burner goes out, then the fuel to it must be isolated automatically. (c) On big installations, the gas line to the oven must be automatically tested for leaks before lighting up. (d) Sufficient combustion air volume must be automatically proved. This point is particularly important for recirculating systems such as Cyclotherm, direct convection and impingement ovens. On these types of ovens it is possible to maintain a flame even with insufficient combustion air, but that flame will produce carbon monoxide. This carbon monoxide is recirculated and builds up until it reaches the explosive limit and is, of course, ignited by the original flame. (e) Much of the safety control of an oven must be hard-wired, unless the programmable logic controller (PLC) running the system has been certified by the authorities. And (f), all oven installations must be inspected regularly, usually yearly, by a specialist.

Most safety control is fairly obvious and should be dealt with as a matter of routine by the bakery production staff and engineers. The following points are included here because they may not be immediately obvious.

First, many ovens do not normally accumulate volatiles. Rarely, however, they do. For example, when new pans are being run through the circuit in a bread oven, they may contain high levels of grease in them for "burning off." The grease does indeed burn off, forming an explosive vapor and risking explosion or, at least, a flash fire. Sometimes, cookie oven belts are cleaned with solvents with potentially the same effect.

Second, flues should be insulated and should not run horizontally. This orientation will help to avoid fats condensing in them, which can provide a future fire hazard.

Third, the interface between the oven's flues and the bakery ceiling must be fire-

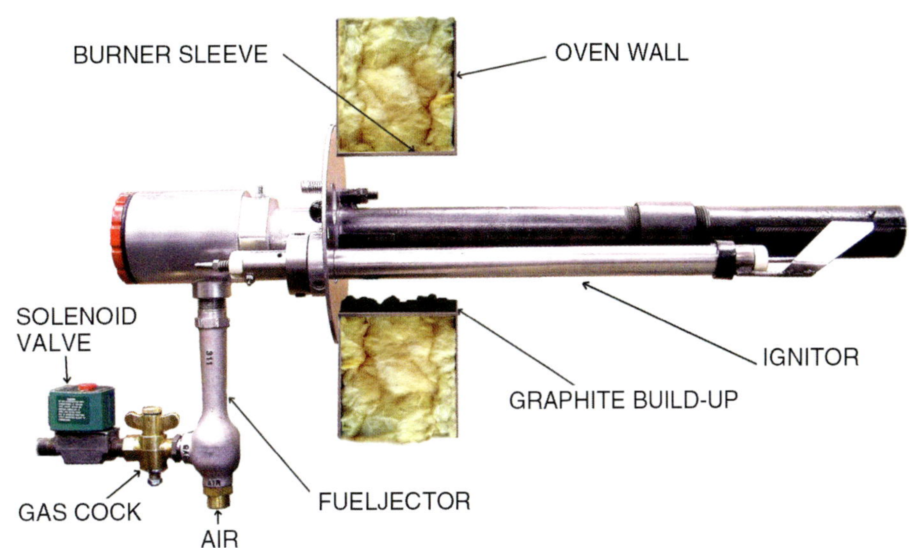

Figure 10.063. Ribbon burner systems now include individual solenoid shut-off valves. (Banner-Day)

Figure 10.064. Automated burner control systems configure the gas train with lockable shut-off valves and other features that enable inspection and testing. (Banner-Day)

proof. Usually, an oven flue is hot, around 200°C (390°F), but it can get much hotter if a fire accidentally occurs in the oven, sending flue temperatures as high as 600°C (1,100°F) or more. If a substantial thermal break does not exist between the flue and the ceiling, the ceiling will catch light. Also, take heed of the material of construction of everything above any inlets into the oven: In a fire situation, flames may come out of the oven inlets.

Finally, if you intend to bake a product in an oven that requires a higher temperature than you have recently been using, make sure that the oven and exhaust flue(s) are clean internally. Any product buildup that had fallen off inside the oven and was only charred before may catch fire now with the higher temperature.

10.B.10. Process control

Modern ovens are usually supplied with programmable logic controllers (PLCs), or industrial computers, that perform all the necessary control and sequencing, house recipes, provide the operator with all current information and store historical information. The process control for an oven comprises five areas: bake time control, temperature control, airflow control, humidity control and zone integrity.

10.B.10.a. Bake time control
An oven for batch baking, for example a rack oven, will have a timer to alert the baker that the bake time has been reached.

An oven for a continuous process will have a frequency controlled variable speed drive motor. By convention, the oven motor is the "master," and the other drive motors in the process are the "slaves" so when the baker alters the bake time, the rest of the production line's speed is altered in harmony.

10.B.10.b. Temperature control
What is really required in an oven to control the degree of bake is heat flux control. Unfortunately, the necessary probes are still being developed so we have to rely on temperature control. In fact, temperature control works fairly well, but the following two chief points need to be borne in mind.

First, in Cyclotherm ovens, historically, temperature control was unsophisticated to the point that "flash heat" (the excessive heat observed on the first few rows of product) was a problem. More recently, however, good positioning of the temperature probes has eliminated this problem.

Second, temperature control on a DGF oven can be problematic. If a temperature probe is situated near a burner and for some reason that burner is switched off, control will be altered. This issue has been overcome by using multiple probes. Also, if the oven hearth allows free airflow through it and a gap occurs in production, all the bottom heat will rise to the top. This issue is resolved by avoiding independent top and bottom temperature control. A form of control called "ratio control" is used. The operator presets a zone temperature and a heat ratio, rather than a top and a bottom temperature. With ratio control, all the top and bottom temperature probes' readings are averaged, providing an average actual temperature, which is compared with the stored average required temperature. The necessary control signal to the top and bottom burners is split according to the ratio preset by the operator.

Most ovens' temperature control systems are fully modulating; in other words, the control system settles out at the desired temperature. Older ovens may still have on-off or high-low-off controls where the temperature oscillates around the set point.

10.B.10.c. Airflow control

Airflow control, in this context, means managing the way heated air flows around the baking product. Such control encompasses top and bottom turbulence, convection or impingement airflows. These airflows are usually controlled by dampers (**Figure 10.065**), which alter in position to rapidly change the relevant airflows and, therefore, heat fluxes. Refer to **Figure 10.025** on Page 496 for a representation of the effect of different damper positions on the heat flux available to the product.

10.B.10.d. Humidity control

Bake chamber humidity is important, particularly in the early stages of baking, so maintaining the correct humidity is important. The primary humidity control element is the extraction fan speed or, if relevant, the extraction damper.

High temperature humidity probes are now available that enable the zone to be held at a fixed humidity no matter what other changes are made. Regular preventative maintenance of the probes is necessary for best operation.

10.B.10.e. Zone integrity

The ability to tightly control the temperature and humidity within a zone is considered a good attribute of an oven. However, a few ovens have effective physical boundaries between the various zones. (These ovens score "reasonable" or "good" for zonal control in the oven type comparisons in **Table 10.06** on Page 513.) For these ovens, it is possible to fit a system of "zone integrity" that maintains the conditions within that zone irrespective of any pressure changes in neighboring zones, which would otherwise have caused a drift of air between them.

Figure 10.065. Oven dampers can be opened or closed to change the heat flux available to products as they bake. (Reading Bakery Systems)

10.B.11. Oven concerns

In past years, deficiencies in oven operation were frequently encountered in such areas as control of the heat supply, occurrence of flash heat, steaming conditions, proper heat distribution and appropriate oven loading. Energy requirements and working conditions for oven operators must also be considered. With improvements in oven design and construction as well as the widespread adoption of advanced electronic control devices and PLCs, the frequency of abnormal oven conditions has been substantially reduced. Nonetheless, errors in judgment and aberrations in oven operation still do occur and result in unsatisfactory baking performance.

10.B.11.a. Operator comfort

Operator comfort is often considered too late in the selection of equipment. Any baker knows that the vicinity of an oven can be uncomfortably hot and noisy. When considering laying out a new bakery line, the bakery engineer would be well advised to (a) reduce the room temperature in the vicinity of the oven and (b) minimize pan noise. The oven is certain to put some heat into the oven room, but high ceilings and vertical baffles hung from rafters around the oven effectively control the flow of heat in this area. Pan noise is not only irritating to the ear, but also it reveals points in the process where pan damage can occur.

10.B.11.b. Energy requirements

A frequently cited theoretical value for the amount of heat needed to bake 1 lb of bread is 235 Btu. Actual heat requirements can differ considerably because they are influenced by factors such as the specific heat of dough, which may range from 0.65 to 0.88; the temperature of the dough entering the oven, which can vary from 32 to 43°C (90 to 110°F); differences in moisture evaporation rates; and variations in oven temperatures. When all these variables are taken into account, the calculated theoretical value for bread will fall anywhere within the range of 150 to 250 Btu per lb.

In actual practice, additional factors such as type of oven, kind of fuel used, method of heat application, amount of steam used and level of efficiency of oven operation all enter importantly into the calculation of energy requirements. Actual measurements have shown that the heat input required per lb of bread will range from a highly efficient 325 to 400 Btu in modern ovens to a rather wasteful 1,780 Btu in old coal-fired brick peel ovens. Some representative data for common fuels and common types of ovens are listed in **Table 10.11**.

10.B.11.c. Insufficient oven heat

Among the causes of cool ovens are faulty temperature controls, defective firing systems and over-loading with product that strains the oven's heat generating capacity. Appropriate corrective steps for all of these faults are self-evident. Failure to correct these situations will result in a loaf that has an excessive volume; coarse grain and harsh texture; a thick, pale crust; and an unacceptable bake-out loss. Bake-out losses generally fall within the range of 7 to 13%, with 10 to 12% representing the commonly accepted norm. They include the normal evaporative moisture loss of about 2% that takes place during product cooling. Because low-temperature baking extends baking time, it may lead to a bake-out loss that exceeds the average by a margin wide enough to result in a short-weight baked product.

10.B.11.d. Excessive oven heat

Ovens that are too hot generally result from defective temperature controls or

Table 10.11. Relative Heat Utilization in Bread Baking

Oven style	Fuel per 100 lb of bake	Btu per lb of bake
Natural gas (1,000 Btu per cu ft)		
Tray ovens (direct fired)	52 cu ft	520
Tray ovens (indirect fired)	80 cu ft	800
Tunnel ovens	82 cu ft	820
Reel ovens	100 cu ft	1,000
Peel ovens (brick)	142 cu ft	1,420
Manufactured gas (546 Btu per cu ft)		
Tray ovens (direct fired)	82 cu ft	445
Tray ovens (indirect fired)	112 cu ft	610
Tunnel ovens	125 cu ft	685
Peel ovens (brick)	264 cu ft	1,440
Fuel oil (140,000 Btu per gal)		
Tray ovens (indirect fired)	0.76 gal	950
Tunnel ovens	1.00 gal	1,250
Peel ovens (brick)	1.03 gal	1,280
Electricity (3,412 Btu per kWhr)		
Tray ovens	13.9 kWhr	475
Rotary ovens (cake)	14.2 kWhr	485
Tunnel ovens	15.0 kWhr	512
Peel ovens (brick)	18.5 kWhr	563

(Harrel and Thelen 1959)

from occasional inadequate product loads that fail to absorb a sufficient amount of the heat supplied by the burners. High baking temperatures tend to yield pan loaves of reduced volume with a dark top crust, under-baked sidewalls and frequently wild break-and-shred. The crumb may exhibit an uneven grain with large, flat holes. All these defects result from the premature formation of a crust that prevents optimal loaf expansion and creates internal stresses that interfere with uniform crumb development.

The crust begins to brown at an early stage and attains its proper bloom long before the crumb has properly baked. Under these circumstances, if the bread is withdrawn from the oven on the basis of an attractive crust color, then its crumb will be gummy and lacking in flavor. Excessively high baking temperatures also tend to produce blisters on the loaf's top crust, particularly in instances where the dough pieces enter the oven in a cool or wet condition or are made from young doughs.

A hot oven may be more acceptable for old and lean doughs where crust coloration needs to be accentuated. It is required for hearth breads and hard crust rolls but then must be supplemented by large amounts of steam.

10.B.11.e. Flash heat

Flash heat is a condition, often localized, of intense heat, which rapidly dissipates on contact with the baking product, and was formerly a relatively common problem. At present, when most ovens are equipped with some system of forced convection, it is rarely if ever encountered.

Flash heat is objectionable because it causes the crust to brown rapidly but fails to bake the crumb adequately within the established baking time because of its rapid dissipation. Where flash heat is still encountered, it usually occurs at the startup of the baking cycle and following idle oven periods.

Once the condition is recognized, it can be readily ameliorated by measures such as (a) rearranging the production schedule to ensure that the oven is never completely empty, (b) "bridging over," or running the oven only partly full, when necessary, either by spacing the pan straps farther apart or by loading every other tray in tray ovens, or (c) making use, at the beginning of an oven run, of "flash pans," which most suitably are old pans filled with heat-absorbing material such as water. A sufficient number of such pans must be used to simulate the load conditions that prevail for the first rows of pans or the first trays during normal baking.

10.B.11.f. Excess steam

Excessive moisture in the oven atmosphere is a principle cause of tough crusts in round-top white pan bread. When the dough piece emerges from the final proofer, its surface temperature will generally be within a range of about 35 to 41°C (95 to 105°F). As it enters a steam-saturated oven chamber maintained at more than 204°C (400°F), moisture will condense on the dough's relatively cool surface. While this action during the first minute or so favors good ovenspring and large loaf volume, extended exposure to steam tends to create a tough crust. However, copious amounts of steam over somewhat longer periods, when associated with elevated temperatures, provide a favorable baking environment for the creation of a smooth, glossy and crispy crust on hearth breads and hard crust rolls.

10.B.11.g. Insufficient steam

When shell tops form on white pan bread, a dry oven is frequently the cause. A similar effect is produced when the dough surface is permitted to dry out too much in the final proofer. In both cases, the shell top, in the form of a separation of the crust from the crumb, is induced by the premature firming of the crust in loaves that would otherwise undergo a vigorous ovenspring. This condition can be effectively corrected by increasing the relative humidity of the final proofer or by steam injection at the oven inlet.

10.B.11.h. Steam quality

The use of the correct type of steam in the oven and, prior to that, in the proof box significantly influences bread quality. The steam intended for both these applications should be low-pressure saturated steam having a boiler gauge pressure of 5 to 15 psi that is subsequently reduced to 2 to 5 psi by the steam injector.

Saturated steam at a pressure of 10 psi has a temperature of 115°C (239°F) and at atmospheric pressure, 100°C (212°F). Hence, as the steam's pressure is reduced so is its temperature and also its moisture-holding capacity. These drops account for the observation when pressurized steam is released to the atmosphere, the loss of heat causes its moisture, present as discrete water molecules in the pressurized state, to condense into visible water droplets, forming a mist.

When such saturated steam is injected into the baking chamber and comes into contact with the cooler surface of the freshly loaded dough pieces, its moisture will condense on the dough surface and produce the desired steam effect. Once the surface temperature of the dough pieces reaches 100°C (212°F), steam is without effect because its moisture will no longer condense.

High-pressure steam is also high-temperature steam. Thus, at a pressure of 50 psi, steam has a temperature of 148°C (298°F). No condensation of such steam can occur on the dough surface because there is insufficient time for its temperature to drop to the steam's dew point before the oven heat has acted to again increase it and that of the dough surface. Not only does high-pressure steam fail to produce the normal steam effect, it actually tends to depress loaf volume, particularly in rye bread.

10.B.11.i. Heat distribution

For the most part, faulty heat distribution in ovens manifests itself in insufficient bottom heat, or the heat conducted through the hearth plate. Such maldistribution of heat produces loaves possessing a well-baked top crust but an under-baked bottom crust and sidewalls. These conditions result in bread whose sides tend to cave in during cooling and to collapse on slicing and stacking on retail shelves. Inadequate bottom heat is particularly troublesome in rye bread baking because the loaves will tend to flatten out and break at the sides or the seam.

10.B.11.j. Pan spacing

Adequate spacing of pans, both within the straps and between the straps, is essential for uniform and thorough baking. Clearance between pans in a strap or on the baking surface should be adequate to allow unimpeded circulation of the hot oven gases for a uniform bake. In general, strapped pans for 1-lb loaves should be spaced no less than 0.75 in. apart at the top rim and preferably more, while pans for 1.5-lb or larger loaves require a minimum separation of 1 in. A reasonable minimum space for 3-lb Pullman pans would be 1.5 in.

10.C. Dryers

Updated by L.A. Gorton

Certain baked foods require application of more heat after the oven but not the extra browning such added oven heat can entail. They need drying. Pretzels, for example, require a 2-stage process (**Figure 10.066**). Initially, the raw pretzel pieces bake in single layers in a hot oven, achieving their signature brown, glazed surface and unique taste after only a few minutes, but their interiors remains doughy. So, a second heating stage is required to dry the pretzels, completing the baking process at a lower temperature that does not foster additional browning. Leaving the oven, pretzels enter the dryer, also called a "kiln," bunched into piles, perhaps 10 layers deep. The kiln's mesh belt moves along slowly, taking 30 or more minutes to fully dry the pretzels to the desired moisture (Moreth 1987b).

Dryers perform toasting operations for preparation of pita and bagel chips as well as croutons, Melba toast, biscotti and zwieback. Popular party mixes that combine several ready-to-eat (RTE) breakfast cereal, cracker and nut components — some baked, others fried — benefit from drying before packaging because components may be at different moisture contents when they enter the mix. If no steps are taken to standardize the moisture level, the mix can lose its crispness and go stale quickly. Without dryers, the entire category of baked-not-fried tortilla chips and potato crisps would not exist.

Figure 10.066. Located below the oven, the dryer, or kiln, on pretzel lines completes the baking process at a lower temperature.
(Reading Bakery Systems)

10.C.1. Function of dryers

Although closely related to ovens in technology, dryers serve a different function: to optimize the moisture profile of baked foods after they leave the oven. Low-moisture products such as cookies and crackers may be 10 to 15% moisture at the oven exit; dryers reduce that concentration to 1 to 2%. Baked tortilla chips can be quite leathery as they leave the oven and require drying to achieve the right texture and crisp snap.

The relatively short baking periods for cookies, crackers, tortilla chips and similar products drive moisture out of product surfaces, leaving interiors may fairly wet. This moisture gradient exerts strain on the surface and causes minute cracks, an undesirable effect called "checking." The result is high breakage during packaging and shipping.

10.C.2. Types

Although dryers resemble ovens, they operate at lower temperatures and higher air velocities. To carry products through the drying process, these machines use open-weave mesh, slotted or perforated belts so that air can pass through easily. All dryers require high volumes of air, necessary to break through the boundary of moist

Figure 10.067. Impingement dryers move products using conveyor belts or vibratory pans.
(The Lanly Co.)

Figure 10.068. "Dielectric dryers" use radio-frequency electromagnetic radiation to penetrate the surfaces of dough pieces or finished baked goods to preferentially heat wet areas.
(Radio Frequency Co.)

air at the surface of the product and sweep it away (Whitaker 2007).

Dryers equal out moisture content, thus reducing the risk of undesirable checking (cracking) during packaging and shipment.

Some dryers combine several technologies. One integrates convection with radio frequency heating, while another employs both radio frequency and impingement methods.

10.C.2.a. Impingement

Impingement systems use a stream of high-velocity air, narrowing its output into the dryer with tubes, slots or nozzles that add even more speed to the air. The tubes or openings project columnated streams of heated high-velocity air onto the product. The fast-moving air strips away the boundary layer of moist, stagnant, cooler air surrounding the product. The trick, though, is to configure the jet to sweep away that air without also deforming the surface of the product, blowing it off the belt or allowing fines to mix back into the returning air flow. The best results come from using a relatively large port with openings roughly the size of a coin, high air velocity and low clearance between the jet opening and the product being dried. Some systems configure the jets as tubes, others as round slots in large plenums. Impingement dryers feature either a conveyor bed or a vibratory pan to advance products, and airflow can range from 800 to 5,000 ft per minute (**Figure 10.067**). Impingement technology is discussed in more detail by Part G of this chapter.

10.C.2.b. Radio frequency (dielectric)

As noted in the discussion of oven types earlier in Part B of this chapter, radio frequency technology effectively heats products from within. Also called "dielectric dryers," these systems (**Figure 10.068**) operate by generating electromagnetic radiation at frequencies of either 27.12 or 40.68 MHz. This energy penetrates the surface of dough pieces to be absorbed by polar molecules, chiefly water. The radiation's electrical field alternates more than 40 million times per second. The rapidly reversing polarity causes synchronous oscillation of the polar material's positive and negative ends, and the friction resulting from this vibration heats the water and the surrounding material. Thus, radio frequency radiation preferentially heats wet areas without affecting the areas already dry. At full loads, efficiency reaches 67 to 72%.

But unlike microwave energy (high-energy electromagnetic radiation), lower-energy radio frequency radiation tends to be self-limiting in low-moisture products such as cookies, crackers and similar baked foods. The action drives water from areas of high concentration to those of lower, with the excess expelled as water vapor.

Low-fat foods, in general, benefit from dielectric drying. When fat is missing from the formula, heat is less efficiently distributed within the dough during baking, and wider swings occur in the moisture content of finished products. Also, crusts color faster, often before optimum moisture levels are achieved. For example, conventional ovens can bring no-fat saltines to 7% moisture, but they will not get to 3% moisture without excessive color and edge-curl problems.

Installed at the end of conventional ovens, dielectric dryers apply "finish" heat to biscuit and cracker products (**Figure 10.069**). This placement allows the baker to set the last zone of the oven to color the product, while using the dryer to drive out excess moisture without risking excessive crust browning. Dielectric dryers can boost line output because they allow the oven to run faster (Moreth 1987b). Some experts peg such productivity increases at 15 to 20%, while others suggest a near doubling of output capacity.

Dielectric dryers (**Figure 10.070**) consist of an emitter-receptor array, housed in an enclosure through which a nonmetallic conveyor belt runs. The emitter-receptor array stretches the length and width of the enclosure. Supplied with high-voltage energy, the emitter sends radio frequency radiation across a gap to the receptor. Products passing through the gap absorb some of the radiation. Metal conveyors cannot be used or else the system would short-circuit. The electromagnetic tubes have a life of 15,000 to 20,000 hours (Smith 1999).

Radio frequency drying is effective for deep-bed dryers. With this procedure, the belt of the post-baking dryer runs slower than the upstream belts so products bunch up and form beds 2 to 6 in. deep. An alternative method for building up the product bed uses a slowly swinging horizontal arm that accepts incoming product from a relatively narrow feed conveyor and deposits it across the wide bed of the dryer (**Figure 10.071**). The thick mass of material provides more cubic area to absorb the dielectric radiation than single-layer systems, thus boosting system efficiency (Earle 1997).

Unlike microwave systems, dielectric heating methods do not require extensive shielding, but they use substantial electrical voltage, so equipment must be safeguarded against the hazard of electric shock. A significant challenge in operation of radio frequency dryers is the problem of arcing, a high-voltage discharge from the electrode to the product. Arcing is generally caused by a gross abnormality in the incoming load such as large lumps of wet dough. Carbonized debris or burned edges can also cause arcing. Systems that operate at 40 MHz frequencies are able to do the same work at 20% lower voltage, which suppresses arcing.

10.C.2.c. Deep bed and fluid bed

Conventional conveyor dryers such as those used by pasta and ready-to-eat (RTE) breakfast cereal processors use deep bed techniques and long, slow drying procedures, although shallow bed techniques are required for some products (**Figure 10.072**). Airflow is typically 100 to 200 ft per minute, while system temperatures range from 65 to 177°C (150 to 350°F). These low-velocity units can be configured vertically with multiple belts to save plant floor space (**Figure 10.073**).

Fluidizing increases heat transfer because more treatment air contacts each particle or product. When properly fluidized, the product being dried looks and behaves like a fluid.

Traditionally, fluid bed dryers have featured an open-mesh vibrating screen. Air pushes upward from below through the screen to lift products as they move through the system. A newer design uses a solid, nonperforated pan or conveyor with air delivery tubes mounted above (**Figure 10.074**). The air moves strongly downward, pushing against the solid surface and rises to lift the product being dried. The air's action fluidizes products, making them airborne before falling gently back onto the conveyor bed, which holds a cushion of air to receive the products. Another design sends air pulses through different portions of the bed in a timed manner.

Figure 10.069. Placed at the end of cookie ovens, a dielectric dryer boosts line output.
(Reading Bakery Systems)

Figure 10.070. An electrode array generated radio frequency radiation that excites polar molecules (primarily water) to generate heat.
(Radio Frequency Corp.)

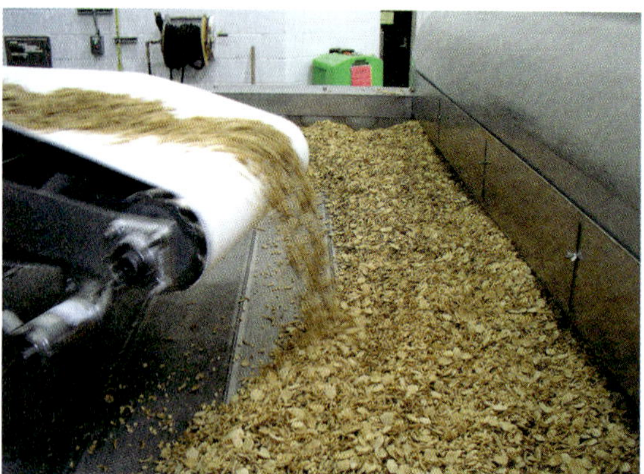

Figure 10.071. Oscillating conveyors spread cereal components on the belt entering the dryer. (Berne 2003)

Figure 10.072. Single-pass dryers can feature different airflow configurations to efficiently dry a product without flipping it. (Aeroglide)

Figure 10.073. This 3-tiered, multi-pass dryer uses forced convection through the product bed to ensure even drying across the belt. (Reading Bakery Systems)

10.D. Frying

Updated by Richard F. Stier

Deep fat frying has been used for thousands of years to cook food; however, it took advances in a number of technologies before frying could become a viable commercial process. These technologies included (a) development of commercial freezing, (b) advances in oil processing and refining, (c) development of packaging technologies, (d) improvements in equipment manufacturing and (e) establishment of distribution networks. Frying has been further enhanced in recent years as oil chemists, engineers, physicists and other scientists have worked to better understand its science and technology (Stier 1997).

Frying and fried foods have been criticized in recent years because these foods contain more fat than those that are baked, boiled, broiled or microwaved. In spite of this disparagement, frying remains a popular cooking method used by consumers, restaurant and food service operators and industrial processors. There are a few basic reasons for these preferences. First and foremost, fried foods taste good. They have a crisp "bite," good flavors and a very desirable texture. The second reason is that frying is a very efficient means of cooking (Stier 2000). Third, heated oil is an excellent heat transfer media. A product that takes 4 to 6 minutes to cook in a fryer might take 25 to 35 minutes in an oven (Stier and Gupta 2006). Fourth, frying will also blanch foods (inactivate enzymes), set coatings and add oil to the food, which enhances mouthfeel (Stier 1996). Ironically, concerns about oil pickup by fried foods may have contributed to a situation where food safety has been compromised. Many nut roasters switched from oil roasting to dry roasting in the 1980s. Dry roasting is simply not as effective at destroying food pathogens as oil roasting. This market-driven change may well have contributed to the 2009 salmonella outbreak linked to peanut butter and other peanut products.

A detailed examination of the equipment used to make doughnuts and fried pies is found in Chapter 12, Part E.

10.D.1. Foods and frying oils

A wide variety of foods are fried. These products include snacks such as potato, corn, tortilla chips, extruded snacks and nuts; bakery items such as doughnuts, beignets, honey buns, filled pies and other items; potato products (french fries and formulated potato products); coated products; and meats. Coated products include vegetables, meats, poultry and fish, potatoes and a wide range of other products. The technology involved in breading and battering foods is a science unto itself. The type of coating selected depends upon the food being fried, the desired flavor and texture profile, and the desired color of the finished product. For example, what works for fried chicken will not work with vegetables.

The type oil in which a food is fried affects a number of issues including food quality (flavor, appearance and mouthfeel), operational efficiencies and how foods are perceived. Doughnuts, beignets and fried pies are traditionally fried in hard fats, that is, fats that are solid at room temperature. Lard and tallow, deep frying's original hard fats, were replaced by all-vegetable partially hydrogenated shortenings, available in a variety of plastic ranges. Such hard fats provide the desired texture and appearance. A doughnut fried in oil that is fluid at room temperature could begin to "weep," thus compromising coating integrity and appearance.

The process of hydrogenation, however, molecularly reshapes some of the fatty acids from the natural *cis* form into the *trans* isomer, and *trans* fats have been linked to raising the risk of coronary heart disease. Food processors began seeking frying oils that did not contain such *trans* fatty acids. The transition to *trans*-free or low-*trans*-fat oils for frying has taken on added impetus in the past few years, especially with local governments mandating that users phase *trans* fats out of their products. The no- or low-*trans* oils being adopted are generally vegetable oils such as modified sunflower or soy oils that have been produced to meet a need. Some operations have made the switch to oils that were traditionally used only as salad oils.

Oils used for frying can create problems for some users. These oils have low levels of saturated fatty acids and relatively high levels of polyunsaturated fatty acids. Useful oil life is reduced, and some operators have reported increases in polymer formation in their fryers. Companies that took the time and made the effort to conduct extensive frying and consumer studies before adopting low- and no-*trans* alternatives have not had such problems (Stier 2007).

Figure 10.074. Air jets push through to reach a solid belt, fluidizing the product. The long tubes create a bed of air, while the open space between them allows smaller pieces and fines to settle out without entering the return process air. (CPM Wolverine Proctor)

10.D.2. Frying systems

Deep-fat frying is more than just cooking the food in hot oil. Frying is a series of unit operations designed to prepare the product for frying, position it for frying, cook the food, remove excess oil, cool the product and package the finished item.

Snack foods such as chips and extruded snacks usually receive seasonings prior to packaging. Fried pies and other pastries go straight to the packaging machines unless they destined as frozen foods. If this is the case, they will be frozen before being packaged.

Because frying is a true system, fryer manufacturers usually supply all the components making up the line (**Figure 10.075**). When purchasing a frying system, the customer must be scrupulously honest with the equipment manufacturer. The information that they need to provide includes type of product or products to be fried, the proposed volumes and how that product will be packaged. It is absolutely essential that the fryer be properly sized. Economies of operation are achieved through running a fryer at maximum capacity. A fryer that is too large will be expensive to operate and maintain. Operating at less than maximum capacity will also cause polymer buildup, which can damage both the oil and the fryer itself.

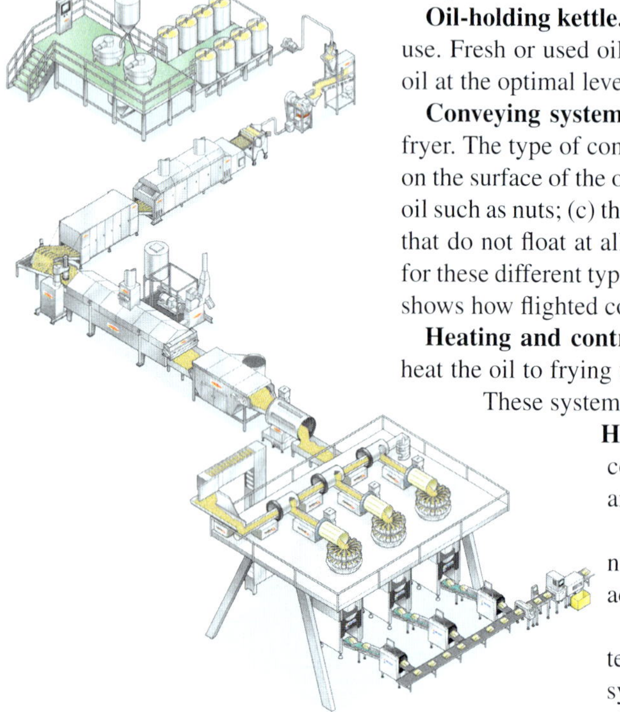

Figure 10.075. Frying lines are typically spec'd and sold as systems such as this tortilla chip line because the unit operations involved must be tailored to sequence products smoothly. (Heat and Control)

10.D.2.a. Components of a frying system

A fryer, whether it is a batch fryer or a continuous cooker, consists of several basic components, listed here.

Oil-holding kettle. The kettle contains the fryer's cooking oil in a state ready for use. Fresh or used oil may be added to the fryer during processing to maintain the oil at the optimal level for cooking.

Conveying system. The conveying system moves products into and out of the fryer. The type of conveyor depends upon the product being fried: (a) those that fry on the surface of the oil such as doughnuts; (b) those that fry while submerged in the oil such as nuts; (c) those that float partially such as tempura and chips; and (d) those that do not float at all such as meat products and french fries. The conveyors used for these different types of food may be seen in **Figure 10.076**, while **Figure 10.077** shows how flighted conveyors move doughnuts move through the fryer.

Heating and control system. The heating and controlling systems are used to heat the oil to frying temperatures and maintain the oil at processing temperatures. These systems will be discussed in greater detail later.

Hood or canopy. The hood or canopy (**Figure 10.078**) covers continuous fryers to conserve energy. Within the hood are ducts and blowers to remove steam and volatiles.

Hoist system. The hoist lifts the hood and conveyor components (**Figure 10.079**) of the fryer for cleaning and maintenance access.

Filter system. Filters remove solids from the oil. Filter systems may be designed to remove solids by sieves (passive filter systems) or incorporate an active material that will affect the chemistry of the oil (active system).

Frying vessel. This large, shallow vat the holds hot oil in which cooking occurs.

Level control. The level control monitors the amount of oil in the fryer and prompts addition of oil to the fryer from the oil holding kettle.

10.D.2.b. Fryer heating systems

Three basic designs characterize systems for heating the oil used for frying: direct, indirect and external (Stier 1996).

Direct. In direct-heated fryers, the heating tubes are immersed directly in the oil (**Figure 10.080**). If fueled by gas or fuel oil, the burner is housed inside the tube (**Figure 10.081**) and supplied with air to maintain combustion. The burner heats the inside surface of the tube, which conducts heat to its exterior and into the frying oil. If electrically heated, the element itself becomes the heating tube. Temperatures are controlled by modulating the fuel input to the burners or switching electrical elements on and off. A controller is linked to a sensor in the fryer that monitors temperature.

The heating tubes may run lengthwise, across the fryer or in an S-shaped configuration that snakes through the fryer. Food processed in direct-heated systems include kettle-style chips, batter and breaded products, oil-roasted nuts, doughnuts and other snack foods.

Indirect. With indirect-heated systems, an external heat source such as a heater

Figure 10.076. Conveyors designed as pusher bars, flights or submerging systems carry foods through the fryer. (Belshaw Adamatic Bakery Group)

or boiler fired with gas, oil or electricity is used to heat a thermal fluid. The heater tube arrangement is similar to that used in direct heated systems. The thermal fluid is set at a temperature slightly above the target temperature of the oil. Temperature control is achieved by regulating the temperature of thermal fluid as it moves through the oil, with 3-way valves usually used to control oil temperature. Feedback from a temperature probe modulates a valve that releases thermal fluid to the fryer tubes or diverts it back to the heat exchanger. Products fried in indirect systems include batter and breaded foods and nuts.

External. The frying oil itself is used by external heating systems to maintain temperature in the fryer. Drawn from the frying vessel, the cooking oil passes through a heat exchanger and is returned directly to the fryer. External heating systems may use steam, gas, fuel oil or electrical heat to maintain oil temperatures in the heat exchanger. A thermocouple at the inlet side of the cooker controls the temperature of the system.

Figure 10.077. Flighted conveyors enable doughnuts to float through the frying oil in regular order. A flipper turns the products over half-way along. (Belshaw Adamatic Bakery Group)

10.D.2.c. Environmental concerns

Other issues that must be considered in today's world are energy and the environment. Fryer manufacturers are working to build systems

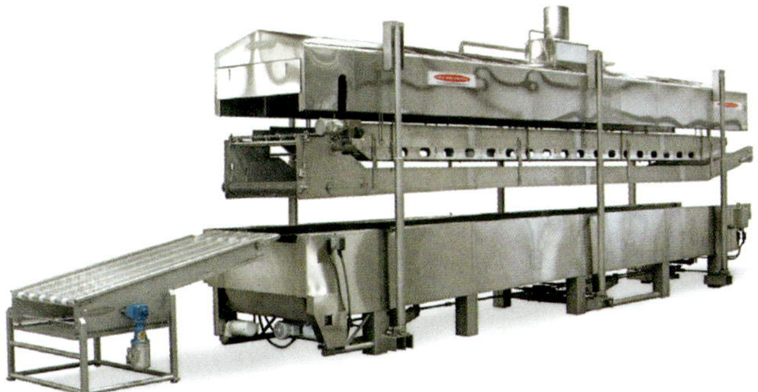

Figure 10.078. While a hood or canopy helps conserve energy during operation of the fryer (top), it should include a hoist that enables full access to the kettle for cleaning and maintenance (bottom). (Heat and Control)

that are both more energy efficient and less polluting. Fryers are built with scrubbers, incinerators and converters in the flues to ensure emissions are clean. Ultimately, the goal is have the only carbon dioxide and water coming out of the stacks. **Figure 10.082** shows a system that incinerates waste gases and particulates. The heat from the incineration process is then routed to the cooking oil heat exchanger, thus reducing energy usage.

10.D.3. Quality control in deep fat frying

Robertson (1967) proposed several basic principles for maintaining frying oil quality: (a) design, build and maintain equipment properly; (b) clean equipment properly; (c) minimize exposure of frying oils to ultraviolet light; (d) keep salt and other sources of metal away from the oil; and (e)

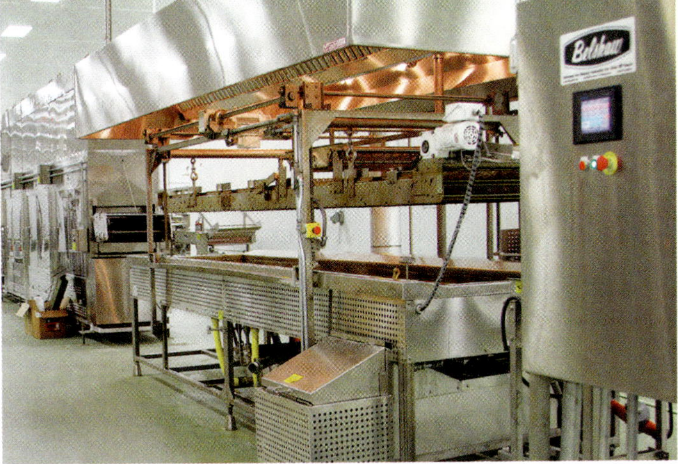

Figure 10.079. Powered conveyor hoists on fryers 10 ft or longer eliminate a dangerous and difficult manual job. (Belshaw Adamatic Bakery Group)

Figure 10.080. The heating tubes in this direct-fired system run across the width of the fryer.
(Belshaw Adamatic Bakery Group)

Figure 10.081. To heat direct-fired fryers, the burners point their jets of flame into the heating tubes.
(Belshaw Adamatic Bakery Group)

filter oils regularly.

His principles remain just as valid today.

10.D.3.a. Oil quality curve

Many also believe that it is important to monitor oil quality and temperature during downtimes as well as active frying. Keeping a fryer at elevated temperatures during extended downtimes can severely damage the cooking oil. Following Robertson's basic principles will maintain oil quality and allow processors to maximize oil life.

Another tool that can help processors better understand frying was developed by Blumenthal (1991): the frying oil quality curve (**Figure 10.083**). The curve describes five stages of oil degradation: break-in, fresh, optimum, degrading and runaway.

If one looks at french fry cooking, these changes can be seen throughout the life of the oil. When frying initiates in a clean fryer with fresh oil, fries are light in color and do not have the rich smell one would expect in the product. This fresh oil has few surfactants, so the oil and food do not remain in contact long enough to properly cook the food. Water escaping from the potato pushes the oil away from the surface of the product so the surface does not brown and the interior does not properly cooked. As surfactants build in the oil, food quality increases to a point at which the oil is considered "optimum." This stage produces the best quality fried foods.

The goal of both industrial and food service frying is to maintain the oil in this optimum condition for the longest possible time. This objective is easier to accomplish in industrial operations, especially when cooking foods that absorb a great deal of oil such as potato chips. Such operations literally reach a steady state and can be maintained.

If users allow the oil to go beyond optimum to the degrading and runaway stages, food quality becomes progressively worse. Products become darker, surfaces are case hardened, coatings are lost, and taste is poor. Operators who fail to maintain their oil will lose customers.

Once oil begins to break down, the process is irreversible. Failure to follow the basic quality guidelines noted above will speed up the process of degradation. Improper cleaning of a fryer will accelerate the breakdown process. The presence of metals, particularly copper and bronze, can destroy oil in a very short time. So, if repairs are required on your fryer, don't use a brass fitting.

10.D.3.b. Oil filtration and treatment

The use of oil treatment or filtration systems is regarded as an essential step for maintaining oil quality. Oil must be treated from the very beginning so that breakdown components of the oil, which act as catalysts for further oil degradation, are continually removed and not allowed to accumulate in the oil.

Two types of oil filtration systems are used: passive and active. Passive systems simply remove particulates; that is, they simple filter the oil. They act as sieves to remove particulates from the oil. These systems include metal screens, rolling (indexing) paper filters, paper cones and plastic cloths. Large-scale frying operations may opt for plate-and-frame systems (**Figure 10.084**), which use diatomaceous earth and leaf filters. All of these systems are routinely used in frying operations today.

Active systems remove specific oil soluble chemical compounds from heated oils.

These active filters or systems remove or trap not only the particulates but also remove or reduce certain nonfilterable chemicals or breakdown compounds. There are a number of these products on the market today.

There are pros and cons to adopting an active filter system. Potential benefits of filtration include reduced energy usage, improved food quality, reduced oil usage, enhanced shelf life, reduced down time, oil life extension, reduced cleanup time, the use of healthier oil for frying and the potential for having a safer and more comfortable work place. When evaluating any filter material, take a look at these benefits and work to put numbers on them.

Potential concerns with oil treatments are leaching of powders into the oil, leaching of metals into the oil, the lack of good filtration equipment, potential legal issues in different countries, the capital expenditures and safety of the system.

Remote oil filtration, done on a continuous basis, involves a relatively new concept. The system (**Figure 10.085**) filters 100% of the cooking oil but does not clog under prolonged operation and keeps its exterior surfaces relatively cool even though its tanks contain 232°C (450°F) oils. The filter accepts oils pumped out of the fryer at rates as high as 400 gal per minute. The system applies centrifugal force to separate the incoming oil into two streams because particulate materials are heavier than the oil. The stream containing the particulates proceeds into the filter, while the other stream returns to the fryer supply tank. State-of-the-art sensors and a PLC control operation of the filtering system, which requires no consumables such as filter material or filter paper. Controls can be programmed to monitor the frying process by reporting the amount of particulates removed and the rate at which they enter the system.

With food service or restaurant frying (doughnut frying, for example), the employees must also be factored into the equation. Any system that is introduced into a restaurant must be easy to use and field rugged. Just as one must look at the benefits, it is essential that one must look at the negatives.

The bottom line is whether the benefits outweigh the costs. The equipment vendor must work closely with the baker, snack food processor or food service operator to evaluate costs and benefits because only the users understand what constitutes quality fried food in their businesses.

10.D.3.c. Cleaning

Proper cleaning of a fryer is essential to ensuring quality frying operations. The first step is to drain the oil from the fryer kettle. The oil should be cooled to approximately 65°C (150°F) using an external cooling system. The used oil should be stored in a designated oil holding tank. These tanks should be designed to allow sediments to precipitate out. The tank design should also allow the oil to be sparged with or blanketed with nitrogen. With trans-fat free oils it is necessary to heat the holding tank and all the pipes. The oil must be stored above 65°C (150°F)

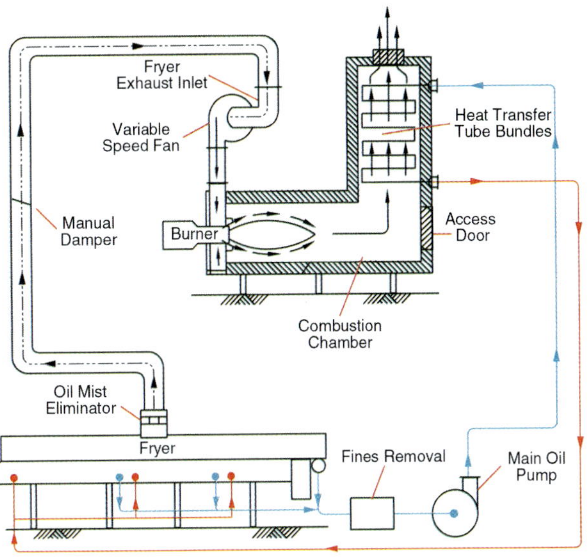

Figure 10.082. A pollution control heat exchanger removes oil, odors and particulates from fryer exhaust while recovering heat to supply the frying line. (Heat and Control)

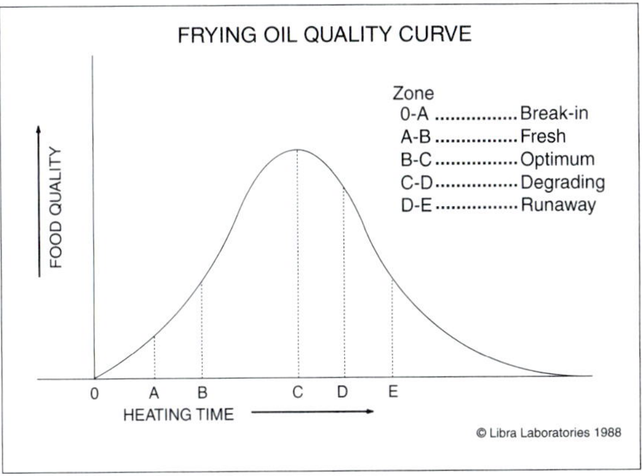

Figure 10.083. Frying oil goes through five distinct quality stages. (Stier and Blumenthal 1993)

Figure 10.084. Plate-and-frame filters remove particulates using diatomaceous earth and leaf filters.
(Star Filters)

Figure 10.085. By filtering 100% of the oil, this remote oil filter monitors particulates not only by amount but also by rate of accumulation.
(GCS Engineering)

to keep the oil in a liquid state. Failure to do this will result in oil solidification and an inability to pump it back into the fryer after cleaning.

The empty oil holding tank and the frying vessel should then be rinsed with water to remove particulates and then filled with cold water. For doughnut operations, the fryer conveyor should be lifted out of the fryer kettle for initial cleaning of sediment and particulates and then lowered back down into the fryer kettle for the boil-out cleaning process.

Caustic is then added to the cold water, and the tank brought up to a boil. Never add caustic to hot water! Once the tank has been boiled out, the caustic should be neutralized and disposed per local regulations. Some locales will not allow discharge of neutralized caustic into public systems.

The empty tank is then rinsed with a mild acid solution to fully neutralize any residual caustic. This mild acid is followed by a water rinse and then another acid treatment. Failure to neutralize the caustic and/or properly rinse can damage the oil later.

It is absolutely essential that water be completely drained from the system prior to introduction of oil. If water remains in the lines or the fryer kettle, it could inadvertently be introduced into the hot oil and cause an explosion. The small amount of water remaining in the open fryer will be boiled off.

10.D.3.d. Startup

Fryer operators should go through a checklist at startup. This checklist should include the following elements (Gupta 2006): (a) Is the quality of the fresh oil quality satisfactory? (b) Does used oil meet specified standards? (c) Have used and fresh oils been appropriately blended for startup? (d) Are the product feed system and product supply to the fryer ready? (e) Are the take-out conveyor, salt and seasoning applicator and product feed to the packaging machine working satisfactorily? And (f), are the filling machines operating satisfactorily?

Operators should also make sure that the fryer has been properly cleaned. The fryer should be filled approximately 2 hours before the start of production. Operators often use a mixture of fresh and used oil to fry, which is why steps must be taken during cleanup to ensure that used oil is protected. Heat the fryer to between 101 and 104°C (215 and 220°F). This temperature will serve to dewater the cooking oil.

If a layer of foam develops on the oil, the entire contents of the fryer should be discarded. Such deposits indicate that there was residual caustic from the cleaning operations. After disposing of the caustic-tainted oil, the fryer should be cleaned again and refilled with a mixture of fresh and properly treated used oil. Bring the fryer up to temperature, and start frying as soon as possible. Operating a fryer at cooking temperatures without introducing food will damage the oil.

10.D.3.e. Operations

Fryers should be operated without interruptions. Stops and starts will compromise both food and oil quality (Gupta 2006). The only time a fryer should be shut down is when repairs are required or there is a product changeover.

Operators should cool the oil slightly whenever there is an extended stoppage. During operations, industrial fryers reach a steady state. Oil turnover — defined as the time it takes for the product being fried to use up the oil in the fryer — is an important key to quality operations. Fryers should be designed with low oil turnover times, as demonstrated in the following example:

If 4,000 lb of oil is required to fill the fryer, which operates at 2,500 lb per hour, and the 20% of the finished product's weight is oil taken up during frying, then:

$$\text{Oil carried out of the system by the product} = 0.2 \times 2{,}500 = 500 \text{ lb per hour}$$
$$\text{Theoretical oil turnover time} = 4{,}000 \div 500 = 8 \text{ hours}$$

10.D.3.f. Shutdown

When production is done for the day, the fryer must be properly shut down. Proper shut down includes the following (Gupta 2006): (a) turning off the heat as soon as the last food enters the fryer, (b) initiating the cooling process for oil as soon as the last bit of food leaves the fryer and (c) cooling the oil in an external cooler to minimize thermal shock to the fryer pan. This last step minimizes the chances of warping the fryer pan.

10.E. Cooling Equipment

Updated by J. Peter Clark

Baked products require cooling to an appropriate temperature before they can be sliced or packaged. The rate at which cooling is carried out exerts a measurable effect on product quality. For example, if the temperature of products like bread is reduced too rapidly, then the products' internal vapor phase will condense into a liquid phase that occupies a much smaller volume, resulting in a proportionate reduction in the product volume. In other words, the products often shrink in volume, which detracts from their quality (Euverard 1972).

According to Gable (1960), the most effective cooling conditions are provided by a temperature of 23.9 ± 1.67°C (75 ± 3°F), a relative humidity (RH) of 85% and an air movement sufficient to produce an 11 C° (20 F°) rise in the temperature at the exhaust point. Given these conditions, a 1.25-lb loaf of bread will cool to an internal temperature of 32°C (90°F) in 90 minutes, to 38°C (100°F) in 65 minutes and to 43°C (110°F) in 52 minutes.

Formerly, the general practice of cooling bread involved placing the hot loaves on the shelves of stationary racks and exposing them to the cooling effect of the bakery's ambient air until their internal temperature had reached an acceptable level.

This method, still used extensively in smaller bakery plants, consumes time, space and labor and can be rather inefficient. Not only does the inevitable heat gradient from the center to the outer loaves on the rack result in non-uniform cooling, but the actual cooling rate may vary on a daily basis with changing atmospheric conditions.

A new method earning increasing use handles cooling as a 2-stage operation in which ambient-temperature pre-cooling is followed by refrigerated final cooling. This method allows much of the product's initial heat, typically around 82°C (180°F), to flash off as it exits the oven, while the final cooler brings internal temperatures of 43°C (110°F) down to 21°C (70°F). Energy efficiency is a major benefit of this system (Gorton 2007a).

10.E.1. Continuous belt coolers

Major improvements in bread cooling — and that of cookies, cakes and sweet goods — came with the introduction of conveyorized coolers because these provide identical cooling conditions for each loaf and, when they are suspended from the ceiling, liberate substantial floor space. The simplest of these coolers, sometimes referred to as "racetrack" conveyors, consists of endless, multiple-tier overhead conveyors that travel in straight flights, with 180° turns at the end of each flight, and that transport the bread through a 60- to 90-minute cooling cycle. They may be either open on all sides, as shown in **Figure 10.086**, with an overhead fan exhausting the heat radiating from the loaves to the exterior, or they may be enclosed with panels to form a tunnel-like structure and use a counter-current air movement to accelerate the cooling action.

Variable-frequency drives regulate unit speed, and some overhead coolers come with digital displays that report cooling times. For weight savings, the framing is constructed from anodized aluminum with aluminum tubing spacers and zinc-plated hardware.

Disk-style turns (**Figure 10.087**) smooth the operation of some overhead coolers. Resembling a multiple-tier cage, the disk system provides low-friction support for conveyors as them make turns of 90 to 180°.

Figure 10.086. The large-diameter drive wheels of this multiple-tier open product cooling conveyor engage the conveyor track for smooth turns. (This bakery installed the cooler on a mezzanine for improved maintenance access.) (Stewart Systems)

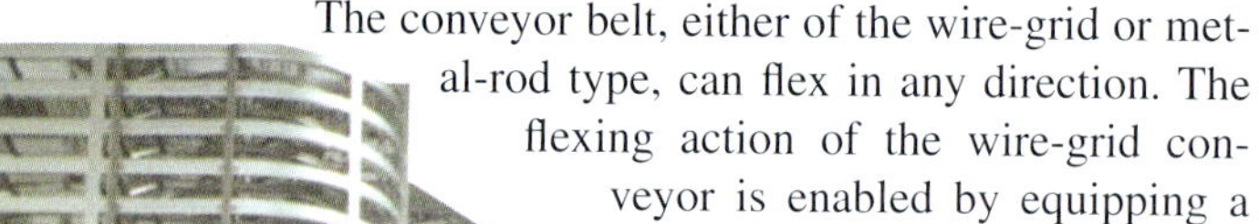

Figure 10.087. Disk turns (the circular assemblies seen at the corners) enable smooth flow of the cooling conveyor through angles of 90 to 180°. (AMF Bakery Systems)

The conveyor belt, either of the wire-grid or metal-rod type, can flex in any direction. The flexing action of the wire-grid conveyor is enabled by equipping a standard roller chain with attachments for mounting the wire grid and, in the case of the rod chain, by using slotted end connectors that allow the rods to close in on each other at the inner radius of a turn (Latendorf 1973). Another design (**Figure 10.088**) for wire-rod conveyors employs a T-shaped assembly that mounts the rods at their center point and supports the outer edges with passive, friction-rail channels. Plastic-link belting has also been successfully used for overhead conveyors, and in-line belt washers are available for continuous or downtime sanitation.

Vinyl under-guards are often installed under the bottom tiers and feed systems for overhead cooling conveyors. Such guards catch bread crumbs falling from conveyed products, and their color, usually yellow, provides a visual reminder of the low headroom underneath.

While the most popular belt path configuration is the overhead racetrack, other forms are available to the baker. Of these, spiral coolers of varying design and featuring either single or double helices have found increasing acceptance. These coolers may range in height from 4 to as many as 28 tiers and have belt widths of 18 to 32 in. Their circular form, as shown in **Figure 10.089**, conserves floor space and at the same time offers wide latitude in belt length to meet any potential cooling time requirements.

A cage-like assembly of vertical bars forms the internal cylinder of the spiral conveyor, while the system's housing supports horizontal bars, topped with low-friction plastic strips. The vertical bars engage the endless conveyor every few inches to power the belt's travel through the system. Wire-rod and plastic-link belting find common use for spiral conveying systems.

The double-spiral cooler consists of two concentric circles, with the outer helix forming the ascending flight and the inner one the descending flight. **Figure 10.090** shows how the conveyor that carries products switches from one side to the other at the top of the system. This low-entrance, low-exit design simplifies line layout.

A triple-conveyor configuration has also been put to work. In this design, all three belts travel around a single spiral cage.

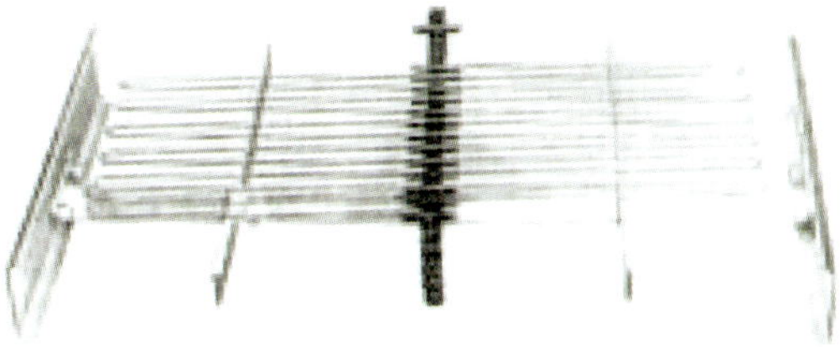

10.E.2. Tray coolers

In tray coolers, the conveyor belt is replaced by trays. These trays usually consist of stainless steel grills mounted on steel frames attached to parallel standard roller chains, with the drive sprockets located at the conveyor loops. The length and height of the tray cooler can be varied to adapt it to the available headroom and floor space. In loading this type of bread cooler, the loaves being fed continuously from the depanner must be grouped and metered for transfer onto the trays or pallets. Some units incorporate a tray washer

Figure 10.088. A cross-section shows the T-assembly of wire rods in a racetrack cooler.
(AMF Bakery Systems)

Figure 10.089. This spiral cooling conveyor features tower-in-tower, or double-helix, design that conserves plant floor space.
(Stewart Systems)

Figure 10.090. On a double-spiral system, the conveyor travels up the outer side, across the top and down the inner side.
(AMF Bakery Systems)

equipped with high-pressure spray nozzles for sanitizing the trays with hot detergent solution and hot water rinses as the need arises.

10.E.3. Rack coolers

The automatic rack cooler represents a third type of bread cooler and, in essence, constitutes an adaptation of the rack proofer to bread cooling. While it may be enclosed and air conditioned, rack coolers frequently omit the exterior panels. Such design facilitates the flow of natural convection air currents through the racks. However, dense concentration of loaves found in rack coolers during operation may require forced air circulation to improve the cooling rate. In this instance, the cooler would be enclosed.

The loading sequence with this unit is the same as with automatic tray coolers. At its loading/unloading station, the rack, with 10 or more shelves, is intermittently indexed upward until all its shelves are loaded. By this time, the rack has reached the upper runway and proceeds on its way toward the back of the cooler to make room for the succeeding loaded racks. At the end of the upper run, it is lowered to the bottom runway and proceeds to the loading/unloading station, where the cooled loaves are unloaded while the freed shelves are loaded with hot loaves. A major advantage of the rack cooler is its potential for space savings.

10.E.4. Cooling tunnels

Refrigerated cooling has long been an essential step in preparation of iced snack cakes and other products with fat-based fillings and toppings, especially those containing cocoa butter (chocolate). When fat crystals set properly, they remain stable during packaging and distribution to deliver an attractive appearance and optimum eating quality to the consumer. Cooling tunnels (**Figure 10.091**) carefully regulate temperature and humidity conditions to achieve proper crystallization.

Newer designs apply impingement methods to speed cooling. This process of heat transfer uses high-velocity, or high pressure, air moving in large-diameter streams to strip away the layer of insulating air at the surface of a product. This enables faster transfer of heat into or, in the case of refrigeration applications, out of the product, yet the action of the impinged air is gentle enough not to disturb the product's surface.

Another efficient heat-dissipation method that supplements the action of refrigerated air in a cooling tunnel is use of chill plates below the conveyor on which products travel (**Figure 10.092**). These plates circulate a refrigerated coolant, creating a cold zone underneath the product.

Figure 10.091. Clamshell construction for this cooling tunnel facilitates access for cleaning and maintenance. (Total Baking Solutions)

10.E.5. Vacuum coolers

A relatively new method for cooling baked foods is the modulated vacuum cooling system, which brings about a very rapid reduction in product temperatures (Bradshaw 1976, Fish 1980, Newbery 1996). As shown in **Figure 10.093**, the system consists of a conveyor within a tunnel that serves as the vacuum chamber and whose ends are provided with vertical doors that form an airtight seal when closed. A pivoting bridge conveyor at each end of the tunnel affects the transfer of the product onto the interior conveyor and to the discharge conveyor.

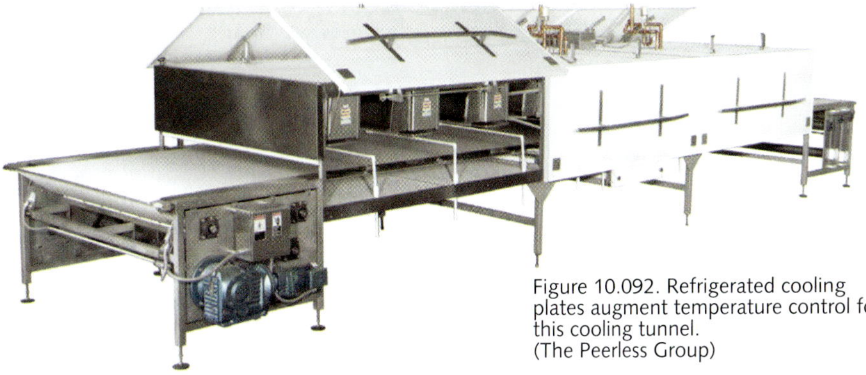

Figure 10.092. Refrigerated cooling plates augment temperature control for this cooling tunnel. (The Peerless Group)

The vacuum system itself consists of a mechanical ring pump or pumps that create a vacuum in the cooler tunnel by removing atmospheric gases and vapors. The gases are entrapped in steam that is injected by a steam-augmenter and enter a water-cooled condenser in which the condensable water vapor is removed by condensation, while the noncondensable gases are discharged to the atmosphere by the pumps.

Vaporization of the moisture in the hot baked product proceeds very rapidly under the partial vacuum conditions thus created in the cooling tunnel and causes a correspondingly rapid decrease in the product's temperature. In one commercial application involving cooling of hard rolls, the temperature of the rolls is drops from about 66 to 71°C (150 to 160°F) down to 41 to 43°C (105 to 110°F) in less than 60 seconds (Fink et al. 1979).

Vacuum cooling involves moisture losses that are higher than those encountered with atmospheric cooling. For this reason, the baking time for products that are to be cooled by the vacuum system must be reduced by about 20% of the normal baking cycle. During the final stage of baking, or the stabilization phase, the product's moisture content is reduced to the desired level. In vacuum cooling, this reduction takes place in the vacuum chamber at a greatly accelerated rate and additionally results in a much more even distribution of moisture within the crumb.

Figure 10.093. A tunnel-type continuous vacuum cooler can be sealed at either end to allow vacuum extraction of heat. (Tweedy of Burnley Ltd.)

The Milton Keynes process (Gorton 1995, Roberts 1997) takes advantage of this phenomenon to produce baked foods that are stable at ambient conditions and are finish-baked at point-of-sale. Products, best described as "pre-formed" rather than "parbaked," get sufficient oven time to deactivate the yeast and gelatinize the starch, but stops just short of full coloration. Now stabilized, the items must be moved quickly to the vacuum cooling chambers, or else the pre-formed loaves will collapse. The method suits both batch and continuous vacuum chamber cooling technologies.

10.F. Refrigeration and Freezing
Updated by J. Peter Clark

Refrigeration accomplishes a variety of objectives for bakers. These may include atmospheric temperature control, cold storage of perishable ingredients, control of dough temperature in the course of production, slowing of the fermentation rate in the retarded dough process and, ultimately, freezing of either raw dough products or baked foods and their frozen storage. The last application has assumed significance as a production control tool because it permits baking of large amounts of both high-volume and low-volume products during slack production periods for subsequent freezing and inventory buildup and can thus serve to level out production schedules.

The importance of temperature control during dough processing and in the production of pastry products has been reviewed in the appropriate sections of this text and will therefore not be considered at this point. Similarly, the requisite conditions for the optimum freezing of bakery products have also been discussed in Chapter 6, Part I.

Mechanical refrigeration systems find the widest use in the bakery, where they reduce temperatures either during processing or for freezing of partially or fully

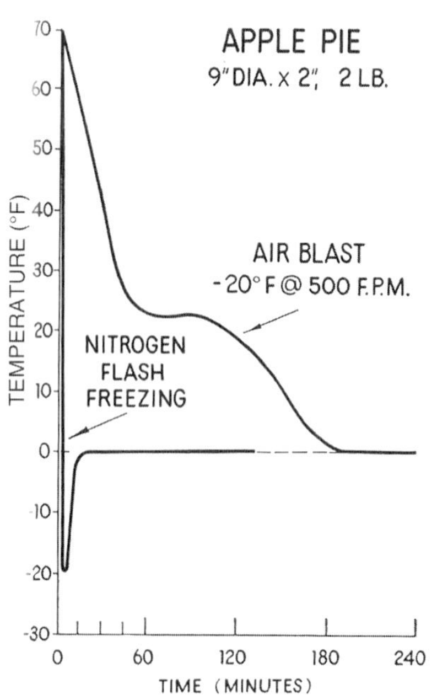

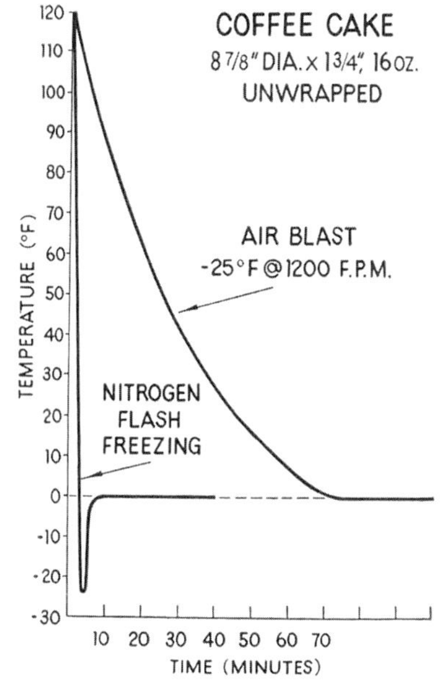

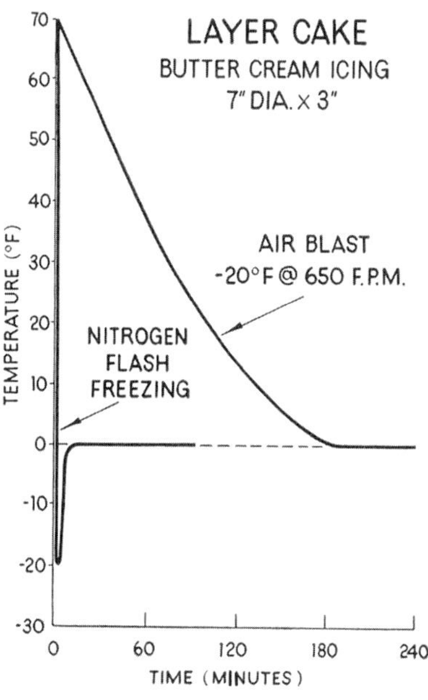

Figure 10.094. Liquid nitrogen's freezing curve, compared with blast freezing, shows the swift pace at which temperatures decrease. (Breyer et al. 1965)

finished baked foods. Cryogenic freezing of bakery products also finds some application, as does the use of carbon dioxide snow for temperature control of such dry ingredients as flour and sugar in pneumatic conveyors and in the batch mixing of cookie doughs (Baron 1983, Richards 1992).

All foods freeze from the outside in. It's the speed of freezing that makes a difference and, thus, determines the choice of mechanical or cryogenic methods. Cryogenic is best suited to freezing finished products and small items. The outer surface freezes almost instantly (**Figure 10.094**), but such speed works against use for frozen dough applications, where blast freezing provides the best results.

To stabilize bread, its temperature must be lowered below its freezing point, or approximately -7°C (20°F). With mechanical freezer temperatures maintained at -23 to -29°C (-10 to -20°F), and with air movements at velocities up to 1,300 linear ft per minute, bread will reach its freezing point in about 45 minutes. Air movement affects times. Freezing with air velocities of only 300 to 500 linear ft will lengthen the freezing time to nearly two hours. Studies have found that although freezing causes an increase in crumb firmness in the first 24 hours, properly frozen and thawed bread, 48 hours after thawing, will be equivalent in crumb firmness to 2-day old unfrozen bread and perhaps better in flavor.

Considerations for freezing dough are unique. Fast freezing is not always the optimum method. Raw yeast-raised dough is a biologically active system that must be preserved. Yeast cells are very sensitive to the rate of freezing. When yeast cells are cooled rapidly to -30°C (-22°F) or below, less than 0.01% of the cells survive, whereas slower cooling rates result in a 70% or greater survival rate (Berne 2006a).

10.F.1. Mechanical refrigeration

The most extensively used mechanical refrigeration system is the vapor-compression system, which consists of a compressor powered by an electric motor and which, as its name implies, compresses a low-density vaporized refrigerant, usually a halogenated hydrocarbon type known as hydrofluorocarbon (HFC) or hydrochlorofluorocarbon (HCFC) into a high pressure vapor. As a result of the mechanical energy imparted by compression, the gas acquires a high temperature.

Also included in the system is a condenser that serves as a heat exchanger in which the heat of the hot vapor is dissipated sufficiently by means of atmospheric or water cooling to cause it to condense into the liquid form for storage in the receiver. An evaporator produces the actual cooling action and is equipped with a thermostatic expansion valve that greatly reduces the pressure on the refrigerant and thereby causes it to vaporize and absorb heat from the environment that represents the insulated cold room.

The refrigerant in this system is thus alternately evaporated in the cooling coil and the resultant vapor compressed and subsequently condensed in the condenser, absorbing heat from the environment in the first instance and dissipating it in the other. In blast freezers, the cooling coil is mounted within the insulated cold box or tunnel with powerful fans that blow the cold air directly over the product to be frozen. Some refrigerants previously used, specifically the chlorofluorocarbons (CFCs), are known to reduce ozone in the atmosphere and are being phased out in favor of HCFCs and HFCs (Stoecker 1995, Clark 2002).

The freezers that employ mechanical refrigeration vary in type based on a bakery's space, products and throughput. These types include simple stationary insulated boxes (**Figure 10.095**) in which the products are exposed on racks to air blasts, generally at a temperature of -29°C (-20°F) as well as tunnel blast freezers through which the product is carried on a conveyor at a speed that is determined by the time needed to freeze the product.

Continuous spiral freezers contain one or two helices of conveyors on which the product is carried through the freezing cycle. Both open wire-mesh and plastic belts (**Figures 10.096** and **10.097**) suit spiral freezers well.

Among the many designs of spiral conveyor freezers is one with a self-stacking

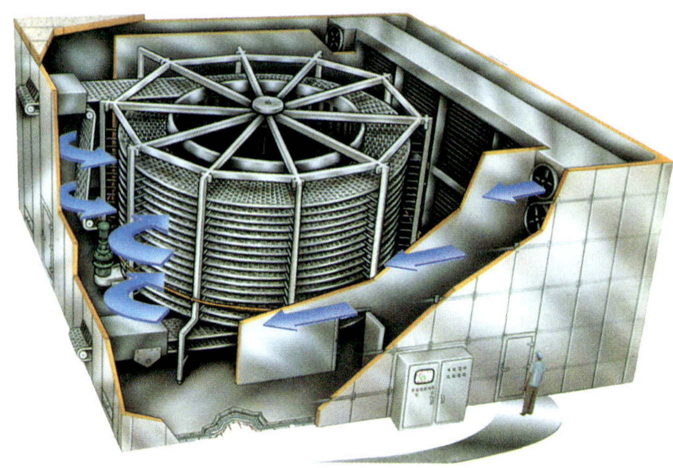

Figure 10.095. Cam locks connect with internal strapping to seal freezer enclosures tightly. This air blast freezer directs low-temperature air at high velocity through the spiral conveyor that carries products.
(I.J. White Corp.)

belt (**Figure 10.098**). The flexible conveyor is constructed with rigid side walls that support the weight of each succeeding tier. Air flows vertically through these freezers to improve operating efficiency.

Continuous multi-tray blast freezers include open-ended wire trays containing the product. These are automatically stacked to a predetermined height, passed through the freezing chamber on a conveyor bed and, on emerging from the freezer after a predetermined time, are automatically unstacked (Ingram 1974). Because the speed of each of the freezer conveyors can be independently controlled, tray freezers permit simultaneous freezing of products with different dwell time requirements. Normally, all these primary freezers are augmented by suitable holding freezers.

Thompson (1974) recommended blast freezing at temperatures of -34 to -40°C (-30 to -40°F), with air velocities of 600 to 700 cu ft per minute, and for a time that will lower the core temperature in the product to -18°C (0°F). The holding freezer should be maintained at an air temperature of -23 to -29°C (-10 to -20°F) and should not be allowed to rise above -18°C (0°F), with the air held at the highest practical relative humidity and circulating freely.

Under these conditions, product quality will stay undiminished for several weeks or months. The optimum freezing conditions for specific bakery products have been summarized by Bamford (1975a, 1975b), and additional aspects of freezing were covered by Thompson (1976), Plante (1995) and Whitaker (2008).

10.F.2. Cryogenic freezers

Cryogenic freezing relies on liquid nitrogen and liquid carbon dioxide, used as a contact freezing medium. Liquid nitrogen has a boiling point of -196°C (-320°F), while that of liquid carbon dioxide is -78°C (-109°F), as noted in **Table 10.12**. Product freezing is achieved both by the low temperature of the cryogens and by their rapid evaporation rates. Thus, in the case of liquid nitrogen, the conversion from the liquid to the gaseous state at -196°C (-320°F) absorbs 80 Btu per lb, and an additional 80 Btu are required raise the vapor temperature raised to -18°C (0°F).

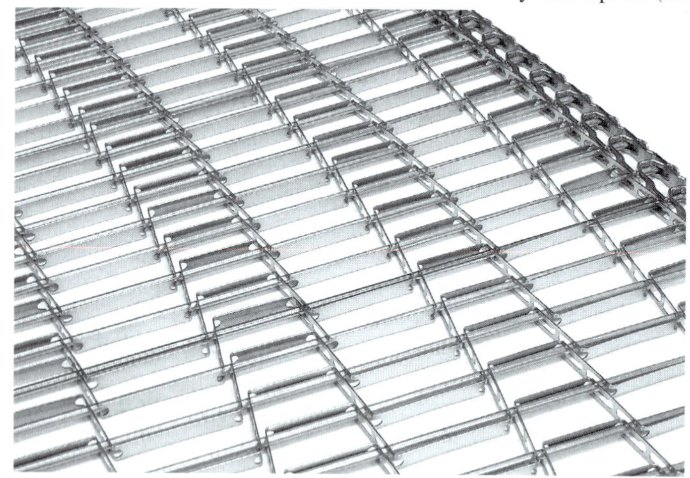

Figure 10.096. Flexible lightweight belting improves air circulation through spiral conveyors during freezing.
(Ashworth Bros.)

Major advantages of cryogenic freezers are their greater simplicity, lower initial investment, reduced maintenance costs and power requirements, and much smaller floor space requirements, compared with mechanical freezers. Also of great significance are their extremely rapid freezing rates, which generally are 10 to 30 times faster than those for blast freezing. Such speeds result in a perceptibly greater retention of quality as the baked product's temperature passes through the zone of 21 to -7°C (70 to 20°F) in which maximum staling occurs — fast enough to minimize starch retrogradation (**Figure 10.099**). For the most part, cryogenic freezers are insulated tunnels that range from 10 to 70 ft in length, through which belt conveyors carry the product to be frozen. Large countercurrent tunnel freezers can readily freeze up to 5,000 lb per hr of product (Byars 1979). The tunnel is normally divided into three temperature zones that serve, respectively, (a) to pre-cool the product in nitrogen gas at about -18°C (0°F) from the entry temperature to the freezing temperature, (b) to freeze the product very quickly with liquid nitrogen at -196°C (-320°F) and (c) to temper the product evenly throughout its mass at the desired exit temperature level with gas at -107°C (-160°F).

Spray heads introduce the liquid nitrogen into the freezing zone at a controlled rate. It vaporizes into a low-temperature gas that circulates at speeds of up to 7,000 ft per minute to the various zones and is eventually exhausted to the atmosphere.

The liquid nitrogen needed for cryogenic freezing is delivered in special tank trucks to the baking facility and stored in well-insulated tanks of various sizes and capacities under specific pressure and temperature conditions that prevent the liquid from boiling. The tanks are provided with controls and vaporizers that permit the withdrawal of the liquid nitrogen either as a liquid or as a medium-pressure gas.

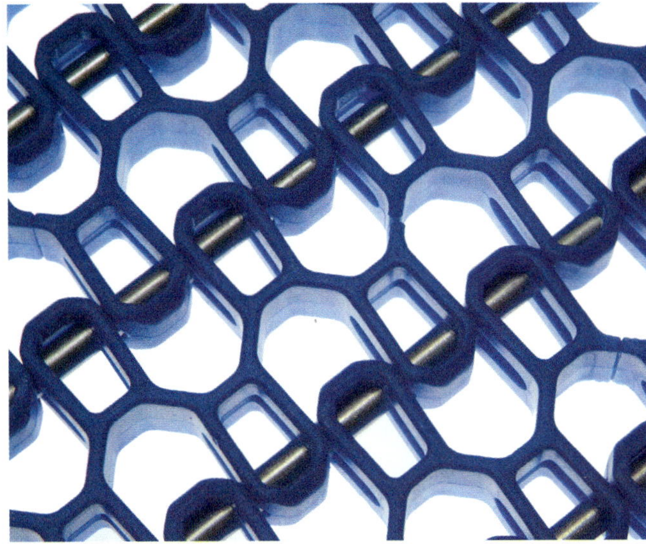

Figure 10.097. Composed of plastic modules and stainless steel rods, this belt for spiral conveyors is both is USDA approved and NSF certified. (Ashworth Bros.)

The refrigerant is piped to the point of use through well-insulated supply lines. Details of the various aspects of cryogenic freezing of bakery products with liquid nitrogen have been provided by Breyer et al. (1965).

When carbon dioxide is the refrigerant, the pressurized liquid, upon exposure to atmospheric pressure, cools and solidifies into a snow-like solid (dry ice) that sublimes, passing directly into gas without melting, at a temperature of -78°C (-109°F), exerting a cooling effect in the process.

Snow-dispensing devices in a wide range of sizes are available to meet the requirements of such varied uses as spot chilling of baked products, temperature control of dry ingredients and during batch mixing, and large volume product freezing in tunnel freezers. The use of carbon dioxide to chill flour is described in Chapter 9, Part A.

When large product volumes are involved, cryogenic spiral-type freezers are frequently employed. They have capacities of 10,000 lb per hour of product and can be accommodated in a relatively small space (Byars 1979, Baron 1983).

10.F.3. Ice builders

Figure 10.098. Self-stacking design enables efficient freezing with vertical air flow in this spiral freezer. (JBT Food Tech)

Freezing technology has another application in bakeries, albeit one that is rapidly disappearing: preparing ice for the doughmaking process and for chilling ingredient water. Addition of refrigerated jackets to dough mixers and the use of inline flour

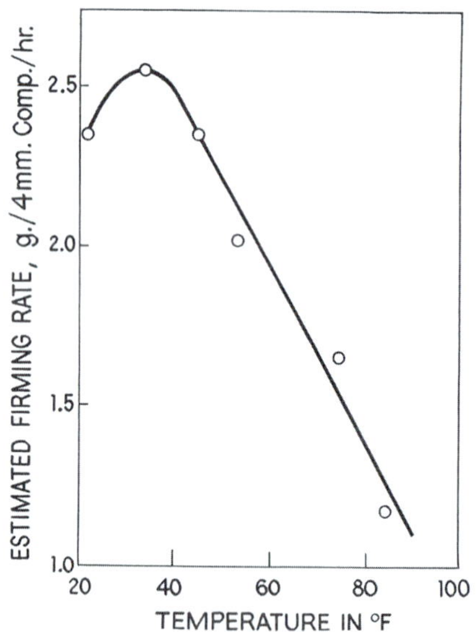

Figure 10.099. Bread firming, as measured by its compressibility, takes place most rapidly at temperatures around 4°C (40°F), the "staling zone." (Breyer et al. 1965)

cooling, as well as chilled water supplies, have made the imprecise method of adding ice to doughs obsolete at most large wholesale bakeries. Some bakers continue to use ice, supplied by conventional ice-making machines capable of making one ton or more of ice daily and installed close to the bakery's mixers. The use of ice in the heat balance of doughmaking is discussed in Chapter 6, Part A.

Ice builders, another application of freezing, address the need for a reliable supply of very cold ingredient water. These systems comprise a form of insulated water reservoir housing a series of refrigerated coils, kept cold enough to cause water in contact with them to freeze and form an ice bank. During periods of dough cooling requirements, ice melts off the ice bank, and the resulting chilled water, at about 0.6°C (33°F), is pumped through the coolant side of a plate heat-exchanger that then supplies the potable chilled ingredient water to the dough mixer.

Once an ice bank has been built up, it can provide a supply of chilled water over many hours in case of a mechanical failure or enforced reduction in electrical power demand. Ice builders, when properly insulated and protected, can be located outside the bakery plant proper, thereby conserving valuable interior space (Thompson 1981).

10.G. Impingement Systems
Updated by J. Peter Clark

An effective means of accelerating heat transfer rates in ovens was devised by Smith (1985), who was granted a patent in 1975 on the use of special air impingement modules. Each such module consists of multiple jet nozzles through which heated air is forced to impinge in narrow air streams on the baking product.

Tests have shown that an air flow of 500 ft per minute, with the air movement parallel to the baking surface, produces a heat transfer rate of 2.4 Btu per hour per sq ft per F° (Smith 1986). When the air speed increases to 3,000 ft per minute, the heat transfer rate rises to 6.0 Btu per hour per sq ft per F°. However, by creating a complex turbulence on the dough piece's surface by means of vertical hot air impingement, also at 3,000 ft per minute, the heat transfer rate may be raised to 23.3 Btu per hour per sq ft per F°.

Such air turbulence is produced by the impingement modules whose tapered jet nozzles are directed both downward and upward close to the oven conveyor. Brunson (1966) had previously demonstrated graphically that the increased efficiency of recirculating, indirect-fired, band ovens resulted from the air circulation within the baking chamber at velocities of 200 to 400 ft per minute.

In the air impingement oven, air flow rates of 3,000 ft per minute are attained in the proximity of the orifices. The nozzles have been so designed that they produce narrow air jet streams that effectively create maximum air turbulence around the baking product. In test bakes, the im-

Table 10.12. Carbon Dioxide vs. Nitrogen

Characteristic	Carbon dioxide (CO$_2$)	Nitrogen (N)
Molecular weight	44.0	14.0
Boiling point	-78.6°C (-109.5°F)	-195.8°C (-320.4°F)
Melting point	-56.6°C (-69.9°F)	-209.9°C (-345.8°F)

pingement oven was shown to require lower baking temperatures and shorter baking times, to yield products with higher moisture contents and slower staling rates, and to be more energy efficient (Smith 1983). A series of American Institute of Baking technical bulletins described impingement systems in great detail (Walker 1987, Walker and Sparman 1989, Walker and Li 1993, Ovadia and Walker 1997). Impingement ovens are discussed earlier in this chapter at Part B.

The same technique for increasing heat transfer rates can be applied in cooling and freezing, with claims that impingement cooling systems are efficient enough to replace nitrogen and refrigerated cooling methods (Gorton 2007a). The impingement units (**Figure 10.100**) cool products traveling on a conveyor by moving chilled air or cryogens (**Figure 10.101**) through a series of pressurized distribution ducts above and below the belt. The hole pattern in the ducts features 75% open area. Depending on the temperatures required, filtered cooling air can be drawn into the tunnel through a series of fans, with the options of evaporation units, refrigeration or chilled water doing the cooling.

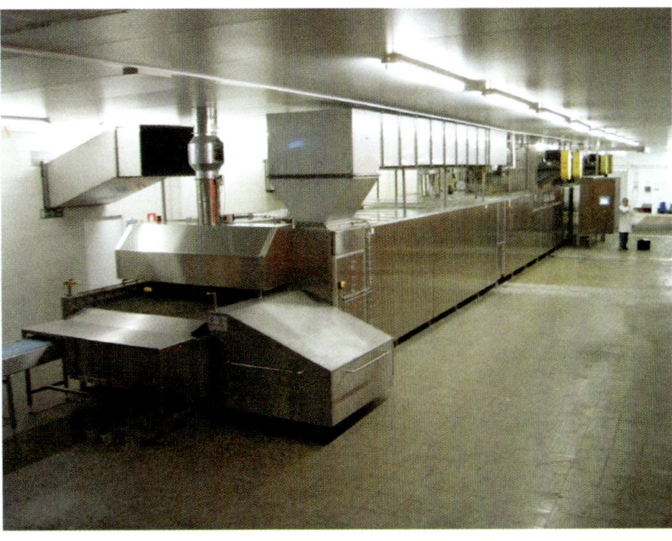

Figure 10.100. This impingement cooler has been integrated with an impingement oven, making one baking system with no transfers. (C.H. Babb Co.)

10.H. Microwave Systems

Updated by J. Peter Clark

Microwave frequencies fall between the ranges of the longer radio waves, on the one hand, and the shorter-wavelength infrared spectrum, on the other. Microwaves applicable to high-frequency processing equipment have a range from 915 to 2,450 megacycles per second, or megaHerz (MHz), for use in microwave heating, and from 13.56 to 27.12 mHz for use in dielectric heating, also termed radio-frequency heating (Spooner 1984). The 47.68 MHz wavelength is also employed by some dielectric systems. Dielectric dryers are discussed in Part C of this chapter.

High-frequency microwaves are generated by a magnetron and create heat in moisture-containing foods by producing a rapid oscillation of the dipolar water molecules in the swiftly alternating electrical field. Because microwaves pass through the product more or less uniformly, heating takes place evenly throughout the product and without the normal temperature gradient from the exterior to the interior that characterizes conventional modes of heating. Hence, doughs baked by dielectric heating do not form a crust and consequently require the supplementary application of either radiant or convection heat to achieve crest coloration.

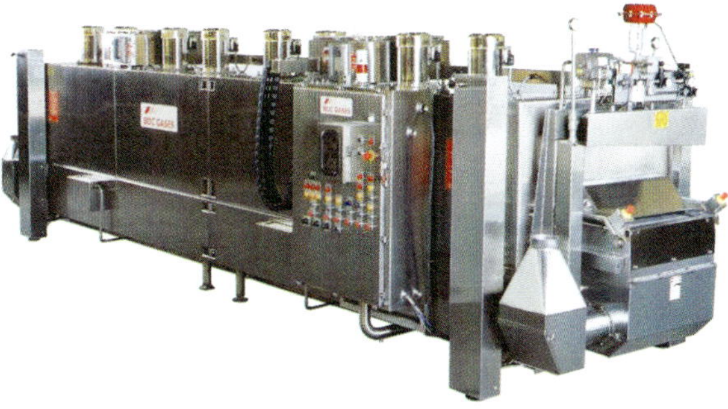

Figure 10.101. Impingement freezers circulate cryogenic gases through plenums to impact on baked foods. (BOC Gases)

Microwave heating, as applied in bakeries, has been found effective in such areas as the rapid defrosting of frozen fruits, eggs and frozen bakery products (Decareau 1967), proofing of yeast-raised doughnuts, accelerating doughnut frying (Schiffmann et al. 1971) and inhibition of mold growth in packaged sliced bread and other bakery products whose exposure to a microwave frequency of 2,450 MHz for about 1 minute will result in a temperature rise to 60°C (140°F) that suffices to inhibit mold growth for periods well beyond 10 days (Olsen 1965).

According to Spooner (1984), temperatures of 66°C (150°F) can be attained within 30 seconds using lower-frequency dielectric heat. Attempts to apply microwave heating to bread baking have thus far failed to achieve commercial success, although research in this area continues (Davis and Gordon 1990, Neufeld 1991). European producers of flatbreads, *Tostbrot* and *Vollkornbrot* developed a unique use for the sterilizing power of microwaves: After slicing and packaging these products, bakers run them through a continuous microwave treatment system that kills any microbes present and prolongs shelf life (Mans 1991).

The most extensive use of dielectric heating (in the range of 30 to 40 MHz) in the baking industry is for the final reduction of moisture in cookies and crackers. Its high efficiency is based on the fact that heat generation in the product does not depend on any temperature differential between the product and the energy source but is proportional to the latter's moisture content. Hence, the higher the moisture content of the product, the more heat is generated to drive off the moisture.

As Spooner (1984) pointed out, an increase in the production capacity of a cookie or cracker band oven normally entails a reduction in the bake time, which, in turn, results in a proportionate increase in the moisture content of the baked product. By inserting one or more appropriately sized dielectric ovens immediately following the band oven, the moisture content of the emerging cookies or crackers can be reduced economically to the desired low level.

Additional benefits that accrue from the use of dielectric heating following regular baking include the elimination of checking of the product surface, a better retention of ingredient and added flavors, a more accurate control over final moisture content, and, ultimately, greater economies.

References

Anonymous. 2003. Food Engr. 75 (3).

Bamford, R. 1975a. Freezing and thawing of bakery products. Proc. Am. Soc. Bakery Engrs. 51: 118.

Bamford, R. 1975b. Freezing and thawing of bakery products. Bakers Digest 49 (3): 40.

Baron, D.L. 1983. Oven energy efficiency. Proc. Am. Soc. Bakery Engrs. 59: 90.

Berne, S. 2003. Walking nature's path. Baking & Snack 25 (10): 28.

Berne, S. 2006a. Cold play. Baking & Snack 28 (3): 51.

Blümel, F., and Boog, W. 1977. 5000 Jahre Backofen. Deutsches Brot-museum E.V.: Ulm/ Donau, West Germany.

Blumenthal, M.M. 1991. A new look at the chemistry and physics of deep fat frying. Food Tech. 45 (1): 68.

Bradshaw, W. 1976. Modulated vacuum cooling for bakery products. Bakers Digest 50 (1): 26.

Breyer, F., Wagner, R.C., and Ryan, J.P. 1965. Application of liquid nitrogen freezing to bakery products. Bakers Digest 39 (6): 56.

Brixey, R. 1998. New bun makeup systems. Proc. Am. Soc. Bakery Engrs. 74: 121.

Brunson, B. 1966. Advanced methods of heat transfer and control in modern band ovens. Bakers Digest 40 (1): 64.

Byars, M. 1979. Cryogenic freezing as applied to the special needs of bakers. Bakers Digest 53 (1): 37.

Campbell, G.P. 1988. Bread production without intermediate proofing. Proc. Am. Soc. Bakery Engrs. 64: 129.

Clark, J.P. 2002. Baking industry deals with refrigeration. Food Tech. 56 (7): 76.

Coffin, M. 1996. Water wash. Proc. Am. Soc. Bakery Engrs. 42: 133.

Davis, D.L. 2000. Biotrickling filter for the control of ethanol emissions. Proc. Am. Soc. Baking 76: 43.

Davis, E.A., and Gordon, J. 1990. Microwave application for bakery products. AIB Tech. Bull. 12 (9).

Day, J. 2001. Automatic ignition systems. Proc. Am. Soc. Baking 77: 170.

Day, J. 2008. Improvements in oven technologies: burner management. Proc. Am. Soc. Baking 84: 100.

Decareau, R.V. 1967. Applications of high frequency energy in the baking field. Bakers Digest 41 (6): 52.

Dersch, J. A. 1989. The use of steam in bread ovens. Am. Soc. Bakery Engrs. Tech. Bull. 218.

Diver, J. 2006. Saving money through thermal oil application. Proc. Am. Soc. Baking 82: 115.

Dorfman, I.A. 1986. Energy developments. Proc. Am. Soc. Bakery Engrs. 62: 96.

Dorfman, I.A. 1996. Ten years after. Baking & Snack 18 (2): 106.

Duffin, D. 1981. Improving cookie and cracker oven efficiency. AIB Tech. Bull. 3 (11).

Earle, G. 1997. Post bake benefits. Baking & Snack 19 (11): 37.

Euverard, M.R. 1972. Bakery product cooling. Bakers Digest 46 (3): 46.

Fink, S., Rosenthal, H., Kurschner, H., and Meyerson, N.R. 1979. Vacuum cooler reduces roll temperature 50° in 60 seconds. Baking Ind. 146 (9): 60.

Fish, A.R. 1980. Vacuum cooling. Proc. Am. Soc. Bakery Engrs. 56: 120.

Gable, H.R. 1960. Bread and roll cooling. Proc. Am. Soc. Bakery Engrs. 36: 175.

Gorton, L. 1995. Bread breakthrough. Baking & Snack 17 (8): 18.

Gorton, L. 1996. Donut power. Baking & Snack 18 (4): 16.

Gorton, L. 2003. Now, that's a bakery! Baking & Snack 25 (11): 30.

Gorton, L. 2007a. Cool progress. Baking & Snack 29 (5): 77.

Gorton, L. 2007b. Powering a solution. Baking & Snack 29 (7): 34.

Grogan, P.E. 1980. Conveyorized proofing and baking systems. Proc. Am. Soc. Bakery Engrs. 56: 113.

Gupta, M.K. 2006. Quality in frying. Presented at Technology and Application of Frying short course held by Institute of Food Technologists, April 5-7, at Chicago, IL.

Harrell, C.G., and Thelen, R.J., eds. 1959. Conversion

Factors and Technical Data for the Food Industry. Burgess Publishing Co.: Minneapolis, MN.

Ingram, C.E. 1974. Automatic freezing system. Bakers Digest 48 (2): 42.

Johnson, A. M. and Walker, C. E. 2003. Humidity inside ovens. AIB Tech. Bull. 25 (6).

Kent, N.L., and Evers, A.D. 1994. Bread-baking technology. In: Kent's Technology of Cereals, 4th ed. Elsevier Science: Oxford, UK.

Kudronowicz, J.A. 1996. Catalytic oxidizers. Proc. Am. Soc. Bakery Engrs. 42: 125.

Lanham, W.E. 1970. A new technology of continuous proofing and baking. Bakers Digest 44 (6): 54.

Latendorf, M.W. 1973. Automatic mechanical coolers in the bakery. Bakers Digest 47 (5): 114.

Lescure, K.P. 1992. Controlling bakery oven emissions. Proc. Am. Soc. Bakery Engrs. 68: 56.

Manley, D.J.R. 2000. Technology of Biscuits, Crackers and Cookies. Woodhead Publishing Ltd.: Cambridge, UK.

Mans, J. 1991. Microwaves and radio frequency. Prepared Foods 160 (11).

Marino, M. 1998. Serpentine systems from Australia. Proc. Am. Soc. Bakery Engrs. 74: 145.

Moreth, N.W. 1987a. Cookie and cracker ovens. I and II. AIB Tech. Bull. 9 (6).

Moreth, N.W. 1987b. Cookie and cracker ovens. I and II. AIB Tech. Bull. 9 (7).

Mottram, D.S., Wedzicha, B. L. and Dodson, T.A. 2002. Food chemistry: Acrylamide is formed in the Maillard reaction. Nature 419: 448.

Mowbray, W.R. 1981. Technology of the 'hot box.' Food Manufacture (Oct.)

Neufeld, K. 1991. Microwave baking. Proc. Am. Soc. Bakery Engrs. 67: 77.

Newbery, D. 1996. Vacuum cooling. Proc. Am. Soc. Bakery Engrs. 72: 81.

Olsen, C.M. 1965. Food Engr. 37 (7): 51.

Ovadia, D.Z., and Walker, C.E. 1997. Opportunities for impingement technology in the baking and allied industries. IV. AIB Tech. Bull. 19 (5).

Plante, D. Two-sided freezing of bakery products. AIB Tech. Bull. 17 (2).

Richards, B. 1992. Refrigeration systems. Proc. Am. Soc. Bakery Engrs. 68: 126.

Roberts, D. 1997. The Milton Keynes process. Proc. Am. Soc. Bakery Engrs. 73: 75.

Robertson, C.J. 1967. The practice of deep-fat trying. Food Tech. 21 (1): 34.

Schack, A. 1965. Industrial Heat Transfer. Chapman and Hall: London, UK.

Schiffmann, R.F., Stein, E.W., and Kaufman, Jr., H.B. 1971. The microwave proofing of yeast-raised doughnuts. Bakers Digest 45 (1): 55.

Smith, B.C. 1999. A cool dry place. Baking & Snack 21 (8): 76.

Smith, D.P. 1985. Jet accelerated convection baking. Presented at Update on Oven Technology seminar held by American Institute of Baking, Sept. 21, at Orlando, FL.

Smith, D.P. 1986. Food Tech. 40: 112.

Smith, L.H. 1983. Rapid baking characteristics and energy efficiency of an impingement air oven compared to a reel oven. Thesis. Texas A&M University, College Station, TX.

Spooner, T.F. 1984. The electromagnetic spectrum and its roles in baking. I, II and III. Baking Equipment 6 (2): BE-34; (3): BE-32; (4): BE-38.

Stier, J.V. 1989. Oven stack emissions. Proc. Am. Soc. Bakery Engrs. 65:80.

Stier, R.F. 1996. Understanding high volume frying. I. Baking & Snack 18 (2): 70.

Stier, R.F. 1997. The history of frying. Baking & Snack, 19 (11): 42.

Stier, R.F. 2000. Chemistry of frying and optimization of deep-fat fried food flavour — an introductory review. Euro. J. Lipid Sci. Tech. 102: 8-9, 507-514.

Stier, R.F. 2007. Ensuring safe and high quality fried goods. Food Safety Magazine 13 (3): 30.

Stier, R.F., and Blumenthal, M.M. 1993. Quality control in deep-fat frying. Baking & Snack 15 (2): 67.

Stier, R.F., and Gupta, M.K. 2006. Treatment of used oil for enhanced shelf life. Presented at Technology and Application of Frying short course held by Institute of Food Technologists, April 5-7, at Chicago, IL.

Stitley, J.W., Kemp, K.E., Kyle, B.G., and Kulp, K. 1987. Bakery oven ethanol emissions, experimental plant and survey results. AIB Tech. Bull. 9 (12).

Stoecker, W.F. 1995. Substitutes for currently-used refrigerants in the baking industry. AIB Tech. Bull. 17 (9).

Thogersen, P. 2001. Environmental mapping for oven and proof box heat distribution. Proc. Am. Soc. Baking 77: 164.

Thompson, D.R. 1976. Refrigeration for the baking industry. Bakers Digest 50 (2): 20.

Thompson, D.R. 1978. Freezing bakery products. Bakers Digest 52 (4): 33.

Thompson, D.R. 1981. Ice builders for bakery use. Bakers Digest 55 (5): 98.

Trate, P.J. 2001. Serpentine baking systems in action. Proc. Am. Soc. Baking 77: 157.

Varilek, P., and Walker, C.E. 1983. Baking and ovens — history of heat technology. I and II. Bakers Digest 57 (5): 52; (6): 24.

Varilek, P., and Walker, C.E. 1984. Baking and ovens — history of heat technology. III, IV and V. Bakers Digest 58 (1): 24; (2): 12; (3): 24.

Wade, P. 1987. Biscuit baking by near-infrared radiation. J. Food Engr. 6: 167.

Walker, C.E. 1987. Impingement oven technology. I: Principles. AIB Tech. Bull. 9 (11).

Walker, C.E., and Li, A. 1993. Impingement oven technology. III: Combining impingement with microwave (hybrid oven). AIB Tech. Bull. 15 (9).

Walker, C.E., and Sparman, A.B. 1989. Impingement oven technology. II: Applications and future. AIB Tech. Bull. 11 (11).

Wells, R.A. 1983. Proofing and bakery systems. Proc. Am. Soc. Bakery Engrs. 59: 119.

Whitaker, S. 2007. Mitigating moisture. Baking & Snack 29 (2): 69.

Whitaker, S. 2008. Deep freeze. Baking & Snack 30 (1): 107.

Recommended reading

Barnes, J., and Grogan, P. 2009. Alternative energy. Proc. Am. Soc. Baking 85: 142.

Berne, S. 2006. The hot seat. Baking & Snack 28 (6): 59.

Bourne, J.K. 2009. Alternative energy sources. Proc. Am. Soc. Baking 85: 82.

Eijsink, J. 2005. Hybrid ovens. Proc. Am. Soc. Baking 81: 109.

Gupta, M.K. 2004. Frying Technology and Practices, AOCS Press: Urbana, IL

Irwin, G. 2007. Practical solutions for blast freezing bakery products. Proc. Am. Soc. Baking 83: 128.

Johnson, C.C. 1968. New baking methods. Proc. Am. Soc. Bakery Engrs. 44: 75.

Knott, K.G. 1994. High turbulence ovens. Proc. Am. Soc. Bakery Engrs. 70: 133.

Knott, K.G. 1996. Ovens: new technology in mass air handling. Proc. Am. Soc. Bakery Engrs. 72: 73.

Kocer, D., Karwe, M.V., and Sumnu, S.G. 2008. Alternative baking technologies. In: In: Food Engineering Aspects of Baking Sweet Goods. S.G. Sumnu and S. Sahin, eds. CRC Press: Boca Raton, FL.

Koch, A. 1983. Oven energy efficiency. Proc. Am. Soc. Bakery Engrs. 59: 90.

Lanham, W.E. Jr. 1994. Efficient oven usage. Proc. Am. Soc. Bakery Engrs. 70: 141.

Lehmann, T.A., and Dreese, P. 1981. Stability of frozen bread dough — effects of freezing temperatures. AIB Tech. Bull. 3 (7).

Lummus, A.D. 1989. Ovens/proofing/cooling. Proc. Am. Soc. Bakery Engrs. 65: 175.

McManus, L.S. 1980. Oven efficiency and alternate fuels. Proc. Am. Soc. Bakery Engrs. 56: 172.

Moore, M. 1988. Humidity effects on baking quality and human comfort. AIB Tech. Bull. 10 (12).

Mowbray, W. 1994. Bakery ovens. In: Cookie Chemistry and Technology. K. Kulp, ed. AIB International: Manhattan, KS.

Padilla, J. 1998. Fryer systems technology: direct- and indirect-heated systems. Cereal Foods World 43 (8): 635.

Spooner, T.F. 1993. Stacking up. Baking & Snack 15 (5): 36.

Spooner, T.F. 1997. Cooking with air. Baking & Snack 19 (8): 58. WPS 17075.

Spooner, T.F. 1998. Emission control: Now and in the future. Baking & Snack 20 (6): 56.

Spooner, T.F. 2000. Omitting emissions. Baking & Snack 22 (3): 74.

Swartz, W.L. 1978. Alternate fuel systems. Proc. Am. Soc. Bakery Engrs. 54: 111.

Weidkamp, M. 2005. Optimizing baking profits through product and process temperature profiling. AIB Tech. Bull. 27 (2).

Zaleski, J.S. Jr. 1999. Improvement of oven heat use. Proc. Am. Soc. Baking 75: 69.

Zhou, W., and Therdthai, N. 2008. Heat and mass transfer during baking of sweet goods. In: In: Food Engineering Aspects of Baking Sweet Goods. S.G. Sumnu and S. Sahin, eds. CRC Press: Boca Raton, FL.

CHAPTER 11

Finishing and Packaging

Updated by Jim Kline

Jim Kline
The Ensol Group LLC
P.O. Box 136, Erwinna, PA 19820
Phone (610) 294-3072; e-mail jkline@theensolgroup.com

INTRODUCTION

We eat with our eyes. How many times have we heard this? However, there is a strong truth behind this. Therefore, going to market requires an appealing appearance. A flawless topping, an attractive coating, an eye-catching package — all and more will be needed to prompt the buying impulse. Not only must a bakery

Appearance plays an important role in the appeal of all baked foods, while automated technology holds down manpower issues and raises output capacity.

Vision systems evaluate product attributes such as count, color, size and/or shape. The inspection system can make adjustments upstream if needed. (Georgia Tech Research Institute, Baking Technology Systems)

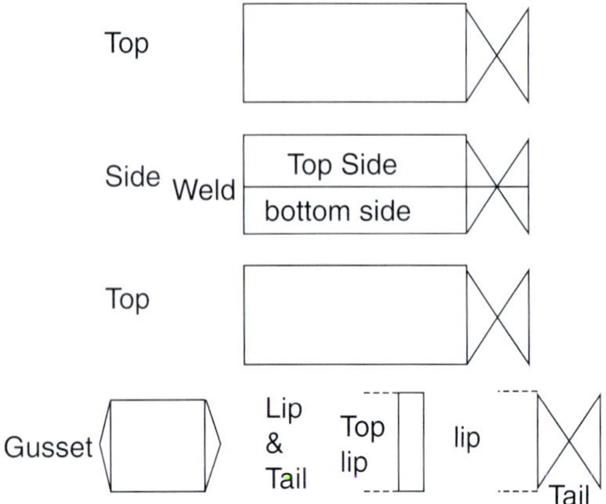

Figure 11.001. The top, sides, bottom, lip and tail of a bread bag each provide a distinct area of display for package graphics.
(Self et al. 1984)

Figure 11.002. The Nutrition Facts panel for a loaf of white bread reports the nutrients provided. The nutrients listed, the type size and font, and the design of the panel are stipulated by FDA regulations.

Nutrition Facts

Serving Size 1 Slice (28g)
Servings Per Container 20

Amount Per Serving		1 Slice	2 Slices
Calories		70	140
Calories from Fat		5	15
	% Daily Value*	1 Slice	2 Slices
Total Fat 1g, 1.5g		2%	2%
Saturated Fat 0g, 0g		0%	0%
Trans Fat 0g, 0g			
Polyunsaturated Fat 0g, 0.5g			
Monounsaturated Fat 0g, 0g			
Cholesterol 0mg, 0mg		0%	0%
Sodium 150mg, 300mg		6%	13%
Total Carbohydrate 14g, 28g	5%	9%	
Dietary Fiber 0g, Less than 1g	0%	2%	
Sugars 2g, 3g			
Protein 2g, 4g			

Vitamin A 0% 0%	• Vitamin C	0%	0%
Calcium 15% 30%	• Iron	4%	8%
Vitamin D 6% 10%	• Thiamine	8%	15%
Riboflavin 4% 8%	• Niacin	4%	10%
Folic Acid 6% 10%			

*Percent Daily Values are based on a 2,000 calorie diet. Your daily values may be higher or lower depending on your calorie needs:

		Calories:	2,000	2,500
Total Fat	Less than		65g	80g
Sat Fat	Less than		20g	25g
Cholesterol	Less than		300mg	300mg
Sodium	Less than		2,400mg	2,400mg
Total Carbohydrate			300g	375g
Dietary Fiber			25g	30g

Figure 11.003. Flexographic printing can now be done on presses offering up to 10 color fountains.
(Bryce)

package be made of a material that can run efficiently on packaging machines, but it must also be able to contain, preserve and communicate. The need to hold and protect the food are self-evident, but what about communication?

Packaging serves as a billboard, advertising its contents, and that function is determined by its graphic design. Product names, brands, images and text comprise the look of a package. Bread bags offer five distinct areas (**Figure 11.001**), each capable of relating information.

Some of the information printed on packaging is discretionary; some is mandatory. In the US, consumer food packages must carry information mandated by the Nutritional Labeling and Education Act of 1990 (NLEA) or the Dietary Supplement Health and Education Act of 1994 (DSHEA). For example, the Nutrition Facts panel (**Figure 11.002**) must be prominently displayed on back or side panels of packaging for consumer foods that travel in interstate commerce. The US Food and Drug Administration (FDA) wrote regulations that carry out NLEA and DSHEA and published them in the Code of Federal Regulation (21 CFR 100 to 199). These rules set forth the specific type fonts and sizes for some label components, while also spelling out the wording for health claims. FDA continues to publish guidance documents concerning labeling issues under NLEA, DSHEA and other laws. Canada and Mexico have similar rules, and the EU is in the final stages of codifying food labeling rules.

Graphic design determines how all these elements fit together. Bakery marketing departments can consult many resources for assistance with the graphic design of a bakery package including advertising and promotion agencies, bakery cooperatives and packaging convertors. Designs may be evaluated by focus groups and consumer intercept methods, while the packaging materials under consideration should be tested to make sure they provide the right barriers, appearance and machining characteristics. Of course, regulatory requirements regarding placement of some elements must be followed.

The flexographic process for printing bakery packaging films can use as many as 8, and recently 10, different inks (referred to as "fountains" in the printing trade) per run (**Figure 11.003**). Limits are based on the number of colors a converter's press holds. Ink choices cover the full spectrum of colors, not just the cyan-magenta-yellow-black (CMYK) protocol of 4-color process printing like that used to prepare this book.

The 4-color process printing lays down inks as dots of varying size, which the human eye and brain combine to view as a colored image. But single inks can be created by blending pigments to achieve a specific color, also called a "manufacturer spot" color. In the 1960s, Pantone (now a subsidiary of X-Rite) developed a color matching method, the Pantone Matching System (PMS) to standardize specification of spot colors, and graphic designers widely adopted the regulated color swatches not only to specify spot colors but also to use CMYK to duplicate those colors. For example, Kansas State University specifies both Pantone 266 and 268 as its signature purple color, with 877 for silver and 467 (optional) for tan, in its logos and secondary trademarks (**Figure 11.004**).

In addition to color, the inks used to print packages come in fluorescent and metallic choices and can provide textures such as glossy and flat (matte) and coverage effects including a full range from transparent to opaque.

Films themselves can be extruded to provide opaque regions and treated with atomized metals to yield a shiny metallic appearance. Printing techniques include reverse printing, which puts the ink on the inside surface of the film to protect it against scuffing during distribution. Because such cases may involve food contact, food-grade inks must be used, or another layer of film can be laminated onto the surface of printed film exposed to food.

Self et al. (1984) and Kale (1987) detailed the graphic design, production and printing of bread bags, advising on proper sizing and in-plant handling of this style of packaging.

Figure 11.004. Use of standardized colors such as those described by the Pantone Matching System (PMS) assure correct reproduction at every printing. (Kansas State University)

11.A. Enrobing, Topping and Finishing Equipment

Top treatment of baked foods can take place at many different stages of the process. Scoring, which slashes the top crust of hearth and artisan products, is best done between the proofer and the oven. Water-splitting and butter toppings should also be applied at this stage, and so, too, is the dispensing of salt, sesame seeds or streusel toppings, which go through the oven to bake along with the dough piece. Other toppings such as cheese powders and/or flavoring slurries for snack crackers go on immediately after baking. Still other materials, in particular, chocolate and confectionery coatings, must wait for the baked item to cool fully before being applied.

11.A.1. Scoring and splitting systems

Scoring, or cutting, the surface of dough pieces not only adds attractive patterns to the finished loaf or roll but also prevents unattractive wild splits of the top crust during baking. In artisan production, the baker takes a sharp blade and slits the top of the dough piece, cutting shallowly through the surface at an angle. The depth of the cut and its length yield characteristic patterns. This manual method is far too slow for commercial wholesale manufacturing, and equipment manufacturers have devised a number of systems that split loaf tops and score crusts.

Figure 11.005. A stream of low pressure water splits the top of the proofed product, and next a stream of melted butter is applied into the split. (Burford Corp.)

Figure 11.006. Rotary blades use a circular saw-like motion that provides clean crisp cuts like those made by hand. (The Perfect Score)

11.A.1.a. Top splitters

"Splitter" methods for treating the tops of bread loaves use narrow, high-velocity jets of water to cut through the surface of the dough piece. Installed between the proofer and the oven, the splitters (**Figure 11.005**) employ sensors to locate the leading edge of the pan strap and thus initiate the water jet. Water splitters can be set to produce multiple diagonal cuts and even wavy lines, and certain systems will produce their split patterns without pan stoppage.

A similar "splitter" technology deposits butter in controlled amounts onto the tops of bread loaves right before the dough pieces enter the oven. The system converts block butter into either a paste or liquid form for application.

11.A.1.b. Scoring systems

Automated scoring systems offer a variety of methods to make the desired slits in a consistent manner, including conveyors that turn to facilitate angled cuts. Various machines can create multiple scoring patterns such as bi-directional, cross-hatch, diamond, straight, angular and angular-entry. Rotary blades (**Figure 11.006**) manage a clean, crisp cut through tough dough skins as well as low-absorption doughs (Burrington 2004). Another approach uses blades cocked at an angle attached to a scoring head that drops to pan level and slits the surface. Blades enter the dough angularly to create a unique look after baking (Bradley 2005). Digitally controlled robots and water-jet systems have also been used for scoring.

11.A.2. Particulate applicators

Whether salt, sesame seed or streusel — particulate materials make interesting toppings for baked foods. Multi-grain mixtures, especially those that add nutritive value such as flaxseed and oats, are becoming increasingly popular. When applied before the oven, such toppings require dispensing equipment that creates an even coating without waste. The baker can choose among topping systems for dispensing dry materials (chopped nuts, candy pieces, sugars, flour, salts, decorettes, jimmies, nonpareils or similar free-flowing dry substances) and moist materials (shredded cheeses, wet onions, streusels, frozen vegetables and other slightly wet textured toppings). Systems have also been specialized for dispensing grated and shredded parmesan and romano cheeses (Clyma 2008). Removable hoppers enable quick changeover on lines that run multiple products.

Topical application of seasonings involves a number of depositing methods: rotary, screen, vein and belt.

11.A.2.a. Rotary systems

Most common is the rotating shaft or mandrel (**Figure 11.007**), where shaft speeds control the volume of seasoning being put down. The surfaces of these mandrels are configured with slots, flutes, ovals and other textures to pull particulates and seeds out of the hopper and drop them onto dough pieces. Flutes can be staggered to more evenly spread the toppings, while smooth sections effectively block deposition and can be placed to prevent material from dropping on pan surfaces instead of products. The operator can easily change topping distribution by pulling out one mandrel and replacing it with another. Electronic chips can be embedded in the mandrel shaft. When the operator inserts such a mandrel into the machine, the system reads the chip and automatically adjusts settings according to the parameters set for the product.

11.A.2.b. Screen and template systems

Screen systems depend on perforated or mesh metal screens and templates that duplicate the shape of the products to be topped. When the pan reaches the dispenser, it is stopped, and the hopper releases seeds or other materials into the screen. The template restricts seed movement so it does not drop on the pan rather than the product. The operator changes out the template when schedules call for a different pan or product style.

Seasonings and toppings such as cinnamon sugar, powdered sugar and corn meal, as well as flour can be handled by duster systems that lay down accurate patterns. The dispenser (**Figure 11.008**) uses a screen and template, swept by a brush, to manage distribution of toppings. Indexing mechanisms on these machines that advance pans row by row allow depositing of these materials only where the product is.

11.A.2.c. Vein and belt systems

Vein is another metering method (**Figure 11.009**), where the size and depth of the veins (open channels that carry the topping to the dispensing point) control the amount of topping being dispensed.

Belt systems address the problem of depositing sticky, moist and hard-to-flow materials at consistent rates that would otherwise have to be applied by hand. For example, compression rolls (**Figure 11.010**) manage the depositing of seed and vegetable pieces. Toasted onion bits present another application best suited to belt systems (Gorton 2009).

Figure 11.007. A mandrel inside the dispensing tube controls the pattern in which the system releases baby oats or other topping ingredients.
(Burford Corp.)

Figure 11.008. The brush inside this duster helps release fine powders such as flour or cinnamon sugar onto products passing below.
(Burford Corp.)

Figure 11.009. This salter uses veins, or channels, to control the rate at which it releases topping salts.
(Axis Automation Group)

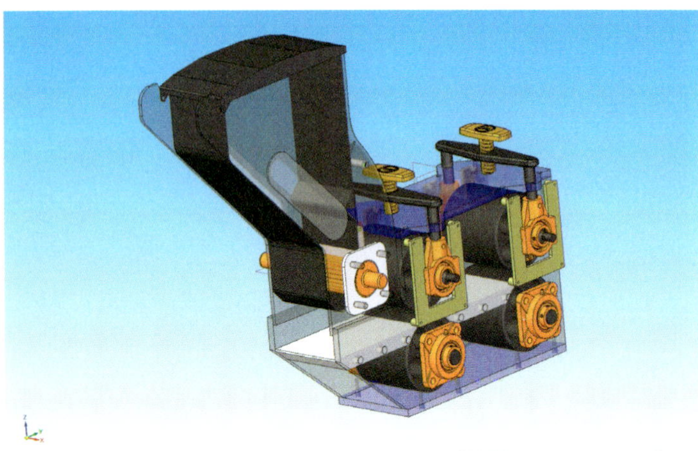

Figure 11.010. To deposit vegetable and seed toppings, this design combines belt feeding with compression rolls. (R&D Machine)

11.A.2.d. Seeders and strewers

Electronically controlled seeders (**Figure 11.011**) apply everything from sesame and poppy seeds to wheat bran to baby oats or other grains on bread, buns and sweet goods. Used in conjunction with a programmable logic controller (PLC) or other industrial computer system that sequences production operations, these seeders automatically switch setups when variety changes occur. Presets manage different types and amounts of toppings and different sizes and amounts of pans. On such modern seeders, a sensor picks up the leading edge of the pan or row, and programming releases toppings only when product is present. For proper adhesion of sesame seeds, the dough pieces must be moist so many seeders are designed with optional water misters ahead of the seed dispenser.

Particulate depositors and strewing systems often include reclaim systems to catch surplus material and return it to the dispenser's hopper. Sifters remove clumps and other extraneous material from reclaimed ingredients. Automatic refill systems (**Figure 11.012**) are also available, which help maintain a constant head pressure in the hopper, thus achieving more consistent application of toppings. Segregated or interchangeable hoppers help better control potential allergens. Another design adaptation provides a double-jacketed hopper, allowing glycol refrigerant to flow through the system to help handle temperature-sensitive materials such as frozen blueberries or chocolate chips (Whitaker 2009).

The cracked grain, bran, seed and nut toppings applied to bread and roll products are usually put on before the oven; however, Sammons (2002) described a system his bakery devised for dispensing such toppings after the breadstuffs leave the depanner. The bakery achieved its goal to eliminate the pan damage, equipment clogging and cleaning expense associated with pre-oven topping methods, while assuring proper adhesion of the sprayed toppings to the finished goods.

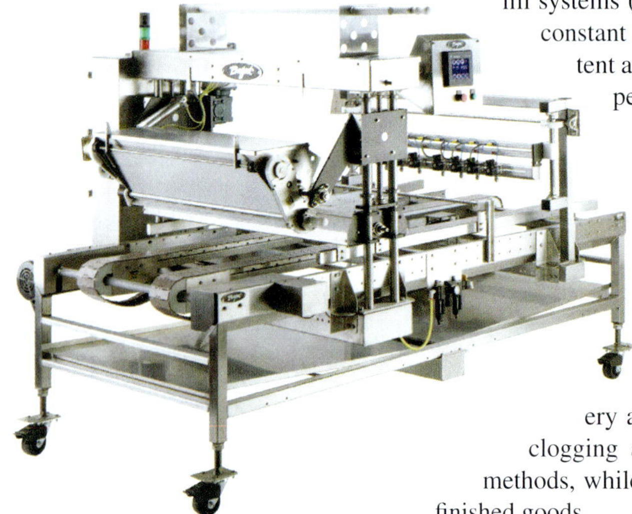

Figure 11.011. This seeder precisely applies a variety of toppings, minimizing waste and helping bakers achieve significant seed and topping savings. (Burford Corp.)

11.A.3. Sprayers and tumblers

Spraying systems in bakery use consist of two types of systems: those that apply release oils to pans (discussed in Chapter 9, Part D) and those that dispense flavorings, colorings, oils and seasonings onto crackers, chips or croutons after baking. Applications vary from protective coatings for frozen pizza crusts (**Figure 11.013**) to flavored slurries for snack crackers. Post-baking spray systems are also used to coat egg wash onto buns, croissants and sweet goods to enhance their appearance.

11.A.3.a. Nozzles and disks

Most spraying systems employ nozzles to dispense liquids, but several designs employ spinning disks (**Figure 11.014**), which permit application of particulated slurries without risk of clogged nozzles. As oils or slurries fall onto a rapidly spinning disk, they are thrown outward and dispersed in fine droplets, and dry powders are quickly distributed, as illustrated by **Figure 11.015**. Hoods and baffles direct and contain materials sprayed from one or more disks to optimize application. Output ranges from a fine mist to a heavy soaking. Custom disk designs — smooth, fluted, flat, conical — provide complete coverage, specific flow patterns. For complete coverage, spinning disks can be set below the product conveyor as well as above it. This method is commonly used for applying a light coating of oil to snack crackers. It is also responsible for placing speckles of colored sugar solutions onto confections.

Spinning disks are well suited to applications that must cover the full width of the band with a high degree of uniformity across the whole band. Known for their ability to handle slurries, these systems can also distribute dry and particulate materials, including salt.

11.A.3.b. Electrostatic methods

Electrostatic sprayers use their nozzles as both metering devices and electrodes. This method establishes a high-voltage DC charge at the nozzle. The nozzles have no moving parts and are made of non-conductive plastic materials. They encapsulate a stainless steel shim that serves as both a metering device and an electrode. As materials pass over the electrode, they receive a charge. As the fluid is propelled from the nozzle, the streams break into equally charged and sized droplets. Like repels like, thus widening the scattering pattern. Liquids dispensed through electrostatic systems tend to divide into smaller droplets than they do when sprayed out of ordinary nozzles. Electrostatically, the droplets seek out and adhere to the surface of the product being sprayed, creating a uniform and controllable coating.

Electrostatic principles have also been applied to salter systems for soda (saltine) and snack crackers. These dispensers induce a negative static charge on the surface of the salt flakes, causing them to mutually repel each other. They are drawn to the dough surface where the charge is neutralized.

11.A.3.c. Tumbling drums

Another technology for coating products involves a rotating drum. Typically used for potato, corn or tortilla chips, slowly rotating drums gently tumble the product while seasonings, oils and other toppings are dispensed via a spray bar or tube (**Figure 11.016**). Some use electrostatic means to control the movement of toppings through the bar; others employ augers and recirculating pump.

Application of doughnut sugar to doughnuts — and toppings to snacks — generally takes place within revolving drums where the finished products tumble together with their toppings to assure coverage on all exterior surfaces.

The powder applicator uses a screw auger and rotary squirrel cage to dispense powder out the length of a tube and spread the product in air before applying to base product. Another method, the scarf feeder uses a small vibratory conveyor to apply an even curtain of seasoning on the product. The electrostatic applicator puts an electric charge on the seasoning, which then attaches to product as it is attracted to a metal drum. The liquid applicator uses a pump and nozzle system to spray oil onto product.

Inside tumbler or coating reel, a spray system delivers the liquid or dry flavorings. Mounted at either end of the coating drum, this tube sits slightly above the drum's

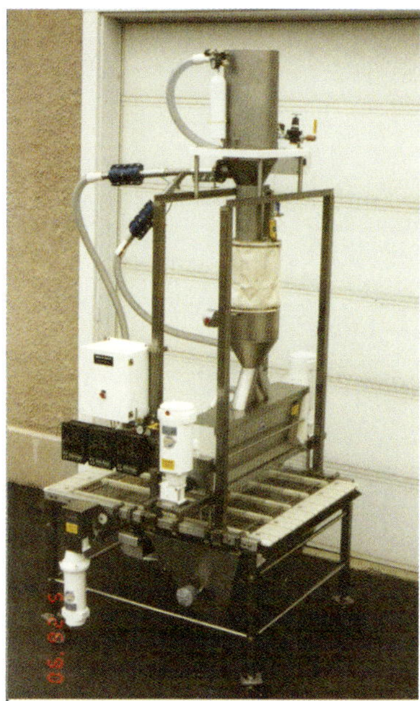

Figure 11.012. A vacuum fill system is mounted on top of this dry material dispenser, which features a mesh conveyor and a reclaim hopper. (Christy Machine Corp.)

Figure 11.013. Protective coatings applied to prepared pizza crusts provide an efficient way to minimize dehydration during freezing and absorption of moisture during later application of sauce and other toppings. (Spraying Systems Co.)

Figure 11.014. This spin disk applicator is fully enclosed to minimize airborne particles and includes four disks above the belt and four below for complete product coverage.
(The Peerless Group)

Figure 11.015. A spinning disk disperses fine powders across the full width of the band below.
(Arcall)

Figure 11.016. A revolving drum gently tumbles tortilla chips through a shower of seasonings, which adhere to the chips' surface.
(Heat and Control)

long axis and remains stationary.

The size of the drum is significant, according to Levine (2007). His analysis indicated that as the drum gets bigger, the energy per unit mass of the material in the drum increases in proportion to the drum diameter. As a consequence, more product damage occurs but the coating effect is more uniform and output capacity larger.

Designed for low- and no-fat products, a 2-stage coating method allows processors to apply tack agents based on starches or food gums as well as conventional spray oils. The method requires use of a coating drum, a tack agent applicator and a dry ingredient dispenser. The system's flighted coating drum is installed at a slight angle, usually between 4 and 7° from horizontal. As the product progresses through the drum, it is slowly flipped over. The tack agent is applied in the first half of the drum, while the dry toppings are dispensed in the second half via a specially designed screw feeder. The physics of this method favor optimum adhesion when the tack agent — usually oil — covers the surface evenly. Small droplets of tack agent offer more total surface area than the same amount of agent deposited in large drops.

For lightweight goods, such as snack foods, the function of the drum is to present all sides of the item to the sprayed oils and flavors. Flights within the drum should lift and gently tumble the goods, so that the spray contacts the food in midair.

Coating heavier foods, such as applying sugar to doughnuts, requires an alternate approach. A perforated cylinder rotates within a solid-surface outer cylinder (**Figure 11.017**). Toppings — powdered sugar (actually powdered dextrose), cinnamon sugar, granulated sugar or crunch coating — are fed into the perforated cylinder along with doughnuts. The inclined drums tumble doughnuts, exposing all surfaces to the toppings, and then drop the covered doughnuts onto the packaging conveyor. Loose sugar falls through the inner drum's perforations to be screened before recycling back into the tumbler.

Breakfast cereals — and more recently snack foods — get their sugar topping by traveling through a long, enclosed trough. The system uses flexible nylon finger-like brushes set in two inverted-pitch spirals that rotate in opposite directions. The spiral brushes create small pockets that carry snacks or cereals through a turbulent storm of seasonings. The action of the soft fibers is gentle but thorough. Application is well-controlled, allowing different materials to be applied over the length of the trough. (This system works well for breakfast cereals because enrichment or fortification is applied first, and then a coating of sugar or other topping seals in and protects the nutrients from loss.)

11.A.3.d. Fire protection

All too many bakers and snack makers know the devastation produced by a fire in an oil sprayer. Even contained to a single location, fire really messes up a line. All a fire hose does is spread the hot flaming fat to other areas of the plant. Externally applied conventional fire-extinguisher foams and carbon dioxide systems cannot be easily contained and can pose risks to nearby staff.

Recently, a spraying systems manufacturer debuted a new way to put out oil fires with water (Gorton 2002a). The fire-suppression system links a series of nozzles to two 20-l (20-qt) pressurized canisters, one filled with water and the other nitrogen. The system is housed within the oiler's hood. When set off, it instantly creates a thick, cold fog, which cuts off the fire's air supply and removes latent heat that would otherwise accelerate combustion. It extinguishes a fire in a typical cracker oiler in five minutes or less. This fire-suppression system employs the same technology used in ships' engine rooms.

11.A.4. Cake decorating systems

Custom-decorating a cake takes time, skill and patience, which specialty bakers readily offer. Many cakes, however, do not require this level of artistry; they can be decorated via assembly line methods. Icing puddlers (depositors) and pump-augmented pastry bags can be found assisting manual cake decorating lines methods. But to supply cakes in high quantities, automation has been adopted, bringing speeds of 20 to 24 cakes per minute to these operations (**Figure 11.018**).

Figure 11.017. Sugar sifts through a perforated, rotating inner drum to coat doughnuts in a gentle turning, tumbling motion to the discharge conveyor. (Moline Machinery LLC)

11.A.4.a. Automated lines

In such systems, the decorator's pastry bag has been replaced with depositors, spreaders and even robotic formers, sequenced by computer (**Figure 11.019**). Servo-driven depositors spread icing on rectangular cakes in a manner equal to that of manual hand dressing. Until recently, sides and tops of round cakes had to be iced separately, but at least one manufacturer developed a strip depositing system with a right-angled head that simultaneously extrudes icing on the top and sides of round cakes (**Figure 11.020**). Other mechanisms and auxiliary equipment can be provided to automatically split cake layers, deposit center fillings and replace the top layer back onto the cake.

These systems will also automatically apply melted chocolate, ganache or caramel drizzles in a range of patterns from spirals and swirls and are fully capable of finishing a base iced cake with rosettes, shell borders, string icing and other specialty toppings (Whitaker 2007a).

Cupcake icing machines feature icing heads that top these products with decorative swirls in loading patterns such as 4-by-3 or 5-by-3 to accommodate packaging. Because the icing heads are interchangeable, each row can ice in a different color and/or swirl style. Separate pumps handle the different colors of icing. The machines can decorate 480 cupcakes per minute.

Crumbers (**Figure 11.021**) have been devised that spray cake crumbs at an iced cake as it rotates on a turntable. The equipment supplies enough velocity to the crumbs that they stick on the cake and can handle particulates ranging from very fine cake crumbs to chocolate chips, sliced almonds and even chocolate flakes. All over-spill is captured in a containment bin and automatically recycled back to the crumber's hopper.

11.A.4.b. Printing techniques

There is even a system that can "print" images onto the tops of cakes (**Figure 11.022**). It uses perforated rotary screens to deposit any granular ingre-

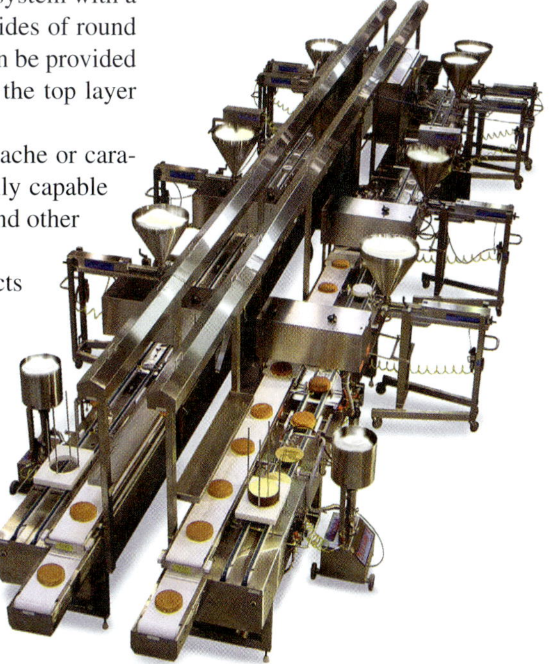

Figure 11.018. Large automated lines can turn out 20 to 24 decorated cakes per minute, taking them from unsliced layers to final package. (Unifiller Systems)

Figure 11.019. Robotic icing systems, sequenced by computer, turn out results indistinguishable from hand-decorated methods.
(Unifiller Systems)

Figure 11.020. A right-angled head simultaneously deposits icing on a cake's top and sides.
(Unifiller Systems)

Figure 11.021. This crumb applicator can mechanically spray a wide range of particulates at high velocity onto the sides of a cake as it spins.
(Unifiller)

dient from seeds to flakes to sugar. Vacuum pressure creates temporary adhesion of the particles to the outside of the screen and releases them onto the product passing below. Another system employs high-speed, industrial ink-jet imaging to apply food-grade inks onto food products, creating high-resolution images that range in style from 4-color process to spot and monochrome.

The finished cakes come off assembly lines as finished products, ready for the customer. Dome- or clam-shell packaging protects the cakes as they go through the freezer.

Changeover from one size or shape of cake to the next, if the icing is similar, requires around 10 minutes. A complete changeover, from chocolate to white icing, for example, would take 30 minutes, although some bigger bakeries invest in back-up depositors to cut changeover time to 5 to 10 minutes (Bradley 2004).

Automated cake decorating lines still require labor but at a greatly reduced level. A certain amount of manual touchup is generally required. Still, automated lines reduce injuries to decorators such as carpal tunnel syndrome and allow better control of icing weights, thus reducing giveaway.

11.A.5. Chocolate and coating equipment

Small cakes, doughnuts, swiss rolls, petit fours, cookies, sugar wafer, pretzels — a broad range of baked foods take their appeal from the chocolate or other fat-based coating applied to the outside of the product. Such coatings also provide an edible form of packaging with good moisture barriers that prevent the product from drying out. But they must be properly handled and tempered, or else the fat (cocoa butter or other fats) will "bloom" on the surface as white, greasy deposits. If finished products are stored at high humidity, sugar blooms may form as well.

11.A.5.a. Tempering systems

Bars of fat-based coating (chocolate, pastel, confectionery) must first be melted, then cooled to a stable crystalline form before being supplied to the enrober at a rate that keeps the system's supply tank at an even level. The coating processor may also supplied these materials in liquid form, which the bakery will store in a hot-water-jacketed tank under slow-moving agitation, sufficient to keep all materials at a uniform temperature but not so fast that air gets whipped into the coating.

Dark sweet and milk chocolates must first undergo the critical process of tempering, which involves melting at 49°C (120°F) for the dark sweet chocolate and 43°C (110°F) for the milk chocolate. The dark chocolate is then tempered by first cooling to 31°C (88°F) under constant agitation (28°C, or 83°F, in the case of milk chocolate), and rewarming to 33°C (91°F) for the enrobing process (31°C, or 88°F, for milk chocolate).

Tempering can be accomplished by several methods (Hofberger 1999). Most commonly in industrial production, the chunk or drip feed systems are employed. In the chunk method, the coating is heated to 43 to 46°C (110 to 115°F), and chunks of tempered chocolate are added. These chunks "seed" the formation of the proper crystalline structure, the stable beta (β) phase. The mass is stirred slowly until its temperature comes down to 30°C (86°F) for milk chocolate or 31°C (88°F) for dark chocolate. Any unmelted pieces of chocolate are removed. In the drip method, a small steady flow of untempered chocolate at 32 to 36°C (90 to 96°F), equaling the rate of consumption by the enrobing system, is added to the tempered chocolate, which seeds the incoming coating. Approximately 2 lb of tempered chocolate should be maintained for every 1 lb used in production.

Automated tempering systems (**Figure 11.023**) consist of tempering kettles, plate heat exchangers, screw-type and bowl-type temperers. Inline temper meters (**Figure 11.024**) automatically monitor the conditions of coatings.

With confectionery, or pastel, coatings, the tempering procedure is quite similar, except that somewhat higher temperatures are generally required. Thus, a coating containing fats with a melting point of 44°C (112°F) or higher must be gradually heated to 54°C (130°F). The temperature is then reduced slowly and under constant agitation until the coating begins to thicken. At this point, the temperature is held constant for some 15 minutes and is then raised to within 1.8 C° (1 F°) of the melting point of the hard butter.

The operator can test the temper of chocolate manually with the following procedure, outlined by Hofberger (1999). (a) Dip a metal spatula or knife blade into the chocolate, leaving a thin film on the spatula. (b) Place the spatula in a cool room (18 to 21°C, or 65 to 70°F). (c) Observe the time required for the chocolate to harden to the touch and record this set-up timing. Set-up timings can be interpreted as follows: < 2 minutes, over-tempered, may have less than optimal gloss; 4 to 6 minutes, good temper, good gloss; 7 to 9 minutes, under-tempered, may still have a soft texture, good gloss, may bloom in 1 to 2 months; > 10 minutes, little or no temper, poor gloss, presence of bloom.

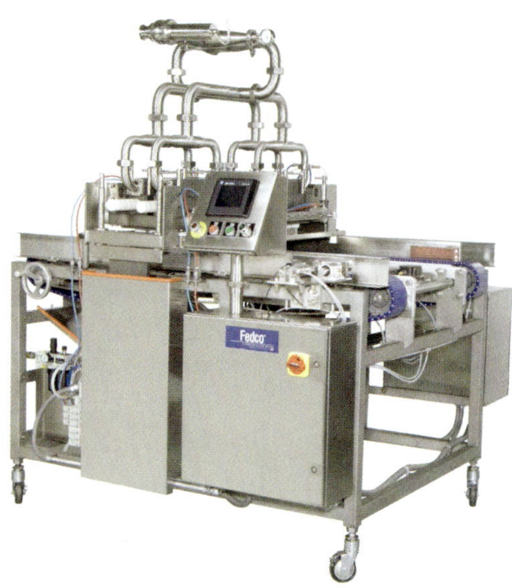

Figure 11.022. This decorating unit places granules onto products in detailed patterns that look as if they have been printed.
(The Peerless Group)

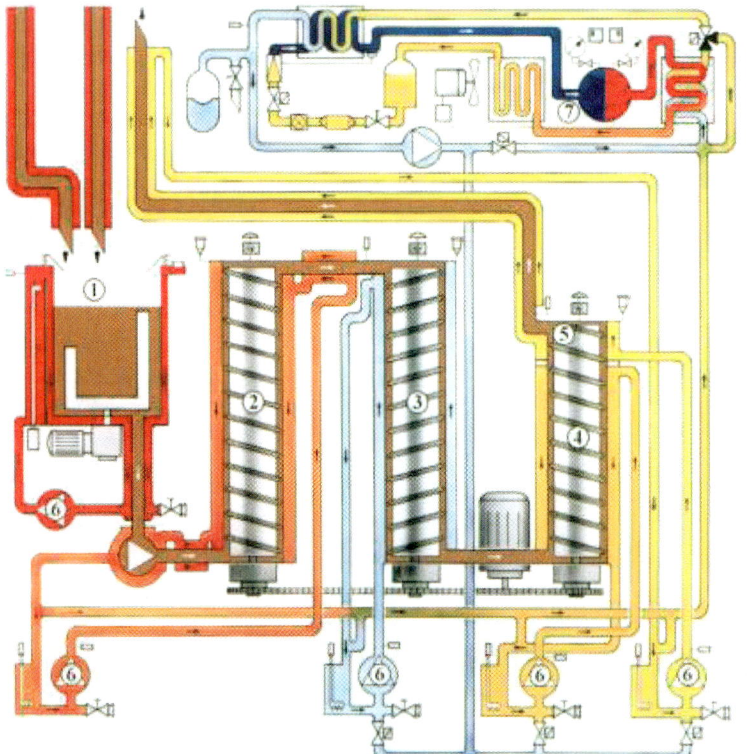

Figure 11.023. This schematic drawing shows how chocolate moves through a tempering system from the built-in buffer tank (1), into the de-crystallizing zone (2), to the cooling zone (3), into the pre-heating zone (4) and to the holding zone (5). Five separate closed water circuits (6), each separately controlled and managed by a heat exchanger (7), regulate temperature throughout the system.
(Hosokawa Kreuter)

Figure 11.024. An inline meter monitors the temper of chocolate by automatically extracting a sample from the production line, testing it and returning it to the line. (Tricor Systems)

Figure 11.025. Tops and bottoms of baked items are covered with chocolate or compound coatings using waterflow and bottoming techniques. (Hosokawa Bepex)

11.A.5.b. Enrobing methods

The products to be enrobed in chocolate should be at a temperature of 21 to 24°C (70 to 75°F), and the ambient temperature should be maintained at 27 to 32°C (80 to 90°F). Cooling tunnel temperatures for conventional confectionery coatings are some 3 C° (5 F°) higher throughout than for chocolate coverings. The packaging and storage temperatures are the same as those for chocolate-covered products (McCloskey et al. 1966).

In the enrobing process, as explained by Wing (1975), the baked items transfer onto a wire-mesh belt to travel through the enrobing machine (**Figure 11.025**). This mesh belt carries them through a waterfall-like curtain of liquid coating, which covers the items' tops and sides. A roller under the belt coats the bottom side. A tank holding a supply of coating is located under the belt, and a pump circulates the coating to a flow pan, which forms the curtain. (If only the bottoms are to be coated, then the waterfall curtain is halted, and wire-mesh conveyor floats products along the surface of the coating tank.) An air blower removes the excess coating, which falls down through the mesh and into the supply tank.

The air blast helps to intensify the gloss on the coating and may leave slight ripples, which reflect light to give it more shine. A vibrator shakes a section of the mesh conveyor belt and smooths out some of the ripples. Both blower and shaker are adjustable, thus allowing control over the amount of coating remaining on the baked foods. All items pass over a detailer rod that controls the amount of coating remaining on the bottom of the product. The rod also removes strings and tails of coating.

As the coating cools, its proper crystal structure is ensured by the cooling tunnel, as explained in Chapter 10, Part E. The cooling tunnel, with countercurrent air movement, generally has several temperature and air-velocity zones to ensure proper setting of the coating. The air enters the cooling tunnel at the discharge end at a temperature of 7°C (45°F) and, by the time it exits at the feed end of the tunnel, it will have warmed to 16 to 18°C (60 to 65°F), and its movement at this point will be relatively slow. In the zone where a visible film begins to form on the coating, air movement is more rapid and the air temperature is lower. Toward the discharge end of the tunnel, the temperature is at the initial 7°C (45°F), and the air velocity is at its maximum to produce complete setting of the coating. The coated products should be packed and stored at a temperature of 18 to 21°C (65 to 70°F).

11.A.6. Glazing equipment

Many baked foods — sweet goods, danish, doughnuts and cookies among them — require specialized equipment that reproduces hand-application methods in automated fashion. For example, a retail baker may hand-dip doughnuts into thick icings or let icing drip off his fingers to drizzle thin strings onto cookies or pastries. Bakery engineers have developed waterfall icers, roll (or "print") icers and stringer systems to replace such hand-decorating methods.

Waterfall icers consist of a supply trough and a manifold mounted over a wire-rod conveyor above a collection basin. During operation, icing or glaze is pumped continually from the trough into the manifold's slit openings, which creates a constant waterfall that covers the top surface of the products carried through it by the conveyor. If the product is to be iced on its bottom as well, then the conveyor is set to run right at or slightly below the surface of the glaze collected in the catch basin. A pump mounted below the heat-jacketed collection basin recirculates the icing to the supply trough.

Roll icers are configured with a supply trough and a medium-diameter roll positioned over a conveyor. The trough pumps icing or glaze onto the roll, which transfers the icing by contact onto the products passing under it. Such systems are also called roller or print icers. Any excess icing is collected below the conveyor to be returned to the supply trough.

String icers (**Figure 11.026**) supply the icing or glaze to a series of nozzles or a manifold with a row of small perforations along its bottom. Products to be iced are carried on a wire-mesh conveyor travelling under the nozzles or manifold. An oscillating mechanism attached causes the depositing mechanism to move or swing back and forth, thus depositing strings of icing in a way that mimics hand stroking. Excess icing is collected below the conveyor for re-use or is scraped off at a transfer point.

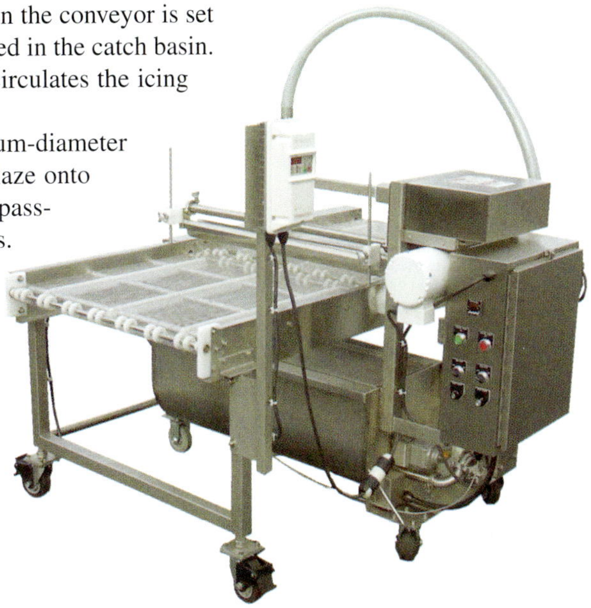

Even the squiggle of white icing on top of chocolate-frosted snack cakes is applied automatically by a specialized machine (**Figure 11.027**). Controlled by specific gearbox configurations, stringer patterns are not limited to single loop designs but also encompass cross-hatch patterns. Excess material is scraped off the belt at a transfer point.

A typical system for finishing snack cakes is shown in **Figure 11.028**. Traveling right to left, snack cakes injected with filling while still in the pan are depanned and turned upside down. Reaching the icing conveyor, they flip over and pass under a curtain of top icing. The cakes transfer to the decorating conveyor, while excess icing is scraped off the belt into a heated hopper for reuse. A squiggle icer applies the top decoration, and cakes proceed to a cooling tunnel.

Glazing equipment designed specifically for doughnuts is described in Chapter 12, Part F.

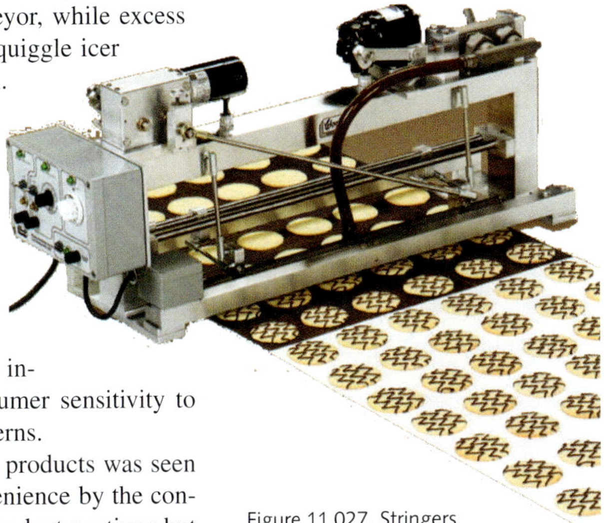

Figure 11.026. An adjustable oscillating head and variable-speed conveyor, both computer controlled, generate a variety of string icing patterns that mimic hand application of icing. (Hinds-Bock)

11.B. Slicing and Cutting Equipment

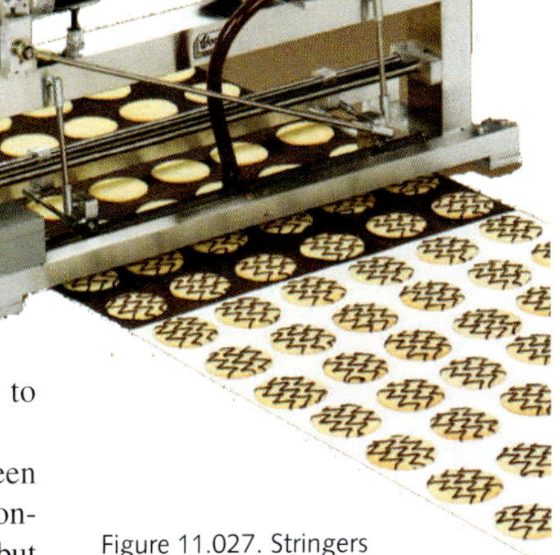

Figure 11.027. Stringers apply single-loop, zig-zag, cross-hatch and even random designs, depending on the gearbox selected. (Woody Associates)

The importance paid to slicing and cutting equipment has increased significantly as a result of changing technology, consumer sensitivity to portion control and their diet, and the impact of regulatory concerns.

At one time, slicing of bread and proportioning other bakery products was seen as a point of marketing differentiation by bakers and as a convenience by the consumer. Slicing not only provided the consumer with uniform product portions but also relieved them of the difficult task of having to slice very soft bread with cutting utensils that were often inadequate for that purpose. While these historical views hold true, today the emphasis is on portion control as it relates to an increasingly

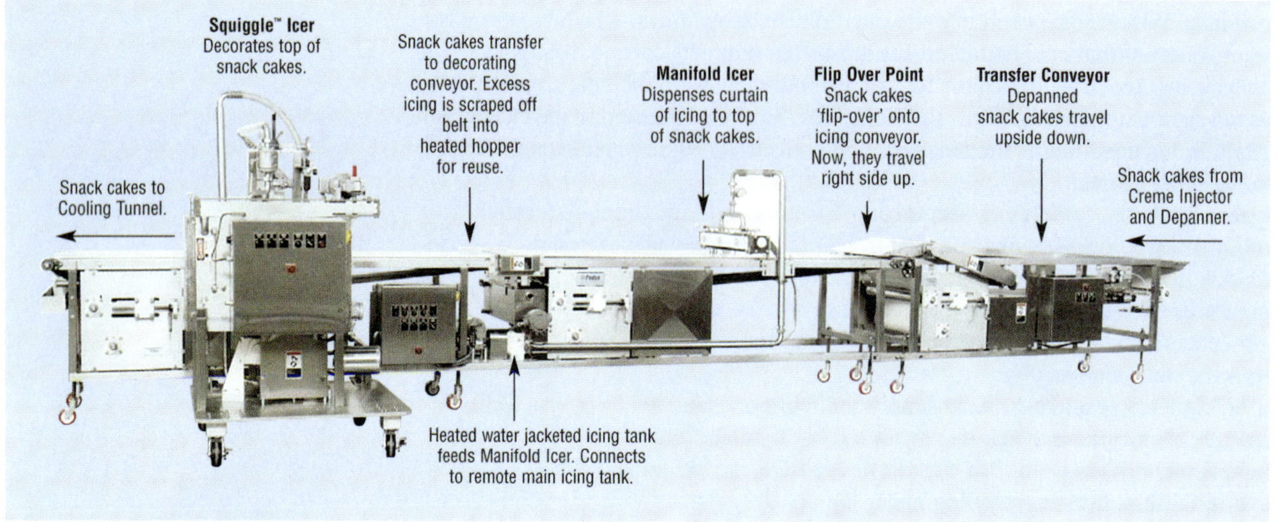

Figure 11.028. With snack cakes traveling from right to left, a typical decorating line combines a top icer (center) and a string icer (left). (The Peerless Group, Fedco)

aware and demanding consumer as well as meeting government-mandated product labeling requirements.

The breadth of slicing and cutting equipment has increased significantly in recent years. Whereas such equipment was used primarily to slice bread and rolls, new entries in this category allow portioning of virtually every bread and cake variety commercially produced today. Automated equipment now proportions pies, cakes, danish, artisan breads and baguettes, and specialty equipment now produces fork-split English muffins, easy opening pita bread pockets, crustless bread and perfectly cubed croutons.

The usual equipment for slicing baked products continues to be reciprocating blade slicers, continuous band slicers and disk or circular blade slicers. Reciprocating slicers are principally used for slicing variety breads containing inclusions as well as iced products, where the items tend to gum or dull the blades. As a result of their flexible design — from single loaf manual feeders to fully automated inline units slicing 55 loaves per minute — reciprocating slicers can be found in operations ranging from small retail shops to large commercial bakeries. Band slicers are principally used by intermediate to large wholesale bakeries and are nearly universally used to slice soft and wide pan breads. Disk and circular blade slicers are principally used to slice buns, rolls, bagels, English muffins and other similar products. A variation of the disk slicer produces the New England style hot dog bun where the circular blades are mounted vertically for a top cut.

Bread slicing speeds have steadily increased. In the 1920s, the machines could handle between 20 and 25 loaves per minute, but that rate has increased to 75 loaves per minute today, with some systems now capable of 90 to 120 loaves per minute. Buns slicing is even faster, and as one packaging equipment manufacturer noted, the speed at which buns can be sliced exceeds the capabilities of speed in packaging (Cornell 1998).

Bastasch (1989) speculated on the future of slicing, describing laser and water-jet technologies. He noted, however, that improved band slicing provided the most attractive approach to production speeds of 100 loaves per minute. Waterjet cutting was also described by Wightman (1989).

11.B.1. Reciprocating slicers

In the reciprocating slicer, straight blades are mounted in frame assemblies constructed to yield the desired slice thickness. When one wants to change slice thickness, it is a simple matter to remove the frame assembly and replace it with one designed for the desired slice thickness. This simple interchangeability helps the reciprocating slicer accommodate applications where gumming or dulling requires frequent changing of the blades. Adjustable scissors-frame blade assemblies are also available from various suppliers and allow on-the-fly slice width adjustments as needed. Common applications for reciprocating slicers include raisin bread, hard crusted breads and rolls (French breads, baguettes, etc.), whole-grain breads containing seeds and nuts, and iced breads and cakes.

The reciprocating slicer (**Figure 11.029**) is designed so that adjacent blades move in opposite directions with a smooth saw-cut motion at high speed. The slicer blades are held in a frame assembly comprised of 2 racks. Each rack, containing half of the blades in a frame assembly, is able to move independent of the other, and the blades of the racks are alternately spaced, thus enabling the described blade movement. The saw-cut, a reciprocating motion, is imparted to the frames by an electric motor through gearing, a crankshaft and levers. Proper tension is maintained on the knife blades by springs that can be individually adjusted. Slicing is performed by gently pushing the loaf through the reciprocating blades. The frames are typically mounted either vertically, in which case the bread conveyor feeding the cutting zone is slanted at a downward angle, or the frames may be tilted toward the feed side, in which case the conveyor is then on a level plane. The purpose of creating a less than perpendicular angle between the conveyor and the slicer blades is to assure that the top crust of the loaf contacts the cutting blades first and thus prevent tearing of the bread.

To serve the needs of smaller retail bakeries, where slicing is normally done one or two loaves at a time, reciprocating slicers are available with hinged blade frames, which enables them to be lifted and allowing a loaf to be placed beneath them into a shallow cradle (**Figure 11.030**). During the slicing operation, the blade frames descend either by gravity or with manual assistance as the blades pass through the loaf to leave the sliced product on the top side, ready for bagging.

11.B.2. Continuous band slicers

Band slicers (**Figure 11.031**) are by far the most common slicer for high-volume bakeries. They use endless band blades driven at high speed by a set of revolving steel drums located at the top and bottom of the machine. The blades are given a 180° twist from one drum to the other and are crossed at the central cutting zone between the drums (**Figure 11.032**). Thus each blade makes two slices through the bread.

Finger-like guides (**Figure 11.033**) above and below the cutting zone stabilize the blades and direct their forward cutting edge at a right angle to the longitudinal center line of the loaf, which is fed sideways through them. Modern band slicers will slice a maximum of 80 loaves per minute with a minimum of crumb production and loaf deformation, and operate at band speeds in excess of 1,000 ft per minute.

Because consumer preferences for slice thickness vary with different markets,

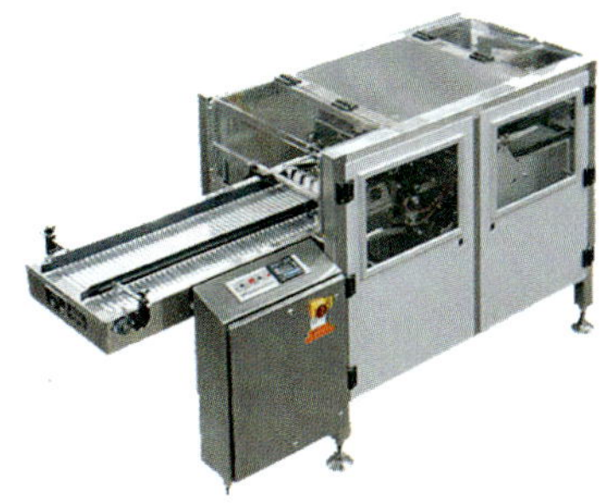

Figure 11.029. Reciprocating slicers use blades that move in opposite directions. (United Bakery Equipment)

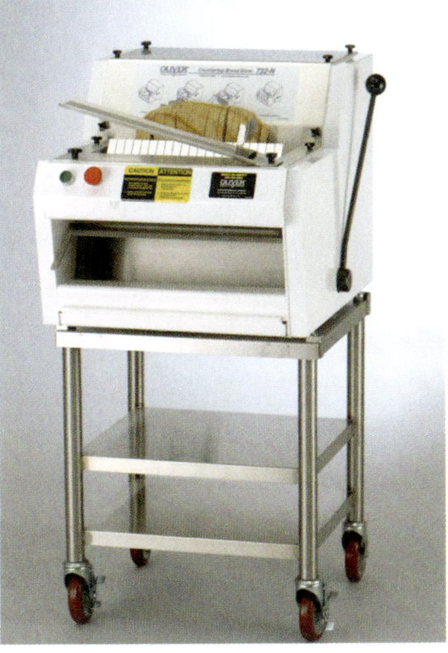

Figure 11.030. On a small reciprocating slicer, the blade frame can be raised and the loaf inserted manually. (Oliver Products)

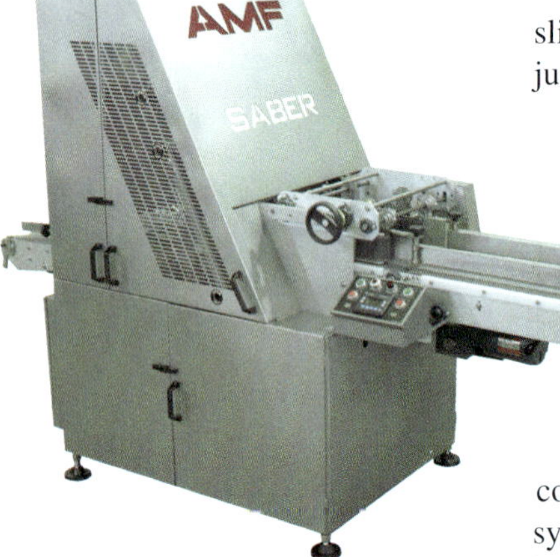

Figure 11.031. Using endless blades, band slicers are the usual choice for slicing pan breads.
(AMF Bakery Systems)

Figure 11.032. Bands twist as they travel between drums so each makes two slices through the bread.
(Treif)

slicing machines are usually provided with slice thickness controls that permit adjustments within a normal range of 0.375 to 0.625 in. (9.5 to 16 mm).

Most commercial slicing of loaf breads is done on slicing units that incorporate an array of band blades (**Figure 11.034**). The product is fed into the blades either by a paddle or through a pair of conveyor belts above and below the product. The array is adjustable for various slice thicknesses through the use of a lattice mechanism that spaces the blades (**Figure 11.035**).

This complex mechanism provides the required adjustability and consistent superior slice quality. Some slicers incorporate programmable logic control (PLC) units that can be used to set up slicer operations and thus control and sequence installed automatic honing units and spraying systems, even to systematically apply compressed air to remove crumb from the interior of the slicing unit. Some advanced units offer variable-speed control over blade speed and/or product feed conveyors so that optimum slicing is achieved on each product.

A variation of band slicing technology is used by the bulk bun slicer (**Figure 11.036**) in which individual or clustered buns are sliced fully in half, creating a top and bottom of approximately even thickness. Such systems can also slice buns horizontally in thirds for double-decker hamburgers and specialty sandwiches. In this application, a single blade band slicer is mounted horizontally. Instead of the blade path following the conventional figure-8 pattern of the bread slicer, the blade is installed between two rotating drums (one of which is driven), and the blades run parallel to one another and to the conveyor belt on which the product is conveyed.

The bulk bun slicer is housed in a frame (**Figure 11.037**) that can be raised and lowered above the product conveyor, thus enabling adjustment of the thickness of the bottom slice. The resulting product is sliced through (**Figure 11.038**).

11.B.2.a. Band slicer operation

The aim in bread slicing is to consistently obtain slices of uniform thickness, with smooth surfaces free of corrugations or torn, ragged cell structure. Such results are generally achieved with modern slicers, provided they are properly maintained, with clean drive drums and correctly aligned and honed band blades.

The installation of blades in a slicer should be done with care to ensure their proper alignment and correct tension — both required to keep frictional wear to a minimum. Whenever the blades are changed, good practice also dictates that the direction of their cutting edge in the guides be reversed to distribute the frictional

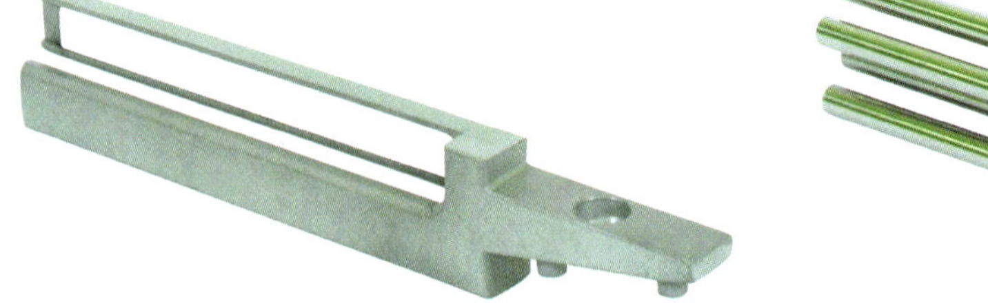

Figure 11.033. Blade guides include 4-prong and ceramic offset styles, among others.
(Hansaloy)

wear on the guides over a greater area. The guides should be inspected for wear on a scheduled basis to avoid the formation of grooves deeper than 0.008 in. (0.2 mm) because these channels will tend to shear off the cutting points of the blades (Stanford 1972). Properly aligned blade guides should have a useful life of 2 to 3 years, depending on the amount of use they receive.

Blade tension can vary with manufacturer; however, this tension is typically maintained within a range of 60 to 75 lb and should be set regularly to the manufacturers' specification using a tension gauge. Insufficient tension will cause the blades to weave in the blade guides and produce uneven slicing. They may also slip on the drive drums and cause drum wear. Excessive tension, on the other hand, increases the possibility of band breakage and intensifies guide wear because of the added pressure that is required to straighten the blades in the slicing area. Most importantly, improper tensioning represents a safety hazard to those operating and maintaining the equipment.

Proper honing not only improves the slicing performance of the blades but also prolongs their life. Modern band slicers offer honing as an optional mechanical feature for the slicer. The honing device uses a hardened material to effectively hone the blade edges on both sides. The honing tool removes burrs and increases blade sharpness, extending the useful life of the blade. The frequency of honing is determined by blade use and product characteristics.

The effectiveness of honing is determined by examining newly installed blades and then monitoring their appearance after 2 or 3 honing cycles. The blades should show even honing on both sides, be free of burrs and show no damage to the blade points. Honing cycles can be activated manually or be scheduled automatically using the slicers control panel.

A basic requirement for proper slicer performance is keeping the equipment thoroughly clean. Allowing crumbs to accumulate on the lower drive drum will eventually lead to excessive blade tension and band breakage. Similarly, if the blade guides are not kept free of crumbs, guide clearance will become restricted and result in increased friction, heating and breakage of the blades. The occasional application of a few drops of divider oil on the guides will provide lubrication and reduce harmful friction.

A persistent slicing problem is the adherence of gummy residues on the blades, which then transfers to the drums, where they build up undesirably. If such buildup remains uncorrected, its presence will interfere with the operation of the slicer. The solution to this problem has been the addition of an attachment that applies controlled amounts of steam, water and/or oil mist to the blades (Stines 1970). The device is coordinated with slicer operation by the control package. The injection tubes are directed at the blades near the top and bottom drums, and a scrapper installed against the bottom drum removes any soft product adhesions from both the blades and the drum. This system reduces the need for frequent stoppages to clean the blades.

Most band slicers now incorporate into their design a spray system for continually applying oil to the slicing bands. This oil is typically mixed with a mold-retarding agent to inhibit mold growth on the sliced product.

11.B.2.b. Slicer blades

Band slicer blades are subjected to severe stress conditions during the slicing circuit that result from (a) their rapid and continual bending and flexing, (b) the frictional abrasion from the blade guides and as they pass through the crust and crumb and (c) the frequent application of honing stones during high-speed slicing. Spooner

Figure 11.034. Blade array shows the scalloped cutting edges of the bands. (Hansaloy)

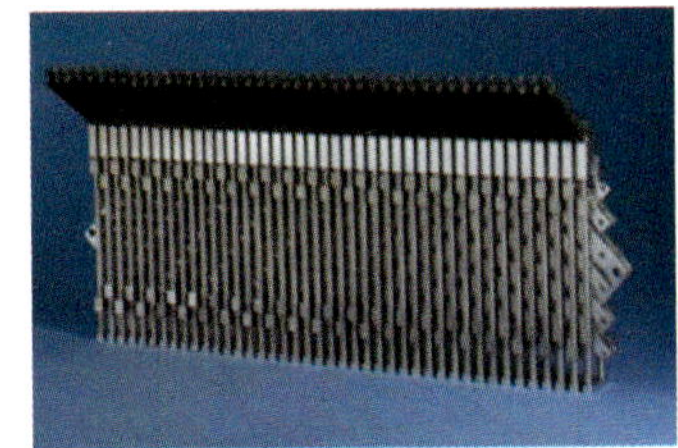

Figure 11.035. A lattice of fingers guides the positions of the slicing blades. (Hansaloy)

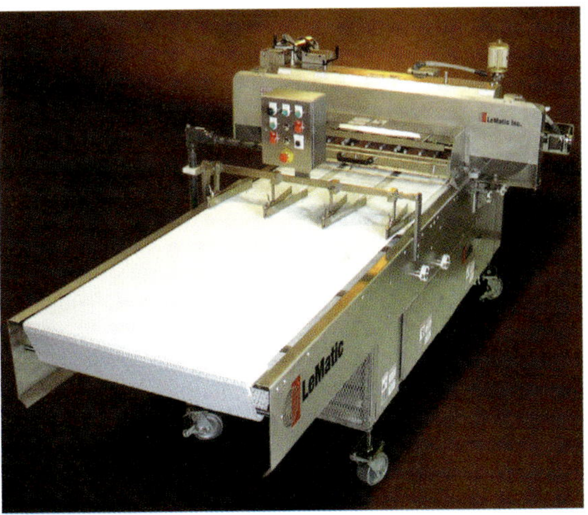

Figure 11.036. Grouped in rows, buns travel through a band slicer for bulk packaging. (LeMatic)

Figure 11.037. The adjustable frame housing a bulk bun band slicer allows the baker to control the thickness of the bottom slice. (LeMatic)

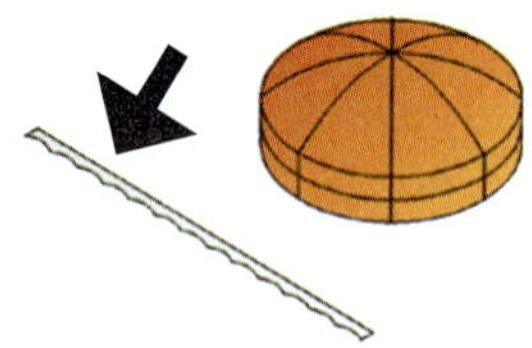

Figure 11.038. Arrow shows the direction of blade movement that creates the horizontal slice. (LeMatic)

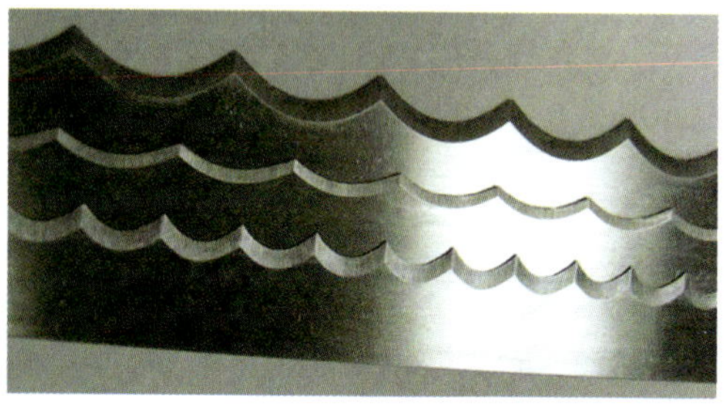

Figure 11.039. Scalloped cutting edges for slicing bands vary in pitch (distance between scallop tips) from 0.5, 0.33 and 0.25 in. (12.7, 9.5 and 6.3 mm). (Hansaloy)

(1986) calculated the total stress on the band as it is bent over the drum to exceed 54,000 lb per sq in. Hence, the useful service life of blades is affected not only by the control exercised over the operating conditions but even more significantly by the type of steel used in their manufacture.

Chrome-vanadium steel alloys yield maximum durability for blades, with chromium imparting the required hardness for the band to maintain a sharp cutting edge and vanadium endowing it with the toughness to withstand the stresses created by the repeated and extremely rapid bending and flexing that are imposed during each cycle (Fitzmaurice 1970).

Great slice quality is achieved through a balance of slicer selection, the correct blade edge, slicer setup and training of personnel. There is not a universal slicer or slicer blade on the market that is excellent for sustained slicing of all products. To achieve superior slice quality means process formulation and parameters, slicer type and blade selection all need to be considered and optimized. Some products will require a durable edge for slicing through hard crust or a very fine finish for supersoft product, some will slice well on band slicers and others on a rack slicer, and still others will require a specialty slicer.

Bakers must balance slice quality with available equipment and the tool life of the blade. A bakery with only one product can fine-tune selection to a specific blade. Those running a wide variety of products must find a slicer setup and one blade that will do well with all of their products. The first place to look when trying to determine which blade to use is product mix; knowing the product mix for a production line will enable blade selection to be narrowed and identify blades that cannot be used. Understanding which product is most difficult to slice normally determines the equipment and blade type that need to be installed in the slicing unit (Cox 2007).

Blades of various widths and cutting edge designs have developed to meet the different slicing needs presented by breads that range in firmness from the hard-crusted varieties to the extremely soft types exemplified by bread made by the continuous-mixing process. The nature of the bevel applied to the cutting edge of the blade — whether it is cross-ground, that is, perpendicular to the cutting edge, or parallel-ground in the direction of blade travel — exerts a significant effect on slicing efficiency and slice surface smoothness.

The general scallop design of the cutting edge on all blade types is basically the same (**Figure 11.039**). The size and depth of the scallop and the thickness of the cutting edge, as affected by its bevel, determine the suitability of any particular blade for slicing bread of a specific character.

A special type of blade, designated as a "throw away" blade, combines cutting tips of exceptional hardness with a measurably enhanced flexibility of the band as a whole. This dual improvement results in a more effective slicing performance and a 2- to 3-fold increase in the blade's useful life. These blades cannot be reground, however.

11.B.3. Blade recommendations

Different bread formulations will affect the way blades wear as well as the quality of the slice obtained. The chart in **Figure 11.040** reports how one manufacturer matches blade type with product variety.

11.B.3.a. Bread types

White. These soft products require a blade with a feathered profile for smooth crust penetration and minimal internal tearing. Consider using a blade with a double bevel, and for the best slicing, both bevels should have a polishing grind in the same direction as blade travels. Make sure the honing equipment is operational, installed correctly and is well maintained. Set honing frequency to approximately every 3,000 loaves. Run the machine at the top of the manufacturers recommended blade speed, normally 1,200 ft per minute.

Wheat. These products are similar to the white products in many cases and normally use the same type of blade. Coarse-grained products and those with multi-grain toppings, however, may require more frequent hone operation than white breads. If these products have a hard crust, look to a single-bevel blade.

Breakfast. Raisin, nut and other breakfast-type breads quickly damage the blades' edges. A single-bevel blade is preferable for longevity. These blades must be honed often to maintain sharpness. The slicing unit needs a spray system installed to apply water to the blades. The sugars in these products can build up on the drum and in the blade guides, causing the blades to stick and resulting in the unit seizing up. Use 4-prong blade guides to limit buildup. Some bakeries reduce blade speed so the water becomes more effective on the blade.

Potato. These loaves are typically the cottage-style wide loaves. The larger loaf size means more internal moisture and higher internal temperature. Blades must be kept lubricated and sharp. Select a double-bevel blade with polished parallel grinds to limit buildup on the blade. Use ceramic honing stones, and hone more frequently to keep the blade edge sharp.

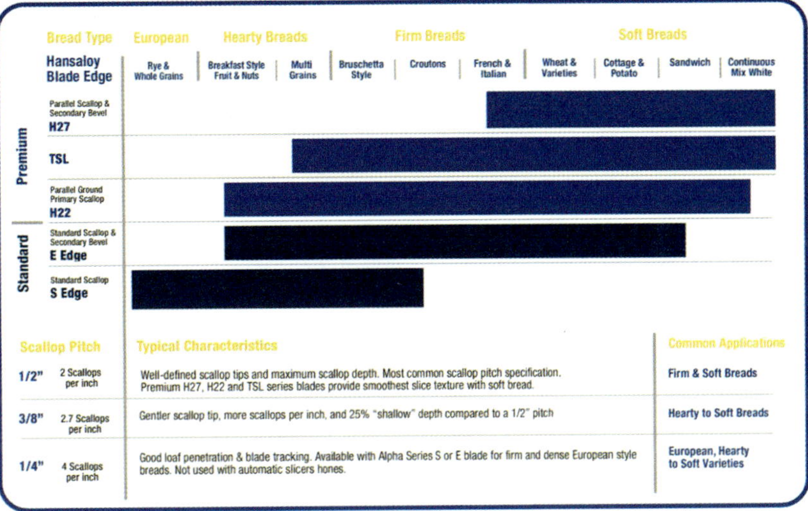

Figure 11.040. Different products cause different rates of wear on slicing blades. (Hansaloy)

Low-fat, no-fat. Products made without significant oil are difficult for blades to slice. The lack of lubrication causes excessive friction, which heats the blade and can cause buildup on the side of the blade. Blade and drum scrapers must be installed in these slicing units. A gravity-fed oiling system is necessary and preferably a spray system as well. Honing frequency must be increased. Use of a single-bevel blade for crust penetration and a parallel grind for interior slice texture is recommended.

Low-carb. New-age formulations that suit the "low carb" market require a blade with a very sharp edge. A single-bevel blade with a parallel grind is preferable. Honing must be done more frequently using a ceramic honing stone. Machinery should have a pressurized spray system supplying intermittent oil spray to the blade and a gravity-fed oil system with blade scrapers on both drums to keep the blades cool and clean.

Hard crust, dense product. Any product with a very hard crust or a very dense texture such as a European rye will require a durable blade edge. Use of a single-bevel blade will maximize blade life. Use of ceramic honing stones can improve the blade edge with frequent honing to provide a superior slice texture.

11.B.3.b. Troubleshooting slice problems

When slicing problems occur or when replacing blades, always save the used blade for inspection. By examining the blade carefully, the bakery engineer may find evidence that some other component on the slicer is the source of the problem. For example, damage on the non-slicing edge is a sign of backing roller wear, and sheared scallop points indicates worn blade guides or that the blade is cutting into something very hard.

Saving the blade lets its manufacturer identify whether the blade was sub-standard before it was installed. If the package in which the blades were shipped is available, the blade manufacturer can glean more information concerning the exact production of the blades. The packaging information should always be kept on hand until a new set of blades has been installed. The packaging and the blade samples allow the manufacturer to identify problems within their own manufacturing process and to analyze the metallurgical properties of the blade. The long-term result of such actions is that bakers get improved blades compared with the first blade that was ever bought.

The next step is to inspect the machine where the blade was installed. Look for any abnormalities that could have damaged the blade such as worn or loose parts. If blades are installed, check their tension and calibration of the tension gauge.

Other indicators can also help find problems before it affects production. Should any of the following problems occur, take time to do a thorough analysis of the slicer as soon as production can accommodate the inspection.

Bread crumb texture. How the slice looks can be a good indicator that something is not right. Crumb consists of two types: (a) the darker, dry particles that come from the crust of the product and (b) the fairer, moist particles from the interior of the bread loaf. Dark crumb is seen before and after the slicing unit, and light crumb appears only after the slicing unit. A high volume of light crumb means that something needs to be corrected. The first places to check are blade tensioning and hone stone positioning.

Slice thickness. If sliced products show both thick and thin slices in the same loaf, something is wrong. In this case, look at blade tensioning, lattice rigidity and blade guides to find which is not properly supporting the blade.

Blade wear. If blades experience accelerated wear, the tension may be too high. Also, blade guides may have worn out, or a honing stone is out of position. Look for anything that may be damaging the blade edge. Any other component that shows accelerated wear is also an indicator that something is not right inside the unit.

Blade tension. Incorrect blade tension is the main reason that blades do not operate correctly, and improper tensioning affects, directly or indirectly, many other components of the slicing unit. Make sure that operators and maintenance personnel set up and operate the slicer's blades at the manufacturer's recommended tension.

Information in this section was adapted from Cox (2007).

11.B.4. Disk slicers

Buns and rolls can be sliced individually or, as is more generally the case, in clusters of 4, 6, 8 and 24 units at rates in excess of 48,000 units per hour. Buns and rolls, bagels and English muffins are traditionally sliced by circular or disk knives mounted horizontally on motor-driven spindles and set parallel to the direction of product travel, as illustrated in **Figure 11.041**'s schematic drawings. Lecrone (1980) provided interesting insight into the development of bun slicing systems from single-lane methods into today's bulk slicing approach.

The circular blades are spaced so that they leave either a center web of uncut bun ("web slice") or a narrow hinge of uncut crumb on the outside edge of the bun or roll ("hinge slice"). Web slicing characterizes bagels and fast food buns because their tops and bottoms must stay together during distribution until use. Hot dog buns are a good example of hinge slicing.

The web slice is made by passing the bun centrally positioned between the knives. The cutting disks rotate in opposite direction, resulting in slicing the bun in the same direction. The space between the knives determines the amount of center web that remains after slicing. To form the hinge cut, a single cutting disk is used, and the size of the hinge is determined by the depth of cut in the bun.

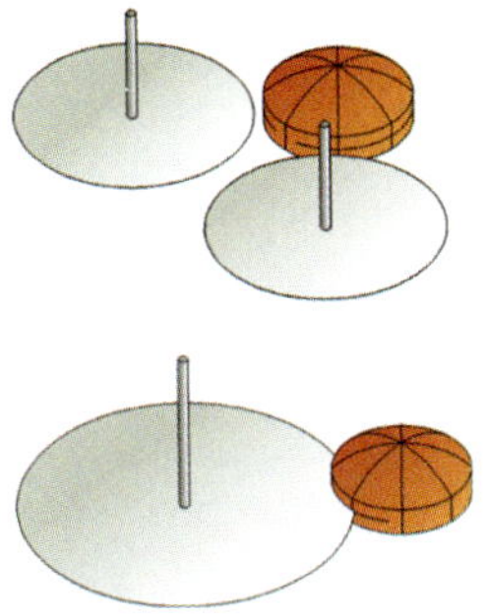

For both styles, the baked product must be in correct position, assured by the line's side guides and lane channels (**Figure 11.042**). The positioned product is held in place by top hold-down conveyors, textured belts for high-friction contact that prevents bun rotation and maintains alignment during slicing. These hold-down belts are synchronized with the bottom conveying belt to ensure a secure grip on the product. The line's conveyor takes products through and past the blades in rows. The hold-down head assembly is adjustable above the product conveyor, allowing the operator to control the depth of the bottom slice. This adjustment is made either mechanically using a hand wheel that rotates a gear set to raise and lower the assembly or from the control panel in which case a motor is used to turn the positioning gear set.

As with band slicers, sanitation is critical to good performance of disk slicers. If crumb buildup occurs on slicer disks, drive spindles or on the top conveyors, slice thickness will vary, and product damage will occur during the slicing. The operator must monitor the quality of slice to determine when blade replacement is necessary. The disk blades can either be sharpened in-house or by outside services that provide exchange programs.

Operators should monitor the amount of crumbs generated as well as the appearance of the finished products. If crumbs accumulate quickly or damaged product occurs, then the slicer blades should be inspected immediately. Material building up on the blades inhibits smooth slicing, as do dull cutting edges. If either of these conditions exist, check internal temperatures of the product and the quality of the bake because under-baked product can result in increased crumb and tearing during the slicing operation.

Figure 11.041. Depending on how the bun encounters disk blades, it is cut with a web (top) or a hinge (middle). (LeMatic)

Figure 11.042. Buns slide down channels that set up lanes for slicing.

11.B.5. Specialty slicers and cutters

Baked foods come in a broad spectrum of styles, some involving intricately different portioning methods. Several systems are described here, highlighting the diversity of styles.

11.B.5.a. English muffin forkers

Open grain is crucial to the quality of English muffins. Disk cutters have been successfully used to slice these products, but the smooth cut surface does not accentuate the muffin's attractive "nooks and crannies." The traditional way that restaurants served English muffins was to fork-split them by puncturing them around their circumference with a fork and then pulling the muffins apart by hand. Bakery engineers devised a specialty cutting device mimics the fork's action: the English muffin forker.

The English muffin forker (**Figure 11.043**) consists of two set of knives or tines, mounted on traveling chains. The two chains are positioned opposite one another, and a conveyor carries the muffin between them. The tines are inserted into the muffin mechanically, although in non-uniform fashion, to slice or tear the internal grain structure. The process does not actually separate the muffin into top and bottom pieces; instead, it creates a field of openings that allow the consumer to easily pull the muffin apart.

11.B.5.b. Ultrasonic cutters

Ultrasonic cutters employ a generator to produce high-frequency radio waves, typically in the range of 20 to 40 kilohertz (kHz), which are imposed on the cutting blade, also called the "cutting horn" or "blade horn." The high-frequency vibration applied to the blade reduces the friction resistance at cutting surface, resulting in an enhanced, clean cut. Champagne and Davis (2001) described the components of ultrasonic cutters in detail.

The ultrasonic cutter is well adapted to frozen and iced products that are difficult, if not impossible, to cut using traditional techniques. The advantages to this high-tech technique are: (a) The cut is extremely clean and sharp, (b) very little crumb forms during cutting, and (c) the knife is self-cleaning due to the ultrasonic frequency on the blade. The cutter's blade typically moves in the vertical plane, with product positioned below the blade. An option to this traditional configuration is the installation of the ultrasonic cutter on a robotic arm (**Figure 11.044**). Using an associated vision system, the blade is positioned by the robotic arm for the required cuts (**Figure 11.045**).

Today, ultrasonic cutters are routinely used to slice cheesecakes, pies, iced cakes and layer cakes. A complementary feature to this and similar cutters is the ability to insert a divider between the slices. The divider or spacer, usually consisting of waxed or coated paper, is inserted between the slices to enable easy separation of the sliced product when serving (**Figure 11.046**). This feature is particularly attractive for items produced for food service or deli customers.

The main limitations to ultrasonic cutting include (a) the size and shape of the cutting blade, which must specifically designed for use with ultrasonics; (b) the initial capital cost, which can be double to triple that of conventional methods; and (c) the need for a more sophisticated maintenance support capability. However, for those baked foods that cannot be efficiently sliced or proportioned without the aid of ultrasonics, it is an excellent solution.

11.B.5.c. Book cutters

Cutting frames for book cutters (also called "harp" slicers) are composed of steel 0.3-mm bands or 0.6-mm wires that portion wafer cookies and petit fours. Both intermittent and continuously operating systems (**Figure 11.047**) are available (Gorton 1998).

The process of making sugar wafer cookies first coats filling onto thin wafer

Figure 11.043. Fork-like tines pierce the sides of English muffins to different depths, thus preserving the product's desirable "nooks and crannies" texture. (LeMatic)

Figure 11.044. Installed on a robotic arm, an ultrasonic cutter can portion a frozen pie or cake into wedge-shaped pieces. (Colborne Foodbotics)

sheets and then stacks the filled sheets until a book is created with a predetermined number of layers. A gauge roll "standardizes" book height with gentle pressure. In some cases, the system stacks multiple books to create a magazine. Pusher bars or overhead feed units move the resulting magazine of wafer stacks through cutting frames at slow speed to slice the wafers in side- and lengthwise fashion, with cutting guided by plates at the side of the machine. Conveyors synchronized to the cutting systems remove the cut wafer fingers and transport them to packaging operations.

Slicing of petits fours (3 to 5 layers of cake and filling) and Dobosh torte (25 layers) uses similar methods, according to Gorton (1983).

11.B.5.d. Loaf decruster

If necessity is the mother of invention, then necessity gave birth to one of the most interesting cutting systems in the bakery: the loaf decruster. Emerging first in Europe, crustless bread has become very popular, especially with time-strapped parents making sandwiches to be packed in their children's lunchboxes. To automate the removal of crusts from sandwich loaves, bakery engineers invented the bread decruster (**Figure 11.048**). This machine, essentially a band slicer, uses two slicing blades, mounted at 90° to each other, i.e., perpendicularly. The bands slice the top, bottom and side crusts from the loaf, which then travels to a conventional band slicer. The end crusts are removed before the now-crustless loaf reaches the bagger. The same guidance for operation and maintenance concerning the band slicer applies to the loaf decruster.

11.B.5.e. Cubing slicer

When making croutons, a cubing slicer is used. After the loaf is sliced in a traditional slicer, it is either conveyed or manually transferred to the cubing slicer. This system, in essence, mounts 2 band slicers perpendicularly to one another and orients them 45° from vertical. The equipment configuration creates the appearance of a giant "X" (**Figure 10.049**). The cubing slicer can produce up to 2,500 lb of croutons per hour. Once again, the same guidance for operation and maintenance for the band slicer applies to the cubing slicer.

11.B.6. Employee safety

The American National Standards Institute (ANSI) Z50.1 Safety Standards stipulate safety requirements for all types of slicers. The general provisions of the standards are: (a) All slicers shall be equipped with a mechanical device for pushing the final loaf through the slicer knives without contacting the moving knives. (b) In reciprocating blade slicers, the cover over the knife frames is to be provided with a safety interlock that will make the slicer inoperative if the cover is not in place. (c) On slicers with endless band knives, the drive motor shall be equipped with automatic braking that will quickly stop the motor. Each door, panel or other point of access to the cutting blades shall be provided with a safety interlock so the drive motor will stop if any such access points are opened and so the motor cannot be restarted while these panels or doors remain open. Restarting shall require manual activation of the start control. (d) On slicers with endless band knives, a safety device shall be

Figure 11.045. Schematic drawings show how a vision system positions the robotic arm to make cuts in the right places. (Colborne Foodbotics)

Figure 11.046. The cutter works in two stages, first cutting the frozen product, then inserting the paper spacers between slices. (Colborne Foodbotics)

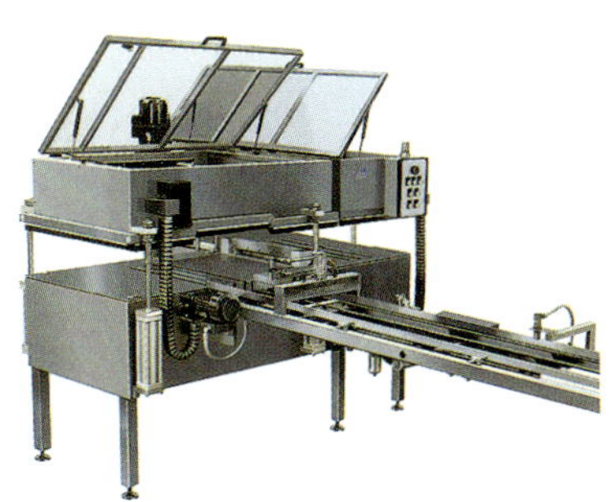

Figure 11.047. Exchangeable cutting frames can vary the size of wafer fingers produced by book cutters. (Franz Haas Waffelmaschinen)

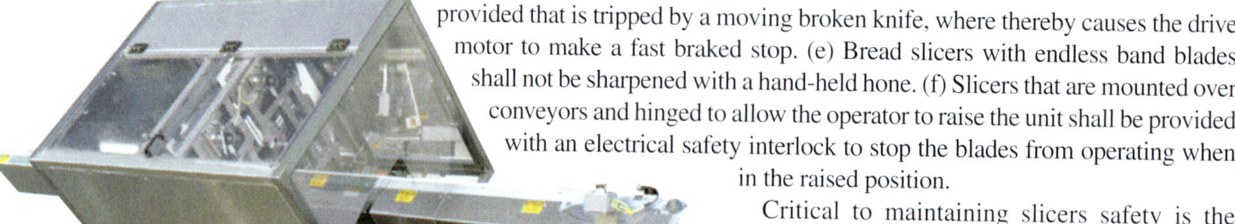

provided that is tripped by a moving broken knife, where thereby causes the drive motor to make a fast braked stop. (e) Bread slicers with endless band blades shall not be sharpened with a hand-held hone. (f) Slicers that are mounted over conveyors and hinged to allow the operator to raise the unit shall be provided with an electrical safety interlock to stop the blades from operating when in the raised position.

Critical to maintaining slicers safety is the periodic inspection and testing of the safety guards, interlocks and sensors. Any slicer having an inoperative or missing safety device must be made inoperative until corrected. Maintenance and sanitation personnel need particular training on slicer equipment because of the inherent dangers associated with the blade assemblies.

The specific safety requirements in Z50.1-2006 that cover slicing, wrapping and bagging equipment are found in section 17. This information is available on the Web at www.ansi.org.

Likewise, the Occupational Health and Safety Administration (OSHA) wrote standards for bakery equipment. Information regarding the operational design of slicers can be found along with other regulations concerning bakery machinery can be found in the Code of Federal Regulation at 29 CFR 1910.263 and is available on the Web at www.osha.gov.

For additional resources, see Appendix 4.

Figure 11.048. Individual band slicers in this "loaf decruster" remove the sides, tops and bottoms of loaves. (Burford)

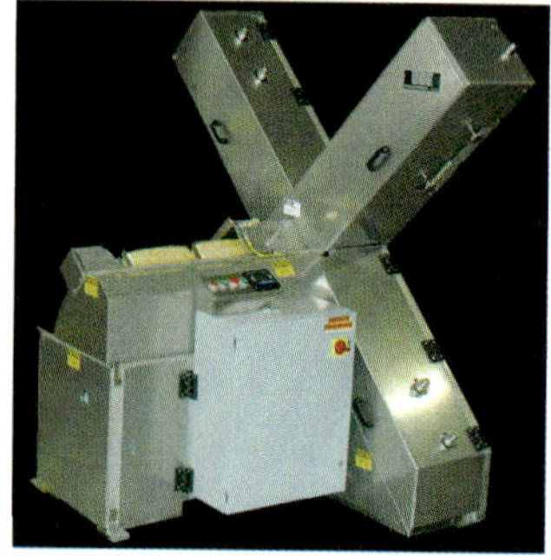

Figure 11.049 A cubing slicer accepts sliced bread and turns it into cubes to be processed into croutons or stuffing. (United Bakery Equipment Co.)

11.C. Product Packaging

Until the 1920s, bakers distributed and marketed their bread products unwrapped. The inventor of the bread slicer, Otto Rohwedder, produced a machine that sliced bread and wrapped it to keep in moisture (Baird 2008). In 1928, Mr. Rohwedder's machine was exhibited at a bakery trade fair in America. Concurrent with the development of the slicer was introduction of the bread overwrapping machine. The origin of the bread overwrapper can be traced to Britain, where, in the early 1900s, a machine was invented for automatically wrapping soap bars (Wenban 1951). The bar wrappers produced a diamond-fold end-seal pattern, the classic pattern that continues to be used by conventional bread wrappers to this day. By 1930, Wonder Bread was being sold un-sliced and overwrapped in waxed paper to preserve freshness, and by 1933, around 80% of bread sold in the US was pre-sliced and wrapped.

While several different bread wrapping machines where developed, they all were based on essentially the same principles of operation. At first, opaque waxed paper served as the primary wrapping material. It was gradually replaced by transparent materials, at first by cellulose film (cellophane) and subsequently by films such as polypropylene. The traditional wrapped package was fully heat-sealed at its bottom overlaps well as at its two ends, which were further augmented by end seals or labels. One of the major drawbacks of this package was, and is, that once the wrapper was opened at one of its ends, it was difficult to reclose tightly.

Bagged bread did not appear on the market until around 1960 (Formost 2009) and, because of its reclosable feature, rapidly increased in popularity after that time. Some bakers, typically those producing premium breads, chose to retain the inner wrap when converting to the ever-popular outer bag because this packaging style solved the problem of reclosing overwrapped product and guaranteed product freshness. In recent years, the practice of overwrapping followed by bagging (**Figure 11.050**) — a practice described as "over-bagging" — has increased as bakers boosted their marketing investment in value-added products (Gorton 2002b).

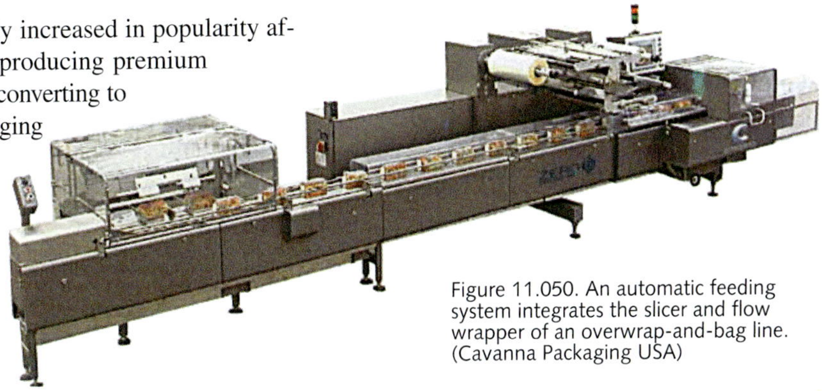

Figure 11.050. An automatic feeding system integrates the slicer and flow wrapper of an overwrap-and-bag line. (Cavanna Packaging USA)

11.C.1. Bread wrapping machines

Two basic methods characterize overwrapping of bread products. The first is the conventional bread wrapping machine that produces the traditional diamond-fold wrap in use since the 1920s. The second is the horizontal flow wrapper that is only recently gaining popularity for overwrapping of bread.

11.C.1.a. Conventional bread overwrappers

Although the conventional bread wrapping machine such as the modern version shown in **Figure 11.051** is a rather complex machine, basic operational assemblies are few in number. The operational assemblies of the wrapper are: the product infeed conveyor, film feed section, product elevator, folding and tucking mechanisms, heat sealing sections, cooling section and the discharge section. PLCs control the modern-day version, governing metering of wrapping material and sequencing the servo drives that control film speed and most other machine functions. Typical of the modern systems, adjustments can be preprogrammed in "recipes" for each product, thus making operator setup simple and repeatable.

The infeed conveyor receives the bread from upstream, usually from the bread slicer, and controls the flow of bread into the bagger, indexing the bread into the elevator section at the proper time. Concurrently, the wrapper cuts a piece of the overwrap film (typically cellophane, waxed paper and polypropylene) to a predetermined length established for the bread product being wrapped. The piece of film is transferred to, and suspended above, the elevator section of the wrapper.

The sliced loaf of bread, having been positioned by the product transfer section of the wrapper onto the elevator below the film, is raised by the elevator section of the wrapper through the film. The lifting action of the elevator results in film draping over the top and sides of the bread. As the bread transfers from the elevator into the heated sealing section, various folding and tucking mechanisms fold the film to cover the ends and bottom of the loaf. The loaf then travels the hard way (that is, leading with its long side) through the heating sections where the end folds and the bottom overlap are heat sealed. The loaf continues through cooling section of the wrapper before being discharged.

The heating section may be as simple as electrically heated polished stainless steel plates across which the overwrapped bread pass, conveyed by a bottom or side pusher. Other types of heating assemblies for sealing the film include heated rollers or belts; direct resistance heating elements, infrared, and hot air; and various combinations of these methods.

Regardless of the heating assembly or method, temperature control of the heaters is critical. In modern wrappers, the operator uses the machine's programmable logic controller (PLC), equipped with temperature control modules. In older units, and those wrappers without PLC-based controls, independent temperature controllers are installed for each heater. Thermocouples in the various heat sealers indicate and govern the individual heater (side or bottom) to the control set-point. The temperature settings for the heating sections are a function of machine speed, the type of film and ambient conditions.

Various methods are used in the cooling section of the wrapper for setting the sealed film. Given sufficient time and space, the cooling section can be as simple as polished stainless steel plates that absorb heat applied during sealing. Other methods include the use of cooling fans, chilled rollers or belts, and chilled side and bottom plates. The advantage to these other methods is that the cooling section can be shorter, thus reducing overall wrapper length and providing a quicker set-time for the seal. When a tight wrap is desired, a quick seal helps to maintain film tightness.

Paper or film packaging materials should be free of any static charge, which can build up under dry ambient conditions. A static charge condition interferes with proper film transfer and alignment, causing defective packages and product jams. It also attracts crumbs, entraining them with the finished wrap or bag. "Static eliminators," devices that dissipate static charges, can be mounted in the film pathway to address this problem.

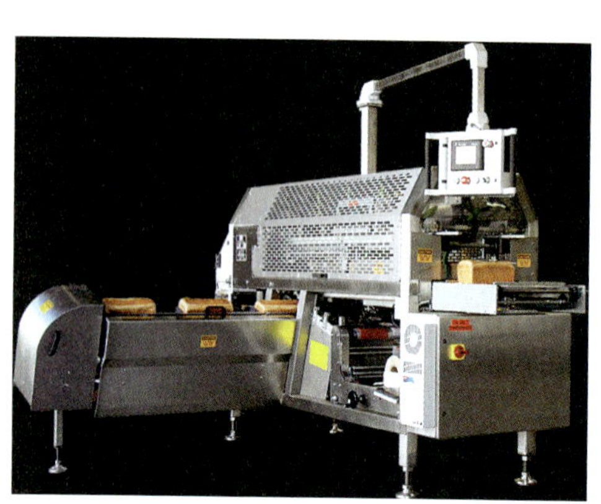

Figure 11.051. This conventional bread wrapper features PLC control over metering of wrapping material, servo drives that control the film speed and tension, machine and conveyor speeds. (United Bakery Equipment)

The film cutter, whether of the shear or the saw-tooth type, must be kept sharp to produce a clean cut without pulling or tearing. The wrapping material should be ordered to provide a minimal, but adequate, overlap on the bottom of the loaf. Machine adjustments enable nominal variation in product size to be accommodated. Modern wrapping machines provide many refinements and control features, such as label applicators, label imprinters, date and price coders, automatic shut-off in cases of product jams or missing film, automated film tensioning, automated film splicers that start a new roll of film when the original roll runs out and automated film tensioning devices. In some modified versions, one set of folding tuckers is eliminated, and a closure device is installed immediately after the discharge of the wrapper that gathers and ties or clips the open package end. This technique greatly facilitates opening and reclosing of the package, thus simulating the features of an outer bag, yet using overwrap technology.

11.C.1.b. Flow wrappers

Horizontal flow wrappers have been gaining in popularity for the overwrap of bread. Until recently, slice control, i.e., maintaining a good and tight alignment of slices, had been a problem with horizontal flow wrappers. Focused R&D efforts by the machinery manufacturers have addressed this problem, and a quality package of sliced bread can now be produced using the horizontal flow wrapper.

The horizontal flow wrapper, also described as a horizontal form/fill/seal (h-f/f/s) system, is a simpler machine then the conventional overwrapper because of the differences in handling the film. Products travel through horizontal flow wrappers the "easy way," leading with narrow end. The wrapper consists of an infeed section, film transfer and forming section, a sealing section, and discharge. As in the conventional wrapper, the infeed receives sliced bread from upstream of the wrapper and times transfer of the loaf into the wrapper's flighted transfer conveyor (**Figure 11.052**). The wrapping material, typically polypropylene, is conveyed overhead of the bread; the film passes over a stainless steel forming box that forms the film into a properly sized tube.

The film threads through a series of heated rollers (under high pressure) located below the forming box, thus closing the bottom seam with a fin-seal. The loaf of bread, assisted by a pusher attached to the transfer conveyor, moves into the tube. The formed tube travels at the same speed as the transfer conveyor, thus carrying the loaf forward to the end sealer. This rotary mechanism produces the fin-seal seal characteristic of the horizontal flow wrapper. During the sealing operation, a knife within the rotary sealer cuts the formed and sealed tube, creating an individual overwrapped loaf of bread. The loaf then leaves the wrapper.

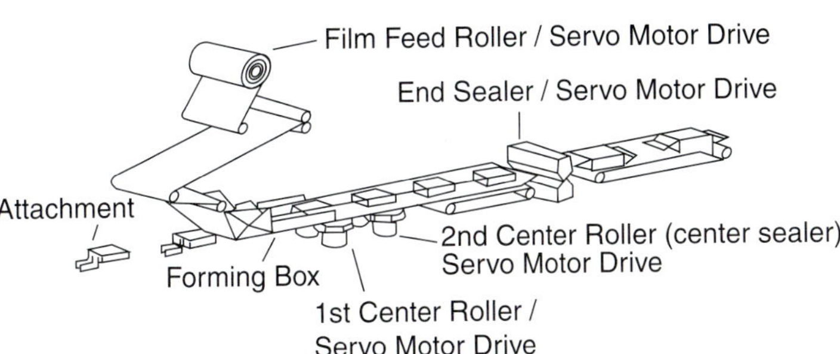

Figure 11.052. The web of film travels through a flow wrapper into the system's forming box, where a loaf of sliced bread awaits. (Formost Fuji Corp.)

The horizontal flow wrapper has several advantages over the conventional wrapper.

For example, a loose piece of film is not being handled during the wrapping operation. In the horizontal flow wrapper, the film travels uncut through the wrapper to the discharge point before being severed from its roll, thus enabling the wrapper to run at higher speeds and greater efficiency than the conventional wrapper.

Another advantage is speed. Horizontal flow wrappers run faster than conventional overwrappers. The conventional machine can wrap 55 to 65 units per minute but is limited by the film transport and mechanical operations of the wrapper. The horizontal flow wrapper's speed is determined by the speed at which the film can be sealed. When heat-sealing polypropylene, its speed can reach 120 ft per minute; therefore, the horizontal flow wrapper can output 80 to 95 loaves per minute, depending upon loaf length.

Also, the flow wrapper is mechanically simpler and therefore easier to maintain and adjust. Typically, a PLC control system governs all functions of the flow wrapper, using built-in feedback loops and servo drives. Product setup can be menu-driven for operational simplicity.

The horizontal flow wrapper can overwrap a wide variety of products, including those using carriers such as U-boards, corrugated and paperboard trays and foils. Therefore, the flow wrapper is the packaging machine of choice among bakers when overwrapping specialty products such as tray-packed English muffins, brown-and-serve rolls, cakes and pies (**Figure 11.053**). The flow-wrap package is also especially good for individual-serve (single portion) items such as cereal bars, snack cakes and pastry, and packages containing these baked products can frequently be found in convenience stores and vending machines.

Figure 11.053. This horizontal flow wrapper operates dual film spindles to ensure continuous film feed. Its adjustable forming box accommodates products of different sizes. The touchscreen control terminal can be seen above the sealing section. (Formost Fuji Corp.)

The one problem that has restricted acceptance of overwrapped product is the difficult opening and the inability to reclose the package. Recently, tear strips have been added to the overwrapped bread package. As can be seen in **Figure 11.054**, the tear strip successfully addresses opening of overwrapped product. Once opened using this technique, a reusable self sticking tab provides closeability. Zipper-style opening and reclosing seals, with and without tamper-evident features, are gaining popularity for bagels,

Figure 11.054. A quick-tear strip simplifies opening of the flow-wrapped package. (Formost Fuji Corp.)

buns and rolls, and English muffins. Also, as with the conventional wrapper, the flow-wrapped package can either be sealed at one or both ends. If sealed only on one end, wire ties, clip locks or tamper-evident closures can be used to seal the open end. Package closures will be reviewed in further detail later in this chapter.

11.C.2. Vertical form/fill/seal machines

Vertical form/fill/seal (v-f/f/s) machines (**Figure 11.055**) use technology similar to the horizontal flow wrapper to form and seal a tube of film. In this case, however, the tube is formed and filled vertically and is the approach used to package the majority, if not all, of salted snack foods commercially produced today.

In the baking industry, products such as mini bagels, mini-muffins and pastry, mini doughnuts, doughnut holes and cookies are distributed in pouches in additional to traditional family-sized cartons. Baked products can be found in pouches in convenience stores and vending machines; they can also be found at supermarkets in multi-pack and variety-pack formats. Perfect for individual portions, the pouch has gained significant presence in lunch boxes, box lunches and wherever snacks are served.

As in horizontal flow wrappers, the film used for the pouch is supplied as roll stock. (A roll of packaging film can be 3,000 to 5,000 ft long, depending on film thickness.) The film threads through a series of powered and idler rollers that feed the film at proper tension and speed to the forming head, also termed a "forming collar" or "shoulders." The film is drawn down around the head, forming into a tube (**Figure 11.056**). The back of the tube is heat sealed by sealer attached to the forming head. The whole tube is drawn downward by the end-seal assembly.

The jaws of the end-seal assembly are heated, and when the jaws clamp the tube, the pressure and heat form and seal the ends of tube, creating the back fin-seal and making the pouch. A knife in the center of the jaw assembly (**Figure 11.057**) cuts along the center line of the seal separating the newly formed pouch from the roll stock.

In the meantime, the products being packaged have either been weighed or counted (**Figures 11.058** and **11.059**). When the tube's back seam and bottom end sealed, product is automatically dropped through the neck of the forming tube into the pouch. The sealing process is then repeated, and for the end-seal, the jaws clamp and seal the tube of film forming the top seal of the filled pouch and the bottom seal for the pouch next to be filled.

With stand-up bags (**Figure 11.060**) getting more attention from cookie and cracker marketers, equipment manufacturers have adapted v-f/f/s machines to this bag style (Whitaker 2007b). To achieve the 4-corner seal required requires addition of creasing wheels and more sealers. The action of the sealing system must also be adjusted: The wrapper is controlled to create an asymmetrical bag, with the back fin very close to the base. The top fin sits further away from the product. Thus, when the bag is set on its bottom end, it looks virtually the same as the former pre-made block-bottom bag.

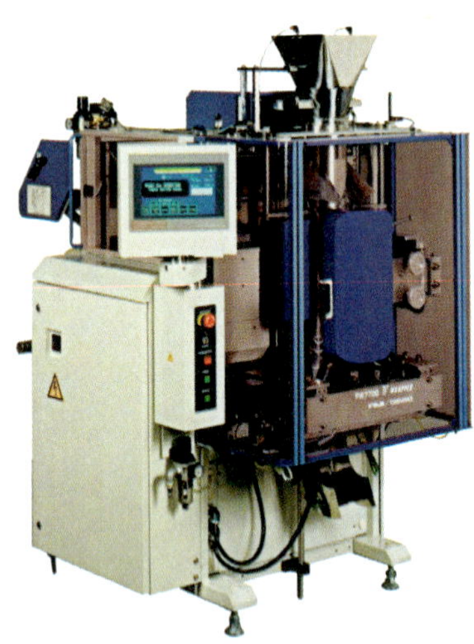

Figure 11.055. This vertical form/fill/seal bagger forms packaging film into a vertical tube to accept products flowing from scales (not shown) above the machine. (Formost Fuji Corp.)

11.C.3. Bread baggers

Two basic designs characterize bread bagging machines: the reciprocating scoop bagger and the paddle bagger (Petrella 1978).

11.C.3.a. Reciprocating bagger

The reciprocating bagger (**Figure 11.061**) is essentially a straight-line unit, and the loaf being bagged does not change its direction of travel through the bagger. Typical rated capacity for such baggers is 60 loaves per minute. As the sliced loaf is conveyed into the bagger, it is sensed by an electric eye that activates an air jet, which then blows open a polyethylene bag supplied on a wicket (**Figure 11.062**). A wicket is a U-shaped stiff wire holding 350 to 500 bags, with number of bags on a wicket determined by bag size and film thickness. A bagger will have 2 to 6 wicket tables staged with loaded wickets. Depending on the model and features of the bagger, the wicket tables are either automatically or manually changed when a wicket of bags runs empty.

Although the complete bagging cycle requires only about one second, product movement stops momentarily in the load position for the bag to be drawn over the loaf. Once the loaf is in the load position, a scoop assembly advances forward, over and past the loaf, to engage the inflated bag and then returns in a reciprocating motion to pull the bag over the loaf of bread. The bagged loaf then transfers to the closing section where the film bag's open end, or "ponytail," is gathered, removing excess air from within the bag and preparing it for closure.

The closure is usually a plastic clip, plastic-covered wire twist tie or tamper-evident tape, automatically applied to the bagged loaf. Bakers select a particular closure based on considerations such as market preference, comparative cost of the closure and the relative complexity of operation and maintenance of the closing device. Installation of a coder that imprints price-and-date information either directly on the bag or on the plastic clips eliminates the need for the baker to purchase pre-printed closures.

11.C.3.b. Paddle bagger

The paddle bagger (**Figure 11.063**) uses a different concept for packaging the loaf, which permits continuous operating speeds of up to 90 loaves per minute. Here, the bread is transferred into the bagger from the slicer by a flighted conveyor. As it enters the bagger, the loaf is engaged by the machine's overhead paddle (pusher), which travels horizontally across the product transfer conveyor. The push imparted by the paddle changes the loaf's direction of the travel by 90° so it now leads end-on rather than broadside as it enters the bagger. Air jets inflate and open the bag just before the arrival of the loaf, which is then pushed into the open bag by the overhead paddle. The pusher continues forward,

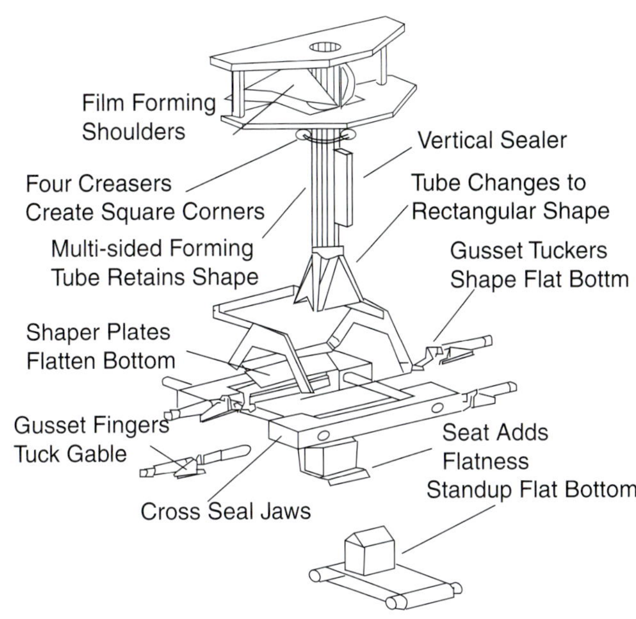

Figure 11.056. The bag-making assembly of a vertical form/fill/seal machine brings roll stock over the forming collar (or "shoulders") and around the tube that conveys the product being packaged. (Triangle Package Machinery Corp.)

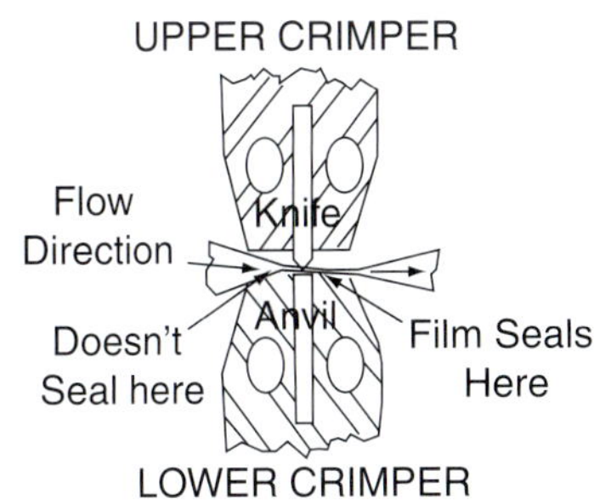

Figure 11.057. The sealing jaws incorporate a knife, located between the upper and lower crimpers, which severs the top of the previous package from the bottom of the current one.

Figure 11.058. The statistical net weighing scale (top) accepts small-sized baked items such as cookies, crackers, pretzels and the like. The control system weighs the contents of each randomly filled bucket, assembling the combination of bucket that best meets the target weight. The selected buckets release their contents into the vertical form/fill/seal baggers below. (Ishida)

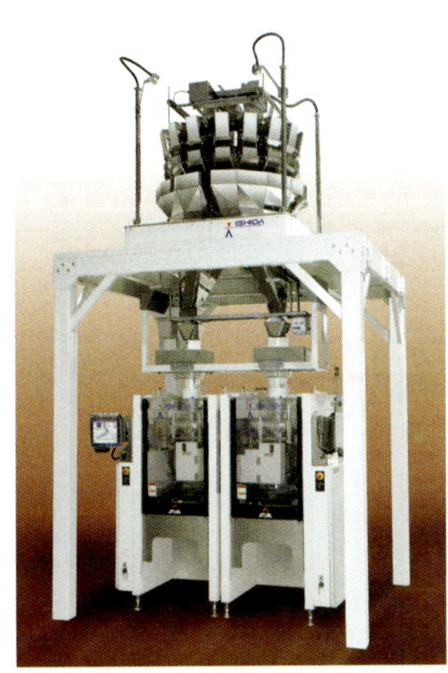

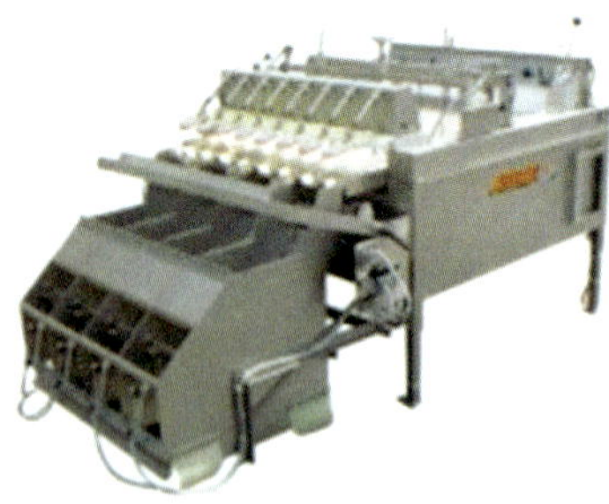

Figure 11.059. This system counts individual pieces to reach the correct number per package before it releases them into the packaging machine. (Affeldt)

Figure 11.060. More styles of bags are being made on vertical form/fill/seal machines than ever before. (Formost Fuji)

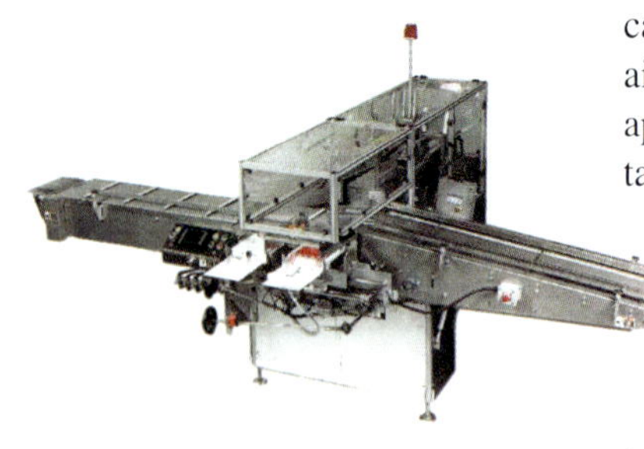

Figure 11.061. As bread flows from right to left, it is inserted into a bag scooped off a wicket and then sealed by a wire-tie closure system mounted above the discharge conveyor (left). (AMF Bakery Systems)

moving the bagged bread onto a flighted discharge conveyor that takes the loaf away (at 90° from the pusher travel) to enter the closure device. Like the reciprocating bagger, the paddle bagger uses closures such as twist ties, plastic clips and tamper-evident tape seals.

The latest models of bread baggers feature microprocessor control of their timed and interrelated functions. This control method can facilitate continuous operation by automatically changing the wickets of bags as each wicket is depleted. Some baggers can be programmed with predetermined package counts, changing wickets automatically once that count is reached. This feature is particularly useful for private label packaging. Kiefer (1989) described how bread baggers can be adapted to regularly run 100 loaves per minute. Self et al. (1984) provided troubleshooting tips (**Table 11.1**).

11.C.4. Bun and roll packaging

Bakers market buns, rolls, bagels and other smaller bakery products in a wide assortment of package sizes, number of units per package and configurations so the equipment required for this purpose is correspondingly varied.

11.C.4.a. Bun and roll baggers

Buns and rolls in 8-, 12- and 16-count retail packages are most frequently bagged. In a fully automatic bagging system, the buns or rolls, either singly or in clusters, are transferred from the cooling conveyor directly onto the infeed conveyor of the bagger where they are aligned into rows prior to slicing. Following slicing, the system indexes or groups buns or rolls into the appropriate package arrangement (product array) for packing. Some systems can also stack buns into 2 layers prior to bagging. The flighted infeed conveyor advances the grouped products into position for paddles to push the group into an inflated bag. Like the bread bagger, photo eyes sense the presence of the buns or rolls and activate air jets to inflate and open the bag just before the arrival of the buns or rolls.

Once bagged, the paddle then pushes the bagged buns or rolls onto a flighted discharge conveyor installed at a right angle to the pusher. The discharge conveyor carries the bagged product a short distance to the closure device, where the excess air in the bag is removed, film at the open end of the bag is gathered, and the closure applied. Again, the most common bag closure devices are twist ties, plastic clips and tamper-evident tape seals.

Some loose-count buns, rolls and bagels are packed "penny stacked" into bags, in other words, loaded on their edges rather than flat on their bottoms. To handle this style, a special loader (**Figure 11.064**) is needed ahead of the bagger's infeed. After slicing, the products are guided into lanes and aligned; the items are released in rows of 6 or 8 each. On release, the buns or bagels drop into a serpentine chute that rotates the product 90°, and at discharge from the chutes, the products are on edge and adjacent to one another. A receiving "trough" or "pocket" made from a series of parallel-spaced round stock maintains product orientation for bagging.

The bun and roll bagger can also handle tray-packed products such as English muffins, muffin tops, sponge cakes and lady fingers. In these applications, the tray (typically paperboard, foil or a thermo-formed polymer) acts as a carrier for the

Table 11.1. Troubleshooting Bagger Operations

Problem	Solution	Variable
Bags not opening properly	Check for sufficient air	• Properly aimed or directed. • Sufficient volume. • Sufficient pressure. • Dry and clean.
	Check the bag table	• Be sure it is free (not binding) and properly loaded with "stock springs to maintain consistent bag height. • Check to see that the bag is held with even tension across the lip.
	Examine the bags	• Check the lip dimension (short lips are troublesome). • Check the wicket holes for proper placement. • The bags may be blocking (sticking together on the inside or outside). • Too many bags on the wicket will cause an oversize hump at the lip.
Scoops not entering the bag efficiently	Check the equipment	• Top scoop is set too tall, does not fully enter the bag. • Lower scoop snags the bag, releasing it prematurely. • Inglated bag is fluttering, causing scoops to snag or miss. • Bag hold-down fingers are not working properly. • Bags are ot opening properly (see above). • On bun baggers, the inflating cycle is too short; bag relaxes before scoops have entered completely. • On bun lines, be sure scoops are matched to the product.
	Check the bags	• Determine that the bags are on the proper width wicket as indicated by the product's width and height. • Determine that there is sufficient uncut material above the wicket hole to prevent premature release. • Too much uncut material will prevent the bag from releasing. • Bags are not on both legs of the wicket. • Check to see that bags have not "shingled." (Bags will not line up with height sensors, setting bag levels too high.) • Folded corners prevent hold-down fingers from reaching the bag. Bag inflates off-center and misses the scoop. • Bags split at the sideweld.
Problems in loading the product		• Determine if bag is properly sized to the product. • Product crust can cut or slit the bag. • Check for excesses in proofing vs. bag size.
Problems closing the bag	Check the equipment	• Check gathering brushes. • Check that the flight, plunger and tyer needle are in synchronization.
	Check the bag	• Check length of bag tail, neither too long nor too short. • Sticky bags with a high coefficient of friction (COF) can causing gathering or tying problems. • Slick bags with a very low COF cause similar problems.

(Self et al. 1984)

Figure 11.062. Pre-made bread bags are mounted on wickets in counts of 350 to 500 bags. The wicket permits quick mounting on the bagger.
(Formost Fuji)

Figure 11.063. This high-speed paddle bagger can package as many as 90 loaves per minute.
(Formost Fuji Corp.)

Figure 11.064. A robotic method for penny stacking uses an end effector to pick up a stack of English muffins (rear) and transfer them to the packaging station (front).
(BluePrint Automation)

product, thus eliminating the need for indexing and grouping. These baggers are, therefore, simpler because no collating or grouping mechanism is needed at the infeed to the bagger. Bagger operations remain the same as for buns and rolls.

Lecrone (1980) offered a short history of bun and roll slicing and packaging, describing the development of packaging techniques and machinery for handling cluster and bulk-packed products.

11.C.4.b. Bulk bun packer

Used principally for products supplied to commercial or food service customers, the bulk bun packer (**Figure 11.065**) typically produces packages that range from 12 to 96 count, with 12 to 48 items in a layer, stacked in single or double layers. The bulk bun packer is a combination machine that unites product aligning and indexing, slicing, accumulating and pattern forming, and overwrapping; some units incorporate tray and carton loading operations.

Products move from the cooling belt and travel through lane systems arranging them 4 to 8 across for slicing. After slicing, buns are briefly accumulated to produce a backlog for indexing. Products are released from the indexer properly arrayed and counted for overwrapping (**Figure 11.066**).

It is most common for the wrapper section to use two rolls of film, with one supplying the bottom sheet and the other roll the top sheet. The wrapper uses hot air, hot wire or heated rotary sealers for sealing the top and bottom sheets together. The resulting package has a relatively loose fit when compared with the retail packaging; therefore, it is quickly loaded into cases or baskets (corrugated or plastic) for shipment. Maximum rated capacities are 40 packs, or up to 1,000 buns, per minute.

11.C.5. Bagging vs. overwrapping

At present, virtually all bread reaches the consumer in polyethylene bags, including those variety breads for which some bakers still use an inner wrap. This method of bread packaging had its inception in wholesale bakeries of the Pacific Northwest. Formo (1981) attributed the nearly universal acceptance of the bread bag by the consumer at that time to the following advantages: (a) Bread packaged in polyethylene bags is perceived to retain its freshness longer than conventionally wrapped bread; (b) the package is more readily opened and reclosed tightly; and (c) its ponytail feature renders it more convenient to handle.

The incentives for the baker to adopt bagging of bread and buns and rolls included the greater simplicity of the bagging machines in their design, operation and maintenance compared with the more complex conventional bread wrapping machines. Other advantages were lower acquisition costs, more economical operation, higher packaging speeds, and greater dependability that lessen the need for standby equipment.

Bagger operating speeds were rated at 65 to 90 loaves per minute, compared with 45 to 55 loaves per minute for conventional overwrapping machines. Today, wrapper costs have dropped as the technology has evolved, and there is no longer is the significant cost difference between baggers and wrappers. With the advances in wrapping technology and the advent of the horizontal flow wrapper, wrappers have caught up with baggers in speed.

Today the principle points of differentiation between baggers and wrappers are: (a) film selection — bags are traditionally made from polyethylene, while overwrapping uses polypropylene or waxed paper; (b) package image — the tradition "bag" vs. the wrapper's diamond-fold or crimp end-seal; and (c) convenience — the bag remains the easy-open, easy-close package of choice among consumers.

Not to be outdone, the manufacturers of horizontal flow wrappers have teamed with film suppliers to create bread packages that are convenient to open and re-seal. Still in its relative infancy, the resealable package's premium cost and reduced manufacturing efficiency have limited its introduction and acceptance.

A point in favor of horizontal flow wrapping is the technology's ability to handle diverse film stocks. While a conventional bread overwrapper used waxed paper or polypropylene, the flow wrapper is not limited to these materials. Film manufacturers can supply coextruded film with properties tailored to specific applications. A coextruded film composed of multiple layers can regulate the movement of moisture, oxygen, odors and air into and out of the package. A layer of nylon, for example, can be added to change film strength and alter its tearability, as described earlier in this chapter at Part B.

11.C.6. Related technologies

Packaging is probably the most diverse process in the bakery as it is in most food processing facilities. More ways to go to market emerge every year — more new package designs, more new package types, more new package configurations. The packaging department, thus, houses an ever-widening range of technologies. Some recent introductions or modifications of existing technologies are noted here.

11.C.6.a. Slug wrapping

Similar to but far more elaborate than bagel penny stackers are the slug wrappers that package many crackers varieties. As saltine crackers emerge from ovens to cool, they pass through breaking stations that separate crackers individually or into blocks of 4 each. Eventually, the cooling conveyors lead into lane systems, which divide the bulk flow into a dozen or more separate long rows. Bakers adjust the speed of the laning conveyors forcing crackers to shingle and eventually stack up to move forward on-edge. Round, oval and shaped crackers need not be separated by breaking, but they also are routed into lanes for stacking.

The rows, or lanes, separate off, each leading to a combination slug former and wrapper (**Figure 11.067**). This machine groups the incoming crackers by length, indexing them into position ahead of a chain-mounted lug. This lug pushes the whole stack into an overwrapper or horizontal form/fill/seal (h-f/f/s) system, where the packaged stack becomes a single slug. The slugs leave the wrapper and enter a cartoning system that boxes them according to the desired pattern, with 2- or 4-across and 4-square being common styles.

Such laning and grouping systems also find application in cookie processing. For example, cookies move into lanes and are stacked before entering sandwich-filling machines. Laning also replaces the manual labor of counting cookies and loading them into trays.

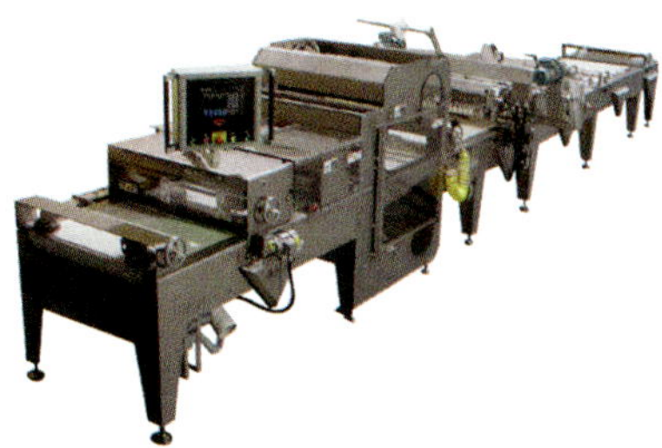

Figure 11.065. An automated bulk packer for buns combines indexing, slicing, pattern forming and overwrapping stages. (AMF Bakery Systems)

Figure 11.066. Adjustable lane guides make changeovers for bulk bun packaging systems easy and quick. (LeMatic)

11.C.6.b. Stand-up pouch baggers

Using roll stock, packaging machines have been developed that form pouches with gussets or special shapes. These systems fill, seal and trim the pouches to meet increasing market demand for cookies, crackers and baked snacks offered in this style of packaging. As shown in the drawing, the line draw from a tensioned roll of film stock and folds the material to achieve the desired bottom characteristics. Grippers on a chain transport the package to the loading station and through sealing operations.

11.C.6.c. Modified atmosphere packaging

A big part of the consumer's definition of "fresh" involves wholesome appearance, or in other words: no mold. Although fresh baked foods emerge from the oven in sterile condition, they can be contaminated by mold spores in the atmosphere, particularly during slicing and post-oven handling.

Sealed bakery packages can provide moist environments for such micro-organisms, hence the baker's use of preservatives and antimicrobial ingredients to prevent mold growth. A growing number of consumers, however, want "natural only" formulations and reject such chemical additives, and the food industry has long searched for alternatives. Controlling the water activity (a_w) of baked foods to keep it low is one approach. Some European bakers lightly mist baked foods with alcohol before packaging. Modified atmosphere packaging (MAP) technologies provides additional options.

The Earth's normal atmosphere mixes 78% nitrogen, 21% oxygen and 1% carbon dioxide with very small amounts of rare gases plus water vapor. Like humans, microbes require oxygen to sustain their life forces. A change in the composition of the gaseous environment within packages that cuts the amount of oxygen present will inhibit growth of microbes — the principle behind MAP methods.

Reporting about studies into the effect of different kinds of gases, Doerry (1985) pointed out that nitrogen (N_2) or carbon dioxide (CO_2), each used alone, inhibited mold growth, although nitrogen did not stop bacterial activity. Pure carbon dioxide was also found to be absorbed by baked foods, thus producing a vacuum within the package, shrinking it. He noted that mixing N_2 to CO_2 in ratios of 1:1 and 2:3 were both effective in stopping mold growth. Lowering of pH was also noticed with some products. Neither gas slowed staling.

MAP techniques modify the atmosphere within packages by (a) direct injection of gases (often CO_2 and/or N_2) into the package, (b) evacuating air from the package or (c) interaction between package contents and the air inside over time. The last describes the natural respiration that happens with fresh fruit and vegetables. Sealed packages made by MAP techniques have an atmosphere different from ambient air, but that atmosphere can change over time because of the moisture, vapor and gas transmission rates of the packaging material itself.

As a packaging method, MAP encloses food products in a film having high gas barrier properties and changes the gaseous environment to retard mold growth. Among the technologies involved are vacuum packaging, gas-flush packaging, use of oxygen absorbents/gas generators and application of ethanol vapor generators. Gas-flush wrappers and oxygen scavengers are the most commonly used.

Figure 11.067. Aligned on edge, cookies move into the h-f/f/s wrapper in a slug. The on-edge wrapper's software monitors the motion of cookies, conveyors and loaders. (Doboy, Inc.)

Gas flushing introduces an inert gas (CO_2 and/or N_2) into bags formed on vertical or horizontal form/fill/seal machines. The gas nozzle extends into the formed tube ending just before the sealing jaws. The injected gas, thus, hits the sealed end and reverses course to flush any entrained atmospheric gases out of the open back end of the tube. The pressure of the remaining gases within the tube should reach about one atmosphere, or equal to the external pressure. This method does not remove all of the "normal" air in the tube but replaces a good portion of it with the inert gas, thus altering the atmosphere sufficiently to restrain mold growth over a normal shelf life period.

Smith (1994) summarized MAP methods and evaluated their use with bread, cake, croissant, doughnut, English muffin, pastry, pie, pizza crust and waffle products, among others.

This technique involves added costs for high-gauge films and the extra gas introduced into the package and thus tends to find use mostly for premium and value-added foods. A good example is par-baked pizza crust sold at ambient temperatures.

Controlled atmosphere packaging (CAP) involves a different approach than modified atmospheric packaging. In CAP, the mix of gases is maintained or controlled over time by some external apparatus or by an internal chemical reaction. Placing an oxygen-absorbing sachet (**Figure 11.068**) inside a barrier package is an example of CAP. The sachet absorbs any oxygen transmitted through the package barrier.

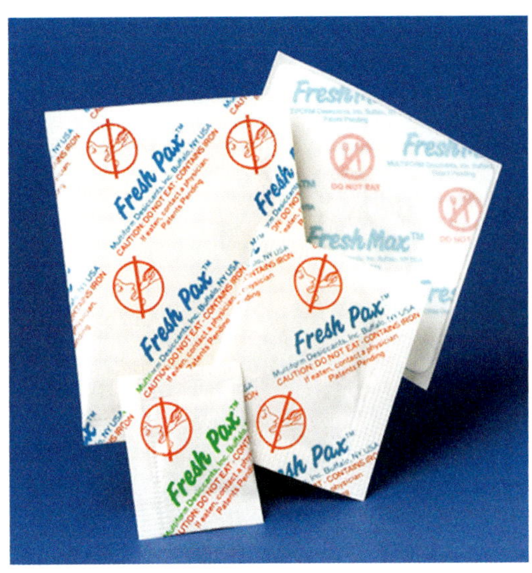

Figure 11.068. Oxygen scavengers inside small sachets absorb oxygen and to remove it from use by spoilage microbes.
(Multisorb Technologies)

11.D. Packaging Materials

Getting baked foods to market generally requires some form of packaging, whether it is a bulk paper bag for supplying a restaurant or an overwrapped structure that protects loaves as they travel to the supermarket and then home with the consumer. Packaged baked foods represented a huge improvement in consumer life styles when introduced in the early 1900s. Today, the package has become as much a billboard for the product contained as it is already a protective device. In the US and Canada, consumer packaged foods carry a mandated Nutrition Facts panel describing the food's nutritional value. Ingredient listings are printed on packaging as well. In recent years, tamper-evident styles of packaging materials have emerged to give consumers another assurance of product purity.

11.D.1. Films

Before the "bread bag," waxed paper served as the preeminent wrapping material for many decades since its introduction in the 1920s. Initially, paraffin wax served as the exclusive coating material for bleached paper stock of suitable weight. Subsequently, the paraffin wax was blended with microcrystalline wax to improve its gloss, flexibility and sealing strength. At the same time, progress in paper processing resulted in a bright, white opaque paper that provided an excellent base for printing. End labels sealed the wrappings.

In the 1930s, cellulose film, or cellophane, was introduced to the baking industry and quickly gained widespread acceptance as a transparent wrapping material. In its original form, the film consisted of a single base sheet of various thicknesses that determined its strength. The application of coatings of nitrocellulose or polyvinylidene chloride (PVdC) greatly improved its oil resistance, gas permeability, heat sealability and moisture proofness. It is an excellent packaging film, but its cost was comparatively high.

By the mid 1950s, plastic polyolefin films in the form of polyethylene and polypropylene began to replace cellulose films as a transparent bread wrapper. Manufacturing of plastic films starts with resins derived by organic chemistry and forms the thin films by either cast or blown extrusion.

Polyethylene and polypropylene differ in properties such as strength, stiffness, temperature sensitivity, permeability, clarity and gloss. Different methods of manufacture result in a broad range of films such as cast oriented, unbalanced oriented, oriented coated and laminated combinations, all with measurably different properties. Their special characteristics and specific suitability to particular applications were discussed at length by Jurist (1964) and Smith (1967). Thomas (1985) provided a summary of packaging as specifically used by the baking industry, along with a comprehensive glossary of commonly used packaging terms.

Polyethylene film, available in low, medium and high densities, is the principal packaging material used for bread and rolls, with the low-density film forming the major base material for preformed bags and roll stock used by flow wrappers and bulk bun lines. The thickness, or gauge, of polyethylene films, as well as other films, is generally measured in mils, with 1 mil equal to 0.001 in.

Polyethylene and polypropylene films cannot be interchanged in flow wrappers and bulk bun packaging equipment because of the differences in sealing methods and technology required by the different sealing properties of these families of films. Sealing polyethylene requires the film be fused together (melted at the closure point), but polypropylene is sealed using a combination of temperature and pressure, while cold seal uses pressure only.

In general, low-density polyethylene offers adequate strength, gas permeability, moisture resistance and low temperature characteristics to satisfy normal packaging needs.

Where improved heat sealability is required, medium-density polyethylene will normally suffice. Polypropylene possesses properties similar to those of polyethylene but is stiffer and tougher at equivalent thicknesses and possesses superior optical characteristics; however, polypropylene is more susceptible to tearing than polyethylene (once torn, it "runs" with its grain, in line with its direction of initial extrusion). Polyethylene can be used as a component in coextruded films where it contributes resilience to the coextrusion. The essential properties and uses of polyolefin and cellulose films are summarized in **Table 11.2.**

To produce finished packages, a converter prepares the film by laminating it with other films, if required by the customer, and applying any needed adhesive coatings. The films are printed and trimmed to the desired size. Some packaging machines (flow wrappers and stand-up pouch systems) require roll stock, while others use pre-formed bags made to the specific size required by the baker. Bagmaking yields gusseted bags, mounted on wickets. Bun bakers generally use wickets of 250 bags because the shorter length gussets cause double thicknesses of film, while wickets of 400 to 500 bags are used for longer bread bags.

Table 11.2. Polyolefin and Cellulose Films: Characteristics and Applications

Description	Key characteristics	Applications
Low-density polyethylene	Low cost Machineability onto bag lines Poor optics	All bread, roll and bun bags
Cast polypropylene	Excellent optics Questionable seal range Very poor low-temperature performance	Bread bags Multi-wall bag liner
Oriented polypropylene	Heat sealable Good machineability Excellent MTVR* Lower cost than cellophane Moderate oxygen barrier	Overwrap for snack cakes Used in lamination and as unsupported web
Cellophane (nitrocellulose coated)	High cost Excellent optics Poor dimensional stability Broad seal range Excellent machineability	Snack cakes, limited by machinery
Cellophane (polyvinylidene chloride coated)	Good MTVR and oxygen barrier	Virtually all baked foods
Glassine	Adequate machineability Very poor MTVR	Fried pies

** MVTR, moisture vapor transmission rate*

(Mobil Chemical Co.)

11.D.1.a. Cellulose

Plain cellulose, or cellophane, is a glossy transparent film that is odorless, tasteless and biodegradable when properly composted. To produce cellophane, cellulose fibers from wood, cotton or hemp are treated with alkali and carbon disulfide. It is tough and puncture resistant, although it tears easily. Cellophane has folding properties that make it suitable for twist-wrapping (as used for small confectioneries); however, it is not heat sealable, and its dimensions and permeability of the film vary with changes in humidity. It is used for foods that do not require a complete moisture or gas barrier, including fresh bread and some types of sugar confectionery. Cellulose acetate is a clear, glossy transparent, sparkling film that is permeable to water vapor, odors and gases and is mainly used as a window material for paperboard cartons.

11.D.1.b. Polyethylene

Low-density polyethylene (LDPE) is heat sealable, inert, odor free and shrinks when heated. Polyethylene resin, extruded to make polyethylene film, is produced by the polymerization of ethylene gas under pressure. LDPE is a good moisture barrier but is relatively permeable to oxygen and is a poor odor barrier. It is less expensive than most films and is therefore widely used for bags, for coating papers or boards and as a component in laminates. In different thicknesses, LDPE is also used for shrink- and stretch-wrapping. Additional strength can be obtained by blending in linear low-density polyethylene (LLDPE).

High-density polyethylene (HDPE) is stronger, thicker, less flexible and more brittle than LDPE and a better barrier to gases and moisture. Bags made from HDPE have high resistance to tears and punctures and have good seal strength. Depending on the application, different densities of polyethylene are used for bread bags and bulk bun wrappers.

11.D.1.c. Polypropylene

Polypropylene (PP) is a clear glossy film with a high strength and good puncture resistance. The resin is made by the polymerization of propylene gas. The film has a moderate barrier to moisture, gases and odors, and it is not affected by changes in humidity. It stretches, although less than polyethylene. Oriented polypropylene (OPP) and biaxially oriented polypropylene (BOPP) are also clear glossy films with good optical properties high tensile strength and improved puncture resistance. These films are widely used to pack baked foods, biscuits, snack foods and dried foods. Polypropylene is frequently used as an inner wrapping and for windows in paperboard bakery cartons.

Perforated polypropylene has been used in Europe to wrap baguettes and rolls. The minute holes (known as micro perfs), spaced in regularly patterns, allow the package to breathe, releasing moisture that would otherwise soften the crust undesirably.

Given a matte finish, polypropylene provides the look of paper to the film with the added advantage of superior barrier qualities and economics.

11.D.1.d. Coextruded films

Coextrusion is the simultaneous extrusion of two or more layers of different polymers to make a single film. Coextruded films have three main advantages compared with other types of film: (a) They have very high barrier properties, similar to laminates but produced at a lower cost; (b) they are thinner than laminates and are therefore easier to use on filling equipment; and (c) the layers do not separate. For baked foods, confectioneries and cereals, low-density and high-density polyethylene, and polypropylene are the polymers of choice. If additional strength or barriers (moisture, oxygen, etc.) are required, more expensive polymers such as nylon are added to the coextrusion.

Typically a coextrusion has three layers — an outside layer with high gloss and printability, a middle bulk layer, which provides stiffness and strength, and an inner layer suitable for heat sealing.

11.D.1.e. Other films

Polyvinyl chloride, a resin produced by the polymerization of vinyl chloride, is very strong and is therefore used in thin films. It has a high barrier to gas and water vapor and is heat shrinkable and heat sealable. However, it has a brown tint, which limits its use in some applications. Polyamides (or nylons) are clear, strong films over a wide temperature range from -60 to +200°C (-76 to +392°F) that have low permeability to gases and are greaseproof; however, the films are expensive to produce, require high temperatures to heat seal, and the permeability changes at different storage humidities. They are used with other polymers to make them heat sealable at lower temperatures, to improve the barrier properties and to reduce film cost.

Films can be coated with other polymers or metals to improve their barrier properties or to impart heat sealability. For example, a nitrocellulose coating on both sides of cellulose film improves the barrier to oxygen, moisture and odors, and enables the film to be heat sealed at lower temperature. A thin coating of aluminum, vacuum deposited in a process termed "metallization," produces a very good barrier to oils, gases, moisture, odors and light; however, the cost of these films is significantly higher than un-coated films.

11.D.2. Closures

Various devices have been developed to close bakery bags. These devices range from wire ties and clips that are easy opening and provide the consumer with re-closeability, to tamper evident closures that safeguard the product.

11.D.2.a. Twist ties

Twist ties (**Figure 11.069**) are the original form of closure, first used by commercial bakeries beyond the simple knotting of the bag. Originally, the twist tie consisted of a fine wire embedded in paper; more recently plastic ties, where the wire is embedded in a polymer material, have become available, as are combination structures that use one layer of paper and a second of plastic film. Twist ties are available in various formats such as pre-cut lengths for hand tying and on rolls for fully automated commercial applications. The automated tyers are capable of closing 100 bags per minute (**Figure 11.070**).

Figure 11.069. A bread bag is closed by a paper-coated twist tie. (Bedford Industries)

A feature — and limitation — of the twist tie is the metal wire embedded in the closure. Because metal detectors can find the wire, bakers have a convenient way of assuring the tie has been installed: Running the finished package through a metal detector can confirm the presence of the twist tie. However, the bakery that wants to run its finished product through a metal detector as a part of its quality program must apply the tie after the metal detector. In this case, a secondary metal detector would be required to ensure the twist tie was in place. To address this problem, a line of formable plastic ties has been developed that do not contain wires, but this tie has seen limited application as a result of inability to achieve as tight a seal as the wire-based twist tie and the premium cost of the material.

Typically, bakers color-code their twist tie supplies so each color represents a different day of the week. Thus, when the bakery's driver-salesmen stock store shelves, they can quickly determine the day of production for baked products and pull the older items for stale return.

In response to environmental concerns, biodegradable ties have been developed (Bedford undated). Testing done by a certified, independent laboratory confirmed an estimated 6-month to 1-year time period for total biodegradation of the tie's paper, plastic and wire in a commercial landfill environment. Tie performance and physical properties are identical to conventional twist ties. Biodegradability is not affected by sunlight or moisture so the tie will not prematurely degrade on the store shelf. Additionally, the "green" ties originate from either recycled post-consumer or post-industrial scrap.

Figure 11.070. A modern twist tyer uses servo drives to synchronize its operations. (Burford Corp.)

Figure 11.071. The tab-lock closure can be printed with date codes, prices and other information. (Kwik Lok)

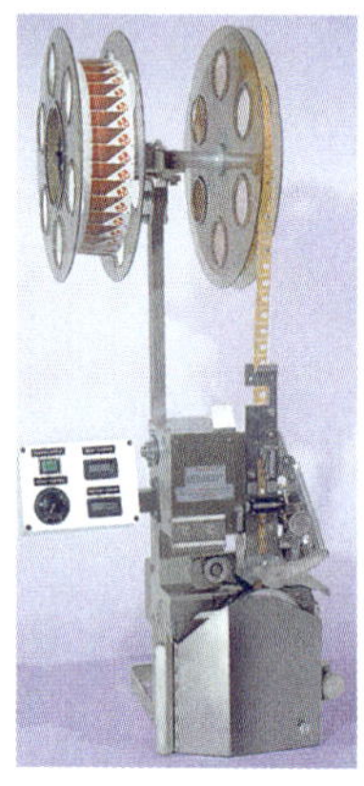

Figure 11.072. A fully automated tab-lock closure machine matches its output with that of the bagger. (Kwik Lok)

Figure 11.073. A tamper-evident tape closure seals this bag. (Burford Corp.)

11.D.2.b. Lock-style closures

The tab lock closure (**Figure 11.071**) has been available to bakers since the 1950s. The small plastic clip was developed as an alternative to the twist tie for bag sealing by the bakery and for simple reclosure by the consumer. Tab locks provide the baker with space to insert product code information (price, code dating, expiration date, etc.) directly on the tab. Other tab locks are manufactured with pre-printed paperboard cards affixed that are used for promotional features such as point-of-sale discount coupons, recipes and suggestions for product use. Fully automated tab applicators (**Figure 11.072**), used by commercial bakers, can close and seal up to 100 bags per minute.

Key to the performance of the lock-style closure is proper sizing of it to match the bag being used. The hole size and lock style are directly related to the size of the bag (the amount of material to be gathered and closed) and weight (thickness) of the film. Improperly sized tab locks will either be too loose, not providing a good closure, or too tight, which can tear the film as the tab is affixed.

11.D.2.c. Tamper-evident closures

Both consumer and manufacturer interest resulted in the development of tamper-evident seals for the bread bag (**Figures 11.073** and **11.074**). A tamper-evident tape is applied in place of the twist tie or lock-style seal and can not be reclosed. When opened, the tape provides a visual indicator of opening that cannot be defeated. Acceptance of this feature has been limited, likely related to its relative newness in the marketplace and a rather lack-luster consumer response.

To make bread bags even more tamper-evident, a machine has been developed to tie the bag with a tape closure, then flatten the pony tail and seal it using a hot air system (**Figure 11.075**). The flattened part runs through a perforator to allow the purchaser to readily open the bag. This system also works with existing twist-tie closers and can handle bag film gauges up to 2 mil.

11.D.3. Other bakery product packaging

Bakers have a variety of other product packaging options for their products. Some are designed to protect toppings and icings during distribution, while others provide both the baking pan and package container.

Packaging provides a "billboard" for marketers, who not only use the front, side and back panels for sales and promotion methods but also attach coupons or insert them into the package itself. If placed inside the package, the coupon must be printed with food-grade inks.

Among the newer aspects for packaging is an anti-microbial inks and coatings composed of silver zeolite and capable of eliminating the growth of bacteria, yeasts and molds inside food packages (Rice 2002). This same author described stand-up pouches for snacks and bulk cookie packages, as well as environmentally friendly biodegradable materials.

11.D.3.a. Paperboard tray

The paperboard or chipboard tray (**Figure 11.076**) and carton have long been used for bakery products. Traditionally, retail bakeries use this style of packaging for all but bread products, while commercial bakeries put these trays and cartons to work handling specialty baked foods (English muffins, par-baked dinner rolls, croutons, etc.) and sweet goods (cakes, pastry, doughnuts, danish, etc.).

Three principle production formats comprise paperboard trays and cartons used in the baking industry: (a) pre-glued trays and cartons that are hand-erected prior to product loading; (b) end-load cartons that are partially glued and are machine opened, loaded and sealed at speeds up to 350 units per minute; and (c) paperboard flats that are machine formed (**Figure 11.077**) using mechanical locks (interlocking corners) or hot melt glue. After forming, the trays are either hand or machine loaded; if a carton, after loading, the carton is automatically closed and sealed by a machine built for this purpose.

An interesting variation in paperboard cartons is used for items prepared at home in microwave ovens (Anon. 1993). Because microwaves do not brown crusts, some other method for achieving the right color was needed. Development of susceptor materials provided the answer. These metal-containing films react to bombardment with microwave energy in three ways: absorption, reflection and transmission. The susceptor is produced through all-over metallized and patterned depositions as well as sputtering methods. The metals used on the polyester films include aluminum, stainless steel and inconel, a chromium and nickel alloy. The whole package is developed by marrying the optimum choice of outer web, laminating method and susceptor, and selecting the desired sealing method. At home, the whole package goes into the microwave, allowing the susceptor to do its work.

11.D.3.b. Release-coated paper

Ovenable paperboard, which includes polyethylene terephthalate (PET), a crystallized polyester, that is used in a modified blend and adhered to 80-lb paper board, can replace aluminum foil for products that are baked and shipped in the same container (Stumpf 1989). Describing a different technology, Percifield (2007) discussed the use of bake-in paperboard trays using a high-tech release coating.

These release-coated corrugated baking trays (**Figure 11.078**) allow sheet cakes, for instance, to be baked, cooled and dumped without the use of pan spray or additional fat. Baking and then shipping baked foods in the same release-coated corrugated container permits wholesale bakers to appeal to an ever-expanding, environmentally conscious clientele. The recyclable trays are 99% derived from renewable resources and reduce refuse by eliminating secondary packaging. They also eliminate water usage for pan washing and energy for heating water to wash the pans.

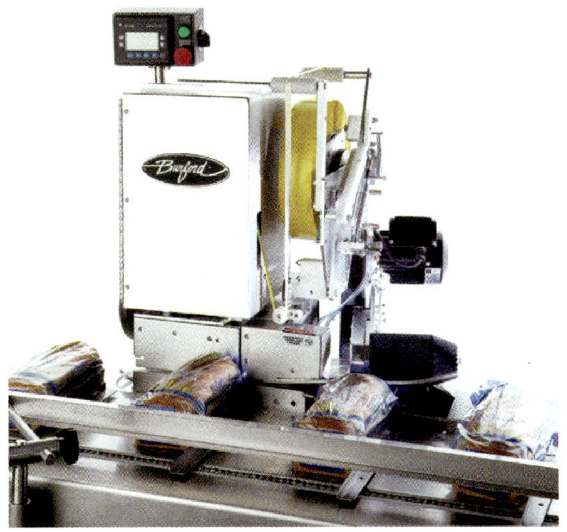

Figure 11.074. Tamper-evident tape-style closures can be applied by this machine at speeds greater than 100 bags per minute.
(Burford Corp.)

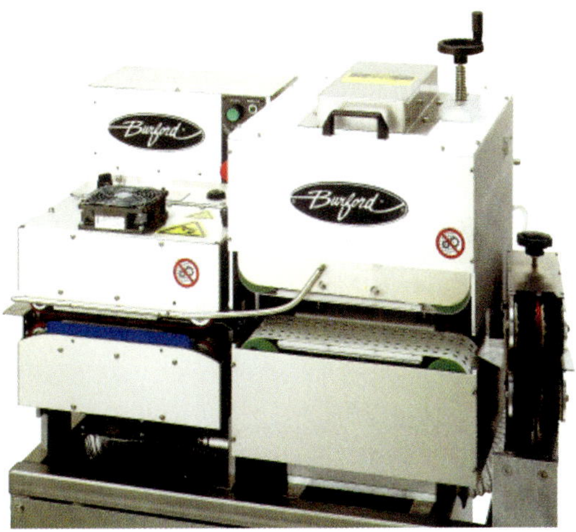

Figure 11.075. By flattening and sealing the pony tail of bread bags, this machine provides tamper-evident closures.
(Burford Corp.)

Figure 11.076. A paperboard "flat" is transformed into a tray. (Eagle Packaging Machinery LLC)

Figure 11.077. Paperboard carton closers can close up to 150 cartons per minute. (Kliklok-Woodman)

Figure 11.078. Pre-sliced products in ovenable trays require only the addition of a lid for transport. Their rigid, heavy duty construction allows them to be stacked on pallets for shipping. Stretch-wrapped, they form a solid stack that protects the product without load-shift. (Traybon Bakeries)

11.D.3.b. Clamshell packaging

Thermo-formed plastic containers for bakery products have become very popular at the retail level and in alternative format stores (Wal-Mart, K-Mart, Target, etc.). There are two basic formats: (a) a 2-piece unit consisting of a base and a separate inter-locking lid and (b) a 1-piece style where the base and lid are cast as a single unit with a hinge joining the two sections (**Figure 11.079**). There are unlimited combinations of dimensions for a wide variety of items (**Figure 11.080**).

Historically, the material of choice was oriented polystyrene (OPS). Its clear, rigid properties allowed development of visual packaging for baked foods as a transition from folding cartons or bags. As the bakery market began to shift from in-store bakery-based manufacturing to the current trend of commercial bakeries providing retailers frozen thaw-and-sell fresh product, the market was forced to provide clamshells with better cold-crack performance. That material based on clarity, cost and structural properties was polyethylene terephthalate (PET). This plastic is synthesized by the esterification reaction between terephthalic acid and ethylene glycol with water as a by-product or by transesterification reaction between ethylene glycol and dimethyl terephthalate with methanol as a by-product. PET yields a clear package, and in some 2-piece designs, the base is opaque and the top clear. PET is also available in blends of up to 100% post consumer recycled material, mainly from recycled pop/soda and water bottles (rPET).

Locks designed into the shell itself give secure closure of clamshells. These seals can range from corner or edge locks to full-perimeter seals (a labyrinth design), which provides a leak-tight seal around the perimeter of the package. Recent developments in lock design as well as other features provided significant improvements in automating the packaging process in commercial bakeries. Automation of the "de-nesting," checkweigh filling and closing of clamshells continue to drive costs down and manufacturing throughput up.

In retail application, a self-sticking band has been the industry standard; however, malicious entry into the side walls of those containers (bypassing the band) motivated the industry to provide higher levels of tamper evidence by creating more positive locks. An extreme application includes actual welding of the outer flanges and providing the consumer with easy opening "tear tabs" that clearly demonstrate tampering. The band is also used for package coding and identification purposes.

Recently, films have been introduced for baked products, snack foods and grocery products that are environmentally friendly. "Green" by manufacture, these films will "de-compost" in a commercial composting facility within months of entombment (Anon. 2006). Analysis completed by Krüger et al. (2009) confirmed that clamshell packaging, made from a unique biopolymer derived from plants rather than oil, emits fewer greenhouse gases and uses less energy when compared to clamshells manufactured with petroleum-based PET or rPET as well as conventional polymers. Proprietary technology processes natural plant sugars to make the biopolymer, which is then used to make finished products.

11.D.3.d. Foil

As a wrapping material, aluminum foil provides excellent barriers to moisture, oxygen and light and gives a bright shiny appearance, but its relatively high cost offsets these advantages. Metallized oriented polypropylene (MOPP) effectively replaces such bakery and snack packaging uses of aluminum foil and adds the benefit of flex-crack resistance.

As a material for disposable baking pans, however, aluminum foil competes well with paperboard and offers several advantages. Aluminum foil pans contribute no taste or odor to products, and although lightweight, they are rigid enough to protect delicate cakes and pastries. Aluminum foil withstands wide temperature variances, allowing bake-in as well as packaging roles, and goes from oven to freezer and back into the oven without altering the integrity of the container.

In the processing operation, aluminum foil pans require no dumping so fewer cripples occur. Because such pans go from makeup to packaging to the super-market and consumer, they eliminate the need for permanent pans. The first products to be produced and sold in aluminum foil pans were frozen cheese-cakes, prepared a 2-piece structure: an ovenable board disk inside a foil pan with a hole in the bottom. Aluminum foil packaging has since been used effectively for many products, including pies, breakfast rolls, danish pastries and cake items such as angel food, sheets and novelty shapes.

Aluminum foil pans can be printed in a wide range of colors and patterns using rotogravure methods. When pie pans are given a black exterior, the crust will bake faster and more evenly than in a plain aluminum pan.

To complete the package, transparent plastic covers and domes as well as clam-shell packaging can be snapped over the foil pans. A crimp closing system will be required, or the whole pan can be slipped into a clamshell.

Foil-laminated paper and paperboard have found use by bakers for many years. Such packages generally allow the consumer to reheat the baked foods in home ov-ens. Although aluminum foil packaging can be used in microwave ovens, if no part of the foil is allowed to touch the oven walls, consumers have been reluctant to take the chance. Aluminum foil packaging, its uses and alternatives were well described by Antoni (1981).

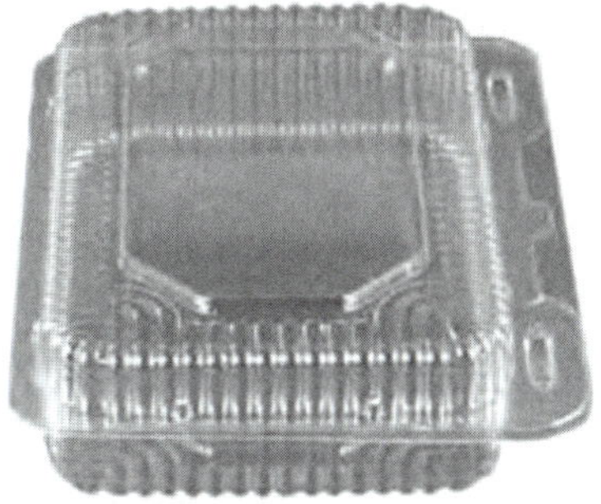

Figure 11.079. A clamshell package protects bakery products from baker to consumer. (CM Packaging)

Figure 11.080. Clamshell packages come in a variety of sizes and shapes. (CM Packaging)

11.D.4. Packaging coding

Price information and production or "use by" dates can be coded di-rectly onto bakery packages. For lock-tab seals, on-bag printing or on-car-ton printing, two principle methods are being used by bakers today: ink-jet (**Figure 11.081**) and laser (**Figure 11.082**) technologies. The ink-jet method uses specially designed printing heads to spray small beads of inks formulated for bakery applications at the surface being coded. Depending on the printing head selected, these beads of ink can be very small, in the micron range, resulting in excellent quality and clarity.

Laser printing systems are very precise and result in coding of high quality when properly adjusted and used with packaging material appro-priate for the laser coding application. In the laser method, the packaging's surface material is burned off to expose the layer of material below. Obvi-ously, to be effective, there must be good color contrast between the layers.

Both methods are capable of producing high-quality print and bar-codes that meet industry standards for coding, and both methods are well suited to the high-speed packaging lines used by commercial bakers. The ink jet method lends itself to printing on polyformed bags, overwrap and lock-tabs.

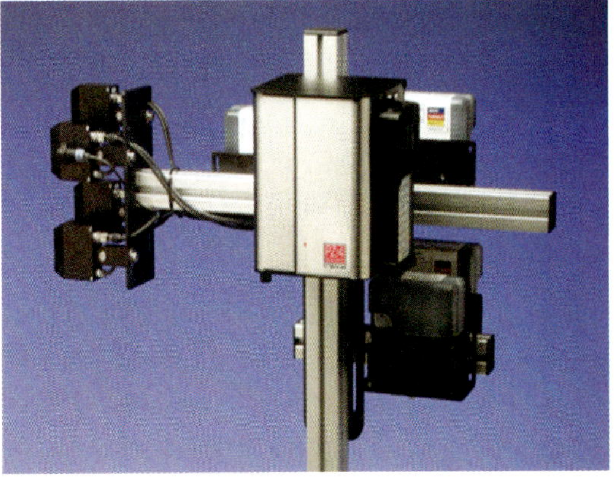

Figure 11.081. Ink-jet coders print on many packaging substrates. (Squid Ink)

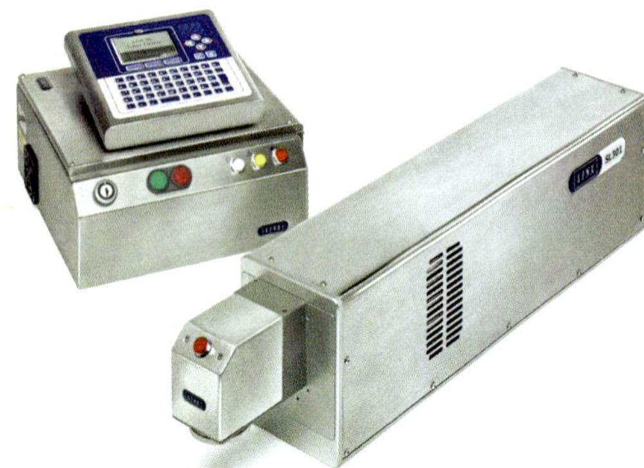

Figure 11.082.Laser systems indelibly "burn" in date codes and other information.
(Diagraph)

The laser coding method lends itself to corrugated cartons and paperboard trays, labeling and coated packaging where the surface layer is designed to be burned-off for coding.

For the most part, ink-jet and laser coding systems have replaced older technologies that stamped information onto tabs using fluid or paste-like inks or hot-stamping with foil ribbons.

11.D.5. Cost analysis

As with any bakery consumable, the cost of packaging materials presents a significant everyday expense. Trausch (2009) provided the following analysis of the materials, preparation, freight and warehousing costs. Several components are involved, not the least of which is the resin from which the packaging film is made. These resins are derivatives of oil and natural gas, and they rise and fall in price along with the base materials. As raw material costs to the petrochemical companies change, they are passed along to the film extruders, thus affecting the price of bakery packaging.

The price paid for packaging is also affected by (a) the size of the package: larger bags cost more; (b) the gauge of the film: heavier gauges have higher prices; (c) the ink percentage: the greater the ink coverage, the greater the cost; (d) the number of colors: each additional color increases press set-up time, adding to costs; (e) the choice of printing style: process vs. line printing adds to the time needed for press set-up and registration; (f) use of 7 and 8 colors: converters charge extra for use of new presses capable of 8 to 10 colors; and (g) quantity of order: press and bagmaking set-up time is pro-rated over the run of the order so the quantity differential is less as order size increases.

Most packaging converters will allow discounts on orders that are combinable. Combinations are a great way to control packaging costs, especially with small quantity orders. These combinations result in less press set-up time, hence the cost savings. Normal combination rules are: (a) All items must be the same size and gauge; (b) orders must be entered together; (c) a maximum of 2 cylinder and 2 color changes are allowed; (d) process images must be the same; and (e) shipping and "have ready" dates may apply. Individual converters may have other restrictions

The majority of the larger converters will pre-pay freight to a bakery location if the freight weight meets their criteria. The majority of the larger converters will offer 90-day warehouse terms. This policy allows bakeries to order at a larger quantity and pull various bag designs as required. The converters will issue "bill to storage" charges if the bags are not shipped within the 90 days.

11.E. Product Inspection

Regulatory compliance puts significant emphasis on product inspection. The requirement for traceability, performance validation and lot tracking all speak to documentation of the process, process parameters and quality assurance programs. Virtually all bakery production lines have some form of inline quality monitoring equipment installed. Checkweighing, metal detection, X-ray inspection and optical scanning are among the various technologies found in modern bakeries. Typically, the equipment installed to monitor process quality has built-in software that provides data collection and analysis, which documents the unit performance and quality attributes being inspected.

11.E.1. Checkweighing

Checkweighing is used principally in two places in the baking process — at make-up to weigh dough pieces and during packaging to check finished product weights. To ensure consistency of dough piece portioning during dividing operations, dough pieces are frequently weighed. However, the more common use of checkweighers in bakeries is during packaging. In either location, the weighing can be done manually with an at-line scale or automatically by an at-line or inline checkweigher.

In manual checkweighing, the operator will weigh individual dough pieces at frequent intervals on a calibrated scale reading out in fractions of an ounce or gram, although some scales indicate simply "under" or "over" weights. When weighing takes place at the divider, the operator can then manually make appropriate volumetric adjustments on the divider, and at most bakeries, the operator records readings and changes in the divider log.

Automatic checkweighers (**Figure 11.083**), on the other hand, will verify the weight of each unit (dough piece or package), ensure that it conforms to the preset values and reject any unit that is outside the established weight range (Benier 1983). An advantage to the inline checkweigher (**Figure 11.084**) after the divider is that rejected dough pieces can be reworked (typically by being tossed back into the divider's dough hopper), resulting in improved yield. Today's checkweighers are computer controlled, some having a feedback loop that automatically adjusts the divider whenever dough weights deviate from the set point by an established variance. All such checkweighers have data logging capability enabling operations to monitor divider performance and yield.

The conveyors that feed into and out of checkweighers automatically create the required separation between units necessary for accuracy in high-speed lines. Inline checkweighers now operate at speeds of up to 165 weighments per minute with an accuracy of ± 1 g.

Figure 11.083. A typical finished product checkweigher operates inline with packaging equipment by passing every item over a computer-monitored weighbelt.
(Mettler-Toledo Hi Speed)

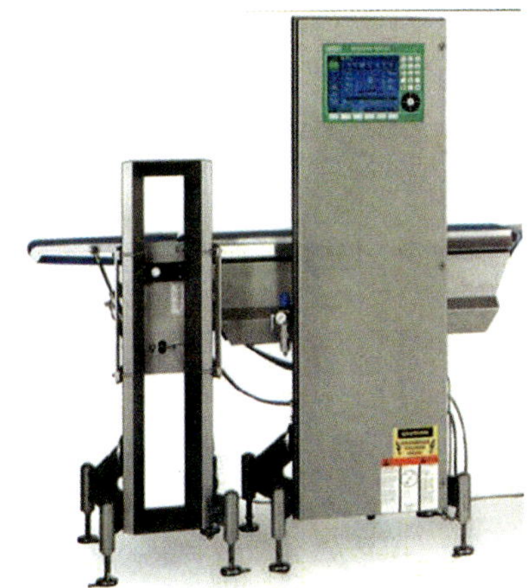

Figure 11.084. This checkweigher monitors dough piece weights and adjusts the divider without operator attention.
(Reiser)

11.E.2. Metal detector

Bakery processes, like the vast majority of food processing operations, are accomplished by equipment and vessels constructed of stainless steel, aluminum and, on occasion, carbon steel. The risk with any metallic construction, although quite remote, is that a dough piece could be contaminated by a scrap of tramp metal. Additionally, tramp metal can damage downstream equipment. Bakers understand these risks and install metal detectors on bakery production lines. Most frequently, the metal detector (**Figure 11.085** and **11.086**) is found at the end of the line, either just prior to or just after the packaging operation.

Metal detectors consist of two or more electrical coils arranged inside a housing so that the electrical fields generated by the coils are balanced with each other (**Figure 11.087**).

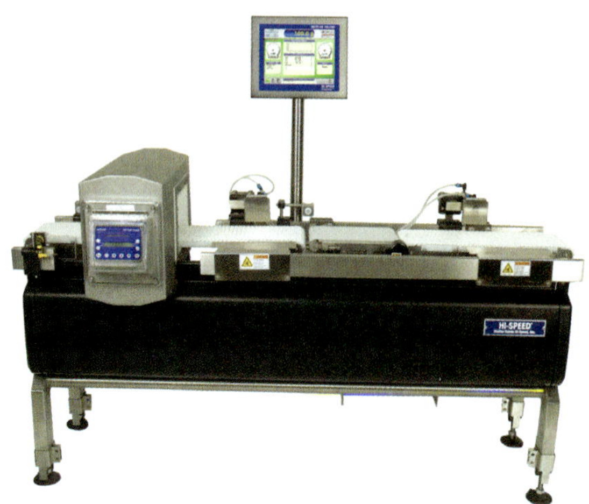

Figure 11.085. A checkweigher and metal detector work in combination, controlled from the large touch-screen user interface. (Mettler-Toledo Safeline and Mettler-Toledo Hi-Speed)

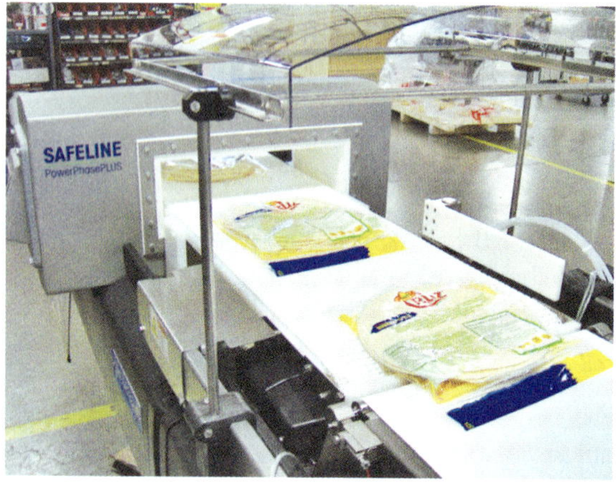

Figure 11.086. In practice, packaged tortillas travel over the checkweigher first, then through the metal detector. The white bar at right is the reject mechanism. (Mettler-Toledo Safeline and Mettler-Toledo Hi-Speed)

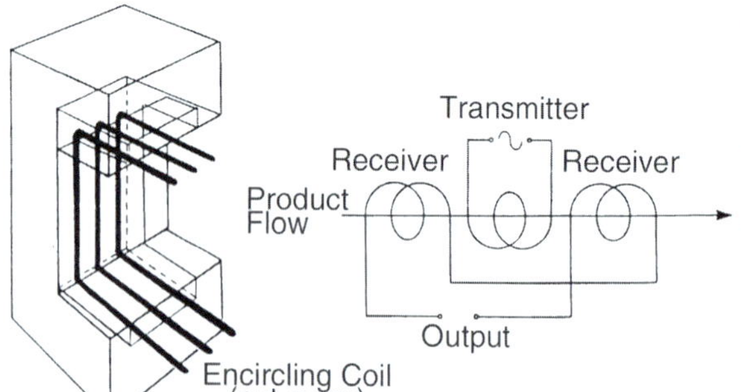

Figure 11.087. Metal detectors are based on the principal that metal moving through an electrical field will disrupt it. (Lock 1992)

When something metallic passes through the fields, they become unbalanced, and this phase shift disturbance is detected as a signal. State-of-the-art metal detectors are sensitive enough to pick up signals from a ferrous sphere of 0.2 mm (0.008 in.). These systems (**Figure 11.088**) detect the presence of ferrous (carbon steel) and nonferrous metals (aluminum, copper and various grades of stainless steel). The sensitivity of the metal detector is determined by the aperture opening (size of the area the product passes through) and the sensing head assembly.

Metal detectors can be programmed for the specific product being produced; some metal detectors have self-calibrating features that allow clusters of products (or product families) to be processed without requiring recalibration. The individual parameters for a number of different products are analyzed and combined automatically into a single optimized product "cluster" setting. As with checkweighers, computers that operate and monitor today's metal detectors collect operating data collection and perform statistical analysis. Recently, digital signal processing has been applied to checkweighers that greatly improves the reliability and flexibility of metal detectors (Gidman 1993). These features further assist the baker in meeting regulatory policies that require monitoring and record-keeping. Periodic testing will keep metal detectors operating properly and should be included in HACCP programs.

Moisture and salt, when combined as in baked foods, or certain forms of iron enrichment can sometimes produce error signals, known as "product effect." The phase shift produced by the product is not the same as that of metal, and by using a phase detection system, product effect can be ignored to a large extent while still allowing detection of small metal contaminants.

Moran (1983) provided guidance on how to best locate metal detectors on processing lines. Lock (1992) updated this topic as it relates to bakery applications and described product reject methods.

An interesting feature of some metal detectors is their ability to communicate directly to key personnel using text messages. Messages can be sent to maintenance and operations personnel on machine status, alerting them to performance issues and even advising on potential nonperformance and quality issues.

11.E.3. X-ray

X-ray technology has made major strides within the baking industry. The cost of X-ray inspection equipment has come into line with the more conventional devices used by the industry. Simply stated, X-ray inspection can distinguish between materials of different densities. The machines operate much the same way as medical or security X-ray systems. X-rays, generated by an electron tube, readily pass through low-density materials but are blocked by dense materials. The low-power X-rays used to inspect food products readily differentiate between glass, rock, bone and some plastics as well as all metals. In the fully shielded machine, the radiation funnels through a columnator to produce a thin curtain of X-rays through which the product passes. The rays are received by a linear detector array and sampled at a high rate by the computer.

Using the information it collects through the product scan, the inspection system creates a virtual image of the product being inspected. A library of material images, as well as operator programming, enables the inspection system to identify foreign material that may have made its way into a baked product. The major advantage to X-ray inspection is its ability to detect both metallic and nonmetallic foreign materials (**Figure 11.089**).

Systems are now available that operate inline at speeds up to 200 ft per minute and can inspect foods packaged in foil and metalized films with no loss of performance. And they have been combined with checkweighers (**Figure 11.090**).

Other uses exist for this technology (Gidman 1993). As a result of its ability to detect nonmetallic materials, X-ray inspection can be used to verify the presence and dispersion of the inclusions such as fruit, nuts or chocolate chips in a product's formulation and intended to be in the product. Because of its ability to differentiate densities, X-ray inspection systems can also be used to examine grain structure of baked products, and in this use, X-ray inspection provides a nondestructive way of assuring product quality.

11.E.4. Optical scanning

Finished product quality attributes can easily be quantified through optical scanning. Optical scanners (**Figure 11.091**) use sophisticated computer programs to analyze product images captured by camera under precise lighting conditions, comparing preprogrammed product standards in real time. Because of the mathematical calculations performed by the software, computers used in optical scanning are industrially hardened high-speed processors.

The optical scanners use 2- and 3-dimensional imaging (**Figure 11.092**) as well as color-based techniques for the data acquisition necessary to discern product characteristics (Scott 2005). Optical scanning is used for bread, buns, muffins, baguettes, cookies and crackers. The continuous monitoring of product provides several benefits: (a) It provides bakeries with real-time information on the performance of its production lines; (b) it enables trends to be identified, thereby assisting plant operations with continuous improvement programs; and

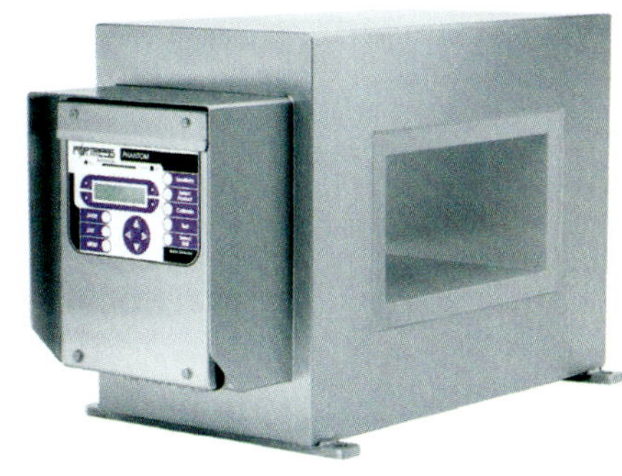

Figure 11.088. Digital signal processing provides fast, accurate detection of ferrous and nonferrous metals, including stainless steel, by this metal detector. (Fortress Technology)

Figure 11.089. An X-ray system can reveal the difference in densities between baked foods and foreign materials. This one is examining pies baked in aluminum tins. (Loma Systems)

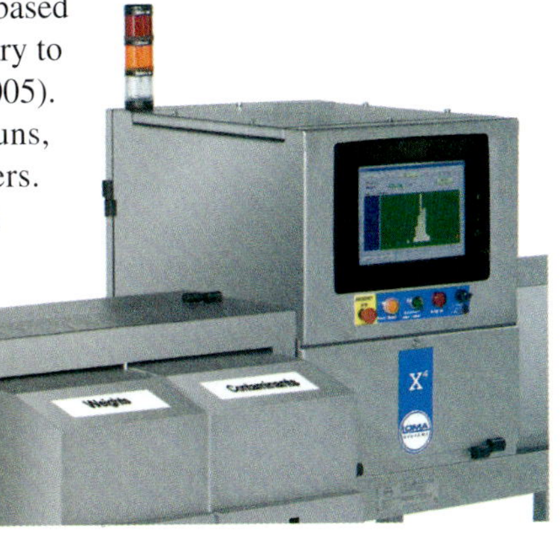

Figure 11.090. This X-ray inspection system also features checkweighing capabilities that enable the unit to inspect, weigh, reject and provide product reports. (Loma Systems)

Figure 11.091. Operating inline, optical scanners examine surface characteristics and can even measure height and volume. (Dipix Technologies)

Figure 11.092. A camera eye's view of the product passing below is recorded and analyzed in real time. (Dipix Technologies)

Figure 11.093. Vision systems can scan up to 1 million units per minute for color, size and shape and report back data on count and conformation. (Dipix Technologies)

(c) the system automatically provides data collection functions for finished product characteristics.

Optical scanners are capable of scanning 50 units per second at speeds of up to 160 ft per minute. Product characteristics such as shape, diameter, height, length, texture and color are all attributes that can be scanned. Over-the-belt systems such as that shown in **Figure 11.093** are in everyday operation at bakeries.

Vision systems, based on cameras linked to computers, for applications such as package inspection are also entering bakery use, and they have found wide acceptance for monitoring color and size of snack foods, particularly potato chips (**Figure 11.094**), although tortillas represent a new application. Miller (1998) explained the components of such systems and how they work, noting that future applications will involve not only quality control but also inventory management and process improvement.

11.F. Pattern Forming, Palletizing and Delivery Systems

Bakery products reach retail outlets or institutional customers in a variety of carriers — baskets, totes, trays or corrugated cartons. These carriers are typically loaded on dollies or pallets for movement within the bakery, in the transporting vehicles and the distribution centers. To an ever-increasing extent, the intra-plant handling of packaged bakery products — loading of the carrier with finished product, stacking the carriers onto their conveyance device (dolly or pallet) in preparation for market delivery — is being converted from a manual to an automated operation.

11.F.1. Product handling

Baskets and totes are permanent containers with sufficiently high side or end walls so that, when filled with loaves or with buns or rolls and stacked or nested in each other, the product remains protected against crushing. Trays, in contrast, have low side walls and require transport racks into which they fit (designed for the particular tray) to support and provide spacing between products.

Baskets, totes and trays are favored in distribution systems where the carrier is returned to the bakery. These carriers have a useful life of 3 years or more and therefore a low cost-per-use when compared with corrugated cartons. Where the transport is one way (the carrier will not be returned to the bakery), corrugated cartons become the carrier of choice.

Among the more popular and versatile designs of basket type containers are the multilevel "basket trays" (**Figures 11.095, 11.096** and **11.097**). This basket, through various means noted in the caption descriptions, can be stacked with different clearances between them to accommodate product height. In their upper position, clearance is provided for bread and other high-profile bakery products (penny packed products, cakes, etc.). Stacked at their intermediate level, clearance is provided for buns and other bakery products having a lower profile (sweet rolls, pies, danish). In its lowest position, the trays are nested for their return trip to the bakery. Thus, the multilevel basket tray enables the cube of a transport vehicle to be maximized.

11.F.2. Automatic basket loading

In intermediate- and large-volume bakeries, the trend is to convert manual loading and transport of the baskets and trays into totally mechanized and highly flexible systems that perform the product pattern forming and transfer operations under programmable computer control.

The first step in the automatic loading of the shipping basket is forming the pattern. Two principal methods are employed in pattern forming. The traditional and more mechanical approach uses a rotating table to position the product and form the array, or pattern. The rotating table method relies on gates and pusher mechanisms to achieve proper product count as well as to position the pattern in the former. The rotating table pattern former is available as a stand-alone unit; however, it is usually an integral part of an automatic tray loader (**Figure 11.098**).

The second method uses pick-and-place technology to form the product pattern. The pick-and-place can be performed using linear motion actuators or robotic units (**Figure 11.099**).

After the pattern is formed, it is loaded into the distribution carrier. Two different techniques characterize loading methods. The first method uses an articulated conveyor, slide or drop-gate to lower the formed pattern into the shipping basket as the basket passes under the discharge of the loader (**Figure 11.100**).

The second approach is robotic, where the pattern is formed and placed by the robot using a vacuum end-arm tool, or end effector, for pickup and placement of the product (**Figures 11.101**, **11.102** and **11.103**).

Robotic pattern forming and loading systems have numerous common components: a controller, a manipulator, an end effector (or hand) and a basket handing system.

The programmable multi-axis controller is either vision based or position based. In the case of a vision based controller, a camera determines product location and position and calculates the pick-and-place motions required to form the product array and load the shipping basket. In a positioned-based robotic system, product is located in a defined queue for the robots pick-and-place actions.

The manipulator represents the physical arm or device required for moving and positioning materials, and the end effector, or hand, can be configured either as a gripper or vacuum lifter that carries out specifically designated tasks of product pick-and-place.

Figure 11.094. All chips pass through a color sorting system that eliminates under- and over-cooked pieces. (Key Technologies)

Figure 11.095. The multi-level baskettrays (foreground, tan color) use repositionable "bails" to achieve variable stack height. Other tray styles can be cross-nested (foreground, green color) to save space on the return trip. Open grid and open sides allow ventilation and product visibility. (Buckhorn)

Figure 11.096. Without a bail mechanism, these basket trays achieve different stack heights (nested, intermediate and full) through positioning of the basket to engage the shoulders cast into the carrier. (Rehrig Pacific)

Figure 11.097. In Europe, the Broban crate, a standard crate design, transports and displays bakery products for sale. A bail provides support for the crate in its proper position, and with the bail lowered, an intermediate tray position suitable for buns and rolls is achieved. Positioned on a dolly, with the rear elevated, the nested crates can be used as the in-store display.
(Van de Windt Verpakking BV)

Figure 11.098. A rotary table accepts product from the bagger and turns to form the correct pattern for loading the carrier basket or tray.
(Turkington USA)

Figure 11.099. Vacuum cups pick up packages and place them in proper orientation for loading the carrier basket or tray.
(AMF Bakery Systems)

The basket handling and positioning system places the basket in position for loading and then discharges the loaded basket to the basket stacker. Usually, some type of sensing device is provided that checks the packages as they arrive at the pattern-forming station to ensure that they are properly secured with either a plastic clip or tie. This verification protects the system against malfunction in case of a faulty package.

In operation, loaves are allowed to accumulate on the infeed conveyor, to be released to the pick-up table in groups and numbers designated by the pattern program. The loader head, operating on the vacuum principle, descends and picks up the packages. As it ascends again, the grouped loaves are gently held together by flaps on either side of the vacuum head. The head then travels to the loading station, rotates to position the loaves according to the preset pattern and then releases the loaves into the waiting basket or tray. The head returns to the pick-up table to complete the cycle, while the full basket or tray is released by the loading station to the take-away conveyor.

Pattern loaders normally will handle 60 to 150 loaves per minute depending upon product patterns, product weight and stability of the package. Robotic units operate at speeds of 12 to 22 cycles per minute. After the initial programming, changes in loading patterns are made to adapt to different bread or bun varieties, and the proper pattern is selected though the man-machine interface (MMI) and is ready to go in a matter of seconds after selection.

A more recent approach to basket loading has been to re-think basket patterns because robots are able to form and load patterns that could not be formed manually without damaging product. For one baker, the application of this technology resulted in a 25% increase in basket fill, as demonstrated by **Figure 11.104**.

Greater detail on robotic theory, design and applications can be found in vendor literature, the robotics handbook prepared by Nof (1999) and online through the Robotic Industries Association (RIA) at www.robots.org.

11.F.3. Basket handling systems

Bakeries put conveying systems to many uses, including movement of the empty baskets and trays to the production lines for loading; transport of loaded product trays to stacking and rack loading operations; and in some instances, for the routing stacks and racks to the shipping and distribution area.

The basket or tray handling system begins with denesting empty baskets and trays. Various robotic, gantry and elevator-based denesters are designed for this purpose. Depending on denester design, unstacking is performed either mechanically (**Figure 11.105** and **11.106**) using grippers to denest the stacked empty baskets and trays or robotically.

The unstacker removes baskets from their nested stack either from the bottom or from the top, with the top unstackers being further differentiated into units that unstack from a constant level or from a variable level.

For handling stacks of cross-nested empty baskets, an unstacker equipped with a turntable is used; the cross-nested basket is sensed using a proximity or photo-eye sensor and then rotated 90° to maintain proper basket orientation. Unstacking rates vary from 15 to 30 baskets per minute depending upon basket style and complexity of the nesting.

Stacking represents essentially the reverse of unstacking. Stackers automatically build up stacks of baskets or trays filled with the product, usually from the bottom up (**Figure 11.107**), to a preselected stack count that typically corresponds to the height limit imposed by the transport vehicle. In one type of stacker, the filled baskets enter the lift section near the bottom of the unit, one at a time. Here, each basket is raised one position, thereby permitting the stacking lip on the lower basket to fit into the corresponding stacking groove on the bottom of the basket above.

While the stacked baskets are held in position by movable horizontal supports, the next basket enters the lifter to repeat the cycle. After the desired stack height is attained, the full stack is lowered onto the discharge conveyor for transfer either to a dolly loader, directly onto the floor, or onto an in-floor conveyor to be transported to the shipping department.

Basket and tray handling and palletizing systems have been described by Rader (1984), Benson (1989) and Higham (1991), among others. Efficient loading of trucks and comparisons of stacked baskets vs. racked trays were discussed by Stritch (1986) and Davis (1999), while McNeely (2001) examined post-order packaging automation methods that included laser-guided vehicles and multiple-tier picking technologies. Examples of bakery shipping systems in action were offered by Richter (1984), who described distribution of cakes and sweet goods, and McGuire (2002), who described updating his bakery's order assembly and distribution system for bread.

11.F.4. Case palletizers

As noted previously, corrugated cases are the preferred shipping method when the product carrier will not be returned to the bakery, as is frequently the case when transporting frozen products as well as fresh products to distribution centers. Automated case-loading using equipment similar to, and some cases identical to, the basket and tray loaders is used to load the corrugated case. After loading, the case proceeds through automatic taping and coding equipment that seals the carton and applies the necessary product codes.

Most caseload product is then palletized for shipment. Palletizing is done manually or automatically using robots (**Figure 11.108**); the decision whether to perform this task manually or to automate it is usually dependent upon case size, volume of product being produced and labor rates.

11.F.5. Conveyors

A distinctive feature of modern baking plants is the integration of the various processing steps into a synchronous system by means of suitable conveyors. In the early days of commercial baking, each step in production constituted an essentially

Figure 11.100. A drop-gate loader shifts the full pattern of assembled products into a basket or tray waiting below. (Turkington USA)

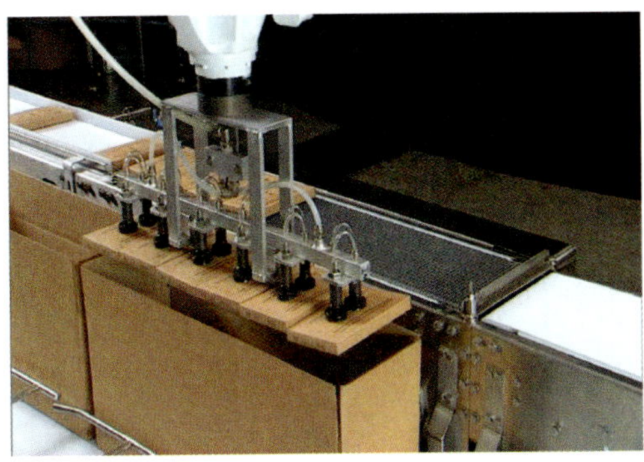

Figure 11.0101. An articulated pick-and-place arm moves the full pattern of assembled products into a carton waiting to the side. (Raque Food Systems)

Figure 11.102. This gantry style robot gathers loaves on its pick-and-place transfer head and lightly compresses the outside packages to yield a tight, attractive pattern in the basket. (AMF Bakery Systems)

Figure 11.103. This system for loading packages of bread or buns into basket delivery trays can integrate with gantry or articulated robot loaders. (Stewart Systems)

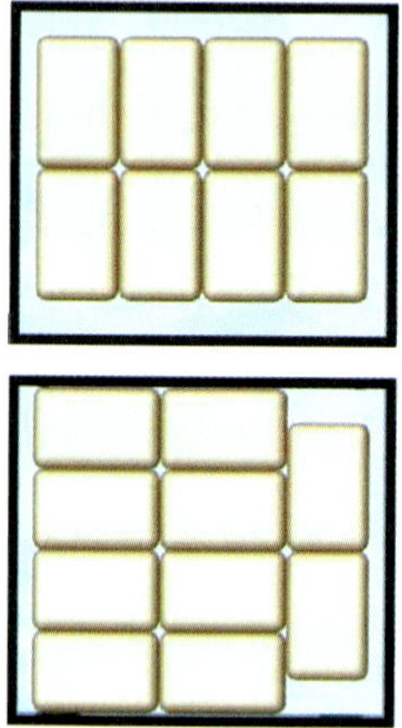

Figure 11.104. The original loading pattern (left) is optimized (right), allowing a 25% increase in basket fill. (Colborne Foodbotics)

Figure 11.105. Mechanical grippers denest basket trays. (Turkington USA)

separate function that required the manual transfer of product or material to the next processing phase. The extensive automation of individual equipment units, notably proofers, ovens, coolers and slicing and packaging machines, imposed the need for equally automated transfer and conveying mechanisms so that the separate production steps could be connected into a smoothly functioning and efficient system. It is in their primary role as connecting links between production steps that conveyors will be considered at this point. Their use as an integral component of conveyorized proofers and ovens, coolers and similar mechanized equipment has been described earlier.

Conveyors perform a wide variety of tasks in the bakery, and each task carries with it different functional requirements for the conveyor. In turn, these requirements must be met by the use of a suitable type of conveyor. Among available types are systems whose carrying surfaces are in the form of table tops, flat tops, free and powered rollers, coated and uncoated fabrics, as well as chains, slats, wire rods and meshed wire.

Heavy duty conveyors of the flat-top type and rough-top belting are generally used for the transport of heavy pan loads. For lighter-weight applications such as product conveying and cooling, various plastic and metal grid or link belts are used.

Recently, extremely low-friction flat-belt modular plastic conveyors (**Figure 11.109**) have been used to convey individual dough pieces within the baking process. Specific applications have included checkweighing and replacement of the intermediate proofer with a continuous run of conveyor that provides the desired dwell time between dividing and proofing.

Materials employed in conveyor construction vary according to the demands of their particular use. Cotton fabric, rubberized cotton and canvas, multi-ply synthetic belting, stainless steel and various types of plastic are used. The use of plastic belting reduces pan wear in pan handling systems and also cuts ambient noise. The introduction of lateral belt flexibility — the ability to make turns — greatly simplified conveyor design and layouts because it eliminated the need for transfers between straight runs and turns.

Variations of the flexing belt design have enabled construction of conveyorized proofers and ovens, as well as spiral product coolers and freezers, where the conveyors travel through multiple tiers in a spiraling pattern. To avoid frictional wear, the belt is preferably supported by a slider rail bed made of a low-friction material such as ultra-high-molecular-weight (UHMW) polyethylene or by a roller chain where supporting roller assemblies provide low friction support of the chain.

In-floor conveyors, once thought to be the leading edge of new distribution methods have not found wide spread acceptance. The in-floor conveying system has been supplanted by distribution centers, pick-to-order systems and direct-ship methods. An innovative application of conveyors, the in-floor conveyors facilitates the transfer of product in stacked baskets or trays from the bakery's packaging department to the shipping department. These conveyors are arranged in interconnecting loops of slowly moving chains that travel at speeds ranging from 40 to 90 ft per minute.

The conveyors consisted of 4 parallel strands of link-style conveyor chain. The 2 outer chain strands, installed 12 to 18 in. apart depending on the basket size, protrude about 0.5 in. above the floor level and serve as the load-carrying segment. The inside strands travel slightly below floor level and constitute the return section of the chain loop. An advantage to the in-floor conveyor is that it does not impede cross traffic by hand trucks, dollies or fork lift trucks while the system is in operation.

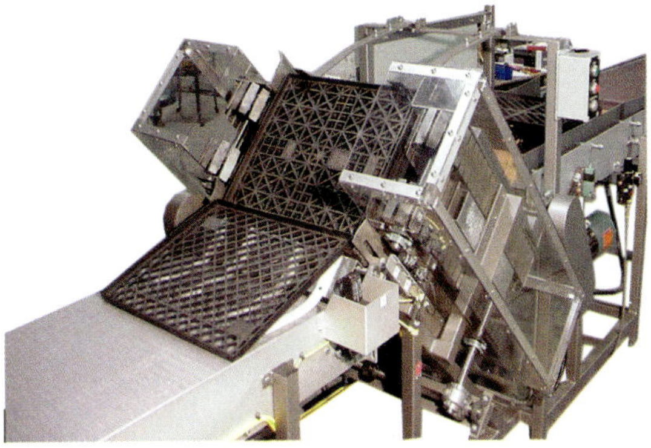

11.G. Pan, Basket and Tray Washers

Various pan cleaners that use brush and air knife assemblies (**Figure 11.110**) are installed in today's production lines. Even though the coating and glazing of pans has improved in recent years, the variety of toppings and glazing applied to various baked foods requires ongoing pan washing. Also, shipping baskets and trays are subjected to various contaminants outside the bakery environment during the course of product distribution. Dirt and debris are frequently found in returned baskets and trays, and the plastic materials from which they are made tend to build up static charges, thus attracting dirt. Pan, basket and tray washing meet these cleaning requirements.

Pan, basket and tray washers (**Figure 11.111**) are essentially the same equipment with minor variation; the exception is the submersible washer used for shipping baskets. The pan, basket and tray washers consist of (a) an infeed section that positions the pan basket or tray in the proper orientation for cleaning, (b) a washing section that sprays the unit being cleaned with high-pressure wash water at 60°C (140°F) and contains an appropriate loaf foaming detergent, (c) a stripping section that uses an air knife or nozzles to remove a majority of the wash water from the unit being cleaned, (d) a rinse section that removes any residual wash water, (e) a drying section that consists of air knives and heated air that dry the basket tray or pan and (f) a discharge section that returns the cleaned unit to its proper orientation.

Pan washers are available in a wide variety of designs, ranging from small batch-type units to straight-line tunnels and return-type tunnels, all of which are capable of cleaning strapped pan sets, bun pans, pots and shipping baskets and trays. All washers subject the soiled items to high-pressure sprays of hot recirculated detergent solution drawn from a supply tank for predetermined durations. This stage is followed by rinsing with heated fresh water and, in some cases, by hot air drying.

Operating parameters such as wash and rinse temperatures and times, spray pressures and conveyor speed are automatically regulated by a control panel. A forced exhaust system vents the vapors generated during washing and rinsing cycles to the outside and assists in the hot-air drying of the washed pans or utensils. The pressure pumps are electrically interlocked with the door by a limit switch that shuts down the sprays when the door is open.

Straight-line tunnel pan washers, designed for bakeries operating continuous high-speed production lines, are often capable of conveyor speeds approaching

Figure 11.106. A denester tips the stack to facilitate removal of individual trays. (Stewart Systems)

Figure 11.107. This bottom-up stacker inserts filled baskets at the bottom and then lowers the completed stack onto a dolly waiting below. (Stewart Systems)

Figure 11.108. This automated case palletizer uses a robot to assemble shipping cartons in a preset pattern onto a pallet. (Stewart Systems)

Figure 11.109. A flat-top belt reduces the number of hinges to allow fast, thorough cleaning. (Intralox)

100 ft per minute. They clean up to 40 pans, baskets or trays per minute. When greater capacity is required, units containing multiple lanes are employed. These units are typically integrated into the production line for pans in the pan return loop and for trays and baskets in the empty basket supply conveyor system.

To reduce the environmental impact of the washer, several washer manufacturers have introduced systems using only 25% of the water traditionally consumed and discharged. These water savings are accomplished by reverse flow of the water within the washer, which significantly reduce the volume discharged. Additionally, rinse water is captured by the washer and used as the supply water in the washing section. Detergent is added to this "gray water," which is then is heated by electric or steam coils to maintain the washing temperature. Only the overflow from the washing section is discharged to the sewer system.

Figure 11.110. A pan cleaner, usually installed inline right after the depanner, removes debris from pans. (The Henry Group)

11.H. Lubrication

Machine lubrication for food industry applications is a highly complex subject. Food-grade, food-plant, USDA-certified, FDA-listed and USDA-registered are just some of the industry standards that must be considered and met by a facility's lubrication program (Eldridge 2007).

Trough greases and release oils should not be considered machine lubricants, although divider oils do provide this effect in a specific part of such machines. The discussion here concerns the lubricants applied to gears, motors, chains and processing equipment in general.

11.H.1. Selection

Lubricants for use in bakeries must provide the same protection and service that conventional lubricants do; however, they must also comply with food regulations and be physiologically inert, tasteless and odorless. Products for the food industry are often referred to as food grade; however, only H1-class lubricants are truly "food grade." Lubricants for the food and beverage industry are reviewed by NSF International and are registered as either H1 or H2. NSF adopted the classification standards of USDA, and FDA lists allowable lubrication substances at 21 CFR 178.3570 (lubricants with incidental food contact). A new standard, ISO 21649 (Safety of Machinery, Lubricants with incidental product contact, hygiene requirements) is being debated, and NSF has already stated that it will certify to that standard when adopted.

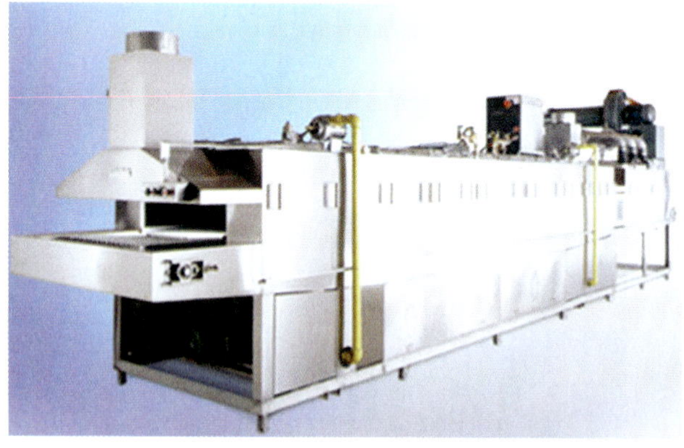

Figure 11.111. A tunnel pan washer prepares plastic baskets and tray to accept their next load. (Douglas Machines)

H1-class lubricants are suitable for incidental, or otherwise technically unavoidable, contact with the food product. These lubricants may be safely used in bakeries for processing equipment and on conveyors, that is, "above the line." On the other hand, H2 lubricants may be used if contact with the food product is absolutely impossible.

Eldridge (2007) observed that a previously common misconception was that performance had to be sacrificed to meet H1 standards, but with modern lubricants, including synthetic varieties, performance and life is the same or better than conventional industrial oils.

Beyond the requirement for food-grade lubricants, other factors affect the choice of a specific lubricant. The user should consider (a) the type of mechanical motion involved such as rolling or sliding, (b) the speed at which the unit operates, (c) temperature and humidity in which it will operate, (d) types of load to which the component will be subjected and (e) the operating environment. Also, the baker needs to consider the expected life of the lubricant as it will be used, its appropriateness of use and its cost. All of these factors need to be quantified and discussed with your supplier during the selection process.

11.H.2. Application

Once the proper lubricants have been selected, the baker should work with the supplier and equipment manufacturers to establish an effective preventive maintenance program that optimizes equipment life and minimizes total cost of lubrication. Costs involve not only the cost of the lubricant but also the labor involved in maintaining the lubrication program, the cost of the inventory and the downtime required for lubrication.

Weekly check sheets should be developed for the lubrication program. The check sheets could list all the lubrication points, the specific lubricant to be used and the method for application. The sheets also should provide space for comments and a check block that indicates lubrication has been performed as defined. The weekly check sheet thus provides a complete reference tool for the lubricator and ensures timely lubricant application and proper lubricant use, and it provides bakery managers with documentation as part of the preventive maintenance program.

Proper lubrication is key to continued standard performance of bakery production equipment. For maintenance and operations management, it is advised to invest in your lubrication program wisely; it will pay back invisible dividends for years to come.

References

Anonymous. 1993. Film advances. Baking & Snack 15 (4): 39.

Anonymous. 2006. Biodegradable plastic made from plants, not oil, is emerging. USA Today, Dec. 26, 2006.

Antoni, P. 1981. Aluminum foil packaging. Proc. Am. Soc. Bakery Engrs. 55: 146.

Baird, B. 2008. Baking Hall of Fame 2008 inductees: Otto Rohwedder. Proc. Am. Soc. Baking 84: 21.

Bastasch, F.J. 1989. Slicing. Proc. Am. Soc. Bakery Engrs. 65: 194.

Bedford. Undated. Biodegradable Ties. Bedford Industries: Worthington, MN.

Benier, J. 1983. Automated checkweighing. Proc. Am. Soc. Bakery Engrs. 59: 113.

Benson, A.R. 1986. Controlled atmosphere packaging. Proc. Am. Soc. Bakery Engrs. 62: 132.

Bradley, H.H. 2004. Cake walk. Baking & Snack 26 (2): 103.

Bradley, H.H. 2005. The final touch. Baking & Snack 27 (9): 69.

Burrington, K.J. 2004. Topping it off. Baking & Snack 26 (5): 87.

Champagne, L., and Davis, S.K. 2001. Applications of ultrasonic technologies in food production. Proc. Am. Soc. Baking 77: 201.

Clyma, K. 2008. Top of the line. Baking & Snack 30 (6): 109.

Cornell, M. 1998. Any way you slice it. Baking & Snack 20 (3): 46.

Cox, P. 2007. Slicer Maintenance and Instruction. Hansaloy: Davenport, IA.

Davis, B. 1999. From bagger to truck — the lost frontier. Proc. Am. Soc. Baking 75: 63.

Doerry, W.T. 1985. Packaging bakery foods in controlled atmospheres. AIB Tech. Bull. 7 (4).

Eldridge, K. 2007. How to make your food or beverage facility successful. Machinery Lubrication. Nov. 2007. Also published online by Klüber Lubrication at www.kluberna.com.

Fitzmaurice, D.T. 1970. Selection and care of slicer blades. Bakers Digest 44 (3): 52.

Formo, A.C. 1981. Bakery packaging in the 1980s. Bakers Digest 55 (5): 88.

Formost. 2009. History. The company: Woodinville, WA. Published online at www.formostpkg.com.

Gidman, S.T. 1993. Contaminant detection technologies. Proc. Am. Soc. Bakery Engrs. 69: 139.

Gorton, L. 1983. The Swiss Colony breaks tradition: manual methods give way to automation. Baking Equipment 5 (5): BE-6.

Gorton, L. 1996. Wafers and beyond. Baking & Snack 18 (9): 56.

Gorton, L. 2002a. Spray and wash, glaze and top. Baking & Snack 24 (5): 74.

Gorton, L. 2002b. Premium bagging. Baking & Snack 24 (8): 93.

Gorton, L. 2009. Season to taste accurately. Baking & Snack 31 (3): 75.

Higham, J.D. 1991. Automation in shipping and packaging. Proc. Am. Soc. Bakery Engrs. 67: 150.

Hofberger, R. 1999. Processing and food uses of chocolate. AIB Tech. Bull. 21 (7).

Jurist, M.A. 1964. Films for baked foods. Bakers Digest 38 (1): 74.

Kale, E.L. 1987. Package power. Proc. Am. Soc. Bakery Engrs. 63: 64.

Kiefer, G.J. 1989. Bagging. Proc. Am. Soc. Bakery Engrs. 65: 197.

Krüger, M., Kauertz, B., and Detzel, A. 2009. Life cycle assessment of food packaging made of Ingeo biopolymer and (r) PET. ifeu – Institüt für Energie- und Umweltforschung GmbH: Heidelberg, Germany. Published online at www.natureworksllc.com.

Lecrone, D.S. 1980. Automated roll slicing and handling into packaging. Proc. Am. Soc. Bakery Engrs. 56: 127.

Lecrone, D.S. 1980. Automated roll slicing and handling into packaging. Proc. Am. Soc. Bakery Engrs. 56: 127.

Levine, L. 2007. Product damage in mixing and coating drums. Cereal Foods World 52 (2): 81.

Lock, A. 1992. Update on metal detectors. AIB Tech. Bull. 14 (3).

McCloskey, K.E., Summy, C.D., and Welch, R.C. 1966. Chocolate and cocoa powders for the baking industry. Bakers Digest 40 (4): 65.

McGuire, B. 2002. From the floor to the door. Proc. Am. Soc. Baking 78: 250.

Miller, K. 1998. Vision systems. Proc. Am. Soc. Bakery Engrs. 74: 153.

Moran, J.M. 1983. Metal detectors. AIB Tech. Bull. 5 (9).

Nof, S.Y. 1999. Handbook of Industrial Robots, 2nd ed. John Wiley & Sons: New York, NY.

Percifield, S. 2007. The paper chase. Baking & Snack 29 (2): 110.

Petrella, G.L. 1978. Automatic packaging of buns, rolls and bread. Bakers Digest 52 (6): 28.

Rader, J.J. 1984. Automated packaged product systems. Proc. Am. Soc. Bakery Engrs. 60: 75.

Rice, J. 2002. Film technologies on the march. Baking & Snack 24 (3): 62.

Richter, R.T. 1984. Distribution of cakes and sweet goods. Proc. Am. Soc. Bakery Engrs. 60: 85.

Sammons, K. 2002. Post oven toppings. Proc. Am. Soc. Baking 78: 160.

Scott, A. 2005. Adaptive vision systems. Proc. Am. Soc. Baking 81: 133.

Self, B., Jensen, C., Horner, P., and Timberlake, N. 1984. The poly bag — A package for bread and rolls. AIB Tech. Bull. 6 (9).

Smith, J.P. 1994. Modified atmosphere packaging for bakery products. AIB Tech. Bull. 16 (3).

Smith, V.O. 1967. Polyolefin films. Bakers Digest 41 (3): 64.

Spooner, T.F. 1986. Problem-free bread slicing a matter of proper blade choice and maintenance. Baking Equipment 8 (1): BE-36.

Stanford, J.D. 1972. Bread slicer maintenance. Proc. Am. Soc. Bakery Engrs. 48: 119.

Stines, H.F. 1970. Slicer innovation. Bakers Digest 44 (1): 80.

Stritch, J.J. 1986. Container designs to reduce distribution costs. Proc. Am. Soc. Bakery Engrs. 62: 83.

Stumpf, S.O. 1989. New high heat materials for bakery use. Proc. Am. Soc. Bakery Engrs. 65: 230.

Thomas, G. 1985. The use of flexible packaging materials in the bakery foods industry. AIB Tech. Bull. 7 (12).

Trausch, T. 2009. Private correspondence.

Wenban, H.J. 1951. The History of Forgrove Machinery Ltd. 1901-1951. The company: Leeds, UK. Summarized by the Baker Perkins Historical Society online at www.bphs.net.

Whitaker, S. 2007a. Icing on the cake. Baking & Snack 29 (7): 69.

Whitaker, S. 2007b. Building better bags. Baking & Snack 29 (7): 107.

Whitaker, S. 2009. Back on top. Baking & Snack 31 (6): 75.

Wing, D.H. 1975. Enrobing of bakery products. Am. Soc. Bakery Engrs. 51: 136.

Wrightman, D.F. 1989. Waterjet cutting of bakery foods. Proc. Am. Soc. Bakery Engrs. 65: 110.

Recommended reading

Benson, A.R. 1986. Controlled atmosphere packaging. Proc. Am. Soc. Bakery Engrs. 62: 132.

Berne, S. 2006. On target. Baking & Snack 28 (3): 45.

Carrigan, T. 2001. Packaging — evolution to innovations. Proc. Am. Soc. Baking 77: 230.

Egan, T.M. Jr. 1988. Vision inspection advances baking. Proc. Am. Soc. Bakery Engrs. 64: 140.

Gales, C. 2002. Robotics in baking. Proc. Am. Soc. Baking 78: 182.

Gorlich, M.P. 2001. Modified atmospheric packaging. Proc. Am. Soc. Baking 77: 151.

Gorton, L. 1993. Coating and topping. Baking & Snack 15 (8): 45.

Hendrix, J. 2007. Cost effective robotics. Proc. Am. Soc. Baking 83: 118.

Hiebert, A.C. 1978. Automated pallet and basket handling systems. Proc. Am. Soc. Bakery Engrs. 54: 132.

Hohenthal, T., and Seguine, E.S. 1987. Selection, specification and use of chocolate in confectionery and baking. AIB Tech. Bull. 9 (9).

Hrdina-Dubsky, D.L. 1993. Packaging, modified. Baking & Snack 15 (5): 49.

McWard, C. 1994. Modify and control. Baking & Snack 16 (9): 40.

Sadwith, H.M. 1979. Machinery for cleaning and drying of plastic trays and baskets. Proc. Am. Soc. Bakery Engrs. 55: 157.

Sagan, B. 2008. Robotics in baking. Proc. Am. Soc. Baking 84: 118.

Salzman, J. 2001. Icing on the cake. Baking & Snack 23 (6): 63.

Steward, C. 2007. Packaging for high speed vertical production. Proc. Am. Soc. Baking 83: 76.

Taylor, R. 2002. From the door to the store. Proc. Am. Soc. Baking 78: 258.

Wilson, R.L. Jr. 1975. Coding systems for bakers. Proc. Am. Soc. Bakery Engrs. 55: 169.

Whitaker, S. 2004. Topping it off. Baking & Snack 26 (5): 87.

CHAPTER 12

Specialty Equipment

Updated by Hans van der Maarel (Parts A-D and G),
L.A. Gorton (Parts E and F)
and Michael Bakhoum, MS (Part H)

Machinery to make cakes, cookies, crackers, pies, sweet goods, flatbreads, muffins, bagels, sugar wafers, ice cream cones and more brings considerable ingenuity onto the bakery shop floor.

Hans van der Maarel
International Bakery Consulting, Ltd.
1070 Beech Hollow Rd., Ambler, PA 19002. Phone (215) 591-3821;
mobile (267) 252-2465; e-mail hvdm@comcast.net

Michael Bakhoum, MS
Bakery R&D Consulting, Inc.
1396 Huntington Dr., Mundelein, IL 60060. Phone (847) 680-1072;
e-mail mbakhoum1@aol.com

Wire-cut chocolate chip cookies slot into lanes leading to the packaging line. (*Baking & Snack*)

INTRODUCTION

If the baking industry produced nothing more than bread and rolls, it could certainly feed the world's consumers adequately and with sufficient variety to satisfy most desires. But the existence of sweet goods in the baker's repertoire makes life all the more pleasurable, while griddled items provide a wakeup that jumpstarts the consumer's morning. Equipment to produce such specialty products can "push the envelope" in terms of engineering creativity.

How can the baker and bakery engineer keep up with all this innovation? By using peer-based communication methods. First, individual membership in organizations such as AACC International, the American Society of Baking and the Institute of Food Technologists gives access to annual technical meetings, short courses and scientific papers, many of which have been used to prepare this book. Corporate membership in the Biscuit & Cracker Manufacturers' Association and the Tortilla Industry Association also enables attendance at annual technical conferences. AIB International not only offers intensive resident education in baking science, technology and maintenance engineering but also short courses and seminars about topics of current concern. These groups and other industry organizations provide networking opportunities as well, and a list of such resources appears in Appendix 4.

Of course, the industry's suppliers intensely track what their bakery customers want in terms of technology and communicate closely about opportunities. These vendors also participate in several large trade fairs that mount enormous exhibitions for the benefit of the baking industry. Currently on a staggered schedule of every 3 years, the International Baking Industry Exposition in the US and the iba World Market for Baking in Germany bring together equipment, ingredient and supplies manufacturers. Packaging is the focus of both Pack Expo in the US and interpack in Germany. These and the many regional and local events throughout the world allow bakers and food processors to get hands-on experience with new systems and to look ahead at trends in equipment and processes.

A number of tightly focused business periodicals, now provided in print and digital formats, serve the industry. *Baking & Snack, Milling & Baking News, Food Business News* and *World Grain* are prepared by Sosland Publishing Co. with the news and technical information needs of industry readers in mind. AIB International produces its *AIB Technical Bulletin*, which gives detailed insight into many technical and formulating trends. The editors and contributing writers of these publications and more report in depth about baking's many technical developments to help readers improve their business operations.

Some of these organizations are even experimenting with Web-based social media on the Internet such as Twitter, LinkedIn and Facebook to network with industry managers and spread the word about trends and new thinking in the grain-based foods industry.

12.A. Pastry and Pie Equipment
Updated by Hans van der Maarel

If only dough sheeting was as simple as what happens in the Saturday morning cartoons: When another attempt to snare the Road Runner fails, the steam roller squashes the Coyote. He peels himself up from the pavement. As he totters off to the next episode, he is intact in structure and thinner in body but definitely no wiser. Rheology has nothing to do with it.

In the real world of bakery processing, rheology has everything to do with it. Rheology is the science that studies how matter deforms under pressure. When it comes to dough rheology, the pressure can be applied by the baker's hand, by a roller, by a stamper and even by the force of gravity. To successfully sheet dough, you must make its rheological characteristics work with you, not against you.

Some doughs — corn masa for corn tortillas and tortilla chips — can be sheeted in a single step. Because such doughs are viscous without being elastic, the dough can be extruded by a constant pressure and sheeted by one set of rollers.

Doughs made with wheat flour, however, have viscoelastic properties because of the flour's gluten proteins. These doughs flow viscously when pressure is applied, yet they resist that flow elastically and partially spring back. The "bounce factor" must be considered throughout the makeup process, from creation of the initial dough blanket, through sheeting, reduction and forming.

Pie doughs tend not to be very elastic, but the opposite is true of danish, puff pastry and croissant doughs, hence the big difference in the machinery with which they are processed.

12.A.1. Pie production

Pies are pastries that consist of two distinct components: a thin, flour-and-shortening-based crust and a filling made of either fruits or some type of custard with or without an aerated cream or meringue topping. While the kind of filling, which generally represents the predominant portion of the finished product, normally establishes the specific character of the pie, the overall quality of the pie is influenced in large measure by the structural and eating properties of the crust. Pies may have only a bottom crust, as is usual with the custard and cream varieties, or both bottom and top crusts, as is generally the case with fruit-filled pies.

12.A.2. Pie production equipment

Pie crust dough involves a relatively simple formula and mixing only enough to develop the desired "flake," generally in an articulated double-arm mixer, which simulates the rubbing action of hand mixing. Vertical mixers with pastry knife attachments or horizontal sigma-arm mixers are used when higher volume is required. Optimum dough-out temperature is 15°C (60°F) or cooler, and 18°C (65°F) is considered too warm by many pie bakers (Gorton 1997).

Because pie dough is not mixed to development, processing lines must be designed to handle the relatively sticky, tacky material. Pie crusts are produced by one of two methods: (a) by pressing the dough into the desired shape between two dies and (b) by the more complex system of sheeting and cutting the dough. The first method uses a special dough press that finds application for the most part in small volume production runs, although high-speed equipment based on the same principle is also available. In its simplest form, the pie press stamps individually scaled and rounded dough pieces into thin sheets that will fit into a pie plate for both bottom and top crusts.

Pie crust forming by the sheeting method is performed by machines of two basic designs: (a) rotary machines, as shown in **Figure 7.11** (on Page 152), that have production rates of up to 15 large 2-crust pies per minute, but substantially greater capacities with small single-crust pies and tarts; and (b) straight-line machines of the type shown in **Figure 12.001**, whose production speeds may reach 300 large pies per minute and as high as 1,200 small pies per minute (Stephens 1972, Engstrom 1981).

Figure 12.001. A straight-line pie system uses sheeting methods to achieve high output rates.
(Colborne Foodbotics)

Moving pie dough from the mixer to the forming line was a manual process in the past, but today pivot dump systems are available to automatically unload mixers into troughs. The 1,000-lb-capacity troughs can be used to retard dough overnight to 2 to 4°C (35° to 40°F) or wheeled directly to the dough input system. The 120° over-tilt dump moves the trough forward, out and over the hopper of the dough delivery system. The manufacturer designed the trough with a controllable guillotine gate at the discharge end to permit the operator to monitor and adjust the dough flow and its height in the hopper to match production.

A specially designed sheeter head supplies the final step in this "hands-off" dough delivery method. Intended for both single- and double-crust lines, the head delivers a steady stream of dough, with its PLC controls matching line speeds for even flow onto the conveyor belt. A typical application would require one or two 4-in. wide, 0.5-in. thick dough sheets, although thickness is adjustable. One recent installation featured a flow rate of 50 640-lb batches per 10-hour shift, thus handling 3,200 lb per hour or 80 10-in. pie crusts per minute.

12.A.2.a. Rotary pie machine

In the rotary pie machine, all required operations are performed on a rotating table that carries the pie plates, held by special plate holders, past the various filling, sealing and trimming devices. Typically, the pie-making process on the rotary machine is as follows. An adjustable roller reduces the mixed dough to the required thickness, which is then cut into 3- by 5-in. pieces. These pieces are cross-rolled twice into thin round shapes. A bottom crust is placed manually into a pie plate and automatically docked and its rim wetted. The filling is then deposited, either manually or automatically, and the top crust placed manually on the filled pie shell. The completed pie is then automatically crimped, sealed, trimmed and lifted for manual removal from the machine.

This machine can also be tooled to run various other pie products such as pressed bottom tarts and crumb-based cream pie shells with varying sequences of operation.

12.A.2.b. Straight-line pie machines

In straight-line pie machines, all sheeting, forming, filling and finishing operations are performed automatically, with large systems capable of producing 1,200 5-in. or 200 8-in. to 9-in. pies per minute. The machine's hopper divides the dough into two batches, which are then fed by endless belts into separate sets of reduction rollers. Following reduction to the appropriate thickness, the dough bands enter a scaling mechanism in which rotary cutters divide the dough into 3- by 4.5-in. pieces (**Figure 12.002**). These pieces transfer onto two belts that convey them to the top and bottom crust rollers. Here, the dough pieces are cross-rolled twice to reduce their thickness by about one-half and to transform them into oval shapes. A second double cross-rolling, this time at right angles, follows and imparts a round shape to the thin sheeted dough pieces preparatory to their depositing in the pie plate.

A dispensing magazine supplies aluminum foil or ovenable paperboard pie plates into plate holders. These holders form part of a carrier system that conveys the pie through various operations by endless drive chains. The operations include inserting the bottom crust into a plate, spray wetting of the upper crust rim to ensure a good seal, depositing the fruit or other filling into the crust, placing of the top crust on the filled bottom shell and, finally, sealing, crimping and trimming off any excess dough. Crimpers offer a variety of edge styles: fancy, fork or plain (**Figure 12.003**). If a lattice top is desired, that pattern is cut or docked into the dough surface before it reaches the filled bottom crust. At the end of the forming line, automatic lifters raise the pies for removal and transfer to the takeaway conveyors that feed freezers or ovens and packing lines.

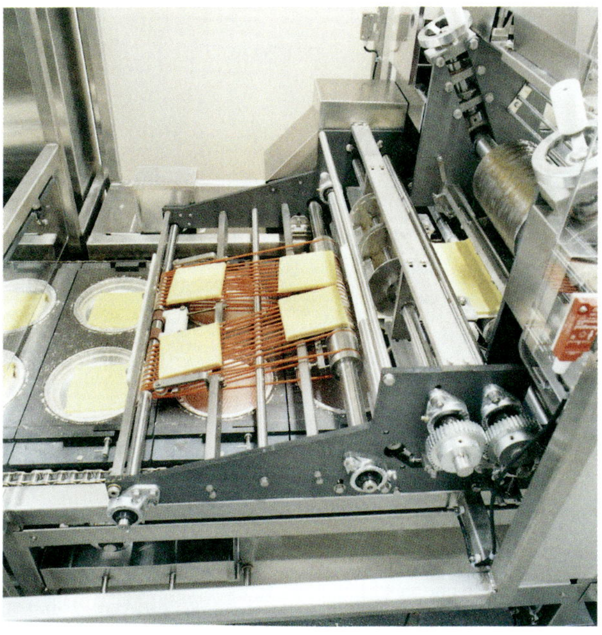

Figure 12.002. A block, or billet, of dough is deposited into a pie pan before moving to the stamping station. (Raque Food Systems)

Also available for higher throughput pie production are strip-sheeting pie systems. This method of sheeting does not include the cross sheeting normally done by straight-line pie machines mentioned above. However, it does allow users to run more than twice as fast because of the inline sheeting process, which runs at a faster pace.

Also, continuous stream lines sheet their doughs across the width of the processing table, currently 300 to 1,200 mm (12 to 48 in.) wide, thus allowing multiple lanes of pie tins to be filled simultaneously. Multiple-roll sheeters, also called satellite heads, gently but quickly reduce the thick dough blanket into a thin sheet properly sized for crusts. As the dough sheet transfers to the forming line, it is gently pressed and tamped into place in foil tins or baking pans held in traveling carriers, or platens. A rotary crimper, driven by the line shaft, runs synchronously to sever excess dough that is pulled off to the scrap return line. At the line exit, the pans are pushed out of their platens so they may continue to the next operation.

Figure 12.003. The stamping operation forms a shell with a crimped edge, but other edge styles are possible. (Raque Food Systems)

To produce pressed pies, such lines employ rotary dough feeders that eliminate weight variation between rows across the line. Some doughs, such as those for quiche, need heat to flow properly into cups so a heated hydraulic press unit is available. Another innovation is the scrap-free lattice top. The top dough is produced on a rotary cutter, using methods similar to rotary-cut cookies. The formed lattice pieces are synchronized with the filled pies passing below the transfer belt.

Figure 12.004. A stamping line forms miniature tart crusts. A stamping line does not create dough scrap that must be reworked.
(Tromp Bakery Equipment)

Equipment for automatic high-volume pie making by the press method has also been described (Frobeen 1960, Gorton 1997b). In one such system, with a capacity of 10,000 tarts per hour, the pie plates are centered by a conveyor under the template of the dough divider to receive extruded and precisely scaled cylindrical pieces of dough. In the next step, the dough pieces are pressed into the shape of the pans (**Figure 12.004**). Blocked, or pressed, pie shells do not generate scrap, and as Whitaker (2008) pointed out, the less scrap, the more tender the final crust.

Filling in predetermined amounts is then deposited into the dough shell, completing the final step in the forming of tarts and single-crust pies. With 2-crust pies, the filled shells proceed to a lidding mechanism, which places top crusts over the filled shells and then seals them via a stamping device. In addition to creating 2-crust filled pies, newer straight-line pie lines also produces pie shells for pumpkin, custard or cream pies. These shells can be made using a traditional trimmer, or to create an appealing high rim deep dish pie, the shell rims can be crimped with an optional rimmer section. These high-volume lines employ carriers with 14-in. centers for maximum output on 8-, 9- or 10-in. pies and shells. They output both standard and deep dish, or "high-pie," styles.

Scrap dough returns to the dough hopper. As Zelch et al. (2004) explained, most bakers incorporate scrap only into the dough for the bottom crust because any textural differences it causes will be less noticeable there. Gates (2005) observed that European pastry products tend not to be as flaky as American items and thus tolerate more rework.

To make cream pies and cheesecakes, the same types of machines, rotary and straight line, are used. In either case, the sequence of operation involves depositing crumb into a pie pan via auger-type fillers. After the crumb is deposited into the foil, a high-speed crumb forming device will spin the crust into its final form. At this point, a series of piston fillers deposit the necessary filling configurations, which can include cream or cheese filling (**Figure 12.005**) and various toppings consisting of whipped cream or some other aerated creme. Rotary systems will produce up to 25 crusts per minute while straight line systems can produce in excess of 150 per minute.

Hoskins (2005) looked into the future of pie processing equipment and predicted development of methods to emboss images onto pie crusts as well as to produce top crust cut-outs to give pies a homemade appearance. Woven lattices and different trim patterns also figured into possible developments.

12.A.3. Fried pie equipment

Figure 12.005. Soft fillings for "oven filled" pies such as pumpkin or custard styles are pumped into stamped crusts.
(Colborne Foodbotics)

Fried fruit pies are produced by automatic equipment derived from regular pie-making machines but which does not require the use of pie plates. As a result, both its design and mode of operation are greatly simplified. The equipment (**Figure 12.006**) first reduces the bulk dough from the hopper into a flattened dough ribbon by passing it through 4 sets of sheeting rollers with progressively narrower spacings. The dough ribbon then transfers to the makeup conveyor belt, which transports it under a filler head. This filler deposits accurately measured amounts of filling on the left-hand side of the dough strip. An assembly of fold-over belts then folds the right-hand side of the dough strip over the filling. The filled and folded dough strip is then crimped into individual pies by a rotating die wheel, which additionally trims and seals them into their finished form. The turnover pies are then transferred onto a take-away conveyor belt to be delivered to the fryer.

In another method, two continuous sheeted dough strips form the top and bottom crusts, with the fruit deposited between them. The filled dough strip is then cut, crimped and sealed into individual pies.

Frying takes place with the help of a twin conveyor, with top and bottom chain belts spaced about 1 in. apart. The conveyor transports the pies fully submersed through the fryer. Except for the constraints imposed by the conveyor belts, the pies float freely in the hot shortening and will absorb some 5 to 8 oz of the fat per dozen fried pies. The frying temperature is held at about 118°C (370°F), and the frying time for 4- to 5-oz pies will approximate 4 to 5 minutes. These frying conditions will ensure a thoroughly fried crust, without bringing the filling to a boil and causing the pies to burst.

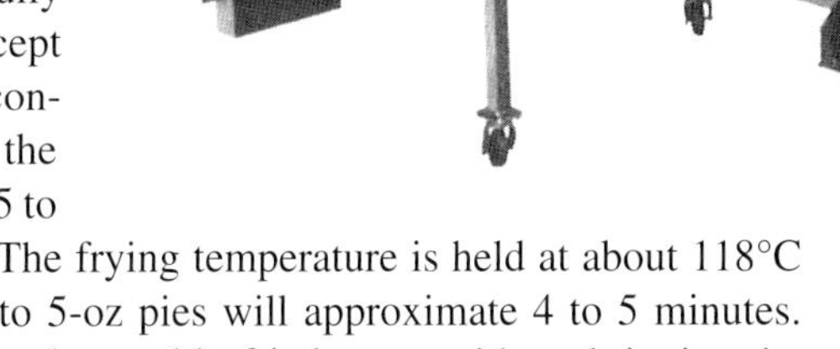

Figure 12.006. An automated fried pie machine can produce up to 200 pies per minute.
(Colborne Foodbotics)

Following discharge from the fryer, the hot pies receive a sugar glaze by passing through a waterfall-style glazing machine and are then transferred to an atmospheric cooler. It requires about 90 to 100 minutes for the filling center of fried pies to reach near-ambient temperatures. Proper cooling is important because pies, if packaged before their centers have cooled adequately, will sweat, thereby causing the crust to lose its desirable crispness. Burris (1979) provided a valuable review of fried pie processing.

12.A.4. Sweet yeast dough equipment

Although most sweet goods are leavened by yeast, their high sugar content and rich ingredients such as shortening, milk solids and whole eggs make them different from bread, and their production equipment must be able to handle these soft, sticky doughs.

Although the term "sweet goods" covers many of the products European bakers would term "patisserie," among American bakers this category tends to cover sweetened, yeast-raised items as diverse as cinnamon rolls, danish pastry, strudel, coffee cakes and turnovers. These products normally contain generous amounts of fillings and toppings and their desirable flaky structure is created by lamination of the dough, usually with a roll-in fat. Cannon (1987) described the highly automated, highly flexible sweet goods line installed at the large bakery she managed.

12.A.4.a. Dough preparation
Dough development for laminated pastry doughs is not done in the mixer but during the sheeting process. (Chapter 6, Part E, provides the scientific explanation of

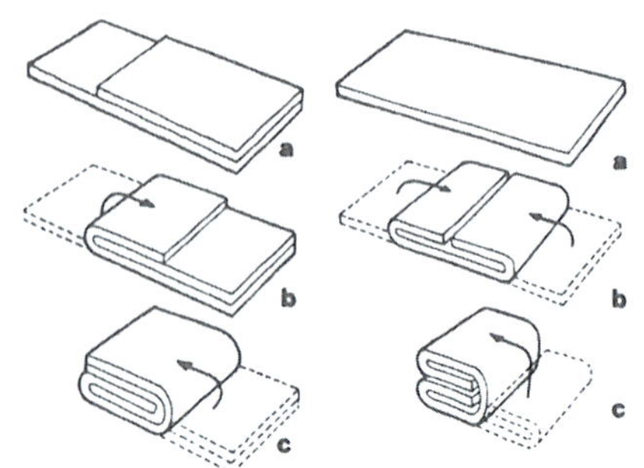

Figure 12.007. The 3-fold or English method of making puff pastry is shown at left; the 4-fold, or book-fold, method is shown at right.
(McGill 1975)

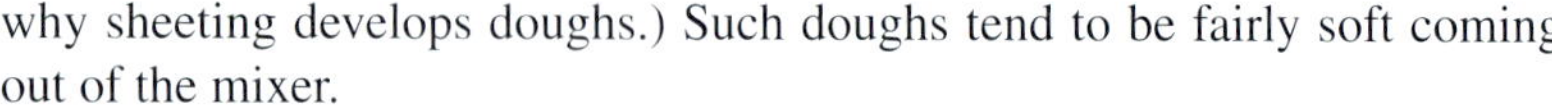

Figure 12.008. The conveyor belt on the table of a reversible sheeter passes dough blocks through a set of gauge rollers. The number of passes and gap settings for the rollers can be programmed to sequence automatically.
(RONDO)

Figure 12.009. Cross rollers sheet the dough across the width of the band.
(RONDO)

why sheeting develops doughs.) Such doughs tend to be fairly soft coming out of the mixer.

The area of preparatory dough handling, prior to final makeup or product forming, has experienced major technical advances in recent decades. Present makeup tables are equipped with varying numbers of sheeting or head rollers, cross, satellite or caterpillar and reduction rollers, extruders, laminating or folding sections, filling depositors, flour sifters, curling arms, rotary and guillotine cutters and trimmers, and transfer belts — all integrated into a synchronized sequence of operations, many phases of which are directed by computers or programmable logic controllers.

12.A.4.b. Booking methods

The production of danish pastry requires the formation of alternating layers of dough and fat. This layering may be accomplished in various ways. The traditional procedure is to scale the dough into 10- to 15-lb pieces, pass them through a reversible sheeter, reduce their temperature to about 13 to 16°C (55 to 60°F) by holding them for 2 to 4 hours in a retarder maintained at temperatures of 1 to 4°C (34 to 40°F), spot two-thirds of their area with pastry fat and then give them a 3-fold (illustrated in **Figure 12.007**), thus forming 5 alternating layers of dough and fat. A variation is a 4-fold or book fold. Depending on the degree of flakiness desired in the final product, the folding process is repeated 2 or 3 times, with each fold-in followed by a 1- to 2-hour rest in the retarder and the final one extending for 12 to 24 hours. The current trend is to limit the fold-in operation to yield 45 to 60 fat-and-dough layers, in contrast with well over 100 in earlier practice (Kunstmann 1969). These resting times allow the yeast to activate, thus giving more flavor to the end product.

The reversible sheeter (**Figure 12.008**) consists of a conveyor table and a transport mechanism that passes the conveyor belt in either direction through a set of centrally mounted gauge rollers. With each pass, the gap between the rolls can be adjusted to reduce dough thickness.

In a modification of this method, the dough is extruded by a pump through a flat nozzle to create a dough strip some 18- to 20-in. wide, which is deposited directly onto the roll-in table. The dough strip is sheeted, cross-rolled (**Figure 12.009**), covered with the roll-in fat by another extruder and cut by a rotary or guillotine cutter into pieces that are then folded and retarded as above.

A second method is to extrude two continuous dough strips with the shortening layer sandwiched between them by another extruder, a process known as coextrusion. The laminated dough band is then reduced in thickness by a pressure roller and cut into 18-in. long pieces that are then lapped in shingle fashion on a cross belt to form a multi-layered structure (**Figure 12.010**). The shingled dough pieces are again reduced to 1-in. thickness, and the shingling and reduction processes repeated. The second reduction is followed by cutting the laminated dough to into pan-sized pieces for retarding for 12 to 24 hours.

The third, or laminating, method resembles the shingle method, except that instead of the flat laminated dough strip being cut and deposited on a cross belt, it is layered in a continuous folding action on a second belt by an advancing and retracting motion of the dough conveyor and is subsequently reduced in thickness by repeated rolling. Here, also, the laminated dough is cut into appropriately-sized pieces and receives the usual rest in the retarder.

12.A.4.c. Automatic laminating

Although many pastry production lines continue to be fed by dough pumps, newer automated lines primarily use a hopper-fed roller system, which handles dough in a gentle fashion (**Figure 12.011**). The rolls may have different diameters that can run at different linear speeds to deliver a strip of dough to the processing belt.

Because this strip of dough has been gently formed, it requires additional development by additional sheeting and cross sheeting before fat or butter can be applied to the dough. The sheeting or reduction must be done as gently as possible in order to protect the gluten structure. Gauge rollers reduce doughs by 2:1 or 4:1 before they disrupt the fat-and-dough layering. Satellite head reduction can give a reduction of 10:1 without damage to the dough.

Satellite sheeting heads comprise of a number of free running rollers between 1.5- and 2-in. diameter that are mounted on a large driven wheels or in oval shape with a chain drive (**Figure 12.012**). These heads contact the dough strip from above with multiple small-diameter rollers running in the direction of the dough flow. As the dough reduces in thickness, it is supported underneath by either 2 variable-speed support rollers or a short belt to allow the high-speed transfer of the continuous dough sheet upon reduction.

All rollers in a satellite system act as individual stretching rollers, and as many as 16 rollers or as few as 8 rollers comprise the satellite head (**Figure 12.013**). Obviously, more rollers allow greater reduction without dough damage.

The dough sheet is then either laminated and again run through a satellite head or run past a cross-roller system for a cross-grain effect that also ensures the correct thickness and width of the dough sheet.

At this point, the fat is delivered in a wide ribbon by a fat pump on half of the dough sheet after which a plow with powered conveyor folds the other half of the dough sheet onto the layer of fat. A 2-plow system is also used (**Figure 12.014**).

Another method is to cut the dough sheet in half with an in-line cutter wheel and redirect the other half of the dough sheet to an overhead belt to top the next fat layer. The combination of dough and fat is again reduced in either a satellite head or reduction rollers to be either manually cut, folded and placed on sheet pans or automatically laminated, followed by a final reduction station before being cut and panned. Retardation follows.

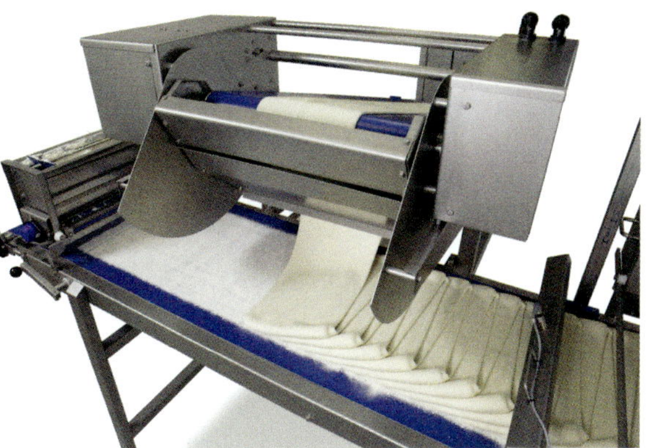

Figure 12.010. This lapping laminator books dough by folding it over itself as a conveyor belt below takes it to the next process.
(Rademaker USA)

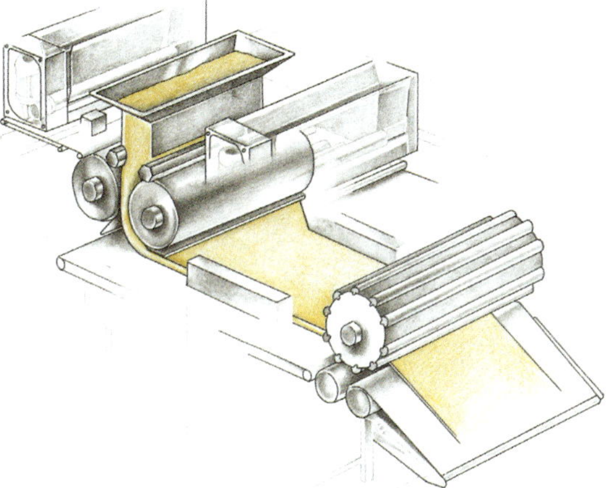

Figure 12.011. Two rolls draw bulk dough from a hopper to create a continuous sheet.
(RONDO)

Figure 12.012. A satellite sheeting head can accomplish reductions of 10:01 in sheet depth without disrupting the layers in the dough.
(RONDO)

Figure 12.013. Small-diameter rolls individually stretch the dough as they contact it. (RONDO)

Figure 12.014. Plows fold both edges of the dough over a strip of fat extruded down the middle. (Rademaker USA)

Figure 12.015. Cut sheets of dough overlap by means of a retracting conveyor. (Baker Perkins)

The final lamination determines the number of layers of fat in the dough and is controlled by the process conveyor speed: slow speeds make for many folds per linear foot, while faster speeds allow fewer laminations. The final reduction station addresses a problem unique to folded layers: The volume of dough at the folds is higher than in the center of the dough sheet. The final reduction step eliminates that difference.

To avoid this difference, some systems employ a cutting and reciprocation system where, instead of folding, sheets of dough are cut and reciprocated into an overlapping sequence of dough sheets (**Figure 12.015**). Here, too, a faster final processing belt speed makes for bigger intervals and fewer layers per linear feet.

12.A.4.d. Continuous line operation

Cutting and "book" style retardation can be eliminated on modern sheeting and lamination systems because the dough sheet is sufficiently relaxed by resting stages built into the line. Pastry production equipment that includes inline retardation now operates at many bakeries. Depending on the final product, a dough sheet prepared on such a line can be cut or formed into its final shape right after the final sheeting stage.

According to product style, filling, folding and topping appliances (**Figure 12.016**) are placed along the makeup section of the line. For example, a cinnamon layered dough for preparing bear claws gets a layer of cinnamon-sugar-and-shortening paste deposited in the center one-third or on one half of the dough sheet, after which it will be folded again once more, patted down with an overhead roller and cut into its final shape or form.

To allow dough to be manipulated many times in sequence, an automated system will often employ a number of flour dusters, which apply a slight dusting of flour on the bottom processing conveyor and on the dough sheet. Excess dusting flour is removed from the belts and the dough sheet after sheeting by rotating brushes and can be well contained by overhead flour dust vacuum systems.

When using booked doughs, the finishing operation starts with taking the chilled dough pieces from the retarder and joining them end-to-end on the makeup table to form a continuous strip. The pieces knit together by passage through one or more head rolls and sheeting roller sets. Depending on the type of final product being produced, the dough sheet may then be cut or stamped into individual pieces for additional forming, finishing and panning, or it may pass under one or more filling depositors and be coiled for final cutting and forming.

At least one bakery figured out how to give automatically produced sweet goods a desirably homemade look. As described by Gorton (1995), the company wanted to duplicate the small differences in sizes of handmade clustered sweet rolls yet assure accurate package weights. The dough, produced on a laminating line and coiled into a log, passes through a specially programmed guillotine cutter. Computer controls time the system to cut five minutely different sizes, which vary at random to duplicate hand-cutting. When 16 such roll pieces are placed in pan, however, the laws of statistics take over and the total weight reaches the proper target setting.

The made-up dough pieces proof at 35 to 38°C (95 to 100°F) or at slightly lower temperatures for those containing roll-in fat. The dough should be brought to room temperature before it enters the proof box to avoid moisture condensation and uneven proofing rates. After the proofing, products receive, when applicable, their final toppings such as cheese, fruit and/or streusel and then go to the oven. Baking is done generally at about 204°C (400°F) (Meigs 1968).

12.A.5. Croissant production

The production of croissants has undergone far-reaching automation with the increasing availability of specialized laminating and dough forming equipment (**Figure 12.017**). Hayashi (1978) described his breakthrough technology for automating production of puff pastry, and Rijkaart (1984) examined automated systems for croissant production.

Figure 12.016. The final makeup section splits a laminated dough sheet to make petite palmiers, folding the dough one last time before it reaches the guillotine cutter. (Baking & Snack)

In one such system, the dough and pastry fat, with starting temperatures of 13 to 16°C (55 to 60°F) and 16°C (60°F), respectively, are extruded in combination as a continuous cylinder in which the dough forms the exterior layer and the shortening the interior layer. This cylinder is next flattened into a laminated dough sheet and then reduced to one-tenth of its original thickness by means of novel stretching rollers as described earlier as a satellite roller system. This stage also applies gentle compression pressure. Next, the dough is folded by a swinging paddle-type mechanism that deposits the dough sheet in a predetermined number and width of folds on a receiving conveyor.

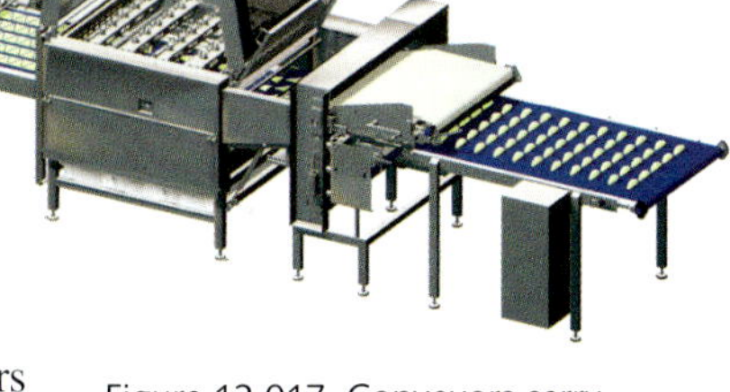

Figure 12.017. Conveyors carry laminated croissant dough through cutters, turners and coilers to produce straight croissants. (Rademaker)

The folded and layered dough sheet is then conveyed into an overhead refrigerated space where the dough sheet, in cascading fashion, is conveyed for up to 2 hours to allow dough retardation to cool the fat layers and allow for additional flavor development. The dough sheet descends from the inline retarder to enter a final stretcher mechanism where its thickness is again reduced to about 0.175 in. It is then ready for the croissant cutting, filling and rolling/coiling machine (Haarsgaard 1980).

Cutting the continuous band of croissant dough into contiguous triangles is efficient and limits scrap to just the edges, but the problem remains of turning the triangles so they all travel to coiling in the same orientation. One machine (**Figure 12.018**) divides this task into punching and turning stages. The first step cuts the laminated dough into long strips, trimming off the edge scrap, and then into triangles. An array of tools equipped with needles separates the triangles from each other and turns them to place the long side in the forward direction. The system described can handle hourly output of 60,000 miniature croissants (each 25 g, or 0.8 oz) or 72,000 micro-croissants (each 15 g, or 0.5 oz).

Figure 12.018. A punch-and-turn system realigns dough pieces so croissants enter the coiling system in uniform orientation. (Fritsch)

Sensors on automated makeup lines can assure no-product, no-deposit operation, thus preventing wastage of costly filling materials. The line shown in **Figure 12.019** deposits chocolate for preparation of chocolate-filled croissants.

In some highly automated systems, the coiled croissant cylinders are deposited on

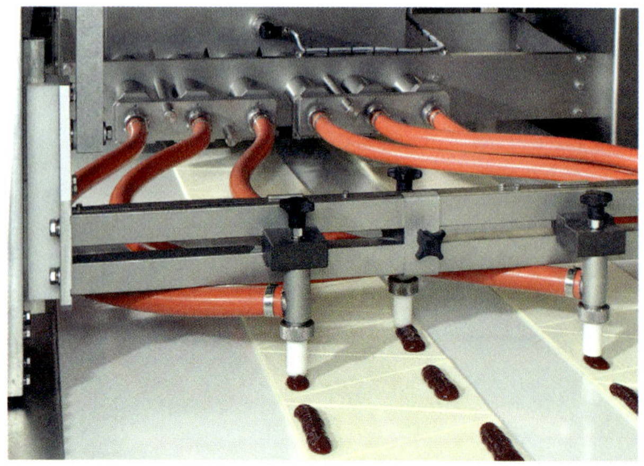

Figure 12.019. In no-product, no-deposit mode, this system senses the presence of dough on the conveyor and releases filling only if it is present. (Rademaker)

a forming belt system where the cylinders are shaped into their distinctive croissant or crescent shape. A distinct advantage of this processing system, which avoids the high pressures normally developed by conventional sheeting rollers, is that the operation is not interrupted by the need for temporary storage of the dough in the retarder box, as is the case with conventional methods of pastry production.

12.B. Cake Equipment

Updated by Hans van der Maarel

(The author acknowledges assistance from Peter and Noel Oakes.)

Cake technology, especially for small items, is currently undergoing tremendous change. Berne (2002, 2006) and Gorton (1993, 1999a, 2001b, 2003) described how various "new tech" cake lines operate in a number of large wholesale bakeries. These articles cover operations at J.W. Allen (2 reports), Morristown, TN; Best Brands, Dallas, TX; The Cheesecake Factory Bakery, Rocky Mount, NC; Flowers Foods, Crossville, TN; and Galaxy Desserts, San Rafael, CA. Producers of snack cakes are under tremendous pressure to control costs and have been willing to invest in technology that saves time and reduces waste. Additionally, like the mini-muffins before them, the very small size of products that fit today's "100 calorie" pack paradigm can only be accurately and efficiently made by automated methods.

The mixing processes for cake batters — creaming, flour-batter, single stage, sugar-and-water, foam, sponge and continuous — are explained earlier in this volume at Chapter 7, Part A. The specialized equipment for icing and finishing of cake products is described in Chapter 11, Part A.

12.B.1. Cake mixers

Cake ingredients must be completely and uniformly dispersed during mixing, with the resulting batter showing homogeneous emulsification. The process entraps air and reduces the size of air cells to ready them to accept the leavening gases generated early during baking. These batters flow readily. Some cake-like products, for example, muffins and scones, require minimal mixing, and their batters are stiffer and stickier.

The vertical mixer has long served bakers in batch preparation of cake, muffin and brownie batters, while continuous shear-style mixers enabled production of finely textured items at high-volume rates. In the past two decades, both kinds of mixers have been made more controllable by the application of PLCs for automatic repeat batching. Recent interest in preparing batters that contain particulates such as fruits, nuts or chocolate chips, chunks or pieces has also prompted improvement in batch systems.

12.B.1.a. Vertical mixers

Cake batters have typically been mixed in vertical mixers of the planetary style

(**Figure 12.020**), which are described in Chapter 9, Part B. The specifics of using such mixers for cake preparation involve a lengthier discussion. Filled bowls require mechanical assistance for emptying, and the column-style bowl dumper shown in **Figure 12.021** can manage loads of 1,000 lb and tilt the bowl it carries at a variable angle up to 45°.

Several changes in planetary mixing technology improve their mixing function. For example, addition of continuous scraper mechanisms that revolve around the sides and bottom of the bowl constantly reincorporate ingredients and prevent formation of stagnant side films and bottoms. Planetary heads of some mixers allow addition of a second tool; for example, a wire whisk for foaming can be combined with a cross-beater for development. The bowl can be closed and pressurized to build air incorporation and also assure uniform specific gravity batch after batch. Another change was to incorporate a pump so the bowl could be emptied directly to depositors, which saves time by eliminating a separate bowl-unloading stage.

These systems (**Figure 12.022**) can support production rates up to 10,000 lb per hour with bowl capacities of abut 250 gal, or 1,000 qt and mix times that allow 5 to 8 batches per hour. Clean-in-place (CIP) systems aid in sanitary performance. Automatic feeding options supply both wet and dry ingredients.

Ruckh (1986) described the practical application of vertical batch mixers for preparation of batters and slurries, while Wilkinson (1987) examined the functioning of multiple-tool vertical batch mixers.

Figure 12.020. An open-bowl planetary vertical mixer features a stainless steel rotating head assembly, beater drive shaft and locking ring.
(AMF Bakery Systems)

12.B.1.b. Continuous mixers

Briefly explained in Chapter 9, Part B, continuous batter mixers are essential to high-volume cake production so this section takes a more detailed look at the equipment and its technology.

The cake batter process employs a pre-mixer or slurry mixer, a holding tank and a continuous mixer, also called an aerating mixer (**Figure 12.023**). Several variants of continuous cake batter mixing systems have appeared on the market. Oakes (1948) described the first prototype unit, while Whitaker (2009b) touched on current developments in the technology. Capacities for these systems now reach 15,000 lb per hour or more. Styles include the compact rotor-stator mixing chamber type (Morine 1975, Egan 1977, Bonavia 1963) and the tubular scraped- or swept-surface mixer (Bolanowski 1966). The latter also finds extensive application in the production of aerated icings and marshmallow.

In the first type of continuous mixer, the shearing, dispersing, emulsifying and aerating actions occur within a compact mixing head consisting of front and back stators that en-

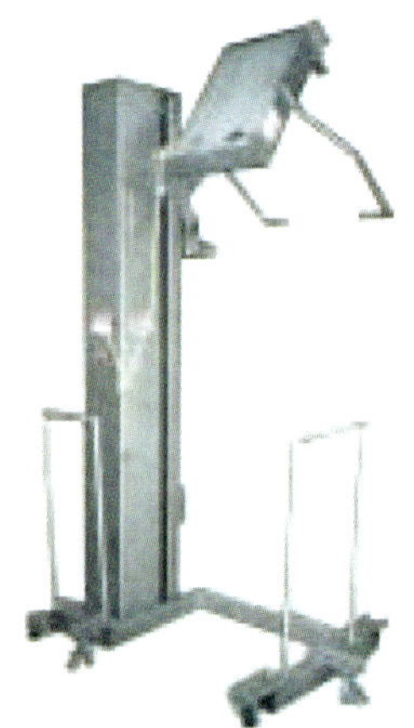

Figure 12.021. Bowl hoists enable rapid emptying of batters into depositors.
(AMF Bakery Systems)

Figure 12.022. Vertical mixing equipment has been improved through use of computer sequencing, multiple tool capacity, bowl scrapers, pressurization and clean-in-place capability.
(Tonelli Group)

Figure 12.023. A slurry mixer blends batters to be sent to the slurry holding tank that supplies the continuous mixer. (The Peerless Group, Fedco)

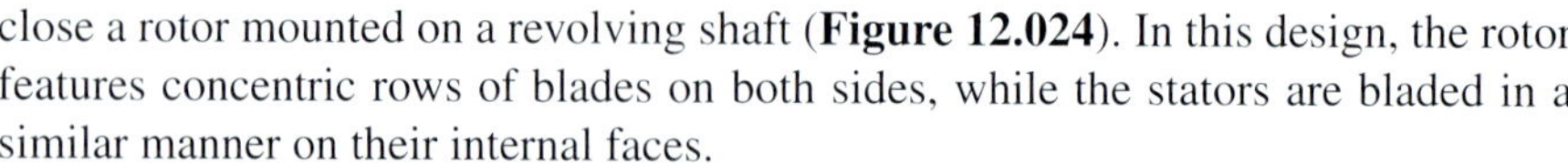

Figure 12.024. Mixing head assembly of a continuous cake batter mixer reveals the two stators and central rotor. Each features rows of shearing blades that homogenize the batter. (E.T. Oakes).

Figure 12.025. A continuous cake batter mixing system consists of (left to right) a continuous mixer, slurry holding tank and slurry mixer. (E.T. Oakes)

close a rotor mounted on a revolving shaft (**Figure 12.024**). In this design, the rotor features concentric rows of blades on both sides, while the stators are bladed in a similar manner on their internal faces.

Depending on batter viscosity and desired final density, these teeth are arranged in patterns that vary the number of teeth per row, as well as the radial thickness and width of the teeth. The total number of teeth governs the number of shear cycles per rotor revolution. The tooth thickness controls the gap between the rotor and fixed stator teeth. The tooth width determines the maximum and minimum opening through which the batter can flow as rotor and stator teeth pass each other. More than 200 tooth patterns have been designed to accommodate many different batter types.

In one variant of this basic design, the blades on both the rotor and the stators are slightly wider at their base to form a pyramidal shape. This modification results in both axial and radial mixing actions, said to produce more effective results. In yet another version, the mixing teeth or blades are located at equal intervals at the periphery of both the rotor and the stator. As the rotor revolves, small openings occur momentarily, forcing the batter through and subjecting it to shearing action. The batter, which enters the mixer at the center of the first rotor-stator assembly, works its way out in a radial direction to the periphery and then flows inward along the front stator before being discharged through the outlet. Batter dwell time is low, only a few seconds (Tireki 2008a).

The basic equipment required for continuous cake batter mixing consists of a premixer or slurry mixer, a holding tank for the slurried batter and the continuous mixer (**Figure 12.025**). The preparation of the slurry is a relatively simple process and is usually accomplished in an automatic slurry mixer into which all the dry and wet ingredients are automatically metered, followed by the manual addition of the shortening and minor ingredients. The ingredients are blended into a homogeneous fluid mixture with little or no aeration within less than 1.5 minutes. Slurries can also be prepared in vertical mixers.

The continuous mixer (**Figure 12.026**) is equipped with a self-contained pump that draws the slurry from the holding tank into the mixing chamber at a controlled rate. Here, the slurry is homogenized and emulsified by the rotor, revolving at speeds of 145 to 300 rpm, and aerated by incorporation of purified air compressed up to 135 psi. The pump speed, rotor speed, air flow and back pressure are all under close control, with PLCs often used to sequence operations.

The specific gravity and flow rate of the batter leaving the continuous mixer can be automatically controlled by accurately measuring the slurry and injection air mass flow being introduced into the continuous mixer. A computer uses this information to control both the product pump speed and the volume of air being metered into the mixer. Batter temperature rise through the mixer is typically held to 1.6 to 5.5°C (3 to 11 F°) by an appropriate adjustment of the rotor speed and by circulating cold water through a jacket surrounding the mixing chamber if necessary.

Because of the very short time batter is actually in the mixing head and optimum mixing head tooth pattern for a particular class of batter, the mixing process becomes very efficient resulting in little and sometimes no measurable frictional heat rise. No prior experience is required to operate the continuous mixer because all the product-specific variables can be programmed into a menu selectable by product name. The computer then continuously monitors and adjusts the mixer as required to pace the production line including automatically starting and stopping.

Some comparisons of the mixing times required to prepare aerated batters in standard vertical cake mixers and the slurries for continuous processing are shown in **Table 8.074** (on Page 290). Also included are the respective batch weights based on equal volumes and their corresponding specific gravities to point up some of the differences that exist between the continuous and the conventional cake-mixing systems.

A second continuous batter mixing system employs a scraped- or swept-surface heat exchanger or mixer whose main feature is a rotating shaft, equipped with a series of mixing blades, housed in a jacketed cylinder. The shaft is positioned either concentrically or eccentrically within the cylinder housing formed by the cylinder heads that enclose the annular product space between the shaft and cylinder walls. The batter slurry is pumped through this space, while its temperature is rapidly and accurately controlled by the heat exchange medium circulated through the cylinder jacket. The slurry is emulsified and whipped by the high-speed rotation of the bladed shaft. Compressed air is introduced during the mixing operation. A back-pressure valve at the discharge end of the cylinder regulates the most appropriate operating air pressure that will ensure optimum cake volume and texture. This type of swept-surface mixer also finds extensive application in the production of aerated icings and marshmallow (Bolanowski 1966).

Wafer batters are a specialty of another continuous aerating mixer (**Figure 12.027**). This machine injects a controlled amount of air on the input side of its rotor-and-stator mixing head. An airflow meter combined with the automatic air input system assures a constant density for the resulting foam. Unique to this system, the mixing head is cut by spark erosion to form the intermeshing teeth, thus avoiding welded or soldered construction.

12.B.2. Batter depositors

Cake batters must move from mixer to oven in a minimum amount of time because leavening agents, now in solution in the batter, have begun to generate carbon dioxide gas. Some carbon dioxide will inevitably escape as the batter rests in the open hopper of the depositor. This loss of aeration can be minimized by use of manifold-type depositors or those that employ pressurized mixing chambers and/or hoppers.

Piston depositors, of single or multiple outlet (**Figure 12.028**) designs, dispense

Figure 12.026. A self-contained pump transfers slurry to this vertical aerating mixer where it is homogenized and emulsified before transfer to the holding tank or depositor manifold.
(Tonelli Group)

Figure 12.027. The mixing head with its numerous teeth is cut by spark erosion, not welded.
(Haas Mondomix)

Figure 12.028. A range of interchangeable outlet nozzles adapt this multiple piston depositor to suit specific requirements. (Unifiller)

Figure 12.029. A turntable moves a tube-style cake pan under the depositor head to fill the pan evenly with batter. (Unifiller)

Figure 12.030. Viscous batters are laid down as a continuous sheet to evenly and smoothly fill the pan to its corners. (Reiser)

cake batter into pans (Gorchow 1992). One style uses a long, cylindrical common sleeve. The piston retracts to draw batter into the cylinder, while a valve seals off the discharge nozzle. The system then seals off the batter supply, opens the valve at the discharge point and dispenses the batter. Another system, consisting of individual pistons, draws the batter into a hollow cylinder of pre-adjusted volume. On the downward stroke, the piston rotates 180° to seal off the cylinder from the rest of the batter and discharges the piston's content through the nozzle into pan cavities.

At this point, pans index forward and stop. The height-adjustable piston heads move the nozzles down into the interior of the pan cavities and deposits the batter as it moves back up. This method eliminates splashing and prevents unwanted tails that occur when filling mechanisms drip upon closing or when sticky batters cling to filler edges. This diving method is one way to address such "tailing." At the end of the cycle, a "suck back" piston, integrated within the outlet nozzle, draws back batter to eliminate tails.

Another approach employs positive cut-off nozzles consisting of large depositing ports that automatically close at the end of the cycle. A third method closes the main piston gate and then moves a second gate in the direction of pan travel to deflect any remaining batter forward onto the batter in the pan.

Many different batter depositor designs have evolved to handle the wide variety of cake and batter styles. For example, a depositor designed specifically to fill bundt and angel food pans (**Figure 12.029**) uses a turntable to rotate the pans under the head, while a sheeter-style attachment (**Figure 12.030**) extrudes thick brownie batters.

Not content with volumetric depositing, a bakery equipment manufacturer chose to control depositing action with coriolis mass flow meters on a new patent-pending depositor (**Figure 12.031**). A coriolis flow meter measures the mass of the product flowing through a tube as opposed to measuring volume as in a traditional piston depositor. Depositing accuracy improved to achieve a standard deviation of less than 0.1 oz on a 14-oz deposit.

Unless preparing cupcakes or muffins in paper liners or sheetcakes in ovenable paperboard, all cake pans must not only carry a permanent glaze but they must also be sprayed with a release oil before the batter is deposited. Modern release-spray dispensers direct the oil selectively into pans or pan cavities (**Figure 12.032**). After depanning, pans will require washing to remove the crumbs that remain.

Most commercially produced cakes are baked in pans, but an increasing number of snack cakes (swiss rolls and cut-shape items), layer cakes and cake rolls bake as continuous bands (**Figure 12.033**). As described by Freihofer (1985), this process uses a continuous mixer to supply batter of a uniform specific gravity, depositing directly onto the oven band as a continuous stream. Depositing style determines whether the batter will be one wide band or several narrow ones.

After baking, the band of cake continues forward to cool before being finished. A variety of cutters and slicers divide the cake band into individual units. Plows, coilers and stackers supplement the fillers, toppers (**Figure 12.034**) and enrobers required to achieve the finished product's desired shape and style.

Different cake products require different depanning methods. In the past, dump cradles were often the only choice: They accepted full pans and rotated them 180° to allow gravity to release the cake items upside down to the cooling belt. This noisy method also resulted in pan damage. A newer approach uses a puff of compressed air to loosen cakes from their pans, and then an invertor releases the cakes upside down onto a take-away conveyor.

Another depanner employs a vacuum head in an array that conforms to the pan configuration: A robotic arm lowers the array to just above the product, activates the vacuum and rises to remove the baked cakes from the pan and transfer them into shipping trays or onto a conveyor. A similar method, suited to items with baked-on particulate toppings typical of muffins, uses an end-effector array of needle-like retracting fingers to pick up baked foods. Because the items are still warm, the needle holes in the crust "heal" quickly and disappear from sight.

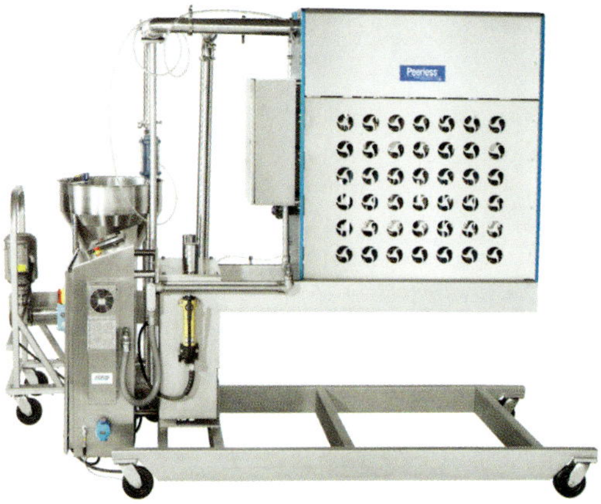

Figure 12.031. A "next generation" depositor, this system uses coriolis mass flow meters and pinch valves to control batter flow, assuring high accuracy. (The Peerless Group, Fedco)

12.B.3. Muffin equipment

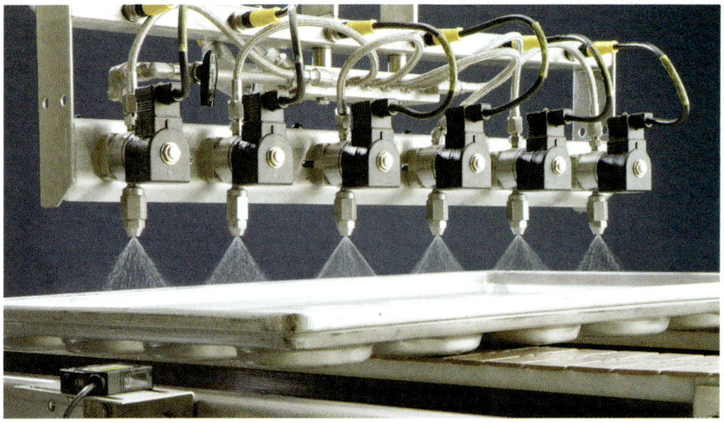

The batters of cake-style muffins often include fruits, nuts, vegetables and even meats and require special handling that maintains the piece integrity of such particulate inclusions. With muffins, Benson (1988) emphasized that care must be taken not to over-mix the batter, or else the finished muffins will become misshapen and tough with poor eating quality. Mixing, generally in an open-bowl vertical batch mixer, will take about 7 to 8 minutes, but no more, and is done in 2 or 3 stages, with particulates added at the end of the mixing cycle. Horizontal mixers equipped with sigma or bar arms have also been used, and most recently, computer-controlled sealed-bowl vertical mixers equipped with two tools and a constant scraper have been adopted for muffin batter preparation. Gorchow (1992) observed that a sealed-bowl mixer, operated by computer, assures double the output of similarly sized open-bowl mixers.

Depositing must not only be accurate but also be done in a way that minimizes damage to particulates. Retail bakers deposit muffin batters by hand or use scoops of different sizes, matched to the desired weight. Small filling machines are also available that deposit 4 muffins at once. Piston depositors are the choice when producing muffins in quantity, provided the system adequately safeguards piece integrity (**Figure 12.035**). In some cases, particulates are not added during mixing but are put into the baking

Figure 12.032. Precise, automated application of release oils increases product quality, reduces waste, improves hygiene and lengthens the life of baking pans. (Burford Corp.)

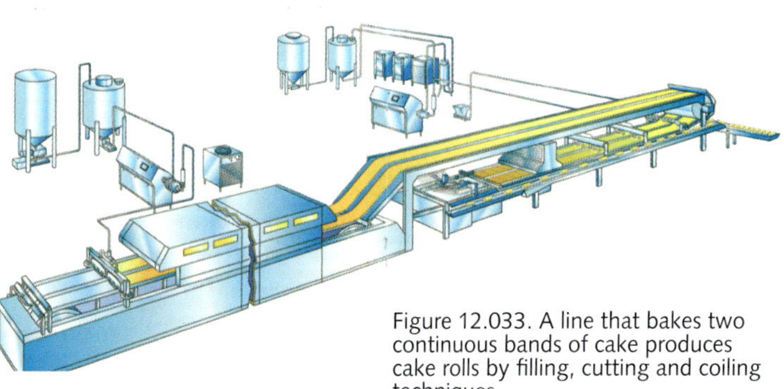

Figure 12.033. A line that bakes two continuous bands of cake produces cake rolls by filling, cutting and coiling techniques. (Haas Mondomix)

Figure 12.034. Custom-designed nozzles allow a wide variety of applications from a single depositor.
(Colborne Foodbotics)

Figure 12.035. Piston depositors handle large particulates such as those found in muffins.
(Hinds-Bock)

cups by target toppers before or after the batter is deposited.

A cup denester will generally also be required for muffin production. These units typically use interchangeable paper cup magazines and articulated vacuum heads to pull individual paper cups out of the stack and place them into pan cavities. The alternative is provide an automatic pan oiler, equipped with moving spray nozzles that project the oiling medium through a template directly into the pan cavities.

Topping systems provide refrigerated hoppers for materials like frozen blueberries. Another design uses interchangeable large-diameter cylinders with adjustable-volume cavities and moving at a speed synchronized with pan movement to dispense particulated toppings in accurate measures. The topping is ejected downward with an air assist that helps broadcast the materials across the entire muffin. Dusting and strewing systems, described in Chapter 11, Part A, can be used as well.

Depanning employs the same style equipment as cake depanning with the exception of vacuum methods, which can clog if used for muffins with heavy top treatment with streusel and similar particulates.

12.C. Cookie and Cracker Equipment
Updated by Hans van der Maarel

Three general methods characterize cookie forming: (a) cutting or stamping their shapes from a sheeted dough; (b) moulding the dough by means of dies engraved in a cylinder and then extracting the dough pieces and (c) extruding the dough through variously-shaped dies and either cutting or depositing the individual pieces on a baking sheet or oven belt. Each of these methods requires a dough that possesses certain physical properties that will render it suitable for the kind of processing that is entailed with each method. (Some experts consider deposited cookies to be a separate category because their doughs tend to be very soft and semi-fluid in contrast with wire-cut doughs, which are quite stiff.)

From a very general standpoint, the doughs intended for extruded wire-cut cookies are relatively stiff and plastic. Doughs and batters for extrusion depositing are softer and more fluid in order to be processed and to yield the desired spread during baking. Doughs that are destined for rotary moulding are mixed relatively stiff and plastic, are devoid of elasticity and contain high fat and/or sugar contents to ensure good cohesive properties that will facilitate the release from the die moulds onto the canvas apron. Finally, doughs that are to be cut or stamped out require adequate tensile strength and elasticity so they can be sheeted to a uniform thickness without tearing.

Cracker forming technologies employ lamination and sheeting as primary methods, with rotary cutting and/or stamping systems to shape dough before baking. As described earlier in Part B of this chapter, the dough sheet is formed by a cut-sheet laminator or a lapper. Encrusting machines, a form of extrusion described in Chapter 9, Part F, earned their place in cookie equipment history as the technology that launched the Cookie Wars of the early 1980s (Burrough and Helyar 1990, Moreth 1994).

12.C.1. Dough feeding systems

In the past, bakers often laid out their plants to use gravity to move in-process materials, particularly doughs, from one stage to another. Operators wheeled heavily laden troughs to chutes built into the floors of second-story mixing rooms and dumped the dough directly into the supply hopper of the cookie or cracker line located just below on the first floor. Some bakeries were configured with 3 or 4 stories so that gravity would assist the movement of (a) ingredients down to the mixing room, (b) doughs down to the makeup and oven floor and (c) baked items down to the packaging and shipping floor.

When bakeries moved to single-floor construction, a new method for transferring the dense doughs had to be devised. Trough hoists and bowl lifts such as those used for handling bread and bun doughs were available, but live-bottom dough feeding systems proved more useful for the dry doughs typical of cookies and crackers. The feeder's large supply bin can handle mixer batch sizes up to 1,500 kg (3,300 lb), acting as a buffer bin to ensure a continuous stream of dough to downstream processes. This method also affords some lay time to rotary-moulded products, allowing the flour to hydrate properly, which assures good machining characteristics.

A belt conveyor, supported on a bed of rollers, forms the bottom of the bin. Dough, deposited in the bin by a built-in bowl lift-and-tilt system, moves forward on the conveyor toward the guillotine gate at the front of the bin. The gate cuts off discrete pieces of dough, which exit onto an inclined conveyor feeding the forming system. A kibbler or tine-style dough feeder (**Figure 12.036**) can be placed at the front of the bin to break up dough lumps, thus assuring more uniform feed to the next processing step.

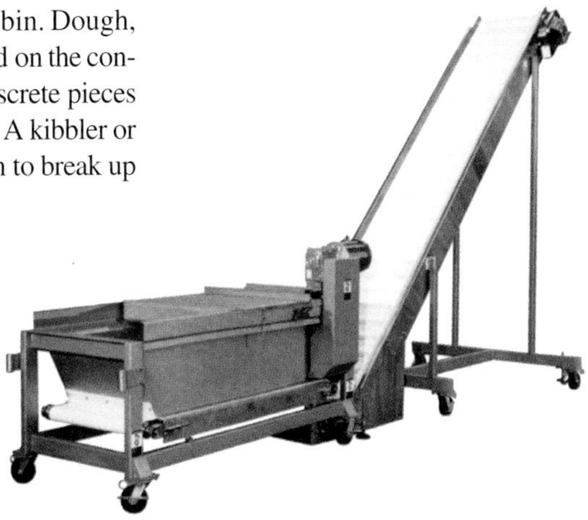

12.C.2. Cutting machines

The sheeting and laminating equipment used to transform bulk cookie or cracker dough into a continuous dough sheet is similar in general design to that employed for processing dough intended for the production of pastry products. The dough is subjected to a series of reductions, optionally interspersed with application of fat (or flour, in the case of cream crackers) and folded where lamination is required, until it attains the desired uniform thickness.

Figure 12.036. A tine-style dough feeder breaks up clumps of dough to provide uniform feeding to forming equipment. (The Peerless Group)

These lines begin the transformation of dough into a sheet using either 2- or 3-roll sheeters, whose action was described by Moreth (1994). The 2-roll dough sheeter consists of a dough hopper and a set of rolls in its base. The rolls, usually about 300 mm (12 in.) in diameter rotate in opposite directions, powered by a variable-speed drive. The dough passes through the gap between the rolls and is transferred to a conveyor belt by scraper knives or pick-off rolls. A 3-roll sheeter employs rolls of about 250 mm (10 in.) in diameter set in triangular fashion, with two rolls on top and one on the bottom. The top rolls turn opposite to each other, with the bottom roll rotating in the same direction as the back grooved roll of the upper two. Dough is pulled into the gap between the top rolls and then down between the forward and bottom rolls. Because the gaps and speeds of these rolls can be controlled and adjusted separately, a 3-roll sheeter can handle many more kinds of dough than a 2-roll system. Moreth (1994) indicated that the extra work provided by the third roll may permit elimination of one or more sets of reduction rolls in downstream processing.

Figure 12.037. Cut-sheet lamination produces doughs that yield flaky, tender texture in cookies and crackers. (DFE Meincke Vuurslag)

Figure 12.038. A reciprocating stamper (No. 30 in illustration) cuts and embosses in the same cycle. (Baker Perkins Historical Society)

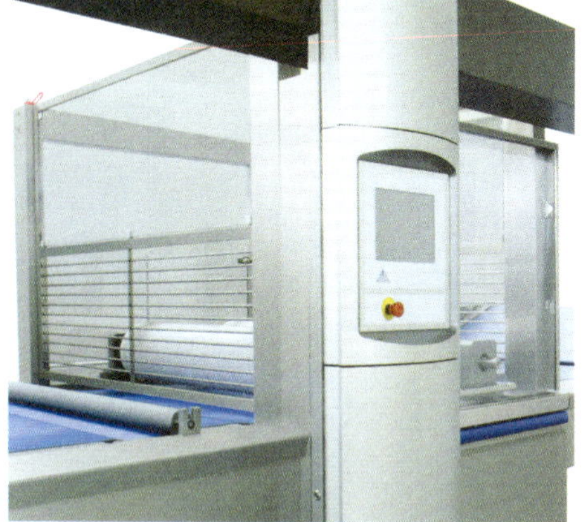

Figure 12.039. A twin-roll cutting machine features independent drives for each cutting roller and optional moistening device. (Franz Haas)

In cracker production, the sheeter is often set at right angles to the main processing line, and the emerging dough sheet runs through either a lapper or a cut-sheet laminator to reach makeup (**Figure 12.037**). When designing a cracker line, the baker must take into account the extra thickness and differing weight at the sheet edges caused by lapping. Cut-sheet laminating developed to solve this problem.

Lamination gives crackers their open, flakey texture and is considered essential to their production. The technology is used for some styles of cookies such as "hard sweet" biscuits; however, such applications are rare.

In cookie production, the sheeter is usually set inline with the forming and baking line, and the dough proceeds to makeup without lamination.

The dough sheet that emerges is relatively thin but still requires reduction in depth before it can be cut into its final shape. It passes through 2 or 3 reducting and gauging stations equipped with sets of rolls about 300 mm (12 in.) thick. Scraper knives or pick-off rolls are again required to transfer the dough sheet to the conveyor. Variable speed drives control the rolls and belts, while the gap between the rolls is also adjustable.

The dough sheet is then fed on a conveyor belt into the stamping and cutting machine of either the reciprocating or the rotary type. In the reciprocating machine (**Figure 12.038**), the cutter dies are mounted on a frame in 1 to 4 horizontal rows, with each row accommodating 6 or more dies, depending on the oven band width. Cutting and embossing are performed simultaneously by the reciprocating up-and-down motion of the cutter head, with the dies fully penetrating the dough sheet that is supported by the canvas belt riding on the surface of the cutting table. However, the reciprocating style is old technology that was not always as accurate as necessary, punished doughs mechanically, required intensive maintenance and generated excessive noise. In some cases, the hard and repeated poundings of the heavy stamper mechanism caused actual damage to building structure.

Cutters of the rotary type (**Figure 12.039**) mount the cutting and embossing dies on rotating cylinders on top of the dough sheet that is transported by a conveyor. The cutting and embossing (or docking, also "dokking") functions may be combined in a single die, or they may be performed by separate dies mounted on two synchronously connected cutter cylinders. The cups that do the cutting can be permanently fixed or engraved into the roll, or the roll can be designed to accept removable cups made of metal or plastic. In 2-roll systems, the dough sheet will be embossed or docked by the first roll and cut by the second, and careful synchronization is required to assure perfect centering of docking and cutting action.

Docker pins have blunt, not sharp, points for a reason. Although docking is commonly believed to help moisture to escape from the interior of the dough piece, the primary function is to "pin" the dough together at each point where there is a hole. Such pinning controls the height of the blisters that can form on top of dough pieces. This method produces finished cookies and crackers that are more even in profile (important for sandwiching applications) and far less likely to crumble and shatter during packaging and distribution.

When cutting squares, rectangles or other nested (or tessellated) shapes, only the edges of the sheet produce any scrap, but when cutting shaped products that do not fully cover the sheet, the excess dough must be removed. Such scrap dough is lifted off in the form of a continuous web for return to the feed hopper, and the die-cut products are transferred to the oven belt.

Rotary cutters for cracker lines have been supplemented with special fans to suppress the tendency of some doughs to wrap around the cutting roll. This fan, as wide as the line's belt blows down onto the dough surface to "skin" it prior to reaching the rotary cutter, thus preventing it from rolling up around the cutter and halting the line.

12.C.3. Rotary moulding machines

Originally, rotary moulding machines were called "Dutch cookie machines" or "shortbread machines," named after the doughs for which the first such systems were designed. Moreth (1994) traced the development and improvement of rotary moulding machines and noted their importance to the emergence of the now very popular creme-filled sandwich cookie.

In the rotary moulding machine, the cookie dough is pressed into dies that are engraved in a brass, bronze or stainless steel cylinder (**Figure 12.040**), then extracted by a canvas belt and transferred to the oven band. A fluted feed roll (or "forcing" roll) at the bottom of the dough hopper presses the dough against the moulding roll that contains the die cavities into which the dough is pushed. Product uniformity requires that the alignment between the die and feed rolls, as well as the pressure of the rubber-coated extraction roll, be controlled with utmost precision.

The die cavities are either cast or engraved into the metal surface of the roll, with engraving yielding finer design details. Their depth ranges a few fractions of an inch, depending on the nature of the cookie product being made. Typically the bronze or brass die is tubular in shape, ¾ to 1¼ in thickness, and mounted on a shaft with cast-iron bell hubs. Many European manufacturers use plastic inserts (**Figure 12.041**) mounted into a blank roll with appropriately sized cutouts.

Die impressions of either identical or of several different designs may be incised on the same roll. Design of the engraved roll may include docker pins, which help hold in doughs that might fall out of impressions prematurely. Die designs that are relatively long compared with their width are best placed with their long edge running across the width of the roll rather than around its circumference, otherwise the turning strain would be relatively high as dough pieces are extracted from the die and subsequently peeled from the transfer belt. Such orientation would tend to break the piece along its narrow width.

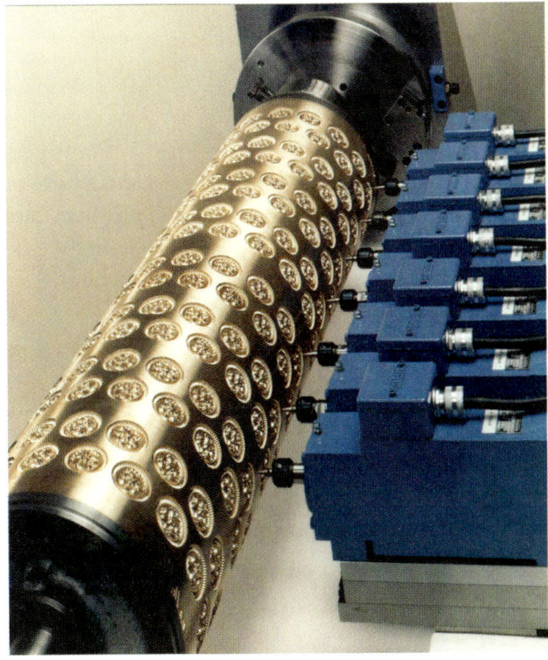

Figure 12.040. A bronze of brass cylinder is engraved with the pattern for a rotary moulded cookie.
(Baker Perkins)

Figure 12.041. Plastic inserts are configured to dock and stamp rotary moulded crackers.
(Baker Perkins)

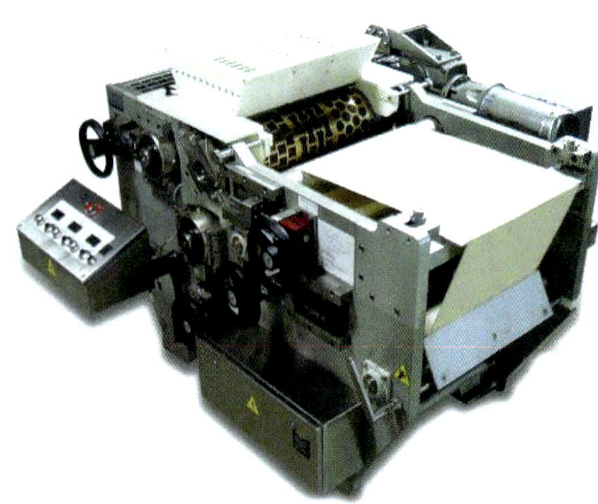

Figure 12.042. Rotary moulding methods have been upgraded with independent drives, heating or cooling of the feed roll, automatic web tensioning, motorized knife adjustment and automatic belt tracking. (Baker Perkins)

Figure 12.043. This rotary moulder forms dough into 3-D shapes by pressing it into engraved cavities and extracting it with a computer-controlled knife. (Reading Bakery Systems)

The nip point, or gap, between the forcing roll and the die roll should be no more than $^{3}/_{16}$ in. Set into the gap, about $^{1}/_{8}$ in. below the centerline of the engraved die roll, is a sharp-edged oscillating scraper blade or knife. It cuts or separates the dough from the cylinder cavities and the bulk of dough in the hopper. The cylinder or drum rotates with the impressed dough in the cavities for another 15 to 20° before it meets the rubber roller covered with an extraction belt. Blades set too high give slightly heavier weights, which can result in tailings or fringes on the cookies.

The extraction belt, in the form of an endless canvas apron, is pressed against the die roll by the rubber-coated extraction roll usually located below the die roll. According to Matz (1968), the removal of the dough pieces from the die cavities is effected by the adhesive action exerted by the canvas belt, rather than by suction, as had long been assumed. The formed cookie dough pieces are then transferred to the oven band or sheetpan. A modern rotary moulder is illustrated in **Figure 12.042**.

Rotary moulders capable of handling soft doughs (those with roughly the same shortening levels but higher moisture content than conventional rotary dough formulations) have been developed. These systems mount their feed roll above and slightly to the rear of the die roll and place extraction rolls and belt immediately after the scraper knife to prevent dough from "wrapping around" the die roll. Extraction, thus, takes place over a longer period of time, using 120° of the belt vs. 70 to 80° on standard systems. A misting of release oil may also be applied to the die roll to assure full extraction.

An important change in rotary moulding design puts separate inverter drives on the die roll, the forcing roll and the extraction belt. Independent operation of these components allows the baker to alter the speed of each to pull shapes more effectively and accurately out of the die.

Design changes also include placement of the scraper knife that releases dough from the rotary die. By locating the knife tangentially to the roller and controlling its movement in all 3 dimensions via computer, the system can release highly complex shapes (**Figure 12.043**).

Another advance in rotary moulding equipment for both cookie and cracker applications makes the machines much more "portable." In other words, these units have been configured with castors so they can serve multiple lines instead of being dedicated to a single location. Rails embedded in the plant floor help guide placement of these heavy machines.

12.C.4. Deposit machines

Deposit machines, as their name implies, deposit a rather soft dough through so-called die cups directly onto the baking surface, which may be either a cookie sheet or an oven band. The dough is forced into the die cups by feed rollers located at the bottom of the dough hopper and then extruded through orifices.

A "squeeze box" design is often used, featuring nesting boxes for the dough reservoir. Pushing up the bottom box decreases the capacity of the reservoir, and allowing the box to descend increases it. When the box rises, it increases the pressure on the dough within, causing it to be extruded through the deposit tubes located on a die plate that forms the bottom of the box. The feed rolls assist in moving dough through the squeeze box but are timed to stop before the box completes its full depositing movement. As a result, the pressure on the dough is released, and a slight "suck back" occurs at the end of the deposit.

During depositing, the baking band is raised close to the extruding orifice to receive the dough, after which it is again lowered. This downward movement, along with the pressure reduction at the nozzles, breaks the dough and completes the deposit.

Some units are provided with an oscillating or rotary head that momentarily follows the oven band during the depositing stage. All these functions are closely synchronized.

With variable frequency drives on the deposit and roller functions, the volume stream can be controlled as an intermittent or continuous stream of dough or batter, thus allowing a large variety of products to be pressed through differently shaped and moving nozzles (**Figure 12.044**). Traveling spritz-style nozzles are also used to create cookies that mimic those hand-deposited in smaller batches using pastry bags. Depositing speeds run from 80 to 120 rows per minute.

The same kind of depositor can deliver continuous strips of batter or dough onto a tunnel oven belt. The batter bakes as a continuous band and is cut by guillotine-style overhead knifes into its final length size. Divider plates placed in the supply hopper facilitate dispensing of co-extruded doughs such as fig- or fruit-paste-filled bars.

A multiple-port extruder (**Figure 12.045**) was developed to manage co-extrusion of a pair of very soft doughs or a combination of dough and a separate jam, jelly or other semi-liquid filling. These systems have 2 or more hoppers,

Figure 12.044. By combining horizontal and vertical movement, depositors can provide a wide range of shapes, placing them directly on the oven band. (Rademaker)

Figure 12.045. Multiple-port extruders can manage different doughs, jams and fillings to create a single deposit or many rows. (DFE Meincke)

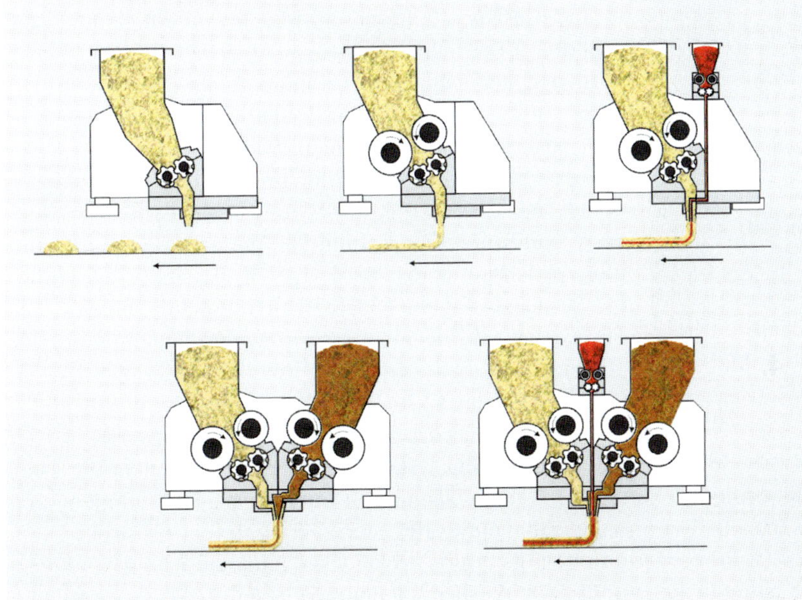

Figure 12.046. Schematic diagrams show how multiple-port extruders manage co-extrusion of one to three different materials. (DFE Meincke)

Figure 12.047. PLC control over wire-cut systems enables rapid changeover and consistent performance.
(Baker Perkins)

Figure 12.048. The filler block above the orifices of this wire-cut depositor guides cookie dough into place.
(Baker Perkins)

one for each of the materials to be deposited (**Figure 12.046**). A set of feed rolls controls the rate at which material reaches the specially designed filler block, which supplies the co-extrusion dies. The system readily manages very stiff doughs for the outside material and very liquid fillings.

12.C.5. Wire-cut machines

Wire-cut machines (**Figure 12.047**) permit processing of somewhat firmer doughs than are used in deposit machines. This method also suits doughs containing particulates such as chocolate drops, nuts or raisins. Before development of wire-cut depositors, bakers portioned such doughs using scoops of established volume.

Dough from the supply hopper is drawn down by a pair of corrugated or grooved feed rolls, rotating in opposite directions, which grip the dough to move it through the gap into the die cups. Knives at the bottom of the feed rolls scrape the dough off and keep it moving downward to the dies. Corrugations can be straight across or at a slight diagonal. In rolls with horizontal grooves, narrow flat areas (called "land areas") encircle the rolls to absorb the pressure of the scraper knife thus preventing it from catching in the grooves. Land areas are not necessary for rolls with diagonal or spiral grooves. Gaps between the feed rolls can be fixed or variable and range from 8 mm (0.32 in.) to 12 mm (0.47 in.), with the larger sizes being less accurate in weight control but better for doughs containing particulates such as chocolate chips.

The orifices of the die may be of the most varied sizes and shapes, permitting the production of a broad range of cookie shapes and styles as well as thickness. The wire-cut device consists of a frame, called a "harp," which holds and supports a thin stainless steel wire (0.020-in., or 0.5-mm, tensioned steel piano wire) at intervals along its length. The wires cut the dough as it is extruded either intermittently or at a constant rate from the die orifices.

Wire-cut depositors typically use filler blocks to guide the dough into the orifices, distributing it across the depositor more uniformly, thus keeping the pressure on the die cups more consistent across the length of the die. A filler block can be seen in **Figure 12.048**, which shows the block pulled out as it would be for cleaning. Sprocket pumps provide another means of transporting dough into the wire-cut, as shown in **Figure 12.049**. Such pumps are also used with the deposit machines described earlier.

Cookie height is established by an adjustment of the speed of the feed rolls in relation to the rate of the cut-off mechanism. The cutting motion permits the wire to travel close to the die orifice face during the cut-off stroke but in a somewhat lowered position on its return stroke. Oscillating the wire can help cut through larger inclusions. Oscillation speeds are normally 400 to 4,000 per minute.

Stopping the wire-cut mechanism and running the feed rollers at a constant, controlled speed produces a continuous ribbon of dough that can be further processed into various snack food products.

To maximize the use of the oven belt, the wire-cut depositor can be set at an angle (**Figure 12.050**) whereby the distance of the deposited cookies can be less than the space between the die orifices.

A different style of cookie dough depositing involves extrusion using unique double conveying screws or augers to move the dough to single or multiple orifices that are configured in the desired cookie shape (**Figure 12.051**). The machine's round hopper includes a rotating scraper to assure complete usage of dough supplies and to facilitate clean-out at changeovers. A guillotine knife over the orifice cuts the stream of cookie dough in short cycle times either onto a retracting belt system or to sheet pans. Such extruders are ideally suited for portioning dough chunks or patties that will be frozen for later baking. Two or more such extruder units, linked together both mechanically as well as electronically can deliver a broad variety of coextruded products.

Technology for forming disk shapes, originating in the meat industry for patty making, has also been adapted to cookie forming. The system (**Figure 12.052**) moves dough into templates with diameters up to 6 in. and walls approximately 0.25 to 1 in. high. These mould openings can also be shaped, for example, in holiday designs. The machine also has a feature for quartering the resulting disks (or "hockey pucks"), yielding 4 semi-attached pieces. Such quarter-disks of cookie dough are then frozen and supplied to instore bakeries and food service operations for bake off. An optional paper feeding system allows depositing and stacking of dough pieces, ready for the blast freezer.

12.C.6. Sandwiching systems

Many popular cookie and cracker styles feature a filling sandwiched between 2 basecakes. Specialty sandwiching equipment makes these styles possible. The sandwicher accepts rows of cookies or crackers, stencils or deposits the filling onto one cake and places the second cake on top. Sandwichers come in two basic styles: inline,

Figure 12.049. A separate sprocket-pump feeds dough to each wire-cut position on this depositor.
(DFE Meincke)

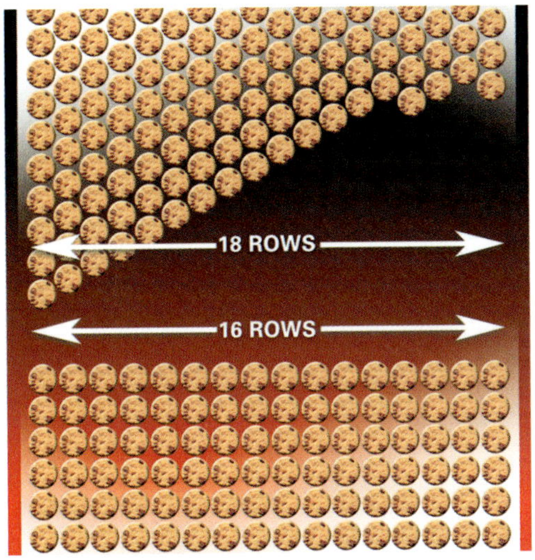

Figure 12.050. By setting the wire-cut depositor at an angle across the oven belt, more cookies can be baked than with straight-across positioning.
(Baker Perkins)

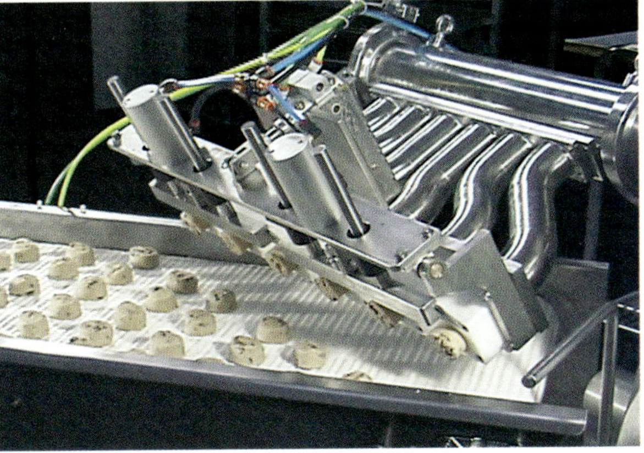

Figure 12.051. Cookie dough pieces are deposited in rows by a multiple-port extrusion system.
(Reiser)

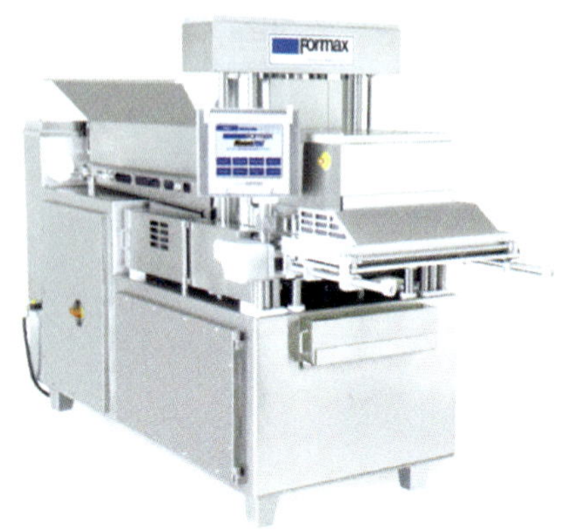

Figure 12.052. Forming dough disks, this system can be equipped with a feature for quartering each disk to produce a dough piece style preferred for bake-off customers.
(Formax)

Figure 12.053. Filling cremes must be aerated to the proper specific gravity to produce the best results in sandwich cookies.
(The Peerless Group)

which produces items in single file, and full-width, which handles items in rows. Inline sandwiching suits the needs for filling "hard" rotary-moulded cookies and snack crackers with readily pumpable fillings, while full-width systems manage the needs of "soft" wire-cut cookies and fillings that are difficult to stencil such as jams, very soft cremes and marshmallow. Each of these systems is supplied from mixing and holding systems that include continuous aeration systems, which tightly control specific gravity (**Figure 12.053**).

12.C.6.a. Inline sandwiching

The inline sandwicher (**Figure 12.054**) accepts products from the cooling line, oriented to present the bottom surface to accept the filling and stacked in a vertical magazine chute. A chain conveyor equipped with short pins strips the basecake from the bottom of the chute and carries it forward through the stencil station and on under the second chute, where a second basecake is stripped off by the same set of pins, thus completing the sandwich. The stencil manifold consists of a rapidly rotating cylinder (**Figure 12.055**) supplied with creme or other fillings by pump. The stencil manifold extrudes filling into an orifice as wide and deep as required for an individual portion. As the cylinder turns, a gate shuts off the filling supply, and a cut-off wire or knife separates the filling from the manifold's stencil and "prints" it onto the basecake moving below. Each cylinder typically has 2 or more despositing orifices.

Inline systems operate at speeds of 600 to 6,000 sandwiches per minute, and they can be configured with 1 to 6 sandwiching lanes. Recent changes include the ability to handle triple-decker styles (also called "3-high," with 3 basecakes and 2 layers of filling of the same or different flavors), as well as a variety of sizes and shapes, and to deposit as many as 3 different fillings per sandwich or produce double-size ("double stuff") deposits. Current technology allows basecake sizes of 40 to 70 mm for standard products and 25 to 30 mm for "mini" sandwiches. Larger products, up to 70 mm in length, can be accommodated, too.

Redesigning the sandwicher, a bakery equipment manufacturer replaced the usual chain-and-pin systems for transporting basecakes through the filler with a vacuum belt instead (**Figure 12.056**). This belt positions the bottom cookie. The new design is said to be easy to clean, particularly under allergen management standards, and the vacuum method draws crumbs away from the product zone.

12.C.6.b. Full-width sandwiching (capping)

After cooling, cookies are aligned into straight rows to enter a full-width filling-and-sandwiching system (**Figure 12.057**). Alternate rows are inverted, usually by a brief jet of air so that one row consists of bases and the next of lids. Rows are re-aligned before the filling is deposited. At the next station, a suction head picks up the row of lids and places it on the following row of filled bases.

A new capping system (**Figure 12.058**) inverts every second row, deposits aerated creme filling through a manifold and aligns bottom and top base-cakes with a pneumatic stopper system. The turning device is interchange-able to accommodate a variety of basecake styles.

12.C.7. Trolley cakes

Production of trolley cakes (soft, cake-like cookies enrobed with layers of marshmallow and chocolate-flavored coatings) involves a novel meth-od. Before the advent of air-conditioned warehouses, bakers encountered considerable difficulty delivering chocolate-coated marshmallow cookies during warm weather months. The trolley cake, with its stable chocolate-flavored coating, was invented to satisfy this need (Moreth 1994).

When a leading cookie company revived this old-fashioned cookie style as a low-fat product in 1992, it received enthusiastic consumer support, especially the devil's food flavor. Although this fad faded a few years later, trolley cake cookies are still being marketed, but only one bakery currently uses this technol-ogy, Interbake Foods, North Sioux City, SD.

The basecakes for this process are produced by conventional depositing meth-ods. After baking, they are hung by hooks onto bars, or "trolleys," attached to endless roller chains. The cookies travel through a series of stations where they are dipped in icings (marshmallow, chocolate and other flavors as required), fol-lowed by drying, or "set up" periods, all while being transported by the trolley. The final stage applies a sugar glaze that adds sheen to the enrobed basecake. Finished trolley cakes have two small holes on the back side from the prongs of the hooks.

More detailed discussions of cookie forming machines, as well as of the many technologies involved in cookie, cracker and biscuit production, have been pro-vided by Matz (1968), Smith (1972) and Kulp (1994). Also recommended is Volume II from the Biscuit and Cracker Manufacturers' Association's corre-spondence course (BCMA 2002).

12.D. Doughnut Equipment

Updated by Hans van der Maarel
(The author acknowledges assistance from John DeMarre.)

Doughnuts differ from other bakery foods because their cooking medium becomes part of the finished food. Doughnuts cook by brief submersion and surface frying in heated edible fat (**Figure 12.059**) rather than baked in supporting containers in ovens. In contrast to oven baking in which the required heat energy is transmitted variously by radiation, convection and conduction, the heating fat in the frying process not only serves as an energy transferring medium but also enters into and becomes an intrinsic part of the finished product. Hence, the ultimate character of fried products is established not only by the quality of their formula ingredients and the method of their processing but also to a substantial degree by the quality of the frying medium.

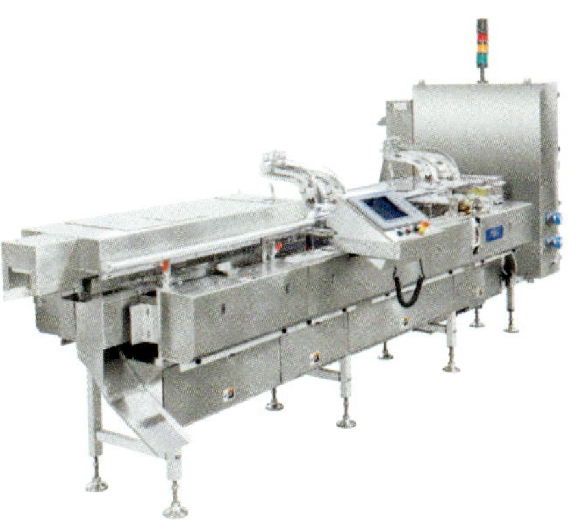

Figure 12.054. This inline sandwiching machine "prints" a stencil of filling onto one basecake and tops it with another. Larger systems can handle up to 4 lanes of product.
(The Peerless Group, Peters Machine)

Figure 12.055. A new design for the rotating manifold can deposit two flavors of sandwich creme filling at once.
(The Peerless Group, Peters Machine)

Figure 12.056. The vacuum belt under the filling manifold holds basecakes in position as they move through a new sandwiching machine.
(Franz Haas)

Figure 12.057. The traveling depositor (right) heads portion filling on every other row of baked crackers before a set of vacuum cups (left) picks and places the corresponding top cracker to complete the sandwich.
(Machine Builders & Design)

Figure 12.058. Operating at up to 150 rows per minute, this system deposits filling on one row of basecakes and them tops them with the second row.
(Franz Haas, Houdijk)

Figure 12.059. The hood over this automated doughnut fryer catches steam and air-borne oils, keeping it out of the plant enviromment.
(Moline Machinery LLC)

12.D.1. Makeup and depositing equipment

12.D.1.a. Cake doughnut equipment

Cake doughnuts are made from batters much like those for layer cakes, but these batters are scaled, or cut, into ring-shaped forms. The batter, scaled into 0.5- to 2-oz portions, is deposited into heated shortening or oil and allowed to fry for 1 to 2.5 minutes or until properly cooked.

Floor time of time of 10 to 15 minutes will help condition the batter by bringing about adequate hydration and activation of the leavening system. Too much or too little floor time can produce specific defects in the finished product such as reduced volume, poor product symmetry, high fat absorption and split crusts (Goodsell 1984). Ash (1979) cautioned that floor time should be counted as bowl time plus hopper time.

Equipment specialized for production of cake doughnuts includes an array of depositors, fryers and icing/glaze applicators.

12.D.1.a.i. Depositors

While doughnut depositors (**Figure 12.060**) operate according to principles similar to cake depositing equipment, the action of the nozzles, or cutters, is quite different. Cake doughnut batter is portioned directly into the frying fat by means of gravity-fed, air-pressure or vacuum-mechanical methods (Fischer 1976, Belshaw 1976, Ash 1979, Dixon 1983).

Gravity-fed depositors. In the first of these devices, the batter flows from the hopper by gravity into a series of feed tubes equipped with plungers whose lower end serves as the cutter. A cycled opening and closing of the cutters extrudes rings of batter for direct depositing into the frying fat.

Pressure-head depositors. In these depositors, a rotary gate forces the batter from the hopper into a chamber that serves as a manifold for several depositor tubes. Air pressure of 4 to 10 lb forces the batter into the tubes from which it extrudes as the cutters open and close in a rhythmic cycle. Doughnut weight is controlled by the amount of air pressure applied, the duration of the cutter opening, the actual size of the opening and the batter viscosity. Cutter overlap — the distance the sleeve of the cutter extends below the lower end of the cutter disk in a totally closed position — is normally about $^{1}/_{32}$ in. Excessive overlap will require more air pressure, resulting in increased spread. An insufficient overlap will cause poor scaling control and problems with the doughnut dropping properly.

Vacuum-mechanical depositors. In the vacuum-mechanical head, product size is established by volumetric measurement of the batter. Here, individual plungers or cutters first create a vacuum that draws the batter from the open hopper into the individual cutter cylinders. When the predetermined amount of batter has entered the cylinders, they are closed off. The premeasured amount of batter is then extruded in the form of a ring through a preset opening. This type of cutter head offers considerable accuracy in controlling the volume of the extruded batter.

In all these depositors, plunger design (**Figure 12.061**) determines the shape of the doughnut, extensively discussed by Belshaw (1976). Cutter size must match doughnut weight targets; simply holding open longer a cutter normally used for a smaller size doughnut will not yield a larger doughnut with the proper symmetry. Ash (1979) matched cutter sizes and with finished product weight in **Table 12.1**. Placement of the cutter is also critical because the extruded batter should be partially supported by the fat before being completely separated from the cutter. Thus, the cutter to fat distance should be minimal, 0.25 to 0.5 in. With larger distances, gravity will elongate the batter piece as it is extruded, resulting in poor symmetry and high fat absorption.

Roth (1975) described a dual-chambered doughnut extruder (**Figure 12.062**) that permits production of jelly-filled, ring-shaped cake doughnuts. The pressure-cut cake doughnut extruder features an annular-shaped chamber that serves as a reservoir for the jelly and is set within the regular chamber holding the doughnut batter. This second chamber is equipped with a pair of flanges or lips that direct the flow of the filling into the enveloping batter during the extrusion process. The ratio of filling to batter, as well as the volume and weight of the individual doughnuts, can be adjusted at will within more or less precise limits.

12.D.1.a.ii. Specialty items

Choux paste specialties. Two additional pieces of equipment are required for the production of so-called "French doughnuts" made by the choux paste process described in Chapter 8, Part L. Steam, generated from the moisture content of eggs as well as the formula water, leavens this style of doughnut. The pâte à choux batter is prepared in a heated kettle, jacketed by steam or placed directly over a gas-fired burner, often called a "candy stove." The second required processing component is the cutter, a specially shaped cutter using a counter-rotating forming die and forming piston. The rotation imparts the twisted, fluted shape to the dough-

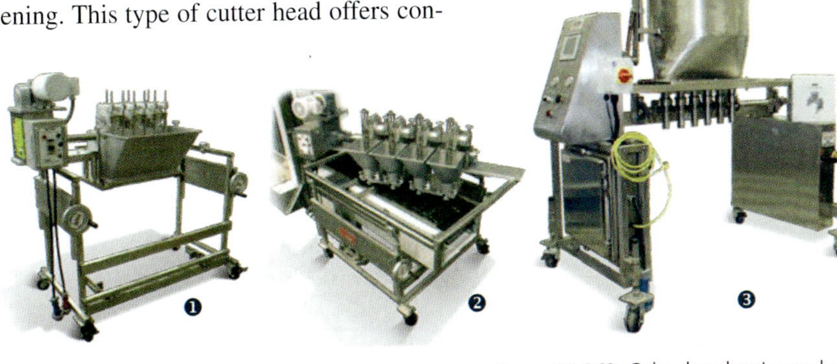

Figure 12.060. Cake doughnuts can be deposited by gravity (1), while vacuum (2) and pressure (3) systems handle yeast-raised doughnut dough. (Belshaw Adamatic Bakery Group)

Figure 12.061. Different plunger designs produce different doughnut styles, including straight and crescent forms. (Belshaw)

Table 12.1. Doughnut Cutter Guidelines

Cutter diameter (in.)	Finished, fried weight (oz per doz)
1.250	4.5 to 6
1.375	6 to 7.5
1.500	7.5 to 11
1.750	10 to 16
1.875	14 to 19
2.000	17 to 20
2.188	19 or more

(Ash 1979)

Figure 12.062. A dual manifold system enables production of filled, ring-shaped cake doughnuts.
(Moline Machinery)

nut. These products usually require a longer frying time, 5 to 6 minutes, than typical cake doughnuts.

Churros. The long, straight doughnut-like Hispanic deep-fried pastries called "churros" require an extrusion system for high-volume production. The crispy "waffle sticks" are made by extruding long ropes of soft batter directly into the fryer. Leaving the hot fat, the strips pass under a guillotine that cuts them to the desired length. The final step is to roll the churro in a cinnamon-sugar mixture.

A depositor-extruder system (**Figure 12.063**) capable of co-extruding multiple doughs and/or fillings provides the automation. This equipment is the same as that developed to deposit Danish-style butter cookies and jelly-spotted swirl-style cookies. The machine consists of multiple depositing heads (**Figure 12.045**) on Page 635), each equipped with feed rollers, and operates continuously or intermittently. Traditional dosing, or metering, systems use the feed rollers' built-up head pressure to push the product through the die or nozzle. On this system, the only job of the feed rollers is to keep a constant supply of dough flowing to the metering pumps. Each nozzle, or die opening, has its own set of dosing pumps, or rotors.

A common splined shaft, operated by an electronic servomotor, controls the rotation of the pumps. To deposit separate pieces, automatic reversal of the dosing pumps creates a vacuum to cut off the dough supply so that no tailing occurs. Because of the short material flow path from the dosing pumps to the nozzle openings, the depositor can handle a wide range of materials.

Funnel cakes. The fried snack known as a funnel cake is most often encountered in a county fair or festival setting, but at least one baking company now makes frozen funnel cakes for the supermarket trade. The specialty equipment involved is relatively simple: a depositor with a narrow nozzle and capable of randomized movement during a lengthy deposit. The batter is deposited directly into the fryer, turned once and removed for finishing.

12.D.1.b. Yeast-raised doughnut equipment

While cake doughnuts use chemical leavening to aerate their batters, yeast-fermented dough is the basis for yeast-raised doughnuts. These products also receive final proofing of approximately 30 minutes instead of the cake products' short 10- to 15-minute floor time. Processing equipment is different and consists of a sheeter and cutter rolls or a pressurized cutter and a proofer. Frying and finishing equipment are much the same as that on a cake line, although the temperatures and other settings will differ.

12.D.1.b.i. Cutting

Sheeting. Fully fermented yeast-raised doughnut dough is transferred to the line's supply hopper where its transformation into a continuous sheet follows the basic principles of dough sheeting but without any lamination stages. The band of dough is then cut into individual pieces using rotary cutters (**Figure 12.064**), designed to yield round, hexagonal, ring, square or rectangular shapes, normally 2¾ to 3 in. in size. According to Braden (1976), round cutters produce about 40% trim dough, whereas hexagonal cutters reduce such scrap to about 20%. The trim dough returns to the final dough mixer for reincorporation.

Extrusion. Yeast-raised doughnuts may also be produced by extrusion methods similar to those employed for cake doughnuts. Either air-pressure or vacuum extrusion systems are used.

With the pressure extrusion method, the dough is placed into a pressure chamber, which extrudes it through a series of cutter dies that deposit the cut pieces directly onto the infeed conveyor of a continuous proofer. Once the dough chamber is empty, old dough must be pulled and the chamber recharged with new dough, a process that causes a major interruption in the production flow. The air pressure required to extrude doughnut dough through the die will generally run between 20 to 24 lb per sq in.

The vacuum extrusion system, on the other hand, uses an open dough hopper so continuous operation may be maintained by merely keeping the hopper filled with dough. Dough is drawn by vacuum from the hopper into the cutter tubes, where the dies then cut and deposit the dough pieces on the automatic proofer tray or infeed conveyor.

Extrusion methods have the advantage of being highly automated and, hence, require a minimum of labor. On the other hand, product flexibility is relatively limited, and greater care must be taken in preparing the doughs for this type of processing. As Wise (1971) pointed out, doughs age rapidly when placed under air pressure, thus their floor time must be carefully controlled. While young doughs cut better because they are less extensively aerated and possess good flow characteristics, they tend to yield smaller product volumes because of insufficient expansion during frying. In contrast, old doughs require less air pressure, but yield non-uniform dough pieces.

Sponge doughs fermented at 27°C (80°F) for 2 to 2.5 hours appear to be best adapted to the extrusion process. The dough is mixed for 15 to 20 minutes to full development, with an absorption that favors optimum extensibility. Floor time should be limited to less than 5 minutes, and the dough should be processed within 15 to 20 minutes.

Figure 12.063. Capable of co-extruding up to three materials at once, a depositor pumps out filled churros ahead of a fryer. (DFE Meincke)

Figure 12.064. Cutters create (from top left) round-with-hole, round-without-hole and strip/rectangular shapes for sheeted yeast-raised doughnuts. (Moline Machinery LLC)

12.D.1.b.ii. Proofing

Yeast-raised doughnut dough pieces require relatively dry and warm proofing conditions (**Figure 12.065**), within a temperature range of 35 to 43°C (95 to 110°F) and a relative humidity of 75 to 80% (Smith (1996). If the baker wishes to form a skin on the dough piece, then proof box temperatures will need to be 48 to 50°C (118 to 122°F), with relatively dry conditions at RH of 61 to 66%, with some experts recommending of 35 to 45% RH.

Proof time will normally run 20 to 30 minutes, but no longer. High humidity proofing

Figure 12.065. Capacity of this industrial proofer ranges from 10,000 to 20,000 standard-sized yeast-raised doughnuts per hour.
(Belshaw Adamatic Bakery Group)

Figure 12.066. Eliminating dusting flour from the proofing of yeast-raised doughnuts minimizes excess particulates in the fryer.
(Belshaw Adamatic Bakery Group)

Figure 12.067. Automated makeup of apple fritters can be accomplished by an extruder with a wide-diameter port fed by a special double screw, thus replacing the normally laborious manual process.
(Reiser)

tends to cause excessive product expansion and can produce blister formation and high fat absorption in the fried product. Automatic proofers feature zone control that permits adjustment of proofing conditions in different sections of the box. The general practice calls for a moist zone at the outset of proofing to promote the spread of the doughnuts and a dry zone toward the discharge end to favor product rise and volume increase, as well as to facilitate product release off the trays (Braden 1976).

Recently, the addition of active release mechanisms to proofers has reduced or eliminated the need for dusting flour normally applied to the proofer baskets to reduce sticking (**Figure 12.066**). As a result, overall sanitation is improved, cleaning time is reduced, and contamination of frying oil with flour is avoided.

An innovative approach to doughnut proofing used microwave energy to accelerate the process (Schiffmann et al. 1971, Moyer 1973). In contrast to conventional proofing, in which the dough piece exhibits a temperature gradient from the exterior to the interior, microwave energy produced an instant, uniform rise in temperature throughout the dough piece. This method reduced the normal proofing times of 25 to 35 minutes down to 2 to 4 minutes. In practice, the cut doughnuts were deposited on a continuous belt conveyor for their passage through a tunnel-like microwave cavity, where microwaves at a frequency of about 2,450 MHz, acted upon them. An environmental control system regulated the relative humidity and ambient temperature within the proofer tunnel. This method of microwave proofing failed, however, to achieve widespread commercial application and is no longer in use.

12.D.1.b.iii. Specialty items

Honey buns. When yeast-raised doughnut dough is sheeted, sprinkled lightly with cinnamon filling, rolled, cut, proofed and fried, the result is the "honey bun," a Southeastern favorite now found at markets nationwide. For makeup of these products, the sheeting line is supplemented with a dry material depositor, a coiling roll, also called a "torpedo roll," and a guillotine cutter. After the dough sheet receives its light sprinkling of cinnamon filling, it encounters the coiler, which turns the sheet into a thick rope. The guillotine cuts the long roll into individual dough pieces, which transfer into the proofer via a transpositor capable of loading full proofer trays at once. Frying and finishing follows the usual methods.

Apple fritters. Preparation of apple fritters (**Figure 12.067**) requires the baker to chop apple chunks and spices into yeast-raised doughnut dough. Automating apple fritter production requires a special touch. Conventional dividers and multilane extruders make the fritters too uniform, when what consumers want are asymmetrical lumpy items that look individually handmade.

Recently, this process has been successfully automated, first, by using a vertical twin-arm mixer to roughly chop the fully fermented dough, apples and spices together and, second, by dividing the lumpy mixture with a double-screw, wide-diameter port extruder equipped with a fast cutoff knife. The double-screw dough transport method maintains optimum piece integrity of both apple pieces and dough chunks. Several extruders, each supplying one lane, enable high-volume production. The formed dough pieces drop onto the belt of the shuttle conveyor feeding an automatic proofer. Like other yeast-raised doughnuts, the fritters move out of the proofer into the fryer and through a glazing system for finishing.

12.D.2. Frying equipment

The proofed pieces are then automatically transferred to the infeed conveyor that passes them into a conveyor-type fryer. For yeast-raised doughnuts, the temperature of the frying medium should be maintained within a range of 191 to 196°C (375 to 385°F), according to Smith (1996). Frying time will normally run from 45 to 60 seconds per side, depending on doughnut size, for a total of 1.5 to 2 minutes.

For cake doughnuts, frying fat temperature is best in the range of 182 to 193°C (360 to 380°F). Frying time varies according to size and variety and ranges from 1 to 2.5 minutes.

The continuous fryers (**Figure 12.068**) for making doughnuts are typically shallow, holding from 1,000 to 5,400 lb of frying shortening. A flight-bar style conveyor transports items through the hot fat from depositing to finishing. All styles of doughnuts are flipped half-way through the frying process. Conveyor systems more than 10 ft long should be configured with a moving drop plate. Such plates prevent distortion of cut doughnuts. The batter falls onto the submerged plate and is moved along until it becomes buoyant and floats free to be controlled by the flight bars.

Figure 12.068. Mini-doughnuts fry in a high-output continuous fryer system. (Belshaw Adamatic Bakery Group)

As explained in Chapter 10, Part D, fryers can be heated by gas or electricity and include a cold zone at the bottom of the tank for isolating extraneous solid matter (flour dust, crumbs and other such debris) from the rest of the fat. Oil filtration systems are also described in that chapter. A live bottom sediment sweep has been added to some fryers (**Figure 12.069**), as a part of a dynamic filtering system.

Most large fryers have separate temperature controls for the front and discharge ends. This design allows the front frying temperature to be set about 5.5 C° (10 F°) higher to equalize the frying time for both sides of the product. Because doughnuts are initially cooler than the fat, the frying rate for the raw product side that enters the hot fat first is comparatively slower than that of the second, or upper, side, which is heated up by the time the product is turned midway through the frying cycle.

Yeast-raised doughnuts tend to float as soon as they reach the frying fat, but when

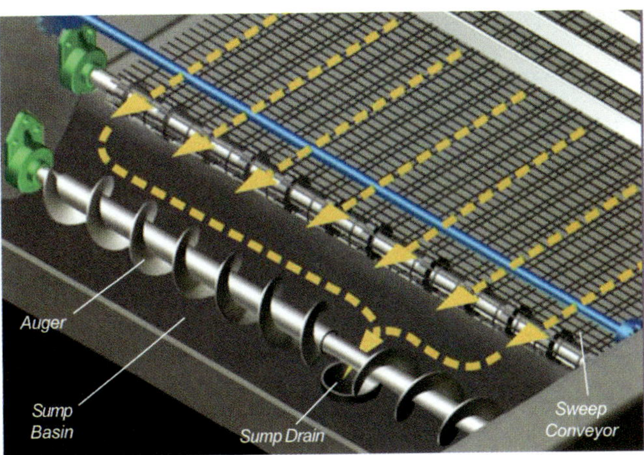

Figure 12.069. A live bottom sediment sweep mechanism continually removes debris by carrying it to a sump its auger. (Moline Machinery LLC)

Figure 12.070. A powered hoist lifts the conveyor system out of a doughnut fryer filled with frying oil. (Belshaw Adamatic Bakery Group)

Figure 12.071. The smallest of the doughnut robots can make 13 doz standard doughnuts per hour. (Belshaw Adamatic Bakery Group)

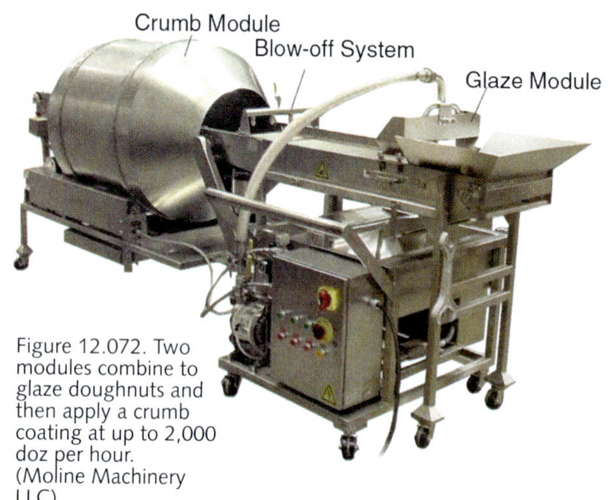

Figure 12.072. Two modules combine to glaze doughnuts and then apply a crumb coating at up to 2,000 doz per hour. (Moline Machinery LLC)

cake doughnuts are first deposited, they sink below the surface and rise 3 to 7 seconds later. This "rise time" can serve as a control factor because it is affected by the leavening level and the conditioning of the batter (Owen 1975). As the doughnuts progress through the fryer, the surface batter flows toward their centers to impart a star shape to the center hole by the time the products reach the turner.

Powered hoists to lift depositors and conveyor systems eliminate the need for manual lifting during cleaning or servicing of the fryer (**Figure 12.070**). Oil mist eliminators help reduce environmental emissions while improving sanitation and working conditions around the fryer.

Just as microwave heating techniques were used to supplement proofing of yeast-raised doughnuts during the mid-1970s, they were also used to improve frying action. Microwave energy was applied during the first half of the frying operation, heating the polar water molecules in the dough but not the nonpolar fat molecules in the frying medium (Moyer 1973). Although the technology claimed to reduce frying time and fat absorption, while increasing production rates, it was never put into commercial use.

The doughnut robot. An interesting piece of doughnut production equipment is the doughnut robot (**Figure 12.071**), a small, table-sized system, capable of producing 13 to 56 doz standard donuts per hour, or 74 to 226 doz mini-doughnuts, per hour. With a single depositor and a small fryer, the conveyorized system catches shopper attention to merchandise doughnut products. It is also well suited to laboratory use.

12.D.3. Glazing and finishing equipment

The fried doughnuts are next subjected to cooling, either on screen loader stackers, screen and tower coolers, continuous ceiling-mounted conveyors or circular continuous conveyors, until they reach an internal temperature of about 32°C (90°F), at which point they are ready for coating with powdered sugar (Belshaw 1970).

Doughnuts are glazed by passing them through a waterfall, but heavier icings are applied from the bottom as the doughnuts travel on wire-rod conveyors through a pool of icing. The doughnuts then flip over onto the discharge conveyor for cooling. (Glazed doughnuts are not flipped.)

Application of glaze and crumbs has been integrated (**Figure 12.072**) by a 2-module system. The glazer consists of a glaze trough and manifold mounted over a wire-rod conveyor with a heat-jacketed glaze reservoir and pump unit mounted below. Excess glaze is captured in drip trays beneath the wire-rod conveyor. Doughnuts fresh from the fryer passes through a continuous waterfall of heated glaze. A blow-off system removes excess glaze and sends the doughnuts along to a bumbling drum to be coated with crumbs. Another conveyor discharges the doughnuts from the drum.

12.E. Tortilla and Flatbread Equipment

Updated by L.A. Gorton

The first bread ever made was likely a flatbread, a Stone Age cereal gruel baked on hot rocks. By the time of the Iron Age (1800 BCE to 1 AD), flat sourdough bread had become the main grain-based food of Europe. Indeed, in much of the world today, the principal form of bread is still a flat loaf made from a simple formula and baked quickly in a high-heat oven or on a griddle.

Eaten the world over, flatbreads go by many different names — balady, bannock, chapatti, glaris, lavash, naan, pita, rye crisp, tandouri and tortilla, among others. In Western cuisine, tortillas are the principal flatbread, although some might argue that pizza crust occupies a similarly important position in American diets.

Both wheat- and corn-based tortillas have become increasingly popular and are now widely available in American markets. These products have even made culinary inroads into Europe and other parts of the world. Corn, or maize, originated in the New World, and tortillas made of corn fed the pre-Columbian civilizations. Tortillas made of corn and later of the wheat introduced by the Spanish remain a culinary mainstay of Central America. As Hispanics migrated northward, tortillas came along with them.

Although corn and wheat are the principal grains used to manufacture tortillas, some are also made from sorghum and other grains. Processing of such products, however, calls for the same kind of equipment as used for corn and wheat tortillas.

The discussion here takes up the technology that produces wheat tortillas first, followed by corn styles. Related products such as pita, pizza crust and cracker bread will also be covered. Ovadia (2008) related the history of pizza, linking it with many other flatbread styles.

The ANSI/BISSC/Z50.2-2003 Sanitary Standards for the Design of Bakery Equipment cover many of the machines used to make tortillas and flatbreads. In addition to the "basic criteria," "definitions" and "general principles of design, construction and cleaning," such machines should also conform to specific standards for ingredient storage and handling systems, mixers, dough forming equipment, proofers, conveyors, ovens, kettles and coolers, among others.

12.E.1. Flatbread science: heat and steam

High heat, steam leavening, quick baking — all characterize the processing methods for preparation of flatbreads such as tortillas, pita and cracker breads. Pizza crust shares some of the same technologies (heat pressing and die cutting) with tortillas but employs unique topping equipment. Baking methods for pizza crusts tend to favor tunnel ovens, even when preparing par-baked or frozen styles. Cracker breads are now commonly made by cooker-extruders that process the dough under pressure, and the leavening power of steam comes into play at the die plate, where it flashes off to puff up the bread's texture.

12.E.2. How tortilla equipment works

Preparation of wheat tortillas employs mixing and makeup methods similar to those used for bread and buns. Wheat flour, shortening, water, yeast and salt are

Figure 12.073. This automated line can output 900 to 4,500 doz heat-pressed wheat tortillas per hour. (Lawrence Equipment)

combined in a bread-style mixer of appropriate size and mixed to full development. Both spiral and horizontal mixers can be used, but the horizontal style suits the large batch sizes of automated wheat tortilla systems. Divider/rounder and intermediate proofing/resting steps follow. **Figure 12.073** depicts a typical heat-press wheat tortilla line.

Corn tortillas, in contrast, consist basically of cooked corn, treated with an alkali solution during cooking, then ground and shaped into individual tortillas. They, too, bake quickly in hot, multi-pass ovens. Corn tortilla systems also yield tortilla chips, taco and tostada shells, and the frying method is used to make corn chips.

The mixing, dividing and intermediate proofing of wheat tortillas use methods and equipment like that for preparation of yeast-raised buns and rolls. The result is cohesive homogeneous dough. Makeup results in flat, pancake-like dough pieces and is accomplished by pressing, sheeting and/or die-cut equipment. Typically, wheat tortilla dough pieces pass directly from makeup to the oven; no final proofing stage is needed.

To set the structure of the tortilla, the pieces pass through an oven. Tortilla and flatbread processing systems differ from other bakery lines in that products bake in high-temperature, 3-pass ovens for very short periods of time, compared with most other forms of bread. An equilibration step often follows baking, particularly for corn tortillas intended for further processing into tortilla chips. Corn tortillas for fresh local distribution are often packaged while still warm. To enhance shelf stability, tortillas can be sprayed with a preservative solution, a step similar to that used for English muffins.

12.E.3. Effect on doughs

During processing of flatbreads such as tortillas, doughs are divided into individual pieces, sometimes rested, sometimes sent directly to the oven, baked quickly and cooled. The process transforms raw dough into finished products, usually light in color with some dark spots. The variegated appearance is considered desirable by consumers, but translucent patches are not because they reveal doughy regions that did not bake properly.

With wheat tortillas, pita and balady, the process also creates a single large interior pocket, yielding a double-layered bread. The oven's extreme heat causes interior moisture to flash off as steam, inflating the dough piece like a hollow ball. The heat of the oven and the steam change the interior crumb sufficiently to allow retention of the hollow pocket even after the piece collapses during cooling. Other flatbreads such as tandoor and chapatti are single-layer breads.

12.E.4. Wheat tortilla methods and equipment

Three methods are used for making up individual tortillas: (a) hand-stretched, (b) heat-pressed and (c) die-cut. Each results in finished products with different characteristics and applications. Hand-stretching and heat-pressing yield the most traditional styles favored for table tortillas, while die-cut flour tortillas find use in entree preparation for food service and frozen foods or fried to make edible salad bowls (Gorton 2008).

In the hand-stretched and heat-pressed systems, tortilla dough runs through a divider-rounder similar to those that handle bread and bun doughs. Die-cut tortillas are produced on a sheeting line, with dough rolled and stretched to the proper depth.

12.E.4.a. Heat press

The main method for preparing wheat tortillas today is heat-pressing, also called "hot press." Here, the scaled and rounded dough pieces, on emerging from the proofer, enter a hydraulic stamping device in which they are pressed into their final thin tortilla form (**Figure 12.074**).

Figure 12.074. A press tortilla line automatically stamps rested dough balls to form tortillas. The press platen is heated to improve dough flow. (Stewart Systems)

Dough for pressed tortillas tends to be under-mixed and is set at 32 to 38°C (90 to 100°F). Tortillas made from over-mixed doughs tend to show larger blisters than the smaller, more-desirable blisters of under-mixed doughs. No floor time is needed (Janson 1990), although another worker (Qarooni 1993) reported resting the dough for 5 minutes before transferring it to the divider/rounder (**Figure 12.075**). Extrusion dividing has recently been applied successfully to wheat tortilla production (**Figure 12.076**), and such systems operate without divider oil. The higher dough temperatures and under-development help the dough pieces relax more quickly after dividing and rounding, thus facilitating pressing and stretching operations. Wheat tortilla dough is like that of hearth bread and roll doughs, and it tends to be very stiff and dry.

Dough ball weight and finished tortilla size are related, with 25 g (0.9 oz) producing the small snack size and 60 g (2.1 oz) for food service tortillas. The divider/rounder and intermediate proofing equipment used to portion the dough balls for heat-pressed and hand-stretched wheat tortillas is the same as that used for hearth buns and rolls. Heat and humidity within the proofer must be controlled to prevent the surface of the dough balls from forming a skin (too dry) or collecting moisture (too wet). Proofing conditions of 32°C (90°F) and 60 to 70% relative humidity are optimum (Qarooni 1993).

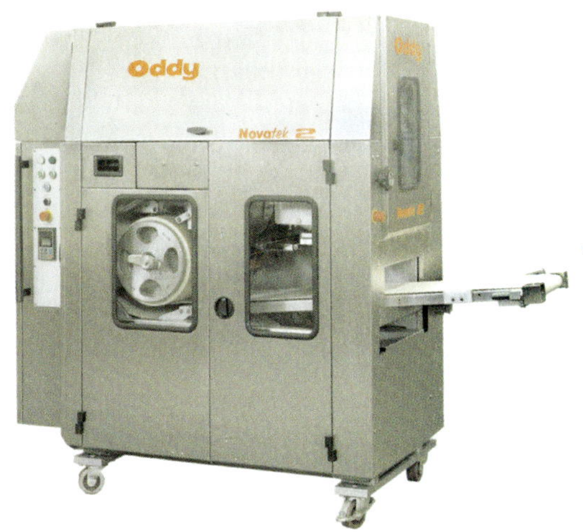

Figure 12.075. The divider/rounder systems for wheat tortillas operate in the same way as systems that divide bun doughs. (Oddy)

Dough balls fall from the overhead proofer down an indexer (**Figure 12.077**), consisting of 4 to 16, or more, chutes connected to a template that positions them correctly on the fluorocarbon-coated pressing belt below. The template head descends to lightly press the dough balls so they don't roll out of place. The press and the plate under it are heated to 177 to 232°C (350 to 450°F), with a dwell time of 1 to 2 seconds. The press operates at 400 to 1,000 lb per sq in. The exact pressure, time and heat depend on the tortilla's formulation, hence the ranges noted here (Janson 1990).

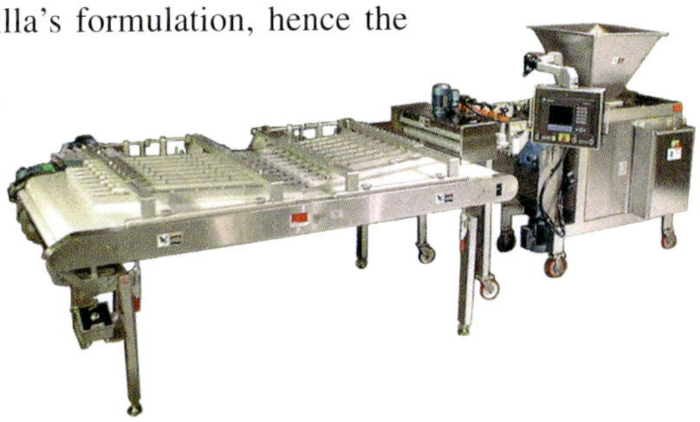

The hot press sears the top and bottom surfaces of the tortilla, creating a skin or membrane on both sides of the dough piece. During baking, the piece expands, but the skin holds the leavening gases inside, resulting in a desirable light, flakey tex-

Figure 12.076. Extrusion dividing technology is also used for wheat tortillas doughs. (AMF Bakery Systems)

ture (Janson 1990).

Until recently, pressing was an intermittent process. The press' conveyor stopped while dough balls were deposited on it and tamped into place to prevent them from rolling out of position. The platen would then descend to flatten the balls and rise out of the way, allowing the belt to start up again, moving the pressed tortillas to the oven. New "flying head" technology uses continuous horizontal and vertical movement of the press to complete more than 20 strokes per minute, without stopping the belt. An automatic dough detection system allows pressing only when dough balls are present, and the press maintains exact product spacing. Such systems can achieve rates of 990 doz per hour for 12-in. tortillas or 2,200 doz per hour for 6-in. tortillas.

Figure 12.077. An indexer positions dough balls for flattening. (Lawrence Equipment)

12.E.4.b. Hand stretch

Compared with pressed tortillas, hand-stretched tortillas tend to have a leaner formula so mixing time is slightly longer. More development is desired for this style of tortilla because each dough piece is actually sheeted twice. Dough-out temperature should be 32 to 38°C (90 to 100°F), and no floor time is needed (Janson 1990).

Dividing, rounding and intermediate proofing are the same as for pressed tortillas. A scaling weight as low as 25 g will yield a 6-in. tortilla, while as much as 60 g are required for 10- and 12-in. tortillas (Schmidt 1985).

In the hand-stretching procedure, the dough is scaled and rounded into individual dough pieces, 1 to 2 oz in weight, and given a brief rest in an intermediate proofer. They are then sheeted into very thin, circular dough sheets that receive an added stretching by hand to their final size as they pass over a heated aluminum plate. The flattened tortillas actually tend to be slightly oval as they come out of the cross-grain sheeter, with the longest dimension parallel to the direction of travel. The stretching gives them a desired homemade appearance.

12.E.4.c. Die cut

A more developed and cooler dough is required for the die-cut tortilla process. Dough-out temperature should be in the range of 27 to 32°C (80 to 90°F), and again, no floor time is necessary (Janson 1990). The dough will be very stiff.

The mixed dough is extruded by a dual auger pump or extruder as a 0.25-in.-thick continuous band onto a conveyor belt for subsequent cross-rolling and sheeting to the desired thickness (0.125 to 0.1875 in.). The dough sheet then passes through the die-cutting machine (**Figure 12.078**) that cuts it into slightly oblong forms that shrink into the conventional circular shape before the dough pieces reach the oven. Scrap dough is recycled back to the hopper at the front of the sheeting line.

12.E.5. Related wheat tortilla equipment

The baking, cooling and packaging of wheat and corn tortillas use similar systems but with a few key differences. Operating parameters, including temperatures and times, will vary with product type.

12.E.5.a. Tortilla ovens

Flour tortillas bake in a compact 3-tier oven (**Figure 12.079**). The tortillas move on a conveyor composed of metal plates or wire mesh band and are, thus, inverted or flipped twice during the baking cycle. A 3-pass oven reflects the home method of placing the dough piece on a hot griddle and flipping it twice. This method sets the starch and bakes the tortilla. To conserve space, the oven conveyors move in opposite directions at each pass.

For pressed tortillas, oven temperatures range from 191 to 260°C (375 to 500°F), and baking time varies from 25 to 40 seconds. Hand-stretched and die-cut tortillas bake for 17 to 25 seconds at a temperature of 218 to 260°C (425 to 500°F) (Janson 1990).

Nearly all of the browning takes place by conduction from the hot (206°C, or 500°F) surface of the oven's baking plates or mesh bands. A certain number of "toast points," as the coin-sized, dark brown spots are known, is desirable. The size and number of toast points depends on the belt temperature, which is controlled by burner settings. Infrared temperature sensors, located outside the heating zones, can be used to "look into" the oven and measure the temperature of both the tortilla and the belt on which it travels.

In the past, tortilla ovens had been notorious for wasting energy. Without the accurate temperature control now available, ovens had to remain idle during reheating after a production shutdown, or else the first products put into the oven during the restart would burn or show excessive toast points.

To get enough oxygen to the burners, some operators would prop open or completely remove the oven's insulated panels. Energy efficiency has come to tortilla oven design. Such ovens can proportionally mix combustion air. Other heating improvements include individual burner controls and pilotless active flame management. Double-walled microporous insulation with an increased intra-layer air gap functions as a heat sink to cut air loss from the oven chamber and reduce the temperature of the outer walls.

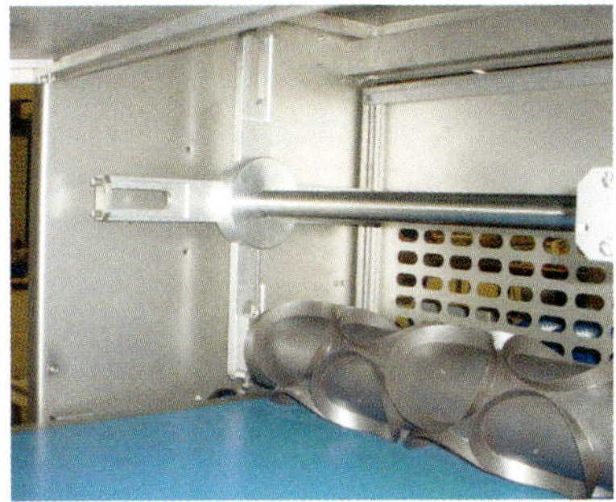

Figure 12.078. This roller die cuts uniform flour tortillas on a sheeting line. (Rademaker)

12.E.5.b. Cooling

When wheat tortillas exit the oven, they sometimes look like half-inflated basketballs, but the heated leavening gasses and steam cool quickly and dissipate within a few seconds, leaving the tortilla in its characteristically flat form.

Released from the oven, tortillas enter a multitier conveyor for room-temperature cooling (**Figure 12.080**). The tortillas travel along one level and flip over as they drop to the next level of the cooler. To conserve space, the conveyors move in opposite directions at each subsequent tier. The cooling action of these conveyors is often augmented by placement of large fans alongside, especially in warmer climates and during summer months when temperature and humidity is high. Insufficient cooling will result in tortillas that stick together.

Wheat tortillas should be as close to plant ambient temperature as possible when packaged. Higher temperatures will cause moisture to condense inside the package, encouraging mold growth.

Figure 12.079. As they bake, tortillas travel through 3 oven tiers to be flipped twice thus mimicking the home method of griddling.
(Heat and Control)

12.E.5.c. Preservative application

The normal water activity (a_w) of corn tortillas is 0.98 or higher and wheat tortillas 0.88, which presents a substantial risk for microbiological spoilage. The preservative system typically used for tortillas consists of a solution of potassium sorbate or calcium propionate. The preservatives require a pH in the range of 5.1 to 5.6.

If used as part of the dough, dry preservatives are blended with the flour and other dry ingredients before the water is added. Such dry materials will compete with the flour for available water so a better way to add it to doughs is to inject it into the water stream as it enters the mixer. Dry preservatives are not recommended for addition to corn masa doughs because the granules will stick to the dough and not disperse evenly. In liquid form, preservatives can be applied to the grinding stones, but the resulting masa should be thoroughly mixed afterward to ensure dispersion of the preservative.

Hickey (1980) introduced the topic of surface spraying of yeast-raised baked foods, including tortillas and pita bread. Sorbates, even at low 0.1% (flour weight basis), inhibit yeast activity so their application as a mold inhibitor had to take place after baking. By placing the sprayer immediately after the oven, proper drying of the solution is assured.

Rolow (2002) presented a thorough discussion of preservatives and how they are added or applied to tortillas.

Figure 12.080. As tortilla travel along the multiple tiers of this cooler, the flip over as they drop a level. (Stewart Systems)

12.E.5.d. Counting, stacking, packaging

Generally, wheat tortillas are bagged 1 to 2 doz per package in polybags sealed with twist ties, plastic tabs or heated bar sealers.

Programmable counter-stackers (**Figure 12.081**) replace the manual task of counting tortillas before packaging. Current designs accommodate 1,800 to 5,400 doz per hour, counting stacks of four to 60 tortillas each. Because consumers prefer different sizes, counter-stackers should be able to accommodate the various diameters. A universal product laning air chute system on one such counter-stacker allows quick changeover between sizes. Other equipment designs use adjustable feed angles and quick-change canisters to allow two, three or four row stacking of flour tortillas.

The bagged tortillas reach market in master shipping containers, but care must be taken not to stack bags more than five high. If stacked too high, the bulk density of the product will compress the bottom bag to the point where tortillas cannot be separated without tearing.

Despite accurate portioning during dividing, both the pressing and hand-stretching processes may produce slight size differences in wheat tortillas. Such dimensional variances can affect packaging operations, and Gelroth et al. (2005) recommended no more than ± 0.5 in. for an 8-in. heat-pressed tortilla.

12.E.5.e. Recent developments

Today's flour tortilla lines have been steadily increasing in output capacity, producing up to 4,500 doz 6-in. tortillas per hour. Sequencing via programmable logic controller (PLC) is a must for such systems. Full control over all processing variables is thus possible. For example, when changing the press cycle rate, the controls automatically adjust divider, proofer and cooler speeds. The press transfer belt speed is automatically calculated to ensure that transfer speeds are kept as low as possible, and controls make it impossible to feed pressed tortillas into the oven faster than it can receive them, thus eliminating folds.

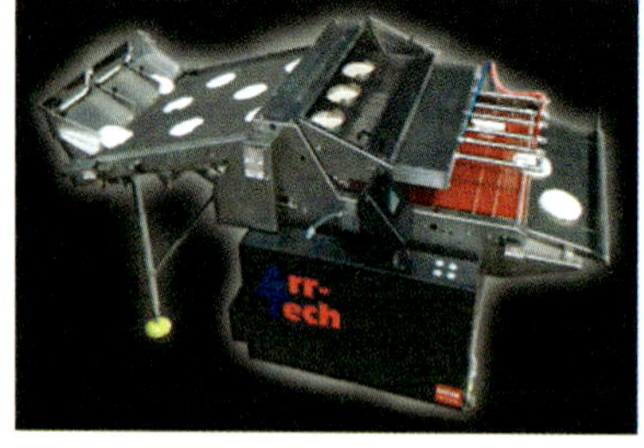

Figure 12.081. A servo-operated counter stacker automates the formerly manual task of counting tortillas for packaging. (ARR-Tech)

The large heated platens of pressed tortilla systems also require precise temperature control. As many as 18 separate heaters per platen can be controlled by PLC on a fully programmable tortilla press.

Research into infrared baking of wheat tortillas (Martínez-Bustos et al. 1999) found the method produced products with good rollability, puffing, layering, color and texture. The system applies infrared radiation at 11 W per cu cm, which produced an effective temperature of 549°C (1,020°F), to the top and bottom surfaces simultaneously, baking the tortillas in 17 seconds. The tortillas showed less dehydration than conventionally baked items, and energy needs amounted to roughly half that of a conventionally heated oven.

Automated inspection is a must for today's high-speed tortilla lines. The human eye cannot keep up with conveyor speeds that reach 250 ft per minute. Electronic vision systems are being added to at least half the new tortilla lines now being installed. The screening system measures every tortilla that passes through it for diameter; determines if holes are present; detects flat edges, raw spots and edge defects; and searches for translucent spots (Whitaker 2004). Such systems can calculate the percentage of toast points and even the thickness of the tortilla. Tortillas that don't measure up are rejected by a jet of compressed air that pushes them off the line.

While inspection generally takes place at the end of the processing line and right before packaging, engineering work is being done with a visual inspection system that looks at hot-pressed tortillas right after the press (**Figure 12.082**).

Finally, engineers of flour tortilla equipment are giving more attention to sanitation. Clean-in-place capability is now part of many designs, with attention given to elimination of standing water and debris collection.

12.E.6. Corn tortilla methods and equipment

Corn tortillas are made from alkali-cooked corn (**Figure 12.083**) and qualify as a whole-grain food. Originally, all corn tortillas were made from raw corn cooked by the nixtamal process (**Figure 12.084**). Dry masa flours, developed during the middle of the 20th century, shortened and simplified tortilla preparation. (These developments are explained in Volume I, Chapter 2, Part A.)

On a raw material basis, dry corn is less expensive than masa flour, but the masa flour process for producing corn tortillas has several benefits. First, the capital cost of corn storage, cooking, steeping and grinding equipment can be avoided. Second, the highly alkali cooking water from this process carries organic material (about 18% of the corn kernel), which creates a high biochemical oxygen demand (BOD) if disposed into municipal water treatment systems. Environmental Protection Agency and local regulations often require that such wastewater be treated on-site at the bakery before disposal.

Cooked corn, on the other hand, tends to yield a softer dough than that made with masa flour and is fully hydrated, which makes it less dense at the sheeter head. In some cases, larger particles can be processed without hanging up on wires and dies (Riley 1991).

Figure 12.082. Automatic inspection of tortillas measures their size, shape and color characteristics, removing defective products based on user-defined criteria. (Dipix Technologies)

12.E.6.a. Nixtamal process

Commercial cooking involves a series a heated cooking vessels (**Figure 12.085**), usually steam-jacketed systems, in which raw corn and an alkali solution combine.

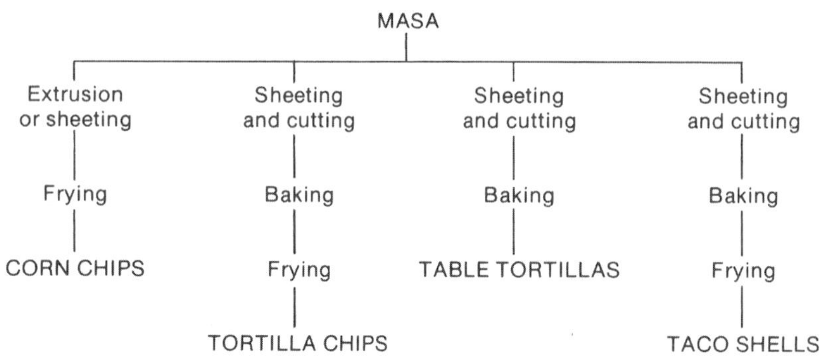

Figure 12.083. Alkaline-cooked corn yields different products based on processing methods.
(Rooney and Serna-Saldivar 1987)

Typical cooking kettles can accommodate 2,000 lb of corn kernels. Steam and recirculating hot water bring the kettles up to temperature. The corn is hydrated with water maintained at 49°C (120°F) and then gelatinized by raising the temperature to 74°C (165°F). Afterwards, the heat is shut off. Cooking takes place under agitation and is closely timed to gelatinize at least half the starch in the corn kernel (**Figure 12.086**). When the heat drops to 140°F, recirculation of water shuts off, and the corn is allowed to steep for about 12 hours (Matz 1988).

Improvements continue to be made in cooking and steeping methods such as that described by Freudenrich et al. (2003). The patented method saves water, wastewater, lime and energy. During the grain cook-and-steep process, the phase-separated supernate is retained for a subsequent batch of grain. In addi-

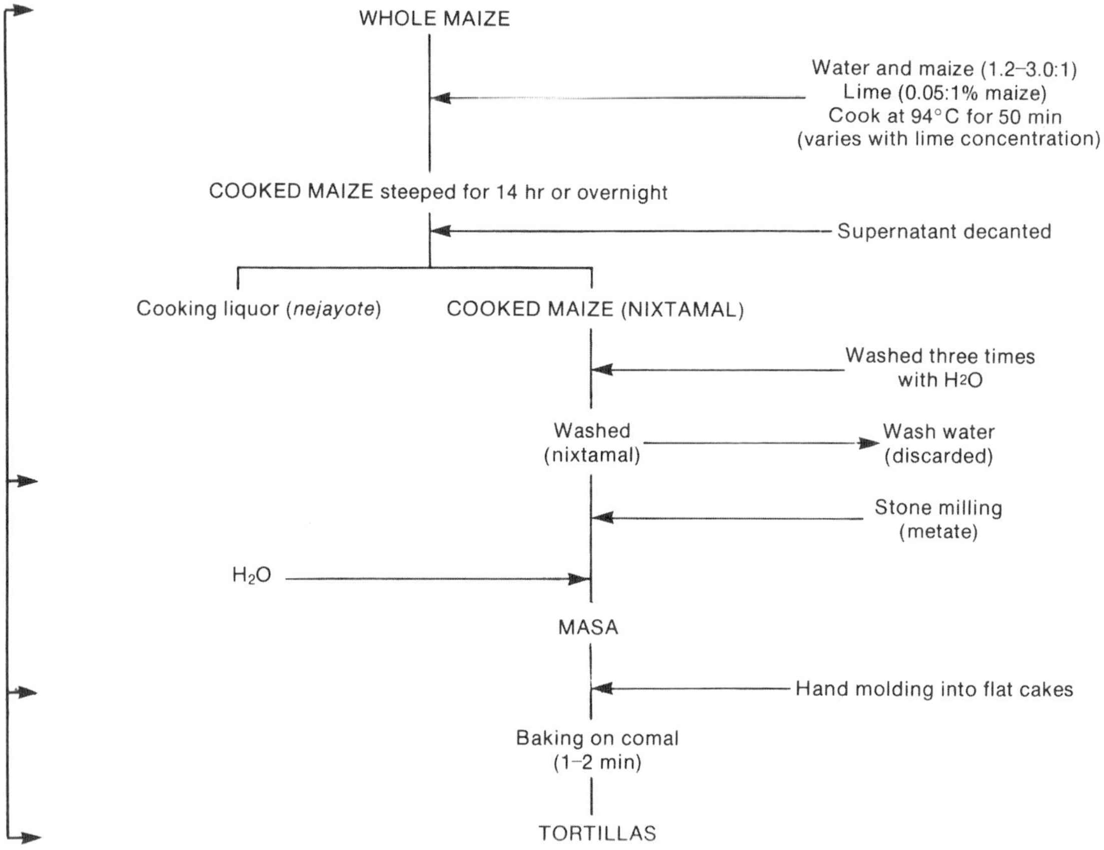

Figure 12.084. The nixtamal process yields masa for preparation of corn tortillas.
(Rooney and Serna-Saldivar 1987)

tion, a fresh water rinse stream is recycled as push water.

The cooked corn is put through a washer to remove extraneous debris, especially the hard pericarp. The extra water is separated out, and the finished masa pumped to the former (**Figure 12.087**). Multiple wash cycles carry away extra lime, free starch and the hard, indigestible pericarp. The drained corn is conveyed to the mill, where it will be ground. The mill uses a stationary lower stone disk and a rotating upper stone.

Grinding disrupts the swollen gelatinized starch granules and distributes the hydrated starch and protein around the ungelatinized portion of the corn endosperm (Rooney and Serna-Saldivar 1987). Grinding establishes the particle size and, because of the friction between the stone and the nixtamal, further damages the starch enabling more gelatinization during baking. The grinding process results in masa (the Spanish word for "dough") ready to go into the roll and die-cut sheeter head or a low-pressure extruder that scales individual corn tortillas.

Figure 12.085. Preparing nixtamaled corn onsite typically involves a series of cooking and steeping kettles. (Heat and Control)

Over-cooking produces sticky masa, which is difficult to handle; under-cooking results in noncohesive masa that produces tortillas of poor texture. Ramirez-Wong et al. (1994) optimized cooking time at 55 minutes and reported that grinding the corn to a medium particle size with a moisture content of 54.6 to 56.2% gave the best masa texture for sheeting and cutting of corn tortillas.

The most traditional style of grinding equipment employs carved lava stones to mill the cooked corn. Water can be added to avoid excessive heat generation. The gap between the stones determines the particle size of the resulting masa. An experienced operator can judge the particle size by squeezing a piece of masa between the fingers.

A "stoneless" grinding system was recently introduced that can produce 2,500 to 5,000 lb of finished masa per hour. It uses a proprietary metal alloy disk, ground parallel within 0.001 in., which is said to last two to three times longer than conventional lava stones. The gap between stones, which can be adjusted in increments of 0.0005 in. by an optional motorized actuator, is shown on a digital indicator.

When properly ground and hydrated, the masa is ready for immediate transfer to forming and sheeting systems.

Figure 12.086. At any given time, some kettles of corn will be filling, cooking, soaking or emptying. (Heat and Control)

12.E.6.b. Masa flour process

With the use of masa flour, or dehydrated nixtamal, the first step in tortilla production is the mixing of the corn flour with sufficient water, usually by means of large horizontal mixers to yield a dough with a consistency essentially similar to that of the original masa.

Doughs made with these flours are sensitive to shear stress (Riley 1991). Corn masa doughs require minimal agitation and mixing. Trevino and Norton (2006) recommended preparation in mixers equipped with sigma blades for their lift-and-drop action.

Figure 12.087. After cooking and steeping, corn must be washed, with the extra water removed, before it can be pumped to the former. (Heat and Control)

Sigma-arm mixers come in sizes to handle 400 to 1,000 lb of dough per batch. Unlike the bread-style mixers used for wheat flour doughs, sigma-arm mixers impart very little work or heat to the dough but produce homogenous dough balls when mixing corn masa flour and water. The ball will be slightly sticky with a rough, non-uniform break when pulled apart and a granular, spongy, non-uniform appearance. Recommended mixing speed is 20 rpm for a total time of 4 to 6 minutes.

12.E.7. Related corn tortilla equipment

12.E.7.a. Sheeting

Originally, corn tortillas were made commercially using forming methods similar to home preparation. The masa was scaled into individual pieces ranging in weight from 1.0 to 2.0 oz, depending on the intended final size of the product. The masa pieces were then rounded and flattened into circular thin sheets with a diameter of 6 to 12 in.

However, it is far more common today to use sheeting and cutting methods. The dough is fed, with a minimum of delay, into an extruder and through circular die cutters, which produce the final flat, round form. The most common sizes for corn tortillas are 6.5, 8.5 and 10.5 in. in diameter.

In the most automated systems, masa supplied by the grinder or mixer transfers to the sheeter via an inclined belt conveyor, bucket elevators or by direct gravity drop into the sheeter's hopper. A dual-auger system in 5- and 9-in. configurations and gooseneck styles for horizontal and vertical layouts can also be used to transfer corn masa. Pumping tends to increase the masa's temperature, making it overly sticky and pasty so this transfer method is typically not used for corn tortillas.

A presheeter takes the non-uniform blocks of masa from the transfer belt and, in a cold extrusion process, creates a thick, uniform curtain of dough that falls into the center of the gap between the sheeter head's rolls. Most corn tortilla sheeter heads have a concave front roll and a matching convex back roll equipped with a high-tensile steel piano wire for stripping and/or transferring product (**Figure 12.088**). One wire on the back roll and two on the front assist in sheeting and releasing the cut product from the roll. Wires may be placed straight or at an angle across the face of the rolls. The head's front roll cuts the tortilla shapes. Recent design improvements place the wire on the back roll to feed the front roll, while other changes do away with wires altogether (Trevino and Norton 2006).

12.E.7.b. Baking and cooling

At home, corn tortillas are generally baked on a griddle, as they have been for centuries, but commercial preparation uses a hot, high-speed, 3-pass oven, with gas burners placed under the conveying belts. The oven's burners should be set to provide a violet internal flame surrounded by a blue flame. The surface of the conveyors that carry corn tortillas through the oven are generally limed, coated with calcium hydroxide. The lime actually cools the belt, and the effect is to spread heat side to side.

The design of most tortilla ovens place the burners across the width of the belt, which means that product travels across multiple heat zones, and the product in the middle receives more heat, drying it more than the tortillas passing through on the sides. A different design, reported by Whitaker (2004), sets burners to run the length of the oven but at a slight angle (**Figure 12.089**). The burners heat the belt in the direction of travel and are said to save 15 to 20% on energy costs.

Oven belts consist of three kinds: a slat belt or an open-weave belt, one of looser design and the other more closely woven. The type of belt determines the baking marks on the product.

The shaped tortillas transfer onto a limed conveyor into the oven where they are baked for 20 to 30 seconds at a temperature of about 260°C (500°F). Ideally, the dough receives no floor time whatever so the rate of production is established by the intervals at which the successive doughs are mixed (Sosland 1984). Baking is accomplished chiefly by conductive heat (Schmidt 1985). Tortilla ovens are equipped with a 3-tier conveyor system whose closely-woven wire mesh belt serves as the baking surface. As the product moves through the oven, it transfers successively from tier to lower tier, being flipped over at each transfer so that it receives three bakes, with two of them on one side.

Oven temperature and residence time vary with the style and weight of the tortilla, and according to the manufacturer's preference. Baking times can range from 20 to 38 seconds at oven temperatures of 288 to 427°C (550 to 800°F). Typically, baked corn tortillas contain 44 to 46% moisture, a reduction of 10 to 14 percentage points from the dough stage (Trevino and Norton 2006).

For best keeping quality, corn tortillas must be cooled before packaging to below the dew point temperature of the production facility, transport vehicles and product display at point of sale. Generally, this cooling point will be below 38°C (100°F) in the center of the stacked corn tortillas. Such cooling allows steam to escape prior to packaging so moisture does not condense inside the bag, a condition that could lead to mold growth.

In-line "cascade" cooling conveyors consist of 3-, 5-, 7-, 9- and 11-tier systems, from 30 to 35 ft long and 6 to 7 ft high. Such coolers have 300 to 500 ft of effective belt. The largest of these systems uses a 52-in.-wide belt and can travel at speeds up to 250 ft per minute. Air that is filtered before it passes though these conveyors will reduce the microbial problems caused by bacteria, yeast and mold. For table tortillas, the longer the cooling time, the lower the packaging temperature and the longer the expected shelf life of the product.

Figure 12.088. A sheeter forms corn tortillas that will be processed into tortilla chips. (Casa Herrera)

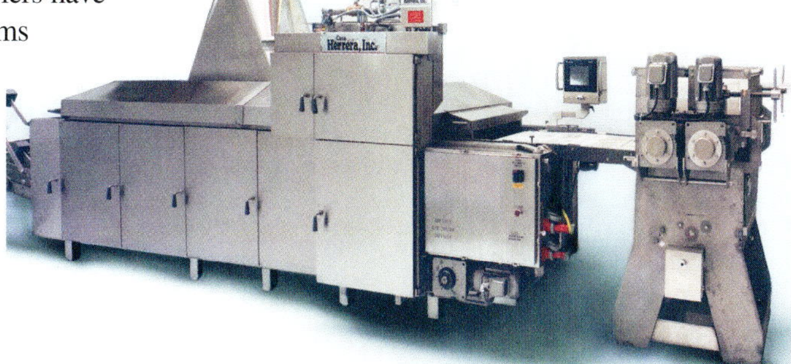

Figure 12.089. The burners in this oven run lengthwise to provide more consistent heat to bake high-moisture corn tortillas. (Casa Herrera)

12.E.8. Related corn products

12.E.8.a. Tortilla chips

Tortilla chips (**Figure 12.090**) are baked first and then held for a period that allows them to equilibrate before being fried. The chips can be cut and formed into the desired shape — round, triangular, strips or rectangles, etc. — at the sheeter head and baked in that form. Or they can be produced as conventional corn tortillas, held under refrigeration and then cut manually or by a hydraulic press into the desired shape. The latter method is older and mimics the way tortilla chips were originally made in restaurants and sometimes still are.

The raw tortilla chip bakes in a multitier oven of the same design as those used

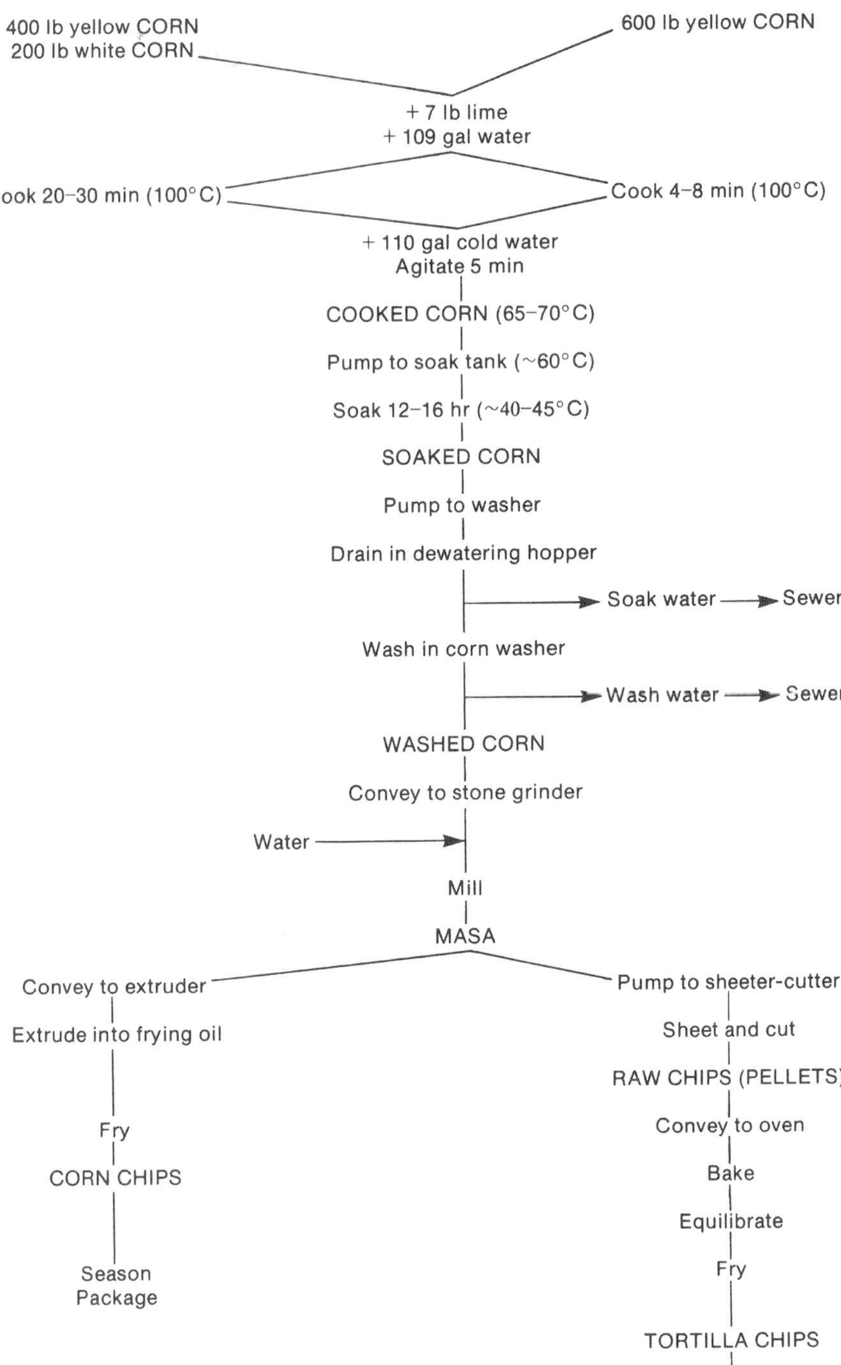

Figure 12.090. Making tortilla chips requires a different process than corn chips, but both start with masa. (Rooney and Serna-Saldivar 1987)

to bake corn tortillas, usually in no more than 18 to 21 seconds at 440 to 454°C (825 to 850°F), which is shorter in time and hotter in temperature than for regular corn tortillas (Riley 1991). The baked chips then enter an equilibration unit, essentially a cooling and resting system that provides sufficient time for the chip's moisture to equalize throughout its body. The now leathery chips move along to the fryer where they are finished (**Figure 12.091**). Equilibration prevents formation of blisters that can trap frying oil or burn undesirably. The longer the equilibration time for tortilla chips, the harder the bite. There will also be less puffiness and less oil pickup.

Continuous and batch fryers are used to produce tortilla chips, with batch fryers handling smaller production requirements.

To make corn chips, no baking stage is required. Instead, the cooked corn dough is either extruded at low pressure through a set of dies or sheeted and die-cut onto a transfer belt and deposited directly into the fryer (Riley 1991). Corn chips can be made from dry masa as well, and a blend of white and yellow corn masa is used. Corn chips made with 100% yellow corn masa often have an undesirable burnt flavor (Riaz 1997).

12.E.8.b. Taco shells and tostadas

To make taco shells, the processor starts with freshly prepared corn tortillas. The tortilla must still be warm from its earlier preparation enough to bend without fracturing. Using a timing conveyor or manual loading methods, the tortillas are placed into a 2-part form, or basket, usually featuring open wire mesh construction. The top section descends to push the tortilla down into the bottom U- or V-shaped form. The form, mounted on a carrying chain with other forms, stays closed as it carries the corn tortilla through the hot oil of a fryer (**Figure 12.092**). At the end of the fryer, the form remains closed for a few moments to help "set" the shape of the taco shell and then releases it to a packaging conveyor.

12.E.9. Pita and flatbreads

Figure 12.091. Tortilla chips emerge from the fryer and are routed into the seasoning system that applies topical flavorings.
(Heat and Control)

The flat breads common to the Middle East, Northern Europe and India exhibit both single- and double-layered style, with the only processing difference being the second proofing period and the practice of docking (also called "dockering" or "dokking"). As Qarooni (1990) observed, in the double-layered type, this period may exceed 30 minutes, during which the dough aerates and its surface dries to form a skin. The skin enables the piece to hold its leavening gasses and puff up during baking. In single-layered products, the second proofing stage is very short, usually only a few seconds, and puffing is prevented by docking the sheeted dough before baking.

Quail (1996) provided a comprehensive review of Arabic bread production, describing the evolution of traditional preparation methods into automated processes.

12.E.9.a. Double-layered flatbreads

Also called Arabic or pocket bread, pita bread features a 2-layered structure, or "pocket," created by steam during baking in a hot oven. Exposure of the flat loaves to the very high temperatures in the oven causes an almost instantaneous formation of top and bottom crusts. As the heat penetrates into the loaf, it transforms the interior moisture into steam within some 30 to 45 seconds. The steam, being confined by the external crust, expands the loaf into a puffed-up form that consists essentially of only the top and bottom crusts. The interior void thus created then forms the "pocket" when the puffed-up loaf collapses on cooling (Gorton 1985).

Figure 12.092. Forming baskets carry corn tortillas through the fryer to form taco shells.
(Heat and Control)

In pita bread production, all the ingredients are mixed using the straight-dough process. Mixed for 2 minutes at slow and 6 minutes at a higher speed, the dough becomes fully developed and very stiff, much like any hearth bread dough. Spiral, horizontal and even high-intensity Chorleywood-process mixers are used (Quail 1996). With a dough-out temperature of 24 to 25°C (76 to 78°F), it is fermented for about 1 hour. The dough is then scaled into units of 3 to 4 oz, rounded by means of a rounding belt with gyratory rounding cups or other types of mechanical rounders and given an intermediate proof of 15 to 20 minutes. Because the dough is relatively dry to the touch, only a small amoung of dusting flour, if any, is needed to avoid sticking (Cooper 1986). The relaxed dough pieces are pressed to 2 to 2.5 cm (about 1 in.) and next enter a double sheeter moulder, where they are first flattened into oblong slabs, which then enter the second sheeter at right angle to be cross-sheeted into thin circular dough sheets about 6 to 9 in. in diameter and 0.0625 in. thick, depending on market preferences.

The sheeted dough pieces then undergo a final proof of 20 to 30 minutes in a cabinet maintained at a temperature of 30°C (86°F) and a relative humidity of 65 to 75% (Quail 1996). Humidity at this relatively low range enables "case hardening" of the dough surface, forming a leathery crust that helps trap the leavening gases (Cooper 1986). The proofing surface is a moving wide flat belt that is arranged in a series of tiers, much like the systems used to cool tortillas. The belt carries the dough pieces through the various tiers, dropping them at the end of each tier to the next lower level and inverting them in the process. The repeated turns helps even out the crust formation so final crust and crumb will be of equal thickness on both top and bottom surfaces. On emerging from the final tier, the dough sheets are deposited on the hot oven hearth for baking.

Pita ovens are hot, heated to around 400°C (753°F) or even as high as 538°C (1,000°F), and loaves bake in 100 seconds or less (**Figure 12.093**). The hot loaves, puffed into hollow spheres by the force of the interior steam, deflate quickly as they cool on a conveyor that leads to packaging operations. The tunnel ovens used for these products, and other commercially made flatbreads, employ steel mesh or steel plate hearths. Mesh surfaces tend to be preferred because they minimize bottom cracking of the flatbread loaves, while the edges of plate-style hearths can act as hot knives, promoting crack formation.

The ovens are usually direct-fired. Some use a single jet-style burner fitted to the oven's back wall above the exit (**Figure 12.094**). High-velocity air impingement ovens are also very successful at baking pita and other flatbreads. To prevent heat loss, ovens may use a "top hat" feature, overhanging the exit end of the oven, thus reducing the amount of air exchanged with the plant environment.

As Cooper (1986) pointed out and Quail (1996) confirmed, for many years, it was thought that pita absolutely required the dough ball process, with its dividing and rounding methods applied to individual dough pieces. Both reported that it is possible, however, to successfully make pita via the die-cut process. The dough can be continually extruded, then rolled into a flat sheet and die-cut into individual pieces that can be processed in the same manner as loaves formed from balls.

12.E.9.b. Single-layered flatbreads

Tanoor, an example of single-layered flatbread, is traditionally baked in a clay oven called a tandoor, from which it gets its name ("tanoor" or "tandoori"). The manual process requires the baker to place the proofed dough piece onto a moistened cushion to manually adhere it to the oven's interior wall. The finished loaves are removed with special metal rods when baking is done, 1 to 2 minutes later. The process for this product and other dockered flatbreads (barbari, lavash and taftoon) has been automated to use modern high-temperature tunnel ovens (Faridi and Finney 1980).

Doughs are generally mixed (usually in spiral mixers but also in horizontal bread mixers) to optimum development and fermented for 30 to 40 minutes. Piece size varies by variety and ranges from 150 to 250 g (5.3 to 8.8 oz) for tandoori, 320 g (11.3 oz) for lavash, 450 g (15.9 oz) for taftoon and 610 g (21.5 oz) for barbari. Resting time for any of these varieties is short: 1 to 5 minutes for most but up to 10 minutes for others. Makeup involves sheeting and dockering, with a short 1- to 2-minute final proof. The loaves travel to short tunnel ovens. Baking temperatures vary from 205 to 425°C (400 to 800°F), and baking times are correspondingly short, from 60 seconds to 2 minutes.

Hashmi and Wootton (2000) provided an interesting discussion of how they developed a method to test bake and evaluate tandoori bread. In this report, they also examined the parameters of commercial processing of this popular bread from the Middle East.

12.E.10. Pizza crusts

Pizza for immediate consumption is usually prepared with toppings placed on top of raw dough and all baked together. Because the crust bakes while having to carry the cheese, meat, vegetables and sauce of the topping, the resulting product is often on the verge of being doughy. But pizza made for sale from a refrigerated case or as a frozen product is typically made by baking the crust (also called a "shell") separately and then applying the topping later (Fischer 1981). New styles to emerge include par-baked, chemically leavened (called "rising crust") and take-and-bake varieties (Valentino 1994, Lehmann 1997, Lehmann 2002). Crust sizes run

Figure 12.093. A 3-zone oven (background) bakes pita for 25 to 35 seconds at 415°C (780°F) before sending them to 35 minutes of ambient cooling. (*Baking & Snack*)

Figure 12.094. The single-jet burner is visible at the top of the pita oven in this view from the exit end of the oven. (*Baking & Snack International*)

from round styles with diameters of 3.5 to 16.5 in., as well as squares and rectangles. Lipped styles include deep-dish, pan-style or crown-style. Even cheese- or sauce-stuffed crusts can be automatically made.

Styles of pizza crust range from thin and crispy (the so-called "cracker" style) to thick and bread-like. Lehmann (1986b) observed that efforts to make more authentic pizzeria-type crusts have included frying, rather than baking, the crust. Lamination in conjunction with specialized ovens designed for rapid baking will open up the laminated cell structure in much the same way as puff pastry structure is formed.

Preparation of pizza crusts follows two different methods: by pressing of individual dough balls or by sheeting and cutting (**Table 12.2**). Pizza doughs are mixed as straight doughs, containing as much as 5% yeast, on a flour weight basis, and given some floor time to allow the dough to mellow and flavors to develop.

Some pizzarias and chain pizza restaurants are organized around commissary preparation of pizza dough and crusts (Lehmann 1986a). These locations handle the skilled tasks of mixing, dividing and rounding and may also prepare the crusts themselves. These raw dough products must be chilled to 7°C (45°F) or lower, and refrigerated trucks distribute the dough balls and crusts to the "satellite" stores and restaurants for preparation. Raw dough skins are extremely sensitive to temperature.

Table 12.2. Pizza Processing Parameters

	Manual pizzeria perparation		Automated stamped or sheeted preparation	
	Thin crust	Thick crust	Thin crust	Thick crust
Dough process	Straight dough	Straight dough	No time	No time
Mixing	7 to 10 minutes at low speed	7 to 10 minutes at low speed	1 minute at low speed 5 minutes at high speed	1 minute at low speed 5 minutes at high speed
Dough temperature	23 to 24°C (74 to 76°F)	23 to 24°C (74 to 76°F)	38°C (100°F)	38°C (100°F)
Bulk fermentation	None	None	None	None
Processing	Divide and round	Divide and round	Divide and round, or sheet and cut	Divide and round, or sheet and cut
Dough retarding	12 to 96 hours	12 to 96 hours	–	–
Floor time	30 to 90 minutes	30 to 60 minutes	–	–
Intermediate proof	–	–	10 to 15 minutes	10 to 15 minutes
Relaxation period after first press	–	–	2 minutes (only if pressed twice)	2 minutes
Second press	–	–	Optional	Optional
Final proof	–	–	None	5 to 10 minutes (optional)
Sheeting	0.175 to 0.1875 in.	0.25 to 0.3125 in.	–	–
Docking	Optional	Yes	Optional	Optional
Proofing	None	15 to 45 minutes at 29°C (85°F) and 85% RH		
Topping	If applicable	If applicable	–	–
Baking	232 to 246°C (450 to 475°F)	218 to 232°C (425 to 450°F)	218°C (425°F)	218°C (425°F)

(Lehmann 1986)

If held above 7°C (45°F), the yeast will begin to ferment, but below that temperature, the skins can be held for up to 3 days after assembly (Lehmann 2002).

12.E.10.a. Pressed pizza crusts

The pressed pizza crust style is made by putting a no-time dough, mixed 3 to 5 minutes or sufficiently to develop a smooth consistency, through dividing, rounding and intermediate proofing stages using equipment similar to that for conventional bread and bun production. Under-mixing is better than over-mixing since excessive mixing results in excessively soft doughs with poor makeup properties and finished shells with poor volume and excessive toughness (Lehmann 1979).

Batch sizes should be arranged so that no dough remains in the divider hopper for more than 8 to 12 minutes. The overhead proofer should be maintained at 35 to 38°C (95 to 100°F), and dwell time will be 10 to 15 minutes. Excessive processing time produces sticky and gassy doughs.

Cold-pressed method. After the first proof, dough balls are deposited into their baking pans and pressed, usually with the help of a spray of release oil, or occasionally olive oil, to prevent sticking. Because the dough's gluten retracts after pressing, in the cold-press method, a second press is usually applied after a short rest period to make sure the crust will assume its final shape. The first press will achieve 75% of the desired diameter. The rest time should be no less than 2 minutes, but Lehmann (1986b) reported that many bakers shorten the interval to 45 seconds to reduce the need for additional conveyors. The slight increase in dough shrinkage is generally controlled through formulation adjustments.

Such "cold press" dies consist of two components: the stripper ring (also called a "damming ring") and the punch. During the pressing cycle, the spring-loaded stripper ring makes first contact with the pan to contain the dough within the pan cavity. The punch section continues to press out the dough, at a pressure of up to 1,000 lb per sq in. Dwell time will vary according to product needs, with larger, lipped or deep-dish styles requiring more time than smaller sizes, but is typically 2 to 4 seconds. After pressing, the punch recedes first, followed by the stripper ring (Valentino 1994).

Cold-pressed pizza is typically flat or has a slight rim on the top. The press baking pan has rings molded into the cavities to prevent dough shrinkage after the press process; these rings are clearly evident after baking on the bottom of the pizza crust.

Heat-pressed method. A second method presses the dough ball with heated platens. When making cracker-style crusts, the platen can be just above room temperature, 24 to 27°C (75 to 80°F), while other styles will require more heat, typically 35 to 38°C (95 to 100°F). Hot press lines generally use only one press. The dies are similar to those used for cold pressing. This method usually presses the dough long enough for the heat to kill the yeast, and this causes the crust to shrink and prevents further proofing, resulting in a somewhat par-baked crust that normally does not require a pan for further handling and needs no final proofing. Valentino (1994) noted that some bakers use less heat in the press, thus keeping yeast active for a final proofing stage.

The pressed crust can be as simple as a rimmed edge crust or a pressed-in logo into the crust. The high temperature of the die sears the skin of the crust into its final shape without the typical dough retraction of the cold press. Press cycles run between 6 and 9 seconds and platen dimension can be up to 54 by 54 in. Formulation and technology has made significant improvements in the quality of the hot pressed crusts in recent years.

Automatic pressing equipment is available for both cold press and hot press methods.

Some thick crust styles may receive an additional 5 to 10 minutes of final proofing at 32°C (90°F) to promote greater crust thickness before baking. Pressed crusts are baked in the pan by traveling through a tunnel or tray oven. Baking time varies with product size and desired end color.

Retail and food service operators bake their pizzas in pans, and Varela (2002) provided a detailed discussion of pizza pans and disks, their construction and how they affect the degree of bake.

12.E.10.b. Sheeted pizza crusts

Depending on the texture and amount of flavor desired, dough for sheeted and die-cut pizza crusts may or may not be fermented in the trough after mixing. Preparation of the sheeted dough follows the principals of sheeting laid out earlier in this volume, and the equipment employed is the same: a conveyorized makeup line equipped with reduction rolls, cutters and other forming stations. Use of a cross-sheeting station helps minimize dough shrinkage from side to side across the belt. Stress-free sheeting systems are particularly gentle to these doughs.

The depth of the dough sheet for thin crusts should be 0.125 to 0.25 in. and 0.25 to 0.375 in. for thick crusts (Lehmann 1979). A variety of effects can be achieved with such lines, including docking and light pressing to give the crust a raised lip (**Figure 12.095**). A web of dough, equal to 30 to 50% of the original sheet, remains after cutting and is stripped away for return to the mixer.

Figure 12.095. To create a pizza crust with a well-developed edge and a thin middle, a hydraulic press compresses the center of the crust yet applies very little pressure to the edge. (Fritsch)

Stamper equipment may be necessary to handle thicker products (**Figure 12.096**). This style of equipment uses a straight, vertical cutting action, and the stamper's "walking" action, advancing with the belt, allows dough pieces to be cut with no lateral action between the dough and the cutting surfaces. Excess dough is stripped as trim scrap and can be sent back to the mixer for reincorporation (**Figure 12.097**).

When a more open-textured crust is desired, the sheeted crust can be proofed after cutting and before baking. Conditions in the final proofer should be maintained at 32 to 35°C (90 to 95°F) and 80 to 85% relative humidity, and dwell time is 8 to 10 minutes for a thin crust and 20 to 40 minutes for a thick crust. Proofed crusts, however, are very sticky and collapse easily. The dough is limp and easily stretched, thus distorting the crust and affecting its ability to be packaged on automated machinery. To reduce the mechanical working of the dough, nonstick surfaces can be employed for the sheeting rolls.

When making cracker-style crusts, the scrap dough can be delivered immediately back to the hopper feeding the extruder. But with proofed crusts, scrap is better added back at the mixer, or else the older dough will show up as streaks in the resulting dough sheet (Fischer 1981).

Pizza crusts travel to a tunnel or band oven heated to 205°C (400°F) in the first zones and as much as 315°C (600°F) in the final zones (Lehmann 1979). Baking times for die-cut pizza crusts are just 3 to 5 minutes, enough to set the structure without overly coloring the crust.

12.E.10.c. Related pizza equipment

Docking. Pizza crusts are sometimes docked before baking. Docking is done with rollers equipped with blunt pins, 3.2 to 4.8 mm (0.125 to 0.1875 in.) in diameter. A blunt, rather than pointed, design is important because effective pin docking consists of forcing the top of the dough down into the bottom of the dough with sufficient force to cause it to adhere together, a process that Gelroth et al. (2005) described as "much like spot-welding two sheets of steel together." Docking limits the formation of bubbles in the thin dough, and it may also help the crust bake faster than undocked dough. The dough structure sets faster as well.

Equilibration. In some bakeries, fresh baked shells are allowed to temper, to reach moisture equilibration and firm up slightly for 24 to 96 hours before being sent to the topping line for finishing.

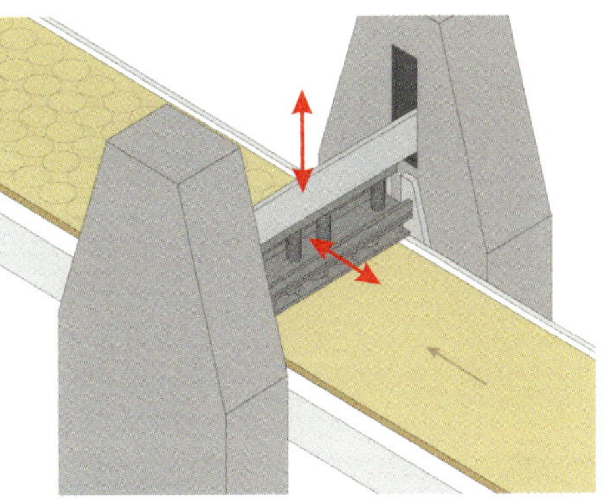

Figure 12.096. The stamping head travels with the belt to produce a straight, vertical cutting action. (Moline Machinery LLC)

12.E.10.d. Packaging considerations

Because the par-baked pizza crusts sold for home preparation still contain a good deal of moisture, they can suffer from mold. A spray of calcium propionate or potassium sorbate solution over the warm crust prior to packaging will hold microbial damage in check. Par-baked crusts may also be frozen before distribution and/or packaged in barrier films under nitrogen or another inert gas in controlled-atmosphere packaging, with vacuum packaging another option (Valentino 1994).

Interleaving and stacking equipment (**Figure 12.098**) for handling crusts and topped pizzas (6- to 18-in. diameter) operates at speeds up to 240 portions per minute.

12.E.11. Cracker breads

Also called crispbreads, cracker breads originated in Europe. They grew in popularity following introduction of extrusion technology to replace older processing methods. Extruded crispbreads can be made in many shapes, colors and textures, as well as different degrees of toasting (Riaz 1997).

Crisp bread, in its original form, describes a hard whole-meal bread for which the dough is rolled out into a thin sheet, about 5 mm (0.2 in.) thick and baked very quickly in less than 10 minutes (Tolle 1985). Some styles are fermented with yeast; others are not. Crisp bread made from fermented dough has a firmer consistency.

The dough, when sheeted, receives dockering (**Figure 12.099**) to prevent blisters and bubbles from forming during baking, and then the dough sheet is cut transversely into strips. Fermented doughs receive final proofing by passing through a temperature- and humidity-controlled tunnel. Either of these styles can also receive a topping of sesame or caraway seeds or other ingredients.

Figure 12.097. Scrap automatically recycles after die-cutting. Low-stress sheeting methods do not over-work doughs, thus permitting scrap reuse without affecting the end product. (RONDO)

Ovens (**Figure 12.100**) for baking crispbread operate at very high temperatures, typically 380°C (716°F) in the first zone. Ten minutes later, when the bread finishes baking, the oven temperature in the Cylotherm system drops to 110 to 169°C (230 to 320°F) to finish drying the product. The air speed within the oven varies, too, with high rates of movement in the early high-temperature zone and lower rates in the second zone, moving along the long drying section, reaching 64°C (147°F) at the end of the oven. Steam dampers within the oven exhaust the water that evaporates during baking, taking moisture content from 55 to 60% in the dough to 6% in the finished baked product.

The strips run through a slicing saw to be cut both across and lengthwise. Scrap from this trimming operation is removed by a suction device or conveyor screw. The

Figure 12.098. Pizza crust stackers automate a formerly manual job. (Packaging Progressions)

Figure 12.099. A pair of dockering rolls prepare the crispbread dough for baking. (Werner & Pfleiderer)

Figure 12.100. Crispbreads require a long bake and a long oven. (Werner & Pfleiderer)

cut crisp bread moves along to be cooled, stacked and packaged.

Using a cooker-extruder system, flatbread doughs are mixed and plasticized by the system's intermeshing and co-rotating screws before being extruded through narrow slit-style die heads (Tolle 1985). Cooked under pressure, the dough flashes off steam at the extruder die, thus leavening the finished product and creating its characteristic texture. A takeaway system moves the puffed strips along to be cut at the proper length. A gauging section may be used to press the bread while still hot to set its depth to the desired dimension. The gauge station can also be used to emboss patterns into the warm crust of the still pliable but fully cooked product. Typical output rates on such systems runs 500 to 700 kg (1,100 to 15,500 lb) per hour.

Crispbreads produced by extrusion are essentially starch melts, in which pressurized water vapor is responsible for expansion as the extrudate leaves the die. The bubbles of water vapor inflate rapidly and then show a small degree of shrinkage, caused by the partial vacuum created when the water vapor pressure in the bubble drops below atmospheric pressure as the product cools. Mitchell et al. (1999) experimented with such systems to study how the viscosity of cell walls affected final product volume.

12.F. Bagel Equipment
Updated by L.A. Gorton

A hard roll with a hole, a shiny chewy crust and a dense texture, the bagel has changed a good deal since first introduced to Americans in the early 1900s by Eastern European Jewish bakers seeking to replicate an Old World ethnic specialty on Western shores. Long before it left home, the bagel's original shape of a stirrup (or *Bügel*, in German, which became "bagel" in Yiddish) morphed into a ring, but it took American ingenuity to produce styles containing blueberries or chocolate chips, to name just two variations. Although sizes range from mini-bagels at ¾ to 1 oz (20 to 28 g) up to "bull" bagels at 4 to 7 oz (110 to 200 g), the most common sizes are in the range of 2.5 to 3.5 oz (70 to 100 g).

When considering the high degree of innovation that characterizes automated bagel lines, it is worthwhile noting that it was a manufacturer of bagel equipment that devised star-wheel chunking as a low-stress way of feeding stiff doughs to dividers. Bagel equipment manufacturers also developed knife-cut dividers that feed dough strips through two rollers as a spinning knife rotates to cut off the dough piece.

Readers interested in how bagel technology developed will find the autobiographical report by Thompson (undated) fascinating. He described the many prototypes, experimental installations and commitment of bakers that were involved in the invention of the bagel machine by him and his father.

12.F.1. Bagel formers

Forming bagels by traditional methods required great skill and much labor. As

Petrofsky (1986) explained, bakers would manually roll 3-oz pieces of dough into 6-in. strips and then wrap those strips around the first 3 fingers of the hand, overlapping the ends of the strip by 1 in. under the palm. Another method found the baker making a single long string-like roll of dough. The baker wrapped the leading end of this strip around his hand and broke off a piece between two fingers.

A quick roll sealed the strip ends. Finished pieces were put onto pans or peels dusted heavily with corn meal, which kept the bagels from sticking to the pans. Handmade bagel doughs were retarded under refrigerated conditions (3 to 4°C, or 38 to 40°F) for 12 to 18 hours. Bagels can be retarded for up to 2 days, and the doughs can be frozen. Manual preparation proceeded at the rate of 40 to 50 doz per hour. This relatively slow production rate is one reason that bakers typically retarded bagel doughs to bake them the next day (Eberts 1998).

All that work prompted invention of bagel formers of two distinct types: (a) vertical forming-cup systems and (b) horizontal belt-and-mandrel designs. Although the inventor of the vertical system experimented with belt systems, he commercialized vertical design instead. Today, automated bagel formers enable bakers to reach typical line speeds of 2,000 doz bagels per hour and higher, and one manufacturer reported a system making more than 8,000 doz bagels per hour

Dough pieces suitable for processing on these systems can be supplied by the knife-cut system described above, by drum-style hard roll dividers and by rotary extrusion dividers.

12.F.1.a. Vertical forming-cup systems

Cup systems (**Figure 12.101**) are composed of a vertical roller chain circuit with a multi-part, or winged, cup attached to the chain. In its closed position, the cup (**Figure 12.102**) forms a round hollow tube, which provides the outer rounding surface. The inner moulding surface is provided by a vertical stationary round rod or mandrel, held concentrically in the tube created by the cups (Genau 1996).

Supplied by a 6- or 8-pocket roll divider, the relaxed dough piece drops into the cup at the top of the machine, and the cup then closes like a clamshell around the dough piece. As chain carries the cup downward, the confined dough piece is rolled against the stationary mandrel, elongating until both ends join in a ring (also called a "toroid"). The cups open at the bottom to release the formed bagel, which drops out still guided by an extension to the mandrel. Different bagel sizes are created by larger and smaller cup-and-mandrel combinations. Because the vertical formers have a relatively narrow width, they can be installed in banks to output formed bagels in rows, depositing them directly onto peels or pans.

12.F.1.b. Horizontal belt-and-mandrel systems

Mandrel-and-belt systems (**Figure 12.103**) use a flat, endless, fabric conveyor belt, which is bent and guided through a stationary round tube, or sleeve, to comprise the outer moulding surface (Genau 1996). The inner moulding surface is a mandrel mounted down the center of the tube. To accommodate different bagel sizes, the belt width and tube size are changed to form larger or smaller outer diameters. The mandrel diameter, as in the vertical system, ranges from 1.125 to 2 in. (30 to 50 mm) and determines the size of the bagel's hole.

Dough pieces drop into the curved lead end of the belt. As the belt moves forward, the tube forces the belt's long edges to curve up and over the dough piece. Contact with the mandrel initiates elongation of the piece, while the curved sides prompt the

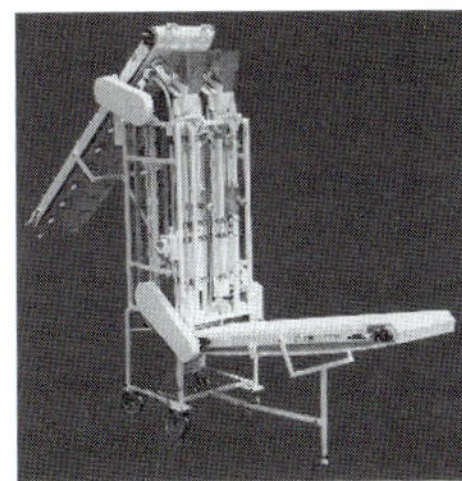

Figure 12.101. A vertical circuit of forming cups travel down a mandrel, releasing the formed bagel at the bottom.
(Thompson Bagel Machine)

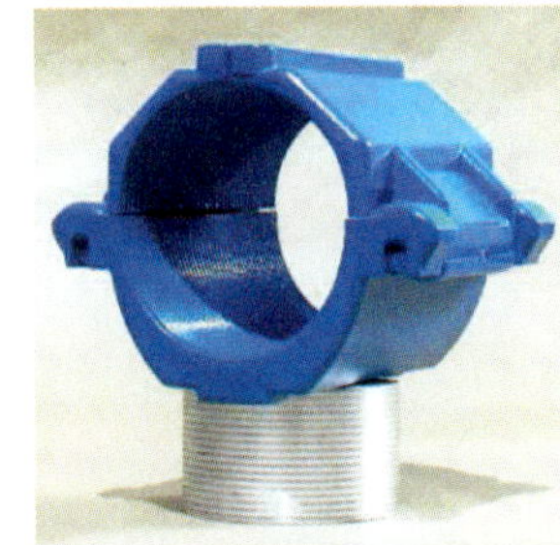

Figure 12.102. The multipart cup opens to accept dough pieces and closes to hold the dough in place as it forms into a ring around a vertical mandrel.
(Thompson Bagel Machine)

piece's ends to come together and join into a ring. As the belt leaves the tube, the bagel reaches the end of the mandrel, and lays over on one side to be discharged from the forming system onto a take-away conveyor. These horizontal forming systems are now available with quick-change mandrels, sleeves and belts.

Such mandrel systems can be installed in banks (**Figure 12.104**) to feed high-speed production lines. Like bagels made on vertical systems, the individual dough pieces can be grouped and transferred, usually by a retracting transpositor conveyor, to pans and peels, dusted with cornmeal (**Figure 12.105**). Standard 18-in.-by-26-in. peel boards can carry 24 3-oz bagels.

Proofing and/or retarding stages follow. Peels can be loaded into mobile racks and enclosed with a zippered fabric covering to sit on the bakery floor for 45 to 60 minutes, or the peels can be loaded into an automated proofer. Because the low temperatures of retarding favor the fermentation of lactic acid bacteria, the bagels develop a better flavor and aroma than bagels subjected to continuous processing, according to Genau (1996).

A recent development in bagel proofing uses rack-style loading and a powered transport system.

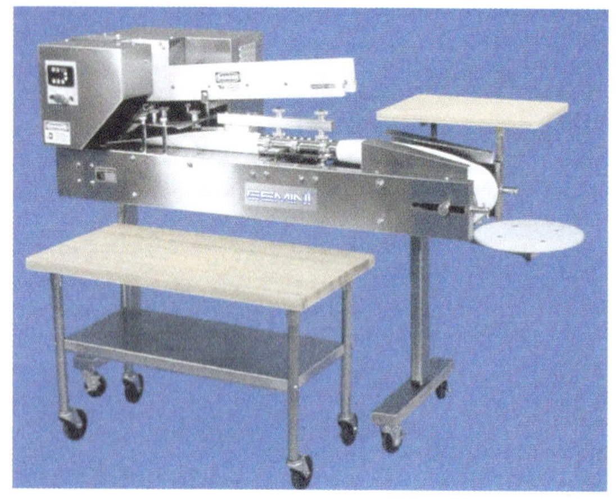

Figure 12.103. A forming belt curls up around a mandrel to form dough pieces running along its length.
(ABI Ltd.)

12.F.2. Bagel boilers

Boiling of the proofed bagels, a unique step in bakery processing, accomplishes two purposes, according to Meloan and Doerry (1988): (a) It fully gelatinizes the starch on the dough's surface, thus giving bagels the gloss that distinguishes them from regular hard rolls, and (b) it sets the outside structure of the roll so that the bagel retains its shape during baking. This boiling process gives the "water bagel" its unique texture, crust characteristics and its name (Petrofsky 1986). Boiling started as a way to preserve the stirrup-like shape during baking. The crust-to-crumb ratio of a bagel is much higher than that of a conventional hard roll, and the crust provides the bagel's primary flavor.

Bagel dough, which is often retarded to allow a slow fermentation, should be at room temperature before going into the boiler. Water bagels are cooked in simmering water (**Figure 12.106**) at 93 to 100°C (200 to 212°F), giving them a hard crusty crust as well as a shiny surface, often studded with desirable "eye" features. The water in the boiler can be plain tap water or supplemented with sugar or malt at 2.5%, or about 4 oz to each 10 lb of water. The addition of the sweetener adds to the shine of the crust (Petrofsky 1986).

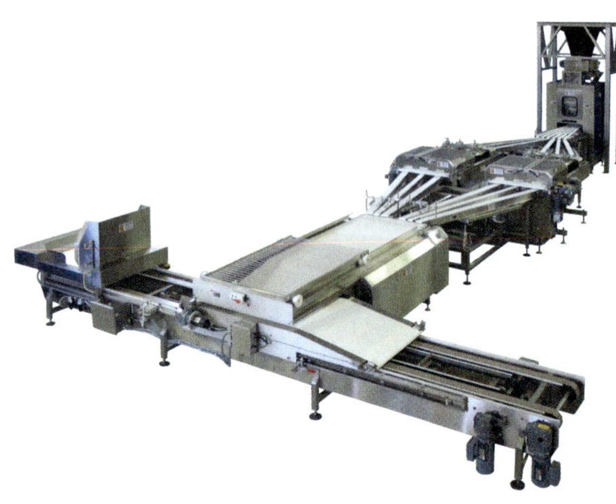

Figure 12.104. This combination bagel line can produce either four lanes of sandwich-sized bagels or six lanes of mini-bagels.
(ABI Ltd.)

Bagels will sink to the bottom of the kettle and then float to the surface. The bagels should cook for 30 to 60 seconds on the first side and then be flipped to cook for about the same time on the other side. Total time varies from 1 to 2 minutes, depending on the baker's preference. The cooked bagels must then be removed from the cooker and allowed to dry briefly.

Submersible-style boilers use top and bottom belts to control the movement of the raw bagels and to eliminate the need to flip them halfway through the process. The top belt holds the buoyant bagel down in the hot water. The bottom belt first brings the bagel into the water and then, after the 1-minute cooking period, carries the bagel out.

The conveyor system can be hoisted out of the tank for sanitation and maintenance. A self-cleaning bottom design drags the kettle, removing fines and debris through a continuous belt filter. Short open-wire mesh belts, called "preloaders," can also be installed right after the proofer; this method helps remove excess flour or corn meal ahead of the cooker. Cooking water is continually recirculated and filtered. Wastewater from bagel cookers will need treatment to remove any remaining organic materials before it reaches the municipal water system.

Waterfall systems have been developed to cook lighter and softer products (Whitaker 2009a). This method carries bagels on a belt through a shallow pan containing approximately 0.5 in. of water. A spillway across the width of the unit pours hot water (93 to 96°C, or 200 to 205°F) over the top of the bagels. An advantage of this method is that it does not leave marks or indentations on bagel surfaces.

Toppings such as sesame or poppy seed can be sprinkled onto bagels as they emerge from the cookers. As bagels climb out of the cooker on the conveyor, they pass through a drying zone for 1 to 1.5 minutes. The dryers feature infrared burners mounted under the conveyor, and indirect heating methods may also be employed. At least one manufacturer offers a dryer with a forced-air system at the unit's entrance. The stream of warm air blow off 75% of the water on the bagel surface before it reaches the dryer.

Only the bottom of the bagel needs to be dried to prevent sticking to the oven hearth (**Figure 12.107**). The dryer belt should run through a continuous belt washer to remove gelatinous material from the wet bagels that adheres to the belt at each cycle. Baking time in a direct-fired oven will be about 17 minutes at 232°C (450°F).

The traditional baking method described by Petrofsky (1986) used long redwood boards that had been washed with water and sprinkled with seeds if desired. The boards carrying a single row of bagels went directly into the oven, set at 205°C (400°F). After about 5 minutes or when the tops were dry to the touch, the baker twisted the board to turn the bagels upside down on the oven shelf to bake another 20 to 25 minutes until golden brown. Without the short drying period, the wet bagels will stick to the oven shelf. Bakers used long peels to remove the bagels after baking.

Meloan and Doerry (1988) cautioned that over-proofed bagels will expand during boiling and collapse as they dry before reaching the oven. To reduce such adverse effects, boiling time should be minimized and drying time also reduced.

A bagel not scalded by hot water will expand excessively in the oven, and the finished results will look more like hard rolls than bagels. However, bakers learned that abundant wet steam in the oven could accomplish almost the same effects as boiling, as could giving the dough an egg wash and baking it like any other hard roll.

Eberts (1998) pointed out that water boiling methods did not travel well when bagel makers from New York migrated to the South and West. Hard water, in par-

Figure 12.105. Four formers shape dough pieces into bagels and deposit them on cornmeal-coated peel boards. (*Baking & Snack*)

Figure 12.106. The hot water in a bagel boiler gelatinizes the starches on the surface and gives the final product its sheen and chewy texture. (Heat and Control)

Figure 12.107. After cooking in an immersion boiler, bagels emerge onto a wire-belt conveyor to dry briefly before baking. (Heat and Control)

ticular, caused problems with shelf life and proper forming.

In the steam-baking process, rack-style ovens, set at 260°C (500°F), inject low-pressure steam for the first 3 to 4 minutes of baking. After this period, the oven damper is opened to release the excess steam, and baking is finished with the damper open. Steaming produces a thinner crust than boiling, and the process also accelerates ovenspring, resulting in a soft, tender bagel. Steaming also allows bakers to use softer particulates in the dough such as chocolate chips, cheese or jalapeño peppers, inclusions that would normally not survive the boiling process.

12.G. Pretzel, Breadstick and Baked Snack Equipment
Updated by Hans van der Maarel

It is believed that the history of pretzels dates back to the 1550s in Europe. During that time, monks rewarded children who had correctly learned their prayers with a baked snack made from scraps of dough formed to resemble a person with arms folded across their chest in prayer or the two wings of an angel (Kazemzadeh 1999). In fact, the name "pretzel" is believed to be derived from the Latin *pretiola*, which means "little reward."

In contrast to these simple beginnings, today's pretzels are made on highly automated production lines throughout the world, capable of producing several thousand pounds of pretzels per hour in a striking variety of formats.

12.G.1. Pretzel systems

Bakers tend to follow proprietary processes, but the steps in pretzelmaking can be broken down into mixing or low-pressure extrusion, followed by proofing, cooking, salting, baking and drying. Kazemzadeh (1999) provided a detailed description of the physical and chemical changes that pretzels undergo during processing.

12.G.1.a. Mixing equipment
Traditionally, the very stiff pretzel doughs have been prepared by horizontal mixers, usually equipped with heavy duty motors and double sigma-style arms. The doughs require 1 to 2 minutes on slow speed, followed by 3 to 5 minutes on fast speed. Finished dough temperatures range between 26 and 38°C (80 and 100°F) for batches weighing 70 to 350 kg (150 to 750 lb). High-speed horizontal mixers are also used to make pretzel dough.

Once mixed, pretzel dough should "set" or "rest" no longer than 30 minutes before being formed. Most bakers today allow little floor time for pretzel doughs, moving it directly to extruders.

In the mid-1990s, continuous mixing was introduced to the pretzel industry. This method virtually eliminated the problem of dough setting too long before machining because the dough is made continuously rather than in large batches and rest time is consistent throughout the production run. In present day, nearly all new pretzel lines in the US have been equipped with continuous mixing equipment (**Figure 12.108**). Additionally, many pretzel manufacturers have retrofitted their existing batch mixing with new, continuous mixing systems.

Streams of dry and liquid ingredients feed continuously into the mixing cylinder. The accuracy of automatic feeders exceeds that of manual scaling, with tolerances of ± 3% to 5% for volumetric systems and ± 0.5% for gravimetric equipment. Hourly output ranges from 500 lb to 20,000 lb, depending on the size of the machine.

Dry materials are wetted and blended before entering the mixer. These materials move forward along an auger-like mixing shaft. The shaft's configuration and speed of rotation determine the extent of work (incorporation, mixing, kneading and developing) applied to the dough. Experts in this technology recommend selection of a mixer that allows the user to vary the work given to the dough without changing the throughput rate of the mixer.

12.G.1.b. Low-pressure extrusion

During the infancy of pretzel manufacturing in the US, many pretzels were hand-tied with a twist-and-flip motion into the traditional 3-ring shape that is known today. This method was replaced by mechanical twisting machines for many years until the low-pressure extruder was developed. These systems operate at pressures of 40 to 120 psi (Romeo 2009). (Doughs extruded at higher pressures may exhibit "crystallization," caused by breakdown of the gluten structure and thus result in a very hard-biting, fragile product. Such pretzels have little product texture and little consumer appeal.) Most commercial pretzel manufacturers today use low pressure extrusion as the primary means of making pretzels. Rows of pretzels up to 80 in. wide can be cut at a rate up to 265 rows a minute.

Automated dough handling equipment represents a big improvement in moving dough from the mixer to the extruder (**Figure 12.109**). These systems deliver dough at a consistent rate to keep the feed hoppers at a constant level.

This machine uses 2 counter-rotating screws to pull dough from a hopper and push it into a compression head with an attached die plate. Co-rotating twin screw extruders are also used. Shapes cut into the die plate form the pretzels (see **Figure 8.110** on Page 344). The presence of a back plate at each die hole equalizes the flow within the hole or shape. In much the same way that wire-cut cookies are made, pretzel dough emerges from the die plate to be cut off by a reciprocating knife, moving from top to bottom, with a single stroke cutting off a full row of deposits at rates that now reach 175 to 265 cuts per minute.

The pieces drop onto a long resting conveyor. In the case of stick-style pretzels, the die lays down long strings of dough, which are cut to the desired length by a guillotine system prior to the cooker.

12.G.1.c. Knotting machines

Recent interest in reviving the knotting method resulted in development of pretzel formers, or "slingers" (**Figure 12.110**). These machines accept a string of dough,

Figure 12.108. By producing pretzel dough in continuous fashion, this mixer assures uniform age of dough going into the extruder.
(Reading Bakery Systems, ExACT Mixing)

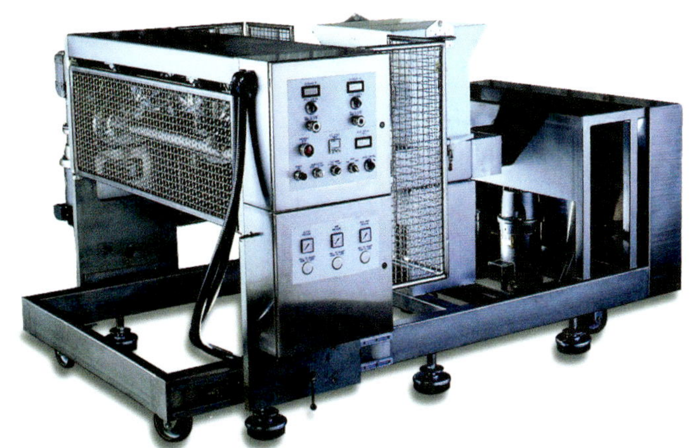

Figure 12.109. This low-pressure extruder can create a variety of structural and flat shapes as well as provide uniform dough flow with soft and hard inclusions.
(Reading Bakery Systems)

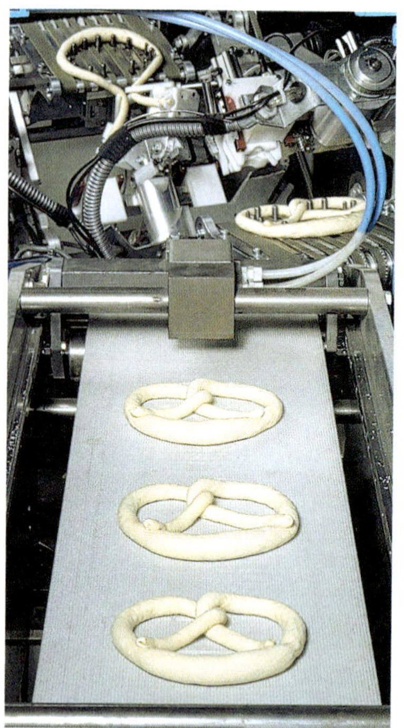

Figure 12.110. As shown in this composit photo, the slinger grips the pretzel dough string by two arms, while the forming table assembly turns perpendicularly and horizontally to form the knot. (Fritsch)

gripping it at either end and looping it around two forming heads or pins. The dough string, moulded under pressure boards like other stringline products, falls off the supply belt, with its center engaged by the work platform. Two arms grasp the ends of the dough string, and the whole assembly turns perpendicularly and horizontally to form the knot and seal the ends of the dough to the main body of the roll. The pins drop down to release the twisted pretzel. A single twisting machine operates at 30 to 35 strokes per minute to produce up to 1,800 pretzels per hour. This machine was developed to makeup soft laugen-style (lye bath) pretzel rolls, also called "brezeln."

12.G.1.d. Proofing

The proofing conveyor is a long belt upon which the formed dough pieces rest after extrusion. This belt is typically made of cotton or a cotton/poly blend to allow the dough piece to breathe on its underside. Proof times range from a few minutes up to an hour, depending on the type of pretzel being produced. Additionally, this proofing time allows the yeast or other leavening agents in the dough time to expand and create air pockets in the dough, which will aid in producing a pleasant texture in the finished pretzel. Most often proofer belts travel through plant ambient conditions, but enclosed proofing tunnels are also available for pretzel production.

12.G.1.e. Cooking

Pretzels, like bagels, are cooked before baking, but instead of traveling through a sweetened bath, they encounter an alkaline solution. The cooker is, perhaps, the most underestimated yet most important part of the pretzel process because it controls the most important characteristics of a pretzel: its color and flavor. The cooker holds a dipping bath that normally consists of a solution of sodium hydroxide (NaOH) and water heated to between 88 and 98°C (190 and 210°F). Kazemzadeh (1999) noted the strength of the solution as 0.5% for sodium or potassium hydroxide and 2% when using sodium carbonate. The cooking solution contains between 0.7 and 2.0 causticity (or 0.7 to 2.0 parts alkali per 100,000 parts water) for most pretzel types.

From the proofing belt, the pretzels transfer directly into the cooker (**Figure 12.111**), where they are dipped into the solution for a specific amount of time, generally less than 15 seconds. A wire-rod conveyor assists movement of the dough pieces in and out of the cooker.

The alkaline cooking step makes pretzels unique. The heat and caustic gelatinize the crust's starch and form a shell around the outside of the dough piece, limiting moisture loss yet allowing the dough to puff slightly during baking to give it a lighter texture. This shell may have a pH as high as 13.0. The combination of an outer alkaline shell and inner slightly acidic core gives the pretzel its unique flavor. Additionally, the overall composite alkaline pH of a pretzel makes it one of the only foods humans eat that is not acidic.

12.G.1.f. Salting

After the above steps are performed in the process, the gelatinized dough piece travels under a curtain of salt before entering the oven. Since the dough's crust is now warm and sticky from the hot cooker dip, the salt will stick to the crust as it falls on top of the dough piece. The salting unit consists of a storage hopper located over a grooved or pocketed roller. The speed of the roller is variable and is set to the desired salt application rate, typically 2%. Salt that does not stick to the pretzel is reclaimed and recycled back into the storage hopper via a vacuum system.

12.G.1.g. Baking

After salting, the dough piece now passes through the oven where the primary baking occurs. Most pretzel ovens are configured as tunnel ovens and can be as long as 150 ft (45 m). Some of these ovens are direct-fired, which means the flame is located inside the baking chamber so the pretzels are subjected to the heat and radiation energy of the actual fire.

Many modern pretzel ovens are of the indirect-fired design, where there is no fire inside of the chamber. In these ovens, hot air is precisely circulated across the product resulting in a very even bake with no flame scorching. Such tunnel ovens may contain several baking zones, and each zone can be customized to a specific baking temperature, air velocity and exhaust. These ovens may also contain radiant burners, in addition to the forced air, to give the operator more baking flexibility. Radiant heat also imparts flavor characteristics to the product. In fact, some bakers still use all-brick ovens as a means of keeping these characteristics.

All of these settings, in total, allow the operator to customize the oven to achieve specific product characteristics. Oven temperatures generally range between 205 and 315°C (400 and 600°F). Baking times are from 1.5 to 5.0 minutes.

12.G.1.h. Drying (kilning)

As pretzels exit the oven, their moisture content is between 8.0 and 15%, but this level must be reduced still further to avoid checking, or spontaneous cracking, hence the use of a separate dryer, or kiln (**Figure 12.112**). The dryer is an independent, low-temperature oven (93 to 149°C, or 220 to 300°F) whose purpose is solely to cut pretzel moisture to 2 and 5%, depending on the pretzel thickness. This very low moisture gives pretzels a shelf life of up to 6 months. The pretzel resides in the dryer between 5 and 50 minutes for most types.

As opposed to the single layer of pretzels that go through the oven, the dryer may have several inches of pretzel bed passing through it. It is this process that allows the residual moisture to escape through the hard caustic pretzel shell before transferring to final packaging. No cooking or coloring functions occur during the drying phase.

Pretzel kilns can be installed as stand-alone driers, but they are more often configured as a second oven tier, this one located below the main oven and traveling in the reverse direction.

12.G.1.i. Related product systems

Soft pretzels. Similar to hard pretzels but with a softer texture, soft pretzels are prepared by mixing dough, extruding or hand tying it and putting the formed dough pieces through proofing. Soft pretzels are often cooked, but a solution of sodium bicarbonate, rather than sodium hydroxide, is used to give the pretzel a milder flavor, more similar to bread. Course white salt, called pretzel "I" salt, is applied to give the

Figure 12.111. Raw pretzel dough pieces pass through the cooker (foreground) before entering the oven's top level to bake and sliding to the bottom level's kiln to dry.
(Lanly)

Figure 12.112. After baking, pretzels slide down to the kiln below the oven to dry further.
(Reading Bakery Systems)

pretzel a saltier flavor. The largest difference between hard and soft pretzels lies in final moisture content. For soft pretzels, it can range from 15 to 25% compared with the 2 to 5.0% of the hard pretzel. This attribute give the soft pretzel its bread-like texture. Fresh shelf life is limited to only a few days but can be lengthened by frozen distribution in a par-baked format.

Typically produced in 3.5-oz sizes for general consumption, soft pretzels are also made in a smaller 2.0 oz size for school lunch programs as a bread alternative. Large 6.0-oz soft pretzels are favorites at food service operations located in sports stadiums and airport terminals, as well as through street vendors.

Groff (1996) detailed the history of this product along with its manufacturing process.

Filled pretzels. These pretzels exhibit the outer shell of a standard hard pretzel but contain a soft interior filling, usually peanut butter, process cheese or chocolate, among others. The pretzel dough runs through a low-pressure co-extruder equipped with a special compression head and die. The dough forms a continuous tube as it exits the die onto the proofer belt. Simultaneously, the extruder pumps a filling through an inner nozzle thereby continuously filling the inside of the tube. The filled rope is then cut on the proofer belt to the desired length and follows the same process as the hard pretzel. The diameters of the ropes can be as small as 2 to 3 mm (filled stick) or as large as 20 mm (filled nugget).

12.G.2. Breadstick systems
Updated by L.A. Gorton

Breadsticks are made from yeast-raised doughs and formed using stringline, sheeting-and-lamination or extrusion methods. Stringline systems output long, thin dough strips, which can be cut to the desired length before proofing and baking. To make a cheese-straw style stick, sheeting and lamination methods are employed to create a layered dough. A guillotine cutter cuts the sticks before proofing and baking.

Because of its productivity, low-pressure extrusion is a common technique for making breadsticks. The dough put through a low-pressure extruder of the same design as pretzel extruders and emerges as long strings, with diameters set by the extruder die. The extruder can also be configured with nozzles that turn to create twists in the dough strings (**Figure 12.113**). While twisted shapes offer the hand-crafted look, embossed styles show an artisan appearance, slightly flattened with rough edges, and there are also plain, flat and ridged choices. The long strings of dough travel along a conveyor for proofing and cutting. Applicators add salt, seeds or other toppings as required. Bread sticks bake in a tunnel oven.

Gorton (2001a) and Berne (2007, 2009) described bakery operations producing breadsticks.

12.G.3. Baked snack systems
Updated by L.A. Gorton

Until the 1990s, pretzels and snack crackers comprised the bulk of baked snacks on the market, but interest in producing "baked not fried" styles of snack foods prompted development of technology to make such items. Two chief methods were introduced: (a) half product (also called "pellet") and (b) sheeting.

12.G.3.a. Half-product methods

Half product gets its name from the fact that it has been partially processed and needs only to be finished by the customer who fries or air-pops the pellet to produce a light, crispy food. The snack's base is more likely to be potato starch or rice flour, although wheat flour is also used. This product style gets its leavening from steam when the customer prepares the final product. Plants that make half product and pellets were described by Gorton (1987, 1999b).

The half-product approach uses techniques and equipment more commonly found in pasta plants. Doughs made of flour, water and oil are mixed and cooked. The raw dough emerges as moist, hot lumps and transfers immediately to a former/extruder. Additional heat, pressure and shear transform the raw dough into a fully hydrated, gelatinized mass. Depending on die selection, the extruder will output strips, twirls, shells or nearly any other shape, as desired. The dough can also be sheeted, stamped and die-cut.

Figure 12.113. A patented process to make breadsticks twists up to 5 strands of dough as they exit the extruder. (*Baking & Snack*)

Shaped or cut, the pellets are still very high in moisture and not yet ready for oven or fryer processing. First, they must be dried, and some producers put them through as many as three separate drying systems, staged one after the other, to reduce the moisture content of the pellets. The first stage, a lapped dryer, accepts pellets onto its belts and carries them into the dryer. Dwell time for most products is 5 to 10 minutes, although the process can be extended to 20 to 30 minutes, if required. The second drying stage uses a shaker bed. As pellets travel through this section, constant gentle agitation keeps them from sticking together. Dwell time averages 20 to 30 minutes. Last, the pieces pass into the final dryer, a stacked system of multiple belts. Pellets take an average of 3 hours to pass through this dryer, which can handle drying times as short as 2 hours or as long as 6. The system is capable of producing up to 1,000 lb of pellets per hour, depending on the water content of the dough.

Pellets emerge from the final dryer onto a vibratory conveyor, which separates and removes any clumps as well as small broken pieces. The pellets drop into bulk containers to be moved to the finishing lines or to other processing locations.

Some pellets are sold to food service operators who prepare it in their kitchen fryers as signature snacks or bar food, but most half product goes to industrial food manufacturers, primarily other snack food processors. At the customer's plant, the pellets are put through fryers such as those used for potato chips, corn chips or tortilla chips, or they are baked in flow-through systems such as the air-poppers used for popcorn.

12.G.3.b. Sheeting

Many of the "baked not fried" snacks found on supermarket shelves are made through sheeting methods, and the technology is the same as sheeting and laminating systems for pastries, described earlier in this chapter. Like half product, the doughs for sheeted snacks are made primarily from potato starch, with rice, wheat and other grains also used.

Sheeting (**Figure 12.114**) is essential to the process because such doughs tend to be fairly fragile and will not tolerate development in the mixer. Instead,

Figure 12.114. The potato-based "dough" for baked potato crisps is sheeted and cut. (*Baking & Snack*)

the repeated reduction stages, often using glycol-chilled rolls, provide sufficient development, as explained in Chapter 6, Part E. The sheeting process also allows laminating one dough on top of another, to create a "potato skin" effect. Rotary cutters turn the continuous dough sheet into individual snack pieces. A short conveyor-rest period is sometimes required. Baking or frying follows.

12.H. Griddled Products Technology
By Michael T. Bakhoum, MS

Baked foods prepared on a griddle present interesting challenges to baker and bakery engineer alike. Pancakes, French toast, English muffins, scones, waffles and wafers cook by conduction of heat through a heavy plate or griddle, yet the results differ markedly in appearance, flavor and texture. Moving products onto and off of that heavy griddle require some ingenuity, as do handling of the slack, sticky doughs.

Bakers have the food service industry, McDonald's Corp., specifically, to thank for the growing prominence of English muffins and, now, pancakes. Seeking to expand its morning business, McDonald's introduced the Egg McMuffin sandwich in 1972 and the McGriddle sandwich in 2003. A flurry of muffin and pancake line installations quickly followed.

Formulation specifics for these products can be found in Chapter 8, Part F.

12.H.1. Frozen pancake systems

In spite of the popularity of the pancake, little technical information has been published on this topic, especially in relation to mass production and high-speed systems. This section outlines a typical automated high-speed process and establishes guidelines for special operating considerations.

In general, an automated pancake line (**Figure 12.115**) consists of an ingredient handling mechanism, batter mixers, batter holding tanks, depositors, griddles with dedicated cooling and retracting conveyors, freezers, stackers, wrappers and case packers. The depositor drops portions of batter across the width of the griddle. Product is griddled for approximately 65 seconds, flipped and griddled for an additional 55 seconds before discharging from the bottom of the griddle onto a cooling conveyor. Pancakes are cooled at around 15°C (60°F) with the aid of cooling fans and conveyed to the freezers. After freezing, pancakes are automatically stacked and wrapped in sleeves, which are automatically cased. Finished cases are palletized before storage in the finished product freezer. Cases are stored at -18°C (0°F) until shipped to distribution centers or direct to customers.

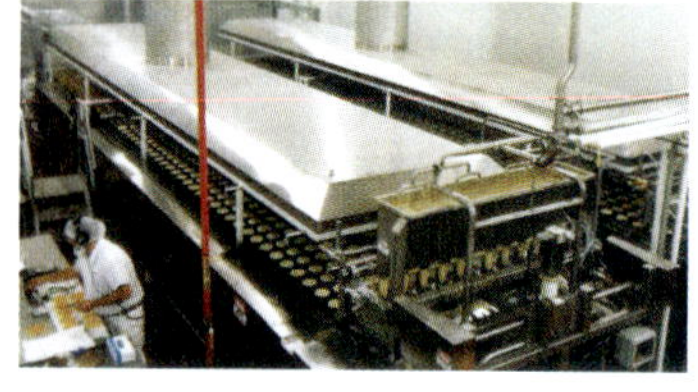

Figure 12.115. A fully automated pancake line consists of a batter system linked to the griddle. (TSA Griddle Systems)

12.H.1.a. Mixing
Batter viscosity influences the spread of the pancake on the griddle and determines the final size, thickness, texture and shape of the product.

Dry mixing. The pancake batter can be produced with either batch or continuous mixing techniques. In batch mixing, all ingredients except flour are added to the water, and when all ingredients are mixed uniformly, the wheat flour is added for further mixing. The finished batter should be smooth and free of lumps.

If a continuous mixer is used, the major ingredients are received in bulk, stored, pneumatically conveyed to a weigh hopper and discharged into a ribbon blender. The remaining dry minor ingredients are received, stored in sacks, hand or automatically weighed and added to the other ingredients in the ribbon blender. All the dry ingredients are blended to a homogeneous dry mix. The oil and minor liquid ingredients are blended in a small tank and sprayed into the dry mix ribbon blender for even distribution. The mixing is completed to achieve a specified mix temperature.

Batter mixing. The batter mixing system (**Figure 12.116**) consists of water, egg and dry mix as well as batter mixers, holding tanks and associated pumps, piping and controls. The water system uses heat exchanger and refrigeration systems to control the water temperature and produce the desired final batter temperature. Mixing is completed to achieve specified batter viscosity and temperature.

The system then transfers the mixed batter to holding tanks, mounted on load cells and refilled automatically from the batter mixers. On demand from the batter depositors, batter is pumped to the depositors as required. Programmable logic controllers (PLCs) or industrial computers sequence the operations of these systems and are tied into the controls on the griddle line, too.

Figure 12.116. A batter blending system brings together pancake ingredients, mixes them and holds the resulting batter for delivery to the griddle. (TSA Griddle Systems)

12.H.1.b. Depositing and griddling

The most common types of depositors for batter are gravity displacement units and air-pressurized tank systems. Using a gravity depositor, control over deposit weight is a function of the nozzle size, height of batter in the hopper and deposit time. The weight of deposits made by a pressurized tank depositor is controlled mainly by the amount of pressure in the tank. Servo-controlled batter depositors are accurate to ± 0.3 g (**Figure 12.117**).

The griddle consists of many plates and a stainless steel hood to exhaust hot air, moisture and combustion gases (**Figure 12.118**). The griddle plates can be made from steel or iron. It is well established that iron absorbs and loses heat slower than steel; therefore, it is more stable in heat retention than steel.

The length and width of the griddle vary, depending on the manufacturer and the desired production rate and capacity. Plates are attached to conveyor roller chains and driven by a variable-speed motor. Heat is provided by numerous completely independent burners. Sensors monitor the temperature of the griddle plates and provide feedback to the automatic temperature control system. Product is turned over halfway through the process by a set of flippers. The types of flippers and the mechanism by which they work vary between manufacturers. Logos or brand symbols can be cooked into the top of the griddle cake's crust (**Figure 12.119**).

Figure 12.117. Pancake batters are deposited onto heated flights of the automatic griddle. (TSA Griddle Systems)

The flippers' position can be moved upstream or downstream to provide some variation in the bake time ratio between first side and second side of the pancake. Usually, the second side bake is less than the first side bake, mainly because the second side surface dries out and gets warmer while the first side is being baked (**Figure 12.120**). Pancakes are removed from the griddle by a set of takeoff knives. Griddle plates turn down and travel below the active griddle section to return to the front of the unit for reloading. A high-temperature brush system located under the griddle cleans the plates during their return.

Figure 12.118. This automated pancake line can make many sizes, ranging from minis to 6-in. diameter pancakes. (TSA Griddle Systems)

Figure 12.119. Pancake systems are capable of cooking symbols onto the cake's crust, including this wafer/waffle style oven designed to bake pancakes for a major food service organization. (Tromp USA, Vanderpol)

Figure 12.120. Pancakes flip to cook on their second side. (TSA Griddle Systems)

Figure 12.121. Released from the griddle by a take-off knife, pancakes slide in rows onto a cooling conveyor. (TSA Griddle Systems)

Ventilation of the griddle room is critical. Currently, most griddles in use are not confined to a chamber or enclosed cover; therefore, the hot surfaces are exposed to the surrounding atmosphere and loose heat easily. Hot, humid conditions allow the product to bake out excessively before flipping, causing white spots and an exceptionally wide white ring around the edge of the second side. Special attention should be considered to eliminate any air drafts or major fluctuation in room temperature because these factors can alter the baking profile of the product and result in substandard finished product and color variations across the width of the griddle (Forrest 2009).

French toast systems use cooker griddle plates almost 1 in. thick. An automated sanitary applicator and slice loader, with a chilled liquid batter holding reservoir, supplies the pieces to the griddle.

12.H.1.e. Cooling and packaging

Removal knives aid release of pancakes from the griddle plates, and the finished pancakes drop in rows onto a cooling conveyor (**Figure 12.121**), which passes from the griddle room into another room held at around 16°C (60°F). Several fans above and below the conveyor circulate air to help cool the products. From the cooling room, the pancakes move along to the spiral blast freezer.

Recommended freezer temperature range around -37°C (-35°F) to freeze the product to the glassy temperature of -18°C (0°F). However, the critical control point is to store the product below its freezing point, which is usually higher than 18°C (0°F) and depends on formulation.

Pancakes leave the freezer in rows, and each row is directed to a stacking head. The stacking head creates a certain number of pancakes in each stack. The stacks enter a wrapper, where a certain numbers of stacks are wrapped together into a sleeve. Sleeves are conveyed through a metal detector and are automatically case packed. Cases are checkweighed, taped closed, coded and conveyed to the palletizer, then from the palletizer to the storage freezer. The flowchart in **Table 12.3** summarizes the pancake process.

12.H.2. English muffin systems

English muffins can be made using a sponge dough, straight dough or pre-ferment process. An automated English muffin line produces between 500 and 2,000 doz units per hour. These highly automated systems have special requirements for formulation and processing, and they require strict control of processing conditions. These conditions are necessary to produce high-absorption dough, which will handle well in highly automated equipment yet be fluid enough to flow in the griddle cup and develop the leavening steam at the proper time in the griddle.

Short-time straight-dough processes have been developed to meet these requirements, and the majority of the high speed systems now utilize this process (Dubois 1979).

12.H.2.a. Mixing

English muffin dough can be mixed with different types of mixers, but the most commonly used equipment for such production is the horizontal bread dough mixer. Mixer size and capacity are determined by production rate of the other equipment; the size should be limited to an amount of dough that can be processed within a

20-minute period.

Excessive processing time produces sticky and "gassy" dough, which is difficult to divide uniformly and which will adhere to the rounder bars, causing production delays. English muffin dough is over-mixed, compared with bread dough, in order to improve its flowability in the griddle cup and the porosity of the finished muffin. The extremely long mixing time required for the high-absorption dough (17 to 22 minutes) can be shortened considerably by withholding a portion of the water and all of the salt until the dough is partially mixed.

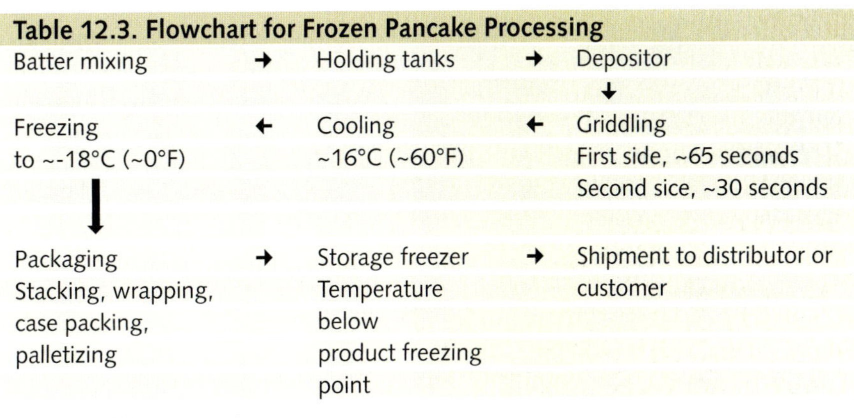

Table 12.3. Flowchart for Frozen Pancake Processing

Batter mixing	→	Holding tanks	→	Depositor
Freezing to ~-18°C (~0°F)	←	Cooling ~16°C (~60°F)	←	Griddling First side, ~65 seconds Second sice, ~30 seconds
Packaging Stacking, wrapping, case packing, palletizing	→	Storage freezer Temperature below product freezing point	→	Shipment to distributor or customer

(TSA Griddle Systems)

Mix time. In general, there are two schools of thought with respect to the mixing time of English muffin dough. The first proposes that dough should be greatly under-mixed. Under-mixing should promote a coarse crumb structure. The second proposes that dough should be greatly over-mixed. The theory here is that the over-mixed dough would have excellent flowability and produce porosity from the breakdown of the gluten network. In practice, the second theory of over-mixing is more prevalent (Pfefer 1976).

Mix order. A recommended procedure is to add all of the ingredients except the salt and 10% of the water, and mix the dough until it has cleaned from the back of the mixer (cleanup). Next, add the remaining water and mix an additional 2 minutes, then add the salt and complete the mixing cycle. This procedure shortens the total mixing time by several minutes and produces more completely hydrated dough. As mentioned previously, the dough temperature at this point should not exceed 20°C (68°F) (Dubois 1979).

One thing that must be taken into consideration when muffin doughs are mixed is the manner in which the doughs are kept cool. Mixers having direct-expansion jackets are, perhaps, most suitable. Mixers having jackets chilled with circulating cold water or brine are equally suitable if the heat absorbing capacity of the jacket can keep pace with the heat generated by the over-mixing.

12.H.2.b. Dividing and rounding

Dividing of the dough pieces can be accomplished with standard roll dividers. However, a divider in good operating condition is a must for cutting and dropping this high-absorption dough. Normal scaling weight is 2.25 to 2.5 oz (65 to 70 g) per dough piece. The rounding of the dough piece is equally as critical as the mixing procedure, and the degree of rounding affects the quality of the muffin. Too much rounding or making a compact dough piece will produce a product having good volume but little or no porosity. A light rounding pressure will produce a muffin having excellent porosity but lacking in volume and having poor symmetry. Therefore, the rounding bar should be adjusted to produce a round, firm dough piece but not so tight that the dough will stick to the bar and cause production delays. At this point, the first dusting is applied to the entire dough piece as it rolls down a zig-zag chute (**Figure 12.122**) to the conveyor that transports the piece to the proofer.

Figure 12.122. Zig-zag lanes assure complete coverage of sticky English muffin doughs with flour. (*Baking & Snack*)

Dusting at proofer entry should completely cover the piece but not be excessive. Insufficient dusting will cause sticking problems in the proofer, while excessive dusting will result in some of the dusting materials dropping into the griddle, causing problems at that point. The amount of dusting is controlled by the feed from the dispenser and by the slope of the zig-zag conveyor.

12.H.2.c. Proofing

Most automatic proofing systems for English muffin are standardized to give 28 to 31 minutes of proofing time. The individual dough pieces are dropped into cups that are usually canvas covered. A small amount of dusting flour is dusted into the cups prior to depositing. The proof box is maintained at a temperature of 46 to 52°C (115 to 125°F) and a 50 to 55% relative humidity — a fairly dry proof box. Juers (1982) recommended a tighter temperature range for the proofer: 43 to 46°C (110 to 115°F).

Too much humidity in the proofer will keep the outer surface of the dough too wet to deposit easily or uniformly into the griddle. Too little humidity in the proofer will result in the dough crusting, which will decrease the flow and result in small, non-uniform muffins with a poor outer appearance. The lower the dough temperature and the higher the proofing temperature, the greater the amount of humidity produced by the dough itself. Thompson (1981) recommended using large differential between the wet bulb and the dry bulb, rather than spraying water in the air within the proofer.

At the end of the proof time, the dough piece should feel slightly dry to the touch but without a dry skin. The piece should be fairly flat and of sufficient diameter to nearly fill the griddle cup when deposited. If the dough piece is too small or crusted, it will not expand properly, and the muffin will be small and lack symmetry. If the dough piece is too large, it will have excessive rise in the cup and have good symmetry but poor porosity.

12.H.2.d. Depositing and griddles

After proofing, the dough pieces are deposited in griddle cups on a moving conveyor heated from the bottom by gas burners. The dough pieces are deposited in the griddle cups by means of a 360° turning mechanism. This turning mechanism keeps the top of the proofed dough piece on the top as it is placed in the griddle.

To achieve the proper dough weight and shape, the depositor may be coated with release agent to reduce stickups. Also, controlling the speed of the depositor by installing a variable-speed motor greatly improves both the weight control and shape of the dough. At most times, the depositor has to be operated at a speed low enough to lay the dough evenly into the griddle cup. Juers (1982) recommended installing of a piece of fiber glass cloth on the slide to decrease dough stickups and better guide the dough pieces uniformly in to the griddle cup. Make sure the back slide is clean and smooth to avoid muffins catching, or hanging up, during the transfer to the bottom flight plates from the cups.

Although the size of the cups may vary, the most common dimensions are 3.875 in. (9.8 cm) across and 1 in. (2.5 cm) deep. At this point, the cups are open at the top, and the griddle plates have not reached full baking temperature. After approximately 2.5 minutes travel time, during which the dough pieces flow to fill the cup, the griddle cups are topped with metal covers.

The final symmetry of the muffin is largely determined at this point by the height and condition of the cup lid or top flight plate. Satisfactory muffins are usually produced with about 0.25-in. (6-mm) space between the top of the cup and this top flight plate.

After a 4-minute bake, the muffins are automatically emptied from the griddle cups and inverted 180° (**Figure 12.123**) for a final 3.5-minute bake on flat griddle plates without rings or lids. The top flight plates must be checked regularly to be certain the height is uniform across the griddle band and that the plates have not become warped through mishandling. For example, accidentally stepping on the plates while maintaining the equipment or accidentally spraying the hot plates with water can cause serious warping problems. The result will be nonsymmetrical English muffins.

Another style of griddle is a double plate, single conveyor type. In this system, the dough piece is deposited by rotating it 180°, and depositing the piece, wet side down, in the griddle cup. Each row of cups has its own plate, which fits on the top for an initial 4-minute bake. The cups are then inverted and the top plate becomes the griddle for the final 3- to 4-minute bake.

Figure 12.123. As English muffins prepare to transfer to the lower return tier of the oven, a top conveyor covers the griddle cups and muffins to keep pieces in place until turning is completed.
(*Baking & Snack*)

The height of the griddle's top flights is critical to the production of porous muffins. When the equipment is new, it is very easy to adjust the top flights above the cups and obtain uniformity. It should be noted that when the equipment is used constantly, the metal frame of the griddle will warp under the extreme temperatures. Most adjustments for the top flights will range from five to six feet between one another.

To maintain a uniform height and decrease warping, bolts can be welded to the lower frame every 18 in. and adjusted upward to stop the flight plates from warping (Pfefer 1976).

Avoid running the griddle empty for too long because this practice will cut the life of the release coating in the cup and subsequent burn the product for at least the first five minutes of production.

Finally, the griddle cups should be constantly blown out with air during production to avoid carbon buildup and black specs on the finished product.

The baked muffins are automatically deposited on a conveyor and cooled 30 to 45 minutes (**Figure 12.124**), preferably in a filtered air atmosphere to reduce the possibility of surface mold contamination. The internal muffin temperature should be about 3 C° (5 F°) above plant ambient temperature for best slicing or splitting.

A similar system produces crumpets and has the capacity to emboss the top side of the product. An option on this system is a corn meal depositor to produce the bottom crust's crunchy texture.

12.H.2.e. Slicing or splitting

English muffins are sold whole, split or sliced. They are generally either sliced or split before packaging, the process being determined by consumer preference.

The original English muffins were usually split by inserting a fork at several points around the circumference of the muffin, then pulling the muffin apart. This procedure produced an irregular and rough surface, having about twice as much surface area as the surface of a sliced muffin. This split muffin exposes a rough surface to the toaster. The flavor of the toasted muffin is enhanced by the variation in degree of toasting

Figure 12.124. Cooling of English muffins must take the hot products to a temperature no more than 3 C° (5 F°) above plant ambient for best packaging results.
(I.J. White Corp.)

Figure 12.125. When English muffins are sliced, rather than forked, they must be lined up accurately before entering the web-slicing system.
(*Baking & Snack*)

in this rough surface, and the rough surface also allows the heat to penetrate further into the muffin, improving the chewiness of the product. The automated forking process is explained in Chapter 11, Part B.

This splitting operation is accomplished in the bakery by one of several types of splitters, producing muffins that may be pulled apart by the consumer, then toasted or broiled. Slicing of muffins (**Figure 12.125**) is accomplished by special muffin slicing equipment that produces a smooth surface similar to the surface of the hamburger bun slice.

If the muffins have to be frozen, a conveyor takes the bagged product from the packaging area to a spiral blast freezer. The muffins emerge in approximately 45 minutes later to be put in to shipping cases, stacked onto pallets and moved into the storage freezer.

12.H.2.f. Product quality and sorting

A new piece of equipment (**Figure 12.126**) was developed to measure and inspect each piece of product before it is packaged. It inspects, rejects and reports on at least 400 pieces per minute. Based on the quality criteria set up in the industrial computer, a camera takes pictures of the muffins and automatically evaluates the piece. Rejections are based on over-size, under-size, odd-shape, over-baked and under-baked. The rejection is done by blowing the rejected items off the line by air.

12.H.2.g. Packaging

English muffins are packaged in several styles, usually 6 to a package (**Figure 12.127**). These packages range from trays overwrapped with cellophane or placed in a polyethylene bag to packaging in a polyethylene bag without any support. This package is currently the most popular, primarily because of lower packaging costs.

An English muffin equipment company developed two types of automatic packers, the penny packer (**Figure 12.128**) and the flat packer (**Figure 12.129**). The penny packer can accommodate a diversity of products and is easily adjusted to various package sizes. It can be integrated with any bagger and adjust to handle 4 to 6 muffins per bag at up to 60 bags per minute. The flat packer is an alternative to penny packing. It has an interchangeable chute and magazine allowing different pack configurations at a rate of 50 bags per minute. Penny packing is explained in more detail in Chapter 11, Part C.

Figure 12.126. English muffins are inspected by an automatic vision system that examines size, shape and crust surface for bake quality.
(Dipix Technologies)

If the muffins have to be frozen, a conveyor takes the bagged product from the packaging area to a spiral blast freezer. The muffins emerge in approximately 45 minutes to be put in to shipping cases, stacked onto pallets, and moved into the storage freezer. **Table 12.4.** summarizes the typical processing procedure for English muffins.

12.H.3. Waffle and wafer equipment

This section will discuss and focus on the two major types of the griddle ovens that produce waffles and wafers products. In the case of wafers, the discussion will also cover equipment that produces related products such as ice cream cones and rolled wafer sticks.

In general, a fully automated waffle/wafer production line consists of an ingredient mixing system, griddle oven and packaging equipment. Because wafers are processed into different shapes with different fillings and coating products, more processing equipment is needed, including ambient coolers, spreading and book-building machine, cooling tunnels, buffer storage and cutting machines. Packaging operations include automated feed into a wrapping machine and a carton erector and loader. All these pieces of equipment must work together to produce the desired finished product (Berne 2001).

12.H.3.a. Mixing

The standard waffle/wafer batter mixing system includes a high-speed, low-shear mixer, use bins located above the mixer, liquid tanks, a batter screen and a holding tank (**Figure 12.130**). In modern waffle/wafer production plants, computer-controlled ingredient handling systems sequence the addition of ingredients into the mixer. An automated system may consist of 5 dry ingredients bins and 4 liquid ingredients tanks, with micro ingredients and other materials added manually.

The basic mixing philosophy in waffle/wafer production is to blend in small batches. Doing so not only reduces the effects of time on the batter but also reduces the risk of batter variability. Automated wafer batter systems can produce batches up to 550 lb (250 kg) per batch, or 4,400 lb (2,000 kg) per hour. High-volume systems usually program mixing operations to prepare new batches every 6 to 10 minutes (Cornell 1999).

Dry ingredients are generally blended first, with water added gradually. Ingredients such as dried eggs and milk powders are included with the first additions of water so they can partially rehydrate before the remaining dry ingredients are added. Shortening should be added during batter blending.

The batter must be lump-free to pass through the dispensing system; thus, after mixing, it is passed through oscillating screens to eliminate any solid material. From the mixer, the batter transfers to a holding tank, where it can be stored for up to 30 minutes (Cornell 1999).

12.H.3.b. Waffle griddle-ovens

An automatic waffle machine is used for both the crispy and soft waffle (Belgian waffle) as well as other special products.

Depending on desired capacity and griddle time, waffle griddle-ovens are available with a varying number of baking plate sets. The most common baking plates are 228 by 340 mm (9 by 13.4 in.) or 280 by 340 mm (11 by 13.4 in.) and made of special iron or gray metal alloys. Each plate has 6 to 8 waffle moulds. The waffle usually is 10 to 20 mm (0.4 to 0.8 in.) thick, but other dimensions are possible. A special mounting system allows quick removal of the baking plates for cleaning.

The griddle-ovens consist of a robust steel frame with two screw-mounted running rails and an endless link chain that carries the baking plates. A ball bearing serves as running wheel. The system of plate closures and wheels is designed to

Figure 12.127. The penny packer can place 4 to 6 English muffins, or more, into bags. It also penny-packs bagels. (Formost Fuji)

Figure 12.128. Lanes set up English muffins on-edge so they can be penny-stacked for packaging. (Formost Fuji)

Figure 12.129. For flat stacking, like that of hamburger buns, lanes keep English muffins moving on their flat sides. (Formost Fuji)

Table 12.4. English Muffin Process

- Place all ingredients, except salt and 10% of water, in mixer
    (total absorption 85%; 75% first addition).
- Mix 30 seconds low speed, then on high speed until dough cleans from back of mixer.
- Add remaining water (10%).
- Mix 15 seconds low speed, 2 minutes high speed.
- Add salt.
- Mix 15 seconds low speed, then on high speed until properly developed.
- Dough temperature, 20°C (68°F).
- Rest dough for 10 to 15 minutes.
- Scale 2.25 to 2.5 oz per dough piece, round, dust and convey to proofer.
- Proof 28 to 31 minutes at 46 to 52°C (115 to 125°F) and 50 to 55% relative humidity.
- Deposit dough piece in griddle, bake 2.5 minutes in preheat zone, 4 minutes in cup with lid,
    invert dough piece and bake 3 minutes without cup or lid.
- Cool 30 to 45 minutes.
- Slice or split and package.

Figure 12.130. Load cells monitor pre-mix, mixing and holding tanks for liquid and solid ingredients. PLC allows direct input and storage of formulations. (Franz Haas Waffelmaschinen)

Figure 12.131. Waffle ovens have designs that accommodate 48 to 110 baking plate pairs, with 4 to 16 moulds per plate. Rotating vacuum drums or needle systems remove the baked waffles from the plates. (Franz Haas Waffelmaschinen)

keep these components out of the heat zone, but a cooling system at the upper running rail is often added. The burners that heat the griddles are located above and below the line, which is enclosed in an insulated housing (**Figure 12.131**).

For Belgian-type waffles, a device turns the griddle plates 180° after batter depositing to distribute the batter quickly and uniformly within the moulds. The griddle plates also can be made of aluminum. In this case, the upper plates will lie on the batter only with their own weight, resulting in baked soft waffles with especially fluffy structure.

Waffle removal. Flat thin waffles are lifted from baking plates by vacuum. The vacuum take-off device consists of a perforated drum connected to a vacuum blower. After removal from the griddle, the product is held to the drum by vacuum. A steel wire mesh belt runs on the drum, which transports the waffles upwards and transfer them to a conveyor.

Thick Belgian-style waffles are taken off the griddle plates by needles. The needle take-off device consists of rotating drum on which needles are mounted. Moving synchronously with the griddle plates, the needles lift the products from the baking moulds and transfer them to the conveyor on the top of the drum. During this process the needles are withdrawn and remain in stand-by till the next take-off.

Waffle finishing. After the waffle is baked, there is the possibility for a waffle make-up machine. Depending on the desired effect, the machine is built with cutting, capping, stacking, decorating and depositing.

12.H.3.c. Wafer griddle-oven

Wafer sheets for production of stacked-and-filled wafer fingers use similar equipment (**Figure 12.132**). Batter is pumped to the oven and deposited between a pair of heated metal plates engraved with fine, medium or deep reeding patterns (**Figure 12.133**). Plate sizes, commonly 290 by 470 mm (11.4 by 18.5 in.), are trending to larger dimensions — up to 350 by 700 mm (13.8 by 27.5 in.) and even 355 by 730 mm (14 by 28.7 in.), providing 80 to 90% more wafer baking capacity than the smaller plates and less waste during cutting.

Like waffle plates, wafer plates are made of special iron or gray metal alloys, selected to provide a homogeneous, dense, bubble-free surface as well as high heat-storage and good stability. Chrome plating protects the engravings and helps release the baked wafers. The edges of the baking plates can be engraved with numbers or codes to allow identification of a baked wafer sheet and its corresponding plate to save time when fine-tuning performance. The number does not affect the end product because it is removed during edge clipping or cutting. Computer-aided design and manufacturing methods are used to engrave plate surfaces for moulded ice cream cone designs (Gorton 1996).

The baking plates, also called a book, are carried by tongs attached to a chain-and-roller mechanism that conveys the whole assembly through the oven.

An intermittent pump deposits the thin aerated batter onto the bottom plate of the open book. The system's controls electronically set the action and position of the batter depositor. One depositor design offers a suck-back feature to eliminate batter dripping. As the chain moves forward, the plates close and lock. Pressure on the plates, generated through the lock and separate pressure bars, maintains the thickness of the finished wafer sheet over its entire surface with a tolerance of ± 0.1 mm (0.004 in.). Locking mechanisms differ among equipment manufacturers (Gorton 1996).

During the 2-minute baking process, steam is generated and acts as the main leavening agent. The steam expands the batter to fill the engraved plates, and the release rate of the steam is controlled by vent strips along the edges of the plate assembly.

Baking plates follow a single-loop path through the oven, traveling long edge forward to maximize oven-loading efficiency. The output volume of a wafer line is determined by oven capacity. The maximum speed of a wafer oven is 55 sheets per minute. System output ranges from 220 to 2,600 lb (100 to 1,200 kg) per hour. Output depends on the number of baking plates that circulate through the oven, and current capacity is between 12 and 120 books. New systems are modularly designed to increase in capacity as needed (Berne 2001).

Wafer griddle ovens (**Figure 12.134**) have two temperature zones: one for the baking plates and a much cooler zone for the chain, wheels and other drive mechanisms to increase their life span. Computer controls automatically regulate the baking temperature in both zones. Ovens are either heated with gas or electricity. One gas oven model has triangular universal burners, arranged in twin rows. Fueled by either natural gas or propane/butane, the burners can swivel to provide even distribution across the entire baking plate surface. With electrical systems, heat is directly transmitted to the baking plates.

When the book reaches the far end of the oven, the chain turns down, moving back to the front of the oven. Just before the plate returns to the home position, the locking mechanism releases, and the plates open as the chain-and-wheel assembly rides up the release rail. The wafer sheet contracts slightly, and air jets located beside and above the bottom of the baking plates gently blow the sheet onto a star wheel, which carries the sheet out of the oven. A vacuum pickup system has been developed to release large-format wafer sheets (**Figure 12.135**). The empty book continues forward, and the

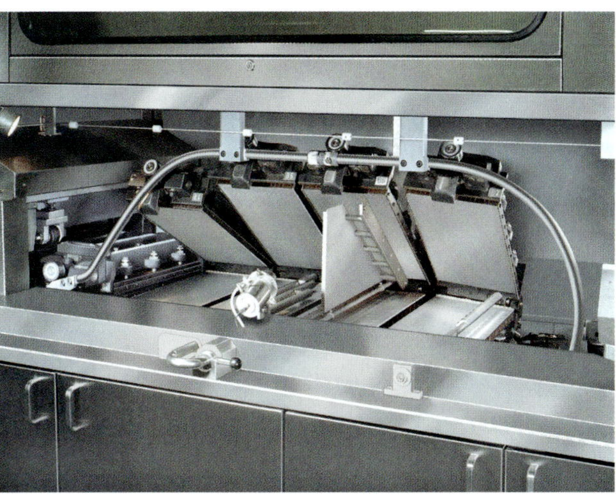

Figure 12.132. Wafer plate sets open to accept portioned doses of batter. (Hebenstreit)

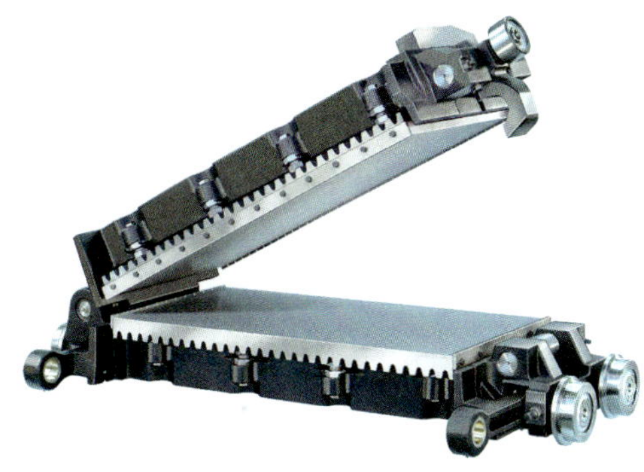

Figure 12.133. A set of wafer plates rides in a lockable tong-style frame. (Hebenstreit)

Figure 12.134. Operating with 32 to 120 pair of self-supporting baking plates, this wafer oven separates the zones through which plates and their support members travel, thus reducing thermal stress on the transport system. (Franz Haas Waffelmaschinen)

Figure 12.135. Large-format wafer sheets are taken off baking plates by a vacuum pickup system on a rotating drum. (Franz Haas Waffelmaschinen)

Figure 12.136. An arch-style ambient cooler is synchronized to the oven, accepting baked wafer sheets. (Franz Haas Waffelmaschinen)

depositor arm releases another dose of batter onto the now-empty, but still warm, bottom plate.

If a wafer sheet hangs up in the baking plate, creating a double deposit, the control program alerts the system to skip that book in the next cycle, cutting off batter flow until the set passes out of range. This book will not be refilled until the previous wafer sheet is removed. To prevent damage to the costly plates, the book remains open while traveling through the oven.

Optical, infrared, photoelectric or video inspection systems placed after oven take-off can verify sheet integrity. Incomplete and discolored sheets are automatically rejected (Berne 2001).

12.H.3.d. Wafer cooling and conditioning

After baking, the wafer sheets feed into an arch-shaped ambient cooler, consisting of closely spaced U-shaped wire brackets anchored to traveling chains (**Figure 12.136**). The brackets are positioned opposite of each other and synchronized with oven output. An infrared sensing system notes when a sheet has been placed in a bracket and signals the chain to advance to accept another sheet. The brackets travel up and over the arch, releasing the wafer sheet onto the conveyor leading into the spreading and filling systems.

The arch design evolved because wafer processing lines can be very long. The high arch permits personnel to walk through. Some are even high and wide enough to allow fork-lift trucks to pass underneath (Gorton 1996).

Wafers to be coated in chocolate or other material pass through conditioning towers or tunnels, which bring the wafers to the desired moisture levels. Spiral conveyors are often used for conditioning wafer sheets and sandwiched wafer-and-creme stacks. The spiral can be configured for ambient cooling or housed in a temperature- and humidity-controlled enclosure. Conditioning the sheets before coating keeps the wafers from expanding from additional moisture absorption and prevents the coating from flaking or cracking.

Depending on the type and thickness of the wafer, relative humidity in the conditioning system is set between 65 and 80%, with a temperature of 40 to 60°C (104 to 140°F). The higher the temperature, the shorter the conditioning time. Time in the conditioner usually varies from 15 to 20 minutes (Berne 2001).

12.H.3.e. Wafer filling and finishing

If the wafers are to be creme-filled, the cooled and conditioned sheets are automatically fed to a spreading machine. Every other wafer sheet is diverted onto an overhead conveyor to avoid coating. These sheets are held until collected by the stacking system to build a stack, also called a "book" or a "block."

The bottom sheets are buffered together and conveyed under the spreader head. The most common spreading system is the film method, in which a continuous ribbon of creme is spread onto the wafer sheets. Because the process is continuous, little if no tailing occurs. When the coated sheets are separated, however, some tailing may happen, dropping the excess creme onto the conveyor belts. Modern lines have smooth belts that are scraped continuously (Berne 2001).

After spreading, the sheets are accelerated to create a gap between each sheet in preparation for book building. One stacking system uses a pair of spiral supports to perform this process. The top sheet of the book is fed into the stacker between tiers of the spirals, which rotate to carry the sheet upward. Next, a creme-covered sheet is fed into the spirals, which rotate again and elevate the sheet so that it comes in contact with the top sheet, forming a sandwich. A second creamed sheet is fed into the spirals and again elevated until it comes in contact with the bottom layer of the sandwich, forming a 3-wafer, 2-creme-layer book. The process is repeated until the desired number of levels is achieved (Berne 2001).

Before cutting, a calibrating roller ensures that the wafer stacks are of uniform thickness and that each block has been properly filled. The thickness of a wafer book depends on the number of wafer sheets, the amount of creme spread between the sheets and the degree of thickness calibration. The simplest calibration device is a roller, and the best device is a pressure plate that is either servo or pneumatically actuated.

Figure 12.137. Books of filled wafers are cut automatically in two directions. Exiting to the left, the individual wafers are separated and sent along to packaging operations. (Hebenstreit)

The wafer books cool in a tower, tunnel or spiral system that sets the creme filling. They are then transported to a book cutting machine (**Figure 12.137**). The books are stacked and pushed through fixed wire frames to be cut in parallel and transverse directions, guided by plates at the side of the machine, thus forming stacked wafer fingers. Intermittent and continuously operating cutters are available. Cut wafers are transported to downstream operations such as enrobing, wrapping and cartooning (Berne 2001).

Hollow wafer sheets and large wafer books are assembled using vacuum and servo technology, which is extremely gentle on the sheets and provides precise thickness control. Hollow wafers also use the film method for filling operations. A knife takes the creme film off a spreading roll and deposits on the inverted wafer sheet, while a second scraper removes the excess filling. Two creme-filled sheets are combined into one sandwich and pressed together before the individual pieces are separated by a punching press. Equipment manufacturers also offer devices that automatically deposit nutmeats into hollow wafers.

12.H.3.f. Related equipment

Wafer technology lends itself to the creation of diverse products, involving a network of machines. The production process differs slightly for rolled wafer sticks, hollow cookie sticks and ice cream cones.

Rolled wafer sticks are baked as a continuous sheet on the broad outer edge of a wheel-shaped griddle that rotates vertically (**Figure 12.138**). A thin layer of batter is deposited on the heated griddle surface. The baked sheet is then released from the griddle by a stationary knife and twisted around a thin mandrel. When cooled, the continuous roll is cut at the end of the mandrel into pre-set lengths. Filled cookie sticks use a hollow forming mandrel through which flavored creme is pumped to fill the cookie as it leaves the end of the mandrel.

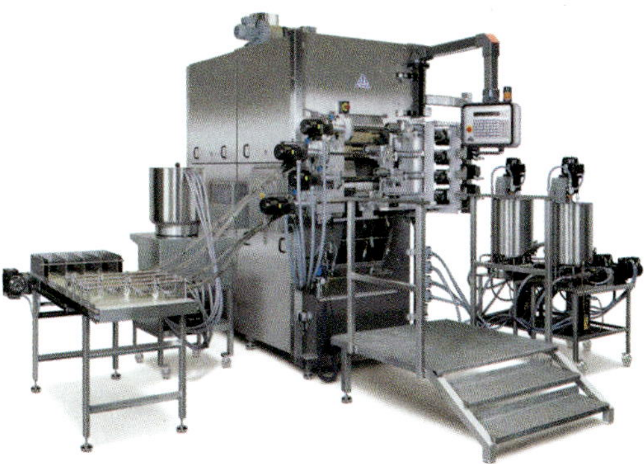

Figure 12.138. Long strips of wafer batter bake on the drum revolving inside this oven, emerging to be rolled into hollow sticks. (Franz Haas Waffelmachinen)

Molded ice cream cone production uses the same technology as wafers, except that the cone mould consists of three pieces spilt longitudinally, with a top component. Molded ice cream cone systems range in size from 12 to 72 sets of baking moulds, and each mold consist of 4 to 10 cones. (**Figure 12.139**) Cones bake for 1 to 4 minutes. From the oven, the moulds are first stripped of any waste batter that comes out of the steam slots

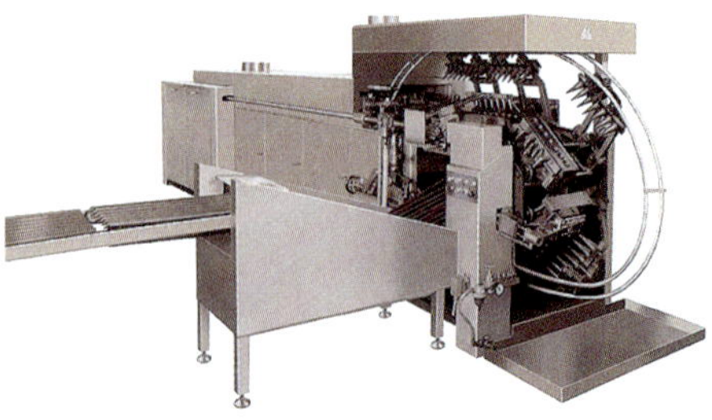

Figure 12.139. This ice cream cone system carries 12 to 36 sets of interchangeable cone baking moulds. Larger systems can handle up to 72 moulds.
(Franz Haas Waffelmaschinen)

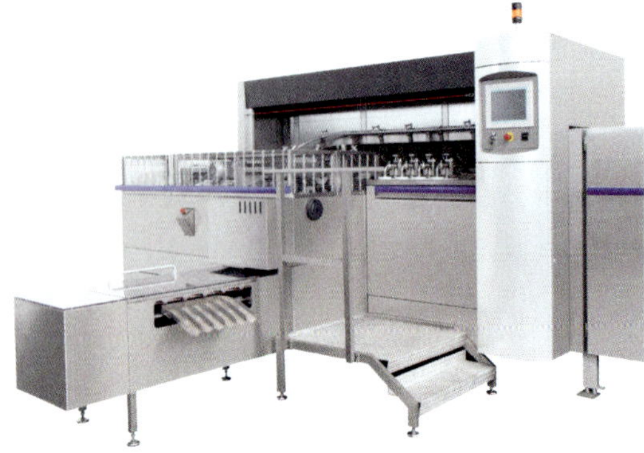

Figure 12.140. Production of ice cream cones with a sugar content up to 50% can be done automatically on this oven, baking up to 8,200 cones per hour.
(Franz Haas Waffelmaschinen)

during baking. The moulds automatically open, and the baked cones are ejected onto the collating and stacking conveyor.

The production process for rolled sugar cones requires two stages (**Figure 12.140**). First, a thin flat wafer is baked between two heated plates. Batter depositing and baking follow the same methods as wafer sheets, although the plate sets are smaller, each sized for one cone. Baking times range from 1 to 2 minutes. The thickness of the sheet is adjustable, and the maximum diameter of the cone depends on the cone's finished height. In the second stage, the cone rollers lift the hot wafer sheet directly off the upper baking plate. The wafer sheets are briefly twisted under pressure. At the same time, a calibrating device creates the rims of the cones, a process taking about 5 seconds. Finished cones leave the system in pairs to be conveyed to an automatic stacker. Rolled cone systems vary in production output from 36 to 140 sets of plates for the oven section and 1 to 2 rolling towers, each with 12 to 20 rolling tools (Gorton 1996).

Spraying systems installed after the cone oven spray cones with fat to make them impenetrable to other fillings or coatings. A chocolate lining can also be sprayed into cones.

Automatic collating, stacking and packaging tables receive the cones or cups on release from the baking moulds. The system electronically counts cones to the required number and passes the grouped cones along the packing table. Packaging line options include a foil wrapper magazine that can be mounted above the automatic stacker to put sugar cones into paper or aluminum foil containers.

References

Ash, D.J. 1979. Cake doughnuts. II. Mix preparation, scaling, mixing and frying. AIB Tech. Bull. 1 (7).

Belshaw, T.E. 1970. Developments in automated doughnut production. Bakers Digest 44 (4): 50.

Belshaw, T.E. 1976. Cutting and frying equipment. Proc. Am. Soc. Bakery Engrs. 52: 112.

Benson, R.C. 1988. Muffin technology. AIB Tech. Bull. 10 (6).

Berne, S. 2001. Pressing advantage. Baking & Snack 23 (10): 61.

Berne, S. 2002. Quest toward value. Baking & Snack 24 (10): 28.

Berne, S. 2006. Into new territory. Baking & Snack 28 (10): 28.

Berne, S. 2007. Sustainable reinvention. Baking & Snack 29 (8): 38.

Berne, S. 2009. Riding high. Baking & Snack 31 (5): 37.

Biscuit and Cracker Manufacturers' Association (BCMA). 2002. Cookie and Cracker Manufacturing, Vol. II. The association: Silver Spring, MD.

Bolanowski, J. 1966. Continuous processing in the cake bakery. Bakers Digest 40 (5): 62.

Bonavia, W. 1963. Practical aspects of continuous cake batter mixing. Bakers Digest 37 (3): 72.

Bonavia, W. 1967. Techniques, operation and engineering aspects of continuous production of cake batter. Proc. Am. Soc. Bakery Engrs. 43: 301.

Braden, B.W. 1976. Yeast-raised doughnuts. Proc. Am. Soc. Bakery Engrs. 52: 127.

Burris, J.B. 1979. Fried pies. Proc. Am. Soc. Bakery Engrs. 55: 111.

Burrough, B., and Helyar, J. 1990. Barbarians at the Gate: The Fall of RJR Nabisco. Harper & Row: New York, NY.

Cannon, A.S. 1987. Automated sweet goods production. Proc. Am. Soc. Bakery Engrs. 63: 107.

Cooper, I. 1986. Pita/pocket bread. Am. Soc. Bakery Engrs. 62: 151.

Cornell, M. June 1999. Hot off the press. Baking & Snack 21 (5): 62.

Dixon, J. 1983. Cake donut production: A controlled process. Bakers Digest 57: (5): 26.

Dubois, D.K. 1979. English muffins, production technology. AIB Tech. Bull. 1 (1).

Eberts, J. 1998. Bagels: formulation and regional differences. Proc. Am. Soc. Bakery Engrs. 74: 99.

Egan, E.J. 1977. For the cake baker: Ultimate efficiency in continuous mixers. Bakers Digest 51 (5): 129.

Engstrom, L.E. 1981. Update on automatic pie production methods. Bakers Digest 55 (5): 92.

Faridi, H.A., and Finney, P.L. 1980. Technical and nutritional aspects of Iranian breads. Bakers Digest 54 (5): 14.

Fischer, H.A. 1981. Pizza crust production. Am. Soc. Bakery Engrs. 57: 170.

Fischer, L.G. 1976. Cake doughnuts. Proc. Am. Soc. Bakery Engrs. 52: 121.

Forrest, K. 2009. From TSA Griddle Systems, Inc., Web site, www.griddlesystems.com.

Freihofer, W.D. 1985. New trends in small cake production. Proc. Am. Soc. Bakery Engrs. 61: 134.

Freudenrich, A.L., Moore Jr., W.A., and Sardeshpandi, I.N. 2003. Nixtamalization process. U.S. Patent No. 6,872,417.

Frobeen, H. 1960. Advances in the automatic production of tarts and pies. Bakers Digest 34 (1): 62.

Gates, R. 2005. Equipment for pie production. Presented at Pie Industry Seminar held by the American Institute of Baking and the American Pie Council, April 21, at Celebration, FL.

Gelroth, J., Glaser, B., Lehmann, T., Moore, T., O'Donnell, K., Pickering, D., Rootring, J., and Sieloff, T. 2005. Technical assistance. AIB Tech. Bull. 27: 1.

Genau, P. 1996. Bagel production line. Proc. Am. Soc. Bakery Engrs. 72: 95.

Goodsell, G.R. 1984. Cake doughnut production. Proc. Am. Soc. Bakery Engrs. 60: 118.

Gorchow, J.J. 1992. Cake muffin production. Proc. Am. Soc. Bakery Engrs. 68: 145.

Gorton, L. 1985. Pita bread: How to get started and how to add capacity. Baking Equipment 7 (2): BE-44.

Gorton, L. 1987. New Tech Snacks' Joliet plant shortens supply lines for "half product" snack foods. Baking Equip. 9 (1): BE-7.

Gorton, L. 1993. Cake expertise. Baking & Snack 15 (8): 10.

Gorton, L. 1995. Sister's secret. Baking & Snack 17 (9): 28.

Gorton, L. 1996. Wafers and beyond. Baking & Snack 18 (9): 56.

Gorton, L. 1997. As easy as pie. Baking & Snack 19 (3): 53.

Gorton, L. 1999a. Small cakes at big volumes. Baking & Snack 21 (7): 36.

Gorton, L. 1999b. Manufacturing push. Baking & Snack 21 (8): 40.

Gorton, L. 2001a. New generation. Baking & Snack 23 (1): 52.

Gorton, L. 2001b. Star quality. Baking & Snack 23 (4): 27.

Gorton, L. 2003. In the sweet spot. Baking & Snack 25 (3): 28.

Gorton, L. 2008. Smooth operations. Baking & Snack 30 (9): 91.

Groff, E.T. 1996. Soft and chewy pretzels. Proc. Am. Soc. Bakery Engrs. 72: 151.

Haarsgaard, N.E. 1980. Automated production of puff pastry. Bakers Digest 54 (1): 16.

Hashmi, I., and Wootton, M. 2000. Test baking and evaluation of tandoori bread. AIB Tech. Bull. 22 (11).

Hayashi, T. 1978. Automated puff pastry production. Proc. Am. Soc. Bakery Engrs. 54: 139.

Hickey, C.S. 1980. Sorbate spray application for protecting yeast-raised bakery products. Bakers Digest 54 (4): 20.

Hoskins, R. 2005. Equipment for pie production. Presented at Pie Industry Seminar held by the American Institute of Baking and the American Pie Council, April 21, at Celebration, FL.

Janson, J.J. 1990. Tortilla manufacturing. Proc. Am. Soc. Bakery Engrs. 66: 110.

Juers, A.A. 1982. English muffins. Proc. Am. Soc. Bakery Engrs. 58: 46.

Kazemzadeh, M. 1999. Technology of producing hard pretzels. AIB Tech. Bull. 21 (9).

Kulp, K., ed. 1994. Cookie Chemistry and Technology. American Institute of Baking: Manhattan, KS.

Kunstmann, W.O. 1969. New production techniques for yeast-raised products. Proc. Am. Soc. Bakery Engrs. 45: 174.

Lehmann, T.A. 1979. Guide to pizza crust production. AIB Tech. Bull. 1 (11).

Lehmann, T.A. 1986a. Commissary methods of processing pizza dough. AIB Tech. Bull. 8 (12).

Lehmann, T.A. 1986b. Pizza crust. Am. Soc. Bakery Engrs. 65: 167.

Lehmann, T.A. 1997. Chemically-leavened pizza crusts. AIB Tech. Bull. 19 (11).

Lehmann, T.A. 2002. Take and bake pizza. AIB Tech. Bull. 24 (10).

Martínez-Bustos, F., Morales, S.E., Chang, Y.K., Herrera-Gómez, A., Martinez, M.J.L., Baños, L., Rodriguez, M.E., and Flores, H.H.E. 1999. Effect of infrared baking on wheat flour tortilla characteristics. Cereal Chem. 76 (4): 491.

Matz, S.A. 1968. Cookie and Cracker Technology. Avi Publishing Co.: Westport, CT.

Matz, S.A. 1988. Equipment for Bakers. Pan-Tech International: McAllen, TX.

McGill, E.A. 1975. Puff pastry production. Bakers Digest 49 (1): 28.

Meigs, H.T. 1968. Sweet doughs. Am. Soc. Bakery Engrs. Bull. 186.

Meloan, E., and Doerry, W.T. 1988. Update on bagel technology. AIB Tech. Bull. 10 (4).

Mitchell, J.R., Fan, J.-T., and Blanshard, J.M.V. 1999. Simulation of bubble growth in heat processed cereal systems. In: Bubbles in Food. G.M. Campbell, C. Webb, S.S. Pandiella and K. Niranjan, eds. AACC: St. Paul, MN.

Moreth, N. 1994. Engineering and processing. In: Cookie Chemistry and Technology. K. Kulp, ed. American Institute of Baking: Manhattan, KS.

Morine, R.L. 1975. Automated cake production. Bakers Digest 49 (2): 18.

Moyer, J. 1973. New developments in doughnut production equipment. Bakers Digest 47 (5): 120.

Oakes, E.T. 1948. Continuous mixing. Bakers Digest 23 (3): 27.

Ovadia, D. 2008. A history of pizza. In: Bubbles in Food 2: Novelty, Health and Luxury. G.M. Campbell, M.G. Scanlon and D.L. Pyle, eds. AACC: St. Paul, MN.

Owen, J.A. 1975. Cake doughnut production. Proc. Am. Soc. Bakery Engrs. 51: 142.

Petrofsky, R. 1986. Bagel production and technology. AIB Tech. Bull. 8 (11).

Pfefer, D. 1976. English muffins. Proc. Am. Soc. Bakery Engrs. 52: 51.

Qarooni, J. 1990. Flat breads. AIB Tech. Bull. 12 (12).

Qarooni, J. 1993. Wheat flour tortillas. AIB Tech. Bull. 15 (5).

Quail, K.J. 1996. Arabic Bread Production. AACC International: St. Paul, MN. [LAG: many good photos and flow charts]

Ramirez-Wong, B., Sweat, V.E., Torres, P.I., and Rooney, L.W. 1994. Cooking time, grinding and moisture content effect on fresh corn masa texture. Cereal Chem. 71 (4): 337.

Riaz, M.N. 1997. Technology of producing snack foods by extrusion. AIB Tech. Bull. 19 (2).

Rijkaart, C. 1984. Croissant production. Proc. Am. Soc. Bakery Engrs. 60: 137.

Riley, J.P. 1991. Corn tortillas, corn chips and tortilla chips. Proc. Am. Soc. Bakery Engrs. 67: 142.

Rolow, A.M. 2002. Preservatives and their applications in flour and corn tortillas. AIB Tech. Bull. 24 (8).

Romeo, J. 2009. Extrusion revolution. Baking & Snack 31 (1): 107.

Rooney, L.W., and Serna-Saldivar, S.O. 1987. Food uses of whole corn and dry-milled fractions. In: Corn: Chemistry and Technology. S.A. Watson and P.E. Ramsted, eds. AACC: St. Paul, MN.

Roth, H. 1975. Extruder for the production of ring-shaped, jelly-filled doughnuts. Bakers Digest 49 (6): 14.

Ruckh, A.B. 1986. Cakes. Proc. Am. Soc. Bakery Engrs. 62: 125.

Schiffmann, R., Stein, E.W., and Kaufman Jr., H.B. 1971. The microwave proofing of yeast-raised doughnuts. Bakers Digest 45 (1): 55.

Schmidt, C.O. 1985. Tortilla production. Proc. Am. Soc. Bakery Engrs. 61: 114. {Pyler 3 reference 25-72}

Smith, R. 1996. Technology of yeast-raised doughnuts. AIB Tech. Bull. 18 (2).

Smith, W.H. 1972. Biscuits, Crackers and Cookies. Vol. 1. Technology, Production and Management. Applied Science Publishers: London, 1972.

Sosland, L.J. 1984. Growth in corn and wheat tortilla demand leads Arga's to open plant in Arizona. Baking Equipment 6 (6): BE-14.

Stephens, C. 1972. Automation in modern pie making operations. Bakers Digest 46 (4): 56.

Thompson, D.T. Undated. History and development of the bagel machine. Published online at www.bagelproducts.com/bagel_formers/history.htm.

Thompson, J.B. 1981. English muffins. Proc. Am. Soc. Bakery Engrs. 55: 141.

Tireki, S. 2008a. Technology of cake production. In: Food Engineering Aspects of Baking Sweet Goods. S.G. Sumnu and S. Sahin, eds. CRC Press: Boca Raton, FL.

Tolle, C.O. 1985. Industrial baking technology: rusks and crisp bread. Presented at the 60th Annual Technical Conference held by the Biscuit & Cracker Manufacturers' Association.

Trevino, E., and Norton, R.C. 2006. Nixtamalized corn tortillas. AIB Tech. Bull. 28 (2).

Valentino, F. 1994. Par-baked pizza. Am. Soc. Bakery Engrs. 70: 153.

Varela, R. 2002. Pizza pans and disks. AIB Tech. Bull. 24 (2).

Whitaker, S. 2004. Tortilla tech. Baking & Snack 26 (8): 111.

Whitaker, S. 2008. Pie wheel. Baking & Snack 30 (5): 89.

Whitaker, S. 2009a. Boiled and baked. Baking & Snack 31 (2): 93.

Whitaker, S. 2009b. Batter up. Baking & Snack 31 (3): 82.

Wilkinson, G. 1987. Cake mixing technology. Proc. Am. Soc. Bakery Engrs. 63: 99.

Wise, C.E. 1971. Production quality control of extruded yeast-raised doughnuts. Bakers Digest 45 (6): 32.

Zelch, R., Sieloff, T., and Lehmann, T. 2004. Production of pie crusts. AIB Tech. Bull. 26 (9).

Recommended reading

Cleven, F., and Weber, L. 1977. A new method for the continuous production of puff and danish pastry doughs. Bakers Digest 51 (5): 138.

Cornell, M. 1999a. Drop in the pan. Baking & Snack 21 (3): 69.

Doerry, W. 1997. Technology of producing danish pastries (sweet rolls and coffee cakes). AIB Tech. Bull. 19 (2).

Fischer, L.G. 1976. Cake doughnuts. Proc. Am. Soc. Bakery Engrs. 52: 121.

Gorton, L. 1997a. Bagel-making muscle. Baking & Snack 19 (3): 53.

Gorton, L. 1997b. Stressing sheeting. Baking & Snack 19 (5): 34.

Gorton, L. 2001. Twists and turns. Baking & Snack 23 (4): 55.

Gorton, L. 2002. Cookie crafting: formative stages. Baking & Snack 24 (9): 71.

Gorton, L. 2008. Improving choices. Baking & Snack 30 (2): 93.

Gorton, L. 2009. Theory and practice. Baking & Snack 31 (1): 101.

Krubert, G.J. 1990. Cracker production. Proc. Am. Soc. Bakery Engrs. 66: 90.

Levine, L. 1998. Principles of sheeting dough. AIB Tech. Bull. 20 (9).

Moyer, J.H. 1986. Doughnuts. Proc. Am. Soc. Bakery Engrs. 62: 120.

Poehlman, R.W. 1979. Premium Danish production. Proc. Am. Soc. Bakery Engrs. 55: 91.

Rooney, L.W., Kirleis, A.W., and Murty, D.S. 1985. Traditional foods from sorghum: their production, evaluation and nutritional value. In: Advances in Cereal Science and Technology, Vol. III. Y. Pomeranz, ed. AACC: St. Paul, MN.

Roth, R.L. 1975. Fried yeast-raised production. Proc. Am. Soc. Bakery Engrs. 51: 149.

Rowe, C. 1985. Croissants. Proc. Am. Soc. Bakery Engrs. 61: 154.

Seiffer, G. 2002. Stress-free dough technology. AIB Tech. Bull. 24 (3).

Shaffer, T. 1977. Automated sweet yeast-raised production. Proc. Am. Soc. Bakery Engrs. 53: 117.

Strouts, B. 2008. Basic cracker technology. II. Processing. AIB Tech. Bull. 30 (6).

Tireki, S. 2008b. Technology of cookie production. In: Food Engineering Aspects of Baking Sweet Goods. S.G. Sumnu and S. Sahin, eds. CRC Press: Boca Raton, FL.

Tweed, A.R. 1979. The production of traditional breads — Iran, Cuba, Syria, Japan. Proc. Am. Soc. Bakery Engrs. 55: 38.

Vey, J.E. 1986. Danish. Proc. Am. Soc. Bakery Engrs. 62: 111.

Volpe, T. 2006. Layered design. Baking & Snack 28 (11): 69.

Whitaker, S. 2004. Knot-bread knowledge. Baking & Snack 26 (7): 79.

Whitaker, S. 2005. Gentle effects. Baking & Snack 27 (2): 71.

Whitaker, S. 2007a. Precision placement. Baking & Snack 29 (5): 69.

Whitaker, S. 2007b. Stress relief. Baking & Snack 29 (10): 59.

Whitaker, S. 2007c. Frying times. Baking & Snack 29 (11): 65.

Whitaker, S. 2009. Batter up. Baking & Snack 31 (3): 82.

Withrow, J. 2005. Hitting the nail on the head. Baking & Snack 27 (11): 65.

Withrow, J. 2006. Perfect pretzels. Baking & Snack 28 (2): 81.

Yankellow, J. 2005. Lamination: layers beyond imagination. San Francisco Baking Institute Newsletter. Spring edition.

Zelch, R. 2001. Batter cakes. II. Mixing. AIB Tech. Bull. 23 (10).

Appendix 2: Bakery Mathematics

Accurate batching of ingredients depends on the operator's familiarity with the formulation's basis.

Working with bakery formulations requires knowledge of mathematics, specifically that of ratio and proportion. The ability to interpret and manipulate fractions and percents is also essential.

In the baking industry, and throughout the food processing and manufacturing industries, the word "formula" (or "formulation," with the plural being "formulations" for both) is preferred to "recipe," which is commonly used in the food service, retail and home sectors. The term "recipe," however, finds frequent use in computer-operated systems where it refers to a group of program settings that govern the processing conditions for a specific application.

Formula reporting methods. Two different methods are used to write formulations for baked products: "bakers percent" and "formula percent" (**Table App.2.1**). Both are based on measuring the weight (not the volume) of ingredients. The two methods are mathematically related, and conversions can be made back and forth between them, according to individual plant practice.

Although most food processors write their formulations in terms of formula percent, a bakery is more likely to follow bakers percent because the formula is reported on the basis of the ingredient used most: flour. In the days when bakers could only get flour in bagged form, those bags weighed 50 or 100 lb. Even today, the common unit of weight for flour is the hundredweight, or cwt, denoting 100 lb.

Table App.2.1. Bakers Percent vs. Formula Percent: White Pan Bread		
Ingredient	Bakers percent	Formula percent
Flour	Always 100	55.558
Water	63.0	35.000
Yeast	2.5	1.380
Mineral yeast foods	0.5	0.280
Salt	2.0	1.115
Sugar	4.0	2.222
Shortening	4.0	2.222
Nonfat dry milk (NFDM)	4.0	2.222
TOTAL	**180.0**	**Always 100**

Mixers, too, are usually calibrated in terms of the optimum flour weight they can manage. A No. 10 mixer, for example, can handle formulations containing up to 10 100-lb bags of flour. This capacity figure may also be used in the machine's description as a 1,000-lb mixer. (It should be noted that the designation "1,000 lb" refers only to the flour portion of the mixer's capacity. The mixer will actually hold between 1,800 and 2,000 lb in total of all dough ingredients.)

Most formulations will indicate their "basis" in their headings or listings. When total flour weight is being used as the formula basis, the phrases "flour weight basis", "per cwt flour", "based on flour" and "bakers percent" may used. When total formula weight is the formula basis, the phrases "conventional percentage," "formula weight basis" and "formula percentage" may be used.

Another way of identifying how a formula has been balanced is to examine the figures given for flour. If the formula contains more than one type of flour, make sure to add all flours together. If the total flour figure sums to 100, then the formula was written in bakers percent. In some situations, all gluten-forming materials are considered in the flour percentage. If gluten is being added to a bread dough at 3% and wheat flour was listed at 97%, together they would add to the 100% flour percentage.

For both methods to work properly, all weights and volumes must be converted into a common measure. One oz equals $^1/_{16}$ (0.0625) lb; thus, 20 lb 8 oz becomes 20.5 lb. Volumetric measurements, too, must be converted. Honey, for example, weighs 12 oz (340 g) per cup; thus, 3 cups of honey weigh 2 lb 4 oz or 2.25 lb (1,020 g). (Volume-to-weight conversions for common bakery ingredients can be found in **Tables 8.002a** and **8.002b** of Chapter 8, Pages 170 and 171.)

Bakers percent. This method measures the weight of individual formula ingredients as a percentage, or portion, of the total flour weight. The total flour is always 100%. Thus, the sum of all ingredient percentages always exceeds 100%.

To change measurements in lb and oz (or g) into bakers percent, first determine the total amount of flour in the formula. If more than one type of flour is needed, add all the flour weights together, and be sure to include any separate gluten additions. This figure becomes the base number for figuring the other percentages.

Then to determine the bakers percent of any other ingredient, divide the weight of that ingredient by the total weight of flour.

To scale ingredients using a formula written in bakers percent, start with the amount of flour. If the mixer is sized to take 400 lb (4 cwt) of flour, then multiply all the percent figures by 4 to determine how much of each ingredient to scale. If you are given the desired weight for the complete batch, then use formula percent methods to determine your flour needs.

Formula percent. This method measures the weight of individual formula ingredients as a percentage, or portion, of the total formula weight. The sum of all ingredient percentages is always equal to 100%.

Parts per million (ppm) and parts per billion (ppb). Some ingredients (oxidants, reductants, vitamins, minerals) are specified by formulations in terms of parts per million (ppm). Mathematically, 1 ppm equals 0.0001% (or 10^{-6}) of the basis. Based on 1 cwt of flour, 100 ppm equals 0.16 oz ($^1/_6$ oz), or 4.54 g. For example, if ascorbic acid is added at 150 ppm, this amounts to 1 oz per 400 lb of flour. In terms of liquid measures, 1 ppm equals 1 mg per liter.

One part per billion (ppb) is only one-thousandth as much as a ppm, or 0.0000001% (or 10^{-9}) of the basis. Scaling by ppb is practically never encountered in bakery formulations, but limits on trace materials are often expressed in terms of maximum ppb allowable.

To give an idea of the relationship between ppm and ppb in a commonplace example, one drop of vermouth in 13 gal of gin would make a 1-ppm martini. Closer to the baking industry's experience, 1 ppb can be represented by one kernel of soft white wheat in a farm's 1,200-bu grain bin filled with hard red wheat.

Editor's note: Appendix 1,
on the topic of molecular drawings,
appears in Volume I at Page 729.

Appendix 3: Automation in the Bakery Industry

Even a cursory knowledge of nomenclature and applications offers insight into automation's uses and benefits to bakery operations.

By Charles Rastle, industry marketing manager, CPG Industry; and Nigel Hitchings, industry marketing manager; Rockwell Automation, 1201 South Second St., Milwaukee, WI 53204; 303.517.8914; dmrastle@ra.rockwell.com, nehitchings@ra.rockwell.com.

Companies in the baking industry are in a highly competitive environment. They strive to manufacture their products with the highest quality and meet the delivery demands of retail outlets and their customers, while at the same time manage operations to satisfy regulatory requirements. These companies must continually invest in their operations to meet the conditions that drive their business, while improving production to reduce cost, improve production flexibility and increase throughput.

App.3.A. Automation in the Plants

One approach that bakeries have taken is to improve the level of automation in their plants. Automation can control everything from mixing of the dough to packaging the final product. The challenge is how to best deploy automation in a bakery to realize the greatest value, when each production area has its own unique automation needs.

The automation system accomplishes this goal by providing control of the machines and equipment on the production floor. This includes conveyor motors, flour delivery systems, oven heating and packaging machines, among other operations. A Human Machine Interface (HMI), which may be a computer in a control room or a flat panel next to a machine, gives operators a view of the process and the capability to change or initiate different operations.

The heart of the automation system is the controller(s) containing the programs that manage operations. These controllers are called Programmable Automation Controllers (PACs), Programmable Logic Controllers (PLCs) or Distributed Control Systems (DCS). PACs are a newer version of PLCs that have greater capabilities and can handle all operations in the bakery. DCS systems can be deployed in the mixing area but are not usually used in oven control or on packaging machinery. Each system is similar, but in the baking industry, the vast majority of facilities use a combination of PLCs and/or PACs.

App.3.A.1. Mixing

The first key processing area in a bakery is mixing, which is most commonly a batch-type operation. In this area, ingredients for the product are brought to the mixer manually and/or in automated fashion and mixed together to produce dough.

To meet consumer demands for new products, bakeries now produce a greater number of different products. Each product will have its own set of ingredients and process parameters requiring the automation system to manage all the different recipes and processing steps. (In this usage, "recipe" refers not to the formulation of the product being made but to a series of machine commands, programmed by the computer to be run in a pre-set sequence to accomplish the manufacturing task.)

The recipes are either maintained in the PAC/PLC or in a computer program that is connected to the controllers. The challenge is to design a system that provides consistent operations, while having the ability to easily incorporate new recipes and processes.

In the past 10 years, the programs in the mixing area have evolved from custom-written software to systems that are designed to industry standards to provide greater flexibility. All of the major automation vendors deliver software for their systems specifically designed for batch operations like those seen in the mixing area.

Key issues in this area consist of connecting the automation system to field instruments, which include weighing operations, valves/pumps for liquid additions and the motors used for material transfer. The mixing control system must monitor and run their operations as well.

App.3.A.2. Baking

Following mixing, the next major operation is baking — a continuous operation. (For the purposes of this discussion of automation, rack and deck ovens are not examined here.)

Dough is formed into its final product shape via dividing, rounding, moulding, sheeting and other intermediate steps then passed through long tunnel ovens to bake the products. The major automation control issue in this area is to monitor and run oven operations to achieve the desired quality standards for products (neither under- nor over-cooked).

The automation system regulates heat in the oven by controlling the heaters (the majority being gas-fired burners) and the conveying system. The gas pressure and flow is adjusted to achieve the desired temperature, and the temperature of the oven is monitored.

The speed of the conveying line is dictates the length of time the product is in the oven and is adjustable. A Variable Frequency Drive (VFD) accomplishes this task by controlling the motors on the conveying line to manage its speed.

App.3.A.3. Packaging

After additional intermediate steps such as cooling and slicing for bread or icing, enrobing, glazing, etc., for cookies and cakes, the last major operation is packaging. In this area, machines take the final product, put them in to containers, case them and palletize the cases. Each part of the packaging process is performed by a machine designed for that particular step. The machines are controlled by a PAC/PLC.

In the past, machine operations were controlled by mechanical means, but today's new machines use servo motors to sequence their moving parts. The servos are operated by motion controllers.

Some of the motion controllers are stand-alone systems that require extra work to integrate with PAC/PLCs. Some automation vendors provide an integrated motion solution with their controllers to reduce complexity and effort by the Original Equipment Manufacturer (OEM). Each machine will have different sensors to detect the product and monitor the packaging operations to identify breakages or jams. The sensors are connected to the controllers and assist in the machine control programming. The machines also rely on VFDs to power the conveying systems through the equipment.

App.3.B. Global Standards

As companies look at investing in automation to improve operations, they can leverage standards that have been developed on a global basis for evaluating the correct solution for their operations

When deploying automation, the International Society of Automation (ISA) has been a leader in defining models for the development of control systems. It has designed a set of standards that define a structure for developing the programming in the control system. The standards include definitions for unit operations, production sequences, types of data and communication parameters.

Relevant standards are:

ISA S88 — Batch standard. Defines the parameters for batch control and the method for control of the system

ISA S95 — Information. Defines production operations, parameters to be monitored and data to be transferred for communication between the operations and business systems

ISA S99 — Security. Sets the standard for deploying security for automation systems.

OMAC — A standard developed by the Organization for Machine Automation and Control (OMAC), a machine manufacturer's users group for equipment control. This group has now merged with ISA and is jointly developing standards based on the OMAC and the ISA S88 efforts.

App.3.C. Information Management

Bakers are realizing big paybacks through the use of information from the automation system to improve operations in the bakery. The automation systems can monitor the value of all key process parameters. This includes mixing speed, weight and delivery of ingredients, oven temperature, conveyor speed, machine conditions and machine or equipment faults and causes. Automation systems also include data historians that record such data for review and reporting purposes. Historians log data into databases (SQL Server, Oracle, etc.) or into compressed file structures that reduce the amount of data storage but include all critical data.

The data monitored and collected by the automation system can be used for a variety of purposes.

Performance monitoring. The data can support development of plant-wide or enterprise-wide Key Performance Indicator (KPI) dashboards. (In this instance, a "dashboard" is a computer screen displaying simple visual graphics such as charts and tables to present a wide variety of different measurements in a consolidated view. The various components of the dashboard assemble the collected data into high-level summaries. They use intuitive indicators like gauges or red and green lights that are instantly understandable.) Historically, these dashboards have been manually created by plant personnel. Automation systems can collect and report this data. Some typical reports include looking at actual vs. planned production, actual throughput, machine uptime, machine faults and root causes of faults.

HACCP and compliance data. In many cases, bakeries are required to collect and report data that demonstrate compliance with regulations. This includes data such as that generated by Hazardous Analysis Critical Control Point (HACCP) programs. It also may include documentation of cleaning operations, conformance to Good Manufacturing Practices (GMPs), etc. Automation systems are capable of monitoring, collecting and reporting this data.

Enterprise Resource Planning systems (ERP). To improve management of order and production activities, better connectivity now exists between ERP or business systems and the plant floor automation system. The ERP system will send the orders to be produced to the automation system. The automation system will execute the production orders and capture associated data (ingredients used, quantity produced, cycle time, etc.) and communicate the information back to the ERP or business system. This provides a better method to manage production operations.

App.3.D. System Suppliers to the Industry

With the reduction in staff at bakeries, most companies now have only a limited number of engineers on-site to plan, conduct and commission large automation system projects. The actual implementation is mainly being outsourced to other groups and managed by engineers from the bakery. Major suppliers to the industry specialize in the following areas:

System integrators (SI). These companies are usually smaller engineering firms located near the bakery. Usually they will have less than 40 employees. Many of these firms will have local offices in different cities, which allow them to support bakeries with multiple manufacturing sites. Several of these firms focus on the food industry and have experience delivering systems for the bakery segment. They are used for new projects, upgrades and system maintenance.

Process SI/OEM. These firms focus on a specific operation in the baking industry. Organizations in this group tend to have capabilities in the mixing/batching area. They will have developed specific applications (using their own software or built on packages from the major automation vendors) for the baking industry. While not in every city, they have experience in delivering bakery-specific applications.

Packaging SI/OEM. These vendors concentrate on building and delivering machines for the bakery industry. This category includes ovens and all of the machines in the packaging area. Bakeries are now contracting with these firms to build, deliver, install and start up the equipment. Firms in this group specialize in providing solutions to the bakery industry.

Automation suppliers. Most of the major automation suppliers have an engineering/solutions team that will design, program, install and start up automation systems for the bakery industry. The teams from the automation supplier will have experience from their relationships with other bakeries. In addition, they will have a global team and can more easily manage deployment of solutions at multiple sites.

App.3.E. Training and Support of Automation

With the reduction of the engineering and maintenance staff in bakeries, proper training on the machines, applications and automation equipment is becoming more critical. Such activities include not only reference manuals but also hands-on training about the systems and knowledge of the automation components. Each of the suppliers to the industry provides different levels of training.

OEM. The Original Equipment Manufacturer (OEM) that provides either a specific application (for example, batching/mixing) or the machine equipment can offer a variety of training and support services. Each group will make available a defined training program for plant engineers/maintenance and operators to understand how to use and troubleshoot their equipment. The machine OEMs in particular will produce a variety of reference manuals, most of which are now available in electronic format. In addition, the bakery may purchase a support contract from the OEM. The scope of the contract varies by OEM.

Automation supplier. These companies offer a variety of training and support. Each firm provides training classes for their equipment. Some of the larger vendors will offer the training in local offices, while others make the training available at a limited number of sites. In addition, several of the vendors will develop site/location-specific training.

All of the major vendors provide support. This includes telephone support and local personnel who can help troubleshoot problems. The number of local resources varies based on the supplier and customer location.

App.3.F. Opportunities for Improvement

Automation suppliers continue to invest in their hardware and software to make them more flexible and reduce the effort needed to install and maintain applications built on their platforms. Some of the features now being provided include:

Reusable engineering. This method is one of the most important trends in the industry. In the past, each application delivered to a bakery was relatively specific. It was developed by a small group of engineers based on their experience. This approach was partially driven by the challenges in replicating programs from previous projects. The automation vendors have invested in their tools and now provide a variety of methods to develop standard applications and code that can be reused.

Automation libraries. The automation vendors make available libraries of programming code that can be used to build applications. These include samples for batch control and material handling systems.

Instrumentation. The instrument vendors are supplying equipment with greater capabilities. These "smart instruments" reduce the time needed to configure and calibrate, while improving troubleshooting activities. The automation suppliers in turn leverage these enhanced capabilities and provide connectivity to the instruments. Such instruments connect to the automation system in specific instrument networks, which include HART, Foundation Fieldbus and Profibus PA. The major vendors enable connectivity to these networks, allowing a person to access information in the instruments. In addition, automation suppliers offer configuration tools and HMI faceplates for these instruments that reduce the time needed to develop configurations and reduce errors.

Appendix 4: Industry Resources and Government Agencies

Knowing where to find information can be almost as valuable as the knowledge itself. The following links cover key domestic and international associations, councils, groups and societies as well as key contact information within government agencies.

AACC Cereals and Europe, Heverlee, Belgium
Phone (+32) 16204035; fax (+32) 16202535; Web *www.cerealsandeurope.net*

AACC International, St. Paul, MN
Phone (651) 454-7250; fax (651) 454-0766; Web *www.aaccnet.org*

American Bakers Association (ABA), Washington, DC
Phone (202) 789-0300; fax: (202) 898-1164; Web *www.americanbakers.org*

American Dairy Products Institute, Elmhurst, IL
Phone (630) 530-8700; fax (630) 530-8707; Web *www.adpi.org*

American Dietetic Association, Chicago, IL
Phone (800) 752-6312; fax (630) 434-1216; Web *www.eatright.org*

American Institute of Baking (AIB), Manhattan, KS
Phone (785) 537-4750 or (800) 633-5137; fax (785) 537-1493; Web *www.aibonline.org*

American National Standards Institute (ANSI), Washington, DC
Phone (202) 293-8020; Web *www.ansi.org*

American Oil Chemists' Society, Urbana, IL
Phone (217) 359-2344; fax (217) 351-8091; Web *www.aocs.org*

American Pie Council, Lake Forest, IL
Phone (847) 920-9905; fax (847) 920-9886; Web *www.piecouncil.org.com*

American Society of Baking (ASB), Petaluma, CA
Phone (707) 762-8800; fax (707) 762-9500; Web *www.asbe.org*

American Society of Brewing Chemists, St. Paul, MN
Phone (651) 454-7250; fax (651) 454-0766; Web *www.asbcnet.org*

American Spice Trade Association, Washington, DC
Phone (202) 367-1127; fax (202) 367-2127; Web *www.astaspice.org*

Association of Official Analytical Chemists International (AOAC), Gaithersburg, MD
Phone (301) 924-7077; fax: (301) 924-4089; Web *www.aoac.org*

ASI Food Safety Consultants, St. Louis, MO
Phone (800) 477-0778; fax (314) 727-2563; Web *www.asifood.com*

Bakery Equipment Manufacturers' Association (BEMA), Overland Park, KS
Phone (913) 338-1300; fax (913) 338-1327; Web *www.bema.org*

Baking Association of Canada, Mississauga, ON
Phone (888) 674-2253 or (905) 405-0288; fax (905) 405-0993; Web *www.baking.ca*

Baking Industry Sanitation Standards Committee (BISSC), Chicago, IL
Phone: (773) 761-4100; fax: (773) 274-3242; Web *www.bissc.org*

Biscuit and Cracker Manufacturers' Association (BCMA), Columbia, MD
Phone (443) 545-1645; fax (410) 290-8585; Web *www.thebcma.org*

Bread Bakers Guild of America, Sonoma, CA
Phone (707) 935-1468; fax (707) 935-1672; Web: *www.bbga.org*

Calorie Control Council, Atlanta, GA
Phone (404) 252-3663; Web *www.caloriecontrol.org*

Campden and Chorleywood Food Research Association, Gloucestershire, UK
Phone (+44) 1386 842000; fax (+44) 1386 842100; Web *www.campden.co.uk*

Canadian Food Inspection Agency
Phone (613) 225-2342; Web *www.inspection.gc.ca*

Canadian Standards Association, Mississaugua, ON
Phone (416) 747-4000; fax (416) 747-2473; Web *www.csa.ca*

Cookie and Snack Bakers Association (CASBA), Cleveland, TN
Phone (423) 472-5856; fax (423) 478-1273; Web *www.casba.us*

Council for Responsible Nutrition, Washington, DC
Phone (202) 204-7700; fax (202) 204-7701; Web *www.crnusa.org*

Culinary Institute of America, Hyde Park, NY
Phone (845) 452-9600; Web *www.ciachef.edu*

Dairy Management Inc., Rosemont, IL
Phone (800) 853-2479; Web *www.dairyinfo.com*

European Snacks Association (ESA), London, UK
Phone (+44) 20 7420 7220; fax (+44) 20 7420 7221; Web *www.esa.org.uk*

Food Allergy and Anaphylaxis Network, Fairfax, VA
Phone (800) 929-4040; fax (703) 691-2713; Web *www.foodallergy.org*

Food Allergy Research and Resource Program, Lincoln, NE
Phone (402) 472-2833; fax (402) 472-1693; Web *www.farrp.org*

Food and Consumer Products of Canada, Toronto, ON
Phone (416) 510-8024; fax (416) 510-8043; Web *www.fpcmc.com*

Food and Drug Administration (FDA), Silver Spring, MD
Phone (888) 463-6332; Web *www.fda.gov*

Food and Drug Law Institute, Washington, DC
Phone (202) 371-1420; fax (202) 371-0649; Web *www.fdli.org*

The Food Institute, Elmwood Park, NJ
Phone (201) 791-5570; fax (201) 791-5222; Web *www.foodinstitute.com*

Food Marketing Institute (FMI), Arlington, VA
Phone (202) 452-8444; fax (202) 429-4519; Web *www.fmi.org*

Food Processing Suppliers Association (FPSA), McLean, VA
Phone (703) 761-2600; fax (703) 761-4334; Web *www.fpsa.org*

Grain and Feed Trade Association, London, UK
Phone (+44) 207 814 9666; fax (+44) 207 814 8383; Web *www.gafta.com*

Grain Elevator and Processing Society, Minneapolis, MN
Phone (952) 928-4640; fax (952) 929-1318; Web *www.geaps.org*

Grain Foods Foundation, Ridgeway, CO
Phone (970) 626-5183; fax (970) 626-5814; Web *www.grainpower.org*

Grain Marketing and Production Research Center, Manhattan, KS
Phone (785) 776-2701; fax (785) 776-2789; Web *www.gmprc.ksu.edu*

Grocery Manufacturers Association (GMA), Washington, DC
Phone (202) 639-5900; fax (202) 639-5932; Web *www.gmaonline.org*

Guelph Food Technology Centre, Guelph, ON
Phone (519) 821-1246; fax (519) 836-1281; Web *www.gftc.ca*

Health Canada, Ottawa, ON
Phone (613) 957-8329; Web *www.hc-sc.gc.ca*

HealthFocus International, St. Petersburg, FL
Phone (727) 821-7499; fax (727) 821-7764; Web *www.healthfocus.com*

Home Baking Association, Topeka, KS
Phone (785) 478-3283; Web *www.homebaking.org*

Illinois Center for Food Safety and Technology (ICFS&T), Summit, IL
Phone (708) 563-8272; fax (708) 563-8274; Web *www.foodsafety.iit.edu*

IMR International, San Diego, CA
Phone (858) 451-6080; fax (858) 451-0428; Web *www.hydrocolloid.com*

Independent Bakers Association (IBA), Washington, DC
Phone (202) 333-8190; fax (202) 337-3809; Web *www.independentbaker.com*

Informa Economics, Inc., Memphis, TN
Phone (901) 202-4600; fax (901) 766-4402; Web *www.informaecon.com*

Information Resources, Inc. (IRI), Chicago, IL
Phone (312) 726-1221; fax (312) 474-2592; Web *www.infores.com*

Institute of Food Technologists (IFT), Chicago, IL
Phone (312) 782-8424; fax (312) 782-8348; Web *www.ift.org*

Institute of Packaging Professionals, Naperville, IL
Phone (630) 544-5050; fax (630) 544-5055; Web *www.iopp.org*

Instituto Sperimentale Cerealicoltura, Rome, Italy
Phone (+39) 6 329 5705 06 07; fax (+39) 6 363 06022; Web *www.cerealicoltura.it*

International Association for Cereal Science and Technology (ICC), Vienna, Austria
Phone (+43) 1 707 7202 0; fax (+43) 1 707 7204 0; Web *www.icc.or.at*

International Association for Food Protection, Des Moines, IA
Phone (515) 276-3344; fax (515) 276-8655; Web *www.foodprotection.org*

International Association of Operative Millers (IAOM), Leawood, KS
Phone (913) 338-3377; fax (913) 338-3553; Web *www.aomillers.org*

International Dairy-Deli-Bakery Association (IDDBA), Madison, WI
Phone (608) 310-5000; fax (608) 238-6330; Web *www.iddanet.org*

International Grains Council, London, UK
Phone (+44) 20 7513 1122; fax (+44) 20 7513 0630; Web *www.igc.org.uk*

International Society of Antioxidant in Nutrition and Health, Paris, France
Phone (+33) 1 55 04 77 55; fax (+33) 1 55 04 77 57; Web *www.isanh.com*

International Union of Food Science & Technology, Oakville, ON
Phone (905) 815-1926; fax (905) 815-1574; Web *www.iufost.org*

Japan Bakery and Confectionery Machinery Manufacturers' Association, Tokyo, Japan
Phone (+81) 3 3862 8478; fax (+81) 3 3862 8470; Web *www.jcbm.or.jp*

Japan Food Machinery Manufacturers' Association, Tokyo, Japan
Phone (+81) 3 5484 0981; fax (+81) 3 5484 0989; Web *www.fooma.or.jp*

Joint Institute for Food Safety and Applied Nutrition (JIFSAN), College Park, MD
Phone (301) 405-8382; fax (301) 405-8390; Web *www.jifsan.umd.edu*

Kansas State University, Dept. of Grain Science and Industry, Manhattan, KS
Phone (800) 355-5531; fax (785) 532-7010; Web *www.grains.ksu.edu*

Leatherhead Food Research, Surrey, UK
Phone (+44) 1372 376761; fax (+44) 1372 386228; Web *www.leatherheadfood.com*

Legal Suites Compliance Network, Mansfield, ON
Phone (705) 435-2041; fax (705) 435-1467; Web *www.legalsuites.com*

The Long Company, Chicago, IL
Phone (312) 726-4606; fax (312) 726-4625; Web *www.thelongco.com*

Master Brewers Association of the Americas, St. Paul, MN
Phone (651) 454-7250; fax (651) 454-0766; Web *www.mbaa.com*

National Association for the Specialty Food Trade (NASFT), New York, NY
Phone (212) 482-6440; fax (212) 482-6459; Web *www.nasft.org*

National Association of Flavors and Food-Ingredient Systems, Neptune, NJ
Phone (732) 922-3218; fax (732) 922-3590; Web *www.naffs.org*

National Association of Flour Distributors, Canfield, OH
Phone (330) 718-6563; fax (877) 573-1230; Web *www.thenafd.com*

National Association of Pizza Operators
Phone (502) 736-9500; Web *www.napo.com*

National Association of Wheat Growers, Washington, DC
Phone (202) 547-7800; fax (202) 546-2648; Web *www.wheatworld.org*

National Confectioners Association, Washington, DC
Phone (202) 534-1440; fax (202) 337-0637; Web *www.candyusa.com*

National Grain and Feed Association, Washington, DC
Phone (202) 289-0873; fax (202) 289-5388; Web *www.ngfa.org*

National Pasta Association, Washington, DC
Phone (202) 637-5888; fax (202)223-9741; Web *www.ilovepasta.org*

National Restaurant Association (NRA), Washington, DC
Phone (202) 331-5900; fax (202) 331-2429; Web *www.restaurant.org*

Natural Products Association, Washington, DC
Phone: (202) 223-0101; fax (202) 223-0250; Web *www.naturalproductsassoc.org*

North American Association of Food Equipment Manufacturers (NAFEM), Chicago, IL
Phone (312) 821-0201; fax (312) 821-0202; Web *www.nafem.org*

North American Millers Association (NAMA), Washington, DC
Phone (202) 484-2200; fax (202) 488-7416; Web *www.namamillers.org*

Occupational Safety and Health Adminstration (OSHA), Washington, DC
Phone (800) 321-OSHA (6742); Web *www.osha.gov*

Oldways Preservation Trust, Boston, MA
Phone (617) 421-5500; fax (617) 421-5511; Web *www.oldwayspt.org*

Organic Trade Association (OTA), Greenfield, MA
Phone (413) 774-7511; fax (413) 774-6432; Web *www.ota.com*

Packaging Association of Canada, Toronto, ON
Phone (416) 490-7860; fax (416) 490-7844; Web *www.pac.ca*

The Packaging Group, Inc., Milltown, NJ
Phone (732) 636-0885; fax (732) 390-1402; Web *www.packaginggroup.com*

Packaging Machinery Manufacturers Institute (PMMI), Arlington, VA
Phone (703) 243-8555; fax (703) 243-8556; Web *www.pmmi.org*

Prime Label Consultants, Inc., Washington, DC
Phone (202) 546-3333; fax (202) 543-4337; Web *www.primelabel.com*

Private Label Manufacturers Association (PLMA), New York, NY
Phone (212) 972-3131; fax (212) 983-1382; Web *www.plma.com*

Private Label Manufacturers Association International Council (PLMA-IC), Amsterdam, The Netherlands
Phone (+31) 20 575 3032; fax (+31) 20 575 3093; Web *www.plmainternational.com*

Prosoy Research and Strategy, Bilthoven, The Netherlands
Phone (+31) 30 225 2060; fax (+31) 30 225 4139; Web *www.prosoy.org*

Research and Development Associates for Military Food and Packaging Systems, Inc., San Antonio, TX
Phone (210) 493-8024; fax (210) 493-8036; Web *www.militaryfood.org*

Research Chefs Association, Atlanta, Georgia
Phone (404) 252-3663; fax (404) 252-0774; Web *www.culinology.com*

Retail Bakers of America (RBA), McLean, VA
Phone (703) 610-9035; fax (703) 610-0239; Web *www.rbanet.com*

Snack Food Association (SFA), Arlington, VA
Phone (703) 836-4500; fax (703) 836-8262; Web *www.sfa.org*

Soyfoods Association of North America, Washington, DC
Phone (202) 659-3520; Web *www.soyfoods.org*

Texas A&M, Food Protein R&D Center, College Station, TX
Phone (979) 845-2741; fax (979) 845-2744; Web *www.tamu.edu/extrusion*

TNO, Quality of Life, Zeist, The Netherlands
Phone (+31) 30 694 41 44; fax (+31) 30 694 42 95; Web *www.tno.nl*

Tortilla Industry Association (TIA), McLean, VA
Phone (703) 610-9036; fax (703) 610-0251; Web *www.tortilla-info.com*

United Soybean Board, Chesterfield, MO
Phone (800) 989-8721; fax (636) 530-1560; Web *www.unitedsoybean.com*

USDA Agricultural Research Service, Washington, DC
Phone (202) 720-3656; fax (202) 720-5427 Web *www.ars.usda.gov*

USDA Economic Research Service, Washington, DC
Phone (202) 694-5050; Web *www.ers.usda.gov*

USDA Food and Nutrition Service, Alexandria, VA
Phone (703) 305-2062; Web *www.fns.usda.gov/fns*

USDA Foreign Agricultural Service, Washington, DC
Web *www.fns.usda.gov/fns*

US Grains Council, Washington, DC
Phone (202) 789-0789; fax (202) 898-0522; Web *www.grains.org*

US Patent and Trademark Office, Washington, DC
Phone (800) 786-9199; Web *www.uspto.gov*

Wheat Foods Council, Parker, CO
Phone (303) 840-8787; fax (303) 940-6877; Web *www.wheatfoods.org*

Whole Grains Council, Boston, MA
Phone (617) 421-5500; fax (617) 421-5511; Web *www.wholegrainscouncil.org*

Afterword

Even at two volumes, containing nearly 1,600 pages, with almost 700,000 words and weighing in at 8 lb, this 4th edition of "Baking Science & Technology" cannot cover everything involved in commercial baking theory and practice. Additionally, its authors and editors know from firsthand experience that the science and industry of grain-based foods will continue to evolve.

Looking ahead, we see the need to keep this book current to reflect those changes. We have begun plans that involve electronic formats for updating this information. Also, we wanted to include some bonus material about several highly specialized topics. Finally, the 3rd edition contained descriptions of systems now best described as legacy technology. We want to make this material available as well to those who need it.

For these reasons and more, we anticipate involving Internet and Web resources in the future of this book.

Readers are encouraged to visit our publishing company's Web site, www.bakingbusiness.com, to stay current about news and happenings throughout the grain-based foods industry. Developments concerning "Baking Science & Technology" will be posted at: www.bakingbusiness.com/resources.

— The editors

Index

Editor's note: Volume I listings are shown in *italic* text.

A

Amylolytic activity, of malt, vI.190

Amylopectin, vI.7-8

Amylopectin, molecular weight, vI.8
    structure, vI.8

Amylose, vI.7-8
    content, by starch types, vI.357 (table)
    molecular weight, vI.7
    structure, vI.7

Amylose-complexing index, of improvers, vI.451 (table)

Anaerobic fermentation, of bacteria, vI.300

Anaerobic respiration, of yeast, vI.284-285

Analysis — see "Composition"

Analysis, cost, of packaging, vII.598
    water quality, vI.693-694

Angel biscuits, vII.292

Angel food cake, baking temperature and time,
    vII.153 (table)
    batter weight, specific gravity, mixing time,
    vII.144 (table)
    cupping of top crust, vII.287
    effect of baking temperature on quality,
    vII.286 (table)
    effect of egg white temperatures, on
        whipping time, batter temperature and
        cake volume, vII.286 (table)
    formula, vII.285 (table)
    formulating, vII.284-287
    pH, vII.146 (table)
    formula balance, vII.279

Anhydrous dry whey, vI.327

Animal extracts, source of exogenous enzymes, vI.405

Animal proteins, as gums, vI.474

Anise, vI.528

ANSI (American National Standards Institute), vII.372

ANSI/BISSC/Z50.2-2003 standards, vII.372

Anstellgut, definition, vII.33

Antimicrobial inks, on packaging, vII.594-595

Antimicrobials, action of Lactobacillus sanfranciscensis,
    vI.302
    as ingredients, vI.452, vI.456-459
    functions, vI.456-459
    in eggs, vI.349

Antioxidants, vI.69-70
    as biologically active materials, vI.452
    as food additives, vI.452
    as ingredients, vI.452-456

    in eggs, vI.349
    in fats and oils, vI.209
    natural, vI.455-456
    role in inhibiting auto-oxidation, vI.454

Anti-staling action, of enzymes, vI.407

AOAC approved methods, vI.614

Apoprotein, in eggs, vI.336

Apple fritter equipment, vII.644

Apples, vI.500
    dehydrated, vI.503-504
    varieties dehydrated, vI.503 (table)

Applicators, vII.558-562
    particulate, equipment, vII.558-560

Apprêt, in French bread formulating, vII.195

Approved methods, AACC, AOAC, vI.614

Approved tests, of flour, vI.615 (table)

Apricots, dried, composition, vI.504 (table), vI.504

Aprotein, in eggs, vI.336

Arabic (gum arabic), vI.467-468

Arabic bread equipment, vII.659-661

Arabinogalactan, as fiber, vI.371

Arabinose, vI.17

Arabinoxylanase, vI.408

Arabinoxylans, in oxidative gelation, vI.83-84

Arachidic acid, vI.60

Aroma, scoring, vI.650

"Artificial" additives, issue in formulating, vII.353

Artificial flavors, vI.520

Ascorbic acid, vI.141-142
    as flour maturing agent, vI.397
    as improver, vI.397
    as reducing agent, vI.400

Ascorbyl palmitate, vI.454

Ash content, of flour, vI.132-133

Ash determination, tests, vI.630-631

Ash value, soft flours, vI.155 (table)

Ash vs. flour extraction, vI.132 (table)

Asparaginase, vI.411
    in preventing acrylamide formation, vI.15

Asparagine, in acrylamide formation, vI.15

Aspergillus (green mold), vI.461

Aspergillus glaucus, vI.461

Aspergillus niger, vI.49, vI.406, vI.411, vI.460-461

Aspergillus oryzae, vI.49, vI.406, vI.411, vI.460

Assays, of nutrient content, vI.487-488

C

F

J

N

X-Y-Z